CHOICE, PREFERENCES, AND PROCEDURES

CHOICE, PREFERENCES, AND PROCEDURES

A RATIONAL CHOICE THEORETIC APPROACH

KOTARO SUZUMURA

Harvard University Press
Cambridge, Massachusetts
London, England ■ 2016

Printed in the United States of America

First printing

Library of Congress Cataloging-in-Publication Data

Suzumura, Kotaro, 1944– author.
Choice, preferences, and procedures : a rational choice theoretic approach / Kotaro Suzumura.
pages cm
Chiefly essays previously published in various sources.
Includes bibliographical references and index.
ISBN 978-0-674-72512-6 (alk. paper)
1. Social choice. 2. Rational choice theory. 3. Welfare economics. 4. Normative economics. I. Title.
HB846.8.S958 2016
302′.1301—dc23 2015030869

Contents

Preface

Over the past four decades, most if not literally all my research on economic theory has been focused on several facets of normative economics, which consists of social choice theory and welfare economics. This volume represents a selection of my essays on normative economics in this sense, chosen in accordance with seven focal issues within this intellectual discipline, viz.,

1. rational choice as rationalizable choice,
2. social choice and welfare economics,
3. equity, efficiency, and intergenerational justice,
4. individual rights and social welfare,
5. consequentialism versus nonconsequentialism,
6. competition, cooperation, and economic welfare, and
7. historically speaking.

To each and every focal issue, I have assigned one part of the volume, each consisting of 4 selected essays arranged in the logical order of evolution rather than the historical order. It amounts to 28 essays altogether, among which 26 essays are based on the essays previously published in academic journals, 1 essay is based on the essay previously published in an edited book, and the last (Essay 28) is newly prepared for the purpose of suggesting the new vista of my immediate future research. There is an introduction to the whole volume, where I explain the reasons I believe that these seven focal issues constitute the main poles of normative economics. There is also an introduction to each part. It is my hope that the reasons these seven issues have been crucial in the evolution of my own work in normative economics, and the reasons these essays are construed to be worth republication in this volume, are thereby made clear.

The oldest among the selected essays were first published as early as 1976. The proof of the pudding is in the eating, and I strongly hope that the reader's tasting will prove that the collection of these essays may be justified for their internal coherence, logical complementarity, and the services they have rendered in the subsequent evolution of the subject.

I am most grateful to my mentors Kenneth Arrow and Amartya Sen, the coauthors of the original jointly written essays, and to the publishers of journals and/or books where my essays were first published. My sincere gratitude will be expressed in more concrete detail in the acknowledgments to follow.

Acknowledgments

My greatest gratitude goes to Kenneth Arrow and Amartya Sen. Not only have they led me to the fascinating frontier of social choice theory and welfare economics, but they have also generously given me several opportunities to collaborate with them.[1] It is my great fortune to have shared these experiences with them. It was also Sen who, at some precarious stages of my academic life, gave me strong encouragement as well as a much-needed intellectual environment and quiet time at All Souls College, Oxford University, in 1988, at Harvard University in 1995, and at Trinity College, Cambridge University, in 2001 and 2011. My indebtedness to him far exceeds the highest words of appreciation that I can possibly find. It is my sincere hope that they would approve my intellectual progress reported in this volume.

I am also grateful to the precious instructions and friendly advice provided by excellent teachers at Hitotsubashi University, Tokyo University, and Kyoto University in Japan, and Cambridge University and London School of Economics in the UK. In particular, I am grateful to Masahiko Aoki, Kenjiro Ara, Terrence Gorman, Frank Hahn, Koichi Hamada, Michio Morishima,

1. These collaborative efforts resulted in K. J. Arrow, A. K. Sen, and K. Suzumura, eds., *Social Choice Reexamined*, Macmillan, 2 vols., 1996/1997; K. J. Arrow, A. K. Sen, and K. Suzumura, eds., *Handbook of Social Choice and Welfare*, Amsterdam: Elsevier, 2 vols., Vol. I in 2002, Vol. II in 2011.

Takashi Negishi, Hukukane Nikaido, Amartya Sen, Miyohei Shinohara, and Yuichi Shionoya.

Another fortune of mine is that I could greatly benefit from friendly communications and academic collaborations with such excellent colleagues and friends as Geir Asheim, Nick Baigent, Salvador Barberà, Timothy Besley, Douglas Blair, Georges Bordes, Walter Bossert, Partha Dasgupta, Marc Fleurbaey, Louis Gevers, Peter Hammond, Motoshige Itoh, Kunio Kawamata, Jerry Kelly, Kazuharu Kiyono, Hideki Konishi, Masahiro Okuno-Fujiwara, Prasanta Pattanaik, Andrew Postlewaite, John Roemer, Yves Sprumont, Koichi Tadenuma, John Vickers, Shlomo Weber, John Weymark, and Yongsheng Xu. Some of the essays in this volume would not have been completed if I could not entertain their frank advice and friendly collaboration. My special gratitude goes to Walter Bossert, who helped me improve the final draft of this work.

Thanks are also due to Trinity College, Cambridge University, where I spent a fruitful six months as a Visiting Fellow Commoner from April 2011 to September 2011 and completed the substance of this volume. If it had not been for this generous hospitality, the completion of this work would have been further delayed.

I am grateful to the following journals and publishers for agreeing to allow my previously published papers to be brought together here: *American Economic Review, Analyse & Kritik, Economica, Economic Journal, Economic Theory, Japanese Economic Review, Journal of Economic Theory, Journal of Public Economics, Review of Economic Studies, Social Choice and Welfare, Spanish Economic Review,* and North-Holland/Elsevier Publishing Company.

Throughout the preparation process of this volume, I have been generously supported by the research project on *Economic Analysis of Intergenerational Issues: Searching for Further Development* through the Grant-in-Aid for Specially Promoted Research from Japan's Ministry of Education, Culture, Sports, Science and Technology (grant number 22000001), to which I am most grateful.

Original Sources

The author and publisher are grateful to the co-authors, journals, and publishers for their kind permission to reproduce the following previously published papers.

PART I

Essay 1: "Rational Choice and Revealed Preference." *Review of Economic Studies* Vol. 43, No. 1 (February 1976), 149–158. Published by Oxford University Press on behalf of Review of Economic Studies, Ltd. © 1976 Review of Economic Studies, Ltd.

Essay 2: "Houthakker's Axiom in the Theory of Rational Choice." *Journal of Economic Theory* Vol. 14, No. 2 (April 1977) 284–290. Published by Elsevier Inc. © 1977 Academic Press, Inc.

Essay 3: "Consistent Rationalizability," with Walter Bossert and Yves Sprumont. *Economica*, New Series, Vol. 72, No. 286 (May 2005), 185–200. Published by Wiley on behalf of London School of Economics and Political Science and Suntory and Toyota International Centres for Economics and Related Disciplines. © 2005 The London School of Economics and Political Science.

Essay 4: "Revealed Preference and Choice under Uncertainty," with Walter Bossert. *SERIEs - Journal of the Spanish Economic Association* Vol. 3, No. 1-2, *Special Issue in Honor of Salvador Barberà. Part II: On Social Choice, Political Economy, and Decision-Making,* edited by Matthew O. Jackson and Hugo F. Sonnenschein (March 2012), 247–258. Published by Springer-Verlag via a Creative Commons Attribution 4.0 International (CC BY 4.0) License.

PART II

ESSAY 5: "Impossibility Theorems without Collective Rationality," with Douglas H. Blair, Georges Bordes, and Jerry S. Kelly. *Journal of Economic Theory* Vol. 13, No. 3 (December 1976), 361–379. Published by Elsevier Inc. © 1976 by Academic Press, Inc.

ESSAY 6: "Remarks on the Theory of Collective Choice." *Economica*, New Series, Vol. 43, No. 172 (November 1976), 381–390. Published by Wiley on behalf of London School of Economics and Political Science and Suntory and Toyota International Centres for Economics and Related Disciplines. © 1976 London School of Economics.

ESSAY 7: "Arrovian Aggregation in Economic Environments: How Much Should We Know about Indifference Surfaces?" with Marc Fleurbaey and Koichi Tadenuma. *Journal of Economic Theory* Vol. 124, No. 1 (September 2005), 22–44. Published by Elsevier Inc. © 2004 Elsevier Inc.

ESSAY 8: "A Characterization of Consistent Collective Choice Rules," with Walter Bossert. *Journal of Economic Theory* Vol. 138, No. 1 (January 2008), 311–320. Published by Elsevier Inc. © 2007 Elsevier Inc.

PART III

ESSAY 9: "On Pareto-Efficiency and the No-Envy Concept of Equity." *Journal of Economic Theory* Vol. 25, No. 3 (December 1981), 367–379. Published by Elsevier Inc. © 1981 Academic Press, Inc.

ESSAY 10: "The Informational Basis of the Theory of Fair Allocation," with Marc Fleurbaey and Koichi Tadenuma. *Social Choice and Welfare* Vol. 24, No. 2 (April 2005), 311–341. Published by Springer Science + Business Media. © 2005 Springer-Verlag.

ESSAY 11: "Ordering Infinite Utility Streams," with Walter Bossert and Yves Sprumont. *Journal of Economic Theory* Vol. 135, No. 1 (July 2007), 579–589. © 2006 Elsevier Inc.

ESSAY 12: "Multi-Profile Intergenerational Social Choice," with Walter Bossert. *Social Choice and Welfare* Vol. 37, No. 3 (September 2011), 493–509. © 2010 Springer-Verlag.

PART IV

Essay 13: "On the Consistency of Libertarian Claims." *Review of Economic Studies* Vol. 45, No. 2 (June 1978), 329–342. Published by Oxford University Press. © 1978 Review of Economic Studies, Ltd.

Essay 14: "Liberal Paradox and the Voluntary Exchange of Rights-Exercising." *Journal of Economic Theory* Vol. 22, No. 3 (June 1980), 407–422. Published by Elsevier Inc. © 1980 by Academic Press, Inc.

Essay 15: "Individual Rights Revisited," with Wulf Gaertner and Prasanta K. Pattanaik. *Economica*, New Series, Vol. 59, No. 234 (May 1992), 161–177. Published by Wiley on behalf of London School of Economics and Political Science and Suntory and Toyota International Centres for Economics and Related Disciplines. © 1992 London School of Economics.

Essay 16: "Welfare, Rights, and Social Choice Procedure: A Perspective." *Analyse & Kritik* Vol. 18, No. 1 (1996), 20–37. © Westdeutscher Verlag, Opladen.

PART V

Essay 17: "Consequences, Opportunities, and Procedures." *Social Choice and Welfare* Vol. 16, No. 1 (January 1999), 17–40. © 1999 Springer-Verlag, Berlin Heidelberg.

Essay 18: "Characterizations of Consequentialism and Nonconsequentialism," with Yongsheng Xu. *Journal of Economic Theory* Vol. 101, No. 2 (December 2001), 423–436. © 2001 Elsevier Science (USA).

Essay 19: "Consequences, Opportunities, and Generalized Consequentialism and Nonconsequentialism," with Yongsheng Xu. *Journal of Economic Theory* Vol. 111, No. 2 (August 2003), 293–304. © 2003 Elsevier Science (USA). All rights reserved.

Essay 20: "Welfarist-Consequentialism, Similarity of Attitudes, and Arrow's General Impossibility Theorem," with Yongsheng Xu. *Social Choice and Welfare*, Vol. 22, No. 1 (February 2004), 237–251. © 2004 Springer-Verlag.

PART VI

Essay 21: "Entry Barriers and Economic Welfare," with Kazuharu Kiyono. *Review of Economic Studies* Vol. 54, No. 1 (January 1987), 157–167. Published by Oxford University Press on behalf of The Society for Economic Analysis Ltd. © 1987 The Society for Economic Analysis Ltd.

Essay 22: "Oligopolistic Competition and Economic Welfare: A General Equilibrium Analysis of Entry Regulation and Tax-Subsidy Schemes," with Hideki Konishi and Masahiro Okuno-Fujiwara. *Journal of Public Economics* Vol. 42, No. 1 (June 1990), 67–88. © 1990 Elsevier Science Publishers B. V., North-Holland.

Essay 23: "Symmetric Cournot Oligopoly and Economic Welfare: A Synthesis," with Masahiro Okuno-Fujiwara. *Economic Theory* Vol. 3, No. 1 (January 1993), 43–59. Published by Springer Science+Business Media. © 1993 Springer-Verlag.

Essay 24: "Cooperative and Noncooperative R & D in an Oligopoly with Spillovers." *American Economic Review* Vol. 82, No. 5 (December 1992), 1307–1320. © 1992 American Economic Association.

PART VII

Essay 25: Introduction to *Handbook of Social Choice and Welfare*, Volume 1, edited by Kenneth J. Arrow, Amartya K. Sen and Kotaro Suzumura, 2002, pp. 1–32. © 2002 Elsevier Science B. V., North-Holland.

Essay 26: "Paretian Welfare Judgements and Bergsonian Social Choice." *Economic Journal* Vol. 109, No. 455 (April 1999), 204–220. Published by Wiley on behalf of the Royal Economic Society. © 1999 Royal Economic Society.

Essay 27: "Presidential Address: Welfare Economics Beyond Welfarist Consequentialism." *Japanese Economic Review* Vol. 51, No. 1 (March 2000), 1–32. Published by Blackwell Publishers on behalf of the Japanese Economic Association. © 2000 Japanese Economic Association.

CHOICE, PREFERENCES, AND PROCEDURES

Introduction

> The man who never alters his opinion is like standing water, and breeds reptiles of the mind.
>
> —WILLIAM BLAKE, "A Memorable Fancy," *The Marriage of Heaven and Hell,* 1791

> One of the most ordinary weaknesses of the human intellect is to seek to reconcile contrary principles, and to purchase peace at the expense of logic.
>
> —ALEXIS DE TOCQUEVILLE, *Democracy in America,* 1835–39

I.1. Some Personal Recollections

Throughout my academic career, I have been keeping a strong innate desire to understand the performance characteristics of democratic methods of collective decision making. At the outset of this introduction, I would like to explain how this innate desire evolved, how it grew into my lifelong commitment to the intellectual disciplines of welfare economics and social choice theory, and what lies behind my concern about *consequentialism* versus *nonconsequentialism,* on the one hand, and about *welfarism* versus *nonwelfarism,* on the other.

The opening section of this introduction depends heavily on an interview I have given to *Social Choice and Welfare,* viz., Walter Bossert and Marc Fleurbaey (2015), and on my *Memoire* [Suzumura (2014)].

The origin of my innate desire may be traced a long way back to my high school days in 1960. The allied occupation of Japan after World War II was ended by the San Francisco Peace Treaty, which was signed on September 8, 1951, and became effective on April 28, 1952. The Security Treaty between the United States and Japan was signed the same day. It was this security treaty that granted the United States the territorial means in Japan to establish a military presence in the Far East. In 1959, bilateral talks on revising the 1951 Security Treaty were started, and the new Treaty of Mutual Cooperation and Security was signed on January 19, 1960, in Washington, DC. When the new treaty pact was submitted to the Japanese Diet for ratification, harsh debates over the Japan-US security relationship were triggered. The leftist opposition, which was based on the fear that the new treaty might lead to the enduring subordinate independence of Japan under US hegemony, made an extensive effort to prevent its passage. The crucial step was taken when the House of Representatives finally approved the new treaty pact on May 20, 1960. The Socialist Party representatives boycotted the Lower House session, and they tried to prevent the Liberal Democratic Party representatives from entering the chamber. They were removed by police force, which led to massive demonstrations and riots by students, trade union activists, and some ordinary citizens. However, the House of Councilors failed to vote on the issue within the required thirty days after the Lower House approval, and the treaty pact was passed by default on June 19, 1960.

The 1960 struggle made a high school boy wonder about the meaning and virtue of democratic methods of collective decision making. Both sides of the struggle, viz., the Liberal Democratic Party government and the opposition, issued stern warnings against the imminent danger of the breakdown of democracy. Although both sides were using the same portmanteau catchword of democracy, it was clear that they were assigning very different meanings to the same term. However, it was impossible for an immature high school boy to crystallize an operational definition of democratic methods of collective decision making. Nevertheless, even a naive youngster could be aware of the precarious status of Japan after independence in the midst of a harsh cold war confrontation between the two major opposing camps. Thus, the *outcome* of the Treaty of Mutual Cooperation and Security seemed to be not only a sensible but also an almost inevitable choice for Japan. However, the *political artifice* used by the Liberal Democratic Party government in their attempt to pass the pact was too hideous to be approved. These observations led me to think that there are two aspects of the methods of collective decision making, viz., the *final outcome* to which it leads, and the *procedure* through which the final outcome is brought about, which may well lead us into sharply contrasting judgments on the virtue of democracy.

With this naive perception in mind, I went on to Hitotsubashi University in 1962, where chances seemed high that I could study social sciences capable of shedding some academic light on my personal agenda. It was the good old days, and we were not trained in the way our students are trained nowadays. Many teachers talked more about their own interests rather than teaching standard courses and following a standard curriculum. I still remember the first day of the class on development economics that was taught by a senior professor, who I later learned was a famous scholar. I was then a third-year undergraduate. His lecture was an extreme example of nonstandard education that was common in these days. Without giving even a word of introduction, he turned his back to us and began to draw a colorful picture on the blackboard, which took little more than thirty minutes. Students were puzzled, and a stir ran through the classroom. When his artistic work was completed, what appeared on the blackboard was Siddhartha Gautama sitting on a lotus calyx. He turned to us and declared that it represented the economic nirvana. Without uttering any further word, he went out of the classroom to take a puff at a pipe. Needless to say, his theatrical performance took us by great surprise. I could have enjoyed it if I had not been pressed by the strong innate desire to pursue my personal agenda on democratic methods of collective decision making. I soon decided to spend more time in libraries than in classrooms if I found that the class was unlikely to help me pursue my personal end.

I was fortunate enough to encounter a few fascinating books on microeconomics and related disciplines in the library, including Takashi Negishi's monograph on *Price and Allocation Theory* and Hukukane Nikaido's fine textbook on *Mathematical Methods of Modern Economics*.[1] Above anything else, it was my great fortune that I had a chance to grapple with Kenneth

1. Negishi's monograph, which was originally published in Japanese in 1965, later formed the core of his classic [Negishi (1972)]. Nikaido's book, which was also originally published in Japanese in 1960, was subsequently translated into English by Kazuo Sato [Nikaido (1970)] and soon established a high international reputation.

Arrow's *Social Choice and Individual Values* [Arrow (1951)]. These books became my lifelong resources

My first encounter with Arrow's monograph, and his general impossibility theorem, was almost accidental. When I was a first-year undergraduate student, I was assigned to a compulsory class of mathematics taught by a professor with a strong commitment to the leftist cause of the Maoist school. Although the heat of the 1960 Security Treaty struggle had already come to an end, he vigorously agitated us to stand against the Liberal Democratic Party government. He said he would assure us the credit of his class on mathematics if only we could write an essay about Chairman Mao's books on practice and on contradiction. I decided to neglect his class, his agitation, and his essay assignment altogether, and spend most of the time thereby vacated in the library to read books that seemed to be relevant to my personal agenda.[2] When I became a third-year undergraduate student, I found in the library an article written by the Maoist professor in his early days, which was on general economic equilibrium and social choice theory. Out of curiosity, I skimmed through his article, and I soon found a statement of Arrow's general impossibility theorem. I was so intrigued by the Arrow theorem that I rushed to another bookshelf and got hold of the first edition of *Social Choice and Individual Values*.

Most of the summer in 1964 was devoted to a lonely struggle with Arrow's classic. Although I was unable to understand it in full detail for the lack of my mathematical knowledge and maturity, I was intoxicated for several weeks to follow the grand vistas suddenly opened in front of me. My persistent interest in democratic methods of collective decision making, coupled with the encounter with Arrow's monograph, made me determined to pursue the research agenda suggested by Arrow.

It was around this time that I also stepped into the field of welfare economics through my reading of Chapter VIII of Paul Samuelson's *Foundations of Economic Analysis* [Samuelson (1947)]. His splendid discourse was a great reading overall, but it was occasionally too cryptic and terse for a beginner to appreciate in full depth. Almost simultaneously, I was exposed to Edward

2. The books I read included Jean-Jacques Rousseau's *Social Contract* [Rousseau (1762)], John Stuart Mill's *On Liberty* [Mill (1859)], Joseph Schumpeter's *Capitalism, Socialism and Democracy* [Schumpeter (1943)], and Max Weber's *The Protestant Ethic and the Spirit of Capitalism* [Weber (1904)].

Mishan's "A Survey of Welfare Economics, 1939–1959" [Mishan (1960)]. It was a useful survey for the purpose of knowing what had been done at the frontier of "new" welfare economics over the past 20 years. To be honest, however, I was perplexed by Mishan's declaration to the following effect: "While it continues to fascinate many, welfare economics does not appear at any time to have wholly engaged the labors of any one economist. It is a subject which, apparently, one dabbles in for a while, leaves and, perhaps, returns to later in response to a troubled conscience—which goes some way to explain why, more than other branches of economics, it suffers from an unevenness in its development, a lack of homogeneity in its treatment and, until very recently, a distressing disconnectedness between its parts."

Mishan's aloof remark on the contemporary state of "new" welfare economics left me with a query: What was the founding philosophy of "old" welfare economics? It is true that the shift from "old" welfare economics created by Arthur Pigou (1920) to "new" welfare economics à la Nicholas Kaldor (1939), John Hicks (1940), Tibor Scitovsky (1941), and Paul Samuelson (1950), on the one hand, and Abram Bergson (1938) and Paul Samuelson (1947, Chapter VIII), on the other hand, was caused by Lionel Robbins's (1932/1935) criticism on Pigou's epistemological basis, but "new" welfare economics need not be the sole route one may follow in the attempt of salvaging the sound upper structure of Pigou's "old" welfare economics. To understand where exactly we were standing, I thought we must carefully re-examine the founding philosophy as well as the logical performance of "old" welfare economics.

Fortunately, I was attending a lecture on the economics of planning delivered by Yuichi Shionoya (1932–2015). His lecture was actually not about economic planning at all, and the whole lecture was devoted to the critical examination of *The Economics of Welfare* [Pigou (1920)]. It gave me an ideal opportunity to study Pigou's classic in full detail. I confess I found the structure of this magnum opus somewhat disorderly, but I was fascinated with the preface to the third edition, which declared as follows: "The complicated analyses which economists endeavour to carry through are not mere gymnastic. They are instruments for the bettering of human life. The misery and squalor that surround us, the injurious luxury of some wealthy families, the terrible uncertainty overshadowing many families of the poor—these are evils too plain to be ignored. By the knowledge that our science seeks it is possible that they may be restrained. Out of the darkness light! To search for it is the task, to find it perhaps the prize, which the 'dismal science of Political Economy' offers to those who face the discipline." The founder's declaration to this effect strongly encouraged me to pursue the path he had cultivated. All the more, I was embarrassed by the deep cleavage that developed between Pigou's ardent preface and Mishan's aloof remark. Ever since, I have been keeping the desire to find a way to account for this deep cleavage. It was my great fortune that I could encounter *Social Choice and Individual Values* and *The Economics of Welfare* in an early stage of my scholarly growth.

As a matter of fact, there is a further background reason for my early interest in social choice theory and welfare economics, which is tightly connected with the contrast between the two rival economic regimes, viz., the *capitalist regime* and the *socialist regime*. Recollect that Japan regained full sovereignty in the midst of the harsh cold war confrontation between these rival regimes. Sometime during my undergraduate years, I came to be aware of a harsh controversy that took place in the 1930s concerning the rational workability of the capitalist regime vis-à-vis the socialist regime. On the one hand, the functioning of the capitalist regime, which once seemed to lead the free market economies to everlasting prosperity, suddenly became seriously doubtful in view of the New York stock market collapse on October 24, 1929, and the subsequent worldwide depression. On the other hand, the socialist regime, which was born by the Russian Revolution in October 1917, seemed to have circumvented its embryo vulnerability and began to grow into the sustainable and eligible alternative to the capitalist regime. The economic planning controversy in the 1930s was not about the *de facto* workability of these rival regimes but about their *rational* workability. The salient players of the controversy were Friedrich Hayek and Oscar Lange, and the focal point of the controversy could be neatly summarized as follows: Can there be an economic regime that is capable of exhibiting a satisfactory performance with respect to the list of characteristics such as (a) Pareto efficiency of outcomes thereby generated; (b) compatibility with the respect for a democratic procedure of collective decision making as well as the respect for individual libertarian rights; and (c) efficiency in the use of dispersed information, which is privately owned, in the promotion of public objectives. If the answer to this basic question turns out to be affirmative, a further question naturally suggests itself: Can the capitalist regime and/or the socialist regime qualify as an eligible regime?

In my perception, the economic planning controversy in the 1930s identified many crucial questions to be pursued by welfare economics and social choice theory even if in a crude and informal way. It was also this controversy that called my attention to a remarkable feature of normative economics in that they treat the economic regimes, not as historically given *constants* that are imposed from outside but as endogenous *variables* to be rationally designed, socially chosen, and implemented. My perennial interest in the performance characteristics of the democratic methods of collective decision making can be construed as a part of this broader agenda of normative economics. This perception of the agenda of our subject is squarely reflected in my introduction to the *Handbook of Social Choice and Welfare,* Vol. I, which I edited 35 years later along with Kenneth Arrow and Amartya Sen [Arrow, Sen, and Suzumura (2002)].[3]

It was with this broad understanding in mind regarding the research agenda of our discipline that I proceeded to the Graduate School of Economics at Hitotsubashi University in 1966, where I began my graduate studies under the guidance of Kenjiro Ara (1925–2002). It was during my second year in the graduate school that I attended—to be more precise, creeped into—a session in the Far Eastern Meeting of the Econometric Society held in Tokyo, where Amartya Sen presented a paper and Ken-Ichi Inada was his discussant.[4] According to my memory, the title of Sen's presentation was "On Pareto Optimality," which was an early version of what came to be called the *Impossibility of a Paretian Liberal* [Sen (1970; 1970a, Chapter 6*)]. The conflict between the welfaristic value of Pareto efficiency and the liberal value of the respect for individual libertarian rights suggested by Sen strongly impressed me. His thesis was reminiscent of an observation by Isaiah Berlin (1958, pp. 15–16) to the effect that "the connexion between democracy and individual liberty is a good deal more tenuous than it seemed to many advocates of both. The desire to be governed by myself, or at least to participate in the process by which my life is to be controlled, may be as deep a wish as that of a free area for action, and perhaps historically older. But it is not a desire for the same thing. So different is it, indeed, as to have led in the end

3. This introduction is reprinted as Essay 25 of this volume.

4. Concerning the history of the Far Eastern Meeting of the Econometric Society, the interested readers are referred to Suzumura (1999a).

to the great clash of ideologies that dominates our world." I was fascinated by the fact that Berlin's thoughtful observation could be logically culminated into Sen's impossibility theorem.

Throughout the 1960s, some important progress was accomplished in several subfields of social choice theory, the most conspicuous among them being the exploration of the logical performance of the simple majority decision (SMD) rule. Capitalizing on the seminal contributions by Duncan Black (1948; 1958) and Arrow (1951, Chapter VII), and fortified by the works by Ken-Ichi Inada (1964), Sen (1966), and many others, the necessary and sufficient conditions for the SMD rule to generate a transitive social preference relation were identified by Inada (1969), on the one hand, and Sen and Prasanta Pattanaik (1969), on the other. Turning to the state of welfare economics in the 1960s, Peter Hammond (1985, p. 405) pointed out that "after the publication of the two major but rather negative textbooks by [Ian Little (1950) and Jan Graaff (1957)], welfare economics seemed to lie mostly dormant and sterile during the 1960s."[5] It was Sen's splendid synthesis [Sen (1970a)], viz., *Collective Choice and Social Welfare,* that opened the gate to a flood of theoretical work in normative economics in the 1970s.

A couple of years after the Far Eastern Meeting, I became aware of Sen's book, thanks to the suggestion by Koichi Hamada. By that time, I was already determined to devote my future academic activities to normative economics. However, I was unable to find out how to kick off my research and in which direction I should step forward within the broad areas I identified through my reading of Arrow, Hayek, Pigou, and Samuelson. It was *Collective Choice and Social Welfare* that helped me draw up a research scenario of my own.[6] Indeed, my initial research program in normative economics was designed to explore the following crucial problems, which I identified through intensive studies of Arrow and Sen: (a) to characterize the concept of *rational choice as*

5. See also Hammond (1993; 1997) for his view on what has happened since 1970 in normative economics.

6. By the time I could draw up my research scenario, Japan's historically unprecedented rapid growth was almost over. The exclusive focus on GDP growth was about to be replaced by concerns about the equity and fairness of income and wealth distributions, and the problems of poverty and gender equality as well as environmental disruptions and intergenerational justice were about to come to the fore. On reflection, this should have provided a favorable wind for normative economics. However, these disciplines have never gained a dominant status in economic studies in Japan.

rationalizable choice by means of the generalized revealed preference axioms à la Samuelson and Houthakker; (b) to explore the less-than-full rationality of social choice functions and "irrational" social choice functions in relation to Arrow's general impossibility theorem; (c) to explore the "irrational" goal of collective decision making with special reference to the no-envy fairness of socially chosen outcomes; and (d) to examine the logical structure of Sen's impossibility of a Paretian liberal for its robustness as well as the intuitive reasonableness of his articulation of individual libertarian rights.

It was in the process of my struggle with issue (a) that I came across a puzzle in the theory of preference or probability relations at Wolfson College, Cambridge University. It was in 1973, and I was then a British Council scholar. Frank Hahn and Michael Farrell were my advisers.[7] I also participated in the research seminar on income and wealth distributions organized by David Champernowne. I came across in his book on *Uncertainty and Estimation in Economics* [Champernowne (1969)] a novel concept of consistency, to be called *Champernowne consistency*, of preference or probability relations. Let X be a universal set of alternatives and R be a binary relation on X. A t-tuple of alternatives $(x^1, x^2, \ldots, x^t)$ in X is a *Champernowne cycle, C-cycle* for short, of order t $(3 \leq t < +\infty)$ if and only if $(x^1, x^2) \in P(R) \cup N(R)$, $(x^h, x^{h+1}) \in R$ $(h = 2, \ldots, t-1)$ and $(x^t, x^1) \in R$ hold, where $P(R)$ is the strict preference or probability relation corresponding to the weak preference or probability relation R, viz., $(x, y) \in P(R)$ holds if and only if $[(x, y) \in R$ and $(y, x) \notin R]$ holds, and $N(R)$ denotes the noncomparability relation, viz., $(x, y) \in N(R)$ holds if and only if $[(x, y) \notin R$ and $(y, x) \notin R]$ holds. R is said to be *Champernowne-consistent* if and only if there exists no C-cycle of any finite order. This concept seemed persuasive, but I found an intriguing puzzle, viz., *a binary relation R is Champernowne-consistent if and only if it is transitive*.[8] Starting from this puzzle, I could formulate a new concept of consistency, which came to be christened *Suzumura consistency*.[9] A t-tuple of alternatives $(x^1, x^2, \ldots, x^t)$

7. In April 1973, I was appointed associate professor of the Institute of Economic Research, Kyoto University. I was also fortunate enough to visit Cambridge University from July 1973 for one year.

8. A binary relation R satisfies the classical coherence property of *transitivity* if and only if, for any alternatives x, y, and z in X, $[(x, y) \in R \ \& \ (y, z) \in R]$ implies $(x, z) \in R$.

9. It was Walter Bossert (2008) who coined this nomenclature.

in X is a *Suzumura cycle, S-cycle* for brevity, of order t $(3 \leq t < +\infty)$ if and only if $(x^1, x^2) \in P(R)$, $(x^h, x^{h+1}) \in R$ $(h = 2, \ldots, t-1)$ and $(x^t, x^1) \in R$ hold. R is said to be *Suzumura-consistent* if and only if there exists no S-cycle of any finite order. Considering the unfortunate fate of the concept of Champernowne consistency, I had every reason to be cautious about the logical properties of Suzumura consistency. It turned out that (i) just like Sen's (1969) concept of *quasi transitivity,* viz., transitivity of the strict preference relation, Suzumura consistency lies strictly between transitivity and acyclicity in their logical strength;[10] (ii) the discrepancy between transitivity and Suzumura consistency disappears if R is reflexive and complete; and (iii) R has an *ordering extension* R^*, viz., there exists an ordering relation R^* such that $R \subseteq R^*$ and $P(R) \subseteq P(R^*)$ hold if and only if R is Suzumura-consistent. The last property is nothing other than the generalization of Szpilrajn's (1930) ordering extension theorem.[11] It turned out that this generalized ordering extension theorem is crucially important in several distinct contexts of individual choice and collective decision making. Further implications of Suzumura consistency were subsequently clarified and synthesized by Bossert and Suzumura (2010).

During my study of issue (d) mentioned previously, I became strongly captured by the issue of informational bases of normative economics. The standard approach in normative economics focused its attention on the *consequences* of the act of choice in neglect of the *procedures* through which consequential outcomes are brought about. It also paid little attention, if any at all, to the *opportunities* that lie behind the consequential outcomes apart from their *instrumental value* in full neglect of their *intrinsic value*. In my perception, this informational parsimony of the standard approach in normative economics may be at least partly held responsible for the persistence of many perplexing paradoxes in welfare economics and social choice theory.

Throughout my work on normative economics, I had never forgotten the first paragraph of Chapter VIII on welfare economics of Samuelson's

10. A binary relation R satisfies *acyclicity* if and only if there exists no finite sequence $x^1, x^2, \ldots, x^t$ in X, where $3 \leq t < +\infty$, such that $(x^1, x^2) \in P(R)$, $(x^2, x^3) \in P(R), \ldots, (x^{t-1}, x^t) \in P(R)$ and $(x^t, x^1) \in P(R)$ hold.

11. A version of Szpilrajn's ordering extension theorem asserts that there exists an ordering extension R^* of a binary relation R if it satisfies *reflexivity* $[(x, x) \in R$ holds for all $x \in X]$ and transitivity.

Foundations of Economic Analysis, which gave me a strong impression in my first reading. It reads as follows: "Beginning as it did in the writings of philosophers, theologians, pamphleteers, special pleaders, and reformers, economics has always been concerned with problems of public policy and welfare. And at least from the time of the physiocrats and Adam Smith there has never been absent from the main body of economic literature the feeling that in some sense perfect competition represented an optimal situation."[12]

The sense in which "perfect competition represented an optimal situation" was neatly rephrased in modern terms by Kenneth Arrow [Arrow (1951a)], Gèrard Debreu [Debreu (1959)], and others under the name of the *fundamental theorems of welfare economics*.[13] It is true that these theorems clarified what perfectly competitive markets can accomplish at equilibrium. However, I had to remain unsatisfied with the message of these theorems on the precise relationship between competition and welfare—for at least two reasons.

In the first place, since my first encounter with the economic planning controversy, I was strongly impressed by Hayek's view on the role of information as well as on the meaning of competition. In particular, I was intrigued by his observation on the concept of perfect competition to the following effect: "[It] assumes that state of affairs already to exist which . . . the process of competition tends to bring about. . . . If the state of affairs assumed by the theory of perfect competition ever existed, it would not only deprive of their scope all the activities which the verb 'to compete' describes but would make them virtually impossible."[14]

In the second place, through the study on the means and ends of Japanese industrial policy in the era of postwar economic growth [Komiya, Okuno, and Suzumura (1988); Itoh, Kiyono, Okuno-Fujiwara, and Suzumura (1991)] as well as the study on the transplantation of antimonopoly law and competition policy to Japan from US soil [Goto and Suzumura (1999)], I became aware of the existence of two pieces of conventional wisdom on the welfare effects of competition, which had been strenuously maintained in

12. Samuelson (1947, p. 203).

13. For the sake of fairness, I should add that it was Ian Little (1950/1957) who introduced the term *Pareto optimality*. I owe this observation to my conversation with Samuelson. See Suzumura (2005).

14. Hayek (1948, pp. 92–96).

Japan by public officials, academic economists, and people at large. According to the first piece of conventional wisdom, the old Confucian maxim to the effect that "too much is as bad as too little" applies to the welfare effect of competition as well. The upshot of this wisdom is the belief that competition can serve to the enhancement of public welfare only under the judicious regulation of competitive forces. According to the second piece of conventional wisdom, competition is nothing but the decentralized mechanism for efficient allocation of scarce resources, so that the unfettered competition could always be welfare-enhancing if it were not for factors that obstruct the proper functioning of competitive forces. It was in view of these conflicting ideas that I pursued a research project on the precise relationship between welfare and competition.

This volume consists of 28 essays edited into seven parts with 4 essays each. The first six parts gather my previously published essays, which represent my persistent focal interests in the theory of normative economics, viz., welfare economics and social choice theory. The last part is of a somewhat different nature. It consists of 4 essays that try to account for the historical evolution of the focal issues of this work.

I retired from Waseda University at the end of March 2014, where I had taught normative economics and the philosophical backgrounds thereof over a six-year period after my long terms at Hitotsubashi University (1971–1973; 1982–2008) and Kyoto University (1973–1982). My valedictory lecture at Waseda University was delivered under the title "In Search of Welfare Economics with Red Corpuscles." It was in his touching tribute to James Meade at his eightieth birthday that Robert Solow (1987, p. 986) wrote as follows: "I suppose Meade's effort could be described as fundamental welfare economics, but welfare economics with red corpuscles, not the sort of attenuated theory that concludes that if only everything were convex and everybody knew everything and there were perfect markets for all future contingent commodities, including contingencies for which no vocabulary now exists, then with costless lump-sum transfers we could make all for the best in this best of imaginable worlds. Meade expects welfare economics to provide advice, not resignation." In my perception, this characterization of Meade's work in welfare economics brings us a long way back to Pigou's preface to *The Economics of Welfare*. It was in search of the resurgence of welfare economics in the spirit of Pigou and Meade that I borrowed this unorthodox circumlocution from Solow as the title of my valedictory lecture.

I am convinced that one of the best aspects of retirement is that one can exercise the full freedom of choice to devote oneself to the research activities of one's strongest concern. I am impatient to kick off my own game of welfare economics with red corpuscles. Before setting about doing this, however, I would like to present the main footsteps of my pilgrimage in normative economics, which started from my youthful desire to understand the instrumental as well as intrinsic value of democratic methods of collective decision making. This is precisely what the present volume of essays is intended to do.

I.2. Scope, Methods, and Informational Bases of Normative Economics

As soon as a group of individuals with differential abilities and idiosyncratic subjective values gather together to form a collectivity, a multitude of social choice problems come to the fore. These problems include the following:

(a) To whom should the collectivity assign which role to play for the sake of the whole group with or without collaboration with other member(s) of the collectivity?
(b) How should outcomes of the collective activities be distributed among those who played their assigned roles?
(c) How should the collectivity choose the public decision-making rules and mechanisms?
(d) To what extent should the collectivity entitle individuals to exercise their freedom of choice within their conferred protected spheres? How should the protected sphere be determined in the first place?
(e) How should the collectivity cope with the infringements on the conferred individual freedom of choice?
(f) How should the collectivity help members who are prevented from participation in the collective activities owing to their innate or imposed handicaps, for which they have no reason to be held personally responsible?

If these assignments, allocations, choice of decision-making rules, entitlements, rectifications, and/or assistances fail to be acceptable to a segment of the group of individuals, there may be an imminent danger of triggering resistance by the dissenting segment of individuals to the collectivity, thereby threatening the sustainability of the collectivity as a unified whole. Social choice theory is one wing of normative economics that is concerned with the resolution of these problems that come to the fore whenever we think of the rational design and effective management of mechanisms for collective decision making and their implementation. Historically speaking, we may trace the origin of social choice theory at least as far back as to Jean-Charles de Borda (1781) and Marie-Jean de Condorcet (1785) in the period of the French Revolution. The modern articulation of social choice theory may be attributable to Black (1948; 1958) and Arrow (1951).

The other wing of normative economics is welfare economics, which is concerned with "the critical scrutiny of the performance of actual and/or imaginary economic systems, as well as with the critique, design and implementation of alternative economic policies" [Suzumura (2002, p. 1)]. The original source of this intellectual tradition may be found in the writings of Jeremy Bentham (1789; 1843) and his principle of *the greatest happiness of the greatest number,* but the first attempt to systematize the long British tradition of moral philosophy into the new intellectual discipline under the title of welfare economics had to wait until Pigou published his *Wealth and Welfare* (1912) and *The Economics of Welfare* (1920).

Pigou's synthesis, which came to be called the "old" welfare economics, experienced a great turmoil in the 1930s when Robbins (1932/1935) harshly criticized the epistemological basis of Pigou's welfare economics. The gist of his criticism was that the utilitarian informational basis of Pigou's edifice, which consists of *cardinal* and *interpersonally comparable* individual utilities, is unscientific in the sense of being unverifiable. Several attempts were made to salvage the wreckage of "old" welfare economics by constructing "new" welfare economics on the basis of *ordinal* and *interpersonally noncomparable* individual utilities and nothing else. The first line of research along this line was based on the so-called compensation principle due to Kaldor (1939), Hicks (1940), Scitovsky (1941), and Samuelson (1950), among others, whereas the second line of research was based on the concept of the *social welfare function* due to Bergson (1938) and Samuelson (1947, Chapter VIII; 1981).

At this juncture, it is worthwhile to observe that the informational basis of the theory of voting à la Borda and Condorcet, social choice theory à la Black and Arrow, and the "new" welfare economics based on the compensation principle and that based on the Bergson-Samuelson social welfare function have one crucial feature in common. Although these various approaches of normative economics are different in many important respects, they share the same feature of basing normative social judgments on ordinal and interpersonally noncomparable individual utilities (or preference orderings), which are defined over the set of all social alternatives.

All essays selected for this volume focus in common on one or the other aspect of collective decision making mechanisms in a "democratic" society that consists of a finite number of individuals.[15] To confine our problems within reasonable bounds, it is assumed that individuals as well as the society they form are "rational" in a well-specified sense. The first problem to be asked and settled, then, is this: *What do we exactly mean by individual and social acts of choice being rational?*

I.3. Rational Choice and Revealed Preference

Rationality of the act of choice is a subject that has been central in economics throughout its evolution. According to Andreu Mas-Colell (1982), Samuelson once observed that, even after a hundred years, we would be talking economics in terms of the concept of rational choice. Just like Samuelson, I am convinced that rational choice is a concept that lies at the heart of economic theory in general, and social choice theory and welfare economics in particular. Having said this, however, I should add that the concept of rational choice has always been highly controversial and will remain so in the future as well. The concept of rationality adopted throughout this work is that of *rationality as rationalizability*.

I.3.1. Traditional Concept of Rationality of the Act of Choice

The concept of rationality as rationalizability seems to be standard in the literature. The origin of this classical rationality concept may well be

15. Exceptions are Essay 11 based on Bossert, Sprumont, and Suzumura (2007) and Essay 12 based on Bossert and Suzumura (2011). The former discusses the issue of ordering infinite utility streams, whereas the latter contains an analysis of the Arrovian social choice problem in an infinite-horizon intergenerational setting.

traced back to antiquity, but it suffices to cite the great German sociologist/economist Max Weber, who explicated his usage of the concept of rationality as follows: "The term 'formal rationality of economic action' will be used to designate the extent of quantitative calculation or accounting which is technically possible and which is actually applied. The 'substantive rationality,' on the other hand, is the degree to which the provisioning of given groups of persons (no matter how delimited) with goods is shaped by economically oriented social action under some criterion (past, present, or potential) of ultimate values (*wertende Postulate*), regardless of the nature of these ends."[16]

In Weber's own admission, "the concept of 'substantive rationality' . . . is full of ambiguities. It conveys only one element common to all 'substantive' analyses: namely, that they do not restrict themselves to note the purely formal and (relatively) unambiguous fact that action is based in 'goal-oriented' rational calculation with the technically most adequate available methods, but apply certain criteria of ultimate ends, whether they be ethical, political, utilitarian, hedonistic, feudal (*ständisch*), egalitarian, or whatever, and measure the results of the economic action, however formally 'rational' in the sense of correct calculation they may be, against these scales of 'value rationality' or 'substantive goal rationality.'"[17] It is this concept of *substantive goal rationality* that I accept and maintain throughout the following analysis of rationality of the act of choice. Observe that the essence of this concept lies in the existence of an underlying criterion of ultimate values, regardless of the nature of these ends.

The choice of this concept of substantive goal rationality is not made fortuitously. Quite to the contrary, it is the orthodox conception of rational choice in economics. To vindicate this assertion, we have only to quote a few passages from *An Essay on the Nature and Significance of Economic Science* by

16. It may not be out of place to make sure of Weber's concept of "goods." He starts from the concept of "utilities." "By 'utilities' (*Nutzleistungen*) will always be meant the specific and concrete, real or imagined, advantages (*Chancen*) of opportunities for present or future use as they are estimated and made an object of specific provision by one or more economically acting individuals. The action of these individuals is oriented to the estimated importance of such utilities as means for the ends of their economic action. . . . Utilities may be the services of non-human or inanimate objects or of human beings. Non-human objects which are the sources of potential utilities of whatever sort will be called 'goods'" [Weber (1978, p. 68)].

17. Weber (1978, pp. 85–86).

Robbins (1932/1935): "There is a sense in which the word rationality can be used which renders it legitimate to argue that at least some rationality is assumed before human behavior has an economic aspect—the sense, namely, in which it is equivalent to 'purposive.' . . . It is arguable that if behavior is not conceived of as purposive, then the conception of the means-end relationships which economics studies has no meaning." However, "to say [that rational choice is tantamount to purposive behavior] is not to say in the least that all purposive action is completely consistent. It may indeed be urged that the more that purposive action becomes conscious of itself, the more it necessarily becomes consistent. But this is not to say that it is necessary to assume *ab initio* that it always is consistent or that the economic generalizations are limited to that, perhaps, tiny section of conduct where all inconsistencies have been resolved."[18]

Three remarks may be in order at this juncture. In the first place, Weber's concept of *goal-oriented rational calculus* per se need not be based on any underlying criterion of goodness of consequences, whereas his concept of *value rationality* or substantive goal rationality hinges crucially on the underlying value of goodness of consequences. It is this feature of the concept of substantive goal rationality that tightly connects Weber with Robbins. In the second place, not only Weber's concept of substantive goal rationality but also Robbins's concept of rational choice as a purposive act says very little, if anything at all, about the substantive contents of values and/or purposes that underlie their substantive concept of rationality. In the third place, having no apparent connection with the work by Weber and Robbins, Samuelson (1938; 1938a) kicked off a salient tradition of *revealed preference theory*, which may be construed as an analytical sophistication of the Weber-Robbins concept of substantive goal rationality and its axiomatic characterization. In the following sections, the meaning of these remarks will be clarified in analytical depth.

I.3.2. Basic Concepts of Binary Relations

Throughout this volume, extensive use will be made of the theory of binary relations on a universal set X of all conceivable alternatives. It may facilitate

---

18. Robbins (1935, p. 93).

our discourse if we list basic concepts and symbols at the outset that will be frequently used in what follows.

A *binary relation* on X is a proposition (R) such that, for each ordered pair (x, y), where $x, y \in X$, we may say that the proposition (R) is true or false. The set of all ordered pairs that satisfy (R) is a well-defined subset, say, R of the Cartesian product $X \times X$. Conversely, given a subset $R \subseteq X \times X$, we may define a binary relation (R) by

$$(R) \text{ is true for } (x, y) \Leftrightarrow (x, y) \in R, \tag{I.1}$$

where a double-headed arrow means logical equivalence. Thus, a binary relation (R) on X may be identified with a subset R of $X \times X$ that satisfies (I.1). For the sake of brevity, we will frequently write, for any $x, y \in X$, xRy if and only if $(x, y) \in R$. The set of all binary relations on X will be denoted by $\mathcal{B}$.

Corresponding to a given binary relation $R \in \mathcal{B}$, the *symmetric part* $I(R)$ and the *asymmetric part* $P(R)$ of R are defined by

$$I(R) = \{(x, y) \in X \times X \mid (x, y) \in R \;\&\; (y, x) \in R\} \tag{I.2}$$

and

$$P(R) = \{(x, y) \in X \times X \mid (x, y) \in R \;\&\; (y, x) \notin R\}, \tag{I.3}$$

respectively. If R is construed to be the *weak preference relation* on the universal set X of alternatives such that $(x, y) \in R$ if and only if x is weakly preferred to y, then $I(R)$ and $P(R)$ stand, respectively, for the *indifference relation* and the *strict preference relation* over the universal set X of alternatives.

Let us now introduce a few standard properties of a binary relation $R \in \mathcal{B}$, which will frequently appear in individual decision theory as well as in social choice theory.

(a) [*Completeness*] $\forall x, y \in X : x \neq y \Rightarrow (x, y) \in R \vee (y, x) \in R$.
(b) [*Reflexivity*] $\forall x \in X : (x, x) \in R$.
(c) [*Irreflexivity*] $\forall x \in X : (x, x) \notin R$.
(d) [*Transitivity*] $\forall x, y, z \in X : [(x, y) \in R \;\&\; (y, z) \in R] \Rightarrow (x, y) \in R$.

(e) [*Symmetry*] $\forall x, y \in X : (x, y) \in R \Rightarrow (y, x) \in R$.
(f) [*Asymmetry*] $\forall x, y \in X : (x, y) \in R \Rightarrow (y, x) \notin R$.
(g) [*Equivalence*] R satisfies (b), (d), and (e).
(h) [*Ordering*] R satisfies (a), (b), and (d).
(i) [*Quasi ordering*] R satisfies (b) and (d).

In addition to these standard properties, we introduce three coherence conditions that are weaker than the most fundamental coherence condition, viz., transitivity.[19] The first property is due to Sen (1969), which requires one of the implications of transitivity of R, viz., transitivity of $P(R)$, and no other implications thereof:

(j) [*Quasi transitivity*] $\forall x, y, z \in X : [(x, y) \in P(R) \;\&\; (y, z) \in P(R)] \Rightarrow (x, y) \in P(R)$.

For each binary relation $R \in \mathcal{B}$, the *transitive closure T(R)* of R is defined as follows: For any $x, y \in X$, $(x, y) \in T(R)$ holds if and only if there exists a natural number t such that $2 \leq t < +\infty$ and a sequence of alternatives $x^0, x^1, \ldots, x^t$ in X satisfying $x^0 = x$, $(x^\tau, x^{\tau+1}) \in R$ $(\tau = 0, 1, \ldots, t-1)$ and $x^t = y$. It is easy to verify that the operator T on the set $\mathcal{B}$ of all binary relations on X satisfies the following axioms of *closure operation* [Berge (1963)]:

(T_1) $T(R) \supseteq R$;
(T_2) $R^1 \supseteq R^2 \Rightarrow T(R^1) \supseteq T(R^2)$;
(T_3) $T[T(R)] = T(R)$;
(T_4) $T(\emptyset) = \emptyset$.

19. Despite its predominance in individual as well as social choice theory, the basic coherence postulate of transitivity tends to be violated in several distinct contexts. Suffice it to quote Duncan Luce's (1956) coffee-sugar example. More often than not, a decision maker may be unable to perceive "small" differences in alternatives, so that he may judge two adjacent alternatives with "small" differences to be indifferent. However, if he compares the first term x of a long chain of paired alternatives with the last term y of the same chain, the difference between x and y may be so conspicuous that he may strictly prefer x to y in violation of the transitivity of indifference relation. However, transitivity of a weak preference relation R implies transitivity of indifference relation $I(R)$, which is a contradiction.

The crucial property of the transitive closure $T(R)$ of $R \in \mathcal{B}$ is the following conspicuous property. See Suzumura (1983, p. 12) for the proof.

THEOREM I.1. For any $R \in \mathcal{B}$, $T(R)$ is the smallest transitive superset of R.

We are now ready to introduce a coherence concept that is weaker than transitivity. This concept is due originally to Suzumura (1976a, Essay 6 of this volume).

(k) [*Suzumura consistency*] $\forall x, y \in X : (x, y) \in T(R) \Rightarrow (y, x) \notin P(R)$.

This coherence concept excludes the existence of a finite chain of alternatives $x^0, x^1, \ldots, x^t$ for some natural number t $(2 \leq t < +\infty)$ such that $x^0 = x$, $(x^\tau, x^{\tau+1}) \in R$ $(\tau = 0, 1, \ldots, t-1)$, $x^t = y$, and $(y, x) \in P(R)$. In other words, it excludes the existence of a weak as well as strong *money pump*.[20]

Yet another coherence concept that is weaker than transitivity is the following:

(l) [*Acyclicity*] $\forall x, y \in X : (x, y) \in T(P(R)) \Rightarrow (y, x) \notin P(R)$.

This coherence concept excludes the existence of a strict preference cycle. As such, acyclicity is a weaker variant of Suzumura consistency.[21]

---

20. Suppose that such a cyclic chain of alternatives happens to exist. Then an agent with cyclic preferences is willing to trade x^t for x^{t-1}, x^{t-1} for x^{t-2}, and so on until we reach x^0 such that the agent strictly prefers retrieving x^t to retaining x^0. Thus, at the end of a cycle of exchanges, the agent is willing to pay a positive amount of money to retrieve the original alternative. This is a typical example of a money pump. See Raiffa (1968, p. 78).

21. To bring the contrast between quasi transitivity and Suzumura consistency into clear relief, suppose that x, y, and z are such that xPy and yPz. Between x and z, there are two possible relationships, which lead to contradictory cycles to be named as *strong money pump case* and *weak money pump case*, respectively: (a) zPx and (b) zIx. There are two possible methods of avoiding both (a) and (b). The first method, which is attributable to Sen (1969), is to require that (xPy and yPz) implies xPz. The second method, which leads to Suzumura consistency, is to require that (xPy and yPz) implies either xPz or xNz, where N stands for noncomparability relation, viz., aNb if and only if neither aRb nor bRa.

To exemplify that xPy, yPz, and xNx are not at all pathological, suppose that x, y, and z denote three cars with different characteristics: (i) speed, (ii) maneuverability, and (iii) design. In terms of speed, x far exceeds y and y far exceeds z, thus x far exceeds z. In terms of

The logical strength of the four coherence concepts, viz., transitivity, quasi transitivity, Suzumura consistency, and acyclicity, vis-à-vis each other may be summarized in the following implication diagram, where a single-headed arrow from the property (A) to the property (B) implies that (A) is logically stronger than (B), where the reverse arrow does not hold in general. See Suzumura (1983, pp. 244–245) or Bossert and Suzumura (2010, p. 37) for the proof of the assertions contained in this implication diagram. We should add that Suzumura consistency and quasi transitivity are logically independent of each other, which can be shown by means of examples. See Suzumura (1983, p. 244).

$$\begin{array}{ccc} \text{Transitivity} & \Rightarrow & \text{Quasi transitivity} \\ \Downarrow & & \Downarrow \\ \text{Suzumura consistency} & \Rightarrow & \text{Acyclicity} \end{array}$$

Before closing this preliminary subsection, an important implication of the property of Suzumura consistency should be noted. For any binary relation $R \in \mathcal{B}$, another binary relation $R^* \in \mathcal{B}$ is said to be an *extension* of R if and only if $R \subseteq R^*$ and $P(R) \subseteq P(R^*)$ hold. If this is the case, R is said to be a *subrelation* of R^*. The following classical theorem due to Szpilrajn (1930) identifies a *sufficient* condition for R to have an ordering R^* that extends R. For mnemonic convenience, such an ordering R^* is called an *ordering extension* of R.

THEOREM I.2 (SZPILRAJN (1930)). A quasi ordering R has an ordering extension R^*.

In many contexts of individual decision making and social choice, it is of great help if we can identify a *necessary and sufficient* condition for $R \in \mathcal{B}$

---

maneuverability, the difference between x and y and that between y and z, are marginal. In this case, we may accept that xPy and yPz. In the third place, although the difference in style between x and y, and that between y and z are marginal, the difference in style between x and z may exceed the threshold of minimum noticeable difference and z may well be judged to exceed x in terms of design. These considerations may well result in the noncomparability of x vis-à-vis z.

to have an ordering extension $R^* \in \mathcal{B}$. The following theorem is due to Suzumura (1976a), which is the exact answer to this crucial question.[22]

Theorem I.3 (Suzumura (1976a, Essay 6 of this volume)). There exists an ordering extension R^* of $R \in \mathcal{B}$ if and only if R satisfies the property of Suzumura consistency.

We are now ready to proceed to the formal analysis of choice functions in general, and rational choice functions in particular.

I.3.3. Rational Choice as Rationalizable Choice

Given the universal set X of alternatives, let $\mathcal{K}_A$ be an arbitrary nonempty family of nonempty subsets of X. A *choice function* C defined on $\mathcal{K}_A$ is a functional relationship that maps each $S \in \mathcal{K}_A$ into a nonempty subset $C(S)$ of S. The intended interpretation is that each $S \in \mathcal{K}_A$ is an *opportunity set* offered to an agent for choice, and $C(S)$ denotes a nonempty subset of S that consists of chosen alternatives from S. In what follows, $C(S)$ will be called the *choice set* from $S \in \mathcal{K}_A$.

We may have occasions to invoke some special domains of a choice function if we want to secure wide relevance of the theory of rational choice as rationalizable choice. The first variant is the *finite domain* $\mathcal{K}_F$, viz., the family of all nonempty *finite* subsets of the universal set X. The choice function C on the domain $\mathcal{K}_F$ is extensively used in the theory of individual choice and collective decision making.

To prepare for the introduction of the second variant, let there be a natural number l $(2 \leq l < +\infty)$ such that $X \subseteq \mathbb{R}^l_+$ holds, where $\mathbb{R}_+$ is the set of all nonnegative real numbers and $\mathbb{R}^l_+$ is the l-fold Cartesian product of $\mathbb{R}_+$. It is intended that X is the *commodity space* and l is the number of commodities that are traded in competitive markets. Let $\mathcal{K}_{CB}$ be such that $S \in \mathcal{K}_{CB}$ holds if and only if there exists a price vector $\boldsymbol{p} = (p_1, p_2, \ldots, p_l) \gg 0$ and a positive income $M > 0$ such that

$$S = B(\boldsymbol{p}, M) := \{\boldsymbol{x} = (x_1, x_2, \ldots, x_l) \in \mathbb{R}^l_+ \mid \boldsymbol{px} \leq M\}, \quad \text{(I.4)}$$

22. Since Suzumura consistency and quasi transitivity are logically independent, it follows from Theorem I.3 that quasi-transitivity of R cannot provide a general guarantee for the existence of an ordering extension thereof.

where $\boldsymbol{px} = \Sigma_{i=1}^{l} p_i x_i$. For mnemonic convenience, $\mathcal{K}_{CB}$ will be christened the *competitive budget domain*.

With these preliminary terminologies and notations at hand, let us go back to the choice function C on an arbitrary domain $\mathcal{K}_A$. Capitalizing on the Weber-Robbins concept of substantive goal rationality, we define the concept of rationality of the act of choice as follows: The act of choice articulated by the choice function C on the arbitrary domain $\mathcal{K}_A$ is *rational* if and only if there exists a binary relation $R \in \mathcal{B}$ such that

$$\forall S \in \mathcal{K}_A : C(S) = G(S, R) := \{x^* \in S \mid \forall x \in S : (x^*, x) \in R\} \quad \text{(I.5)}$$

holds, where R is interpreted as a *weak preference relation* that underlies the choice function C and $G(S, R)$ is the set of *R-greatest elements* of S. In this case, the choice set $C(S)$ is generated by optimizing the underlying weak preference relation R over S for each $S \in \mathcal{K}_A$. In what follows, R that satisfies (I.5) is called a *rationalization* of C.[23]

Observe that the concept of rationality as rationalizability does *not* impose any constraint whatsoever on the coherence property to be satisfied by the rationalization per se. This observation naturally leads us into further analyses of the rational choice as rationalizable choice by means of various *grades of coherence*, which are required of the rationalization. These concepts are introduced and analyzed in what follows.

I.3.4. Rational Choice Functions on Competitive Budget Domains

Historically speaking, the first attempt to introduce and axiomatically characterize the concept of rational choice as rationalizable choice was kicked off by Samuelson (1938; 1938a; 1947, Chapter V) in the special context of the

---

23. An alternative definition of rationality as rationalizability can be introduced by

$$\forall S \in \mathcal{K}_A : C(S) = M(S, R) := \{x^* \in S \mid \forall x \in S : (x, x^*) \notin P(R)\}. \quad \text{(I.5*)}$$

This alternative definition uses the *R-maximal set* $M(S, R)$ instead of the R-greatest set $G(S, R)$. The main body of this volume uses the R-greatest definition of rationality. The readers who are interested in the concept to be called the R-maximality definition of rationality are referred to Suzumura (1976, Essay 1 of this volume), Sen (1997), and Bossert, Sprumont, and Suzumura (2005a).

pure theory of consumer's behavior.[24] The point of departure of his theory was an acute observation that "from its very beginning the theory of consumer's choice has marched steadily toward greater generality, sloughing off at successive stages unnecessarily restrictive conditions. [However,] much of even the most modern [as of the time of his writing] analysis shows vestigial traces of the utility concept" [Samuelson (1938, pp. 61–62)]. To drop off the last vestige of the utility concept, Samuelson started his analysis from a *demand function* of a competitive consumer, which is a *single-valued choice function* c on the competitive budget domain $\mathcal{K}_{CB}$. For each $S = B(\boldsymbol{p}, M) \in \mathcal{K}_{CB}$ for some $(\boldsymbol{p}, M) \gg 0$, $c(S)$ is the commodity bundle that the agent purchases from the budget set $S = B(\boldsymbol{p}, M)$. In this familiar framework, Samuelson (1938) introduced his choice-functional coherence postulate, which came to be called the *weak axiom of revealed preference* in the later literature, viz., Samuelson (1950a, p. 370):

$$\exists\, B(\boldsymbol{p}, M) \in \mathcal{K}_{CB} : \boldsymbol{x} = c(B(\boldsymbol{p}, M))\ \&\ \boldsymbol{y} \in B(\boldsymbol{p}, M) \setminus \{c(B(\boldsymbol{p}, M))\}$$
$$\Rightarrow \forall\, B(\boldsymbol{p}^*, M^*) \in \mathcal{K}_{CB} : [\boldsymbol{y} = c(B(\boldsymbol{p}^*, M^*)) \Rightarrow \boldsymbol{x} \notin B(\boldsymbol{p}^*, M^*)] \tag{I.6}$$

The meaning of this postulate is simple and intuitive. If $\boldsymbol{x}$ is chosen from $B(\boldsymbol{p}, M)$ that also contains $\boldsymbol{y}$, but $\boldsymbol{y}$ is *not* chosen from $B(\boldsymbol{p}, M)$, then there should not exist a budget set $B(\boldsymbol{p}^*, M^*)$ from which $\boldsymbol{y}$ is chosen in the presence of $\boldsymbol{x} \in B(\boldsymbol{p}^*, M^*)$. In simple words, the weak axiom of revealed preference means that if $\boldsymbol{x}$ is revealed preferred to $\boldsymbol{y}$, then $\boldsymbol{y}$ should not be revealed preferred to $\boldsymbol{x}$. Equipped with this weak axiom and nothing else, Samuelson (1938; 1938a) could derive almost all properties of the demand function c of a competitive consumer, which the Pareto-Slutsky-Hicks-Allen theory of consumer's behavior could derive from the constrained maximization of the ordinal utility function.

---

24. According to Nicolas Georgescu-Roegen (1954; 1966), it was Vilfredo Pareto (1906/1920) and Ragnar Frisch (1926/1971) who laid the foundations of modern theories of rational choice. However, Samuelson (1950a, pp. 369–370) himself attributed the original inspiration of the so-called revealed preference theory to his discussion with Gottfried von Haberler and to Wassily Leontief's analysis of indifference curves. The interested readers are referred to Bossert and Suzumura (2010, pp. 7–8) for further analytical and bibliographical details.

Although Samuelson's tour de force is highly praiseworthy, it falls short of dropping off the last vestige of the utility concept altogether. In Samuelson's own parlance (1950a, p. 370), "I soon realized that this could carry us almost all the way along the path of providing new foundations for utility theory. But not quite all the way. The problem of integrability, it soon became obvious, could not yield to this weak axiom alone. I held up publication on the conjecture that if the axiom were strengthened to exclude non-contradictions of revealed preference for a chain of three or more situations, then non-integrability could indeed be excluded. At scientific meetings and in correspondence this problem was proposed, both to economists and mathematicians. But no proof was forthcoming for all these years, until Mr. Houthakker's paper arrived in the daily mail. Not only had he provided the missing proof, but in addition he had independently arrived at precisely the same strong axiom as I had hoped would save the day."

Houthakker's (1950) important contribution appeared in *Economica* (Vol. 17, 1950), where the *semitransitivity axiom* in his own wording was proposed, which reads as follows: Suppose that there exists a positive integer K, consumption bundles $\boldsymbol{x}^0, \boldsymbol{x}^1, \ldots, \boldsymbol{x}^K \in X$, among which at least two bundles are distinct, positive price vectors $\boldsymbol{p}^0, \boldsymbol{p}^1, \ldots, \boldsymbol{p}^K$, and positive incomes $M^0, M^1, \ldots, M^K$ such that $\boldsymbol{x}^k = c(B(\boldsymbol{p}^k, M^k)), \boldsymbol{p}^k\boldsymbol{x}^k = M^k$ for all $k \in \{0, 1, \ldots, K\}$, and $\boldsymbol{p}^{k-1}\boldsymbol{x}^{k-1} \geq \boldsymbol{p}^{k-1}\boldsymbol{x}^k$ for all $k = \{1, 2, \ldots, K\}$ hold. Then $\boldsymbol{p}^K\boldsymbol{x}^K < \boldsymbol{p}^K\boldsymbol{x}^0$ must be true.

In the same volume of *Economica,* Samuelson (1950a, pp. 370–371) rephrased the rather complicated semitransitivity axiom as follows: "If A reveals itself to be 'better than' B, and if B reveals itself to be 'better than' C, and if C reveals itself to be 'better than' D, etc., then I extend the definition of 'revealed preference' and say that A can be defined to be 'revealed to be better than' Z, the last in the chain. In such cases it is postulated that Z must never *also* be 'revealed to be better than' A." As an axiom of coherence imposed on the single-valued choice function c defined on the competitive budget domain $\mathcal{K}_{CB}$, the semitransitivity axiom and the strong axiom are indeed equivalent, but not necessarily otherwise.[25]

25. The possible discrepancy between Houthakker's semitransitivity axiom and Samuelson's strong axiom will prove very crucial in the context of the *multivalued* choice function C on an arbitrary domain, viz., $\mathcal{K}_A$. See Section I.4.3.

Capitalizing on the path-breaking contribution by Samuelson, Houthakker succeeded in establishing the existence of a utility function u defined on the commodity space such that $c(B(\boldsymbol{p}, M))$ can be rationalized by the maximization of u over $B(\boldsymbol{p}, M)$ for each $B(\boldsymbol{p}, M) \in \mathcal{K}_{CB}$ if c satisfies the semitransitivity axiom of revealed preference. This is the first major result in the theory of rational choice as rationalizable choice in the context of a single-valued choice function c on the competitive budget domain $\mathcal{K}_{CB}$. Although Houthakker's accomplishment is worthy of the highest praise, the fact remains that it applies only to the special case of a competitive consumer with a single-valued demand function. Is there room for generalizing the Samuelson-Houthakker theory of rationalizability beyond this narrow cage?

To bring the theory of rationality along the line of Samuelson and Houthakker to its completion, two responses soon evolved in the literature. The first response came from Arrow (1959) and Sen (1971), whereas the second response came from Marcel Richter (1966; 1971) and Bengt Hansson (1968). On the one hand, Arrow and Sen developed a theory of rationality as rationalizability for a multivalued choice function whose domain contains the family $\mathcal{K}_F$ of nonempty *finite* subsets of an arbitrary universal set X of alternatives.[26] On the other hand, Richter and Hansson developed a theory for a choice function whose domain consists of arbitrary nonempty subsets of the universal set, viz., $\mathcal{K}_A$. It was about this time that I arrived in this field of research with two contributions, "Rational Choice and Revealed Preference" [Suzumura (1976, Essay 1 of this volume)] and "Houthakker's Axiom in the Theory of Rational Choice" [Suzumura (1977, Essay 2 of this volume)]. These approaches expanded the reach of revealed preference theory pioneered by Samuelson and Houthakker beyond the act of choice of a competitive consumer. Let us briefly discuss these extended theories of the act of choice one by one.

I.3.5. Rational Choice Functions on Finite Domains

It was Arrow (1959) who started the operation to go beyond the narrow cage of competitive consumer theory. When his *Economica* 1959 paper was

26. As a matter of fact, there is a delicate difference between Arrow's theory and Sen's theory in that, while Arrow assumed the domain $\mathcal{K}_F$, Sen showed that Arrow's theory can be extended beyond this domain in the sense that all we need is that the domain contains all pairs and triples taken from the universal set of all alternatives.

republished in *Collected Papers of Kenneth J. Arrow* (Vol. 3, *Individual Choice under Certainty and Uncertainty,* Harvard University Press, 1984), he added an introduction to the following effect: "The development of my work on social choice depended in part on an understanding of the relation between the choices from varying sets of alternatives and an underlying ordering of preferences. The ideas were indeed related to Paul Samuelson's concept of revealed preference, but unlike that work mine took an abstract view of the domains of choice instead of confining them to budget sets. This led to a different perspective and indeed to a different set of results. When only budget sets are considered, the weak axiom of revealed preference is not sufficient to imply the existence of an ordering; but it is sufficient when choice from all finite sets is considered." Thus, "the demand-function point of view would be greatly simplified if the range over which the choice functions are considered to be determined is broadened to include all finite sets."[27]

Arrow's original insight enticed Sen (1971), Charles Plott (1973), Douglas Blair, Georges Bordes, Jerry Kelly and Kotaro Suzumura (1976, Essay 5 of this volume), Thomas Schwartz (1976), and many others to follow suit. The preponderance of successsive work, together with Arrow's (1959, p. 107) observation to the effect that "requiring the choice functions to be defined for finite sets is thoroughly consistent with the intuitive arguments underlying revealed preference," seems to have paved the way toward overwhelming dominance of the theory of rational choice as rationalizable choice along the lines of Arrow and Sen.

Having said this, however, there are at least two reasons to think that it is premature to subscribe to this point of view without reservation. In the first place, suppose that the convexity assumption is imposed on each opportunity set belonging to the domain of the choice function C, which is not at all a pathological assumption to make in many parts of economic theory. Suppose that two alternatives x and y are available for choice. Then the whole closed interval $[x, y]$, and not just the pair set $\{x, y\}$, must be contained in the opportunity set. Thus, there exists no possibility of having a pair set $\{x, y\}$ in the domain of the choice function under convexity. In the second place, we would like to establish the theory of rational choice as rationalizable choice that is general enough not to hinge squarely on special

27. Arrow (1959, p. 122).

structural assumptions on the domain of choice functions, but to be based only on the logic of choice per se. In other words, the theory that we seek should treat the class of choice functions defined on an arbitrary domain $\mathcal{K}_A$. If such a theory can be constructed, any verdict brought about by the general theory of rational choice can be applied not only to the single-valued choice function c on the competitive budget domain $\mathcal{K}_{CB}$ as well as to the multivalued choice function C on the finite domain $\mathcal{K}_F$, but also to whatever choice function on any domain that we may care to specify. It is to this general theory of rational choice as rationalizable choice that we now turn.

I.3.6. Rational Choice Functions on Arbitrary Domains

As Nigel Howard (1971, p. xvii) pointed out in a different context, "cold winds blow through unstructured sets." This aphorism applies above all to the theory of rational choice functions C on an arbitrary domain $\mathcal{K}_A$. Reflecting this difficulty, the general theory of rational choice as rationalizable choice has been rather slow to unfold. Although Richter (1966; 1971), Hansson (1968), and Suzumura (1976, Essay 1 of this volume; 1977, Essay 2 of this volume) made their early contributions with basic importance from the late 1960s until the late 1970s, further results on the theory of rational choice as rationalizable choice on the general domain had to wait until Walter Bossert, Yves Sprumont, and Kotaro Suzumura (2005, Essay 3 of this volume; 2005a; 2006) and Bossert and Suzumura (2009; 2010) succeeded in pushing forward the theory of rational choice functions on general domains so as to cover various grades of rationalizability.

To begin with, a succinct summary of the classical contributions by Richter, Hansson, and Suzumura may be in order. Let C be a choice function on an arbitrary domain $\mathcal{K}_A$. The *direct revealed preference relation* R_C and the *direct revealed strict preference relation* R_C^S are defined by

$$R_C = \{(x, y) \in X \times X \mid \exists\, S \in \mathcal{K}_A : x \in C(S) \ \&\ y \in S\} \qquad \text{(I.7)}$$

and

$$R_C^S = \{(x, y) \in X \times X \mid \exists\, S \in \mathcal{K}_A : x \in C(S) \ \&\ y \in S \setminus C(S)\}, \quad \text{(I.8)}$$

respectively. The *indirect revealed preference relation* of a choice function C is the transitive closure $T(R_C)$ of R_C, whereas the *indirect revealed strict preference relation* of a choice function C is the transitive closure $T(R_C^S)$ of R_C^S.

We are now ready to introduce three revealed preference axioms.

WEAK AXIOM OF REVEALED PREFERENCE (WARP). $\forall\, x, y \in X : (x, y) \in R_C^S \Rightarrow (y, x) \notin R_C$

STRONG AXIOM OF REVEALED PREFERENCE (SARP). $\forall\, x, y \in X : (x, y) \in T(R_C^S) \Rightarrow (y, x) \notin R_C$

HOUTHAKKER'S AXIOM OF REVEALED PREFERENCE (HARP). $\forall\, x, y \in X : (x, y) \in T(R_C) \Rightarrow (y, x) \notin R_C^S$

It is easy to confirm that these axioms defined for the choice function C on $\mathcal{K}_A$ are natural generalizations of the axioms introduced by Samuelson (1938; 1938a; 1950a) and Houthakker (1950) in the specific context of the single-valued choice function c on $\mathcal{K}_{CB}$. It can also be verified that these axioms are arranged in descending order of logical strength as follows:

$$\text{(HARP)} \Rightarrow \text{(SARP)} \Rightarrow \text{(WARP)}.$$

In this logical implication diagram, the reverse arrow does not hold in general.[28]

In addition to these axioms, we introduce two further axioms due to Richter (1966; 1971).

DIRECT REVELATION COHERENCE (DRC). $\forall\, S \in \mathcal{K}_A, \forall\, x \in S : [\forall\, y \in S : (x, y) \in R_C \Rightarrow x \in C(S)]$

TRANSITIVE CLOSURE COHERENCE (TCC). $\forall\, S \in \mathcal{K}_A, \forall\, x \in S : [\forall\, y \in S : (x, y) \in T(R_C) \Rightarrow x \in C(S)]$

The meaning of these axioms should be straightforward to spell out.

28. In the presence of some special assumptions either on the properties of choice functions or on the domains thereof, some of these axioms may turn out to be equivalent. Indeed, we have already noted that (HARP) and (SARP) coincide for a single-valued choice function c defined on the competitive budget domain $\mathcal{K}_{CB}$. It is also true that (HARP), (SARP) and (WARP) coincide for the choice function C defined on the finite domain $\mathcal{K}_F$.

At this juncture of our analysis, let us formally introduce the concept of *grades of rationality* of the choice function C on an arbitrary domain $\mathcal{K}_A$.

Rationality (R). The choice function C on an arbitrary domain $\mathcal{K}_A$ has a rationalization $R \subseteq X \times X$.

Acyclic Rationality (AR). The choice function C on an arbitrary domain $\mathcal{K}_A$ has an acyclic rationalization $R \subseteq X \times X$.

Quasitransitive Rationality (QTR). The choice function C on an arbitrary domain $\mathcal{K}_A$ has a quasi-transitive rationalization $R \subseteq X \times X$.

Suzumura-Consistent Rationality (SCR). The choice function C on an arbitrary domain $\mathcal{K}_A$ has a Suzumura-consistent rationalization $R \subseteq X \times X$.

Full Rationality (FR). The choice function C on an arbitrary domain $\mathcal{K}_A$ has a rationalization $R \subseteq X \times X$ that is an ordering.

It is easy to verify that there is some order of logical strength among these axioms. Indeed, we have (i) (FR) $\Rightarrow$ (QTR) $\Rightarrow$ (AR) $\Rightarrow$ (R) and (ii) (FR) $\Rightarrow$ (SCR) $\Rightarrow$ (AR) $\Rightarrow$ (R), where the reverse arrow does not hold in general, and (iii) (QTR) and (SCR) are logically independent.[29]

The classical theorems due to Richter (1966), Hansson (1968), and Suzumura (1977) focused on the axiomatic characterization of full rational choice functions C on an arbitrary domain $\mathcal{K}_A$ by means of one or the other of the revealed preference axioms.

The main theorem of the Richter-Hansson-Suzumura theory can be stated as follows:

Theorem I.4 (Richter (1966); Hansson (1968); Suzumura (1977)). A choice function C on an arbitrary domain $\mathcal{K}_A$ is full rational if and only if it satisfies Houthakker's axiom of revealed preference (HARP).[30]

---

29. See Suzumura (1983) and Bossert and Suzumura (2010) for the proof of these implications.

30. Richter's axiom of transitive closure coherence (TCC) can replace Houthakker's axiom of revealed preference (HARP) in Theorem I.4 to obtain Richter's characterization theorem. The readers who are interested in Hansson's axiom for alternative characterization are referred to Hansson (1968) and Suzumura (1983, Appendix A to Chapter 2).

In addition to this main theorem, Richter (1971) could identify the necessary and sufficient condition for a choice function C on an arbitrary domain $\mathcal{K}_A$ to be rational.

THEOREM I.5 (RICHTER (1971)). A choice function C on an arbitrary domain $\mathcal{K}_A$ is rational if and only if it satisfies direct revelation coherence (DRC).

Enough has been said of the Richter-Hansson-Suzumura theory of rational choice as rationalizable choice in the early phase of its evolution. Although their theory could characterize the polar extreme cases of full rationality and rationality per se in terms of revealed preference axioms, the intermediate grades of rationality, viz., SCR, QTR and AR, were left unaccounted for. It was not until the work by Bossert, Sprumont, and Suzumura (2005, Essay 3 of this volume; 2005a; 2006) and Bossert and Suzumura (2009; 2010) that these lacunae were filled in. To illustrate the nature of their work by means of an example, we introduce an auxiliary concept and a new revealed preference axiom. According to Theorem I.1, the transitive closure $T(R)$ of a binary relation R is the smallest transitive superset of R. Analogously, we define the *Suzumura-consistent closure* $SC(R)$ of R as the smallest Suzumura-consistent superset of R. As Bossert, Sprumont, and Suzumura (2005, Essay 3 of this volume) and Bossert and Suzumura (2010, p. 39) confirmed, the Suzumura-consistent closure $SC(R)$ of R has an explicit representation, which reads as follows:

$$SC(R) = R \cup \{(x, y) \in X \times X \mid (x, y) \in T(R) \;\&\; (y, x) \in R\}. \quad \text{(I.9)}$$

It should also be noted that, just as a binary relation R is transitive if and only if $R = T(R)$, R is Suzumura-consistent if and only if $R = SC(R)$. For the proof, see Bossert and Suzumura (2010, Theorem 2.1 and Theorem 2.4). The concept of the Suzumura-consistent closure is instrumental to introduce the following revealed preference axiom for the choice function C defined on an arbitrary domain $\mathcal{K}_A$.

SUZUMURA-CONSISTENT CLOSURE COHERENCE (SCCC). $\forall\, S \in \mathcal{K}_A \;\&\; \forall\, x \in S: [\forall\, y \in S : (x, y) \in SC(R_C) \Rightarrow x \in C(S)]$

It should be clear that SCCC is closely parallel to DRC and TCC, which we have introduced in relation to Richter's characterization of rationality (R) and full rationality (FR).

We are now ready to present the characterization theorem for Suzumura-consistent rationalizability.

THEOREM I.6 (BOSSERT, SPRUMONT, AND SUZUMURA (2005, ESSAY 3 OF THIS VOLUME); BOSSERT AND SUZUMURA (2010)). A choice function C on an arbitrary domain $\mathcal{K}_A$ is Suzumura-consistent rational if and only if C satisfies the axiom of Suzumura-consistent closure coherence (SCCC).

So much for the brief overview of the theory of rationality as rationalizaility, which should suffice as an introduction to Part I of this volume. We are now ready to proceed to the theory of collective decision making along the passage paved by Arrow in his great classic, *Social Choice and Individual Values*.

I.4. Social Choice Theory with or without Collective Rationality

The institutional framework of a society consists of the rules of social decision making, the rules of remuneration and compensation, and the rules of conflict resolution. Some of these rules are spontaneously evolved and legally authorized, whereas other rules are based on the deliberate human design. Arrow's social choice theory is focused on the possibility of the rational design of social decision making rule that embodies the idea of democracy.

I.4.1. Social Choice and Individual Values

Suppose that there are a finite number n of *individuals,* where $2 \leq n < +\infty$, who form a collectivity called *society* $N = \{1, 2, \ldots, n\}$. By judicious collaboration, the society can attain a consequential outcome in an opportunity set, which is unattainable if individuals cannot but act in isolation. Let X be the universal set of consequential outcomes, which contains at least three *social alternatives,* viz., $3 \leq \#X$. Let $\mathcal{S}$ be the family of potential opportunity sets. A typical member of $\mathcal{S}$ will be denoted by S that satisfies $\emptyset \neq S \subseteq X$. Throughout what follows, we assume that individuals are fully rational in the sense specified in Section I.3. For each individual $i \in N$, let R_i denote a full rationalization of his/her act of choice from each opportunity set $S \in \mathcal{S}$, together forming a profile $\boldsymbol{R} = (R_1, R_2, \ldots, R_n)$ of individual preference orderings.[31]

We are interested in a society based on the democratic method of collective decision making, so that the social choice should take due account of the individuals' wishes expressed by the profile $\boldsymbol{R}$ of individual preference orderings. It follows that the social choice function C defined on the family $\mathcal{S}$ of potential opportunity sets must be responsive to the specification of the profile $\boldsymbol{R}$. This basic idea can be neatly articulated as follows. The social choice function C on $\mathcal{S}$ hinges parametrically on $\boldsymbol{R}$. Thus:

$$\forall S \in \mathcal{S} : [C(S, \boldsymbol{R}) \subseteq S \ \& \ C(S, \boldsymbol{R}) \neq \emptyset]. \tag{I.10}$$

In *Social Choice and Individual Values,* Arrow assumed that the social choice function should also be fully rationalized by means of a social preference ordering R that depends on the profile $\boldsymbol{R} = (R_1, R_2, \ldots, R_n)$. The function f that maps each profile $\boldsymbol{R}$ into a social preference ordering R is called the *Arrovian social welfare function*.[32] Thus, $R = f(\boldsymbol{R})$ for each admissible profile $\boldsymbol{R}$. Equipped with Arrovian concepts, we are in the position to express the social choice function $C(S, \boldsymbol{R})$ as follows:

$$C(S, \boldsymbol{R}) = G(S, f(\boldsymbol{R})) \text{ for all } S \in \mathcal{S}$$
$$\text{and for all admissible } \boldsymbol{R} = (R_1, R_2, \ldots, R_n). \tag{I.11}$$

31. No individual $i \in N$ is in the position of choosing a social alternative from each opportunity set $S \in \mathcal{S}$ by him/herself unless he/she is a *dictator*. However, the counterfactual preference in the sense of what he/she would choose if he/she were in the position to choose on behalf of the society seems to be a perfectly legitimate epistemological basis for the analysis of social choice.
32. The social welfare function f is called *Arrovian* because Bergson (1938) and Samuelson (1947, Chapter VIII) introduced the concept of a social welfare function of their own, which is related to, but distinct from Arrow's concept. Let g be a *Bergson-Samuelson social welfare function*. For each profile $\boldsymbol{R} = (R_1, R_2, \ldots, R_n)$ of individual preference orderings, the Arrow social welfare function f and the Bergson-Samuelson social welfare function g are related as follows:

$$\forall x, y \in X : g(x) \geq g(y) \Leftrightarrow xRy,$$

where $R = f(\boldsymbol{R})$. Thus, the Bergson-Samuelson social welfare function g is nothing other than the numerical representation of the social preference ordering R generated for each profile $\boldsymbol{R}$ by the Arrow social welfare function f.

Arrow is concerned with the characterization of democratic methods of collective decision making by means of a set of axioms imposed on the Arrovian social welfare function f.

I.4.2. Arrow's General Impossibility Theorem

Arrow's axioms imposed on f are meant to capture the spirit of democratic methods of collective decision making without requiring too much information on individual preference orderings. These axioms are listed as follows.[33]

Axiom U (unrestricted domain). The domain of f consists of all logically possible profiles of individual preference orderings.

Axiom P (Pareto principle). For any pair of social alternatives $x, y \in X$ and for any admissible profile $\boldsymbol{R} = (R_1, R_2, \ldots, R_n)$ of individual preference orderings, if $x P(R_i) y$ holds for all $i \in N$, then $x P(R) y$ must also hold, where $R = f(\boldsymbol{R})$.

Axiom I (independence of irrelevant alternatives). Let $x, y \in X$ be any two social alternatives, and let $\boldsymbol{R} = (R_1, R_2, \ldots, R_n)$ and $\boldsymbol{R}^* = (R_1^*, R_2^*, \ldots, R_n^*)$ be any two admissible profiles of individual preference orderings. If R_i and R_i^* coincide on the set $\{x, y\}$ for all $i \in N$, then R as well as R^* must also coincide on $\{x, y\}$, where $R = f(\boldsymbol{R})$ and $R^* = f(\boldsymbol{R}^*)$.[34]

Axiom D (nondictatorship). There should be no dictator in the society with the Arrow social welfare function f, where an individual $d \in N$ is called a *dictator* for f if and only if

$$x P(R_d) y \Rightarrow x P(R) y \tag{I.12}$$

holds for any pair of social alternatives $x, y \in X$ and any admissible profile $\boldsymbol{R} = (R_1, R_2, \ldots, R_n)$ of individual preference orderings, where $R = f(\boldsymbol{R})$.

---

33. As a matter of fact, Arrow (1951) introduced a more sophisticated set of axioms, but we do not go into this version throughout this work.

34. Two binary relations Q and R on X are said to coincide on the set $\{x, y\} \subseteq X$ if and only if $Q \cap (\{x, y\} \times \{x, y\}) = R \cap (\{x, y\}\} \times \{x, y\})$ holds.

Arrow's axioms are easy to interpret. Axiom U requires that all individuals are free to express whatever preference orderings they may care to specify as long as they are logically admissible in the sense of being complete, reflexive, and transitive. Since we are concerned with the design of a democratic method of collective decision making, the social welfare function under consideration should be such that individuals are conferred the full freedom of expressing their preferences.

Arrow's axiom P is the familiar *Pareto principle*. Although Section I.6 is devoted to the conflict between the classical Pareto principle and the requirement of individual libertarian rights, we should be carefully on guard if we wish to escape from the cage of the Pareto principle in view of its almost invincible status in "new" welfare economics.

Arrow's axiom I is a requirement of *informational efficiency* of the method of collective decision making. To decide on the relative worth of the two social alternatives x and y for the society, we have only to know the restriction of each profile $\boldsymbol{R} = (R_1, R_2, \ldots, R_n)$ to the set $\{x, y\}$ if the method of collective decision making satisfies Arrow's axiom I, thereby greatly saving on the informational inputs required for making social choice.

Finally, Arrow's axiom D requires that the extreme inequality of decision making power in the form of a dictatorship should not be allowed in a democratic society.

Although each one of these axioms imposes a constraint on the admissible class of the rules of collective decision making, it is hard to imagine that the admissible class of collective decision making rules will be substantially reduced by means of Arrow's innocuous-looking four axioms. Indeed, the total number of the methods of collective decision making is astronomically large even in the small society where $n = 2$ and $\#X = 3$.[35] This being the case, the following result established by Arrow (1963) and known as the *Arrow general impossibility theorem* was a real bombshell.

Theorem I.7 (Arrow (1963/2012)). Suppose that the number of individuals is finite and at least two, and the number of social alternatives is at least three.

35. For the sake of simplicity, let us assume that the admissible class of individual and social preference orderings does not allow indifference. Then the total number of admissible preference orderings over three alternatives is 6, so that the total number of admissible profiles of individual preference orderings is $6 \times 6 = 36$. Thus, the total number of Arrow's social welfare functions is 6^{36}, which can be verified to exceed the Avogadro constant.

Then there exists no Arrovian social welfare function that satisfies axiom U, axiom P, axiom I, and axiom D.

How, then, can we find reasonable escape routes from Arrow's impasse?

I.4.3. Social Choice Theory with Less-Than-Full Collective Rationality

From the point of view of this volume, the most relevant step in examining possible escape routes from Arrow's impasse is the one that was explored by Sen (1969; 1970a, Chapter 4*), who retained everything of Arrow's framework as well as his axioms except for making a small concession on Arrow's collective rationality requirement. Instead of full collective rationality that Arrow required, Sen replaced it with quasi-transitive rationality and obtained a rule of collective decision making satisfying all of axiom U, axiom P, axiom I, and axiom D. Sen proved this possibility theorem by means of a concrete example, which he christened the *Pareto extension rule*. Let R^P be defined for any $x, y \in X$ and any profile $\boldsymbol{R} = (R_1, R_2, \ldots, R_n)$ by

$$xR^P y \Leftrightarrow \forall i \in N : xR_i y, \tag{I.13}$$

which enables us to define R^E by $xR^E y \Leftrightarrow \neg\, yR^P x$. This R^E is demonstrably quasi-transitive, but not necessarily transitive. Sen's *Pareto extension rule* f^{PE} associates this R^E with each profile $\boldsymbol{R}$: $R^E = f^{PE}(\boldsymbol{R})$. It is easy to verify that f^{PE}, thus defined, satisfies all of the axioms that Arrow required except for full rationality of social choice functions.

This is a remarkable result, but we should not forget that Sen himself intended his possibility theorem to bear testimony to the conspicuous delicacy of the Arrow general impossibility theorem. Although even a minor concession on Arrow's requirement of collective rationality can secure the existence of an eligible rule, it was far from Sen's intention to advocate the Pareto extension rule per se as a "good" rule of democratic decision making.

Soon after Sen had caused a stir in the social choice circle, Andreu Mas-Colell and Hugo Sonnenschein (1972) effectively closed the door Sen opened by showing that the social welfare functions are incapable of satisfying a slightly strengthened version of Arrow's axioms that are still democratic in nature. It is worthwhile to emphasize that the impossibility theorems due to Mas-Colell and Sonnenschein covered not only the replacement of Arrow's full rationality with Sen's quasi-transitive rationality but also the replacement of Arrow's full rationality with a weaker requirement of acyclic rationality. In effect, then, Mas-Colell and Sonnenschein called back the negative impact of Arrow's general impossibility theorem.[36] The main message of their work is straightforward. The phantom uncovered by Arrow cannot be exorcised so easily by a straightforward weakening of his requirement of collective full rationality.

However, it is premature to conclude that the escape route via the weakening of collective rationality à la Arrow is a complete blind alley. It is true that the potential escape route from Arrow's impasse through the successive weakening of the requirement of collective rationality, starting from full rationality through quasi-transitive rationality, and finishing with acyclic rationality, is essentially closed by Mas-Colell and Sonnenschein.[37] However, we should recollect that there exists an alternative route of successively weakening the requirement of collective rationality, starting from full rationality, going through Suzumura-consistent rationality, and finishing with acyclic rationality. Along this alternative route, both ends of the route are known to be incompatible with the rest of Arrow's axioms by virtue of Arrow's impossibility theorem and the Mas-Colell and Sonnenschein impossibility theorem. That leaves us with a single possibility that is open for our challenge, which is to ask whether or not there exists an Arrovian social welfare function that satisfies Suzumura-consistent rationality. Since a Suzumura-consistent relation R reduces to a full ordering if it satisfies reflexivity and completeness, the attempt to find an escape route from Arrow's impasse through the weakening of his full rationality to Suzumura-consistent rationality makes sense only when we are ready to discard the requirement of reflexivity and

---

36. It should be noted that Arrow's axiom U, axiom P, axiom I, and axiom D are meant to form a set of *minimal necessary conditions* for his social welfare function to be democratic. The Mas-Colell and Sonnenschein strengthenings of Arrow's minimal necessary conditions seem to retain reasonableness as necessary (but not *minimally necessary*) conditions for Arrow's social welfare function to be democratic.

37. It may be asked, Why should we stop at the requirement of collective acyclic rationality when there is an even weaker requirement of collective rationality pure and simple? The answer lies in the original Arrovian scenario of expounding social *choice* by means of social *preference*. As was shown by Sen (1970a, Lemma 1*1), in order for a choice function $C(S) = G(S, R)$ to be well defined for each nonempty *finite* set $S \subseteq X$ and a reflexive and complete social preference relation R, it is necessary and sufficient that R be acyclic over X.

completeness of rationalization. The search for escape routes along this scenario was raised and answered by Bossert and Suzumura (2008, Essay 8 of this volume) in the affirmative. The Arrovian axioms of social welfare functions required by Bossert and Suzumura are axiom U, axiom SP (strong Pareto principle), axiom A (anonymity), and axiom N (neutrality) along with Suzumura-consistent rationality. Axiom SP, axiom A, and axiom N are formulated as follows.

Axiom SP (strong Pareto principle). For any pair of social alternatives $x, y \in X$, and for any admissible profile $\boldsymbol{R} = (R_1, R_2, \ldots, R_n)$ of individual preference orderings,

(a) if xR_iy holds for all $i \in N$, then xRy must also hold, where $R = f(\boldsymbol{R})$;
(b) if xR_iy holds for all $i \in N$ and $xP(R_j)y$ holds for some $j \in N$, then $xP(R)y$ must also hold, where $R = f(\boldsymbol{R})$.

Axiom A (anonymity). For any one-to-one mapping $\sigma : N \to N$ and for any admissible profiles $\boldsymbol{R} = (R_1, R_2, \ldots, R_n)$ and $\boldsymbol{R}^* = (R_1^*, R_2^*, \ldots, R_n^*)$ of individual preference orderings, if $R_i = R_{\sigma(i)}^*$ holds for all $i \in N$, then $R = R^*$ must also hold, where $R = f(\boldsymbol{R})$ and $R^* = f(\boldsymbol{R}^*)$.[38]

Axiom N (neutrality). For any social alternatives $x, y, z, w \in X$ and for any admissible profiles $\boldsymbol{R} = (R_1, R_2, \ldots, R_n)$ and $\boldsymbol{R}^* = (R_1^*, R_2^*, \ldots, R_n^*)$ of individual preference orderings, if $xR_iy \Leftrightarrow zR_i^*w$ and $yR_ix \Leftrightarrow wR_i^*z$ hold for all $i \in N$, then $xRy \Leftrightarrow zR^*w$ and $yRx \Leftrightarrow wR^*z$ must also hold, where $R = f(\boldsymbol{R})$ and $R^* = f(\boldsymbol{R}^*)$.[39]

Since axiom SP is a natural strengthening of the familiar axiom P, we have only to give an intuitive meaning of axiom A and axiom N. Axiom A just requires that the social preference relation R corresponding to a profile $\boldsymbol{R} = (R_1, R_2, \ldots, R_n)$, viz., $R = f(\boldsymbol{R})$, should remain invariant even when we reshuffle the individual preference orderings among individuals. Thus, a social welfare function that satisfies axiom A treats all individuals in the

38. It should be clear that axiom A is a stronger requirement than axiom D.
39. It should be observed that axiom N is a stronger requirement than axiom I.

society anonymously. Likewise, a social welfare function that satisfies axiom N treats all alternatives neutrally. These axioms seem reasonable enough to impose on the admissible class of social welfare functions.

To prepare for the main theorem of Bossert and Suzumura (2008, Essay 8 of this volume), let a set $\mathcal{M} \subseteq \{0, 1, \ldots, n\} \times \{0, 1, \ldots, n\}$ be defined by

$$\mathcal{M} = \{(w, l) \in \{0, \ldots, n\}^2 \mid 0 \leq l \,\#X < w + l \leq n\} \cup \{(0, 0)\}. \quad \text{(I.14)}$$

Making use of (I.14), we can further define a family $\mathcal{F}_{\mathcal{M}}$ of the subsets of $\mathcal{M}$ by

$$\mathcal{F}_{\mathcal{M}} = \{M \subseteq \mathcal{M} \mid \forall w \in \{0, \ldots, n\} : (w, 0) \in M\}. \quad \text{(I.15)}$$

As an auxiliary step in defining what we christen the *M-rule*, where $M \in \mathcal{F}_{\mathcal{M}}$, let us define, for any social alternatives $x, y \in X$, and any profile $\boldsymbol{R} = (R_1, R_2, \ldots, R_n)$ of individual preference orderings, a subset $B(x, y; \boldsymbol{R}) \subseteq N$ as the set of individuals who strictly prefer x to y under $\boldsymbol{R}$. We are now ready to define the M-rule, which we denote f^M, by $R^M = f^M(\boldsymbol{R})$ for each profile $\boldsymbol{R}$, where R^M is defined by

$$xR^My \Leftrightarrow \exists\ (w, l) \in M : \#B(x, y; \boldsymbol{R}) = w \ \&\ \#B(y, x; \boldsymbol{R}) = l \quad \text{(I.16)}$$

for each and every $x, y \in X$. The Bossert and Suzumura theorem reads as follows.

Theorem I.8 (Bossert and Suzumura (2008, Essay 8 of this volume)). A Suzumura-consistent social welfare function f satisfies axiom U, axiom SP, axiom A, and axiom N if and only if there exists $M \in \mathcal{F}_{\mathcal{M}}$ such that $f = f^M$ holds.

This is clearly a possibility theorem as well as a characterization theorem rather than an impossibility theorem. A further question to be asked and answered is the following: How strong is the possibility thereby secured? As an auxiliary step to answer this question, let us formally define the *Pareto rule* f^P as a social welfare function f^P that maps each profile $\boldsymbol{R}$ into R^P, where R^P is defined by (I.13). It is clear that the Pareto rule is the special case of Suzumura-consistent social welfare function f^{M_0}, where $M_0 = \{(w, 0) \mid w \in \{0, \ldots, n\}\}$. If $\#X \geq n$, this f^{M_0} is the *only* M-rule.

This is the case because only pairs (w, l) with $l = 0$ are in M under $\#X \geq n$. To verify this fact, suppose to the contrary that there exists $(w, l) \in M$ such that $l > 0$. It follows from $(w, l) \in M$ that $n \geq w + l > l\#X > 0$. If we combine this with $\#X \geq n$, we obtain $n > nl$, which is impossible if $l > 0$. It follows that our characterization of the class of M-rules provides an alternative characterization of the Pareto rule in the case where $\#X \geq n$.[40] However, if $\#X < n$, the class of M-rules is much wider than the Pareto rule. Thus, in applications where there are many voters and relatively few candidates, it follows from Theorem I.8 that it is possible to go considerably beyond the limitations of unanimity imposed by the Pareto rule.

We have thus identified the real escape route from the Arrow impossibility theorem by weakening Arrow's full rationality postulate into Suzumura-consistent rationality at the cost of disposing reflexivity and completeness of social preference relations. This result may fall short of dissipating the gloomy cloud of Arrow's general impossibility theorem by one stroke. However, the arena of welfare economics and social choice theory is slippery, and even small progress may be worthwhile to keep on record.

We are now in the stage of going one further step and making a search for more radical resolutions of Arrow's impasse.

I.4.4. "Irrational" Social Goals and Robustness of Impossibility Theorems

Among Arrow's incompatible axioms on democratic social welfare functions, one of the most debatable and harshly debated axioms is that of collective full rationality. The earliest criticism came from James Buchanan (1954), who argued as follows: "The mere introduction of the idea of social rationality suggests the fundamental philosophical issues involved. Rationality or irrationality as an attribute of the social group implies the imputation to the group of an organic existence apart from that of its individual components. . . . We may adopt the philosophical bases of individualism in which

40. Our characterization of the Pareto rule for the case where $\#X \geq n$ may be compared with the standard characterization result due to John Weymark (1984), which was proved with no constraint on $\#X$ vis-à-vis n. The crucial difference lies in the fact that we weaken Weymark's transitivity condition that he imposed on the social preference relation to Suzumura consistency, and we strengthen his axiom I into axiom N.

the individual is the only entity possessing ends or values. In this case no question of social or collective rationality may be raised. A social value scale simply does not exist. Alternatively, we may adopt some variant of the organic philosophical assumption in which the collectivity is an independent entity possessing its own value ordering. It is legitimate to test the rationality or irrationality of this entity only against this value ordering."[41] Thus, Buchanan claimed in effect that the use of the concept of collective rationality in the individualistic conceptual framework is an illegitimate transplantation of a property that makes sense only for individuals.

When I interviewed Paul Samuelson on behalf of *Social Choice and Welfare,* one of the questions I asked his opinion about was his response to Buchanan's criticism on Arrow's collective rationality postulate. Samuelson's answer was a categorical rejection of Buchanan's stance: "I don't at all agree with [Buchanan's] position. It boils down to the claim that, if it is a social choice in an individualistic society that is being analyzed, then you should not be interested in any degree of rationality, consistency, or transitivity at the social level. This would be like an answer from fallacy. It seems to be a Humpty-Dumptyism. Humpty Dumpty says: 'If I say a thing twice, then it is true.' I see no reason to think that there is any cogent force in Buchanan's argument. What he says boils down to the statement: 'I, Buchanan, have no interest in that.' He gives no reason why other reasonable men should go along with him."[42]

Arrow's own reply to Buchanan took a different course. Indeed, he presented the first serious argument in support of the requirement of collective full rationality. In his own parlance, "collective rationality in the social choice mechanism is not . . . merely an illegitimate transfer from the individual to society, but an important attribute of a genuinely democratic system capable of full adaptation to varying environments," because it avoids the "democratic paralysis—failure to act, not because of desire for inaction but because of inability to agree on the proper action—by guaranteeing 'the independence of the final choice from the path to it.'"[43] Thus, Arrow's defense of collective rationality boils down to the claim that it ensures the *path*

41. Buchanan (1954, p. 116).
42. Suzumura (2005, p. 341).
43. Arrow (1963, p. 120).

independence of social choice procedures. Is this a legitimate justification of Arrow's requirement of collective full rationality?

It was Charles Plott (1973) who succeeded in formalizing the concept of path independence, which enabled us to scrutinize the validity of Arrow's defense of collective full rationality. The formal articulation of Plott's concept of path independence goes as follows:

Axiom PI (path independence). For all $S_1, S_2 \in \mathcal{S}$, $C(S_1 \cup S_2) = C(C(S_1) \cup C(S_2))$.

To understand the intuitive meaning of axiom PI, suppose that we are in the position of choosing from a "large" opportunity set $S \in \mathcal{S}$. To facilitate the social choice from S, we may take recourse to the conventional wisdom of "divide and conquer." Suppose that there are two methods—two alternative paths—of dividing the original "large" problem S into the tractable "small" subproblems, viz., $S = S_1 \cup S_2$ and $S = S_1^* \cup S_2^*$. The tractable problems $\{S_1, S_2\}$ and $\{S_1^*, S_2^*\}$ can be solved by invoking the choice mechanism C to obtain $\{C(S_1), C(S_2)\}$ and $\{C(S_1^*), C(S_2^*)\}$, respectively. If we want to secure "the independence of the final choice from the path to it," we must be assured of the following equality:

$$C(S) = C(C(S_1) \cup C(S_2)) = C(C(S_1^*) \cup C(S_2^*)). \tag{I.17}$$

This is, in essence, what the path independence axiom requires.

Can Arrow's argument by means of path independence justify his postulate of collective full rationality? It is easy to verify that the full rationality property—indeed even the weaker property of quasi-transitive rationality—implies the path-independence property, but not necessarily vice versa. Besides, the path independence property does not guarantee rationality per se of a choice function, to say nothing of its transitive rationality or full rationality.[44] Thus, Arrow's defense of the axiom of collective full rationality by means of the path independence property is not valid in general. As a matter of fact, if we replace Arrow's collective full rationality axiom by Plott's path-independence property, Arrow's original impossibility impasse can be circumvented, viz., there exists a method of constructing path-independent

44. See Suzumura (1983/2009, Chapter 2) for the proof of these assertions.

social choice functions that satisfies the Arrovian axioms of democracy. See Plott (1973) for further details.

Observe that the Arrow-Plott path independence property opened Pandora's box for identifying and exploring the class of interesting "irrational" choice functions with reasonable choice coherence properties. In order to avoid unjustifiable optimism, however, we must hasten to add that there is by now a large literature on nonbinary social choice theory, where essentially Arrovian impossibility results strenuously reemerge. Those who are interested in this development are cordially referred to Blair, Bordes, Kelly, and Suzumura (1976, Essay 5 of this volume), Sen (1977), and Rajat Deb (2011). No general escape route from Arrow's labyrinth seems open in this direction.

I.4.5. Multiprofile Intergenerational Social Choice

Throughout this section, the method of democratic decision making at stake has been that of direct democracy, where all individuals simultaneously participate in the social choice procedure. A conspicuous feature of this timeless conceptual framework is that there is no explicit consideration of sequential decision making. Time flows only in one direction, so that individuals, who belong to different generations, have no way of meeting, let alone interacting, with each other.[45] To capture the essence of intergenerational problems, we must go beyond traditional social choice models of the Arrow type.

It was John Ferejohn and Talbot Page (1978) who kicked off intergenerational social choice theory by identifying a set of axioms under which an Arrow social welfare function, *if one ever exists,* cannot but empower generation one to be the dictator of intergenerational social choice. Edward Packel (1980) answered the question Ferejohn and Page left open in the

45. Since there is no natural upper limit on the time horizon of intergenerational social choice problems, there will be a countably infinite number of generations to be included in the model of intergenerational social choice. Recollect that the Arrow general impossibility theorem hinges squarely on the finiteness of the society. Indeed, Peter Fishburn (1970), Amartya Sen (1979), and Kotaro Suzumura (2000, Essay 27 of this volume) made crucial use of this assumption of the finiteness of population to prove Arrow's general impossibility theorem. For timeless society with infinite populations, there exist nondictatorial social welfare functions satisfying Arrow's axioms, and they can be described by their corresponding collections of decisive coalitions.

negative by establishing a strong impossibility theorem: *Even without independence of irrelevant alternatives and without assuming social preferences to be transitive, no social aggregation function can satisfy unrestricted domain, weak Pareto, and the Koopmans-Ferejohn-Page stationarity axiom.* The Koopmans-Ferejohn-Page stationarity axiom, which was introduced in the intergenerational social choice context by Ferejohn and Page, reads as follows:[46] *If a common first-period alternative is eliminated from two infinite streams of per-period alternatives, then the resulting continuation streams must be ranked in the same way as the original streams in accordance with the social ranking obtained for the original profile.* It is true that Ferejohn and Page kicked off the multi-profile theory of intergenerational social choice, but their reformulation of the Koopmans stationarity in the intergenerational context invoked only a single profile of generational evaluation orderings. The impossibility theorem due to Packel pushed this single-profile nature even further by excluding the multi-profile axiom of independence of irrelevant alternatives altogether. As Bossert and Suzumura have shown, the Packel single-profile impossibility theorem can be strengthened much further: *Even without reflexivity and completeness, there exists no social aggregation function that satisfies unrestricted domain, weak Pareto, and single-profile stationarity.*

Although these negative verdicts on intergenerational social choice theory are not without interest, the crucial single-profile stationarity may lose intuitive appeal if the preferences of each generation are *selfish* in the sense that they depend only on the outcome for this generation. However, we may introduce a suitable version of *multi-profile* stationarity axiom to the following effect: For any two streams of per-period alternatives and for any preference profile, if the first-period alternatives are the same in the two streams, then the social ranking of the two streams according to this profile is the same as the social ranking that results if the common first-period alternative is removed *together with the preference ordering of generation one*. The main result of Bossert and Suzumura states that *a social welfare function f satisfies selfish domain, weak Pareto, Pareto indifference, independence of irrelevant alternatives, and multiprofile stationarity if and only if f is the lexi-*

46. Koopmans (1960) analyzed the problem of intergenerational resource allocation, where each generation has a *fixed* utility function. In this sense, Koopmans's problem has no direct and necessary connection with Arrow's multiprofile social choice theory.

cographic dictatorship in which the generations are taken into consideration in chronological order. Thus, although the infinite-population version of the Arrow social choice problem may permit nondictatorial rules, these additional possibilities cannot but vanish if multi-profile stationarity is imposed. It is in this sense that Arrow's phantom is alive and kicking even in the context of intergenerational social choice.[47]

I.5. Extended Sympathy and Fairness-as-No-Envy Approach

Two crucial features of Arrow's social choice scenario deserve special attention. In the first place, his original scenario of social choice in the first edition of *Social Choice and Individual Values* articulated the social decision making in an individualistic society in two steps. The first step was to aggregate the profile of individual preference orderings into the social preference ordering, whereas the second step was to generate the social choice from the set of feasible social alternatives by means of the optimization of social preference ordering subject to feasibility constraint. Keeping this dichotomous scenario due to Arrow intact, a string of subsequent work tried to discover an escape route from Arrow's impasse by weakening his stringent requirement of social full-rationality into weaker variants thereof. It was Arrow himself who, in the second edition of his classic, kicked off the attempt to go beyond the dichotomous social choice scenario altogether by focusing on the social choice function defined for each profile of individual preference orderings without the intermediation of social preference judgments. The first attempt to this effect was introduced with reference to the path independence of social choice procedures, but there is a large room for accommodating coherence properties of social choice function other than the path independence property. One of the major candidates of social coherence property is the equity and fairness of social choice to be made, which is the central focus of Part III of this volume.

In the second place, a remarkable feature of Arrow's social choice framework is his modest requirement of information about individual preference

47. See Bossert and Suzumura (2015) for a succinct survey of some relevant literature.

orderings. This is a virtue rather than a vice from the viewpoint of the social cost of information gathering and processing, as well as of the social respect for privacy of individuals. However, too much parsimony on the use of information may hinder the effective performance of social choice procedures. Let us begin with the examination of this problem by means of the pros and cons of Arrow's axiom of independence of irrelevant alternatives.

I.5.1. Informational Parsimony of the Arrovian Social Choice Theory

An insidious feature of social choice theory created by Arrow is the *informational parsimony* that prevails throughout his research program. On the one hand, the utilitarian tradition of maximizing the sum total of individual utilities was outlawed by the ordinalist revolution of microeconomic theory promoted in the 1930s by John Hicks (1939/1946) and Paul Samuelson (1938; 1938a; 1947), among others. The harsh criticism on the epistemological basis of Pigou's "old" welfare economics by Lionel Robbins (1932/1935) may be construed as the last straw in the attempt to leave the cardinal and interpersonally comparable informational basis and land on the ordinal and interpersonally noncomparable informational basis. Arrow's social choice theory was even more exacting in the parsimonious use of ordinal information in that it invoked the controversial axiom of the independence of irrelevant alternatives, which restricted the use of ordinal and interpersonally noncomparable individual preference information even further. Indeed, for any pair of social alternatives $\{x, y\} \subseteq X$, the information about *individual* preference orderings on the social alternatives lying outside $\{x, y\}$ should not exert any influence whatsoever on the *social* preference ordering over $\{x, y\}$.

There are two possible views one may take on the persuasiveness of axiom I. On the one hand, if our focal task is to make a social choice from $\{x, y\}$ on the basis of individual values, it seems *minimally necessary* to gather information about individual values over $\{x, y\}$, since otherwise the social choice from $\{x, y\}$ is made in full neglect of individual wishes for x (resp. y) against y (resp. x), thereby disqualifying the social choice procedure to be democratic. If the Arrow social welfare function satisfies axiom I, the social decision can be made only with this *minimally necessary* informational input and nothing else. For this reason, axiom I can be interpreted as the requirement of *informational efficiency* of the Arrow social welfare function. This positive view on the use and usefulness of axiom I seems to have appealed to many social choice theorists in the tradition of Marquis de Condorcet (1785), who used the simple majority decision rule as a standard of reference in thinking about democratic methods of collective decision making. For the sake of later reference, let us define the *simple majority decision relation* $M(\boldsymbol{R})$, the SMD relation for short, for each profile $\boldsymbol{R} = (R_1, R_2, \ldots, R_n)$ of individual preference orderings by

$$\forall\, x, y \in X : xM(\boldsymbol{R})y \Leftrightarrow B(x, y; \boldsymbol{R}) \geq B(y, x; \boldsymbol{R}). \qquad \text{(I.18)}$$

We may then define the *Condorcet selection function* $Con(S, \boldsymbol{R})$ on $\mathcal{S}$ as follows:

$$\forall\, S \in \mathcal{S} : Con(S, \boldsymbol{R}) := \{x^* \in S \mid \forall\, x \in S \setminus \{x^*\} : x^* P(M(\boldsymbol{R}))x\}. \qquad \text{(I.19)}$$

If $(S, \boldsymbol{R})$ is such that $Con(S, \boldsymbol{R}) \neq \emptyset$, the sole element in $Con(S, \boldsymbol{R})$, which defeats all other alternatives in S by the simple majority decision contest, is called the *Condorcet winner.* See Duncan Black (1958), among many others, for the role and appeal of the Condorcet winner in the theory of voting.

On the other hand, there are some others who are strongly attracted by the *rank-order method of collective decision making* proposed by Jean-Charles de Borda (1781), which may be formulated as follows: Given a profile $\boldsymbol{R} = (R_1, R_2, \ldots, R_n)$ of individual preference orderings and an opportunity set $S \in \mathcal{S}$, the *Borda count* for each $x \in S$ and each $i \in N$ is defined by

$$\beta_i(x : S, \boldsymbol{R}) := \#\, \{y \in S \mid xP(R_i)y\}, \qquad \text{(I.20)}$$

in terms of which the *Borda choice function* $Bor(S, \boldsymbol{R})$ on $\mathcal{S}$ is defined by

$$Bor(S, \boldsymbol{R}) := \{x \in S \mid \forall\, y \in S : \Sigma_{i \in N} \beta_i(x : S, \boldsymbol{R}) \geq \Sigma_{i \in N} \beta_i(y : S, \boldsymbol{R})\} \qquad \text{(I.21)}$$

for all $S \in \mathcal{S}$. It should be clear that the Borda choice function makes use of much richer information about individual preference orderings than the Condorcet selection function. From this point of view, axiom I may be construed to be excessively parsimonious in the use of ordinal preference information, thereby unduly precipitating Arrovian impossibility theorems. See Duncan Black (1958) and Peyton Young (1974), among many others, on the pros and cons of the Borda rule.

The informational parsimony of the Arrovian social choice theory is conspicuous and ubiquitous indeed. One of the focuses of the post-Arrow social choice theory was to reinstate the interpersonal comparisons of individual values as a crucial ingredient of the extended informational basis of social choice theory. It goes without saying that the simple atavism to the utilitarian sum total of individual utilities does not make sense in view of the historical evolution of ordinalist welfare economics and social choice theory. Can we find a sensible method of using interpersonal comparability of individual values without falling into this impasse?

I.5.2. Extended Sympathy: Adam Smith, Patrick Suppes, and Kenneth Arrow

The point of departure is nobody other than Adam Smith, whose major work on moral philosophy, viz., *The Theory of Moral Sentiments* [Smith (1739/2009)], started off with a simple observation to the following effect: "How selfish soever man may be supposed, there are evidently some principles in his nature, which interest him in the fortune of others, and render their happiness necessary to him, though he derives nothing from it except the pleasure of seeing it. Of this kind is pity or compassion, the emotion which we feel for the misery of others, when we either see it, or are made to conceive it in a very lively manner. That we often derive sorrow from the sorrow of others, is a matter of fact too obvious to require any instances to prove it; for this sentiment, like all the original passions of human nature, is by no means confined to the virtuous and humane, though they perhaps may feel it with the most exquisite sensibility. The greatest ruffian, the most hardened violator of the laws of society, is not altogether without it." However, "as we have no immediate experience of what other men feel, we can form no idea of the manner in which they are affected, but by conceiving what we ourselves should feel in the like situation." Indeed, we can place ourselves through the imaginary exchange of circumstances in the position of others and form some idea of their sensations. Smith continues: "That this is the source of our fellow-feeling for the misery of others, that it is by changing places in fancy with the sufferer, that we come either to conceive or to be affected by what he feels, may be demonstrated by many obvious observations, if it should not be thought sufficiently evident of itself."

The modern resurgence of the Smithian principle of sympathy was pioneered by Patrick Suppes (1957; 1966). Arrow (1963, Section IV; 1977/1983) eagerly endorsed Suppes's proposal and gave it the name *extended sympathy approach*: "People seem prepared to make comparisons of the form: State x is better (or worse) for me than state y is for you. This is certainly one way of approaching the notion of an appropriate income distribution; if I am richer than you, I may find it easy to make the judgment that it is better for you to have the marginal dollar than for me. The ordinalist would ask what possible meaning the comparison could have to anyone; a comparison should represent at least a conceivable choice among alternative actions. Interpersonal comparisons of the extended sympathy type can be put in operational form; the judgment takes the form: It is better (in my judgment) to be myself in state x than to be you in state y."

Not only did Arrow see through the potential relevance of the extended sympathy approach, but he also observed the important feature of this approach: "In this approach, the characteristics that define an individual are included in the comparison. In effect, these characteristics are put on a par with the items usually regarded as constituting an individual's wealth. The possession of tools would ordinarily be regarded as part of the social state; why not the possession of the skills to use the tools and the intelligence which lies behind those skills? Individuals, in appraising each other's states of well-being, consider not only material possessions but also find themselves 'desiring this man's scope and that man's art.'" This is where Arrow left the ground, as he recognized that "it is not easy to see how to construct a theory of social choice from this principle [of extended sympathy]." It was Sen (1970a, Chapter 9*) who succeeded him and developed a full-fledged social choice theory on the basis of the Smith-Suppes-Arrow extended sympathy approach.

Let x and y be two conventionally defined social alternatives, and i, j, and k be three individuals in the society. The pair (x, i) denotes the situation of being in the position of individual i when the social alternative x prevails. If i prefers x to y, keeping his own personal identity whichever alternative in $\{x, y\}$ prevails in the society, then we say that i prefers (x, i) to (y, i). If i prefers being in the position of j when x prevails to being in the position of k when y prevails, then we say that i prefers (x, j) to

(y, k). These preferences held by i are still not *interpersonal* comparisons of individual well-being, but *intrapersonal* and *intersituational* comparisons of him/herself. In this approach, nothing prevents us from encountering the situation where i prefers x to y, keeping his/her own identity intact whichever social alternative in $\{x, y\}$ may happen to prevail, whereas j, where $i \neq j$, prefers y to x even if he/she identifies him/herself with i by means of imaginary exchanges of *objective* circumstances under x as well as under y. In other words, no sympathy among individuals is assured to prevail in this framework of intrapersonal and intersituational comparisons.

It was in this context that Sen introduced what he christened the Axiom of Identity, Axiom ID for short, to the effect that j's (resp. i's) preference over the set of extended alternatives $\{(x, i), (y, i)\}$ (resp. $\{(x, j), (y, j)\}$) should be in full concordance with i's (resp. j's) preference over the same set $\{(x, i), (y, i)\}$ (resp. $\{(x, j), (y, j)\}$). In other words, when i (resp. j) places him/herself through imaginary exchanges of circumstances in j's (resp. i's) position, he/she should accept j's (resp. i's) *subjective* personal identities along with his/her *objective* circumstances. This seems a reasonable axiom to be required of intrapersonal and intersituational comparisons, but a further problem surfaces. By the imposition of Axiom ID, what started as intrapersonal and intersituational comparisons of well-being is turned into interpersonal comparisons thereof. It is our judgment that the interpersonal comparisons of the extended sympathy type thus formulated seem to be not only sensible but also fruitful in many important respects. To substantiate this judgment, the services rendered by this approach are illustrated in the next subsection by means of the issues of equity and justice in the simple context of a cake division.

Before leaving this subsection, it may not be superfluous to compare the informational basis of the Arrovian social choice approach, say, approach A, with that of the extended sympathy approach, say, approach E. For the sake of simplicity, suppose that there are two conventionally defined social alternatives x and y, and two individuals 1 and 2 in the society. It follows that there are altogether 4 extended social alternatives, viz., $(x, 1)$, $(y, 1)$, $(x, 2)$, and $(y, 2)$. In approach A, individual 1 (resp. individual 2) is asked to submit his/her preference ordering over $\{(x, 1), (y, 1)\}$ (resp. $\{(x, 2), (y, 2)\}$) and nothing else, whereas in approach E, individual 1 as well as individual 2 is asked to submit his/her preference ordering over $\{(x, 1), (y, 1), (x, 2), (y, 2)\}$. If axiom ID is assumed in approach E, individual preference orderings in approach A are coherently subsumed in the individual preference orderings in approach E. In this sense, approach E under axiom ID is a natural extension of approach A, viz., Arrow's social choice theory. The extended sympathy approach, which enlarges the informational basis of social choice theory in this sense, serves as the *principle of communication between individuals* [Morrow (1923, p. 29)] that will bring about coordination of the interests of the various individuals through the mutual adaptation of individual concerns.

I.5.3. Fairness-as-No-Envy Approach in the Theory of Social Choice

To motivate our succeeding analyses, let us begin with a simple cake division problem.

Example I.1 (Problem of a Cake Division). Let there be three persons 1, 2, and 3, among whom a homogeneous cake should be divided. There exist four possible divisions, viz., $\boldsymbol{x} = (1/2, 1/2, 0)$, $\boldsymbol{y} = (1/2, 0, 1/2)$, $\boldsymbol{z} = (0, 1/2, 1/2)$, and $\boldsymbol{w} = (1/3, 1/3, 1/3)$, where the component h of each division $\boldsymbol{s} \in S$, where $S := \{\boldsymbol{w}, \boldsymbol{x}, \boldsymbol{y}, \boldsymbol{z}\}$, denotes the proportion of the cake to be distributed to each person $h \in N := \{1, 2, 3\}$ under $\boldsymbol{s}$. The subjective preference ordering over S by each person $h \in N$, say, R_h, denotes h's preference ranking over S from his/her personal point of view, which is given by[48]

$$R_1 : [\boldsymbol{x}, \boldsymbol{y}], \boldsymbol{w}, \boldsymbol{z} \qquad R_2 : [\boldsymbol{x}, \boldsymbol{z}], \boldsymbol{w}, \boldsymbol{y} \qquad R_3 : [\boldsymbol{y}, \boldsymbol{z}], \boldsymbol{w}, \boldsymbol{x}. \quad \text{(I.22)}$$

Given the profile $\boldsymbol{R} = (R_1, R_2, R_3)$ of intrapersonally ordinal and interpersonally noncomparable preference orderings, which alternative in S should the society N choose? Suppose that we invoke the simple majority decision (SMD) rule. Then $\boldsymbol{x}$ and $\boldsymbol{y}$, $\boldsymbol{y}$ and $\boldsymbol{z}$, and $\boldsymbol{z}$ and $\boldsymbol{x}$ tie with each other, whereas each alternative in $\{\boldsymbol{x}, \boldsymbol{y}, \boldsymbol{z}\} \subsetneq S$ beats $\boldsymbol{w}$. Several other methods of collective decision making recommend the choice of $\{\boldsymbol{x}, \boldsymbol{y}, \boldsymbol{z}\}$ as the solution to the

48. Preference orderings are written horizontally with the more preferred alternative to the left of the less preferred, the indifferent alternatives being gathered together by square brackets.

cake division problem. For example, the Borda method of rank-order decision making also declares that each element of $\{\boldsymbol{x}, \boldsymbol{y}, \boldsymbol{z}\}$ is strictly better than $\boldsymbol{w}$, whereas all elements of $\{\boldsymbol{x}, \boldsymbol{y}, \boldsymbol{z}\}$ are declared socially indifferent to each other.[49] However, a single element must be eventually chosen from $\{\boldsymbol{x}, \boldsymbol{y}, \boldsymbol{z}\}$ through some tie-breaking rule. Whatever tie-breaking rule one may use, the fact remains that it is judged best, according to these methods, to sacrifice an unlucky person to benefit the lucky majority of persons, *even if there exists a perfectly egalitarian division,* viz., $\boldsymbol{w}$, *of the cake in question.*

It is in this arena that the extended sympathy approach makes a sensible contribution. Suppose that all individuals share the following extended preference ordering over the extended set of all alternatives $\{(\boldsymbol{x}, 1), (\boldsymbol{y}, 1), (\boldsymbol{z}, 1), (\boldsymbol{w}, 1), (\boldsymbol{x}, 2), (\boldsymbol{y}, 2), (\boldsymbol{z}, 2), (\boldsymbol{w}, 2), (\boldsymbol{x}, 3), (\boldsymbol{y}, 3), (\boldsymbol{z}, 3), (\boldsymbol{w}, 3)\}$, which seems to make good sense in the context of distributing a homogeneous cake among three persons:[50]

$$\begin{array}{c} \mathfrak{R}_1 = \mathfrak{R}_2 = \mathfrak{R}_3 \\ \hline [(\boldsymbol{x}, 1), (\boldsymbol{x}, 2), (\boldsymbol{y}, 1), (\boldsymbol{y}, 3), (\boldsymbol{z}, 2), (\boldsymbol{z}, 3)] \\ [(\boldsymbol{w}, 1), (\boldsymbol{w}, 2), (\boldsymbol{w}, 3)] \\ [(\boldsymbol{x}, 3), (\boldsymbol{y}, 2), (\boldsymbol{z}, 1)] \end{array} \tag{I.23}$$

where $\boldsymbol{\mathfrak{R}} = (\mathfrak{R}_1, \mathfrak{R}_2, \mathfrak{R}_3)$ is the profile of extended individual preference orderings. It should be clear that axiom ID is satisfied by each person's extended preference ordering. If we are equipped with this extended informational basis, there are two reasonable methods of circumventing the dilemma identified in the previous paragraph.

(a) According to the profile $\boldsymbol{\mathfrak{R}}$, $(\boldsymbol{x}, 1)$ is better than $(\boldsymbol{x}, 3)$, $(\boldsymbol{y}, 3)$ is better than $(\boldsymbol{y}, 2)$, and $(\boldsymbol{z}, 2)$ is better than $(\boldsymbol{z}, 1)$, so that person 3 envies person 1 if alternative $\boldsymbol{x}$ prevails, person 2 envies person 3 if alternative $\boldsymbol{y}$ prevails, and person 1 envies person 2 if alternative $\boldsymbol{z}$ prevails. It follows that there is only one alternative in the opportunity set

49. See also Georges Bordes (1976; 1979) for the use of transitive closure of the SMD rule.

50. Preference orderings are written vertically with the more preferred alternative above the less preferred, the indifferent alternatives being gathered together by square brackets.

$S = \{\boldsymbol{x}, \boldsymbol{y}, \boldsymbol{z}, \boldsymbol{w}\}$, viz., $\boldsymbol{w}$, which is *equitable* in the sense of generating no instance of interpersonal envy.

(b) According to the profile $\mathfrak{R}$, it is better to be in any person's position under $\boldsymbol{w}$ than to be in the position of the worst-off person under $\boldsymbol{x}$, $\boldsymbol{y}$, and $\boldsymbol{z}$. Following John Rawls's (1971) *A Theory of Justice,* a social alternative $\boldsymbol{a}$ is judged to be more *just* than another alternative $\boldsymbol{b}$ if the welfare level of the worst-off person under $\boldsymbol{b}$ is less than the welfare level of the worst-off person under $\boldsymbol{a}$. It follows that $\boldsymbol{w}$ is the only just alternative contained in the opportunity set $S = \{\boldsymbol{x}, \boldsymbol{y}, \boldsymbol{z}, \boldsymbol{w}\}$.

Capitalizing on the message of Example I.1, let us formalize the extended sympathy approach in social choice theory on the informational basis of the profile of extended preference orderings $\mathfrak{R} = (\mathfrak{R}_1, \mathfrak{R}_2, \ldots, \mathfrak{R}_n)$. For each individual $i \in N$, let his/her subjective preference ordering $\Sigma(\mathfrak{R}_i)$ on X be defined by

$$\forall\, x, y \in X : x\Sigma(\mathfrak{R}_i)y \Leftrightarrow (x, i)\mathfrak{R}_i(y, i), \tag{I.24}$$

which helps us define the *Paretian quasi ordering* $R_N(\mathfrak{R})$ by $R_N(\mathfrak{R}) = \cap_{i \in N}\Sigma(\mathfrak{R}_i)$. The set of all *Pareto-efficient* alternatives in $S \in \mathcal{S}$ is defined by

$$E_f(S, \mathfrak{R}) = \{x \in S \mid \forall\, y \in S : \neg\, yP(R_N(\mathfrak{R}))x\}. \tag{I.25}$$

We may also introduce the set of all *no-envy equitable* alternatives in $S \in \mathcal{S}$ by

$$E_q(S, \mathfrak{R}) = \{x \in S \mid \forall\, i, j \in N : (x, i)\mathfrak{R}_i(x, j)\}. \tag{I.26}$$

An alternative that satisfies Pareto efficiency as well as no-envy equity is called *fair,* and the set of all fair alternatives in the opportunity set $S \in \mathcal{S}$ is defined by

$$F(S, \mathfrak{R}) = E_f(S, \mathfrak{R}) \cap E_q(S, \mathfrak{R}). \tag{I.27}$$

Recollect that the extended sympathy approach was introduced as a possible escape route from Arrow's impasse by widening his parsimonious informational basis. However, the efficacy of this escape route is not automatically guaranteed. Indeed, this approach may generate a logical impasse of its own.

It is all too easy to discover an instance of the *equity-efficiency trade-off* within this approach.

EXAMPLE I.2 (EQUITY-EFFICIENCY TRADE-OFF). Let there be two persons 1 and 2, and two social alternatives $\boldsymbol{x}$ and $\boldsymbol{y}$. Consider the following profile $\boldsymbol{\mathfrak{R}} = (\mathfrak{R}_1, \mathfrak{R}_2)$ of extended preference orderings:

$$\mathfrak{R}_1 : (\boldsymbol{y}, 2), (\boldsymbol{y}, 1), (\boldsymbol{x}, 1), (\boldsymbol{x}, 2);$$

$$\mathfrak{R}_2 : (\boldsymbol{y}, 2), (\boldsymbol{y}, 1), (\boldsymbol{x}, 2), (\boldsymbol{x}, 1). \tag{I.28}$$

It is easy to verify that $E_f(S, \boldsymbol{\mathfrak{R}}) = \{\boldsymbol{y}\}$ and $E_q(S, \boldsymbol{\mathfrak{R}}) = \{\boldsymbol{x}\}$ hold for this profile, so that we cannot but conclude that $F(S, \boldsymbol{\mathfrak{R}}) = \emptyset$.

It deserves emphasis that the profile (I.28) of Example I.2 satisfies axiom ID, so that the discovered equity-efficiency trade-off cannot be attributed to the lack of sympathetic identification among individuals.

To sum up, there are two routes that are worth exploring by means of the extended sympathy approach in normative economics. On the one hand, it may provide us with a potential escape route from the Arrow impossibility theorems through the concept of no-envy equity.[51] On the other hand, it presents a clear manifestation of the equity-efficiency trade-off that requires logical scrutiny and calls for workable resolution schemes. The first three essays in Part III of this volume are devoted to my struggle with these tasks.[52] The last essay in Part III is also on the issue of equitable allocation of resources, but the focus of the essay is on the issue of *intergenerational equity*

---

51. An alternative role of the extended sympathy approach is to provide an analytical vehicle for formulating the Rawlsian theory of maximin justice. See, among others, Arrow (1977/1983), Peter Hammond (1976), Kevin Roberts (1980; 1980a; 1995), and Sen (1977a).

52. The origin of the basic concept of equity-as-no-envy may be traced back to Jan Tinbergen (1953), according to whom *two individuals are treated justly with respect to each other if they would not want to change places.* By places he meant their whole situations—not only their occupations and incomes but also their personal conditions such as health, size and health of their families, levels of education, abilities, and so forth. The modern resurgence of this equity concept is due to Duncan Foley (1967) and Serge-Christophe Kolm (1972). See, among many others, Marc Fleurbaey, Kotaro Suzumura, and Koichi Tadenuma (2005, Essay 7 of this volume; 2005a, Essay 10 of this volume), Kolm (1996), Elisha Pazner and David Schmeidler (1974; 1978), Suzumura (1981, Essay 9 of this volume; 1983a), William Thomson (2011), and Hal Varian (1974; 1975) for further analyses of this and related equity concepts.

in the tradition of Henry Sidgwick (1907, p. 414), who observed that "the time at which a man exists cannot affect the value of his happiness from a universal point of view; and [. . .] the interests of posterity must concern a utilitarian as much as those of his contemporaries." In the 1960s, Tjalling Koopmans (1960) and Peter Diamond (1965) kicked off an extensive investigation into a new aspect of equity-efficiency trade-off by crystallizing the logical incompatibility between intergenerational equity à la Sidgwick and Pareto efficiency in the form of an impossibility theorem on ordering infinite utility streams.[53] Essay 12 is devoted to this infinite generational equity-efficiency trade-off from the viewpoint of the *Pigou-Dalton transfer principle*[54] due originally to Arthur Pigou (1912) and Hugh Dalton (1920) rather than the *Sidgwick-Koopmans-Diamond anonymity principle.*

I.5.4. Outcome Fairness and Procedural Fairness

There are two related but distinct concepts of fairness, which should be precisely identified and carefully examined. Let us begin our analysis with two auxiliary concepts. Consider a society that consists of n individuals, where $2 \leq n < +\infty$. X denotes the set of all social alternatives, where $3 \leq \#X$. The first auxiliary concept is that of a *selection function* μ, which is defined as a function that maps $\boldsymbol{R}$ into a subset $\mu(\boldsymbol{R})$ of X for each profile of individual preference orderings $\boldsymbol{R} = (R_1, R_2, \ldots, R_n)$. The second auxiliary concept is that of a *game form*, which serves us as a model of a social decision procedure. A game form in the society N is a triplet $\theta = (N; \boldsymbol{\Sigma} = \{\Sigma_1, \Sigma_2, \ldots, \Sigma_n\}; g)$, where Σ_i is the set of individual i's *admissible strategies* for each $i \in N$ and g is the concept of *outcome function* that associates an outcome $g(\boldsymbol{\sigma}) \in X$ with each strategy profile $\boldsymbol{\sigma} = (\sigma_1, \sigma_2, \ldots, \sigma_n) \in \times_{i \in N} \Sigma_i$. When a profile

53. Notable contributions on the problem posed by Koopmans and Diamond include, among many others, Kaushik Basu and Tapan Mitra (2003; 2007), Chiaki Hara, Tomoichi Shinotsuka, Kotaro Suzumura, and Yongsheng Xu (2008), John Roemer and Kotaro Suzumura (2007), and Lars-Gunner Svensson (1980).

54. The Pigou-Dalton transfer principle, which is adapted to the infinite-horizon framework by Hara, Shinotsuka, Suzumura, and Xu (2008), is defined as follows. A *Pigou-Dalton transfer* is a transfer of a positive amount of utility from a better-off generation to a worse-off generation so that the relative ranking of the two generations in the posttransfer utility stream remains the same as their relative ranking in the pretransfer stream. The Pigou-Dalton transfer principle requires that any Pigou-Dalton transfer brings about a utility stream that is strictly preferred to the pretransfer stream.

of individual preference orderings $\boldsymbol{R} = (R_1, R_2, \ldots, R_n)$ is specified, the pair $(\theta, \boldsymbol{R})$ becomes a full-fledged game, where the game form θ can be construed as the *rules of the game.* In what follows, $\mathcal{E}$ denotes the equilibrium concept prevailing in the society. The set of all equilibrium outcomes of the game $(\theta, \boldsymbol{R})$ is denoted by $g(\mathcal{E}(\theta, \boldsymbol{R}))$, where $\mathcal{E}(\theta, \boldsymbol{R}) \subseteq \times_{i \in N} \Sigma_i$ stands for the set of equilibrium strategy profiles.

Equipped with these auxiliary concepts, we are now ready to define the concept of *outcome fairness* and that of *procedural fairness.* The point of departure for the analysis of outcome fairness is the notion of *outcome morality,* which may be exemplified by no-envy fairness, viz., the simultaneous satisfaction of Pareto efficiency and no-envy equity. The specification of the outcome morality, say, κ, determines the selection function μ_κ in such a way that $x \in \mu_\kappa(\boldsymbol{R})$ holds if and only if x conforms to the outcome morality κ when the profile $\boldsymbol{R}$ prevails. The social decision procedure represented by the game form θ is judged fair as a reflection of the outcome fairness if and only if

$$g(\mathcal{E}(\theta, \boldsymbol{R})) \subseteq \mu_\kappa(\boldsymbol{R}) \tag{I.29}$$

holds for each profile $\boldsymbol{R}$. In the terminology of Leonid Hurwicz (1960; 1972; 1996), the game form θ that satisfies (I.29) is *nonwasteful* in the sense that all equilibrium outcomes of the game $(\theta, \boldsymbol{R})$ conform to the outcome morality κ. On the other hand, if

$$g(\mathcal{E}(\theta, \boldsymbol{R})) \supseteq \mu_\kappa(\boldsymbol{R}) \tag{I.30}$$

holds for each profile $\boldsymbol{R}$, the game form θ is *unbiased* in the sense of Hurvicz, viz., any outcome that conforms to the outcome morality κ under the profile $\boldsymbol{R}$ is realizable as an equilibrium outcome of the game $(\theta, \boldsymbol{R})$. It deserves emphasis that, according to the concept of outcome fairness, the social decision procedure does not have any *intrinsic* value; the value that it carries is nothing other than its *instrumental* usefulness in bringing about an outcome that conforms to the preassigned outcome morality. In contrast, the point of departure for the analysis of procedural fairness is the a priori definition of the intrinsic value of procedures. If θ conforms to the intrinsic value of procedures, then for each realized profile $\boldsymbol{R}$, any outcome that is generated by playing the game $(\theta, \boldsymbol{R})$, viz., any outcome belonging to $g(\mathcal{E}(\theta, \boldsymbol{R}))$, is regarded as a fair outcome as a reflection of the a priori procedural fairness of θ.

The concept of outcome fairness and that of procedural fairness are two idealized prototypes of the concept of fairness that are actually prevailing in the literature of welfare economics and social choice theory. We will have several occasions to invoke these alternative perspectives on the fairness of procedures and outcomes in this volume of selected essays.

I.6. Between Welfare and Rights

It is worthwhile to emphasize that Arrow's mutually incompatible axioms on the social choice procedure are meant to be a set of necessary conditions for a democratic method of collective decision making to be satisfactory, and there is no claim that they exhaust all desiderata to be desired for. Among other conspicuous desideratum is the libertarian claim of the social respect for individual rights to the effect that there ought to exist a certain minimum sphere of individual autonomy, which should not be interfered with by anyone other than the individual in question.

Needless to say, just to add the desiderata of libertarian claim to Arrow's mutually incompatible axioms will make no sense in that doing so simply overkills the possibility of reasonable social choice procedure. Besides, it is not obvious how the desiderata of libertarian claim should be articulated in the social choice framework. It was Amartya Sen (1970; 1970, Chapter 6*) who articulated the desiderata of libertarian claim within Arrow's social choice framework, and posed the problem of incompatibility between the social respect for libertarian claim of rights and the Pareto principle. The present Section I.6 is devoted to the meaning and role of *welfarism,* which has dominated most, if not literally all, approaches in welfare economics and social choice theory. It was Sen's theorem on the *impossibility* of a *Paretian liberal* that posed the problematic nature of welfarism to the fore.

I.6.1. Beyond Welfarism

According to Arrow (1987, p. 124), "economic or any other social policy has consequences for the many and diverse individuals who make up the society or economy. It has been taken for granted in virtually all economic policy discussions since the time of Adam Smith, if not before, that alternative policies should be judged on the basis of their consequences for individuals." As a matter of fact, the informational parsimony of traditional normative economics in general, and the standard social choice theory in particular, is even more exacting than consequentialism as such. Indeed, welfare economics, old and new, as well as social choice theory in the form that Arrow laid its foundation allows the description of consequences only through the looking glass of individual welfare resulting from consequential outcomes. This subcategory of consequentialist informational bases is commonly called *welfarist consequentialism,* or *welfarism* for short. Although the dependence on welfaristic informational bases is ubiquitous in the literature on normative economics, there are several acute criticisms as well, some of which deserve careful scrutiny.

To begin with, consider a fable of *The Fox and the Grapes,* which is one of Aesop's fables made popular by La Fontaine:

> The fox who longed for grapes, beholds with pain
> The tempting clusters were too high to gain;
> Grieved in his heart he forced a careless smile,
> And cried, 'They're sharp and hardly worth my while.

It was Jon Elster (1982; 1983, Chapter III) who tried to throw light on a foundational problem of utilitarian, or more generally welfaristic, theory by means of the fable of *sour grapes*. He asks: "Why should individual want satisfaction be the criterion of justice and social choice when individual wants themselves may be shaped by a process that preempts the choice? And in particular, why should the choice between feasible options only take account of individual preferences if people tend to adjust their aspirations to their possibilities?" Invoking the fable of sour grapes, he elaborates his point further: "For the utilitarian [and the welfarist more generally], there would be no welfare loss if the fox were excluded from consumption of the grapes, since he thought them sour anyway. But of course the cause of his holding them to be sour was his conviction that he would be excluded from consuming them, and then it is difficult to justify the allocation by invoking his preferences" [Elster (1982, p. 109)].

The difficulty of exclusively using welfaristic informational bases in normative economics may be further highlighted by a parable of a millionaire introduced by Ronald Dworkin (1981; 2000). Simplifying his parable, suppose that a millionaire with two sons wants to draw his will. One son has an innate handicap from his unlucky birth, for which he has no reason to be held personally responsible. He needs expensive medical assistance for a decent subsistence. Another son is a playboy with expensive tastes for champagne, which he has nourished for himself through his own luxurious life. In this situation, how shall the millionaire draw his will? Dworkin's reasoning goes as follows: "If we want genuinely to treat people as equals . . . then we must contrive to make their lives equally desirable to them, or give them the means to do so. . . . When the question arises how wealth should be distributed, . . . those who are seriously physically or mentally handicapped do seem to have, in all fairness, a claim to more than others. . . . [However,]most people would resist the conclusion that those who have expensive tastes are . . . entitled to a larger share than others. Someone with champagne tastes . . . [may] also need more resources to achieve welfare equal to those who prefer beer. But it does not seem fair that he should have more resources on that account" [Dworkin (1981, p. 189)]. Nevertheless, to tell the handicapped person from the person with champagne tastes for making better allocation, we must go behind the veil of utility or welfare and dig deeper into nonwelfaristic or even nonconsequentialist informational bases.

In the third and last place, let us refer to another parable introduced earlier by Sen (1970; 1970a), which is meant to cast a new light on the nature of welfarism. It goes as follows. There is one copy of *Lady Chatterley's Lover*. There are three alternatives: Mr. P reads it (x), Mr. L reads it (y), and no one reads it (z). Mr. P is a prude, who prefers most that no one reads it, but given the choice between either of the two reading it, he prefers reading it himself rather than exposing lascivious Mr. L to the literary work of Lawrence. In decreasing order of preference, his ranking is z, x, y. Mr. L prefers that either of them should read it rather than neither. Furthermore, he takes delight in the thought that Mr. P may have to be exposed to Lawrence, and his first preference is that Mr. P should read it, next best that he himself should read it, and worst that neither should. His ranking is, therefore, x, y, z. If the choice is precisely between the pair $\{x, z\}$, i.e., between Mr. P reading the book and no one reading it, someone with liberal values may argue it is Mr. P's preference that should count. Thus, the society should prefer z to x. Similarly, in the choice between Mr. L reading the book

(y) and no one reading it (z), liberal values require that Mr. L's preference should be decisive. Hence y should be judged socially better than z. Thus, according to liberal values it is better that no one reads it rather than Mr. P being forced to read it, and it is still better that Mr. L is permitted to read the book rather than no one reading it. That is, the society should prefer y to z, and z to x. Thus, it may seem that the book should be handed over to Mr. L, save for the fact that x is Pareto superior to y. It follows that every social choice that we can think of is bettered by some other social alternative as long as we respect the Pareto principle and the principle of liberalism. This is why this parable is called the *Pareto libertarian paradox*.

Observe that the Pareto principle is clearly a *welfaristic* outcome morality, whereas the libertarian claim articulated by Sen is nothing other than a *nonwelfaristic* claim of individual rights in the sense that Mr. P (resp. Mr. L) can impose his preference for z against x (resp. for y against z) by preferring z to x (resp. y to z) on the social choice from $\{x, z\}$ (resp. $\{y, z\}$) in view of the fact that the sole difference between x and z (resp. y and z) is Mr. P's (resp. Mr. L's) own personal matter. Thus, the Pareto libertarian paradox goes against the universal appeal of the welfaristic Pareto principle if only the nonwelfaristic libertarian claim of rights is found widely appealing.

I.6.2. Impossibility of a Paretian Liberal

To bring the main message of the Pareto libertarian paradox into clearer relief, let $N = \{1, 2, \dots, n\}$ $(2 \leq n < +\infty)$ be the set of all individuals in the society, and let X be the set of all social alternatives, where each social alternative is defined as "a complete description of society including every individual's position in it" [Sen (1970, p. 152)]. For each $i \in N$, R_i denotes individual i's preference ordering on X, together forming a profile $\boldsymbol{R} = (R_1, R_2, \dots, R_n)$ of individual preference orderings. Let $\mathcal{R}$ be the family of all logically possible profiles. A *social choice rule* is a function φ that maps each profile $\boldsymbol{R} \in \mathcal{R}$ into a social choice function $C^{\boldsymbol{R}} = \varphi(\boldsymbol{R})$ such that, for each set of feasible alternatives $S \in \mathcal{S}$, $C^{\boldsymbol{R}}(S) \subseteq S$ denotes the set of social alternatives that the society chooses from S reflecting the profile $\boldsymbol{R}$ of individual preference orderings, where $\mathcal{S}$ denotes the family of all nonempty *finite* subsets of X. It is assumed that φ satisfies the following:

AXIOM U (UNRESTRICTED DOMAIN). The social choice rule φ is capable of determining a social choice function $C^{\boldsymbol{R}} = \varphi(\boldsymbol{R})$ with the full domain $\mathcal{S}$ for each profile $\boldsymbol{R} \in \mathcal{R}$.

To give an analytical substance to Sen's concept of individual libertarian rights, let x and y be two social alternatives, which are identical except for the specification of some private features of an individual $i \in N$. Suppose that i him/herself prefers x to y, yet the society chooses y from some opportunity set $S \in \mathcal{S}$ containing x. In Sen's perception, this represents a clear infringement on i's libertarian rights, as the society does not respect i's preference for x against y, even when the sole difference between x and y is a feature that belongs to i's *private sphere*. Capitalizing on this intuitive perception, define, for each $i \in N$, a subset $D_i \subseteq X \times X$ such that the only difference between x and y is i's private feature of the world if and only if $(x, y) \in D_i$. The social choice rule φ is said to respect i's *individual libertarian rights* over his/her *protected sphere* D_i if and only if

$$(x, y) \in D_i \cap P(R_i) \Rightarrow [x \in S \Rightarrow y \notin C^{\boldsymbol{R}}(S)] \quad \text{for all } S \in \mathcal{S} \qquad \text{(I.31)}$$

holds for all $\boldsymbol{R} \in \mathcal{R}$, where $C^{\boldsymbol{R}} = \varphi(\boldsymbol{R})$. Sen's requirement of the social respect for individual libertarian rights and the Pareto principle may be stated as follows.

AXIOM SML (SEN'S MINIMAL LIBERTARIANISM). There exist at least two individuals, say, j and k, each endowed with a nonempty protected sphere D_j and D_k, respectively, such that φ bestows on j and k the libertarian rights in the sense of Sen over D_j and D_k, respectively.

AXIOM P (PARETO PRINCIPLE). For any $x, y \in X$ and any $\boldsymbol{R} \in \mathcal{R}$,

$$(x, y) \in \cap_{i \in N} P(R_i) \Rightarrow [x \in S \to y \notin C^{\boldsymbol{R}}(\boldsymbol{R})] \text{ for all } S \in \mathcal{S} \qquad \text{(I.32)}$$

holds, where $C^{\boldsymbol{R}} = \varphi(\boldsymbol{R})$.

Considered in isolation, both axiom SML and axiom P seem to be noncontroversial, yet in combination, axiom U, axiom SML and axiom P turn out to be logically incompatible. This is nothing other than Sen's *impossibility of a Paretian liberal*.

Theorem I.9 (Sen (1970; 1970a, Chapter 6*) and Suzumura (2011, pp. 615–616)). No social choice rule φ satisfies axiom U, axiom SML and axiom P.

Observe that Arrow's theorem and Sen's theorem have two conspicuous differences. In the first place, there is no requirement of collective rationality in Sen's theorem in sharp contrast with Arrow's theorem. In the second place, axiom I (independence of irrelevant alternatives), which plays a crucial role in Arrow's theorem, has no role to play in Sen's theorem. Thus, two usual suspects, who are widely held responsible for the counterintuitive conclusion of Arrow's theorem, are altogether missing from the list of potential culprits. Together with the fact that Sen's theorem forces us to face up to the conflict between the welfaristic Pareto principle and the nonwelfaristic claim of individual libertarian rights, there is no wonder that Sen's theorem caused a great stir in the social choice circle.

There is, by now, a substantial body of literature on the Impossibility of a Paretian liberal, among which two lines of research deserve special emphasis. The first line of research accepts Sen's original formulation of libertarian rights and attempts to resolve the impossibility by weakening either the libertarian claim of individual rights, or the weak welfaristic claim of the Pareto principle, or both. Essay 13 [Suzumura (1978)] and Essay 14 [Suzumura (1980)] in Part IV of this volume constitute my representative work along this line of research.[55] The second and heated line of research is devoted to the critical scrutiny of Sen's articulation of libertarian rights per se. Although Sen (1976; 1979a; 1982; 1983; 1992; 1996) has painstakingly tried to answer most of these criticisms, the field is still in need of conceptual clarifications and further analyses. The next subsection is devoted to these debates with a view of highlighting the *game form approach to individual rights,* which was introduced and promoted as an alternative articulation of libertarian rights by Robert Sugden (1985) and Wulf Gaertner, Prasanta Pattanaik, and Kotaro Suzumura (1992, Essay 15 of this volume).

55. See also Sen (1976) and Suzumura (1996, Essay 16 of this volume; 2011, Chapter 23) for succinct surveys and critical evaluations of the relevant literature.

I.6.3. Rights: Amartya Sen versus Robert Nozick

One of the earliest criticisms on Sen's formulation of libertarian rights came from Robert Nozick (1974) in his thought-provoking book *Anarchy, State, and Utopia*. Both Sen and Nozick agree with John Stuart Mill (1859/1977) that every person in the society should be warranted a *personal protected sphere,* with which the rest of the society should not interfere. However, the difference comes to the fore when they try to formalize the concept of a personal protected sphere, and to show how the society's respect for personal protected spheres gets reflected in social choice. According to Nozick (1974, p. 166), "a more appropriate view of individual rights [than Sen's view articulated by means of social choice rules] goes as follows. Individual rights are co-possible; each person may exercise his rights as he chooses. The exercise of these rights fixes some features of the world. Within the constraints of these fixed features, a choice may be made by a social choice mechanism based upon a social ordering; if there are any choices left to make! Rights do not determine a social ordering but instead set the constraints within which a social choice is to be made, by excluding certain alternatives, fixing others, and so on." That is to say, instead of formulating rights on a par with the weak welfaristic claim such as the Pareto principle, Nozick proposes to assign libertarian rights a completely different role of specifying some personal features of the world *before* the social choice rule starts its function as a preference aggregation mechanism. As such, Nozick's formulation of libertarian rights has nothing to do with individual preferences over consequential social outcomes. It should be emphasized that Nozick's view of rights is deeply rooted in the libertarian tradition of respecting the freedom of choice in private spheres along the line of John Stuart Mill. It is in this sense that Nozick's criticism on Sen's view of rights seems to carry heavy weight in the context of libertarian rights. Not only are there differences of opinion between Sen's view of rights and Nozick's view of rights, but the latter view of rights in fact constitutes a serious criticism on the former view of rights. To scrutinize Nozick's view of rights with a view of crystallizing its logical conflict with Sen's view of rights is one of the main purposes of Essay 15 [Gaertner, Pattanaik, and Suzumura (1992)] in Part IV of this volume.

So far, so good. However, Nozick's view of rights, which may be traced all the way back to Mill's classical view of rights, has at least two problems of its own.

In the first place, the problem of demarcating protected personal spheres, viz., that of drawing "a frontier . . . between the area of private life and that of public authority" [Berlin (1958)] goes all the way back to Mill (1859/1977), who posed it as follows: "What . . . is the rightful limit to the sovereignty of the individual over himself? Where does the authority of society begin? How much of human life should be assigned to individuality, and how much to society?" Mill's answer to his own question is a famous, and deceptively simple, principle to the following effect: "Each will receive its proper share, if each has that which more particularly concerns it. To individuality should belong the part of life in which it is chiefly the individual that is interested; to society, the part which chiefly interests society." Unfortunately, Mill's simple principle poses more problems than it settles, as "men are largely interdependent, and no man's activity is so completely private as never to obstruct the lives of others in any way. 'Freedom for the pike is death for the minnows'; the liberty for some must depend on the restraint of others" [Berlin (1958)]. To the best of our knowledge, this first problem related to Nozick's view of rights is largely left unresolved to date.

In the second place, Nozick's view of rights, the characteristic feature of which is expressed by Nozick himself in the statement that "individual rights are co-possible; each person may exercise his rights as he chooses," cannot be sustained as it is. This point can be made unambiguous by means of the following.

Example I.3 (Secondary Smoking Case). There are two passengers, Ann and Fred, in the same compartment of a train. Ann cannot stand cigarette smoke, whereas Fred is a cigarette addict. In the compartment is an authorized notice by the train company to the effect that "if your fellow passengers object, please refrain from smoking." The set of feasible social alternatives is given by $X = \{x, y, z\}$, where x = "Ann objects, and Fred does not smoke," y = "Ann does not object, and Fred smokes," and z = "Ann does not object, but Fred does not smoke anyway." In this situation, if the decision making is completely decentralized and individuals are left free to choose from the sets of private options—{to object, not to object} for Ann and {to smoke, not to smoke} for Fred—directly, nothing prevents a culmination outcome, where Ann objects and Fred smokes, from occurring.

The second purpose of Essay 15 of this volume is to show how the logical sustainability of Nozick's view of rights could be secured by elaborating his view of rights into the game form articulation of rights, which is a full-fledged alternative to Sen's original view of rights.[56] To avoid possible misunderstanding, it deserves emphasis that the game form approach to rights is meant to cast reasonable doubt on Sen's articulation of libertarian rights and to propose a meaningful alternative articulation that seems to be firmly rooted in the tradition of J. S. Mill on liberty. It is *not* our claim that the game form articulation of libertarian rights dissipates the impossibility of a Paretian liberal by one stroke. Essay 15 makes this point unambiguously, and the subsequent paper by Rajat Deb, Prasanta Pattanaik, and Laura Razzolini (1997) established that Sen's impossibility theorem strenuously comes back within the new framework of the game form approach to rights.

A final remark on the theory of libertarian rights might be in order. In the interview by Jerry Kelly on behalf of *Social Choice and Welfare,* Arrow was asked of his first response to the impossibility of a Paretian liberal. He recalled as follows: "I thought that [Sen's theorem] was stunning and penetrating to a very important issue. But . . . why do we have rights? . . . The one thing I retain from utilitarianism is that, basically, judgments are based on consequences. . . . I view rights as arrangements that may help you in achieving a higher utility level. For example, if you are much better informed about a certain choice, because it's personal to you and not to me, I don't really know anything about it, I should delegate the choice to you. . . . But who settles what rights are legitimate? The consequentialist view—I won't say that fully settles it either, but at least you have something to argue about. So this is why I'm a little unsympathetic to the rights issue—everybody just multiplies the rights all over the place and you get total paralysis. . . . Unless somebody produces a logic of rights in terms of which we can argue, I really find the whole issue is unfocused" [Arrow, Sen and Suzumura (2011, p. 642)]. Thus, what made Arrow skeptical about social choice analyses of rights is the conspicuous lack of the raison d'être of libertarian rights. In all

56. The game form approach to individual rights has been further developed by Rajat Deb (1994; 2004), Deb, Prasanta Pattanaik, and Laura Razzolini (1997), Peter Gärdenfors (1981), Pattanaik (1996), Pattanaik and Suzumura (1996), Bezalel Peleg (1998), Robert Sugden (1985; 1994), and Martin van Hees (1999).

fairness and despite several serious attempts, Arrow's anxiety remains to be clarified in the successive work of social choice theory.

I.7. Consequentialism versus Nonconsequentialism: An Axiomatic Approach

It is hard to deny that the contemporary microeconomic theory is deeply rooted in the informational basis of welfarism. It is slightly ironic that John Hicks, who is one of the major proponents of the contemporary microeconomic theory in the 1930s, kicked off a serious criticism on the welfaristic informational basis of welfare economics towards the end of 1950s. It is true that Hicks's criticism could not receive a proper attention until recently, his criticism in fact applies not simply to welfarism as such, but also to consequentialism in general. It seems fair to say that the time is ripe now to pay due attention to the nonconsequentialist judgments along with the consequentialist judgments in our normative economics.

I.7.1. John Hicks's Farewell to "Economic Welfarism"

As far as I am aware, it was John Hicks who first declared an explicit farewell to the welfaristic informational basis of normative economics. In his esoteric "Preface—and a Manifesto" attached to his *Essays in World Economics* (1959), Hicks flatly declared his denial of what he christened "Economic Welfarism" as follows: "The view which, now, I do not hold I propose . . . to call 'Economic Welfarism'; for it is one of the tendencies which has taken its origin from that great and immensely influential work, the *Economics of Welfare* of Pigou. But the distinction which I am about to make has little to do with the multifarious theoretical disputes to which the notion of Welfare Economics has given rise to. One can take any view one likes about measurability, or additivity, or comparability of utilities; and yet it remains undetermined whether one is to come down to one side or other of the Welfarist fence. The line between Economic Welfarism and its opposite is not concerned with what economists call utilities; it is concerned with the transition from Utility to the more general good, Welfare (if we like) itself."

The reasons behind, and the substantial contents of, Hicks's *Manifesto* are carefully examined in Essay 28 of this volume. On the basis of this scrutiny, I contend that Hicks was opposed not only to welfarist consequentialism (welfarism) but also to consequentialism as such. To substantiate this interpretation, we have only to cite the following statement by Hicks (1981, p. 137): "One of the issues that can be dealt with most elaborately by Welfarist methods is that of Monopoly and Competition: the theory of the social optimum which would be reached in a (practically unattainable) condition of all-round perfect competition, and of the departures from the optimum which may occur under any form in which a system of free enterprise can in practice be organized, is one of the chief ways in which the Welfarist has left its mark. I do not question that we have learned a great deal from these discussions; but they leave me with an obstinate feeling that they have failed to penetrate to the centre of the problem with which they are concerned. Why is it . . . that antimonopoly lcgislation (and litigation) get so little help, as they evidently do, from the textbook theory? Surely the answer is that the main issues of principle—security on the one side, freedom and equity on the other, the issues that lawyers, and law-makers, can understand—have got left right out." Thus, by invoking such nonconsequentialist values as security, freedom, and equity on a par with the consequentialist values, Hicks was ready to go beyond the consequentialist informational basis of normative economics.

How do we proceed in the attempt to explore the possible use of nonconsequentialist informational bases of normative economics? Can we accommodate this apparently novel approach within the traditional approach by means of a simple device of expanding the definition of conventional notion of consequential outcomes? To answer these questions and to find a way to proceed, let us consider two nonconsequentialist features of the world, viz., *procedures* for social decision making and *opportunity sets* from which consequential outcomes should be chosen. The rest of this subsection is devoted to exemplifying that we cannot accommodate nonconsequentialist features of the world within the conventional framework of normative analysis through the simple change of conceptual definitions. The remaining two subsections are devoted to bringing the contrast between consequentialism and nonconsequentialism into clear relief by means of an extended conceptual framework where we focus on the opportunity to choose culmination outcomes.

To fix ideas, let N be a society that consists of n individuals. X denotes the set of all conventionally defined social alternatives. As a model of social decision-making procedure, a game form in the society N is defined by a triplet $\theta = (N; \boldsymbol{\Sigma} = \{\Sigma_1, \Sigma_2, \ldots, \Sigma_n\}; g)$, where Σ_i is the set of individual i's admissible strategies for each $i \in N$, and g is the *outcome function* that associates an outcome $g(\boldsymbol{\sigma}) \in X$ with each strategy profile $\boldsymbol{\sigma} = (\sigma_1, \sigma_2, \ldots, \sigma_n) \in \times_{i \in N} \Sigma_i$, one strategy for each individual. Let Θ be the set of all feasible game forms. A pair (x, θ), where $x \in X$ and $\theta \in \Theta$, stands for an extended social alternative where a conventionally defined social alternative x is attained through the medium of a game form θ. Consider an extended individual preference ordering ER_i of $i \in N$, which is defined by

$$(x, \theta) ER_i (y, \omega) \Leftrightarrow \text{According to } i\text{'s judgments, attaining } x \text{ through } \theta \text{ is at least as good as attaining } y \text{ through } \omega, \tag{I.33}$$

where $(x, \theta), (y, \omega) \in X \times \Theta$. Let $\boldsymbol{ER} = (ER_1, ER_2, \ldots, ER_n)$ be the profile of extended individual preference orderings, one extended ordering for each individual. There seem to exist widely held beliefs that by replacing X by $X \times \Theta$, and $\boldsymbol{R}$ by $\boldsymbol{ER}$, the classical social choice framework can neatly accommodate the procedural considerations, and the basic theoretical results may be kept essentially intact. To show that this is *not* the case, let $S \subseteq X$ be the set of conventionally defined *feasible* social alternatives. Recollect that a conventionally defined social alternative $x \in X$ is feasible if and only if $x \in S$ holds. In contrast, an extended social alternative $(x, \theta) \in X \times \Theta$ is feasible if and only if

$$x \in g(\mathcal{E}(\theta, \rho_X(\boldsymbol{ER}))) \tag{I.34}$$

holds, where $\rho_X(\boldsymbol{ER})$ stands for the projection of $\boldsymbol{ER}$ onto X and $\mathcal{E}$ stands for the equilibrium concept prevailing in the society. In the case of conventionally defined social alternatives, the profile of individual preference orderings has nothing to do with the definition of feasibility, whereas the definition of feasibility of extended social alternatives hinges squarely on the profile of extended individual preference orderings. As in the case of the New Testament (Matthew 9:14–17), it is not advisable to put new wine into old wineskins in the arena of the nonconsequentialist approach to social choice theory.

I.7.2. Consequentialism versus Nonconsequentialism: Characterization

Let us now turn to the extended informational framework where individuals care not only about the *instrumental* value but also about the *intrinsic* value, of opportunities to choose. Although most people may be consequential—even welfaristic—in their personal conviction, it seems undeniable that there are some people who care not only about the value of consequences and the instrumental value of opportunities but also about the intrinsic value of opportunities. Thus, scholars in normative economics may be in need for an analytical framework that is flexible enough to accommodate nonconsequentialists along with consequentialists. To prepare for such a framework, we assume that individuals form extended preference orderings of the following type: Choosing an alternative x from an opportunity set A is at least as good as choosing an alternative y from an opportunity set B. By means of this analytical vehicle, Essay 18, which is based on Kotaro Suzumura and Yongsheng Xu (2001), and Essay 19, which is based on Suzumura and Xu (2003), provide an axiomatic characterization of a *consequentialist* and a *nonconsequentialist*.

Let me begin with a simple case where no trade-off exists between consequential considerations, which focus on the individual's preferences over culmination outcomes, and nonconsequential considerations, which focus on the individual's concern about the richness of opportunities. Let X be the set of all mutually exclusive and jointly exhaustive alternatives. Let $\mathcal{S}$ denote the family of all nonempty *finite* subsets of X. Representative elements of $X \times \mathcal{S}$ are denoted by (x, A), (y, B), (z, C), . . . , and they are called *extended alternatives*. Let Ω be defined by

$$\Omega = \{(x, A) \in X \times \mathcal{S} \mid x \in A \text{ and } A \in \mathcal{S}\}. \qquad \text{(I.35)}$$

For all $(x, A) \in X \times \mathcal{S}$, $(x, A) \in \Omega$ holds if and only if x is chosen from A.

Let $\succcurlyeq$ be a reflexive, complete, and transitive binary relation over Ω. Its symmetric part and asymmetric part are denoted by $\sim$ and $\succ$, respectively. For any $(x, A), (y, B) \in \Omega$, $(x, A) \succcurlyeq (y, B)$ means that "choosing x from A is at least as good as choosing y from B." In this framework, the decision maker recognizes the intrinsic value of the opportunity for choice if there is an extended alternative $(x, A) \in \Omega$ satisfying $(x, A) \succ (x, \{x\})$. We are now ready to define two versions of consequentialism, viz., *extreme consequentialism* and *strong consequentialism*.

Definition EC (extreme consequentialism). $\succcurlyeq$ is *extremely consequential* if $(x, A) \sim (x, B)$ holds true for all $(x, A), (x, B) \in \Omega$.

DEFINITION SC (STRONG CONSEQUENTIALISM). $\succsim$ is *strongly consequential* if

(a) $(x, \{x\}) \sim (y, \{y\})$ implies $[(x, A) \succsim (y, B) \Leftrightarrow \#A \geq \#B]$; and
(b) $(x, \{x\}) \succ (y, \{y\})$ implies $(x, A) \succ (y, B)$

hold true for all $(x, A), (y, B) \in \Omega$.

Thus, an extreme consequentialist's judgments on (x, A) vis-à-vis (y, B) are based exclusively on the two consequences x and y, the richness of opportunities in A and B being completely irrelevant. In contrast, according to the judgments of a strong consequentialist, the richness of opportunities in A and B does not matter at all whenever he/she has a strict preference for $(x, \{x\})$ against $(y, \{y\})$. It is only when he/she is indifferent between $(x, \{x\})$ and $(y, \{y\})$ that the richness of opportunities measured by means of the cardinalities of A and B becomes relevant. Essay 18 is devoted to a full axiomatic characterization of extreme consequentialism and that of strong consequentialism.

We now turn to the *extreme nonconsequentialism* and *strong nonconsequentialism.*

DEFINITION ENC (EXTREME NONCONSEQUENTIALISM). $\succsim$ is *extremely nonconsequential* if $(x, A) \succ (y, B) \Leftrightarrow \#A > \#B$ holds for all $(x, A), (y, B) \in \Omega$.

DEFINITION SNC (STRONG NONCONSEQUENTIALISM). $\succsim$ is *strongly nonconsequential* if, for all $(x, A), (y, B) \in \Omega$, the following holds:

(a) $\#A > \#B \Rightarrow (x, A) \succ (y, B)$; and
(b) $\#A = \#B \Rightarrow [(x, \{x\}) \succsim (y, \{y\}) \Leftrightarrow (x, A) \succsim (y, B)]$.

Thus, an extreme nonconsequentialist orders two extended alternatives, viz., (x, A) and (y, B), exclusively according to the cardinality of A and that of B, so that the consequences x and y do not have any say at all. In its complete neglect of the value of consequences, extreme nonconsequentialism is indeed extreme. In contrast, a strong nonconsequentialist pays proper attention to the value of consequences in that, when $\#A = \#B$ holds, his/her ranking between (x, A) and (y, B) faithfully mirrors his/her ranking between $(x, \{x\})$ and $(y, \{y\})$. Essay 18 presents a full axiomatic characterization of extreme nonconsequentialism and that of strong nonconsequentialism.

So much for the analysis of the simple case, where no trade-off relationship exists between consequential considerations and nonconsequential considerations. Essay 19 generalizes the analysis of consequentialism versus nonconsequentialism by allowing for the existence of active interactions between the concern about consequences and the concern about opportunities for choice.

We assume that the following basic axioms are satisfied by $\succsim$ on $X \times \mathcal{S}$:[57]

Axiom IND (independence). For all $(x, A), (y, B) \in \Omega$, and all $z \in X - A \cup B$,

$$(x, A) \succsim (y, B) \Leftrightarrow (x, A \cup \{z\}) \succsim (y, B \cup \{z\}) \qquad \text{(I.36)}$$

holds true.

Axiom SI (simple indifference). For all $x \in X$, and all $y, z \in X - \{x\}$, $(x, \{x, y\}) \sim (x, \{x, z\})$ holds truc.

Axiom SM (simple monotonicity). For all $(x, A), (x, B) \in \Omega$, if $B \subseteq A$, then $(x, A) \succsim (x, B)$ holds true.

Axiom IND requires that, for all opportunity sets A and B, if an alternative z is not in both A and B, then the extended preference ranking over $(x, A \cup \{z\})$ and $(y, B \cup \{z\})$ should follow the extended preference ranking over (x, A) and (y, B), regardless of the nature of the added alternative z.[58] Axiom SI requires that the agent judges $(x, \{x, y\})$ and $(x, \{x, z\})$ indifferent as long as x and y, and x and z, are distinct.[59] Finally, axiom SM

57. As a matter of fact, Axiom IND, axiom SI and axiom SM also underlie the analysis of the simple case.

58. This axiom is *not* completely free from criticism. For instance, one may argue that freedom of choice offered by an opportunity set $A \in \mathcal{S}$ depends crucially on how diverse the alternatives are in A. Suppose that the added alternative z is very similar to some alternative in A but quite different from any alternative in B. Then the addition of z to A may not change the degree of freedom of choice, whereas the addition of z to B may vastly increase the degree of freedom of choice offered by B. Thus, the agent in charge of choice may rank $(y, B \cup \{z\})$ strictly higher than $(x, A \cup \{z\})$ even when the same agent ranks (x, A) and (y, B) to be indifferent.

59. Axiom SI is also vulnerable to the similar criticism that is raised against axiom IND.

requires that choosing an alternative x from the opportunity set A cannot be worse than choosing the same alternative x from the subset B of A. In other words, the agent in charge of choice is not averse to richer opportunities.[60] Although axiom IND, axiom SI, and axiom SM may not be universally appealing, they are not pathological either, and they help us circumscribe a situation where generalized consequentialism and nonconsequentialism can be analyzed.

$\mathbb{N}$ and $\mathbb{R}$ stand for the set of all natural numbers and the set of all real numbers, respectively. Let us begin with the complete characterization of the class of all extended preference orderings satisfying axiom IND, axiom SI, and axiom SM.

Theorem I.10 (Suzumura and Xu (2003, Theorem 3.3)). The extended preference ordering $\succsim$ satisfies axiom IND, axiom SI, and axiom SM if and only if there exists a function $u\colon X \to \mathbb{R}$ and a function $f\colon \mathbb{R} \times \mathbb{N} \to \mathbb{R}$ such that

(a) For all $x, y \in X$, $u(x) \geq u(y) \Leftrightarrow (x, \{x\}) \succsim (y, \{y\})$;
(b) For all $(x, A), (y, B) \in \Omega$, $(x, A) \succsim (y, B) \Leftrightarrow f(u(x), \#A) \geq f(u(y), \#B)$; and
(c) f is nondecreasing in each of its arguments and has the following property:
For all integers $i, j, k \geq 1$ and all $x \in X$, if $i + k, j + k \leq \#X$, then

$$f(u(x), i) \geq f(u(y), j) \Leftrightarrow f(u(x), i + k) \geq f(u(y), j + k).$$

Observe that Theorem I.10 allows us to treat all the cases where the utility of consequential outcomes and the value of richness of opportunities actively interact. In particular, extreme consequentialism (EC), strong consequentialism (SC), extreme nonconsequentialism (ENC), and strong nonconsequentialism (SNC) can be obtained as special cases of Theorem I.10.

---

60. This axiom may be widely supported, but it is argued that there are cases where richer opportunities for choice may be a liability rather than a virtue; see, for example, Gerald Dworkin (1982).

EC: For all $(x, A) \in \Omega$, $f(u(x), \#A) = u(x)$.

SC: For all $(x, A), (y, B) \in \Omega$, $(x, A) \succcurlyeq (y, B) \Leftrightarrow [u(x) > u(y)$ or $(u(x) = u(y)$ and $\#A \geq \#B)]$.

ENC: For all $(x, A) \in \Omega$, $f(u(x), \#A) = \#A$.

SNC: For all $(x, A), (y, B) \in \Omega$, $(x, A) \succcurlyeq (y, B) \Leftrightarrow [\#A > \#B$ or $(\#A = \#B$ and $u(x) \geq u(y))]$.

I.7.3. Implications of Consequentialism versus Nonconsequentialism

An axiomatic characterization of complex ideas may bring about a bright illumination, by means of which we can understand what is involved in these ideas much better than otherwise. What about a rich fruit of having an axiomatic characterization of consequentialism and nonconsequentialism? The best arena for exemplifying the services thereby rendered is the perennial conundrum of social choice theory, viz., Arrow's general impossibility theorem. Recollect that Arrow unambiguously based his social choice theory on the informational basis of welfarist consequentialism. How much do we affect his general impossibility result if we widen the informational basis beyond welfarist consequentialism?

Let $N = \{1, 2, \ldots, n\}$ $(2 \leq n < +\infty)$ be the set of all individuals in the society. Each individual $i \in N$ has an extended preference ordering $\succcurlyeq_i$, together forming a profile $\succcurlyeq = (\succcurlyeq_1, \succcurlyeq_2, \ldots, \succcurlyeq_n)$ of individual extended preference orderings on $X \times \Omega$. Let $\mathcal{D}$ be the set of all profiles of individual extended preference orderings. An *extended social welfare function* (ESWF) is a function ζ that maps each profile $\succcurlyeq$ in some domain $D_\zeta \subseteq \mathcal{D}$ into an extended social preference ordering $\zeta(\succcurlyeq)$ on $X \times \Omega$. The symmetric part and the asymmetric part of $\zeta(\succcurlyeq)$ will be denoted by $\sim(\zeta(\succcurlyeq))$ and $\succ(\zeta(\succcurlyeq))$, respectively.

Our assumptions on the extended social welfare function ζ are two-fold. In the first place, we assume that the domain D_ζ consists of all profiles subject to the assumption that all extended individual preference orderings satisfy axiom IND, axiom SI, and axiom MON. In the second place, we assume that ζ satisfies the naturally modified versions of the strong Pareto principle (SP), independence of irrelevant alternatives (I), and nondictatorship (ND).

Essay 20, which is based on Suzumura and Xu (2004), introduces two frameworks of extended social choice theory. The first framework is broader than welfarist consequentialism, which Arrow used in his social choice theory, yet it remains within the boundary of consequentialism. The second framework goes further and is in the territory of nonconsequentialism.

Let us begin with the consequentialist framework. Capitalizing on the axiomatization in Section I.7.2, we introduce two special categories of consequentialists, viz., the extreme consequentialist and the strong consequentialist. Recollect that an extreme consequentialist ranks two extended alternatives (x, A) and (y, B) simply in terms of the consequences x and y, allowing no relevance to the two opportunity sets A and B, from which x and y are respectively chosen. In contrast, a strong consequentialist ranks two extended alternatives (x, A) and (y, B) in full accordance with their consequences x and y only if he/she has a strict preference between $(x, \{x\})$ and $(y, \{y\})$. If he/she is indifferent between $(x, \{x\})$ and $(y, \{y\})$, his/her preference ranking between (x, A) and (y, B) is in accordance with the cardinality comparison between A and B.

There are three theorems we may assert on the possibility of an ESWF within the consequentialist framework.

Theorem I.11 (Suzumura and Xu (2004, Theorem 1; Essay 20 of this volume)). Suppose that all individuals in the society are extreme consequentialists. Then there exists no extended social welfare function satisfying SP, I, and ND.

Theorem I.12 (Suzumura and Xu (2004, Theorem 2; Essay 20 of this volume)). Suppose that there exists at least one extreme consequentialist and at least one strong consequentialist in the society. Then there exists an extended social welfare function satisfying SP, I, and ND.

Theorem I.13 (Suzumura and Xu (2004, Theorem 3; Essay 20 of this volume)). Suppose that all individuals in the society are strong consequentialists. Then there exists no extended social welfare function satisfying SP, I, and ND.

The message of these three theorems taken together seems clear. Within the consequentialist framework, if all individuals in the society are either extreme consequentialists or strong consequentialists, Arrow's general impossibility theorem cannot but resurge. However, if the society becomes so diverse as to accommodate at least one extreme consequentialist and at least one strong consequentialist, it is possible to design an extended social welfare function that satisfies the Arrovian axiom SP, axiom IIA, and axiom ND.

Let us now turn to the nonconsequentialist framework. In what follows, a mention will be made only to the concept of strong nonconsequentialist defined in Section I.7.2. The following theorem neatly summarizes the effect of having a strong nonconsequentialist in the society.

Theorem I.14 (Suzumura and Xu (2004, Theorem 4; Essay 20 of this volume)). Suppose that there is at least one strong nonconsequentialist in the society. Then there exists an extended social welfare function satisfying SP, I, and ND.

It may be worthwhile to point out that, unlike an extreme consequentialist and a strong consequentialist in Theorem I.12, a strong nonconsequentialist in Theorem I.14 is able to assure the existence of an Arrovian extended social welfare function *all by him/herself*, and his ability to turn an impossibility into a possibility is not nullified even in the homogeneous society.

I.8. Welfare and Competition, or Can Competition Ever be Socially Excessive?

It was Harold Demsetz (1982, p. 1) who began his lectures on economic, legal, and political dimensions of competition with the following thoughtful remark: "Competition occupies so important a position in economics that it is difficult to imagine economics as a social discipline without it. Stripped of competition, economics would consist largely of the maximizing calculus of an isolated Robinson Crusoe economy. Few economists complete a major work without referring to competition, and the classical economists found in competition a source of regularity and scientific propositions." Not many economists would dare to disagree with Demsetz on the central place he assigns to competition, yet there may remain a broad spectrum of disagreements among economists and, a fortiori, the public at large concerning the precise meaning of competition, the exact role competition plays as a decentralized resource allocation mechanism, and the social values attainable through the unconstrained working of competition.

I.8.1. The Suzumura-Kiyono Excess Entry Theorem

Almost thirty years ago, Suzumura and Kiyono (1987, Essay 21 of this volume) established a theorem that came to be called the *excess entry theorem*. It casts serious doubt on the validity of traditional belief in the welfare-improving effect of increasing competitiveness within the partial equilibrium model of an industry with three features.[61] The first feature is that the industry is subject to *economies of scale due to the existence of fixed costs*. The second feature is that firms in the industry produce a *homogeneous product*. The third feature is that firms in the industry engage in *oligopolistic competition*.[62] Since "a widespread belief that increasing competition will increase welfare" [Joseph Stiglitz (1981, p. 184)] has been strenuously held, the very phrase that competition may be "socially excessive" sounds almost self-contradictory. There is no wonder that the excess entry theorem caused a stir in the profession.

The point of departure of the Suzumura-Kiyono excess entry theorem is the insightful observation by William Baumol (1982, p. 2) to the effect that "the standard analysis [of industrial organization] leaves us with the impression that there is a rough continuum, in terms of desirability of industry performance, ranging from unregulated pure monopoly as the pessimal [sic] arrangement to perfect competition as the ideal, with relative efficiency in resource allocation increasing monotonically as the number of firms expands." It was this observation that provided us with a workable test

61. The message of the Suzumura-Kiyono excess entry theorem has strong resemblance to the result of N. Gregory Mankiw and Michael Whinston (1986), but the Suzumura-Kiyono theorem is completely independent of their result. We should also refer to two earlier contributions, viz., Richard Schmalensee (1976) and Carl Christian von Weizsäcker (1980; 1980a), both of which showed the essence of the excess entry theorem by means of simple examples. See also Martin Perry (1984) for a related result.

62. In Japan, from the end of World War II through today, one of the guiding principles for the formulation of industrial policy has always been the prevention of "excessive competition" in industries having these three features as common idiosyncrasies. Some salient examples of these industries include iron and steel, petroleum refining, petrochemicals, certain other chemicals, cement, and paper and pulp. See Ryutaro Komiya, Masahiro Okuno-Fujiwara, and Kotaro Suzumura (1988) for further details.

hypothesis in the attempt to verify whether or not there is a sense in which we can meaningfully talk about social excessiveness of competition.

The prototype model of an oligopolistic industry is formulated as follows. Consider an industry with n firms engaging in oligopolistic competition by means of a homogeneous product. Let f be the inverse demand function that associates the market price p of the product with the industry output Q, viz.,

$$p = f(Q), \text{ where } Q = \Sigma_{j=1}^{n} q_j, \tag{I.37}$$

and q_j is the firm j's output ($j = 1, 2, \ldots, n$). It is assumed that

A(1). $f(Q)$ is twice continuously differentiable with $f'(Q) < 0$ for all $Q \geq 0$ such that $f(Q) > 0$.

All firms are assumed to be identical in technology as well as in behavior. Let $C(q_i)$ be the cost function of the firm i, where $i = 1, 2, \ldots, n$. We assume that

A(2). $C(q_i)$ is twice continuously differentiable with $C(q_i) > 0$, $C'(q_i) > 0$ and $C''(q_i) > 0$ for all $q_i \geq 0$.

The profit function of the firm i is defined by

$$\pi_i(q_i; Q_{-i}) = q_i f(q_i + Q_{-i}) - C(q_i), \tag{I.38}$$

where Q_{-i} denotes the aggregate output of all firms other than i taken together, viz., $Q_{-i} = \Sigma_{j \neq i} q_j = Q - q_i$. As an auxiliary step in introducing our assumptions on the strategic interdependence of firms, let us define

$$\mu_i(q_i, Q_{-i}) = (\partial/\partial q_i)Q = 1 + (\partial/\partial q_i)Q_{-i} \quad (i = 1, 2, \ldots, n), \tag{I.39}$$

$$\alpha_i(q_i, Q_{-i}) = (\partial^2/\partial q_i^2)\pi_i(q_i, Q_{-i}) \quad (i = 1, 2, \ldots, n), \tag{I.40}$$

$$\beta_{ij}(q_i, Q_{-i}) = (\partial^2/\partial q_i \partial q_j)\pi_i(q_i, Q_{-i}) \quad (i \neq j; i, j = 1, 2, \ldots, n). \tag{I.41}$$

Note that μ_i is nothing other than the *coefficient of conjectural variation* that measures the extent by which rival firms will adjust their outputs in response to a change in i's output. We are now ready to introduce the following crucial assumptions.

A(3). The *Cournot conjecture* prevails, viz., $\mu_i(q_i, Q_{-i}) = 1$ holds for all $i = 1, 2, \ldots, n$.

A(4). The *strategic substitutability* prevails, viz., $\beta_{ij}(q_i, Q_{-i}) < 0$ holds for all i and j such that $i \neq j$ and $i, j = 1, 2, \ldots, n$.[63]

Under A(1), A(2), A(3), and A(4), the profit-maximizing output q_i of the firm i that corresponds to the output of all other firms taken together, Q_{-i}, is characterized by

$$f(q_i + Q_{-i}) + q_i f'(q_i + Q_{-i}) - C'(q_i) = 0 \quad (i = 1, 2, \ldots, n), \tag{I.42}$$

namely, by the equality of marginal revenue and marginal cost. For each number n of firms, $\boldsymbol{q}^N(n) = (q^N(n), q^N(n), \ldots, q^N(n))$ denotes the *symmetric Cournot-Nash equilibrium,* which satisfies (I.42) simultaneously for all firms. It can be verified that A(1), A(2), A(3), and A(4) assure us that $(d/dn)q^n < 0$, $(d/dn)Q^N(n) > 0$, and $(d/dn)p^N(n) < 0$ hold for any n, where $p^N(n) = f(Q^N(n))$.

Let us turn to the long-run properties of the Cournot-Nash model of oligopolistic competition. A key concept of this analysis is the equilibrium profit $\pi^N(n)$ that each incumbent firm earns at the Cournot-Nash equilibrium among n firms, viz.,

$$\pi^N(n) = q^N(n) f(nq^N(n)) - C(q^N(n)). \tag{I.43}$$

If $\pi^N(n) >$ (resp. $<$) 0 holds, potential competitors (resp. incumbent firms) will be induced to enter into (resp. exit from) this profitable (resp. unprofitable) industry. This entry-exit dynamics will halt if the *equilibrium number of firms,* n_e, which is defined by

$$\pi^N(n_e) = 0, \tag{I.44}$$

is attained.

63. The concepts of *strategic substitutes* and *strategic complements* are due to Jeremy Bulow, John Geanakoplos, and Paul Klemperer (1985). See Suzumura (1995, Prologue) for the meaning of, and services rendered by, these concepts in the theory of oligopolistic competition.

Let us now turn from the description of the oligopolistic equilibrium to the evaluation of welfare performance thereof. The focus of our analysis is to verify whether or not the conventional belief in the welfare-enhancing effect of increasing competitiveness can be sustained. Following the conventional welfare measure of partial equilibrium analysis, let the *net market surplus function* $W(n, \boldsymbol{q})$ be defined by

$$W(n, \boldsymbol{q}) = \int_0^Q f(Z)dZ - \Sigma_{j=1}^n C(q_j), \tag{I.45}$$

where $\boldsymbol{q} = (q_1, q_2, \ldots, q_n)$ is the output configuration of firms and $Q = \Sigma_{j=1}^n q_j$. It is clear that (I.45) is nothing other than the sum of consumer's surplus and producer's surplus, which enables us to introduce the *second-best market surplus function* by

$$W^S(n) = W(n, \boldsymbol{q}^N(n)). \tag{I.46}$$

Clearly, $W^S(n)$ is the conventional welfare measure of oligopolistic competition among n firms. We are now ready to define the *second-best number of firms,* n_s, by

$$n_s = \text{arg max } W^S(n) \text{ over all } n > 0. \tag{I.47}$$

There are two versions of what we christen the prototypical *second-best excess entry theorem*. The first version is concerned with the direct comparison between the equilibrium number of firms n_e and the second-best number of firms n_s.

THEOREM I.15 (SECOND-BEST EXCESS ENTRY THEOREM). Suppose that A(1), A(2), A(3) and A(4) are satisfied. Then the equilibrium number of firms n_e exceeds the second-best number of firms n_s.

The message of Theorem I.15 should be clear. If left unfettered, oligopolistic competition among Cournot competitors will settle in the long-run Cournot-Nash equilibrium $\boldsymbol{q}^N(n_e)$ among n_e firms, where the equilibrium number of firms n_e is excessive in comparison with the second-best number of firms n_s. As a theoretical verdict, Theorem I.15 is impeccable, but it does not provide the helmsman of industrial policy with any clear-cut prescription in search of welfare improvement. The second version of the second-best excess entry theorem is more down-to-earth in its policy implication.

THEOREM I.16 (SECOND-BEST EXCESS ENTRY THEOREM AT THE MARGIN). Suppose that A(1), A(2), A(3), and A(4) are satisfied. Then the equilibrium number of firms n_e is socially excessive at the margin in the second-best sense, viz., a marginal decrease in the number of firms at n_e increases the second-best market surplus $W^S(n)$ marginally.

In combination, Theorem I.15 and Theorem I.16 tell us that there is a strong tendency toward social excessiveness of unfettered competition in the Cournot market satisfying A(1), A(2), A(3), and A(4). In view of these theoretical verdicts, should we prescribe that competition must not be left uncontrolled and had better be subject to the deliberate regulation by government bureaus in charge of industrial policy?

Throughout this subsection, we have been exclusively concerned with the second-best performance of an oligopolistic industry. There are first-best counterparts of the excess entry theorem, which go as follows. Let $\boldsymbol{q}^F(n)$ be the socially first-best output profile, which is defined by

$$\boldsymbol{q}^F(n) = \text{ arg max } W(n, \boldsymbol{q}) \text{ over all } \boldsymbol{q} > 0,$$

by means of which the *first-best market surplus function* is defined by

$$W^F(n) = W(n, \boldsymbol{q}^F(n)),$$

which measures the welfare performance of the oligopolistic industry on the assumption that all incumbent firms follow the socially first-best marginal cost principle. The first-best number of firms n_f is then defined by

$$n_f = \text{ arg max } W^{F(n)} \text{ over all } n > 0.$$

We are now ready to state the *first-best excess entry theorem* and the *first-best excess entry theorem at the margin* as follows.

THEOREM 1* (FIRST-BEST EXCESS ENTRY THEOREM). Suppose that A(1), A(2), A(3), and A(4) are satisfied, and the equilibrium number of firms n_e exceeds 1. Then n_e exceeds the first-best number of firms n_f as far as n_f exceeds 1.

THEOREM 2* (FIRST-BEST EXCESS ENTRY THEOREM AT THE MARGIN). Suppose that A(1), A(2), A(3), and A(4) are satisfied. Then the equilibrium number of firms n_e is socially excessive at the margin in the first-best sense, viz., a marginal decrease in the number of firms at n_e increases the first-best market surplus $W^F(n)$ marginally.

However, the first-best welfare ideal is hard to attain for an actual down-to-earth government, as it presupposes that the government can enforce the marginal cost principle to firms even in the presence of economies of scale due to the existence of fixed costs.

I.8.2. Generalizations and Qualifications of the Excess Entry Theorem

Before trying to confront this crucial question, careful examinations of the robustness of excess entry theorems may be in order. Essay 22 [Konishi, Okuno-Fujiwara, and Suzumura (1990)] and Essay 23 [Okuno-Fujiwara and Suzumura (1993)] in Part VI of this volume are devoted to some of these examinations.

It is a standard practice in the theories of international trade, tax incidence, and industrial organization that we try the depth of the water by means of a simple partial equilibrium framework before we take recourse to the heavier apparatus of a general equilibrium framework. It is in this spirit that Essay 22 introduces a simple two-sector model of general economic equilibrium to verify if the main message of excess entry theorems can be sustained in the presence of interactions between the two sectors. In this model of a closed economy, there are two sectors producing two goods, X and Y, and two factors of production, capital K and labor L. The good X is produced under increasing returns to scale due to the existence of fixed costs, whereas the good Y is competitively produced under constant returns to scale. The industry X consists of identical firms engaging in the Cournot-Nash quantity competition, whereas the industry Y consists of perfectly competitive firms producing the good Y. It is assumed that both factors of production are in fixed supply, and they are freely mobile between sectors. It is assumed that both factor markets are perfectly competitive. There is a single representative consumer, whose income consists of factor rewards and profits earned in the industry X, profits earned in the industry Y being driven down to zero by perfect competition.

The focus of the analysis is the effect of an exogenous decrease in the number of firms in the industry X, viz., n, from the equilibrium number of firms n_e, where the equilibrium profits earned in the industry X is driven down to zero, on the utility of the representative consumer. The main result of Essay 22 is the identification of a clear condition under which we may assert the resurgence of the excess entry theorem in general equilibrium at the margin.

To identify the condition that supports the validity of the excess entry theorem in general equilibrium at the margin, let us introduce three concepts of factor intensities, paying due attention to the fact that the existence of economies of scale in the industry X forces us to distinguish the *marginal factor intensity* and the *average factor intensity* in the industry X. Let us define

k_M^X = marginal capital intensity in the industry X,

k^X = average capital intensity in the industry X,

k^Y = marginal as well as average capital intensity in the industry Y.

In terms of these concepts of factor intensities, we may define the following crucial condition.

$$\textit{No Capital Intensity Twist} \Leftrightarrow (k_M^X - k^Y)(k^X - k^Y) \geq 0. \qquad \text{(I.48)}$$

THEOREM I.17 (EXCESS ENTRY THEOREM IN GENERAL EQUILIBRIUM AT THE MARGIN). Suppose that there is no capital intensity twist. Then the long-run free entry equilibrium number n_e of oligopolistic firms is socially excessive at the margin in the sense that a marginal decrease in the number of oligopolistic firms from n_e marginally improves the welfare level of the representative consumer.

Recollect that the relative size of capital intensity in one sector and that in another sector plays an essential role in virtually all two-sector models that are widely used in international trade theory, such as Wolfgang Stolper and Paul Samuelson (1941), Paul Samuelson (1948), and Ronald Jones (1965; 2002); two-sector growth theory, such as Yoichi Shinkai (1960) and Hirofumi Uzawa (1961; 1963); and the theory of tax incidence, such as Arnold Harberger (1962) and Charles McLure (1975). However, most, if not all, preceding analyses presupposed that both industries are perfectly competitive, so that there is no need to distinguish between the marginal capital intensity and the average capital intensity. In the general equilibrium model in Essay 22, one of the two industries is engaged in oligopolistic competition, so that there is a clear conceptual distinction between the marginal capital intensity and the average capital intensity. In this context, no capital intensity twist seems to be a natural condition to require.

Another direction to explore with the purpose of examining the robustness of the prototypical excess entry theorem is the introduction of a further stage of competition in the model of oligopolistic interactions. Recollect that the original model of Suzumura and Kiyono has only two stages of interfirm interactions, viz., the stage of entry-exit decision and the stage of market competition in quantities. The additional stage that we introduce is that of strategic R&D commitments, where those firms that have decided either to enter into or to stay within the industry decide on the cost-reducing R&D investments. Essay 23 of this volume, which is based on the paper by Masahiro Okuno-Fujiwara and Kotaro Suzumura (1993), introduces a three-stage model of oligopolistic competition. In the first stage, firms decide whether or not to enter into or stay within the market. In the second stage, firms make an irrevocable commitment to cost-reducing R&D investment. In the third stage, firms compete for the market by means of quantities produced. There are three equilibrium concepts to be examined in this model. Thinking backward, given an arbitrary number of firms and the profile of R&D commitments, the *third-stage Cournot-Nash equilibrium in quantities* is defined. Given an arbitrary number of firms, the *second-stage subgame perfect equilibrium* is defined. Finally, the *first-stage free-entry equilibrium* is defined as a subgame perfect equilibrium of the entire three-stage game. The crucial question to be asked is the welfare effect of an exogenous change in the number of firms from the free-entry number of firms. To keep our analysis within tractable bounds, we return to the partial equilibrium analysis and invoke the net market surplus function to be defined as our welfare measure as follows:

$$W(n; \boldsymbol{x}; \boldsymbol{q}) = \int_0^Q f(Z)dZ - \Sigma_{j=1}^n \{c(x_j)q_j + x_j\}, \qquad \text{(I.49)}$$

where $\boldsymbol{x} = (x_1, x_2, \ldots, x_n)$ is the profile of R&D commitments, $\boldsymbol{q} = (q_1, q_2, \ldots, q_n)$ is the output profile, and $Q = \Sigma_{j=1}^n q_j$. The inverse demand function f is assumed to satisfy

A*(1). $f(Q)$ is twice continuously differentiable with $f'(Q) < 0$ for all $Q \geq 0$ such that $f(Q) > 0$. Besides, the elasticity of the slope of the inverse demand function, which is defined by $\delta(Q) = Qf''(Q)/f'(Q)$, is constant.[64]

In defining the welfare measure (I.49), we are assuming that the cost-reducing R&D commitments are measured by means of the fixed costs thereby incurred. We also assume that the marginal cost function $c(x)$ satisfies the following:

A*(2). $c(x)$ is twice continuously differentiable and satisfies $c(x) > 0$, $c'(x) < 0$ and $c''(x) > 0$ for all $x > 0$.

As in the case of the Suzumura-Kiyono prototype model, we assume the following:

A*(3). The third-stage quantity strategies are strategic substitutes.

The main result of Essay 23 may be stated as follows.

THEOREM I.18 (EXCESS ENTRY THEOREM WITH STRATEGIC COMMITMENT AT THE MARGIN). Suppose that A*(1), A*(2), and A*(3) are satisfied. Then a small reduction in the number of firms at the first-stage, free-entry equilibrium unambiguously improves the second-best social welfare as long as $n_e \geq 1 - \delta$.

On the basis of Theorem I.13, the essence of the simple partial equilibrium version of the Suzumura-Kiyono excess entry theorem at the margin may be kept intact even when we introduce a further stage of R&D commitment.

There are many other directions to explore with the purpose of checking the robustness of excess entry theorems. Some of these directions may bring us into the contrary verdicts on the welfare effects of increasing competitiveness. For example, suppose that we get rid of the basic assumption A(1) or

---

64. The admissible class of inverse demand functions under A*(1) consists of

$$f(Q) = a - b \cdot Q^{\epsilon} \text{ if } \epsilon = \delta + 1 \neq 0, \text{ and } f(Q) = a - b \cdot \log Q \text{ if } \delta = -1,$$

where a is a non-negative constant and b is another constant such that $b > 0$ (resp. $b < 0$) if $\delta \geq -1$ (resp. $\delta < -1$).

A*(1) and allow the industry to produce a wide spectrum of differentiated products. Then the entry of a new firm, more often than not, accompanies a widening of the product spectrum, which endows consumers with the wider freedom of choice in the market and may increase rather than decrease social welfare.[65] Besides, if firms are heterogeneous in the sense that their technologies, viz., cost functions, are different from each other, the degree of competitiveness among firms cannot be captured by means of a simple index such as the number of firms in the industry in question.[66] Another good case in point is the situation where oligopolistic firms are producing *intermediate* goods rather than *final* goods. It was Arghya Ghosh and Hodaka Morita (2007) who analyzed a model of successive vertical oligopoly and demonstrated that free entry of firms into an industry producing a homogeneous intermediate product may lead to a socially insufficient, rather than socially excessive, number of firms if its vertical relationships to the other industry are taken into explicit account. It is also shown by Ghosh and Morita (2007a) that a similar insufficient entry result can hold in a bilateral oligopoly model.

Essay 24, the last essay of Part VI, is based on Suzumura (1992) and casts a new light on the effects of competition on social welfare in the two-stage model of oligopolistic competition. In the first stage, firms make strategic commitments with cost-reducing R&D investment either noncooperatively or cooperatively. It is assumed that the cost-reducing benefits of R&D investment have spillover effects among firms. In the second stage, firms engage in noncooperative competition in quantities. The mixed cooperative and non-cooperative equilibrium is compared with the subgame perfect noncooperative equilibrium in terms of social welfare with the purpose of

65. It may not be totally irrelevant to recollect that the automobile industry, where product differentiation plays a crucial role as one of the strategic measures in interfirm competition, has never experienced the so-called excessive competition throughout the post–World War II history of Japan.

66. However, not everything is lost. Indeed, Suzumura (1995, Chapter 9) invoked the method of analysis developed by Gérard Debreu and Herbert Scarf (1963) and Koji Okuguchi (1973) and established the generalized excess entry theorem in a Cournot-Nash oligopoly model, where interfirm differences in cost functions are properly admitted. It is assumed that there exist an identical number of firms having each type of conceivable cost function, and we let the number of firms increase uniformly over all types of cost functions whenever we talk about the entry of new firms. It is shown by Suzumura (1995, Theorem 9.1 and Theorem 9.2) that the second-best excess entry theorems hold within this generalized class of Cournot-Nash oligopolies. See also Suzumura (2012) for the overall evaluation of the excess entry theorem.

identifying the conditions under which R&D collaborations may be socially beneficial vis-à-vis noncooperative R&D.

I.8.3. Instrumental Value and Intrinsic Value of Competition

There is no rule without exception. Likewise, there is no theorem without assumptions. Outside the territory circumscribed by the set of assumptions, no theorem has any legitimate claim to assert, and the excess entry theorem is no exception. Indeed, it is the existence of exceptional cases that sheds light on the reach, meaning, and relevance of the excess entry theorem. At least within the circumscribed territory, it casts serious doubt on the universal validity of a conventional belief, which may be traced all the way back to Adam Smith's *The Wealth of Nations,* to the effect that "in general, if any branch of trade, or any division of labor, be advantageous to the public, the freer and more general the competition, it will always be the more so."

We are now in the stage of answering the question, which was raised but left open at the end of Section I.8.1, to the following effect: Should we acquiesce in a resigned view that "regulation by enlightened, but not omniscient, regulators could in principle achieve greater efficiency than deregulation" [John Panzar (1980, p. 313)]? It is in this context that we should examine the meaning and role of competition more in detail.

There are three instrumental roles of competition, which seem to underlie the traditional belief. In the first place, competition abhors waste, just as nature abhors a vacuum. The existence of waste sends a signal that there are underexploited opportunities for earning profits, and unfettered competition will sooner or later drive them out. Thus, competition plays an *instrumental* role in promoting an *intrinsic* value of economic efficiency. In the second place, competition is a spontaneous mechanism, through which new innovations are introduced into economic processes. Both for aggressive and protective purposes, firms in competitive environments are motivated to transform scientific inventions into industrial innovations. Thus, competition plays an *instrumental* role in promoting an *intrinsic* value of long-run economic progress. In the third place, competition is a *discovery procedure* in the sense of Friedrich von Hayek (1948; 1978) to the effect that it is through competition that the market economy finds a way of making the efficient use of dispersed and privately owned information. Thus, competition plays an *instrumental* role in promoting an *intrinsic* value of privacy-respecting and decentralized decision making.

In addition to these *instrumental* values, competition has an *intrinsic* value of its own. Recollect that the competitive market mechanism is the unique mechanism that enables each economic agent to try out his/her own life chances on his/her own initiative and responsibility. There is no guarantee that his/her attempt will be successful in bringing about favorable consequential outcomes, but those who had an opportunity to pursue their life chances autonomously may well feel happier than those who are deprived of autonomy to try out their life chances. It is this *intrinsic* value of competition that goes against the use of excess entry theorems as a reason for justifying "regulation by enlightened, but not omniscient, regulators" in the name of keeping socially excessive competition under control. There are at least two further reasons for this verdict.

On the one hand, the welfare criterion that underlies the partial equilibrium version of the excess entry theorem is insidious, to say the least. Recollect that the net market surplus consists of the consumer's surplus and the producer's surplus. When we decrease the number of firms marginally from the equilibrium number of firms, the producer's surplus surely increases by virtue of the better exploitation of residual economies of scale due to the existence of fixed costs, whereas the consumer's surplus unambiguously decreases due to the increase of monopoly power held by incumbent firms. It can easily be verified that the latter effect is of higher order infinitesimal vis-à-vis the former effect, so that the net market surplus becomes larger by a marginal decrease in the number of firms. It follows that the use of net market surplus cannot but imply that the social priority is implicitly conferred to the producer's benefit vis-à-vis the consumer's benefit. Unless there exists a priori social agreement on this conferment of priority to producers, it is hard to justify the use of net market surplus as a welfare criterion for choosing between competition and regulation.

On the other hand, even if it is theoretically possible that deliberate regulation by enlightened—but less-than-perfect—government may outperform the uncontrolled competition, the social cost of regulation must be weighed against the social cost of competition. In this context, a thoughtful observation by Ryutaro Komiya (1975, p. 214) on the "excessive competition in investment" in postwar Japan may be worthwhile to cite: "The 'excessive competition in investment' in an industry appears to me to depend on the following three factors: (i) the products of the industry are homogeneous, not differentiated; (ii) the size of productive capacity can be expressed readily by a single index such as monthly output in standard tons, daily refining capacity in barrels, number of spindles, etc.; and (iii) such an index of productive capacity is used by the supervising *genkyoku* [viz., the government office having the primary responsibility for the industry in question] or by the industry association for administrative or allocative purposes. . . . That productive capacity has actually been used or referred to for administrative or allocative purposes in direct controls, administrative guidance, or cartelization, and the companies rightly or wrongly expect this to be repeated in the future, seems to be the real cause of the 'excessive competition in investment.'"

The purpose of the four essays in Part VI of this volume would be served if they could call the reader's attention to these complex relationships that hold between competition and welfare.

I.9. A Closing Remark and a Disclaimer

Let us conclude this overall introduction with a closing remark and a disclaimer. The identified seven pillars are meant to pitch a tent that covers almost all areas within normative economics where I aspired for making contributions of my own. It is my hope that each part of these selected essays, together with some other essays that could not be accommodated in this volume, but are briefly expounded in this overall introduction, crystallizes my contributions to normative economics with some relevance for the evolution of the subject. There is no claim that the area covered by this volume of selected essays is wide enough to accommodate all the relevant issues of normative economics. My modest purpose would be served if those issues that are covered by the tent spanned by these seven pillars could be recognized as an integral part of the important issues in their own right.

It is obvious that the issues covered by this volume are theoretical in nature even if they are partly motivated by the historical experience in Japan and elsewhere. Pigou once observed that "there will, I think, be general agreement that in the sciences of human society, be their appeal as bearers of light never so high, it is the promise of fruit and not of light that chiefly merits our regard" [Pigou (1932, p. 4)]. I am hoping that the time is ripe for me to step into a new pilgrimage in search of real fruit and not just light of normative economics.

I.10. References

[1] Arrow, K. J., *Social Choice and Individual Values,* New York: John Wiley & Sons, 1st ed., 1951; Expanded 2nd ed., 1963. Third edn. with an Introduction by Eric Maskin, New Haven, Conn: Yale University Press, 2012.

[2] Arrow, K. J., "An Extension of the Basic Theorems of Classical Welfare Economics," in J. Neyman, ed., *Proceedings of the Second Berkeley Symposium on Mathematical Statistics and Probability,* Berkeley and Los Angeles: University of California Press, 1951a, 507–532. Reprinted in *Collected Papers of Kenneth J. Arrow,* Vol. 2, *General Equilibrium,* Cambridge, Mass.: Belknap Press of Harvard University Press, 1983, 13–45.

[3] Arrow, K. J., "Rational Choice Functions and Orderings," *Economica* **26**, 1959, 121–127. Reprinted in *Collected Papers of Kenneth J. Arrow,* Vol. 1, *Social Choice and Justice,* Cambridge, Mass.: Belknap Press of Harvard University Press, 1984, 100–108.

[4] Arrow, K. J., "Extended Sympathy and the Possibility of Social Choice," *American Economic Review: Papers and Proceedings* **67**, 1977, 219–225. Reprinted in *Collected Papers of Kenneth J. Arrow,* Vol. 1, *Social Choice and Justice*, Cambridge, Mass.: Belknap Press of Harvard University Press, 1983, 147–161.

[5] Arrow, K. J., "Arrow's Theorem," in J. Eatwell, M. Milgate, and P. Newman, eds., *The New Palgrave: A Dictionary of Economics,* Vol. I, London: Macmillan, 1987, 124–126.

[6] Arrow, K. J., A. K. Sen, and K. Suzumura, eds., *Handbook of Social Choice and Welfare,* Vol. I, Amsterdam: North-Holland, 2002.

[7] Arrow, K. J., A. K. Sen, and K. Suzumura, eds., *Handbook of Social Choice and Welfare,* Vol. II, Amsterdam: Elsevier, 2011.

[8] Basu, K., and T. Mitra, "Aggregating Infinite Utility Streams with Intergenerational Equity: The Importance of Being Paretian," *Econometrica* **71**, 2003, 1557–1563.

[9] Basu, K., and T. Mitra, "Utilitarianism for Infinite Utility Streams: A New Welfare Criterion and Its Axiomatic Characterization," *Journal of Economic Theory* **133**, 2007, 350–373.

[10] Baumol, W. J., "Contestable Markets: An Uprising in the Theory of Industry Structure," *American Economic Review*: *Papers and Proceedings* **72**, 1982, 1–15.

[11] Bentham, J., *An Introduction to the Principles of Morals and Legislation,* London: Payne, 1789. Reprinted in 1907 by Oxford: Clarendon Press.

[12] Bentham, J., "Anarchical Fallacies." First published in English in J. Bowring, ed., *The Works of Jeremy Bentham,* Vol. 2, Edinburgh: William Tait, 1843, 489–534.

[13] Berge, C., *Topological Spaces,* London: Oliver & Boyd, 1963.

[14] Bergson, A., "A Reformulation of Certain Aspects of Welfare Economics," *Quarterly Journal of Economics* **52**, 1938, 310–334.

[15] Berlin, I., *Two Concepts of Liberty,* Oxford: Oxford University Press, 1958.

[16] Black, D., "On the Rationale of Group Decision Making," *Journal of Political Economy* **56**, 1948, 23–34.

[17] Black, D., *The Theory of Committees and Elections,* Cambridge, UK: Cambridge University Press, 1958.

[18] Blair, D. H., G. Bordes, J. S. Kelly, and K. Suzumura, "Impossibility Theorems without Collective Rationality," *Journal of Economic Theory* **13**, 1976, 361–379. Essay 5 of this volume.

[19] Borda, J.-C. de, "Mémoire sur les èlections par scrutin," *Mémoires de l'Acadèmie Royale des Sciences Annèe,* 1781, 657–665. English translation by A. de Grazia, "Mathematical Derivation of the Election System," *Isis* **44**, 1953, 42–51.

[20] Bordes, G., "Consistency, Rationality and Collective Choice," *Review of Economic Studies* **43**, 1976, 451–457.

[21] Bordes, G., "Some More Results on Consistency, Rationality and Collective Choice," in J.-J. Laffont, ed., *Revelation and Aggregation of Preferences,* Amsterdam: North-Holland, 1979, 175–197.

[22] Bossert, W., "Suzumura Consistency," in P. K. Pattanaik, K. Tadenuma, Y. Xu, and N. Yoshihara, eds., *Rational Choice and Social Welfare: Theory and Applications,* New York: Springer, 2008, 159–179.

[23] Bossert, W., and M. Fleurbaey, "An Interview with Kotaro Suzumura," *Social Choice and Welfare* **44**, 2015, 179–208.

[24] Bossert, W., Y. Sprumont, and K. Suzumura, "Consistent Rationalizability," *Economica* **72**, 2005, 185–200. Essay 3 of this volume.

[25] Bossert, W., Y. Sprumont, and K. Suzumura, "Maximal-Element Rationalizability," *Theory and Decision* **58**, 2005a, 325–350.

[26] Bossert, W., Y. Sprumont, and K. Suzumura, "Rationalizability of Choice Functions on General Domains without Full Transitivity," *Social Choice and Welfare* **27**, 2006, 435–458.

[27] Bossert, W., and K. Suzumura, "A Characterization of Consistent Collective Choice Rules," *Journal of Economic Theory* **138**, 2008, 311–320. Editor, "Erratum," *Journal of Economic Theory* **140**, 2008, 355. Essay 8 of this volume.

[28] Bossert, W., and K. Suzumura, "Rational Choice on General Domains," in K. Basu and R. Kanbur, eds., *Arguments for a Better World: Essays in Honor of Amartya Sen,* Vol. I, *Ethics, Welfare, and Measurement,* Oxford: Oxford University Press, 2009, 103–152.

[29] Bossert, W., and K. Suzumura, *Consistency, Choice, and Rationality,* Cambridge, Mass.: Harvard University Press, 2010.

[30] Bossert, W., and K. Suzumura, "Multiprofile Intergenerational Social Choice," *Social Choice and Welfare* **37**, 2011, 493–509. Essay 12 of this volume.

[31] Bossert, W., and K. Suzumura, "Multiprofile Intertemporal Social Choice: A Survey," in C. Binder, G. Codognato, M. Teschl, and Y. Xu, eds., *Individual and Collective Choice and Social Welfare,* Berlin, Heidelberg: Springer, 2015.

[32] Buchanan, J. M., "Social Choice, Democracy, and Free Markets," *Journal of Political Economy* **62**, 1954, 114–123.

[33] Bulow, J. I., J. D. Geanakoplos, and P. D. Klemperer, "Multimarket Oligopoly: Strategic Substitutes and Complements," *Journal of Political Economy* **93**, 1985, 488–511.

[34] Champernowne, D. G., *Uncertainty and Estimation in Economics,* 3 vols., San Francisco: Holden-Day, 1969.

[35] Condorcet, M. J. A. N. de, *Essai sur l'application de l'analyse à la probabilité des décisions rendues à la pluralité des voix,* Paris: Imprimerie Royale, 1785. Facsimile published in 1972 by Chelsea Publishing Company, New York.

[36] Dalton, H., "The Measurement of the Inequality of Income," *Economic Journal* **30**, 1920, 348–361.

[37] Deb, R., "Waiver, Effectivity and Rights as Game Forms," *Economica* **61**, 1994, 167–178.

[38] Deb, R., "Rights as Alternative Game Forms," *Social Choice and Welfare* **22**, 2004, 83–111.

[39] Deb, R., "Nonbinary Social Choice," in K. J. Arrow, A. K. Sen, and K. Suzumura, eds., *Handbook of Social Choice and Welfare,* Vol. II, Amsterdam: Elsevier, 2011, 335–366.

[40] Deb, R., P. K. Pattanaik, and L. Razzolini, "Game Forms, Rights, and the Efficiency of Social Outcomes," *Journal of Economic Theory* **72**, 1997, 74–95.

[41] Debreu, G., *Theory of Value,* New York: John Wiley and Sons, Inc., 1959.

[42] Debreu, G., and H. Scarf, "A Limit Theorem on the Core of an Economy," *International Economic Review* **4**, 1963, 235–246.

[43] Demsetz, H., *Economic, Legal, and Political Dimensions of Competition,* Amsterdam: North-Holland, 1982.

[44] Diamond, P., "The Evaluation of Infinite Utility Streams," *Econometrica* **33**, 1965, 170–177.

[45] Dworkin, G., "Is More Choice Better Than Less?" in P. A. French, T. E. Uehling, Jr., and H. K. Wettstein, eds., *Midwest Studies in Philosophy* VII: *Social and Political Philosophy*, Minneapolis: University of Minnesota Press, 1982.

[46] Dworkin, R., "What Is Equality? Part 1: Equality of Welfare," *Philosophy & Public Affairs* **10**, 1981, 185–246.

[47] Dworkin, R., *Sovereign Virtue: The Theory and Practice of Equality,* Cambridge, Mass.: Harvard University Press, 2000.

[48] Elster, J., "Sour Grapes—Utilitarianism and the Genesis of Wants," in A. Sen and B. Williams, eds., *Utilitarianism and Beyond,* Cambridge, UK: Cambridge University Press, 1982.

[49] Elster, J., *Sour Grapes: Studies in the Subversion of Rationality,* Cambridge, UK: Cambridge University Press, 1983.

[50] Ferejohn, J., and T. Page, "On the Foundations of Intertemporal Choice," *American Journal of Agricultural Economics* **60**, 1978, 269–275.

[51] Fishburn, P. C., "Arrow's Impossibility Theorem: Concise Proof and Infinite Voters," *Journal of Economic Theory* **2**, 1970, 103–106.

[52] Fleurbaey, M., K. Suzumura, and K. Tadenuma, "Arrovian Aggregation in Economic Environments: How Much Should We Know about Indifference Surfaces?" *Journal of Economic Theory* **124**, 2005, 22–44. Essay 7 of this volume.

[53] Fleurbaey, M., K. Suzumura, and K. Tadenuma, "The Informational Basis of the Theory of Fair Allocations," *Social Choice and Welfare* **24**, 2005a, 311–341. Essay 10 of this volume.

[54] Foley, D., "Resource Allocation in the Public Sector," *Yale Economic Essays* **7**, 1967, 45–98.

[55] Frisch, R., "Sur un Probléme d'Economie Pure," *Norsk Matematisk Forening Skrifter* **1**, 1926, 1–40. English translation: "On a Problem in Pure Economics," in J. S. Chipman, L. Hurwicz, M. K. Richter, and H. F. Sonnenschein, eds., *Preferences, Utility, and Demand,* New York: Harcourt Brace Jovanovich, 1971, 386–354.

[56] Gärdenfors, P., "Rights, Games and Social Choice," *Noûs* **15**, 1981, 341–356.

[57] Gaertner, W., P. K. Pattanaik, and K. Suzumura, "Individual Rights Revisited," *Economica* **59**, 1992, 161–177. Essay 15 of this volume.

[58] Georgescu-Roegen, N., "Choice and Revealed Preference," *Southern Economic Journal* **21**, 1954, 119–130.

[59] Georgescu-Roegen, N., *Analytical Economics: Issues and Problems,* Cambridge, Mass.: Harvard University Press, 1966.

[60] Ghosh, A., and H. Morita, "Free Entry and Social Efficiency under Vertical Oligopoly," *Rand Journal of Economics* **38**, 2007, 541–554.

[61] Ghosh, A., and H. Morita, "Social Desirability of Free Entry: A Bilateral Oligopoly Analysis," *International Journal of Industrial Organization* **25**, 2007a, 925–934.

[62] Goto, A., and K. Suzumura, eds., *Competition Policy of Japan,* Tokyo: University of Tokyo Press, 1999. In Japanese.

[63] Graaff, J. de V., *Theoretical Welfare Economics,* Cambridge, UK: Cambridge University Press, 1957.

[64] Hammond, P. J., "Equity, Arrow's Conditions, and Rawls' Difference Principle," *Econometrica* **44**, 1976, 793–804.

[65] Hammond, P. J., "Welfare Economics," in G. R. Feiwel, ed., *Issues in Contemporary Microeconomics and Welfare,* London: Macmillan Press, 1985, 405–434.

[66] Hammond, P. J., "Credible Liberalization: Beyond the Three Theorems of Neoclassical Welfare Economics," in D. Bös, ed., *Economics in a Changing World,* Vol. 3, *Public Policy and Economic Organization,* London: St. Martin's Press, 1993, 21–39.

[67] Hammond, P. J., "Progress in the Theory of Social Choice and Distributive Justice," in S. Zandvalkili, ed., *Research on Economic Inequality,* Vol. 7, London: JAI Press, 1997, 87–106.

[68] Hansson, B., "Choice Structures and Preference Relations," *Synthese* **18**, 1968, 443–458.

[69] Hara, C., T. Shinotsuka, K. Suzumura and Y. Xu, "Continuity and Egalitarianism in the Evaluation of Infinite Utility Streams," *Social Choice and Welfare* **31**, 2008, 179–191.

[70] Harberger, A. C., "The Incidence of the Corporation Income Tax," *Journal of Political Economy* **70**, 1962, 21–214.

[71] Hayek, F. A., *Individualism and Economic Order,* Chicago: University of Chicago Press, 1948.

[72] Hayek, F. A., "Competition as a Discovery Procedure," in his *New Studies in Philosophy, Politics, Economics and the History of Ideas,* London: Routledge & Kegan Paul, 1978, 179–190.

[73] Hicks, J. R., *Value and Capital,* London: Oxford University Press, 1st edn., 1939, 2nd edn., 1946.

[74] Hicks, J. R., "The Valuation of Social Income," *Economica* **7**, 1940, 105–124.

[75] Hicks, J. R., *Essays in World Economics,* Oxford: Oxford University Press, 1959.

[76] Hicks, J. R., "A Manifest," in his *Wealth and Welfare,* Vol.1 of *Collected Essays on Economic Theory,* Oxford: Basil Blackwell, 1981, 135–141.

[77] Houthakker, H. S., "Revealed Preference and the Utility Function," *Economica* **17**, 1950, 159–174.

[78] Howard, N., *Paradoxes of Rationality: Theory of Metagames and Political Behavior,* Cambridge, Mass.: MIT Press, 1971.

[79] Hurwicz, L., "Optimality and Informational Efficiency in Resource Allocation Processes," in K. J. Arrow, S. Karlin and P. Suppes, eds., *Mathematical Methods in the Social Scences 1959,* Stanford: Stanford University Press, 1960, 27–46. Reprinted in K. J. Arrow, and L. Hurwicz, eds., *Studies in Resource Allocation Processes,* New York: Cambridge University Press, 1977, 393–412.

[80] Hurwicz, L., "On Informationally Decentralized Systems," in R. Radner and C. B. McGuire, eds., *Decision and Organization,* Amsterdam: North-Holland, 1972, 297–336.

[81] Hurwicz, L., "Institutions as Families of Game Forms," *Japanese Economic Review* **47**, 1996, 113–132.

[82] Hurwicz, L., "But Who Will Guard the Guardians?" *American Economic Review* **98**, 2008, 577–585.

[83] Inada, K., "A Note on the Simple Majority Decision Rule," *Econometrica* **32**, 1964, 525–531.

[84] Inada, K., "The Simple Majority Decision Rule," *Econometrica* **37**, 1969, 490–506.

[85] Itoh, M., K. Kiyono, M. Okuno-Fujiwara and K. Suzumura, *The Economic Theory of Industrial Policy,* San Diego: Academic Press, 1991. English translation of the Japanese original published in 1988 by The University of Tokyo Press.

[86] Jones, R. W., "The Structure of Simple General Equilibrium Models," *Journal of Political Economy* **73**, 1965, 557–572.

[87] Jones, R. W., "Trade Theory and Factor Intensities: An Interpretive Essay," *Review of International Economics* **10**, 2002, 581–603.

[88] Kaldor, N., "Welfare Propositions in Economics and Interpersonal Comparisons of Utility," *Economic Journal* **49**, 1939, 549–552.

[89] Kolm, S.-Ch., *Justice et Equite,* Paris: Editions du Centre National de la Recherche Scientifique, 1972; English translation, *Justice and Equity,* Cambridge, Mass.: The MIT Press, 1997.

[90] Kolm, S.-Ch., *Modern Theories of Justice,* Cambridge, Mass.: MIT Press, 1996.

[91] Komiya, R., "Planning in Japan," in M. Bornstein, ed., *Economic Planning: East and West,* Cambridge, Mass.: Ballinger, 1975, 189–227.

[92] Komiya, R., M. Okuno, and K. Suzumura, eds., *Industrial Policy of Japan,* San Diego: Academic Press, 1988. English translation of the Japanese original published in 1984 by The University of Tokyo Press.

[93] Konishi, H., M. Okuno-Fujiwara and K. Suzumura, "Oligopolistic Competition and Economic Welfare: A General Equilibrium Analysis of Entry Regulation and Tax-Subsidy Schemes," *Journal of Public Economics* **42**, 1990, 67–88.

[94] Koopmans, T. C., "Stationary Ordinal Utility and Impatience," *Econometrica* **28**, 1960, 287–309.

[95] Little, I. M. D., *A Critique of Welfare Economics,* Oxford: Clarendon Press, 1st edn., 1950; 2nd edn., 1957.

[96] Luce, R. D., "Semiorders and the Theory of Utility Discrimination," *Econometrica* **24**, 1956, 178–191.

[97] Mankiw, N. G. and M. D. Whinston, "Free Entry and Social Efficiency," *Rand Journal of Economics* **17**, 1986, 48–58.

[98] Mas-Colell, A., "Revealed Preference after Samuelson," in G. R. Feiwel, ed., *Samuelson and Neoclassical Economics,* Amsterdam: Kluwer, 1982, 72–82.

[99] Mas-Colell, A., and H. Sonnenschein, "General Possibility Theorems for Group Decisions," *Review of Economic Studies* **39**, 1972, 185–192.

[100] McLure, C. E., Jr., "General Equilibrium Incidence Analysis: The Harberger Model after Ten Years," *Journal of Public Economics* **4**, 1975, 125–161.

[101] Mill, J. S., *On Liberty,* London: Parker, 1859. Reprinted in *The Collected Works of John Stuart Mill,* Vol. XVIII, J. M. Robson, ed., Toronto: University of Toronto Press, 1977.

[102] Mishan, E. J., "A Survey of Welfare Economics, 1939–1959," *Economic Journal* **70**, 1960, 197–265.

[103] Morrow, G., *The Ethical and Economic Theories of Adam Smith,* New York: Longmans Green, 1923.

[104] Negishi, T., *General Equilibrium Theory and International Trade,* Amsterdam: North-Holland, 1972.

[105] Nikaido, H., *Introduction to Sets and Mappings in Modern Economics,* Amsterdam: North-Holland, 1970. English translation of the Japanese original published in 1960.

[106] Nozick, R., *Anarchy, State, and Utopia,* Oxford: Basil Blackwell, 1974.

[107] Okuguchi, K., "Quasi Competitiveness and Cournot Oligopolies," *Review of Economic Studies* **40**, 1973, 145–148.

[108] Okuno-Fujiwara, M., and K. Suzumura, "Symmetric Oligopoly and Economic Welfare: A Synthesis," *Economic Theory* **3**, 1993, 43–59. Essay 23 of this volume.

[109] Packel, E., "Impossibility Results in the Axiomatic Theory of Intertemporal Choice," *Public Choice* **35**, 1980, 219–227.

[110] Panzar, J. C., "Regulation, Deregulation, and Economic Efficiency: The Case of CAB," *American Economic Review: Papers and Proceedings* **70**, 1980, 311–319.

[111] Pareto, V., *Manuale di Economia Politica,* Milano: Societa Editrice Libraria, 1906. English translation: *Manual of Political Economy,* New York: A. M. Kelley, 1920.

[112] Pattanaik, P. K., "On Modelling Individual Rights: Some Conceptual Issues," in K. J. Arrow, A. K. Sen, and K. Suzumura, eds., *Social Choice Reexamined,* London: Macmillan, 1996/1997.

[113] Pattanaik, P. K., and K. Suzumura, "Individual Rights and Social Evaluation: A Conceptual Framework," *Oxford Economic Papers* **48**, 1996, 194–212.

[114] Pazner, E., and D. Schmeidler, "A Difficulty in the Concept of Fairness," *Review of Economic Studies* **41**, 1974, 441–443.

[115] Pazner, E. and D. Schmeidler, "Egalitarian Equivalent Allocations: A New Concept of Economic Equity," *Quarterly Journal of Economics* **92**, 1978, 671–687.

[116] Peleg, B., "Effectivity Functions, Game Forms, Games, and Rights," *Social Choice and Welfare* **15**, 1998, 67–80.

[117] Perry, M. K., "Scale Economies, Imperfect Competition, and Public Policy," *Journal of Industrial Economics* **32**, 1984, 313–330.

[118] Pigou, A. C., *Wealth and Welfare,* London: Macmillan, 1912.

[119] Pigou, A. C., *The Economics of Welfare,* London: Macmillan, 1st edn., 1920; 4th edn., 1932.

[120] Plott, C. R., "Path Independence, Rationality, and Social Choice," *Econometrica* **41**, 1973, 1075–1091.

[121] Raiffa, H., *Decision Analysis,* Reading, Mass.: Addison-Wesley, 1968.

[122] Rawls, J., *A Theory of Justice,* Cambridge, Mass.: Harvard University Press, 1971.

[123] Richter, M. K., "Revealed Preference Theory," *Econometrica* **34**, 1966, 635–645.

[124] Richter, M. K., "Rational Choice," in J. S. Chipman, L. Hurwicz, M. K. Richter, and H. F. Sonnenschein, eds., *Preferences, Utility, and Demand,* New York: Harcourt Brace Jovanovich, 1971, 29–58.

[125] Robbins, L., *An Essay on the Nature and Significance of Economic Science,* London: Macmillan, 1st edn., 1932; 2nd edn., 1935.

[126] Roberts, K. W. S., "Possibility Theorems with Interpersonally Comparable Welfare Levels," *Review of Economic Studies* **47**, 1980, 409–420.

[127] Roberts, K. W. S., "Interpersonal Comparability and Social Choice Theory," *Review of Economic Studies* **47**, 1980a, 421–439.

[128] Roberts, K. W. S., "Valued Opinions or Opinionized Values: The Double Aggregation Problem," in K. Basu, P. Pattanaik, and K. Suzumura, eds., *Choice, Welfare, and Development: A Festschrift in Honour of Amartya K. Sen,* Oxford: Clarendon Press, 1995, 141–165.

[129] Roemer, J. E., and K. Suzumura, *Intergenerational Equity and Sustainability,* Amsterdam: Palgrave, 2007.

[130] Rousseau, J.-J., *Du Contrat Social,* 1762. English translation: "*The Social Contract or Principle of Political Right,*" in *Social Contract: Essays by Locke, Hume and Rousseau* (with an introduction by Sir Ernest Barker), London: Oxford University Press, 1947.

[131] Samuelson, P. A., "A Note on the Theory of Consumer's Behaviour," *Economica* **5**, 1938, 61–71.

[132] Samuelson, P. A., "A Note on the Pure Theory of Consumer's Behaviour: An Addendum," *Economica* **5**, 1938a, 353–354.

[133] Samuelson, P. A., *Foundations of Economic Analysis,* Cambridge, Mass.: Harvard University Press, 1947; Enlarged 2nd edn., 1983.

[134] Samuelson, P. A., "International Trade and Equalization of Factor Prices," *Economic Journal* **58**, 1948, 163–184.

[135] Samuelson, P. A., "Evaluation of Real National Income," *Oxford Economic Papers* **2**, 1950, 1–29.

[136] Samuelson, P. A., "The Problem of Integrability in Utility Theory," *Economica* **17**, 1950a, 355–385.

[137] Samuelson, P. A., "Bergsonian Welfare Economics," in S. Rosefielde, ed., *Economic Welfare and the Economics of Soviet Socialism: Essays in Honor of Abram Bergson,* Cambridge, Mass.: Cambridge University Press, 1981, 223–266.

[138] Schmalensee, R., "Is More Competition Necessarily Good?" *Industrial Organization Review* **4**, 1976, 120–121.

[139] Schumpeter, J. A., *Capitalism, Socialism and Democracy,* London: George Allen & Unwin, 1943.

[140] Schwartz, T., "Choice Functions, 'Rationality' Conditions, and Variations of the Weak Axiom of Revealed Preference," *Journal of Economic Theory* **13**, 1976, 414–427.

[141] Scitovsky, T., "A Note on Welfare Propositions in Economics," *Review of Economic Studies* **9**, 1941, 77–88.

[142] Sen, A. K., "A Possibility Theorem on Majority Decisions," *Econometrica* **34**, 1966, 491–499.

[143] Sen, A. K., "Quasi Transitivity, Rational Choice and Collective Decisions," *Review of Economic Studies* **36**, 1969, 381–393.

[144] Sen, A. K., "The Impossibility of a Paretian Liberal," *Journal of Political Economy* **78**, 1970, 152–157.

[145] Sen, A. K., *Collective Choice and Social Welfare,* San Francisco: Holden-Day, 1970a. Republished, Amsterdam: North-Holland, 1979.

[146] Sen, A. K., "Choice Functions and Revealed Preference," *Review of Economic Studies* **38**, 1971, 307–317.

[147] Sen, A. K., "Liberty, Unanimity and Rights," *Economica* **43**, 1976, 217–245.

[148] Sen, A. K., "Social Choice Theory: A Reexamination," *Econometrica* **45**, 1977, 53–89.

[149] Sen, A. K., "On Weights and Measures: Informational Constraints in Social Welfare Analysis," *Econometrica* **45**, 1977a, 1539–1572.

[150] Sen, A. K., "Personal Utilities and Public Judgements: Or What's Wrong with Welfare Economics?" *Economic Journal* **89**, 1979, 537–558.

[151] Sen A. K., "Utilitarianism and Welfarism," *Journal of Philosophy* **76**, 1979a, 463–489.

[152] Sen, A. K., "Liberty as Control: An Appraisal," *Midwest Studies of Philosophy* **7**, 1982, 207–221.

[153] Sen, A. K., "Liberty and Social Choice," *Journal of Philosophy* **80**, 1983, 5–28.

[154] Sen, A. K., "Minimal Liberty," *Economica* **59**, 1992, 139–159.

[155] Sen, A. K., "Rights: Formulation and Consequences," *Analyse & Kritik* **18**, 1996, 153–170.

[156] Sen, A. K., "Maximization and the Act of Choice," *Econometrica* **65**, 1997, 745–779.

[157] Sen, A. K., and P. K. Pattanaik, "Necessary and Sufficient Conditions for Rational Choice under Majority Decisions," *Journal of Economic Theory* **1**, 1969, 178–202.

[158] Shinkai, Y., "On Equilibrium Growth of Capital and Labor," *International Economic Review* **1**, 1960, 107–111.

[159] Sidgwick, H., *The Methods of Ethics*, London: Macmillan, 7th edn., 1907.

[160] Smith, A., *The Theory of Moral Sentiments,* first published in Great Britain by London: A. Millar, and Edinburgh: A. Kincaid & J. Bell, 1759. Penguin Classics edn.: Introduction by A. Sen and edited with notes by R. P. Hanley, London: Penguin Books Ltd., 2009.

[161] Smith, A., *An Inquiry into the Nature and Causes of the Wealth of Nations,* R. H. Campbell and A. K. Skinner, eds., Oxford: Oxford University Press, 1976. Originally printed for London: W. B. Strahan and T. Cadell, 1776.

[162] Solow, R. M., "James Meade at Eighty," *Economic Journal* **97**, 1987, 986–988.

[163] Stiglitz, J. E., "Potential Competition May Reduce Welfare," *American Economic Review: Papers and Proceedings* **71**, 1981, 184–193.

[164] Stolper, W. F. and P. A. Samuelson, "Protection and Real Wages," *Review of Economic Studies* **9**, 1941, 58–73.

[165] Sugden, R., "Liberty, Preference, and Choice," *Economics and Philosophy* **1**, 1985, 213–229.

[166] Sugden, R., "Rights: Why Do They Matter, and To Whom?" *Constitutional Political Economy* **4**, 1993, 127–152.

[167] Suppes, P., "Two Formal Models for Moral Principles," Technical Report No. 15, Office of Naval Research Contract Nonr 225(17), Applied Mathematics and Statistics Laboratory, Stanford University, Stanford, California, November 1, 1957.

[168] Suppes, P., "Some Formal Models of Grading Principles," *Synthese* **6**, 1966, 284–306.

[169] Suzumura, K., "Rational Choice and Revealed Preference," *Review of Economic Studies* **43**, 1976, 149–158. Essay 1 of this volume.

[170] Suzumura, K., "Remarks on the Theory of Collective Choice," *Economica* **43**, 1976a, 381–390. Essay 6 of this volume.

[171] Suzumura, K., "Houthakker's Axiom in the Theory of Rational Choice," *Journal of Economic Theory* **14**, 1977, 284–290. Essay 2 of this volume.

[172] Suzumura, K., "On the Consistency of Libertarian Claims," *Review of Economic Studies* **45**, 1978, 329–342. "A Correction," *Review of Economic Studies* **46**, 1979, 743. Essay 13 of this volume.

[173] Suzumura, K., "Liberal Paradox and the Voluntary Exchange of Rights-Exercising," *Journal of Economic Theory* **22**, 1980, 407–422. Essay 14 of this volume.

[174] Suzumura, K., "On Pareto-Efficiency and the No-Envy Concept of Equity," *Journal of Economic Theory* **25**, 1981, 367–379. Essay 9 of this volume.

[175] Suzumura, K., *Rational Choice, Collective Decisions and Social Welfare,* New York: Cambridge University Press, 1983. Reissued in paperback in 2009.

[176] Suzumura, K., "Resolving Conflicting Views of Justice in Social Choice," in P. K. Pattanaik and M. Salles, eds., *Social Choice and Welfare,* Amsterdam: North-Holland, 1983a, 125–149.

[177] Suzumura, K., "Cooperative and Noncooperative R&D in Oligopoly with Spillovers," *American Economic Review* **82**, 1992, 1307–1320. Essay 24 of this volume.

[178] Suzumura, K., *Competition, Commitment, and Welfare,* Oxford: Clarendon Press, 1995.

[179] Suzumura, K., "Welfare, Rights, and Social Choice Procedure: A Perspective," *Analyse & Kritik* **18**, 1996, 20–37. Essay 16 of this volume.

[180] Suzumura, K., "Consequences, Opportunities, and Procedures," *Social Choice and Welfare* **16**, 1999, 17–40. Essay 17 of this volume.

[181] Suzumura, K., "Report on the Far Eastern Activities of the Econometric Society," *Econometrica* **67**, 1999a, 221–233.

[182] Suzumura, K., "Welfare Economics beyond Welfarist Consequentialism," *Japanese Economic Review* **51**, 2000, 1–32. Essay 27 of this volume.

[183] Suzumura, K., "Introduction," in K. J. Arrow, A. K. Sen, and K. Suzumura, eds., *Handbook of Social Choice and Welfare,* Vol. I, Amsterdam: North-Holland/Elsevier, 2002, 1–32. Essay 25 of this volume.

[184] Suzumura, K., "An Interview with Paul Samuelson: Welfare Economics, 'Old' and 'New,' and Social Choice Theory," *Social Choice and Welfare* **25**, 2005, 327–356. Reprinted in J. Murray, ed., *The Collected Scientific Papers of Paul A. Samuelson,* Vol. 6, Cambridge, Mass.: MIT Press, 2011, 843–872.

[185] Suzumura, K., "Welfarism, Individual Rights, and Procedural Fairness," in K. J. Arrow, A. K. Sen, and K. Suzumura, eds., *Handbook of Social Choice and Welfare,* Vol. II, Amsterdam: Elsevier, 2011, 605–685.

[186] Suzumura, K., "Excess Entry Theorems after 25 Years," *Japanese Economic Review* **63**, 2012, 152–170.

[187] Suzumura, K., *Between Welfare and Rights,* Kyoto: Minerva Publishing Co., 2014. In Japanese.

[188] Suzumura, K., and K. Kiyono, "Entry Barriers and Economic Welfare," *Review of Economic Studies* **54**, 1987, 157–167. Essay 21 of this volume.

[189] Suzumura, K., and Y. Xu, "Characterizations of Consequentialism and Nonconsequentialism," *Journal of Economic Theory* **101**, 2001, 423–436. Essay 18 of this volume.

[190] Suzumura, K., and Y. Xu, "Consequences, Opportunities, and Generalized Consequentialism and Nonconsequentialism," *Journal of Economic Theory* **111**, 2003, 293–304. Essay 19 of this volume.

[191] Suzumura, K., and Y. Xu, "Welfarist Consequentialism, Similarity of Attitudes, and Arrow's General Impossibility Theorem," *Social Choice and Welfare* **22**, 2004, 237–251. Essay 20 of this volume.

[192] Svensson, L.-G., "Equity among Generations," *Econometrica* **48**, 1980, 1251–1256.

[193] Szpilrajn, E., "Sur l'Extension de l'Ordre Partiel," *Fundamenta Mathematicae* **16**, 1930, 386–389.

[194] Thomson, W., "Fair Allocation Rules," in K. J. Arrow, A. K. Sen, and K. Suzumura, eds., *Handbook of Social Choice and Welfare,* Vol. II, Amsterdam: Elsevier, 2011, 393–506.

[195] Tinbergen, J., *Redelijke Incomensverdeling,* Haarlem, Netherlands: De Gulden Pers, 1953.

[196] Uzawa, H., "On a Two-Sector Model of Economic Growth," *Review of Economic Studies* **29**, 1961, 40–47.

[197] Uzawa, H., "On a Two-Sector Model of Economic Growth II," *Review of Economic Studies* **30**, 1963, 105–118.

[198] van Hees, M., "Liberalism, Efficiency, and Stability: Some Possibility Results," *Journal of Economic Theory* **88**, 1999, 294–309.

[199] Varian, H. R., "Equity, Envy and Efficiency," *Journal of Economic Theory* **9**, 1974, 61–91.

[200] Varian, H. R., "Distributive Justice, Welfare Economics, and the Theory of Fairness," *Philosophy and Public Affairs* **4**, 1975, 223–247.

[201] von Weizsäcker, C. C., "A Welfare Analysis of Barriers to Entry," *Bell Journal of Economics* **11**, 1980, 399–420.

[202] von Weizsäcker, C. C., *Barriers to Entry: A Theoretical Treatment,* Berlin: Springer-Verlag, 1980a.

[203] Weber, M., *The Protestant Ethic and the Spirit of Capitalism,* T. Parsons (trans.) and A. Giddens (intro.), London: Routledge, 1905. English translation of the German original (published in 1904).

[204] Weber, M., *Economy and Society: An Outline of Interpretive Sociology,* G. Roth and C. Wittich, eds., Berkeley and Los Angeles: University of California Press, 1978. English translation of the 4th edn. of *Wirtschaft und Gesellschaft: Grundriss der verstehenden Soziologie,* J. Winckelmann, ed., Tübingen, Germany: J. C. B. Mohr (Paul Siebeck), 1956.

[205] Weymark, J. A., "Arrow's Theorem with Social Quasi-Orderings," *Public Choice* **42**, 1984, 235–246.

[206] Young, H. P., "An Axiomatization of the Borda Rule," *Journal of Economic Theory* **9**, 1974, 43–52.

PART I

RATIONAL CHOICE AS RATIONALIZABLE CHOICE

Introduction to Part I

Man is a gaming animal. He must be always trying to get the better in something or other.

—CHARLES LAMB, "Mrs. Battle's Opinions on Whist," *Essays of Elia,* 1823

We do what we can, and then make a theory to prove our performance the best.

—EMERSON, *Journals*, 1834

There's nothing people can't contrive to praise or condemn and find justification for doing so.

—MOLIÈRE, *The Misanthrope,* 1666 (English translation by John Wood)

One of the most widely invoked concepts in economics is that of *rationality* of the act of choice. It is also one of the basic concepts that is frequently criticized for the wrong reasons. Since this volume hinges squarely on the rationality of individual as well as collective acts of choice, we would like to make at the outset the sense of a rational act of choice as unambiguous as possible.

An agent in charge of making choices is said to be acting rationally if he or she chooses an alternative within each specified opportunity set of alternatives that brings him/her to the "optimal" position with reference to an underlying objective.[1] This definition, according to which the rational choice is identified with the purposive choice, will be sustained throughout

1. There are at least two meanings of "optimality" that make important sense in the context of the theory of rational choice. The first meaning is that of *greatestness*: An alternative x^* in S is said to be *R-greatest* in S if and only if x^*Rx holds true for all $x \in S$, where R is the binary relation that represents the underlying purpose of the act of choice. The second meaning is that of *maximality*: An alternative x^* in S is said to be *R-maximal* in S if and only if there is no x^{**} in S that satisfies $x^{**}P(R)x^*$, where $P(R)$ stands for the asymmetric part of R, viz.,

this work. On reflection, this notion of rationality is deeply rooted in the evolution of economic theory.[2]

To bring this concept of the rational act of choice into clear relief, let X and $\mathcal{S}$ stand, respectively, for the *universal set of alternatives* and the *family of opportunity sets*, each set $S \in \mathcal{S}$ being a nonempty subset of X. C denotes the *choice function* defined on the family $\mathcal{S}$ such that, for each $S \in \mathcal{S}$, $C(S)$ is a nonempty subset of S. The intended interpretation is that $C(S)$ stands for the set of alternatives that are chosen from the opportunity set $S \in \mathcal{S}$. We say that the choice function is *rational* if and only if there exists an underlying purpose in the form of a binary relation R on X such that, for all $x, y \in X$, xRy means that x is at least as good as y, and that $C(S)$ consists of $x^* \in S$ that optimizes R over S in the sense of R-greatestness for all $S \in \mathcal{S}$. If this is the case, the underlying purpose $R \subseteq X \times X$ is said to be a *rationalization* of C.

At this juncture of our discourse, consider the following two statements, which are often invoked when one criticizes the rationality of the act of choice.

(A) Rationality of the act of choice is a narrowly circumscribed view in the sense that it construes human acts only through the optimization of *selfish interest*.

(B) A rational agent is one whose act of choice is motivated by a preference *ordering*, viz., a preference relation R that satisfies *completeness* (viz., for all $x, y \in X$, xRy or yRx holds) and *transitivity* (viz., for all $x, y, z \in X$, if xRy and yRz hold, xRz must also hold).

We contend that the concept of a rational act in the sense of being a rationalizable act by means of an underlying purpose intrinsically has nothing to

---

[For all $x, y \in X$, $xP(R)y$ if and only if (xRy and not yRx)]. The optimality in the sense of greatestness is familiar in the context of the theory of consumer's behavior, whereas the optimality in the sense of maximality is familiar in the context of the Pareto optimal allocation of resources. Part I is focused mostly on the greatestness version of optimality, although some analysis is made on the maximality version of optimality in Essay 1 and Essay 4. Those who are interested in the maximality version of optimality should refer to Bossert, Sprumont and Suzumura [3], Sen [21], and Suzumura [23, Chapter 1], among others.

2. A brief historical account of the evolution of the concept of rationality of the act of choice may be found in Bossert and Suzumura [6, Chapter 1].

do either with (A) or with (B). To dissociate the rational act as rationalizable act from the statement (A), we have only to observe that the underlying purpose of the rationalizable act need not be selfish at all. Indeed, an act of choice from the purely altruistic purpose is a perfectly rationalizable act. To dissociate the rational act as a rationalizable act from the statement (B), we have only to reconfirm that the definition of the concept of a rational act as a rationalizable act simply requires the existence of an underlying purpose in the form of a binary preference relation R with no additional regularity properties, such as completeness and transitivity, being imposed on R.

After having said this, however, nothing prevents us from introducing some further regularity properties of R with the purpose of identifying the wide spectrum of rational acts as rationalizable acts. Along with completeness and transitivity, we may invoke the following regularity properties:[3]

Quasi transitivity. For all $x, y, z \in X$, if $xP(R)y$ and $yP(R)z$, then $xP(R)z$.

Suzumura consistency. For any positive integer t, where $3 \leq t < +\infty$, and for all $x^1, x^2, \ldots, x^t \in X$, if $x^h R x^{h+1}$ holds for all $h \in \{1, 2, \ldots, t-1\}$ with at least one instance of R being $P(R)$, then $x^t R x^1$ should not hold.

Acyclicity. For any natural number t, where $3 \leq t < +\infty$, and for all $x^1, x^2, \ldots, x^t \in X$, if $x^h P(R) x^{h+1}$ holds for all $h \in \{1, 2, \ldots, t-1\}$, then $x^t P(R) x^1$ should not hold.

Among these properties, quasi transitivity due to Sen [18; 19, Chapter 1*] requires that the strict preference part $P(R)$ of the weak preference relation R should be transitive, but the indifference part $I(R)$ of R need not be transitive. In view of many experimental results, which go squarely against the hypothesis of transitive indifference, the concept of quasi transitivity has strong intuitive appeal.[4] Observe that it lies in between full transitivity and

3. Among these regularity properties, the property of quasi transitivity was originally introduced by Sen [18; 19, Chapter 1*], whereas the concept of Suzumura consistency was originally introduced by Suzumura [22]. See also Bossert [2] and Bossert and Suzumura [6, Chapter 2; 7] for further analysis of Suzumura consistency and the crucial implications thereof, and Champernowne [8] for a related but distinct concept of consistency.

4. See Luce [12] and Raiffa [13, Chapter 4, Section 8] for illuminating examples.

acyclicity in its logical strength. Suzumura consistency and acyclicity share a crucial property of being capable of excluding the occurrence of *a money pump*.[5] Besides, R being Suzumura-consistent is necessary and sufficient for the existence of an ordering R^* that satisfies $R \subseteq R^*$ and $P(R) \subseteq R^*$.[6] This *ordering extension theorem* is a generalization of the classical extension theorem due to Szpilrajn [24], which plays crucial roles in many contexts of individual and social choice theory.

Turning to the logical strength among these regularity properties of binary relations, we have (a) transitivity implies Suzumura consistency, but not vice versa in general; (b) Suzumura consistency implies acyclicity, but not vice versa in general; (c) Suzumura consistency, coupled with completeness, implies full transitivity;[7] and (d) Suzumura consistency and quasi transitivity are logically independent.

With these properties of binary relations close at hand, we are ready to introduce the wide spectrum of the concept of rationality as rationalizability:

Full rationalizability. C on $\mathcal{S}$ is rationalizable by an ordering on X.

Quasi-transitive rationalizability. C on $\mathcal{S}$ is rationalizable by a quasi-transitive binary relation on X.

Acyclic rationalizability. C on $\mathcal{S}$ is rationalizable by an acyclic binary relation on X.

Suzumura-consistent rationalizability. C on $\mathcal{S}$ is rationalizable by a Suzumura-consistent binary relation on X.

The first step in the development of the theory of rationality as rationalizability was taken by Paul Samuelson [16; 17] in the special case where X is the finite dimensional Euclidean space, $\mathcal{S}$ consists of the budget sets in the commodity space X, and C is the single-valued demand function of a competitive consumer. If there are l commodities altogether, where $2 \leq l < +\infty$, each opportunity set S in $\mathcal{S}$ can be represented as

$$S = B(\boldsymbol{p}, M) := \{\boldsymbol{x} \in X \mid \boldsymbol{p} \cdot \boldsymbol{x} \leq M\}$$

5. See Raiffa [13, Chapter 4, Section 8] for an eye-catching example.

6. For the proof of this extension theorem, the readers are referred to Essay 6 of this volume.

7. Thus, a complete and Suzumura-consistent binary relation is nothing other than an ordering.

for some price vector $\boldsymbol{p} = (p_1, p_2, \cdots, p_l) \gg 0$ and income $M > 0$. Instead of starting from a utility function or a preference ordering of the competitive consumer, Samuelson [16] started from the individual demand function as the primitive concept of his pure theory of consumer's behavior. He identified a simple property, to be called the *weak axiom of revealed preference*, and derived almost all, if not literally all, of the classical propositions in demand theory synthesized by John Hicks's classic, *Value and Capital* (Hicks [10]). What Samuelson could not derive from his revealed preference axiom could be retrieved by the subsequent contribution à la Hendrik Houthakker [11], who strengthened Samuelson's weak axiom into the semitransitivity axiom of his own. Although the revealed preference theory à la Samuelson [16; 17] and Houthakker [11] was concerned only with a special case of the rational act of a competitive consumer, there is no doubt that they have opened the gate wide toward a general theory of choice functions and rationalizability thereof.

An important next step was taken by Kenneth Arrow [1], who left the restricted arena of a competitive consumer, and widened the reach of revealed preference theory to a choice function C on the general family $\mathcal{S}$ of opportunity sets. Conceptually speaking, Arrow took an important step toward a generalized theory of rational choice as rationalizable choice. However, his own analysis introduced a restriction of a different nature. Unlike the Samuelson-Houthakker theory, Arrow assumed that each $S \in \mathcal{S}$ is a nonempty *finite* subset of the abstract universal set X. It is true that Arrow's analysis could greatly simplify the Samuelson-Houthakker revealed preference theory, but this simplification was purchased at a price that is rather high. Amartya Sen [20] and many others followed Arrow's suit, and there are by now a plethora of revealed preference analyses à la Arrow and Sen in the literature. It should be observed, however, that the Samuelson-Houthakker theory as well as the Arrow-Sen theory are *not* general theories of rational choice as rationalizable choice for their imposed domain restrictions.

Part I consists of four essays on the general theory of rational choice as rationalizable choice, where *no* restrictive assumption is imposed on the universal set X and the family $\mathcal{S}$ of opportunity sets. Essay 1 ("Rational Choice and Revealed Preference") is one of the earliest papers on the general theory of rational choice and revealed preference along with Marcel Richter [14; 15] and Bengt Hansson [9]. Essay 2 ("Houthakker's Axiom in the Theory of Rational Choice") shows in the general framework of rational choice theory that the Houthakker axiom of revealed preference is necessary and sufficient for full rationalizability of a choice function. Coupled with Richter's [15] characterization of the concept of rationality as rationalizability per se, two polar extremes of the spectrum of rationality concepts, viz., full rationality and rationality per se, are made crystal-clear. What is left wide open is the characterization of rationality concepts lying in between those polar extremes. Bossert, Sprumont, and Suzumura [4] and Bossert and Suzumura [5; 6] gained a lot of mileage in this project. Essay 3 ("Suzumura-Consistent Rationalizability") is devoted to the characterization of general choice functions with Suzumura-consistent rationalization. Finally, Essay 4 ("Revealed Preference and Choice under Uncertainty") extends the theory of revealed preference and rational choice to uncertain environments.

References

[1] Arrow, K. J., "Rational Choice Functions and Orderings," *Economica* **26**, 1959, 121–127.

[2] Bossert, W., "Suzumura Consistency," in P. K. Pattanaik, K. Tadenuma, Y. Xu, and N. Yoshihara, eds., *Rational Choice and Social Choice: Theory and Applications*, New York: Springer, 2008, 159–179. Collected papers in honor of Kotaro Suzumura.

[3] Bossert, W., Y. Sprumont, and K. Suzumura, "Maximal-Element Rationalizability," *Theory and Decision* **58**, 2005, 325–350.

[4] Bossert, W., Y. Sprumont, and K.Suzumura, "Rationalizability of Choice Functions on General Domains without Full Transitivity," *Social Choice and Welfare* **27**, 2006, 435–458.

[5] Bossert, W., and K. Suzumura, "Rational Choice on General Domains," in K. Basu and R. Kanbur, eds., *The Oxford Handbook of Arguments for a Better World: Essays in Honor of Amartya Sen*, Vol. I, *Ethics, Welfare and Measurement*, Oxford: Oxford University Press, 2009, 103–135.

[6] Bossert, W., and K. Suzumura, *Consistency, Choice, and Rationality*, Cambridge, Mass.: Harvard University Press, 2010.

[7] Bossert, W., and K. Suzumura, "Quasi-Transitive and Suzumura-Consistent Relations," *Social Choice and Welfare* **39**, 2012, 323–334. Special issue in honor of Maurice Salles.

[8] Champernowne, D. G., *Uncertainty and Estimation in Economics*, Vol. I, San Francisco: Holden-Day, 1969.

[9] Hansson, B., "Choice Structures and Preference Relations," *Synthese* **18**, 1968, 443–458.

[10] Hicks, J. R., *Value and Capital*, Oxford: Clarendon Press, 1st edn., 1939; 2nd edn., 1946.

[11] Houthakker, H. S., "Revealed Preference and the Utility Function," *Economica* **17**, 1950, 159–174.

[12] Luce, R. D., "Semiorders and the Theory of Utility Discrimination," *Econometrica* **24**, 1956, 178–191.

[13] Raiffa, H., *Decision Analysis*, Reading, Mass.: Addison-Wesley, 1968.

[14] Richter, M. K., "Revealed Preference Theory," *Econometrica* **34**, 1966, 635–645.

[15] Richter, M. K., "Rational Choice," in J. S. Chipman, L. Hurwicz, M. K. Richter, and H. F. Sonnenschein, eds., *Preferences, Utility, and Demand*, New York: Harcourt Brace Jovanovich, 1971, 29–58.

[16] Samuelson, P. A., "A Note on the Pure Theory of Consumer's Behaviour," *Economica* **5**, 1938, 61–71.

[17] Samuelson, P. A., "The Problem of Integrability in Utility Theory," *Economica* **17**, 1950, 355–385.

[18] Sen, A. K., "Quasi-Transitivity, Rational Choice and Collective Decisions," *Review of Economic Studies* **36**, 1969, 381–393.

[19] Sen, A. K., *Collective Choice and Social Welfare*, San Francisco: Holden-Day, 1970.

[20] Sen, A. K., "Choice Functions and Revealed Preference," *Review of Economic Studies* **38**, 1971, 307–317.

[21] Sen, A. K., "Maximization and the Act of Choice," *Econometrica* **65**, 1997, 745–779.

[22] Suzumura, K., "Remarks on the Theory of Collective Choice," *Economica* **43**, 1976, 381–390. Essay 6 of this volume.

[23] Suzumura, K., *Rational Choice, Collective Decisions and Social Welfare*, New York: Cambridge University Press, 1983. Reprinted in paperback, 2009.

[24] Szpilrajn, E., "Sur l'Extension de l'Ordre Partiel," *Fundamenta Mathematicae* **16**, 1930, 386–389.

ESSAY 1

Rational Choice and Revealed Preference

1.1. Introduction

According to the currently dominant view, the choice behavior of an agent is construed to be rational if there exists a preference relation R such that, for every set S of available states, the choice therefrom is the set of "R-optimal" points in S.[1] There are at least two alternative definitions of R-optimality—R-maximality and R-greatestness. On the one hand, an x in S is said to be R-maximal in S if there exists no y in S that is strictly preferred to x in terms of R. On the other, an x in S is said to be R-greatest in S if, for all y in S, x is at least as preferable as y in terms of R. The former viewpoint can claim its relevance in view of the prevalent adoption of the concept of Pareto efficiency in the theory of resource allocation processes.[2]

First published in *Review of Economic Studies* **43**, 1976, pp. 149–158. Thanks are due to the editors of this journal for their helpful comments on the original version of this essay.

1. Arrow's seminal works [1; 2] are the main sources of the current theory of rational choice. Notable contributions in this field include Bengt Hansson [4], Marcel Richter [9; 10], and Amartya Sen [13], among others. See also Hans Herzberger [5], Dean Jamison and Lawrence Lau [7], and Robert Wilson [16]. In his recent paper [8], Charles Plott axiomatized the concept of path-independent choice, which is related to, but distinct from, the concept of rational choice. See Kotaro Suzumura [15].

The latter standpoint is deeply rooted in the well-developed theories of the integrability problem, revealed preference and social choice theory. The difference between these two definitions of rational choice is basically as follows. Any two states in a choice function that is R-maximal rational are either R-indifferent or R-incomparable, while any two states in a choice function that is R-greatest rational are R-indifferent.

A condition for rational choice has been put forward in terms of the R-greatestness interpretation of optimality (Hansson [4] and Richter [9; 10]). In this essay, a condition for rational choice in its R-maximality interpretation will be presented. The condition in question will, in a certain sense, synthesize both concepts of rationality, because it can be seen that the rational choice in terms of R-maximality is rational in terms of R-greatestness as well. The role of various axioms of revealed preference and congruence in the theory of rational choice will also be clarified.

In this analysis, special care should be taken with the domain of the choice function. It was Arrow [1] who first suggested that "the demand-function point of view would be greatly simplified if the range over which the choice functions are considered to be determined is broadened to include all finite sets." This line of inquiry was recently completed by Sen [13].[3] As was persuasively discussed by Sen [13, Section 6], there is no convincing reason for *restricting* the domain of the choice function to the class of convex polyhedras representing budget sets in the commodity space. At the same time, however, there is no specific reason for our *extending* the domain so as to include *all* finite sets. This being the case, no restriction will be placed on the domain of the choice function except that it should be a nonempty family of nonempty sets.

Section 1.2 introduces our conceptual framework. The main results are stated in Section 1.3, the proofs being given in Section 1.4. Section 1.5 presents some examples that negate the converse of our theorems. Finally,

---

2. See also Herzberger [5, pp. 196–199], who calls an agent a *liberal maximizer* (resp. stringent maximizer), if he chooses R-maximal points (resp. R-greatest points) from the points available and favors the liberal maximizer as a model of rational agent.

3. As was carefully noted by Sen [13, p. 312], the Arrow-Sen theory works well even if the domain includes all pairs and all triples, but not all finite sets.

Section 1.6 compares our results with the Arrow-Sen theory, on the one hand, and the Richter-Hansson theory, on the other.

1.2. Definitions

Let X be the basic set of all alternatives and let $\mathcal{S}$ stand for the nonempty family of nonempty subsets of X. A suggested interpretation is that each and every $S \in \mathcal{S}$ is the set of available alternatives that could possibly be presented to the agent.

DEFINITION 1.1 (PREFERENCE RELATION). A *preference relation* is a binary relation R on X, that is to say, a subset of $X \times X$. If $(x, y) \in R$, we say that x is at least as preferable as y. A *strict preference relation* associated with R is a binary relation

$$P_R = \{(x, y) \in X \times X \mid (x, y) \in R \ \&\ (y, x) \notin R\}.$$

An *indifference relation* associated with R is a binary relation

$$I_R = \{(x, y) \in X \times X \mid (x, y) \in R \ \&\ (y, x) \in R\}.$$

R is said to be

(a) *complete* if and only if $\{(x, y), (y, x)\} \cap R \neq \emptyset$ for all $x, y \in X$,
(b) *acyclic* if and only if $(x, x) \notin T(P_R)$ for all $x \in X$,[4]
(c) *transitive* if and only if $[(x, y) \in R \ \&\ (y, z) \in R \Rightarrow (x, z) \in R]$ for all $x, y, z \in X$, and
(d) an *ordering* if and only if it is complete as well as transitive.

DEFINITION 1.2 (MAXIMAL-POINT SET AND GREATEST-POINT SET). Let R and S be, respectively, a preference relation and an arbitrary subset of X. The

4. For any binary relation Q on X, $T(Q)$ stands for the *transitive closure* of Q: $T(Q) = \{(x, y) \in X \times X \mid (x, y) \in Q \text{ or } [(x, z^1), (z^k, z^{k+1}), (z^n, y) \in Q \ (k = 1, \ldots, n-1) \text{ for some } \{z^1, \ldots, z^n\} \subseteq X]\}$. If R is acyclic, there exists no strict preference cycle.

subsets $M(S, R)$ and $G(S, R)$ of S, to be called the *R-maximal-point set* and the *R-greatest-point set* of S, respectively, are defined by

$$M(S, R) = \{x \in X \mid x \in S \;\&\; (y, x) \notin P_R \text{ for all } y \in S\}$$

and

$$G(S, R) = \{x \in X \mid x \in S \;\&\; (x, y) \in R \text{ for all } y \in S\}.$$

Remark 1.1. (i) For any $S \subseteq X$ and $R \subseteq X \times X$, $G(S, R) \subseteq M(S, R)$, and (ii) if R is complete, $G(S, R) = M(S, R)$.[5] For any $x, y \in G(S, R)$, we have $(x, y) \in I_R$, while for any $x, y \in M(S, R)$, we have either $(x, y) \in I_R$ or $[(x, y) \notin R \;\&\; (y, x) \notin R]$.

Definition 1.3 (choice function). A *choice function* is a function C on $\mathcal{S}$ such that $C(S)$ is a nonempty subset of S for all $S \in \mathcal{S}$.

The intended interpretation is that, for any set S of available alternatives, the subset $C(S)$ thereof represents the set of alternatives that are chosen from S. Associated with the given choice function C on $\mathcal{S}$, we can define various concepts of revealed preference.

Definition 1.4 (revealed preference relations). Two preference relations R^* and R_* on X such that

(a) $(x, y) \in R^* \Leftrightarrow [x \in C(S) \;\&\; y \in S]$ for some $S \in \mathcal{S}$ and
(b) $(x, y) \in R_* \Leftrightarrow [x \notin S \text{ or } x \in C(S) \text{ or } y \notin C(S)]$ for all $S \in \mathcal{S}$

are called the *revealed preference relations.*

In simple words, x is said to be revealed R^*-preferred to y if x is chosen when y is also available, and x is said to be revealed R_*-preferred to y if there exists no choice situation in which y is chosen and x is available but rejected. In order to connect these revealed preference relations to the revealed preference axioms, we introduce the following auxiliary concept.

5. For the proof of this well-known result, see Herzberger [5, Proposition P1] and Sen [12, Chapter 1*].

Definition 1.5 (C-connectedness). A sequence of sets $(S_1, \ldots, S_n)$ in $\mathcal{S}$ is said to be C-connected if and only if $S_k \cap C(S_{k+1}) \neq \emptyset$ for all $k \in \{1, \ldots, n-1\}$ and $S_n \cap C(S_1) \neq \emptyset$.

It turns out that for our present purpose the following rather abstract formulation of the revealed preference axioms is the most convenient.

Definition 1.6 (revealed preference axioms). A choice function C on $\mathcal{S}$ is said to satisfy

(a) *weak axiom of revealed preference*—WARP for short—if and only if, for any C-connected pair (S_1, S_2) in $\mathcal{S}$, $S_1 \cap C(S_2) = C(S_1) \cap S_2$ holds,
(b) *strong axiom of revealed preference*—SARP for short—if and only if, for any C-connected sequence $(S_1, \ldots, S_n)$ in $\mathcal{S}$, $S_k \cap C(S_{k+1}) = C(S_k) \cap S_{k+1}$ for some $k \in \{1, \ldots, n-1\}$ holds, and
(c) *Hansson's axiom of revealed preference*—HARP for short—if and only if, for any C-connected sequence $(S_1, \ldots, S_n)$ in $\mathcal{S}$, $S_k \cap C(S_{k+1}) = C(S_k) \cap S_{k+1}$ for all $k \in \{1, \ldots, n-1\}$ holds.

At first sight, WARP and SARP in Definition 1.6, which are due originally to Hansson [4], might seem rather different from their traditional formulation, such as in Sen [13], but they are equivalent. In order to substantiate this claim, let us define another revealed preference relation R^{**} by $(x, y) \in R^{**}$ if and only if $[x \in C(S)\ \&\ y \in S \backslash C(S)]$ for some $S \in \mathcal{S}$ holds. By definition, we have $R^{**} \subseteq R^*$. (In words, x is said to be revealed R^{**}-preferred to y if x is chosen and y is available but rejected.) In terms of R^* and R^{**}, the common version of WARP is given by

$$(x, y) \in R^{**} \Rightarrow (y, x) \notin R^*. \tag{1.1}$$

Similarly, the traditional formulation of SARP is given by

$$(x, y) \in T(R^{**}) \Rightarrow (y, x) \notin R^*. \tag{1.2}$$

It is shown in the appendix that (1.1) and (1.2) are equivalent to WARP and SARP, respectively, in Definition 1.6.

We are now in the position to introduce the concepts coined by Richter [9] and Sen [13].

Definition 1.7 (congruence axioms). A choice function C on $\mathcal{S}$ is said to satisfy

(a) *weak congruence axiom*—WCA for short—if and only if for any $S \in \mathcal{S}$, $(x, y) \in R^*$, $x \in S$ and $y \in C(S)$ imply $x \in C(S)$, and
(b) *strong congruence axiom*—SCA for short—if and only if for any $S \in \mathcal{S}$, $(x, y) \in T(R^*)$, $x \in S$ and $y \in C(S)$ imply $x \in C(S)$.

The central concepts of this essay are given by the following definition.

Definition 1.8 (rational choice function). A choice function C on $\mathcal{S}$ is said to be

(a) *G-rational* if and only if there exists a preference relation R such that $C(S) = G(S, R)$ for all $S \in \mathcal{S}$, and
(b) *M-rational* if and only if there exists a preference relation R such that $C(S) = M(S, R)$ for all $S \in \mathcal{S}$.

A preference relation R that rationalizes the choice function C is called the *rationalization* of C.[6]

Intuitively, a choice function is said to be rational if we can interpret the stipulated choice behavior as that of preference optimization. Two possible interpretations of this idea are formulated in Definition 1.8(a) and

6. It should be noted that (i) there exists an irrational choice and (ii) the rationalization of the rational choice function is not necessarily unique. The following examples will establish these points.

Example 1. $X = \{x, y, z\}$, $\mathcal{S} = \{S_1, S_2\}$, $S_1 = X$, $S_2 = \{x, y\}$, $C(S_1) = \{y\}$, and $C(S_2) = \{x\}$. It is easy to see that this choice function is neither G-rational nor M-rational.

Example 2. $X = \{x, y, z\}$, $\mathcal{S} = \{S_1, S_2\}$, $S_1 = \{x, y\}$, $S_2 = \{y, z\}$, $C(S_1) = \{x\}$ and $C(S_2) = \{y, z\}$. This choice function has two G-rationalizations

$$R_1 = \{(x, y), (y, z), (z, y)\},\ R_2 = \{(x, y), (y, z), (z, y), (x, z), (z, x)\}$$

and two M-rationalizations $R_1' = \{(x, y), (y, z), (z, y)\}$ and $R_2' = \{(x, y)\}$.

1.8(b). It should be noted that the *M-rational choice function is G-rational but not vice versa.* This can be seen as follows. Let C on $\mathcal{S}$ be M-rational with the rationalization R. We define a binary relation R' on X by $[(x, y) \in R' \Leftrightarrow (y, x) \notin P_R]$ for all x and y in X. From Definition 1.2, we then have $M(S, R) = G(S, R')$ for all $S \in \mathcal{S}$, so that C is G-rational with the rationalization R'. In order to see that the G-rational choice function is not necessarily M-rational, let us consider an example where $X = \{x, y, z\}$, $\mathcal{S} = \{S_1, S_2, S_3\}$, $S_1 = \{x, y\}$, $S_2 = \{x, z\}$, $S_3 = X$, $C(S_1) = S_1$, $C(S_2) = S_2$ and $C(S_3) = \{x\}$. This choice function is G-rational with the rationalization $R = \{(x, y), (y, x), (x, z), (z, x)\}$. Assume that this C is M-rational with the rationalization R'. From $C(S_1) = S_1$ we obtain

$$(x, y) \in I_{R'} \quad \text{or} \quad [(x, y) \notin R' \ \& \ (y, x) \notin R']. \tag{1.3}$$

From $C(S_2) = S_2$ we obtain

$$(x, z) \in I_{R'} \quad \text{or} \quad [(x, z) \notin R' \ \& \ (z, x) \notin R']. \tag{1.4}$$

From $C(S_3) = \{x\}$ we obtain

$$[(x, y) \in P_{R'} \text{ or } (z, y) \notin P_{R'}] \ \& \ [(x, z) \in P_{R'} \text{ or } (y, z) \in P_{R'}]. \tag{1.5}$$

From (3), (4), and (5) we obtain $(z, y), (y, z) \in P_{R'}$, which contradicts Definition 1.1. Thus the choice function in question is not M-rational.

In view of Definition 1.2 and the associated remark, it is clear that both concepts of rationality coincide if the rationalization is complete. If this complete rationalization satisfies the transitivity axiom as well, we say that the choice function is *full rational.*

Finally, let us introduce the concept of normality.

DEFINITION 1.9 (NORMAL CHOICE FUNCTION). Let two functions G^* and M^* on $\mathcal{S}$ be defined by $G^*(S) = G(S, R^*)$ and $M^*(S) = M(S, R^*)$ for all $S \in \mathcal{S}$. A choice function C on $\mathcal{S}$ is said to be

(a) *G-normal* if and only if $C(S) = G^*(S)$ for all $S \in \mathcal{S}$, and
(b) *M-normal* if and only if $C(S) = M^*(S)$ for all $S \in \mathcal{S}$.

1.3. Theorems

We are now ready to investigate the structure of rational choice functions. At the outset, we set down the equivalence that holds between revealed preference axioms and congruence axioms.

THEOREM 1.1. (i) WARP, WCA, and the property ($R^* \subseteq R_*$) are mutually equivalent. (ii) HARP and SCA are equivalent.

Our concept of G-normality is identical to Richter's V-axiom, which he proposed as a necessary and sufficient condition for G-rationality in [10, p. 33]. The role of our M-rationality is made clear by the following.

THEOREM 1.2. An M-normal choice function is G-normal.

In view of Richter's theorem and our Theorem 1.2, it is important to find an economically meaningful condition that assures the M-normality of the choice function. This is where the revealed preference axioms come in.

THEOREM 1.3. A choice function satisfying WARP is M-normal.

By combining Theorem 1.2 and Theorem 1.3, we can see the role played by WARP in the theory of rational choice.

THEOREM 1.4. A choice function satisfying WARP is M- as well as G-normal.

We have seen that the concept of M-rationality and that of G-rationality coincide if the rationalization satisfies completeness. This being the case, it is important to have the following:

THEOREM 1.5. An M-rational choice function is complete rational.

Hansson [4] and Richter [9] showed that the necessary and sufficient condition for full rationality of the choice function is HARP or, equivalently, SCA. On the other hand, Theorem 1.4 shows us the relevance of WARP in the theory of rational choice. Why do we need SARP? Our answer is given by the following theorem.

THEOREM 1.6. A choice function satisfying SARP is acyclic and complete rational.

These theorems are proved in the next section.

1.4. Proofs

PROOF OF THEOREM 1.1 (I).

STEP 1. [(WARP) $\Rightarrow$ ($R^* \subseteq R_*$)]. If ($R^* \subseteq R_*$) does not hold, we have $(x, y) \in R^* \backslash R_*$ for some $x, y \in X$. Then there exist $S, S' \in \mathcal{S}$ such that $x \in C(S)$, $y \in S$, $x \in S'$, $x \notin C(S')$, and $y \in C(S')$, so that we have $x \in S' \cap C(S)$, $y \in C(S') \cap S$, and $x \notin C(S') \cap S$. Thus WARP does not hold. Hence WARP implies ($R^* \subseteq R_*$).

STEP 2. [($R^* \subseteq R_*$) $\Rightarrow$ (WCA)]. Suppose ($R^* \subseteq R_*$) and let $(x, y) \in R^*$, $x \in S$, and $y \in C(S)$ for some $S \in \mathcal{S}$. Then we have $(x, y) \in R_*$, $x \in S$, and $y \in C(S)$, which imply $x \in C(S)$ by virtue of Definition 1.4(b). Thus WCA holds.

STEP 3. [(WCA) $\Rightarrow$ (WARP)]. Let C satisfy WCA. Let (S_1, S_2) be a C-connected pair in $\mathcal{S}$ and let x and y be taken arbitrarily from $S_1 \cap C(S_2)$ and $C(S_1) \cap S_2$, respectively. Because of $x \in C(S_2)$ and $y \in S_2$, we have $(x, y) \in R^*$, which, coupled with $x \in S_1$ and $y \in C(S_1)$, implies $x \in C(S_1)$ thanks to WCA. Thus we have $S_1 \cap C(S_2) \subseteq C(S_1) \cap S_2$.

Similarly, we can verify that $S_1 \cap C(S_2) \supseteq C(S_1) \cap S_2$. Thus WARP holds. ■

PROOF OF THEOREM 1.1 (II).

STEP 1. [(HARP) $\Rightarrow$ (SCA)]. Let $(x, y) \in T(R^*)$, $x \in S$, and $y \in C(S)$ for some $S \in \mathcal{S}$. Then either (α) $(x, y) \in R^*$, or (β) there exist $\{z^1, \ldots, z^{n-1}\} \subseteq X$ and $\{S_1, \ldots, S_n\} \subseteq \mathcal{S}$ such that $x \in C(S_1)$, $z^k \in S_k \cap C(S_{k+1}) (k = 1, \ldots, n-1)$, and $y \in S_n$. In case (α), we have $x \in C(S)$, since HARP implies WARP, which is equivalent to WCA. In case (β), taking $x \in S$ and $y \in C(S)$ into consideration, $(S, S_1, \ldots, S_n)$ is C-connected, so that we obtain $S \cap C(S_1) = C(S) \cap S_1$ by virtue of HARP. Thus $x \in C(S)$. In any case, SCA holds.

STEP 2. [(SCA) $\Rightarrow$ (HARP)]. Let a sequence $(S_1, \ldots, S_n)$ in $\mathcal{S}$ be C-connected and let z^k and z^n be taken arbitrarily from $S_k \cap C(S_{k+1})$ and $S_n \cap C(S_1)$, respectively $(k = 1, \ldots, n-1)$. We show that $S_1 \cap C(S_2) = C(S_1) \cap S_2$. By definition, we have $z^1 \in S_1$, $(z^1, z^n) \in T(R^*)$ and $z^n = C(S_1)$, so that SCA entails $z^1 \in C(S_1)$. Noting $z^1 \in C(S_2) \subseteq S_2$, we have $S_1 \cap C(S_2) \subseteq C(S_1) \cap S_2$. Next, let z be an arbitrary point of $C(S_1) \cap S_2$. Then $z \in S_2$, $(z, z^1) \in R^* \subseteq T(R^*)$ and $z^1 \in C(S_2)$, so that we have $z \in C(S_2)$, thanks to SCA. Thus we have $C(S_1) \cap S_2 \subseteq S_1 \cap C(S_2)$, yielding $S_1 \cap C(S_2) = C(S_1) \cap S_2$. In a similar way, we can show $C(S_k) \cap S_{k+1} = S_k \cap C(S_{k+1})$ for all $k \in \{1, \ldots, n-1\}$. Thus HARP is implied. ■

PROOF OF THEOREM 1.2. Let us establish:

$$C(S) \subseteq G^*(S) \subseteq M^*(S) \quad \text{for all } S \in \mathcal{S}. \tag{1.6}$$

For any $S \in \mathcal{S}$, let $x \in C(S)$. Then for all $y \in S$, $(x, y) \in R^*$, so that $x \in G^*(S)$. The other part follows from Remark 1. Thanks to (1.6) and Definition 1.9, the assertion of the theorem holds. ■

PROOF OF THEOREM 1.3. In view of (1.6), we have only to show that WARP implies

$$M^*(S) \subseteq C(S) \quad \text{for all } S \in \mathcal{S}. \tag{1.7}$$

Let an $S \in \mathcal{S}$ be fixed once and for all and let $x \in M^*(S)$. ($M^*(S) \neq \emptyset$ for all $S \in \mathcal{S}$ because of (1.6) and Definition 1.3.) Then $x \in S$ and for all $y \in S$, either (α) [$y \notin C(S')$ or $\notin S'$] for all $S' \in \mathcal{S}$, or (β) [$x \in C(S'')$ & $y \in S''$] for some $S'' \in \mathcal{S}$. Let $y \in C(S)$. Then (α) cannot hold for $S' = S$, so that (β) must hold for $y \in C(S)$. By virtue of WARP, $x \in C(S)$ follows from $x \in S \cap C(S'')$ and $y \in C(S) \cap S''$, entailing (1.7). ■

PROOF OF THEOREM 1.4. By virtue of Theorem 1.3, WARP implies the M-normality of C, which implies its G-normality, thanks to Theorem 1.2. The assertion of the theorem then follows from Definitions 1.8 and 1.9. ■

Proof of Theorem 1.5. By M-normality, we have $C(S) = M^*(S)$ for all $S \in \mathcal{S}$. Let R^0 be defined on X by

$$[(x, y) \in R^0 \Leftrightarrow (y, x) \notin P_{R^*}] \quad \text{for all } x, y \in X. \tag{1.8}$$

Then R^0 is a complete relation and, by its very definition, $M^*(S) = G(S, R^0)$ for all $S \in \mathcal{S}$. Taking Remark 1 into consideration, the assertion of the theorem follows. ■

Proof of Theorem 1.6. SARP implies WARP, so that we have $C(S) = G(S, R^0) = M(S, R^0)$ for all $S \in \mathcal{S}$ by virtue of Theorems 1.3 and 1.5, where R^0 is a complete relation defined by (1.8). Noticing $P_{R^*} = P_{R^0}$, we have only to show $(x, x) \notin T(P_{R^*})$ for all $x \in X$. Suppose, to the contrary, that there exists an $x \in X$ such that $(x, x) \in T(P_{R^*})$ does hold. Then there exist $\{z^1, \ldots, z^{n-1}\} \subseteq X$ and $\{S_1, \ldots, S_n\} \subseteq \mathcal{S}$ satisfying $x \in C(S_1)$, $z^k \in [S_k \backslash C(S_k)] \cap C(S_{k+1})$ $(k = 1, \ldots, n-2)$ and $x \in S_n \backslash C(S_n)$. Then $(S_1, \ldots, S_n)$ is a C-connected sequence in $\mathcal{S}$ but $S_k \cap C(S_{k+1}) \neq C(S_k) \cap S_{k+1}$ for all $k \in \{1, \ldots, n-1\}$, so that SARP does not hold. Thus under SARP, R^0 must be acyclic. ■

1.5. Counterexamples

In this section, counterexamples are given for the converse of our theorems. The set of all alternatives is always taken as $X = \{x, y, z\}$.

(a) By Definition 1.6, HARP implies SARP, which, in turn, implies WARP. The converse does not hold, as was shown by Hansson [4, Theorem 5 and Theorem 6]. By Definition 1.7, SCA implies WCA. The converse does not hold as is shown by the following:

Example 1.1. $\mathcal{S} = \{S_1, S_2, S_3\}$, $S_1 = \{x, y\}$, $S_2 = \{y, z\}$, $S_3 = \{x, z\}$, $C(S_1) = S_1$, $C(S_2) = S_2$ and $C(S_3) = \{x\}$. This C has a revealed preference relation

$$R^* = \{(x, x), (y, y), (z, z), (x, y), (y, x), (y, z), (z, y), (x, z)\}.$$

SCA is not satisfied, because $(z, x) \in T(R^*)$, $x \in C(S_3)$, $z \in S_3$ but $z \notin C(S_3)$. On the other hand, WCA is easily seen to be satisfied.

(b) The converse of Theorem 1.2 does not hold in general; that is to say, there exists a G-normal choice function that is not M-normal.

EXAMPLE 1.2. $\mathcal{S} = \{S_1, S_2\}$, $S_1 = X$, $S_2 = \{x, z\}$, $C(S_1) = \{z\}$, and $C(S_2) = \{x, z\}$. In this case, $R^* = \{(z, z), (z, x), (z, y), (x, z), (x, x)\}$, so that we have $G^*(S_1) = \{z\}$ and $G^*(S_2) = \{x, z\}$. Thus C is G-normal. But $M^*(S_1) = \{x, z\} \neq C(S_1)$, so that C is not M-normal.

(c) The converse of Theorem 1.3 does not hold in general. An example of a choice function that is M-rational but does not satisfy WARP will do.

EXAMPLE 1.3. $\mathcal{S} = \{S_1, S_2\}$, $S_1 = X$, $S_2 = \{y, z\}$, $C(S_1) = \{x, y\}$, and $C(S_2) = S_2$. For this C, $R^* = \{(x, x), (y, y), (z, z), (x, y), (x, z), (y, x), (y, z), (z, y)\}$. This C is M-normal as can easily be verified. WARP is, however, not satisfied, because $S_1 \cap C(S_2) = \{y, z\}$ and $C(S_1) \cap S_2 = \{y\}$.

(d) The converse of Theorem 1.4 is not true in general, as the following example testifies.

EXAMPLE 1.4. $\mathcal{S} = \{S_1, S_2\}$, $S_1 = X$, $S_2 = \{x, y\}$, $C(S_1) = \{x\}$, and $C(S_2) = S_2$. Corresponding to this C, we have $R^* = \{(x, x), (y, y), (x, y), (x, z), (y, x)\}$. Therefore, $M^*(S_1) = \{x, y\} \neq C(S_1)$. This C is not M-normal, hence WARP does not hold, thanks to Theorem 1.3. But we have $C(S) = G(S, R_1) = M(S, R_2)$ for all $S \in \mathcal{S}$, where $R_1 = \{(x, x), (y, y), (x, y), (y, x), (x, z)\}$ and $R_2 = \{(z, y), (x, z)\}$.

(e) The converse of Theorem 1.5 is falsified by the following example.

EXAMPLE 1.5. $\mathcal{S} = \{S_1, S_2, S_3\}$, $S_1 = X$, $S_2 = \{x, y\}$, $S_3 = \{y, z\}$, $C(S_1) = \{y\}$, $C(S_2) = S_2$, and $C(S_3) = \{y\}$. For this C, $R^* = \{(x, x), (y, y), (x, y), (y, x), (y, z)\}$. This C is not M-normal, because $M^*(S_1) = \{x, y\} \neq C(S_1)$. But

$$R = \{(x, y), (y, x), (y, z), (z, x), (x, x), (y, y), (z, z)\}$$

has the property $C(S) = G(S, R)$ for all $S \in \mathcal{S}$ and R is complete, so that C is complete rational.

(f) The converse of Theorem 1.6 is falsified by the following example.

Example 1.6. $\mathcal{S} = \{S_1, S_2, S_3\}$, $S_1 = \{x, y\}$, $S_2 = \{y, z\}$, $S_3 = \{x, z\}$, $C(S_1) = \{x\}$, $C(S_2) = \{y\}$ and $C(S_3) = S_3$. As can be verified,

$$R = \{(x, x), (y, y), (z, z), (x, y), (y, z), (z, x), (x, z)\}$$

is an acyclic and complete relation such that $C(S) = G(S, R)$ for all $S \in \mathcal{S}$. SARP, however, is not satisfied, because $S_1 \cap C(S_2) = \{y\}$, $S_2 \cap C(S_3) = \{z\}$, $S_3 \cap C(S_1) = \{x\}$, $C(S_1) \cap S_2 = \emptyset$, and $C(S_2) \cap S_3 = \emptyset$.

(g) WARP is not strong enough to assure the acyclic and complete rationality of the choice function.

Example 1.7. $\mathcal{S} = \{S_1, S_2, S_3\}$, $S_1 = \{x, y\}$, $S_2 = \{y, z\}$, $S_3 = \{x, z\}$, $C(S_1) = \{x\}$, $C(S_2) = \{y\}$, and $C(S_3) = \{z\}$. In this case, $R^* = \{(x, y), (y, z), (z, x)\}$. We are going to show that $R^* \subseteq R_*$. We have $(x, y) \in R_*$, because $x \in C(S_1)$, $x \notin S_2$ and $y \notin C(S_3)$. Similarly, $z \notin C(S_1)$, $y \in C(S_2)$, and $y \notin S_3$ entail $(y, z) \in R_*$, while $z \notin S_1$, $x \notin C(S_2)$, and $z \in C(S_3)$ show $(z, x) \in R_*$. Thus, thanks to Theorem 1.1 (i), this choice function satisfies WARP. The unique complete rationalization thereof is, however, a cyclic one, viz.,

$$R^* = \{(x, y),\ (y, z),\ (z, x)\}.$$

1.6. Concluding Remarks

In conclusion, let us compare our results with the Arrow-Sen theory, on the one hand, and the Richter-Hansson theory, on the other. We are concerned with a choice function C on the family $\mathcal{S}$. The choice mechanism C is said to be G-rational (resp. M-rational) if there exists a preference relation R such that the choice set $C(S)$ can be identified with the set of all R-greatest points (resp. R-maximal points) in S for any possible choice situation $S \in \mathcal{S}$. Note here that the concepts of G-rationality and M-rationality have nothing to do with the transitivity of the rationalization R. If R happens to satisfy the ordering axiom of completeness and transitivity, C is said to be full rational. Arrow [1] and Sen [13] showed that

(α) SCA, WCA, SARP, *and* (WARP) *are mutually equivalent necessary and sufficient conditions for full rationality if* $\mathcal{S}$ *includes all the pairs and all the triples taken from the universal set* X.

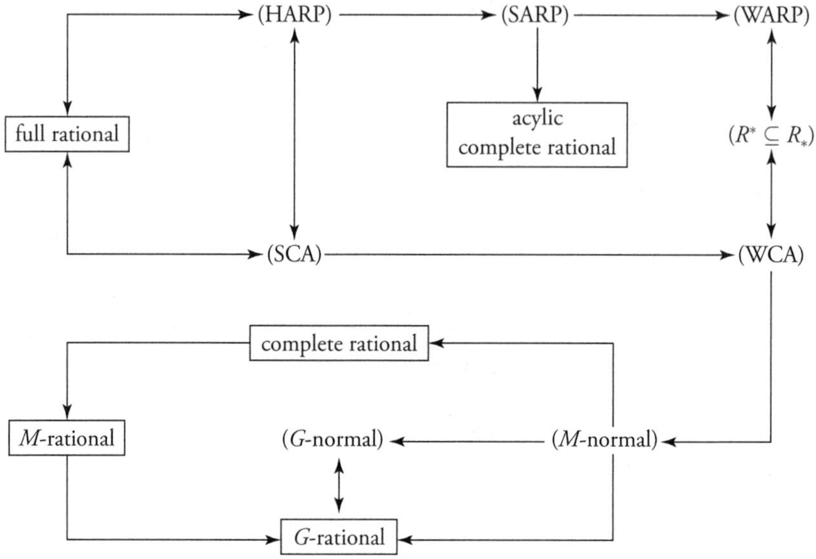

Figure 1.1. Logical Implications

It seems to us that the cost paid for the neat result (α) is rather high. Their assumption on the content of $\mathcal{S}$ might not generally be admissible, hence depriving their result of its general applicability. On the other hand, Richter [9] and Hansson [4] made virtually no restrictions on the content of $\mathcal{S}$ and established that

(β) SCA *and* HARP *are mutually equivalent necessary and sufficient conditions for full rationality.*

Later, Richter [10] extended his conceptual framework and established the following characterization of G-rational choice functions.

(γ) *G-normality is a necessary and sufficient condition for G-rationality.*

In this essay, we have systematically examined the structure of G-rational and M-rational choice functions. The domain of the choice function is assumed simply to be a nonempty family of nonempty sets. Thus we may reasonably claim the general applicability of our results. The role of SARP, WARP, WCA, and M-normality are clarified in this general setting.

Our results, together with (β) and (γ), are summarized in Figure 1.1. A single-headed arrow indicates logical implication, which cannot in general be reversed. A double-headed arrow indicates logical equivalence. The contrast with the Arrow-Sen result (α) is clear.

Appendix 1.A. Equivalence among Axioms

1.A.1. The Equivalence between (1.1) and WARP

[(WARP) $\Rightarrow$ (1)] Let us assume that $(x, y) \in R^{**}$ and $(y, x) \in R^*$ for some x and y in X. Then there exist S_1 and S_2 in $\mathcal{S}$ such that $x \in C(S_1)$, $y \in S_1 \backslash C(S_1)$, $x \in S_2$, and $y \in C(S_2)$. It follows that (S_1, S_2) is a C-connected pair in $\mathcal{S}$ but $y \notin C(S_1) \cap S_2$ and $y \in S_1 \cap C(S_2)$ so that WARP does not hold.

[(1.1) $\Rightarrow$ (WARP)] Let (S_1, S_2) be a C-connected pair in $\mathcal{S}$ such that $x \in S_1 \cap C(S_2)$ and $x \notin C(S_1) \cap S_2$ for some x in X. Then $(y, x) \in R^{**}$ and $(x, y) \in R^*$ for any $y \in C(S_1) \cap S_2$, negating (1.1).

1.A.2. The Equivalence between (1.2) and SARP

[(SARP) $\Rightarrow$ (1.2)] Suppose that $(x, y) \in T(R^{**})$ and $(y, x) \in R^*$ for some x and y in X. Then either $(x, y) \in R^{**}$ or $(x, z^1), (z^1, z^2), \ldots, (z^n, y) \in R^{**}$ for some $z^1, \ldots, z^n \in X$. In view of (a) and Definition 1.6, we have only to consider the latter case. In this case, there exist $S_1, \ldots, S_n$ and S in $\mathcal{S}$ such that $x \in C(S_1)$, $z^1 \in S_1 \backslash C(S_1)$, $z^1 \in C(S_2)$, $z_2 \in S_2 \backslash C(S_2), \ldots$, $z^n \in C(S_{n+1})$, $y \in S_{n+1} \backslash C(S_{n+1})$, $y \in C(S)$, and $x \in S$. Then $(S_1, \ldots, S_{n+1}, S)$ is a C-connected sequence in $\mathcal{S}$. But

$$z^1 \in [S_1 \cap C(S_2)] \backslash [C(S_1) \cap S_2],\ z^2 \in [S_2 \cap C(S_3)] \backslash [C(S_2) \cap S_3], \ldots,$$
$$y \in [S_{n+1} \cap C(S)] \backslash [C(S_{n+1}) \cap S],$$

so that SARP does not hold.

[(1.2) $\Rightarrow$ (SARP)] Let $(S_1, \ldots, S_n)$ be any C-connected sequence in $\mathcal{S}$. If

$$S_{n-1} \cap C(S_n) = C(S_{n-1}) \cap S_n,$$

there remains nothing to be proved. Suppose, then, that $S_{n-1} \cap C(S_n) \neq C(S_{n-1}) \cap S_n$. First, suppose that there exists an $x \in X$ such that $x \in C(S_{n-1}) \cap C(S_n)$ and $x \notin S_{n-1} \cap C(S_n)$. In this case, for any $y \in S_{n-1} \cap C(S_n)$, we have $(x, y) \in R^*$ and $(y, x) \in R^{**}$ in contradiction to (1.2). Second, suppose that we have $x \notin C(S_{n-1}) \cap S_n$, $x \in S_{n-1} \cap C(S_n)$, and $y \in C(S_{n-1}) \cap S_n$ for some x and y in X. Here again we have $(x, y) \in R^*$ and $(y, x) \in R^{**}$ in contradiction to (1.2). Finally, suppose that $C(S_{n-1}) \cap$

$S_n = \emptyset$. $(S_1, \dots, S_n)$ being a C-connected sequence in $\mathcal{S}$, $x \in S_{n-1} \cap C(S_n)$ for some x in X. If $x \in C(S_{n-1})$, we have $x \in C(S_{n-1}) \cap C(S_n) \subseteq C(S_{n-1}) \cap S_n$, a contradiction. Thus we obtain $x \in S_{n-1} \backslash C(S_{n-1})$. If $S_{n-2} \cap C(S_{n-1}) = C(S_{n-2}) \cap S_{n-1}$, there remains nothing to be proved. Otherwise, we repeat the above procedure to obtain a

$$z^{n-1} \in [S_{n-2} \backslash C(S_{n-2})] \cap C(S_{n-1}).$$

This algorithm leads us either to

$$S_k \cap C(S_{k+1}) = C(S_k) \cap S_{k+1} \quad \text{for some } k \in \{1, \dots, n-1\} \quad (1.1^*)$$

or to the following:

There exist $z^2, \dots, z^{n-1}$ such that $z^2 \in [S_1 \backslash C(S_1)] \cap C(S_2)$,

$$z^3 \in [S_2 \backslash C(S_2)] \cap C(S_3), \dots, z^{n-1} \in [S_{n-2} \backslash C(S_{n-2})] \cap C(S_{n-1}). \quad (1.2^*)$$

In the latter case, take a $z^1 \in C(S_1) \cap S_n$. Then we obtain $(z^1, x) \in T(R^{**})$ and $(x, z^1) \in R^*$, in contradiction with (1.2).

1.7. References

[1] Arrow, K. J., "Rational Choice Functions and Orderings," *Economica* NS **26**, 1959, 121–127.

[2] Arrow, K. J., *Social Choice and Individual Values,* New York: John Wiley & Sons, 1951; 2nd edn., 1963.

[3] Fishburn, P. C., *The Theory of Social Choice,* Princeton, N.J.: Princeton University Press, 1973.

[4] Hansson, B., "Choice Structures and Preference Relations," *Synthese* **18**, 1968, 443–458.

[5] Herzberger, H. G., "Ordinal Preference and Rational Choice," *Econometrica* **41**, 1973, 187–237.

[6] Houthakker, H. S., "Revealed Preference and the Utility Function," *Economica* NS **17**, 1950, 159–174.

[7] Jamison, D. T., and L. J. Lau, "Semiorders and the Theory of Choice," *Econometrica* **41**, 1973, 901–912.

[8] Plott, C. R., "Path Independence, Rationality and Social Choice," *Econometrica* **41**, 1973, 1075–1091.

[9] Richter, M. K., "Revealed Preference Theory," *Econometrica* **34**, 1966, 635–645.

[10] Richter, M. K., "Rational Choice," in J. Chipman, L. Hurwicz, M. Richter, and H.Sonnenschein, eds., *Preferences, Utility, and Demand,* New York: Harcourt Brace Jovanovich, 1971, 29–58.

[11] Samuelson, P. A., *Foundations of Economic Analysis,* Cambridge, Mass.: Harvard University Press, 1947.

[12] Sen, A. K., "Quasi-Transitivity, Rational Choice, and Collective Decisions," *Review of Economic Studies* **36**, 1969, 381–393.

[13] Sen, A. K., *Collective Choice and Social Welfare,* San Francisco: Holden-Day, 1970.

[14] Sen, A. K., "Choice Functions and Revealed Preference," *Review of Economic Studies* **38**, 1971, 307–317.

[15] Suzumura, K., "General Possibility Theorems for Path-Independent Social Choice," Kyoto Institute of Economic Research, Kyoto University, Discussion Paper 77, 1974.

[16] Wilson, R. B., "The Finer Structure of Revealed Preference," *Journal of Economic Theory* **2**, 1970, 348–353.

ESSAY 2

Houthakker's Axiom in the Theory of Rational Choice

2.1. Introduction

In his celebrated classic paper [4], Houthakker strengthened Samuelson's weak axiom of revealed preference [7, 8] into what he called *semitransitivity*, and showed that the Lipschitz continuous demand function of a competitive consumer satisfying his axiom does possess a generating utility function.[1] Uzawa [11], Arrow [1], and others extended the conceptual framework of revealed preference theory so as to make it applicable to a wider class of problems. Instead of confining our attention to a demand function of a competitive consumer, we are now concerned with a *choice function* over a family of nonempty subsets of the nonempty universal set. A natural question suggests itself: What property of a choice function guarantees the existence of a rationalizing preference ordering (RPO)? In particular, does Houthakker's axiom, if suitably reformulated, qualify as such? It is this problem of the existence of an RPO that constitutes the problem of *rationalizability* of a choice function, which is a choice-functional counterpart of the integrability problem in demand theory.

First published in *Journal of Economic Theory* **14**, 1977, pp. 284–290. Thanks are due to Professors William Gorman and Amartya Sen for their helpful comments. However, they should not be held responsible for any defects that may remain in this essay.

1. Further results on this problem are found in Chipman, Hurwicz, Richter, and Sonnenschein [2]. See, especially, Uzawa [2, Chapter 1] and Hurwicz and Richter [2, Chapter 3].

In the literature we have two answers to this question, depending on the extent of the domain of a choice function. On the one hand, if the family over which a choice function is defined contains all finite subsets of the universal set, the weak axiom ensures the existence of an RPO and that the *strong axiom of revealed preference* (which was so named by Samuelson [8] and attributed to Houthakker) is equivalent to the weak axiom [1, 9]. On the other hand, if we do not impose any such additional assumption on the domain, the strong axiom is necessary but not sufficient for the existence of an RPO [3, 10].[2] Richter [5] and Hansson [3] proposed in this general setting a necessary and sufficient condition for the existence of an RPO, which was called the *congruence axiom* by Richter.

The purpose of this essay is to show that Houthakker's semitransitivity axiom, if suitably formalized in the choice-functional context, is in fact necessary and sufficient for the existence of an RPO. Therefore, it follows that, contrary to the prevailing interpretation, the strong axiom is *not* a legitimate formalization of Houthakker's axiom, which is *equivalent* to the congruence axiom. In other words, Houthakker's axiom, unlike the strong axiom, provides us with the precise restriction on a choice function for the rationalizability thereof, just as it provided us with the precise restriction on a Lipschitz continuous demand function for the integrability thereof.

2.2. Rationalizability

2.2.1. Choice Function and Preference Relation

Let X be a nonempty set that stands for a fixed universe of alternatives. We assume that there is a well-specified family $\mathcal{S}$ of nonempty subsets of X. The pair $(X, \mathcal{S})$ will be called a *choice space.* A *choice function* on a choice space $(X, \mathcal{S})$ is a function C defined on $\mathcal{S}$ that assigns a nonempty subset (*choice set*) $C(S)$ of S to each $S \in \mathcal{S}$.

A *preference relation* R on X is a binary relation on X, namely, a subset of a Cartesian product $X \times X$. Associated with a given preference relation R, an infinite sequence of binary relations $\{R^{(\tau)}\}_{\tau=1}^{\infty}$ is defined

2. This statement is true for one version of the strong axiom, which is used by Arrow [1], Hansson [3], Sen [9], and Suzumura [10]. More about this in the final section of this essay.

by $R^{(1)} = R$, $R^{(\tau)} = \{(x, y) \in X \times X \mid (x, z) \in R^{(\tau-1)} \text{ \& } (z, y) \in R$ for some $z \in X\}(\tau \geq 2)$. The *transitive closure* of R is then defined by $T(R) = \cup_{\tau=1}^{\infty} R^{(\tau)}$.[3] The *strict preference relation* P_R corresponding to a preference relation R is an asymmetric component of R:

$$P_R = \{(x, y) \in X \times X \mid (x, y) \in R \text{ \& } (y, x) \notin R\}. \tag{2.1}$$

We say that a preference relation R is *transitive* if $(x, y) \in R$ and $(y, z) \in R$ imply $(x, z) \in R$, *acyclic* if $(x, x) \notin T(P_R)$, and *complete* if either $(x, y) \in R$ or $(y, x) \in R$ for all x and y in X. R is said to be an *ordering* if it is transitive and complete. For every $S \in \mathcal{S}$, we define

$$G(S, R) = \{x \in X \mid x \in S \text{ \& } (x, y) \in R \text{ for all } y \in S\}, \tag{2.2}$$

which is the set of all R-greatest points in S.

2.2.2. Rationality as Rationalizability

A preference relation R on X is said to rationalize a choice function C on $(X, \mathcal{S})$ if we have

$$C(S) = G(S, R) \quad \text{for every } S \in \mathcal{S}. \tag{2.3}$$

A choice function C is said to be *rational* if there exists a preference relation R that rationalizes C. (R is then called a *rationalization* of C.) If a choice function C is rational with an acyclic rationalization, we say that C is *acyclic rational.* Similarly, if C is rational with an ordering rationalization, we say that C is *full rational.*

2.2.3. Revealed Preference Relations and Revealed Preference Axioms

Let C be a choice function on $(X, \mathcal{S})$ that is fixed once and for all. Two revealed preference relations R^* and R^{**} are induced from C as follows. We

---

3. It is easy to see that T satisfies the axiom of *closure operations:* (α) $R \subseteq T(R)$ for every R, (β) $R \subseteq R'$ implies $T(R) \subseteq T(R')$ for every R and R', (γ) $T[T(R)] = T(R)$ for every R, and (δ) $T(\emptyset) = \emptyset$.

define a binary relation R^* on X by

$$R^* = \{(x, y) \in X \times X \mid x \in C(S) \;\&\; y \in S \text{ for some } S \in \mathcal{S}\} \quad (2.4)$$

and, when $(x, y) \in R^*$, we say that x is *revealed R^*-preferred to* y. Similarly, we define

$$R^{**} = \{(x, y) \in X \times X \mid x \in C(S) \;\&\; y \in S \backslash C(S) \text{ for some } S \in \mathcal{S}\} \quad (2.5)$$

and, when $(x, y) \in R^{**}$, we say that x is *revealed R^{**}-preferred to* y. It is easy to see that R^* and R^{**} are related by the following relation:

$$P_{R^*} \subseteq P_{R^{**}} \subseteq R^{**} \subseteq R^*. \quad (2.6)$$

We have only to show that $P_{R^*} \subseteq P_{R^{**}}$, the remaining inclusions in (2.6) being obvious by definition. If $(x, y) \in P_{R^*}$, then we have

$$x \in C(S) \;\&\; y \in S \quad \text{for some } S \in \mathcal{S}, \quad (2.7)$$

and

$$y \notin C(S') \quad \text{or} \quad x \notin S' \text{ for all } S' \in \mathcal{S}. \quad (2.8)$$

If we apply (2.8) for $S' = S$, this (coupled with (2.7)) yields

$$x \in C(S) \;\&\; y \in S \backslash C(S) \quad \text{for some } S \in \mathcal{S}, \quad (2.9)$$

while (2.8) implies

$$y \notin C(S') \quad \text{or} \quad x \notin S' \quad \text{or} \quad x \in C(S') \text{ for all } S' \in \mathcal{S}. \quad (2.10)$$

It follows from (2.9) and (2.10) that $(x, y) \in P_{R^{**}}$.

We now turn from our revealed preference relations to revealed preference axioms. A finite sequence $\{x^1, x^2, \ldots, x^t\}$ $(t \geq 2)$ in X is called an *H-cycle of order t* if we have $(x^1, x^2) \in R^{**}$, $(x^\tau, x^{\tau+1}) \in R^*(\tau = 2, \ldots, t-1)$, and $(x^t, x^1) \in R^*$. Similarly, a finite sequence $\{x^1, x^2, \ldots, x^t\}$ $(t \geq 2)$ in X is called an *SH-cycle of order t* if we have $(x^1, x^2) \in R^*$, $(x^\tau, x^{\tau+1}) \in R^{**}(\tau = 2, \ldots, t-1)$, and $(x^t, x^1) \in R^{**}$. In view of (2.6) it is clear that *an SH-cycle of some order* is *an H-cycle of the same order.* This being the case, the exclusion of an H-cycle of any order excludes, a fortiori, the existence of an SH-cycle of any order. We now introduce the following two revealed preference axioms.

HOUTHAKKER'S REVEALED PREFERENCE AXIOM. *There exists no H-cycle of any order.*

STRONG AXIOM OF REVEALED PREFERENCE. *There exists no SH-cycle of any order.*

Clearly, Houthakker's axiom is stronger than the strong axiom. We have shown in [2.10] that the strong axiom is necessary but not sufficient for full rationality and that it is sufficient but not necessary for acyclic rationality. In the final section we will argue that the above-stated Houthakker's axiom is a proper choice-functional counterpart of Houthakker's semitransitivity in demand theory.

2.2.4. Rationalizability Theorem

We are now ready to put forward our theorem.

RATIONALIZABILITY THEOREM. *A choice function C is full rational if and only if it satisfies Houthakker's axiom of revealed preference.*

PROOF OF NECESSITY. If C is full rational with an ordering rationalization R, then we have (2.3). Suppose that there exists a sequence $\{x^1, x^2, \ldots, x^t\}$ $(t \geq 2)$ such that $(x^1, x^2) \in R^{**}$ and $(x^\tau, x^{\tau+1}) \in R^*(\tau = 1, 2, \ldots, t-1)$. Then there exists a sequence $\{S^1, S^2, \ldots, S^{t-1}\}$ in $\mathcal{S}$ such that $x^1 \in C(S^1)$, $x^2 \in S^1 \backslash C(S^1)$, $x^\tau \in C(S^\tau)$, and $x^{\tau+1} \in S^\tau (\tau = 2, \ldots, t-1)$. Since C is full rational we then have $(x^1, x^2) \in P_R$ and $(x^\tau, x^{\tau+1}) \in R(\tau = 2, \ldots, t-1)$, which entails $(x^1, x^t) \in P_R$, thanks to the transitivity of R. But this result excludes the possibility that $(x^t, x^1) \in R^*$, so that there exists no H-cycle of any order. ∎

PROOF OF SUFFICIENCY. Let a *diagonal* Δ be defined by

$$\Delta = \{(x, x) \in X \times X \mid x \in X\}, \tag{2.11}$$

and define a binary relation Q by

$$Q = \Delta \cup T(R^*). \tag{2.12}$$

It is easy to see that Q is transitive and *reflexive:* $(x, x) \in Q$ for all x in X. Thanks to a corollary of Szpilrajn's theorem [3, Lemma 3] there exists an ordering R that subsumes Q; namely, there exists an ordering R such that

$$Q \subseteq R, \tag{2.13}$$

and

$$P_Q \subseteq P_R. \tag{2.14}$$

We are going to show that this R in fact satisfies

$$R^* \subseteq R, \tag{2.15}$$

and

$$P_{R^*} \subseteq P_R. \tag{2.16}$$

The former is obvious in view of $R^* \subseteq T(R^*)$, (2.12), and (2.13). To prove the latter we have only to show that $P_{R^*} \subseteq P_Q$, thanks to (2.14). Assume $(x, y) \in P_{R^*}$, which means $(x, y) \in R^*$ and $(y, x) \notin R^*$. From $(x, y) \in R^*$ it follows that $(x, y) \in Q$. It only remains to be shown that $(y, x) \notin Q$. Assume, therefore, that $(y, x) \in Q$. Clearly, $(y, x) \notin \Delta$, else we cannot have $(x, y) \in P_{R^*}$. It follows that $(y, x) \in T(R^*)$, which, in combination with $(x, y) \in P_{R^*} \subseteq R^{**}$, implies the existence of an H-cycle of some order, a contradiction. Therefore, (2.15) and (2.16) are valid.

Let $S \in \mathcal{S}$ be chosen and let $x \in C(S)$. Then $(x, y) \in R^*$ for all $y \in S$. In view of (2.15) we then have $x \in G(S, R)$. It follows that

$$C(S) \subseteq G(S, R). \tag{2.17}$$

Next let $x \in S \backslash C(S)$ and take $y \in C(S)$, so that $(y, x) \in R^{**}$. If we have $(x, y) \in R^*$, it turns out that $\{x, y\}$ is an H-cycle of order 2, a contradiction. Therefore, we must have $(x, y) \notin R^*$, which, in view of $(y, x) \in R^{**} \subseteq R^*$, implies $(y, x) \in P_{R^*}$. Thanks to (2.16), we then have $(y, x) \in P_R$, entailing $x \in S \backslash G(S, R)$. Therefore, we obtain

$$G(S, R) \subseteq C(S). \tag{2.18}$$

As (2.17) and (2.18) are valid for any $S \in \mathcal{S}$, we have shown that C is full rational with an ordering rationalization R. This completes the proof. ■

2.3. Comments on the Literature

It only remains to make some comments on the existing literature.

(i) Houthakker [4, pp. 162–163] introduced his semitransitivity axiom in terms of a demand function h on the family of competitive budgets. Let Ω, $\boldsymbol{p}$, and M be the commodity space, a competitive price vector, and an income. Then h is a function on the family of all budget sets

$$B(\boldsymbol{p}, M) = \{x \in \Omega \mid \boldsymbol{p}x \leq M\}. \tag{2.19}$$

We consider a sequence $\{\boldsymbol{p}^\tau\}_{\tau=1}^T$ in Ω satisfying

$$\boldsymbol{x}^\tau = h(\boldsymbol{p}^\tau, \boldsymbol{p}^\tau \boldsymbol{x}^\tau) \quad \text{for every } \tau \in \{1, 2, \ldots, T\}, \tag{2.20}$$

$$\boldsymbol{x}^{\tau+1} \in B(\boldsymbol{p}^\tau, \boldsymbol{p}^\tau \boldsymbol{x}^\tau) \quad \text{for every } \tau \in \{1, 2, \ldots, T-1\}, \tag{2.21}$$

and

$$\boldsymbol{x}^{\tau+1} \neq h(\boldsymbol{p}^\tau, \boldsymbol{p}^\tau \boldsymbol{x}^\tau) \quad \text{for } \textit{at least one } \tau \in \{1, 2, \ldots, T-1\}. \tag{2.22}$$

Houthakker's semitransitivity then requires that $\boldsymbol{x}^1 \notin B(\boldsymbol{p}^T, \boldsymbol{p}^T \boldsymbol{x}^T)$. It will be noticed that what we called Houthakker's axiom of revealed preference in Section 2.3 is a natural reformulation of this requirement in terms of a choice function C.

(ii) What Samuelson [8, pp. 370–371] called the strong axiom is the same requirement as Houthakker's, save for the replacement of (2.22) by

$$\boldsymbol{x}^{\tau+1} \neq h(\boldsymbol{p}^\tau, \boldsymbol{p}^\tau \boldsymbol{x}^\tau) \quad \text{for } \textit{every } \tau \in \{1, 2, \ldots, T-1\}. \tag{2.23}$$

Our strong axiom of revealed preference in Section 2.2.3 is, it will be noticed, a natural extension of Samuelson's axiom in the context of a choice function.

(iii) We have shown in [2.10] that Hansson's strong axiom of revealed preference [2.3] is, despite its apparent difference, equivalent to that of ours in Section 2.2.3.

(iv) Richter [5, p. 637] argued that "the revealed preference notions employed in [the weak axiom of Samuelson and the strong axiom of Houthakker] are relevant only to the special case of competitive consumers, so that axioms also have meaning only in that limited context." However, these axioms can be and have been generalized beyond the narrow confinement of competitive consumers. Besides, Richter himself defined in [2.6] the weak and the strong axioms for a *single-valued* choice function. There is no reason, furthermore, that we should not consider these axioms in terms of a set-valued choice function.

In conclusion, it is hoped that our result will help to clarify the central role played by Houthakker's axiom in the whole spectrum of revealed preference theory.

2.4. References

[1] Arrow, K. J., "Rational Choice Functions and Orderings," *Economica* NS **26**, 1959, 121–127.

[2] Chipman, J. S., L. Hurwicz, M. K. Richter, and H. F. Sonnenschein, eds., *Preferences, Utility, and Demand,* New York: Harcourt Brace Jovanovich, 1971.

[3] Hansson, B., "Choice Structures and Preference Relations," *Synthese* **18**, 1968, 443–458.

[4] Houthakker, H. S., "Revealed Preference and the Utility Function," *Economica* NS **17**, 1950, 159–174.

[5] Richter, M. K., "Revealed Preference Theory," *Econometrica* **34**, 1966, 635–645.

[6] Richter, M. K., "Rational Choice," in J. Chipman, L. Hurwicz, M. Richter, and H. Sonnenschein, eds., *Preferences, Utility, and Demand,* New York: Harcourt Brace Jovanovich, 1971, 29–58.

[7] Samuelson, P. A., "A Note on the Pure Theory of Consumer's Behaviour," *Economica* NS **5**, 1938, 61–71, 353–354.

[8] Samuelson, P. A., "The Problem of Integrability in Utility Theory," *Economica* NS **17**, 1950, 355–385.

[9] Sen, A. K., "Choice Functions and Revealed Preference," *Review of Economic Studies* **38**, 1971, 307–317.

[10] Suzumura, K., "Rational Choice and Revealed Preference," *Review of Economic Studies* **43**, 1976, 149–158. Essay 1 of this volume.

[11] Uzawa, H., "Note on Preference and Axioms of Choice," *Annals of the Institute of Statistical Mathematics* **8**, 1957, 35–40.

ESSAY 3

Suzumura-Consistent Rationalizability

3.1. Introduction

Rationalizability is an important issue in the analysis of economic decisions. It provides a means to test theories of choice, including—but not limited to—traditional consumer demand theory. The central question to be addressed is as follows: Are the observed choices of an economic agent compatible with our standard theories of choice as being motivated by optimizing behavior? More precisely, can we find a preference relation with suitably defined properties that generates the observed choices as the choice of greatest or maximal elements according to this relation? This question has its origin in the theory of consumer demand but has since been explored in more general contexts, including both individual and collective choice. By formulating necessary and sufficient conditions for the existence of a rationalizing relation, testable restrictions on observable choice behavior implied by the various theories are established.

Samuelson [12] began his seminal work on revealed preference theory with a remark that "from its very beginning the theory of consumer's choice

---

First published in *Economica* **72**, 2005, pp. 185–200. Joint paper with W. Bossert and Y. Sprumont. Financial support through grants from the Social Sciences and Humanities Research Council of Canada, the Fonds pour la Formation de Chercheurs et l'Aide à la Recherche of Québec, and a Grant-in-Aid for Scientific Research for Priority Areas Number 603 from the Ministry of Education, Culture, Sports, Science and Technology of Japan is gratefully acknowledged. It was presented at Bocconi University. We thank three referees assigned by *Economica* for comments and suggestions.

has marched steadily toward greater generality, sloughing off at successive stages unnecessarily restrictive conditions" (Samuelson [12, p. 61]). Even after Samuelson [12; 13, Chapter V; 14; 15] laid the foundations of "the theory of consumer's behaviour freed from any vestigial traces of the utility concept" (Samuelson [12, p. 71]), the exercise of Ockham's Razor persisted within revealed preference theory. According to Georgescu-Roegen [5, p. 125], the intuitive justification of the axioms of revealed preference theory has nothing to do with the special form of budget sets, but is based on the implicit consideration of choices from two-element sets. Arrow [2] expanded the analysis of rational choice and revealed preference beyond consumer choice problems. He pointed out that "the demand-function point of view would be greatly simplified if the range over which the choice functions are considered to be determined is broadened to include all finite sets" (Arrow, [2, p. 122]). Sen [16, p. 312] defended Arrow's domain assumption by posing two important questions: "Why assume the axioms [of revealed preference] to be true only for 'budget sets' and not for others?" and "are there reasons to expect that some of the rationality axioms will tend to be satisfied in choices over 'budget sets' but not for other choices?"

While it is certainly desirable to liberate revealed preference theory from the narrow confinement of budget sets, the admission of all finite subsets of the universal sets into the domain of a choice function may well be unsuitable for many applications. In this context, two important groups of contributions stand out. In the first place, Richter [10; 11], Hansson [7], and Suzumura [17; 19; 20, Chapter 2] developed the theory of rational choice and revealed preference for choice functions with general nonempty domains that do not impose any extraneous restrictions whatsoever on the class of feasible sets. In the second place, Sen [16] showed that Arrow's results (as well as others with similar features) do not hinge on the full power of the assumption that *all* finite sets are included in the domain of a choice function—it suffices if the domain contains all two-element and three-element sets.

It was in view of this state of the art that Bossert, Sprumont, and Suzumura [3] examined two crucial types of general domains in an analysis of several open questions in the theory of rational choice. The first is the general domain à la Richter, Hansson, and Suzumura, and the second is the class of *base domains,* which include all singletons and all two-element subsets of the universal set. The status of the general domain seems to be impeccable, as the theory developed on this domain is relevant in whatever choice situations we may care to specify. The base domains also seem to be on safe ground, as the concept of rational choice as maximizing choice is intrinsically connected with pairwise comparisons: singletons can be viewed as pairs with identical components, whereas two-element sets represent pairs of distinct alternatives. As Arrow [1, p. 16] put it, "one of the consequences of the assumptions of rational choice is that the choice in any environment can be determined by a knowledge of the choices in two-element environments."

In this essay, we focus on the rationalizability of choice functions by means of *Suzumura-consistent* relations. The concept of Suzumura consistency—*S-consistency* for short—was first introduced by Suzumura [18], and it is a weakening of transitivity requiring that *any preference cycle should involve indifference only*. As was shown by Suzumura [18; 20, Chapter 1], S-consistency is necessary and sufficient for the existence of an ordering extension of a binary relation. For that reason, S-consistency is a central property for the analysis of rational choice as well: in order to obtain a rationalizing relation that is an ordering, an extension procedure is, in general, required in order to ensure that the rationalization is complete. Violations of transitivity are quite likely to be observed in practical choice situations. For instance, Luce's [9] well-known coffee-sugar example provides a plausible argument against assuming that indifference is always transitive: the inability of a decision maker to perceive 'small' differences in alternatives is bound to lead to intransitivities. As this example illustrates, transitivity frequently is too strong an assumption to impose in the context of individual choice. In collective choice problems, it is even more evident that the plausibility of transitivity can be questioned. On the other hand, it is difficult to interpret observed choices as "rational" if they do not possess any coherence property. Because of Suzumura's [18] result, S-consistency can be considered a weakening of transitivity that is *minimal* in the sense that it cannot be weakened further without abandoning all hope of finding a rationalizing ordering extension.

To further underline the importance of S-consistency, note that this property is precisely what is required to prevent the problem of a "money pump." If S-consistency is violated, there exists a preference cycle with at least one strict preference. In this case, the agent under consideration is willing to trade an alternative x_0 for another alternative x_1 (where "willingness to trade" is to be interpreted as being at least as well off after the trade as before), x_1

for an alternative x_2, and so on until we reach an alternative x_K such that the agent *strictly prefers* getting back x_0 to retaining possession of x_K. Thus, at the end of a chain of exchanges, the agent is willing to pay a positive amount in order to get back the alternative it had in its possession in the first place—a classical example of a money pump.

We examine S-consistent rationalizability under two domain assumptions. The first is, again, the general domain assumption where no restrictions whatsoever are imposed, and the second weakens the base domain hypothesis: we merely require the domain to contain all two-element sets but not necessarily all singletons, and we refer to those domains as *binary domains.* Thus, our results are applicable in a wide range of choice problems. Unlike many contributions to the theory of rational choice, we do not have to assume that triples are part of the domain. Especially the first domain assumption—the general domain—is highly relevant because it can accommodate any choice situation that arises in the analysis of both individual and collective choice. For instance, our results are applicable in traditional demand theory but in more general environments as well.

Depending on the additional properties that can be imposed on rationalizations (reflexivity and completeness), different notions of S-consistent rationalizability can be defined. We characterize all but one of those notions in the general case, and all of them in the case of binary domains. It is worth noting that we obtain full characterization results on binary domains (in particular, on domains that do not have to contain any triples), even though S-consistency imposes a restriction on possible cycles of any length.

In Section 3.2, the notation and our basic definitions are presented, along with some preliminary lemmas. Section 3.3 develops the theory of S-consistent rationalizability on general domains, whereas Section 3.4 expounds the corresponding theory on binary domains. Some concluding remarks are collected in Section 3.5.

3.2. Preliminaries

The set of positive (resp. nonnegative) integers is denoted by $\mathbb{N}$ (resp. $\mathbb{N}_0$). For a set S, $|S|$ is the cardinality of S. Let X be a universal nonempty set of alternatives. $\mathcal{X}$ is the power set of X excluding the empty set. A choice function is a mapping $C\colon \mathcal{S} \rightarrow \mathcal{X}$ such that $C(S) \subseteq S$ for all $S \in \mathcal{S}$, where

$\mathcal{S} \subseteq \mathcal{X}$ with $\mathcal{S} \neq \emptyset$ is the domain of C. Note that C maps $\mathcal{S}$ into the set of all *nonempty* subsets of X. Thus, using Richter's [11] terminology, the choice function C is assumed to be *decisive*. Let $C(\mathcal{S})$ denote the image of $\mathcal{S}$ under C, that is, $C(\mathcal{S}) = \cup_{S \in \mathcal{S}} C(S)$. In addition to arbitrary nonempty domains, to be called *general domains*, we consider *binary domains*, which are domains $\mathcal{S} \subseteq \mathcal{X}$ such that $\{S \in \mathcal{X} | S| = 2\} \subseteq \mathcal{S}$.

Let $R \subseteq X \times X$ be a (binary) relation on X. The asymmetric factor $P(R)$ of R is given by $(x, y) \in P(R)$ if and only if $(x, y) \in R$ and $(y, x) \notin R$ for all $x, y \in X$. The symmetric factor $I(R)$ of R is defined by $(x, y) \in I(R)$ if and only if $(x, y) \in R$ and $(y, x) \in R$ for all $x, y \in X$. The noncomparable factor $N(R)$ of R is given by $(x, y) \in N(R)$ if and only if $(x, y) \notin R$ and $(y, x) \notin R$ for all $x, y \in X$.

A relation $R \subset X \times X$ is (i) *reflexive* if, for all $x \in X$, $(x, x) \in R$; (ii) *complete* if, for all $x, y \in X$ such that $x \neq y$, $(x, y) \in R$ or $(y, x) \in R$; (iii) *transitive* if, for all $x, y, z \in X$, $[(x, y) \in R$ and $(y, z) \in R]$ implies $(x, z) \in R$; (iv) *S-consistent* if, for all $K \in \mathbb{N} \setminus \{1\}$ and for all $x^0, \ldots, x^K \in X$, $(x^{k-1}, x^k) \in R$ for all $k \in \{1, \ldots, K\}$ implies $(x^K, x^0) \notin P(R)$; and (v) *acyclic* if, for all $K \in \mathbb{N} \setminus \{1\}$ and for all $x^0, \ldots, x^K \in X$, $(x^{k-1}, x^k) \in P(R)$ for all $k \in \{1, \ldots, K\}$ implies $(x^K, x^0) \notin P(R)$.

The *transitive closure* of $R \subseteq X \times X$ is denoted by $T(R)$, that is, for all $x, y \in X$, $(x, y) \in T(R)$ if there exist $K \in \mathbb{N}$ and $x^0, \ldots, x^K \in X$ such that $x = x^0$, $(x^{k-1}, x^k) \in R$ for all $k \in \{1, \ldots, K\}$ and $x^K = y$. Clearly, $T(R)$ is transitive and, because we can set $K = 1$, it follows that $R \subseteq T(R)$. For future reference, we state the following well-known result. The proof is straightforward and thus omitted (see Suzumura [20, pp. 11–12]).

LEMMA 3.1. Let R and Q be binary relations on X. If $R \subseteq Q$, then $T(R) \subseteq T(Q)$.

The *direct revealed preference relation* $R_C \subseteq X \times X$ of a choice function C with an arbitrary domain $\mathcal{S}$ is defined as follows. For all $x, y \in X$, $(x, y) \in R_C$ if there exists $S \in \mathcal{S}$ such that $x \in C(S)$ and $y \in S$. The *(indirect) revealed preference relation* of C is the transitive closure $T(R_C)$ of the direct revealed preference relation R_C.

For $S \in \mathcal{S}$ and a relation $R \subseteq X \times X$, the set of R-greatest elements in S is $\{x \in S \mid (x, y) \in R$ for all $y \in S\}$, and the set of R-maximal elements in

S is $\{x \in S \mid (y, x) \notin P(R)$ for all $y \in S\}$. A choice function C is *greatest-element rationalizable* if there exists a relation R on X, to be called a *G-rationalization,* such that $C(S)$ is equal to the set of R-greatest elements in S for all $S \in \mathcal{S}$. C is *maximal-element rationalizable* if there exists a relation R on X, to be called an *M-rationalization,* such that $C(S)$ is equal to the set of R-maximal elements in S for all $S \in \mathcal{S}$. We use the term *rationalization* in general discussions where it is not specified whether greatest-element rationalizability or maximal-element rationalizability is considered.

If a rationalization is required to be reflexive and complete, the notions of greatest-element rationalizability and maximal-element rationalizability coincide. Without these properties, however, this is not necessarily the case. Greatest-element rationalizability is based on the idea of chosen alternatives weakly dominating all alternatives in the feasible set under consideration, whereas maximal-element rationalizability requires chosen elements not to be strictly dominated by any other feasible alternative. Specific examples illustrating the differences between those two concepts will be discussed later.

Depending on the properties that we might want to impose on a rationalization, different notions of rationalizability can be defined. For simplicity of presentation, we use the following notation. G (resp. RG; CG; RCG) stands for greatest-element rationalizability by means of an S-consistent (resp. reflexive and S-consistent; complete and S-consistent; reflexive, complete, and S-consistent) G-rationalization. Analogously, M (resp. RM; CM; RCM) is maximal-element rationalizability by means of an S-consistent (resp. reflexive and S-consistent; complete and S-consistent; reflexive, complete, and S-consistent) M-rationalization. Note that we do not identify S-consistency explicitly in these acronyms even though it is assumed to be satisfied by the rationalization in question. This is because S-consistency is required in all of the theorems presented in this essay, so that the use of another notation would be redundant and likely increase the complexity of our exposition. However, note that the two lemmas stated in the following do not require S-consistency. In particular, the implication of part (i) of Lemma 3.3 does not apply to rationalizability by an S-consistent relation; see also Theorem 3.1.

We conclude this section with two further preliminary results. We first present the following lemma, the first part of which is due to Samuelson [12; 14]; see also Richter [11]. It states that the direct revealed preference relation must be contained in any G-rationalization and, moreover, that if an alternative x is directly revealed preferred to an alternative y, then y cannot be strictly preferred to x by any M-rationalization.

LEMMA 3.2. (i) If R is a G-rationalization of C, then $R_C \subseteq R$.
(ii) If R is an M-rationalization of C, then $R_C \subseteq R \cup N(R)$.

PROOF. (i) Suppose that R is a G-rationalization of C and $x, y \in X$ are such that $(x, y) \in R_C$. By definition of R_C, there exists $S \in \Sigma$ such that $x \in C(S)$ and $y \in S$. Because R is a G-rationalization of C, we obtain $(x, y) \in R$.

(ii) Suppose R is an M-rationalization of C and $x, y \in X$ are such that $(x, y) \in R_C$. By way of contradiction, suppose $(x, y) \notin R \cup N(R)$. Therefore, $(y, x) \in P(R)$. Because R maximal-element rationalizes C, this implies $x \notin C(S)$ for all $S \in \mathcal{S}$ such that $y \in S$. But this contradicts the hypothesis that $(x, y) \in R_C$. ■

Our final preliminary observation concerns the relationship between maximal-element rationalizability and greatest-element rationalizability when no further restrictions are imposed on a rationalization. This applies, in particular, when consistency is not imposed. Moreover, an axiom that is necessary for either form of rationalizability is presented. This requirement is referred to as the V-axiom in Richter [11]; we call it direct revelation coherence in order to have a systematic terminology throughout this essay.

DIRECT REVELATION COHERENCE. For all $S \in \mathcal{S}$, for all $x \in S$, if $(x, y) \in R_C$ for all $y \in S$, then $x \in C(S)$.

Suzumura [17] establishes that, in the absence of any requirements on a rationalization, maximal-element rationalizability implies greatest-element rationalizability. Furthermore, Richter [11] shows that direct revelation coherence is necessary for greatest-element rationalizability by an arbitrary G-rationalization on an arbitrary domain. We summarize these observations in the following lemma. For completeness, we provide a proof.

LEMMA 3.3. (i) If C is maximal-element rationalizable, then C is greatest-element rationalizable.
(ii) If C is greatest-element rationalizable, then C satisfies direct revelation coherence.

Proof. (i) Suppose R is an M-rationalization of C. It is straightforward to verify that $R' = \{(x, y) \mid (y, x) \notin P(R)\}$ is a G-rationalization of C.

(ii) Suppose R is a G-rationalization of C, and let $S \in \mathcal{S}$ and $x \in S$ be such that $(x, y) \in R_C$ for all $y \in S$. By part (i) of Lemma 3.2, $(x, y) \in R$ for all $y \in S$. Because R is a G-rationalization of C, this implies $x \in C(S)$. ■

There are alternative notions of rationality, such as that of Kim and Richter [8], who proposed the concept of *motivated choice:* C is a motivated choice if there exists a relation R on X, which is to be called a *motivation* of C, such that

$$C(S) = \{x \in S \mid (y, x) \notin R \text{ for all } y \in S\}$$

for all $S \in \mathcal{S}$. This property is implied by maximal-element rationalizability but the converse implication is not true. Moreover, C is a motivated choice if and only if C is greatest-element rationalizable. Indeed, R greatest-element rationalizes C if and only if its dual R^d, which is defined by

$$(x, y) \in R^d \Leftrightarrow (y, x) \notin R$$

for all $x, y \in X$, is a motivation of C.

Richter [11] shows that direct revelation coherence is not only necessary but also sufficient for greatest-element rationalizability on an arbitrary domain, without any further restrictions imposed on the G-rationalization. Moreover, the axiom is necessary and sufficient for greatest-element rationalizability by a reflexive (but otherwise unrestricted) rationalization on an arbitrary domain. The requirement remains, of course, necessary for greatest-element rationalizability if we restrict attention to binary domains. As shown below, if we add S-consistency as a requirement on a rationalization, direct revelation coherence by itself is sufficient for neither greatest-element rationalizability nor maximal-element rationalizability, even on binary domains.

3.3. General Domains

In this section, we impose no restrictions on the domain $\mathcal{S}$. We begin our analysis by providing a full description of the logical relationships between the different notions of rationalizability that can be defined, given our S-consistency assumption imposed on a rationalization. The possible definitions of rationalizability that can be obtained depend on whether reflexivity or completeness are added to S-consistency. Furthermore, a distinction between greatest-element rationalizability and maximal-element rationalizability is made. For convenience, a diagrammatic representation is employed: all axioms that are depicted within the same box are equivalent, and an arrow pointing from one box b to another box b' indicates that the axioms in b imply those in b', and no further implications are true without additional assumptions regarding the domain of C.

THEOREM 3.1. Suppose $\mathcal{S}$ is a general domain. Then

$$\begin{array}{ccc} & \boxed{\text{RCG, CG, RCM, CM}} & \\ \swarrow & & \searrow \\ \boxed{\text{RG, G}} & & \boxed{\text{RM, M}} \end{array}$$

PROOF. We proceed as follows. In step 1, we prove the equivalence of all axioms that appear in the same box. In step 2, we show that all implications depicted in the theorem statement are valid. In step 3, we provide examples demonstrating that no further implications are true in general.

STEP 1. For each of the three boxes, we show that all axioms listed in the box are equivalent.

STEP 1a. We first prove the equivalence of the axioms in the top box.

Clearly, RCG implies CG and RCM implies CM. Moreover, if a relation R is reflexive and complete, it follows that the set of R-greatest elements in S is equal to the set of R-maximal elements in S for any $S \in \mathcal{S}$. Therefore, RCG and RCM are equivalent.

To see that CM implies RCM, suppose R is an S-consistent and complete M-rationalization of C. Let

$$R' = R \cup \{(x, x) \mid x \in X\}.$$

Clearly, R' is reflexive. R' is S-consistent and complete because R is. That R' is an M-rationalization of C follows immediately from the observation that R is.

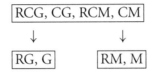

To complete step 1.a of the proof, it is sufficient to show that CG implies RCG. Suppose R is an S-consistent and complete G-rationalization of C. Let

$$R' = [R \cup \Delta \cup \{(y, x) \mid x \notin C(\mathcal{S}) \ \& \ y \in C(\mathcal{S})\}] \setminus \{(x, y) \mid x \notin C(\mathcal{S}) \ \& \ y \in C(\mathcal{S})\},$$

where $\Delta = \{(x, x) \mid x \in X\}$. Clearly, R' is reflexive by definition.

To show that R' is complete, let $x, y \in X$ be such that $x \neq y$ and $(x, y) \notin R'$. By definition of R', this implies

$$(x, y) \notin R \text{ and } [x \notin C(\mathcal{S}) \text{ or } y \in C(\mathcal{S})]$$

or

$$x \notin C(\mathcal{S}) \text{ and } y \in C(\mathcal{S}).$$

If the former applies, the completeness of R implies $(y, x) \in R$ and, by definition of R', we obtain $(y, x) \in R'$. If the latter is true, $(y, x) \in R'$ follows immediately from the definition of R'.

Next, we show that R' is S-consistent. Let $K \in \mathbb{N} \setminus \{1\}$ and $x^0, \ldots, x^K \in X$ be such that $(x^{k-1}, x^k) \in R'$ for all $k \in \{1, \ldots, K\}$. Clearly, we can, without loss of generality, assume that $x^{k-1} \neq x^k$ for all $k \in \{1, \ldots, K\}$. We distinguish two cases.
(i) $x^0 \notin C(\mathcal{S})$. In this case, it follows that $x^1 \notin C(\mathcal{S})$; otherwise we would have $(x^1, x^0) \in P(R')$ by definition of R', contradicting our hypothesis. Successively applying this argument to all $k \in \{1, \ldots, K\}$, we obtain $x^k \notin C(\mathcal{S})$ for all $k \in \{1, \ldots, K\}$. By definition of R', this implies $(x^{k-1}, x^k) \in R$ for all $k \in \{1, \ldots, K\}$. By the S-consistency of R, we must have $(x^K, x^0) \notin P(R)$. Because $x^K \notin C(\mathcal{S})$, this implies, according to the definition of R', $(x^K, x^0) \notin P(R')$.
(ii) $x^0 \in C(\mathcal{S})$. If $x^K \notin C(\mathcal{S})$, $(x^K, x^0) \notin P(R')$ follows immediately from the definition of R'. If $x^K \in C(\mathcal{S})$, it follows that $x^{K-1} \in C(\mathcal{S})$; otherwise we would have $(x^{K-1}, x^K) \notin R'$ by definition of R', contradicting our hypothesis. Successively applying this argument to all $k \in \{1, \ldots, K\}$, we obtain $x^k \in C(\mathcal{S})$ for all $k \in \{1, \ldots, K\}$. By definition of R', this implies $(x^{k-1}, x^k) \in R$ for all $k \in \{1, \ldots, K\}$. By the S-consistency of R, we must have $(x^K, x^0) \notin P(R)$. Because $x^0 \in C(\mathcal{S})$, this implies, according to the definition of R', $(x^K, x^0) \notin P(R')$.

Finally, we show that R' is a G-rationalization of C. Let $S \in \mathcal{S}$ and $x \in S$.

Suppose first that $(x, y) \in R'$ for all $y \in S$. If $|S| = 1$, $x \in C(S)$ follows immediately because $C(S)$ is nonempty. If $|S| \geq 2$, we obtain $x \in C(\mathcal{S})$. Because R is a G-rationalization of C, this implies $(x, x) \in R$. By definition of R', $(x, z) \in R$ for all $z \in C(S)$. Therefore, $(x, z) \in R$ for all $z \in C(S) \cup \{x\}$. Suppose, by way of contradiction, that $x \notin C(S)$. Because R is a G-rationalization of C, it follows that there exists $y \in S \setminus (C(S) \cup \{x\})$ such that $(x, y) \notin R$. The completeness of R implies $(y, x) \in P(R)$. Let $z \in C(S)$. It follows that $(z, y) \in R$ because R is a G-rationalization of C and, as established earlier, $(x, z) \in R$. This contradicts the S-consistency of R.

To prove the converse implication, suppose $x \in C(S)$. Because R is a G-rationalization of C, we have $(x, y) \in R$ for all $y \in S$. In particular, this implies $(x, x) \in R$ and, according to the definition of R', we obtain $(x, y) \in R'$ for all $y \in S$.

Step 1b. The proof that RM and M are equivalent is analogous to the proof of the equivalence of RCM and CM in step 1.a.

Step 1c. Clearly, RG implies G. Conversely, suppose R is an S-consistent G-rationalization of C. Let

$$R' = (R \cup \Delta) \setminus \{(x, y) \mid x \notin C(\mathcal{S}) \;\&\; x \neq y\}.$$

Clearly, R' is reflexive.

Next, we prove that R' is S-consistent. Let $K \in \mathbb{N} \setminus \{1\}$ and $x^0, \ldots, x^K \in X$ be such that $(x^{k-1}, x^k) \in R'$ for all $k \in \{1, \ldots, K\}$. Again, we can assume that $x^{k-1} \neq x^k$ for all $k \in \{1, \ldots, K\}$. By definition of R', $x^0 \in C(\mathcal{S})$. The rest of the proof follows as in part (ii) of the S-consistency of the relation R' in step 1.a.

It remains to be shown that R' is a G-rationalization of C. Let $S \in \mathcal{S}$ and $x \in S$.

First, suppose $(x, y) \in R'$ for all $y \in S$. By definition of R', $(x, y) \in R$ for all $y \in S \setminus \{x\}$. Analogously to the corresponding argument in step 1.a, the assumption $x \notin C(S)$ implies the existence of $y \in S \setminus (C(S) \cup \{x\})$ such that $(x, y) \notin R$, a contradiction.

Finally, suppose $x \in C(S)$. This implies $(x, y) \in R$ for all $y \in S$ because R is a G-rationalization of C. Furthermore, because $C(S) \subseteq C(\mathcal{S})$, we have $x \in C(\mathcal{S})$. By definition of R', this implies $(x, y) \in R'$ for all $y \in S$.

Step 2. The implications corresponding to the arrows in the theorem statement are straightforward.

Step 3. Given steps 1 and 2, to prove that no further implications are valid, it is sufficient to provide examples showing that (a) M does not imply G: and (b) G does not imply M. Note that this independence of M and G in the presence of S-consistency does not contradict part (i) of Lemma 3.3—S-consistency is not required in the lemma.

Step 3a. M does not imply G.

Example 3.1. Let $X = \{x, y, z\}$ and $\mathcal{S} = \{\{x, y\}, \{x, z\}, \{y, z\}\}$. For future reference, note that $\mathcal{S}$ is a binary domain. Define the choice function C by letting $C(\{x, y\}) = \{x, y\}$, $C(\{x, z\}) = \{x, z\}$, and $C(\{y, z\}) = \{y\}$. This choice function is maximal-element rationalizable by the S-consistent (and reflexive) rationalization

$$R = \{(x, x), (y, y), (y, z), (z, z)\}.$$

Suppose C is greatest-element rationalizable by an S-consistent rationalization R'. Because $C(\mathcal{S}) = X$, greatest-element rationalizability implies that R' is reflexive. Therefore, because $y \in C(\{y, z\})$ and $z \notin C(\{y, z\})$, we must have $(y, z) \in R'$ and $(z, y) \notin R'$. Therefore, $(y, z) \in P(R')$. Because R' is a G-rationalization of C, $z \in C(\{x, z\})$ implies $(z, x) \in R'$ and $x \in C(\{x, y\})$ implies $(x, y) \in R'$. This yields a contradiction to the assumption that R' is S-consistent.

Step 3b. To prove that G does not imply M, we employ an example due to Suzumura [17, pp. 151–152].

Example 3.2. Let $X = \{x, y, z\}$ and $\mathcal{S} = \{\{x, y\}, \{x, z\}, \{x, y, z\}\}$, and define $C(\{x, y\}) = \{x, y\}$, $C(\{x, z\}) = \{x, z\}$ and $C(\{x, y, z\}) =$

$\{x\}$. This choice function is greatest-element rationalizable by the S-consistent (and reflexive) rationalization

$$R = \{(x, x), (x, y), (x, z), (y, x), (y, y), (z, x), (z, z)\}.$$

Suppose R' is an M-rationalization of C. Because $z \in C(\{x, z\})$, maximal-element rationalizability implies $(x, z) \notin P(R')$ and, consequently, $z \notin C(\{x, y, z\})$ implies $(y, z) \in P(R')$. Analogously, $y \in C(\{x, y\})$ implies, together with maximal-element rationalizability, $(x, y) \notin P(R')$ and, consequently, $y \notin C(\{x, y, z\})$ implies $(z, y) \in P(R')$. But this contradicts the preceding observation that we must have $(y, z) \in P(R')$. Note that S-consistency (or any other property) of R' is not invoked in the preceding argument. Moreover, R is reflexive. Thus, RG does not even imply maximal-element rationalizability by an arbitrary rationalization.

This completes the proof of Theorem 3.1. ■

We now provide characterizations of two of the three notions of rationalizability identified in the above theorem. The first is a straightforward consequence of Richter's [10] result and the observation that S-consistency is equivalent to transitivity in the presence of reflexivity and completeness. Richter [10] shows that the *congruence* axiom is necessary and sufficient for greatest-element rationalizability by a transitive, reflexive, and complete rationalization. Congruence is defined as follows.

Congruence. For all $x, y \in X$, for all $S \in \mathcal{S}$, if $(x, y) \in T(R_C)$, $y \in C(S)$, and $x \in S$, then $x \in C(S)$.

We obtain the following.

Theorem 3.2. C satisfies RCG if and only if C satisfies congruence.

Proof. As is straightforward to verify, a relation is S-consistent, reflexive, and complete if and only if it is transitive, reflexive, and complete. The result now follows immediately from the equivalence of congruence and greatest-element rationalizability by a transitive, reflexive, and complete rationalization established by Richter [10]. ■

In order to characterize G (and, therefore, RG; see Theorem 3.1), we employ the *S-consistent closure* of the direct revealed preference relation R_C. The S-consistent closure of a relation R is analogous to the transitive closure: the idea is to add all pairs to the relation R that must be in a G-rationalizing relation due to the requirement that the rationalization be S-consistent. Define the S-consistent closure $SC(R)$ of R by

$$SC(R) = R \cup \{(x, y) \mid (x, y) \in T(R) \;\&\; (y, x) \in R\}.$$

Clearly, $R \subseteq SC(R)$. To illustrate the definition of the consistent closure and its relationship to the transitive closure, consider the following examples.

Example 3.3. Let $X = \{x, y, z\}$ and $R = \{(x, x), (x, y), (y, y), (y, z), (z, x), (z, z)\}$. We obtain $SC(R) = T(R) = X \times X$.

Example 3.4. Let $X = \{x, y, z\}$ and $R = \{(x, y), (y, z)\}$. We have $SC(R) = R$ and $T(R) = \{(x, y), (y, z), (x, z)\}$.

In Example 3.3, the S-consistent closure coincides with the transitive closure, whereas in Example 3.4, the S-consistent closure is a strict subset of the transitive closure. More generally, $SC(R)$ is always a subset of $T(R)$; see Lemma 3.4 that follows. Moreover, the lemma establishes an important property of $SC(R)$: just as $T(R)$ is the smallest transitive relation containing R, $SC(R)$ is the smallest S-consistent relation containing R.

Lemma 3.4. Let R be a binary relation on X.

(i) $SC(R) \subseteq T(R)$.

(ii) $SC(R)$ is the smallest S-consistent relation containing R.

Proof. (i) Suppose that $(x, y) \in SC(R)$. By definition, $(x, y) \in R$ or $[(x, y) \in T(R) \;\&\; (y, x) \in R]$. If $(x, y) \in R$, $(x, y) \in T(R)$ follows because $R \subseteq T(R)$. If $[(x, y) \in T(R) \;\&\; (y, x) \in R]$, $(x, y) \in T(R)$ is implied trivially.

(ii) We first prove that $SC(R)$ is S-consistent. Suppose $K \in \mathbb{N} \setminus \{1\}$ and $x^0, \ldots, x^K \in X$ are such that $(x^{k-1}, x^k) \in SC(R)$ for all $k \in \{1, \ldots, K\}$. We show that $(x^K, x^0) \notin P(SC(R))$. By part (i) of the lemma, $(x^{k-1}, x^k) \in T(R)$ for all $k \in \{1, \ldots, K\}$, and the transitivity of $T(R)$ implies

$$(x^0, x^K) \in T(R). \tag{3.1}$$

If $(x^K, x^0) \notin SC(R)$, we immediately obtain $(x^K, x^0) \notin P(SC(R))$ and we are done. Now suppose that $(x^K, x^0) \in SC(R)$. By definition of $SC(R)$, we must have

$$(x^K, x^0) \in R \text{ or } [(x^K, x^0) \in T(R) \,\&\, (x^0, x^K) \in R].$$

If $(x^K, x^0) \in R$, (3.1) and the definition of $SC(R)$ together imply $(x^0, x^K) \in SC(R)$ and, thus, $(x^K, x^0) \notin P(SC(R))$. If $(x^K, x^0) \in T(R)$ and $(x^0, x^K) \in R$, $(x^0, x^K) \in SC(R)$ follows because $R \subseteq SC(R)$. Again, this implies $(x^K, x^0) \notin P(SC(R))$ and the proof that $SC(R)$ is S-consistent is complete.

To show that $SC(R)$ is the smallest S-consistent relation containing R, suppose that Q is an arbitrary S-consistent relation containing R. To complete the proof, we establish that $SC(R) \subseteq Q$. Suppose that $(x, y) \in SC(R)$. By definition of $SC(R)$,

$$(x, y) \in R \text{ or } [(x, y) \in T(R) \,\&\, (y, x) \in R].$$

If $(x, y) \in R$, $(x, y) \in Q$ follows because R is contained in Q by assumption. If $(x, y) \in T(R)$ and $(y, x) \in R$, Lemma 3.1 and the assumption $R \subseteq Q$ together imply that $(x, y) \in T(Q)$ and $(y, x) \in Q$. If $(x, y) \notin Q$, we obtain $(y, x) \in P(Q)$ in view of $(y, x) \in Q$. Since $(x, y) \in T(Q)$, this contradicts the S-consistency of Q. Therefore, we must have $(x, y) \in Q$. ∎

Analogously to Lemma 3.2(i), we obtain the following:

Lemma 3.5. If R is an S-consistent G-rationalization of C, then $SC(R_C) \subseteq R$.

Proof. Suppose that R is an S-consistent G-rationalization of C and $(x, y) \in SC(R_C)$. By definition,

$$(x, y) \in R_C \text{ or } [(x, y) \in T(R_C) \,\&\, (y, x) \in R_C].$$

If $(x, y) \in R_C$, Lemma 3.2 implies $(x, y) \in R$. If $(x, y) \in T(R_C)$ and $(y, x) \in R_C$, Lemmas 3.2 and 3.1 together imply $(x, y) \in T(R)$ and $(y, x) \in R$. If $(x, y) \notin R$, it follows that $(y, x) \in P(R)$ in view of $(y, x) \in R$. Because $(x, y) \in T(R)$, this contradicts the S-consistency of R. Therefore, $(x, y) \in R$. ∎

Part (ii) of Lemma 3.2 does not generalize in an analogous fashion. To see this, consider again Example 3.1. We have $SC(R_C) = X \times X$ and, therefore, $(z, y) \in SC(R_C)$. But $(y, z) \in P(R)$ according to the S-consistent M-rationalization R defined in the example, and it follows that $SC(R_C) \nsubseteq R \cup N(R)$.

The following axiom is a strengthening of direct revelation coherence which we call S-consistent closure coherence. It is obtained by replacing R_C with its S-consistent closure $SC(R_C)$ in the definition of direct revelation coherence.

S-Consistent Closure Coherence. For all $S \in \mathcal{S}$, for all $x \in S$, if $(x, y) \in SC(R_C)$ for all $y \in S$, then $x \in C(S)$.

We may now assert the following:

Theorem 3.3. C satisfies G if and only if C satisfies S-consistent closure coherence.

Proof. To prove the only-if part, suppose R is an S-consistent G-rationalization of C, and let $S \in \mathcal{S}$ and $x \in S$ be such that $(x, y) \in SC(R_C)$ for all $y \in S$. By Lemma 3.5, $(x, y) \in R$ for all $y \in S$. Thus, because R is a G-rationalization of C, $x \in C(S)$.

Now suppose C satisfies S-consistent closure coherence. We complete the proof by showing that $SC(R_C)$ is an S-consistent G-rationalization of C. That $SC(R_C)$ is S-consistent follows from Lemma 3.4. To prove that $SC(R_C)$ is a G-rationalization of C, suppose first that $S \in \mathcal{S}$ and $x \in S$. Suppose $(x, y) \in SC(R_C)$ for all $y \in S$. S-consistent closure coherence implies $x \in C(S)$. Conversely, suppose $x \in C(S)$. By definition, this implies $(x, y) \in R_C$ for all $y \in S$ and, because $R_C \subseteq SC(R_C)$, we obtain $(x, y) \in SC(R_C)$ for all $y \in S$. ■

3.4. Binary Domains

We now turn to the special case of binary domains. These domains are of interest because they represent a natural weakening of some domains studied in the earlier literature on rational choice. In particular, the binary domain assumption is implied by the requirement that $\mathcal{S}$ contains all nonempty and finite subsets of X, by the assumption that the domain contains all pairs and all triples, and by the requirement that $\mathcal{S}$ is a base domain. Moreover, binary domains occur naturally in applications such as tournaments where a pairwise comparison of all agents is performed; consider, for example, a round-robin tournament.

In the case of binary domains, the presence of all two-element sets in $\mathcal{S}$ guarantees that every G-rationalization must be complete and, as a consequence, all rationality requirements involving greatest-element rationalizability and S-consistency become equivalent. In contrast, maximal-element rationalizability by an S-consistent and complete rationalization remains a stronger requirement than maximal-element rationalizability by a consistent and reflexive rationalization. These observations are summarized in the following theorem.

THEOREM 3.4. Suppose $\mathcal{S}$ is a binary domain. Then

$$\boxed{\text{RCG, CG, RCM, CM, RG, G}}$$
$$\downarrow$$
$$\boxed{\text{RM, M}}$$

PROOF. We divide the proof into the same three steps as in Theorem 3.1.

STEP 1. We prove the equivalence of the axioms for each of the two boxes.

STEP 1a. Using Theorem 3.1, the equivalence of the axioms in the top box follows from the observation that any S-consistent G-rationalization of C must be complete, given that $\mathcal{S}$ is binary.

STEP 1b. This part is already proven in Theorem 3.1.

STEP 2. Again, the implication corresponding to the arrow in the theorem statement is straightforward.

STEP 3. To prove that the reverse implication is not valid, Example 3.1 can be employed. ■

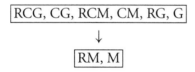

As shown in Theorem 3.4, there are only two different versions of rationalizability for binary domains. Consequently, we can restrict attention to the rationalizability axioms G and M in this case, keeping in mind that, by Theorem 3.4, all other rationalizability requirements involving S-consistent rationalizations are covered as well. Although there are some analogies between the results in this section and some of the theorems established in Bossert, Sprumont, and Suzumura [3], our characterizations are novel because, unlike the earlier paper, they employ S-consistency and they apply to binary domains rather than base domains.

First, we show that G (and all other axioms that are equivalent to it according to Theorem 3.4) is characterized by the following weak congruence axiom (see Bossert, Sprumont, and Suzumura, [3]).

WEAK CONGRUENCE. For all $x, y, z \in X$, for all $S \in \mathcal{S}$, if $(x, y) \in R_C$, $(y, z) \in R_C$, $x \in S$, and $z \in C(S)$, then $x \in C(S)$.

In contrast to congruence, weak congruence applies not to chains of direct revealed preference of an arbitrary length but merely to chains involving three elements. For binary domains, weak congruence is necessary and sufficient for all forms of greatest-element rationalizability involving an S-consistent G-rationalization.

THEOREM 3.5. Suppose $\mathcal{S}$ is a binary domain. C satisfies G if and only if C satisfies weak congruence.

PROOF. By Theorem 3.4, G is equivalent to RCG given that $\mathcal{S}$ is a binary domain. Moreover, as mentioned earlier, S-consistency is equivalent to transitivity in the presence of reflexivity and completeness. Theorem 3.3 in Bossert, Sprumont, and Suzumura [3] states that greatest-element rationalizability by a reflexive, complete, and transitive relation is equivalent to weak congruence, provided that $\mathcal{S}$ is a binary domain. The result follows immediately as a consequence of this observation. ■

Finally, we establish that direct revelation coherence and acyclicity of R_C together are necessary and sufficient for M (and RM) on a binary domain. This result is analogous to the characterization of greatest-element rationalizability by an acyclic, reflexive, and complete rationalization on base domains (domains that contain all singletons in addition to all two-element sets) in Bossert, Sprumont, and Suzumura [3, Theorem 5].

THEOREM 3.6. Suppose $\mathcal{S}$ is a binary domain. C satisfies M if and only if C satisfies direct revelation coherence and R_C is acyclic.

PROOF.

STEP 1. We first show that M implies that R_C is acyclic (that direct revelation coherence is implied follows from Lemma 3.3). Suppose R is an S-consistent M-rationalization of C. By way of contradiction, suppose R_C is not acyclic. Then there exist $K \in \mathbb{N} \setminus \{1\}$ and $x^0, \ldots, x^K \in X$ such that $(x^{k-1}, x^k) \in P(R_C)$ for all $k \in \{1, \ldots, K\}$ and $(x^K, x^0) \in P(R_C)$. Because $\mathcal{S}$ is a binary domain, $\{x^{k-1}, x^k\} \in \mathcal{S}$ for all $k \in \{1, \ldots, K\}$ and $\{x^0, x^K\} \in \mathcal{S}$. By definition of R_C, it follows that $x^k \notin C(\{x^{k-1}, x^k\})$ for all $k \in \{1, \ldots, K\}$ and $x^0 \notin C(\{x^0, x^K\})$. Because R is an M-rationalization of C, it follows that $(x^{k-1}, x^k) \in P(R)$ for all $k \in \{1, \ldots, K\}$ and $(x^K, x^0) \in P(R)$, contradicting the S-consistency of R.

STEP 2. We show that direct revelation coherence and the acyclicity of R_C together imply M. Define $R = P(R_C)$. Clearly, $P(R) = R = P(R_C)$ and, consequently, R is S-consistent because R_C is acyclic.

It remains to be shown that R is an M-rationalization of C. Let $S \in \mathcal{S}$ and $x \in S$. Suppose first that x is R-maximal in S, that is, $(y, x) \notin P(R)$ for all $y \in S$. If $S = \{x\}$, $x \in C(S)$ follows from the nonemptiness of $C(S)$. Now suppose $S \neq \{x\}$, and let $y \in S \setminus \{x\}$. Because $\mathcal{S}$ is a binary domain, $\{x, y\} \in \mathcal{S}$. If $x \in C(\{x, y\})$, we obtain $(x, y) \in R_C$ by definition. If $x \notin C(\{x, y\})$, it follows that $(y, x) \in R_C$ and, because $(y, x) \notin P(R) = P(R_C)$ by assumption, we again obtain $(x, y) \in R_C$. By direct revelation coherence, it follows that $x \in C(S)$.

Now suppose $x \in C(S)$. This implies $(x, y) \in R_C$ for all $y \in S$ and, therefore, $(y, x) \notin P(R_C) = P(R)$ for all $y \in S$. Therefore, x is R-maximal in S. ∎

3.5. Concluding Remarks

The only notion of S-consistent rationalizability that is not characterized in this essay is maximal-element rationalizability by means of an S-consistent (and reflexive) rationalization on a general domain. The reason why it is difficult to obtain necessary and sufficient conditions in that case is the existential nature of the requirements for maximal-element rationalizability. It is immediately apparent that the revealed preference relation must be respected by any greatest-element rationalization, whereas this is not the case for maximal-element rationalizability (see Lemma 3.3). In order to exclude an element from a set of chosen alternatives according to maximal-element rationalizability, it merely is required that there exists (at least) *one* element in that set that is strictly preferred to the alternative to be excluded. The problem of identifying necessary and sufficient conditions for that kind of rationalizability is closely related to the problem of determining the *dimension* of a quasi ordering; see, for example, Dushnik and Miller [4]. Because this is an area that is still quite unsettled, it is not too surprising that characterizations of maximal-element rationalizability on general domains are difficult to obtain. To the best of our knowledge, this is a feature that is shared by *all* notions of maximal-element rationalizability that are not equivalent to one of the notions of greatest-element rationalizability on general domains: we are not aware of any characterization results for maximal-element rationalizability on general domains unless the notion of maximal-element rationalizability employed happens to coincide with one of the notions of greatest-element rationalizability. Thus, there are important open questions to be addressed in future work in this area of research.

3.6. References

[1] Arrow, K. J., *Social Choice and Individual Values,* New York: John Wiley & Sons, 1951; second edn., 1963.

[2] Arrow, K. J., "Rational Choice Functions and Orderings," *Economica* **26**, 1959, 121–127.

[3] Bossert, W., Y. Sprumont, and K. Suzumura, "Rationalizability of Choice Functions on General Domains without Full Transitivity," *Social Choice and Welfare* **27**, 2006, 435–458.

[4] Dushnik, B., and E. W. Miller, "Partially Ordered Sets," *American Journal of Mathematics* **63**, 1941, 600–610.

[5] Georgescu-Roegen, N., "Choice and Revealed Preference," *Southern Economic Journal* **21**, 1954, 119–130.

[6] Georgescu-Roegen, N., *Analytical Economics: Issues and Problems,* Cambridge, Mass.: Harvard University Press, 1966.

[7] Hansson, B., "Choice Structures and Preference Relations," *Synthese* **18**, 1968, 443–458.

[8] Kim, T., and M. K. Richter, "Nontransitive-Nontotal Consumer Theory," *Journal of Economic Theory* **38**, 1986, 324–363.

[9] Luce, R. D., "Semiorders and a Theory of Utility Discrimination," *Econometrica* **24**, 1956, 178–191.

[10] Richter, M. K., "Revealed Preference Theory," *Econometrica* **34**, 1966, 635–645.

[11] Richter, M. K., "Rational Choice," in J. Chipman, L. Hurwicz, M. Richter, and H. Sonnenschein, eds., *Preferences, Utility, and Demand,* New York: Harcourt Brace Jovanovich, 1971, 29–58.

[12] Samuelson, P. A., "A Note on the Pure Theory of Consumer's Behaviour," *Economica* **5**, 1938, 61–71.

[13] Samuelson, P. A., *Foundations of Economic Analysis,* Cambridge, Mass.: Harvard University Press, 1947.

[14] Samuelson, P. A., "Consumption Theory in Terms of Revealed Preference," *Economica* **15**, 1948, 243–253.

[15] Samuelson, P. A., "The Problem of Integrability in Utility Theory," *Economica* **17**, 1950, 355–385.

[16] Sen, A. K., "Choice Functions and Revealed Preference," *Review of Economic Studies* **38**, 1971, 307–317.

[17] Suzumura, K., "Rational Choice and Revealed Preference," *Review of Economic Studies* **43**, 1976, 149–158. Essay 1 of this volume.

[18] Suzumura, K., "Remarks on the Theory of Collective Choice," *Economica* **43**, 1976, 381–390. Essay 6 of this volume.

[19] Suzumura, K., "Houthakker's Axiom in the Theory of Rational Choice," *Journal of Economic Theory* **14**, 1977, 284–290. Essay 2 of this volume.

[20] Suzumura, K., *Rational Choice, Collective Decisions and Social Welfare,* New York: Cambridge University Press, 1983.

ESSAY 4

Revealed Preference and Choice under Uncertainty

4.1. Introduction

The choice behavior of an economic agent can be considered more fundamental than the optimization of his/her preference ordering or utility function. An agent's act of choice can be observed directly, and one may seek an axiom for rationalizing an act of choice such as that of preference optimization. Recognizing this possibility early on in the development of demand analysis, Samuelson [17; 18] laid the foundations of what has come to be known as revealed preference theory; see also Houthakker [11], among others. Although these early contributions restricted attention to consumer choice in perfectly competitive markets, the theory of rational choice progressed rapidly, and more general choice scenarios were analyzed in contributions such as those of Richter [15], Hansson [10], and Suzumura [20; 22]. Initially, the analysis of rational choice behavior focused on models where a rationalizing relation was assumed to be an ordering. More recently, however, weaker coherence properties of a rationalization have been considered; see, for instance, Richter [16] and Suzumura [21] for an early contribution in this spirit. A detailed review of rational choice and revealed preference theory can be found in Bossert and Suzumura [7].

First published in *Spanish Economic Review* **3**, 2012, pp. 247-258. Joint paper with W. Bossert, which was our contribution to the Special Issue of this *Review* in Honor of Salvador Barberà.

Numerous theories of choice under uncertainty have emerged over the years; prominent examples include proposals by von Neumann and Morgenstern [24], Milnor [14], Savage [19], Barberà, Barrett, and Pattanaik [2], Barberà and Pattanaik [4], and Kannai and Peleg [12]. Both probabilistic and nonprobabilistic choice models (such as set-based models) are covered by these and other contributions. In this essay, we aim at combining the theory of rational choice with a general approach to choice situations under uncertainty.

In decision problems under certainty, the revealed preference approach typically does not try to uncover a specific objective, the optimization of which may be revealed through the observed choices; rather, the fundamental question is whether these choices are consistent with *some* objective in the sense that the choices from each feasible set are the greatest elements according to a rationalizing relation. Analogously, we do not want to restrict ourselves to a specific theory of choice under uncertainty. Our basic question is whether observable choices can be consistent with *some* coherent way of making decisions in the presence of uncertainty. We therefore use as our primitive a set of *prospects*. Suppose there is a universal set X (with at least two members) of certain outcomes and a finite number (at least two) of possible states of the world. A prospect assigns to each possible state an outcome in X. We can think of a prospect as the result of an action taken by an agent before the uncertainty regarding the state that actually occurs is resolved. The reason why we choose prospects to provide a fundamental description of our choice situations is the generality we aim to achieve: if we were, for instance, to use lotteries as the objects to be chosen from, we would already be committed to a probabilistic choice model. Because we do not want to rule out nonprobabilistic models such as those examined by Milnor [14] and Barberà and Pattanaik [4], for instance, we choose to use prospects as our basic representation of choice situations under uncertainty. However, models that do endow a decision maker with a probability distribution are included as special cases in our approach.

The definition of a decision rule that we use in this essay is based on what we think is a minimal requirement. Given a choice function defined on a domain of sets of feasible prospects, we first demand that there be a relation that rationalizes the observable choices in the usual sense of generating them as greatest elements in the requisite feasible set. In addition, we ask that the rationalization satisfy a *dominance* property so as to be interpretable as a choice rule under uncertainty. The dominance condition is easily described: if two prospects $\mathbf{x} = (x_1, \ldots, x_m)$ and $\mathbf{y} = (y_1, \ldots, y_m)$ are such that, for *every* state i and for *every* state j, the certain prospect $(x_i, \ldots, x_i)$ that repeats outcome x_i in $\mathbf{x}$ over all states is revealed to be at least as good as the certain prospect $(y_j, \ldots, y_j)$ that repeats outcome y_j in $\mathbf{y}$ over all states, then prospect $\mathbf{x}$ must be at least as good as prospect $\mathbf{y}$. This is a very weak requirement because we do not demand state-by-state dominance to be respected but, instead, merely unambiguous dominance where the worst possible certain outcome in $\mathbf{x}$ is at least as good at the best possible certain outcome in $\mathbf{y}$. Although this condition that we impose in addition to rationalizability per se is rather mild, it does impose further restrictions, as is shown once our formal framework is introduced.

There is a resemblance to the analysis carried out by Bossert [5], who also examines rationalizability in the context of uncertainty. However, Bossert [5] restricts attention to set-based models whereas our approach is considerably more general. Because of the more specialized framework, Bossert's [5] restrictions differ from our dominance property.

In the next section, we define the fundamentals of the problem to be addressed in this essay, namely, the notions of prospects and choice functions. Section 4.3 provides necessary and sufficient conditions for dominance rationalizability (that is, rationalizability by a relation that respects the previosly described dominance requirement). In Sections 4.4 and 4.5, we add the coherence properties of transitivity and of Suzumura consistency, respectively, to the list of requirements imposed on a rationalization. Section 4.6 concludes.

4.2. Prospects and Choice Functions

Suppose there is a set of alternatives or outcomes X with at least two elements. X could be finite or infinite. There are $m \in \mathbb{N} \setminus \{1\}$ possible states of the world and a *prospect* $\mathbf{x} = (x_1, \ldots, x_m)$ with $x_i \in X$ for all $i \in \{1, \ldots, m\}$ specifies, for each state, the alternative that materializes in this state. The set of all prospects is denoted by X^m. Important special cases of prospects are the *certain* prospects in which the same outcome emerges in all possible states. For any $x \in X$, the certain prospect associated with alternative x is the m-tuple $(x, \ldots, x)$ and we will denote this m-tuple by $x\mathbf{1}_m$. The set of all nonempty subsets of X^m is $\mathcal{X}$.

A (binary) relation on X^m is a subset R of the Cartesian product $X^m \times X^m$ and the asymmetric part of R is $P(R)$. The *transitive closure* $T(R)$ of a relation R on X^m is

$$T(R) = \Big\{(\mathbf{x}, \mathbf{y}) \in X^m \times X^m \mid \text{there exist } K \in \mathbb{N} \text{ and } \mathbf{x}^0, \ldots, \mathbf{x}^K \in X^m \text{ such that } [\mathbf{x} = \mathbf{x}^0 \text{ and } (\mathbf{x}^{k-1}, \mathbf{x}^k) \in R \text{ for all } k \in \{1, \ldots, K\} \text{ and } \mathbf{x}^K = \mathbf{y}]\Big\}.$$

The transitive closure of a relation R is the smallest transitive superset of R.

A relation R is *Suzumura-consistent* if and only if, for all $K \in \mathbb{N}$ and for all $\mathbf{x}, \mathbf{y} \in X^m$,

$$(\mathbf{x}, \mathbf{y}) \in T(R) \Rightarrow (\mathbf{y}, \mathbf{x}) \notin P(R).$$

The *Suzumura-consistent closure* $SC(R)$ of a relation R is given by

$$SC(R) = R \cup \{(\mathbf{x}, \mathbf{y}) \in X^m \times X^m \mid (\mathbf{x}, \mathbf{y}) \in T(R) \text{ and } (\mathbf{y}, \mathbf{x}) \in R\}.$$

Suzumura consistency was first introduced in Suzumura [21]. Analogous to the transitive closure of a relation, the Suzumura-consistent closure of R is the smallest Suzumura consistent superset of R. The notion of a Suzumura-consistent closure is due to Bossert, Sprumont, and Suzumura [6]. See Bossert and Suzumura [7] for a detailed discussion of Suzumura consistency and its use in individual and collective choice.

We assume that, in the presence of uncertainty, a decision maker faces a set of feasible actions and that each action leads to a prospect in X^m. Rather than working with actions and their induced prospects, we work with prospects directly in order to simplify our exposition. Thus, a choice rule under uncertainty can be expressed by means of a *choice function* that selects, from each feasible set of prospects in its domain, a nonempty subset of this feasible set. The only assumption (other than nonemptiness) that we make about the domain $\mathcal{S}$ of a choice function is that it includes all singletons and pairs of certain prospects. Formally, a *choice function with a certainty-inclusive domain* is a mapping $C: \mathcal{S} \to \mathcal{X}$ such that $\{\{x\mathbf{1}_m, y\mathbf{1}_m\} \subseteq$

$X^m \mid x, y \in X\} \subseteq \mathcal{S} \subseteq \mathcal{X}$ and $C(S) \subseteq S$ for all $S \in \mathcal{S}$. Because the certainty inclusiveness assumption will be maintained throughout the essay, we will simply refer to C as a choice function with the understanding that this function has a certainty-inclusive domain.

4.3. Dominance Rationalizability

A choice function C is *rationalizable* by a binary relation R on X^m if and only if, for each feasible set of prospects S in the domain $\mathcal{S}$, C selects the R-greatest elements in S. However, in the present context of choice under uncertainty, we might want to impose more than just the standard rationalizability property in order to think of a choice function as representing a plausible method of selecting from sets of available prospects. Clearly, there are many theories of choice under uncertainty, such as those pioneered and discussed by von Neumann and Morgenstern [24], Milnor [14], Savage [19], Fishburn [8], Arrow and Hurwicz [1], Gärdenfors [9], Kim and Roush [13], Barberà, Barrett, and Pattanaik [2], Barberà and Pattanaik [4], Kannai and Peleg [12], and Barberà, Bossert, and Pattanaik [3], to name but a few.

The main purpose of the approach advocated in this essay is not the identification of a specific theory of choice under uncertainty but, rather, to define a more general criterion that subsumes many of the models proposed so far. Clearly, this means that our definition of possible choice rules is quite permissive. In addition to probabilistic choice rules such as those proposed by von Neumann and Morgenstern [24] or Savage [19], our class of choice rules includes many others that are not based on (objective or subjective) probabilities, such as those discussed by Milnor [14] or Kannai and Peleg [12], for instance. Of course, our definition of possible choice rules still has *some* bite in that it allows us to eliminate rules that we consider unacceptable given our interpretation; this is illustrated below via a simple example. As we discuss in the concluding section, our approach can be amended in a straightforward and intuitive manner if one desires to come up with a more stringent definition. What we think of as the major contribution of this essay is the method we propose to incorporate notions of uncertainty into a model of rational choice.

Coming back to our definition of rationalizability in the current context, we propose as a minimal requirement that, in addition to rationalizability per se, a weak dominance property be respected. More precisely, we demand that observed choices involving *certain* prospects be respected in the following sense. Consider two prospects $\mathbf{x} = (x_1, \ldots, x_m)$ and $\mathbf{y} = (y_1, \ldots, y_m)$. If *every* certain prospect $x_i \mathbf{1}_m$ with $i \in \{1, \ldots, m\}$ is revealed to be weakly preferred to *every* certain prospect $y_j \mathbf{1}_m$ with $j \in \{1, \ldots, m\}$ in the sense that $x_i \mathbf{1}_m$ is chosen in a situation where $y_j \mathbf{1}_m$ is feasible, then the relation rationalizing C must declare $\mathbf{x}$ to be at least as good as $\mathbf{y}$. Formally, we say that a choice function C is *dominance rationalizable* if and only if there exists a relation R on X^m such that

$$C(S) = \{\mathbf{x} \in S \mid (\mathbf{x}, \mathbf{y}) \in R \text{ for all } \mathbf{y} \in S\} \quad \text{for all } S \in \mathcal{S} \tag{4.1}$$

and

$$\left[(x_i \mathbf{1}_m, y_j \mathbf{1}_m) \in R \text{ for all } i, j \in \{1, \ldots, m\} \Rightarrow (\mathbf{x}, \mathbf{y}) \in R\right]$$
$$\text{for all } \mathbf{x}, \mathbf{y} \in X^m. \tag{4.2}$$

If C and R are such that (4.1) and (4.2) are satisfied, we also say that R is a *dominance rationalization* of C or that C is *dominance rationalized* by R.

Property (4.1) represents the standard rationalizability requirement: for any feasible set S in the domain $\mathcal{S}$ of a choice function C, the set of chosen elements $C(S)$ must coincide with the set of R-greatest elements in S according to a (dominance) rationalization R.

That (4.2) imposes additional restrictions on C can be seen by considering the following example. Suppose that the set of certain alternatives is $X = \{x, y, z\}$, that there are $m = 2$ possible states of the world, and the certainty-inclusive domain of C is given by

$$\begin{aligned}\mathcal{S} = \{&\{(x, x)\}, \{(y, y)\}, \{(z, z)\},\\ &\{(x, x), (y, y)\}, \{(x, x), (z, z)\}, \{(y, y), (z, z)\},\\ &\{(x, y), (y, z)\}\}.\end{aligned}$$

Now define the choice function C by letting

$$\begin{aligned}C(\{(x, x)\}) &= \{(x, x)\}, C(\{(y, y)\}) = \{(y, y)\}, C(\{(z, z)\})\\ &= \{(z, z)\}, C(\{(x, x), (y, y)\}) = \{(x, x)\}, C(\{(x, x), (z, z)\})\\ &= \{(x, x)\}, C(\{(y, y), (z, z)\}) = \{(y, y)\}, C(\{(x, y), (y, z)\})\\ &= \{(y, z)\}.\end{aligned}$$

Consider the relation R on X^m defined by

$$R = \{((x, x), (x, x)), ((y, y), (y, y)), ((z, z), (z, z)),$$
$$((x, x), (y, y)), ((x, x), (z, z)), ((y, y), (z, z)),$$
$$((y, z), (x, y))\}.$$

It is straightforward to verify that (4.1) is satisfied for C and R. However, there exists no relation R' such that, for C and R', (4.2) is satisfied in addition to (4.1). By way of contradiction, suppose R' is such a relation. First of all, as a consequence of (4.1) and the definition of C, we must have $((x, x), (y, y)) \in R'$, $((y, y), (y, y)) \in R'$, $((x, x), (z, z)) \in R'$, and $((y, y), (z, z)) \in R'$. Thus, (4.2) implies $((x, y), (y, z)) \in R'$. Therefore, the prospect (x, y) is an R'-greatest element in $\{(x, y), (y, z)\}$ and (4.1) demands that $(x, y) \in C(\{(x, y), (y, z)\})$, in contradiction to the definition of C. Thus, even though the additional property that we require of a rationalization in the context of choice under uncertainty is very weak, it is not redundant and can be used to eliminate rules that are in violation of the basic dominance condition (4.2).

Richter [16] characterizes rational choice in a general setting where no additional requirements such as that expressed by (4.2) are imposed. In our framework, an analogous result can be obtained by modifying his necessary and sufficient condition in a suitable manner. To do so, we first introduce the notion of the *direct revealed preference relation* R_C^d associated with a choice function C. This relation is defined by letting, for all $\mathbf{x}, \mathbf{y} \in X^m$,

$$(\mathbf{x}, \mathbf{y}) \in R_C^d \Leftrightarrow \text{ there exists } S \in \mathcal{S} \text{ such that } \left[\mathbf{x} \in C(S) \text{ and } \mathbf{y} \in S\right].$$

Because we have to take into account the dominance property in addition to mere rationalizability, we consider the following relation that incorporates this requirement. The *direct revealed preference and dominance relation* R_C corresponding to C is defined by letting, for all $\mathbf{x}, \mathbf{y} \in X^m$,

$$(\mathbf{x}, \mathbf{y}) \in R_C \Leftrightarrow (\mathbf{x}, \mathbf{y}) \in R_C^d$$
$$\text{or} \quad \left[(x_i \mathbf{1}_m, y_j \mathbf{1}_m) \in R_C^d \text{ for all } i, j \in \{1, \ldots, m\}\right].$$

Following Samuelson's [17; 18] observation in the context of rationality in consumer choice problems, Richter [16] establishes that the direct revealed preference relation R_C^d associated with a choice function C must be respected by any rationalizing relation R in the sense that R_C^d is contained in R. An analogous result is valid in our setting. However, because of the additional dominance requirement we impose, the relation R_C rather than R_C^d must be respected when choices are made from sets of feasible prospects. This leads to the following result, which is analogous to the aforementioned observation due to Richter [16].

Lemma 4.1. If a choice function C is dominance rationalized by a relation R, then $R_C \subseteq R$.

Proof. Suppose that R is a dominance rationalization of C and that $(\mathbf{x}, \mathbf{y}) \in R_C$. By definition of R_C, there are two possible cases:

(a) $(\mathbf{x}, \mathbf{y}) \in R_C^d$;
(b) $(x_i \mathbf{1}_m, y_j \mathbf{1}_m) \in R_C^d$ for all $i, j \subset \{1, \ldots, m\}$.

In case (a), the definition of R_C^d implies that there exists $S \in \mathcal{S}$ such that $\mathbf{x} \in C(S)$ and $\mathbf{y} \in S$. Thus, $\mathbf{x}$ is an R-greatest element in S by (4.1), which, together with $\mathbf{y} \in S$, implies $(\mathbf{x}, \mathbf{y}) \in R$.

In case (b), the result just established for case (a) implies that $(x_i \mathbf{1}_m, y_j \mathbf{1}_m) \in R$ for all $i, j \in \{1, \ldots, m\}$. By (4.2), it follows that $(\mathbf{x}, \mathbf{y}) \in R$. ■

We can now use this lemma to characterize dominance rationalizability. Again, the method of proof is based on that employed by Richter [16]. In our framework, however, some additional steps are needed as a consequence of imposing the dominance requirement. The following property of a choice function C turns out to be necessary and sufficient for dominance rationalizability.

Direct Dominance Revelation Coherence. For all $S \in \mathcal{S}$ and for all $\mathbf{x} \in X^m$,

$$(\mathbf{x}, \mathbf{y}) \in R_C \quad \text{for all } \mathbf{y} \in S \Rightarrow \mathbf{x} \in C(S).$$

Direct dominance revelation coherence requires that the relation R_C be respected by the choice function C. It is relatively straightforward to see that this is indeed necessary for dominance rationalizability. As established in the following theorem, the property is also sufficient.

THEOREM 4.1. A choice function C is dominance rationalizable if and only if C satisfies direct dominance revelation coherence.

PROOF. We first prove the "only if" part of the equivalence stated in the theorem. Suppose R is a dominance rationalization of C. Let $S \in \mathcal{S}$ and $\mathbf{x} \in S$ be such that $(\mathbf{x}, \mathbf{y}) \in R_C$ for all $\mathbf{y} \in S$. By Lemma 4.1, it follows that $(\mathbf{x}, \mathbf{y}) \in R$ for all $\mathbf{y} \in S$. Because R is a dominance rationalization of C, this implies $\mathbf{x} \in C(S)$ and direct dominance revelation coherence is established.

To prove the "if" part of the theorem, suppose that C satisfies direct dominance revelation coherence. We now show that $R = R_C$ is a dominance rationalization of C.

To establish that (4.1) is satisfied for $R = R_C$, suppose first that $S \in \mathcal{S}$ and $\mathbf{x} \in S$ are such that $(\mathbf{x}, \mathbf{y}) \in R_C$ for all $\mathbf{y} \in S$. Direct dominance revelation coherence immediately implies $\mathbf{x} \in C(S)$.

Now suppose that $S \in \mathcal{S}$ and $\mathbf{x} \in S$ are such that $\mathbf{x} \in C(S)$. By definition, this implies $(\mathbf{x}, \mathbf{y}) \in R^d_C$ for all $\mathbf{y} \in S$ and, because $R^d_C \subseteq R_C$, we obtain $(\mathbf{x}, \mathbf{y}) \in R_C$ for all $\mathbf{y} \in S$.

Finally, we show that (4.2) is satisfied for $R = R_C$. Suppose $\mathbf{x}, \mathbf{y} \in X^m$ are such that $(x_i \mathbf{1}_m, y_j \mathbf{1}_m) \in R_C$ for all $i, j \in \{1, \ldots, m\}$. For $g \in \{1, \ldots, m\}$, let $(x_i \mathbf{1}_m)_g$ denote the gth component of the m-tuple $(x_i, \ldots, x_i)$. By definition of R_C, for each $i, j \in \{1, \ldots, m\}$, there are two possible cases:

(a) $(x_i \mathbf{1}_m, y_j \mathbf{1}_m) \in R^d_C$;
(b) $((x_i \mathbf{1}_m)_g, (y_j \mathbf{1}_m)_h) \in R^d_C$ for all $g, h \in \{1, \ldots, m\}$.

Because $(x_i \mathbf{1}_m)_g = x_i$ and $(y_j \mathbf{1}_m)_h = y_j$ for all $g, h \in \{1, \ldots, m\}$, $(x_i \mathbf{1}_m, y_j \mathbf{1}_m) \in R^d_C$ follows in both cases. Thus, by definition of R_C, we obtain $(\mathbf{x}, \mathbf{y}) \in R_C$ and the proof is complete. ■

Note that the preceding proof does not make use of the assumption that C is a choice function with a certainty-inclusive domain; the conclusion of Theorem 4.1 remains true if $\mathcal{S}$ can be any arbitrary nonempty domain.

However, the certainty inclusiveness of $\mathcal{S}$ is crucial for the results to be established in the following two sections.

4.4. Transitive Dominance Rationalizability

In traditional choice models that do not involve uncertainty, demanding rationalizability without any further restrictions on the rationalizing relation can be considered somewhat unsatisfactory. If, for instance, all rationalizations of a choice function generate strict preference cycles, it is difficult to think of the choice behavior thus revealed as coherent. The same reasoning applies to dominance rationalizability in the context of choosing from feasible sets of prospects: in addition to (4.1) and (4.2), one may want to demand that a dominance rationalization possesses some coherence property such as the well-established transitivity requirement. In this section, we show how transitivity can be incorporated into our model of choice under uncertainty. Interestingly, as mentioned at the end of the previous section, the certainty inclusiveness assumption on the domain of a choice function is important for the main result of this section.

Lemma 4.1 has a natural counterpart in the transitive setting (see Richter [16]). All that needs to be done is to replace the relation R_C with its transitive closure $T(R_C)$ so that we obtain the following result.

Lemma 4.2. If a choice function C is dominance rationalized by a transitive relation R, then $T(R_C) \subseteq R$.

Proof. Suppose that R is a transitive dominance rationalization of C and that $(\mathbf{x}, \mathbf{y}) \in T(R_C)$. Thus, there exist $K \in \mathbb{N}$ and $\mathbf{x}^0, \ldots, \mathbf{x}^K \in X^m$ such that $\mathbf{x} = \mathbf{x}^0$, $(\mathbf{x}^{k-1}, \mathbf{x}^k) \in R_C$ for all $k \in \{1, \ldots, K\}$, and $\mathbf{x}^K = \mathbf{y}$. By Lemma 4.1, it follows that $\mathbf{x} = \mathbf{x}^0$, $(\mathbf{x}^{k-1}, \mathbf{x}^k) \in R$ for all $k \in \{1, \ldots, K\}$, and $\mathbf{x}^K = \mathbf{y}$. Because R is transitive, we obtain $(\mathbf{x}, \mathbf{y}) \in R$. ■

Our characterization of dominance rationalizability by a transitive relation relies on the assumption that the domain of C is certainty inclusive. Adapting direct dominance revelation coherence to the transitive framework considered in this section is straightforward, and the requisite necessary and sufficient condition is obtained by replacing R_C with its transitive closure $T(R_C)$.

Transitive Dominance Revelation Coherence. For all $S \in \mathcal{S}$ and for all $\mathbf{x} \in X^m$,

$$(\mathbf{x}, \mathbf{y}) \in T(R_C) \text{ for all } \mathbf{y} \in S \Rightarrow \mathbf{x} \in C(S).$$

The main result of this section characterizes dominance rationalizability by a transitive relation.

Theorem 4.2. A choice function C is dominance rationalizable by a transitive relation if and only if C satisfies transitive dominance revelation coherence.

Proof. The proof of the "only if" part of the theorem is a straightforward adaptation of the proof of the "only if" part of Theorem 4.1; we leave it to the reader to verify that all that is required is to replace R_C with $T(R_C)$ and Lemma 4.1 with Lemma 4.2.

To prove the if part of the theorem, suppose that C satisfies transitive dominance revelation coherence. We show that $R = T(R_C)$ is a transitive dominance rationalization of C.

Clearly, $R = T(R_C)$ is transitive by definition.

To establish that (4.1) is satisfied for $R = T(R_C)$, suppose first that $S \in \mathcal{S}$ and $\mathbf{x} \in S$ are such that $(\mathbf{x}, \mathbf{y}) \in T(R_C)$ for all $\mathbf{y} \in S$. By transitive dominance revelation coherence, $\mathbf{x} \in C(S)$.

Now suppose that $S \in \mathcal{S}$ and $\mathbf{x} \in S$ are such that $\mathbf{x} \in C(S)$. By definition, this implies $(\mathbf{x}, \mathbf{y}) \in R_C^d$ for all $\mathbf{y} \in S$ and, because $R_C^d \subseteq R_C \subseteq T(R_C)$, we obtain $(\mathbf{x}, \mathbf{y}) \in T(R_C)$ for all $\mathbf{y} \in S$.

Finally, we show that (4.2) is satisfied for $R = T(R_C)$. Suppose $\mathbf{x}, \mathbf{y} \in X^m$ are such that

$$(x_i \mathbf{1}_m, y_j \mathbf{1}_m) \in T(R_C) \text{ for all } i, j \in \{1, \ldots, m\}. \tag{4.3}$$

Because $\mathcal{S}$ is a certainty-inclusive domain, $\{x_i \mathbf{1}_m, y_j \mathbf{1}_m\} \in \mathcal{S}$ for all $i, j \in \{1, \ldots, m\}$. Because $T(R_C)$ dominance rationalizes C, (4.3) implies $x_i \mathbf{1}_m \in C(\{x_i \mathbf{1}_m, y_j \mathbf{1}_m\})$ for all $i, j \in \{1, \ldots, m\}$. Thus, by definition of the direct revealed preference relation, we have $(x_i \mathbf{1}_m, y_j \mathbf{1}_m) \in R_C^d$ for all $i, j \in \{1, \ldots, m\}$. By definition of R_C^d, we obtain $(\mathbf{x}, \mathbf{y}) \in R_C$ and, because $R_C \subseteq T(R_C)$, it follows that $(\mathbf{x}, \mathbf{y}) \in T(R_C) = R$. ∎

4.5. Suzumura-Consistent Dominance Rationalizability

Full transitivity is often considered too demanding a requirement, especially in (but not restricted to) the context of collective choice. Thus, it is worthwhile to study the possibility of obtaining characterization results that employ notions of dominance rationalizability that are weaker than transitive dominance rationalizability and stronger than mere dominance rationalizability. One possibility to do so is to explore dominance rationalizability by a Suzumura-consistent relation. The reason why we focus on Suzumura consistency as a suitable weakening of transitivity rather than on alternative properties such as quasi transitivity or acyclicity is discussed in the concluding section of the essay.

As in the previous section, our starting point is an analogue of Lemma 1 where R_C is replaced with its Suzumura-consistent closure $SC(R_C)$.

Lemma 4.3. If a choice function C is dominance rationalized by a Suzumura-consistent relation R, then $SC(R_C) \subseteq R$.

Proof. Suppose that R is a Suzumura-consistent dominance rationalization of C and that $(\mathbf{x}, \mathbf{y}) \in SC(R_C)$. By definition, we can distinguish two cases.

(a) $(\mathbf{x}, \mathbf{y}) \in R_C$;
(b) $(\mathbf{x}, \mathbf{y}) \in T(R_C)$ and $(\mathbf{y}, \mathbf{x}) \in R_C$.

In case (a), Lemma 4.1 implies $(\mathbf{x}, \mathbf{y}) \in R$.

In case (b), there exist $K \in \mathbb{N}$ and $\mathbf{x}^0, \ldots, \mathbf{x}^K \in X^m$ such that $\mathbf{x} = \mathbf{x}^0$, $(\mathbf{x}^{k-1}, \mathbf{x}^k) \in R_C$ for all $k \in \{1, \ldots, K\}$, and $\mathbf{x}^K = \mathbf{y}$. Moreover, $(\mathbf{y}, \mathbf{x}) \in R_C$. By Lemma 4.1, it follows that $\mathbf{x} = \mathbf{x}^0$, $(\mathbf{x}^{k-1}, \mathbf{x}^k) \in R$ for all $k \in \{1, \ldots, K\}$, and $\mathbf{x}^K = \mathbf{y}$. Therefore, $(\mathbf{x}, \mathbf{y}) \in T(R_C)$. Furthermore, $(\mathbf{y}, \mathbf{x}) \in R$ as a consequence of Lemma 4.1. If $(\mathbf{x}, \mathbf{y}) \notin R$, it follows that $(\mathbf{y}, \mathbf{x}) \in P(R)$. Because $(\mathbf{x}, \mathbf{y}) \in T(R_C)$, this contradicts the Suzumura consistency of R. Thus, $(\mathbf{x}, \mathbf{y}) \in R$. ■

A necessary and sufficient condition for dominance rationalizability by a Suzumura-consistent relation is obtained by employing Suzumura-consistent closure instead of transitive closure when formulating the requisite coherence property.

Suzumura-Consistent Dominance Revelation Coherence. For all $S \in \mathcal{S}$ and for all $\mathbf{x} \in X^m$,

$$(\mathbf{x}, \mathbf{y}) \in SC(R_C) \quad \text{for all } \mathbf{y} \in S \Rightarrow \mathbf{x} \in C(S).$$

The proof of our final characterization result is analogous to that of Theorem 4.2; we leave it to the reader to verify that all that is required is to replace the transitive closure with the Suzumura-consistent closure and Lemma 4.2 with Lemma 4.3.

Theorem 4.3. A choice function C is dominance rationalizable by a Suzumura-consistent relation if and only if C satisfies Suzumura-consistent dominance revelation coherence.

4.6. Concluding Remarks

In traditional models of rational choice on general domains without uncertainty, rationalizability by a transitive relation is equivalent to rationalizability by a reflexive, complete, and transitive relation; see Richter [15]. The same observation applies to the current framework. Richter's [15] proof technique employs a variant of Szpilrajn's [23] extension theorem and proceeds by showing that *any* extension of the transitive closure of the direct revealed preference relation to a reflexive, complete, and transitive relation also rationalizes C. That the dominance property does not change this result follows from the assumption that we operate on certainty-inclusive domains. As a consequence of this property, the restriction of the direct revealed preference relation (and, thus, the restriction of R_C) to the set of certain prospects is already reflexive and complete. Therefore, no new pairs need to be added to the original relation as a consequence of the dominance requirement. However, the same argument does not apply to arbitrary domains because the aforementioned reflexivity and completeness property of the restriction of R_C is not guaranteed without assuming that $\mathcal{S}$ is certainty inclusive. This means that there may exist extensions that do not obey the restrictions imposed by the definition of dominance rationalizability by a transitive relation, and existential clauses may have to be invoked to formulate necessary and sufficient conditions. See Bossert [5] for analogous observations in the more restricted framework of set-based decision rules.

In contrast, Suzumura-consistent dominance revelation coherence is not sufficient for dominance rationalizability by a reflexive, complete, and Suzumura-consistent relation. This is an immediate consequence of the observation that Suzumura consistency and transitivity coincide in the presence of reflexivity and completeness; see Suzumura [21].

The reason why we focus on Suzumura consistency as the weakening of transitivity to be considered is that properties such as quasi transitivity or acyclicity cannot be treated in an analogous fashion. This is the case because there is no such thing as a quasi-transitive or acyclic closure: if a relation fails to be quasi-transitive or acyclic, there is no unique way of defining a unique superset of this relation that possesses the requisite property. For instance, if $\mathbf{x}$ is strictly preferred to $\mathbf{y}$, $\mathbf{y}$ is strictly preferred to $\mathbf{z}$, and $\mathbf{z}$ is strictly preferred to $\mathbf{x}$, the resulting relation clearly is not acyclic (and, of course, not quasi-transitive). In order to obtain a superset of this relation that is acyclic, one of the pairs $(\mathbf{y}, \mathbf{x})$, $(\mathbf{z}, \mathbf{y})$, or $(\mathbf{x}, \mathbf{z})$ has to be added to the original relation, but *any one* of the three possibilities will do. Analogously, to obtain a quasi-transitive superset of the relation, two of the three pairs need to be added, but, again, *any two* will do the job. Thus, there is no well-defined closure operation for these properties and, as a consequence, a condition that demands such a closure to be respected cannot be formulated. This observation also applies to dominance rationalizability by itself: because there does not exist a complete closure of a relation, our condition does not work if we want to obtain dominance rationalizability by a reflexive and complete relation. See Bossert and Suzumura [7] for a detailed discussion of these issues in the traditional rational choice framework without uncertainty.

Our definition of the class of possible decision rules is very permissive—the dominance requirement appears to be quite uncontroversial. If one intends to come up with more restrictive notions of suitable decision models, the method suggested here may be applied to this alternative setting. Because of this observation, we think of this essay as providing two contributions: in addition to the results that we consider to be of interest in themselves, we propose a general method that can be employed when applying theories of rational choice to the analysis of decision making under uncertainty.

4.7. References

[1] Arrow, K. J., and L. Hurwicz, "An Optimality Criterion for Decision Making under Ignorance," in C. F. Carter and J. L. Ford, eds., *Uncertainty and Expectations in Economics: Essays in Honour of G. L. S. Shackle,* Oxford: Basil Blackwell, 1972, 1–11.

[2] Barberà, S., C. R. Barrett, and P. K. Pattanaik, "On Some Axioms for Ranking Sets of Alternatives," *Journal of Economic Theory* **33**, 1984, 301–308.

[3] Barberà, S., W. Bossert, and P. K. Pattanaik, "Ranking Sets of Objects," in S. Barberà, P. Hammond, and C. Seidl, eds., *Handbook of Utility Theory,* Vol. 2: *Extensions,* Dordrecht, Netherlands: Kluwer, 2004, 893–977.

[4] Barberà, S., and P. K. Pattanaik, "Extending an Order on a Set to the Power Set: Some Remarks on Kannai and Peleg's Approach," *Journal of Economic Theory* **32**, 1984, 185–191.

[5] Bossert, W., "Choices, Consequences, and Rationality," *Synthese* **129**, 2001, 343–369.

[6] Bossert, W., Y. Sprumont, and K. Suzumura (2005), "Consistent Rationalizability," *Econometrica* **72**, 2005, 185–200. Essay 3 of this volume.

[7] Bossert, W., and K. Suzumura, *Consistency, Choice, and Rationality,* Cambridge, Mass.: Harvard University Press, 2010.

[8] Fishburn, P. C., *Utility Theory for Decision Making,* New York: John Wiley & Sons, 1970.

[9] Gärdenfors, P., "Manipulation of Social Choice Functions," *Journal of Economic Theory* **13**, 1976, 217–228.

[10] Hansson, B., "Choice Structures and Preference Relations," *Synthese* **18**, 1968, 443–458.

[11] Houthakker, H. S., "Revealed Preference and the Utility Function," *Economica* **17**, 1950, 159–174.

[12] Kannai, Y., and B. Peleg, "A Note on the Extension of an Order on a Set to the Power Set," *Journal of Economic Theory* **32**, 1984, 172–175.

[13] Kim, K. H., and F. R. Roush, "Preferences on Subsets," *Journal of Mathematical Psychology* **21**, 1980, 279–282.

[14] Milnor, J., "Games against Nature," in R. Thrall, C. Coombs, and R. Davis, eds., *Decision Processes,* New York: John Wiley & Sons, 1954, 49–59.

[15] Richter, M. K., "Revealed Preference Theory," *Econometrica* **41**, 1966, 1075–1091.

[16] Richter, M. K., "Rational Choice," in J. S. Chipman, L. Hurwicz, M. K. Richter, and H. F. Sonnenschein, eds., *Preferences, Utility, and Demand,* New York: Harcourt Brace Jovanovich, 1971, 29–58.

[17] Samuelson, P. A., "A Note on the Pure Theory of Consumer's Behaviour," *Economica* **5**, 1938, 61–71.

[18] Samuelson, P. A., "Consumption Theory in Terms of Revealed Preference," *Economica* **15**, 1948, 243–253.

[19] Savage, L. J., *The Foundations of Statistics,* New York: John Wiley & Sons, 1954.

[20] Suzumura, K., "Rational Choice and Revealed Preference," *Review of Economic Studies* **43**, 1976, 149–158. Essay 1 of this volume.

[21] Suzumura, K., "Remarks on the Theory of Collective Choice," *Economica* **43**, 1976, 381–390. Essay 6 of this volume.

[22] Suzumura, K., "Houthakker's Axiom in the Theory of Rational Choice," *Journal of Economic Theory* **14**, 1977, 284–290. Essay 2 of this volume.

[23] Szpilrajn, E., "Sur l'extension de l'ordre partiel," *Fundamenta Mathematicae* **16**, 1930, 386–389.

[24] von Neumann, J., and O. Morgenstern, *Theory of Games and Economic Behavior,* Princeton, N.J.: Princeton University Press, 1944.

PART II

SOCIAL CHOICE AND WELFARE ECONOMICS

Introduction to Part II

There are as many preferences as there are men.
—HORACE, *Satires*, 35–30 BC

Paradoxes are useful to attract attention to ideas.
—MANDELL CREIGHTON, *Life and Letters*, 1904

Constitutions are checks upon the hasty action of the majority. They are the self-imposed restraints of a whole people upon a majority of them to secure sober action and a respect for the rights of the minority.
—WILLIAM HOWARD TAFT, veto of Arizona Enabling Act, August 22, 1911

Social choice theory is the science on social choice rules and/or procedures. It was Jean-Jacques Rousseau (1712-1778) who foretold the main concern of this science as follows:[1] "The social order is a sacred right which serves as a foundation for all other rights. And as it is not a natural right, it must be one founded on covenants. The problem is to determine what those covenants are." Arrow's social choice theory may be construed as a formal framework for analyzing what Rousseau's covenants are.

At the outset of such an analysis, we must make a choice on the informational bases of our discourse. According to Arrow [2, p. 124]: "Economic or any other social policy has consequences for the many and diverse individuals who make up the society or economy. It has been taken for granted in virtually all economic policy discussions since the time of Adam Smith, if not before, that alternative policies should be judged on the basis of their consequences for individuals." Arrow showed no hesitation to accommodate

1. Rousseau, J.-J., *Du Contrat Social*, 1763. English translation by M. Cranston, *The Social Contract*, Harmondsworth, England: Penguin Books, 1968.

this convention of judging rules and/or procedures by means of their consequences:[2] "What I am after all is a kind of utilitarian manqué. That is to say, I'd like to be a utilitarian but the only problem is I have nowhere those utilities come from. The problem I have with utilitarianism is not that it is excessively rational, but that the epistemological foundations are weak. My problem is: What are those objects we are adding up? I have no objection to adding them up if there's something to add. But the one thing I retain from utilitarianism is that, basically, judgments are based on consequences." Thus, Arrow made a commitment of basing his social choice theory on the epistemological basis of *consequentialism*, if not of utilitarianism. To be more explicit, the point of departure of Arrow's social choice theory is the profile of individual preference *orderings* defined over the set of *consequences* of social choice rules and/or procedures.

It is often said that Arrow's general impossibility theorem for social choice rules and/or procedures is a generalization of the *Condorcet paradox* on the simple majority decision rule. It is true that the Condorcet paradox was one of the driving forces of Arrow's theorem, but the relation between these two intellectual accomplishments seems to be rather subtle. To bring this point into clear relief, suppose that there are m social alternatives, where $3 \leq m < +\infty$, and n individuals, where $2 \leq n < +\infty$, in the society. For the sake of simplicity, suppose further that individuals express only linear preference orderings without indifference. It is clear that there are $m! := \prod_{k=1}^{m} k$ possible linear preference orderings, so that the total number of profiles of individual linear preference orderings is given by $(m!)^n$. What we christen the *social aggregator* of individual linear preference orderings is a function that maps each profile of individual linear preference orderings into one social linear preference ordering. Since a social aggregator designates, for each and every profile, a social linear preference ordering, the total number $\mu(m, n)$ of social aggregators can be obtained by multiplying $m!$ as many times as $(m!)^n$, viz., $\mu(m, n) := m!$ of the power $(m!)^n$, which is an astronomically large number. Even in the smallest conceivable society, where $m = 3$ and $n = 2$, the total number of social aggregators is given by $\mu(3, 2) = 6^{36}$, which far exceeds the Avogadro number. The class of Arrow social welfare functions is a special subset of the class of social aggregators, which satisfy Arrow's axioms of the

2. Arrow and Kelly [3, pp. 21–22].

Pareto principle and the independence of irrelevant alternatives. Needless to say, it is out of the question to enumerate all social aggregators in turn with the purpose of checking their eligibility under Arrow's list of desiderata. In conspicuous comparison, the Condorcet paradox is concerned with the single rule of preference aggregation, viz., the simple majority decision rule. As such, the Arrow impossibility theorem and the Condorcet paradox are on different analytical plateaus.

Arrow's innovation in this context is the axiomatic method of analysis. In addition to the axiom of the *Pareto principle* and the axiom of the *independence of irrelevant alternatives*, he invoked the axiom of *unrestricted domain* of the social aggregators and the axiom of *collective rationality.* He could thereby curtail the permissible class of social aggregators to the set $\{f_1, f_2, \ldots, f_n\}$, where f_k $(k = 1, 2, \ldots, n)$ is the social aggregator that allows the individual k to be a *dictator*. For each profile of individual linear preference orderings and for each pair $\{x, y\}$ of social alternatives, if k is a dictator and he/she prefers x (resp. y) to y (resp. x), then the associated social linear preference ordering should judge that x (resp. y) is socially preferred to y (resp. x). Thus, if we add the last axiom of *nondictatorship*, we end up with the Arrow general impossibility theorem.[3]

Part II contains four essays. Essay 5 ("Impossibility Theorems without Collective Rationality") starts from the exchange of views among James Buchanan [6, p. 116], Kenneth Arrow [1, p. 120], and Charles Plott [12]. It was Buchanan who starkly criticized Arrow's use of the axiom of collective rationality as an illegitimate transplantation of a property that can be appropriate only in the context of individual choice. As an auxiliary step in defending his own use of the axiom of collective rationality, Arrow introduced a novel concept of *path-independence*: "Collective rationality in the social choice mechanism is not . . . merely an illegitimate transfer from the individual to society, but an important attribute of a genuinely democratic system capable of full adaptation to varying environment . . . ," which avoids the "democratic paralysis" by guaranteeing "the independence of the final choice from the path to it." However, it was not until Plott [12] gave

3. This exposition presupposed that the individual preference relations as well as social preference relations are linear orderings. The Arrow theorem holds true even if we get rid of this simplifying assumption of no indifference.

a precise formulation to the intuitive concept of path-independence that we could verify if the Arrow concept of path-independence could cope with the Buchanan criticism on the axiom of collective rationality. In fact, the Buchanan-Arrow-Plott exchange of views opened the Pandora's box of *nonbinary social choice theory*.[4] It was Essay 5, viz., "Impossibility Theorems without Collective Rationality" by Douglas Blair, Georges Bordes, Jerry Kelly, and Kotaro Suzumura, that kicked off a large number of subsequent works in this arena.[5] It is shown in Essay 5 that the shift from Arrow's binary framework to a nonbinary framework à la Plott and others is incapable of dissipating the impossibility cloud.

Essay 6 ("Remarks on the Theory of Collective Choice") has two focal issues. The first focal issue is the question of how much we must weaken Arrow's axiom of collective rationality to avoid his general impossibility theorem. We identify the gulf that separates possibility from impossibility in between the two versions of revealed preference axioms. The second focal issue is the comparison between the Arrow social welfare function[6] and the Bergson-Samuelson social welfare function (Bergson [5]; Samuelson [14, Chapter VIII; 16]). It is asserted that the Bergson-Samuelson social welfare ordering satisfying the unrestricted domain and the Pareto principle exists even when the Arrow social welfare function does not exist. It is in this context that the concept of *Suzumura consistency* was first introduced, and the Szpilrajn ordering extension theorem (see Szpilrajn [20]) was generalized to the effect that a binary relation R can be extended into an ordering R^* if and only if R satisfies Suzumura consistency.[7]

---

4. Formally speaking, Arrow's axiom of collective rationality just requires that the range of the preference aggregators is the set of *social preference orderings*. The *social choice* is derived from the *social preference* through the additional assumption of preference optimization within the opportunity set. The shift of emphasis from collective rationality to path-independence means that there is an implicit shift from the *binary* social choice framework, which was initiated by Arrow [1], to the *nonbinary* social choice framework.
5. See Deb [7], Sen [18], and Suzumura [19, Chapter 3] for an extensive overview of this broad area of research.
6. The Arrow social welfare function is the social preference aggregator that satisfies the axiom of unrestricted domain, the axiom of the Pareto principle, and the axiom of the independence of irrelevant alternatives.
7. In many essays of this volume and elsewhere, Suzumura's extension theorem plays crucial roles. See Essay 2, Essay 7, and Essay 13.

Throughout this work up until Essay 7 ("Arrovian Aggregation in Economic Environments: How Much Should We Know about Indifference Surfaces?"), no special structure such as *linear structure* or *topological structure* was assumed on the universal set of social alternatives. Essay 7 retains an analytical framework with purely ordinal and interpersonally noncomparable preferences. However, we focus on the shapes of indifference surfaces defined in the orthodox commodity space, and ask how much we need to strengthen our knowledge about their shapes to escape from impossibility results of the Arrow type. To make our problem at all reasonable, we make use of the model of allocating infinitely divisible commodities among a finite number of agents, which allows a finely grained analysis of information about preferences. Within such an economic model, we can make a sensible use of information about marginal rates of substitution and other local notions about indifference surfaces.[8]

In Essay 8 ("A Characterization of Suzumura-Consistent Collective Choice Rules"), we go back to the arena of abstract social choice theory with no linear or topological structure and ask the effects of replacing the Arrow full rationality with the Suzumura-consistent rationality on the sustainability of Arrovian impossibility theorems. This is a meaningful avenue to explore if only we are ready to sacrifice completeness of social judgments. This essay characterizes a class of social choice rules that generates social preference relations satisfying Suzumura consistency. The axioms on social choice rules used in our characterization are unrestricted domain, strong Pareto, anonymity, and neutrality. If there are at most as many individuals as there are alternatives, the axioms provide an alternative characterization of the Pareto rule. If there are more individuals than alternatives, however, further rules become available. It follows that the concept of Suzumura consistency leads to a possibility theorem in the Arrovian arena where impossibility theorems abound.

Four essays in Part II represent a small part of possible directions one can explore for the purpose of finding escape routes from the Arrow impossibility impasse. Some other directions that are worthwhile to explore are discussed in Part III and Part V.

8. Those who are interested in Arrovian impossibility theorems on economic domains are invited to consult Kalai, Muller, and Satterthwaite [9] and Le Breton and Weymark [11] among many others for further information.

References

[1] Arrow, K. J., *Social Choice and Individual Values*, New York: John Wiley & Sons, 1st edn., 1951; Enlarged 2nd edn., 1963. Republished with an introduction by E. Maskin, New Haven: Yale University Press, 2012.

[2] Arrow, K. J., "Arrow's Theorem," in Eatwell, J., M. Milgate, and P. Newman, eds., *The New Palgrave: A Dictionary of Economics,* Vol. I, London: Macmillan, 1987, 124–126.

[3] Arrow, K. J., and J. S. Kelly, "An Interview with Kenneth J. Arrow," in Arrow, Sen, and Suzumura [4, Vol. II, pp. 3–27].

[4] Arrow, K. J., A. K. Sen, and K. Suzumura, eds., *Handbook of Social Choice and Welfare*, Amsterdam: North-Holland/Elsevier, Vol. I in 2002; Vol. II in 2011.

[5] Bergson, A., "A Reformulation of Certain Aspects of Welfare Economics," *Quarterly Journal of Economics* **52**, 1938, 310–334.

[6] Buchanan, J. M., "Social Choice, Democracy, and Free Markets," *Journal of Political Economy* **62**, 1954, 114–123.

[7] Deb, R., "Nonbinary Social Choice," Arrow, Sen, and Suzumura [4, Vol. II, pp. 335–366].

[8] Hicks, J. R., "The Valuation of the Social Income," *Economica* **7**, 1940, 105–124.

[9] Kalai, E., E. Muller, and M. A. Satterthwaite, "Social Welfare Functions When Preferences Are Convex, Strictly Monotone, and Continuous," *Public Choice* **34**, 1979, 87–97.

[10] Kaldor, N., "Welfare Propositions in Economics and Interpersonal Comparisons of Utility," *Economic Journal* **49**, 1939, 549–552.

[11] Le Breton, M., and J. A. Weymark, "Arrovian Social Choice Theory on Economic Domains," in Arrow, Sen, and Suzumura [4, Vol. II, pp. 191–299].

[12] Plott, C. R., "Path Independence, Rationality, and Social Choice," *Econometrica* **41**, 1973, 1075–1091.

[13] Robbins, L., *An Essay on the Nature and Significance of Economic Science*, London: Macmillan, 1st edn., 1932; 2nd edn., 1935.

[14] Samuelson, P. A., *Foundations of Economic Analysis*, Cambridge, Mass.: Harvard University Press, 1947. Enlarged edition, 1983.

[15] Samuelson, P. A., "Evaluation of Real National Income," *Oxford Economic Papers* **2**, 1950, 1–29.

[16] Samuelson, P. A., "Bergsonian Welfare Economics," in Rosefielde, S., *Economic Welfare and the Economics of Soviet Socialism: Essays in Honor of Abram Bergson*, Cambridge, UK: Cambridge University Press, 1981, 223–266.

[17] Scitovsky, T., "A Note on Welfare Proposition in Economics," *Review of Economic Studies* **9**, 1941, 77–88.

[18] Sen, A. K., "Social Choice Theory: A Re-examination," *Econometrica* **45**, 1977, 53–89.

[19] Suzumura, K., *Rational Choice, Collective Decisions and Social Welfare*, New York: Cambridge University Press, 1983. Reprinted in paperback, 2009.

[20] Szpilrajn, E., "Sur l'Extension de l'Ordre Partiel," *Fundamenta Mathematicae* **16**, 1930, 386–389.

ESSAY 5

Impossibility Theorems without Collective Rationality

5.1. Introduction

Arrow's general impossibility theorem [2] demonstrated the incompatibility of five conditions on collective choice rules: *unrestricted domain, nondictatorship, the Pareto condition, independence of irrelevant alternatives,* and *transitive rationality* of the social choice function. The last condition requires the existence of a social preference ordering such that, given a set of alternatives, the chosen elements are those that are best with respect to that ordering. Since the publication of Arrow's theorem, an extensive body of literature has appeared seeking to circumvent the difficulty. This essay focuses on attempts to resolve the paradox by weakening the collective rationality requirement.

For our purpose, it is convenient to decompose Arrow's collective rationality requirement into two parts:

(a) *Rationality*. There exists a social preference relation R such that the elements chosen out of a set of available alternatives S are those that are best in S with respect to R. (R will be referred to as a *rationalization*.)

First published in *Journal of Economic Theory* **13**, 1976, pp. 361–379. Joint paper with D. H. Blair, G. Bordes, and J. S. Kelly. Reprinted in Arrow, K. J., and G. Debreu, eds., *The Foundations of 20th Century Economics,* Vol. 3, *Landmark Papers in General Equilibrium Theory, Social Choice and Welfare,* Cheltenham, Glos, UK: Edward Elgar, 2001, pp. 660–678. This paper represents a consolidation of overlapping work done independently by the four authors [3; 5; 13; 26]. The authors are indebted to the referees of the *Journal of Economic Theory,* the *Review of Economic Studies,* and *Econometrica* for seeing the possibility of such a consolidation. Thanks are also due to Donald J. Brown, John A. Ferejohn, Robert P. Parks, and Amartya K. Sen.

(b) *Transitivity and completeness of the rationalization.*

The sensitivity of Arrow's result to the specification of the degree of rationality was first noticed by Sen [22]. He continued to impose rationality but relaxed the second component to require only completeness and quasi transitivity (that is, transitivity of strict preference), and showed that this weakened collective rationality requirement is compatible with the remainder of Arrow's conditions. Gibbard [10] subsequently proved that any society whose collective choice rule meets Sen's conditions contains an *oligarchy,* a class of individuals who are jointly decisive for exclusion of an alternative from the social choice out of a two-element set and each of whose members is individually decisive for inclusion of an element in the choice from such a set. Any individual who by strictly preferring x to y can ensure that y is not socially preferred to x is called a *weak dictator;* every member of an oligarchy is clearly a weak dictator. Mas-Colell and Sonnenschein [14] provided the first published proof of Gibbard's theorem and proved an alternative impossibility result: even if weak dictators are to be countenanced, their multiplicity causes quasi-transitive rational (and otherwise Arrovian) collective choice rules to violate a decisiveness condition they call *positive responsiveness.* Thus, demanding merely quasi-transitive rationality of social choice provides no satisfactory resolution of Arrow's antidemocratic result. Even the smallest nondictatorial oligarchy (of two) fails a requirement of responsiveness (which is admittedly quite strong) when there are more than two voters; enlarging and "democratizing" the oligarchy aggregates the heterogeneity of individual preferences into widespread social indifference rather than intransitivity.

Further weakening of the consistency requirement imposed by Arrow's collective rationality (while continuing to insist on the existence of a rationalization) is entailed by requiring acyclicity (nonexistence of a strict preference cycle) instead of quasi transitivity of the social preference relation. The importance of this substitution comes from the observation that acyclicity is necessary and sufficient to guarantee that society is able to make a nonempty rational choice from any *finite* subset of the set of alternatives. In the case of individuals with acyclic preferences choosing over an *infinite* set of alternatives, Brown [7] has shown that the only acyclic collective choice rules that satisfy the remainder of Arrow's conditions and are not oligarchic are those of what he calls *collegial polities.* Under such a procedure, there exists a *quasi oligarchy,* a subset of individuals whose unanimous assent is a necessary condition for the exclusion of an alternative from the social choice out of a two-element set. In contrast with the Gibbardian oligarchy, consensus within the quasi oligarchy, though necessary, is not sufficient for exclusion. For this class of decision rules, at least one individual outside the quasi oligarchy must also prefer x to y to ensure a similar social preference. Thus, weakening Arrow's transitive rationality to require only acyclic rationality is a step in the democratic direction. The complete asymmetry between the power of individuals within and outside the oligarchy is diluted when quasi transitivity is abandoned. Some nonquasi oligarchs do have power: they are pivotal to the success of some winning coalitions. Nevertheless, the trade-offs remain between heterogeneity of preferences, decisiveness, and inequalities in the distribution of power, as is shown by another Mas-Colell-Sonnenschein theorem, which asserts that no acyclic collective choice rules exist satisfying both their no-weak-dictators and positive responsiveness conditions along with the remainder of Arrow's conditions. This proposition imposes no restrictions on the size of the alternatives set. In the case of individuals with acyclic preferences choosing over a finite set, Brown [6] has obtained a precise characterization of acyclic Arrovian collective choice rules that indicates clearly how they violate the positive responsiveness requirement. Collegial polities are of course acyclic even on a finite set, and nontrivial ones are obviously unresponsive to changes in the preferences of some voters. The only anonymous acyclic procedures in the finite case, as Brown shows, are rules satisfying the following condition: if M is the number of alternatives, every M-tuple of decisive coalitions of individuals must have nonempty intersection. This class of procedures includes simple special-majority rules (e.g., $\frac{2}{3}$ majority) and representative systems with a special-majority rule at each stage. For alternative sets that are large relative to the size of the set of individuals, these procedures are close to the unanimity rule.

Given all these results involving the weakening of Arrow's transitivity requirement, it is not surprising to find attacks focusing directly on rationality itself. Both Schwartz [21] and Plott [16; 17; 18] have criticized the demand for the existence of rationalizations. Plott [18] argues that a major reason for Arrow's insistence on transitive rationality was that it ensured that social choice would be invariant under arbitrary manipulations of the agenda, that is, the order and method by which alternatives are compared and inferior ones discarded (see Arrow [2, p. 120]). He proposes a consistency requirement for choice functions, which he calls *path independence:*

> The alternatives are "split up" into smaller sets, a choice is made over each of these sets, the chosen elements are collected, and then a choice is made from them. Path independence, in this case, would mean that the final result would be independent of the way the alternatives were initially divided up for consideration.[1] (Plott [17, pp. 1079–1080])

A fairly natural question now arises: What happens to impossibility theorems when path independence is substituted for transitive rationality and the remaining Arrovian conditions prevail? Plott [17; 18] observes, citing Sen [22] as a source, that the collective choice rule that chooses the Pareto optimal subsets from available alternative sets serves as a counterexample to a proposed impossibility result. Unfortunately, this collective choice rule runs afoul of Gibbard's theorem; it is also too undiscriminating in the face of heterogeneous individual preferences. It is important to notice that there exist path-independent choice functions that have no rationalization. Plott's position on impossibility results *with* path independence but *without* rationality is ambiguous. He has said that "some of the standard constructions in welfare economics such as social welfare functions and social preference relations unduly restrict the set of admissible policies and consequently induce impossibility results" (Plott [16, p. 182]) and that, with the relaxation of rationality, "the immediate impossibility result discovered by Arrow is avoided" (Plott [17, p. 1075]). He has been careful, however, to observe that "the lines which separate rationality properties, which induce immediate impossibility results, from path independence properties are very thinly drawn" [17, p. 1075]. Blair [4] and Parks [15] have exhibited examples of collective choice rules that can result in path-independent but not quasi-transitive choices; both, however, suffer from the defect that they can generate choice functions that are not very selective.

We prove in this essay several impossibility theorems in which we do not require social choices to have a rationalization. One of our results shows

1. For procedures aggregating preferences over many alternatives, which must of necessity be multistage processes due to computational costs, path independence is a desirable property for two reasons. First, it rules out certain forms of institutional arbitrariness, such as bias in favor of the status quo. Second, it precludes strategic behavior at the agenda-determination stage.

the incompatibility of nonweak dictatorship, the Pareto condition, independence of irrelevant alternatives, and path independence. Thus the replacement of Arrow's collective rationality with Plott's path independence does not help us to escape from the Arrovian dilemma. Still weaker consistency properties for social choice functions than path independence will be proposed. They too, however, fail to provide us with a means of avoiding impossibility results. As Arrow has written, "the paradox of social choice cannot be so easily exorcised" [2, p. 109].

5.2. The Structures of Choice Functions

Before presenting our impossibility theorems, we will clarify in this section the relationships between, on one hand, the rationality conditions used in the existing impossibility theorems and, on the other, path independence and some weaker conditions.

Let X denote the set of (mutually exclusive) alternatives. $\mathcal{S}$ stands for a family of nonempty subsets of X. Each element $S \in \mathcal{S}$ is an *admissible agenda;* it contains the currently feasible alternatives in a given choice situation. We assume throughout this essay that $\mathcal{S}$ contains all nonempty finite elements of $\mathcal{P}(X)$, the power set of X. A *choice function* C on $\mathcal{S}$ is a function that maps each $S \in \mathcal{S}$ into a nonempty subset $C(S)$ of S; note that $C(S)$ is not required to be a one-element set. Five properties of choice functions will be of interest here:

Path independence (PI). $C(S_1 \cup S_2) = C(C(S_1) \cup C(S_2))$ for all S_1, $S_2 \in \mathcal{S}$.

Chernoff condition (C). $S_1 \subseteq S_2 \Rightarrow C(S_2) \cap S_1 \subseteq C(S_1)$ for all S_1, $S_2 \in \mathcal{S}$. That is, every element chosen out of a set must also be chosen in every subset of the set containing the element.[2]

Property β. $[S_1 \subseteq S_2 \;\&\; C(S_1) \cap C(S_2) \neq \emptyset] \Rightarrow C(S_1) \subseteq C(S_2)$ for all S_1, $S_2 \in \mathcal{S}$. That is, if some chosen element from a set is chosen from a

2. This condition, first introduced by Chernoff [8], has appeared in the literature under a variety of names, including, unhappily, "independence of irrelevant alternatives." It is discussed extensively by Arrow in [1].

superset of that set, then *every* such element is chosen from the superset. (See Sen [24].)

SUPERSET PROPERTY (S). $S_1 \subseteq S_2 \Rightarrow$ not $[C(S_2) \subsetneq C(S_1)]$. That is, the choice out of the superset of a set is not strictly contained in the choice out of the set.

GENERALIZED CONDORCET PROPERTY (GC). $(x \in S \,\&\, x \in C(\{x, y\})$ for all $y \in S) \Rightarrow x \in C(S)$ for all $S \in \mathcal{S}$. That is, if no element in a set beats a given element x in a binary choice, then x must be among the elements chosen from the set.[3]

A *preference relation* R is a binary relation on X having the interpretation that xRy if and only if x is at least as good as y from the point of view of the person or group in question. In the usual way we define from R the subrelations P of strict preference and I of indifference. R is *complete* if and only if xRy of yRx, *transitive* if and only if $xRy \,\&\, yRz \Rightarrow xRz$, *quasi-transitive* if and only if P is transitive, and *acyclic* if and only if $(x_1Px_2P \ldots Px_tPx_1)$ for no finite subset $\{x_1, \ldots, x_t\}$ of X. A transitive and complete relation will be called a *transitive* ordering.

Choice functions induce preference relations in two ways. If there exists a preference relation R satisfying $C(S) = \{x \in S \mid xRy$ for all $y \in S\}$ for all $S \in \mathcal{S}$, the choice function C will be called *rational* (R); in that event R is a *rationalization* of C. A choice function is *transitive rational* (TR), *quasi-transitive rational* (QTR), or *acyclic rational* (AR) if it has a rationalization with the requisite property.

Alternatively, a preference relation may be derived from choice functions restricted to two-element agenda sets. Even if C has no rationalization, we can always define, following Herzberger [12], the *base relation* R^* as follows: xR^*y if and only if $x \in C(\{x, y\})$ for all $\{x, y\} \in \mathcal{S}$. Strict preference P^* may be defined in the obvious way. A choice function will then be said to satisfy *base quasi transitivity* (BQT) if and only if R^* is quasi-transitive, *base acyclicity* (BA) if and only if R^* is acyclic, and *base triple acyclicity* (BTA) if and only if $xP^*y \,\&\, yP^*z \Rightarrow xR^*z$.

3. The Condorcet condition in its usual form is stated in terms of pairwise comparisons by simple majority rule. Our condition is a weaker version of Sen's property γ, discussed in [24].

We turn now to comparing these consistency conditions by decomposing several of them into more basic parts. Sen [24] has proven that a choice function has a transitive rationalization if and only if it satisfies both property β and the Chernoff condition. Plott [17], in turn, has shown that quasi-transitive rationality is equivalent to the conjunction of path independence and the generalized Condorcet property. The relationship between these results becomes more apparent when we further decompose path independence.

THEOREM 5.1. A choice function is path independent if and only if it satisfies the Chernoff condition and the superset property.

PROOF. First we show that path independence implies the Chernoff condition. Let $S_1 \subseteq S_2$, and let $x \in S_1 \cap C(S_2)$. By path independence, $C(S_2) = C[C(S_2 \setminus S_1) \cup C(S_1)] \subseteq C(S_2 \setminus S_1) \cup C(S_1)$. Since $x \in S_1$, $x \notin S_2 \setminus S_1$, so $x \notin C(S_2 \setminus S_1)$. Hence $x \in C(S_1)$; therefore, $S_1 \cap C(S_2) \subseteq C(S_1)$.

Next we show that path independence implies the superset property. Suppose, contrary to that condition, that $S_1 \subseteq S_2$ and $C(S_2) \subsetneq C(S_1)$. By path independence, $C(S_2) = C[C(S_2) \cup C(S_1)] = C[C(S_1)]$. By the first part of this proof, the Chernoff condition holds, so that from $C(S_1) \subseteq S_1$ we can derive $C(S_1) \cap C(S_1) \subseteq C[C(S_1)]$; thus $C[C(S_1)] = C(S_1)$. This yields $C(S_1) = C(S_2)$, a contradiction.

Finally, we obtain path independence from the superset property and the Chernoff condition. Suppose $x \in C(S_1 \cup S_2)$. If $x \in S_1$, the Chernoff condition implies $x \in C(S_1)$; if $x \in S_2$, then $x \in C(S_2)$. Hence $x \in C(S_1) \cup C(S_2) \subseteq S_1 \cup S_2$. By another application of the Chernoff condition, $x \in C[C(S_1) \cup C(S_2)]$. Thus $C(S_1 \cup S_2) \subseteq C[C(S_1) \cup C(S_2)]$. The inclusion cannot be strict, however, because of the superset property and the fact that $C(S_1 \cup S_2) \subseteq C[C(S_1) \cup C(S_2)]$. Therefore, $C(S_1 \cup S_2) = C[C(S_1) \cup C(S_2)]$. ∎

What we now know is that quasi-transitive rationality is equivalent to the conjunction of the Chernoff condition, the superset property, and the generalized Condorcet property, and that if the generalized Condorcet property is no longer required we have path independence. Suppose we retain the Chernoff condition and the generalized Condorcet property but do not require that the superset property hold. Theorem 5.2 demonstrates that what remains is acyclicity.

THEOREM 5.2. If a choice function C on $\mathcal{S}$ satisfies the Chernoff condition and the generalized Condorcet property and if $\mathcal{S}$ contains all finite nonempty subsets of X, it has a unique, complete, reflexive, acyclic rationalization. If a choice function is induced by an acyclic relation, it satisfies the Chernoff condition and the generalized Condorcet property.

PROOF. Beginning with the first proposition, we assume C satisfies the conditions stated. Each two-element subset of X belongs to $\mathcal{S}$, so the only possible rationalization is the base relation R^*:

$$xR^*y \Leftrightarrow x \in C(\{x, y\}).$$

If $x \in C(S)$, then, by the Chernoff condition, $x \in C(\{x, y\})$ for each $y \in S$. On the other hand, if $x \in C(\{x, y\})$ for all $y \in S$, then $x \in C(S)$ by the generalized Condorcet property. Thus,

$$\begin{aligned} C(S) &= \{x \in S \mid x \in C(\{x, y\}) \text{ for all } y \in S\} \\ &= \{x \in S \mid xR^*y \text{ for all } y \in S\}, \end{aligned}$$

that is, R^* is in fact a rationalization of C. Completeness and reflexivity of R^* are obvious: it remains to show that R^* is acyclic. Suppose that $x_1P^*x_2P^* \dots P^*x_n$, that is, $x_i \notin C(\{x_{i-1}, x_i\})$ for $i = 2, \dots, n$. By the Chernoff condition, $x_i \notin C(\{x_1, x_2, \dots, x_n\})$ for $i = 2, \dots, n$. By our assumption about the content of $\mathcal{S}$, $C(\{x_1, x_2, \dots, x_n\}) \neq \emptyset$, so $C(\{x_1, x_2, \dots, x_n\}) = \{x_1\}$. By another application of the Chernoff condition, $x_1 \in C(\{x_1, x_n\})$, that is, *not* $x_nP^*x_1$, as was to be shown.

Turning now to the second assertion, for each $S \in \mathcal{S}$,

$$C(S) = \{x \in S \mid xRy \text{ for all } y \in S\} = \{x \in S \mid \text{not } (\exists y)(y \in S \;\&\; yPx)\},$$

where R is acyclic. Suppose $x \in C(\{x, y\})$ for all $y \in S$. Then xRy for all $y \in S$, that is, $x \in C(S)$; the generalized Condorcet property therefore holds. Suppose $x \in C(S_2)$ and $x \in S_1 \subseteq S_2$. Now $x \in C(S_2)$ implies xRy for all $y \in S_2$, which implies xRy for all $y \in S_1$. Hence $x \in C(S_1)$, and the Chernoff condition holds. ■

Theorems 5.1 and 5.2, coupled with Plott's theorem, imply that the only path-independent choice functions that are acyclic rational are those that are quasi-transitive rational as well. We have earlier remarked that path-independent choice functions exist which are not rational (see Plott [17]). It should now be clear that there exist rational choice functions that violate path independence; indeed, the choice function induced by any acyclic but not quasi-transitive preference relation falls in this category.

The following example shows that the Chernoff condition implies neither path independence nor the existence of a rationalization.

EXAMPLE 5.1. Let $X = \{x, y, z\}$ and $\mathcal{S} = \mathcal{P}(X) \setminus \{\emptyset\}$. The choice function defined by $C(X) = \{x\}$ and $C(S) = S$ for all $S \subsetneq X$ is easily shown to satisfy the Chernoff condition. It is not path independent, however, since $C(\{x, y, z\}) = \{x\} \subsetneq \{x, y\} = C(\{x, y\})$, which contradicts the superset property. If C has any rationalization it must be universal indifference, given $C(S) = S$ for all two-element S, but this contradicts $C(X) = \{x\}$.

Finally, we relate path independence and the Chernoff condition to the properties of the base relation.

LEMMA 5.1. Path independence implies base quasi transitivity. The Chernoff condition implies base acyclicity.

PROOF. Suppose that C is path independent and that xP^*yP^*z for some $x, y, z \in X$. By path independence,

$$\begin{aligned}\{x\} = C(\{x, y\}) &= C[C(\{x\}) \cup C(\{y, z\})] = C(\{x, y, z\}) \\ &= C[C(\{x, y\}) \cup C(\{z\})] = C(\{x, z\}).\end{aligned}$$

Hence xP^*z, so R^* is quasi-transitive.

The second proposition is established by an argument already given in the first part of the proof of Theorem 5.2. ■

Counterexamples to the converse of Lemma 5.1's assertions are left for the reader to construct.

We conclude this section with an implication diagram, which summarizes the results presented here and other relationships that follow easily from the definitions. The properties in parentheses are jointly equivalent to the conditions above them. Note that the equivalence of rationality and acyclic rationality is dependent on our assumption that $\mathcal{S}$ includes all finite nonempty subsets of X.

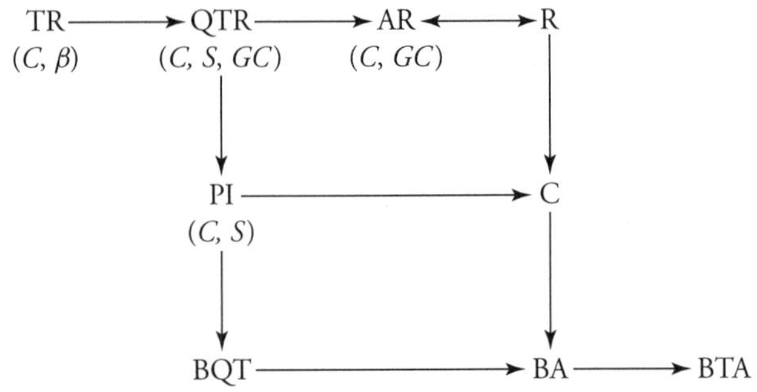

Figure 5.1. Logical Implications

5.3. Impossibility Theorems

Suppose that there are n individuals and let $N = \{1, 2, \ldots, n\}$; it is assumed that $2 \leq n < \infty$. X stands for the set of social alternatives, now taken to have at least three elements. The problem at hand is to characterize the institutionally and ethically "acceptable" collective choice rules; such a rule f is a function that maps each *profile,* or n-tuple, of individual transitive preference orderings of X into the set of choice functions on $\mathcal{S}$. (Note that what is called here a collective choice rule is analogous to Arrow's [2] *social welfare function,* and that choice functions play in this analysis the same role as Arrow's *social preference ordering*.) The domain of f is the set of all logically possible profiles. Formally, given a profile k, society's choice function C is given by $C = f(k)$. However, the function f will be fixed throughout the proof of each of the subsequent theorems. We will therefore frequently not refer explicitly to f but rather will simply write $C^k(S)$ for the choice out of agenda set S under profile k, given the fixed collective choice rule. When the profile is invariant, we will suppress the superscript as well and merely write $C(S)$.

All of the rationality and consistency requirements studied in Section 5.2 are properties of choice functions, that is, of elements of the range of collective choice rules. Each of these conditions will also be attributed to a collective choice rule f in the event that, for every profile, the choice function determined by f satisfies the given condition. For example, we will call a collective choice rule path independent if the image of every profile under the rule is a path independent choice function.

A further set of definitions is necessary before proceeding to the results of this section.

A set of individuals $J \subseteq N$ is *decisive for x against y* (resp. *weakly decisive for x against y*) if and only if $x P_i y$ for all $i \in J$ and $j P_i x$ for all $i \notin J$ implies $\{x\} = C(\{x, y\})$ (resp. $x \in C(\{x, y\})$).

If V is decisive for some a against some b, and W being decisive for some x against some y implies that the number of individuals in W is at least as great as the number of individuals in V, then V is a *smallest decisive set*.

Individual i is a *dictator* (resp. *weak dictator*) if and only if for all $x, y \in X$, $x P_i y$ implies $\{x\} = C(\{x, y\})$ (resp. $x \in C(\{x, y\})$).

A collective choice rule is said to satisfy

The Pareto condition if and only if for any profile k such that $x P_i y$ for all $i \in N$, we have $\{x\} = C^k(\{x, y\})$.

Nondictatorship if and only if there exists no dictator.

Nonweak dictatorship if and only if there exists no weak dictator.

Positive responsiveness if and only if k is a profile resulting in $x \in C^k(\{x, y\})$ and l is another profile with $R_j^k = R_j^l$ for all $j \neq i$, and either $(y P_i^k x \ \& \ x I_i^l y)$ or $(y I_i^k x \ \& \ x P_i^l y)$ implies $\{x\} = C^l(\{x, y\})$, where $i \in N$ is any specified individual.

Independence of irrelevant alternatives if and only if for any two profiles $j = (R_1, \ldots, R_n)$ and $k = (R'_1, \ldots, R'_n)$ such that $(x R_i y \Leftrightarrow x R'_i y \ \& \ y R_i x \Leftrightarrow y R'_i x)$ for all $i \in N$, we have $C^j(\{x, y\}) = C^k(\{x, y\})$.

Notice that our independence condition restricts its attention to choices from two-element sets, in contrast with Arrow's independence axiom. Although the two conditions are equivalent for rational collective choice rules, our axiom is strictly weaker if rationality is not imposed.

Profiles will be written horizontally with more preferred alternatives to the left; indifference will be indicated by parentheses. For example, the expression

$$V: \qquad x, (y, z)$$

means that every individual in V prefers x to both y and z, between which indifference prevails.

We now proceed to establish an impossibility theorem using only path independence rather than Arrow's transitive rationality. The theorem is otherwise Arrovian except for a slight strengthening of the nondictatorship condition.

THEOREM 5.3. If there are at least three voters, there is no collective choice rule satisfying all of (1) path independence, (2) the Pareto condition, (3) independence of irrelevant alternatives, and (4) nonweak dictatorship.

In view of Lemma 5.1, we can establish this proposition by proving the following stronger result, which utilizes the weaker condition of base quasi transitivity. An alternative proof of Theorem 5.4 is given by Fishburn [9, Theorem 16.2].

THEOREM 5.4. If there are at least three voters, there is no collective choice rule satisfying all of (1) base quasi transitivity, (2) the Pareto condition, (3) independence of irrelevant alternatives, and (4) nonweak dictatorship.

This proposition follows immediately from the following three lemmas.

LEMMA 5.2. If a collective choice rule satisfies the Pareto condition, independence of irrelevant alternatives, and base quasi transitivity, and if i is decisive for some $x, y \in X$, then i is a dictator; that is,

$$(x P_i y \ \&\ y P_j x \text{ for all } j \neq i \Rightarrow \{x\} = C(\{x, y\}))$$
$$\Rightarrow (\text{for all } s, t \in X : s P_i t \Rightarrow \{s\} = C(\{s, t\})).$$

PROOF. We first show

$$(x P_i y \ \&\ y P_j x \text{ for all } j \neq i \Rightarrow \{x\} = C(\{x, y\})) \tag{5.1}$$
$$\Rightarrow (\text{for all } s \in X : s P_i y \Rightarrow \{s\} = C(\{s, y\})).$$

Suppose not. Then there exists a profile such that $x P_i y$ and $y P_j x$ for all $j \neq i$ implies $\{x\} = C(\{x, y\})$, $s P_i y$, and $\{s\} \neq C(\{s, y\})$:

$$i : s, x, y,$$
$$N \setminus \{i\} : (\text{some } (n-1)\text{-tuple of orderings of } y \text{ and } s), x.$$

By assumption, $\{x\} = C(\{x, y\})$. By the Pareto condition $\{s\} = C(\{s, x\})$. Base quasi transitivity then implies that, under this profile, $\{s\} = C(\{s, y\})$. By independence, $\{s\} = C(\{s, y\})$ under *every* profile in which $s P_i y$, since no specification has been made of other voters' preferences between these alternatives. This contradiction establishes (5.1). Next we show

$$\text{(for all } s \in X : sP_iy \ \& \ yP_js \text{ for all } j \neq i \Rightarrow \{s\} = C(\{s, y\})) \qquad (5.2)$$

$$\Rightarrow \text{(for all } s, t \in X : sP_it \Rightarrow \{s\} = C(\{s, t\})).$$

The antecedent of (5.2) is implied by (5.1). Suppose (5.2) is false. Then there exists a profile such that sP_iy and yP_js for all $j \neq i \Rightarrow \{s\} = C(\{s, y\})$, sP_it, and $\{s\} \neq C(\{s, t\})$:

$$i : s, y, t,$$

$$N \setminus \{i\} : y, \text{(some } (n-1)\text{-tuple of orderings of } s \text{ and } t).$$

By assumption, $\{s\} = C(\{s, y\})$ and by the Pareto condition, $\{y\} = C(\{y, t\})$. Base quasi transitivity shows that under this profile $\{s\} = C(\{s, t\})$. By independence, the social choice is the same for all profiles in which sP_it holds, contradicting our assumption and establishing (5.2). ■

Lemma 5.3. If a collective choice rule satisfies independence of irrelevant alternatives, the Pareto condition, and base quasi transitivity, and if i is weakly decisive for some $x, y \in X$, then i is a weak dictator; that is,

$$(xP_iy \ \& \ yP_jx \text{ for all } j \neq i \Rightarrow x \in C(\{x, y\}))$$

$$\Rightarrow \text{(for all } s, t \in X : sP_it \Rightarrow s \in C(\{s, t\})).$$

The proof of this lemma is virtually identical to that of Lemma 5.2 and is omitted.

Lemma 5.4. If V is a smallest decisive set with respect to a and b under a collective choice rule satisfying base quasi transitivity, the Pareto condition, nondictatorship, and independence of irrelevant alternatives, then

V contains at least two individuals, (5.3)

and every $i \in V$ is a weak dictator. (5.4)

Proof. Assertion (5.3) is obvious from Lemma 5.2 and nondictatorship. To establish (5.4), we must show that

$$\text{if } i \in V, xP_iy \Rightarrow x \in C(\{x, y\}) \text{ for some } x, y \in X.$$

Suppose not. Then for some $a, z \in X$, there exists a profile of the form

$$i: \quad a, z,$$
$$N \setminus \{i\}: \quad \text{(some } (n-1)\text{-tuple of orderings of } a \text{ and } z)$$

such that $\{z\} = C(\{a, z\})$. Let $W \subseteq V$ and $V \setminus W = \{i\}$. Consider the following further specification of the previous profile:

$$i: \quad a, b, z,$$
$$W: \quad \text{(same individual orderings as before between } a \text{ and } z), b,$$
$$N \setminus V: \quad b, \text{ (same individual orderings as before between } a \text{ and } z).$$

We know $C(\{a, z\}) = \{z\}$ and, because of V's decisiveness for a over b, $C(\{a, b\}) = \{a\}$. By base quasi transitivity, $\{z\} = C(\{b, z\})$ under the profile in question. But this implies that W is decisive for z against b, which contradicts the minimality of V. Thus, if $i \in V$, i is weakly decisive for some x against y, $x, y \in X$. By Lemma 5.3, such an individual is a weak dictator, establishing (5.4). ■

Proof of Theorem 5.4. Every dictator is a weak dictator, so prohibiting weak dictators rules out dictators too. If a collective choice rule satisfies base quasi transitivity, independence of irrelevant alternatives, and the Pareto condition and it has no weak dictators (and thus no dictator either), then Lemma 5.4 yields the conclusion that there must exist a weak dictator. This contradiction proves the theorem. ■

Mas-Colell and Sonnenschein's [14] result on the inconsistency of quasi transitivity and positive responsiveness in the presence of the Arrovian conditions carries over in a straightforward manner to the case of irrational path independence, and thence to base quasi transitivity.

Theorem 5.5. If there are at least three voters, there is no collective choice rule satisfying all of (1) base quasi transitivity, (2) the Pareto condition, (3) nondictatorship, (4) independence of irrelevant alternatives, and (5) positive responsiveness.

Proof. By Lemma 5.4, there exist at least two weak dictators; call them 1, 2. Suppose under some profile xP_1y and yP_2x for some $x, y \in X$; by weak dictatorship, $\{x, y\} = C(\{x, y\})$, regardless of the preferences of other voters, of whom there exists at least one. This violates positive responsiveness. ■

In view of the impossibility theorems discussed in the introduction and the new results just presented, one might be tempted to retreat and demand the imposition only of the Chernoff condition which, as we have seen, is strictly weaker than both acyclicity and path independence. This condition is an appealing one to impose on collective choice rules. It is clearly desirable in piecemeal choice mechanisms where choices are made from unions of choices over subsets. If an alternative fails to be chosen in some subset, it need not be considered again at a later stage, for the contra-positive of the Chernoff condition ensures that the alternative will not be among the final choices. Arrow's justification [2, pp. 26–27] for his independence axiom is obviously instead an argument for this condition. See also Sen [23, p. 17]. Nevertheless, as the following theorems demonstrate, the Chernoff condition standing alone as a rationality condition must also be rejected, at least if the Arrovian conditions are found compelling.[4]

Theorem 5.6. If there are at least four voters, there is no collective choice rule satisfying all of (1) the Chernoff condition, (2) the Pareto condition, (3) nonweak dictatorship, (4) independence of irrelevant alternatives, and (5) positive responsiveness.

As in the case of Theorem 5.3, we will establish this result by proving an even stronger proposition. By Lemma 5.1, the Chernoff condition implies base acyclicity, and it is obvious from the definitions that base acyclicity implies base triple acyclicity.

Theorem 5.7. If there are at least four voters, there is no collective choice rule satisfying all of (1) base triple acyclicity, (2) the Pareto condition,

4. The existence of collective choice rules that satisfy the Chernoff condition but are neither path independent nor rational is guaranteed by the following proposition, which is easily verified: the rule that makes the collective choice equal to the union of individuals' choices from the feasible set satisfies the Chernoff condition, if the individuals' preferences satisfy that condition as well. The group's choice function is precisely the one given in Example 5.1 if the group has two members with the following acyclic preferences: $x P_1 y$, $y P_1 z$, $x I_1 z$, $x P_2 z$, $z P_2 y$, $x I_2 y$ and the collective choice rule is the union rule just described.

(3) nonweak dictatorship, (4) independence of irrelevant alternatives, and (5) positive responsiveness.

PROOF. We will proceed in two steps. First, assuming all of the conditions in the theorem except nonweak dictatorship, we will show that there exists a voter who is weakly decisive for some pair of alternatives. We will then show that individual is a weak dictator, contradicting the third condition in the theorem.

STEP 1. We must show that if a collective choice rule satisfies base triple acyclicity, the Pareto condition, independence, and positive responsiveness, there exists an individual $i \in N$ and alternatives $x, y \in X$ such that

$$(x P_i y \ \& \ y P_j x \text{ for all } j \neq i) \Rightarrow x \in C(\{x, y\}). \qquad (5.5)$$

Suppose (5.5) is false. Then for all $x, y \in X$ and all $i \in N$, if a profile a is such that under it $x P_i y$ and $y P_j x$ for all $j \in N \setminus \{i\}$, then $C^a(\{x, y\}) = \{y\}$. Let V be a smallest decisive set; V is decisive for some x against y. Our assumption implies that V contains at least two individuals, say, 1 and 2. Partition V as $V = \{1, 2\} \cup V^*$. Consider profile b:

1:	x, y, z
$\{2\} \cup V^*$:	z, x, y
$N \setminus V$:	y, z, x.

By the definition of V, $\{x\} = C^b(\{x, y\})$, and by assumption, $C^b(\{x, z\}) = \{z\}$. By base triple acyclicity, $z \in C^b(\{y, z\})$. Now consider profile c:

1:	x, y
2:	y, x
V^*:	x, y
$N \setminus V$:	y, x.

Since V is a smallest decisive set, $y \in C^c(\{x, y\})$. Next consider profile d:

$$\begin{array}{ll} 1: & (x, y, z) \\ 2: & z, y, x \\ V^*: & x, z, y \\ N \setminus V: & y, x, z. \end{array}$$

Comparing profiles c and d, and noting the conclusion drawn from the former, positive responsiveness and independence require that $\{y\} = C^d(\{x, y\})$. Comparing profiles b and d, the same two axioms require that $\{z\} = C^d(\{y, z\})$. Base triple acyclicity then yields $z \in C^d(\{x, z\})$. Next examine profile e:

$$\begin{array}{ll} 1: & z, x \\ 2: & z, x \\ V^*: & x, z \\ N \setminus V: & x, z. \end{array}$$

Comparing profiles d and e, positive responsiveness and independence require that $\{z\} = C^e(\{x, z\})$. This conclusion and independence imply that $\{1, 2\}$ is decisive for z against x, so that $V = \{1, 2\}$. Finally, examine profile f:

$$\begin{array}{ll} 1: & x, y, z \\ 2: & z, x, y \\ N \setminus V: & y, z, x. \end{array}$$

Since V is decisive for x against y, $\{x\} = C^f(\{x, y\})$, while our assumption yields $\{y\} = C^f(\{y, z\})$. By base triple acyclicity, $x \in C^f(\{x, z\})$, in contradiction to our assumption. Thus we have shown that voter 1 is weakly decisive for x against z.

Step 2. In this step we show that if voter 1 is weakly decisive for x against y, then he or she is a weak dictator if there are at least four voters. In the presence of positive responsiveness, this can be established by proving that for all $s, t \in X$,

$$(s P_1 t \ \& \ t P_j s \text{ for all } j \in N \setminus \{1\}) \Rightarrow s \in C(\{s, t\}). \qquad (5.6)$$

We will prove only that for all $t \in X$,

$$(x P_1 t \ \& \ t P_j x \text{ for all } j \in N \setminus \{1\}) \Rightarrow s \in C(\{x, t\}). \qquad (5.7)$$

The steps from (5.7) to (5.6) are sufficiently similar to the ones we use in establishing (5.7) that they may safely be skipped. To prove (5.7), we first examine profile a:

1:	x, y, t
2:	$(x, y), t$
3:	y, t, x
4:	y, t, x
$N \setminus \{1, 2, 3, 4\}$:	y, t, x.

By step 1 and positive responsiveness, $C^a(\{x, y\}) = \{x\}$. By the Pareto condition, $C^a(\{y, t\}) = \{y\}$. By base triple acyclicity, $x \in C^a(\{x, t\})$. Now consider profile b:

1:	y, x, t
2:	y, x, t
3:	t, y, x
4:	$y, (x, t)$
$N \setminus \{1, 2, 3, 4\}$:	t, y, x.

Comparing profiles a and b, positive responsiveness and independence require that $C^b(\{x, t\}) = \{x\}$. By the Pareto condition, $C^b(\{x, y\}) = \{y\}$. Base triple acyclicity then implies $y \in C^b(\{y, t\})$. Next examine profile c:

1:	x, y, t
2:	y, t, x
3:	(x, y, t)
4:	y, t, x
$N \setminus \{1, 2, 3, 4\}$:	t, y, x.

By Step 1 and positive responsiveness, $C^c(\{x, y\}) = \{x\}$. Comparing profiles b and c, positive responsiveness and independence require that $C^c(\{y, t\}) = \{y\}$. Another application of base triple acyclicity yields $x \in C^c(\{x, t\})$. Next consider profile d:

1:	y, x, t
2:	t, y, x
3:	y, x, t
4:	t, y, x
$N \setminus \{1, 2, 3, 4\}$:	t, y, x.

Comparing profiles c and d, positive responsiveness and independence require $C^d(\{x, t\}) = \{x\}$; by the Pareto condition $\{y\} = C^d(\{x, y\})$. Base triple acyclicity then yields $y \in C^d(\{y, t\})$. Finally, consider profile e:

1:	x, y, t
2:	$t, (x, y)$
3:	y, t, x
4:	$(y, t), x$
$N \setminus \{1, 2, 3, 4\}$:	t, y, x.

Comparing profiles d and e, positive responsiveness and independence again require $\{y\} = C^e(\{y, t\})$. By step 1 and positive responsiveness, $C^e(\{x, y\}) = \{x\}$. A final application of base triple acyclicity yields $x \in C^e(\{x, t\})$. In view of the independence axiom, this proves (5.7).

■

Concluding Remarks

Arrow and subsequent writers have modeled the output of collective decision-making institutions as binary social preference relations, both by analogy with consumers' preferences in demand theory and as a generalization of Condorcet's proposal that any alternative that receives a majority of votes against every other candidate should be chosen. Such a view, as the well-known series of impossibility theorems demonstrates, is inconsistent with a set of several democratic requirements. In this essay we have shown that binary rationality per se is not the culprit in these theorems.

We have taken a more general view, and required only that the group makes a nonempty choice from every finite feasible set of alternatives. Several weak conditions imposed on the resultant choice functions are each shown to contradict one or more of the same democratic requirements, even if the choices have no binary rationalization.

5.4. References

[1] Arrow, K. J., "Rational Choice Functions and Orderings," *Economica NS* **26**, 1959, 121–127.
[2] Arrow, K. J., *Social Choice and Individual Values,* New York: Wiley, 1951; 2nd edn., 1963.
[3] Blair, D. H., "Possibility Theorems for Non-binary Social Choice Functions," unpublished manuscript.
[4] Blair, D. H., "Path-Independent Social Choice Functions: A Further Result," *Econometrica* **43**, 1975, 173–174.
[5] Bordes, G., "Alpha-Rationality and Social Choice: A General Possibility Theorem," unpublished manuscript.
[6] Brown, D. J., "Acyclic Aggregation over a Finite Set of Alternatives," unpublished manuscript, 1973.
[7] Brown, D. J., "Aggregation of Preferences," *Quarterly Journal of Economics* **89**, 1975, 456–469.
[8] Chernoff, H., "Rational Selection of Decision Functions," *Econometrica* **22**, 1954, 423–443.
[9] Fishburn, P. C., *The Theory of Social Choice,* Princeton, N.J.: Princeton University Press, 1973.
[10] Gibbard, A., "Social Choice and the Arrow Conditions," unpublished manuscript. Published subsequently in *Economics and Philosophy* **30**, 2014, 269–284.
[11] Hansson, B., "Choice Structures and Preference Relations," *Synthese* **18**, 1968, 443–458.
[12] Herzberger, H. G., "Ordinal Preference and Rational Choice," *Econometrica* **41**, 1973, 187–237.
[13] Kelly, J. S., "Two Impossibility Theorems on Independence of Path," unpublished manuscript.

[14] Mas-Colell, A., and H. Sonnenschein, “General Possibility Theorems for Group Decision Functions,” *Review of Economic Studies* **39**, 1972, 185–192.

[15] Parks, R. P., “Choice Paths and Rational Choice,” unpublished manuscript.

[16] Plott, C. R., “Ethics, Social Choice Theory, and the Theory of Economic Policy,” *Journal of Mathematical Sociology* **2**, 1972, 181–208.

[17] Plott, C. R., “Path Independence, Rationality and Social Choice,” *Econometrica* **41**, 1973, 1075–1091.

[18] Plott, C. R., “Rationality and Relevance in Social Choice Theory,” Social Science Working Paper, 5, California Institute of Technology, Pasadena, 1971.

[19] Richter, M. K., “Revealed Preference Theory,” *Econometrica* **34**, 1966, 635–645.

[20] Richter, M. K., “Rational Choice,” J. Chipman, M. K. Richter, and H. Sonnenschein, eds., *Preferences, Utility, and Demand,* New York: Harcourt Brace Jovanovich, 1971, 29–58.

[21] Schwartz, T., “On the Possibility of Rational Policy Evaluation,” *Theory and Decision* **1**, 1970, 89–106.

[22] Sen, A. K., “Quasi-Transitivity, Rational Choice and Collective Decisions,” *Review of Economic Studies* **36**, 1969, 381–393.

[23] Sen, A. K., *Collective Choice and Social Welfare,* San Francisco: Holden-Day, 1970.

[24] Sen, A. K., “Choice Functions and Revealed Preference,” *Review of Economic Studies* **38**, 1971, 307–317.

[25] Suzumura, K., “Rational Choice and Revealed Preference,” *Review of Economic Studies* **43**, 1976, 149–158. Essay 1 of this volume.

[26] Suzumura, K., “General Possibility Theorems for Path-Independent Social Choice,” Kyoto Institute of Economic Research, Discussion Paper 77, 1974.

ESSAY 6

Remarks on the Theory of Collective Choice

Ever since the so-called paradox of voting was generalized by Arrow [2] to every democratic method of collective decision making, a vast literature has appeared (a) trying to circumvent Arrow's difficulty by weakening some of his conditions (Bordes [6]; Hansson [12]; Plott [15]; Sen [20]); (b) proposing some other paradoxes in the theory of collective choice (Batra and Pattanaik [3]; Hansson [11]; Schwartz [19]; Sen [21]), and (c) casting doubts about the relevance of Arrow's theorem to the theory of Paretian welfare economics (Bergson [4]; Little [14], Samuelson [17; 18]). The purpose of this essay is to make some remarks on these recent developments in the theory of collective choice.

The first part of the essay deals with the question of how much one needs to weaken Arrow's collective rationality condition in order to avoid his impossibility result. As is well known, Arrow [2] imposed the collective rationality condition that the society can arrange all conceivable alternatives in order of preference and that, if some available set of alternatives is specified, the society must choose therefrom the best alternative(s) with respect to that preference ordering. We will consider two conditions of consistent choice that are weaker than that of Arrow. The first condition requires that, if an alternative x is chosen over another alternative y in binary choice, y should

First published in *Economica* **43**, 1976, pp. 381–390. Thanks are due to Professors A. K. Sen and G. Bordes for their comments. They are, of course, not responsible for any remaining deficiencies of this essay. Thanks are also due to an anonymous referee and the editor of *Economica* for their helpful comments.

never be chosen from any set of alternatives that contains x; the second condition requires that, if x is chosen over y in binary choice, there exists no choice situation in which y is chosen and x is available but rejected. (In the second case y can be chosen if x is also chosen, while in the first case y cannot be chosen anyway.) There seems to be a gulf that separates possibility from impossibility in between these two seemingly similar consistency conditions. It will be shown that the first consistency requirement is *incompatible* with essentially Arrovian conditions on the collective choice rule, while the second consistency condition is *compatible* with the same conditions. Although the difference between these consistency requirements is rather subtle, the implication thereof in the context of the impossibility result is therefore dramatically different.

Lest we should be too satisfied, we must hasten to add that no collective choice rule satisfying our second consistency requirement can be free from the paradox of a Paretian liberal (Sen [21]; Batra and Pattanaik [3]).

The Arrow-Sen theory is then contrasted with the Bergson-Samuelson "new" welare economics. In view of doing this, it is convenient to remember that Arrow's incompatible conditions on collective choice rules can be classified into two categories. The first category consists of statements that apply to any *fixed* profile of individual preference relations, while the second category refers to the responsiveness of the collective choice to the *variations* in profiles. (The first category embraces the *Pareto rule,* while the second category consists of the condition of *collective rationality,* the *independence of irrelevant alternatives,* and *nondictatorship*. See Sections 6.1 and 6.2 below for the definition of these conditions.) Bergson [4], Little [14], and Samuelson [17; 18] agreed with Arrow as far as his conditions of the first category were concerned. It was only when Arrow went on to introduce some conditions of the second category that Bergson, Little, and Samuelson came to deny the reasonableness and/or necessity thereof. Let us, therefore, fix a profile of individual preference relations. What we call the *Bergson-Samuelson social welfare ordering* is an ordering R on the set X of all social alternatives such that, if a state x is Pareto-noninferior (resp. Pareto-superior) to a state y with respect to the given profile, then x is not less preferred (resp. preferred) to y in terms of R. (Incidentally, the Bergson-Samuleson social welfare function is a numerical function u such that $u(x) \geq u(y)$ if and only if xRy for all states x and y in X.) Now we raise the problem of whether we can define such a social welfare ordering corresponding to a given profile. The answer is in the affirmative if each and every individual preference relation satisfies the strong consistency condition of transitivity. The major result in this section establishes that a social welfare ordering exists if and only if the Paretian unanimity rule corresponding to the given profile satisfies what we call the *axiom of Suzumura consistency*. (Thus, even if intransitive individual preference is countenanced, we may still have a well-defined social welfare ordering.) This will be done by proving a general theorem on the extension of a binary relation.

What emerges as a result of our investigation is an ever sharper contrast between the *variable* profile framework of the Arrow-Sen theory, on the one hand, and the *fixed* profile framework of the Bergson-Little-Samuelson theory, on the other.

All the proofs are relegated to the final section, which can be neglected by those who are not interested in technical details.

6.1. Rationality and Revealed Preference

For the sake of logical clarity, we discuss in this section the concept of rationality and that of revealed preference in abstraction from the problem of collective decision. The heart of our argument is the implication diagram given at the end of this section.

Let X be the set of all alternatives that are mutually exclusive. We assume that X contains at least three distinct elements. Also let $\mathcal{S}$ stand for the family of nonempty subsets of X, containing all the pairs and all the triples taken from X (and possibly more). A preference relation is a binary relation on X. Let R be a binary relation. By xRy (or, equivalently, $(x, y) \in R$) we mean that x is at least as good as y. By xPy and xIy we mean, respectively, (xRy and *not* yRx) and (xRy and yRx). An R is said to be *reflexive* if (xRx for all $x \in X$), *complete* if (xRy and/or yRx for all $x, y \in X$), *transitive* if (xRy and $yRz \Rightarrow xRz$ for all $x, y, z \in X$), and *acyclic* if ($x^1Px^2 \ldots x^tPx^1$ for no finite subset $\{x^1, x^2, \ldots, x^t\}$ of X). A *quasi ordering* is a reflexive and transitive relation and an *ordering* is a complete quasi ordering.

Given a preference relation R and an $S \in \mathcal{S}$, we define

$$G_R(S) = \{x \in S \mid xRy \text{ for all } y \in S\}. \tag{6.1}$$

Clearly, $G_R(S)$ is a subset of S such that $x^* \in G_R(S)$ has the following property: x^* is at least as good as any alternative in S.

A *choice function* on $\mathcal{S}$ is a function C that assigns a nonempty subset $C(S)$ of S to each $S \in \mathcal{S}$. (It is intended that $S \in \mathcal{S}$ represents a set of available alternatives and $C(S)$ represents the set of chosen elements from S.) We say that C is *rational* (R) if there exists a preference relation R, to be called a *rationalization* of C, such that

$$C(S) = G_R(S) \quad \text{for all } S \in \mathcal{S}. \tag{6.2}$$

In other words, a choice function is rational if it can be construed as a result of preference optimization. (It should be noted that the concept of rational choice in itself has nothing to do with the transitivity of rationalization.) We say, in particular, that C is *full rational* FR if (a) C is rational and (b) a rationalization thereof is an ordering. Arrow [1] has shown that C is FR if and only if, for all S_1 and S_2 in $\mathcal{S}$ such that $S_1 \subseteq S_2$ and $S_1 \cap C(S_2) \neq \emptyset$, $S_1 \cap C(S_2) = C(S_1)$ holds true. (In other words, it is required that if some elements are chosen out of S_2, and then the range of alternatives is narrowed to S_1 but still contains some previously chosen elements, no previously rejected element becomes chosen and no previously chosen element becomes unchosen.) This *Arrovian property* A is to be decomposed into what we call the *Bordes's property* B and the *Chernoff's property* C. We say that C satisfies B (resp. C) if and only if, for all S_1 and S_2 in $\mathcal{S}$ such that $S_1 \subseteq S_2$ and $S_1 \cap C(S_2) \neq \emptyset$, $S_1 \cap C(S_2) \supseteq C(S_1)$ (resp. $S_1 \cap C(S_2) \subseteq C(S_1)$). Property B requires that if some elements are chosen out of S_2 and then the range of alternatives is narrowed to S_1 but still contains some previously chosen elements, no previously unchosen element becomes chosen. Property C requires, on the other hand, that if some elements of subset S_1 of S_2 are chosen from S_2, then they should be chosen from S_1. Property B is due to Bordes [6], while property C is named after Chernoff [8], although in the present context it is better known as Sen's condition α (see Sen, [20; 22]).

An alternative formulation of the concept of rational choice goes as follows. Given a preference relation R and an $S \in \mathcal{S}$, we define

$$M_R(S) = \{x \in S \mid \textit{not } yPx \text{ for all } y \in S\}.$$

We say that a choice function C is *M-rational* if there exists a preference relation R, to be called an *M-rationalization,* such that $C(S) = M_R(S)$ for all $S \in \mathcal{S}$. In view of some arguments by Herzberger [13] and Schwartz [19] in favor of the M-rationality concept, it may be worth our while to investigate how M-rationality will fare in the context of the impossibility results. In order to do so, let C be M-rational with an M-rationalization R. Let us define a binary relation R' by $\{xR'y \Leftrightarrow (xRy \text{ or } not\ yRx)\}$ for all x and y in X. It can easily be shown that $M_R(S) = G_{R'}(S)$ for all $S \in \mathcal{S}$. Therefore, *if C is M-rational, it is rational*. This being the case, the concept of M-rationality has no special role to play in the impossibility exercises (see, however, Suzumura [24]).

So much for rational choice functions. Let us now introduce some axioms of revealed preference. Our *first axiom of revealed preference* (FARP) and *second axiom of revealed preference* (SARP) consider the binary choice of x over $y : \{x\} = C(\{x, y\})$. In this case, FARP requires that there should be no choice situation $S \in \mathcal{S}$ such that $x \in S$ and $y \in C(S)$, while SARP requires that there should be no choice situation $S \in \mathcal{S}$ such that $x \in S \setminus C(S)$ and $y \in C(S)$. What these two axioms essentially say is that the choice pattern revealed in binary choice should never be contradicted in nonbinary choice. Our third revealed preference axiom, which we called in Blair et al. [5] *base triple acyclicity* (BTA), is concerned solely with binary choices. It requires that if x is chosen over y in binary choice and y is chosen over z in binary choice, x should never be rejected in the binary choice between x and z : $\{x\} = C(\{x, y\})$ and $\{y\} = C(\{y, z\}) \Rightarrow x \in C(\{x, z\})$ for all $x, y, z \in X$. Finally, we introduce the *weak axiom of revealed preference* (WARP), due originally to Samuelson [16], who introduced it in the context of consumers' behavior. It says that, if $\{x \in C(S)$ and $y \in S \setminus C(S)\}$ for some $S \in \mathcal{S}$, then $\{x \in S'$ and $y \in C(S')\}$ for no $S' \in \mathcal{S}$. Namely, if in some choice situation x is chosen while y, though available, is rejected, then y should never be chosen in the presence of x.

Essential for our present purpose is an implication network among these various requirements on the choice function, which is summarized in the implication diagram of Figure 6.1. Here, a double-headed arrow indicates equivalence and a single-headed arrow indicates implication. Some of these arrows have been established by Arrow [1] and Sen [20], while the remaining ones will be proved in Section 6.5.

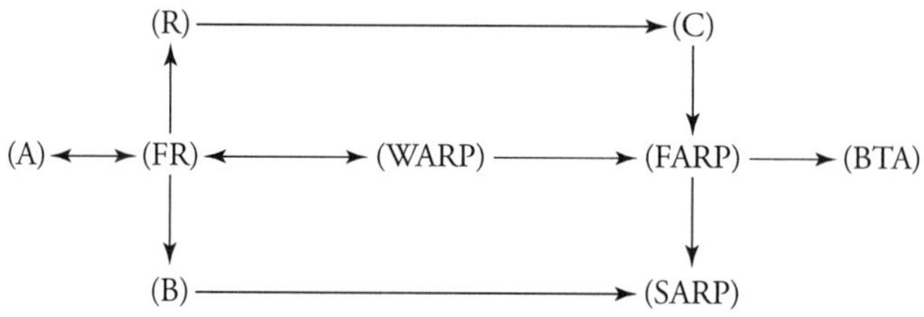

Figure 6.1. Logical Implications

6.2. Arrow's Theorem and Collective Rationality

We are ready to discuss the problem originally posed by Arrow [2]. Suppose that there exist n individuals in the society and let $N = \{1, \dots, i, \dots, n\}$ stand for the index set of the individuals. In order to exclude a trivial case, we assume that $2 \leq n < +\infty$. An n-tuple of preference orderings $(R_1, \dots, R_n)$, one ordering for each individual, will be called a *profile* (of individual preference orderings). Corresponding to R_i, we define P_i by $x P_i y \Leftrightarrow (x R_i y$ and *not* $y R_i x)$. The problem of collective choice is to find a function f, to be called a *collective choice rule* (CCR), which aggregates a profile into a collective choice function:

$$C = f(R_1, \dots, R_n). \tag{6.3}$$

If an $S \in \mathcal{S}$ is specified as a set of available alternatives, $C(S)$ represents the set of socially chosen elements from S when the profile $(R_1, \dots, R_n)$ prevails. In what follows, we will always assume *universal domain* (U) for f: f should be able to aggregate all logically possible profiles. As a matter of terminology, we say that f satisfies the property ω if f always yields a choice function having the property ω. (For example, if C determined by (6.3) is always rational, we say that f is rational in itself.) Some other conditions on CCR will be introduced when and where necessity dictates.

Arrow [2] has shown that *there exists no* CCR *that satisfies universal domain* (U), *full rationality* (FR), *the independence of irrelevant alternatives* (IIA), *the Pareto rule* (P), and *nondictatorship* (ND). Here the conditions IIA, P, and ND are defined as follows. Let x and y be any two alternatives. A CCR f is said to satisfy condition IIA if, for any two profiles $(R_1, \dots, R_n)$ and $(R'_1, \dots, R'_n)$ such that $(x R_i y \Leftrightarrow x R'_i y$ and $y R_i x \Leftrightarrow y R'_i x)$ for all

$i \in N$, we have $C(\{x, y\}) = C'(\{x, y\})$; condition P if, for any profile $(R_1, \ldots, R_n)$ such that $x P_i y$ for all $i \in N$, we have $\{x\} = C(\{x, y\})$ and condition ND if there exists no individual $i \in N$ such that, for any profile $(R_1, \ldots, R_n)$, $x P_i y \Rightarrow \{x\} = C(\{x, y\})$. Throughout in what follows, we let $C = f(R_1, \ldots, R_n)$ and $C' = f(R'_1, \ldots, R'_n)$.

Among these incompatible conditions on CCR, P and ND can hardly be objectionable, so that the culprit for Arrow's phantom should be sought among U, FR, and IIA. In what follows, our attention will be focused upon condition FR. (The relevance of condition U is extensively discussed in Sen [21, Chapter 10] in the context of simple majority decision, while condition IIA is critically examined by Hansson [12].) Can we circumvent Arrow's difficulty by weakening FR to some reasonable extent?

In order to prepare for our answer to this question, it is necessary to introduce some more conditions on CCR. First, there is the condition of the *nonweak dictatorship* (NWD). Let x and y be any two alternatives. We say that f satisfies condition NWD if there exists no $i \in N$ such that, for any profile $(R_1, \ldots, R_n)$, $x P_i y \Rightarrow x \in C(\{x, y\})$. Clearly, NWD is a stronger version of ND. Second, there is the condition of *positive responsiveness* PR. Let $i \in N$ be any prescribed individual and let x and y be any two alternatives. We say that f satisfies condition PR if (a) $(R_1, \ldots, R_n)$ is a profile resulting in $x \in C(\{x, y\})$, and (b) $(R'_1, \ldots, R'_n)$ is another profile with $R_j = R'_j$ for all $j \in N \setminus \{i\}$ and $\{(y P_i x \text{ and } x I'_i y) \text{ or } (x I_i y \text{ and } x P'_i y)\}$, then $\{x\} = C'(\{x, y\})$.

We now put forward two theorems that are relevant in the context of the question raised in this section.

Theorem 6.1. If $n \geq 4$, there exists no CCR that satisfies U, FARP, P, IIA, NWD, and PR.

Theorem 6.2. There exists a CCR that satisfies U, SARP, P, IIA, NWD, and PR.

Note that the impossibility in Theorem 6.1 is turned into the possibility in Theorem 6.2 by simply replacing condition FARP by condition SARP. Put differently, in the presence of U, P, IIA, NWD, and PR, the gulf that separates possibility from impossibility is located by Theorem 6.1 and Theorem 6.2 as being in between FARP and SARP.

6.3. Paradise Lost

It is now time to make some observations by comparing Arrow's theorem, Theorem 6.1 and Theorem 6.2. First, let us compare Theorem 6.1 with Arrow's theorem. In Theorem 6.1, Arrow's rationality condition FR is substantially weakened into FARP, but ND is strengthened into NWD and PR (which does not appear in Arrow's theorem). Therefore, strictly speaking, Theorem 6.1 is not a generalization of Arrow's theorem. It may, however, be claimed that NWD and PR are still reasonable conditions on a democratic collective choice rule and our Theorem 6.1 may be taken to mean that Arrow's difficulty cannot be gotten rid of even if his rationality condition FR is substantially weakened.

Let us next compare Theorem 6.1 with Theorem 6.2. We have noticed already that, although FARP and SARP look quite similar, their implications in the context of collective choice are very disparate. The contrast being sharp, we might be tempted to say that Arrovian impossibility depended squarely on an unjustifiably strong collective rationality requirement such as FARP and that if we replaced FARP by a weaker SARP, the Arrovian phantom would go. Life would be happier, then, for democrats if this could really be the end of the story. Unfortunately, however, this is not the case. The gist is that the theory of collective choice is full of disturbing paradoxes and Arrow's theorem is only one eminent example.

Two more conditions on the CCR are to be introduced. The first one is a strengthened version of the Pareto rule (P). Let S be any set in $\mathcal{S}$ and let $(R_1, \ldots, R_n)$ be any profile. Let y be any point in S. We say that f satisfies the *weak Pareto rule* (WP) if $\{(x P_i y \text{ for all } i \in N) \text{ for some } x \in S\} \Rightarrow y \notin C(S)$. In words, y should not be chosen out of S if there exists an x in S that is unanimously preferred to y. The second condition is what Sen [21] called the condition of *minimal liberalism* (ML), which reads as follows. There are at least two individuals such that for each of them there is at least one pair of alternatives over which he is decisive; that is, there is a pair of x, y such that if he prefers x (resp. y) to y (resp. x), then society should prefer x (resp. y) to y (resp. x) (Sen [21, p. 154]).

Sen [21] has shown that *there exists no CCR that satisfies universal domain (U), rationality (R), the weak Pareto rule (WP) and minimal liberalism (ML).* This so-called liberal paradox has been generalized by Batra and Pattanaik [3], from which it follows that *there exists no CCR that satisfies U, SARP, WP and ML.* This being the case, we cannot but say that, although the replacement of FARP by SARP fares quite well in exorcising the Arrovian phantom, it cannot let the CCR be free from Sen's liberal paradox. The cloud is thicker here because the independence condition IIA (which has also been suspected to be a possible culprit for Arrow's difficulty) does not play any role at all in establishing Sen's paradox. Our conclusion is that, even if the collective rationality condition is substantially weakened, we cannot eradicate the paradoxes of collective decision.

6.4. Bergson-Samuelson Social Welfare Ordering

We now discuss the logical foundation of the Bergson-Samuelson theory of Paretian welfare economics. It has long been lamented that Arrow gave his collective choice rule, which is, in our terminology, a full rational CCR, the name *social welfare function*. Clearly, it is completely different from the Bergson-Samuelson social welfare function, which, according to Little, is "a 'process or rule' which would indicate the best economic state as a function of a changing environment (i.e., changing sets of possibilities defined by different economic transformation functions), *the individual tastes being given*" (Little [14, p. 423], Little's italics). It is also claimed that "the only axiom restricting Bergson social welfare function (of individualistic type) is a 'tree' property of Pareto-optimality type" (Samuelson [17, p. 49]). The purpose of the rest of this essay is to examine the possibility of this *fixed* profile theory of Paretian welfare economics.

Let us, therefore, fix a profile $(R_1, \ldots, R_n)$ of the individual preference relations. Let a binary relation Q, to be called the *Pareto unanimity relation,* be defined by $(xQy \Leftrightarrow xR_iy$ for all $i \in N)$ for all $x, y, \in X$. The asymmetric component P_Q and the symmetric component I_Q of Q are defined, respectively, by $(xP_Qy \Leftrightarrow xQy$ and *not* $yQx)$ and $(xI_Qy \Leftrightarrow xQy$ and $yQx)$.

A *social welfare ordering* (SWO) in the sense of Bergson and Samuelson is an ordering R such that $\{(xQy \Rightarrow xRy)$ and $(xP_Qy \Rightarrow (xRy$ and *not* $yRx))\}$ for all $x, y \in X$. (In words, an SWO is an ordering that preserves whatever information the Pareto unanimity relation can tell us about the wishes of the individuals.) A *social welfare function* (SWF) in the sense of Bergson and Samuelson is a numerical representation u of $R : u(x) \geq u(y) \Leftrightarrow xRy$ for all $x, y \in X$.

Our problem is to examine the existence of an SWO for a fixed profile. Thanks to the work of Debreu [9] and others, we know that an SWO may not have an SWF representing it. It may, however, be said that what is important is an SWO but not its numerical representation.

Suppose that $R_1, \ldots, R_n$ are orderings. In this case Q is a quasi ordering, so that a corollary of Szpilrajn's theorem (Fishburn [10, Lemma 15.4]) assures us of the existence of an SWO corresponding to the given profile. How about the case where $R_i (i \in N)$ is not necessarily transitive? Generally speaking, we cannot have an SWO in this case, as the following examples where $n = 3$ and $X = \{x, y, z\}$ exhibit.

$$\text{(A)}\ \begin{array}{l} xI_1y,\ yI_1z,\ zP_1x \\ yI_2z,\ zI_2x,\ xP_2y \\ zI_3x,\ xI_3y,\ yP_3z \end{array} \qquad \text{(B)}\ \begin{array}{l} xP_1y,\ yI_1z,\ zI_1x \\ yI_2z,\ zI_2x,\ xP_2y \\ zI_3x,\ xI_3y,\ yP_3z \end{array}$$

(Notice here that in both profiles individual strict preference is transitive but individual indifference is not.) In case A, we have xP_Qy, yP_Qz and zP_Qx, so that Q is cyclic and there exists no ordering that can subsume this Q. In case B, we have xP_Qy, yP_Qz, and xI_Qz. Although this Q is acyclic, we cannot still have an ordering subsuming it. Under what condition can Q have an ordering that subsumes it?

Our answer will be given via a general theorem on the extension of a binary relation. Let R be a given binary relation. A t-tuple of alternatives $(x^1, x^2, \ldots, x^t)$ is called a *PR-cycle* of order t if we have $x^1Px^2R \ldots Rx^tRx^1$, where P is the asymmetric component of R. We say that R is *Suzumura-consistent*—*S-consistent* for short—if there exists no *PR*-cycle of any finite order. It is clear that an S-consistent binary relation is acyclic but not vice versa. An ordering R^* is said to be an *ordering extension* of R if $\{(xRy \Rightarrow xR^*y)$ and $(xPy \Rightarrow xP^*y)\}$ for all $x, y \in X$, where P^* is the asymmetric component of R^*. We can now state a theorem on the existence of an extended ordering.

THEOREM 6.3. A binary relation R has an ordering extension R^* if and only if R is S-consistent.

In passing we note that Champernowne [7] introduced a concept of consistent preference (or probability) relations, which is similar to but distinct from ours. We say that a t-tuple $(x^1, x^2, \ldots, x^t)$ is a *C-cycle* of order t if $x^1(P \cup N)x^2R \ldots Rx^tRx^1$, where $\{x^1(P \cup N)x^2 \Leftrightarrow (x^1Px^2 \text{ or } x^1Nx^2)\}$

and $\{x^1 N x^2 \Leftrightarrow (\textit{not } x^1 R x^2 \text{ and } \textit{not } x^2 R x^1)\}$. R is said to be *Champernowne-consistent* if there exists no C-cycle of any finite order. Unfortunately it turns out that R is Champernowne-consistent if and only if it is transitive. Clearly we have only to show that Champernowne consistency implies transitivity. Suppose that R is not transitive. Then we have xRy, yRz but not xRz for some $x, y, z \in X$. Therefore we have $z(P \cup N)xRyRz$ so that (z, x, y) is a C-cycle of order 3. In order to show that our concept of consistency does not reduce to transitivity, we give an example. Let $X = \{x, y, z\}$ and let R be defined by xPy, yRz and xNz.

It follows from Theorem 6.3 that a social welfare ordering exists for a profile $(R_1, \ldots, R_n)$ if and only if the Pareto unanimity relation Q corresponding to this profile is S-consistent. In this context, it is worth our while to notc that the transitivity of an R_i implies that of strict preference P_i and of indifference I_i, and cases against transitive indifference are plenty. This being the case, it is interesting to see that we can define an SWO corresponding to a profile $(R_1, \ldots, R_n)$ even if R_i is not necessarily transitive so far as Q satisfies the axiom of S-consistency. The contrast between the *variable* profile framework of the Arrow-Sen theory, which leads us to logical impossibility even under weakened rationality requirements, and the *fixed* profile framework of the Bergson-Samuelson theory, which can even accommodate some individual preference intransitivity, is made sharper than ever.

6.5. Proofs

Proof of the Implication Diagram. First, we show that C implies FARP. Let x and y be such that $C(\{x, y\}) = \{x\}$ and take a superset $S \in \mathcal{S}$ of $\{x, y\}$. By virtue of C, we have $\{x, y\} \cap C(S) \subseteq C(\{x, y\})$, so that $y \notin C(S)$.

Second, we show that FARP implies BTA. If BTA is not satisfied by C, there exist x, y, and z in X such that $C(\{x, y\}) = \{x\}$, $C(\{y, z\}) = \{y\}$ and $C(\{x, z\}) = \{z\}$. Suppose that C satisfies FARP. Then x does not belong to $C(\{x, y, z\})$ because $\{z\} = C(\{x, z\})$. Similarly, neither y nor z belong to $C(\{x, y, z\})$. Thus $C(\{x, y, z\}) = \emptyset$, a contradiction. Therefore FARP implies BTA.

Third, it will be shown that B implies SARP. If C does not satisfy SARP, there exist $x, y \in X$ and $S \in \mathcal{S}$ such that $C(\{x, y\}) = \{x\}$, $x \in S \setminus C(S)$ and $y \in C(S)$. Let $S' = \{x, y\}$. Then $S' \subseteq S$, $S' \cap C(S) \neq \emptyset$, but $x \notin S' \cap C(S)$ and $x \in C(S')$, so that B does not hold. Therefore, B implies SARP.

In order to show that a single-headed arrow in the diagram cannot in general be reversed, we put forward the following examples.

EXAMPLE 6.1. $X = \{x, y, z\}$, $\mathcal{S} = \{S_1, \ldots, S_7\}$, $S_1 = \{x\}$, $S_2 = \{y\}$, $S_3 = \{z\}$, $S_4 = \{x, y\}$, $S_5 = \{y, z\}$, $S_6 = \{x, z\}$, $S_7 = X$, $C(S_t) = S_t$ $(t = 1, 2, 3)$, $C(S_4) = S_1$, $C(S_5) = S_2$, $C(S_6) = S_3$, and $C(S_7) = S_7$.

EXAMPLE 6.2. The same as Example 6.1 except $C(S_6) = S_6$ and $C(S_7) = S_2$.

EXAMPLE 6.3. The same as Example 6.1 except $C(S_6) = S_6$ and $C(S_7) = S_1$.

EXAMPLE 6.4. The same as Example 6.1 except $C(S_6) = S_1$.

EXAMPLE 6.5. The same as Example 6.1 except $C(S_4) = S_4$, $C(S_5) = S_5$, $C(S_6) = S_6$, and $C(S_7) = S_1$.

EXAMPLE 6.6. $X = \{w, x, y, z\}$, $\mathcal{S} = \{S_1, \ldots, S_{15}\}$, $S_1 = \{x\}$, $S_2 = \{y\}$, $S_3 = \{z\}$, $S_4 = \{w\}$, $S_5 = \{w, x\}$, $S_6 = \{w, y\}$, $S_7 = \{w, z\}$, $S_8 = \{x, y\}$, $S_9 = \{x, z\}$, $S_{10} = \{y, z\}$, $S_{11} = \{w, x, y\}$, $S_{12} = \{w, x, z\}$, $S_{13} = \{w, y, z\}$, $S_{14} = \{x, y, z\}$, $S_{15} = X$, $C(S_t) = S_t$ $(t = 1, \ldots, 10)$, $C(S_{11}) = S_8$, $C(S_{12}) = S_1$, $C(S_{13}) = S_2$, $C(S_{14}) = S_1$, and $C(S_{15}) = S_2$.

The choice function in Example 6.1 satisfies SARP but not FARP, so that SARP does not necessarily imply FARP. The choice function in Example 6.2 satisfies BTA but not FARP, so that BTA does not imply FARP in general. (Incidentally, Example 6.1 gives a choice function that satisfies SARP but not BTA, while the choice function in Example 6.2 satisfies BTA but not SARP. It follows, therefore, that SARP and BTA are generally independent.) The choice function in Example 6.3 satisfies R without satisfying FR, so that R does not imply FR. This choice function does not satisfy B, so that R does not imply B. The choice function in Example 6.4 satisfies B but not R, so that a fortiori it does not satisfy FR. Thus FR is not implied by B. The choice function given by Example 6.5 satisfies C without satisfying R, so that C does not necessarily imply R. It can be seen that the choice function in Example 6.6 satisfies FARP but not C, neither does it satisfy WARP. Therefore, FARP does not imply C in general, neither does FARP imply WARP. Finally, we note that the choice function in Example 6.6 satisfies SARP but not B, so that SARP does not imply B in general. ∎

PROOF OF THEOREM 6.1. It has been shown by Blair et al. [5] that, if $n \geq 4$, there exists no CCR that satisfies U, BTA, P, IIA, WD, and PR (see also Sen [23]). Our implication diagram shows that FARP is a stronger requirement on CCR than BTA, so that a fortiori it is incompatible with U, P, IIA, WD, and PR, establishing Theorem 6.1. ■

Let R and S be, respectively, a binary relation on X and a subset of X. A sequence of relations $\{R_S^{(n)}\}_{n=1}^{\infty}$ is then defined recursively by $R_S^{(1)} = R$, $R_S^{(n)} = RR_S^{(n-1)} = \{(x, y): (x, z) \in R, \text{ and } (z, y) \in R_S^{(n-1)} \text{ for some } z \in S\}$ $(n \geq 2)$. The *transitive closure of R relative to S* is a binary relation that is defined by $T(R \mid S) = \cup_{n=1}^{\infty} R_S^{(n)}$. For simplicity, we let $T(R) = T(R \mid X)$.

PROOF OF THEOREM 6.2. For any profile $(R_1, \ldots, R_n)$, let $N(xR_iy)$ be the number of individuals who regard x to be at least as good as y. We define an R by $[xRy \Leftrightarrow N(xR_iy) \geq N(yR_ix)]$ for all $x, y \in X$ and define a CCR F by associating a choice function $C(S) = G_{T(R|S)}(S)$ with $(R_1, \ldots, R_n)$. It is easy to verify that this CCR satisfies U, B, P, IIA, WD, and PR (see Bordes [6]). Our implication diagram shows that SARP is a weaker requirement on CCR than B, so that a fortiori it is compatible with the requirements U, P, IIA, WD, and PR. Hence Theorem 6.2. ■

PROOF OF THEOREM 6.3. (a) *Necessity proof.* Suppose that R has an ordering extension R^*. Let t be any finite positive integer and suppose that we have $x^1Px^2R \ldots Rx^t$ for some $x^1, x^2, \ldots, x^t$ in X. Then we have $x^1P^*x^2R^* \ldots R^*x^t$, which yields $x^1P^*x^t$, thanks to the transitivity of R^*. Thus we have (*not* $x^tR^*x^1$), which implies (*not* x^tRx^1). It follows that if R has an ordering extension, R has to be S-consistent.

(b) *Sufficiency proof*. Let the identity Δ be defined by $\Delta = \{(x, x) : x \in X\}$. We define a binary relation Q by

$$Q = \Delta \cup T(R). \tag{6.4}$$

We show that Q is a quasi ordering. Reflexivity is obvious. In order to show its transitivity, let $(x, y), (y, z) \in Q$. If $(x, y), (y, z) \in T(R)$, we have $(x, z) \in T(R) \subseteq Q$. If $(x, y) \in \Delta$ (resp. $(y, z) \in \Delta$), we have $x = y$ (resp. $y = z$), so that $(x, z) \in Q$ follows from $(y, z) \in Q$ (resp. $(x, y) \in Q$). Q being a quasi ordering, it has an ordering extension R^* (see, for example, Fishburn [10, Lemma 15.4]). If we can show that Q is an extension of R, we are home. For that purpose, we have to show that R is included in Q and P in P_Q (asymmetric component of Q). The former is obvious. To prove the latter, assume $(x, y) \in P$, which means $(x, y) \in R$ and $(y, x) \notin R$. From $(x, y) \in R$ it follows that $(x, y) \in Q$, so that we have only to prove that $(y, x) \notin Q$. Assume, therefore, that $(y, x) \in Q$. Clearly, $(y, x) \notin \Delta$, otherwise we cannot have $(x, y) \in P$. It follows that $(y, x) \in T(R)$. When $(x, y) \in P$ is added to this, we obtain a PR-cycle, and this contradiction proves the theorem. ■

6.6. References

[1] Arrow, K. J., "Rational Choice Functions and Orderings," *Economica* **26**, 1959, 121–127.

[2] Arrow, K. J., *Social Choice and Individual Values,* New York: Wiley, 1951; 2nd edn., 1963.

[3] Batra, R. N. and P. K. Pattanaik, "On Some Suggestions for Having Non-binary Social Choice Functions," *Theory and Decision* **3**, 1972, 1–11.

[4] Bergson, A., *Essays in Normative Economics,* Cambridge, Mass.: Harvard University Press, 1966.

[5] Blair, D. H., G. Bordes, J. S. Kelly, and K. Suzumura, "Impossibility Theorems without Collective Rationality," *Journal of Economic Theory* **13**, 1976, 361–379. Essay 5 of this volume.

[6] Bordes, G., "Consistency, Rationality, and Collective Choice," *Review of Economic Studies* **43**, 1976, 451–457.

[7] Champernowne, D. G., *Uncertainty and Estimation in Economics,* Vol. I, San Francisco: Holden-Day, 1969.

[8] Chernoff, H., "Rational Selection of Decision Functions," *Econometrica* **22**, 1954, 422–443.

[9] Debreu, G., *Theory of Value,* New York: Wiley, 1959.

[10] Fishburn, P. C., *The Theory of Social Choice,* Princeton: Princeton University Press, 1973.

[11] Hansson, B., "Group Preferences," *Econometrica* **37**, 1969, 50–54.

[12] Hansson, B., "The Independence Condition in the Theory of Social Choice," *Theory and Decision* **4**, 1973, 25–49.

[13] Herzberger, H. G., "Ordinal Preference and Rational Choice," *Econometrica* **41**, 1973, 187–237.

[14] Little, I. M. D., "Social Choice and Individual Values," *Journal of Political Economy* **60**, 1952, 422–432.

[15] Plott, C. R., "Path Independence, Rationality and Social Choice," *Econometrica* **41**, 1973, 1075–1091.

[16] Samuelson, P. A., *Foundations of Economic Analysis,* Cambridge, Mass.: Harvard University Press, 1947.

[17] Samuelson, P. A., "Arrow's Mathematical Politics," in S. Hook, ed., *Human Values and Economic Policy,* New York: New York University Press, 1967, 41–51.

[18] Samuelson, P. A., "Reaffirming the Existence of 'Reasonable' Bergson-Samuelson Social Welfare Functions," *Economica* **44**, 1977, 81–88.

[19] Schwartz, T., "On the Possibility of Rational Policy Evaluation," *Theory and Decision* **1**, 1970, 89–106.

[20] Sen, A. K., "Quasi-Transitivity, Rational Choice and Collective Decision," *Review of Economic Studies* **36**, 1969, 381–393.

[21] Sen, A. K., "The Impossibility of a Paretian Liberal," *Journal of Political Economy* **78**, 1970, 152–157.

[22] Sen, A. K., *Collective Choice and Social Welfare,* San Francisco: Holden-Day, 1970.

[23] Sen, A. K., "Social Choice Theory: A Re-examination," *Econometrica* **45**, 1977, 53–89.

[24] Suzumura, K., "Rational Choice and Revealed Preference," *Review of Economic Studies* **43**, 1976, 149–158. Essay 1 of this volume.

[25] Suzumura, K., "Houthakker's Axiom in the Theory of Rational Choice," *Journal of Economic Theory* **14**, 1977, 284–290. Essay 2 of this volume.

ESSAY 7

Arrovian Aggregation in Economic Environments: How Much Should We Know about Indifference Surfaces?

7.1. Introduction

From Arrow's celebrated theorem of social choice, it is well known that the aggregation of individual preferences into a social ordering cannot make the social ranking of any pair of alternatives depend only on individual preferences over that pair (this is the famous axiom of independence of irrelevant alternatives). Or, more precisely, it cannot do so without trespassing basic requirements of unanimity (the Pareto principle) and anonymity (even in the very weak version of nondictatorship). This raises the following question: What additional information about preferences would be needed in order to make aggregation of preferences possible, and compatible with the basic requirements of unanimity and anonymity?

In the last decades, the literature on social choice has explored several paths and given interesting answers to this question. The main avenue of

First published in *Journal of Economic Theory* **124**, 2005, pp. 22–44, as a joint paper with M. Fleurbaey and K. Tadenuma. We thank A. Leroux for a stimulating discussion, A. Trannoy and anonymous referees of *Journal of Economic Theory* for helpful comments, and participants at seminars in Cergy, Rochester, Waseda, and Hitotsubashi, and the 5th International Meeting of the Society for Social Choice and Welfare in Alicante. Financial support from the Ministry of Education, Culture, Sports, Science and Technology of Japan through Grant-in-Aid for Scientific Research No.10045010 ("Economic Institutions and Social Norms: Evolution and Transformation") and the 21st Century Center of Excellence Project on the Normative Evaluation and Social Choice of Contemporary Economic Systems is gratefully acknowledged.

research has been, after Sen [18] and d'Aspremont and Gevers [7], the introduction of information about utilities, and it has been shown that the classical social welfare functions, and less classical ones, could be obtained with the Arrovian axiomatic method by letting the social preferences take account of specific kinds of utility information with interpersonal comparability.

In this essay, we focus on the introduction of additional information about preferences that is not of the utility sort. In other words, we retain a framework with purely ordinal and interpersonally noncomparable preferences. The kind of additional information that we study is about the shapes of indifference surfaces, and we ask how much one needs to know about indifference surfaces so as to be able to aggregate individual preferences while respecting the unanimity and anonymity requirements. The introduction of this additional information is formulated in terms of weakening Arrow's axiom of independence of irrelevant alternatives.

The model adopted here is an economic model, namely, the canonical model of division of infinitely divisible commodities among a finite set of agents. We choose to study an economic model rather than the abstract model that is now commonly used in the theory of social choice[1] for two reasons. First, it allows a more fine-grained analysis of information about preferences, because it makes it sensible to talk about marginal rates of substitution and other local notions about indifference surfaces. Second, in an economic model preferences are naturally restricted, and by considering a restricted domain we can hope to obtain positive results with less information than under an unrestricted domain.

Our first extension of informational basis is to take account of marginal rates of substitution. It turns out that such infinitesimally local information would not be enough to escape from dictatorship, and we establish an extension of Arrow's theorem. Then, it is natural to take account of the portions of indifference surfaces in some finitely sized neighborhoods of the allocations. Based on this additional information, we can construct a nondictatorial aggregation rule or *social ordering function*—SOF for short—but still anonymity cannot be attained.

The second direction of extending informational basis focuses on indifference surfaces within the corresponding "Edgeworth box." More precisely,

1. Recollect, however, that Arrow's initial presentations [1; 2] dealt with this economic model of division of commodities.

for any two allocations, we define the smallest vector of total resources that makes both allocations feasible, and take the portion of the indifference surface through each allocation in the region below the vector. The introduction of this kind of information, however, does not help us avoid dictatorship.

The third avenue relies on some fixed monotone path from the origin in the consumption space, and focuses on the points of indifference surfaces that belong to this path. The idea of referring to such a monotone path is due to Pazner and Schmeidler [16], and may be justified if the path contains relevant benchmark bundles. Making use of this additional information, and following Pazner and Schmeidler's [16] contribution, we can construct a Paretian and anonymous SOF.

Our final, the largest, extension of informational basis is to take whole indifference surfaces. Given the preceding result, a Paretian and anonymous SOF can be constructed on this informational basis.

The motivation for our research builds on many works in recent and less recent literature. Attempts to construct SOFs and similar objects embodying unanimity and equity requirements were made by Suzumura [19; 20] and Tadenuma [21]. The idea that information about whole indifference surfaces is sufficient, hinted at by Pazner and Schmeidler [16] and Maniquet [14], was made more precise in Pazner [15] and was revived by Bossert, Fleurbaey, and Van de gaer [4] and Fleurbaey and Maniquet [8; 9], who were able to construct nicely behaved SOFs on this basis. Campbell and Kelly [5] recently studied essentially the same issue in an abstract model of social choice and showed that limited information about preferences may be enough. However, their model does not have the rich structure of economic environments, and they focus only on nondictatorship and do not study how much information is needed for the stronger requirement of anonymity.

The essay is organized as follows. Section 7.2 introduces the framework and the main notions. Sections 7.3–7.5 consider the four types of extensions of the informational basis of social orderings, and present the results. Section 7.6 concludes. The appendixes contain some proofs.

7.2. Basic Definitions and Arrow's Theorem

The *population* is fixed. Let $N := \{1, \ldots, n\}$ be the set of *agents,* where $2 \leq n < \infty$. There are l *goods* indexed by $k = 1, \ldots, l$, where $2 \leq l < \infty$. Agent i's *consumption bundle* is a vector $x_i := (x_{i1}, \ldots, x_{il})$. An *allocation* is denoted $x := (x_1, \ldots, x_n)$. The *set of allocations* is $\mathbb{R}^{nl}_{+}$. The set of allocations such that no individual bundle x_i is equal to the zero vector is denoted X. Vector inequalities are denoted as usual: $\geq$, $>$, and $\gg$.

A *preordering* is a reflexive and transitive binary relation. Agent i's *preferences* are described by a complete preordering R_i (strict preference P_i, indifference I_i) on $\mathbb{R}^{l}_{+}$. A *profile of preferences* is denoted $\boldsymbol{R} := (R_1, \ldots, R_n)$. Let $\mathcal{R}$ be the set of continuous, convex, and strictly monotonic preferences over $\mathbb{R}^{l}_{+}$.

A SOF is a mapping $\bar{R}$ defined on $\mathcal{R}^n$ such that, for all $\boldsymbol{R} \in \mathcal{R}^n$, $\bar{R}(\boldsymbol{R})$ is a complete preordering on the set of allocations $\mathbb{R}^{nl}_{+}$. Let $\bar{P}(\boldsymbol{R})$ (resp. $\bar{I}(\boldsymbol{R})$) denote the strict preference (resp. indifference) relation associated to $\bar{R}(\boldsymbol{R})$.

Let π be a bijection on N. For each $x \in \mathbb{R}^{nl}_{+}$, define $\pi(x) := (x_{\pi(1)}, \ldots, x_{\pi(n)}) \in \mathbb{R}^{nl}_{+}$, and for each $\boldsymbol{R} \in \mathcal{R}^n$, define $\pi(\boldsymbol{R}) := (R_{\pi(1)}, \ldots, R_{\pi(n)}) \in \mathcal{R}^n$. Let Π be the set of all bijections on N. The basic requirements of unanimity and anonymity on which we focus in this essay are the following.

Weak Pareto. $\forall \boldsymbol{R} \in \mathcal{R}^n, \forall x, y \in \mathbb{R}^{nl}_{+}$, if $\forall i \in N$, $x_i P_i y_i$, then $x \bar{P}(\boldsymbol{R}) y$.

Anonymity. $\forall \boldsymbol{R} \in \mathcal{R}^n, \forall x, y \in \mathbb{R}^{nl}_{+}, \forall \pi \in \Pi$:

$$x \bar{R}(\boldsymbol{R}) y \Leftrightarrow \pi(x) \bar{R}(\pi(\boldsymbol{R})) \pi(y).$$

Concerning the nondictatorship form of anonymity, we only define here what dictatorship means, for convenience. Notice that it has to do only with allocations in X, that is, without the zero bundle for any agent.

Dictatorial SOF. A SOF $\bar{R}$ is *dictatorial* if there exists $i_0 \in N$ such that

$$\forall \boldsymbol{R} \in \mathcal{R}^n, \forall x, y \in X : x_{i_0} P_{i_0} y_{i_0} \Rightarrow x \bar{P}(\boldsymbol{R}) y.$$

The traditional, Arrovian, version of independence of irrelevant alternatives is as follows.

Independence of Irrelevant Alternatives (IIA). $\forall \boldsymbol{R}, \boldsymbol{R}' \in \mathcal{R}^n, \forall x, y \in \mathbb{R}^{nl}_{+}$, if $\forall i \in N$, R_i and R'_i agree on $\{x_i, y_i\}$, then $\bar{R}(\boldsymbol{R})$ and $\bar{R}(\boldsymbol{R}')$ agree on $\{x, y\}$.

IIA requires that the social ranking of any pair of allocations depends only on agents' binary preferences *over that pair*. Hence, the informational basis of construction of social orderings is very restricted.

The version of Arrow's theorem for the present canonical model of division of commodities is due to Bordes and Le Breton [3].

PROPOSITION 7.1. (Bordes and Le Breton [3]). If a SOF $\bar{R}$ satisfies weak Pareto and IIA, then it is dictatorial.

7.3. Local Extension of Informational Basis

The IIA axiom can be weakened by strengthening the premise: that is, for any two preference profiles and any pair of allocations, only when some properties about indifference surfaces associated with the two allocations coincide in addition to pairwise preferences, it is required that the social ranking over the two allocations should agree. This amounts to allowing the SOF to make use of more information about indifference surfaces when ranking each pair of allocations.

In this essay, we consider four types of extensions of the informational basis of social orderings. First, we use information about marginal rates of substitution. Economists are used to focusing on marginal rates of substitution when assessing the efficiency of an allocation, especially under convexity, since for convex preferences the marginal rates of substitution determine the half space in which the upper contour set lies. Moreover, for efficient allocations, the shadow prices enable one to compute the relative implicit income shares of different agents, thereby potentially providing a relevant measure of inequalities in the distribution of resources. Therefore, taking account of marginal rates of substitution is a natural extension of the informational basis of social choice in economic environments.

Let $C(x_i, R_i)$ denote the cone of price vectors that support the upper contour set for R_i at x_i :

$$C(x_i, R_i) := \{p \in \mathbb{R}^l \mid \forall y \in \mathbb{R}^l_+, py = px_i \Rightarrow x_i R_i y\}.$$

When preferences R_i are strictly monotonic, one has $C(x_i, R_i) \subseteq \mathbb{R}^l_{++}$ whenever $x_i \gg 0$.

IIA except Marginal Rates of Substitution (IIA-MRS). $\forall \boldsymbol{R}, \boldsymbol{R}' \in \mathcal{R}^n$, $\forall x, y \in \mathbb{R}_+^{nl}$, if $\forall i \in N$, R_i and R_i' agree on $\{x_i, y_i\}$, and

$$C(x_i, R_i) = C(x_i, R_i'),$$

$$C(y_i, R_i) = C(y_i, R_i'),$$

then $\bar{R}(\boldsymbol{R})$ and $\bar{R}(\boldsymbol{R}')$ agree on $\{x, y\}$.

It is clear that IIA implies IIA-MRS. The converse does not hold as an example in Appendix 7.D shows. It turns out, unfortunately, that weakening IIA into IIA-MRS cannot alter the dictatorship conclusion of Arrow's theorem. Introducing information about marginal rates of substitution, in addition to pairwise preferences, does not make room for satisfactory SOFs.

Proposition 7.2. If a SOF $\bar{R}$ satisfies weak Pareto and IIA-MRS, then it is dictatorial.

The proof of Proposition 7.2 is long and is relegated to Appendix 7.A, but here we sketch the main line of the proof. Since IIA implies IIA-MRS, Proposition 7.2 is a generalization of the theorem by Bordes and Le Breton [3, Theorem 3]. An essential idea of the proofs of Arrow-like theorems in economic environments (Kalai, Muller, and Satterthwaite [13], Bordes and Le Breton [3], and others) is as follows: First, we find a "free triple," that is, three allocations for which any ranking is possible in each individual's preferences satisfying the standard assumptions in economics. By applying Arrow's theorem for these three allocations, it can be shown that there exists a "local dictator" for each free triple. Then, we "connect" free triples in a suitable way to show that these local dictators must be the same individual.

Turning to IIA-MRS, notice first that for each free triple, IIA-MRS works just as IIA, only in the class of preference profiles for which individuals' marginal rates of substitution at the three allocations do not change from one profile to another and satisfy certain "supporting conditions." Invoking Arrow's Theorem, we can only show that there exists a "local dictator" for each free triple in this much-restricted class of preference profiles (Lemmas 7.A.1 and 7.A.2). The difficulty in the proof of Proposition 7.2 lies in extending "local dictatorship" over the class of all preference profiles. This requires much work to do. See Lemmas 7.A.3 and 7.A.4 in Appendix 7.A.

Inada [12] also considered marginal rates of substitution in an IIA-like axiom, but the difference from our work is that he looked for a local aggregator of preferences, namely, a mapping defining a social marginal rate of substitution between goods and individuals, on the basis of individual marginal rates of substitution. Hence, Inada requires that, for each allocation, social preferences *in an infinitely small neighborhood of the allocation* should not change whenever every agent's marginal rates of substitution at the allocation remain the same. By contrast, our IIA-MRS requires that, for each pair of allocations, social preferences *over that pair* should not change whenever every agent's marginal rates of substitution at each of the two allocations remain the same. There is no logical relation between Inada's axiom and ours.

Marginal rates of substitution give an infinitesimally local piece of information about indifference surfaces at given allocations. A natural extension of the informational basis would be to take account of the indifference surfaces in some finitely sized neighborhoods of the two allocations. Define, for any given real number $\varepsilon > 0$,

$$B_\varepsilon(x_i) := \{v \in \mathbb{R}^l_+ \mid \max_{k \in \{1,\ldots,l\}} |x_{ik} - v_k| \leq \varepsilon\}.$$

Define

$$I(x_i, R_i) := \{z \in \mathbb{R}^l_+ \mid z \, I_i \, x_i\}.$$

The set $I(x_i, R_i)$ is called the *indifference surface* at x_i for R_i.

The next axiom is defined for any given $\varepsilon > 0$.

IIA EXCEPT INDIFFERENCE SURFACES IN ε-NEIGHBORHOODS (IIA-ISεN). $\forall \boldsymbol{R}, \boldsymbol{R}' \in \mathcal{R}^n$, $\forall x, y \in \mathbb{R}^{nl}_+$, if $\forall i \in N$, R_i and R'_i agree on $\{x_i, y_i\}$, and

$$I(x_i, R_i) \cap B_\varepsilon(x_i) = I(x_i, R'_i) \cap B_\varepsilon(x_i),$$

$$I(y_i, R_i) \cap B_\varepsilon(y_i) = I(y_i, R'_i) \cap B_\varepsilon(y_i),$$

then $\bar{R}(\boldsymbol{R})$ and $\bar{R}(\boldsymbol{R}')$ agree on $\{x, y\}$.

It is clear that for any given $\varepsilon > 0$, IIA-MRS implies IIA-ISεN. Notice also that the larger the value of ε, the weaker the condition IIA-ISεN becomes.

The next proposition shows that as soon as one switches from IIA-MRS to IIA-ISεN, the dictatorship result is avoided *even if* ε *is arbitrarily small*. However, it remains impossible to achieve anonymity *even for an arbitrarily large* ε.

Proposition 7.3. For any given $\varepsilon > 0$, there exists a SOF that satisfies weak Pareto, IIA-ISεN, and is not dictatorial. However, for any given $\varepsilon > 0$, there exists no SOF that satisfies weak Pareto, IIA-ISεN, and anonymity.

Proof. The proof of the impossibility part is in Appendix 7.B. Here we prove the possibility part. Define $\bar{R}$ as follows: $x\bar{R}(\boldsymbol{R})y$ if either $x_1 R_1 y_1$ and $[I(x_1, R_1) \not\subseteq B_\varepsilon(0)$ or $I(y_1, R_1) \not\subseteq B_\varepsilon(0)]$, or $x_2 R_2 y_2$ and $[I(x_1, R_1) \subseteq B_\varepsilon(0)$ and $I(y_1, R_1) \subseteq B_\varepsilon(0)]$. For brevity, let $\Gamma(v)$ denote $[I(v, R_1) \subseteq B_\varepsilon(0)]$. Weak Pareto and the absence of a dictator are straightforwardly satisfied. IIA-ISεN is also satisfied because when $\Gamma(x_1)$ and $\Gamma(y_1)$ hold, we have $B_\varepsilon(0) \subseteq B_\varepsilon(x_1) \cap B_\varepsilon(y_1)$, and therefore $\Gamma(x_1)$ and $\Gamma(y_1)$ remain true if the indifference surfaces are kept fixed on $B_\varepsilon(x_1)$ and $B_\varepsilon(y_1)$. It remains to check transitivity of $\bar{R}(\boldsymbol{R})$. First, note the following property: If $\Gamma(v)$ holds and vR_1v', then $\Gamma(v')$ also holds. Assume that there exist $x, y, z \in \mathbb{R}^{nl}_+$ such that $x\bar{R}(\boldsymbol{R})y\bar{R}(\boldsymbol{R})z\bar{P}(\boldsymbol{R})x$. If $\Gamma(x_1)$, $\Gamma(y_1)$, and $\Gamma(z_1)$ all hold, this is impossible because one should have $x_2R_2y_2R_2z_2P_2x_2$. If only one of the three conditions $\Gamma(x_1)$, $\Gamma(y_1)$, $\Gamma(z_1)$ is satisfied, it is similarly impossible because one should have $x_1R_1y_1R_1z_1P_1x_1$. Assume $\Gamma(x_1)$ and $\Gamma(y_1)$ hold but not $\Gamma(z_1)$. Then $y\bar{R}(\boldsymbol{R})z\bar{P}(\boldsymbol{R})x$ requires $y_1R_1z_1P_1x_1$, which implies $\Gamma(z_1)$, a contradiction. Assume $\Gamma(x_1)$ and $\Gamma(z_1)$ hold but not $\Gamma(y_1)$. Then $x\bar{R}(\boldsymbol{R})y\bar{R}(\boldsymbol{R})z$ requires $x_1R_1y_1R_1z_1$, which implies $\Gamma(y_1)$, a contradiction. Assume $\Gamma(y_1)$ and $\Gamma(z_1)$ hold but not $\Gamma(x_1)$. Then $z\bar{P}(\boldsymbol{R})x\bar{R}(\boldsymbol{R})y$ requires $z_1P_1x_1R_1y_1$, which implies $\Gamma(x_1)$, a contradiction. ■

7.4. Extension of Informational Basis to "Edgeworth Boxes"

Our second type of extension of informational basis is to focus on the portions of indifference surfaces, associated with each pair of allocations, that lie within the corresponding "Edgeworth box": namely, the set of bundles that are achievable by redistributing the two allocations under consideration. However, for a given pair of allocations, the two allocations may need different amounts of total resources to be feasible. Therefore we need to introduce the following notions. For each good $k \in \{1, \ldots, l\}$, define

$$\omega_k(x, y) := \max \left\{ \sum_{i \in N} x_{ik}, \sum_{i \in N} y_{ik} \right\}.$$

Let $\omega(x, y) := (\omega_1(x, y), \ldots, \omega_l(x, y))$. The vector $\omega(x, y) \in \mathbb{R}^l_+$ represents the smallest amount of total resources that makes two allocations x and y feasible. Figure 7.1 illustrates the construction of $\omega(x, y)$. Then, define

$$\Omega(x, y) := \left\{ z \in \mathbb{R}^l_+ \mid z \leq \omega(x, y) \right\}.$$

The set $\Omega(x, y) \subseteq \mathbb{R}^l_+$ is the set of consumption bundles that are feasible with $\omega(x, y)$. The following axiom captures the idea that the ranking of any two allocations should depend only on the indifference surfaces over the region satisfying the corresponding feasibility constraint.

IIA EXCEPT INDIFFERENCE SURFACES OVER FEASIBLE ALLOCATIONS (IIA-ISFA). $\forall \boldsymbol{R}, \boldsymbol{R}' \in \mathcal{R}^n$, $\forall x, y \in \mathbb{R}^{nl}_+$, if $\forall i \in N$,

$$I(x_i, R_i) \cap \Omega(x, y) = I(x_i, R'_i) \cap \Omega(x, y),$$

$$I(y_i, R_i) \cap \Omega(x, y) = I(y_i, R'_i) \cap \Omega(x, y),$$

then $\bar{R}(\boldsymbol{R})$ and $\bar{R}(\boldsymbol{R}')$ agree on $\{x, y\}$.

The left panel in Figure 7.1 illustrates the relevant portions of indifference surfaces under IIA-ISFA, which are indicated by thick curves, while the right panel shows the relevant parts under IIA-ISεN. One can see that, in general, there is no inclusion relation between the relevant portions of indifference surfaces under IIA-ISFA and those under IIA-ISεN. Hence, there is no logical relation between the axioms IIA-ISFA and IIA-ISεN. See counterexamples in Appendix 7.D.

The introduction of information about indifference surfaces over the region satisfying the corresponding feasibility constraint, however, cannot help us avoid a dictatorial SOF.

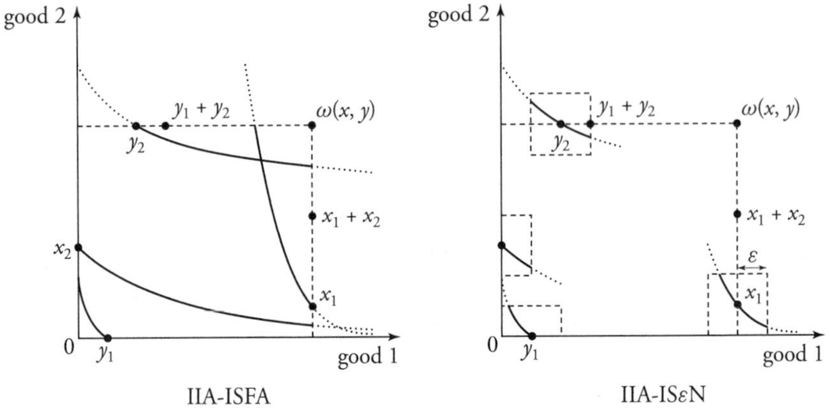

Figure 7.1. Relevant Portions of Indifference Surfaces under IIA-ISFA and IIA-ISεN

Proposition 7.4. If a SOF satisfies weak Pareto and IIA-ISFA, then it is dictatorial.

The proof relies on the following lemmas. First, we define a weak form of IIA.

Weak Independence of Irrelevant Alternatives (WIIA). $\forall \boldsymbol{R}, \boldsymbol{R}' \in \mathcal{R}^n$, $\forall x, y \in X$, if $\forall i \in N$, R_i and R_i' agree on $\{x_i, y_i\}$, and for no i, $x_i \, I_i \, y_i$, then $\bar{R}(\boldsymbol{R})$ and $\bar{R}(\boldsymbol{R}')$ agree on $\{x, y\}$.

A key lemma to prove Proposition 7.4 is the following:

Lemma 7.1. If a SOF $\bar{R}$ satisfies weak Pareto and IIA-ISFA, then it satisfies WIIA.

The proof of this lemma is long and relegated to Appendix 7.C. We also define a weak form of dictatorship: Given a SOF $\bar{R}$, $Y \subseteq X$ and $\mathcal{R}' \subseteq \mathcal{R}^n$, we say that agent $i_0 \in N$ is a *quasi dictator for* $\bar{R}$ *over* $(Y, \mathcal{R}')$ if, for all $x, y \in Y$, and all $\boldsymbol{R} \in \mathcal{R}'$, whenever $x_{i_0} P_{i_0} y_{i_0}$ and there is no $i \in N$ with $x_i I_i y_i$, we have $x \, \bar{P}(\boldsymbol{R}) y$.

Quasi-Dictatorial SOF. A SOF $\bar{R}$ is quasi dictatorial if there exists a quasi-dictator $i_0 \in N$ for $\bar{R}$ over $(X, \mathcal{R}^n)$.

Lemma 7.2. If a SOF $\bar{R}$ satisfies weak Pareto and WIIA, then it is quasi-dictatorial.

Proof. Let $\bar{R}$ be a SOF that satisfies weak Pareto and WIIA. By an adaptation of a standard proof of Arrow's theorem (for instance, Sen [18]), we can show that for every free triple $Y \subseteq X$, there exists a quasi dictator over $(Y, \mathcal{R}^n)$. Then a direct application of Bordes and Le Breton [3] establishes the quasi-dictatorship of $\bar{R}$. ■

It is interesting that, in our economic environments, quasi dictatorship is equivalent to dictatorship, as the next lemma shows.

Lemma 7.3. If a SOF $\bar{R}$ is quasi-dictatorial, then it is dictatorial.

Proof. Let $\bar{R}$ be a quasi-dictatorial SOF. Let $x, y \in X$ and $\boldsymbol{R} \in \mathcal{R}^n$ be such that $x_{i_0} P_{i_0} y_{i_0}$. By continuity and strict monotonicity of preferences, there exists $x' \in X$ such that $x_{i_0} P_{i_0} x'_{i_0} P_{i_0} y_{i_0}$ and for all $i \in N$, either $x_i P_i x'_i P_i y_i$ or $y_i R_i x_i P_i x'_i$. Since $\bar{R}$ is quasi-dictatorial, it follows that $x \bar{P}(\boldsymbol{R}) x'$ and $x' \bar{P}(\boldsymbol{R}) y$. By transitivity, $x \bar{P}(\boldsymbol{R}) y$. ■

Given these lemmas, the proof of Proposition 7.4 is straightforward.

Proof of Proposition 7.4. Let $\bar{R}$ be a SOF that satisfies weak Pareto and IIA-ISFA. By Lemma 7.1, $\bar{R}$ satisfies WIIA. Then, by Lemmas 7.2 and 7.3, $\bar{R}$ is dictatorial. ■

One may define a weaker axiom than IIA-ISFA by considering a radial expansion of the corresponding "Edgeworth box", namely $\lambda\Omega(x, y)$ for a given $\lambda \geq 1$, where λ can be arbitrarily large. With this version, however, the same impossibility still holds as Proposition 7.4.

7.5. Extension of Informational Basis with a Monotone Path

The previous sections have shown that nonlocal information about indifference surfaces is needed to construct a satisfactory SOF. This does not mean, however, that a lot of information is needed. In this section we show that knowing one point in each indifference surface may be enough.

Our third way of extending information about indifference surfaces is to rely on a path

$$\Lambda_{\omega_0} := \{\lambda\omega_0 \in \mathbb{R}^l_{++} \mid \lambda \in \mathbb{R}_+\},$$

where $\omega_0 \in \mathbb{R}^l_{++}$ is fixed, and to focus on the point of each indifference surface that belongs to this path. The idea of referring to such a path is due to Pazner and Schmeidler [16] and may be justified if the path contains relevant benchmark bundles. Although the choice of ω_0 is not discussed here, it need not be arbitrary. For instance, one may imagine that it could reflect an appropriate equity notion, or it could be the bundle of the total available resources.

IIA except Indifference Surfaces on Path ω_0 (IIA-ISPω_0). $\forall \boldsymbol{R}, \boldsymbol{R}' \in \mathcal{R}^n$, $\forall x, y \in \mathbb{R}^{nl}_+$, if $\forall i \in N$,

$$I(x_i, R_i) \cap \Lambda_{\omega_0} = I(x_i, R_i') \cap \Lambda_{\omega_0},$$

$$I(y_i, R_i) \cap \Lambda_{\omega_0} = I(y_i, R_i') \cap \Lambda_{\omega_0},$$

then $\bar{R}(\boldsymbol{R})$ and $\bar{R}(\boldsymbol{R}')$ agree on $\{x, y\}$.

Following Pazner and Schmeidler's [16] contribution, we can derive the next result, which means that not much information is needed to have an anonymous SOF if only we are prepared to accept an externally specified reference bundle.

Proposition 7.5. For any given $\omega_0 \in \mathbb{R}^l_{++}$, there exists a SOF that satisfies weak Pareto, IIA-ISPω_0, and anonymity.

Proof. For each $i \in N$, each $R_i \in \mathcal{R}$, and each $x_i \in \mathbb{R}^l_+$, let $\alpha(x_i, R_i) \in \mathbb{R}_+$ be the scalar such that $\alpha(x_i, R_i)\omega_0 I_i x_i$. By continuity and strict monotonicity of preferences, $\alpha(x_i, R_i)$ always exists uniquely. Let $\bar{R}$ be defined by

$$x\bar{R}(\boldsymbol{R})y \Leftrightarrow \min_{i\in N} \alpha(x_i, R_i) \geq \min_{i\in N} \alpha(y_i, R_i).$$

This SOF clearly satisfies weak Pareto and anonymity. It also satisfies IIA-ISPω_0 because whenever $I(x_i, R_i) \cap \Lambda_{\omega_0} = I(x_i, R_i') \cap \Lambda_{\omega_0}$, we have $\alpha(x_i, R_i) = \alpha(x_i, R_i')$. ■

By relying on the leximin criterion rather than the maximin for the SOF defined in the preceding proof, we could have the strong Pareto property as well: $\forall x, y \in \mathbb{R}_+^{nl}, \forall \boldsymbol{R} \in \mathcal{R}^n$ if $\forall i \in N, x_i R_i y_i$, then $x \bar{R}(\boldsymbol{R}) y$, and if, in addition, $\exists i \in N, x_i P_i y_i$, then $x \bar{P}(\boldsymbol{R}) y$.

The final extension of informational basis that we consider is to introduce whole indifference surfaces. This condition was already introduced and studied by Hansson [11] in the abstract model of social choice, who showed that the Borda rule, which does not satisfy the Arrow IIA condition, satisfies this constrained variant thereof. Pazner [15] also proposed it, in a study of social choice in economic environments.

IIA EXCEPT WHOLE INDIFFERENCE SURFACES (IIA-WIS). $\forall \boldsymbol{R}, \boldsymbol{R}' \in \mathcal{R}^n$, $\forall x, y \subset \mathbb{R}_+^{nl}$, if $\forall i \in N$,

$$I(x_i, R_i) = I(x_i, R_i'),$$

$$I(y_i, R_i) = I(y_i, R_i'),$$

then $\bar{R}(\boldsymbol{R})$ and $\bar{R}(\boldsymbol{R}')$ agree on $\{x, y\}$.

Since IIA-ISPω_0 (as well as every other IIA-type axiom introduced so far) implies IIA-WIS, we have the following corollary.

COROLLARY 7.1. There exists a SOF that satisfies weak Pareto, IIA-WIS, and anonymity.

There are many examples of SOFs satisfying weak Pareto, IIA-WIS, and anonymity. Thus, in addition to these three axioms, we may add other requirements embodying various equity principles. Notice that strong Pareto and anonymity already entail a version of the *Suppes grading principle:* for all $\boldsymbol{R} \in \mathcal{R}^n$, and all x, y, if there are i, j such that $R_i = R_j$, $x_i P_i y_j$ and $x_j P_i y_i$, and for all $h \neq i, j, x_h = y_h$, then $x \bar{P}(\boldsymbol{R}) y$. We can also construct SOFs satisfying strong Pareto, IIA-WIS (or IIA-ISPω_0), anonymity, and the following version of the *Hammond equity axiom* (Hammond [10]): for all $\boldsymbol{R} \in \mathcal{R}^n$, and all $x, y \in \mathbb{R}_+^{nl}$, if there are i, j such that $R_i = R_j$, $y_i P_i x_i P_i x_j P_i y_j$, and for all $h \neq i, j, x_h = y_h$, then $x \bar{P}(\boldsymbol{R}) y$.

Let us summarize in Figure 7.2 the various IIA-type axioms that we have introduced, and the main results in this essay. The arrows indicate logical

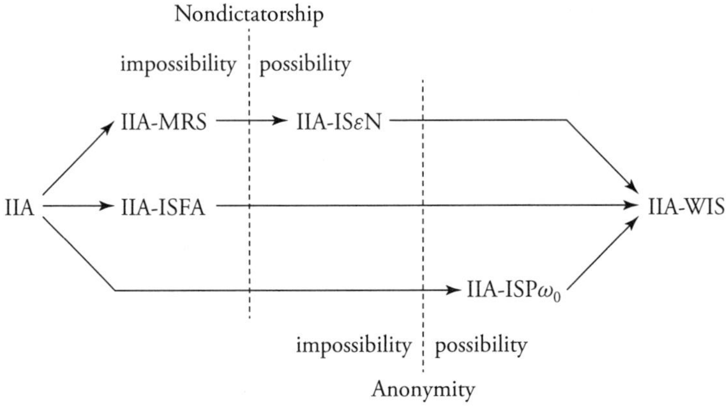

Figure 7.2. Various IIA Axioms and Summary of the Main Results

relations between the axioms. Weaker axioms allow SOFs to depend on more information about indifference surfaces. In the appendixes we show that all the implications are strict (the converse relations do not hold). The dotted lines in the figure indicate borderlines between possibility and impossibility, under weak Pareto, of nondictatorship and of anonymity.

7.6. Conclusion

The construction of a nondictatorial Arrovian SOF in a framework with purely ordinal, interpersonally noncomparable preferences requires information about the shape of indifference surfaces that goes well beyond infinitesimally local data such as marginal rates of substitution or data within the corresponding "Edgeworth box." On the basis of information in some finitely sized neighborhoods, one can construct a nondictatorial SOF but still cannot have an anonymous one. Only substantially nonlocal information about indifference surfaces enables one to construct a Paretian and anonymous SOF. These are the main messages of this essay, in which we proved two extensions of Arrow's impossibility theorem and several possibility results. We hope that this essay, more broadly, contributes to clarifying the informational foundations in the theory of social choice.

There are limits to our work, which may be noticed here and which call for further research. First, we study a particular economic model, and it would be worth analyzing the same issues in models such as the standard abstract model of social choice or other economic models, in particular models with public goods (the case of consumption externalities in our model could also be subsumed under the case of public goods). Second, the information about indifference surfaces is a complex set of objects, and our analysis is far from being exhaustive on the pieces of data that can be extracted from this set. We have focused on what seemed to us the most natural parts of indifference surfaces to which one may want to refer in social evaluation of allocations, namely, the marginal rates of substitution, the Edgeworth box (bundles that are achievable by redistributing the considered allocations), and reference rays. But there may be other ways of considering indifference surfaces. For instance, it would be nice to have a measure of the degree to which a given piece of information is local, and the connection between this work and topological social choice (e.g., Chichilnisky [6]) might be worth exploring. Third, there may be other kinds of interesting additional information. For instance, Roberts [17] considered introducing information about utilities and about nonlocal preferences at the same time, and was able to characterize the Nash social welfare function on this basis. There certainly are many avenues of research along these lines. The purpose of this essay would be well served if it could open the gate toward these enticing avenues.

Appendix 7.A. Proof of Proposition 7.2

The proof of Proposition 7.2 relies on the following lemmas.

Let $Y \subseteq X$ be a given finite subset of X. Let $i \in N$ be given. Define $Y_i := \{y_i \in \mathbb{R}^l_+ \mid \exists y_{-i} \in \mathbb{R}^{(n-1)l}_+, (y_i, y_{-i}) \in Y\}$. Let $\mathcal{Q}$ denote the set of convex cones in $\mathbb{R}^l_{++}$. For each $y_i \in Y_i$, let $Q(y_i) \in \mathcal{Q}$ be given. We say that the set Y_i satisfies the *supporting condition* with respect to $\{Q(y_i) \mid y_i \in Y_i\}$ if for all $y_i \in Y_i$, all $q \in Q(y_i)$, and all $y'_i \in Y_i$ with $y'_i \neq y_i$, $q \cdot y_i < q \cdot y'_i$. Define

$$\mathcal{R}(Y_i, \{Q(y_i) \mid y_i \in Y_i\}) := \{R_i \in \mathcal{R} \mid \forall y_i \in Y_i, C(y_i, R_i) = Q(y_i)\}.$$

The set of all complete preorderings on Y_i is denoted by $\mathcal{O}(Y_i)$. For all $R_i \in \mathcal{R}$, $R_i \mid_{Y_i}$ denotes the restriction of R_i on Y_i. Namely, $R_i \mid_{Y_i}$ is the complete preordering on Y_i such that for all $x_i, y_i \in Y_i$, $x_i R_i \mid_{Y_i} y_i \Leftrightarrow x_i \ R_i \ y_i$. For all $\mathcal{R}' \subseteq \mathcal{R}$, let $\mathcal{R}' |_{Y_i} := \{R_i |_{Y_i} | R_i \in \mathcal{R}'\}$. For all $x_i \in X$ and all $R_i \in \mathcal{R}$, let $U(x_i, R_i) := \{x_i' \in X \mid x_i' \, R_i \, x_i\}$ denote the (closed) upper contour set of x_i for R_i.

Lemma 7.A.1. If a finite set $Y_i \subseteq \mathbb{R}^l_+$ satisfies the supporting condition with respect to $\{Q(y_i) \mid y_i \in Y_i\}$, then $\mathcal{R}(Y_i, \{Q(y_i) \mid y_i \in Y_i\}) |_{Y_i} = \mathcal{O}(Y_i)$.

Proof. We have only to show that $\mathcal{O}(Y_i) \subseteq \mathcal{R}(Y_i, \{Q(y_i) \mid y_i \in Y_i\}) |_{Y_i}$. Let $R' \in \mathcal{O}(Y_i)$ be any preordering on Y_i. Construct a complete preordering $R_i \in \mathcal{R}$ so that the upper contour set of each $y_i \in Y_i$ is defined as follows. Let $x_i \in Y_i$ be such that for all $y_i \in Y_i$, $y_i R_i' x_i$. Define $Y_i^1 := \{y_i \in Y_i \mid y_i I_i' x_i\}$. For each $a \in \mathbb{R}^l_+$ and each $q \in \mathbb{R}^l_{++}$, define $H(a, q) := \{b \in \mathbb{R}^l_+ \mid q \cdot b \geq q \cdot a\}$. Let

$$U(x_i, R_i) := \bigcap_{y_i \in Y_i^1} \left[\bigcap_{q \in Q(y_i)} H(y_i, q) \right].$$

Let $I(x_i, R_i)$ be the boundary of $U(x_i, R_i)$. Clearly, for all $y_i \in Y_i^1$, $C(y_i, R_i) = Q(y_i)$. We also have that, for all $y_i \in Y_i \backslash Y_i^1$, and for all $x_i' \in I(x_i, R_i)$, $y_i P_i x_i'$. Given $\delta > 0$, let $(1+\delta)U(x_i, R_i) := \{x_i' \in \mathbb{R}^l_+ \mid \exists a_i \in U(x_i, R_i), x_i' = (1+\delta)a_i\}$, and let $(1+\delta)I(x_i, R_i)$ be the boundary of $(1+\delta)U(x_i, R_i)$. For sufficiently small δ, we have that for all $y_i \in Y_i \backslash Y_i^1$ and all $x_i' \in (1+\delta)I(x_i, R_i)$, $y_i P_i x_i'$ by continuity of preferences. Let $z_i \in Y_i \backslash Y_i^1$ be such that for all $y_i \in Y_i \backslash Y_i^1$, $y_i R_i' z_i$. Define $Y_i^2 := \{y_i \in Y_i \backslash Y_i^1 \mid y_i I_i' z_i\}$. Let

$$U(z_i, R_i) := (1+\delta)U(x_i, R_i) \bigcap \left(\bigcap_{y_i \in Y_i^2} \left[\bigcap_{q \in Q(y_i)} H(y_i, q) \right] \right).$$

Let $I(z_i, R_i)$ be the boundary of $U(z_i, R_i)$. By definition, for all $y_i \in Y_i^2$, $C(y_i, R_i) = Q(y_i)$. We have that, for all $y_i \in Y_i \backslash \left(Y_i^1 \cup Y_i^2\right)$ and all $x_i' \in I(z_i, R_i)$, $y_i P_i x_i'$. Similarly, we can construct the upper contour set of each $y_i \in Y_i \backslash \left(Y_i^1 \cup Y_i^2\right)$. By its construction, $R_i \in \mathcal{R}(Y_i, \{Q(y_i) \mid y_i \in Y_i\})$ and $R_i |_{Y_i} = R'$. Thus, $R' \in \mathcal{R}(Y_i, \{Q(y_i) \mid y_i \in Y_i\}) |_{Y_i}$. ■

Let $\bar{R}$ be a SOF. Let $Y \subseteq X$ and $\mathcal{R}' \subseteq \mathcal{R}^n$ be given. We say that agent $i_0 \in N$ is a *local dictator for $\bar{R}$ over* $(Y, \mathcal{R}')$ if, for all $x, y \in Y$ and all $\boldsymbol{R} \in \mathcal{R}'$, $x_{i_0} P_{i_0} y_{i_0}$ implies $x \bar{P}(\boldsymbol{R}) y$.

Given a set A, let $|A|$ denote the cardinality of A.

Lemma 7.A.2. Let $\bar{R}$ be a SOF satisfying weak Pareto and IIA-MRS. Let $Y \subseteq X$ be a finite subset of X such that $|Y| \geq 3$. Suppose that for all $i \in N$, Y_i satisfies the supporting condition with respect to $\{Q(y_i) \mid y_i \in Y_i\}$. Then there exists a local dictator $i_0 \in N$ for $\bar{R}$ over $(Y, \prod_{i \in N} \mathcal{R}(Y_i, \{Q(y_i) \mid y_i \in Y_i\}))$.

Proof. For all $\boldsymbol{R}, \boldsymbol{R}' \in \prod_{i \in N} \mathcal{R}(Y_i, \{Q(y_i) \mid y_i \in Y_i\})$, all $y \in Y$, and all $i \in N$, $C(y_i, R_i) = C(y_i, R_i')$. Since $\bar{R}$ satisfies IIA-MRS, we have that, for all $x, y \in Y$, and all $\boldsymbol{R}, \boldsymbol{R}' \in \prod_{i \in N} \mathcal{R}(Y_i, \{Q(y_i) \mid y_i \in Y_i\})$, if R_i and R_i' agree on $\{x_i, y_i\}$ for all $i \in N$, then $\bar{R}(\boldsymbol{R})$ and $\bar{R}(\boldsymbol{R}')$ agree on $\{x, y\}$. By Lemma 7.A.1, for all $i \in N$, $\mathcal{R}(Y_i, \{Q(y_i) \mid y_i \in Y_i\}) |_{Y_i} = \mathcal{O}(Y_i)$. Hence, by Arrow's theorem, there exists a local dictator for $\bar{R}$ over $(Y, \prod_{i \in N} \mathcal{R}(Y_i, \{Q(y_i) \mid y_i \in Y_i\}))$. ■

We say that a subset Y of X is *free for agent i* if $\mathcal{R} |_{Y_i} = \mathcal{O}(Y_i)$. It is *free* if it is free for all $i \in N$. If Y contains two elements, it is a *free pair*. If Y contains three elements, it is a *free triple*. Note that a set $\{x, y\}$ is a free pair for $i \in N$ if and only if, for some $k, k' \in \{1, \ldots, l\}$, $x_{ik} > y_{ik}$ and $y_{ik'} > x_{ik'}$. Given two consumption bundles $x_i, y_i \in \mathbb{R}^l_+$, define $x_i \wedge y_i \in \mathbb{R}^l_+$ as $(x_i \wedge y_i)_k = \min \{x_{ik}, y_{ik}\}$ for all $k \in \{1, \ldots, l\}$.

Lemma 7.A.3. Let $\bar{R}$ be a SOF satisfying weak Pareto and IIA-MRS. If $\{x, y\} \subseteq X$ is a free pair, then there exists a local dictator for $\bar{R}$ over $(\{x, y\}, \mathcal{R}^n)$.

Proof. Let $\bar{R}$ be a SOF satisfying weak Pareto and IIA-MRS. Let $\{x, y\} \subseteq X$ be a free pair. Let

$$K_1 := \{k \in \{1, \ldots, l\} \mid x_{ik} > y_{ik}\}$$

$$K_2 := \{k \in \{1, \ldots, l\} \mid x_{ik} < y_{ik}\}.$$

Since $\{x, y\}$ is a free pair, $K_1, K_2 \neq \emptyset$.

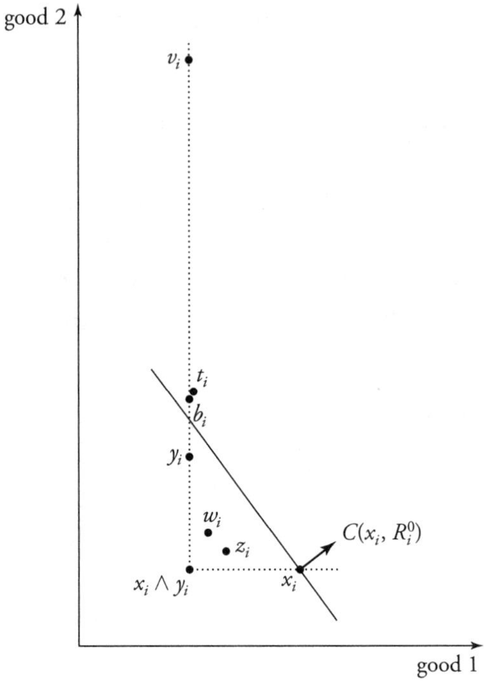

Figure 7.3. Proof of Lemma 7.A.3

STEP 1. For each $i \in N$, we define two consumption bundles $z_i, w_i \in X$ as follows:

$$z_i := x_i \wedge y_i + \frac{1}{2}\left[\frac{2}{3}(x_i - x_i \wedge y_i) + \frac{1}{3}(y_i - x_i \wedge y_i)\right] \quad (7.1)$$

$$w_i := x_i \wedge y_i + \frac{1}{2}\left[\frac{1}{3}(x_i - x_i \wedge y_i) + \frac{2}{3}(y_i - x_i \wedge y_i)\right]. \quad (7.2)$$

Figure 7.3 illustrates the bundles $x_i, y_i, x_i \wedge y_i, z_i, w_i$, and also b_i, v_i, t_i, which are defined in the next step. Let $q \in \mathbb{R}^l_{++}$. Then, $q \cdot y_i < q \cdot w_i$ if and only if

$$\frac{2}{3} \sum_{k \in K_2} q_k(y_{ik} - x_{ik}) < \frac{1}{6} \sum_{k \in K_1} q_k(x_{ik} - y_{ik}). \quad (7.3)$$

Since $K_1 \neq \emptyset$, the right-hand side of (7.3) can be arbitrarily large as $(q_k)_{k \in K_1}$ become large, $(q_k)_{k \in K_2}$ being constant. Hence, there exists a price vector

$q(y_i) \in \mathbb{R}^l_{++}$ that satisfies inequality (7.3). With some calculations, it can be shown that $q(y_i) \cdot y_i < q(y_i) \cdot z_i$ and $q(y_i) \cdot y_i < q(y_i) \cdot x_i$.

Similarly, for each $a \in \{x_i, z_i, w_i\}$, we can find a price vector $q(a) \in \mathbb{R}^l_{++}$ such that, for all $a' \in \{x_i, z_i, w_i, y_i\}$ with $a' \neq a$, $q(a) \cdot a < q(a) \cdot a'$. Hence, the set $Y_i^0 = \{x_i, z_i, w_i, y_i\}$ satisfies the supporting condition with respect to $\{q(x_i), q(z_i), q(w_i), q(y_i)\}$.[2]

Let $z := (z_i)_{i \in N}$ and $w := (w_i)_{i \in N}$. Let $Y^0 := \{x, z, w, y\}$. By Lemma 7.A.2, there exists a local dictator $i_0 \in N$ for $\bar{R}$ over

$$\left(Y^0, \prod_{i \in N} \mathcal{R}(Y_i^0, \{q(x_i), q(z_i), q(w_i), q(y_i)\})\right).$$

Step 2. We will show that agent i_0 is a local dictator for $\bar{R}$ over $(\{x, y\}, \mathcal{R}^n)$.

Suppose, on the contrary, that there exists a preference profile $\boldsymbol{R}^0 \in \mathcal{R}^n$ such that (i) $x_{i_0} P^0_{i_0} y_{i_0}$ and $y \bar{R}(\boldsymbol{R}^0) x$ or (ii) $y_{i_0} P^0_{i_0} x_{i_0}$ and $x \bar{R}(\boldsymbol{R}^0) y$. Without loss of generality, suppose that (i) holds. Let $Y^1 := \{z, w, y\}$. Since agent i_0 is the local dictator for $\bar{R}$ over

$$\left(Y^0, \prod_{i \in N} \mathcal{R}(Y_i^0, \{q(x_i), q(z_i), q(w_i), q(y_i)\})\right),$$

he is also the local dictator for $\bar{R}$ over

$$\left(Y^1, \prod_{i \in N} \mathcal{R}(Y_i^1, \{q(z_i), q(w_i), q(y_i)\})\right).$$

(Otherwise, by Lemma 7.A.2, there exists a local dictator $j \neq i_0$ for $\bar{R}$ over $(Y^1, \prod_{i \in N} \mathcal{R}(Y_i^1, \{q(z_i), q(w_i), q(y_i)\}))$, and we can construct a preference profile

$$\begin{aligned} \boldsymbol{R} &\in \prod_{i \in N} \mathcal{R}(Y_i^0, \{q(x_i), q(z_i), q(w_i), q(y_i)\}) \\ &\subseteq \prod_{i \in N} \mathcal{R}(Y_i^1, \{q(z_i), q(w_i), q(y_i)\}) \end{aligned}$$

2. With a slight abuse of notation, we write $q(\cdot)$ for $Q(\cdot) = \{\alpha q(\cdot) \mid \alpha > 0\}$.

such that $z_{i_0} P_{i_0} w_{i_0}$ and $w_j P_j z_j$. Hence we must have $z \bar{P}(\boldsymbol{R}) w$ and $w \bar{P}(\boldsymbol{R}) z$, which is a contradiction.)

We define two allocations $v, t \in X$ in the following steps. Let $i \in N$. First, define $b_i \in \mathbb{R}^l_+$ as follows: If, for all $q \in C(x_i, R_i^0)$, $q \cdot (y_i - x_i) \geq 0$, then let $b_i := y_i$. If, for some $q \in C(x_i, R_i^0)$, $q \cdot (y_i - x_i) < 0$, then let $\theta > 0$ be a positive number such that, for all $q \in C(x_i, R_i^0)$, $q \cdot \left[y_i + \theta(y_i - x_i \wedge y_i) - x_i\right] > 0$. Since $q \in \mathbb{R}^l_{++}$ by strict monotonicity of preferences, and $y_i - x_i \wedge y_i > 0$, such a number θ exists. Then define $b_i := y_i + \theta(y_i - x_i \wedge y_i)$. By definition, $b_i > y_i$, and, for all $q \in C(x_i, R_i^0)$, $q \cdot (b_i - x_i) > 0$. Define

$$v_i := b_i + 2(b_i - x_i \wedge y_i).$$

Then $v_i > b_i > y_i$ and, for all $q \in C(x_i, R_i^0)$, $q \cdot (v_i - x_i) > 0$.

Next, define

$$t_i := x_i \wedge y_i + \frac{1}{2}\left[\frac{2}{3}(v_i - x_i \wedge y_i) + \frac{1}{3}(w_i - x_i \wedge y_i)\right].$$

Then

$$t_i = b_i + \frac{1}{6}(w_i - x_i \wedge y_i) > b_i$$

and, for all $q \in C(x_i, R_i^0)$, $q \cdot x_i < q \cdot t_i$.

As in step 1, we can find price vectors $q(v_i), q(t_i) \in \mathbb{R}^l_{++}$ such that $q(v_i) \cdot v_i < q(v_i) \cdot a$ for all $a \in \{x_i, z_i, w_i, t_i\}$ and $q(t_i) \cdot t_i < q(t_i) \cdot a$ for all $a \in \{x_i, z_i, w_i, v_i\}$.

On the other hand, because $v_i > y_i$ and $t_i > y_i$, we have $q(z_i) \cdot z_i < q(z_i) \cdot a$ for all $a \in \{t_i, v_i\}$ and $q(w_i) \cdot w_i < q(w_i) \cdot a$ for all $a \in \{t_i, v_i\}$.

So far we have shown that

(i) the set $Y_i^2 := \{x_i, t_i, v_i\}$ satisfies the supporting condition with respect to $\{C(x_i, R_i^0), q(t_i), q(v_i)\}$.

(ii) the set $Y_i^3 := \{z_i, w_i, t_i, v_i\}$ satisfies the supporting condition with respect to $\{q(z_i), q(w_i), q(t_i), q(v_i)\}$.

Let $v := (v_i)_{i \in N}$ and $t := (t_i)_{i \in N}$. Let $Y^2 := \{x, t, v\}$ and $Y^3 := \{z, w, t, v\}$. By Lemma 7.A.2, there exist a local dictator

$$i_1 \in N \text{ for } \bar{R} \text{ over } (Y^2, \textstyle\prod_{i \in N} \mathcal{R}(Y_i^2, \{C(x_i, R_i^0), q(t_i), q(v_i)\}))$$

and a local dictator

$$i_2 \in N \text{ for } \bar{R} \text{ over } (Y^3, \textstyle\prod_{i \in N} \mathcal{R}(Y_i^3, \{q(z_i), q(w_i), q(t_i), q(v_i)\})).$$

Recall that agent $i_0 \in N$ is the local dictator for $\bar{R}$ over

$$(Y^1, \prod_{i \in N} \mathcal{R}(Y_i^1, \{q(z_i), q(w_i), q(y_i)\})).$$

Let $\boldsymbol{R}^1 \in \mathcal{R}^n$ be a preference profile such that for all $i \in N$, $C(x_i, R_i^1) = C(x_i, R_i^0)$, and for all $a_i \in \{t_i, v_i, w_i, y_i, z_i\}$, $C(a_i, R_i^1) = \{q(a_i)\}$, and such that

$$x_{i_0} P_{i_0}^1 z_{i_0} P_{i_0}^1 w_{i_0} P_{i_0}^1 t_{i_0} P_{i_0}^1 v_{i_0} P_{i_0}^1 y_{i_0}$$

and, for all $i \in N$ with $i \neq i_0$,

$$x_i P_i^1 v_i P_i^1 t_i P_i^1 w_i P_i^1 z_i P_i^1 y_i.$$

Since $\boldsymbol{R}^1 \in \prod_{i \in N} \mathcal{R}(Y_i^1, \{q(z_i), q(w_i), q(y_i)\})$ and agent i_0 is the local dictator for $\bar{R}$ over $(Y^1, \prod_{i \in N} \mathcal{R}(Y_i^1, \{q(z_i), q(w_i), q(y_i)\}))$, we have $z \bar{P}(\boldsymbol{R}^1) w$. Because $\boldsymbol{R}^1 \in \prod_{i \in N} \mathcal{R}(Y_i^3, \{q(z_i), q(w_i), q(t_i), q(v_i)\})$, this implies that $i_0 = i_2$. Hence, we have $t \bar{P}(\boldsymbol{R}^1) v$. Since

$$\boldsymbol{R}^2 \in \prod_{i \in N} \mathcal{R}(Y_i^2, \{C(x_i, R_i^0), q(t_i), q(v_i)\}),$$

it follows that $i_0 = i_1$.

Let $\boldsymbol{R}^2 \in \mathcal{R}^n$ be a preference profile such that $x_{i_0} P_{i_0}^2 v_{i_0}$ and, for all $i \in N$, $R_i^2 |_{\{x_i, y_i\}} = R_i^0 |_{\{x_i, y_i\}}$, and $C(x_i, R_i^2) = C(x_i, R_i^0)$, $C(t_i, R_i^2) = \{q(t_i)\}$, $C(v_i, R_i^2) = \{q(v_i)\}$, and $C(y_i, R_i^2) = C(y_i, R_i^0)$. Since agent $i_0 \in N$ is the local dictator for $\bar{R}$ over

$$\left(Y^2, \prod_{i \in N} \mathcal{R}(Y_i^2, \{C(x_i, R_i^0), q(t_i), q(v_i)\})\right)$$

and

$$\boldsymbol{R}^2 \in \prod_{i \in N} \mathcal{R}(Y_i^2, \{C(x_i, R_i^0), q(t_i), q(v_i)\}),$$

we have that $x \bar{P}(\boldsymbol{R}^2) v$. Recall that, for all $i \in N$, $v_i > y_i$. Hence, by strict monotonicity of preferences, $v_i P_i^2 y_i$ for all $i \in N$. Because the SOF $\bar{R}$ satisfies weak Pareto, we have $v \bar{P}(\boldsymbol{R}^2) y$. By transitivity of $\bar{R}$, $x \bar{P}(\boldsymbol{R}^2) y$. However, since $\bar{R}$ satisfies IIA-MRS, and $C(x_i, R_i^2) = C(x_i, R_i^0)$, $C(y_i, R_i^2) = C(y_i, R_i^0)$, and $y \bar{R}(\boldsymbol{R}^0) x$, we must have $y \bar{R}(\boldsymbol{R}^2) x$. This is a contradiction. ■

LEMMA 7.A.4. Let $\bar{R}$ be a SOF satisfying weak Pareto and IIA-MRS. If $\{x, y, z\} \subseteq X$ is a free triple, then there exists a local dictator for $\bar{R}$ over $(\{x, y, z\}, \mathcal{R}^n)$.

PROOF. By Lemma 7.A.3, there exist a local dictator i_0 over $(\{x, y\}, \mathcal{R}^n)$, a local dictator i_1 over $(\{y, z\}, \mathcal{R}^n)$, and a local dictator i_2 over $(\{x, z\}, \mathcal{R}^n)$. Suppose that $i_0 \neq i_1$. Let $\boldsymbol{R} \in \mathcal{R}^n$ be a preference profile such that $x_{i_0} P_{i_0} y_{i_0}$, $y_{i_1} P_{i_1} z_{i_1}$, and $z_{i_2} P_{i_2} x_{i_2}$. Then we have $x \bar{P}(\boldsymbol{R}) y \bar{P}(\boldsymbol{R}) z \bar{P}(\boldsymbol{R}) x$, which contradicts the transitivity of $\bar{R}(\boldsymbol{R})$. Hence, we must have $i_0 = i_1$. By the same argument, we have $i_0 = i_1 = i_2$. ■

PROOF OF PROPOSITION 7.2. Let $\bar{R}$ be a SOF satisfying weak Pareto and IIA-MRS. By Lemma 7.A.3, for every free pair $\{x, y\} \subseteq X$, there exists a local dictator over $(\{x, y\}, \mathcal{R}^n)$. By Lemma 7.A.4 and Bordes and Le Breton [3, Theorem 2], these dictators must be the same individual. Denote this individual by i_0. It remains to show that, for any pair $\{x, y\}$ that is not free, i_0 is the local dictator over $(\{x, y\}, \mathcal{R}^n)$. Suppose, on the contrary, that there exist $\{x, y\} \subseteq X$ and $\boldsymbol{R} \in \mathcal{R}^n$ such that $\{x, y\}$ is not a free pair, and $x_{i_0} P_{i_0} y_{i_0}$ but $y \bar{R}(\boldsymbol{R}) x$. Define $z_{i_0} \in \mathbb{R}_+^l$ as follows.

CASE 1. $\{x, y\}$ is a free pair for i_0.

For all $\lambda \in]0, 1[$, $\{\lambda x + (1 - \lambda) y, x\}$ and $\{\lambda x + (1 - \lambda) y, y\}$ are free pairs for i_0. By continuity, there exists λ^* such that $x_{i_0} P_{i_0} [\lambda^* x_{i_0} + (1 - \lambda^*) y_{i_0}] P_{i_0} y_{i_0}$. Then, let $z_{i_0} := \lambda^* x_{i_0} + (1 - \lambda^*) y_{i_0}$.

CASE 2. $\{x, y\}$ is not a free pair for i_0.

Then, for all $k \in \{1, \ldots, l\}$, $x_{i_0 k} \geq y_{i_0 k}$ with at least one strict inequality. Note that $y \neq 0$.

CASE 2-1. There exists k' such that for all $k \in \{1, \ldots, l\}$ with $k \neq k'$, $x_{i_0 k} = y_{i_0 k}$, and $y_{i_0 k'} > 0$.

Then $x_{i_0k'} > y_{i_0k'} > 0$. Given $\varepsilon > 0$, define $w_{i_0} \in \mathbb{R}^l_+$ as $w_{i_0k'} := y_{i_0k'}$ and, for all $k \neq k'$, $w_{i_0k} := y_{i_0k} + \varepsilon$. For sufficiently small ε, we have $x_{i_0} P_{i_0} w_{i_0} P_{i_0} y_{i_0}$ by continuity and strict monotonicity of preferences. Given $\delta > 0$, define $t_{i_0} \in \mathbb{R}^l_+$ as $t_{i_0k'} := w_{i_0k'} - \delta$ and, for all $k \neq k'$, $t_{i_0k} := w_{i_0k}$. For sufficiently small δ, we have $x_{i_0} P_{i_0} t_{i_0} P_{i_0} y_{i_0}$, again by continuity and strict monotonicity of preferences. Moreover, $\{t, x\}$ and $\{t, y\}$ are free pairs for i_0. Then let $z_{i_0} := t_{i_0}$.

Case 2-2. There exists k' such that, for all $k \in \{1, \ldots, l\}$ with $k \neq k'$, $x_{i_0k} = y_{i_0k}$ and $y_{i_0k'} = 0$.

Then, for all $k \in \{1, \ldots, l\}$ with $k \neq k'$, $x_{i_0k} = y_{i_0k} > 0$. Let $k'' \neq k'$. Given $\varepsilon > 0$, define $w_{i_0} \in \mathbb{R}^l_+$ as $w_{i_0k''} := x_{i_0k''} - \varepsilon$ and, for all $k \neq k''$, $w_{i_0k} := x_{i_0k}$. For sufficiently small ε, we have $x_{i_0} P_{i_0} w_{i_0} P_{i_0} y_{i_0}$. Given $\delta > 0$, define $t_{i_0} \in \mathbb{R}^l_+$ as $t_{i_0k'} := w_{i_0k'} + \delta$ and, for all $k \neq k'$, $t_{i_0k} := w_{i_0k}$. For sufficiently small δ, we have $x_{i_0} P_{i_0} t_{i_0} P_{i_0} y_{i_0}$. Moreover, $\{t, x\}$ and $\{t, y\}$ are free pairs for i_0. Then let $z_{i_0} := t_{i_0}$.

Case 2-3. There exist $k', k'' \in \{1, \ldots, l\}$ with $k' \neq k''$, $x_{i_0k'} > y_{i_0k'}$ and $x_{i_0k''} > y_{i_0k''}$.

Let k^* be such that $y_{i_0k^*} > 0$. Given $\varepsilon > 0$, define $w_{i_0} \in \mathbb{R}^l_+$ as $w_{i_0k^*} := y_{i_0k^*} - \varepsilon$ and, for all $k \neq k^*$, $w_{i_0k} := x_{i_0k}$. For sufficiently small ε, we have $x_{i_0} P_{i_0} w_{i_0} P_{i_0} y_{i_0}$. Let $k^{**} \neq k^*$. Given $\delta > 0$, define $t_{i_0} \in \mathbb{R}^l_+$ as $t_{i_0k^{**}} := w_{i_0k^{**}} + \delta$ and, for all $k \neq k^{**}$, $t_{i_0k} := w_{i_0k}$. For sufficiently small δ, we have $x_{i_0} P_{i_0} t_{i_0} P_{i_0} y_{i_0}$. Moreover, $\{t, x\}$ and $\{t, y\}$ are free pairs for i_0. Then let $z_{i_0} = t_{i_0}$.

Next, for each $i \neq i_0$, let $z_i \in \mathbb{R}^l_+$ be such that $\{z, x\}$ and $\{z, y\}$ are free pairs for i. By the same construction as before, we can find such $z_i \in \mathbb{R}^l_+$ for each i. Let $z = (z_i)_{i \in N} \in \mathbb{R}^{nl}_+$. Since i_0 is the dictator over all free pairs, we have that $x \bar{P}(\boldsymbol{R}) z$ and $z \bar{P}(\boldsymbol{R}) y$. By transitivity of $\bar{R}$, we have $x \bar{P}(\boldsymbol{R}) y$, which contradicts the supposition that $y \bar{R}(\boldsymbol{R}) x$. ■

Appendix 7.B. Proof of Proposition 7.3

In order to prove the impossibility part, it is convenient to consider various possible sizes of the population. Let $\varepsilon > 0$ be given. Suppose, to the contrary, that there exists a SOF $\bar{R}$ that satisfies weak Pareto, IIA-ISεN, and anonymity.

CASE $n = 2$. Consider the consumption bundles $x := (10\varepsilon, \varepsilon, 0, \ldots, 0)$, $y := (20\varepsilon, \varepsilon, 0, \ldots, 0)$, $z := (\varepsilon, 20\varepsilon, 0, \ldots, 0)$, $w := (\varepsilon, 10\varepsilon, 0, \ldots, 0)$. Define preference relations $R_1 \in \mathcal{R}$ and $R_2 \in \mathcal{R}$ as follows.

(i) On the subset

$$S_1 := \{v \in R^l_+ \mid \forall i \in \{3, \ldots, l\}, v_i = 0 \text{ and } v_2 \leq \min\{v_1, 2\varepsilon\}\},$$

we have

$$vR_1v' \Leftrightarrow v_1 + 2v_2 \geq v'_1 + 2v'_2,$$

and on the subset

$$S_2 := \{v \in R^l_+ \mid \forall i \in \{3, \ldots, l\}, v_i = 0 \text{ and } v_1 \leq \min\{v_2, 2\varepsilon\}\},$$

we have

$$vR_1v' \Leftrightarrow 2v_1 + v_2 \geq 2v'_1 + v'_2.$$

(ii) On $B_\varepsilon(x) \cup B_\varepsilon(y)$,

$$vR_1v' \Leftrightarrow v_1 + 2v_2 + \sum_{k=3}^{l} v_k \geq v'_1 + 2v'_2 + \sum_{k=3}^{l} v'_k,$$

and on $B_\varepsilon(z) \cup B_\varepsilon(w)$,

$$vR_1v' \Leftrightarrow 2v_1 + v_2 + \sum_{k=3}^{l} v_k \geq 2v'_1 + v'_2 + \sum_{k=3}^{l} v'_k.$$

(iii) Note that the projection of $B_\varepsilon(x) \cup B_\varepsilon(y)$ on the subspace of good 1 and good 2, namely, $[B_\varepsilon(x) \cup B_\varepsilon(y)] \cap \{v \in R^l_+ \mid \forall i \in \{3, \ldots, l\}, v_i = 0\}$, is included in S_1, and the projection of $B_\varepsilon(z) \cup B_\varepsilon(w)$ on the subspace of good 1 and good 2 is included in S_2.

Since

$$(w_1 + \varepsilon) + 2(w_2 - 2\varepsilon) > x_1 + 2x_2$$

and

$$2(y_1 - 2\varepsilon) + (y_2 + \varepsilon) > 2z_1 + z_2,$$

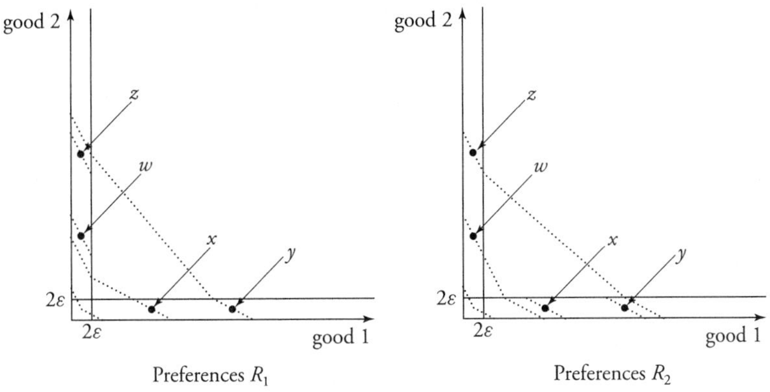

Figure 7.4. Proof of Proposition 7.3

it is possible to complete the definition of R_1 so that wP_1x and yP_1z. Then define R_2 so that it coincides with R_1 on S_1, on S_2, and on $B_\varepsilon(a)$ for all $a \in \{x, y, z, w\}$. Similarly, it is possible to complete the definition of R_2 so that xP_2w and zP_2y. Figure 7.4 illustrates this construction.

If the profile of preferences is $\boldsymbol{R} := (R_1, R_2)$, by weak Pareto we have

$$(y, x)\bar{P}(\boldsymbol{R})(z, w) \quad \text{and} \quad (w, z)\bar{P}(\boldsymbol{R})(x, y).$$

If the profile of preferences is $\boldsymbol{R}' := (R_1, R_1)$, by anonymity we have

$$(y, x)\bar{I}(\boldsymbol{R}')(x, y) \quad \text{and} \quad (w, z)\bar{I}(\boldsymbol{R}')(z, w).$$

Since R_1 and R_2 coincide on $B_\varepsilon(a)$ for all $a \in \{x, y, z, w\}$, it follows from IIA-ISεN that

$$(y, x)\bar{I}(\boldsymbol{R}')(x, y) \Leftrightarrow (y, x)\bar{I}(\boldsymbol{R})(x, y),$$
$$(w, z)\bar{I}(\boldsymbol{R}')(z, w) \Leftrightarrow (w, z)\bar{I}(\boldsymbol{R})(z, w).$$

By transitivity, $(x, y)\bar{P}(\boldsymbol{R})(x, y)$, which is impossible.

Case $n = 3$. Consider the consumption bundles $x := (10\varepsilon, \frac{2\varepsilon}{3}, 0, \ldots, 0)$, $y := (20\varepsilon, \frac{2\varepsilon}{3}, 0, \ldots, 0)$, $t := (15\varepsilon, \frac{2\varepsilon}{3}, 0, \ldots, 0)$, $z := (\frac{2\varepsilon}{3}, 20\varepsilon, 0, \ldots, 0)$, $w := (\frac{2\varepsilon}{3}, 10\varepsilon, 0, \ldots, 0)$, $r := (\frac{2\varepsilon}{3}, 15\varepsilon, 0, \ldots, 0)$. Define preference relations R_1, R_2, and R_3 as before on the subset S_1, on S_2, and on $B_\varepsilon(a)$ for all $a \in \{x, y, z, w, t, r\}$. Complete their definitions so that yP_1z, wP_1x, tP_2r, zP_2y, xP_3w, and rP_3t.

If the profile of preferences is $\boldsymbol{R} := (R_1, R_2, R_3)$, then by weak Pareto we have

$$(y, t, x)\bar{P}(\boldsymbol{R})(z, r, w) \quad \text{and} \quad (w, z, r)\bar{P}(\boldsymbol{R})(x, y, t).$$

If the profile of preferences is $\boldsymbol{R}' := (R_1, R_1, R_1)$, by anonymity we have

$$(y, t, x)\bar{I}(\boldsymbol{R}')(x, y, t) \quad \text{and} \quad (w, z, r)\bar{I}(\boldsymbol{R}')(z, r, w).$$

Since R_1, R_2, and R_3 coincide on $B_\varepsilon(a)$ for all $a \in \{x, y, t, z, w, r\}$, it follows from IIA-IS$\varepsilon$N that

$$(y, t, x)\bar{I}(\boldsymbol{R}')(x, y, t) \Leftrightarrow (y, t, x)\bar{I}(\boldsymbol{R})(x, y, t),$$

$$(w, z, r)\bar{I}(\boldsymbol{R}')(z, r, w) \Leftrightarrow (w, z, r)\bar{I}(\boldsymbol{R})(z, r, w).$$

By transitivity, $(x, y, t)\bar{P}(\boldsymbol{R})(x, y, t)$, which is impossible.

Case $n = 2k$. Partition the population into k pairs, and construct an argument similar to case $n = 2$, with the consumption bundles $x = (10\varepsilon, \frac{2\varepsilon}{n}, 0, \ldots, 0)$, $y = (20\varepsilon, \frac{2\varepsilon}{n}, 0, \ldots, 0)$, $z = (\frac{2\varepsilon}{n}, 20\varepsilon, 0, \ldots, 0)$, $w = (\frac{2\varepsilon}{n}, 10\varepsilon, 0, \ldots, 0)$, and the allocations $(y, x, y, x, \ldots, 0)$, $(x, y, x, y, \ldots, 0)$, $(z, w, z, w, \ldots, 0)$ and $(w, z, w, z, \ldots, 0)$.

Case $n = 2k + 1$. Partition the population into $k - 1$ pairs and one triple, and construct an argument combining cases $n = 2$ and $n = 3$, with the consumption bundles $x = (10\varepsilon, \frac{2\varepsilon}{n}, 0, \ldots, 0)$, $y = (20\varepsilon, \frac{2\varepsilon}{n}, 0, \ldots, 0)$, $t = (15\varepsilon, \frac{2\varepsilon}{n}, 0, \ldots, 0)$, $z = (\frac{2\varepsilon}{n}, 20\varepsilon, 0, \ldots, 0)$, $w = (\frac{2\varepsilon}{n}, 10\varepsilon, 0, \ldots, 0)$, $r = (\frac{2\varepsilon}{n}, 15\varepsilon, 0, \ldots, 0)$, and the allocations $(y, x, y, x, \ldots, y, t, x)$, $(x, y, x, y, \ldots, x, y, t)$, $(z, w, z, w, \ldots, z, r, w)$, and $(w, z, w, z, \ldots, w, z, r)$. ∎

Remark. One may consider a condition that is weaker than both IIA–ISεN and IIA-ISFA by allowing the social ranking of any two allocations x, y to depend on the portions of indifference surfaces in the union of the ε-neighborhoods of x_i and y_i, and the set $\Omega(x, y)$. With this weaker condition, the same impossibility still holds as in Proposition 7.3. The preceding proof can be applied without any changes to derive this result.

Appendix 7.C. Proof of Lemma 7.1

To prove Lemma 7.1, we need an auxiliary lemma. Define

$$X_1 := \{x_i \in \mathbb{R}^l_+ \setminus \{0\} \mid \forall k \geq 2, x_{ik} = 0\}$$

$$X_2 := \{x_i \in \mathbb{R}^l_+ \setminus \{0\} \mid \forall k \neq 2, x_{ik} = 0\}.$$

LEMMA 7.A.5. For all $R_i \in \mathcal{R}$, and all $x, y \in X$, there exists $R_i^* \in \mathcal{R}$ such that

$$I(x_i, R_i) \cap \Omega(x, y) = I(x_i, R_i^*) \cap \Omega(x, y)$$

$$I(y_i, R_i) \cap \Omega(x, y) = I(y_i, R_i^*) \cap \Omega(x, y)$$

$$I(x_i, R_i^*) \cap X_1 \neq \emptyset$$

$$I(y_i, R_i^*) \cap X_1 \neq \emptyset.$$

PROOF. Let $R_i \in \mathcal{R}$ and $x, y \in X$ be given. Without loss of generality, assume that $y_i R_i x_i$. Define $A := I(x_i, R_i) \cap \Omega(x, y)$ and

$$U(x_i, R_i^*) := \bigcap_{a \in A} \left[\bigcap_{q \in C(a, R_i)} H(a, q) \right],$$

where we recall that $H(a, q) = \{b \in \mathbb{R}^l_+ \mid q \cdot b \geq q \cdot a\}$. Let $I(x_i, R_i^*)$ be the boundary of $U(x_i, R_i^*)$.

Define a function $g : A \to \mathbb{R}_+$ as follows: for every $a \in A$, if $(a_1 + 1, 0, \ldots, 0) P_i a$, then let $g(a) = 0$, and otherwise, let $g(a) \in \mathbb{R}$ be such that $(a_1 + 1, g(a)a_2, \ldots, g(a)a_l) I_i a$. By continuity and strict monotonicity of R_i, $g(a)$ exists uniquely and $0 \leq g(a) < 1$. By continuity of R_i, g is continuous. For every $a \in A$, let $b(a) := (a_1 + 1, g(a)a_2, \ldots, g(a)a_l)$. Define $f : A \to X_1$ by

$$f(a) := a + \frac{1}{1 - g(a)} [b(a) - a]$$

$$= \left(a_1 + \frac{1}{1 - g(a)}, 0, \ldots, 0 \right).$$

Since $b(a) R_i a$, it follows that for every $q \in C(a, R_i)$, $q \cdot b(a) \geq q \cdot a$, and so $q \cdot f(a) \geq q \cdot a$. Hence, $f(a) \in H(a, q)$.

The function f is continuous, and the set A is compact and nonempty. Hence, the set $f(A)$ is compact and nonempty. Therefore, there exists $a^* \in A$ such that $||f(a^*)|| = \max_{a \in A} ||f(a)|| = \max_{a \in A} \left[a_1 + \frac{1}{1-g(a)}\right]$. Then, for all $a \in A$, and all $q \in C(a, R_i)$, since $f(a) \in H(a, q)$ and $f(a^*) \geq f(a)$, we have $f(a^*) \in H(a, q)$. Thus, $f(a^*) \in U(x_i, R_i^*)$, which proves that $U(x_i, R_i^*) \cap X_1 \neq \emptyset$. By continuity and strict monotonicity of preferences, $I(x_i, R_i^*) \cap X_1 \neq \emptyset$.

If $y_i I_i x_i$, then we are done. Assume that $y_i P_i x_i$. Define

$$U(y_i, R_i^*) := \bigcap_{a \in I(y_i, R_i) \cap \Omega(x,y)} \left[\bigcap_{q \in C(a, R_i)} H(a, q) \right].$$

By continuity of preferences, there exists $\delta > 0$ such that for all $z_i \in [(1+\delta) I_i(x_i, R_i)] \cap \Omega(x, y)$, $y_i P_i z_i$. Define

$$\tilde{U}(y_i, R_i^*) := U(y_i, R_i^*) \cap (1+\delta) U(x_i, R_i^*).$$

Then let $I(y_i, R_i^*)$ be the boundary of $\tilde{U}(y_i, R_i^*)$. Note that $I(x_i, R_i^*) \cap I(y_i, R_i^*) = \emptyset$. A similar argument as before shows that $U(y_i, R_i^*) \cap X_1 \neq \emptyset$. Since $U(x_i, R_i^*) \cap X_1 \neq \emptyset$, we have $[(1+\delta) U(x_i, R_i^*)] \cap X_1 \neq \emptyset$. Thus, $\tilde{U}(y_i, R_i^*) \cap X_1 \neq \emptyset$. By continuity and strict monotonicity of preferences, $I(y_i, R_i^*) \cap X_1 \neq \emptyset$. ■

Proof of Lemma 7.1. Let $\boldsymbol{R}, \boldsymbol{R}' \in \mathcal{R}^n$, $x, y \in X$ be such that for all $i \in N$, R_i and R_i' agree on $\{x_i, y_i\}$, and for no $i \in N$, $x_i I_i y_i$. Assume that $x \bar{P}(\boldsymbol{R}) y$.

By Lemma 7.A.5, there exists $\boldsymbol{R}^* \in \mathcal{R}^n$ such that for all $i \in N$,

$$I(x_i, R_i) \cap \Omega(x, y) = I(x_i, R_i^*) \cap \Omega(x, y)$$

$$I(y_i, R_i) \cap \Omega(x, y) = I(y_i, R_i^*) \cap \Omega(x, y)$$

$$I(x_i, R_i^*) \cap X_1 \neq \emptyset$$

$$I(y_i, R_i^*) \cap X_1 \neq \emptyset,$$

and similarly there exists $\boldsymbol{R}'^* \in \mathcal{R}^n$ such that for all $i \in N$,

$$I(x_i, R_i') \cap \Omega(x, y) = I(x_i, R_i'^*) \cap \Omega(x, y)$$
$$I(y_i, R_i') \cap \Omega(x, y) = I(y_i, R_i'^*) \cap \Omega(x, y)$$
$$I(x_i, R_i'^*) \cap X_2 \neq \emptyset$$
$$I(y_i, R_i'^*) \cap X_2 \neq \emptyset.$$

By strict monotonicity of preferences, each of $I(x_i, R_i^*) \cap X_1$, $I(y_i, R_i^*) \cap X_1$, $I(x_i, R_i'^*) \cap X_2$, and $I(y_i, R_i'^*) \cap X_2$ is a singleton. Define $x^1, y^1 \in X_1^n$ by $\{x_i^1\} := I(x_i, R_i^*) \cap X_1$ and $\{y_i^1\} := I(y_i, R_i^*) \cap X_1$ for all $i \in N$. Notice that for all $i \in N$, $x_{i1}^1 > 0$, $y_{i1}^1 > 0$ because $x, y \in X$ and preferences are strictly monotonic. Construct $x^{1*}, y^{1*} \in X_1^n$ as follows: for all $i \in N$,

$$x_{i1}^{1*} := x_{i1}^1 + \frac{1}{3}\left|x_{i1}^1 - y_{i1}^1\right|$$
$$y_{i1}^{1*} := \max\left\{\frac{1}{2}y_{i1}^1, y_{i1}^1 - \frac{1}{3}\left|x_{i1}^1 - y_{i1}^1\right|\right\}.$$

Notice that, for all $i \in N$,

$$x_{i1}^{1*} > y_{i1}^{1*} \Leftrightarrow x_i P_i y_i$$
$$y_{i1}^{1*} > x_{i1}^{1*} \Leftrightarrow y_i P_i x_i.$$

By weak Pareto, $x^{1*}\bar{P}(\boldsymbol{R}^*)x$ and $y\bar{P}(\boldsymbol{R}^*)y^{1*}$. By IIA-ISFA, $x\bar{P}(\boldsymbol{R}^*)y$. Therefore, by transitivity,

$$x^{1*}\bar{P}(\boldsymbol{R}^*)y^{1*}.$$

Now define $x^2, y^2 \in X_2^n$ by $\{x_i^2\} := I(x_i, R_i'^*) \cap X_2$ and $\{y_i^2\} := I(y_i, R_i'^*) \cap X_2$ for all $i \in N$. Again, $x_{i2}^2 > 0$, $y_{i2}^2 > 0$ for all $i \in N$. Construct $x^{2*}, y^{2*} \in X_2^n$ as follows: for all $i \in N$,

$$x_{i2}^{2*} := \max\left\{\frac{1}{2}x_{i2}^2, x_{i2}^2 - \frac{1}{3}\left|x_{i2}^2 - y_{i2}^2\right|\right\}$$
$$y_{i2}^{2*} := y_{i2}^2 + \frac{1}{3}\left|x_{i2}^2 - y_{i2}^2\right|.$$

Notice that, for all $i \in N$,

$$x_{i2}^{2*} > y_{i2}^{2*} \Leftrightarrow x_i P_i' y_i \Leftrightarrow x_i P_i y_i \Leftrightarrow x_{i1}^{1*} > y_{i1}^{1*}$$

$$y_{i2}^{2*} > x_{i2}^{2*} \Leftrightarrow y_i P_i' x_i \Leftrightarrow y_i P_i x_i \Leftrightarrow y_{i1}^{1*} > x_{i1}^{1*}.$$

By weak Pareto, $x \bar{P}(\boldsymbol{R}'^*) x^{2*}$ and $y^{2*} \bar{P}(\boldsymbol{R}'^*) y$.

Let $\boldsymbol{R}^{**} \in \mathcal{R}^n$ be such that, for all $i \in N$,

$$x_i^{2*} P_i^{**} x_i^{1*} \quad \text{and} \quad y_i^{1*} P_i^{**} y_i^{2*}.$$

Notice that, for all $i \in N$,

$$I(x_i^{1*}, R_i^{**}) \cap \Omega(x^{1*}, y^{1*}) = I(x_i^{1*}, R_i^*) \cap \Omega(x^{1*}, y^{1*}) = \{x_i^{1*}\},$$

$$I(y_i^{1*}, R_i^{**}) \cap \Omega(x^{1*}, y^{1*}) = I(y_i^{1*}, R_i^*) \cap \Omega(x^{1*}, y^{1*}) = \{y_i^{1*}\}.$$

Therefore, by IIA-ISFA, $x^{1*} \bar{P}(\boldsymbol{R}^{**}) y^{1*}$. By weak Pareto, $x^{2*} \bar{P}(\boldsymbol{R}^{**}) x^{1*}$ and $y^{1*} \bar{P}(\boldsymbol{R}^{**}) y^{2*}$, so that by transitivity, $x^{2*} \bar{P}(\boldsymbol{R}^{**}) y^{2*}$.

Now, we also have that, for all $i \in N$,

$$I(x_i^{2*}, R_i^{**}) \cap \Omega(x^{2*}, y^{2*}) = I(x_i^{2*}, R_i'^*) \cap \Omega(x^{2*}, y^{2*}) = \{x_i^{2*}\},$$

$$I(y_i^{2*}, R_i^{**}) \cap \Omega(x^{2*}, y^{2*}) = I(y_i^{2*}, R_i'^*) \cap \Omega(x^{2*}, y^{2*}) = \{y_i^{2*}\}.$$

By IIA-ISFA again, $x^{2*} \bar{P}(\boldsymbol{R}'^*) y^{2*}$. By transitivity, we deduce $x \bar{P}(\boldsymbol{R}'^*) y$. Finally, by IIA-ISFA,

$$x \bar{P}(\boldsymbol{R}') y.$$

We have proved that $x \bar{P}(\boldsymbol{R}) y$ implies $x \bar{P}(\boldsymbol{R}') y$, It follows from symmetry of the argument that $y \bar{P}(\boldsymbol{R}) x$ implies $y \bar{P}(\boldsymbol{R}') x$ and that $x \bar{I}(\boldsymbol{R}) y$ implies $x \bar{I}(\boldsymbol{R}') y$. ∎

Appendix 7.D. Logical Relations between the IIA Axioms

1. IIA-MRS implies neither IIA-ISFA nor IIA.
   Consider the following SOF: $\forall \boldsymbol{R} \in \mathcal{R}^n$, $\forall x, y \in \mathbb{R}_+^{nl}$, $x \bar{R}(\boldsymbol{R}) y$ if and only if (i) $\exists p \in \mathbb{R}_+^l$ such that $\forall i \in N$, $p \in C(x_i, R_i)$, and $\forall i, j \in$

N, $p \cdot x_i = p \cdot x_j$, or (ii) $\nexists p \in \mathbb{R}^l_+$ such that $\forall i \in N$, $p \in C(y_i, R_i)$, and $\forall i, j \in N$, $p \cdot y_i = p \cdot y_j$.

This SOF satisfies IIA-MRS but violates IIA-ISFA and hence IIA.

2. IIA-ISεN implies neither IIA-ISFA nor IIA.
   This is derived from fact 1 above and the fact that IIA-MRS implies IIA-ISεN.

3. IIA-ISεN does not imply IIA-MRS.
   This is derived from Propositions 7.2 and 7.3.

4. IIA-WIS implies neither IIA-ISεN nor IIA-ISFA.
   This is derived from Propositions 7.3 and 7.4 and Corollary 7.1.

5. IIA-ISFA implies none of IIA-ISεN, IIA-MRS, and IIA.
   Fix $\omega_0 := (1, \ldots, 1) \in \mathbb{R}^l$. For each $i \in N$, each $R_i \in \mathcal{R}$, and each $x_i \in \mathbb{R}^l_+$, let $\alpha(x_i, R_i) \in \mathbb{R}_+$ be defined as in the proof of Proposition 7.5. Consider the following SOF: $\forall \boldsymbol{R} \in \mathcal{R}^n$, $\forall x, y \in \mathbb{R}^{nl}_+$, $x \bar{R}(\boldsymbol{R})\, y$ if and only if (i) $\nexists \lambda \in \mathbb{R}_+$ such that $\sum_{i \in N} y_i = \lambda \omega_0$ or (ii) $\exists \lambda, \lambda' \in \mathbb{R}_+$ such that $\sum_{i \in N} x_i = \lambda \omega_0$ and $\sum_{i \in N} y_i = \lambda' \omega_0$, and $\min_{i \in N} \alpha(x_i, R_i) \geq \min_{i \in N} \alpha(y_i, R_i)$. This SOF satisfies IIA-ISFA, but it violates IIA-ISεN and hence IIA-MRS and IIA.

6. IIA-ISPω_0 implies none of IIA-ISεN, IIA-MRS, IIA-ISFA, and IIA.
   This is derived from Propositions 7.3–7.5.

7. IIA-WIS does not imply IIA-ISPω_0.
   Fix $p := (1, \ldots, 1) \in \mathbb{R}^l$. For each $i \in N$, each $R_i \in \mathcal{R}$, and each $x_i \in \mathbb{R}^l_+$, define $e(x_i, R_i) := \min \{p \cdot y_i \mid y_i \in I(x_i, R_i)\}$. (That is, $e(x_i, R_i)$ is the minimum expenditure to attain $I(x_i, R_i)$ at p.) Consider the following SOF: $\forall \boldsymbol{R} \in \mathcal{R}^n$, $\forall x, y \in \mathbb{R}^{nl}_+$, $x \bar{R}(\boldsymbol{R}) y$ if and only if $\min_{i \in N} e(x_i, R_i) \geq \min_{i \in N} e(y_i, R_i)$. This SOF satisfies IIA-WIS but violates IIA-ISPω_0.

7.7. References

[1] Arrow, K. J., "A Difficulty in the Concept of Social Welfare," *Journal of Political Economy* **58**, 1950, 328–346.

[2] Arrow, K. J., *Social Choice and Individual Values,* New York: John Wiley & Sons, 1951; 2nd edn., 1963.

[3] Bordes, G., and M. Le Breton, "Arrovian Theorems with Private Alternatives Domains and Selfish Individuals," *Journal of Economic Theory* **47**, 1989, 257–281.

[4] Bossert, W., M. Fleurbaey, and D. Van de gaer, "Responsibility, Talent, and Compensation: A Second-Best Analysis," *Review of Economic Design* **4**, 1999, 35–55.

[5] Campbell, D. E., and J. S. Kelly, "Information and Preference Aggregation," *Social Choice and Welfare* **17**, 2000, 3–24.

[6] Chichilnisky, G., "A Unified Perspective on Resource Allocation: Limited Arbitrage Is Necessary and Sufficient for the Existence of a Competitive Equilibrium, the Core and Social Choice," in K. J. Arrow, A. K. Sen and K. Suzumura, eds., *Social Choice Reexamined,* Vol. 1, London: Macmillan, and New York: St. Martin's Press, 1997, 121–174.

[7] d'Aspremont, C., and L. Gevers, "Equity and the Informational Basis of Collective Choice," *Review of Economic Studies* **44**, 1977, 199–209.

[8] Fleurbaey, M., and F. Maniquet, "Utilitarianism versus Fairness in Welfare Economics," in M. Fleurbaey, M. Salles, and J. A. Weymark, eds., *Justice, Political Liberalism and Utilitarianism: Themes from Harsanyi and Rawls,* New York: Cambridge University Press, 1996, 263–280.

[9] Fleurbaey, M. and F. Maniquet, "Fair Social Orderings with Unequal Production Skills," *Social Choice and Welfare* **24**, 2005, 1–35.

[10] Hammond, P., "Equity, Arrow's Conditions, and Rawls' Difference Principle," *Econometrica* **44**, 1976, 793–804.

[11] Hansson, B., "The Independence Condition in the Theory of Social Choice," *Theory and Decision* **4**, 1973, 25–49.

[12] Inada, K.-I., "On the Economic Welfare Function," *Econometrica* **32**, 1964, 316–338.

[13] Kalai, E., E. Muller, and M. A. Satterthwaite, "Social Welfare Functions When Preferences Are Convex, Strictly Monotonic, and Continuous," *Public Choice* **34**, 1979, 87–97.

[14] Maniquet, F., *On Equity and Implementation in Economic Environments,* PhD thesis, University of Namur, Belgium, 1994.

[15] Pazner, E., "Equity, Nonfeasible Alternatives and Social Choice: A Reconsideration of the Concept of Social Welfare," in J. J. Laffont, ed., *Aggregation and Revelation of Preferences,* Amsterdam: North-Holland, 1979.

[16] Pazner, E. and D. Schmeidler, "Egalitarian-Equivalent Allocations: A New Concept of Economic Equity," *Quarterly Journal of Economics* **92**, 1978, 671–687.

[17] Roberts, K., "Interpersonal Comparability and Social Choice Theory," *Review of Economic Studies* **47**, 1980, 421–439.

[18] Sen, A. K., *Collective Choice and Social Welfare,* San Francisco: Holden-Day, 1970. Republished, Amsterdam: North-Holland, 1979.

[19] Suzumura, K., "On Pareto Efficiency and the No-Envy Concept of Equity," *Journal of Economic Theory* **25**, 1981, 367–379. Essay 9 of this volume.

[20] Suzumura, K., "On the Possibility of 'Fair' Collective Choice Rule," *International Economic Review* **22**, 1981, 351–364.

[21] Tadenuma, K., "Efficiency First or Equity First? Two Principles and Rationality of Social Choice," *Journal of Economic Theory* **104**, 2002, 462–472.

ESSAY 8

A Characterization of Suzumura-Consistent Collective Choice Rules

8.1. Introduction

Arrow's [1] theorem regarding the impossibility of defining a collective choice rule possessing some seemingly innocuous properties is one of the most fundamental results in the theory of collective decision making. There have been numerous attempts to modify his framework in order to avoid impossibilities, such as weakening some of his original axioms or departing from the stringent informational assumption that only ordinally measurable and interpersonally noncomparable information on individual well-being is available.

The route of escape from the negative conclusion of Arrow's theorem that we follow in this essay consists of relaxing the requirement that the social ranking be an ordering for all preference profiles under consideration. In this spirit, Sen [5; 6, Theorem 5*3] characterized the Pareto extension rule under the assumption that social preferences are quasi-transitive but not necessarily transitive while retaining the completeness assumption. Weymark [10, Theorem 3] allowed social preferences to be incomplete but imposed full transitivity and, as a result, obtained a characterization of the Pareto rule.

First published in *Journal of Economic Theory* **138**, 2008, pp. 311-320. Joint paper with Walter Bossert. Thnaks are due to the editor in charge and referees of *Journal of Economic Theory* for their helpful comments.

An interesting question that emerges in this context is what happens if transitivity is weakened to *S-consistency.* S-consistency, a property introduced by Suzumura [8], is intermediate in strength between transitivity and acyclicity and coincides with transitivity in the presence of reflexivity and completeness. It is logically independent of quasi transitivity and requires that there be no preference cycles with at least one strict preference.

S-consistency is of importance because, as Suzumura [8] demonstrated, it is *necessary and sufficient* for the existence of an *ordering extension;* that is, a binary relation R can be extended to an ordering respecting all (weak and strict) preferences according to R if and only if R is S-consistent. This fundamental insight represents a significant strengthening of the classical extension theorem and its variants due to Szpilrajn [9], establishing that the transitivity of an incomplete relation is *sufficient* for the existence of an ordering extension. Because S-consistency constitutes the weakest possible coherence property that needs to be satisfied if we do not want to give up all hope of compatibility with an ordering, S-consistency appears to be *the* natural weakening of the transitivity requirement, particularly in the absence of completeness. It is also worthwhile to observe that S-consistency of a weak preference relation R is precisely the requirement that the holder of R is not a "money pump" in the classical illustration of incoherent preferences. See, for example, Raiffa [4, p. 78].

In spite of its intuitive appeal, S-consistency has received relatively little attention in the past (see Bossert [2] for an overview of its application, such as in the analysis of rational choice due to Bossert, Sprumont, and Suzumura [3]). In this essay, we examine the consequences of weakening transitivity to consistency in the context of Arrow's theorem. It turns out that, in some circumstances, S-consistency permits a larger class of possible collective choice rules as compared to those that are available if completeness is dropped as a requirement on a social relation but the full force of transitivity is retained.

The axioms we impose on collective choice rules are unrestricted domain, strong Pareto, anonymity, and neutrality. If there are at least as many alternatives as there are agents, an alternative characterization of the Pareto rule is obtained. The difference between this characterization and Weymark's [10] is that we weaken the transitivity requirement imposed on the social relation to S-consistency and strengthen independence of irrelevant alternatives to neutrality. However, if there are fewer alternatives than agents, additional rules satisfy the preceding axioms. We characterize all of them and obtain the aforementioned new axiomatization of the Pareto rule as a special case. Especially in applications where there are many voters and relatively few candidates (this is the case for political elections, to name a prominent and important example), our result shows that it is possible to go considerably beyond the limitations of unanimity imposed by the Pareto rule. This is achieved at relatively little cost because S-consistency still ensures the existence of an ordering coherent with the social relation.

In addition, this essay develops a new approach to the analysis of collective choice rules in the sense that it does not rely on previously applied proof techniques. In particular, tools such as Sen's [7] *field expansion lemma,* which allows one to extend "local" observations to arbitrary collections of alternatives, crucially rely on transitivity (or quasi transitivity), and S-consistency is not sufficient to obtain these types of results. Therefore, a novel approach to identifying the class of collective choice rules compatible with standard axioms is called for when working with S-consistency.

The following section provides our basic definitions along with a preliminary observation. Section 8.3 introduces the notion of an S-consistent collective choice rule along with some examples. Section 8.4 contains the statement and proof of our characterization result, followed by a discussion and some concluding remarks.

8.2. Preliminaries

Suppose there is a set of alternatives X containing at least three elements, that is, $|X| \geq 3$ where $|X|$ denotes the cardinality of X. The population is $N = \{1, \ldots, |N|\}$ with $|N| \in \mathbb{N} \setminus \{1\}$, where $\mathbb{N}$ denotes the set of all natural numbers. Let $R \subseteq X \times X$ be a binary relation. For simplicity, we write xRy instead of $(x, y) \in R$ and $\neg xRy$ instead of $(x, y) \notin R$. The *asymmetric factor* P of R is defined by

$$xPy \Leftrightarrow [xRy \text{ and } \neg yRx]$$

for all $x, y \in X$. The *symmetric factor* I of R is defined by

$$xIy \Leftrightarrow [xRy \text{ and } yRx]$$

for all $x, y \in X$. If R is interpreted as a *weak preference relation,* that is, xRy means that x is considered at least as good as y, then P and I are the *strict preference relation* and the *indifference relation,* respectively, corresponding to R.

A binary relation R is *reflexive* if and only if, for all $x \in X$,

$$xRx$$

and R is *complete* if and only if, for all $x, y \in X$ such that $x \neq y$,

$$xRy \text{ or } yRx.$$

Furthermore, R is *transitive* if and only if, for all $x, y, z \in X$,

$$[xRy \text{ and } yRz] \Rightarrow xRz$$

and R is *quasi-transitive* if and only if P is transitive. R is *Suzumura-consistent—S-consistent* hereafter—if and only if, for all $M \in \mathbb{N} \setminus \{1, 2\}$ and for all $x^1, \ldots, x^M \in X$,

$$x^{m-1}Rx^m \quad \forall m \in \{2, \ldots, M\} \Rightarrow \neg x^M P x^1$$

and, finally, R is *acyclic* if and only if, for all $M \in \mathbb{N} \setminus \{1, 2\}$ and for all $x^1, \ldots, x^M \in X$,

$$x^{m-1}Px^m \quad \forall m \in \{2, \ldots, M\} \Rightarrow \neg x^M P x^1.$$

Transitivity implies S-consistency, which, in turn, implies acyclicity, but the reverse implications are not true in general. Analogously, transitivity implies quasi transitivity and quasi transitivity implies acyclicity. If R is reflexive and complete, transitivity and S-consistency are equivalent, whereas transitivity remains stronger than quasi transitivity. To see that, in general, quasi transitivity and S-consistency are independent, consider the following examples. Let $X = \{x, y, z\}$. The relation given by xPy and yPz is S-consistent but not quasi-transitive, whereas the relation defined by xIy, yIz, and zPx is quasi-transitive but not S-consistent.

An *ordering* is a reflexive, complete, and transitive relation. If R is an ordering, there is no ambiguity in using chains of individual preferences involving more than two alternatives; for instance, $xPyPz$ means that x is better than y, which, in turn, is better than z and, by the transitivity of R, x is better than z.

The set of all orderings on X is denoted by $\mathcal{R}$ and its $|N|$-fold Cartesian product is $\mathcal{R}^{|N|}$. The set of all reflexive and transitive relations on X is $\mathcal{T}$, and the set of all reflexive and S-consistent relations on X is denoted by $\mathcal{C}$. The set of all binary relations on X is $\mathcal{B}$. A *profile* is a $|N|$-tuple $\boldsymbol{R} = (R_1, \ldots, R_{|N|}) \in \mathcal{R}^{|N|}$.

A *collective choice rule* is a mapping $f\colon \mathcal{D} \to \mathcal{B}$ where $\mathcal{D} \subseteq \mathcal{R}^{|N|}$ is the *domain* of this function, assumed to be nonempty. An *S-consistent collective choice rule* is a collective choice rule f such that $f(\boldsymbol{R}) \in \mathcal{C}$ for all $\boldsymbol{R} \in \mathcal{D}$, and a *transitive collective choice rule* is a collective choice rule f such that $f(\boldsymbol{R}) \in \mathcal{T}$ for all $\boldsymbol{R} \in \mathcal{D}$. Note that, because $\mathcal{D} \subseteq \mathcal{R}^{|N|}$, we retain the assumption that all admissible profiles are composed of individual preferences, which are orderings. On the other hand, we allow social preferences to be incomplete and we permit violations of transitivity as long as S-consistency is satisfied. For each profile $\boldsymbol{R} \in \mathcal{D}$, $R = f(\boldsymbol{R})$ is the social preference corresponding to $\boldsymbol{R}$, and P and I are the strict preference relation and the indifference relation, respectively, corresponding to R.

An example of a transitive (and, thus, S-consistent) collective choice rule is the *Pareto rule* $f^p\colon \mathcal{R}^{|N|} \to \mathcal{B}$ defined by $R^p = f^p(\boldsymbol{R})$, where

$$xR^p y \Leftrightarrow [xR_i y \ \ \forall i \in N]$$

for all $x, y \in X$ and for all $\boldsymbol{R} \in \mathcal{R}^{|N|}$. The *Pareto extension rule* $f^e\colon \mathcal{R}^{|N|} \to \mathcal{B}$ is defined by $R^e = f^e(\boldsymbol{R})$, where

$$xR^e y \Leftrightarrow \neg yP^p x$$

for all $x, y \in X$ and for all $\boldsymbol{R} \in \mathcal{R}^{|N|}$. $R^e = f^e(\boldsymbol{R})$ is quasi-transitive, reflexive, and complete for all $\boldsymbol{R} \in \mathcal{R}^{|N|}$. However, R^e is not necessarily S-consistent (and, thus, not necessarily transitive).

We use $B(x, y; \boldsymbol{R})$ to denote the set of individuals such that $x \in X$ is better than $y \in X$ in the profile $\boldsymbol{R} \in \mathcal{R}^{|N|}$; that is, for all $x, y \in X$ and for all $\boldsymbol{R} \in \mathcal{R}^{|N|}$, $B(x, y; \boldsymbol{R}) = \{i \in N \mid xP_i y\}$. The following simple lemma, which will be of use in the proof of our main result, establishes that the cardinalities of these sets satisfy a *triangle inequality*.

LEMMA 8.1. For all $x, y, z \in X$ and for all $\boldsymbol{R} \in \mathcal{R}^{|N|}$,

$$|B(x, z; \boldsymbol{R})| \leq |B(x, y; \boldsymbol{R})| + |B(y, z; \boldsymbol{R})|.$$

PROOF. Let $x, y, z \in X$ and $\boldsymbol{R} \in \mathcal{R}^{|N|}$. First, we prove that

$$B(x, z; \boldsymbol{R}) \subseteq B(x, y; \boldsymbol{R}) \cup B(y, z; \boldsymbol{R}). \tag{8.1}$$

Suppose $i \notin B(x, y; \boldsymbol{R}) \cup B(y, z; \boldsymbol{R})$. Because individual preferences are complete, this implies yR_ix and zR_iy. By transitivity, zR_ix and, thus, $i \notin B(x, z; \boldsymbol{R})$, which proves (8.1).

Clearly, (8.1) implies

$$|B(x, z; \boldsymbol{R})| \leq |B(x, y; \boldsymbol{R}) \cup B(y, z; \boldsymbol{R})|.$$

Furthermore, we obviously must have

$$|B(x, y; \boldsymbol{R}) \cup B(y, z; \boldsymbol{R})| \leq |B(x, y; \boldsymbol{R})| + |B(y, z; \boldsymbol{R})|.$$

Combining the last two inequalities yields the desired result. ∎

The following axioms are standard in the literature on Arrovian social choice theory.

UNRESTRICTED DOMAIN. $\mathcal{D} = \mathcal{R}^{|N|}$.

STRONG PARETO. For all $x, y \in X$ and for all $\boldsymbol{R} \in \mathcal{D}$,

(i) $xR_iy \ \forall i \in N \Rightarrow xRy$;

(ii) $[xR_iy \ \forall i \in N$ and $\exists j \in N$ such that $xP_jy] \Rightarrow xPy$.

ANONYMITY. For all bijections $\rho: N \to N$ and for all $\boldsymbol{R}, \boldsymbol{R}' \in \mathcal{D}$,

$$R_i = R'_{\rho(i)} \ \forall i \in N \Rightarrow R = R'.$$

INDEPENDENCE OF IRRELEVANT ALTERNATIVES. For all $x, y \in X$ and for all $\boldsymbol{R}, \boldsymbol{R}' \in \mathcal{D}$,

$$[xR_iy \Leftrightarrow xR'_iy \text{ and } yR_ix \Leftrightarrow yR'_ix] \quad \forall i \in N$$

$$\Rightarrow [xRy \Leftrightarrow xR'y \text{ and } yRx \Leftrightarrow yR'x].$$

NEUTRALITY. For all $x, y, z, w \in X$ and for all $\boldsymbol{R}, \boldsymbol{R}' \in \mathcal{D}$,

$$[xR_iy \Leftrightarrow zR_i'w \text{ and } yR_ix \Leftrightarrow wR_i'z] \quad \forall i \in N$$

$$\Rightarrow [xRy \Leftrightarrow zR'w \text{ and } yRx \Leftrightarrow wR'z].$$

As is straightforward to verify, the Pareto rule and the Pareto extension rule satisfy all of the axioms introduced above.

8.3. S-Consistent Collective Choice Rules

Sen [5; 6, Theorem 5*3] characterized the Pareto extension rule by weakening the transitivity of the social ranking to quasi transitivity while retaining the completeness assumption. Weymark [10, Theorem 3] has shown that the Pareto rule is the only transitive collective choice rule satisfying unrestricted domain, strong Pareto, anonymity, and independence of irrelevant alternatives. As a corollary to our main result, we will obtain an alternative characterization of the Pareto rule that is obtained by strengthening independence of irrelevant alternatives to neutrality and weakening transitivity to S-consistency. This special case is obtained whenever $|X| \geq |N|$. If $|X| < |N|$, however, further S-consistent collective choice rules are possible. This is in contrast to Sen's [5; 6, Theorem 5*3] and Weymark's [10] results, which are valid for any $|N| \geq 2$ and any $|X| \geq 3$.

To describe all collective choice rules satisfying our requirements, we introduce some additional definitions. Let

$$\mathcal{S} = \left\{(w, l) \in \{0, \ldots, |N|\}^2 \mid 0 \leq |X|l < w + l \leq |N|\right\} \cup \{(0, 0)\}\}$$

and, furthermore, define

$$\Sigma = \{S \subseteq \mathcal{S} \mid (w, 0) \in S \; \forall w \in \{0, \ldots, |N|\}\}.$$

For $S \in \Sigma$, define the *S-rule* $f^S \colon \mathcal{R}^{|N|} \to \mathcal{B}$ by $R^S = f^S(\boldsymbol{R})$, where

$$xR^Sy \Leftrightarrow [\exists (w, l) \in S \text{ such that } |B(x, y; \boldsymbol{R})| = w \text{ and } |B(y, x; \boldsymbol{R})| = l]$$

for all $x, y \in X$ and for all $\boldsymbol{R} \in \mathcal{R}^{|N|}$. The set S specifies the pairs of numbers of agents who have to consider an alternative x better (resp. worse) than an alternative y in order to obtain a weak preference of x over y according to the profile under consideration. Clearly, because only the number of individuals matters and not their identities, the resulting rule is anonymous. Analogously, neutrality is satisfied because these numbers do not depend on the alternatives to be ranked. Strong Pareto follows from the requirement that the pairs $(w, 0)$ be in S in the definition of Σ. Reflexivity of the social relation follows from the reflexivity of the individual preferences and the observation that $(0, 0) \in S$ for all $S \in \Sigma$. As will be shown in the proof of our characterization result, the social relation R^S is consistent due to the restrictions imposed on the pairs (w, l) in the definition of $\mathcal{S}$.

Clearly, the Pareto rule is the special case that is obtained for $S = \{(w, 0) \mid w \in \{0, \ldots, |N|\}\}$. If $|X| \geq |N|$, this is the *only* S-rule. This is the case because only pairs (w, l), where $l = 0$, are in S in the presence of this inequality. To see this, suppose, to the contrary, that there exists $(w, l) \in S$ such that $l > 0$. Because $(w, l) \in S$, it follows that $|N| \geq w + l > |X|l > 0$. Combined with $|X| \geq |N|$, this implies $|N| > |N|l$, which is impossible if $l > 0$. Thus, if $|X| \geq |N|$, our characterization of the class of S-rules presented in the following section provides an alternative characterization of the Pareto rule. This axiomatization differs from Weymark's in that independence of irrelevant alternatives is strengthened to neutrality and transitivity is weakened to S-consistency. Note that if $|X| \geq |N|$, transitivity is implied by the conjunction of S-consistency and the axioms employed in our theorem. However, if $|X| < |N|$, the Pareto rule is not the only S-rule. For example, consider f^S corresponding to the set $S = \{(w, 0) \mid w \in \{0, \ldots, |N|\}\} \cup \{(|N| - 1, 1)\}$. For $(w, l) = (|N| - 1, 1)$, we have $|N| = |N| - 1 + 1 = w + l = |N| \cdot 1 > |X|l > 0$, and the relevant inequalities are satisfied.

Once rules other than the Pareto rule are available, transitivity is no longer guaranteed (but, of course, all S-rules are S-consistent as we establish in the following section). For example, suppose $X = \{x, y, z\}$, $N = \{1, 2, 3, 4\}$, $S = \{(0, 0), (1, 0), (2, 0), (3, 0), (4, 0), (3, 1)\}$, and consider the profile $\boldsymbol{R}$ defined by

$$x P_1 y P_1 z, \qquad x P_2 y P_2 z, \qquad z P_3 x P_3 y, \qquad y P_4 z P_4 x.$$

According to $R^S = f^S(\boldsymbol{R})$, we have $x P^S y$ and $y P^S z$ because $|B(x, y; \boldsymbol{R})| = |B(y, z; \boldsymbol{R})| = 3$ and $|B(y, x; \boldsymbol{R})| = |B(z, y; \boldsymbol{R})| = 1$. But $|B(x, z; \boldsymbol{R})| = |B(z, x; \boldsymbol{R})| = 2$ and, thus, $\neg x R^S z$ so that R^S is not transitive (not even quasi-transitive).

An interesting feature of the S-rules is that there may be "gaps" in the set of possible values of w or l within a rule. For instance, suppose $X = \{x, y, z\}$, $N = \{1, 2, 3, 4, 5, 6, 7\}$, and $S = \{(0, 0), (1, 0), (2, 0), (3, 0), (4, 0), (5, 0), (6, 0), (7, 0), (5, 2)\}$. Consider the pair $(w, l) = (5, 2)$. We have $|N| = w + l = 7 > 6 = 3 \cdot 2 = |X|l > 0$ and, thus, f^S is well defined. In addition to the rankings generated by unanimity, five agents can ensure a superior ranking of an alternative over another against two agents with the opposite preference but, on the other hand, if six agents prefer x to y and one agent prefers y to x, noncomparability results.

8.4. A Characterization

We now show that the S-rules are the only rules satisfying our axioms. This characterization theorem is the main result of the essay.

Theorem 8.1. An S-consistent collective choice rule f satisfies unrestricted domain, strong Pareto, anonymity, and neutrality if and only if there exists $S \in \Sigma$ such that $f = f^S$.

Proof. "If." As mentioned before the theorem statement, that the S-rules satisfy unrestricted domain, strong Pareto, anonymity, and neutrality is straightforward to verify. Because reflexivity is obvious, it remains to establish that $R^S = f^S(\boldsymbol{R})$ is S-consistent for all $S \in \Sigma$ and for all $\boldsymbol{R} \in \mathcal{R}^{|N|}$. Let $S \in \Sigma$ and suppose, by way of contradiction, that there exist $\boldsymbol{R} \in \mathcal{R}^{|N|}$, $M \in \mathbb{N} \setminus \{1, 2\}$, and $x^1, \ldots, x^M \in X$ such that $x^{m-1} R^S x^m$ for all $m \in \{2, \ldots, M\}$ and $x^M P^S x^1$. Clearly, we can assume $M \leq |X|$ because redundant elements in the cycle can be eliminated. By definition of R^S, there exist $(w_1, l_1), \ldots, (w_M, l_M) \in S$ such that $|B(x^{m-1}, x^m; \boldsymbol{R})| = w_{m-1}$ and $|B(x^m, x^{m-1}; \boldsymbol{R})| = l_{m-1}$ for all $m \in \{2, \ldots, M\}$. Furthermore, we must have $|B(x^M, x^1; \boldsymbol{R})| = w_M$ and $|B(x^1, x^M; \boldsymbol{R})| = l_M$ with w_M positive; if $w_M = 0$, we have $(w_M, l_M) = (0, 0)$ by definition of $\mathcal{S}$, and it follows that $x^1 I^S x^M$, contrary to our hypothesis $x^M P^S x^1$.

If $\max \{l_1, \ldots, l_M\} = 0$, application of Lemma 8.1 (repeated if necessary) yields

$$|B(x^3, x^1; \boldsymbol{R})| \leq |B(x^3, x^2; \boldsymbol{R})| + |B(x^2, x^1; \boldsymbol{R})|,$$

$$\vdots$$

$$|B(x^M, x^1; \boldsymbol{R})| \leq |B(x^M, x^{M-1}; \boldsymbol{R})| + \ldots + |B(x^2, x^1; \boldsymbol{R})| = 0.$$

But this contradicts our earlier observation that $|B(x^M, x^1; \boldsymbol{R})| = w_M > 0$.

If $\max\{l_1, \ldots, l_M\} > 0$, suppose this maximum is achieved at l_m for some $m \in \{1, \ldots, M\}$. By definition of $\mathcal{S}$, $|X| \geq 3 > 0$ and $w_m + l_m > |X| l_m$ together rule out the possibility that $w_m + l_m > |X| w_m$ and, therefore, we must have $(l_m, w_m) \notin S$, and the preference corresponding to the mth element in the chain is strict. This, in turn, allows us to assume, without loss of generality, that $m = M$; this can be achieved with a simple relabeling of the elements in our chain if required. Invoking Lemma 8.1 again and using the maximality of l_M, we obtain

$$|B(x^3, x^1; \boldsymbol{R})| \leq |B(x^3, x^2; \boldsymbol{R})| + |B(x^2, x^1; \boldsymbol{R})| \leq 2l_M$$

$$\vdots$$

$$|B(x^M, x^1; \boldsymbol{R})| \leq |B(x^M, x^{M-1}; \boldsymbol{R})| + \ldots + |B(x^2, x^1; \boldsymbol{R})| \leq (M-1)l_M.$$

Because $M \leq |X|$, this implies

$$|B(x^M, x^1; \boldsymbol{R})| \leq (|X| - 1)l_M. \tag{8.2}$$

By assumption and by the definition of $\mathcal{S}$, we have $|B(x^M, x^1; \boldsymbol{R})| = w_M > (|X| - 1)l_M$, a contradiction to (8.2).

"Only if." Suppose f is an S-consistent collective choice rule satisfying the axioms of the theorem statement. Let

$$S = \{(w, l) \mid \exists\, x, y \in X \text{ and } \boldsymbol{R} \in \mathcal{R}^{|N|} \text{ such that}$$
$$|B(x, y; \boldsymbol{R})| = w,\ |B(y, x; \boldsymbol{R})| = l \text{ and } xRy\}.$$

By anonymity and neutrality, S is such that the relation R is equal to R^S. It remains to show that $S \in \Sigma$. That $(w, 0) \in S$ for all $w \in \{0, \ldots, |N|\}$ follows from strong Pareto. Clearly, for all $(w, l) \in S$, $|X| l \geq 0$ and $w + l \leq |N|$.

As an auxiliary result, we show that

$$w > l \tag{8.3}$$

for all $(w, l) \in S \setminus \{(0, 0)\}$. By way of contradiction, suppose that $w \leq l$ for some $(w, l) \in S \setminus \{(0, 0)\}$. Because $(w, l) \neq (0, 0)$ by assumption, this implies $l > 0$ and, by strong Pareto, $w > 0$. By unrestricted domain and the assumption $|X| \geq 3$, we can choose $x, y, z \in X$ and $\boldsymbol{R} \in \mathcal{R}^{|N|}$ so that

$$x P_i y P_i z \ \forall i \in \{1, \ldots, w\}$$

and

$$y P_i z P_i x \ \forall i \in \{l+1, \ldots, l+w\}.$$

Furthermore, if $w < l$, let

$$y P_i x P_i z \ \forall i \in \{w+1, \ldots, l\}$$

and if $w + l < |N|$, let

$$x I_i y I_i z \ \forall i \in \{w+l+1, \ldots, |N|\}.$$

Because $|B(z, x; \boldsymbol{R})| = |B(x, y; \boldsymbol{R})| = w$ and $|B(x, z; \boldsymbol{R})| = |B(y, x; \boldsymbol{R})| = l$, we must have zRx and xRy. By strong Pareto, it follows that yPz, and we obtain a contradiction to the S-consistency of R. This establishes (8.3).

To complete the proof, we have to show that $w + l > |X|l$ for all $(w, l) \in S \setminus \{(0, 0)\}$. By way of contradiction, suppose this is not true. Then there exists a pair $(w_0, l_0) \in S \setminus \{(0, 0)\}$ such that $w_0 + l_0 \leq |X|l_0$ or, equivalently,

$$w_0 \leq (|X| - 1)l_0. \tag{8.4}$$

Combining (8.3), which is true for all $(w, l) \in S \setminus \{(0, 0)\}$ and thus for (w_0, l_0), with (8.4), we obtain

$$l_0 < w_0 \leq (|X| - 1)l_0. \tag{8.5}$$

Clearly, $l_0 = 0$ is inconsistent with (8.5). Thus, $l_0 > 0$.

It follows from (8.3) that, for any $(w, l) \in S \setminus \{(0, 0)\}$, $(l, w) \notin S$. Thus, in particular, whenever $|B(x, y; \boldsymbol{R})| = w_0$ and $|B(y, x; \boldsymbol{R})| = l_0$, we must have xPy and not merely xRy.

We now distinguish two cases. The first of these occurs whenever w_0 is a positive multiple of l_0. That is, given (8.5), there exists $\beta \in \{3, \ldots, |X|\}$

such that $w_0 = (\beta - 1)l_0$ (and, thus, $w_0 + l_0 = \beta l_0$). By unrestricted domain, we can choose β alternatives $x^1, \ldots, x^\beta \in X$ and a profile $\boldsymbol{R} \in \mathcal{R}^{|N|}$ such that

$$x^1 P_i x^2 P_i \ldots P_i x^{\beta-1} P_i x^\beta \ \forall i \in \{1, \ldots, l_0\},$$

$$x^2 P_i x^3 P_i \ldots P_i x^\beta P_i x^1 \ \forall i \in \{l_0 + 1, \ldots, 2l_0\},$$

$$\vdots$$

$$x^{\beta-1} P_i x^\beta P_i x^1 P_i \ldots P_i x^{\beta-2} \ \forall i \in \{(\beta - 2)l_0 + 1, \ldots, (\beta - 1)l_0\},$$

$$x^\beta P_i x^1 P_i \ldots P_i x^{\beta-2} P_i x^{\beta-1} \ \forall i \in \{(\beta - 1)l_0 + 1, \ldots, \beta l_0\}$$

and, if $|N| > w_0 + l_0 = \beta l_0$,

$$x^1 I_i x^2 I_i \ldots I_i x^{\beta-1} I_i x^\beta \ \forall i \in \{w_0 + l_0 + 1, \ldots, |N|\}.$$

We have $|B(x^{m-1}, x^m; \boldsymbol{R})| = (\beta - 1)l_0 = w_0$ and $|B(x^m, x^{m-1}; \boldsymbol{R})| = l_0$ for all $m \in \{2, \ldots, \beta\}$ and, furthermore, $|B(x^\beta, x^1; \boldsymbol{R})| = (\beta - 1)l_0 = w_0$ and $|B(x^1, x^\beta; \boldsymbol{R})| = l_0$. Therefore, $x^{m-1} P x^m$ for all $m \in \{2, \ldots, \beta\}$ and $x^\beta P x^1$, contradicting the S-consistency of R.

Finally, we consider the case in which w_0 is not a positive multiple of l_0. Clearly, this is only possible if $l_0 > 1$. By (8.5), there exists $\alpha \in \{3, \ldots, |X|\}$ such that

$$(\alpha - 2)l_0 < w_0 < (\alpha - 1)l_0. \tag{8.6}$$

By unrestricted domain, we can consider α alternatives $x^1, \ldots, x^\alpha \in X$ and a profile $\boldsymbol{R} \in \mathcal{R}^{|N|}$ such that

$$x^2 P_i x^3 P_i \ldots P_i x^\alpha P_i x^1 \ \forall i \in \{1, \ldots, l_0\},$$

$$\vdots$$

$$x^{\alpha-1} P_i x^\alpha P_i x^1 P_i \ldots P_i x^{\alpha-2} \ \forall i \in \{(\alpha - 3)l_0 + 1, \ldots, (\alpha - 2)l_0\},$$

$$x^\alpha P_i x^1 P_i \ldots P_i x^{\alpha-2} P_i x^{\alpha-1} \ \forall i \in \{(\alpha - 2)l_0 + 1, \ldots, w_0\},$$

$$x^1 P_i x^2 P_i \ldots P_i x^{\alpha-1} P_i x^\alpha \ \forall i \in \{w_0 + 1, \ldots, 2w_0 - (\alpha - 2)l_0\},$$

$$x^1 P_i x^\alpha P_i x^2 P_i \ldots P_i x^{\alpha-1} \ \forall i \in \{2w_0 - (\alpha - 2)l_0 + 1, \ldots, w_0 + l_0\}$$

and, if $|N| > w_0 + l_0$,

$$x^1 I_i x^2 I_i \ldots I_i x^{\alpha-1} I_i x^\alpha \ \forall i \in \{w_0 + l_0 + 1, \ldots, |N|\}.$$

This profile is well defined because (8.6) implies

$$w_0 < 2w_0 - (\alpha - 2)l_0 < w_0 + l_0.$$

We have $|B(x^{m-1}, x^m; \boldsymbol{R})| = w_0$ and $|B(x^m, x^{m-1}; \boldsymbol{R})| = l_0$ for all $m \in \{2, \ldots, \alpha\}$ and, furthermore, $|B(x^\alpha, x^1; \boldsymbol{R})| = w_0$ and $|B(x^1, x^\alpha; \boldsymbol{R})| = l_0$. Therefore, $x^{m-1} P x^m$ for all $m \in \{2, \ldots, \alpha\}$ and $x^\alpha P x^1$, again contradicting the S-consistency of R. ■

As is the case for most of the literature on social choice, we assume that there are at least three alternatives. The case $|X| = 1$ is trivial and the case $|X| = 2$ is not of much interest in our context, particularly because transitivity and S-consistency are vacuously satisfied and, thus, equivalent in the two-alternative case.

The conclusion of Theorem 8.1 does not hold if merely independence of irrelevant alternatives rather than neutrality is imposed. Suppose $x^0, y^0 \in X$ are two distinct alternatives. Define a collective choice rule by letting

$$xRy \Leftrightarrow [xR^p y \text{ or } (\neg xR^p y \text{ and } \neg yR^p x \text{ and } \{x, y\} = \{x^0, y^0\})]$$

for all $x, y \in X$ and for all $\boldsymbol{R} \in \mathcal{R}^{|N|}$. This is an S-consistent collective choice rule satisfying unrestricted domain, strong Pareto, anonymity, and independence of irrelevant alternatives. However, neutrality is clearly violated.

S-consistency cannot be weakened to acyclicity in our characterization result. The collective choice rule defined by letting

$$xRy \Leftrightarrow [xR^p y \text{ or } |B(x, y; \boldsymbol{R})| = |B(y, x; \boldsymbol{R})| = 1]$$

for all $x, y \in X$ and for all $\boldsymbol{R} \in \mathcal{R}^{|N|}$ produces acyclic social preferences and satisfies the axioms of Theorem 8.1. However, social preferences are not always consistent. For example, suppose $X = \{x, y, z\}$ and $N = \{1, 2, 3\}$, and consider the profile $\boldsymbol{R}$ defined by

$$xP_1yP_1z, \qquad zP_2xP_2y, \qquad xI_3yI_3z.$$

According to $R = f(\boldsymbol{R})$, we obtain yIz, zIx, and xPy, a social preference relation that is not S-consistent.

That the remaining axioms unrestricted domain, strong Pareto, and anonymity cannot be dispensed with can be shown as in the traditional (transitive) case.

8.5. References

[1] Arrow, K. J., *Social Choice and Individual Values,* New York: John Wiley and Sons, 1951; 2nd edn., 1963.

[2] Bossert, W., "Suzumura Consistency," in P. K. Pattanaik, K. Tadenuma, Y. Xu, and N. Yoshihara, eds., *Rational Choice and Social Welfare: Theory and Applications, A Volume in Honor of Kotaro Suzumura,* New York: Springer, 2008, 159-179.

[3] Bossert, W., Y. Sprumont, and K. Suzumura, "Consistent Rationalizability," *Economica* **72**, 2005, 185–200.

[4] Raiffa, H., *Decision Analysis,* Reading, Mass.: Addison-Wesley, 1968.

[5] Sen, A. K., "Quasi-Transitivity, Rational Choice and Collective Decisions," *Review of Economic Studies* **36**, 1969, 381–393.

[6] Sen, A. K., *Collective Choice and Social Welfare,* San Francisco: Holden-Day, 1970.

[7] Sen, A. K., "Personal Utilities and Public Judgements: Or What's Wrong with Welfare Economics?" *Economic Journal* **89**, 1979, 537–558.

[8] Suzumura, K., "Remarks on the Theory of Collective Choice," *Economica* **43**, 1976, 381–390. Essay 6 of this volume.

[9] Szpilrajn, E., "Sur l'Extension de l'Ordre Partiel," *Fundamenta Mathematicae* **16**, 1930, 386–389.

[10] Weymark, J. A., "Arrow's Theorem with Social Quasi-Orderings," *Public Choice* **42**, 1984, 235–246.

PART III

EQUITY, EFFICIENCY, AND INTERGENERATIONAL JUSTICE

Introduction to Part III

> When quarrels and complaints arise, it is when people who are equal have not got equal shares, or vice versa.
>
> —ARISTOTLE, *The Nicomachean Ethics*, fourth century BC, English translation by J. A. K. Thomson

> All things whatever ye would that men should do to you, do ye even so to them: for this is the law and the prophets.
>
> —Bible, Matthew 7:12

> Do not do unto others as you would that they should do unto you. Their tastes may not be the same.
>
> —GEORGE BERNARD SHAW, "Maxims for Revolutionists," *Man and Superman*, 1903

In sharp contrast with the Arrow social choice theory, where the target of analysis is to amalgamate the profile of individual preference orderings over the set X of social alternatives into the social preference ordering over X, the equity-as-no-envy approach in the theory of resource allocation focuses on the set of acceptable alternatives with respect to the stipulated equity and efficiency criteria without aspiring to construct a rationalizing social preference ordering over the set of all alternatives. This clear contrast notwithstanding, we can reformulate the equity-as-no-envy approach as an extended social choice framework and examine the social choice theoretic performance of the equity-as-no-envy approach.

Suppose that we are allocating given resources $\boldsymbol{\omega} \in \mathbb{R}^l_+$ among n individuals, where $2 \leq l, n < +\infty$. A *feasible allocation* is an n-tuple of l-dimensional vectors $\boldsymbol{x} = (\boldsymbol{x}_1, \boldsymbol{x}_2, \ldots, \boldsymbol{x}_n) \in \mathbb{R}^{ln}_+$, where $\boldsymbol{x}_i$ stands for resources allocated to individual $i \in N := \{1, 2, \ldots, n\}$, such that $\sum_{i \in N} \boldsymbol{x}_i = \boldsymbol{\omega}$ holds. Let $A(\boldsymbol{\omega})$ be the set of all feasible allocations. If we are prepared to assume cardinality and interpersonal comparability of utilities, a feasible and equitable allocation $\mathbf{x}^* = (\boldsymbol{x}_1^*, \boldsymbol{x}_2^*, \ldots, \boldsymbol{x}_n^*) \in A(\omega)$ is such that

$$u_1(\boldsymbol{x}_1^*) = u_2(\boldsymbol{x}_2^*) = \ldots = u_n(\boldsymbol{x}_n^*) \qquad \text{(CE)}$$

is satisfied, where u_i is the utility function of individual $i \in N$. The problem with the cardinal equity (CE) principle is that the cardinality and interpersonal comparability of individual utilities go squarely counter to the currently prevailing views of ordinal and interpersonally noncomparable utilities.

Capitalizing on an early suggestion by Jan Tinbergen [28], Duncan Foley [8], Serge-Christophe Kolm [12], and Hal Varian [29; 30] introduced the concept of an ordinal equity (OE) principle without cardinality and interpersonal comparability of utilities, according to which an allocation $\mathbf{x}^* = (\boldsymbol{x}_1^*, \boldsymbol{x}_2^*, \ldots, \boldsymbol{x}_n^*) \in A(\omega)$ is *no-envy equitable* if and only if the following system of simultaneous inequalities holds:

$$\forall i, j \in N : u_i(\boldsymbol{x}_i) \geq u_i(\boldsymbol{x}_j). \qquad \text{(OE)}$$

The essence of this equity concept lies in the fact that "[it] is founded in the notion of 'extended sympathy' and in the idea of 'symmetry' in the treatment of agents. . . . In effect, we are asking each agent to put himself in the position of each other agent to determine if that is a better or a worse position than the one he is now in" (Varian [30, p. 240]). Allan Feldman and Alan Kirman [6], Elisha Pazner and David Schmeidler [16; 17], and many others follow suit on of this ordinal approach to equity and efficiency. Pazner [15] gives us thoughtful reflections on this fascinating area of research, and William Thomson [27] provides us with an extensive and careful survey of the whole area of equity and efficiency in resource allocation models. The first two essays in Part III are concerned with this ordinal equity concept in the generalized framework of social choice theory.

Within the theory of resource allocation, many scholars juxtapose the equity-as-no-envy principle and the Pareto efficiency principle, and expose several compatibility results between them in the context of allocating fixed commodity bundles among perfectly competitive consumers, as well as many incompatibility results between them in the context of production economies where productivity differentials prevail among those who contribute to productive activities. See, among others, Pazner and Schmeidler [16] and Varian [29] in particular. Essay 9 ("On Pareto Efficiency and the No-Envy

Concept of Equity") works with a social choice model, in which the aggregation problem is to map each profile of individual extended preference orderings on $X \times N$ into the corresponding social choice function. Just as in the production economies version of the Foley-Kolm-Varian type of models, our social choice model reveals that the equity-as-no-envy principle and the Pareto efficiency principle may easily conflict with each other. In full awareness of this possible conflict between equity and efficiency, we introduce several axioms that can accommodate the situation of conflict as well as the situation of coherence between the two basic principles, and explore the performance characteristics of the generalized social choice framework.

Essay 10 ("The Informational Basis of the Theory of Fair Allocation") tries to dig deeper into the contrast between the theory of no-envy equity and Pareto efficiency in resource allocation models à la Foley, Kolm, and Varian and the theory of extended sympathy approach in social choice theory. The novel feature of this essay is to focus on the informational requirements to obtain possibility results from the combination of equity and efficiency. Among others, it is argued that the theory of resource allocation based on the principles of no-envy equity and Pareto efficiency can generate social preference ordering à la Arrow, so that the Arrow general impossibility theorem cannot but apply to this induced rule of generating social preference orderings. The introduction of additional information about marginal rates of substitution or about indifference surfaces on possible redistributions of the proposed resource allocations is shown to be sufficient for the existence of satisfactory rules for social preference orderings.

In Essay 11 ("Ordering Infinite Utility Streams"), we turn to a different aspect of the theory of equity, which goes all the way back to Henry Sidwick and his principle of intergenerational equity. According to Sidwick [21, p. 414], who writes in the long utilitarian tradition of moral philosophy, "the time at which a man exists cannot affect the value of his happiness from a universal point of view; and . . . the interests of posterity must concern a utilitarian as much as those of his contemporaries." The view endorsed by Sidgwick, which was widely accepted by many subsequent scholars with utilitarian conviction, is formally expressed by the *anonymity* axiom. Following Tjalling Koopmans's [13] thought-provoking work on the phenomenon that he called *impatience*, viz., preference for advancing the consumption of a preferred good along the time axis, Peter Diamond [5] established that the anonymity axiom is incompatible with the strong

Pareto principle when ordering *infinite* utility streams. He also showed that if anonymity is weakened to *finite* anonymity, which restricts the application of the anonymity axiom to situations where utility streams differ in at most a finite number of generational utilities, and a continuity axiom is imposed on the social evaluation ordering, an impossibility theorem strenuously comes back. Among many works that followed suit, Kaushik Basu and Tapan Mitra [2] showed that strong Pareto, finite anonymity, and *representability* by a real-valued function of the social evaluation ordering are incompatible. On the other hand, Lars-Gunnar Svensson [26] proved that strong Pareto and finite anonymity are compatible by showing that any ordering extension of an infinite horizon variant of Suppes's [22] *grading principle of justice* satisfies the two axioms in question. In view of these impossibility theorems and a possibility theorem, it seems to us that the most natural assumption to drop is that of continuity or representability. Along this line, Essay 11 establishes two possibility theorems. The first theorem characterizes all orderings satisfying strong Pareto, anonymity à la Sidgwick, and the strict transfer principle à la Pigou and Dalton, which are extensions of an infinite-horizon formulation of the generalized Lorenz quasi ordering. The second theorem establishes that a social evaluation ordering satisfies strong Pareto, finite anonymity, and equity preference in the spirit of Hammond [9] if and only if it is an ordering extension of an infinite-horizon version of the leximin criterion.

Observe that the infinite-horizon model à la Diamond focused on the evaluation of infinite utility streams by a social evaluator standing at the beginning of the time axis, whereas John Ferejohn and Talbot Page [7] formulated an intergenerational social choice model, where generation t^* appears in the society only after generation t does if and only if $t < t^*$ holds true. Besides, each generation holds its own evaluation on the infinite-horizon generational utility streams. The focal issue of the analysis is the Arrovian aggregation of infinite profile of generational evaluation orderings into the society's generational evaluation ordering. Thus, Ferejohn and Page opened up the possibility of combining Arrovial social choice theory and the theory of evaluating infinite intergenerational utility streams à la Koopmans and Diamond. Unlike Arrow's impossibility theorem, which hinges on the finiteness of population, the Ferejohn-Page social choice problem hinges squarely on the existence of infinite generations. In this context, Ferejohn and Page [7] proposed a suitably modified version of the stationarity axiom, which is due originally to Koopmans in his related but distinct context, and showed that *if* a social welfare function that satisfies their version of the stationarity axiom in addition to the other Arrow axioms exists, *then* generation one must be a dictator. Edward Packel [14] pursued the problem left open by Ferejohn and Page and showed a stronger impossibility theorem in the intergenerational social choice problem. Essay 12 ("Multiprofile Intergenerational Social Choice"), which is based on Bossert and Suzumura [4], identifies an inappropriate feature of the Ferejohn-Page stationality axiom. By proposing the multi-profile stationarity axiom, which is a more suitable formulation of the stationarity axiom for the problem at stake, it is shown that the impossibility impasse in the intergenerational social choice issue turns out to be much deeper than otherwise.

References

[1] Arrow, K. J., "Extended Sympathy and the Possibility of Social Choice," *American Economic Review: Papers and Proceedings* **67**, 1977, 217–225.
[2] Basu, K., and T. Mitra, "Aggregating Infinite Utility Streams with Intergenerational Equity: The Importance of Being Paretian," *Econometrica* **71**, 2003, 1557–1563.
[3] Basu, K., and T. Mitra, "Utilitarianism for Infinite Utility Streams: A New Welfare Criterion and Its Axiomatic Characterization," *Journal of Economic Theory* **133**, 2007, 350–373.
[4] Bossert, W. and K. Suzumura, "Multiprofile Intergenerational Social Choice," *Social Choice and Welfare* **37**, 2011, 493–509. Essay 12 of this volume.
[5] Diamond, P., "The Evaluation of Infinite Utility Streams," *Econometrica* **33**, 1965, 170–177.
[6] Feldman, A., and A. Kirman, "Fairness and Envy," *American Economic Review* **64**, 1974, 995–1005.
[7] Ferejohn, J., and T. Page, "On the Foundations of Intertemporal Choice," *American Journal of Agricultural Economics* **60**, 1978, 269–275.
[8] Foley, D., "Resource Allocation and the Public Sector," *Yale Economic Essays* **7**, 1967, 45–98.
[9] Hammond, P. J., "Equity, Arrow's Conditions and Rawls' Difference Principle," *Econometrica* **44**, 1976, 793–804.
[10] Hara, C., T. Shinotsuka, K. Suzumura, and Y. Xu, "Continuity and Egalitarianism in the Evaluation of Infinite Utility Streams," *Social Choice and Welfare* **31**, 2008, 179–191.
[11] Harsanyi, J. C., "Cardinal Welfare, Individualistic Ethics and Interpersonal Comparisons of Utility," *Journal of Political Economy* **63**, 1955, 309–321.
[12] Kolm, S.-Ch., *Justice et Equité*, Paris: Editions du Centre National de la Recherche Scientifique, 1972. English translation, *Justice and Equity*, Cambridge, Mass.: MIT Press, 1997.
[13] Koopmans, T. C., "Stationary Ordinal Utility and Impatience," *Econometrica* **28**, 1960, 287–309.
[14] Packel, E., "Impossibility Results in the Axiomatic Theory of Intertemporal Choice," *Public Choice* **35**, 1980, 219–227.
[15] Pazner, E., "Recent Thinking on Economic Justice," *Journal of Peace Science* **2**, 1976, 143–153.

[16] Pazner, E., and D. Schmeidler, "A Difficulty in the Concept of Fairness," *Review of Economic Studies* **41**, 1974, 441–443.

[17] Pazner, E., and D. Schmeidler, "Egalitarian Equivalent Allocations: A New Concept of Economic Equity," *Quarterly Journal of Economics* **92**, 1978, 671–687.

[18] Roemer, J., and K. Suzumura, eds., *Intergenerational Equity and Sustainability*, Basingstoke, England: Palgrave Macmillan, 2007.

[19] Sen, A. K., *Collective Choice and Social Welfare*, San Francisco: Holden-Day, 1970. Republished Amsterdam: North-Holland, 1979.

[20] Sen, A. K., "On Weights and Measures: Informational Constraints in Social Welfare Analysis," *Econometrica* **45**, 1977, 1539–1572.

[21] Sidgwick, H., *The Methods of Ethics*, 7th edn., London: Macmillan, 1907.

[22] Suppes, P., "Some Formal Models of Grading Principles," *Synthese* **6**, 1966, 284–306.

[23] Suzumura, K., *Rational Choice, Collective Decisions, and Social Welfare*, New York: Cambridge University Press, 1983. Reissued in paperback, 2009.

[24] Suzumura, K., "On the Possibility of 'Fair' Collective Choice Rule," *International Economic Review* **22**, 1981, 307-320.

[25] Suzumura, K., "Equity, Efficiency and Rights in Social Choice," *Mathematical Social Sciences* **3**, 1982, 131–155.

[26] Svensson, L.-G., "Equity among Generations," *Econometrica* **48**, 1980, 1251–1256.

[27] Thomson, W., "Fair Allocation Rules," in K. J. Arrow, A. K. Sen, and K. Suzumura, eds., *Handbook of Social Choice and Welfare*, Vol. II, Amsterdam: North-Holland/Elsevier, 2011, 393–506.

[28] Tinbergen, J., *Redelike Inkomensverdeling*, Haarlem, Netherlands: N. V. DeGulden Pers, 2nd edn., 1953.

[29] Varian, H. R., "Equity, Envy, and Efficiency," *Journal of Economic Theory* **9**, 1974, 61–91.

[30] Varian, H. R., "Distributive Justice, Welfare Economics, and the Theory of Fairness," *Philosophy and Public Affairs* **4**, 1975, 223–247.

ESSAY 9

On Pareto-Efficiency and the No-Envy Concept of Equity

9.1. Introduction

In dividing some fixed amount of resources among a fixed number of individuals, the exclusive reliance on the Pareto efficiency criterion will be of little help, since *too many* feasible divisions will be Pareto-efficient under the standard environmental conditions. The introduction of an additional criterion of equity to the effect that a division is *equitable* if and only if no individual envies the position of another individual when the specified division is implemented will substantially narrow down the range of eligible divisions.[1] But the joint use of Pareto efficiency and the no-envy concept of equity encounters difficulty when the amount to be divided depends upon the contribution made by individuals, among whom ability differential prevails, since there may then be *no* eligible division even under the standard environmental conditions.[2] One possible response to

First published in *Journal of Economic Theory* **25**, 1981, pp. 367–379. This essay was written while I was visiting Stanford University in 1979–1980. I am deeply indebted to Kenneth Arrow, Peter Coughlin, Peter Hammond, Steve Goldman, and David Starrett for their helpful comments on an earlier draft. Thanks are also due to the anonymous referees of *Journal of Economic Theory,* whose incisive comments were instrumental in preparing the final version. Needless to say, I am solely responsible for any defects that may still remain.

1. This concept of equity is due originally to Foley [7, Section IV]. See also Pazner and Schmeidler [10] and Varian [20].
2. This dilemma was first exposed by Pazner and Schmeidler [10].

this dilemma would be to observe that, from the viewpoint of moral philosophy, it is not altogether clear whether a concept of equity based on envy can be ethically relevant in the first place and to wash one's hands of the business. The second and arguably more "fruitful" response would be to propose a modified definition of equity, which, coupled with Pareto efficiency, provides us with an alternative definition of eligibility. In the literature, we have abundantly many proposals to this effect: *wealth fairness* (Varian [20; 21]), *income fairness* (Varian [20] and Pazner [9]), *balanced-with-respect-to-envy justice* (Daniel [5]), *egalitarian equivalence* (Pazner and Schmeidler [11]), and *fairness equivalence* (Pazner [9]).[3] The third response would be to embed the proposed concept of fairness as equity-cum-efficiency into the conceptual framework of social choice theory with a view of evaluating how the identified difficulty would be located in the perennial enigma of designing "satisfactory" collective choice mechanisms. The present essay is an attempt in this third category of exercises, which are related to equity, envy, and efficiency. We work with a model of social choice along the lines of Arrow [3, Chapter VIII, Section IV.4], Sen [16, Chapter 9*] and Suppes [18], in which the aggregation problem is to map each profile of individuals' extended orderings of $X \times N$ into a choice function on the family of subsets of X, where X and N denote the set of social states and the set of individuals, respectively. In this set up, the viability of Foley's [7] original definition of fairness will be critically examined.

9.2. Fairness as No-Envy-cum-Efficiency and a Generalized Collective Choice Rule

9.2.1. Extended Sympathy Approach in Social Choice Theory

As Varian [21, p. 240] has aptly observed, "the theory of fairness . . . is founded in the notion of 'extended sympathy' and in the idea of 'symmetry' in the treatment of agents. . . . In effect, we are asking each agent to put

3. These proposals were succinctly surveyed and critically evaluated by Pazner [9] and Sen [17, Section 5].

himself in the position of each other agent to determine if that is a better or a worse position than the one he is now in." To formalize this foundation of the theory of fairness, let X and $N = \{1, 2, \ldots, n\}$ $(2 \leq n < +\infty)$ stand, respectively, for the set of all conceivable social states and the set of individuals, a social state being the complete description of the relevant aspects of the world. For each $i \in N$, we describe his/her views on the society by an extended preference ordering $\widetilde{R}_i$ on the Cartesian product $X \times N$,

$$((x, j), (y, k)) \in \widetilde{R}_i,$$

denoting the fact that being in the position of individual j in the social state x is at least as good as being in the position of individual k in the social state y according to i's view.[4] A list of extended preference orderings, one ordering for each individual, will be called a *profile,* and alternative profiles will be indexed by $\alpha, \beta, \ldots,$ like $\alpha = (\widetilde{R}^\alpha_1, \widetilde{R}^\alpha_2, \ldots, \widetilde{R}^\alpha_n)$, $\beta = (\widetilde{R}^\beta_1, \widetilde{R}^\beta_2, \ldots, \widetilde{R}^\beta_n)$, and so on. The set of all logically possible profiles will be denoted by $\mathcal{A}$, while the set of all nonempty finite subsets of X will be written as $\mathcal{S}$, each $S \in \mathcal{S}$ being construed to represent a set of available states under the specified environmental conditions.

9.2.2. Pareto-Efficiency and No-Envy Equity

Take a profile $\alpha = (\widetilde{R}^\alpha_1, \widetilde{R}^\alpha_2 \ldots, \widetilde{R}^\alpha_n) \in \mathcal{A}$ and $S \in \mathcal{S}$, and fix them for the time being. For each individual $i \in N$, let i's *subjective preference ordering* R^α_i be defined by

$$R^\alpha_i = \{(x, y) \in X \times X \mid ((x, i), (y, i)) \in \widetilde{R}^\alpha_i\}, \tag{9.1}$$

in terms of which the α-*Paretian quasi ordering* R^α_N will be defined by

$$R^\alpha_N = \cap_{i \in N} R^\alpha_i. \tag{9.2}$$

The set of all α-Pareto-efficient states in S will then be denoted by

$$E^\alpha_f(S) = \{x \in S \mid \sim [\exists y \in S : (y, x) \in P(R^\alpha_N)]\}, \tag{9.3}$$

4. Being an ordering, $\widetilde{R}_i$ is a complete, reflexive, and transitive binary relation on $X \times N$.

where and hereafter $P(\cdot)$ will denote an operator giving the asymmetric part of the binary relation in the parenthesis and $\sim$ denotes logical negation.

Following Foley's [7] classical definition, we say that individual $i \in N$ envies individual $j \in N$ at $x \in X$ when the profile α prevails if and only if $((x, j), (x, i)) \in P(\widetilde{R}_i^{\alpha})$ holds true. We say that x is *α-equitable* if and only if nobody envies other individuals at x when the profile α prevails. The set of all α-equitable states in $S \in \mathcal{S}$ may be denoted by

$$E_q^{\alpha}(S) = \{x \in S \mid \forall i, j \in N : ((x, i), (x, j)) \in \widetilde{R}_i^{\alpha}\}. \tag{9.4}$$

If a state in S is simultaneously α-Pareto-efficient and α-equitable, it is said to be *α-fair* in S. The set of all α-fair states in S, to be called the α-fair set in S, will be denoted by

$$F^{\alpha}(S) = E_f^{\alpha}(S) \cap E_q^{\alpha}(S). \tag{9.5}$$

9.2.3. Equity-Efficiency Tradeoff and Axiom of Identity

The first point to be clarified about the α-fair set in S is that it may well be empty. Indeed, it is even possible that $E_q^{\alpha}(X) = \varnothing$ for some $\alpha \in \mathcal{A}$, viz., there may exist no α-equitable state wheresoever. Even if α-Pareto efficiency and α-equity are *individually* self-consistent (in the sense that they may respectively be satisfied), they may well be *jointly* incompatible. This may be easily exemplified as follows.

Example 9.1. Let $X = \{x, y\}$ and $N = \{1, 2\}$. Let a profile $\alpha \in \mathcal{A}$ be specified by[5]

$$\widetilde{R}_1^{\alpha} : (y, 2), (y, 1), (x, 1), (x, 2),$$

$$\widetilde{R}_2^{\alpha} : (y, 2), (y, 1), (x, 2), (x, 1).$$

Clearly, $E_q^{\alpha}(\{x, y\}) = \{x\}$ and $P(R_N^{\alpha}) = \{(y, x)\}$, so that we have $F^{\alpha}(\{x, y\}) = \varnothing$.

5. Preference orderings will be written horizontally with more preferred state-individual combinations to the left of less preferred, indifferent combinations (if any) being put together by square brackets.

Simple though this example is, it may serve us well to expose several important features of the α-fairness concept. As an auxiliary step, let R^{α}_{ij} be defined by

$$R^{\alpha}_{ij} = \{(x, y) \in X \times X \mid ((x, j), (y, j)) \in \widetilde{R}^{\alpha}_{i}\}. \tag{9.6}$$

Clearly, it is true that $R^{\alpha}_{i} = R^{\alpha}_{ii}$ for all $\alpha \in \mathcal{A}$ and all $i \in N$. Notice that $(x, y) \in R^{\alpha}_{i}$ means that individual i thinks that x is no worse for him than y, while $(x, y) \in R^{\alpha}_{ij}$ means that i thinks that it is no worse for j to be in x rather than in y. With this interpretation of R^{α}_{i} and R^{α}_{ij}, it seems fairly natural in the context where we talk about the welfare judgments based on the extended sympathy that we require the fulfillment of the following axiom, which is due to Sen [16, p. 156].[6]

Axiom of Identity. $\forall i, j \in N : R^{\alpha}_{ij} = R^{\alpha}_{j}$.

It is well recognized that the lack of the sympathetic acceptance of other's subjective preferences, viz., the invalidity of the axiom of identity, causes many logical difficulties in the exercise of aggregating profiles of extended preference orderings.[7] Observe, however, that the profile specified in Example 9.1 does satisfy the axiom of identity, so that the problem identified by this example emerges even if the sympathetic identification prevails among individuals.

Our second remark on the α-fairness concept concerns the contrast between the justice concept thereby implied and the traditional rival justice concepts, i.e., *Rawlsian leximin justice* and *Benthamite utilitarian justice*. Notice that in the situation specified by Example 9.1 *both* a Rawlsian and a Benthamite would assert that y is more just than x—assuming for the sake of gaining comparability that 1 and 2 have interpersonally fully comparable cardinal representation of $\widetilde{R}^{\alpha}_{1}$ and $\widetilde{R}^{\alpha}_{2}$, respectively, while $E^{\alpha}_{q}(\{x, y\}) = \{x\}$

6. What the axiom of identity requires is that "placing oneself in the position of the other should involve not merely having the latter's objective circumstances but also identifying oneself with the other in terms of his subjective features" (Sen [16, pp. 149–150]). It is debatable, however, if indeed we need literal transformation of subjective features so as to comply with the requirement of the axiom. On this and related points, the interested readers are referred to Suzumura [19].

7. See, for example, Sen [16, pp. 149–150] and Suzumura [19].

would force one to say that x is more equitable than y. The ethical appeal of the equity-as-no-envy approach seems to be rather fragile indeed.

9.3. On the Possibility of Foley-Fair Collective Choice Rules

9.3.1. Choosing a Fair State—If Ever One Exists

Our problem is to design a "fair" generalized collective choice rule Ψ, GCCR for short, that amalgamates each profile $\alpha \in \mathcal{A}$ of extended preference orderings into a social choice function $C^{\alpha} = \Psi(\alpha)$ on $\mathcal{S}$ such that, for each set $S \in \mathcal{S}$ of available social states, $C^{\alpha}(S)$ denotes the nonempty set of chosen states reflecting a "fair" amalgamation of the α we have started from. In view of the possible nonexistence of α-fair states for some $\alpha \in \mathcal{A}$, care should be taken with the sense in which we mean a GCCR to be "fair." One sense that naturally suggests itself is to require that Ψ satisfies the following condition.

FAIRNESS EXTENSION (FE). For each admissible profile $\alpha \in \mathcal{A}$, $C^{\alpha} = \Psi(\alpha)$ satisfies $F^{\alpha}(S) = C^{\alpha}(S)$ whenever $S \in \mathcal{S}$ is such that $F^{\alpha}(S) \neq \varnothing$.

9.3.2. Choice-Consistency Properties

Collective choice is a repeated exercise in changing environments, and one naturally feels that successive choices made should satisfy some "reasonable" choice-consistency condition. A choice-consistency condition that is deeply rooted in the Arrovian social choice theory is that of collective full rationality (FR), which requires that we may construe a choice function C to describe a behavior of optimizing fully consistent, viz., complete and transitive, collective preference relations. Formally, C satisfies the condition FR if and only if there exists a preference ordering R_C on X satisfying

$$\forall S \in \mathcal{S} : C(S) = \{x \in S \mid \forall y \in S : (x, y) \in R_C\}.$$

It was shown by Arrow [2] that a choice function C on $\mathcal{S}$ satisfies the condition FR if and only if C satisfies the following axiom.

ARROW'S AXIOM (AA).

$$\forall S_1, S_2 \in \mathcal{S} : S_1 \subseteq S_2 \Rightarrow [S_1 \cap C(S_2) = \varnothing \vee S_1 \cap C(S_2) = C(S_1)].$$

The following two axioms, which were found useful in various social and individual choice contexts, provide a natural decomposition of Arrow's axiom.

Chernoff's Axiom (CA).

$$\forall S_1, S_2 \in \mathcal{S} : S_1 \subseteq S_2 \Rightarrow [S_1 \cap C(S_2) = \varnothing \vee S_1 \cap C(S_2) \subseteq C(S_1)].$$

Dual Chernoff Axiom (DCA).

$$\forall S_1, S_2 \in \mathcal{S} : S_1 \subseteq S_2 \Rightarrow [S_1 \cap C(S_2) = \varnothing \vee S_1 \cap C(S_2) \supseteq C(S_1)].$$

Another class of important choice-consistency conditions is that of path independence, due originally to Arrow [3, Chapter VIII, Section V] and Plott [12], and various variants thereof. They essentially require that the choice from a set should be independent of the path to be followed en route to the global choice.

Path-Independence (PI).

$$\forall S_1, S_2 \in \mathcal{S} : C(S_1 \cup S_2) = C(C(S_1) \cup S_2).$$

Weak Path-Independence α [WPI(α)].

$$\forall S_1, S_2 \in \mathcal{S} : C(S_1 \cup S_2) \subseteq C(C(S_1) \cup S_2).$$

Weak Path-Independence β [WPI(β)].

$$\forall S_1, S_2 \in \mathcal{S} : C(S_1 \cup S_2) \supseteq C(C(S_1) \cup S_2).$$

Finally, we introduce two very weak choice-consistency conditions that still have bites.

Superset Axiom (SUA).

$$\forall S_1, S_2 \in \mathcal{S} : [S_1 \subseteq S_2 \ \& \ C(S_2) \subseteq C(S_1)] \Rightarrow C(S_1) = C(S_2).$$

Stability Axiom (ST).

$$\forall S \in \mathcal{S} : C(C(S)) = C(S).$$

To facilitate recollection and later reference, we summarize the logical relationship that holds true among these choice-consistency axioms in the following theorem, where an arrow indicates a logical implication that cannot be reversed in general, while the axioms in square brackets are equivalent to the axiom preceding them.

THEOREM 9.1.

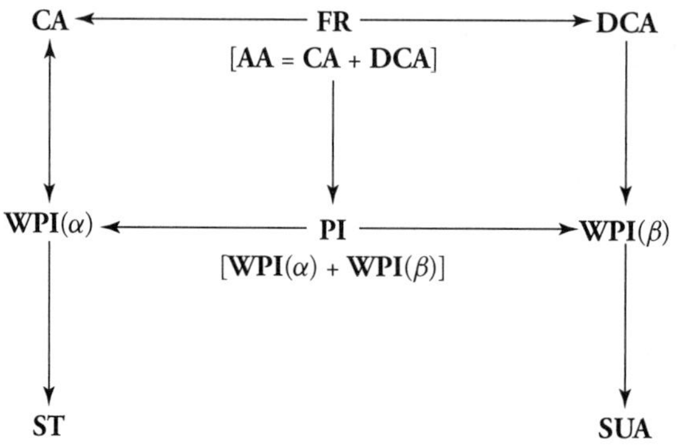

PROOF. Most of the assertions being either immediate results of the definitions or already established in Blair et al. [4], Ferejohn and Grether [6] and Plott [12], we have only to prove that (a) DCA *implies* WPI (β) and (b) WPI (β) *implies* SUA.

(a) Assume that C satisfies the condition DCA on $\mathcal{S}$ and take any $S_1, S_2 \in \mathcal{S}$. Since $C(S_1) \cup S_2 \subseteq S_1 \cup S_2$ is obviously true, we may invoke DCA to assert that either

$$C(S_1 \cup S_2) \cap [C(S_1) \cup S_2] = \varnothing \tag{9.7}$$

or

$$C(S_1 \cup S_2) \cap [C(S_1) \cup S_2] \supseteq C(C(S_1) \cup S_2) \tag{9.8}$$

is true. If (9.8) is indeed the case, we have $C(S_1 \cup S_2) \supseteq C(C(S_1) \cup S_2)$ and we are home. Assume, therefore, that (9.7) is true. Since $S_1 \subseteq S_1 \cup S_2$ is true, the second use of DCA yields either

$$C(S_1 \cup S_2) \cap S_1 = \varnothing \tag{9.9}$$

or

$$C(S_1 \cup S_2) \cap S_1 \supseteq C(S_1). \tag{9.10}$$

It follows from (9.7) that $C(S_1 \cup S_2) \cap C(S_1) = C(S_1 \cup S_2) \cap S_2 = \varnothing$, so that we obtain

$$C(S_1 \cup S_2) \subseteq S_1 \backslash C(S_1), \tag{9.11}$$

which negates the validity of (9.9). Therefore, (9.10) must be true, which contradicts (9.11). This concludes our proof of (a).

(b) Assume that C satisfies WPI(β) and let $S_1, S_2 \in \mathcal{S}$ be such that $S_1 \subseteq S_2$ and $C(S_2) \subseteq C(S_1)$. Thanks to WPI(β), we then have

$$C(S_2) = C(S_1 \cup S_2) \supseteq C(C(S_2) \cup S_1) = C(S_1),$$

which, coupled with $C(S_2) \subseteq C(S_1)$, yields $C(S_1) = C(S_2)$, as desired. ■

Notice that these choice-consistency axioms are properties of a choice function, but they may be regarded as properties of a generalized collective choice rule that generates a choice function having the designated properties. With this understanding in mind, we will talk about choice consistency of a GCCR in the following.

9.3.3. Impossibility of Fairness-Extending Generalized Collective Choice Rule

Let us introduce a rather mild unrestricted domain condition on Ψ, which requires that the class of admissible profiles be rich enough to the following extent.

Unrestricted Domain under the Axiom of Identity (UID). The domain of Ψ consists of all logically possible profiles satisfying the axiom of identity.

We are now ready to present our first negative theorem on the "fair" GCCRs.

Theorem 9.2. Suppose that there exist at least three social states. Then there exists no GCCR that satisfies UID (unrestricted domain under the axiom of identity), FE (fairness extension), and SUA (superset axiom of choice consistency).

Proof. Take three distinct social states x, y, and z and let $S_1 = \{x, y\}$ and $S_2 = \{x, y, z\}$. Let a profile $\alpha = (\widetilde{R}_1^{\alpha}, \widetilde{R}_2^{\alpha}, \ldots, \widetilde{R}_n^{\alpha}) \in \mathcal{A}$ be such that

$$\widetilde{R}_1^\alpha(S_2 \times \{1, 2\}) : (x, 1), (z, 2), (z, 1), (y, 1), (y, 2), (x, 2),$$

$$\widetilde{R}_2^\alpha(S_2 \times \{1, 2\}) : (z, 2), (y, 2), (x, 2), (x, 1), (z, 1), (y, 1),$$

$$\forall i \in N \backslash \{1, 2\} : \widetilde{R}_i^\alpha(S_2 \times \{1, 2\}) = \widetilde{R}_1^\alpha(S_2 \times \{1, 2\}),$$

where $\widetilde{R}_j^\alpha(S_2 \times \{1, 2\})$ denotes the restriction of $\widetilde{R}_j^\alpha$ on $S_2 \times \{1, 2\}$ for all $j \in N$, and that

$$\forall (v, j) \in (X \times N) \backslash (S_2 \times \{1, 2\}) : \begin{cases} ((x, 2), (v, j)) \in P(\widetilde{R}_1^\alpha), \\ ((y, 1), (v, j)) \in P(\widetilde{R}_2^\alpha), \\ \forall i \in N \backslash \{1, 2\} : ((v, j), (x, 1)) \\ \qquad \in P(\widetilde{R}_i^\alpha), \end{cases}$$

$$\forall i \in N, \forall (v^1, j^1), (v^2, j^2) \in (X \times N) \backslash (S_2 \times \{1, 2\}) :$$

$$((v^1, j^1), (v^2, j^2)) \in I(\widetilde{R}_i^\alpha).$$

It is clearly the case that this profile satisfies the axiom of identity. Notice that $E_q^\alpha(S_2) = \{x, y\}$ and $P(R_N^\alpha) \cap (S_2 \times S_2) = \{(z, y)\}$. Therefore, $C^\alpha(S_1) = F^\alpha(S_1) = S_1$ and $C^\alpha(S_2) = F^\alpha(S_2) = \{x\}$, where use is made of the condition FE. We then obtain $S_1 \subseteq S_2$, $C^\alpha(S_2) \subseteq C^\alpha(S_1)$ and $C^\alpha(S_1) \neq C^\alpha(S_2)$. Therefore, a GCCR satisfying UID and FE cannot possibly satisfy SUA. ∎

9.3.4. Impossibility of Fairness-inclusive Generalized Collective Choice Rule

The condition FE demands that the fair state and only the fair state should be chosen when one exists. What if there exists no fair state? To consider this situation, let us define an auxiliary relation R_E^α on X for each $\alpha \in \mathcal{A}$ by

$$R_E^\alpha = \{(x, y) \in X \times X \mid x \in E_q^\alpha(X) \;\&\; y \notin E_q^\alpha(X)\}. \qquad (9.12)$$

Now if we really care about the appeal of equity-as-no-envy as well as Pareto efficiency, the following requirement may seem to be appealing, which says basically that a state that is either "more equitable" or "more efficient" than a state that is chosen should itself be among chosen states.

Fairness Inclusion (FI). If $\alpha \in \mathcal{A}$ and $S \in \mathcal{S}$ are such that $F^{\alpha}(S) = \varnothing$, then

(a) $[x \in S, (x, y) \in R_E^{\alpha} \; \& \; y \in C^{\alpha}(S)] \Rightarrow x \in C^{\alpha}(S)$ and
(b) $[x \in S, (x, y) \in P(R_N^{\alpha}) \; \& \; y \in C^{\alpha}(S)] \Rightarrow x \in C^{\alpha}(S)$, where $C^{\alpha} = \Psi(\alpha)$.

We also introduce a variant of the Pareto unanimity requirement on a GCCR, but we need to step forward carefully in this slippery area. To require the exclusion of a state y from a choice set for a binary choice environment $\{x, y\}$ just because x happens to Pareto-dominate y would be grossly inappropriate in the context where we care about equity and the like, since doing so means to empower the Pareto dominance relation to always outweigh the equity consideration in the binary choice situation. But this lopsided sanctification of Pareto dominance quite simply contradicts the emphasis put on the equity consideration in the fairness approach. This argument, if accepted, would lead us to the following conditional variant of the Pareto rule.

Conditional Binary Exclusion Pareto (CBEP). If an admissible profile $\alpha \in \mathcal{A}$ and $x, y \in X$ are such that $E_q^{\alpha}(\{x, y\}) = \varnothing$ and $(x, y) \in \bigcap_{i \in N} P(R_i^{\alpha})$, then $\{x\} = C^{\alpha}(\{x, y\})$, where $C^{\alpha} = \Psi(\alpha)$.

What emerges out of these mild-looking conditions on a GCCR is another impossibility theorem, which reads as follows.

Theorem 9.3. Suppose that there exist at least three social states. Then there exists no GCCR that satisfies UID (unrestricted domain under the axiom of identity), FI (fairness inclusion), CBEP (conditional binary exclusion Pareto), and CA (Chernoff's axiom of choice consistency).

Proof. Take three distinct social states x, y, and $z \in X$ and let $S_1 = \{x, y\}$ and $S_2 = \{x, y, z\}$. Let a profile $\alpha = (\widetilde{R}_1^{\alpha}, \widetilde{R}_2^{\alpha}, \ldots, \widetilde{R}_n^{\alpha}) \in \mathcal{A}$ be such that

$$\widetilde{R}_1^{\alpha}(S_2 \times \{1, 2\}) : (x, 2), (x, 1), (y, 2), (y, 1), (z, 1), (z, 2),$$

$$\widetilde{R}_2^{\alpha}(S_2 \times \{1, 2\}) : (x, 1), (x, 2), (y, 1), (y, 2), (z, 2), (z, 1),$$

$$\forall i \in N \backslash \{1, 2\} : \widetilde{R}_i^{\alpha}(S_2 \times \{1, 2\}) = \widetilde{R}_1^{\alpha}(S_2 \times \{1, 2\}),$$

where $\widetilde{R}^{\alpha}_{j}(S_2 \times \{1, 2\}) = \widetilde{R}^{\alpha}_{j} \cap [(S_2 \times \{1, 2\}) \times (S_2 \times \{1, 2\})]$ for all $j \in N$, and that

$$\forall (v, j) \in (X \times N) \backslash (S_2 \times \{1, 2\}) : \begin{cases} ((z, 2), (v, j)) \in P(\widetilde{R}^{\alpha}_{1}), \\ ((z, 1), (v, j)) \in P(\widetilde{R}^{\alpha}_{2}), \\ \forall i \in N \backslash \{1, 2\} : ((v, j), (x, 2)) \\ \qquad \in P(\widetilde{R}^{\alpha}_{i}), \end{cases}$$

$$\forall i \in N, \forall (v^1, j^1), (v^2, j^2) \in (X \times N) \backslash (S_2 \times \{1, 2\}) :$$

$$((v^1, j^1), (v^2, j^2)) \in I(\widetilde{R}^{\alpha}_{i}).$$

It is easy to verify that this profile satisfies the axiom of identity. Note that $E^{\alpha}_{q}(S_2) = \{z\}$ and $P(R^{\alpha}_{N}) \cap (S_2 \times S_2) = \{(x, y), (y, z), (x, z)\}$, so that we have $C^{\alpha}(S_1) = \{x\}$ by virtue of CBEP. Consider now $C^{\alpha}(S_2)$. If x or y belongs to $C^{\alpha}(S_2)$, then $z \in C^{\alpha}(S_2)$ by virtue of FI(a). If $z \in C^{\alpha}(S_2)$, then x as well as y belong to $C^{\alpha}(S_2)$, thanks to FI(b). $C^{\alpha}(S_2)$ being nonempty, we should then conclude that $C^{\alpha}(S_2) = S_2$. Then we have $S_1 \subseteq S_2$, $S_1 \cap C^{\alpha}(S_2) = \{x, y\} \nsubseteq C^{\alpha}(S_1) = \{x\}$, which implies that a GCCR satisfying UID, FI, and CBEP cannot possibly satisfy CA. ■

9.3.5. Fairness-Extending and Fairness-Including Generalized Collective Choice Rule: An Example

Several remarks seem to be in order here.

First, let us point out that there exists a concrete example of fairness-extending as well as fairness-including GCCR, which is due essentially to Goldman and Sussangkarn [8]. For any profile $\alpha \in \mathcal{A}$ and any $S \in \mathcal{S}$, let a binary relation R^{α} on X be defined by $R^{\alpha} = P(R^{\alpha}_{N}) \cup R^{\alpha}_{E}$, and let $R^{\alpha}(S)$ stand for the restriction of R^{α} on $S : R^{\alpha}(S) = R^{\alpha} \cap (S \times S)$. We then define a choice set $C^{\alpha}_{GS}(S)$ for S by

$$C^{\alpha}_{GS}(S) = \{x \in S \mid \forall y \in S : (x, y) \in T(R^{\alpha}(S)) \vee (y, x) \notin T(R^{\alpha}(S))\}, \tag{9.13}$$

where $T(R^{\alpha}(S))$ denotes the transitive closure of $R^{\alpha}(S)$. Associating the well-defined choice function C^{α}_{GS} on $\mathcal{S}$ thereby constructed with the profile $\alpha \in \mathcal{A}$ we have started from, we have a complete description of a GCCR

$\Psi_{GS} : \Psi_{GS}(\alpha) = C^{\alpha}_{GS}$ for all $\alpha \in \mathcal{A}$. It is easy, if tedious, to show that Ψ_{GS} satisfies the condition FE as well as the condition FI for all $\alpha \in \mathcal{A}$. Thanks to Theoerem 9.2, we can assert without further ado that Ψ_{GS} cannot possibly satisfy the superset axiom of choice consistency. We may also prove that Ψ_{GS} fails to satisfy Chernoff's axiom of choice consistency as well, but it does satisfy the stability axiom, although the latter property may presumably be too weak to celebrate Ψ_{GS} for its success in this arena. The power of Theorem 9.2 is such that it asserts by one stroke that we cannot possibly improve the performance of Ψ_{GS} unless we renounce the wide applicability of our GCCR or the nice choice-consistency property thereof.

Second, we may assert the following simple corollaries of Theorems 9.1, 9.2, and 9.3. In view of the strong intuitive appeal of the path-independence argument, these corollaries may better crystallize the logical difficulty identified by Theorems 9.2 and 9.3.

Corollary 9.1. Suppose that there exist at least three social states. Then there exists no GCCR that satisfies UID (unrestricted domain under the axiom of identity), FE (fairness extension), and WPI(β) (weak path independence β).

Corollary 9.2. Suppose that there exist at least three social states. Then there exists no GCCR that satisfies UID (unrestricted domain under the axiom of identity), FI (fairness inclusion), CBEP (conditional binary exclusion Pareto), and WPI(α) (weak path independence α).

Third, we should note that Theorem 9.2 as well as Theorem 9.3 do not invoke any interprofile independence conditions, which has often been nominated as *the* culprit of Arrovian impossibility theorems. Indeed, only a single profile is made effective use of in proving Theorems 9.2 and 9.3, so that the *profile richness condition,* UID, is in fact much stronger than is needed.[8] Instead of requiring UID, we may do throughout with the following *state richness condition* suggested by Pollak [13] and Roberts [15], which is the single-profile analogue of the multiple-profile requirement UID. Let $\alpha \in \mathcal{A}$ denote the given fixed profile.

8. In this respect, our Theorems 9.2 and 9.3 are similar in nature to Sen's [16, Chapter 6*] impossibility of a Paretian liberal.

State Richness Condition (SRC). Let $\beta(S_0)$ denote any logically possible subprofile over the hypothetical triple set S_0. Then there exists a one-to-one correspondence γ_β from S_0 into X such that

$$((\gamma_\beta(x), i), (\gamma_\beta(y), j)) \in \widetilde{R}_k^\alpha \Leftrightarrow ((x, i), (y, j)) \in \widetilde{R}_k^\beta$$

for all $x, y \in S_0$ and for all $i, j, k \in N$.[9]

It should be clear that the condition SRC, which essentially requires that the set of states X is rich enough, may replace the condition UID, which is the requirement to the effect that the set of profiles $\mathcal{A}$ is rich enough, to generate a single-profile analogue of Theorems 9.2 and 9.3 and Corollaries 9.1 and 9.2.

9.4. Concluding Remarks

It is hoped that our results reported in this essay, which are largely negative, will help clarify the nature and potentiality of the equity-as-no-envy approach in the theory of fairness and justice. In concluding this essay, a few remarks are due.

(a) According to Varian [20, p. 65], "social decision theory asks for too much out of the [preference aggregation] process in that it asks for an entire *ordering* of the various social states. . . . The original question asked only for a good allocation; there was no requirement to rank all allocations. The fairness criterion in fact limits itself to answering the original question. It is limited in that it gives no indication of the merits of two nonfair allocations, but by restricting itself in this way it allows for a reasonable solution to the original problem." This contrast between "social decision theory" and "fairness criterion" is no doubt a useful one, but it seems to us that the two approaches may well be subsumed in a more general choice-functional collective choice framework. In doing so, we may enrich our understanding of one theory in light of the implications of the other theory on common ground and vice versa. This is precisely the kind of exercise we tried to perform in this essay.

9. More explicitly, $\beta(S_0) = (\widetilde{R}_1^\beta(S_0 \times N), \widetilde{R}_2^\beta(S_0 \times N), \ldots, \widetilde{R}_n^\beta(S_0 \times N))$.

(b) It is often suggested that the prime virtue of the theory of fairness is that it requires no such things as *externally imposed* interpersonal welfare comparisons, hypothetical welfare functions, or fictitious original position. Notice that our analysis of the concept of fairness in the framework of social choice theory fully retains this alleged prime virtue of the theory of fairness. One may even claim, following Alchian [1], that what is involved in our GCCR framework is not an interpersonal welfare comparison but an intrapersonal, intersituational comparison.

9.5. References

[1] Alchian, A. A., "The Meaning of Utility Measurement," *American Economic Review* **43**, 1953, 26–50.

[2] Arrow, K. J., "Rational Choice Functions and Orderings," *Economica* **26**, 1959, 121–127.

[3] Arrow, K. J., *Social Choice and Individual Values,* New York: John Wiley & Sons, 1951; 2nd edn., 1963.

[4] Blair, D. H., G. Bordes, J. S Kelly, and K. Suzumura, "Impossibility Theorems without Collective Rationality," *Journal of Economic Theory* **13**, 1976, 361–379. Essay 5 of this volume.

[5] Daniel, T. E., "A Revised Concept of Distributional Equity," *Journal of Economic Theory* **11**, 1975, 94–109.

[6] Ferejohn, J. A., and D. M. Grether, "Weak Path Independence," *Journal of Economic Theory* **14**, 1977, 19–31.

[7] Foley, D. K., "Resource Allocation and the Public Sector," *Yale Economic Essays* **7**, 1967, 45–98.

[8] Goldman, S. M., and C. Sussangkarn, "On the Concept of Fairness," *Journal of Economic Theory* **19**, 1978, 210–216.

[9] Pazner, E. A., "Pitfalls in the Theory of Fairness," *Journal of Economic Theory* **14**, 1977, 458–466.

[10] Pazner, E. A., and D. Schmeidler, "A Difficulty in the Concept of Fairness," *Review of Economic Studies* **41**, 1974, 441–443.

[11] Pazner, E. A., and D. Schemeidler, "Egalitarian Equivalent Allocations: A New Concept of Economic Equity," *Quarterly Journal of Economics* **92**, 1978, 671–687.

[12] Plott, C. R., "Path Independence, Rationality, and Social Choice," *Econometrica* **41**, 1973, 1075–1091.

[13] Pollak, R. A., "Bergson-Samuelson Social Welfare Functions and the Theory of Social Choice," *Quarterly Journal of Economics* **93**, 1979, 73–90.

[14] Rawls, J., *A Theory of Justice,* Cambridge, Mass.: Harvard University Press, 1971.

[15] Roberts, K. W. S., "Social Choice Theory: The Single-Profile and Multiprofile Approaches," *Review of Economic Studies* **47**, 1980, 441–450.

[16] Sen, A. K., *Collective Choice and Social Welfare,* San Francisco: Holden-Day, 1970.

[17] Sen, A. K., "Social Choice Theory," in K. J. Arrow and M. Intriligator, eds., *Handbook of Mathematical Economics,* Vol. 3, Amsterdam: North-Holland, 1986, 1073–1181.

[18] Suppes, P., "Some Formal Models of Grading Principles," *Synthese* **6**, 1966, 284–306.

[19] Suzumura, K., "Equity, Utility and Majority: Extended Sympathy Approach," Department of Economics, Stanford University, Stanford, Calif., July 1980. Revised and subsequently published under the title "Resolving Conflicting Views of Justice in Social Choice," in P. K. Pattanaik and M. Salles, eds., *Social Choice and Welfare,* Amsterdam: North-Holland, 1983, 125–149.

[20] Varian, H. R., "Equity, Envy, and Efficiency," *Journal of Economic Theory* **9**, 1974, 63–91.

[21] Varian, H. R., "Distributive Justice, Welfare Economics, and the Theory of Fairness," *Philosophy and Public Affairs* **4**, 1975, 223–247.

[22] Varian, H. R., "Two Problems in the Theory of Fairness," *Journal of Public Economics* **5**, 1976, 249–260.

ESSAY 10

The Informational Basis of the Theory of Fair Allocation

10.1. Introduction

The theory of fair allocation studies allocation rules, which select, for every economy in a given class, a subset of feasible allocations on the basis of efficiency and fairness properties. It was initiated by Foley [14], Kolm [16], and Varian [31], among others, who focused on the concept of no-envy. Since then it has been extended to cover many other notions of fairness and a great variety of economic contexts (production, public goods, etc.) by many authors.[1] This theory contains some negative results, because it is usually impossible to find solutions that satisfy all conceivable requirements of efficiency and equity simultaneously, but its hallmark is a richness of positive results. By now, not only are there many interesting *allocation rules* uncovered in the literature, but also they are fully characterized as the only rules satisfying some sets of reasonable axioms.

First published in *Social Choice and Welfare* **24**, 2005, pp. 311–341. Joint paper with M. Fleurbaey and K. Tadenuma. This essay is derived from part of an earlier draft of our paper entitled "Informational Requirements for Social Choice in Economic Environments." Thanks are due to A. Trannoy, an associate editor, and three referees of *Social Choice and Welfare* for comments, and to participants in seminars at the University of Cergy-Pontoise, the University of Rochester, Hitotsubashi University, Waseda University, and the 5th International Meeting of the Society for Social Choice and Welfare in Alicante, Spain. Financial support from the Ministry of Education of Japan through Grant-in-Aid No. 10045010 ("Economic Institutions and Social Norms: Evolution and Transformation") is gratefully acknowledged.

1. For a survey, see Moulin and Thomson [19].

Compared to the theory of social choice, this makes a great contrast. In social choice theory, Arrow's impossibility theorem has been shown to remain valid in most economic or abstract contexts. This theorem, like all theory of social choice, is about *social preferences,* which rank all options in a given set on the basis of individual preferences over these options. The theorem states that there is no way to construct social preferences as a function of individual preferences if this function is required to satisfy basic principles of unanimity (weak Pareto: if everybody prefers x to y, so does society), impartiality (nondictatorship: no individual can always impose his strict preferences), and informational parsimony (independence of irrelevant alternatives: social preferences over any subset of alternatives depend only on individual preferences over this subset).

Impossibilities in social choice theory, possibilities in fair allocation theory—this contrast requires an explanation. Such an explanation not only is interesting from a purely theoretical viewpoint, but bears on the ability of social choice theorists to provide helpful concepts and tools to public economists and decision makers. The possibility of social choice is at stake.

The starting point of this essay is a simple observation: the main explanation that can be found in the literature is not satisfactory. It says that the theory of social choice seeks full-fledged orderings of all alternatives, whereas the theory of fair allocation is satisfied with a selection of efficient and equitable allocations in the feasible set. In other words, Arrow's impossibility theorem applies to *social preferences* and does not apply to *allocation rules*. The problem with this explanation is that an allocation rule is formally equivalent to an ordering of all allocations. It is a coarse ordering, with only two indifference classes, the "good" and the "bad." But a coarse ordering is an ordering. And there is nothing in Arrow's framework that requires social preferences to have more than two indifference classes. Therefore, Arrow's theorem does apply to allocation rules, and the theory of fair allocation is essentially a part of the theory of social choice.

This simple point raises a question and suggests an answer. The question is, What, then, is the explanation for the possibility results in fair allocation theory? The answer is, Allocation rules must violate some of the axioms of Arrow's theorem. It is indeed a simple exercise to show that the prominent solutions in the theory of fair allocation, viewed as social preferences, do violate the axioms of weak Pareto and independence of irrelevant alternatives. It is even quite easy to see why weak Pareto is violated by allocation rules. This axiom requires strict social preference in favor of any Pareto-dominating allocation, and since there are many (chained) instances of Pareto domination in relevant domains, it entails that social preferences must have more than two indifference classes. Allocation rules can at best satisfy the Pareto efficiency condition (requiring the selected allocations not to be Pareto-dominated).

In this essay, we generalize these observations and show why all reasonable (i.e., minimally impartial) allocation rules in fair allocation theory must also violate the axiom of independence of irrelevant alternatives. Moreover, we examine how much weakening of this axiom (i.e., introducing more information about individual preferences) is required for a reasonable allocation rule to be possible. In particular, we find that less weakening of independence of irrelevant alternatives is needed for allocation rules, thanks to the fact that weak Pareto is weakened into the Pareto efficiency condition (so as to be compatible with social preferences having two indifference classes only), than for social preferences satisfying weak Pareto. In other words, there is a trade-off between Pareto conditions and independence conditions.

In summary, the main lessons of this essay are the following. First, *the theory of fair allocation succeeds in obtaining possibility results mainly because it relaxes the axiom of independence of irrelevant alternatives.* Second, in order to obtain possibility results, *the theory of social choice (with social preferences satisfying weak Pareto) needs more information about individual preferences (more weakening of independence of irrelevant alternatives) than the theory of fair allocation (with coarse social preferences satisfying only the Pareto efficiency condition).*

This essay is organized as follows. Section 10.2 briefly examines the explanation of the possibility results in fair allocation theory as given by the literature. This examination seems in order because, in all fairness, the literature is not as simple-minded as the preceding summary suggests. Section 10.3 presents some simple examples in order to show how allocation rules can be viewed as social preferences and what axioms of Arrow's theorem they respect or violate. Then Section 10.4 introduces the model and the main formal notions. The reason why allocation rules must violate independence of irrelevant alternatives is studied in Section 10.5. In Section 10.6 we then discuss some weak variants of independence of irrelevant alternatives, and examine how such variants can be satisfied by allocation rules. Section 10.7 compares the informational basis of the theory of fair allocation to that of social choice theory (with Paretian social preferences), delineating the trade-off between Pareto conditions and independence conditions. In Section 10.8 we come back to the assertion that the theory of fair allocation is just a part of the theory of social choice, and discuss various possible unifications of these theories and their relative merits. Section 10.9 concludes.

10.2. Explanations from the Literature

Most authors have stressed two differences between the two theories. The one most often mentioned is about preferences versus selection. Varian [31] argues as follows:

> Social [choice] theory asks for too much out of the process in that it asks for an entire *ordering* of the various social states (allocations in this case). The original question asked only for a "good" allocation; there was no requirement to rank all allocations. The fairness criterion in fact limits itself to answering the original question. It is limited in that it gives no indication of the merits of two nonfair allocations, but by restricting itself in this way it allows for a reasonable solution to the original problem. (p. 65)

Similarly, Kolm [17] is ironic about social preferences:

> The requirement of a social ordering is indeed problematic at first sight: Why would we want to know the 193th best alternative? Only the first best is required for the choice. (p. 439)

In his famous survey on social choice theory, Sen [25] also emphasizes this contrast:

> The specified subset is seen as good, but there is no claim that they represent the "best" alternatives, all *equally* choosable. There is no attempt to give an answer to the overall problem of social choice, and the exercise is quite different from the specification of a social preference over X. (p. 1106)

And most recently, Moulin and Thomson [19] have compared the two theories in these terms:

> In social choice theory, the focus is commonly on obtaining a complete ranking of the set of feasible alternatives as a function of the profile of

individual preferences. . . . Consider now the axiomatic investigations of resource allocation. As their counterparts in the theory of cooperative games, their focus is on the search for allocation rules, no attempt being made at obtaining a complete ranking of the entire feasible set. (p. 104)

The second difference noticed by these authors is that economic models enable the analyst to take account of the structure of allocations. Varian mentions only the fact that the theory of fair allocation can focus on self-centered preferences (individuals being interested only in their own consumption), while Sen has written about the fairness literature:

First, it has shown the relevance of informational parameters that the traditional social choice approaches have tended to ignore in the single-minded concern with individual orderings of complete social states. Comparisons of different persons' positions within a state have been brought into the calculation, enlarging the informational basis of social judgments. Second, in raising rather concrete questions regarding states of affairs, the fairness literature has pushed social choice theory in the direction of more structure. (p. 1111)

Similarly, Moulin and Thomson have argued that

the models of resource allocation take full account of the microeconomic structure of the problems to be solved. . . . This descriptive richness permits a great deal of flexibility at two levels. First, properties of allocation rules can be formulated directly in terms of the physical attributes of the economy. . . . Second, the rich mathematical structure of microeconomic models gives rise to a host of variations on each general principle. (p. 105)

However, this second difference is about additional requirements formulated in a richer framework, and can hardly explain the relative success of the theory of fair allocation. This was noted by Moulin and Thomson, who have concluded:

Note that social choice theory itself has recently developed in a similar direction, widening its framework by incorporating information about economic environments. . . . But as its objective has remained to obtain complete rankings of sets of feasible alternatives, its conclusions have so far remained largely negative. (p. 105)

Actually, Arrow's initial presentation of his theorem (Arrow [1; 2]) was already formulated in an economic setting, with self-centered preferences. He indeed considered the possibility that a more concrete framework, with a domain restricted to standard consumer preferences, might alter the general outlook of social choice, and he concluded negatively. This conclusion has been fully confirmed by the more recent research alluded to by Moulin and Thomson.

All in all, one can safely conclude that the common explanation for the possibility results in the theory of fair allocation is that it does not seek a full-fledged ordering.

10.3. Allocation Rules as Social Preferences

As explained in the introduction, an allocation rule, in effect, splits the set of allocations in two parts, the good and the bad. Even though the intention of particular authors in this field may not have been to give an ordering of allocations, this twofold partition is, *formally,* an ordering. Now, in view of the preceding quotations from the literature, one may wonder whether the best interpretation of allocation rules is to view them as partial orderings (quasi orderings) or as complete orderings. An allocation rule may be viewed as a partial ordering if the good allocations are deemed noncomparable, and similarly for the bad ones, as suggested previously by Varian and Sen. But this would not save the thesis that Arrow's theorem does not apply to allocation rules. First, the social choice literature has extended the bulk of Arrow's theorem to quasi orderings.[2] Second, nothing prevents one from deriving a complete ordering from any allocation rule. This means that the theory of fair allocation is, willy nilly, able to provide complete orderings, and the puzzle of this success, contrasted to Arrow's impossibility, remains.

In this section we examine some examples in order to provide more intuition about how allocation rules can be viewed as social preferences, and as such may be submitted to the test of Arrow's axioms. Let us for

2. In particular, Weymark [33] has studied the application of Arrow's axioms to partial orderings and obtained oligarchy results. More interestingly, by adding anonymity to the axioms, he characterized the Pareto partial ordering. Although his results are obtained in an abstract framework with unrestricted preferences, they strongly suggest that little can be gained by abandoning completeness. See, however, Essay 8 of this volume.

the moment consider a simple Edgeworth box setting with two goods and two individuals. Every individual has self-centered preferences about his own bundles of these two goods. The set of feasible alternatives contains all allocations for which total consumption does not exceed a fixed available amount of the two goods. From individual self-centered preferences over bundles one can derive individual preferences over allocations, simply by considering that an individual prefers one allocation to another whenever he prefers his own bundle in this allocation to his own bundle in the other allocation. Therefore, we are essentially in a particular version of Arrow's framework, with individual preferences over a given set of allocations, and the question is whether one can derive social preferences over this same set of allocations from any profile of individual preferences.

Arrow's theorem does apply to such a simple setting, as shown by Bordes, Campbell, and Le Breton [4]. More precisely, they assume that the domain of individual preferences contains all continuous, strictly monotonic, and strictly convex preference relations over bundles, and they study social ordering functions defining a complete ordering for any profile of preferences. They show that any such function satisfying weak Pareto and independence of irrelevant alternatives must be such that one particular individual imposes her own strict preferences over all interior allocations.[3]

A prominent solution from the theory of fair allocation, in this simple setting, is the egalitarian Walrasian allocation rule, which selects the competitive equilibrium allocations with equal budgets. (One may describe it as first dividing all available resources equally among individuals and then letting them trade in a competitive market.) This allocation rule defines simple two-tier social preferences, such that any equal-budget competitive equilibrium is ranked above any other type of allocation, all equal-budget competitive equilibria are socially indifferent, and all other allocations are socially indifferent. This is a complete ordering of all the allocations of the relevant set.

Since such an ordering is defined for every profile of individual preferences in the preceding domain, one obtains a social ordering *function,* which satisfies all requirements of Arrow's framework. But it does not satisfy all axioms of Arrow's theorem, and to this we now turn.

3. This is not a full dictator, since this individual is not able to impose his/her strict preferences over all allocations. But this result is sufficiently "dictatorial" to be interpreted as preserving the bulk of Arrow's theorem.

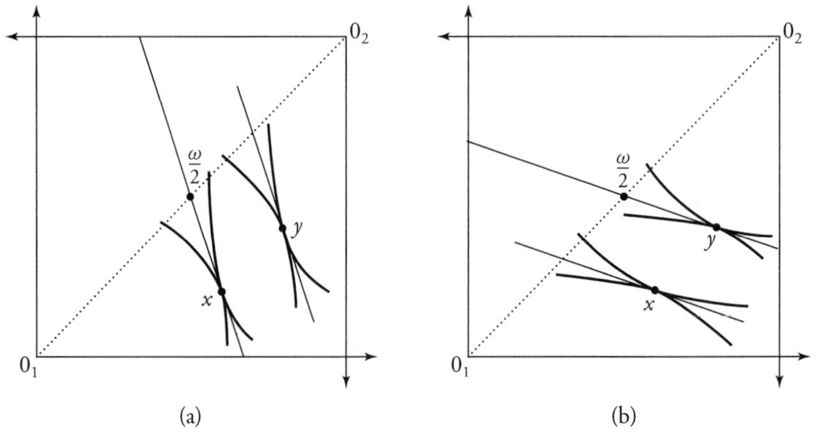

Figure 10.1. The Egalitarian Walrasian Allocation Rule Violates IIA

This social ordering function does not satisfy weak Pareto, for an obvious reason already explained: all nonselected allocations are deemed socially indifferent, in spite of the fact that some of them Pareto-dominate others. Nonetheless, a weaker Pareto condition is satisfied, since the preferred allocations are never Pareto-dominated by the other allocations. Pareto efficiency of the selected allocations is indeed the relevant condition for allocation rules. But it is important to reckon that this is weaker than weak Pareto.

More interestingly, this social ordering function does not satisfy independence of irrelevant alternatives. This is illustrated in Figure 10.1, which features two allocations, x and y. Two different profiles are shown on panel (a) and panel (b). In both profiles, the first individual prefers allocation y (since she receives more of both goods in y), and the other individual has the opposite preferences. By independence of irrelevant alternatives, the fact that individual preferences about x and y are the same in the two profiles implies that social preferences about the two allocations should be identical for the two cases. But this is not satisfied with the social preferences derived from the egalitarian Walrasian allocation rule. Indeed, in panel (a), x is an equal-budget competitive equilibrium allocation and y is not, so that x is socially preferred to y. The reverse occurs in panel (b).

It remains to check that there is no dictator with such social preferences. This is again illustrated in Figure 10.1, since social preferences go against the first individual's preferences on panel (a) and against the other's preferences

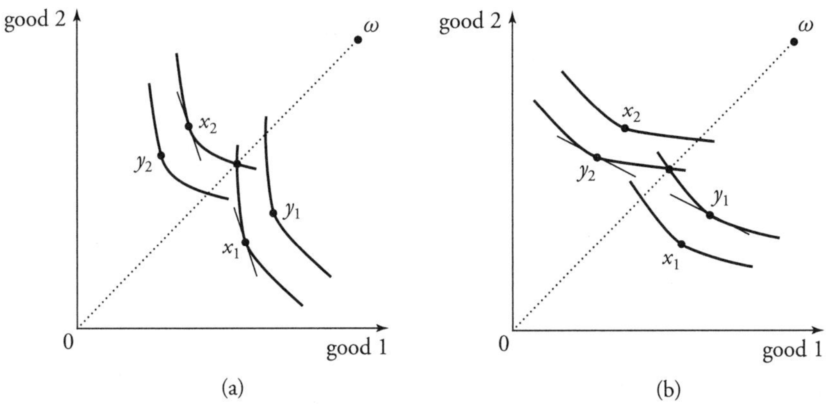

Figure 10.2. The Egalitarian-Equivalent Allocation Rule Violates IIA

on panel (b). It is actually easy to generalize from this example, and see that an allocation rule cannot have a dictator in Bordes, Campbell, and Le Breton's [4] sense. Indeed, when individual preferences are strictly monotonic, a dictator has fine-grained preferences, which cannot be obeyed by a coarse social ordering with only two indifference classes. Therefore, an allocation rule, viewed as social preferences, always trivially satisfies the nondictatorship condition of Arrow's theorem.

Let us now consider a second example. Another prominent solution in fair allocation theory is Pazner and Schmeidler's [22] egalitarian-equivalent allocation rule. This allocation rule selects the Pareto-efficient allocations such that every individual is indifferent between her own bundle and a common reference bundle that is proportional to the total available resources. Similarly as before, one can derive two-tier social preferences from this allocation rule. Again, it does not satisfy weak Pareto and does satisfy the nondictatorship condition, for the same obvious reasons as previously noted. The fact that it does not satisfy independence of irrelevant alternatives is illustrated in Figure 10.2. In panel (a), allocation x is egalitarian-equivalent and allocation y is not, while the reverse holds for panel (b). By independence of irrelevant alternatives, however, social preferences should be the same in the two cases, since individual preferences about x and y are identical.

Figures 10.1 and 10.2 provide intuition for the reason why it is unlikely that an allocation rule, viewed as a social ordering function, will satisfy independence of irrelevant alternatives. In these two examples, information about whether any individual prefers x or y is not sufficient to judge how good the allocations are. In the case of the egalitarian Walrasian allocation rule, one needs to know at least the marginal rates of substitution at the relevant bundles. In the case of the egalitarian-equivalent allocation rule, one needs to know the intersection of the relevant indifference curves with a particular ray in the space of goods. The next sections study how stringent, in all generality, the independence condition is for allocation rules viewed as social ordering functions.

10.4. Model and Definitions

Before going into technicalities, let us take stock and see what remains to be clarified. The previous sections have established the following: (a) the standard explanation for the possibility results in fair allocation, in view of Arrow's impossibility theorem, is that allocation rules are not orderings, so that Arrow's theorem does not apply to them; (b) actually, allocation rules do provide complete orderings, so that Arrow's theorem does apply to them, which means the correct explanation must be that allocation rules violate some of Arrow's axioms; (c) allocation rules, due to the fact that they yield coarse (two-tier) social preferences, always violate weak Pareto and satisfy nondictatorship; and (d) prominent examples of allocation rules violate independence of irrelevant alternatives.

What remains to be seen, at this stage, is whether any reasonable allocation rule may satisfy independence of irrelevant alternatives. What we have to do, therefore, is to examine the implications, for an allocation rule (viewed as two-tier social preferences), of satisfying this axiom. For this we must formally define the concept of an allocation rule, the concept of social preferences, and, more importantly, the concept of two-tier social preferences associated with an allocation rule, so that Arrow's axioms may be correctly applied to an allocation rule.

10.4.1. The Model

The model adopted here is just an immediate extension of the simple framework of the previous section.

The *population* is fixed. Let $N = \{1, \ldots, n\}$ be the set of *agents* where $2 \leq n < \infty$. There are l *goods* indexed by $k = 1, \ldots, l$ where $2 \leq l < \infty$. Agent i's *consumption bundle* is a vector $x_i = (x_{i1}, \ldots, x_{il}) \in \mathbb{R}^l_+$. An *allocation* is denoted $x = (x_1, \ldots, x_n) \in \mathbb{R}^{nl}_+$.

A *preordering* is a reflexive and transitive binary relation. Agent i's *preferences* are described by a complete preordering R_i (strict preference P_i, indifference I_i) on $\mathbb{R}^l_+$. A *profile of preferences* is denoted $\boldsymbol{R} = (R_1, \ldots, R_n)$. Let $\mathcal{R}$ be the set of continuous, convex, and strictly monotonic preferences over $\mathbb{R}^l_+$.

Let π be a bijection on N. For each $x \in \mathbb{R}^{nl}_+$, define $\pi(x) = (x'_1, \ldots, x'_n) \in \mathbb{R}^{nl}_+$ by $x'_i = x_{\pi(i)}$ for all $i \in N$, and for each $\boldsymbol{R} \in \mathcal{R}^n$, define $\pi(\boldsymbol{R}) = (R'_1, \ldots, R'_n) \in \mathcal{R}^n$ by $R'_i = R_{\pi(i)}$ for all $i \in N$. Let Π be the set of all bijections on N.

There is no production in our model, and the amount of *total resources* is fixed and represented by the vector $\omega \in \mathbb{R}^l_{++}$. An allocation $x \in \mathbb{R}^{nl}_+$ is *feasible* if $\sum_{i \in N} x_i \leq \omega$.[4] Let F be the set of all feasible allocations.

For each $\boldsymbol{R} \in \mathcal{R}^n$, let $E(\boldsymbol{R})$ denote the set of *Pareto-efficient allocations*. Because of strict monotonicity of preferences, there is no need to distinguish Pareto efficiency in the strong sense and in the weak sense.

A *social ordering function* (SOF) is a function $\bar{R}$ defined on $\mathcal{R}^n$, such that for all $\boldsymbol{R} \in \mathcal{R}^n$, $\bar{R}(\boldsymbol{R})$ is a complete preordering on the set of allocations F. Let $\bar{P}(\boldsymbol{R})$ (resp. $\bar{I}(\boldsymbol{R})$) denote the strict preference (resp. indifference) relation derived from $\bar{R}(\boldsymbol{R})$.

An *allocation rule* (AR) is a set-valued mapping S defined on $\mathcal{R}^n$, such that[5] for all $\boldsymbol{R} \in \mathcal{R}^n$, $S(\boldsymbol{R})$ is a nonempty subset of F. An AR S is *essentially single-valued* if all selected allocations are Pareto-indifferent:

$$\forall x, y \in S(\boldsymbol{R}), \forall i \in N, x_i I_i y_i.$$

We may now provide precise definitions for the two ARs informally introduced in the previous section. The first one is the egalitarian Walrasian

4. Vector inequalities are denoted as usual: $\geq$, $>$, and $\gg$.

5. An alternative definition of SOFs and ARs makes them a function of ω as well as $\boldsymbol{R}$. This is useful when changes in ω are studied, but here we focus only on the information about preferences, and since ω is kept fixed throughout this essay, we omit this argument.

AR S_W, which is defined as follows: $x \in S_W(\boldsymbol{R})$ if $x \in F$ and there is $p \in \mathbb{R}^l_{++}$ such that for all $i \in N$,

$$\forall y \in \mathbb{R}^l_+, \, p \cdot y \leq p \cdot \frac{\omega}{n} \Rightarrow x_i R_i y.$$

The second allocation rule is the Pazner-Schmeidler AR S_{PS}, which is defined as follows: $x \in S_{PS}(\boldsymbol{R})$ if $x \in E(\boldsymbol{R})$ and there is $\alpha \in \mathbb{R}_+$ such that for all $i \in N$,

$$x_i I_i \alpha\omega.$$

With each AR S one can associate the (two-tier) SOF $\bar{R}_S$ defined as follows: for all $\boldsymbol{R} \in \mathcal{R}^n$, and all $x, y \in F$,

$$x \bar{R}_S(\boldsymbol{R}) y \Leftrightarrow x \in S(\boldsymbol{R}) \text{or } y \notin S(\boldsymbol{R}).$$

One then has the following: for all $\boldsymbol{R} \in \mathcal{R}^n$, and all $x, y \in F$,

$$x \bar{P}_S(\boldsymbol{R}) y \Leftrightarrow \text{not } [y \bar{R}_S(\mathbf{R}) x] \Leftrightarrow x \in S(\boldsymbol{R}) \text{ and } y \notin S(\boldsymbol{R}).$$

Conversely, with each SOF $\bar{R}$ one can associate the AR $S_{\bar{R}}$ defined as follows: for all $\boldsymbol{R} \in \mathcal{R}^n$,

$$S_{\bar{R}}(\boldsymbol{R}) = \{x \in F \mid \forall y \in F, x \bar{R}(\boldsymbol{R}) y\}.$$

Notice that for each AR S,[6]

$$S_{\bar{R}_S} = S,$$

6. One has, for all $\boldsymbol{R} \in \mathcal{R}^n$:

$$\begin{aligned} S_{\bar{R}_S}(\boldsymbol{R}) &= \{x \in F \mid \forall y \in F, x \bar{R}_S(\boldsymbol{R}) y\} \\ &= \{x \in F \mid \forall y \in F, x \in S(\boldsymbol{R}) \quad \text{or } y \notin S(\boldsymbol{R})\} \\ &= \{x \in F \mid \forall y \in S(\boldsymbol{R}), x \in S(\boldsymbol{R})\} \\ &= \{x \in F \mid x \in S(\boldsymbol{R})\} \\ &= S(\boldsymbol{R}). \end{aligned}$$

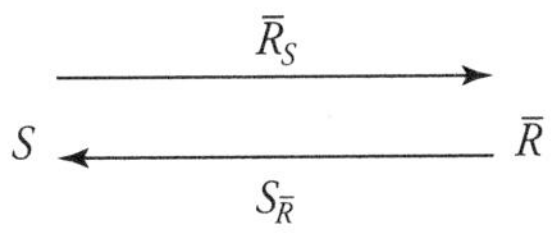

Figure 10.3. One-to-One Correspondence between ARs and SOFs with at Most Two Indifference Classes

and for each SOF $\bar{R}$ that has at most two indifference classes,[7]

$$\bar{R}_{S_{\bar{R}}} = \bar{R}.$$

Hence, there exists a precise one-to-one correspondence between the class of all ARs and the class of all SOFs that have at most two indifference classes. Figure 10.3 illustrates this correspondence.

What we want to study here is the application of Arrow's axioms to a particular class of SOFs, namely, the SOFs that are associated with allocation rules. It is therefore convenient to give them a special name. Let an ARSOF be a SOF that has at most two indifference classes and is therefore associated with an AR. Formally, an ARSOF is a SOF $\bar{R}$ for which there exists an AR S such that $\bar{R} = \bar{R}_S$.

We will say that an ARSOF is *essentially single-valued* if its associated AR is essentially single-valued.

10.4.2. Arrow's Axioms

We are now ready to give precise definitions of Arrow's three conditions.

Weak Pareto. $\forall \boldsymbol{R} \in \mathcal{R}^n$, $\forall x, y \in F$, if $\forall i \in N$, $x_i P_i y_i$, then $x \bar{P}(\boldsymbol{R}) y$.

---

7. One has, for all $\boldsymbol{R} \in \mathcal{R}^n$ and all $x, y \in F$:

$$x\ \bar{R}_{S_{\bar{R}}}(\boldsymbol{R})\ y \Leftrightarrow x \in S_{\bar{R}}(\boldsymbol{R}) \text{ or } y \notin S_{\bar{R}}(\boldsymbol{R})$$

$$\Leftrightarrow [\forall z \in F, x \bar{R}(\boldsymbol{R})\ z] \text{ or } [\exists z \in F, z\ \bar{P}(\boldsymbol{R})\ y].$$

In the former case, we obtain $x \bar{R}(\boldsymbol{R}) y$ by choosing $z = y$. In the latter case, y belongs to the lower indifference class of $\bar{R}(\boldsymbol{R})$, so that we have $x \bar{R}(\boldsymbol{R}) y$ irrespective of whether x belongs to the higher or lower indifference class.

Independence of Irrelevant Alternatives (IIA). $\forall \boldsymbol{R}, \boldsymbol{R}' \in \mathcal{R}^n, \forall x, y \in F$, if $\forall i \in N$,

$$x_i R_i y_i \Leftrightarrow x_i R_i' y_i$$

$$y_i R_i x_i \Leftrightarrow y_i R_i' x_i,$$

then $x \bar{R}(\boldsymbol{R}) y \Leftrightarrow x \bar{R}(\boldsymbol{R}') y$.

In economic domains, it is common to refine the definition of nondictatorship so as to allow for slight strengthenings of the usual axiom. Let $X \subseteq F$ be given.[8]

Nondictatorship (over X). There does not exist $i_0 \in N$ such that

$$\forall \boldsymbol{R} \in \mathcal{R}^n, \forall x, y \in X, x_{i_0} P_{i_0} y_{i_0} \Rightarrow x \bar{P}(\boldsymbol{R}) y.$$

In addition to these axioms, it will be useful to refer to a full anonymity condition, which is stronger than nondictatorship but quite appealing on grounds of impartiality:[9]

Anonymity. $\forall \boldsymbol{R} \in \mathcal{R}^n, \forall x, y \in F, \forall \pi \in \Pi$,

$$x \bar{R}(\boldsymbol{R}) y \Leftrightarrow \pi(x) \bar{R}(\pi(\boldsymbol{R})) \pi(y).$$

10.4.3. Arrow's Axioms and Allocation Rules

Our purpose is to examine the implications of Arrow's axioms for the allocation rules of fair allocation theory. Arrow's axioms, as defined previously for SOFs, can be applied directly to ARSOFs, which are just a particular kind of SOF. But it is quite illuminating to see the exact constraints the axioms impose on the AR associated with an ARSOF. That is, one can directly rewrite

8. For instance, as explained previously, the relevant set for the nondictatorship condition may be the set of interior allocations.

9. Notice that the standard "public good" anonymity condition (stating that social preferences should be invariant to permutations of individual preferences over allocations) would not make sense in the current "private good" setting, since individual i's preferences focus on his own bundle. A permutation of preferences over allocations would mean that he would focus on another individual's bundle, which is not permitted in the domain.

Arrow's axioms in terms of the constraints they impose on an AR. This is just a simple exercise in substituting definitions, but it appears quite useful for the intuition. In addition, the obtained formulations are helpful when one comes to think about weakening the axioms, which will be an important topic in this essay.

When $\bar{R}$ is an ARSOF, $x\ \bar{R}(\boldsymbol{R})\ y$ is logically equivalent to $[x \in S_{\bar{R}}(\boldsymbol{R})$ or $y \notin S_{\bar{R}}(\boldsymbol{R})]$, and $x\ \bar{P}(\boldsymbol{R})y$ is equivalent to $[x \in S_{\bar{R}}(\boldsymbol{R})$ and $y \notin S_{\bar{R}}(\boldsymbol{R})]$. Substituting these expressions, we obtain the following. The direct translation of weak Pareto yields the following:

Weak Pareto (for ARSOF). $\forall \boldsymbol{R} \in \mathcal{R}^n, \forall x, y \in F$, if $\forall i \in N, x_i P_i y_i$, then $x \in S_{\bar{R}}(\boldsymbol{R})$ and $y \notin S_{\bar{R}}(\boldsymbol{R})$.

Formulated in this way, it is immediately seen that weak Pareto is too strong for ARSOFs. If one takes $x, y, z \in F$ such that for all i, $x_i P_i y_i P_i z_i$, the axiom requires $y \in S_{\bar{R}}(\boldsymbol{R})$ and also $y \notin S_{\bar{R}}(\boldsymbol{R})$, a contradiction. The standard weakening of this axiom, for applications to ARs, is the following:

Pareto Efficiency (for ARSOF). $\forall \boldsymbol{R} \in \mathcal{R}^n, \forall x, y \in F$, if $\forall i \in N, x_i P_i y_i$, then $y \notin S_{\bar{R}}(\boldsymbol{R})$.

We are actually more familiar with the following, equivalent, formulation:

Pareto Efficiency (for ARSOF). $\forall \boldsymbol{R} \in \mathcal{R}^n$, $S_{\bar{R}}(\boldsymbol{R}) \subseteq E(\boldsymbol{R})$.

Interestingly, however, this is not the only conceivable weakening of weak Pareto for ARSOFs. Another sensible condition, which is logically weaker than Pareto efficiency, is the following:

Partial Pareto (for ARSOF). $\forall \boldsymbol{R} \in \mathcal{R}^n$, $\forall x, y \in F$, if $\forall i \in N$, $x_i P_i y_i$, then $x \in S_{\bar{R}}(\boldsymbol{R})$ or $y \notin S_{\bar{R}}(\boldsymbol{R})$.

This is equivalent to the following condition: $\forall \boldsymbol{R} \in \mathcal{R}^n$, $\forall x, y \in F$, if $\forall i \in N$, $x_i P_i y_i$, then $y \in S_{\bar{R}}(\boldsymbol{R}) \Rightarrow x \in S_{\bar{R}}(\boldsymbol{R})$. If an ARSOF $\bar{R}$ satisfies this condition, then for each $\boldsymbol{R} \in \mathcal{R}^n$, there exists a subset $T \subseteq F$ such that

$$S_{\bar{R}}(\boldsymbol{R}) \supseteq \bigcup_{y \in T} [\{y\} \cup \{x \in F \mid \forall i \in N, x_i P_i y_i\}].$$

Pareto efficiency and partial Pareto have been introduced in Suzumura [26], under the names exclusion Pareto and inclusion Pareto, respectively. There are interesting ARSOFs satisfying partial Pareto but not Pareto efficiency. For instance, define

$$S_{\bar{R}}(\boldsymbol{R}) \equiv \left\{ x \in F \mid \forall i \in N, x_i R_i \frac{\omega}{n} \right\},$$

that is, $S_{\bar{R}}(\boldsymbol{R})$ is the set of individually rational allocations from the equal division of resources. This rule satisfies partial Pareto.

Let us now consider IIA. The immediate translation is as follows:

IIA (FOR ARSOF). $\forall \boldsymbol{R}, \boldsymbol{R}' \in \mathcal{R}^n, \forall x, y \in F,$ if $\forall i \in N,$

$$x_i R_i y_i \Leftrightarrow x_i R_i' y_i$$

$$y_i R_i x_i \Leftrightarrow y_i R_i' x_i,$$

then $[x \in S_{\bar{R}}(\boldsymbol{R})$ or $y \notin S_{\bar{R}}(\boldsymbol{R})] \Leftrightarrow [x \in S_{\bar{R}}(\boldsymbol{R}')$ or $y \notin S_{\bar{R}}(\boldsymbol{R}')]$.

Interestingly, notice that, since SOFs yield complete orderings, the original IIA axiom can equivalently be written with the conclusion

$$x \bar{R}(\boldsymbol{R}) y \Leftrightarrow x \bar{R}(\boldsymbol{R}') y$$

or the conclusion

$$x \bar{P}(\boldsymbol{R}) y \Leftrightarrow x \bar{P}(\boldsymbol{R}') y.$$

As a consequence, the preceding IIA for ARSOF could equivalently be concluded by

$$[x \in S_{\bar{R}}(\boldsymbol{R}) \text{ and } y \notin S_{\bar{R}}(\mathbf{R})] \Leftrightarrow [x \in S_{\bar{R}}(\boldsymbol{R}') \text{ and } y \notin S_{\bar{R}}(\boldsymbol{R}')],$$

which makes it transparent how demanding it is. It requires that if an allocation is selected while another is not, this does not change when individual preferences relative to these two allocations remain the same, independently of preferences over other allocations.

The translation of nondictatorship is as follows. Let $X \subseteq F$ be given.

NONDICTATORSHIP (OVER X) (FOR ARSOF). There does not exist $i_0 \in N$ such that

$$\forall \boldsymbol{R} \in \mathcal{R}^n, \forall x, y \in X, x_{i_0} P_{i_0} y_{i_0} \Rightarrow x \in S_{\bar{R}}(\boldsymbol{R}) \text{ and } y \notin S_{\bar{R}}(\boldsymbol{R}).$$

It is obvious that this axiom will be trivially satisfied by ARSOFs. For any i_0, one can find $x_{i_0}, y_{i_0}, z_{i_0}$ such that $x_{i_0} P_{i_0} y_{i_0} P_{i_0} z_{i_0}$, and if i_0 were a dictator, this would imply $y \in S_{\bar{R}}(\boldsymbol{R})$ and also $y \notin S_{\bar{R}}(\boldsymbol{R})$, a contradiction.

More interestingly, the anonymity axiom then boils down to the following standard condition:

ANONYMITY (FOR ARSOF).
$\forall \pi \in \Pi, \forall \boldsymbol{R} \in \mathcal{R}^n, \forall x \in S_{\bar{R}}(\boldsymbol{R}), \pi(x) \in S_{\bar{R}}(\pi(\boldsymbol{R}))$.

10.5. IIA and Allocation Rules

It is known from Wilson's theorem (Wilson [34]) that IIA is a very strong axiom. When applied to allocation rules, the fact that IIA is very strong is captured in the following result, which implies that social preferences are totally independent of individual preferences.

PROPOSITION 10.1. An ARSOF $\bar{R}$ satisfies IIA if and only if $\bar{R}$ is a constant function.

The proof is based on a simple argument, which may be summarized as follows. Consider allocation $x^0 \in F$, which gives ω to agent i_0 and 0 to all other agents. Let $x \in F$ be another feasible allocation. Due to the strict monotonicity of preferences, individual preferences over x and x^0 are the same on the whole domain $\mathcal{R}$. Therefore, by IIA, if x is selected while x^0 is not for some $\boldsymbol{R} \in \mathcal{R}^n$, this must also hold for all $\boldsymbol{R} \in \mathcal{R}^n$, and similarly if x^0 is selected while x is not.

PROOF. It is obvious that a constant ARSOF satisfies IIA. For the converse, choose $i_0 \in N$ and define $x^0 \in F$ by $x^0_{i_0} = \omega$ (and $x^0_i = 0$ for all $i \neq i_0$). If for all $\boldsymbol{R} \in \mathcal{R}^n$ one has $S_{\bar{R}}(\boldsymbol{R}) = F$, then $S_{\bar{R}}$ is a constant function. Suppose then that this is not the case, and let $\boldsymbol{R} \in \mathcal{R}^n$ be such that $S_{\bar{R}}(\boldsymbol{R}) \neq F$.

CASE 1. $x^0 \in S_{\bar{R}}(\boldsymbol{R})$. Take any $y \notin S_{\bar{R}}(\boldsymbol{R})$. By monotonicity of preferences, for all $\boldsymbol{R}' \in \mathcal{R}^n$,

$$\forall i \in N, x_i^0 R_i y_i \Leftrightarrow x_i^0 R_i' y_i \quad \text{and} \quad y_i R_i x_i^0 \Leftrightarrow y_i R_i' x_i^0.$$

Therefore, $x^0 \in S_{\bar{R}}(\boldsymbol{R}')$ and $y \notin S_{\bar{R}}(\boldsymbol{R}')$. The latter implies $F \setminus S_{\bar{R}}(\boldsymbol{R}) \subseteq F \setminus S_{\bar{R}}(\boldsymbol{R}')$. Since $x^0 \in S_{\bar{R}}(\boldsymbol{R}')$, one can show by a symmetrical argument that $F \setminus S_{\bar{R}}(\boldsymbol{R}') \subseteq F \setminus S_{\bar{R}}(\boldsymbol{R})$, implying $S_{\bar{R}}(\boldsymbol{R}') = S_{\bar{R}}(\boldsymbol{R})$.

CASE 2. $x^0 \notin S_{\bar{R}}(\boldsymbol{R})$. Take any $x \in S_{\bar{R}}(\boldsymbol{R})$. By monotonicity of preferences, for all $\boldsymbol{R}' \in \mathcal{R}^n$,

$$\forall i \in N, x_i^0 R_i x_i \Leftrightarrow x_i^0 R_i' x_i \text{and} x_i R_i x_i^0 \Leftrightarrow x_i R_i' x_i^0.$$

Therefore, $x^0 \notin S_{\bar{R}}(\boldsymbol{R}')$ and $x \in S_{\bar{R}}(\boldsymbol{R}')$. Hence, $S_{\bar{R}}(\boldsymbol{R}) \subseteq S_{\bar{R}}(\boldsymbol{R}')$. Similarly, by a symmetrical argument based on $x^0 \notin S_{\bar{R}}(\boldsymbol{R}')$, one can show that $S_{\bar{R}}(\boldsymbol{R}') \subseteq S_{\bar{R}}(\boldsymbol{R})$. ■

Contrary to what one might expect, this does not exactly entail an Arrovian impossibility. In fact, there are ARSOFs satisfying IIA and Pareto conditions (and trivially, nondictatorship).

Let us first examine the implication of IIA together with the weakest of our Pareto conditions, viz., partial Pareto. The message of the following proposition is that even with the weakest version of the Pareto conditions, under IIA we are not allowed much room to consider various ARSOFs.

One may get an intuition for the following proposition by considering how an ARSOF $\bar{R}$ may satisfy Pareto efficiency (which is stronger than partial Pareto) and IIA. By the previous result, it must be constant. Now, the only allocations which are Pareto-efficient independently of individual preferences are the allocations like x^0 before, in which one agent receives all of the available resources. With partial Pareto, a few other possibilities are permitted. Either one selects only allocations in which one agent receives all of the available resources, or one must select all of the allocations in which everyone receives some amount of the resources. Let F^* be the set of feasible allocations with no zero bundle:

$$F^* = \{x \in F \mid \forall i \in N, x_i \neq 0\}.$$

Proposition 10.2. If an ARSOF $\bar{R}$ satisfies partial Pareto and IIA, then either for all $\boldsymbol{R} \in \mathcal{R}^n$,

$$S_{\bar{R}}(\boldsymbol{R}) \subseteq \{x \in F \mid \exists i \in N, x_i = \omega\}$$

or for all $\boldsymbol{R} \in \mathcal{R}^n$,

$$F^* \subseteq S_{\bar{R}}(\boldsymbol{R}).$$

Proof. Let $\boldsymbol{R} \in \mathcal{R}^n$ be given. Suppose that

$$S_{\bar{R}}(\boldsymbol{R}) \nsubseteq \{x \in F \mid \exists i \in N, x_i = \omega\},$$

that is, there exists $y \in S_{\bar{R}}(\boldsymbol{R})$ such that for all $i \in N$, $y_i < \omega$. We may assume that $y \neq 0$. For if $y = 0$, then there exists $y' \in F$ such that $y' \gg 0$, and hence for all $j \in N$, $y'_j P_j y_j$. Since $\bar{R}$ satisfies partial Pareto, we have $y' \in S_{\bar{R}}(\boldsymbol{R})$.

Thus, without loss of generality, assume that $0 < y_1 < \omega$. We need to show that $F^* \subseteq S_{\bar{R}}(\boldsymbol{R})$.

Step 1. We show that $\text{int}\, F \equiv \{x \in F \mid \forall i \in N, x_i \gg 0\} \subseteq S_{\bar{R}}(\boldsymbol{R})$.

Since $0 < y_1 < \omega$, there are $k, m \in \{1, \ldots, l\}$, $k \neq m$ such that $y_{1k} > 0$ and $y_{1m} < \omega_m$. Without loss of generality, assume that $y_{11} > 0$ and $y_{12} < \omega_2$.

Define $z \in F$ as follows:

$$z_{11} = 0 \quad \text{and} \quad z_{12} = \omega_2, \tag{1}$$

$$\text{for all } i \in N \text{ with } i \neq 1,\ z_{i1} = y_{i1} + \frac{y_{11}}{n-1} \text{ and } z_{i2} = 0, \text{ and} \tag{2}$$

$$\text{for all } j \in N \text{ and all } k \in \{1, \ldots, l\} \text{ with } k \neq 1, 2,\ z_{ik} = y_{ik}. \tag{3}$$

Let $\boldsymbol{R}^0 = (R^0_1, \ldots, R^0_n)$ be the profile of preferences represented by the following utility functions:

$$u^0_1(x_1) = x_{12} + \frac{1}{r_1} \sum_{m \neq 2} x_{1m},$$

$$\forall i \in N, i \neq 1, u^0_i(x_i) = x_{i1} + \frac{1}{r_i} \sum_{m \neq 1} x_{im},$$

with

$$r_1 > \frac{y_{11}}{\omega_2 - y_{12}}$$

$$\forall i \in N, i \neq 1, r_i > (n-1)\frac{y_{i2}}{y_{11}}.$$

Then, for all $j \in N$, $z_j P_j^0 y_j$. Since $\bar{R}$ satisfies IIA, from Proposition 10.1, it is a constant function. Hence, $y \in S_{\bar{R}}(\boldsymbol{R}^0) = S_{\bar{R}}(\boldsymbol{R})$. Then, by partial Pareto, $z \in S_{\bar{R}}(\boldsymbol{R}^0)$.

To show that int $F \subseteq S_{\bar{R}}(\boldsymbol{R})$, let $t \in$ int F. Let $\boldsymbol{R}^1 = (R_1^1, \ldots, R_n^1)$ be the profile of preferences represented by the following utility functions:

$$u_1^1(x_1) = x_{11} + \frac{1}{s_1}\sum_{m \neq 1} x_{1m},$$

$$\forall i \in N, i \neq 1, u_i^1(x_i) = x_{i2} + \frac{1}{s_i}\sum_{m \neq 2} x_{im},$$

with

$$s_1 > \frac{\sum_{m \neq 1}\left(z_{1m} - t_{1m}\right)}{t_{11}}$$

$$\forall i \in N, i \neq 1, s_i > \frac{\sum_{m \neq 2}\left(z_{im} - t_{im}\right)}{t_{i2}}.$$

For all $j \in N$, $t_j P_j^1 z_j$. Because $z \in S_{\bar{R}}(\boldsymbol{R}^0)$ and $S_{\bar{R}}$ is constant, we have $z \in S_{\bar{R}}(\boldsymbol{R}^1)$. Then, by partial Pareto, $t \in S_{\bar{R}}(\boldsymbol{R}^1)$. Hence, $t \in S_{\bar{R}}(\boldsymbol{R})$.

Step 2. We show that $F^* \subseteq S_{\bar{R}}(\boldsymbol{R})$.

Let $y \in F^*$. Then, for all $i \in N$, $y_i \neq 0$. Let $t \in$ int F be chosen so that for each $i \in N$, there is $k(i) \in \{1, \ldots, l\}$ such that $0 < t_{ik(i)} < y_{ik(i)}$. Let $\boldsymbol{R}' = (R_1', \ldots, R_n')$ be the profile of preferences represented by the following utility functions:

$$u_i(x_i) = x_{ik(i)} + \frac{1}{v_i}\sum_{m \neq k(i)} x_{im},$$

with

$$v_i > \frac{\sum_{m \neq k(i)} \left(t_{im} - y_{im}\right)}{y_{ik(i)} - t_{ik(i)}}.$$

For all $i \in N$, $y_i P_i' t_i$. Because $t \in S_{\bar{R}}(\boldsymbol{R})$ and $S_{\bar{R}}$ is constant, we have $t \in S_{\bar{R}}(\boldsymbol{R}')$. Then, by partial Pareto, $y \in S_{\bar{R}}(\boldsymbol{R}')$. Hence, since $S_{\bar{R}}$ is constant, $y \in S_{\bar{R}}(\boldsymbol{R})$. ■

A direct implication of Proposition 10.2 is that if one requires essential single-valuedness of an ARSOF $\bar{R}$ in addition to partial Pareto and IIA, then the associated AR $S_{\bar{R}}$ must be the usual "dictatorial" AR considered in the fair allocation literature, viz., the AR that always gives all resources to the same individual. It should then be noted that, even with the weakest version of the Pareto conditions, which does *not* require selected allocations to be Pareto-efficient, IIA and essential single-valuedness together lead us to the version of "dictatorship" in fair allocation theory. Notice that this "dictatorship" is different from the Arrovian dictatorship as defined in our nondictatorship condition. A "dictator" in fair allocation theory can impose his strict preferences only for his top choice in relation to all other alternatives. Again, this is because ARSOFs have at most two indifference classes.

Corollary 10.1. An ARSOF $\bar{R}$ satisfies partial Pareto and IIA and is essentially single-valued if and only if

$$\exists i \in N, \forall \boldsymbol{R} \in \mathcal{R}^n, S_{\bar{R}}(\boldsymbol{R}) = \{x \in F \mid x_i = \omega\}.$$

If one requires Pareto efficiency, which is stronger than partial Pareto, then, without requiring essential single-valuedness, one can only get ARSOFs that select allocations in which someone gets all resources. However, this does not contradict anonymity. In fact, together with anonymity, one gets a full characterization of an ARSOF, as stated in the following theorem. The ARSOF thus characterized is anonymous in the sense that no agent is excluded from the chance to get all resources.

Theorem 10.1. If an ARSOF $\bar{R}$ satisfies Pareto efficiency and IIA, then

$$\forall \boldsymbol{R} \in \mathcal{R}^n, S_{\bar{R}}(\boldsymbol{R}) \subseteq \{x \in F \mid \exists i \in N, x_i = \omega\}.$$

An ARSOF $\bar{R}$ satisfies Pareto efficiency, IIA, and anonymity if and only if

$$\forall \boldsymbol{R} \in \mathcal{R}^n, S_{\bar{R}}(\boldsymbol{R}) = \{x \in F \mid \exists i \in N, x_i = \omega\}.$$

Proof. By Proposition 10.2 and Pareto efficiency, for all $\boldsymbol{R} \in \mathcal{R}^n$,

$$S_{\bar{R}}(\boldsymbol{R}) \subseteq \{x \in F \mid \exists i \in N, x_i = \omega\}.$$

Since $\bar{R}$ is a constant, for all $\boldsymbol{R}, \boldsymbol{R}' \in \mathcal{R}^n$,

$$\{i \in N \mid \exists x \in S_{\bar{R}}(\boldsymbol{R}), x_i = \omega\} = \{i \in N \mid \exists x \in S_{\bar{R}}(\boldsymbol{R}'), x_i = \omega\}.$$

Therefore, anonymity requires

$$\{i \in N \mid \exists x \in S_{\bar{R}}(\boldsymbol{R}), x_i = \omega\} = N. \blacksquare$$

Even though the allocation rule characterized in Theorem 10.1 is fully anonymous, it is not appealing because it selects only extremely unequal allocations. A minimal requirement of equality is the following:

Equal Treatment of Equals (for ARSOF). $\forall \boldsymbol{R} \in \mathcal{R}^n$, $\forall x \in S_{\bar{R}}(\boldsymbol{R})$, $\forall i, j \in N$, if $R_i = R_j$, then $x_i I_i x_j$.

One may notice that any ARSOF $\bar{R}$ satisfying anonymity and essential single-valuedness necessarily satisfies equal treatment of equals.

From Theorem 10.1 we immediately deduce

Corollary 10.2. There is no ARSOF satisfying Pareto efficiency, IIA, and equal treatment of equals.[10] There is no essentially single-valued ARSOF satisfying Pareto efficiency, IIA, and anonymity.

Theorem 10.1 is interesting not only in its content but also in what it implies about all allocation rules of the fair allocation literature. Since these rules typically satisfy Pareto efficiency and anonymity, and do not give all

10. A slightly different proof obtains by showing that the only constant ARSOF satisfying equal treatment of equals selects the egalitarian allocation giving ω/n to every agent, which is not Pareto-efficient in general.

resources to one individual, they must all violate IIA. Proposition 10.1 gave the same conclusion even more immediately, since these allocation rules are not constant.

More importantly, the analysis in this section reveals that the possibility results of the theory of fair allocation are not due to the weakening of weak Pareto into Pareto efficiency. Since it is this weakening that allows social preferences to be coarse, this means that the explanation we are looking for does not lie in the fact that allocation rules yield only coarse social preferences. The preceding results show that the only way for allocation rules to be minimally satisfactory is to violate IIA. *Violation of IIA by ARs is therefore the desired explanation for the contrast between the Arrovian theory of social choice and the theory of fair allocation.*

10.6. Weakening Independence of Irrelevant Alternatives

At this stage, one may ask in what sense IIA is violated in the theory of fair allocation or, more precisely, what additional information is taken into account by ARSOFs that is forbidden by IIA.

In the theory of social choice, the main approach with respect to information has been, following Sen [23; 24] in particular, to introduce richer information about utilities. The theory of fair allocation, in contrast, has remained faithful to Arrow's initial project and usually retains only ordinal and interpersonally noncomparable information about preferences. If it introduces more information, it is about preferences, not about utilities. That is, preferences about "irrelevant" alternatives are taken into account by ARs.

It is possible to weaken IIA so as to take account of "irrelevant" alternatives (but not utilities) by strengthening the premise of the axiom in an appropriate way. This attempts brings us into several variants of the axiom, which will be introduced now. In so doing we rely here on previous works by Hansson [15], Fleurbaey and Maniquet [10], and the companion paper by Fleurbaey, Suzumura, and Tadenuma [13].

A first kind of additional information is contained in the marginal rates of substitution at the allocations to be compared. For efficient allocations, shadow prices enable one to compute the relative implicit income shares of different agents, thereby potentially providing a relevant measure of inequalities in the distribution of resources. Therefore, taking account of marginal rates of substitution is a natural extension of the informational basis of social choice theory in economic environments. Let $C(x_i, R_i)$ denote the cone of price vectors that support the upper contour set for R_i at x_i :

$$C(x_i, R_i) = \{p \in \mathbb{R}^l \mid \forall y \in \mathbb{R}^l_+, py = px_i \Rightarrow x_i R_i y\}.$$

When preferences R_i are strictly monotonic, one has $C(x_i, R_i) \subseteq \mathbb{R}^l_{++}$ whenever $x_i \gg 0$.

One then can require the ranking of two allocations to depend on individual preferences between these two allocations and also on marginal rates of substitution at these allocations, but on nothing else:

IIA except Marginal Rates of Substitution (IIA-MRS). $\forall x, y \in F$, $\forall \boldsymbol{R}, \boldsymbol{R}' \in \mathcal{R}^n$, if $\forall i \in N$,

$$x_i R_i y_i \Leftrightarrow x_i R'_i y_i$$

$$y_i R_i x_i \Leftrightarrow y_i R'_i x_i$$

$$C(x_i, R_i) = C(x_i, R'_i)$$

$$C(y_i, R_i) = C(y_i, R'_i),$$

then $x \bar{R}(\boldsymbol{R}) y \Leftrightarrow x \bar{R}(\boldsymbol{R}') y$.

Marginal rates of substitution give an infinitesimally local piece of information about preferences at given allocations. A further extension of the informational basis allows the SOF to take account of finite parts of indifference hypersurfaces. The *indifference sets* are defined as

$$I(x_i, R_i) = \{z \in \mathbb{R}^l_+ \mid z I_i x_i\}.$$

It is natural to focus on the part of indifference sets that lies within the feasible set. However, when considering any pair of allocations, the two allocations may need different amounts of total resources to be feasible and the global set F need not be relevant in its entirety. Therefore, we need to introduce the following notions. The smallest amount of total resources that makes two allocations x and y feasible can be defined by $\omega(x, y) = (\omega_1(x, y), \ldots, \omega_l(x, y))$, where for all $k \in \{1, \ldots, l\}$

$$\omega_k(x, y) = \max \left\{ \sum_{i \in N} x_{ik}, \sum_{i \in N} y_{ik} \right\}.$$

For each vector $t \in \mathbb{R}^l_+$, define the set $\Omega(t) \subseteq \mathbb{R}^l_+$ by

$$\Omega(t) = \left\{ z \in \mathbb{R}^l_+ \mid z \leq t \right\}.$$

The following axiom captures the idea that the ranking of two allocations should depend only on the indifference sets and on preferences over the minimal subset in which the two allocations are feasible.

IIA EXCEPT INDIFFERENCE SETS ON FEASIBLE ALLOCATIONS (IIA-ISFA). $\forall x, y \in F, \forall \boldsymbol{R}, \boldsymbol{R}' \in \mathcal{R}^n$, if $\forall i \in N$,

$$I(x_i, R_i) \cap \Omega(\omega(x, y)) = I(x_i, R_i') \cap \Omega(\omega(x, y))$$

$$I(y_i, R_i) \cap \Omega(\omega(x, y)) = I(y_i, R_i') \cap \Omega(\omega(x, y)),$$

then $x \bar{R}(\boldsymbol{R}) y \Leftrightarrow x \bar{R}(\boldsymbol{R}') y$.

It is immediately apparent from the definitions that

$$\begin{array}{ccc} \text{IIA} & \Rightarrow & \text{IIA-MRS} \\ \Downarrow & & \\ \text{IIA-ISFA} & & \end{array}$$

Notice that IIA-MRS does not imply IIA-ISFA because the set $I(x_i, R_i) \cap \Omega(\omega(x, y))$ does not always provide enough information to determine $C(x_i, R_i)$.[11]

It is also worthwhile here to introduce a couple of independence conditions for ARs, which are closely related to IIA and its variants. Such conditions are quite common in the fair allocation literature. We will formulate them here for ARSOFs.

The first one, dealing with marginal rates of substitution, is essentially Nagahisa's [20] "local independence":[12]

11. It does, however, when every good is consumed by at least two agents in x.

12. See also Yoshihara [35].

Independence of Preferences except MRS (IP-MRS). $\forall x \in F$, $\forall \boldsymbol{R}, \boldsymbol{R}' \in \mathcal{R}^n$, if $\forall i \in N$,

$$C(x_i, R_i) = C(x_i, R_i'),$$

then $x \in S_{\bar{R}}(\boldsymbol{R}) \Leftrightarrow x \in S_{\bar{R}}(\mathbf{R}')$.

The next axiom says that only the parts of indifference sets concerning feasible allocations should matter.

Independence of Preferences except Indifference Sets on Feasible Allocations (IP-ISFA). $\forall x \in F$, $\forall \boldsymbol{R}, \boldsymbol{R}' \in \mathcal{R}^n$, if $\forall i \in N$,

$$I(x_i, R_i) \cap \Omega(\omega) = I(x_i, R_i') \cap \Omega(\omega),$$

then $x \in S_{\bar{R}}(\boldsymbol{R}) \Leftrightarrow x \in S_{\bar{R}}(\mathbf{R}')$.

Although these independence conditions may seem restrictive, they are actually not really stronger than the previous IIA axioms.

Proposition 10.3. On the class of ARSOFs that never select the null allocation $0 = (0, \ldots, 0)$, IIA-MRS $\Rightarrow$ IP-MRS, and IIA-ISFA $\Rightarrow$ IP-ISFA.

Proof. IIA-MRS $\Rightarrow$ IP-MRS. Let $x \in S_{\bar{R}}(\boldsymbol{R})$ and $\boldsymbol{R}'$ be such that for all $i \in N$, $C(x_i, R_i') = C(x_i, R_i)$. Notice that $0 = (0, \ldots, 0) \notin S_{\bar{R}}(\boldsymbol{R})$. Since for all $i \in N$, $C(0, R_i') = C(0, R_i) = \mathbb{R}^l_+$, and $x_i \; R_i \; 0 \Leftrightarrow x_i \; R_i' \; 0$, and $0 \; R_i \; x_i \Leftrightarrow 0 \; R_i' \; x_i$, it follows from IIA-MRS that $x \in S_{\bar{R}}(\boldsymbol{R}')$ and $0 \notin S_{\bar{R}}(\boldsymbol{R}')$.

IIA-ISFA$\Rightarrow$IP-ISFA. Let $x \in S_{\bar{R}}(\boldsymbol{R})$ and $\boldsymbol{R}'$ be such that for all $i \in N$, $I(x_i, R_i) \cap \Omega(\omega) = I(x_i, R_i') \cap \Omega(\omega)$. Notice that for all $i \in N$, $I(0, R_i') = I(0, R_i) = \{0\}$. Then, by IIA-ISFA, $x \in S_{\bar{R}}(\boldsymbol{R}')$. ■

It is also easy to check that IP-MRS implies IIA-MRS, and that, for ARSOFs that never select allocations x such that $\sum_{i \in N} x_i \neq \omega$, IP-ISFA implies IIA-ISFA. In other words, for all practical purposes, the distinction between the IP axioms introduced here and their IIA counterparts is negligible.

The question we may now consider is how much IIA needs to be weakened, or how much additional information is needed in order to obtain the existence of a satisfactory AR (or ARSOF).

Our first result is that with IIA-MRS, a possibility is obtained, but there remains a difficulty about essential single-valuedness. As can be expected from the examples in Section 10.3, IIA-MRS is satisfied by the egalitarian Walrasian ARSOF $\bar{R}_{S_W}$, along with many good properties. But, as is well known, the egalitarian Walrasian AR is not essentially single-valued. Now, in the proof that follows we find a subdomain on which any ARSOF satisfying Pareto efficiency, IIA-MRS, and equal treatment of equals coincides exactly with $\bar{R}_{S_W}$ on this subdomain, even though $\bar{R}_{S_W}$ is still not essentially single-valued on this subdomain.

THEOREM 10.2. There exists an ARSOF satisfying Pareto efficiency, IIA-MRS, equal treatment of equals, and anonymity. There is no essentially single-valued ARSOF satisfying Pareto efficiency, IIA-MRS, and equal treatment of equals. There is no essentially single-valued ARSOF satisfying Pareto efficiency, IIA-MRS, and anonymity.

PROOF. The possibility is illustrated by the egalitarian Walrasian ARSOF $\bar{R}_{S_W}$.

The second impossibility is implied by the first impossibility because essential single-valuedness and anonymity imply equal treatment of equals. To show the first impossibility, suppose, to the contrary, that there exists an essentially single-valued ARSOF $\bar{R}$ satisfying Pareto efficiency, IIA-MRS, and equal treatment of equals. By Pareto efficiency, for all $\boldsymbol{R} \in \mathcal{R}^n$, $0 = (0, \ldots, 0) \notin S_{\bar{R}}(\boldsymbol{R})$. Hence, from Proposition 10.3, $\bar{R}$ satisfies IP-MRS.

Let $\mathcal{R}^*$ be the subset of $\mathcal{R}$ such that any $R \in \mathcal{R}^*$ is representable by a utility function of the following kind:

$$u(x_1, \ldots, x_l) = f_1(x_1) + \ldots + f_l(x_l),$$

where for all $k \in \{1, \ldots, l\}$, f_k is continuous, increasing, concave, and differentiable over $\mathbb{R}_{++}$, with $\lim_{x \to 0} f_k'(x) = +\infty$. The relevant property of this domain is that for all $\boldsymbol{R} \in (\mathcal{R}^*)^n$,

$$E(\boldsymbol{R}) \subseteq \{x \in \mathbb{R}^l_+ \mid \forall i \in N, x_i \gg 0 \text{ or } x_i = 0\}.$$

Let $\boldsymbol{R} \in (\mathcal{R}^*)^n$ be given.

First, suppose that there is $x \in S_{\bar{R}}(\boldsymbol{R}) \setminus S_W(\boldsymbol{R})$. By Pareto-Efficiency $x \in E(\boldsymbol{R})$. Hence, we have $x_i \gg 0$ or $x_i = 0$ for all $i \in N$, and by differentiability of preferences there is a shadow price vector $p \in \mathbb{R}^l_{++}$ such that

$$\forall i \in N, C(x_i, R_i) = \{\lambda p \mid \lambda \in \mathbb{R}_{++}\} \text{ or } x_i = 0.$$

For this p, define $R^p \in \mathcal{R}$ by

$$\forall z, z' \in \mathbb{R}^l_+, zR^pz' \Leftrightarrow p \cdot z \geq p \cdot z'.$$

Let $\boldsymbol{R}^p = (R^p, \ldots, R^p) \in \mathcal{R}^n$. By IP-MRS, $x \in S_{\bar{R}}(\boldsymbol{R}^p)$. Since $x \notin S_W(\boldsymbol{R})$, there exist $i, j \in N$ such that $x_i P^p x_j$, in contradiction to equal treatment of equals. As a consequence, $S_{\bar{R}}(\boldsymbol{R}) \subseteq S_W(\boldsymbol{R})$.

Second, suppose that there is $x \in S_W(\boldsymbol{R}) \setminus S_{\bar{R}}(\boldsymbol{R})$. For all $i \in N$, let $\boldsymbol{R}' \in \left(\mathcal{R}^*\right)^n$ be a profile of homothetic (a given R in $\mathcal{R}^*$ is homothetic if all its component functions f_k are homogeneous of the same degree) and strictly convex preferences satisfying

$$\forall i \in N, C(x_i, R_i') = C(x_i, R_i).$$

We have $x \in S_W(\boldsymbol{R}')$. Moreover, by Theorem 1 in Eisenberg [7], all allocations in $S_W(\boldsymbol{R}')$ are Pareto-indifferent. By strict convexity of preferences, one therefore has $S_W(\boldsymbol{R}') = \{x\}$. Since, by the previous argument, $S_{\bar{R}}(\boldsymbol{R}') \subseteq S_W(\boldsymbol{R}')$, we have $S_{\bar{R}}(\boldsymbol{R}') = \{x\}$. By IP-MRS, $x \in S_{\bar{R}}(\boldsymbol{R})$, which is a contradiction. Therefore, $S_W(\boldsymbol{R}) \subseteq S_{\bar{R}}(\boldsymbol{R})$.

In conclusion, $S_{\bar{R}}(\boldsymbol{R}) = S_W(\boldsymbol{R})$ for all $\boldsymbol{R} \in \left(\mathcal{R}^*\right)^n$. But S_W is not essentially single-valued on the whole domain $\left(\mathcal{R}^*\right)^n$. This contradicts the essential single-valuedness of $S_{\bar{R}}$. ∎

Only with IIA-ISFA do we really obtain a full possibility result, with the Pazner-Schmeidler ARSOF $\bar{R}_{S_{PS}}$.

THEOREM 10.3. There exists an essentially single-valued ARSOF satisfying Pareto efficiency, IIA-ISFA, anonymity, and equal treatment of equals.

PROOF. Consider the Pazner-Schmeidler ARSOF $\bar{R}_{S_{PS}}$, defined at the end of section 10.4.1. It obviously satisfies Pareto efficiency, anonymity and equal treatment of equals. To check that it satisfies IIA-ISFA, let $x, y \in F$ and $\boldsymbol{R}, \boldsymbol{R}' \in \mathcal{R}^n$ be such that for all $i \in N$,

$$I(x_i, R_i) \cap \Omega(\omega(x, y)) = I(x_i, R_i') \cap \Omega(\omega(x, y))$$

$$I(y_i, R_i) \cap \Omega(\omega(x, y)) = I(y_i, R_i') \cap \Omega(\omega(x, y)),$$

and $x \in S_{PS}(\boldsymbol{R})$ and $y \notin S_{PS}(\boldsymbol{R})$. Let $\alpha \in \mathbb{R}_+$ be such that for all $i \in N$, $x_i \; I_i \; \alpha\omega$. Then it necessarily follows that $\alpha < 1$. Notice that $\sum_{i \in N} x_i = \omega$ because $x \in E(\boldsymbol{R})$. Hence, $\Omega(\omega(x, y)) = \Omega(\omega)$ and $\alpha\omega \in \Omega(\omega(x, y))$. Together with the preceding equalities, we deduce that $x \in S_{PS}(\boldsymbol{R}')$ and $y \notin S_{PS}(\boldsymbol{R}')$. ■

10.7. Under Weak Pareto, Social Ordering Functions Need More Information

From the previous results, we now know that violation of IIA is crucial for the possibility results of fair allocation, and that introducing additional information about marginal rates of substitution is almost sufficient, while information about indifference surfaces on feasible allocations is fully sufficient. Such results are obtained for ARSOFs, that is, under the condition that social preferences are coarse and satisfy only Pareto efficiency. The question we now want to examine is whether SOFs satisfying the full weak Pareto condition, and therefore corresponding to fine-grained social preferences, are possible with the same additional information, or whether they need more information, i.e., further weakenings of IIA. In other words, is there a trade-off between Pareto conditions and independence conditions?

Fleurbaey and Maniquet [10], in this model, showed that there exist many SOFs satisfying weak Pareto, anonymity, and the following weak version of IIA:

IIA EXCEPT WHOLE INDIFFERENCE SETS (IIA-WIS). $\forall x, y \in F$, $\forall \boldsymbol{R}, \boldsymbol{R}' \in \mathcal{R}^n$, if $\forall i \in N$,

$$I(x_i, R_i) = I(x_i, R_i')$$

$$I(y_i, R_i) = I(y_i, R_i'),$$

then $x \bar{R}(\boldsymbol{R}) y \Leftrightarrow x \bar{R}(\boldsymbol{R}') y$.

This axiom is weaker than all IIA axioms considered previously, and one may ask what is the minimal amount of information needed by a SOF in order to satisfy weak Pareto and anonymity (or nondictatorship). In Fleurbaey, Suzumura, and Tadenuma [13], we showed that no SOF $\bar{R}$

satisfies weak Pareto, nondictatorship (over the subset X of allocations in which no agent has a zero bundle), and either IIA-MRS or IIA-ISFA.

But these results were obtained in the particular case of unbounded resources $F = \mathbb{R}^{nl}_{+}$. The bounded case on which we focus here has attracted less attention in the social choice literature,[13] and here we have the following result.

THEOREM 10.4. There is no SOF $\bar{R}$ satisfying weak Pareto, IIA-MRS, and anonymity. There is no SOF $\bar{R}$ satisfying weak Pareto, IIA-ISFA, and anonymity.

PROOF. For simplicity of exposition, we assume that $\omega > (20, 20, 0, \ldots, 0)$. When this does not hold, a suitable renormalization of goods allows the rest of the proof to work out. For each $a \in \mathbb{R}^{l}_{+}$, define

$$B(a) = \left\{ b \in \mathbb{R}^{l}_{+} \mid \max_{k \in \{1,\ldots,l\}} \mid b_k - a_k \mid \leq \frac{1}{10} \right\}$$

In order to prove the impossibilities, it is convenient to consider different possible sizes of the population.

CASE $n = 2$. Consider the bundles $x = (8, 1/2, 0, \ldots, 0)$, $y = (12, 1/2, 0, \ldots, 0)$, $z = (1/2, 12, 0, \ldots, 0)$, $w = (1/2, 8, 0, \ldots, 0)$. Let preferences R_1 and R_2 be defined as follows. On the subset

$$S_1 = \{v \in \mathbb{R}^{l}_{+} \mid \forall i \in \{3, \ldots, l\}, v_i = 0, \text{ and } v_2 \leq \min\{v_1, 1\}\},$$

one has

$$vR_1v' \Leftrightarrow v_1 + 2v_2 \geq v'_1 + 2v'_2,$$

and on the subset

$$S_2 = \{v \in \mathbb{R}^{l}_{+} \mid \forall i \in \{3, \ldots, l\}, v_i = 0, \text{ and } v_1 \leq \min\{v_2, 1\}\},$$

one has

$$vR_1v' \Leftrightarrow 2v_1 + v_2 \geq 2v'_1 + v'_2.$$

13. Exceptions are Bordes, Campbell, and Le Breton [4], already quoted, and also Bone [3].

On $B(x) \cup B(y)$, one has

$$vR_1v' \Leftrightarrow v_1 + 2v_2 + \sum_{k=3}^{l} v_k \geq v'_1 + 2v'_2 + \sum_{k=3}^{l} v'_k,$$

and on $B(z) \cup B(w)$,

$$vR_1v' \Leftrightarrow 2v_1 + v_2 + \sum_{k=3}^{l} v_k \geq 2v'_1 + v'_2 + \sum_{k=3}^{l} v'_k.$$

Since

$$w_1 + \left(1 - w_1\right) + 2\left[w_2 - 2\left(1 - w_1\right)\right] > x_1 + 2x_2$$

and

$$2\left[y_1 - 2\left(1 - y_2\right)\right] + y_2 + \left(1 - y_2\right) > 2z_1 + z_2,$$

it is possible to complete the definition of R_1 such that wP_1x and yP_1z. Then define R_2 so that it coincides with R_1 on $S_1 \cup S_2$, and on $B(a)$ for all $a \in \{x, y, z, w\}$. Similarly, it is possible to complete the definition of R_2 such that xP_2w and zP_2y. Figure 10.4 illustrates this construction.

If the profile of preferences is $\boldsymbol{R} = (R_1, R_2)$, by weak Pareto one has

$$(y, x)\bar{P}(\boldsymbol{R})(z, w) \text{ and } (w, z)\bar{P}(\boldsymbol{R})(x, y).$$

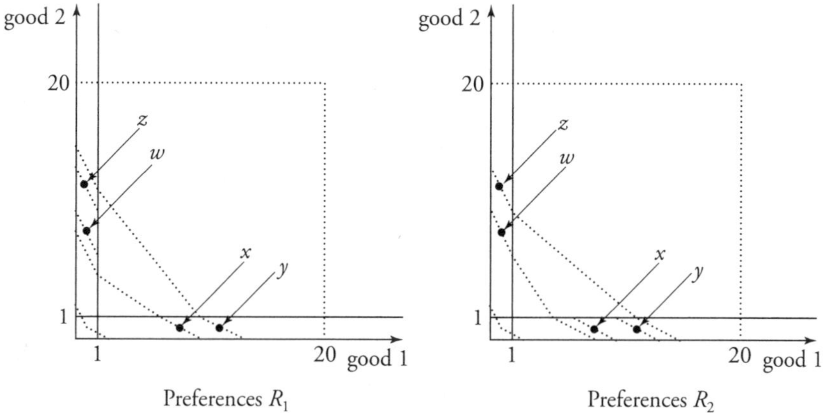

Figure 10.4. Construction of R_1 and R_2

If the profile of preferences is $\boldsymbol{R}' = (R_1, R_1)$, by anonymity one has

$$(y, x)\bar{I}(\boldsymbol{R}')(x, y) \text{ and } (w, z)\bar{I}(\boldsymbol{R}')(z, w).$$

Since R_1 and R_2 coincide on $S_1 \cup S_2$, and on $B(a)$ for all $a \in \{x, y, z, w\}$, by IIA-MRS or IIA-ISFA one has

$$(y, x)\bar{I}(\boldsymbol{R}')(x, y) \Leftrightarrow (y, x)\bar{I}(\boldsymbol{R})(x, y)$$

$$\text{and } (w, z)\bar{I}(\boldsymbol{R}')(z, w) \Leftrightarrow (w, z)\bar{I}(\boldsymbol{R})(z, w).$$

By transitivity, one gets $(x, y)\bar{P}(\boldsymbol{R})(x, y)$, which is impossible.

Case $n = 3$. Consider the bundles $x = (8, 1/3, 0, \ldots, 0)$, $y = (12, 1/3, 0, \ldots, 0)$, $t = (10, 1/3, 0, \ldots, 0)$, $z = (1/3, 12, 0, \ldots, 0)$, $w = (1/3, 8, 0, \ldots, 0)$, $r = (1/3, 10, 0, \ldots, 0)$. Let preferences R_1, R_2, and R_3 be defined as before on the subset $S_1 \cup S_2$, and on $B(a)$ for all $a \in \{x, y, z, w\}$. Complete their definition so that yP_1z, wP_1x, tP_2r, zP_2y, xP_3w, and rP_3t.

If the profile of preferences is $\boldsymbol{R} = (R_1, R_2, R_3)$, by weak Pareto one has

$$(y, t, x)\bar{P}(\boldsymbol{R})(z, r, w) \text{ and } (w, z, r)\bar{P}(\boldsymbol{R})(x, y, t).$$

If the profile of preferences is $\boldsymbol{R}' = (R_1, R_1, R_1)$, by anonymity one has

$$(y, t, x)\bar{I}(\boldsymbol{R}')(x, y, t) \text{ and } (w, z, r)\bar{I}(\boldsymbol{R}')(z, r, w).$$

Since R_1, R_2, and R_3 coincide on $S_1 \cup S_2$, and on $B(a)$ for all $a \in \{x, y, z, w\}$, by IIA-MRS or IIA-ISFA one has

$$(y, t, x)\bar{I}(\boldsymbol{R}')(x, y, t) \Leftrightarrow (y, t, x)\bar{I}(\boldsymbol{R})(x, y, t)$$

$$\text{and } (w, z, r)\bar{I}(\boldsymbol{R}')(z, r, w) \Leftrightarrow (w, z, r)\bar{I}(\boldsymbol{R})(z, r, w).$$

By transitivity, one gets $(x, y, t)\bar{P}(\boldsymbol{R})(x, y, t)$, which is impossible.

Case $n = 2k$. Partition the population into k pairs, and construct an argument similar to the case $n = 2$, with the bundles $x = (8, 1/n, 0, \ldots, 0)$, $y = (12, 1/n, 0, \ldots, 0)$, $z = (1/n, 12, 0, \ldots, 0)$, $w = (1/n, 8, 0, \ldots, 0)$, and the allocations $(y, x, y, x, \ldots, 0)$, $(x, y, x, y, \ldots, 0)$, $(z, w, z, w, \ldots, 0)$, and $(w, z, w, z, \ldots, 0)$.

Case $n = 2k + 1$. Partition the population into $k - 1$ pairs and one triple, and construct an argument combining the cases $n = 2$ and $n = 3$, with the bundles $x = (8, 1/n, 0, \ldots, 0)$, $y = (12, 1/n, 0, \ldots, 0)$, $t = (10, 1/n, 0, \ldots, 0)$, $z = (1/n, 12, 0, \ldots, 0)$, $w = (1/n, 8, 0, \ldots, 0)$, $r = (1/n, 10, 0, \ldots, 0)$, and the allocations $(y, x, y, x, \ldots, y, t, x)$, $(x, y, x, y, \ldots, x, y, t)$, $(z, w, z, w, \ldots z, r, w)$, and $(w, z, w, z, \ldots, w, z, r)$. ■

This result proves that under weak Pareto, more information about preferences is needed than under Pareto efficiency. In that sense, it is true that *the theory of fair allocation, with its coarse orderings, is less demanding in information than the theory of social choice.*

As explained in Essay 7, however, one should not conclude from this analysis that full knowledge of indifference curves is needed under weak Pareto. Define the Pazner-Schmeidler SOF $\bar{R}_{PS}$ as follows: $x\bar{R}(\boldsymbol{R})y$ if and only if

$$\min\{\alpha \in \mathbb{R}_+ \mid \exists i \in N, \alpha\omega R_i x_i\} \geq \min\{\alpha \in \mathbb{R}_+ \mid \exists i \in N, \alpha\omega R_i y_i\}.$$

This SOF satisfies weak Pareto and anonymity, even though it only requires knowledge of the intersection of indifference curves with a ray from the origin. In addition, although this SOF does not satisfy IIA-ISFA in the current framework, it can be shown to satisfy IIA-ISFA when only allocations of the subset

$$\left\{x \in \mathbb{R}_+^{nl} \mid \sum_{i \in N} x_i = \omega\right\}$$

with no free disposal, instead of F, are ranked.

10.8. Toward a Unified Theory

There have been many attempts to import fairness concepts into social choice and thereby build a unified theory, such as Feldman and Kirman [8], Varian [32], Suzumura [27; 28; 29], and Tadenuma [30]. But they did not focus on the informational requirements to obtain positive results.

Our approach provides a unified framework that covers the theory of social choice and the theory of fair allocation. Because ARs in the theory of fair allocation are isomorphic to ARSOFs in the theory of social choice, and ARSOFs are just a particular kind of SOF, the concept of a SOF is comprehensive enough to encompass all relevant notions. This shows how the theory of fair allocation is, rigorously, a part of the theory of social choice.

As a consequence, the way in which possibility results are obtained with ARs, by broadening the informational basis, can be adopted for SOFs, albeit, as shown above, the amount of additional information needed is greater under weak Pareto. From this perspective, there is no longer any reason to view the theory of social choice as plagued with impossibilities, and no longer any reason for social choice theorists to envy fairness theorists and their positive results. The same recipe for success can be adopted by social choice theorists.[14]

In this section we examine two possible objections to this proposed integration of fair allocation theory into social choice theory. The first objection would be posed by recollecting that the celebrated Arrow program of social choice theory consists of two separate steps, viz., (1) the construction of a social preference ordering corresponding to each profile of individual preference orderings; and (2) the construction of a social choice function by means of optimization of social preferences within each set of feasible social alternatives. The first step, which may be called the *preference aggregation stage,* is to determine the *uniform* social objective before the set of feasible social alternatives is revealed. The second step, which may be called the *rational choice stage,* is to determine the rational social choice after the set of feasible social alternatives is revealed. Even though we may construct a coarse social ordering in terms of the fair allocations versus unfair allocations, such an ordering hinges squarely on the specification of the set of feasible allocations. In other words, no social preference ordering, which can be applied *uniformly* to all feasible sets of alternatives, can thereby be generated. Thus, the objection would go, in view of the basic scenario of the Arrow program of social choice theory, the theory of fair allocation does not really offer much to the preference aggregation stage of social choice theory.

Our response to this objection is that what is called "social choice theory" in this essay actually encompasses the preference aggregation stage of the

---

14. For characterizations of SOFs based on fairness axioms, see, e.g., Fleurbaey and Maniquet [11; 12].

Arrow program, as presented in the preceding , as a special case. We believe that it is quite convenient to see the common formal structure in all exercises of construction of a preference ordering over a set of alternatives, whether this set is determined by feasibility constraints or not. In this essay, the need to compare the social choice approach and the fair allocation approach has led us to retain

$$F = \{x \in \mathbb{R}^l_+ \mid x_1 + \ldots + x_n \leq \omega\}$$

as the relevant set of alternatives. An orthodox vision of the Arrow program of social choice theory might possibly require the construction of the social preference ordering to be made on the full set $\mathbb{R}^{nl}_+$, rather than F, but we do not think that the construction of a social preference ordering over F should be excluded from social choice theory for that reason.[15] Moreover, the notion of feasibility itself is multifaceted. Although F is determined by some feasibility constraints, the set of actually feasible alternatives, in practical applications, is likely to be a strict subset of F. For instance, the political system may give special value to a status quo x_0, and restrict attention to another particular alternative x, introduced as a proposed reform of the status quo. In order to decide whether x is better than x_0 or not, a fine-grained ranking of all members of F is quite useful, and a ranking of all members of $\mathbb{R}^{nl}_+$ would be perfectly adequate as well, but would be more than needed.

The second objection to our unification would rely on an alternative way of unifying the two theories, which has been elegantly formulated in Fishburn [9] and adapted to economic environments by Le Breton [18]. It consists of broadening the concept of AR, as done in the theory of social choice based on social decision rules.

Let $\mathcal{F}$ denote the set of nonempty subsets of F, and let $\mathcal{A} \subseteq \mathcal{F}$. A *social decision rule* (SDR) is a mapping $\bar{S}$ from $\mathcal{R}^n \times \mathcal{A}$ to $\mathcal{F}$ such that for all

15. Arrow [2] himself was actually vague about the set of alternatives in his monograph on social choice. For instance, in the economic example he introduces in Chapter 6, Section 4, he simply states: "Suppose that among the *possible* alternatives there are three, none of which gives any individual at least as much of both commodities as any other" (Arrow [2, p. 68]; emphasis added). Bordes, Campbell, and Le Breton [4] study Arrow's theorem on F as a relevant social choice exercise.

$\boldsymbol{R} \in \mathcal{R}^n$, all $A \in \mathcal{A}$, $\bar{S}(\boldsymbol{R}, A) \subseteq A$ and $\bar{S}(\boldsymbol{R}, A) \neq \emptyset$. Each set A is called an *agenda,* and $\mathcal{A}$ is the class of agendas.

In this approach, an AR is just a particular kind of SDR for which $\mathcal{A} = \{F\}$. By contrast, if $\mathcal{A}$ contains all pairs of allocations $\{x, y\} \subseteq F$, one can recover an SOF from an SDR whenever the SDR satisfies a choice-consistency condition. The derived SOF $\bar{R}_{\bar{S}}$ is then defined by

$$x \bar{R}_{\bar{S}}(\boldsymbol{R}) y \Leftrightarrow x \in \bar{S}(\boldsymbol{R}, \{x, y\}).$$

From this perspective, the specificity of the theory of fair allocation is that it has a very restricted class of agendas. This expresses the fact that the theory of fair allocation only seeks the good allocations among all feasible ones, whereas the theory of social choice wants to make fine-grained selections in most conceivable agendas.

The fact that possibility results are obtained in the theory of fair allocation is likely to be interpreted, in this approach, as due to the restricted agendas, and this reinforces the usual explanation, which opposes fine-grained social preferences and selection. But this would be a hasty conclusion. Arrow's independence condition, applied to SDRs, is formulated as follows in Le Breton [18]:

Independence of Infeasible Alternatives (IIF). $\forall \boldsymbol{R}, \boldsymbol{R}' \in \mathcal{R}^n$, $\forall A \in \mathcal{A}$, if

$$\forall i \in N, \forall x, y \in A : x_i \; R_i \; y_i \Leftrightarrow x_i \; R_i' \; y_i,$$

then $\bar{S}(\boldsymbol{R}, A) = \bar{S}(\boldsymbol{R}', A)$.

When the class of agendas is restricted, the amount of information about preferences that may be used by $\bar{S}$ when considering to choose x as against y increases automatically, because the subset A on which preference information is retained becomes larger. Therefore, going to restricted agendas has two consequences. First, it makes one go from fine-grained preferences to coarse preferences, as emphasized by the usual explanation of the possibility results in fair allocation theory. Second, and we believe more importantly, it increases the amount of relevant information about preferences, as delineated by IIF. And in the limit where $\mathcal{A} = \{F\}$, the amount of relevant information is maximal. Hence, in this approach, all ARs are indistinguishable in terms of informational basis since all have the same maximal basis.

It is true that in order to identify all the "good" allocations among all feasible allocations, we need anyway to know information about preferences of individuals over the full set F. However, often in reality, we are faced with a different question: Given two allocations x and y, can we say whether one of the two allocations is good while the other is not? In fact, ARs can answer this type of question. For instance, if x is an egalitarian Walrasian allocation and y is not, one can say that x is good while y is not. As shown in previous sections, information about preferences necessary to derive such an evaluation is much different among various ARs. For example, the egalitarian Walrasian AR only needs knowledge of marginal rates of substitution at the given two allocations whereas the Pazner-Schmeidler AR needs more global knowledge about indifference surfaces. Such distinctions can be captured by the IIA-MRS axiom, the IIA-ISFA axiom, and other axioms in the SOF approach developed in this essay. We are thus inclined to think that the SOF approach is more suitable to the analysis of the informational basis of the various theories.[16]

10.9. Conclusion

Let us briefly summarize the conclusions of this essay.

(a) The allocation rules from the theory of fair allocation do provide social ordering functions, so that Arrow's impossibility theorem of social choice does apply to them.
(b) No satisfactory allocation rule satisfies independence of irrelevant alternatives, so that violation of this axiom is the explanation for the possibility results in fair allocation theory, as compared to impossibility results in social choice theory.

16. The literature does, however, contain some examples of finer informational axioms in the SDR setting. In an abstract model with a fixed agenda, Denicolò [5; 6] introduces a pairwise independence axiom on SDRs in order to obtain impossibility results of the Arrovian sort. This axiom says that if two profiles coincide on $\{x, y\}$, and x is selected and y is not under one profile, then y is still not selected under the other profile.

Table 10.1. Summary of the results

	Weak Pareto	*Pareto Efficiency*
IIA	Arrovian dictatorship (Arrow's theorem)	ARSOFs giving someone all resources (Theorem 10.1)
IIA-MRS	Violation of anonymity (Theorem 10.4)	Anonymous ARSOFs with equal treatment of equals (Theorem 10.2)
IIA-ISFA	Violation of anonymity (Theorem 10.4)	Essentially single-valued, anonymous ARSOFs with equal treatment of equals (Theorem 10.3)
IIA-WIS	Anonymous SOFs (Pazner-Schmeidler [22])	Essentially single-valued, anonymous ARSOFs with equal treatment of equals (Theorem 10.3)

(c) In the process of weakening the independence axiom, the introduction of additional information about marginal rates of substitution or about indifference surfaces on possible redistributions of the contemplated allocations is sufficient for satisfactory allocation rules to be obtained.

(d) Requiring weak Pareto, not just Pareto efficiency, which implies that social preferences must be more fine-grained than allocation rules, makes it necessary to introduce more information about preferences.

More precisely, the results in this essay may be summarized as shown in Table 10.1.

As the table makes clear, weakening weak Pareto into Pareto efficiency, and therefore allowing coarse orderings alone, does not make room for satisfactory ARs. Weakening IIA, and thus expanding the informational basis for social evaluation of allocations, is essential for positive results in fair allocation theory.

However, as is also clear in the table, whether we seek fully Paretian social orderings or only coarse orderings satisfying Pareto efficiency does make a difference in *how much expansion* of informational basis is indeed necessary beyond what Arrow's original IIA allows.

We hope that this essay, more broadly, contributes to clarifying the informational foundations in the theory of social choice and in the theory of fair allocation, and also to clarifying the links and differences between these two theories. Our proposal for a unified theory of social choice, where possibility results from the fairness part can be extended to SOFs, should shake off the negative fame of social choice theory.

10.10. References

[1] Arrow, K. J., "A Difficulty in the Concept of Social Welfare," *Journal of Political Economy* **58**, 1950, 328–346.

[2] Arrow, K. J., *Social Choice and Individual Values,* New York: John Wiley & Sons, 1951; 2nd edn., 1963.

[3] Bone, J., "Simple Arrow-Type Propositions in the Edgeworth Domain," *Social Choice and Welfare* **20**, 2003, 41–48.

[4] Bordes, G., D. E. Campbell, and M. Le Breton, "Arrow's Theorems for Economic Domains and Edgeworth Hyperboxes," *International Economic Review* **36**, 1995, 441–454.

[5] Denicolò, V., "Independent Social Choice Correspondences Are Dictatorial," *Economics Letters* **19**, 1985, 9–12.

[6] Denicolò, V., "Fixed Agenda Social Choice Theory: Correspondence and Impossibility Theorems for Social Choice Correspondences and Social Decision Functions," *Journal of Economic Theory* **59**, 1993, 324–332.

[7] Eisenberg, E., "Aggregation of Utility Functions," *Management Science* 7, 1961, 337–350.

[8] Feldman, A. M., and A. Kirman, "Fairness and Envy," *American Economic Review* **64**, 1974, 996–1005.

[9] Fishburn, P., *The Theory of Social Choice,* Princeton, N.J.: Princeton University Press, 1973.

[10] Fleurbaey, M., and F. Maniquet, "Utilitarianism versus Fairness in Welfare Economics," in M. Fleurbaey, M. Salles, and J. A. Weymark, eds., *Justice, Political Liberalism and Utilitarianism: Themes from Harsanyi and Rawls,* Cambridge, N.Y.: Cambridge University Press, 1996, 263–280.

[11] Fleurbaey, M., and F. Maniquet, "Fair Social Orderings with Unequal Production Skills," *Social Choice and Welfare* **24**, 2005, 93–127.

[12] Fleurbaey, M., and F. Maniquet, "Fair Social Orderings," mimeo., University of Pau, France, 2001.

[13] Fleurbaey, M., K. Suzumura, and K. Tadenuma, "Arrovian Aggregation in Economic Environments: How Much Should We Know about Indifference Surfaces?" *Journal of Economic Theory* **124**, 2005, 22–44. Essay 7 of this volume.

[14] Foley, D., "Resource Allocation and the Public Sector," *Yale Economic Essays* 7, 1967, 45–98.

[15] Hansson, B., "The Independence Condition in the Theory of Social Choice," *Theory and Decision* **4**, 1973, 25–49.

[16] Kolm, S. C., *Justice et Equité,* Paris: Ed. du CNRS, 1972; English translation, *Justice and Equity,* Cambridge, Mass.: MIT Press, 1997.

[17] Kolm, S. C., *Modern Theories of Justice,* Cambridge, Mass.: MIT Press, 1996.

[18] Le Breton, M., "Arrovian Social Choice on Economic Domains," in K. J. Arrow, A. Sen, and K. Suzumura, eds., *Social Choice Reexamined,* Vol. 1, London: Macmillan, and New York: St. Martin's Press, 1997.

[19] Moulin, H., and W. Thomson, "Axiomatic Analysis of Resource Allocation Problems," in K. J. Arrow, A. Sen, and K. Suzumura, eds., *Social Choice Reexamined,* Vol. 1, London: Macmillan, and New York: St. Martin's Press, 1997.

[20] Nagahisa, R.-I., "A Local Independence Condition for Characterization of Walrasian Allocation Rule," *Journal of Economic Theory* **54**, 1991, 106–123.

[21] Nagahisa, R.-I., and S. C. Suh, "A Characterization of the Walras Rule," *Social Choice and Welfare* **12**, 1995, 335–352.

[22] Pazner, E., and D. Schmeidler, "Egalitarian-Equivalent Allocations: A New Concept of Economic Equity," *Quarterly Journal of Economics* **92**, 1978, 671–687.

[23] Sen, A. K., "Interpersonal Aggregation and Partial Comparability," *Econometrica* **38**, 1970, 393–409.

[24] Sen, A. K., *Collective Choice and Social Welfare,* San Francisco: Holden-Day, 1970. Republished, Amsterdam: North-Holland, 1979.

[25] Sen, A. K., "Social Choice Theory," in K. J. Arrow and M. D. Intriligator, eds., *Handbook of Mathematical Economics,* Vol. 3, Amsterdam: North-Holland, 1986.

[26] Suzumura, K., "Liberal Paradox and the Voluntary Exchange of Rights Exercising," *Journal of Economic Theory* **22**, 1980, 407–422. Essay 14 of this volume.

[27] Suzumura, K., "On Pareto Efficiency and the No-Envy Concept of Equity," *Journal of Economic Theory* **25**, 1981, 367–379. Essay 9 of this volume.

[28] Suzumura, K., "On the Possibility of 'Fair' Collective Choice Rule," *International Economic Review* **22**, 1981, 351–364.

[29] Suzumura, K., *Rational Choice, Collective Decisions, and Social Welfare,* New York: Cambridge University Press, 1983.

[30] Tadenuma, K., "Efficiency First or Equity First? Two Principles and Rationality of Social Choice," *Journal of Economic Theory* **104**, 2002, 462–472.

[31] Varian, H., "Equity, Envy, and Efficiency," *Journal of Economic Theory* **9**, 1974, 63–91.

[32] Varian, H., "Two Problems in the Theory of Fairness," *Journal of Public Economics* **5**, 1976, 249–260.

[33] Weymark, J., "Arrow's Theorem with Social Quasi-Orderings," *Public Choice* **42**, 1984, 235–246.

[34] Wilson, R. B., "Social Choice without the Pareto Principle," *Journal of Economic Theory* **5**, 1972, 478–486.

[35] Yoshihara, N., "Characterizations of the Public and Private Ownership Solutions," *Mathematical Social Sciences* **35**, 1998, 165–184.

ESSAY **11**

Ordering Infinite Utility Streams

11.1. Introduction

Treating generations equally is one of the basic principles in the utilitarian tradition of moral philosophy. As Sidgwick [19, p. 414] observes, "the time at which a man exists cannot affect the value of his happiness from a universal point of view; and . . . the interests of posterity must concern a utilitarian as much as those of his contemporaries." This view, which is formally expressed by the anonymity condition, is also strongly endorsed by Ramsey [16].

Following Koopmans [14], Diamond [9] establishes that anonymity is incompatible with the strong Pareto principle when ordering *infinite* utility streams. Moreover, he shows that if anonymity is weakened to *finite* anonymity—which restricts the application of the standard anonymity requirement to situations where utility streams differ in at most a finite number of components—and a continuity requirement is added, an impossibility results again. Hara, Shinotsuka, Suzumura, and Xu [12] adapt the well-known

First published in *Journal of Economic Theory* **135**, 2007, pp. 579–589, as a joint paper with W. Bossert and Y. Sprumont. We thank Geir Asheim for comments and suggestions on an earlier draft. We are also grateful to an anonymous referee of *Journal of Economic Theory* whose helpful comments gave us an opportunity to improve the paper. Financial support through grants from the Social Sciences and Humanities Research Council of Canada, the Fonds pour la Formation de Chercheurs et l'Aide à la Recherche of Québec, and a Grant-in-Aid for Scientific Research from the Ministry of Education, Culture, Sports, Science and Technology of Japan is gratefully acknowledged.

strict transfer principle due to Pigou [15] and Dalton [7] to the infinite-horizon context. They show that this principle is incompatible with strong Pareto and continuity even if the social preference is merely required to be acyclical. Basu and Mitra [5] show that strong Pareto, finite anonymity, and representability by a real-valued function are incompatible.

Faced with these impossibilities, it seems to us that the most natural assumption to drop is that of continuity or representability. We view the strong Pareto principle and finite anonymity as being on much more solid ground than axioms such as continuity or representability, especially in the context of the ranking of infinite utility streams where these conditions may be considered to be overly demanding. Svensson [21] proves that strong Pareto and finite anonymity are compatible by showing that any ordering extension of an infinite-horizon variant of Suppes's [20] grading principle satisfies the required axioms. The Suppes grading principle is a quasi ordering that combines Pareto quasi ordering and finite anonymity. Given Arrow's [1] version of Szpilrajn's [22] extension theorem, this establishes the compatibility result. As noted by Asheim, Buchholz, and Tungodden [2], Svensson's possibility result is easily converted into a characterization: ordering extensions of the Suppes grading principles are the *only* orderings satisfying strong Pareto and finite anonymity.

Once the possibility of satisfying these two fundamental axioms is established, another natural question to ask is what orderings satisfy additional desirable properties. Asheim and Tungodden [3] provide a characterization of an infinite-horizon version of the leximin principle by adding an equity preference condition (the infinite-horizon equivalent of Hammond equity; see Hammond [10]) and a preference continuity property to strong Pareto and finite anonymity. An infinite-horizon version of utilitarianism is characterized by Basu and Mitra [6] by adding an information invariance condition to the two fundamental axioms. Furthermore, they narrow down the class of infinite-horizon utilitarian orderings to those resulting from the overtaking criterion (von Weizsäcker [23]). This is accomplished by using a consistency condition in addition to the three axioms characterizing their utilitarian orderings.

In this essay, we focus on equity properties. One of the most fundamental equity properties (if not *the* most fundamental) is the Pigou-Dalton transfer principle, adapted to the infinite-horizon framework by Hara, Shinotsuka,

Suzumura, and Xu [12]. Our first result characterizes all orderings that satisfy strong Pareto, anonymity, and the strict transfer principle. They are extensions of an infinite-horizon formulation of the well-known generalized Lorenz quasi ordering (Shorrocks [18]).

In the presence of strong Pareto, the axiom of equity preference (the infinite-horizon version of Hammond equity) is a strengthening of the strict transfer principle. We use it to identify a subclass of the class of orderings satisfying the three axioms just mentioned. These orderings are extensions of a particular infinite-horizon incomplete version of leximin. This second result leaves a larger class of orderings than that identified by Asheim and Tungodden [3] because they employ an additional axiom. The relationship between our leximin characterization and that of Asheim and Tungodden is analogous to the relationship between Basu and Mitra's [6] characterizations of infinite-horizon utilitarianism and of the overtaking criterion.

11.2. Basic Definitions

The set of infinite utility streams is $X = \mathbb{R}^{\mathbb{N}}$, where $\mathbb{R}$ denotes the set of all real numbers and $\mathbb{N}$ denotes the set of all natural numbers. A typical element of X is an infinite-dimensional vector $x = (x_1, x_2, \ldots, x_n, \ldots)$ and, for $n \in \mathbb{N}$, we write $x^{-n} = (x_1, \ldots, x_n)$ and $x^{+n} = (x_{n+1}, x_{n+2}, \ldots)$. The standard interpretation of $x \in X$ is that of a countably infinite utility stream where x_n is the utility experienced in period $n \in \mathbb{N}$. Of course, other interpretations are possible—for example, x_n could be the utility of an individual in a countably infinite population.

Our notation for vector inequalities on X is as follows. For all $x, y \in X$, (i) $x \geq y$ if $x_n \geq y_n$ for all $n \in \mathbb{N}$; (ii) $x > y$ if $x \geq y$ and $x \neq y$; (iii) $x \gg y$ if $x_n > y_n$ for all $n \in \mathbb{N}$. For $n \in \mathbb{N}$ and $x \in X$, $(x_{(1)}^{-n}, \ldots, x_{(n)}^{-n})$ is a rank-ordered permutation of x^{-n} such that $x_{(1)}^{-n} \leq \ldots \leq x_{(n)}^{-n}$, ties being broken arbitrarily.

$R \subseteq X \times X$ is a weak preference relation on X with strict preference $P(R)$ and indifference relation $I(R)$. A quasi ordering is a reflexive and transitive relation, and an ordering is a complete quasi ordering. Analogously, a partial order is an asymmetric and transitive relation, and a linear order is a complete partial order. Let R and R' be relations on X. R' is an extension of R if $R \subseteq R'$ and $P(R) \subseteq P(R')$. If an extension R' of R is an ordering, we call it an ordering extension of R, and if R' is an extension of R that is a linear order, we refer to it as a linear order extension of R.

A finite permutation of $\mathbb{N}$ is a bijection $\rho\colon \mathbb{N} \to \mathbb{N}$ such that there exists $m \in \mathbb{N}$ with $\rho(n) = n$ for all $n \in \mathbb{N} \setminus \{1, \ldots, m\}$. $x^{\rho} = (x_{\rho(1)}, x_{\rho(2)}, \ldots, x_{\rho(n)}, \ldots)$ is the finite permutation of $x \in X$ that results from relabeling the components of x in accordance with the finite permutation ρ.

Two of the most fundamental axioms in this area are the strong Pareto principle and finite anonymity, defined as follows.

Strong Pareto. For all $x, y \in X$, if $x > y$, then $(x, y) \in P(R)$.

Finite Anonymity. For all $x \in X$ and for all finite permutations ρ of $\mathbb{N}$,

$$(x^{\rho}, x) \in I(R).$$

Szpilrajn's [22] fundamental result establishes that every partial order has a linear order extension. Arrow [1, p. 64] presents a variant of Szpilrajn's theorem stating that every quasi ordering has an ordering extension; see also Hansson [11]. This implies that the sets of orderings characterized in the theorems of the following sections are nonempty.

11.3. Transfer-Sensitive Infinite-Horizon Orderings

Now we examine the consequences of adding the strict transfer principle to strong Pareto and finite anonymity. A Pigou-Dalton transfer is a transfer of a positive amount of utility from a better-off agent to a worse-off agent so that the relative ranking of the two agents in the posttransfer utility stream is the same as their relative ranking in the pretransfer stream. The strict transfer principle requires that any Pigou-Dalton transfer leads to a utility stream that is strictly preferred to the pretransfer stream.

Strict Transfer Principle. For all $x, y \in X$ and for all $m, n \in \mathbb{N}$, if $x_k = y_k$ for all $k \in \mathbb{N} \setminus \{m, n\}$, $y_m > x_m \geq x_n > y_n$ and $x_n + x_m = y_n + y_m$, then $(x, y) \in P(R)$.

The strict transfer principle is the natural analogue of the corresponding condition for finite streams; see also Hara, Shinotsuka, Suzumura, and Xu

[12]. An alternative (equivalent) formulation of the strict transfer principle involves the explicit expression of the amount transferred from m to n when moving from y to x (this amount is $\delta = y_m - x_m = x_n - y_n$ and is readily obtained from our statement of the axiom). Although this alternative may be more standard in the literature, we use the version introduced here because it is parallel in structure to the equity preference axioms to be defined in the following section.

To define the class of orderings satisfying the three axioms introduced thus far, we begin with a statement of Shorrocks' [18] generalized Lorenz quasi ordering R^n_g for a society consisting of $n \in \mathbb{N}$ individuals. This quasi ordering generalizes the standard Lorenz quasi ordering by extending the relevant dominance criterion to comparisons involving different average (or total) utilities. For all $x, y \in X$,

$$(x^{-n}, y^{-n}) \in R^n_g \Leftrightarrow \sum_{i=1}^{k} x^{-n}_{(i)} \geq \sum_{i=1}^{k} y^{-n}_{(i)} \text{ for all } k \in \{1, \ldots, n\}.$$

The relation $R^n_G \subseteq X \times X$ is defined by letting, for all $x, y \in X$,

$$(x, y) \in R^n_G \Leftrightarrow (x^{-n}, y^{-n}) \in R^n_g \text{ and } x^{+n} \geq y^{+n}.$$

Clearly, R^n_G is a quasi ordering for all $n \in \mathbb{N}$. The infinite-horizon extension of the generalized Lorenz quasi ordering that is of interest in this essay is defined by $R_G = \cup_{n \in \mathbb{N}} R^n_G$. The relation R_G can be shown to be a quasi ordering, and we characterize the class of its ordering extensions in the following theorem.

Theorem 11.1. An ordering R on X satisfies strong Pareto, finite anonymity, and the strict transfer principle if and only if R is an ordering extension of R_G.

Proof. "If."

Step 1. We show that the relations R^n_G and their associated strict preference relations $P(R^n_G)$ are nested, that is, for all $n \in \mathbb{N}$,

$$R^n_G \subseteq R^{n+1}_G \tag{11.1}$$

and

$$P(R^n_G) \subseteq P(R^{n+1}_G). \tag{11.2}$$

To prove (11.1), suppose that $(x, y) \in R^n_G$. By definition, $(x^{-n}, y^{-n}) \in R^n_g$ and $x^{+n} \geq y^{+n}$ and, thus,

$$\sum_{i=1}^{k} x^{-n}_{(i)} \geq \sum_{i=1}^{k} y^{-n}_{(i)} \text{ for all } k \in \{1, \ldots, n\}, \tag{11.3}$$

$$x_{n+1} \geq y_{n+1}, \tag{11.4}$$

and

$$x^{+(n+1)} \geq y^{+(n+1)}. \tag{11.5}$$

Because of (11.5), it is sufficient to prove that

$$\sum_{i=1}^{k} x^{-(n+1)}_{(i)} \geq \sum_{i=1}^{k} y^{-(n+1)}_{(i)} \text{ for all } k \in \{1, \ldots, n+1\}. \tag{11.6}$$

If $k = n + 1$, we have

$$\sum_{i=1}^{n+1} x^{-(n+1)}_{(i)} = \sum_{i=1}^{n} x^{-n}_{(i)} + x_{n+1}$$

and

$$\sum_{i=1}^{n+1} y^{-(n+1)}_{(i)} = \sum_{i=1}^{n} y^{-n}_{(i)} + y_{n+1}.$$

Adding (11.3) for $k = n$ and (11.4), we obtain (11.6) for $k = n + 1$.

Now let $k \in \{1, \ldots, n\}$. We distinguish the following four cases, which cover all possibilities.

Case 1. $x_{n+1} \geq x^{-n}_{(k)}$ and $y_{n+1} \geq y^{-n}_{(k)}$. This implies $x^{-(n+1)}_{(i)} = x^{-n}_{(i)}$ and $y^{-(n+1)}_{(i)} = y^{-n}_{(i)}$ for all $i \in \{1, \ldots, k\}$, and (11.6) for this k follows immediately from (11.3).

Case 2. $x_{n+1} \leq x^{-n}_{(k)}$ and $y_{n+1} \leq y^{-n}_{(k)}$. This implies

$$\sum_{i=1}^{k} x^{-(n+1)}_{(i)} = \sum_{i=1}^{k-1} x^{-n}_{(i)} + x_{n+1}$$

and

$$\sum_{i=1}^{k} y_{(i)}^{-(n+1)} = \sum_{i=1}^{k-1} y_{(i)}^{-n} + y_{n+1}.$$

Adding (11.3) and (11.4), we obtain (11.6) for this k.

CASE 3. $x_{n+1} < x_{(k)}^{-n}$ and $y_{n+1} > y_{(k)}^{-n}$. This implies

$$\sum_{i=1}^{k} x_{(i)}^{-(n+1)} = \sum_{i=1}^{k-1} x_{(i)}^{-n} + x_{n+1}$$

and

$$\sum_{i=1}^{k} y_{(i)}^{-(n+1)} = \sum_{i=1}^{k-1} y_{(i)}^{-n} + y_{(k)}^{-n}.$$

Combining (11.4) and the inequality $y_{n+1} > y_{(k)}^{-n}$ (which is valid by definition of the present case), it follows that $x_{n+1} \geq y_{(k)}^{-n}$. Adding this inequality and (11.3), we obtain (11.6) for this k.

CASE 4. $x_{n+1} > x_{(k)}^{-n}$ and $y_{n+1} < y_{(k)}^{-n}$. This implies

$$\sum_{i=1}^{k} x_{(i)}^{-(n+1)} = \sum_{i=1}^{k-1} x_{(i)}^{-n} + x_{(k)}^{-n}$$

and

$$\sum_{i=1}^{k} y_{(i)}^{-(n+1)} = \sum_{i=1}^{k-1} y_{(i)}^{-n} + y_{n+1}.$$

The inequality $y_{n+1} < y_{(k)}^{-n}$ (which is satisfied by definition of the present case) implies

$$\sum_{i=1}^{k-1} y_{(i)}^{-n} + y_{(k)}^{-n} \geq \sum_{i=1}^{k-1} y_{(i)}^{-n} + y_{n+1}.$$

Combining this inequality with (11.3) yields (11.6) for this k.

To establish (11.2), suppose that $(x, y) \in P(R_G^n)$. By definition, at least one of the following two statements is true:

$$(x^{-n}, y^{-n}) \in P(R_g^n) \text{ and } x^{+n} \geq y^{+n}; \tag{11.7}$$

$$(x^{-n}, y^{-n}) \in R_g^n \text{ and } x^{+n} > y^{+n}. \tag{11.8}$$

If (11.7) is true, it follows that the inequalities in (11.3) are satisfied and at least one of them is strict. Now $(x, y) \in P(R_G^{n+1})$ follows from noting that, in all cases distinguished in the proof of (11.1), the presence of a strict inequality in (11.3) yields (11.6) with at least one strict inequality.

If (11.8) is true, it follows as in the proof of (11.1) that the inequalities in (11.6) are satisfied. If $x_{n+1} > y_{n+1}$, it follows immediately that one of these inequalities must be strict and, together with $x^{+(n+1)} \geq y^{+(n+1)}$, we obtain $(x, y) \in P(R_G^{n+1})$. If $x_{n+1} = y_{n+1}$, we must have $x^{+(n+1)} > y^{+(n+1)}$, which, together with (11.6), establishes that $(x, y) \in P(R_G^{n+1})$.

Step 2. We now show that, for all $x, y \in X$,

$$(x, y) \in P(R_G) \Leftrightarrow \exists n \in \mathbb{N} \text{ such that } (x, y) \in P(R_G^n). \tag{11.9}$$

Suppose first that $(x, y) \in P(R_G)$. By definition, there exists $n \in \mathbb{N}$ such that $(x, y) \in R_G^n$. Moreover, $(y, x) \notin R_G^n$ because otherwise we obtain $(y, x) \in R_G$ by definition and thus a contradiction to our hypothesis that $(x, y) \in P(R_G)$. Hence $(x, y) \in P(R_G^n)$.

Conversely, suppose that there exists $n \in \mathbb{N}$ such that $(x, y) \in P(R_G^n)$ and that there exists $m \in \mathbb{N}$ such that $(y, x) \in R_G^m$. Clearly, $m \neq n$; otherwise we immediately obtain a contradiction. If $m > n$, $(x, y) \in P(R_G^n)$ and application of (11.2) (repeated if necessary) together imply $(x, y) \in P(R_G^m)$, contradicting the assumption $(y, x) \in R_G^m$. If $m < n$, $(y, x) \in R_G^m$ and application of (11.1) (repeated if necessary) together imply $(y, x) \in R_G^n$, contradicting the hypothesis $(x, y) \in P(R_G^n)$. We conclude that $(x, y) \in R_G^n$ and $(y, x) \notin R_G^m$ for all $m \in \mathbb{N}$. By definition, this implies $(x, y) \in P(R_G)$.

STEP 3. Next, we prove that R_G is a quasi ordering. Reflexivity is immediate because, for all $x \in X$, $(x, x) \in R_G^n$ for all $n \in \mathbb{N}$ and hence $(x, x) \in R_G$. To prove that R_G is transitive, suppose that $(x, y), (y, z) \in R_G$. By definition, there exist $m, n \in \mathbb{N}$ such that $(x, y) \in R_G^n$ and $(y, z) \in R_G^m$. Let $k = \max\{m, n\}$. By application of (11.1) (repeated if necessary), $(x, y), (y, z) \in R_G^k$ and by the transitivity of R_G^k, $(x, z) \in R_G^k$, which, in turn, implies $(x, z) \in R_G$.

STEP 4. Now let R be an ordering extension of R_G. We complete the proof of the "if" part by showing that R satisfies the required axioms.

To establish that strong Pareto is satisfied, suppose that $x, y \in X$ are such that $x > y$. Let $n = \min\{m \in \mathbb{N} \mid x_m > y_m\}$. By definition, $(x, y) \in P(R_G^n)$. By (11.9), $(x, y) \in P(R_G)$ and, because R is an ordering extension of R_G, we obtain $(x, y) \in P(R)$.

Next, we show that finite anonymity is satisfied. Let $x \in X$ and let ρ be a finite permutation of $\mathbb{N}$. By definition, there exists $m \in \mathbb{N}$ such that $\rho(n) = n$ for all $n \in \mathbb{N} \setminus \{1, \ldots, m\}$. By definition of R_G^m, $(x^\rho, x) \in I(R_G^m)$. By definition of R_G, this implies $(x^\rho, x) \in I(R_G)$. Because R is an ordering extension of R_G, we obtain $(x^\rho, x) \in I(R)$.

Finally, we show that the strict transfer principle is satisfied. Consider $x, y \in X$ and $m, n \in \mathbb{N}$ such that $x_k = y_k$ for all $k \in \mathbb{N} \setminus \{m, n\}$, $y_m > x_m \geq x_n > y_n$ and $x_n + x_m = y_n + y_m$. Let $j = \max\{m, n\}$. By definition of R_G^j, we obtain $(x, y) \in R_G^j$. By (11.9), $(x, y) \in R_G$ and, because R is an ordering extension of R_G, $(x, y) \in R$.

"Only if." Suppose R is an ordering on X satisfying the three axioms of the theorem statement. To prove that R is an ordering extension of R_G, we have to establish the set inclusions $R_G \subseteq R$ and $P(R_G) \subseteq P(R)$.

Suppose $x, y \in X$ are such that $(x, y) \in R_G$. By definition, there exists $n \in \mathbb{N}$ such that

$$\sum_{i=1}^{k} x_{(i)}^{-n} \geq \sum_{i=1}^{k} y_{(i)}^{-n} \text{ for all } k \in \{1, \ldots, n\}$$

and $x^{+n} \geq y^{+n}$. By anonymity, we can without loss of generality assume that $x_{(i)}^{-n} = x_i$ and $y_{(i)}^{-n} = y_i$ for all $i \in \{1, \ldots, n\}$. Employing an argument analogous to that used by Shorrocks [18, Theorem 2], we let $w \in X$ be such that $w_j = y_j$ for all $j \in \{1, \ldots, n-1\}$, $w_n = y_n +$

$\sum_{i=1}^{n} x_i - \sum_{i=1}^{n} y_i$, and $w^{+n} = x^{+n}$. We have $w \geq y$ and thus $(w, y) \in R$ by reflexivity (if $w = y$) or by strong Pareto (if $w > y$). Furthermore, $(x^{-n}, w^{-n}) \in R_g^n$ and $\sum_{i=1}^{n} x_i = \sum_{i=1}^{n} w_i$. If $x^{-n} = w^{-n}$, $(x, w) \in R$ follows from reflexivity (note that $x^{+n} = w^{+n}$ by definition). If $x^{-n} \neq w^{-n}$, it follows that x^{-n} can be reached from w^{-n} through a finite sequence of Pigou-Dalton transfers (see Hardy, Littlewood, and Pólya [13]). Thus, by application (repeated if necessary) of the strict transfer principle (and transitivity if necessary), we obtain $(x, w) \in R$ (note again that $x^{+n} = w^{+n}$). Transitivity now implies $(x, y) \in R$.

Now let $x, y \in X$ be such that $(x, y) \in P(R_G)$. Because $P(R_G) \subseteq R_G$ by definition and $R_G \subseteq R$ as just established, it follows that $(x, y) \in R$. If $(y, x) \in R$, there exists $m \in \mathbb{N}$ such that $(y, x) \in R_G^m$. By (11.9), there exists $n \in \mathbb{N}$ such that $(x, y) \in P(R_G^n)$. We now obtain a contradiction using the same argument as in the proof of (11.9) and, thus, the hypothesis $(y, x) \in R$ must be false. Together with $(x, y) \in R$, it follows that $(x, y) \in P(R)$. ■

11.4. Infinite-Horizon Leximin

An equity property that has received a considerable amount of attention in finite settings is the Hammond equity and some of its variations. The infinite-horizon version we use is defined as follows.

Equity Preference. For all $x, y \in X$ and for all $m, n \in \mathbb{N}$, if $x_k = y_k$ for all $k \in \mathbb{N} \setminus \{m, n\}$ and $y_m > x_m > x_n > y_n$, then $(x, y) \in R$.

Equity preference is the extension of Hammond's [10] equity axiom to the infinite-horizon environment. The axiom is used in Asheim and Tungodden [3]; see also Asheim, Mitra, and Tungodden [4] for an alternative version, which they call the Hammond equity for the future. A condition that is stronger than Hammond's equity axiom is used by d'Aspremont and Gevers [8], who require $(x, y) \in P(R)$ rather than merely $(x, y) \in R$ in the conclusion of the axiom. In the presence of strong Pareto, the two axioms are equivalent. Moreover, strong Pareto and equity preference together imply the following property, which, in turn, obviously implies the strict transfer principle.

Strict Equity Preference. For all $x, y \in X$ and for all $m, n \in \mathbb{N}$, if $x_k = y_k$ for all $k \in \mathbb{N} \setminus \{m, n\}$ and $y_m > x_m \geq x_n > y_n$, then $(x, y) \in P(R)$.

To see that strict equity preference is implied by strong Pareto and equity preference, suppose that R satisfies the first two axioms, and let $x, y \in X$ and $m, n \in \mathbb{N}$ be such that $x_k = y_k$ for all $k \in \mathbb{N} \setminus \{m, n\}$ and $y_m > x_m \geq x_n > y_n$. Let $z \in X$ be such that $z_k = x_k = y_k$ for all $k \in \mathbb{N} \setminus \{m, n\}$ and $x_n > z_m > z_n > y_n$. By strong Pareto, $(x, z) \in P(R)$ and by equity preference, $(z, y) \in R$. Thus, transitivity implies $(x, y) \in P(R)$ and strict equity preference is satisfied.

If the strict transfer principle is replaced by equity preference (which, in the presence of strong Pareto, is a strengthening), the only remaining orderings are infinite-horizon versions of the leximin criterion. For each $n \in \mathbb{N}$, we denote the usual leximin ordering on $\mathbb{R}^n$ by R^n_ℓ, that is, for all $x, y \in X$,

$$(x^{-n}, y^{-n}) \in R^n_\ell \Leftrightarrow x^{-n} \text{ is a permutation of } y^{-n} \text{ or there exists } m \in \{1, \ldots, n\} \text{ such that } x^{-n}_{(k)} = y^{-n}_{(k)} \text{ for all } k \in \{1, \ldots, n\} \setminus \{m, \ldots, n\} \text{ and } x^{-n}_{(m)} > y^{-n}_{(m)}.$$

Again, let $n \in \mathbb{N}$ and define a relation $R^n_L \subseteq X \times X$ by letting, for all $x, y \in X$,

$$(x, y) \in R^n_L \Leftrightarrow (x^{-n}, y^{-n}) \in R^n_\ell \text{ and } x^{+n} \geq y^{+n}.$$

This relation can be shown to be a quasi ordering for all $n \in \mathbb{N}$. Finally, let $R_L = \cup_{n \in \mathbb{N}} R^n_L$. This relation is a quasi ordering, but it is not complete—some infinite utility streams are not ranked by R_L. Our next result characterizes all ordering extensions of R_L.

Theorem 11.2. An ordering R on X satisfies strong Pareto, finite anonymity, and equity preference if and only if R is an ordering extension of R_L.

Proof. "If." As in the proof of Theorem 11.1, we begin by showing that the relations R_L^n and their associated strict preference relations $P(R_L^n)$ are nested, that is, for all $n \in \mathbb{N}$,

$$R_L^n \subseteq R_L^{n+1} \tag{11.10}$$

and

$$P(R_L^n) \subseteq P(R_L^{n+1}). \tag{11.11}$$

To prove (11.10), suppose that $(x, y) \in R_L^n$. By definition, $(x^{-n}, y^{-n}) \in R_\ell^n$ and $x^{+n} \geq y^{+n}$. Then either x^{-n} is a permutation of y^{-n} and $x^{+n} \geq y^{+n}$, or there exists $j \in \{1, \ldots, n\}$ such that $x_{(k)}^{-n} = y_{(k)}^{-n}$ for all $k \in \{1, \ldots, n\} \setminus \{j, \ldots, n\}$, $x_{(j)}^{-n} > y_{(j)}^{-n}$ and $x^{+n} \geq y^{+n}$. In both cases, $(x^{-(n+1)}, y^{-(n+1)}) \in R_\ell^{n+1}$ and $x^{+(n+1)} \geq y^{+(n+1)}$, that is, $(x, y) \in R_L^{n+1}$.

To establish (11.11), suppose that $(x, y) \in P(R_L^n)$. By definition, at least one of the following two statements is true:

$$(x^{-n}, y^{-n}) \in P(R_\ell^n) \text{ and } x^{+n} \geq y^{+n}; \tag{11.12}$$

$$(x^{-n}, y^{-n}) \in R_\ell^n \text{ and } x^{+n} > y^{+n}. \tag{11.13}$$

By (11.10), it follows that $(x, y) \in R_L^{n+1}$. To prove that $(x, y) \in P(R_L^{n+1})$, suppose, by way of contradiction, that $(y, x) \in R_L^{n+1}$. Then, by definition,

$$(x^{-n}, y^{-n}) \in I(R_\ell^n) \text{ and } x^{+n} = y^{+n},$$

contradicting (11.12) and (11.13).

Using the same arguments as in the proof of (11.9) in Theorem 11.1 (replacing R_G and R_G^n with R_L and R_L^n), it follows that, for all $x, y \in X$,

$$(x, y) \in P(R_L) \Leftrightarrow \exists n \in \mathbb{N} \text{ such that } (x, y) \in P(R_L^n) \tag{11.14}$$

and, furthermore, that R_L is a quasi ordering and that any ordering extension of R_L satisfies strong Pareto and finite anonymity.

We complete the proof of the "if" part by showing that any ordering extension R of R_L satisfies equity preference. Consider $x, y \in X$ and $m, n \in \mathbb{N}$ such that $x_k = y_k$ for all $k \in \mathbb{N} \setminus \{m, n\}$ and $y_m > x_m > x_n > y_n$. Let $j = \max\{m, n\}$. By definition of R_L^j, we obtain $(x, y) \in R_L^j$. By (11.14), $(x, y) \in R_L$ and, because R is an ordering extension of R_L, $(x, y) \in R$.

"Only if." Suppose R is an ordering on X satisfying the three axioms of the theorem statement. Fix $n \in \mathbb{N}$ and $z \in X$ and define the relation $Q^n(z) \subseteq \mathbb{R}^n \times \mathbb{R}^n$ as follows. For all $x, y \in X$,

$$(x^{-n}, y^{-n}) \in Q^n(z) \Leftrightarrow ((x^{-n}, z^{+n}), (y^{-n}, z^{+n})) \in R.$$

$Q^n(z)$ is an ordering because R is. Furthermore, it is clear that

$$(x^{-n}, y^{-n}) \in P(Q^n(z)) \Leftrightarrow ((x^{-n}, z^{+n}), (y^{-n}, z^{+n})) \in P(R) \quad (11.15)$$

for all $x, y \in X$. The three axioms imply that $Q^n(z)$ must satisfy the n-person versions of the axioms and, using Hammond's [10, Theorem 7.2] characterization of n-person leximin (see also d'Aspremont and Gevers [8, Theorem 5]), it follows that

$$Q^n(z) = R^n_\ell. \quad (11.16)$$

Because n and z were chosen arbitrarily, (11.16) is true for all $n \in \mathbb{N}$ and for any $z \in X$.

To prove that R is an ordering extension of R_L, we first establish the set inclusion $R_L \subseteq R$. Suppose that $x, y \in X$ are such that $(x, y) \in R_L$. By definition of R_L, there exists $n \in \mathbb{N}$ such that $(x, y) \in R^n_L$, that is,

$$(x^{-n}, y^{-n}) \in R^n_\ell \text{ and } x^{+n} \geq y^{+n}.$$

Hence, by (11.16),

$$(x^{-n}, y^{-n}) \in Q^n(z) \text{ and } x^{+n} \geq y^{+n}$$

for all $z \in X$. Choosing $z = y$ and using the definition of $Q^n(z)$, we obtain $((x^{-n}, y^{+n}), (y^{-n}, y^{+n})) \in R$. Because $x^{+n} \geq y^{+n}$, reflexivity (if $x^{+n} = y^{+n}$) or the conjunction of strong Pareto and transitivity (if $x^{+n} > y^{+n}$) implies $((x^{-n}, x^{+n}), (y^{-n}, y^{+n})) = (x, y) \in R$.

We complete the proof by establishing the set inclusion $P(R_L) \subseteq P(R)$. Let $x, y \in X$ be such that $(x, y) \in P(R_L)$. By (11.14), there exists $n \in \mathbb{N}$ such that $(x, y) \in P(R^n_L)$. Thus, (11.12) or (11.13) is true.

If (11.12) holds, (11.16) implies

$$(x^{-n}, y^{-n}) \in P(Q^n(z)) \text{ and } x^{+n} \geq y^{+n}$$

for all $z \in X$. Setting $z = y$ and using (11.15), we obtain $((x^{-n}, y^{+n}), (y^{-n}, y^{+n})) \in P(R)$ and, using reflexivity or strong Pareto and transitivity as in the proof of the set inclusion $R_L \subseteq R$, we obtain $(x, y) \in P(R)$.

If (11.13) holds, (11.16) implies

$$(x^{-n}, y^{-n}) \in Q^n(z) \text{ and } x^{+n} > y^{+n}$$

for all $z \in X$. Setting $z = y$, it follows that $((x^{-n}, y^{+n}), (y^{-n}, y^{+n})) \in R$ as a consequence of the definition of $Q^n(z)$ and, by strong Pareto and transitivity, $((x^{-n}, x^{+n}), (y^{-n}, y^{+n})) = (x, y) \in P(R)$. ■

11.5. Concluding Remarks

The results of this essay reinforce the findings of earlier contributions regarding the existence of orderings of infinite utility streams with attractive properties. In particular, we provide characterizations of two classes of such orderings. Given the existential nature of the proofs, we do not provide explicit constructions of these orderings. However, this feature is by no means unique to our approach. Extending quasi orderings to orderings often requires nonconstructive techniques; see, for example, Richter's [17] use of Szpilrajn's [22] extension theorem in the context of rational choice.

A plausible conclusion to be drawn is that impossibility results such as those of Diamond [9], Basu and Mitra [5], and Hara, Shinotsuka, Suzumura, and Xu [12] can be avoided if continuity or representability assumptions are dispensed with. Because continuity and representability can be considered rather demanding in infinite-horizon settings, this confirms, in our view, that the state of affairs in this area is not as disappointing and negative as has been suggested by the impossibility results of many earlier contributions.

The techniques employed to characterize infinite-horizon versions of the generalized Lorenz criterion and of leximin appear to be very powerful and applicable to the extension of other finite-population social choice rules; see also the characterization of infinite-horizon utilitarianism by Basu and Mitra [6]. We hope that our approach will stimulate further research in the area of intergenerational social choice by identifying alternative sets of attractive axioms and characterizing the social orderings that satisfy them.

The classes of orderings characterized in this essay are relatively large: there are many comparisons of utility streams that are not determined by the axioms employed. An issue to be addressed in future work is to examine to what extent the ranking of more pairs of streams can be determined by employing plausible additional axioms.

11.6. References

[1] Arrow, K. J., *Social Choice and Individual Values,* New York: John Wiley & Sons, 1951; 2nd edn., 1963.

[2] Asheim, G. B., W. Buchholz, and B. Tungodden, "Justifying Sustainability," *Journal of Environmental Economics and Management* **41**, 2001, 252–268.

[3] Asheim, G. B., and B. Tungodden, "Resolving Distributional Conflicts between Generations," *Economic Theory* **24**, 2004, 221–230.

[4] Asheim, G. B., T. Mitra, and B. Tungodden, "A New Equity Condition for Infinite Utility Streams and the Possibility of Being Paretian," in J. Roemer and K. Suzumura, eds., *Intergenerational Equity and Sustainability,* Macmillan: London, 2007, 55–68.

[5] Basu, K., and T. Mitra, "Aggregating Infinite Utility Streams with Intergenerational Equity: The Impossibility of Being Paretian," *Econometrica* **71**, 2003, 1557–1563.

[6] Basu, K., and T. Mitra, "Utilitarianism for Infinite Utility Streams: A New Welfare Criterion and Its Axiomatic Characterization," *Journal of Economic Theory* **133**, 2007, 350–373.

[7] Dalton, H., "The Measurement of the Inequality of Incomes," *Economic Journal* **30**, 1920, 348–361.

[8] d'Aspremont, C., and L. Gevers, "Equity and the Informational Basis of Collective Choice," *Review of Economic Studies* **44**, 1977, 199–209.

[9] Diamond, P., "The Evaluation of Infinite Utility Streams," *Econometrica* **33**, 1965, 170–177.

[10] Hammond, P., "Equity, Arrow's Conditions, and Rawls' Difference Principle," *Econometrica* **44**, 1976, 793–804.

[11] Hansson, B., "Choice Structures and Preference Relations," *Synthese* **18**, 1968, 443–458.

[12] Hara, C., T. Shinotsuka, K. Suzumura, and Y. Xu, "Continuity and Egalitarianism in the Evaluation of Infinite Utility Streams," *Social Choice and Welfare* **31**, 2008, 179–191.

[13] Hardy, G., J. Littlewood, and G. Pólya, *Inequalities,* Cambridge, UK: Cambridge University Press, 1934.

[14] Koopmans, T. C., "Stationary Ordinal Utility and Impatience," *Econometrica* **28**, 1960, 287–309.

[15] Pigou, A., *Wealth and Welfare,* London: Macmillan, 1912.

[16] Ramsey, F. P., "A Mathematical Theory of Saving," *Economic Journal* **38**, 1928, 543–559.

[17] Richter, M. K., "Revealed Preference Theory," *Econometrica* **34**, 1966, 635–645.

[18] Shorrocks, A. F., "Ranking Income Distributions," *Economica* **50**, 1983, 3–17.

[19] Sidgwick, H., *The Methods of Ethics,* London: Macmillan, 1907.

[20] Suppes, P., "Some Formal Models of Grading Principles," *Synthese* **6**, 1966, 284–306.

[21] Svensson, L.-G., "Equity among Generations," *Econometrica* **48**, 1980, 1251–1256.

[22] Szpilrajn, E., "Sur l'Extension de l'Ordre Partiel," *Fundamenta Mathematicae* **16**, 1930, 386–389.

[23] von Weizsäcker, C. C., "Existence of Optimal Programs of Accumulation for an Infinite Time Horizon," *Review of Economic Studies* **32**, 1965, 85–104.

ESSAY 12

Multi-Profile Intergenerational Social Choice

12.1. Introduction

As is well known, the validity of Arrow's celebrated general impossibility theorem hinges squarely on the finiteness of population. Fishburn [11], Sen [17], and Suzumura [20] presented their respective methods of proving Arrow's theorem and highlighted the crucial role played by the assumption that the population is finite. Kirman and Sondermann [14] and Hansson [12] cast a new light on the structure of an Arrovian social welfare function with an infinite population, revealing the structure of decisive coalitions for such a function as an *ultrafilter*. In their analysis, however, there was no explicit consideration of a sequential relationship among the members of an infinite population. It was a pioneering analysis due to Ferejohn and Page [10] that introduced time explicitly. Time flows only unidirectionally, and two members t and t' of the society, to be called generation t and generation t', are such that generation t' appears in the society after generation t if and only if t is smaller than t'. As a result of introducing this time structure of infinite population, Ferejohn and Page opened a new gate toward combining Arrovian social choice theory and the theory of evaluating infinite intergenerational utility streams, which was initiated by Koopmans [15] and Diamond [9]. In the traditional Koopmans-Diamond framework, the

First published in *Social Choice and Welfare* **37**, 2011, pp. 493–509. Joint paper with Walter Bossert. Thanks are due to the editor in charge and referees of *Social Choice and Welfare* for their helpful comments.

focus is on resource allocations among different generations with fixed utility functions, one for each generation. Thus, multiprofile considerations do not arise. This essay is an attempt to reexamine the Ferejohn-Page analysis of intergenerational social choice theory in a multi-profile setting.

Starting out with Hansson's [12] result on the ultrafilter structure of the set of decisive coalitions, Ferejohn and Page [10] proposed a *stationarity* condition in an infinite-horizon multi-profile social choice model and showed that *if* a social welfare function satisfying Arrow's conditions and stationarity exists, generation one must be a dictator. Stationarity as defined by Ferejohn and Page demands that if a common first-period alternative is eliminated from two infinite streams of per-period alternatives, then the resulting continuation streams must be ranked in the same way as the original streams according to the social ranking obtained *for the original profile.* The reason why generation one is the only candidate for a dictator is the unidirectional nature of the flow of time—and, thus, the unequal treatment of generations in the stationarity property. Dictatorships of later generations fail to satisfy stationarity because we cannot reassess our social evaluation after a later period has passed but an earlier period is still present: we can only move forward, not backward, in time.

As Ferejohn and Page noted themselves, the question whether such a social welfare function exists at all was left open by their analysis; what they showed was that *if* a function with the required properties exists, it must be dictatorial with generation one being the dictator. Packel [16] answered the question Ferejohn and Page left open by establishing a strong impossibility result: *even without independence of irrelevant alternatives and without assuming social preferences to be transitive, no collective choice rule can satisfy unlimited domain, weak Pareto, and stationarity.* Note that Packel operates within the same framework as Ferejohn and Page to establish the impossibility. Thus, his result is not an observation in a different setting but, rather, an answer to the question left open by Ferejohn and Page.

In this essay, we first prove that the negative implications of the Ferejohn-Page stationarity condition are actually more far-reaching: *even without reflexivity and completeness, there exists no collective choice rule that satisfies unlimited domain, weak Pareto, and stationarity.* The same conclusion holds if individual preferences are restricted to those that are history-independent. No restrictions whatsoever are imposed on social preferences—they need not be reflexive, complete, or transitive. By dropping reflexivity and completeness, we strengthen Packel's impossibility result substantially. It will become clear once we establish the proof of this impossibility theorem why all collective choice rules (including dictatorships) fail to satisfy the required axioms.

Packel's approach to resolve the impossibility consisted of restricting the domain of a social welfare function to profiles where generation one's preferences are themselves stationary. This domain assumption, which is plausible if social preferences are required to be stationary in Ferejohn and Page's sense, allowed him to obtain possibility results in that setting. However, there are alternative domain restrictions that may be considered suitable for which the Ferejohn-Page variant of stationarity may not be the best match. In particular, we think that a natural domain assumption in the intertemporal context is one in which the preferences of each generation are *selfish*—that is, they depend on the outcome for this generation only. In that case, there do exist social welfare functions that satisfy weak Pareto and stationarity, but all of them violate Pareto indifference.

In response, we propose what we consider a suitable multi-profile version of stationarity when individual preferences are assumed to be selfish. *Multi-profile stationarity* requires that, for any two streams of per-period alternatives and for any preference profile, if the first-period alternatives are the same in the two streams, then the social ranking of the two streams according to this profile is *the same* as the social ranking that results if the common first-period alternative is removed *along with the preference ordering of generation one.* Our main result uses multi-profile stationarity to characterize the lexicographic dictatorship in which the generations are taken into consideration in chronological order. The main conclusion is that, although the infinite-population version of Arrow's social choice problem permits, in principle, nondictatorial rules, these additional possibilities all but vanish if multi-profile stationarity is imposed.

12.2. Infinite-Horizon Social Choice

Suppose there is a set of per-period alternatives X containing at least three elements, that is, $|X| \geq 3$ where $|X|$ denotes the cardinality of X. These per-period alternatives could be consumption bundles, for example, but we do not restrict attention to one particular interpretation. Let X^{∞} be the set of all infinite streams of per-period alternatives $\boldsymbol{x} = (x_1, x_2, \ldots)$ where, for each generation $t \in \mathbb{N}$, $x_t \in X$ is the period-t alternative experienced by generation t.

The set of all binary relations on X^∞ is denoted by $\mathcal{B}$, and $\mathcal{C}$ is the set of all complete relations on X^∞. Furthermore, the set of all orderings on X^∞ is denoted by $\mathcal{R}$, where an ordering is a reflexive, complete, and transitive relation. We assume that each generation $t \in \mathbb{N}$ has an ordering $R_t \in \mathcal{R}$. A (preference) profile is a stream $\boldsymbol{R} = (R_1, R_2, \ldots)$ of orderings on X^∞. The set of all such profiles is denoted by $\mathcal{R}^\infty$.

Let $t \in \mathbb{N}$. For $\boldsymbol{x} \in X^\infty$, we define the *period-t continuation of* $\boldsymbol{x}$ as

$$\boldsymbol{x}_{\geq t} = (x_t, x_{t+1}, \ldots),$$

that is, $\left(\boldsymbol{x}_{\geq t}\right)_\tau = x_{\tau+t-1}$ for all $\tau \in \mathbb{N}$. Analogously, for $\boldsymbol{R} \in \mathcal{R}^\infty$, the *period-t continuation of* $\boldsymbol{R}$ is

$$\boldsymbol{R}_{\geq t} = (R_t, R_{t+1}, \ldots).$$

The preceding definition of continuation of streams of per-period alternatives is that used by Ferejohn and Page and Packel. Ferejohn and Page [10, p. 272] interpret $\boldsymbol{x}_{\geq 2}$ and $\boldsymbol{y}_{\geq 2}$ as the streams that are obtained if $\boldsymbol{x}$ and $\boldsymbol{y}$ are "shifted forward one period," and Packel [16, p. 220] assumes that if $(x_1, x_2, x_3, \ldots)$ is an admissible stream, then so is $(x_2, x_3, \ldots)$, saying that "if a certain overall intergenerational program is possible, then moving the program up one generation is also possible."

Two subsets of the *unlimited domain* $\mathcal{R}^\infty$ are of importance in this essay. We define the *forward-looking domain* $\mathcal{R}_F^\infty$ by letting, for all $\boldsymbol{R} \in \mathcal{R}^\infty$, $\boldsymbol{R} \in \mathcal{R}_F^\infty$ if and only if, for each $t \in \mathbb{N}$, there exists an ordering Q_t on X^∞ such that, for all $\boldsymbol{x}, \boldsymbol{y} \in X^\infty$,

$$\boldsymbol{x} R_t \boldsymbol{y} \Leftrightarrow \boldsymbol{x}_{\geq t} Q_t \boldsymbol{y}_{\geq t}.$$

Analogously, the *selfish domain* $\mathcal{R}_S^\infty$ is obtained by letting, for all $\boldsymbol{R} \in \mathcal{R}^\infty$, $\boldsymbol{R} \in \mathcal{R}_S^\infty$ if and only if, for each $t \in \mathbb{N}$, there exists an ordering $\succcurlyeq_t$ on X such that, for all $\boldsymbol{x}, \boldsymbol{y} \in X^\infty$,

$$\boldsymbol{x} R_t \boldsymbol{y} \Leftrightarrow x_t \succcurlyeq_t y_t.$$

Clearly, we have $\mathcal{R}_S^\infty \subseteq \mathcal{R}_F^\infty \subseteq \mathcal{R}^\infty$. The relation R_t is an ordering on the set of streams X^∞, whereas $\succcurlyeq_t$ is an ordering on the set of per-period alternatives X. On selfish domains, the two can be used interchangeably because, by definition, each generation only cares about its own per-period alternatives. Note that the definition of selfish preferences by itself does not prevent *social* preferences from, for example, using $\succcurlyeq_1$ to compare per-period alternatives such as x_t and y_t for periods t that are different from period one. This observation justifies the use of the example following the proof of Theorem 12.1, and just before the statement of Theorem 12.2.

For a relation $R \in \mathcal{B}$, the *asymmetric part* $P(R)$ of R is defined by

$$\boldsymbol{x} P(R) \boldsymbol{y} \Leftrightarrow [\boldsymbol{x} R \boldsymbol{y} \text{ and } \neg \boldsymbol{y} R \boldsymbol{x}]$$

for all $\boldsymbol{x}, \boldsymbol{y} \in X^\infty$. The *symmetric part* $I(R)$ of R is defined by

$$\boldsymbol{x} I(R) \boldsymbol{y} \Leftrightarrow [\boldsymbol{x} R \boldsymbol{y} \text{ and } \boldsymbol{y} R \boldsymbol{x}]$$

for all $\boldsymbol{x}, \boldsymbol{y} \in X^\infty$. Furthermore, for all $\boldsymbol{x}, \boldsymbol{y} \in X^\infty$ and for all $R \in \mathcal{B}$, $R|_{\{\mathbf{x},\mathbf{y}\}}$ is the restriction of R to the set $\{\boldsymbol{x}, \boldsymbol{y}\}$.

In the infinite-horizon context studied in this essay, a *collective choice rule* is a mapping $f: \mathcal{D} \to \mathcal{B}$, where $\mathcal{D} \subseteq \mathcal{R}^\infty$ with $\mathcal{D} \neq \emptyset$ is the domain of f. The interpretation is that, for a profile $\boldsymbol{R} \in \mathcal{D}$, $f(\boldsymbol{R})$ is the social ranking of streams in X^∞. If $f(\mathcal{D}) \subseteq \mathcal{C}$, f is a *complete collective choice rule.* If $f(\mathcal{D}) \subseteq \mathcal{R}$, f is a *social welfare function.*

Arrow imposed the axioms of *unlimited domain, weak Pareto,* and *independence of irrelevant alternatives* and showed that, in the case of a finite population, the resulting social welfare functions are *dictatorial:* there exists an individual such that, whenever this individual strictly prefers one alternative over another, this strict preference is reproduced in the social ranking, irrespective of the preferences of other members of society. This result is quite robust with respect to the domain considered. For example, replacing unlimited domain with various alternative domain assumptions (such as the free-triple assumption and others that apply to economic environments) preserves Arrow's impossibility result. In this essay, it turns out that a specific domain restriction (particularly, the selfish domain assumption defined in the following) allows us to circumvent impossibilities.

The axioms relevant in our context are defined as follows.

UNLIMITED DOMAIN. $\mathcal{D} = \mathcal{R}^{\infty}$.

FORWARD-LOOKING DOMAIN. $\mathcal{D} = \mathcal{R}_F^{\infty}$.

SELFISH DOMAIN. $\mathcal{D} = \mathcal{R}_S^{\infty}$.

WEAK PARETO. For all $\boldsymbol{x}, \boldsymbol{y} \in X^{\infty}$ and for all $\boldsymbol{R} \in \mathcal{D}$,

$$\boldsymbol{x} P(R_t) \boldsymbol{y} \forall t \in \mathbb{N} \Rightarrow \boldsymbol{x} P(f(\boldsymbol{R})) \boldsymbol{y}.$$

PARETO INDIFFERENCE. For all $\boldsymbol{x}, \boldsymbol{y} \in X^{\infty}$ and for all $\boldsymbol{R} \in \mathcal{D}$,

$$\boldsymbol{x} I(R_t) \boldsymbol{y} \ \forall t \in \mathbb{N} \Rightarrow \boldsymbol{x} I(f(\boldsymbol{R})) \boldsymbol{y}.$$

INDEPENDENCE OF IRRELEVANT ALTERNATIVES. For all $\boldsymbol{x}, \boldsymbol{y} \in X^{\infty}$ and for all $\boldsymbol{R}, \boldsymbol{R}' \in \mathcal{D}$,

$$R_t\big|_{\{\mathbf{x},\mathbf{y}\}} = R'_t\big|_{\{\mathbf{x},\mathbf{y}\}} \ \forall t \in \mathbb{N} \Rightarrow f(\boldsymbol{R})|_{\{\mathbf{x},\mathbf{y}\}} = f(\boldsymbol{R}')\big|_{\{\mathbf{x},\mathbf{y}\}}.$$

Let $f: \mathcal{D} \to \mathcal{R}$ be a social welfare function and let $\boldsymbol{x}, \boldsymbol{y} \in X^{\infty}$. A set $T \subseteq \mathbb{N}$ (also referred to as a *coalition*) is *decisive for* $\boldsymbol{x}$ *over* $\boldsymbol{y}$ *for* f if and only if, for all $\boldsymbol{R} \in \mathcal{D}$,

$$\boldsymbol{x} P(R_t) \boldsymbol{y} \ \forall t \in T \Rightarrow \boldsymbol{x} P(f(\boldsymbol{R})) \boldsymbol{y}.$$

Furthermore, a set $T \subseteq \mathbb{N}$ is *decisive for* f if and only if T is decisive for $\boldsymbol{x}$ over $\boldsymbol{y}$ for f for all $\boldsymbol{x}, \boldsymbol{y} \in X^{\infty}$. Clearly, $\mathbb{N}$ is decisive for any social welfare function f that satisfies weak Pareto. If there is a generation $t \in \mathbb{N}$ such that $\{t\}$ is decisive for f, generation t is a *dictator for* f.

Hansson [12] has shown that if a social welfare function f satisfies unlimited domain, weak Pareto, and independence of irrelevant alternatives, then the set of all decisive coalitions for f must be an *ultrafilter.* An ultrafilter on $\mathbb{N}$ is a collection $\mathcal{U}$ of subsets of $\mathbb{N}$ such that

(F_1) $\emptyset \notin \mathcal{U}$;
(F_2) $\forall T \subseteq \mathbb{N}$, $[T \in \mathcal{U}$ or $\mathbb{N} \setminus T \in \mathcal{U}]$;
(F_3) $\forall T, T' \in \mathcal{U}$, $T \cap T' \in \mathcal{U}$.

The conjunction of properties F_1 and F_2 implies that $\mathbb{N} \in \mathcal{U}$ and, furthermore, the conjunction of properties F_1 and F_3 implies that the disjunction in property F_2 is exclusive—that is, T and $\mathbb{N} \setminus T$ cannot both be in $\mathcal{U}$.

An ultrafilter $\mathcal{U}$ is *principal* if and only if there exists a $t \in \mathbb{N}$ such that, for all $T \subseteq \mathbb{N}$, $T \in \mathcal{U}$ if and only if $t \in T$. Otherwise, $\mathcal{U}$ is a *free* ultrafilter. It can be verified easily that if $\mathbb{N}$ is replaced with a finite set, then the only ultrafilters are principal and, therefore, Hansson's theorem reformulated for finite populations reduces to Arrow's theorem—that is, there exists an individual (or a generation) t that is a dictator. In the infinite-population case, a set of decisive coalitions that is a principal ultrafilter corresponds to a dictatorship just as in the finite case. Unlike in the finite case, there also exist free ultrafilters, but they cannot be defined explicitly; the proof of their existence relies on nonconstructive methods in the sense of using variants of the axiom of choice. These free ultrafilters are nondictatorial. However, social preferences associated with sets of decisive coalitions that form free ultrafilters fail to be continuous with respect to most standard topologies; see, for instance, Campbell [6; 7; 8].

12.3. Stationarity

None of the axioms defined in Section 12.2 invoke the intertemporal structure imposed by our intergenerational interpretation. In contrast, the following *stationarity* property proposed by Ferejohn and Page is based on the unidirectional nature of time. The intuition underlying stationarity is that if two streams of per-period alternatives agree in the first period, their relative social ranking is the same as that of their respective period-two continuations. To formulate a property of this nature in a multi-profile setting, the profile under consideration for each of the two comparisons must be specified. In Ferejohn and Page's and Packel's contributions, the same profile is employed before and after the common first-period alternative is removed. Ferejohn and Page's stationarity axiom, the underlying idea of which is due originally to Koopmans in a related but distinct context, is defined as follows.

Stationarity. For all $\boldsymbol{x}, \boldsymbol{y} \in X^{\infty}$ and for all $\boldsymbol{R} \in \mathcal{D}$, if $x_1 = y_1$, then

$$\boldsymbol{x} f(\boldsymbol{R}) \boldsymbol{y} \Leftrightarrow \boldsymbol{x}_{\geq 2} f(\boldsymbol{R}) \boldsymbol{y}_{\geq 2}.$$

Ferejohn and Page's result establishes that *if* there exists a social welfare function f that satisfies unlimited domain, weak Pareto, independence of irrelevant alternatives, and stationarity, then f must be such that generation one is a dictator for f. The existence issue itself remained unresolved by their analysis, as they clearly acknowledge. It was Packel [16, Theorem 1] who answered this open question in the negative by showing that there does not exist any complete collective choice rule that satisfies unlimited domain, weak Pareto, and stationarity. Neither transitivity nor independence of irrelevant alternatives is needed to establish this impossibility result. That even dictatorships do not work under the unlimited domain assumption can be seen by examining the proof of our strengthening of Packel's impossibility result reported in the following theorem; in fact, our proof is modeled after Packel's own proof, but it uses fewer assumptions to establish the impossibility. We show that, in addition to transitivity, reflexivity and completeness can be dropped and, moreover, the impossibility persists even on the forward-looking domain. Note that, however, the result is not true under the selfish domain, as we establish with an example after proving the theorem.

Theorem 12.1. There exists no collective choice rule that satisfies forward-looking domain, weak Pareto, and stationarity.

Proof. Suppose f is a collective choice rule that satisfies the axioms of the theorem statement. Let $x, y \in X$ and let, for each generation t, $\succcurlyeq_t$ be an antisymmetric ordering on X such that $yP(\succcurlyeq_t)x$ for all odd t and $xP(\succcurlyeq_t)y$ for all even t. Define a forward-looking profile $\boldsymbol{R}$ as follows. For all $\boldsymbol{x}, \boldsymbol{y} \in X^\infty$, let

$$\boldsymbol{x}P(R_1)\boldsymbol{y} \Leftrightarrow x_1P(\succcurlyeq_1)y_1 \text{ or } [x_1 = y_1 \text{ and } x_3P(\succcurlyeq_1)y_3].$$

Now let, for all $\boldsymbol{x}, \boldsymbol{y} \in X^\infty$, $\boldsymbol{x}R_1\boldsymbol{y}$ if and only if $\neg\boldsymbol{y}P(R_1)\boldsymbol{x}$. For all $t \in \mathbb{N} \setminus \{1\}$ and for all $\boldsymbol{x}, \boldsymbol{y} \in X^\infty$, let

$$\boldsymbol{x}R_t\boldsymbol{y} \Leftrightarrow x_t \succcurlyeq_t y_t.$$

Clearly, the profile thus defined is in $\mathcal{R}_F^\infty$. Now consider the streams

$$\boldsymbol{x} = (x, y, x, y, x, y, \ldots) = (x, \boldsymbol{y});$$

$$\boldsymbol{y} = (y, x, y, x, y, x, \ldots);$$

$$\boldsymbol{z} = (x, x, y, x, y, x, \ldots) = (x, \boldsymbol{x}).$$

Thus, $\boldsymbol{x}_{\geq 2} = \boldsymbol{y}$ and $\boldsymbol{z}_{\geq 2} = \boldsymbol{x}$. We have $\boldsymbol{z}P(R_t)\boldsymbol{x}$ for all $t \in \mathbb{N}$ and, by weak Pareto, $\boldsymbol{z}P(f(\boldsymbol{R}))\boldsymbol{x}$. Stationarity implies $\boldsymbol{x}P(f(\boldsymbol{R}))\boldsymbol{y}$. But $\boldsymbol{y}P(R_t)\boldsymbol{x}$ for all $t \in \mathbb{N}$, and we obtain a contradiction to weak Pareto. ■

Clearly, replacing forward-looking domain with unlimited domain does not affect the validity of the theorem. Furthermore, there is but a single profile used in the proof and, thus, the conclusion of Theorem 12.1 is preserved by domain expansion; this is not always the case for results in the spirit of Arrow's fundamental impossibility theorem.

The impossibility can be resolved by replacing forward-looking domain with selfish domain. To construct an explicit example, consider any selfish profile $\boldsymbol{R} \in \mathcal{R}_S^\infty$. Recall that, by definition of selfish domain, the profile $\boldsymbol{R}$ of individual orderings defined on the set X^∞ of *streams of per-period alternatives* is in $\mathcal{R}_S^\infty$ if and only if, for each $t \in \mathbb{N}$, there exists an ordering $\succcurlyeq_t$ defined on the set X of *per-period alternatives* such that the relative ranking of two streams $\boldsymbol{x}$ and $\boldsymbol{y}$ in X^∞ according to R_t is identical to the relative ranking of the period-t alternatives x_t and y_t according to $\succcurlyeq_t$. Thus, the selfish profile $\boldsymbol{R}$ of orderings defined on X^∞ is completely specified once the profile $(\succcurlyeq_1, \succcurlyeq_2, \ldots)$ consisting of orderings on X is specified. Suppose $(\succcurlyeq_1, \succcurlyeq_2, \ldots)$ is the profile of orderings on X associated with the selfish profile $\boldsymbol{R} \in \mathcal{R}_S^\infty$ of orderings on X^∞. We now define a social welfare function f by letting, for all $\boldsymbol{x}, \boldsymbol{y} \in X^\infty$ and for all $\boldsymbol{R} \in \mathcal{R}_S^\infty$, $\boldsymbol{x}f(\boldsymbol{R})\boldsymbol{y}$ if and only if

$$\left[x_\tau I(\succcurlyeq_1)y_\tau \forall \tau \in \mathbb{N}\right] \quad \text{or}$$

$$\left[\exists t \in \mathbb{N} \text{ such that } \{x_\tau I(\succcurlyeq_1)y_\tau \forall \tau < t \text{ and } x_t P(\succcurlyeq_1)y_t\}\right].$$

This social welfare function f satisfies selfish domain, weak Pareto, and stationarity. However, it does not satisfy Pareto indifference. Intuitively, this is the case because, at the *social* level, generation one's per-period preferences are consulted not only in period one but also in *later* periods, whereas the per-period preferences of other generations do not influence the social comparisons at all. More generally, replacing forward-looking domain with selfish domain and adding Pareto indifference in Theorem 12.1 produces another impossibility.

THEOREM 12.2. There exists no collective choice rule that satisfies selfish domain, weak Pareto, Pareto indifference, and stationarity.

Proof. Suppose f is a collective choice rule that satisfies the axioms of the theorem statement. Let $x, y, z \in X$ and let, for each $t \in \mathbb{N}$, $\succcurlyeq_t$ be an ordering on X such that $zP(\succcurlyeq_t)xI(\succcurlyeq_t)y$ for all odd t and $zI(\succcurlyeq_t)xP(\succcurlyeq_t)y$ for all even t. Define a profile $\boldsymbol{R}$ as follows. For all $\boldsymbol{x}, \boldsymbol{y} \in X^\infty$ and for all $t \in \mathbb{N}$, let

$$\boldsymbol{x}R_t\boldsymbol{y} \Leftrightarrow x_t \succcurlyeq_t y_t.$$

Clearly, the profile thus defined is in $\mathcal{R}_S^\infty$. Now consider the streams

$$\boldsymbol{x} = (z, x, z, x, z, x, \ldots);$$

$$\boldsymbol{y} = (x, y, x, y, x, y, \ldots);$$

$$\boldsymbol{z} = (z, z, x, z, x, z, x, \ldots) = (z, \boldsymbol{x});$$

$$\boldsymbol{w} = (z, x, y, x, y, x, y, \ldots) = (z, \boldsymbol{y}).$$

Thus, $\boldsymbol{z}_{\geq 2} = \boldsymbol{x}$ and $\boldsymbol{w}_{\geq 2} = \boldsymbol{y}$. We have $\boldsymbol{z}I(R_t)\boldsymbol{w}$ for all $t \in \mathbb{N}$ and, by Pareto indifference, $\boldsymbol{z}I(f(\boldsymbol{R}))\boldsymbol{w}$. Stationarity implies $\boldsymbol{x}I(f(\boldsymbol{R}))\boldsymbol{y}$. But $\boldsymbol{x}P(R_t)\boldsymbol{y}$ for all $t \in \mathbb{N}$, and we obtain a contradiction to weak Pareto. ■

Packel's response to his impossibility result consisted of restricting the domain to profiles that only contain generation-one preferences that are themselves stationary, thus ruling out the type of profile that he used in his impossibility theorem (and that we use in our Theorem 12.1). However, we think that the selfish domain represents a plausible restriction of preferences in an intergenerational setting, and we therefore propose to amend Ferejohn and Page's stationarity condition in accordance with this domain assumption.

12.4. Multiprofile Stationarity

In Ferejohn and Page's stationarity axiom, the same profile $\boldsymbol{R}$ is applied both before and after the common period-one alternative is eliminated. While this property is plausible if individual preferences are themselves stationary, its appeal is less obvious under alternative domain restrictions. Specifically, if individual preferences are selfish, it seems natural to eliminate the (common) first-period component not only from the streams but also from the profile. This leads us to the following alternative version of the axiom.

Multiprofile Stationarity. For all $\boldsymbol{x}, \boldsymbol{y} \in X^\infty$ and for all $\boldsymbol{R} \in \mathcal{D}$, if $x_1 = y_1$, then

$$\boldsymbol{x} f(\boldsymbol{R}) \boldsymbol{y} \Leftrightarrow \boldsymbol{x}_{\geq 2} f(\boldsymbol{R}_{\geq 2}) \boldsymbol{y}_{\geq 2}.$$

Note that the continuation profile $\boldsymbol{R}_{\geq 2}$ is only used in comparing the continuation streams $\boldsymbol{x}_{\geq 2}$ and $\boldsymbol{y}_{\geq 2}$ in the definition of multi-profile stationarity. Thus, there is no conflict with the selfish domain assumption.

We now examine the implications of our multi-profile stationarity axiom. In particular, it allows us to characterize the *chronological dictatorship.* This variant of a lexicographic dictatorship consults *generation one* first but, in the case of its indifference, moves on to consult *generation two* regarding the ranking of two streams, and so on. Thus, there still is a strong dictatorship component, but it is not as extreme as that generated by stationarity—and it is compatible with Pareto indifference. Moreover, the chronological dictatorship is a social welfare function and not merely a collective choice rule.

The chronological dictatorship f^{CD} is defined as follows (again, recall that the orderings $\succcurlyeq_t$ on X are sufficient to identify the corresponding selfish orderings R_t on X^∞). For all $\boldsymbol{x}, \boldsymbol{y} \in X^\infty$ and for all $\boldsymbol{R} \in \mathcal{R}_S^\infty$, $\boldsymbol{x} f^{CD}(\boldsymbol{R}) \boldsymbol{y}$ if and only if

$$\left[x_\tau I(\succcurlyeq_\tau) y_\tau \forall \tau \in \mathbb{N}\right] \quad \text{or}$$

$$\left[\exists t \in \mathbb{N} \text{ such that } \{x_\tau I(\succcurlyeq_\tau) y_\tau \forall \tau < t \text{ and } x_t P(\succcurlyeq_t) y_t\}\right].$$

In order to prove a version of Hansson's theorem that applies to the selfish domain, we require Pareto indifference as an additional axiom. A modification of this nature is required because the selfish domain is not sufficiently rich to generate arbitrary rankings of all streams of alternatives. For instance, whenever we have two streams of per-period alternatives $\boldsymbol{x}$ and $\boldsymbol{y}$ such that $x_t = y_t$ for some selfish generation $t \in \mathbb{N}$, this selfish generation *must* declare $\boldsymbol{x}$ and $\boldsymbol{y}$ indifferent: a per-period alternative cannot be strictly preferred to itself; in fact, indifference is forced by the conjunction of selfish domain and reflexivity. More precisely, this addition of Pareto indifference to the list of axioms is necessitated by the observation that a fundamental preliminary result—an adaptation of Sen's [18, p. 4] *field expansion lemma* to our selfish domain setting—fails to be true if merely selfish domain, weak Pareto, and independence of irrelevant alternatives are imposed.

Our version of the field expansion lemma is stated below. Because we invoke Pareto indifference in addition to the remaining axioms of the statement of the lemma, its proof varies from that of the standard formulation.

LEMMA 12.1. Let f be a social welfare function that satisfies selfish domain, weak Pareto, Pareto indifference and independence of irrelevant alternatives, and let $T \subseteq \mathbb{N}$. If there exist $\boldsymbol{x}, \boldsymbol{y} \in X^{\infty}$ such that $x_t \neq y_t$ for all $t \in \mathbb{N}$ and T is decisive for $\boldsymbol{x}$ over $\boldsymbol{y}$ for f, then T is decisive for f.

PROOF. Let f be a social welfare function that satisfies the axioms of the lemma statement, and let $T \subseteq \mathbb{N}$. Suppose that $\boldsymbol{x}, \boldsymbol{y} \in X^{\infty}$ are such that $x_t \neq y_t$ for all $t \in \mathbb{N}$ and that T is decisive for $\boldsymbol{x}$ over $\boldsymbol{y}$ for f. In order to cover all possible cases, we have to establish that T is decisive:

(i) for $\boldsymbol{x}$ over $\boldsymbol{z}$ for f for all $\boldsymbol{z} \in X^{\infty} \setminus \{\boldsymbol{x}, \boldsymbol{y}\}$;
(ii) for $\boldsymbol{z}$ over $\boldsymbol{y}$ for f for all $\boldsymbol{z} \in X^{\infty} \setminus \{\boldsymbol{x}, \boldsymbol{y}\}$;
(iii) for $\boldsymbol{z}$ over $\boldsymbol{x}$ for f for all $\boldsymbol{z} \in X^{\infty} \setminus \{\boldsymbol{x}, \boldsymbol{y}\}$;
(iv) for $\boldsymbol{y}$ over $\boldsymbol{z}$ for f for all $\boldsymbol{z} \in X^{\infty} \setminus \{\boldsymbol{x}, \boldsymbol{y}\}$;
(v) for $\boldsymbol{z}$ over $\boldsymbol{w}$ for all distinct $\boldsymbol{z}, \boldsymbol{w} \in X^{\infty} \setminus \{\boldsymbol{x}, \boldsymbol{y}\}$;
(vi) for $\boldsymbol{y}$ over $\boldsymbol{x}$ for f.

First, note that if there exists $t \in T$ such that $z_t = x_t$ (or $z_t = y_t$ or $z_t = w_t$, depending on which case applies), T is trivially decisive for $\boldsymbol{x}$ over $\boldsymbol{z}$ (or for $\boldsymbol{z}$ over $\boldsymbol{y}$ or for $\boldsymbol{z}$ over $\boldsymbol{x}$ or for $\boldsymbol{y}$ over $\boldsymbol{z}$ or for $\boldsymbol{z}$ over $\boldsymbol{w}$, respectively) because, by reflexivity and the assumption that preferences are selfish, we must have that $\boldsymbol{x}$ and $\boldsymbol{z}$ (or $\boldsymbol{z}$ and $\boldsymbol{y}$ or $\boldsymbol{z}$ and $\boldsymbol{w}$) are indifferent for any generation $t \in T$ such that $z_t = x_t$ (or $z_t = y_t$ or $z_t = w_t$) and, thus, the implication defining decisiveness is vacuously satisfied for any selfish profile. Thus, we can suppose that, for all $t \in \mathbb{N}$, $z_t \neq x_t$ in (i) and (iii), $z_t \neq y_t$ in (ii) and (iv), and $z_t \neq w_t$ in (v). Furthermore, observe that $x_t \neq y_t$ is assumed throughout (and, in particular, in (vi)) due to the hypothesis of the lemma.
(i) Define an alternative $\boldsymbol{z}' \in X^{\infty}$ by letting

$$z'_t = \begin{cases} z_t & \text{if } z_t \neq y_t; \\ z'_t \in X \setminus \{x_t, y_t\} & \text{if } z_t = y_t \end{cases}$$

for all $t \in \mathbb{N}$. By selfish domain, we can define three profiles $\boldsymbol{R}, \boldsymbol{R}', \boldsymbol{R}'' \in \mathcal{R}_S^\infty$ such that

$$\begin{aligned}
\left[\boldsymbol{x} P(R_t)\boldsymbol{z} \text{ and } \boldsymbol{x} P(R_t')\boldsymbol{y}\right] \quad & \forall t \in T; \\
\left[\boldsymbol{y} P(R_t')\boldsymbol{z}' \text{ and } \boldsymbol{z}' I(R_t'')\boldsymbol{z}\right] \quad & \forall t \in \mathbb{N}; \\
R_t''\big|_{\{\mathbf{x},\mathbf{z}'\}} = R_t'\big|_{\{\mathbf{x},\mathbf{z}'\}} \quad & \forall t \in \mathbb{N}; \\
R_t''\big|_{\{\mathbf{x},\mathbf{z}\}} = R_t\big|_{\{\mathbf{x},\mathbf{z}\}} \quad & \forall t \in \mathbb{N}.
\end{aligned}$$

Because T is decisive for $\boldsymbol{x}$ over $\boldsymbol{y}$ for f by assumption, we have $\boldsymbol{x} P(f(\boldsymbol{R}'))\boldsymbol{y}$. By weak Pareto, $\boldsymbol{y} P(f(\boldsymbol{R}'))\boldsymbol{z}'$. By transitivity, $\boldsymbol{x} P(f(\boldsymbol{R}'))\boldsymbol{z}'$. By independence of irrelevant alternatives, $\boldsymbol{x} P(f(\boldsymbol{R}''))\boldsymbol{z}'$. Pareto indifference implies $\boldsymbol{z}' I(f(\boldsymbol{R}''))\boldsymbol{z}$ and, by transitivity, $\boldsymbol{x} P(f(\boldsymbol{R}''))\boldsymbol{z}$. By independence of irrelevant alternatives, it follows that $\boldsymbol{x} P(f(\boldsymbol{R}))\boldsymbol{z}$ and that T is decisive for $\boldsymbol{x}$ over $\boldsymbol{z}$ for f.
(ii) Define an alternative $\boldsymbol{z}' \in X^\infty$ by letting

$$z_t' = \begin{cases} z_t & \text{if } z_t \neq x_t; \\ z_t' \in X \setminus \{x_t, y_t\} & \text{if } z_t = x_t \end{cases}$$

for all $t \in \mathbb{N}$. By selfish domain, we can define three profiles $\boldsymbol{R}, \boldsymbol{R}', \boldsymbol{R}'' \in \mathcal{R}_S^\infty$ such that

$$\begin{aligned}
\left[\boldsymbol{z} P(R_t)\boldsymbol{y} \text{ and } \boldsymbol{x} P(R_t')\boldsymbol{y}\right] \quad & \forall t \in T; \\
\left[\boldsymbol{z}' P(R_t')\boldsymbol{x} \text{ and } \boldsymbol{z}' I(R_t'')\boldsymbol{z}\right] \quad & \forall t \in \mathbb{N}; \\
R_t''\big|_{\{\mathbf{y},\mathbf{z}'\}} = R_t'\big|_{\{\mathbf{y},\mathbf{z}'\}} \quad & \forall t \in \mathbb{N}; \\
R_t''\big|_{\{\mathbf{y},\mathbf{z}\}} = R_t\big|_{\{\mathbf{y},\mathbf{z}\}} \quad & \forall t \in \mathbb{N}.
\end{aligned}$$

By weak Pareto, the decisiveness of T for $\boldsymbol{x}$ over $\boldsymbol{y}$ for f, transitivity, and independence of irrelevant alternatives, we obtain $\boldsymbol{z}' P(f(\boldsymbol{R}''))\boldsymbol{y}$. Applying Pareto indifference, transitivity, and independence of irrelevant alternatives, it follows that $\boldsymbol{z} P(f(\boldsymbol{R}))\boldsymbol{y}$ and that T is decisive for $\boldsymbol{z}$ over $\boldsymbol{y}$ for f.
(iii) Define an alternative $\boldsymbol{z}' \in X^\infty$ by letting

$$z_t' = \begin{cases} z_t & \text{if } z_t \neq y_t; \\ z_t' \in X \setminus \{x_t, y_t\} & \text{if } z_t = y_t \end{cases}$$

for all $t \in \mathbb{N}$. By selfish domain, we can define three profiles $\boldsymbol{R}, \boldsymbol{R}', \boldsymbol{R}'' \in \mathcal{R}_S^\infty$ such that

$$\left[\boldsymbol{z} P(R_t)\boldsymbol{x} \text{ and } \boldsymbol{z}' P(R_t')\boldsymbol{y}\right] \quad \forall t \in T;$$

$$\left[\boldsymbol{y} P(R_t')\boldsymbol{x} \text{ and } \boldsymbol{z}' I(R_t'')\boldsymbol{z}\right] \quad \forall t \in \mathbb{N};$$

$$R_t''\big|_{\{\mathbf{x},\mathbf{z}'\}} = R_t'\big|_{\{\mathbf{x},\mathbf{z}'\}} \quad \forall t \in \mathbb{N};$$

$$R_t''\big|_{\{\mathbf{x},\mathbf{z}\}} = R_t\big|_{\{\mathbf{x},\mathbf{z}\}} \quad \forall t \in \mathbb{N}.$$

By the decisiveness of T for $\boldsymbol{z}'$ over $\boldsymbol{y}$ for f (see (ii)), weak Pareto, transitivity, and independence of irrelevant alternatives, we obtain $\boldsymbol{z}' P(f(\boldsymbol{R}''))\boldsymbol{x}$. Pareto indifference, transitivity, and independence of irrelevant alternatives together imply that $\boldsymbol{z} P(f(\boldsymbol{R}))\boldsymbol{x}$ and that T is decisive for $\boldsymbol{z}$ over $\boldsymbol{x}$ for f.
(iv) Define an alternative $\boldsymbol{z}' \in X^\infty$ by letting

$$z_t' = \begin{cases} z_t & \text{if } z_t \neq x_t; \\ z_t' \in X \setminus \{x_t, y_t\} & \text{if } z_t = x_t \end{cases}$$

for all $t \in \mathbb{N}$. By selfish domain, we can define three profiles $\boldsymbol{R}, \boldsymbol{R}', \boldsymbol{R}'' \in \mathcal{R}_S^\infty$ such that

$$\left[\boldsymbol{y} P(R_t)\boldsymbol{z} \text{ and } \boldsymbol{x} P(R_t')\boldsymbol{z}'\right] \quad \forall t \in T;$$

$$\left[\boldsymbol{y} P(R_t')\boldsymbol{x} \text{ and } \boldsymbol{z}' I(R_t'')\boldsymbol{z}\right] \quad \forall t \in \mathbb{N};$$

$$R_t''\big|_{\{\mathbf{y},\mathbf{z}'\}} = R_t'\big|_{\{\mathbf{y},\mathbf{z}'\}} \quad \forall t \in \mathbb{N};$$

$$R_t''\big|_{\{\mathbf{y},\mathbf{z}\}} = R_t\big|_{\{\mathbf{y},\mathbf{z}\}} \quad \forall t \in \mathbb{N}.$$

By weak Pareto, the decisiveness of T for $\boldsymbol{x}$ over $\boldsymbol{z}'$ for f (see (i)), transitivity, and independence of irrelevant alternatives, we obtain $\boldsymbol{y} P(f(\boldsymbol{R}''))\boldsymbol{z}'$. Pareto indifference, transitivity, and independence of irrelevant alternatives together imply that $\boldsymbol{y} P(f(\boldsymbol{R}))\boldsymbol{z}$ and that T is decisive for $\boldsymbol{y}$ over $\boldsymbol{z}$ for f.
(v) Let two alternatives $\boldsymbol{z}', \boldsymbol{w}' \in X^\infty$ be such that

$$z_t' = \begin{cases} z_t & \text{if } z_t \neq x_t; \\ z_t' \in X \setminus \{x_t, w_t\} & \text{if } z_t = x_t \end{cases}$$

for all $t \in T$ and

$$w_t' = \begin{cases} w_t & \text{if } w_t \neq x_t; \\ w_t' \in X \setminus \{x_t, z_t\} & \text{if } w_t = x_t \end{cases}$$

for all $t \in T$. Note that, because $z_t \neq w_t$ for all $t \in T$ in this case, x_t, z'_t, and w'_t are pairwise distinct for all $t \in T$. By selfish domain, we can define three profiles $\boldsymbol{R}, \boldsymbol{R}', \boldsymbol{R}'' \in \mathcal{R}_S^\infty$ such that

$$\left[\boldsymbol{z} P(R_t) \boldsymbol{w} \text{ and } \boldsymbol{z}' P(R'_t) \boldsymbol{x} P(R'_t) \boldsymbol{w}'\right] \quad \forall t \in T;$$

$$\left[\boldsymbol{z}' I(R''_t) \boldsymbol{z} \text{ and } \boldsymbol{w}' I(R''_t) \boldsymbol{w}\right] \quad \forall t \in \mathbb{N};$$

$$R''_t\big|_{\{\mathbf{z}',\mathbf{w}'\}} = R'_t\big|_{\{\mathbf{z}',\mathbf{w}'\}} \quad \forall t \in \mathbb{N};$$

$$R''_t\big|_{\{\mathbf{z},\mathbf{w}\}} = R_t\big|_{\{\mathbf{z},\mathbf{w}\}} \quad \forall t \in \mathbb{N}.$$

By the decisiveness of T for $\boldsymbol{z}'$ over $\boldsymbol{x}$ (see (iii)) and for $\boldsymbol{x}$ over $\boldsymbol{w}'$ (see (i)) for f, transitivity, and independence of irrelevant alternatives, we obtain $\boldsymbol{z}' P(f(\boldsymbol{R}''))\boldsymbol{w}'$. Now Pareto indifference, transitivity, and independence of irrelevant alternatives together imply that $\boldsymbol{z} P(f(\boldsymbol{R}))\boldsymbol{w}$ and that T is decisive for $\boldsymbol{z}$ over $\boldsymbol{w}$ for f.

(vi) Let $\boldsymbol{z} \in X^\infty$ be such that $z_t \notin \{x_t, y_t\}$ for all $t \in T$. By selfish domain, we can consider two profiles $\boldsymbol{R}, \boldsymbol{R}' \in \mathcal{R}_S^\infty$ such that

$$\boldsymbol{y} P(R'_t) \boldsymbol{z} P(R'_t) \boldsymbol{x} \quad \forall t \in T;$$

$$R'_t\big|_{\{\mathbf{x},\mathbf{y}\}} = R_t\big|_{\{\mathbf{x},\mathbf{y}\}} \quad \forall t \in \mathbb{N}.$$

By the decisiveness of T for $\boldsymbol{y}$ over $\boldsymbol{z}$ (see (iv)) and for $\boldsymbol{z}$ over $\boldsymbol{x}$ (see (iii)) for f and transitivity, we obtain $\boldsymbol{y} P(f(\boldsymbol{R}'))\boldsymbol{x}$. By independence of irrelevant alternatives, $\boldsymbol{y} P(f(\boldsymbol{R}))\boldsymbol{x}$ and T is decisive for $\boldsymbol{y}$ over $\boldsymbol{x}$ for f. ■

Our version of Hansson's theorem is formulated for the selfish domain. Again, Pareto indifference is added so as to be able to apply Lemma 12.1.

Theorem 12.3. If a social welfare function f satisfies selfish domain, weak Pareto, Pareto indifference, and independence of irrelevant alternatives, then the set of all decisive coalitions for f is an ultrafilter on $\mathbb{N}$.

Proof. Suppose f satisfies selfish domain, weak Pareto, Pareto indifference, and independence of irrelevant alternatives. We need to show that the set of all decisive coalitions for f has the three properties of an ultrafilter.

1. If $\emptyset$ is decisive for f, we obtain $\boldsymbol{x}P(f(\boldsymbol{R}))\boldsymbol{y}$ and $\boldsymbol{y}P(f(\boldsymbol{R}))\boldsymbol{x}$ for any two alternatives $\boldsymbol{x}, \boldsymbol{y} \in X^{\infty}$ and for any profile $\boldsymbol{R} \in \mathcal{R}_S^{\infty}$ such that all generations are indifferent between $\boldsymbol{x}$ and $\boldsymbol{y}$, which is impossible. Thus, $\emptyset$ cannot be decisive for f.
2. Let $T \subseteq \mathbb{N}$. Let $\boldsymbol{x}, \boldsymbol{y}, \boldsymbol{z} \in X^{\infty}$ be such that x_t, y_t, z_t are pairwise distinct for all $t \in \mathbb{N}$. By selfish domain, we can define a profile $\boldsymbol{R} \in \mathcal{R}_S^{\infty}$ such that

$$\boldsymbol{x}P(R_t)\boldsymbol{y} \text{ and } \boldsymbol{x}P(R_t)\boldsymbol{z} \quad \forall t \in T;$$

$$\boldsymbol{x}P(R_t)\boldsymbol{y} \text{ and } \boldsymbol{z}P(R_t)\boldsymbol{y} \quad \forall t \in \mathbb{N} \setminus T.$$

If $\boldsymbol{x}P(f(\boldsymbol{R}))\boldsymbol{z}$, T is decisive for $\boldsymbol{x}$ over $\boldsymbol{z}$ for f. Lemma 12.1 implies that T is decisive for f.

If $\neg\boldsymbol{x}P(f(\boldsymbol{R}))\boldsymbol{z}$, we have $\boldsymbol{z}f(\boldsymbol{R})\boldsymbol{x}$ by completeness. Furthermore, $\boldsymbol{x}P(f(\boldsymbol{R}))\boldsymbol{y}$ by weak Pareto. Transitivity implies $\boldsymbol{z}P(f(\boldsymbol{R}))\boldsymbol{y}$. Thus, $\mathbb{N} \setminus T$ is decisive for $\boldsymbol{y}$ over $\boldsymbol{z}$ and, by Lemma 12.1, $\mathbb{N} \setminus T$ is decisive for f.
3. Suppose T and T' are decisive for f. Let $\boldsymbol{x}, \boldsymbol{y}, \boldsymbol{z} \in X^{\infty}$ be such that x_t, y_t, z_t are pairwise distinct for all $t \in \mathbb{N}$. By selfish domain, we can define a profile $\boldsymbol{R} \in \mathcal{R}_S^{\infty}$ such that

$$\boldsymbol{x}P(R_t)\boldsymbol{y} \text{ and } \boldsymbol{x}P(R_t)\boldsymbol{z} \quad \forall t \in T \setminus T';$$

$$\boldsymbol{z}P(R_t)\boldsymbol{x}P(R_t)\boldsymbol{y} \quad \forall t \in T \cap T';$$

$$\boldsymbol{y}P(R_t)\boldsymbol{x} \text{ and } \boldsymbol{z}P(R_t)\boldsymbol{x} \quad \forall t \in T' \setminus T.$$

Because T is decisive for f, we have $\boldsymbol{x}P(f(\boldsymbol{R}))\boldsymbol{y}$. Because T' is decisive for f, we have $\boldsymbol{z}P(f(\boldsymbol{R}))\boldsymbol{x}$. By transitivity, $\boldsymbol{z}P(f(\boldsymbol{R}))\boldsymbol{y}$. This implies that $T \cap T'$ is decisive for $\boldsymbol{z}$ over $\boldsymbol{y}$ for f. By Lemma 12.1, $T \cap T'$ is decisive for f. ■

The next step toward our characterization result consists of showing that Ferejohn and Page's dictatorship result is true on a selfish domain when Pareto indifference is added and multi-profile stationarity is used instead of stationarity.

Theorem 12.4. If a social welfare function f satisfies selfish domain, weak Pareto, Pareto indifference, independence of irrelevant alternatives, and multi-profile stationarity, then generation one is a dictator for f.

Proof. Suppose f satisfies selfish domain, weak Pareto, Pareto indifference, independence of irrelevant alternatives, and multi-profile stationarity. By Theorem 12.3, the set of decisive coalitions for f is an ultrafilter on $\mathbb{N}$. Suppose $\mathbb{N} \setminus \{1\}$ is decisive for f.

Let x and y be two distinct elements of the set X of per-period alternatives and let $\succcurlyeq$ be an ordering on X such that $x\,P(\succcurlyeq)\,y$. By selfish domain, we can define a profile $\boldsymbol{R} \in \mathcal{R}_S^{\infty}$ by letting, for all $t \in \mathbb{N}$ and for all $\boldsymbol{x}, \boldsymbol{y} \in X^{\infty}$,

$$\boldsymbol{x} R_t \boldsymbol{y} \Leftrightarrow x_t \succcurlyeq y_t.$$

Now consider the streams

$$\boldsymbol{x} = (x, x, y, x, y, x, \ldots) = (x, \boldsymbol{y});$$

$$\boldsymbol{y} = (x, y, x, y, x, y, \ldots) = (x, \boldsymbol{z});$$

$$\boldsymbol{z} = (y, x, y, x, y, x, \ldots).$$

Recall that $\mathbb{N} \setminus \{1\}$ is decisive for f.

If $\{2, 4, 6, \ldots\}$ is decisive for f, we have $\boldsymbol{x} P(f(\boldsymbol{R}))\boldsymbol{y}$. By multi-profile stationarity,

$$\boldsymbol{y} = \boldsymbol{x}_{\geq 2} P(f(\boldsymbol{R}_{\geq 2}))\boldsymbol{y}_{\geq 2} = \boldsymbol{z},$$

contradicting the decisiveness of $\{2, 4, 6, \ldots.\}$ for$f$.

If $\{2, 4, 6, \ldots\}$ is not decisive for f, property F_2 of an ultrafilter implies that

$$\mathbb{N} \setminus \{2, 4, 6, \ldots\} = \{1, 3, 5, \ldots\}$$

is decisive for f. Because, in addition, $\mathbb{N} \setminus \{1\}$ is decisive for f, property F_3 of an ultrafilter implies that

$$\{3, 5, 7, \ldots\} = \{1, 3, 5, \ldots\} \cap (\mathbb{N} \setminus \{1\})$$

is decisive for f. By virtue of the decisiveness of $\{3, 5, 7, \ldots\}$ for f, we have $\boldsymbol{y} P(f(\boldsymbol{R}))\boldsymbol{x}$. By multi-profile stationarity,

$$\boldsymbol{z} = \boldsymbol{y}_{\geq 2} P(f(\boldsymbol{R}_{\geq 2}))\boldsymbol{x}_{\geq 2} = \boldsymbol{y},$$

contradicting the decisiveness of $\{3, 5, 7, \ldots.\}$ for f.

Thus, in all cases, we obtain a contradiction to the assumption that $\mathbb{N} \setminus \{1\}$ is decisive for f. Therefore, because of property F_2 of an ultrafilter, $\{1\}$ is decisive for f and, thus, generation one is a dictator for f. ■

The reason that generation one must be the generation that dictates is, again, a consequence of the unidirectional nature of the flow of time—and, thus, the unequal manner in which multiprofile stationarity treats generations. The example constructed in the preceding proof involving the streams $\boldsymbol{x}$, $\boldsymbol{y}$, and $\boldsymbol{z}$ can be used to make this point: just as the assumption that the coalition $\{2, 4, 6, \ldots\}$ is decisive for f leads to a contradiction in the relevant step of the proof, the same reasoning regarding the assumption that generation two is a dictator leads to a contradiction. Clearly, the example is easily amended so as to apply to any generation other than generation one.

The final result of this essay characterizes f^{CD}.

THEOREM 12.5. A social welfare function f satisfies selfish domain, weak Pareto, Pareto indifference, independence of irrelevant alternatives, and multi-profile stationarity if and only if $f = f^{CD}$.

PROOF. That f^{CD} satisfies the axioms can be verified by the reader. To prove the converse implication, suppose f satisfies the required axioms. It is sufficient to show that, for all $\boldsymbol{x}, \boldsymbol{y} \in X^\infty$ and for all $\boldsymbol{R} \in \mathcal{R}_S^\infty$,

$$\boldsymbol{x} I(f^{CD}(\boldsymbol{R}))\boldsymbol{y} \Rightarrow \boldsymbol{x} I(f(\boldsymbol{R}))\boldsymbol{y} \tag{12.1}$$

and

$$\boldsymbol{x} P(f^{CD}(\boldsymbol{R}))\boldsymbol{y} \Rightarrow \boldsymbol{x} P(f(\boldsymbol{R}))\boldsymbol{y}. \tag{12.2}$$

(12.1) follows immediately from Pareto indifference. To prove (12.2), suppose $t \in \mathbb{N}$, $\boldsymbol{x}, \boldsymbol{y} \in X^\infty$ and $\boldsymbol{R} \in \mathcal{R}_S^\infty$ are such that

$$x_\tau I(\succcurlyeq_\tau) y_\tau \forall \tau < t \text{ and } x_t P(\succcurlyeq_t) y_t.$$

If $t = 1$, let $\boldsymbol{z} = \boldsymbol{y}$; if $t \geq 2$, let $\boldsymbol{z} = (x_1, \ldots, x_{t-1}, \boldsymbol{y}_{\geq t})$. By Pareto indifference, $\boldsymbol{y} I(f(\boldsymbol{R}))\boldsymbol{z}$. Transitivity implies

$$\boldsymbol{x} f(\boldsymbol{R}) \boldsymbol{y} \Leftrightarrow \boldsymbol{x} f(\boldsymbol{R}) \boldsymbol{z}.$$

Together with the application of multi-profile stationarity $t-1$ times and noting that $\boldsymbol{z}_{\geq t} = \boldsymbol{y}_{\geq t}$, we obtain

$$\boldsymbol{x} f(\boldsymbol{R})\boldsymbol{y} \Leftrightarrow \boldsymbol{x} f(\boldsymbol{R})\boldsymbol{z} \Leftrightarrow \boldsymbol{x}_{\geq t} f(\boldsymbol{R}_{\geq t})\boldsymbol{z}_{\geq t} \Leftrightarrow \boldsymbol{x}_{\geq t} f(\boldsymbol{R}_{\geq t})\boldsymbol{y}_{\geq t}. \quad (12.3)$$

By Theorem 12.4, the relative ranking of $\boldsymbol{x}_{\geq t}$ and $\boldsymbol{y}_{\geq t}$ according to $\boldsymbol{R}_{\geq t}$ is determined by the strict preference for $\boldsymbol{x}$ over $\boldsymbol{y}$ according to the first generation in the profile $\boldsymbol{R}_{\geq t}$ (which is generation t in $\boldsymbol{R}$), so that $\boldsymbol{x}_{\geq t} P(f(\boldsymbol{R}_{\geq t}))\boldsymbol{y}_{\geq t}$ and, by (12.3), $\boldsymbol{x} P(f(\boldsymbol{R}))\boldsymbol{y}$. ■

12.5. Concluding Remarks

In concluding this essay, it may be worthwhile to clarify the relationship between the multiprofile version of intergenerational social choice theory analyzed in this essay, on the one hand, and the theory of evaluating infinite intergenerational utility streams, on the other. The latter theory capitalizes on the Koopmans [15] analysis of impatience and the Diamond [9] impossibility theorem on the existence of continuous social evaluation orderings on the set of infinite utility streams satisfying the Sidgwick [19] anonymity principle and the Pareto principle. Among many contributions that appeared after Diamond, those that are most relevant in the present context include Svensson [21], Basu and Mitra [3; 4], Asheim, Mitra, and Tungodden [2], Bossert, Sprumont, and Suzumura [5], and Hara, Shinotsuka, Suzumura, and Xu [13]. Although these two lines of inquiry are related in the sense that both are concerned with aggregating generational evaluations of their well-being into an overall social evaluation, they contrast sharply in at least two respects. In the first place, the latter investigation is *welfaristic* in the sense of basing the overall social evaluation on the infinite generational utility streams, whereas the former exercise is free from such an early commitment to this informational basis. In the second place, while the latter approach hinges squarely on the continuity assumption even in a vestigial form, the former has nothing to do with any continuity assumption on social evaluation orderings. More substantially, the Sidgwick anonymity principle, which plays a crucial role in establishing the Diamond impossibility theorem and related results, has nothing to do with our impossibility theorems. Since continuity is a requirement that is rather technical in nature, getting rid of the dependence on this assumption may be counted as a virtue rather than a vice. Although the Sidgwick anonymity principle has an obvious intuitive appeal, it is fortunate that we need not go against this plausible axiom in defending our approach. This principle can surely be added to the list of axioms, but all that is thereby obtained is another set of Arrow-type impossibility results, some of which will even contain logical redundancies.

12.6. References

[1] Arrow, K. J., *Social Choice and Individual Values,* New York: John Wiley & Sons, 1951; 2nd edn., 1963.

[2] Asheim, G. B., T. Mitra, and B. Tungodden, "A New Equity Condition for Infinite Utility Streams and the Possibility of Being Paretian," in J. Roemer and K. Suzumura, eds., *Intergenerational Equity and Sustainability,* Basingstoke, England: Palgrave Macmillan, 2007, 55–68.

[3] Basu, K., and T. Mitra, "Aggregating Infinite Utility Streams with Intergenerational Equity: The Impossibility of Being Paretian," *Econometrica* **71**, 2003, 1557–1563.

[4] Basu, K., and T. Mitra, "Utilitarianism for Infinite Utility Streams: A New Welfare Criterion and Its Axiomatic Characterization," *Journal of Economic Theory* **133**, 2007, 350–373.

[5] Bossert, W., Y. Sprumont, and K. Suzumura, "Ordering Infinite Utility Streams," *Journal of Economic Theory* **135**, 2007, 579–589. Essay 11 of this volume.

[6] Campbell, D. E., "Intergenerational Social Choice without the Pareto Principle," *Journal of Economic Theory* **50**, 1990, 414–423.

[7] Campbell, D. E., "Quasitransitive Intergenerational Social Choice for Economic Environments," *Journal of Mathematical Economics* **21**, 1992, 229–247.

[8] Campbell, D. E., *Equity, Efficiency, and Social Choice,* Oxford: Clarendon Press, 1992.

[9] Diamond, P., "The Evaluation of Infinite Utility Streams," *Econometrica* **33**, 1965, 170–177.

[10] Ferejohn, J., and T. Page, "On the Foundations of Intertemporal Choice," *American Journal of Agricultural Economics* **60**, 1978, 269–275.

[11] Fishburn, P. C., "Arrow's Impossibility Theorem: Concise Proof and Infinite Voters," *Journal of Economic Theory* **2**, 1970, 103–106.

[12] Hansson, B., "The Existence of Group Preference Functions," *Public Choice* **38**, 1976, 89–98.

[13] Hara, C., T. Shinotsuka, K. Suzumura, and Y. Xu, "Continuity and Egalitarianism in the Evaluation of Infinite Utility Streams," *Social Choice and Welfare* **31**, 2008, 179–191.

[14] Kirman, A. P., and D. Sondermann, "Arrow's Theorem, Many Agents, and Invisible Dictators," *Journal of Economic Theory* **5**, 1972, 267–277.

[15] Koopmans, T. C., "Stationary Ordinal Utility and Impatience," *Econometrica* **28**, 1960, 287–309.

[16] Packel, E., "Impossibility Results in the Axiomatic Theory of Intertemporal Choice," *Public Choice* **35**, 1980, 219–227.

[17] Sen, A. K., "Personal Utilities and Public Judgements: Or What's Wrong with Welfare Economics?" *Economic Journal* **89**, 1979, 537–558.
[18] Sen, A. K., "Rationality and Social Choice," *American Economic Review* **85**, 1995, 1–24.
[19] Sidgwick, H., *The Methods of Ethics,* 7th edn., London: Macmillan and Co., 1907.
[20] Suzumura, K., "Welfare Economics beyond Welfarist Consequentialism," *Japanese Economic Review* **51**, 2000, 1–32. Essay 27 of this volume.
[21] Svensson, L.-G., "Equity among Generations," *Econometrica* **48**, 1980, 1251–1256.

PART IV

INDIVIDUAL RIGHTS AND SOCIAL WELFARE

Introduction to Part IV

> The liberty of the individual must be thus far limited: he must not make himself a nuisance to other people.
>
> —JOHN STUART MILL, *On Liberty*, 1859

> Liberty is not a means to a higher political end. It is itself the highest political end.
>
> —LORD ACTON, address, "The History of Freedom in Antiquity," February 26, 1877

> Liberty means responsibility. That is why most men dread it.
>
> —GEORGE BERNARD SHAW, "Maxims for Revolutionists," *Man and Superman*, 1903

It was in the session chaired by Lawrence Klein at the 1948 Cleveland meeting of the Econometric Society that Kenneth Arrow made the first presentation of his *general impossibility theorem* on democratic methods of collective decision making. According to Arrow's recollection (Arrow and Kelly [1, p. 18]): "In the audience was this contentious Canadian, David McCord Wright, who objected because among the objectives, [Arrow] hadn't mentioned freedom as one of the essential values in social choice, and apparently he went out of the room saying that Klein and Arrow were communists." As a matter of fact, this objection could have been settled easily by saying: "If you could give me your formal articulation of freedom as an essential value in social choice, I would surely add it to my list of values and end up with an impossibility theorem all the more."

However, the Wright saga is not altogether without interest. In the first place, as Isaiah Berlin acutely observed, "the connexion between democracy and individual liberty is a good deal more tenuous than it seemed to many advocates of both. The desire to be governed by myself, or at any rate to participate in the process by which my life is to be controlled, may be as deep a wish as that of a free area for action, and perhaps historically older.

But it is not a desire for the same thing. So different is it, indeed, as to have led in the end to the great clash of ideologies that dominates our world" (Berlin [4, pp. 15–16]). Thus, it is all too natural to ask if a democratic and liberal social choice rule could be designed at the cost of compromising some other values introduced by Arrow. Wright should be congratulated for having made a positive contribution to push the Arrow social choice theory forward by bringing this basic problem to the fore.

In the second place, "a formal articulation of freedom as an essential value in social choice" is easier said than done, and the introduction of a value of freedom into the formal framework of social choice theory was left unattended for quite some time after the Wright saga. Indeed, it was not until 1970 that Amartya Sen [10; 11, Chapter 6*] gave a precise articulation of the liberal value in terms of social choice rules: If two social alternatives x and y differ only in the specification of personal characteristics of an individual, say, Ian, and Ian himself prefers x to y, then the social choice rule should be such that society never chooses y from any opportunity set of social alternatives that contains x. Sen requires that the special say guaranteed for Ian should likewise be guaranteed for all other individuals. The fruit of Sen's tour de force was the well-known impossibility theorem to the effect that *there exists no social choice rule that satisfies the democratic value in the form of the Pareto principle as well as the liberal value in the sense of Sen.*

Part IV of this volume consists of four essays. The first two essays, viz., Essay 13 ("On the Consistency of Libertarian Claims") and Essay 14 ("Liberal Paradox and the Voluntary Exchange of Rights Exercising"), are written by accepting Sen's articulation of the liberal value and focusing *either* on the resolution of his impossibility theorem[1] *or* on the examination of the logical robustness thereof. In sharp contrast with the first two essays, the third essay, viz., Essay 15 ("Individual Rights Revisited"), is meant to cast serious doubts on the appropriateness of Sen's articulation of the liberal value and to propose an alternative game form approach to individual liberty. In conspicuous contrast with Sen's method of articulation, which captured the essence of the liberal value by means of a certain specific property of social choice rules, the game form articulation proposes to capture the essence of the liberal value by means of the *freedom of choice* that the involved individual entertains with

1. See Gibbard [8], Sen [12], and Suzumura [16, Chapter 7; 17; 18, Section 4] for alternative resolution schemes for Sen's impossibility theorem.

respect to the decision on his/her private characteristic of social alternatives.[2] The final essay, Essay 16 ("Welfare, Rights, and Social Choice Procedure: A Perspective"), provides a succinct overview of the meaning and relevance of the issue of liberal values in social choice theory.[3]

As an auxiliary step in bringing the importance of Sen's contribution into sharp relief, let us tersely compare Arrow's general impossibility theorem with Sen's impossibility of a Paretian liberal. The focus of our comparison is threefold: *formal structure*, *implication*, and *raison d'être* of the liberal rights. In the first place, there is a conspicuous contrast between the formal structure of Arrow's theorem and that of Sen's theorem. Indeed, while the validity of the former theorem hinges squarely on the axiom of collective rationality and the axiom of independence of irrelevant alternatives, the validity of the latter theorem is free from these controversial axioms altogether. To crystallize this contrast, it is often said that Arrow's theorem belongs to the class of *multiple-profile impossibility theorems*. This is why the theorem hinges crucially on the axiom that involves multiple profiles of individual preference orderings. In contrast, Sen's theorem belongs to the class of *single-profile impossibility theorems*, where there is no explicit reference to more than one profile of individual preference orderings.

In the second place, Arrow's impossibility theorem is a logical consequence of the parsimonious use of ordinal welfare information at the individual level in the process of forming collective welfare judgments. Not only is the admissible welfare information at the individual level restricted to ordinal welfare without interpersonal comparability, but also the axiom of independence of irrelevant alternatives imposes further requirements on the parsimonious use of information to the following effect: For any pair $\{x, y\}$ of social alternatives, over which we must form welfare judgments at the social level, the admissible use of welfare information at the individual level is confined to the individual welfare comparisons between x and y, and nothing else. Contrary to the parsimonious use of welfare information in the Arrow theorem, even the use of richer welfare information at the individual level admitting cardinality and/or interpersonal comparability of

2. Those who are interested in further developments of the game form approach to individual liberty are referred to Deb [5; 6], Deb, Pattanaik, and Razzolini [7], Peleg [9], Sen [14], Sugden [15], and Suzumura [17; 18].

3. In this volume, I have decided to include this brief overview rather than the more extensive survey and evaluation of the relevant literature on welfare and liberty, viz., Suzumura [18].

individual welfare does *not* provide us with a surefire escape route from Sen's impossibility theorem. Thus, both Arrow and Sen uncovered serious logical difficulties of democratic methods of social choice, but they shed light on different corners by their respective searchlights.

In the third place, Arrow expressed his skepticism about the raison d'être of liberal rights à la Sen. In an interview for *Social Choice and Welfare*, Arrow was asked about Sen's Paretian liberal approach and responded by saying: "I thought that was stunning and penetrating to a very important issue. But . . . why do we have rights? . . . I view rights as arrangements that may help you in achieving a higher utility level" (Arrow and Kelly [1, p. 22]). This is an instrumental view on liberal rights. If this view could be coherently pursued to its logical end in accordance with the plan, no separate room would be left for liberal rights. Recollect that Jeremy Bentham, a harsh critic of the concept of inviolable natural rights, is known for this famous criticism: "Natural rights is simple nonsense: natural and imprescriptible rights, rhetorical nonsense—nonsense upon stilts" (Bentham [3, p. 501]). In one way or the other, the concept of liberal rights seems to be in need of the raison d'être for the sake of its defense. Such a defense does not seem to be made available up until now.

References

[1] Arrow, K. J., and J. S. Kelly, "An Interview with Kenneth J. Arrow," Part II of K. J. Arrow, A. K. Sen, and K. Suzumura, "Kenneth Arrow on Social Choice Theory," in Arrow, Sen, and Suzumura [2, pp. 3–27].

[2] Arrow, K. J., A. K. Sen, and K. Suzumura, eds., *Handbook of Social Choice and Welfare*, Vol. II, Amsterdam: North-Holland/Elsevier, 2011.

[3] Bentham, J.,"Anarchical Fallacies." First published in English in J. Bowring, ed., *The Works of Jeremy Bentham*, Vol. II, Edinburgh: William Tait, 1843. Reprinted in Bristol, UK: Theommes Press, 1955, 489-534.

[4] Berlin, I., *Two Concepts of Liberty*, Oxford: Clarendon Press, 1958.

[5] Deb, R., "Waiver, Effectivity and Rights as Game Forms," *Economica* **61**, 1994, 167–178.

[6] Deb, R., "Rights as Alternative Game Forms," *Social Choice and Welfare* **22**, 2004, 83–111.

[7] Deb, R., P. K. Pattanaik, and L. Razzolini, "Game Forms, Rights, and the Efficiency of Social Outcomes," *Journal of Economic Theory* **72**, 1997, 74–95.

[8] Gibbard, A., "A Pareto-Consistent Libertarian Claim," *Journal of Economic Theory* 7, 1974, 388–410.

[9] Peleg, B., "Effectivity Functions, Game Forms, Games, and Rights," *Social Choice and Welfare* **15**, 1998, 67–80.

[10] Sen, A. K., "The Impossibility of a Paretian Liberal," *Journal of Political Economy* **78**, 1970, 152–157.

[11] Sen, A. K., *Collective Choice and Social Welfare*, San Francisco: Holden-Day, 1970. Republished, Amsterdam: North-Holland, 1979.

[12] Sen, A. K., "Liberty, Unanimity and Rights," *Economica* **43**, 1976, 217–245.

[13] Sen, A. K., "Personal Utilities and Public Judgments: Or What's Wrong with Welfare Economics?" *Economic Journal* **89**, 1979, 537–558.

[14] Sen, A. K., "Minimal Liberty," *Economica* **59**, 1992, 139–159.

[15] Sugden, R., "Liberty, Preference, and Choice," *Economics and Philosophy* **1**, 1985, 213–229.

[16] Suzumura, K., *Rational Choice, Collective Decisions and Social Welfare*, New York: Cambridge University Press, 1983. Reissued in paperback, 2009.

[17] Suzumura, K., "Alternative Approaches to Libertarian Rights in the Theory of Social Choice," in K. J. Arrow, ed., *Markets and Welfare: Issues in Contemporary Economics*, Vol. I, London: Macmillan, 1990, 215–242.

[18] Suzumura, K., "Welfarism, Individual Rights, and Procedural Fairness," in Arrow, Sen, and Suzumura [2, pp. 605–685].

ESSAY 13

On the Consistency of Libertarian Claims

13.1. Introduction

If one social state is unanimously preferred to another, it is difficult to argue that the former state should not be socially chosen over the latter, and, as a result, the claim that the collective choice rule should be Pareto-inclusive has seldom been challenged. It may also be claimed that certain matters are purely personal, and our collective choice rule should empower each person to decide what should be socially chosen, no matter what others may think, in choices over personal matters. Sen [8] has shown that these two principles conflict, namely, there exists no Pareto-inclusive collective choice rule (with an unrestricted applicability) satisfying a mild libertarian claim.

Since the logical correctness of Sen's argument is beyond any doubt, we are forced to weaken either the Pareto rule or the libertarian claim in order to avoid this difficulty, unless we renounce the general applicability of our collective choice procedure. Although many subsequent contributions have modified libertarian claims in favor of the Pareto rule, one of the lessons Sen [8; 9] has drawn from his *paradox of a Paretian liberal* is that a mechanical use of the Pareto rule (irrespective of the motivation behind

First published in *Review of Economic Studies* **45**, 1978, pp. 329–342. A flaw in the original proof of Theorem 13.1 was rectified in "A Correction," *Review of Economic Studies* **46**, 1979, p. 743. We are indebted to A. K. Sen and J. Wise for their comments and discussions on an early draft of this work. Thanks are also due to the editor, Peter Hammond, and the anonymous referees of *Review of Economic Studies*. We retain sole responsibility for remaining opaqueness and errors.

people's preferences) seems unsound. In line with this observation, Sen [10, Section XI] has proposed a resolution of this paradox that restricts the use of the Pareto rule. We will succinctly reconstruct his resolution with some clarifications of the structure of his rights assignment (in Section 13.2) and then show (in Section 13.3) that one of the Gibbard paradoxes [4, Section 3] can be solved by essentially the same line of argument. This might be of some importance, because Sen's paradox and that of Gibbard are essentially different in nature. Suffice it to quote a passage from Gibbard [4, p. 394]: "[Sen's libertarianism] guarantees each person a special voice on only one pair of alternatives, but the special voice is a strong one: the alternative he prefers is to be preferable, no matter what his other preferences. [Gibbard's libertarianism] guarantees each person a special voice on many pairs of alternatives . . . but the voice is limited. The one he prefers is to be preferable if indeed he prefers its distinguishing feature unconditionally; otherwise his preference may be overridden."

In Section 13.4, we examine the possibility of introducing information on interpersonal welfare comparisons into the conceptual framework. It will be shown that, if the rights exercising is restricted by the Rawlsian maximin justice consideration (which is now available to us by the stronger informational basis we are working on), the modified libertarian claim is made compatible with the Pareto principle. This is in sharp contrast with Sen's [10, p. 228] assertion that "for this class of impossibility results, introducing interpersonal comparisons is not much of a cure (in contrast with the impossibility results of the Arrow type)," which he has drawn from Kelly's [6] *impossibility of a just liberal*.

In Section 13.5, we briefly summarize our conclusions. Some basic concepts and lemmas are put forward in the appendix at the end of the essay.

13.2. A Resolution of Sen's Paradox

13.2.1. Pareto Rule and Sen's Libertarian Claim

Let X be the set of all *conceivable* social states, and N a set of n individuals, each of whom has a preference ordering R_i on X, together forming a *profile* of individual preference orderings. We say that $i \in N$ weakly prefers x to y

if and only if $(x, y) \in R_i$. The strict preference relation corresponding to R_i is denoted by $P(R_i) : (x, y) \in P(R_i)$ if and only if

$$[(x, y) \in R_i \; \& \; (y, x) \notin R_i].$$

$\mathcal{S}$ stands for the set of all nonempty *finite* subsets of X. (An intended interpretation is that each $S \in \mathcal{S}$ is the set of available states.) A *collective choice rule* (CCR) is a method of choosing, for each profile, a *social choice function* (SCF) on $\mathcal{S}$. Given a profile $\boldsymbol{R} = (R_1, R_2, \ldots, R_n)$, a CCR f amalgamates this into an SCF:

$$C = f(R_1, R_2, \ldots, R_n). \tag{13.1}$$

Given an $S \in \mathcal{S}$, $C(S)$ represents the set of socially chosen states from S when the profile $\boldsymbol{R} = (R_1, R_2, \ldots, R_n)$ prevails. We want our CCR to be generally applicable and Pareto-inclusive:

Condition U (unrestricted domain). The domain of CCR consists of all logically possible profiles of individual preference orderings.

Condition P (Pareto rule). For all $x, y \in X$, $(x, y) \in \bigcap_{i \in N} P(R_i)$ implies

$$[x \in S \; \& \; y \in C(S)]$$

for no $S \in \mathcal{S}$.

Our third requirement is that CCR should respect some personal liberty. Let Ω be the set of all nonempty subsets of $X \times X$ and denote by Ω^n the n-fold product of Ω. Then the requirement reads as follows:

Condition SL (Sen's libertarian claim).[1] There exists a *symmetric*

$$\boldsymbol{D} = (D_1, D_2, \ldots, D_n) \in \Omega^n$$

1. Sen's condition of *minimal liberalism* is still weaker than this one. In his formulation, D_i may be empty for at most $n - 2$ individuals. See Sen [9, p. 87].

such that, for each $i \in N$, D_i contains at least one *nondiagonal* member and that, for all profile $\boldsymbol{R} = (R_1, R_2, \ldots, R_n)$,[2]

$$(x, y) \in D_i \cap P(R_i) \Rightarrow [x \in S \;\&\; y \in C(S)] \text{ for no } S \in \mathcal{S}. \quad (13.2)$$

D_i is meant to be the set of all protected personal pairs of the individual i. In what follows, D_i will be referred to as i's *protected sphere*. $\boldsymbol{D} = (D_1, D_2, \ldots, D_n)$ will be called a *rights assignment*. Using these terms, condition SL may be interpreted that the individual i can get his own way in choices over his protected sphere irrespective of what others may think.

Taken in isolation, these requirements seem to be rather reasonable. A disturbing fact is that, given condition U, condition P and condition SL cannot *simultaneously* be satisfied by *any* CCR. It is this *paradox of a Paretian liberal* established by Sen [9, pp. 81–82; 10, Theorem 7] that necessitates a closer examination of condition P and condition SL.

13.2.2. On the Concept of Coherent Libertarian Claim

Let us begin with condition SL. Our first task is to introduce the concept of *coherent rights assignment,* which goes as follows.

Let $\boldsymbol{D} = (D_1, D_2, \ldots, D_n)$ be an n-tuple of subsets of $X \times X$. A *critical loop* in $\boldsymbol{D}$ is a sequence of ordered pairs $\{(x^\mu, y^\mu)\}_{\mu=1}^t (t \geq 2)$ such that (i) $(x^\mu, y^\mu) \in \cup_{i=1}^n D_i$ for all $\mu = 1, 2, \ldots, t$, (ii) there exists no $i^* \in \{1, 2, \ldots, n\}$ such that $(x^\mu, y^\mu) \in D_{i^*}$ for all $\mu = 1, 2, \ldots, t$, and (iii) $x^1 = y^t$ and $x^\mu = y^{\mu-1}$ for all $\mu = 2, \ldots, t$.[3] We say that $\boldsymbol{D} = (D_1, D_2, \ldots, D_n)$ is *coherent* if and only if there exists no critical loop in $\boldsymbol{D}$.

From the analytical viewpoint, the importance of the concept of coherence in our present context stems from the following basic lemma, the proof of which will be given in the appendix.

LEMMA 13.1. $\boldsymbol{D} = (D_1, D_2, \ldots, D_n)$ is coherent if and only if, for each profile of individual preference orderings $\boldsymbol{R} = (R_1, R_2, \ldots, R_n)$, there exists an ordering extension R of each and every $D_i \cap R_i$ $(i = 1, 2, \ldots, n)$.

---

2. $\boldsymbol{D}$ is symmetric if, for each $i \in N$, $(x, y) \in D_i$ if and only if $(y, x) \in D_i$. A member $(x, y) \in D_i$ is nondiagonal if and only if $x \neq y$.
3. The concept of the critical loop is due to Farrell [3].

It was Farrell [3] and Gibbard [4] who showed that (i) if the rights assignment $\boldsymbol{D}$ is not coherent, condition U and condition SL conflict by themselves (without invoking condition P), and that (ii) if $\boldsymbol{D}$ is coherent, condition U and condition SL are compatible. It follows that we should restrict condition SL by requiring $\boldsymbol{D}$ to be coherent if we wish to make condition SL compatible with condition U and some version of the Pareto rule. Furthermore, an existential statement of condition SL, though ideal for an impossibility exercise, is ill suited for our present purpose. The doctored version of condition SL we are going to work with is as follows.

Condition CL (coherent libertarian claim). For any coherent rights assignment $\boldsymbol{D} = (D_1, D_2. \dots, D_n) \in \Omega^n$, (13.2) holds for each $i \in N$.

13.2.3. Conditional Pareto Rule and the Concept of a Liberal Individual

Let us now turn to condition P. Let $\boldsymbol{R} = (R_1, R_2, \dots, R_n)$ be any profile and let R_i^* be a transitive subrelation of R_i that individual i wants to count in collective decision. Thus $(x, y) \in P(R_i)$ means that i prefers x to y personally, while $(x, y) \in P(R_i^*)$ means that he wants his preference for x over y to count in social choice. The basic idea here is that "the guarantee of a minimal amount of personal liberty may require that certain parts of individual rankings should not count in some specific social choices, and in some cases even the persons in question may agree with this" (Sen [10, pp. 237–238]). Armed with this important distinction, we now introduce a version of the *conditional* (strong) Pareto rule.

Condition CP (conditional Pareto rule). Let $R^* = \cap_{i \in N} R_i^*$. For all $x, y \in X$,

(a) $(x, y) \in R^* \Rightarrow [x \in S \setminus C(S)\ \&\ y \in C(S)]$ for no $S \in \mathcal{S}$, and
(b) $(x, y) \in P(R^*) \Rightarrow [x \in S\ \&\ y \in C(S)]$ for no $S \in \mathcal{S}$.

The efficacy of condition CP as a resolvent of Sen's paradox depends squarely on the extent that $\boldsymbol{R}^* = (R_1^*, R_2^*, \dots, R_n^*)$ is restrictive vis-à-vis $\boldsymbol{R} = (R_1, R_2, \dots, R_n)$. For example, if $R_i^* = R_i$ for all $i \in N$, then the paradox clearly remains intact. If $R_i^* = \emptyset$ for all $i \in N$, however, condition CP becomes vacuous and the paradox is "resolved." The problem really is to formalize a "reasonable" way of restricting R_i into R_i^* so as to avoid Sen's difficulty. Sen's [10, Section XI] proposal to this effect is now to be recapitulated. Let $\boldsymbol{D} = (D_1, D_2, \ldots, D_n) \in \Omega^n$ be any coherent rights assignment and let $\boldsymbol{R} = (R_1, R_2, \ldots, R_n)$ be any profile. Thanks to Lemma 13.1, we then have an ordering R that subsumes each and every individual preference over respective protected spheres. There may well be multiple ordering extensions, so let $\mathcal{R}$ stand for the set of all such orderings. Let an individual $j \in N$ be called a *liberal* if and only if

$$R_j^* = R_j \cap R \quad \text{for some } R \in \mathcal{R}. \tag{13.3}$$

Namely, an individual j is liberal if and only if he/she claims only those parts of his/her preferences to count that are compatible with others' preferences over their respective protected spheres.

Some remarks on this basic concept might be in order. First, it should be emphasized that a liberal never drops his preferences over his own protected sphere, so that a liberal need not die a martyr for his faith in liberalism. Second, a liberal need not really care very much how the order extension R is constructed from $Q = \cup_{i \in N}(R_i \cap D_i)$. An "active" liberal would hold a clear idea of the part of his preference ordering that he wants to count in the collective decision. (Obviously, he needs lots of information as to the structure of rights assignment and the wishes of individuals.) A "passive" liberal, on the other hand, does not know his R_i^*; instead, he knows only his R_i and that he knows he wants to be liberal. A well-informed umpire then comes in, who constructs an order extension R of Q and thereby constrains the preference ordering of an individual who is wishing to be liberal. Our concept of a liberal individual admits both species.[4]

13.2.4. A Pareto Consistent Libertarian Claim

Now the theorem.

THEOREM 13.1 (SEN [10, THEOREM 9]). If there exists at least one liberal individual, a rational CCR that satisfies U, CL, and CP exists.[5]

---

4. Thanks are due to Peter Hammond for his comment on this point.

5. To be precise, Sen showed that U, CL, and CP are made compatible by a CCR f, but he did not show that f is rational. Theorem 13.1 is an extension of Sen's Theorem 9 in this sense.

PROOF. Let N_1 stand for the set of all liberal individuals. By assumption, N_1 is a nonempty subset of N. Let $\boldsymbol{D} = (D_1, D_2, \ldots, D_n)$ be a given coherent rights assignment and let $\boldsymbol{R} = (R_1, R_2, \ldots, R_n)$ be a given profile. Let $\mathcal{R}$ be the set of all ordering extensions of $Q = \cup_{i \in N}(R_i \cap D_i)$. We define

$$R_i^* = \begin{cases} R_i \cap R^i \text{ for some } R^i \in \mathcal{R} & \text{if } i \in N_1 \\ R_i & \text{otherwise.} \end{cases}$$

Denoting $R^* = \cap_{i \in N} R_i^*$ and $P = \cap_{i \in N_1} P(R^i)$, we define

$$R_0 = \{(x, y) \in X \times X \mid (y, x) \notin P \cup P(R^*)\}. \tag{13.4}$$

Let us establish that R_0 is complete. Suppose that there are x and y in X such that $(x, y) \notin R_0$ and $(y, x) \notin R_0$, so that we have $(x, y) \in P \cup P(R^*)$ and $(y, x) \in P \cup P(R^*)$. There are four possible cases to consider:

(i) $(x, y) \in P \;\&\; (y, x) \in P$,

(ii) $(x, y) \in P(R^*) \;\&\; (y, x) \in P(R^*)$,

(iii) $(x, y) \in P \;\&\; (y, x) \in P(R^*)$,

and

(iv) $(x, y) \in P(R^*) \;\&\; (y, x) \in P$.

Case (i) and case (ii) contradict, respectively, the asymmetry of P and that of $P(R^*)$. Take any $i_0 \in N_1$. Then we have $P \subseteq P(R^{i_0})$ and $P(R^*) \subseteq R_{i_0}^* \subseteq R^{i_0}$, so that case (iii) and the case (iv) contradict the fact that R^{i_0} is an ordering. Therefore, R_0 must be complete.

Next we establish that

$$P(R_0) = P \cup P(R^*). \tag{13.5}$$

If $(x, y) \in P(R_0)$, then $(y, x) \notin R_0$, which implies $(x, y) \in P \cup P(R^*)$ by definition. Therefore, $P(R_0) \subseteq P \cup P(R^*)$. To show the converse, suppose there exists an ordered pair (x, y) such that $(x, y) \in P \cup P(R^*)$ but $(x, y) \notin P(R_0)$. But this contradicts the completeness of R_0 just established. Therefore, (13.5) must be true.

Our next task is to establish the acyclicity of R_0. If there exists a $\{x^1, x^2, \ldots, x^t\} \in \mathcal{S}$ such that $(x^\mu, x^{\mu+1}) \in P(R_0)$ $(\mu = 1, 2, \ldots, t-1)$ and $(x^t, x^1) \in P(R_0)$, we have a contradiction with the transitivity of R_i $(i \in N_1)$ or that of R^*, thanks to the fact that $P(R^*) \subseteq R^i$ $(i \in N_1)$. This contradiction establishes the acyclicity of R_0. Now that R_0 is complete and acyclic,

$$C(S) = G(S, R_0)$$

for all $S \in \mathcal{S}$ is a well-defined rational choice function by virtue of Lemma 13.2* in the appendix. Associating this C with the given profile $\boldsymbol{R} = (R_1, R_2, \ldots, R_n)$, we obtain a rational CCR.

What remains to be shown is that this CCR satisfies CP and CL.

In order to show that it satisfies CP(a), suppose that there exist x and y such that $(x, y) \in R^*$, $x \in S \setminus C(S)$, and $y \in C(S)$ for some $S \in \mathcal{S}$. We will bring out a contradiction by showing that $(x, z) \in R_0$ for all $z \in S$. Take, therefore, any $z \in S$. Since $y \in C(S)$, we have $(z, y) \notin P \cup P(R^*)$, so that $(z, y) \notin P$ and $[(z, y) \notin R^*$ or $(y, z) \in R^*]$. Thanks to the definition of P, we have $(z, y) \notin P$ if and only if $(y, z) \in R^i$ for some $i \in N_1$. By assumption we have $(x, y) \in R^*$ so that we obtain $(x, y) \in R_i^* \subseteq R^i$ for this $i \in N_1$. R^i being transitive, $(x, y) \in R^i$ and $(y, z) \in R^i$ yield $(x, z) \in R^i$. It then follows that $(z, x) \notin P(R^i)$, which implies that

$$(z, x) \notin P. \tag{13.6}$$

Suppose now that $(z, y) \notin R^*$, which implies $(z, y) \notin R_i^*$ for some $i \in N$. If $i \in N \setminus N_1$, then we have $(y, z) \in P(R_i)$. As $(x, y) \in R_i$ follows from $(x, y) \in R^*$, we obtain $(x, z) \in P(R_i)$, namely, $(z, x) \notin R_i$. Therefore, $(z, x) \notin R^*$. If $i \in N_1$, then $[(z, y) \notin R_i$ or $(z, y) \notin R^i]$, namely, $[(y, z) \in P(R_i)$ or $(y, z) \in P(R^i)]$ holds true, which implies $(x, z) \in P(R_i) \cup P(R^i)$ in view of $(x, y) \in R^*$. Therefore, we again obtain $(z, x) \notin R^*$. Consider the case where $(y, z) \in R^*$. Coupled with $(x, y) \in R^*$ this implies that $(x, z) \in R^*$, hence $(z, x) \notin P(R^*)$. Therefore, in every conceivable case we obtain that

$$(z, x) \notin P(R^*). \tag{13.7}$$

It follows from (13.6) and (13.7) that $(z, x) \notin P \cup P(R^*)$, so that we have arrived at $(x, z) \in R_0$ as desired. The proof of CP(a) is thereby complete.

Next CP(b). If there are x and y satisfying $(x, y) \in P(R^*)$, $x \in S$, and $y \in C(S)$ for some $S \in \mathcal{S}$, we have $(y, x) \in R_0$ entailing $(x, y) \notin P \cup P(R^*)$. But this contradicts $(x, y) \in P(R^*)$.

Finally, we show that our CCR satisfies CL. Suppose to the contrary that there are an $i \in N$ and $S \in \mathcal{S}$ satisfying $(x, y) \in D_i \cap P(R_i)$, $x \in S$, and $y \in C(S)$. Then we obtain $(y, x) \in R_0$, entailing $(x, y) \notin P \cup P(R^*)$. By definition of $\mathcal{R}$, we have $P(Q) \subseteq \cap_{i \in N_1} P(R^i) = P$, so that if we can show

$$D_i \cap P(R_i) \subseteq P(Q), \tag{13.8}$$

we are home. (Because, then, we have $(x, y) \in D_i \cap P(R_i) \subseteq P$, in contradiction with $(x, y) \notin P \cup P(R^*)$.) To show (13.8), let $(w, z) \in D_i \cap P(R_i)$. Clearly, $(w, z) \in Q$, so that if $(w, z) \notin P(Q)$ then $(z, w) \in Q = \cup_{i \in N} Q_i$. Then there exists a $j \in N$ $(j \neq i)$ such that $(z, w) \in D_j \cap R_j$. If follows that $\boldsymbol{D}$ contains a critical loop, a contradiction. ■

The gist of this resolution is very simple and intuitive. The Pareto principle is enforced only by unanimous agreement. Its use can therefore be vetoed by any one person, and a liberal may well serve as a vetoer. Notice that a liberal is, by definition, one who always (for every profile) exercises the veto in favor of every expressed protected right, of every consequence of all of these, and of further arbitrary additions.

13.2.5. Modus Operandi of the Resolution Scheme for Sen's Dilemma

It might help if we exemplify how this resolution works.

EXAMPLE 13.1 (LADY CHATTERLEY'S LOVER CASE (SEN [9, PP. 80–81])). There is a single copy of *Lady Chatterley's Lover*. The set of social states consists of three alternatives: Mr. A (the prude) reading it (x), Mr. B (the lascivious) reading it (y), and no one reading it (z). Mr. A prefers z most, next x (wishing thereby to take the hurt on himself), and lastly y (for fear of the possible misbehavior of Mr. B), while Mr. B prefers x most (in order to educate the reactionary Mr. A), y next, and lastly z. Therefore, $R_A = \Delta \cup \{(z, x), (x, y), (z, y)\}$ and $R_B = \Delta \cup \{(x, y), (y, z), (x, z)\}$, where Δ denotes the diagonal binary relation on the space in question. (In our present context, $\Delta = \{(x, x), (y, y), (z, z)\}$.) The protected sphere of Mr. A is $D_A = \{(x, z), (z, x)\}$ and that of Mr. B is $D_B = \{(y, z), (z, y)\}$.

(Notice that this rights assignment $\boldsymbol{D} = (D_A, D_B)$ is coherent.) No Pareto-inclusive CCR can realize this rights assignment, however.

In this case $Q_A = R_A \cap D_A = \{(z, x)\}$ and $Q_B = R_B \cap D_B = \{(y, z)\}$, so that $Q = Q_A \cup Q_B = \{(z, x), (y, z)\}$. The ordering extension of this Q is unique, and it is given by

$$R = \Delta \cup \{(y, z), (z, x), (y, x)\}.$$

Suppose that Mr. A is liberal while Mr. B is not, so that $R_A^* = R \cap R_A = \Delta \cup \{(z, x)\}$ and $R_B^* = R_B$, entailing $R^* = \Delta$. By definition we then have

$$R_0 = \Delta \cup \{(y, z), (z, x), (y, x)\},$$

so that $G(\{x, y, z\}, R_0) = \{y\}$. Therefore our suggested solution for the *Lady Chatterley's Lover* case is: Give that copy to the lascivious.

A few remarks might be in order. First, in line with the statement of Sen's libertarian claim (SL), we supposed that D_A and D_B were symmetric in the *Lady Chatterley's Lover* case. Sen's paradox still works, however, even if $D_A = \{(z, x)\}$ and $D_B = \{(y, z)\}$. It is easy to verify that our resolution still applies without any change. Second, our solution to the *Lady Chatterley's Lover* case does not hinge on our supposing that it is Mr. A who is liberal. Mr. B being liberal leads us to the same solution. Is this a general feature of our solution procedure? To show that it is not, we put forward the following.

Example 13.2 (Two Meddlers Case (Blau [2])). There are two individuals, Mr. A and Mr. B, and four distinct alternatives x, y, z, and w. The rights assignment is $D_A = \{(x, y), (y, x)\}$ and $D_B = \{(z, w), (w, z)\}$. Mr. A prefers w to x to y to z, while Mr. B prefers y to z to w to x. Mr. A is meddlesome in that his preference over his protected pair is weaker (in the ordinal intensity sense) than his opposition to the other's preference over that individual's protected pair. Mr. B is also a meddler in the same sense. In this case the unadulterated exercise of rights, coupled with the mechanical use of the Pareto rule, brings us to the impasse of social indecision.

Let us see how our solution procedure will fare in coping with this situation. It is easy to see that, in this case, $Q = \{(x, y), (z, w)\}$. There are multiple ordering extensions of this Q, thirteen altogether, from which we pick out

$$R^{\alpha} = \Delta \cup \{(x, y), (x, z), (x, w), (y, z), (y, w), (z, w)\},$$
$$R^{\beta} = \Delta \cup \{(z, w), (z, x), (z, y), (w, x), (w, y), (x, y)\}, \text{ and}$$
$$R^{\gamma} = \Delta \cup \{(x, z), (z, x), (x, y), (x, w), (z, y), (z, w), (y, w)\}.$$

Depending on who is liberal and which ordering extension is to be used, there are different solution schemes. Let the scheme where Mr. A is liberal with the ordering extension R^{α} be denoted by (A, α). It is easy, if tedious, to verify that the solution in the scheme (A, α) is $\{x\}$, that in the scheme (B, β) is $\{z\}$, and that in the scheme $(\{A, B\}, \gamma)$ is $\{x, z\}$.

13.3. A Resolution of Gibbard's Paradox

13.3.1. Idiosyncracies of Sen's Rights Assignment

We start with an observation that condition SL and condition CL share two important peculiarities. First, the rights assignment in SL as well as that in CL is *independent* in the sense that, whenever $(x, y) \in D_i$ and i strictly prefers x to y, she can get her way *whatever her preference over* $X \setminus \{x, y\}$ *happens to be*. Second, apart from our *interpretation,* there is nothing in the *formal statement* of SL and CL that assures us that, whenever $(x, y) \in D_i$, the difference between x and y is i's purely personal concern. Gibbard's [4] libertarian claim differs from SL and CL in these respects and, as a result, a paradox he arrived at is essentially different from that of Sen. We will show in this section that this different paradox can nevertheless be resolved along the similar line of reasoning as we used previously.

13.3.2. Gibbard's Decomposable Rights Assignment

The social state is now construed as a list of impersonal and personal features of the world. Let X_0 be the set of all impersonal features and X_i the set of all personal features of individual $i \in N$. X, the set of all social states, is represented as

$$X = X_0 \times X_1 \times \ldots \times X_n.$$

We assume that X_0 and X_i $(i \in N)$ are finite with at least two elements each. Our notational convention is that, for each $i \in N$ and each $x = (x_0, x_1, \ldots, x_n) \in X$,

$$X_{)i(} = X_0 \times X_1 \times \ldots \times X_{i-1} \times X_{i+1} \times \ldots \times X_n$$

and $x_{)i(} = (x_0, x_1, \ldots, x_{i-1}, x_{i+1}, \ldots, x_n)$. Furthermore, if $x_i \in X_i$ and $z = (z_0, z_1, \ldots, z_{i-1}, z_{i+1}, \ldots, z_n) \in X_{)i(}$, $(x_i; z) = (z_0, z_1, \ldots, z_{i-1}, x_i, z_{i+1}, \ldots, z_n)$. Finally, we define D'_i by

$$D'_i = \{(x, y) \in X \times X \mid x_{)i(} = y_{)i(}\} (i \in N).$$

Therefore, if $(x, y) \in D'_i$, then x and y can possibly differ only in the specification of i's personal feature.

13.3.3. Gibbard's Unconditional Libertarian Claim

Now Gibbard's [4, p. 393] version of a libertarian claim.

CONDITION GL (GIBBARD'S LIBERTARIAN CLAIM). For each $i \in N$, if $(x, y) \in D'_i$ and $((x_i; z), (y_i; z)) \in P(R_i)$ for all $z \in X_{)i(}$, then $[x \in S \;\&\; y \in C(S)]$ for no $S \in \mathcal{S}$.

In words, it is required that, if x and y differ only in i's personal feature and if i prefers x_i *unconditionally* to y_i, then her personal choice should be socially respected. Gibbard [4, Theorem 2] has shown that there exists no CCR satisfying U, GL, and P. Notice that $\boldsymbol{D}' = (D'_1, D'_2, \ldots, D'_n) \in \Omega^n$ is *not* independent and it is *not* coherent by construction.

13.3.4. Resolution of Gibbard's Dilemma

As a first step in resolving Gibbard's dilemma, we show that a binary relation Q' defined by

$$Q'_i = \{(x, y) \in D'_i \mid ((x_i; z), (y_i; z)) \in P(R_i) \quad \text{for all } z \in X_{)i(}\} (i \in N)$$

and

$$Q' = \cup_{i \in N} Q'_i$$

is S-consistent for any profile $(R_1, R_2, \ldots, R_n)$. Suppose to the contrary that there exists a $\{x^1, x^2, \ldots, x^t\} \in \mathcal{S}$ such that $(x^1, x^2) \in P(Q')$, $(x^\mu, x^{\mu+1}) \in Q'$ for all $\mu = 2, \ldots, t-1$, and $(x^t, x^1) \in Q'$. Then there exists an $i \in N$ such that

$$(x^1, x^2) \in D'_i \tag{13.9}$$

and

$$((x_i^1; z), (x_i^2; z)) \in P(R_i) \quad \text{for all } z \in X_{)i(}. \tag{13.10}$$

Corresponding to the sequence $\{x^\mu\}_{\mu=1}^t$, define a sequence $\{x_*^\mu\}_{\mu=1}^t$ by

$$x_*^\mu = (x_i^\mu; x_{)i(}^1), \ (\mu = 1, 2, \ldots, t). \tag{13.11}$$

By virtue of Gibbard's lemma [4, p. 396] we then have $(x_*^\mu, x_*^{\mu+1}) \in R_i$ $(\mu = 2, \ldots, t-1)$ and $(x_*^t, x_*^1) \in R_i$, while (13.10) entails that $(x_*^1, x_*^2) \in P(R_i)$. But this contradicts the transitivity of R_i. Now that Q' is S-consistent, there exists an ordering R' subsuming Q' by virtue of Lemma 13.1* in the appendix. Let $\mathcal{R}'$ be the set of all ordering extensions of Q'. Call an individual $j \in N$ a G-*liberal* if and only if

$$R_j^* = R_j \cap R' \quad \text{for some } R' \in \mathcal{R}'. \tag{13.12}$$

In words, j is G-liberal if and only if he claims only those parts of his preferences to count that are compatible with others' unconditional preferences over their personal variations. Our remarks on the nature of a liberal individual presented in 13.2.3 apply to a G-liberal individual as well.

Now the following theorem is true.

Theorem 13.2. If there exists at least one G-liberal individual, a rational CCR satisfying U, GL, and CP exists.

A slight modification of the proof of Theorem 13.1 (replacing $\mathcal{R}$ by $\mathcal{R}'$) establishes Theorem 13.2, the detail of which may be safely skipped.

13.3.5. Modus Operandi of the Resolution Scheme for Gibbard's Dilemma

Let us analyze an example and contrast our solution with that of Gibbard [4].

Example 13.3 (Wall Color Case (Gibbard [4, pp. 394–395])). There are two individuals, Mr. A and Mr. B, and four alternative states, all of which are identical with respect to the impersonal features of the world. They differ only in the color of their respective bedroom walls. Let these alternative states be (w, w), (y, w), (w, y), and (y, y), dropping for the sake of simplicity the coordinate of impersonal features. (The first coordinate designates the color of Mr. A's walls and the second that of Mr. B's, w and y standing respectively for "white" and "yellow.") In this case,

$$D'_A = \{((w, w), (y, w)), ((y, w), (w, w)), ((w, y), (y, y)), ((y, y), (w, y))\}$$

and

$$D'_B = \{((y, y), (y, w)), ((y, w), (y, y)), ((w, y), (w, w)), ((w, w), (w, y))\}.$$

It is clear that $\boldsymbol{D}' = (D'_A, D'_B)$ is not coherent. Suppose that their preferences are such that

$$R_A : (w, w), (y, w), (w, y), (y, y)$$

and

$$R_B : (y, y), (y, w), (w, y), (w, w).$$

namely, Mr. A prefers w to y unconditionally and he wants Mr. B to choose as he does. Mr. B in turn prefers y to w unconditionally and he wants Mr. A to choose as he does. In this case, the rights exercising of Mr. A and Mr. B, coupled with the naive use of the Pareto rule, kicks out all alternatives from social choice, and no CCR can be satisfactory if we stick to U, GL, and P.

Now our solution procedure. Corresponding to the given profile $\boldsymbol{R} = (R_A, R_B)$, we have $Q'_A = \{((w, w), (y, w)), ((w, y), (y, y))\}$ and $Q'_B = \{((y, y), (y, w)), ((w, y), (w, w))\}$. An ordering extension R' of $Q'_A \cup Q'_B$ is then given by[6]

$$R' : (w, y), (y, y), (w, w), (y, w).$$

6. There are two other ordering extensions of $Q'_A \cup Q'_B$, namely,

$$R'^{\alpha} : (w, y), (w, w), (y, y), (y, w)$$

$$R'^{\beta} : (w, y), [(w, w), (y, y)], (y, w).$$

Suppose that Mr. A is G-liberal while Mr. B is not, so that

$$R_A^* = R' \cap R_A = \Delta \cup \{((w, y), (y, y)), ((w, w), (y, w))\}$$

and $R_B^* = R_B$, yielding $R^* = \Delta$. We then have

$$R_0 = \Delta \cup \{((w, y), (y, y)), ((w, y), (w, w)), ((w, y), (y, w)), ((y, y), (w, w)), ((y, y), (y, w)), (w, w), (y, w))\},$$

so that $G(\{(w, w), (y, w), (w, y), (y, y)\}, R_0) = \{(w, y)\}$. Therefore, our solution is: Let people choose whatever color they unconditionally prefer. (Our conclusion remains intact if Mr. B is G-liberal and Mr. A is not.)

Gibbard's [4, Section 4] way out of his paradox is to make his libertarian claim *alienable* and goes typically as follows. Although Mr. A prefers (w, w) to (y, w), and could avoid (y, w) by exercising his right to (w, w) over (y, w), Mr. B claims his right to (w, y) over (w, w), and Mr. A prefers (y, w) to (w, y). By exercising his right to avoid (y, w), Mr. A ends up with what he likes no better, so that, Gibbard argues, his right to (w, w) over (y, w) is waived. By the same token, Mr. B's right to (y, y) over (y, w) is waived. Following this reasoning we arrive at the conclusion that Gibbard's suggested social choice from $\{(w, w), (y, w), (w, y), (y, y)\}$ is (y, w). It seems to us that this is a suggestion that is rather hard to swallow. Why on earth *should* people be assigned the color of their bedroom walls that they unconditionally dislike?[7]

We have thus shown that restricting the use of the Pareto rule is a workable way out of Gibbard's paradox and that, in some cases at least, it provides us with a more "reasonable" solution than Gibbard's own resolution via the alienability of rights.

(In R'^{β}, (w, w) and (y, y) are deemed to be indifferent, so that they are put together by square brackets.) Nothing will be changed even if we use R'^{α} or R'^{β} instead of R' in the rest of our argument: (w, y) will still be chosen.

7. It is true that our way of solving the paradox ignores what Gibbard [4] has called "a strong libertarian tradition of free contract," according to which "a person's rights are his own to use or bargain away as he sees fit" [4, p. 397]. This argument does not seem to deprive our resolution of its reasonableness in the present example, however.

13.4. Justice and Liberty: Interpersonal Welfare Comparisons

13.4.1. Interpersonal Comparisons of the Extended Sympathy Type

Let us go back to Sen's paradox in Section 13.2. The problem at hand is to find a way around the difficulty by making use of information on the interpersonal welfare comparisons. More explicitly, we make use of the information available from "extended sympathy" (Arrow [1, p. 114]), in the form of placing oneself in the position of another. In the literature there are assertions that this additional information does not provide us with a way out of Sen's dilemma (Kelly [6] and Sen [10]). We will show, however, that if the rights exercising is restricted by the maximin justice consideration along the line of Rawls [7] and Sen [9, Chapter 9], the *constrained* libertarian claim is made compatible with the Pareto rule, so that (as in the case of Arrovian impossibility theorems) the possibility of the interpersonal welfare comparisons does help us circumvent Sen's paradox.

13.4.2. Sen's Axiom of Identity

Interpersonal comparisons of the extended sympathy type are of the following form: it is better to be an individual i in state x than to be an individual j in state y. This is formally put by an ordering $\tilde{R}$ (to be called an *extended ordering*) on $X \times N$ with $(x, i) \in X \times N$ standing for being in the position of individual i in social state x. We will work exclusively with the extended orderings satisfying Sen's *axiom of complete identity* (Sen [9, p. 156]) in the sense that we assume that all individuals in the society share identical extended orderings. Needless to say, this still allows each individual to have full freedom in judging social states placing him/herself in his/her own shoes, so that if we define

$$R_i = \{(x, y) \in X \times X \mid ((x, i), (y, i)) \in \tilde{R}\}(i \in N), \quad (13.13)$$

each R_i is an ordering on X and $\boldsymbol{R} = (R_1, R_2, \ldots, R_n)$ is a profile (in the sense of Section 13.2) on which no restriction is placed. We are now concerned with a *generalized collective choice rule* (GCCR), which is a method of choosing, for each extended ordering, an SCF on $\mathcal{S}$:[8]

$$C = \Psi(\tilde{R}). \tag{13.14}$$

The requirement of general applicability of GCCR reads as follows.

Condition GU (unrestricted domain). The domain of GCCR consists of all logically possible extended orderings.

Notice that we can reinterpret condition P, condition SL, and condition CL as requirements on GCCR with the understanding that R_i there now stands for (13.13).

13.4.3. Rawls's Maximum Justice and Suppes's Grading Principle

Let Π be the set of all one-to-one correspondences between N and N. Given an extended ordering $\tilde{R}$, the *maximin relation of justice* $M(\tilde{R})$ and the *Suppes grading principle of justice* $J(\tilde{R})$ are defined respectively by

$$(x, y) \in M(\tilde{R}) \Leftrightarrow \exists k \in N : [\forall i \in N : ((x, i), (y, k)) \in \tilde{R}] \tag{13.15}$$

and

$$(x, y) \in J(\tilde{R}) \Leftrightarrow \exists \pi \in \Pi: \begin{cases} \forall j \in N: & ((x, j), (y, \pi(j))) \in \tilde{R} \\ \exists k \in N: & ((x, k), (y, \pi(k))) \in P(\tilde{R}). \end{cases} \tag{13.16}$$

In words, x is more just than y in the maximin sense if and only if it is no worse to be anyone in state x than to be some specified individual in state y, while x is more just than y in Suppes's sense if and only if there exists

8. This is a *functional* CCR analogue of what Hammond [5] called the *generalized social welfare function*.

a one-to-one transformation of N into itself such that (a) being in state x in someone's position is better than being in state y in the position of the corresponding individual and (b) being in the position of each individual in x is no worse than being the corresponding individual in y. It is known that, for each $\tilde{R}$, $M(\tilde{R})$, is an ordering on X (Sen [9, Theorem 9*4]) and $J(\tilde{R})$ is an asymmetric and transitive relation on X (Sen [9, Theorem 9*1]). Furthermore, the following inclusions are true for each $\tilde{R}$:

$$\cap_{i\in N} P(R_i) \subseteq J(\tilde{R}) \subseteq M(\tilde{R}), \tag{13.17}$$

where R_i is defined by (13.13).

13.4.4. Inefficacy of Suppes's Grading Justice Rule

Consider now the following requirement on GCCR.

Condition SJ (Suppes's justice rule). For all $x, y \in X$ if $(x, y) \in J(\tilde{R})$, then $[x \in S \;\&\; y \in C(S)]$ for no $S \in \mathcal{S}$.

A little reflection convinces us that there is no hope for our obtaining a GCCR satisfying GU, SJ, and SL. (Suffice it to notice that condition SJ implies condition P by virtue of (13.17) and condition GU implies condition U (trivially rephrased as a condition on GCCR), while Sen's liberal paradox tells us that U, P, and SL conflict.) Kelly [6, Theorem 3] has strengthened this observation in that even if we weaken SL so that (13.2) is constrained in such a way that

$$(x, y) \in D_i \cap P(R_i) \;\&\; (y, x) \notin J(\tilde{R}) \Rightarrow$$
$$[x \in S \;\&\; y \in C(S)] \quad \text{for no } S \in \mathcal{S} \tag{13.18}$$

we still cannot break the impasse. This is what he called the *impossibility of a just liberal*.

13.4.5. Efficacy of Rawls's Maximum Justice Rule

The libertarian claim we are going to work with is a constrained version of the previous condition CL.

CONDITION ML (MAXIMIN LIBERTARIAN CLAIM). For any coherent rights-assignment $\boldsymbol{D} = (D_1, D_2, \ldots, D_n) \in \Omega^n$,

$$(x, y) \in D_i \cap P(R_i) \,\&\, (y, x) \notin M(\tilde{R}) \Rightarrow$$
$$[x \in S \,\&\, y \in C(S)] \quad \text{for no } S \in \mathcal{S} \tag{13.19}$$

holds for each $i \in N$.

In words, an individual i can get his/her way for x against y if (x, y) is his/her protected pair and y is not more just than x in the maximin sense. Therefore, rights exercising is restricted in ML by the maximin justice consideration.

The following theorem is true, which sharply contrasts with Kelly's impossibility theorem.

THEOREM 13.3. There exists a rational GCCR satisfying GU, ML, and SJ.

Before proving this proposition, we refer to a simple corollary thereof.

COROLLARY. There exists a rational GCCR satisfying GU, ML, and P.

The message of this proposition is clear: the possibility of the interpersonal welfare comparisons does help us in finding a way around Sen's impossibility theorem as it helped us in avoiding Arrow's impossibility theorem. Kelly's and Sen's contrary statement is due to their insufficient use of the information that is actually available from extended sympathy.

13.4.6. Proof of Theorem 13.3

Let $\tilde{R}$ be any given extended ordering and let R_i $(i \in N)$ be defined by (13.13). R_i being an ordering for all $i \in N$, there exists an ordering extension R of $Q = \cup_{i \in N}(R_i \cap D_i)$ as in Section 13.2.2. Let $\tilde{\mathcal{R}}$ be the set of all such orderings. Take an $R \in \tilde{\mathcal{R}}$ (which is fixed once and for all) and let R_0 be defined by

$$R_0 = \{(x, y) \in X \times X \mid (y, x) \notin J(\tilde{R}) \cup [P(R) \cap P(M(\tilde{R}))]\}. \tag{13.20}$$

We show that this R_0 is complete. Suppose to the contrary that $(x, y) \notin R_0$ and $(y, x) \notin R_0$ for some x and y in X. By definition we then have four cases to consider:

$$\text{(i)}\quad (x, y), (y, x) \in J(\tilde{R}),$$

$$\text{(ii)}\quad (x, y), (y, x) \in P(R) \cap P(M(\tilde{R})),$$

$$\text{(iii)}\quad (x, y) \in J(\tilde{R}) \;\&\; (x, y) \notin P(R) \cap P(M(\tilde{R})),$$

$$\& \; (y, x) \notin J(\tilde{R})(y, x) \in P(R) \cap P(M(\tilde{R})),$$

and

$$\text{(iv)}\quad (x, y) \notin J(\tilde{R}) \;\&\; (x, y) \in P(R) \cap P(M(\tilde{R})) \;\&\; (y, x) \in J(\tilde{R})$$

$$\& \; (y, x) \notin P(R) \cap P(M(\tilde{R})).$$

Case (i) and case (ii) contradict, respectively, the asymmetry of $J(\tilde{R})$ and that of $P(R)$. Case (iii) cannot occur because $(x, y) \in J(\tilde{R})$ and (13.17) imply $(x, y) \in M(\tilde{R})$, while $(y, x) \in P(M(\tilde{R}))$ if and only if $(y, x) \in M(\tilde{R})$ & $(x, y) \notin M(\tilde{R})$. Similarly, case (iv) leads us to a contradiction. Therefore, R_0 is complete. Next we show that

$$P(R_0) = J(\tilde{R}) \cup [P(R) \cap P(M\tilde{R})]. \tag{13.21}$$

If $(x, y) \in P(R_0)$, then $(y, x) \notin J(\tilde{R}) \cup [P(R) \cap P(M(\tilde{R}))]$ and

$$(x, y) \in J(\tilde{R}) \cup [P(R) \cap P(M(\tilde{R}))]$$

by definition, so that we have $P(R_0) \subseteq J(\tilde{R}) \cup [P(R) \cap P(M(\tilde{R}))]$. On the other hand, if there are x and y in X such that $(x, y) \in J(\tilde{R}) \cup [P(R) \cap P(M(\tilde{R}))]$ and $(x, y) \notin P(R_0)$, a contradiction with the completeness of R_0 ensues. Therefore, (13.21) is true. Then we show the acyclicity of R_0. Suppose to the contrary that there exists a $\{x^1, x^2, \ldots, x^t\} \in \mathcal{S}$ such that $(x^\mu, x^{\mu+1}) \in P(R_0)$ $(\mu = 1, 2, \ldots, t-1)$ and $(x^t, x^1) \in P(R_0)$. Noticing (13.17) and (13.21), this leads us to a contradiction with the transitivity of either $J(\tilde{R})$ or $M(\tilde{R})$.

Now that R_0 is complete and acyclic, $C(S) = G(S, R_0)$ for all $S \in \mathcal{S}$ is a well-defined rational choice function on $\mathcal{S}$. Associating this C with the given $\tilde{R}$, we obtain a rational GCCR. To show that this GCCR satisfies condition SJ, suppose that there exist x and y in X such that $(x, y) \in J(\tilde{R})$ and $[x \in S \;\&\; y \in C(S)]$ for some $S \in \mathcal{S}$. We then have

$$(x, y) \notin J(R) \cup [P(R) \cap P(M(\tilde{R}))],$$

thanks to the construction of C, in contradiction with $(x, y) \in J(\tilde{R})$. Thus condition SJ is satisfied. Condition ML is also satisfied. To see this, suppose that there are x and y in X and $i \in N$ such that $(x, y) \in D_i \cap P(R_i)$, $(y, x) \notin M(\tilde{R})$ and $[x \in S \;\&\; y \in C(S)]$ for some $S \in \mathcal{S}$. We then have $(x, y) \notin J(\tilde{R}) \cup [P(R) \cap P(M(\tilde{R}))]$. On the other hand, we have $(x, y) \in D_i \cap P(R_i) \subseteq P(Q) \subseteq P(R)$, while $(y, x) \notin M(\tilde{R})$ implies $(x, y) \in P(M(\tilde{R}))$. Therefore, we obtain $(x, y) \in P(R) \cap P(M(\tilde{R}))$, a contradiction. This completes the proof. ∎

13.4.7. Modus Operandi of the Rawlsian Resolution Scheme

The simplest possible case that is of interest is provided by the following.

Example 13.4 (Two Meddlers Case with Extended Sympathy). This is the same as Example 13.2 save for the fact that Mr. B is physically handicapped and it is commonly reckoned that Mr. B's welfare is lower in whatever social state than that of Mr. A in any social state. Mr. A should realize, then, that by exercising his holy right, the worse-off Mr. B would become worst off of all and, as a socially conscious creature, Mr. A might refrain from exercising his right. Put formally, we may assume in this example that

$$\tilde{R} : (w, A), (x, A), (y, A), (z, A), (y, B), (z, B), (w, B), (x, B).$$

It follows, therefore, that

$$M(\tilde{R}) = \Delta \cup \{(y, x), (w, x), (z, x), (y, w), (z, w), (y, z)\}$$

and

$$J(\tilde{R}) = \{(w, x), (y, z)\}.$$

Let $S = \{x, y, z, w\}$. Thanks to the Pareto rule, we have $x \notin C(S)$ and $z \notin C(S)$. We also have $w \notin C(S)$ because $(z, w) \in D_B \cap P(R_B)$ and $(w, z) \notin M(\tilde{R})$. Although we have $(x, y) \in D_A \cap P(R_A)$, his right for x against y is waived because $(y, x) \in M(\tilde{R})$. It follows that the social choice from S is determinate and we have $C(S) = \{y\}$.

This example poses an interesting problem concerning the use of information in resolving social conflict. Recall that our resolution of the Two Meddlers case in Example 13.2 under the scheme (A, α) was $\{x\}$. It follows that if the interpersonal welfare comparison is possible but it is not made use of in resolving the conflict in question, the outcome might well be the worst possible one relative to the extended sympathy ordering! We may suggest that failure to make efficient use of available information could be extremely costly.

It should be clear that Gibbard's paradox can similarly be resolved along the same line of argument if we are armed with the stronger informational basis allowing interpersonal welfare comparisons.

13.5. Concluding Remarks

In this essay we have shown that if *either* certain parts of individual preferences are refrained from being counted in social choice (thereby constraining the applicability of the Pareto rule) *or* the individual's rights exercising is constrained by the maximin justice considerations, a minimal amount of personal liberty in a Paretian society may be guaranteed. As a conclusion we may suggest that one of the prerequisites for a liberal Paretian society is to develop individual attitudes that respect and care for each other's liberty and well-being. From a slightly different angle, we may put the general implication of our analysis as follows. Just as we needed stronger informational basis (than what is compatible with the independence of irrelevant alternatives axiom) in circumventing Arrow's impossibility theorem, it is necessary to look beyond the set of individual preference orderings and to secure stronger informational basis for collective decision if we wish to be successful in reconciling the libertarian claim with the Paretian ethics.

Appendix 13.A. Auxiliary Concepts and Basic Lemmata

13.A.1. Basic Concepts

Let X be the set of all alternatives and let $\mathcal{S}$ denote the set of all nonempty *finite* subsets of X. A binary relation R is a subset of $X \times X$. The *asymmetric component* of R is defined by

$$P(R) = \{(x, y) \in X \times X \mid (x, y) \in R \;\&\; (y, x) \notin R\}.$$

R is said to be

(a) *complete* if and only if $(x, y) \in R$ or $(y, x) \in R$ for all x and y in X,
(b) *acyclic* if and only if there exists no $\{x^1, x^2 \ldots, x^t\} \in \mathcal{S}$ such that $(x^\mu, x^{\mu+1}) \in P(R)$ for all $\mu = 1, 2, \ldots, t-1$ and $(x^t, x^1) \in P(R)$,
(c) *S-consistent* if and only if there exists no $\{x^1, x^2 \ldots, x^t\} \in \mathcal{S}$ such that $(x^1, x^2) \in P(R)$, $(x^\mu, x^{\mu+1}) \in R$ for all $\mu = 2, \ldots, t-1$ and $(x^t, x^1) \in R$,
(d) *transitive* if and only if $(x, y) \in R$ and $(y, z) \in R$ imply $(x, z) \in R$ for all x, y, and z in X,
(e) *asymmetric* if and only if $R = P(R)$, and
(f) an *ordering* if and only if it is complete and transitive.

13.A.2. Acyclicity and S-Consistency

It might help if we give an alternative formulation for acyclicity and S-consistency. For any two binary relations R^1 and R^2 on X, we define the *composition* of R^1 and R^2 by

$$R^1R^2 = \{(x, y) \in X \times X \mid (x, z) \in R^1 \;\&\; (z, y) \in R^2 \text{ for some } z \in X\}.$$

Given a binary relation R, we define a sequence $\{R^{(n)}\}_{n=1}^{\infty}$ of binary relations by

$$R^{(1)} = R,\ R^{(n)} = RR^{(n-1)} (n \geq 2).$$

The *transitive closure* of R is then defined by

$$T(R) = \cup_{n=1}^{\infty} R^{(n)},$$

which allows us to assert that R is acyclic if and only if $T(P(R)) \cap \Delta = \emptyset$, whereas R is S-consistent if and only if $P(R)T(R) \cap \Delta = \emptyset$, where Δ is the diagonal binary relation on X. Since $T(P(R)) \subseteq P(R)T(R)$ holds true, it immediately follows that an S-consistent binary relation is acyclic.

13.A.3. S-Consistency and the Existence of Ordering Extensions

Let R^1 and R^2 be two binary relations. We say that R^2 is an *extension* of R^1 if and only if (i) $R^1 \subseteq R^2$ and (ii) $P(R^1) \subseteq P(R^2)$. In this case we also say that R^1 is a *subrelation* of R^2. If R^2 is an extension of R^1 and if R^2 is an ordering, we say that R^2 is an *ordering extension* of R^1. In view of the subtle difference between transitivity and S-consistency, it seems quite intuitive that the following extension theorem is true, although it is nontrivial in its full generality.

LEMMA 1* (SUZUMURA [13, THEOREM 3]). A binary relation R has an ordering extension if and only if R is S-consistent.

This proposition generalizes Szpilrajn's basic theorem to the effect that *every quasi ordering has an ordering extension.*[9] It should be noticed that there may well exist multiple ordering extensions of a given S-consistent binary relation.

13.A.4. On the Existence of R-Greatest Points

Let R be any binary relation on X. For any $S \in \mathcal{S}$, the set of all *R-greatest points of S* is defined by

$$G(S, R) = \{x \in X \mid x \in S \;\&\; (x, y) \in R \text{ for all } y \in S\}.$$

9. See Szpilrajn [15]. As a matter of fact Szpilrajn was concerned with partial orderings (rather than quasi orderings), but the proposition referred to is a simple corollary of his theorem. See also Arrow [1, p. 64].

The following neat result is important.

LEMMA 2* (SEN [9, LEMMA 1*l]. $G(S, R)$ is nonempty for all $S \in \mathcal{S}$ if and only if R is complete and acyclic.

13.A.5. Rationality and Full Rationality of Choice Functions

A choice function C on $\mathcal{S}$ maps any $S \in \mathcal{S}$ into a nonempty subset $C(S)$ of S. Thanks to Lemma 13.2*, a complete and acyclic binary relation R generates a choice function C on $\mathcal{S}$ defined by

$$C(S) = G(S, R) \quad \text{for all } S \in \mathcal{S}. \tag{13.1*}$$

Conversely, a choice function C on $\mathcal{S}$ is said to be *rational* if and only if there exists a binary relation R satisfying (13.1*). In this case, R is called a *rationalization* of C. A rational choice function whose rationalization is an ordering is said to be *full rational*. See Suzumura [12; 14] for the characterization of rational and full rational choice functions.

13.A.6. Coherent Rights Assignment

Just as we defined the composition of binary relations in Section 13.A.2, we may define the composition of protected spheres, which enables us to present a less loaded definition of the coherent rights assignment. Namely, the rights assignment $\boldsymbol{D} = (D_1, D_2, \ldots, D_n)$ is coherent if and only if

$$(x, x) \notin D_{i_1} D_{i_2} \ldots D_{i_k} \quad \text{for all} x \in X$$

for every nonconstant sequence $\{i_1, i_2, \ldots, i_k\}$ with $i_\mu \in N$ $(\mu = 1, 2, \ldots, k)$.

13.A.7. Proof of Lemma 13.1

Finally, we prove our basic Lemma 13.1.

PROOF OF LEMMA 13.1. Let $\boldsymbol{D} = (D_1, D_2. \ldots, D_n)$ be coherent and take any profile $\boldsymbol{R} = (R_1, R_2, \ldots, R_n)$ of individual preference orderings. Define Q by

$$Q_i = D_i \cap R_i \ (i = 1, 2, \ldots, n) \ \text{ and } \ Q = \cup_{i=1}^{n} Q_i. \tag{13.2*}$$

We show that Q is an S-consistent binary relation. Suppose to the contrary that there exists $\{x^1, x^2, \dots, x^t\} \in \mathcal{S}$ such that $(x^1, x^2) \in P(Q)$, $(x^\mu, x^{\mu+1}) \in Q$ for all $\mu = 2, \dots, t-1$ and $(x^t, x^1) \in Q$. By definition, $(x^1, x^2) \in P(Q)$ if and only if $(x^1, x^2) \in Q_i$ for some i, and $(x^2, x^1) \notin Q_i$ for all i, so that we have $(x^1, x^2) \in P(Q_i)$ for some i. Therefore, there exists an i^μ for each $\mu = 1, 2, \dots, t$ such that $(x^1, x^2) \in P(Q_{i^1})$, $(x^\mu, x^{\mu+1}) \in Q_{i^\mu}$ $(\mu = 2, \dots, t-1)$, and $(x^t, x^1) \in Q_{i^t}$. It follows that (i) $\{i^1, i^2, \dots, i^t\}$ is not a singleton set and (ii) $(x^\mu, x^{\mu+1}) \in D_{i^\mu}$ $(\mu = 1, 2, , \dots, t-1)$ and $(x^t, x^1) \in D_{i^t}$. Therefore, $\boldsymbol{D}$ contains a critical loop, a contradiction. Now that Q turns out to be S-consistent, there exists an ordering extension R of Q by virtue of our Lemma 13.1*. By construction we have $Q_i \subseteq Q \subseteq R$ and $P(Q) \subseteq P(R)$. If we can show that $P(Q_i) \subseteq P(Q)$, we are home. Suppose, therefore, that there exists $(x, y) \in P(Q_i)$ such that $(y, x) \in Q_{i'}$ for some i'. But then $\boldsymbol{D}$ contains a critical loop, a contradiction.

To prove the converse, suppose to the contrary that $\boldsymbol{D}$ is not coherent. Then we have a critical loop in D: $(x^1, x^2) \in D_{i^1}$, $(x^2, x^3) \in D_{i^2}, \dots, (x^t, x^1) \in D_{i^t}$. Let $\boldsymbol{R} = (R_1, R_2, \dots, R_n)$ be an n-tuple of orderings satisfying

$$(x^1, x^2) \in P(Q_{i^1}), (x^2, x^3) \in Q_{i^2}, \dots, (x^t, x^1) \in Q_{i^t}. \quad (13.3^*)$$

Since $\{i^1, i^2, \dots, i^t\}$ cannot be a singleton set, there is no contradiction in supposing (13.3*). Let R be an ordering extension of Q_i $(i = 1, 2, \dots, n)$. Then (13.3*) implies that

$$(x^1, x^2) \in P(R), (x^2, x^3) \in R, \dots, (x^t, x^1) \in R,$$

in contradiction with the transitivity of R. This completes the proof. ■

13.6. References

[1] Arrow, K. J., *Social Choice and Individual Values,* New York: John Wiley & Sons, 1951; 2nd edn., 1963.

[2] Blau, J. H., "Liberal Values and Independence," *Review of Economic Studies* **42**, 1975, 395–401.

[3] Farrell, M., "Liberalism in the Theory of Social Choice," *Review of Economic Studies* **43**, 1976, 3–10.

[4] Gibbard, A., "A Pareto-Consistent Libertarian Claim," *Journal of Economic Theory* **7**, 1974, 388–410.

[5] Hammond, P. J., "Equity, Arrow's Conditions, and Rawls's Difference Principle," *Econometrica* **44**, 1976, 793–804.

[6] Kelly, J. S., "The Impossibility of a Just Liberal," *Economica* **43**, 1976, 67–75.

[7] Rawls, J., *A Theory of Justice,* Cambridge, Mass.: Harvard University Press, 1971.

[8] Sen, A. K., "The Impossibility of a Paretian Liberal," *Journal of Political Economy* **78**, 1970, 152–157.

[9] Sen, A. K., *Collective Choice and Social Welfare,* San Francisco: Holden-Day, 1970.

[10] Sen, A. K., "Liberty, Unanimity and Rights," *Economica* **43**, 1976, 217–245.

[11] Suppes, P., "Some Formal Models of Grading Principles," *Synthese* **16**, 1966, 284–306.

[12] Suzumura, K., "Rational Choice and Revealed Preference," *Review of Economic Studies* **43**, 1976, 149–158. Essay 1 of this volume.

[13] Suzumura, K., "Remarks on the Theory of Collective Choice," *Economica* **43**, 1976, 381–390. Essay 6 of this volume.

[14] Suzumura, K., "Houthakker's Axiom in the Theory of Rational Choice," *Journal of Economic Theory* **14**, 1977, 284–290. Essay 2 of this volume.

[15] Szpilrajn, E., "Sur l'Extension de l'Ordre Partiel," *Fundamenta Mathematicae* **16**, 1930, 386–389.

ESSAY 14

Liberal Paradox and the Voluntary Exchange of Rights Exercising

14.1. Introduction

Among many recent contributions on the logical (in)compatibility of Paretian ethics and libertarian claims, initiated by Sen's [11, Chapter 6*] theorem on the *impossibility of a Paretian liberal,* Gibbard's [3] analysis, which culminates in the edifice of the alienable rights system, deserves particular scrutiny. It tries, among other things, to call due attention to "a strong libertarian tradition of free contract," according to which "a person's rights are his to use or bargain away as he sees fit."[1] Searching examinations of Gibbard's system have already been put forward by Karni [7], Kelly [8; 9, Chapter 9], Sen [12, Sect. IV], and Suzumura [14], but it seems to us that there remain many important points to be made on this interesting contribution. The purpose of this essay is to point out that Gibbard's system of alienable rights in a revised version proposed by Kelly [8; 9, Chapter 9] represents a standard for individual liberty that cannot be met by any universal collective choice rule. That is to say, it is logically impossible to construct a collective choice rule with unrestricted domain that realizes the Gibbard-Kelly system of alienable

First published in *Journal of Economic Theory* **22**, 1980, pp. 407–422. Reprinted in C. K. Rowley, ed., *The International Library of Critical Writings in Economics,* **27**, *Social Justice and Classical Liberal Goals,* Cheltenham, Glos., UK: Edward Elgar, 1993, pp. 483–498. I am grateful to Professors Kiyoshi Kuga and Jerry S. Kelly, whose incisive comments on Suzumura [14] led me to reexamine Gibbard's system of alienable rights. Thanks are also due to an anonymous referee of *Journal of Economic Theory* for his/her helpful suggestions.

1. Gibbard [3, p. 397]. See also Barry [1, p. 166].

rights. This clearly contradicts Kelly's assertion to the effect that "[the revision] causes no significant changes in the theorems that make up Gibbard's libertarian claim."[2] This is unfortunate, since Kelly's revision seems to be rather persuasive. To the extent that Kelly's proposed revision is acceptable, therefore, the workability and reasonableness of Gibbard's scheme seem to be in serious doubt. At the very least, the edifice of the alienable rights system should be evaluated with this subtlety in mind. In passing, we will examine the possibility and limitation of resolving the liberal paradox via the meta-rational exercising of rights à la Howard [4; 5; 6] in view of the similarity between the prisoners' dilemma and the Paretian liberal paradox, which was pointed out by Fine [2].

14.2. Gibbard's Consistent Libertarian Claim and Kelly's Revision Thereof

14.2.1. Conceptual Framework

Let $N = \{1, 2, \ldots, n\}$ denote the finite set of individuals ($n \geq 2$) and let X stand for the set of all conceivable social states. What we call a social state is a list of impersonal and personal features of the world. Let X_0 and X_i stand, respectively, for the set of all impersonal features of the world and the set of all personal features of the individual $i \in N$. The set of all social states, X, is then defined by $X = X_0 \times (\Pi_{i \in N} X_i)$. It is assumed that X_0 and X_i are finite with at least two elements each. R_i denotes a weak preference (at least as good as) relation of the individual $i \in N$. We assume that R_i is an ordering on X, being *complete* [for all x and y, $(x, y) \in R_i$ and/or $(y, x) \in R_i$] and *transitive* [for all x, y, and z, $(x, y) \in R_i$ and $(y, z) \in R_i$ imply $(x, z) \in R_i$]. The strict preference relation $P(R_i)$ is defined as usual by $(x, y) \in P(R_i) \Leftrightarrow [(x, y) \in R_i \ \& \ (y, x) \notin R_i]$. The indifference relation $I(R_i)$ is defined by $(x, y) \in I(R_i) \Leftrightarrow [(x, y) \in R_i \ \& \ (y, x) \in R_i]$. A list $\boldsymbol{R} = (R_1, R_2, \ldots, R_n)$ of individual weak preference orderings will be called a *profile*. A *collective choice rule* (CCR) is a function f that represents a method of amalgamating each profile $\boldsymbol{R} = (R_1, R_2, \ldots, R_n)$ into a *social*

2. Kelly [8, p. 144; 9, p. 148].

choice function C on the family $\mathcal{S}$ of all finite nonempty subsets of X : $C = f(\boldsymbol{R})$. When an $S \in \mathcal{S}$ is specified as a set of realizable states, $C(S)$ denotes the nonempty set of socially chosen states. In what follows, we will be concerned with constructing a CCR that may amalgamate *every* logically possible profile.

CONDITION U (UNRESTRICTED DOMAIN). The domain of CCR consists of all logically possible profiles.

14.2.2. Impossibility of the Naive Gibbardian Rights System

As a matter of notational convention, we let $X_{)i(} = X_0 \times X_1 \times \ldots \times X_{i-1} \times X_{i+1} \times \ldots \times X_n$ and, for each $i \in N$ and each $x = (x_0, x_1, \ldots, x_n) \in X$, $x_{)i(} = (x_0, x_1, \ldots, x_{i-1}, x_{i+1}, \ldots, x_n)$. Furthermore, if $x_i \in X_i$ and $z = (z_0, z_1, \ldots, z_{i-1}, z_{i+1}, \ldots, z_n) \in X_{)i(}$, then $(x_i; z) = (z_0, z_1, \ldots, z_{i-1}, x_i, z_{i+1}, \ldots, z_n)$. We define D_i by

$$D_i = \{(x, y) \in X \times X | x_{)i(} = y_{)i(}\} (i \in N). \tag{14.1}$$

Therefore, if $(x, y) \in D_i$, x and y may possibly differ only in the specification of i's personal feature. Call $\boldsymbol{D} = (D_1, D_2, \ldots, D_n)$ the *Gibbardian rights system* or the *decomposable rights system*.

14.2.3. Gibbard's First Libertarian Claim

The CCR should also be so designed, a naive libertarian might claim, so that it endows the special say to the ith individual over each and every pair $(x, y) \in D_i$ in the following sense:

CONDITION GL(1) (GIBBARD'S FIRST LIBERTARIAN CLAIM). For every profile $\boldsymbol{R} = (R_1, R_2, \ldots, R_n)$, every $i \in N$, and every $x, y \in X$, if $(x, y) \in D_i \cap P(R_i)$, then $[x \in S \Rightarrow y \notin C(S)]$ for all $S \in \mathcal{S}$, where $C = f(\boldsymbol{R})$.

An unfortunate fact is that *there exists no* CCR *that satisfies this naive libertarian claim together with condition* U. This is Gibbard's first impossibility theorem [3, Theorem 1] on the libertarianism.

14.2.4. Exclusion Pareto and Inclusion Pareto

It is now time we formulate two versions of the Pareto rule.

Condition EP (exclusion Pareto). For every profile $\boldsymbol{R} = (R_1, R_2, \ldots, R_n)$ and every $x, y \in X$, if $(x, y) \in \bigcap_{i \in N} P(R_i)$, then $[x \in S \Rightarrow y \notin C(S)]$ for all $S \in \mathcal{S}$, where $C = f(\boldsymbol{R})$.

Condition IP (inclusion Pareto). For every profile $\boldsymbol{R} = (R_1, R_2, \ldots, R_n)$ and every $x, y \in X$, if $(x, y) \in \bigcap_{i \in N} P(R_i)$, then $[\{x \in S \ \& \ y \in C(S)\} \Rightarrow x \in C(S)]$ for all $S \in \mathcal{S}$, where $C = f(\boldsymbol{R})$.

Let x and y be such that everyone in the society strictly prefers x to y. Then condition EP requires that the CCR prohibits y from being chosen from every environment where x is available, while condition IP requires that the CCR should be such that x is chosen from every environment where x is available and y is chosen. Clearly, EP, which is a common formulation of the Pareto rule, is a stronger requirement on CCR than IP.[3]

14.2.5. Gibbard's Second Libertarian Claim

Turn now to Gibbard's second libertarian claim, which goes as follows.

Condition GL(2) (Gibbard's second libertarian claim). For every profile $\boldsymbol{R} = (R_1, R_2, \ldots, R_n)$, every $S \in \mathcal{S}$, every $i \in N$, and every $x, y \in X$, if $(x, y) \in D_i \cap P(R_i)$ and $((x_i; z_{)i(}), (y_i; z_{)i(})) \in P(R_i)$ for all $z_{)i(}$ such that $(x_i; z_{)i(}), (y_i; z_{)i(}) \in S$, then $[x \in S \Rightarrow y \notin C(S)]$, where $C = f(\boldsymbol{R})$.

In condition GL(1), it is required that the CCR allow each individual to exercise his/her right $(x, y) \in D_i$ whenever he/she happens to prefer x

3. It might be of some interest to present a concrete CCR that satisfies condition IP but does not satisfy condition EP. The simplest example is a rule that assigns to each profile $\boldsymbol{R} = (R_1, R_2, \ldots, R_n)$ a choice function C such that $C(S) = S$ for all $S \in \mathcal{S}$. An intrinsically more interesting example is the *majority closure method* (Sen [13, pp. 56, 74]). Let $M_{\boldsymbol{R}}$ be the simple majority relation corresponding to a given profile $\boldsymbol{R}$. Take any $S \in \mathcal{S}$ and let $T(M_{\boldsymbol{R}} \mid S)$ be the transitive closure of $M_{\boldsymbol{R}}$ on S. A choice set $C^*_{\boldsymbol{R}}(S)$ represents a subset of S consisting of the $T(M_{\boldsymbol{R}} \mid S)$-greatest points in S. The majority closure method is a CCR that assigns to each $\boldsymbol{R}$ the choice function $C^*_{\boldsymbol{R}}(S)$. It is easy to see that this CCR satisfies IP but not EP.

to y. In contrast, condition GL(2) does not necessarily allow the de facto individual preferences to rule the roost: it is required in GL(2) that the CCR protect the right $(x, y) \in D_i$ only when the ith individual prefers the distinguishing feature x_i of x *unconditionally* to the corresponding feature y_i of y. Clearly, GL(2) represents a milder libertarian claim than GL(1). Nevertheless, *there exists no* CCR *that satisfies* GL(2), EP, *and* U. This is Gibbard's second impossibility theorem [3, Theorem 2] on libertarianism. A slight generalization thereof is the following.

THEOREM 14.1. There exists no CCR that satisfies GL(2), IP, and U.

PROOF. Suppose that there exists such a CCR. Take any $a_0 \in X_0$ and $a_i \in X_i$ $(i \in N\backslash\{1, 2\})$ and fix them for the rest of this proof. Take $x_i, x_i' \in X_i$, $x_i \neq x_i'$, where $i = 1, 2$, and define

$$x^1 = (a_0, x_1, x_2, a_3, \ldots, a_n),$$

$$x^2 = (a_0, x_1, x_2', a_3, \ldots, a_n),$$

$$x^3 = (a_0, x_1', x_2, a_3, \ldots, a_n),$$

and

$$x^4 = (a_0, x_1', x_2', a_3, \ldots, a_n).$$

Let $S = \{x_1, x_2, x_3, x_4\} \in \mathcal{S}$ and let a profile $\boldsymbol{R} = (R_1, R_2, \ldots, R_n)$ be such that

$$R_1(S) : x^1, x^3, x^2, x^4,$$

$$R_2(S) : x^4, x^3, x^2, x^1,$$

and, for all $i \in N\backslash\{1, 2\}$,

$$R_i(\{x^2, x^3\}) : x^3, x^2,$$

where $R_i(S)$ denotes the restriction of R_i on the set $S : R_i(S) = R_i \cap (S \times S)$.[4] Clearly, then, $(x^1, x^3) \in D_1$, $(x^2, x^4) \in D_1$, and $(x^2, x^1) \in D_2$. No

4. Preference orderings are written horizontally with the less preferred states appearing to the right of the more preferred states, indifferent states, if any, being put together by square brackets.

other individual has a right over these states. Since individual 1 prefers x_1 to x_1' unconditionally and individual 2 prefers x_2' to x_2 unconditionally, condition GL(2) implies that $x^3 \notin C(S)$, $x^4 \notin C(S)$, and $x^1 \notin C(S)$ for a choice set $C(S)$ that corresponds to the specified $\boldsymbol{R}$ and S. Suppose now $x^2 \in C(S)$. Then we have $(x^3, x^2) \in \cap_{i \in N} P(R_i)$, $x^3 \in S$, and $x^2 \in C(S)$, so that condition IP requires that $x^3 \in C(S)$, a contradiction. Therefore, we must have $C(S) = \emptyset$, which negates the existence of a CCR satisfying GL(2), IP, and U. ■

14.2.6. Gibbard's Third Libertarian Claim: Alienability of Libertarian Rights

A salient common feature of GL(1) and GL(2) deserves particular mention: It is supposed that the ith individual's right is exercised in complete negligence of any repercussion from the rest of the society, guided solely by individual rational calculus. From this viewpoint, the gist of the Gibbardian impossibility theorems mentioned so far may be interpreted as the *failure of isolated rational rights exercising*. An ingenious proposal crystallized in Gibbard's third libertarian claim is to make the individual's libertarian rights *alienable* in cases where the exercise of one's libertarian rights brings him into a situation he likes no better than the situation that would otherwise have been brought about. Gibbard observes that, given an $\boldsymbol{R} = (R_1, R_2, \ldots, R_n)$ and an $S \in \mathcal{S}$, an individual $i \in N$ has the will as well as the right to exclude y from $C(S)$ if $x \in S$ and $(x, y) \in D_i \cap P(R_i)$, but his right for the pair (x, y) had better be *waived* if there exists a sequence $\{y_1, y_2, \ldots, y_\lambda\}$ in S such that

$$y_\lambda = x, (y, y_1) \in R_i \ \& \ y \neq y_1 \qquad (14.2)$$

and

$$(\forall t \in \{1, 2, \ldots, \lambda - 1\}): \quad (y_t, y_{t+1}) \in (\cap_{j \in N} P(R_j)) \cup (\cup_{j \in N \setminus \{i\}} [D_j \cap P(R_j)]). \qquad (14.3)$$

Let us define a subset $W_i(\boldsymbol{R} \mid S)$ of D_i, to be called the *waiver set*, by $(x, y) \in W_i(\boldsymbol{R} \mid S)$ if and only if (13.2) and (13.3) are true for some sequence $\{y_\mu\}_{\mu=1}^{\lambda}$ in S.

Condition GL(3) (Gibbard's third libertarian claim). For every profile $\boldsymbol{R} = (R_1, R_2, \ldots, R_n)$, every $S \in \mathcal{S}$, every $i \in N$, and every $x, y \in X$, if $(x, y) \in D_i \cap P(R_i)$ and $(x, y) \notin W_i(\boldsymbol{R} \mid S)$, then $[x \in S \Rightarrow y \notin C(S)]$, where $C = f(\boldsymbol{R})$.

Clearly, this is a claim that differs essentially from GL(1) and GL(2) in that it is explicitly recognized that an individual's rights exercising may induce unfavorable responses from others, which might well nullify the benefit for which the initial exercising was intended. Gibbard has shown that GL(3) represents a *Pareto-consistent libertarian claim*; i.e., *there exists a* CCR *that satisfies* GL(3), EP, *and* U.[5]

14.2.7. Kelly's Rectifications of Gibbard's Alienable Libertarian Claim

Kelly [8; 9, Chapter 9] claims to have found some "flaws" in Gibbard's definition of the rights-waiving rule and proposes two revisions thereof, the first of which goes as follows.[6] Let a profile $\boldsymbol{R} = (R_1, R_2, \ldots, R_n)$ and a set of realizable states $S \in \mathcal{S}$ be given. An individual i waives his right for $(x, y) \in D_i$, viz., $(x, y) \in W_i^*(\boldsymbol{R} \mid S)$, if and only if there exists a sequence $\{y_1, y_2, \ldots, y_\lambda\}$ in S satisfying (14.2) and

$$y_\lambda = x \ \& \ (y, y_1) \in P(R_i). \tag{14.4}$$

Condition KL(1) (Kelly's first libertarian claim). For every profile $\boldsymbol{R} = (R_1, R_2, \ldots, R_n)$, every $S \in \mathcal{S}$, every $i \in N$, and every $x, y \in X$, if $(x, y) \in D_i \cap P(R_i)$ and $(x, y) \notin W_i^*(\boldsymbol{R} \mid S)$, then $[x \in S \Rightarrow y \notin C(S)]$, where $C = f(\boldsymbol{R})$.

The only difference between GL(3) and KL(1) lies in the contrast between (14.1) and (14.3). The reason behind this revision is that "in forcing the move from y to x by exercising $[(x, y) \in D_i,$ the individual $i]$ does not seem to have gotten into trouble if he is forced in the end to take a y_1 where he is indifferent between y_1 and y. Waiving might be appropriate for a cautious

5. Gibbard [3, Theorem 4].

6. As a matter of fact, Kelly proposes the third revised version. For our purpose it is not necessary to get into this complicated proposal, however.

exerciser if $[(y, y_1) \in P(R_i)]$ for some [sequence $\{y_1, y_2, \ldots, y_\lambda\}$], but not if only $[(y, y_1) \in R_i$ as in (14.1)]" (Kelly [8, p. 141; 9, pp. 146–147]).

Going one step further, Kelly proposes his second revised libertarian claim. Suppose that a profile $\boldsymbol{R} = (R_1, R_2, \ldots, R_n)$ and an $S \in \mathcal{S}$ are given. This time, an individual i is supposed to waive his right for $(x, y) \in D_i$, viz., $(x, y) \in W_i^{**}(\boldsymbol{R} \mid S)$ holds, if and only if

(a) there exists a sequence $\{y_1, y_2, \ldots, y_\lambda\}$ in S such that

$$y_\lambda = x \;\&\; (y, y_1) \in P(R_i) \tag{14.5}$$

and

$$(\forall t \in \{1, 2, \ldots, \lambda - 1\}):$$
$$(y_t, y_{t+1}) \in (\cap_{j \in N} P(R_j)) \cup (\cup_{j \in N \setminus \{i\}}[D_j \cap P(R_j)]); \tag{14.6}$$

and (b) for any sequence $\{z_1, z_2, \ldots, z_{\lambda^*}\}$ in S such that

$$z_{\lambda^*} = y_1 \;\&\; (z_1, y) \in P(R_i) \tag{14.7}$$

and

$$(\forall t \in \{1, 2, \ldots, \lambda^* - 1\}):$$
$$(z_t, z_{t+1}) \in (\cap_{j \in N} P(R_j)) \cup (\cup_{j \in N}[D_j \cap P(R_j)]), \tag{14.8}$$

there exists correspondingly a sequence $\{w_1, w_2, \ldots, w_{\lambda^{**}}\}$ in S such that

$$w_{\lambda^{**}} = z_1 \;\&\; (y, w_1) \in P(R_i) \tag{14.9}$$

and

$$(\forall t \in \{1, 2, \ldots, \lambda^{**} - 1\}):$$
$$(w_t, w_{t+1}) \in (\cap_{j \in N} P(R_j)) \cup (\cup_{j \in N \setminus \{i\}}[D_j \cap P(R_j)]). \tag{14.10}$$

Condition KL(2) (Kelly's second libertarian claim). For every profile $\boldsymbol{R} = (R_1, R_2, \ldots, R_n)$, every $S \in \mathcal{S}$, every $i \in N$, and every $x, y \in X$, if $(x, y) \in D_i \cap P(R_i)$ and $(x, y) \notin W_i^{**}(\boldsymbol{R} \mid S)$, then $[x \in S \Rightarrow y \notin C(S)]$, where $C = f(\boldsymbol{R})$.

The difference between KL(1) and KL(2) is the addition of (b) when we define $W_i^{**}(\boldsymbol{R} \mid S)$, which says basically that any sequence $\{z_1, z_2, \ldots, z_{\lambda^*}\}$

that seems to repair in the eyes of the individual i the damage caused upon him/her by a sequence $\{y_1, y_2, \ldots, y_\lambda\}$ will be made ineffective by some other, out-of-control sequence $\{w_1, w_2, \ldots, w_{\lambda^{**}}\}$.

14.3. Impossibility Theorems

14.3.1. Impossibility of Kelly's Revised Alienable Libertarian Claims

Taken by themselves, these proposed revisions may seem to be fairly persuasive and, according to Kelly [8, p. 144; 9, p. 148], "it causes no significant changes in the theorems that make up Gibbard's libertarian claim." The truth is, however, that Kelly's reasonable-looking revisions to Gibbard's libertarian claim change it into a standard for individual liberty that cannot possibly be met, as the following impossibility theorems show.

Theorem 14.2. There exists no CCR that satisfies KL(1) and U.

Theorem 14.3. There exists no CCR that satisfies KL(2) and U.

To prove these theorems, note first that, for every profile $\boldsymbol{R} = (R_1, R_2, \ldots, R_n)$ and every $S \in \mathcal{S}$, the following set inclusions are true.

$$W_i^{**}(\boldsymbol{R} \mid S) \subseteq W_i^{*}(\boldsymbol{R} \mid S) \subseteq W_i(\boldsymbol{R} \mid S) \qquad (14.11)$$

for all $i \in N$. Clearly, then, KL(2) is a *stronger* libertarian claim than KL(1), so that we have only to prove Theorem 14.2, Theorem 14.3 being a corollary thereof.

Proof of Theorem 14.2. Suppose that f is a CCR that satisfies KL(1) and U. Let $S = \{x^1, x^2, x^3, x^4\} \in \mathcal{S}$ be defined as in the proof of Theorem 14.1 and let a profile $\boldsymbol{R} = (R_1, R_2, \ldots, R_n)$ be such that

$$R_1(S) : x^1, x^4, [x^2, x^3],$$

$$R_2(S) : x^3, x^2, [x^1, x^4].$$

There is no restriction on R_i for $i \in N \backslash \{1, 2\}$ whatsoever. It is clear that $(x^1, x^3) \in D_1$, $(x^4, x^2) \in D_1$, $(x^3, x^4) \in D_2$, and $(x^2, x^1) \in D_2$. No other individual has a right over these pairs of states. Consider the pair of states $(x^1, x^3) \in D_1 \cap P(R_1)$. The worst that could happen to individual 1 after his exercise of $(x^1, x^3) \in D_1$ is the counterexercise by 2 of $(x^2, x^1) \in D_2$ in view of $(x^2, x^1) \in P(R_2)$. (Note that there is no state in S that strictly Pareto-dominates x^1.) Since x^2 and x^3 are indifferent to individual 1 and $x^2 \neq x^3$, GL(3) would let 1 waive his right over (x^1, x^3). However, KL(1) does allow 1 to exercise his right over (x^1, x^3), viz., $(x^1, x^3) \in W_1(\boldsymbol{R} \mid S) \backslash W_1^*(\boldsymbol{R} \mid S)$. Similar reasoning leads us to $(x^4, x^2) \in W_1(\boldsymbol{R} \mid S) \backslash W_1^*(\boldsymbol{R} \mid S)$, $(x^3, x^4) \in W_2(\boldsymbol{R} \mid S) \backslash W_2^*(\boldsymbol{R} \mid S)$, and $(x^2, x^1) \in W_2(\boldsymbol{R} \mid S) \backslash W_2^*(\boldsymbol{R} \mid S)$. By virtue of condition KL(1), it then follows that $C(S) = \emptyset$, a contradiction. ■

14.3.2. Impossibility of Gibbard-Kelly Alienable Libertarian Claim

Kelly's first revised libertarian claim thus brings back an impossibility. A fortiori, his second (and stronger) revised libertarian claim is inconsistent with the existence of a universal CCR. One may thereby be tempted to conclude that the system of alienable rights is something like a fragile glasswork that may be easily smashed to pieces while giving the last finish to it. To be fair, however, one should not forget to examine whether the finishing touch was an appropriate one.

Back, then, to the contrast between GL(3) and KL(1), viz., the contrast between (14.2) and (14.4). Stipulation (14.4) was recommended in place of (14.2), because, in forcing the move from y to x by exercising $(x, y) \in D_i$, individual i does not *lose* anything even if he is forced in the end to take a y_1 such that $(y, y_1) \in I(R_i)$ and $y \neq y_1$. Note, however, that he does not *gain* anything either. Note also that the rights exercising in Gibbard's system places very heavy demands on information gathering and processing,[7] so that the rights exercising would be unwise unless it were to yield a positive gain. This argument, if accepted, would favor (14.2) rather than (14.4) and would necessitate the following modification of KL(2). Given a profile $\boldsymbol{R} = (R_1, R_2, \ldots, R_n)$ and an $S \in \mathcal{S}$, define the waiver set $W_i^0(\boldsymbol{R} \mid S)$ by $(x, y) \in W_i^0(\boldsymbol{R} \mid S)$ if and only if

(a) there exists a sequence $\{y_1, y_2, \ldots, y_\lambda\}$ in S such that

$$y_\lambda = x, (y, y_1) \in R_i \;\&\; y \neq y_1 \tag{14.12}$$

7. Kelly [8, p. 141; 9, p. 146].

and

$$(\forall t \in \{1, 2, \ldots, \lambda - 1\}):$$
$$(y_t, y_{t+1}) \in (\cap_{j \in N} P(R_j)) \cup (\cup_{j \in N \setminus \{i\}} [D_j \cap P(R_j)]); \quad (14.13)$$

and (b) for any sequence $\{z_1, z_2, \ldots, z_{\lambda^*}\}$ in S such that

$$z_{\lambda^*} = y_1 \ \& \ [(z_1, y) \in P(R_i) \vee z_1 = y] \quad (14.14)$$

and

$$(\forall t \in \{1, 2, \ldots, \lambda^* - 1\}):$$
$$(z_t, z_{t+1}) \in (\cap_{j \in N} P(R_j)) \cup (\cup_{j \in N} [D_j \cap P(R_j)]), \quad (14.15)$$

there exists correspondingly a sequence $\{w_1, w_2, \ldots, w_{\lambda^{**}}\}$ in S such that

$$w_{\lambda^{**}} = z_1, (y, w_1) \in R_i \ \& \ y \neq w_1 \quad (14.16)$$

and

$$(\forall t \in \{1, 2, \ldots, \lambda^{**} - 1\}):$$
$$(w_t, w_{t+1}) \in (\cap_{j \in N} P(R_j)) \cup (\cup_{j \in N \setminus \{i\}} [D_j \cap P(R_j)]), \quad (14.17)$$

for all $i \in N$. Utilizing this modified definition of the waiver set, we now put forward the following.

Condition GKL (Gibbard-Kelly libertarian claim). For every profile $\boldsymbol{R} = (R_1, R_2, \ldots, R_n)$, every $S \in \mathcal{S}$, every $i \in N$, and every $x, y \in X$, if $(x, y) \in D_i \cap P(R_i)$ and $(x, y) \notin W_i^0(\boldsymbol{R} \mid S)$, then $[x \in S \Rightarrow y \notin C(S)]$, where $C = f(\boldsymbol{R})$.

How does GKL fare in the context of universal CCRs? That it fares no better than KL(1) and KL(2) is the thrust of the next theorem.

Theorem 14.4. There exists no CCR that satisfies GKL and U.

Proof. Suppose that f is an eligible CCR. Assume $S = \{x^1, x^2, x^3, x^4\} \in \mathcal{S}$ and $\boldsymbol{R} = (R_1, R_2, \ldots, R_n)$ are the same as in the proof of Theorem 14.2. Consider now the pair of states $(x^2, x^3) \in D_1 \cap P(R_1)$. The worst situation that individual 1's exercise of $(x^1, x^3) \in D_1$ may induce is the counterexercise by 2 of $(x^2, x^1) \in D_2$ in view of $(x^2, x^1) \in P(R_2)$. Individual 1 may then exercise $(x^4, x^2) \in D_1 \cap P(R_1)$ to secure x^4, which 1 prefers to x^3. Is there any nullifying sequence? The worst that could happen to 1 is the exercise by 2 of $(x^3, x^4) \in D_2$, which does not require 1 to waive his right $(x^1, x^3) \in D_1$ according to the definition of $W_1^0(\boldsymbol{R} \mid S)$.[8] Therefore, GKL ensures that $x^3 \notin C(S)$. By the same token, we may verify that

$$[(x^4, x^2) \in D_1 \cap P(R_1) \;\&\; (x^4, x^2) \notin W_1^0(\boldsymbol{R} \mid S)] \Rightarrow x^2 \notin C(S),$$

$$[(x^2, x^1) \in D_2 \cap P(R_2) \;\&\; (x^2, x^1) \notin W_2^0(\boldsymbol{R} \mid S)] \Rightarrow x^1 \notin C(S),$$

and

$$[(x^3, x^4) \in D_2 \cap P(R_2) \;\&\; (x^3, x^4) \notin W_2^0(\boldsymbol{R} \mid S)] \Rightarrow x^4 \notin C(S),$$

so that we obtain $C(S) = \emptyset$, a contradiction. ∎

14.3.3. Protection of Libertarian Rights Contingent on Unconditional Preferences

If we examine the profile we utilized in proving Theorems 14.2, 14.3, and 14.4, it turns out that *both* 1 and 2 are expressing preferences that are conditional on the other's selection of his personal feature: 1 prefers x_1 to x_1' if 2 has x_2, while he prefers x_1' to x_1 if 2's choice is x_2' and vice versa. It is probably too much to ask for the existence of a universal CCR that

---

8. Two clarifications might be in order here. First, from x^2, something else may happen (besides 1 exercising his right $(x^4, x^2) \in D_1$) *if* the Pareto dominance relation is weakened from $\cap_{i \in N} P(R_i)$ to $P(\cap_{i \in N} R_i)$. That is to say, *if* $(x^3, x^2) \in R_i$ for all $i \in N \backslash \{1, 2\}$ and *if* in (14.13), (14.15), and (14.17) all instances of $\cap_{i \in N} P(R_i)$ are replaced by $P(\cap_{i \in N} R_i)$, x^3 might be picked over x^2 by a Pareto dominance. It is clear, however, that this possibility does not affect our conclusion that $(x^1, x^3) \notin W_1^0(\boldsymbol{R} \mid S)$. Second, in arriving at the conclusion that $(x^1, x^3) \notin W_1^0(\boldsymbol{R} \mid S)$, we have followed the "path" $x^3 \to x^1 \to x^2 \to x^4 \to x^3$ generated by the successive rights exercising of 1 and 2. Namely, we started from x^3 and came back to x^3 again! It might be asked, why don't we let 1 waive his right $(x^1, x^3) \in D_1$ in this case? Put differently, why do we stipulate the condition $y \neq y_1$ in (14.12)? The reason is that there exists an important difference between (i) the travel from x^3 (via a sequence of states) back to x^3 again and (ii) the travel from x^3 to an $x^* \in S$ such that $(x^3, x^*) \in I(R_1)$. In the former case, individual 1 comes back to x^3 *without losing his right over* x^3, while in the latter case, 1 may well be stuck at x^* *without having any right over* x^*. This is also the reason why we modified (14.7) into (14.14).

protects individuals' mere conditional preferences. On reflection, we need only require the existence of a CCR that protects individuals' libertarian rights so far as the relevant individual expresses unconditional preference for his personal features. Therefore, let $N(\boldsymbol{R} \mid S)$ be the set of individuals having unconditional preferences, given a profile $\boldsymbol{R}$ and an available set $S \in \mathcal{S}$, viz., $i \in N(\boldsymbol{R} \mid S)$ if and only if $(x, y) \in D_i \cap (S \times S) \cap P(R_i)$ always implies that $((x_i; z_{)i(}), (y_i; z_{)i(})) \in P(R_i)$ for all $z_{)i(}$ such that $(x_i; z_{)i(}) \in S$ and $(y_i; z_{)i(}) \in S$. The relevant waiver set can be specified thus: $(x, y) \in D_i$ will be waived, viz., $(x, y) \in W_i^{00}(\boldsymbol{R} \mid S)$ if and only if *either* (i) $i \in N \backslash N(\boldsymbol{R} \mid S)$ *or* (ii) the following conditions hold true:

(a) there exists a sequence $\{y_1, y_2, \ldots, y_\lambda\}$ in S such that

$$y_\lambda = x, (y, y_1) \in R_i \;\&\; y \neq y_1$$

and

$$(\forall t \in \{1, 2, \ldots, \lambda - 1\}):$$
$$(y_t, y_{t+1}) \in (\cap_{j \in N} P(R_j)) \cup (\cup_{j \in N(R|S) \backslash \{i\}} [D_j \cap P(R_j)]);$$

and (b) for any sequence $\{z_1, z_2, \ldots, z_{\lambda^*}\}$ in S such that

$$z_{\lambda^*} = y_1 \;\&\; [(z_1, y) \in P(R_i) \vee z_1 = y]$$

and

$$(\forall t \in \{1, 2, \ldots, \lambda^* - 1\}):$$
$$(z_t, z_{t+1}) \in (\cap_{j \in N} P(R_j)) \cup (\cup_{j \in N(R|S)} [D_j \cap P(R_j)]),$$

there exists correspondingly a sequence $\{w_1, w_2, \ldots, w_{\lambda^{**}}\}$ in S such that

$$w_{\lambda^{**}} = z_1, (y, w_1) \in R_i \;\&\; y \neq w_1$$

and

$$(\forall t \in \{1, 2, \ldots, \lambda^{**} - 1\}):$$
$$(w_t, w_{t+1}) \in (\cap_{j \in N} P(R_j)) \cup (\cup_{j \in N(R|S) \backslash \{i\}} [D_j \cap P(R_j)]).$$

Our final version of the libertarian claim in the spirit of Gibbard and Kelly goes as follows.

Condition GKL*. For every profile $\boldsymbol{R} = (R_1, R_2. \ldots, R_n)$, every $S \in \mathcal{S}$, every $i \in N$, and every $x, y \in X$, if $(x, y) \in D_i \cap P(R_i)$ and $(x, y) \notin W_i^{00}(\boldsymbol{R} \mid S)$, then $[x \in S \Rightarrow y \notin C(S)]$, where $C = f(\boldsymbol{R})$.

Clearly, GKL* is *weaker* than GL(2). Unfortunately, this modest version of the libertarian claim still may not break the impasse if there are at least three individuals in the society.

Theorem 14.5. Suppose that $n \geq 3$. Then there exists no CCR that satisfies GKL*, IP, and U.

Proof. Suppose that an eligible CCR f does exist. Take any $a_0 \in X_0$ and $a_i \in X_i$ $(i \in N\backslash\{1, 2, 3\})$ and fix them for the rest of this proof. Take $x_i, x_i' \in X_i$, $x_i \neq x_i'$ for $i \in \{1, 2, 3\}$ and define

$$x^0 = (a_0, x_1, x_2, x_3', a_4, \ldots, a_n),$$

$$x^1 = (a_0, x_1, x_2, x_3, a_4, \ldots, a_n),$$

$$x^2 = (a_0, x_1, x_2', x_3, a_4, \ldots, a_n),$$

$$x^3 = (a_0, x_1', x_2, x_3, a_4, \ldots, a_n),$$

and

$$x^4 = (a_0, x_1', x_2', x_3, a_4, \ldots, a_n).$$

Let $S = \{x^0, x^1, x^2, x^3, x^4\} \in \mathcal{S}$ and let a profile $\boldsymbol{R} = (R_1, R_2, \ldots, R_n)$ be such that

$$R_1(S) : x^1, x^3, x^2, x^4, x^0,$$

$$R_2(S) : [x^3, x^4], x^2, x^1, x^0,$$

$$R_3(S) : x^3, x^2, x^0, x^4, x^1,$$

and, for all $i \in N\backslash\{1, 2, 3\}$,

$$R_i(\{x^0, x^2, x^3\}) : x^3, x^2, x^0.$$

By definition we see that $(x^1, x^3) \in D_1$, $(x^2, x^4) \in D_1$, $(x^3, x^4) \in D_2$, $(x^2, x^1) \in D_2$, and $(x^0, x^1) \in D_3$. Note that individual 1 prefers x_1 to x_1'

unconditionally and individual 3 prefers x_3' to x_3 unconditionally. On the other hand, individual 2 prefers x_2' to x_2 if 1 chooses x_1, while he is indifferent between x_2 and x_2' if 1 chooses x_1' instead. In view of this conditional nature of 2's preferences, his rights exercising will be made ineffective by a CCR subject to GKL*. Consider now the pair of states $(x^1, x^3) \in D_1 \cap P(R_1)$. The worst contingency that could be induced by the exercise of $(x^1, x^3) \in D_1$ is the counterexercise of $(x^0, x^1) \in D_3 \cap P(R_3)$. Since $(x^3, x^0) \in \cap_{i \in N} P(R_i)$ holds true, and there exists no nullifying sequence in S, we may conclude from GKL* that

$$[(x^1, x^3) \in D_1 \cap P(R_1) \,\&\, (x^1, x^3) \notin W_1^{00}(\boldsymbol{R} \mid S)] \Rightarrow x^3 \notin C(S).$$

Similarly, we may verify that

$$[(x^2, x^4) \in D_1 \cap P(R_1) \,\&\, (x^2, x^4) \notin W_1^{00}(\boldsymbol{R} \mid S)] \Rightarrow x^4 \notin C(S)$$

and

$$[(x^0, x^1) \in D_3 \cap P(R_3) \,\&\, (x^0, x^1) \notin W_3^{00}(\boldsymbol{R} \mid S)] \Rightarrow x^1 \notin C(S).$$

We may then invoke condition IP (as we did in the proof of Theorem 14.1) to conclude that $x^2 \notin C(S)$ and $x^0 \notin C(S)$. It then follows that $C(S) = \emptyset$, a contradiction. ■

14.4. Metarational Exercising of Rights

14.4.1. Naive Rights-Exercising versus Sophisticated Rights-Exercising

Among the libertarian claims we have examined in the preceding sections, GL(3), KL(1), KL(2), GKL, and GKL* differ substantially from GL(1) and GL(2) in that due attention is paid in the former category of claims to the fact that, in deciding whether to exercise one's right or not, one should take into consideration the others' response via their rights exercising and/or Pareto dominance. Notice, however, that it is commonly assumed in these claims that each individual, in predicting the others' response to his rights exercising, presumes that *the others follow the naive rights-exercising rule without making* *any effort of prediction on their part*.[9] It might be asked, what can we make of the libertarian claims if we assume instead the complete mutual prediction?

14.4.2. Meta-Game Theoretic Articulation of Rights-Exercising Behavior

The situation of complete mutual prediction may be modeled after the metagame theory of Howard [4; 5; 6]. For simplicity let there be only two individuals in the society and let an impersonal feature vector $s_0 \in X_0$ be fixed for the rest of this essay. S_1 and S_2 denote the set of all available personal feature alternatives of individual 1 and individual 2, respectively. Given a profile $\boldsymbol{R} = (R_1, R_2)$, we may construe the 4-tuple $\Gamma = (S_1, S_2; R_1, R_2)$ as a *basic game* played by 1 and 2. Each individual $k \in \{1, 2\}$ wishes to choose such an $s_k \in S_k$ as to yield, coupled with the fixed s_0 and the choice $s_{\sim k} \in S_{\sim k}$ of the other individual $\sim k$, a state $(s_0, s_k, s_{\sim k}) \in \{s_0\} \times S_1 \times S_2 \equiv S$ that "optimizes" his preference R_k over S.[10] In a liberal society, k obviously lacks the power to regulate the choice by $\sim k$ of his personal feature, so that the best k can do is to predict the choice by $\sim k$ and to form a *metastrategy*, which is a function g^k from $S_{\sim k}$ into S_k such that, for each $s_{\sim k} \in S_{\sim k}$, $(s_0, g^k(s_{\sim k}), s_{\sim k}) \in S$ is the best state in S with respect to R_k. In effect, then, k is thinking in terms of the first-level metagame $k\Gamma = (G^k, S_{\sim k}; R_k, R_{\sim k})$, where G^k denotes the set of all functions from $S_{\sim k}$ into S_k. In doing this, however, k should be aware that $\sim k$ may be able to, and should rationally try to, predict k's choice of his metastrategy. The subjective game of k in the situation of complete mutual prediction is the second-level metagame $(\sim k)k\Gamma = (G^k, F^{\sim k}; R_k, R_{\sim k})$, where $F^{\sim k}$ denotes the set of all functions from G^k into $S_{\sim k}$. We repeat for emphasis: The metagame $(\sim k)k\Gamma$ represents a model in which $\sim k$ is able to predict k's choice in the metagame $k\Gamma$, while the metagame $k\Gamma$ represents a model in which k is able to predict $\sim k$'s choice in the basic game Γ. Thus in the metagame $(\sim k)k\Gamma$ there is a complete mutual prediction.

---

9. This point was duly stressed by Kelly. He has shown that a serious difficulty of *correctable miscalculation* emerges from this peculiarity of the Gibbardian rights-exercising rule. See Kelly [8; 9, Chapter 9].

10. It is assumed here that the set of realizable states S satisfies Kelly's [8; 9, Chapter 9] *agenda-closedness* and Seidl's [10] *technological separability*.

14.4.3. Meta-Rational Outcomes of Rights-Execising

Let us say, following Howard, that an outcome $(g_*^k, f_*^{\sim k})$ of the metagame $(\sim k)k\Gamma$ is *metarational for k via* $(\sim k)k\Gamma$ if and only if

$$[(g_*^k(f_*^{\sim k}(g_*^k)), f_*^{\sim k}(g_*^k)), (g_*^k(f_*^{\sim k}(g_*^k)), f_*^{\sim k}(g^k))] \in R_k \quad (14.18)$$

for all $g^k \in G^k$. In this case the corresponding basic outcome is given by $(s_0, g_*^k(f^{\sim k}(g_*^k)), f^{\sim k}(g_*^k)) \in S$, which will be called hereafter the *metarational basic outcome for k via* $(\sim k)k\Gamma$. Let $M_k[(\sim k)k\Gamma]$ denote the set of all metarational basic outcomes for k via $(\sim k)k\Gamma$. We may also define $M_{\sim k}[(\sim k)k\Gamma]$, $M_k[k(\sim k)\Gamma]$, and $M_{\sim k}[k(\sim k)\Gamma]$. We may now define the concept of *metasolutions*. In the present context, two possibilities suggest themselves. First we have

$$M^*(\Gamma) = M_k[(\sim k)k\Gamma] \cap M_{\sim k}[k(\sim k)\Gamma], \quad (14.19)$$

which is appealing for the following reason. In general, "there will be a strong tendency for player i's subjective metagame to be one in which he follows all the others last. For such a metagame is precisely one in which he can predict the others' basic strategies, they cannot predict his, and they are possibly able to predict his [metastrategy]. Indeed, if we add the condition that i believes there is complete mutual prediction . . . , then this precisely describes the complete metagames in which he follows all others last."[11] It then follows that, if $s^* \in M^*(\Gamma)$, then s^* is a metarational basic outcome for *both* individuals via their *respective* "natural" subjective metagames with complete mutual prediction. The second metasolution concept of our concern is

$$M_*(\Gamma) = \{M_k[(\sim k)k\Gamma] \cap M_{\sim k}[(\sim k)k\Gamma]\} \cup \{M_k[k(\sim k)\Gamma] \cap M_{\sim k}[k(\sim k)\Gamma]\}. \quad (14.20)$$

By definition, $s^* \in M_*(\Gamma)$ holds true if and only if s^* is a metarational basic outcome for *both* individuals via a *common* metagame with complete mutual prediction. Remember that an $s^* \in M^*(\Gamma)$, however "natural" it may be, cannot be an equilibrium via voluntary bargaining or negotiation except

11. Howard [6, p. 106].

as a result of some kind of misunderstanding: each individual behaves as if he can predict the other's basic strategy while the other can at best predict his metastrategy choice, but they cannot both be correct. In contrast, a metasolution $s^* \in M_*(\Gamma)$ is the basic outcome that constitutes an equilibrium when both individuals have agreed on the same subjective metagame.

14.4.4. Meta-Rational Solutions to Liberal Paradoxes

We now examine these metasolution concepts in the context of the liberal paradoxes.

EXAMPLE 14.1. Let $\Gamma = (S_1, S_2; R_1, R_2)$ be such that $S_1 = \{s_1, s_1'\}$, $S_2 = \{s_2, s_2'\}$ and

$$R_1(S): s^1, s^3, s^2, s^4,$$

$$R_2(S): s^4, s^3, s^2, s^1,$$

where $s^1 = (s_0, s_1, s_2)$, $s^2 = (s_0, s_1, s_2')$, $s^3 = (s_0, s_1', s_2)$, and $s^4 = (s_0, s_1', s'_2)$. Note that this profile is the same as the one used in the proof of Theorem 14.1. In the game theoretic context, this situation is known as the *prisoners' dilemma*.[12] It is easy, if tedious, to verify for this game Γ that $M_1[21\Gamma] = M_2[21\Gamma] = M_1[12\Gamma] = M_2[12\Gamma] = \{s^2, s^3\}$, so that we have

$$M^*(\Gamma) = M_*(\Gamma) = \{s^2, s^3\}.$$

Let $O_{\boldsymbol{R}}(S)$ be the set of Pareto-optimal states in S when the profile $\boldsymbol{R}$ prevails. Note, then, that $\{s^3\} = O_{\boldsymbol{R}}(S) \cap M^*(\Gamma) = O_{\boldsymbol{R}}(S) \cap M_*(\Gamma)$. Therefore, it may duly be said that the metarational exercising of rights brings about a Pareto-optimal state in the case of the prisoners' dilemma profile, thereby resolving the *Paretian liberal paradox*.

An important feature of this scheme should be stressed: each individual need not know the other's preference in this scheme, since $M_k[(\sim k)k\Gamma]$ as well as $M_k[k(\sim k)\Gamma]$ are definable solely in terms of k's own preferences. This is certainly a nice feature, but the real force of this resolution scheme

12. Fine [2] pointed out the similarity between the prisoners' dilemma and the liberal paradox.

is revealed if we examine the next example, which relates to the internal inconsistency of rights.[13]

Example 14.2. Let Γ^* be the same as Γ in Example 1 save for the following specification of the profile $\boldsymbol{R}^* = (R_1^*, R_2^*)$:

$$R_1^*(S): [s^1, s^4], [s^2, s^3],$$

$$R_2^*(S): [s^2, s^3], [s^1, s^4].$$

Consider the metagames $(\sim k)k\Gamma^*$ and $k(\sim k)\Gamma^*$. We may verify that $M_1[21\Gamma^*] = M_1[12\Gamma^*] = \{s^1, s^4\}$ and $M_2[21\Gamma^*] = M_2[12\Gamma^*] = \{s^2, s^3\}$.[14] It then follows that $M^*(\Gamma^*) = M_1[21\Gamma^*] \cap M_2[12\Gamma^*] = \emptyset$, and $M_*(\Gamma^*) = \{M_1[21\Gamma^*] \cap M_2[12\Gamma^*]\} \cup \{M_1[12\Gamma^*] \cap M_2[12\Gamma^*]\} = \emptyset$. Therefore, both metasolution concepts fail to resolve the liberal paradox embodied in the game Γ^*.

14.4.5. Relevance of Meta-Rational Exercising of Libertarian Rights

There are two classes of liberal paradox that we should cope with: the *Paretian liberal paradox* and the *paradox of the internal inconsistency of rights*. We have shown in the preceding that the metarational exercising of rights in the situation of complete mutual prediction may systematically resolve the former class of paradoxes, while the latter difficulty may not be resolved in this manner.

14.5. Concluding Remarks

In reviewing a number of contributions to the Paretian liberal paradox, Sen [12, p. 224] argued that "[Kelly] identifies a number of difficulties with Gibbard's system [which are] essentially arising from problems in deciding *when*

13. See Gibbard's wall color case [3, p. 389] and Sen's Zubeida-Rehana case [12, p. 234]. In the game theoretic literature, the game Γ^* in Example 14.2 is called the game of matching pennies. See Howard [4, p. 182].

14. Howard's *characterization theorem for metarational outcomes* [6, pp.89–96] is useful in verifying these results.

a right is useful for a person. . . . Some of these difficulties are eliminated by modifications of the Gibbard system proposed by Kelly." We have examined in this essay Gibbard's system of alienable rights in light of Kelly's proposed modifications thereof. It was shown that the difficulties identified by Kelly are more serious than Kelly and Sen have thought them to be, and they are *not* eliminated by Kelly's proposed modifications. We have also examined the possibility and limitation of resolving the liberal paradox via metarational rights exercising. In conclusion, it is hoped that the negative results reported in this essay will serve to clarify the nature and stubbornness of the paradox of a Paretian liberal.

14.6. References

[1] Barry, B., *The Liberal Theory of Justice,* London: Oxford University Press, 1973.
[2] Fine, B., "Individual Liberalism in a Paretian Society," *Journal of Political Economy* **83**, 1975, 1277–1281.
[3] Gibbard, A., "A Pareto-Consistent Libertarian Claim," *Journal of Economic Theory* **7**, 1974, 388–410.
[4] Howard, N., "The Theory of Meta-Games," *General Systems* **11**, 1966, 167–186.
[5] Howard, N., "The Mathematics of Meta-Games," *General Systems* **11**, 1966, 187–200.
[6] Howard, N., *Paradoxes of Rationality: Theory of Metagames and Political Behavior,* Cambridge, Mass.: MIT Press, 1971.
[7] Karni, E., "Collective Rationality, Unanimity and Liberal Ethics," *Review of Economic Studies* **45**, 1978, 571–574.
[8] Kelly, J. S., "Rights Exercising and a Pareto-Consistent Libertarian Claim," *Journal of Economic Theory* **13**, 1976, 138–153.
[9] Kelly, J. S., *Arrow Impossibility Theorems,* New York: Academic Press, 1978.
[10] Seidl, C., "On Liberal Values," *Zeitschrift für Nationalökonomie* **35**, 1975, 257–292.
[11] Sen, A. K., *Collective Choice and Social Welfare,* San Francisco: Holden-Day, 1970.
[12] Sen, A. K., "Liberty, Unanimity and Rights," *Economica* **43**, 1976, 217–245.
[13] Sen, A. K., "Social Choice Theory: A Re-Examination," *Econometrica* **45**, 1977, 53–89.
[14] Suzumura, K., "On the Consistency of Libertarian Claims," *Review of Economic Studies* **45**, 1978, 329–342. Essay 13 of this volume.

ESSAY 15

Individual Rights Revisited

15.1. Introduction

Ever since the publication of Sen's [13; 14, Chapter 6*] seminal contributions, the subject of individual libertarian rights has attracted much attention from economists, and Sen's paradox of the impossibility of a Paretian liberal has inspired a large volume of literature that has spanned several disciplines, including economics, philosophy, and politics.[1] Not surprisingly, Sen's contributions have provoked controversies. One of the most fundamental questions raised in this context relates to the very formulation of the concept of libertarian rights due to Sen. It has been contended by Nozick [11], Bernholz [1], Gärdenfors [5], and Sugden [18], among others, that this formulation

First published in *Economica* **59**, 1992, pp. 161–177, as a joint paper with W. Gaertner and P. K. Pattanaik. Reprinted in C. K. Rowley, ed., *The International Library of Critical Writings in Economics,* Vol. 27, *Social Justice and Classical Liberal Goals,* Cheltenham, Glos., UK: Edward Elgar, 1993, pp. 592–608. Our greatest debt is to Amartya Sen. Not only were we introduced to the problem of rights by his writings, but also we have benefited immensely from many discussions we have had with him over the years. We are also grateful to P. Gärdenfors, S. Hansson, S. Kanger, M. Kaneko, I. Levi, D. Parfit, R. Sugden, and the editor and two referees of *Economica* for their helpful comments and discussions. The generosity of the British Council, Wissenschaftskolleg zu Berlin, the Murphy Institute of Political Economy (Tulane), the University of Osnabrück, the University of Birmingham, and All Souls College (Oxford) made this collaborative research possible. We would like to express our sincere gratitude to all these institutions for their support and hospitality, which far exceeded what we had any right to expect. An early draft was presented at the Sixth World Congress of the Econometric Society, Barcelona, August 22–28, 1990.

1. For a partial survey of the literature, see Sen [15], Suzumura [20, Chapter 7], and Wriglesworth [22].

does not capture our intuitive notion of rights.[2] In an important paper, Sen [15] responded to some of these criticisms. This, however, led to further debates (see Sugden [19]). In this essay we seek to highlight some important strands in this debate, and to achieve some clarification of the different and often incompatible views of individual rights that have generated this controversy.

It may be worth clarifying at the outset that our basic concern is the formulation of the notion of individual rights per se, and not the conflict between individual rights and the weak welfarisitic requirement of Pareto optimality. This conflict is a fundamental problem in the theory of social choice and has rightly received much attention, thanks to the path-breaking analysis of Sen. It is our belief that this problem persists under virtually every plausible concept of individual rights that we can think of. However, we do not discuss this issue of incompatibility between individual rights and the Pareto principle, nor do we seek to provide a solution to this problem. Instead, we focus on the conceptual problem of formulating the notion of individual rights in the theory of social choice, and the extent to which our intuition about individual rights is captured by the different formulations in the literature.

The structure of this essay is as follows. In Section 14.2 we discuss some of the main features of Sen's [13; 14; 15; 16] formulation of individual rights. In Section 14.3 we put forward an example, the analysis of which reveals that our intuitive notion about certain types of individual rights is not properly captured by Sen's formulation. In Section 14.4 we generalize our criticism of Sen's formulation of individual rights, and argue that the intuitive difficulties discussed in Section 14.3 affect his formulation in the context of most rights one can think of. In Section 14.5 an alternative formulation of individual rights in terms of game forms is introduced, and its relative merit vis-à-vis Sen's formulation is considered. Section 14.6 concludes with a brief account of the historical background of our analysis.

15.2. Sen's Formulation of Individual Rights

The basic intuitive idea of individual rights, which Sen [13; 14; 15] as well as many of his critics have sought to capture, can perhaps be best stated in

2. See also Gibbard [8].

the language of J. S. Mill [10, Book 5, Chapter 11]: "There is a circle around every individual human being which no government, be it that of one, of a few, or of the many, ought to be permitted to overstep."

Thus, both Sen and his critics would agree with Mill that each individual should have a "recognized personal sphere" (RPS) with which the rest of the society should not be allowed to interfere. Differences, however, arise when they seek to provide a precise formulation of this personal sphere and of how the recognition of the personal spheres of different individuals should get reflected in the choices made by the society.

Sen's [13; 14] original formulation was in terms of social preferences. Recollect that the notion of social preferences, so widely used in the theory of social choice, can bear alternative interpretations, depending on the exact nature of the problem in which one is interested (see Sen [16]). In this essay we concentrate on the normative problem of social choice, and Sen's notion of individual rights will be discussed exclusively in terms of social choice.

For our purpose, a social state will be interpreted as a complete description of all aspects of the society that may be considered relevant, such as the color of individual i's bedroom walls, the number of hospital beds available, the consumption of wheat by each individual, and so on. Every individual is assumed to have a preference ordering over all social states.

The notion of an individual's RPS constitutes the intuitive foundation of Sen's [13; 14] condition of liberalism, which embodies his conception of individual rights. Recollect that individual i is said to be *decisive* over $\{x, y\}$, where $x \neq y$, if y (resp. x) will never be socially chosen when x (resp. y) is available and i strictly prefers x (resp. y) to y (resp. x). Sen's condition of liberalism can then be stated as follows:

(1.1) For every individual i, there exist distinct social alternatives x and y such that i is decisive over $\{x, y\}$.

Implicit in (1.1) is the interpretation that the two alternatives, x and y, differ only with respect to some aspect (e.g., the color of i's bedroom walls) that comes within i's RPS; otherwise the condition (1.1) can hardly be associated with the notion of libertarian rights.

Sen's condition of liberalism can be interpreted in a somewhat weaker sense. Let us say that i is *locally decisive* over $\{x, y\}$, where $x \neq y$, if y (resp. x) will never be socially chosen when x and y are only two available social alternatives and i strictly prefers x (resp. y) to y (resp. x). Then a weaker interpretation of Sen's condition can read as follows:

(1.2) For every individual i, there exist distinct social alternatives x and y such that i is locally decisive over $\{x, y\}$.[3]

Thus, under Sen's conception of individual rights, individual i has a right if (1.1) or (1.2) is satisfied.[4] For convenience, Sen's formulation of individual rights in general will be called formulation S, while the distinction between his formulation in terms of (1.1), (1.2), and similar conditions will be indicated by using terms such as formulation S(1.1), formulation S(1.2), and so on.

Clearly, (1.1) is much stronger than (1.2). It can be easily seen that (1.1) follows from the conjunction of (1.2) and the following property of social "rationality":

(1.3) For all social alternatives z and w, if z is socially chosen in rejection of w when z and w are the only available social alternatives, then the society should never choose w when z is available.

It is worth noting that Sen [16] explicitly adopts interpretation (1.1) in the context of the normative problem of social choice, and therefore we shall concentrate mainly on (1.1) in our subsequent discussion.

Note that (1.1) is stated in terms of the individual's preferences, but it is easy to formulate a counterpart of (1.1) in terms of the individual's (actual or hypothetical) choice. Consider the following assumption:

---

3. As Sen [16] points out, the question of how the social choice is actually made, as distinct from the question of what alternative society chooses, may be of considerable importance in the context of individual rights. Thus, individual i, left to himself, may always choose vegetarian food. If, however, instead of i choosing vegetarian food for himself, he is given vegetarian food by someone else, without his having a choice, it does seem to make a difference to his rights. This aspect is ignored in (1.1) and (1.2).

4. Sen's condition of liberalism admits both of these interpretations, since the condition is stated in terms of social preference rather than social choice, and the strict social preference for x against y can be translated into the terminology of social choice in at least two ways. It can be interpreted to mean that y should not be chosen by the society in any choice situation where x is available. Alternatively, it can be interpreted to mean that, when x and y are the only two available alternatives, society should choose x and reject y. Depending on which of these two interpretations we adopt, we have either (1.1) or (1.2).

(1.4) For all distinct social alternatives, z and w, if individual i has to choose from the available set $\{z, w\}$, then he would choose z and reject w if and only if he prefers z to w.

This is a highly plausible assumption, especially when z and w are assumed to differ only with respect to something in i's RPS. In the presence of (1.4), (1.1) becomes equivalent to the following:

(1.5) For every individual i, there exist distinct social alternatives x and y such that, if i would choose x (resp. y) and reject y (resp. x) when asked to choose from $\{x, y\}$, then y (resp. x) should never emerge as the social choice when x (resp. y) is available.

Sen [13; 14] has shown that, if the social choice procedure satisfies (1.1), then the procedure will sometimes fail to satisfy the Pareto principle.[5] Recollect that the Pareto principle requires that, if all individuals in the society strictly prefer a social alternative z to another social alternative w, then w should never emerge as a social outcome when z is available. While this impossibility result is of crucial importance in several different ways, our basic concern is not with the impossibility result but with formulation S of individual rights embodied in (1.1).

Before concluding this section, let us note several distinguished features of formulation S.

First, in both (1.1) and (1.2), it is an individual's preference over two *complete descriptions of the society* (i.e., over two social states), differing only with respect to that individual's RPS, that constrains social choice. In (1.2) the constraint is imposed "locally" on social choice when two complete descriptions of the society constitute the only feasible social alternatives. In contrast, the constraint on social choice is imposed "globally" in (1.1). (As we have noted earlier, it is possible to restate the stipulations regarding individual rights in terms of the individual's choice rather than the individual's preference. However, even when the formulation is in terms of the individual's choice, it refers to the individual's choice from among complete descriptions

5. For this impossibility theorem, it is not even necessary to require that (1.1) is satisfied. It is sufficient if at least two individuals are decisive over one pair of social alternatives each. This weaker condition is called by Sen [13; 14] the condition of *minimal liberalism*.

of the society, which constitute the different feasible social alternatives, just as the formulation in terms of the individual's preference refers to the individual's preference over complete descriptions of the society, which constitute the relevant social alternatives.)

Second, it is important to remember that Sen intended (1.1) to be only a *necessary* condition for individual i to have a right; it was not meant to be a *necessary and sufficient* condition, which would capture the entire content of the notion of individual rights. This being the case, it would be quite unreasonable if, in evaluating formulation S of individual rights, one were to criticize it on the grounds that it failed to capture some part of our intuition about individual rights, however important that part may happen to be. On the other hand, it would be a shortcoming of formulation S if it turns out to be inconsistent with some important aspects of our intuition about individual rights. In the following sections, we argue that formulation S suffers from this type of logical flaw.

Third, it is of interest to note that a somewhat stronger version of (1.1) has been suggested by Gibbard [7]. Pursuing Sen's concept of an individual's RPS, he stipulated the following condition:

(1.6) For every individual i and for all distinct social alternatives x and y, if x and y differ only with respect to something in i's RPS, then i is decisive over $\{x, y\}$.

Although (1.6) seems to be much stronger than (1.1), it is not clear why one should object to (1.6) if one is ready to accept (1.1). At the very least, they seem to have much in common as far as the underlying motivation goes.

15.3. Critique of Sen's Formulation: A Counterexample

In this section, we consider a simple example to show that there is an important category of individual rights that do not lend themselves to formulation S(1.1). The right that we discuss is the right of an individual to choose the color of his own shirt.[6] We shall later argue that this example has some special features that may not be shared by many other rights. However,

6. This example is due originally to Gibbard [7], though he used it for an entirely different purpose.

we shall also argue that the intuitive problems that arise when we seek to formulate this right in terms of (1.1) arise in the context of a very wide range of rights, and are not at all dependent on these special features. Besides, there are several fundamental rights, such as the right to choose one's own religion, the right to believe and to profess one's belief in the theory of evolution, and so on, which have a structure similar to that of our example.

Now the example. There are two individuals, the conformist (individual 1) and the nonconformist (individual 2). Each individual has the right to choose his shirt from the shirts he owns. Each individual has two shirts: white (w) and blue (b). The two individuals are completely ignorant of each other's preferences, and at the time of making his choice each individual is ignorant about the other's choice. Everything else being fixed, there are only four social states, (w, w), (b, b), (w, b), and (b, w), where (w, b) denotes white shirt for 1 and blue shirt for 2, and similarly for other social states. The two individuals' preference orderings are as follows:

1	2
(w, w)	(b, w)
(b, b)	(w, b)
(b, w)	(w, w)
(w, b)	(b, b)

In words, 1 would like to have w rather than b if 2's choice is w, whereas he would like to have b rather than w if 2's choice is b instead. On the other hand, 2 would like to have w rather than b if 1's choice is b, while he would rather have b if 1's choice is w.

If we want to formulate the right of each individual to choose his shirt in Sen's terms, then (1.1) must hold for $i = 1, 2$, so that, given our intuition about each individual's RPS in this case, at least one of the conditions (2.1) and (2.2) and also at least one of the conditions (2.3) and (2.4) must be satisfied:

(2.1) 1 is decisive over $\{(w, w), (b, w)\}$;
(2.2) 1 is decisive over $\{(b, b), (w, b)\}$;
(2.3) 2 is decisive over $\{(b, w), (b, b)\}$;

and

(2.4) 2 is decisive over $\{(w, b), (w, w)\}$.

We shall now argue that three serious intuitive difficulties arise in the context of formulation S(1.1) and some of its natural extensions. For lack of convenient names, we shall call these problems A, B, and C, respectively. Note that problem A affects formulation S(1.1) as well as its extensions, whereas problems B and C affect the extensions of formulation S(1.1) but not necessarily formulation S(1.1) itself.

Problem A. Suppose that (2.1) holds. Let the two individuals freely choose their shirts without knowing anything about the other individual's choice and preferences. Suppose, given such ignorance, 1 follows the maximin principle and chooses *b*. Similarly, suppose 2 follows the maximin principle and chooses *w*. Then (*b*, *w*) will emerge as the social outcome. This would, of course, be inconsistent with (2.1). However, given that (*b*, *w*) arose from the two individuals' free choices of their respective shirts, very few people would be willing to say that there was a violation of the right of any individual to choose his shirt. The fact that each individual is free to choose his shirt without any external constraint seems to capture the entire intuitive content of our conception of the right under consideration. Even if, as a result of exercising this freedom of choice, (2.1) is violated, it does not justify our saying that there has been a violation of the right of either individual.

In a similar way, for each of the conditions (2.2), (2.3), and (2.4), it is possible to specify the individuals' preference orderings in such a way that, given the maximin behavior on the part of each individual, the free choice of the individuals would give rise to a social outcome that would contradict the condition under consideration. Since Sen's formulation implies that at least one of the four conditions, (2.1), (2.2), (2.3), and (2.4), must be satisfied, it is clear that there are cases where the Sen right of some individual will be violated, even though, from our intuitive point of view, there is no violation of any individual's right.

Note that the assumption of maximin behavior under uncertainty is not crucial to our reasoning. However, given complete ignorance about each other's preferences, there is no compelling reason why the two individuals should not follow the maximin principle either. Indeed, given any rule of choice under uncertainty, we can modify the features of our example suitably to get the same inconsistency between formulation S(1.1) and our intuition about the right under consideration.

PROBLEM B. Problem A arises irrespective of whether 1 is decisive over only one of $\{(w, w), (b, w)\}$ and $\{(b, b), (w, b)\}$ or over each of the two sets. However, given that the pair (w, w) and (b, w), as well as the pair (b, b) and (w, b), differs only with respect to the color of individual 1's shirt, it is not clear why 1 should be decisive over one of the two-element sets, $\{(w, w), (b, w)\}$ and $\{(b, b), (w, b)\}$, but not the other. In fact, the appeal to the notion of 1's RPS may suggest that it would be more natural to assume that 1 is decisive over both the two-element sets. Presumably, it might have been such considerations that led Gibbard [7] and several other writers to replace (1.1) by the more stringent (1.6). However, if we assume that both (2.1) and (2.2) are satisfied, then we have another serious intuitive problem in addition to the one discussed earlier. Put differently, (2.1) and (2.2) together imply a type of power for individual 1 that is completely inconsistent with our intuition.

Consider the type of power that 1 enjoys under our intuitive conception of the right to choose his shirt. He can choose b, thereby securing that the final social outcome will not lie in the set $\{(w, w), (w, b)\}$. Alternatively, he can choose w, thereby securing that the final social outcome will not lie in the set $\{(b, w), (b, b)\}$. Thus, 1 has the power to ensure that the final social outcome will never lie in the set $\{(w, w), (w, b)\}$ and also the power to ensure that the final social outcome will never lie in the set $\{(b, w), (b, b)\}$. Under our intuitive concept of the right, however, there is no way in which 1 can secure that the final social outcome will never lie in the set $\{(b, w), (w, b)\}$. Yet this is exactly the power that 1 has under (2.1) and (2.2), given 1's preference ordering as specified earlier. Given that preference ordering for 1, (2.1) and (2.2) imply that neither (b, w) nor (w, b) must be the social outcome. Thus, in addition to creating problem A, (2.1) and (2.2) together give to 1 a *preference-based* power, which runs strongly counter to our intuition.

PROBLEM C. We have considered the anomalies that arise when, by strengthening formulation S(1.1) in a very natural fashion, we assume that both (2.1) and (2.2) hold. However, if one assumes both (2.1) and (2.2), then it would be natural to assume (2.3) and (2.4) as well. Indeed, why should we give 1 the Sen rights without giving 2 the corresponding Sen rights? Suppose we do this, and consider the implications of assuming that all four conditions are satisfied.

Suppose (2.1), (2.2), (2.3), and (2.4) are all satisfied and the two individuals' preferences are as specified earlier. Then it is easy to check that, irrespective of the final social outcome that emerges, one of the four conditions is bound to be violated. Thus, if we accept this very plausible extension of formulation S(1.1), we would have to accept the inevitability of the violation of someone's right. This is nothing other than an instance of the so-called Gibbard paradox. However, whatever may be the final outcome, it is not at all intuitively clear why we should say that anybody's right is violated; after all, every individual is choosing completely freely.

As we emphasized earlier, the entire intuitive content of the right in our example seems to consist of each individual's freedom to choose a blue shirt or a white shirt for himself. If each individual freely chooses one of the two shirts available to him, then some social outcome will emerge from this process of free choice. No matter what shirt each individual chooses, and no matter what social outcome finally emerges from their separate choices, there would be no violation of the right under consideration.[7]

7. A referee maintained that, while this notion of freedom of choice may capture our intuition about the right involved in the example at hand, it may leave out some important aspects of other types of rights. For example, he pointed out that we have ignored the rights such as the "right to conform" and the "right to be different," which may be associated with Gibbard's example.

There are two points we would like to make in this context. First, our example is intended to be a counterexample to show that our intuition about a certain right, i.e., the right to choose one's own shirt, can come into direct conflict with formulation S(1.1). Since we are interested in providing a counterexample, we have not analyzed other possible rights mentioned by the referee. Second, it is not clear that the "right to conform" and the "right to be different" (as distinct from the "right to choose one's own shirt") can be captured in terms of (1.1) either. To see this, it is necessary to interpret the "right to be different" carefully. When someone says in a liberal society that "I should have the right to be different in my own dress," we should not interpret this statement as a claim that he should have the power to ensure that he should dress differently from the rest of the society. Rather, we would interpret it as a claim that he has no obligation *not* to be different from the rest of society in his dress, and that nobody should penalize him if he manages to be different in his dress. (See Kanger and Kanger [9] for an illuminating formal discussion of the notion of the rights involving absence of obligations as distinct from the rights involving power.) Hence we would not normally say that the right of the person concerned to be different in his dress has been violated if only he was left free to choose his dress and to try to be different, even if he ended up finally with the same dress as the rest of society. His lack of foresight may be lamented, but not his lack of the right.

Let us now examine the origin of all these intuitive difficulties in which formulation S(1.1) and its extensions seem to be enmeshed. Concentrating on formulation S(1.1), consider problem A. The root of this problem is to be found in the following. Under our intuitive conception of the right to choose one's own shirt, the individual enjoys the power to determine a particular *aspect* or *feature* (i.e., the color of his own shirt) of the social alternative; and when he makes his choice with respect to this particular aspect, his choice imposes a restriction on the final social outcome in so far as, in the final social outcome, that particular aspect must be exactly as he chose it to be. In contrast, formulation S(1.1) does not mention the individual's ability to determine a particular aspect of the social alternative. Instead, the constraint on social choice is linked to the individual's preference over some pair(s) of social states or complete descriptions of all aspects of the society.

Of course, if each possible choice by an individual with respect to the aspect of the social state, coming within his RPS, was linked to exactly one social state, there would be an obvious and tight connection between such choice by the individual and his preferences over the social states or complete descriptions of the society. However, in our example no such tight connection exists. Thus, the choice of w by 1 can, depending on 2's choice, lead to either (w, w) or (w, b). In the absence of a tight link between the social states and the alternative options that the individual can choose with respect to the aspect of social states that falls within his RPS, there arises a tension between our intuition, which focuses on the choice of such options, and formulation S(1.1), which focuses on the individuals' preferences over social states.

To see this clearly, consider what would happen if we had exactly two feasible alternatives, say, (w, w) and (b, w), differing with respect to the color of 1's shirt; in other words, 1 had two shirts, w and b, but 2 had only one shirt, w. If information about the feasible set constitutes a part of common knowledge, then 1's preference over $\{(w, w), (b, w)\}$ will have an obvious link to 1's choice from the set of two options relating to the color of his shirt: if (and only if) he strictly prefers (w, w) to (b, w), he will choose (w, w) and reject (b, w); similarly, if (and only if) he prefers (b, w) to (w, w), he will choose (b, w) and reject (w, w). Therefore, in this simple case where (w, w) and (b, w) are assumed to be the only two feasible alternatives, problem A cannot possibly arise, since there is no plausible way in which it can happen that 1 will choose a color only to regret that choice in light of the (trivial) choice made by 2.

However, when all four alternatives, (w, w), (w, b), (b, w), and (b, b), are feasible, the choice of w by 1 is no longer uniquely linked to a single outcome: instead, it is associated with two possible outcomes, (w, w) and (w, b). Each option of each individual is, in this fashion, linked to two possible social states. This is what gives rise to problem A. Note that 1 does not know whether, if he chooses w, (w, w) or (w, b) will finally arise as the social outcome, although he does know that neither (b, w) nor (b, b) can arise, given his choice of w. Likewise, 1 does not know whether, if he chooses b, (b, w) or (b, b) will emerge as the social outcome. Therefore, it is perfectly possible that he will choose w even though he prefers (b, w) to (w, w). Similarly, it is perfectly possible for 2 to choose b. Thus, it is perfectly possible that the two individuals, through their free and unconstrained choice of a shirt, will end up with the final social outcome (w, b), when there exists another feasible outcome, (b, b), where the color of 2's shirt is the same as in (w, b) but that 1 strictly prefers to (w, b). Even if this happens, we do not see any reason whatsoever to say that 1's right has been violated.

We have shown that formulation S(1.1) runs into serious problems in our example. What about the much weaker formulation S(1.2)? It seems to us that no such problem arises for (1.2), provided that a knowledge assumption to be specified below is satisfied and that one makes a very plausible assumption to the following effect:

(2.5) For any individual i, and for any social alternatives z and w, if z and w are the only available social alternatives and if i strictly prefers z to w, i will choose z and reject w whenever he is empowered to act on behalf of the society.

To substantiate this assertion, remember that (1.2) requires that, if (w, b) and (b, b) are the only two feasible social alternatives, and if 1 prefers (w, b) to (b, b), then (b, b) must not be the social outcome. However, in this case each option available to 1 is linked to a unique social outcome. Then it is clear from our earlier reasoning that, given the very plausible assumption (2.5), and given that 1 knows the feasible set to be $\{(w, b), (b, b)\}$, there cannot be any conflict between our intuition about the right and formulation S(1.2).

So far we have assumed that the information as to what constitutes the feasible set of social alternatives is available to both individuals. What happens if the feasible set is really $\{(w, b), (b, b)\}$, but 1 does not know this and mistakenly thinks that the feasible set is $\{(w, b), (b, b), (w, w), (b, w)\}$? This, of course, means that 1 believes that 2 has two options, w and b, when actually 2 has only one option, b. Then 1 may adopt the maximin strategy of choosing a white shirt. In that case, (w, b) will be the social outcome, and this will violate 1's right according to formulation S(1.2). However, given that 1 was free to choose whatever shirt he wanted, we would not want to say that 1's right has been violated in any way. Thus, if the knowledge assumption is relaxed, even S(1.2) may turn out to be inconsistent with our intuition about the right.

Although the counterexample we have considered so far is a representative specimen from a class of rights that many people would consider to be very basic, the specific right discussed has some special features that are not necessarily shared by many other rights.

First, under the right discussed in our example, the individual, through his *actual* choices, *directly* controls the matters coming within his RPS. Sen [16; 17] has argued very convincingly against viewing rights exclusively in terms of such direct control. If i is a Hindu, it may be thought that i has a right to be cremated after his death according to Hindu rituals. However, i can hardly control this aspect of the social state directly through his actual choice, even though it may be conceded that it comes within his RPS. To accommodate such instances, however, we have only to broaden the framework so that matters relating to the RPS of the individual are determined either by the free *actual* choice of the individual concerned or by the choice of some other agent acting on behalf of the individual in accordance with the individual's *hypothetical* choice, i.e., the choice that the individual would make if he were in a position to choose.

Second, the right of the individual in our example consists of his freedom to choose any one of several options. However, there are many rights that can hardly be expressed in this way. For example, the case of Mr. A, who has a right not to be persecuted by the state because he is a Hindu, cannot be articulated through Mr. A's freedom to make certain actual choices. Is it possible to articulate it through his hypothetical choices? The answer seems to be in the negative. Suppose, in order to achieve martyrdom, Mr. A would very much like to be executed by the government for being a Hindu—indeed, if he could influence the government, he would see to it that this would be done. However, even in this case the government would violate Mr. A's rights if, in deference to Mr. A's hypothetical choice, it decided to execute him.

Lastly, in our example, what actions are or are not permissible for the individual do not depend on the prior actions of other agents. (In fact, they do not depend on the prior fulfillment of any condition.) In contrast, there are many rights where what actions are permissible for the agent concerned depend crucially on the prior actions of other agents. In the next section we discuss rights of this type in some detail. Here we would just like to note that there are important rights that do not share this feature of our example.

Thus, the right discussed in this section has some special features that may not be shared by other rights. However, we do believe that many basic rights are structurally similar to this right. In the next section, we go beyond our counterexample with the purpose of assessing the applicability of S(1.1) in general, and argue that, in the context of most rights, formulation S(1.1) and stronger versions of it run into intuitive difficulties exactly similar to the ones we have discussed here.

15.4. Critique of Sen's Formulation: Generalization

How widespread is the difficulty that arose in our example? With the purpose of settling this question, let us try to identify systematically the types of rights that do indeed lend themselves to formulation S. Since our discussion of rights is mainly in the context of social choice theory, we shall concentrate on constitutional and legal rights.

To begin with, we note that (1.1) needs some modification. This is called for if it is to be applicable to the wide class of individual rights that are contingent on the fulfillment of certain conditions, as well as to the class of individual rights that are not contingent on any such condition.

Individual rights are indeed often contingent on the prior fulfillment of certain conditions: an individual i's right to go to j's party is contingent on the condition that j has invited i to come to j's party; an individual's right to criticize the state may be contingent on "normal circumstances" prevailing and may be restricted when the country is engaged in a war; an individual's right to travel by a public bus may be subject to the availability of a vacant seat; and so on. On the other hand, some categories of rights, e.g., the right to believe or not to believe in the existence of God, may not be contingent on the prior fulfillment of any condition. The number of such noncontingent rights is perhaps rather small. To be able to take into account rights that are contingent on the prior fulfillment of a certain set of conditions, let $\Gamma = \{\gamma_1, \gamma_2, \ldots\}$ be the set of alternative contingencies under which a given right can be invoked. Then (1.1) should be modified as follows:

> (3.1) If a certain contingency in Γ occurs, then, for every individual i, there exist distinct alternatives, x and y, such that i is decisive over $\{x, y\}$.

Clearly, the noncontingent rights can be included in (3.1), where the set Γ covers all conceivable contingencies.

To what extent is (3.1) consistent with our intuition about individual rights? In discussing this issue, it seems convenient to invoke the familiar distinction between *passive rights* and *active rights*.[8] A passive right r_i of an individual i just implies certain obligations of other agent(s) (individuals, groups, the society, the state) to do or to refrain from doing something without providing i with any power to do, to have, or to be anything specific. For example, the right of an individual i not to be arrested without a proper warrant implies an obligation of the state not to arrest i without a proper warrant; but it does not provide i with any power to do, to have, or to be anything specific. In contrast, an active right r_i of an individual i provides i (or some other agent acting on behalf of i under suitably specified conditions)[9] with a certain power to do, to have or to be something specific, which usually accompanies certain obligations of other agents to do or to refrain from doing something. For example, the right of an individual i to criticize the state in normal circumstances is an active right. It provides i with a power to do something that expresses her criticism, which is accompanied

---

8. See Feinberg [3; 4] for a very lucid discussion of this important distinction.

9. Strictly speaking, whenever we talk about the power or freedom of an individual i under an active right, we should refer to the power or freedom that she, *or some other agent acting on her behalf under suitably specified conditions,* enjoys. In what follows, we shall leave out the lengthy phrase "or some other agent acting on her behalf under suitably specified conditions" for the sake of expositional convenience, but it should not be construed to imply that we subscribe to a narrow view of active rights, which visualizes these rights only in terms of direct choice made by the individual concerned.

by an obligation of the state not to imprison, interfere with, persecute, or execute i for her doing that act. We shall argue that formulation S(3.1) is consistent neither with passive rights nor with active rights unless certain very restrictive conditions are fulfilled.

Consider passive rights first. By definition, a passive right r_i of an individual i simply imposes certain obligations on other agents without paying any particular attention to i's preferences; neither does it provide i with any power to choose anything in accordance with i's preferences. It should be clear, therefore, that the category of passive rights cannot properly be captured by formulation S, which postulates a link between the final social choice and the right-holder's preferences over certain pairs of social alternatives.

In order to avoid possible misunderstandings, let us examine once again the passive right against arrest without a proper warrant. It is true that this right might have been conferred originally with a certain presumption about people's "usual" preferences, which would go against arrest without a warrant. However, whatever may be the reason that lies behind the introduction of such a right in the first place, the formal structure of this right, once introduced, seems to be independent of the individuals involved. In other words, i's right against arrest without a proper warrant prohibits a specific action of the state, which remains in force even if i would like to be arrested without a warrant for reasons of her own. Likewise, the origin of passive rights, such as the protection from being robbed, the provision of fire-fighting service in case one's house catches fire, and so on, may be traced back to the presumption that people usually prefer the state to provide these services. However, once these passive rights come into existence, their structure may often be independent of the preferences of specific individuals involved. In such cases, it is clear that passive rights would not lend themselves to the preference-based formulation S(3.1).

How about active rights? To be specific, suppose that r_i is an active right of an individual i, which becomes effective under any contingency in a subset $\Gamma(r_i)$ of Γ. (Needless to say, if r_i is a noncontingent active right, then $\Gamma(r_i)$ covers all conceivable contingencies.) Since r_i is an active right, i is endowed with a power to choose (to do, to have, to be) something from, say, a set $\Omega(\gamma) = \{\omega_1, \omega_2, \ldots\}$ of options when a contingency $\gamma \in \Gamma(r_i)$ obtains. Given the right r_i, and given $\gamma \in \Gamma(r_i)$, the choice of $\omega \in \Omega(\gamma)$ by i may imply certain obligations $\sigma_q(\gamma, \omega)$ for another agent q in a set $Q(\gamma, \omega)$.

It may help if we illustrate these notions in terms of an example. Consider an individual i's active right r_i of going or not going to j's party, assuming that j has invited i in the first place. Here $\Gamma(r_i) = \{j$ invites i to his party$\}$. Given that j has invited i, i is free to go or not to go. Thus, $\Omega(j$ invites i to his party$)= \{$to go, not to go$\}$. If j invites i and i chooses to go (resp. not to go), then every other individual q has an obligation not to harass i for going to j's party (resp. not to harass i for not going to j's party). Hence, $Q(j$ invites i, to go) as well as $Q(j$ invites i, not to go) is the set of all individuals other than i. For all $q \in Q(j$ invites i, to go), $\sigma_q(j$ invites i, to go$) = \{$don't harass i for going$\}$. Similarly, for all $q \in Q(j$ invites i, not to go), $\sigma_q(j$ invites i, not to go$) = \{$don't harass i for not going$\}$.

We are now ready to argue that active rights, in general, cannot be properly articulated through formulation S(3.1).

Let $F = \{f_1, f_2, \ldots\}$ be the set of all feature indices involved in the formal description of the social alternatives. In relation to an active right r_i of an individual i, suppose that $\gamma \in \Gamma(r_i)$ obtains, so that r_i becomes effective, and i knows that this has happened. This fact, in itself, will specify some features of the social alternatives. If i exercises r_i and chooses an option $\omega \in \Omega(\gamma)$, some other features of the social alternatives will be thereby specified. The agents $q \in Q(\gamma, \omega)$ are constrained by their obligations $\sigma_q(\gamma, \omega)$ under r_i. The fulfillment of these obligations will specify still further features of the social alternatives. If i understands the nature of his endowed active right r_i, it is not unreasonable to presume that i knows all these specifications of the features of the social alternatives which follow from the invocation of his active right r_i.

Let $F(\gamma, \omega)$ stand for the set of all feature indices that are thus specified by $\gamma \in \Gamma(r_i)$, $\omega \in \Omega(\gamma)$, and $\sigma_q(\gamma, \omega)$ $(q \in Q(\gamma, \omega))$, and known as such by i. The crucial question is whether or not $F(\gamma, \omega)$ exhausts all the feature alternatives.

Suppose, for some $\gamma \in \Gamma(r_i)$ and some $\omega \in \Omega(\gamma)$, that $F \setminus F(\gamma, \omega)$ is nonempty. Then, given γ, the option $\omega \in \Omega(\gamma)$ of i will be associated not with one unique social outcome but with several possible outcomes, any one of which may materialize depending on the exact fashion in which the residual features $f \in F \setminus F(\gamma, \omega)$ are determined. If these residual features matter at all for i's preferences, we shall have exactly the same difficulties that we encountered in our previous example.

The general reasoning presented in the preceding may be illustrated by referring to the example of the party. To keep our reasoning transparent, let us assume that it is physically impossible for anyone to harass anyone else for going or not going to someone's party. While this assumption is not at all essential, it greatly simplifies our reasoning by enabling us to ignore the implied obligations of other agents.

Assume now that j has decided to invite both i and k, and this fact is known to both i and k. This clearly determines a feature of the social alternatives as far as j's invitation to i and k is concerned. Individual i can now decide whether or not to go to j's party. Suppose that he has to make his decision without knowing whether or not k has decided to go to the party. If i decides to go to j's party, a further feature of the social alternatives will be determined, i.e., whether i goes or does not go to j's party. However, there remains a residual feature relating to k's choice, and i has decided whether or not to go to j's party without knowing how this feature is going to be decided. Therefore, in i's own mind, the option of his going to j's party is associated with two possible social outcomes: (i goes to j's party, k goes to j's party) and (i goes to j's party, k does not go to j's party). Similarly for i's option of not going. Given this leeway, it can now be easily shown that, irrespective of whether formulation S(3.1) gives to i decisiveness over {(i goes to j's party, k goes to j's party), (i does not go to j's party, k goes to j's party)} or over {(i goes to j's party, k does not go to j's party), (i does not go to j's party, k goes to j's party)} or over {(i goes to j's party, k does not go to j's party), (i does not go to j's party, k does not go to j's party)}, formulation S(3.1) contradicts our intuition just as in our previous example.

It should now be clear that the problem with formulation S(3.1) can be avoided only under a very restrictive condition, which reads as follows:

(3.2) For all i, all $\gamma \in \Gamma(r_i)$, and all $\omega \in \Omega(\gamma)$, the features in $F \setminus F(\gamma, \omega)$, if any, do not affect the relative desirability for i of the options in $\Omega(\gamma)$.

It seems to us that (3.2) is a quite stringent condition that is likely to be violated in many important cases. If this is the price we have to pay in order to articulate active rights through formulation S(3.1), then it would seem necessary to search for a better alternative. Such an alternative formulation of rights will be discussed in the next section.

15.5. An Alternative Formulation of Individual Rights: Game Form Approach

In discussing individual rights, we have emphasized that every active right of i implies the freedom of i (or someone acting on i's behalf) to choose from a certain set of options or actions; and i's choice of one of these options, in turn, implies obligations of certain other agents to do or not do something. On the other hand, every passive right of i just implies the obligation of certain other agents to do or not do something. Thus, in general, a right of i implies certain restrictions on the set of permissible actions, any one of which may be chosen by individuals, including i himself. This basic idea suggests a very natural formal framework for articulating rights, where the notion of game form plays the central role.[10]

Formally, a game form is a specification of

(a) a set N of n players;
(b) a set S_k of strategies for each player $k \in N$;
(c) a set X of all feasible outcomes;

and

(d) an outcome function that specifies exactly one outcome for each element of $\Pi_{k \in N} S_k$ (i.e., for each $|N|$-tuple of strategies, one strategy for each player).

Given a game form, when we specify the preferences of the players, we have a game.

The content of individual rights in this framework lies in a specification of the admissible strategies for each player $k \in N$, and the complete freedom

10. The concept of a game form is due originally to Gibbard [6]. The formulation of rights in terms of game forms originates in Gärdenfors [5] and Sugden [19].

of each player to choose any of the admissible strategies and/or the obligation of the agent not to choose a nonadmissible strategy.

Let us illustrate this formulation in terms of the party example.[11] Individual j has two admissible strategies,

y_j : to invite i,
y'_j : not to invite i,

whereas individual i has two admissible strategies:

y_i : if j does not invite him, he stays at home, and if j invites him, he declines and stays at home;
y'_i : if j does not invite him, he stays at home, and if j invites him, he accepts and goes to the party.

Note that we have expressed the relevant game form in its normal form. Note also that (y_i, y_j) leads to j's inviting i and j's invitation being declined by i who stays at home; (y'_i, y_j) leads to j's inviting i and j's invitation being accepted by i; and so on. It is clear that our intuitive notion of j's right to invite or not to invite i to her party and i's right to accept or not accept j's invitation is reflected in the specification of the admissible strategies for the two individuals. For example, it is not an admissible strategy for i to extract an invitation at gunpoint if j does not invite i in the first instance, nor is it admissible for i to go to j's party without receiving an invitation from j in the first place. It is, however, possible to specify the game form in such a way that the strategy

y''_i: If j does not invite i, then i forces his way into the party with a gun, and if j invites i on her own, then i goes to j's party

is a feasible strategy for i, but the outcome function is such that the combination (y''_i, y_j) leads to i's spending some time in prison. Thus, in general, the content of individual rights in this framework is reflected in the specification of the sets of admissible strategies and the outcome function that reflects, so to speak, the "rules of the game."

---

11. Many other illustrations of this approach can be found in Suzumura [21].

This formulation of individual rights via a game form (referred to as game form formulation) accommodates most instances of what we would intuitively think of as individual rights, which cannot be so easily accommodated by formulation S. For example, readers can easily check that both the right to choose one's own shirt and the right to decide whether or not to go to the invited party, which we have shown to create so much difficulty for formulation S, can be articulated through the game form formulation without any difficulty whatsoever. In each case, an appropriate specification of the set of permissible strategies for each player can completely capture the intuitive content of the right concerned.

Several general remarks on the nature of game form formulation seem to be in order.

First, it is obvious that the notion of a game form, by itself, has very little to do with rights. All that we are claiming is that rights are best modeled as game forms, with strategy sets being interpreted as the sets of legally or socially admissible strategies for each agent. Of course, one can think of numerous game forms in various other contexts (e.g., feuds between two mafia families, with murder, abduction, and arson being the strategies), where the question of rights does not arise at all. It is the specific *interpretation* of the strategies and the outcome function that determines whether the game form is intended to capture some rights in the sense of game form formulation. Note that, in formulation S of individual rights as well, it is not the formal specification of decisiveness of an individual over a pair of social states as such, but the specific *interpretation* of the intuitive basis of such decisiveness that brings rights into the picture.[12]

Second, how does the society decide which strategies should or should not be admissible for a specific player in a given context? In other words, how are rights granted in the first place in the framework of game form formulation of individual rights? This is an important question, but we ignore it here, since we are not addressing the problem of how or why rights

12. Indeed, Sen [14, p. 89] was careful enough to point out that the acceptability of formulation S will "depend on the nature of the alternatives that are offered for choice," and "if the choices are all non-personal, e.g., whether or not to outlaw untouchability, to declare war against another country," formulation S "should not have much appeal." It is only when two social alternatives are interpreted as differing solely with respect to someone's personal life that formulation S was intended to apply.

come into existence. Our purpose is to discuss the relatively limited issue of the *formal structure* of individual rights and the implications thereof, assuming that the society, for some reason or other, has decided to grant certain rights to some agents. From the formal point of view, the important aspect is that the rights of an individual i in game form formulation always take the form of i's freedom to choose a strategy from the set of all *admissible* strategies for him and/or a specification of the admissible strategies for some other agent(s). Depending on the situation, the intuitive interpretation of such specification can be in terms of either a prohibition of certain strategies for these other agents or their obligation to adopt certain types of strategies.

Lastly, it is worth noting that our game form formulation is modeled in terms of normal game forms, and to that extent it suffers from the usual drawbacks of normal game forms. Thus, it is well known that the intuition of certain extensive games cannot be adequately captured in terms of games in normal form. By relying on the normal game form, our formulation also suffers from this problem.[13] However, despite this, it would seem to provide a far more flexible and adequate framework for analyzing a wide range of rights than is provided by the classical formulation in Sen's terms.

15.6. Historical Background

In this essay, we have concentrated on the problem of formulating, formally, the notion of individual rights, as distinct from the problems of compatibility of individual rights and other social values and possible ethical justifications for individual rights. No attempt will be made here to summarize our arguments. Instead, we shall give a brief historical account of the ways in which different writers have tried to capture the intuition about individual rights in an analytical framework.

Sen [13; 14] was, of course, the first writer to introduce the concept of individual rights into the formal theory of social choice and welfare economics, and to analyze the implications of such rights. Much of the literature on rights in social choice theory and welfare economics over the last

13. For a discussion of some of these issues, see Deb [2].

two decades has evolved around Sen's formulation, which we have discussed in detail in the preceding sections.

One of the earliest critiques of Sen's formulation of individual rights came from Nozick [11]. According to him, "[i]ndividual rights are co-possible; each person may exercise his rights as he chooses. *The exercise of these rights fixes some features of the world*. Within the constraints of these fixed features, a choice can be made by a social choice mechanism based on a social ordering, if there are any choices left to make!" (Nozick [11, p. 166], emphasis added). These lines have several nuances. However, what seems to be particularly important in the context of our analysis is that Nozick, unlike Sen, does not visualize individual rights in terms of restrictions on social choice that are linked to the individual's preference over pairs of social alternatives or complete descriptions of the society. Instead, Nozick visualizes the right of an individual in terms of the individual's freedom to choose from among several available options relating to some specific aspect of the social states, and the constraints on social choice are imposed when the individual, exercising her right, does choose one of the options. (Recall Nozick's [11, p. 166] well-known example of his choosing to live in Massachusetts or New York.) Note that, under Nozick's conception, the individual's act of choice from among the alternative options fixes only some features of the social states; and this, rather than the individual's preferences over some pairs of social states, imposes the constraint on social choice. The similarity of all this to our discussion of the individual's right to choose his own shirt is obvious and does not need any further elaboration. It is of interest to note that Bernholz [1] seems to have taken a similar view of the formal structure of individual rights.

The explicit formulation of rights in terms of game forms was given in an important paper by Gärdenfors [5]. However, Gärdenfors chose to provide the formal representation of rights in terms of "effectivity functions" rather than in terms of game forms.[14] As far as we are aware, the explicit use of normal game forms for representing rights was first suggested by Sugden [19].

---

14. For the notion of effectivity functions, see Peleg [12]. See Deb [2] for an illuminating discussion of various issues relating to the representation of rights in terms of effectivity functions.

15.7. References

[1] Bernholz, P., "Is a Paretian Liberal Really Impossible?" *Public Choice* **20**, 1974, 99–107.

[2] Deb, R., "Rights as Alternative Game Forms: Is There a Difference of Consequences?" *Economica* **61**, 1994, 167–178.

[3] Feinberg, J., *Social Philosophy,* Englewood Cliffs, N.J.: Prentice Hall, 1973.

[4] Feinberg, J., *Rights, Justice, and the Bounds of Liberty: Essays in Social Philosophy,* Princeton, N.J.: Princeton University Press, 1980.

[5] Gärdenfors, P., "Rights, Games and Social Choice," *Noûs* **15**, 1981, 341–356.

[6] Gibbard, A., "Manipulation of Voting Schemes: A General Result," *Econometrica* **41**, 1973, 587–601.

[7] Gibbard, A., "A Pareto-Consistent Libertarian Claim," *Journal of Economic Theory* **7**, 1974, 388–410.

[8] Gibbard, A., "Rights in the Theory of Social Choice," in I. J. Cohen, J. Los, H. Pfeiffer, and K.-P. Podewski, eds., *Logic, Methodology and the Philosophy of Sciences,* Vol. IV, Amsterdam: North-Holland, 1982, 595–605.

[9] Kanger, S., and H. Kanger, "Rights and Parliamentarism," in R. E. Olson and A. M. Paul, eds., *Contemporary Philosophy in Scandinavia,* Baltimore, Md.: Johns Hopkins University Press, 1972.

[10] Mill, J. S., *On Liberty,* London: John W. Parker and Son, 1848.

[11] Nozick, R., *Anarchy, State and Utopia,* Oxford: Basil Blackwell, 1974.

[12] Peleg, B., *Game Theoretic Analysis of Voting in Committees,* Cambridge, UK: Cambridge University Press, 1984.

[13] Sen, A. K., "The Impossibility of a Paretian Liberal," *Journal of Political Economy* **78**, 1970, 152–157.

[14] Sen, A. K., *Collective Choice and Social Welfare,* London: Olivier & Boyd, 1970.

[15] Sen, A. K., "Liberty, Unanimity and Rights," *Economica* **43**, 1976, 217–245.

[16] Sen, A. K., "Liberty and Social Choice," *Journal of Philosophy* **80**, 1983, 5–28.

[17] Sen, A. K., "Well-Being, Agency and Freedom: The Dewey Lectures 1984," *Journal of Philosophy* **82**, 1985, 169-221.

[18] Sugden, R., *The Political Economy of Public Choice,* New York: John Wiley, 1981.

[19] Sugden, R., "Liberty, Preference and Choice," *Economics and Philosophy* **1**, 1985, 185-205.

[20] Suzumura, K., *Rational Choice, Collective Decisions and Social Welfare,* New York: Cambridge University Press, 1983. Reissued in paperback, 2009.

[21] Suzumura, K., "Alternative Approaches to Libertarian Rights in the Theory of Social Choice," in K. J. Arrow, ed., *Markets and Welfare,* Vol. 1, *Issues in Contemporary Economics,* London: Macmillan, 1990, 215–242.

[22] Wriglesworth, J. L., *Libertarian Conflicts in Social Choice,* Cambridge, UK: Cambridge University Press, 1985.

ESSAY 16

Welfare, Rights, and Social Choice Procedure: A Perspective

16.1. Introduction

It is slightly ironic that the *Bergson-Samuelson social welfare function* and the *Arrow social welfare function,* which have so much to contrast with each other in many important respects, have a basic feature in common.[1] Despite the fact that it is the Arrow impossibility theorem and nothing else that

First published in *Analyse & Kritik* **18**, 1996, 20–37. For many helpful discussions on this and related issues over many years, I am most grateful to Kenneth J. Arrow, Peter J. Hammond, Prasanta K. Pattanaik, and Amartya K. Sen.

1. At the risk of reminding readers of what is obvious to them, note that the Bergson-Samuelson social welfare function is "a function of all the economic magnitudes of a system which is supposed to characterize some ethical belief . . . . Any possible opinion is admissible . . . . We only require that the belief be such as to admit of an unequivocal answer as to whether one configuration of the economic system is 'better' or 'worse' than any other or 'indifferent,' and that these relationships are transitive . . . . The function need only be ordinally defined . . . . A more extreme assumption . . . states that individuals' preferences are to 'count.' If any movement leaves an individual on the indifference curve, then the social welfare function is unchanged, and similarly for an increase or decrease" (Samuelson [27, pp. 221–228]). In contrast, "*by* [*the Arrow*] *social welfare function will be meant a process or rule, which for each set of individual orderings* $R_1, \ldots, R_n$ *for alternative social states* (*one ordering for each individual*), *states a corresponding social ordering of alternative social states,* R. . . . [The Arrow] social welfare function . . . is a method of choosing which social welfare function of the Bergson type will be applicable . . . . Since we are trying to describe social welfare and not some sort of illfare, we must assume that the social welfare function is such that the social ordering responds positively to alterations in individual values, or at least not negatively. Hence, if one alternative social state rises or remains still in the ordering of every individual without any other change in those orderings, we expect that it rises, or at least does not fall, in the social ordering" (Arrow [1, pp. 23–25]).

poses a devastating criticism against the possibility of the *democratic* Bergson-Samuelson social welfare function, both concepts hinge on the informational basis that is *welfaristic* in nature.[2]

In the case of the Bergson-Samuelson social welfare function, this fact is quite explicit. For each profile $\boldsymbol{u} = (u_1, u_2, \ldots, u_n)$ of ordinal individual utilities, where u_i $(i = 1, 2, \ldots, n)$ denotes person i's ordinal utility and n denotes the number of persons in the society, the Bergson-Samuelson social welfare function f maps $\boldsymbol{u}$ into an ordinal index of social welfare: $u = f(\boldsymbol{u})$.[3] Thus, social welfare judgments in accordance with the Bergson-Samuelson social welfare function depend on the information of individual utilities and nothing else. In the case of the Arrow social welfare function F, which maps each profile $\boldsymbol{R} = (R_1, R_2, \ldots, R_n)$ of individual preference orderings over the set X of all conceivable social states, where $R_i (i = 1, 2, \ldots, n)$ denotes person i's individual preference ordering, into a social preference ordering $R = F(\boldsymbol{R})$, this fact is less conspicuous.[4] However, it is known that the Arrow social welfare function satisfies the following property with strong welfaristic flavor:[5]

> *Strong neutrality:* For any pairs $\{x, y\}$ and $\{a, b\}$ of social states and for any profiles $\boldsymbol{R}^1 = (R_1^1, R_2^1, \ldots, R_n^1)$ and $\boldsymbol{R}^2 = (R_1^2, R_2^2, \ldots, R_n^2)$ of individual preference orderings, if xR_i^1y holds if and only if aR_i^2b holds for all $i = 1, 2, \ldots, n$, then xR^1y holds if and only if aR^2b holds, where $R^1 = F(\boldsymbol{R}^1)$ and $R^2 = F(\boldsymbol{R}^2)$.

2. According to Sen [33, p. 464], "welfarism implies that any two states of affairs that are identical in terms of individual utility characteristics must be judged to be equally good no matter how different they are in nonutility respects, and also that any state that has more utility for someone and no less utility for anyone in comparison with another state is a better state than the other." The latter property, which is called the *Pareto principle,* is also shared by the Bergson-Samuelson social welfare function and the Arrow social welfare function.
3. See Samuelson [27, p. 228].
4. An *ordering* R on a set X is a binary relation defined over X satisfying (a) [*completeness*]: for any x, y in X, either xRy or yRx holds; and (b) [*transitivity*]: for any x, y, and z in X, xRy and yRz imply xRz. *A preference ordering* R on X is defined to mean that xRy holds if and only if x is at least as preferable as y. When x is strictly preferred to y, viz., when xRy holds but yRx does not hold, we write $xP(R)y$.
5. See Sen [31; 32] for the formal proof of this important fact.

Thus, social welfare judgments in accordance with the Arrow social welfare function depend on the information of relative positions of social states in the individual preference orderings, and all other characteristic features of social states are deemed completely irrelevant. It is against this common welfaristic feature that underlies traditional welfare economics and social choice theory that Sen's "Impossibility of a Paretian Liberal" was meant to cast serious doubt. Whatever else we may say for or against Sen's impossibility theorem, it is in this arena that the value of his contribution should be tested in the final analysis. *Hic Rhodus, hic salta.*

The structure of this essay is as follows. In Section 16.2, Sen's original formulation of the concept of individual liberty and his impossibility theorem are briefly recapitulated. Section 16.3 examines Sen's formulation of individual liberty in light of several criticisms raised against it. In Section 16.4, we identify three crucial problems that should be squarely examined by any theoretical approach to the concept of individual liberty. Section 16.5 is devoted to the evaluation of Sen's criticism against the welfaristic foundation of normative economics. Section 16.6 concludes.

16.2. Sen's Concept of Individual Liberty and the Impossibility of a Paretian Liberal

Sen's concept of individual liberty is phrased in the context of a social choice framework that is slightly more general than that of Arrow [1]. Let X and $N = \{1, 2, \ldots, n\}$, where n is a finite integer no less than 2, be the set of all conceivable social states and the set of all persons in the society, respectively. $\mathcal{S}$ denotes a family of nonempty subsets of X. Each element of $\mathcal{S}$ is meant to denote an *opportunity set,* which the society faces under suitably specified conditions. It is assumed that there exists no restriction on how the individual evaluates social states from his/her idiosyncratic point of view. Thus, each person can have any preference ordering over X he/she cares to express. Given a profile $\boldsymbol{R} = (R_1, R_2, \ldots, R_n)$ of individual preference orderings, and given any opportunity set S in $\mathcal{S}$, the society must choose something from S, paying proper attention to the distribution of persons' wishes as summarized by $\boldsymbol{R}$. Let $C(S, \boldsymbol{R})$ be the nonempty subset of S consisting of all social states that the society chooses from S when $\boldsymbol{R}$ summarizes peoples' wishes. $C(S, \boldsymbol{R})$ is called the *social choice set* for $(S, \boldsymbol{R})$. A function C, which is defined on the Cartesian product of $\mathcal{S}$ and $\mathcal{R}^n$, where $\mathcal{R}^n$ stands for the set of all logically conceivable profiles, and maps each $(S, \boldsymbol{R})$ into $C(S, \boldsymbol{R})$, is called the *collective choice rule*.

Let us say that a group D of persons is *decisive* over a pair $\{x, y\}$ of social states if D can secure that y (resp. x) does not belong to $C(S, \boldsymbol{R})$ as long as x (resp. y) is available in S by expressing unanimous preference within D for x (resp. y) against y (resp. x). If it so happens that a singleton set $\{i\}$ is decisive over $\{x, y\}$ for some person i in N, we say that the person i is decisive over $\{x, y\}$. We are now ready to state the following:[6]

> *Sen's minimal liberty:* There are at least two persons such that for each of them there is at least one pair of social states over which he/she is decisive.

The intended meaning of this condition is illustrated by Sen as follows: "Given other things in the society, if you prefer to have pink walls rather than white, then [the] society should permit you to have this, even if a majority of the community would like to see your walls white. Similarly, whether you should sleep on your back or on your belly is a matter in which the society should permit you absolute freedom, even if a majority of the community is nosey enough to feel that you must sleep on your back" (Sen [29, p. 152]).

Note that, to be concordant with this intuitive justification, the pair of social states that are mentioned in Sen's condition should be such that they differ only in the mentioned person's personal matter.

To make this crucial point explicit, let X_0 denote the set of all *impersonal* features of the society, and let X_i, where $i \in N$, denote the set of all *personal* features of person i. Then X is the Cartesian product of $X_0, X_1, \ldots, X_n$, and each and every social state x is represented by an $(n+1)$-tuple of feature alternatives: $x = (x_0, x_1, \ldots, x_n)$, where x_0 is taken from X_0 and x_i for each $i \in N$ is taken from X_i. For convenience, let x_{-i} for each $i \in N$ be defined by $x_{-i} = (x_0, x_1, \ldots, x_{i-1}, x_{i+1} \ldots, x_n)$ and let x be denoted alternatively

6. There are many versions of Sen's condition of minimal liberty, depending on how we specify the social choice framework as well as on how we define *social preference*. See, among others, Sen [30; 33; 35; 36] and Pattanaik [23; 24]. The version used in the text is taken from Sen [29, p. 156, footnote 4]. Whichever version we may pick from among the many alternatives, the following points basically hold mutatis mutandis.

as $x = (x_i; x_{-i})$. Let j and k be two persons mentioned in Sen's condition and let $\{x^i, y^i\}(i = j, k)$ be the pair of social states over which person i is decisive. In order for Sen's formulation to be consistent with his intuitive concept of individual liberty, we must have $x^i_{-i} = y^i_{-i}$ for $i = j, k$, so that x^i and y^i differ only in person i's personal feature.

Turning to the other requirement of the collective choice rule, let us now introduce a widely known condition that is welfaristic in nature:[7]

> *Pareto principle:* If every person in the society prefers any social state x to another social state y, then y should never be socially chosen from any opportunity set S that contains x.

Since the Pareto principle has seldom been seriously challenged as a reasonable requirement on social welfare judgments, there is no wonder that Sen's impossibility theorem to the effect that *there exists no collective choice rule satisfying Sen's minimal liberty as well as the Pareto principle* caused a stir. As Sen [29, p. 157] put it in his first paper on the impossibility of a Paretian liberal, "the moral [of this impossibility theorem] is that in a very basic sense liberal values conflict with the Pareto principle. . . . If someone does have certain liberal values, then he may have to eschew his adherence to Pareto optimality." A truly devastating criticism against the welfaristic basis of normative economics indeed.

Before proceeding to the critical examination of Sen's condition of minimal liberty, it may be worth examining Gibbard's [14] extension of this condition. The gist of his extension is that if a person, say, i, is warranted by the society's collective choice rule to be decisive over $\{x^i, y^i\}$, where $x^i = (x^i_i; x^i_{-i})$ and $y^i = (y^i_i; x^i_{-i})$, it does not make much intuitive sense to deny i's decisiveness over $\{z^i, w^i\}$, where $z^i = (x^i_i; z_{-i})$ and $w^i = (y^i_i; z_{-i})$. After all, if Ian is empowered to paint his bedroom walls pink rather than white when all other persons paint theirs yellow, why should we not empower him to use pink rather than white when all other persons are using blue instead? Likewise, why should we not empower John, Kevin, and Liz to choose the color of their bedroom walls freely when we empower Ian in

7. This version of the Pareto principle is also taken from Sen [29, p. 156].

this way? Presumably, it was these considerations that led Gibbard [14] to formulate the following natural extension of Sen's condition:

> *Gibbard's libertarianism*: Each person $i \in N$ is decisive over the pair of social states $\{x^i, y^i\}$, where $x^i = (x_i; x_{-i})$ and $y^i = (y_i; x_{-i})$, whatever may be the specification of x_i, y_i, and x_{-i}.

Despite the common intuitive root of Sen's minimal liberty and Gibbard's libertarianism, the logical consequence of Gibbard's libertarianism is even more disturbing than Sen's impossibility of a Paretian liberal. Indeed, it is shown by Gibbard [14] that *there exists no collective choice rule satisfying Gibbard's libertarianism*. The gist of this result can be illustrated by the situation where $N = \{1, 2\}$, $X_0 = \{x_0\}$, and $X_i = \{a, b\}$ for $i = 1, 2$. Let $x = (x_0, a, a)$, $y = (x_0, a, b)$, $z = (x_0, b, a)$, and $w = (x_0, b, b)$. Suppose that the two persons have the following preference orderings: $xP(R_1)z$, $zP(R_1)w$, and $wP(R_1)y$ for person 1 and $zP(R_2)w$, $wP(R_2)y$, and $yP(R_2)x$ for person 2. Given this profile $\boldsymbol{R} = (R_1, R_2)$ and an opportunity set $S = \{x, y, z, w\}$, Gibbard's libertarianism dictates that the social choice set $C(S, \boldsymbol{R})$ cannot but be empty, given the decisiveness of person 1 (resp. person 2) over $\{x, z\}$ and $\{y, w\}$ (resp. $\{x, y\}$ and $\{z, w\}$). Whichever state in S the society chooses, it cannot but violate either person 1's or person 2's decisiveness. The moral is that Sen's concept of liberty in the form generalized by Gibbard generates a system of individual claim rights to collective choice rule, which is self-contradictory.

The Gibbard impossibility theorem leads us to an interesting further question. Under what conditions can we assure the existence of a collective choice rule that materializes a system of individual claim rights generated by Sen's requirement of individual liberty? A complete answer to this question may be found in Suzumura ([42]; [43]; [46, Chapter 7]), but the essence of the answer is simple, which can be intuitively illustrated in terms of Figure 16.1. Note that person 1 is decisive over $\{x, z\}$ and $\{y, w\}$ and person 2 is decisive over $\{x, y\}$ and $\{z, w\}$. Thus, we can start from any state in S, say, x, and follow a path along the edges of the rectangle in Figure 16.1, say, from x to y to w to z, and come back to x again. Along this loop, each edge consists of a pair of social states over which either person 1 or person 2 has decisiveness. It is the existence of such a critical loop that underlies the Gibbard impossibility theorem. Excluding the occurrence of

Figure 16.1. Gibbard's Impossibility Theorem. Person 1 has decisiveness over $\{x, z\}$ and $\{y, w\}$, while person 2 has decisiveness over $\{z, w\}$ and $\{x, y\}$.

such a critical loop is necessary and sufficient for the existence of a collective choice rule that materializes a system of individual claim rights generated by Sen's requirement of individual liberty.

16.3. Sen's Formulation of Individual Liberty: Critical Examination

Given the basic nature of Sen's criticism, it is all too natural that the impossibility of a Paretian liberal has been under careful scrutiny along several lines.[8] Given our present purpose, we have only to focus on the way in which Sen crystallized his intuition on individual liberty in terms of the analytical framework of social choice theory.

The first misgivings, which are frequently expressed in the literature, criticize Sen's formulation of individual liberty as having failed to consider "a strong libertarian tradition of free contract," according to which "a person's rights are for him to use or to bargain away as he finds fit" (Gibbard [14, p. 397]). This viewpoint was most conspicuously formulated by Harel and Nitzan [19]. It is through the careful examination of their proposal that we can pinpoint the crucial problem underlying this escape route from Sen's impossibility theorem.[9]

8. For surveys of some of these works, see Sen [30; 35; 36], Suzumura [46, Chapter 7], and Wriglesworth [50].

9. The following analysis is based on Suzumura [48]. See also Breyer [6].

The gist of the Harel-Nitzan proposal can be crystallized in terms of a simple example due to Sen [29]. There is a single copy of *Lady Chatterley's Lover*. Everything else being the same, there are three social states: Mr. P (the prude) reading it (r_P), Mr. L (the lascivious) reading it (r_L), and no one reading it (r_0). Mr. P ranks them in the descending order of r_0, r_P, r_L, whereas Mr. L ranks them in the descending order of r_P, r_L, r_0. Since to read a book or not is ordinarily construed as a person's private matter and no other person's business, Sen endows Mr. P (resp. Mr. L) with decisiveness over $\{r_P, r_0\}$ (resp. $\{r_L, r_0\}$).[10] Given this system of claim rights based on the decisiveness of persons, and given the profile $\boldsymbol{R} = (R_P, R_L)$ of individual preference orderings we have specified, the social choice set $C(\{r_P, r_L, r_0\}, \boldsymbol{R})$ cannot but be empty, vindicating Sen's impossibility theorem. In this situation, Harel and Nitzan call our attention to the fact that Mr. P (resp. Mr. L) has an *ordinally stronger preference* for r_0 against r_L than that for r_0 against r_P (resp. for r_P against r_0 than that for r_L against r_0).[11] Thus, so the Harel-Nitzan argument goes, Mr. P has an incentive to exchange his claim right based on his decisiveness over $\{r_0, r_P\}$ with the claim right of Mr. L based on his decisiveness over $\{r_L, r_0\}$. Mr. L is similarly motivated. If this mutually beneficial exchange of claim rights is in fact realized between Mr. P and Mr. L, bringing Mr. P (resp. Mr. L) to be decisive over $\{r_L, r_0\}$ (resp. $\{r_0, r_P\}$), then the impossibility result identified by Sen evaporates. Indeed, the social choice after the realization of a voluntary exchange of claim rights $\{r_P\}$.

Note, however, that this "resolution" of the impossibility of a Paretian liberal has very little to commend itself to a person with liberal belief in the ordinary sense of the word. Indeed, to enable Mr. A to choose whether Mr. B should or should not read a book, not in view of Mr. B's own preferences but in view of Mr. A's preferences, is not liberalism but paternalism, and a liberal may well regard paternalism as the worst form of despotism imaginable.

---

10. Note that there exists no critical loop in the distribution of decisiveness in this example, so that the Gibbard impossibility theorem does not have any bite in this context.

11. When a preference ordering R is such that $x P(R) y$, $y P(R) z$, and $x P(R) z$ hold, we say that the preference for x against z is ordinally stronger than that for x against y. Likewise, the preference for x against z is ordinally stronger than that for y against z. It was Blau [5] who introduced this concept into social choice theory, but the origin of the concept goes back at least as far as to Luce and Raiffa [21].

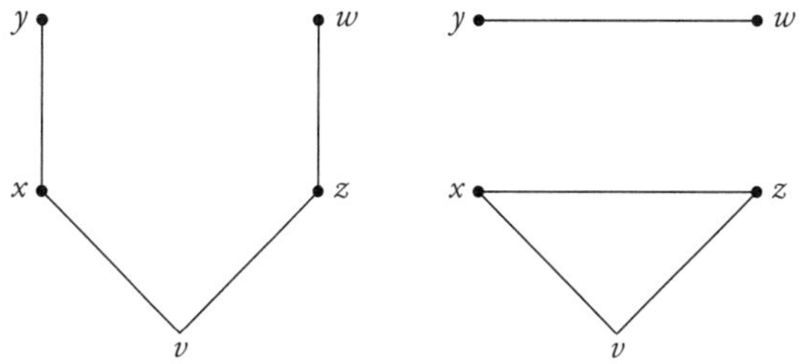

Figure 16.2. Logical Difficulty of Harel-Nitzan Libertarian Claim. On the left 1 (resp. 2) has decisiveness over $\{x, y\}$ and $\{v, z\}$ (resp. $\{v, x\}$ and $\{w, z\}$), while on the right, 1 (resp. 2) has decisiveness over $\{x, z\}$ and $\{v, z\}$ (resp. $\{w, y\}$ and $\{v, x\}$).

The problem with the Harel-Nitzan scheme does not end there. Consider the situation where $N = \{1, 2\}$, $X = \{v, w, x, y, z\}$, and person 1 (resp. person 2) is decisive over $\{x, y\}$ and $\{v, z\}$ (resp. $\{v, x\}$ and $\{w, z\}$). As is clear from Figure 16.2 (left), there is no critical loop in the system of claim rights generated by this distribution of decisive powers. Suppose that the profile of individual preference orderings are as follows: $xP(R_1)v$, $vP(R_1)w$, $wP(R_1)y$, $yP(R_1)z$, $vP(R_2)y$, $yP(R_2)z$, $zP(R_2)x$, and $xP(R_2)w$. It is clear that person 1 has an ordinally stronger preference for x against z than that for x against y. Likewise, person 2 has an ordinally stronger preference for y against w than that for z against w. In a situation like this, Harel and Nitzan allow the two persons to realize the mutually beneficial exchange of *social states* y and z to *create* a new pair $\{x, z\}$ for 1 and $\{w, y\}$ for 2, over which they are decisive. This is obviously bizarre. To exchange a pair of social states, over which a person has a claim right, with another pair of social states, over which the exchange partner has a claim right, has a clear meaning, but to exchange social states between persons so as to concoct new decisive pairs of social states does not make any sense at all. Worse still, if this bizarre exchange is somehow enforced, the resulting assignment of claim rights may have a critical loop, even though such a loop did not exist before the exchange. See Figure 16.2 (right). We cannot but conclude that the criticism against Sen's formulation of individual liberty along this line has serious problems of its own and does not succeed in presenting a meaningful alternative concept of individual liberty, let alone a "resolution" of the impossibility of a Paretian liberal.

There is another string of critics who also find Sen's articulation of individual liberty in terms of decisiveness rather at odds with what an ordinary liberal would claim. To bring his point home, recollect Sen's motivation for his minimal liberty condition to the following effect: "If you prefer to have pink walls rather than white, then [the] society should permit you to have this" and also that "whether you should sleep on your back or on your belly is a matter in which the society should permit you absolute freedom." Not many people with liberal belief would have anything to say against Sen's intuitive motivation. However, the actual formulation of this intuition in terms of the relevant person's decisiveness in social choice may make such a person raise an eyebrow. He/she may well ask: Why don't we simply leave the matter of choosing the color of one's bedroom walls, or choosing one's sleeping posture, to the relevant person's warranted individual choice, rather than articulating such a right through his/her decisiveness in *social choice?*

It was in this vein that Nozick made the following famous remark on Sen's impossibility of a Paretian liberal:

> A more appropriate view of individual rights is as follows. Individual rights are co-possible; each person may exercise his rights as he chooses. The exercise of these rights fixes some features of the world. . . . If l have a right to choose to live in New York or in Massachusetts, and I choose Massachusetts, then alternatives involving my living in New York are not appropriate objects to be entered in a social ordering. [22, p. 166]

Capitalizing on, and generalizing Nozick's observation, Sugden [38; 39; 40] and Gaertner, Pattanaik, and Suzumura [12] developed an alternative approach to individual libertarian rights, which came to be known as the *game form approach* to individual rights.[12] This approach articulates individual libertarian rights as (i) the complete freedom of each player to choose any

12. A *game form* is a specification of a set N of *players,* a set S_i of *admissible strategies* for each player $i \in N$, a set A of *feasible outcomes,* and an *outcome function* g, which maps each strategy profile $\boldsymbol{s} = (s_1, s_2, \ldots, s_n)$, where $s_i \in S_i$ for each $i \in N$, into a social outcome $g(\boldsymbol{s}) \in A$. Given a game form $G = (N, \{S_i\}, g)$, if a profile $\boldsymbol{R} = (R_1, R_2, \ldots, R_n)$ of preference orderings of the players is specified, we have a *game* $(G, \boldsymbol{R})$. Gärdenfors [13] developed a related but distinct game theoretic approach to individual liberty. See also Bernholz [4], Deb [7], Gibbard [15], Hammond [17; 18], Pattanaik [23; 24], Sen [34; 36], and Suzumura [47] for a more detailed

admissible strategy and (ii) the obligation of each player not to choose an inadmissible strategy for him/herself, and not to prevent anyone from choosing an admissible strategy.

In the case of Nozick's counterargument against Sen, for example, the game form that captures Nozick's right to choose to live in New York or Massachusetts can be formulated neatly as follows: Nozick's set of admissible strategies, say, S_{Nozick}, should contain "to live in New York" and "to live in Massachusetts," and the set of admissible strategies for all other persons should not contain such strategies as "to harass Nozick if he chooses to live in Massachusetts," "to force Nozick to live in New York at gunpoint," and so forth, and the outcome function g should be such that $g(\boldsymbol{s})$ is a social state in which Nozick lives in Massachusetts (resp. lives in New York) if s_{Nozick} (viz., Nozick's component of $\boldsymbol{s}$) is "to live in Massachusetts" (resp. "to live in New York").[13]

Two remarks are in order at this juncture. First, unlike the first alternative approach based on the voluntary exchange of libertarian rights, which not only accused Sen's approach of being out of line with traditional liberal values but also asserted that the impossibility of a Paretian liberal could be resolved by appropriately reformulating what a liberal should claim, the game form approach does not claim to be a resolvent of Sen's impossibility theorem. Quite to the contrary, it was conjectured that the Sen impossibility problem "persists under virtually every plausible concept of individual right" (Gaertner, Pattanaik, and Suzumura [12, p. 161]). We will have more to say on this point in the next section.

Second, the game form articulation of individual libertarian rights based on the intuitive concept of freedom of choice is not just an alternative approach to Sen's classical articulation of individual liberty. It is also meant

---

account of the alternative approaches to individual liberty. The exposition of the game form approach that follows is based on Pattanaik and Suzumura [25; 26].

13. Lest we should be misunderstood that the game form approach hinges on the supposition that each person is empowered to control some aspects of social states *directly*, let us emphasize that no such unwarranted restriction is needed for the workability of this approach. Those who are interested are referred to Gaertner, Pattanaik, and Suzumura [12], Pattanaik [24], and Suzumura [47], where many examples are worked out in order to illustrate and substantiate this claim.

to cast serious doubt on Sen's approach. To bring this point home, let us examine a modified version of the *Lady Chatterley's Lover* case. Suppose that both Mr. P and Mr. L own a copy of this book. Everything else remaining the same, there exist four social states: (r, r), (r, n), (n, r), and (n, n), where r (resp. n) stands for "to read it" (resp. "not to read it"). Suppose further that their preference orderings over $\{(r, r), (r, n), (n, r), (n, n)\}$ are described as follows:[14]

$$R_P : (n, n), (r, r), (n, r), (r, n)$$

$$R_L : (n, r), (r, n), (r, r), (n, n).$$

Following the game form approach and the intuitive concept of freedom of choice, let us entrust each person to choose either to read this book or not to read it in accordance with his/her individual preference. However, this is not a straightforward problem of preference optimization. The effect on a person of his/her choice from the set of options $\{r, n\}$ hinges squarely on what the other person chooses from the same set of options, and no one is within his/her right to know the other's choice beforehand. In this sense, the problem of choice faced by Mr. P and Mr. L is that of choice under uncertainty. If they follow the maximin principle of choice under uncertainty, the maximin choice of Mr. P (resp. Mr. L) is n (resp. r), thereby generating a social state (n, r) through unhindered exercise of their respective freedom of choice. However, since (r, r) and (n, r) differ only in Mr. P's reading or not reading this book, and Mr. P prefers (r, r) to (n, r), the realization of (n, r) cannot but be regarded as Mr. P's liberty being violated if we subscribe to Sen's articulation of individual liberty, even though nobody's freedom of choice is violated in this case.

We have thus shown that the game form articulation of individual liberty is a viable alternative to Sen's formulation, and it poses serious doubt on the compatibility of Sen's approach with our intuition about the freedom of choice. In the next section, we will identify three crucial problems in the theory of individual rights within the conceptual framework of the game form approach.

14. Preference orderings are represented horizontally, with the less preferred alternative to the right of the more preferred alternative.

16.4. Articulation, Realization, and Initial Conferment of Rights

In discussing individual libertarian rights, three distinct issues should be addressed. The first issue is the *formal structure* of rights. The second issue is the *realization* of conferred rights. The third issue is the *initial conferment* of rights. In the previous section, we looked at the first issue, contrasting Sen's articulation of the formal structure of individual libertarian rights and the game form articulation of rights. In Sen's approach, the second issue, viz., the realization of conferred rights, boils down to the existence of a collective choice rule that realizes the conferred individual decisiveness in social choice; Sen never addressed the third issue, that of the initial conferment of rights.[15] The rest of this section is devoted to explaining how the game form approach treats the second and third issues.[16]

The issue of the realization of conferred rights is treated by the game form approach as follows. Let A be the set of feasible social states. Given a game form $G_A = (N, \{S_i\}, g_A)$, which articulates the conferred individual rights when A prevails, and given a profile $\boldsymbol{R} = (R_1, R_2, \ldots, R_n)$ of individual preference orderings over the set of social states, we have a game $(G_A, \boldsymbol{R})$. Let $T(G_A, \boldsymbol{R})$ be the set of all social states the society predicts to appear when the game $(G_A, \boldsymbol{R})$ is played.[17] It is clear that the conferred rights G_A will be realized through the play of the game $(G_A, \boldsymbol{R})$ and a social state in $T(G_A, \boldsymbol{R})$ will materialize as a result of the play of this game.

The issue of the initial conferment of rights requires us to expand our conceptual framework rather substantially. To ask and answer how and why

15. Since Sen's interest was focused on the basic conflict between nonwelfaristic claims of individual rights and welfaristic claims of Pareto optimality, it was unnecessary for him to provide a full characterization of rights, neither was it necessary for him to develop a theory of the initial conferment of rights.

16. The analysis that follows is essentially based on Pattanaik and Suzumura [25; 26]. Those who are interested in some technical details are referred to these original sources.

17. If the prevailing concept of equilibrium is given by $\mathcal{E}$ and the set $B_{\mathcal{E}}(G_A, \boldsymbol{R})$ of pure strategy equilibria is nonempty, then it is natural to assume that $T(G_A, \boldsymbol{R}) = \{x^* \in A | x^* = g_A(\boldsymbol{s})$ for some $\boldsymbol{s} \in B_{\mathcal{E}}(G_A, \boldsymbol{R})\}$. The case where there exists no pure strategy equilibrium, but a mixed strategy equilibrium does exist, and the case where there exists no equilibrium are discussed in Pattanaik and Suzumura [26].

a game form representing individual rights comes to be conferred in the first place, it is not enough that we are informed of the individual preference orderings over the set of social outcomes. To bring this point home, consider the following simple problem.

A father is to divide a cake fairly among three children. Method 1 is that the father divides this cake into three equal pieces, and tells them to take a piece each or leave it. Method 2 is that the children are given the opportunity to discuss how this enticing cake should be divided fairly among them, and cut it into three pieces in accordance with the conclusion they arrive at. If they happen to conclude that equal division should be the outcome, and if we are informed only of the outcomes, we cannot but conclude that these two methods are the same. It is clear, however, that this is certainly inappropriate. In the case of method 1, three children are not provided with any right to participate in the process through which their dividend is determined, whereas in the case of method 2 they are endowed with such a right. To capture this important difference, we must enlarge the description of the social state in such a way that not only the social *outcomes* but also the procedure through which such outcomes are brought about is included.[18]

This conceptual expansion can be attained as follows. Let x and y be two (conventionally defined) social states and let θ and η be two decision-making mechanisms. The ordered pair (x, θ) [resp. (y, η)] denotes an extended social state in which the outcome x (resp. y) is attained through the decision-making mechanism θ (resp. η). It is assumed that people are prepared to make judgments of the following type: it is better to attain an outcome x through a mechanism θ than to attain an outcome y through a mechanism η. In what follows, we focus on the situation where the decision-making mechanism is specified by the *rights system* $\boldsymbol{G}$, which specifies a game form G_A for each set of feasible outcomes A. Let $\boldsymbol{Q} = (Q_1, Q_2, \ldots, Q_n)$ be the profile of extended individual preference orderings over the pairs $(x, \boldsymbol{G}^1)$, $(y, \boldsymbol{G}^2)$, etc. Note in passing that, for any fixed rights-system $\boldsymbol{G}$, the profile $\boldsymbol{Q}$ induces a profile $\boldsymbol{Q}_G = (Q_{1\mathbf{G}}, Q_{2\mathbf{G}}, \ldots, Q_{n\mathbf{G}})$ over the set of conventionally defined social states by $x Q_{i\mathbf{G}} y$ if and only if $(x, \boldsymbol{G}) Q_i (y, \boldsymbol{G})$ for all x, y in X and all i in N.

18. See Arrow [1, Chapter 7, Section 6] and Sen [37] for further forceful endorsement of this viewpoint.

Suppose that a feasible set of outcomes A, rights-system $\boldsymbol{G}$, and a profile of extended individual preference orderings $\boldsymbol{Q}$ are given. We then obtain a game $(G_A, \boldsymbol{Q_G})$, the play of which will determine a set $T(G_A, \boldsymbol{Q_G})$ of realizable social states. For the sake of simplicity in exposition, it is assumed in what follows that $T(G_A, \boldsymbol{Q_G})$ consists only of a single element, say, $\tau(G_A, \boldsymbol{Q_G})$.[19] In this case, a feasible extended social state is given by $(\tau(G_A, \boldsymbol{Q_G}), \boldsymbol{G})$.

We are now ready to explain how this framework treats the issue of the initial conferment of rights. Let Ψ be the *extended social welfare function,* which maps each profile $\boldsymbol{Q} = (Q_1, Q_2, \ldots, Q_n)$ of extended individual preference orderings into an extended social welfare ordering: $Q = \Psi(\boldsymbol{Q})$. Given a set A of feasible social states, the socially optimal conferment of rights is nothing but the rights-system $\boldsymbol{G}^*$ such that

$$(\tau(G_A^*, \boldsymbol{Q_{G^*}}), \boldsymbol{G}^*)\Psi(\boldsymbol{Q})(\tau(G_A, \boldsymbol{Q_G}), \boldsymbol{G})$$

holds for any feasible rights-system $\boldsymbol{G}$.

Before closing this summary account of the game form approach to individual libertarian rights, two remarks are due. First, unlike Sen's classical articulation of rights, the game form articulation of rights does *not* assign any role whatsoever to individual preferences. However, in the realization of rights articulated by the rights-system, as well as in the initial conferment of rights, this theory does assign a crucial role to the profile of extended individual preference orderings. In the former case, it is the induced preference profile $\boldsymbol{Q_G}$, together with the set A of feasible social states, that determines the game $(G_A, \boldsymbol{Q_G})$ to be played as well as the outcome of the play $\tau(G_A, \boldsymbol{Q_G})$. In the latter case, it is the extended social welfare ordering $Q = \Psi(\boldsymbol{Q})$ that determines the rights-system to be conferred. Thus, in the full theory of the game form approach to rights, there are important niches for individual preference orderings. To recapitulate, although the formal contents of the conferred game form rights are independent of individual preferences, the extended individual preferences play a crucial role in deciding the rights-system to be conferred, as well as in socially realizing the individual freedom of choice thus conferred.

---

19. See Pattanaik and Suzumura [26] for a fuller exposition without this simplifying assumption.

Second, unlike in the context of the Sen-Gibbard rights, the game form approach to rights does not have any counterpart in the Gibbard impossibility theorem. In other words, the problem of internal inconsistency of rights never surfaces in the game form approach. To the extent that the initial conferment of rights is performed in accordance with the scenario of the game form approach, the conferred rights will be realized through the actual play of the game, thereby excluding any possibility of internal inconsistency of rights.

16.5. Sen's Criticism against Welfarism: An Evaluation

Back, then, to the central focus of this essay. What does the game form approach clarify about the impossibility of a Paretian liberal? Does it fortify, or qualify, or even nullify Sen's criticism against welfarism, which is based on the basic conflict between the welfaristic Pareto principle and the nonwelfaristic claim of individual liberty? In what follows, we will contend that the main thrust of Sen's criticism against welfarism remains intact even if Sen's articulation of individual liberty is rejected and replaced by the game form articulation.

To begin with, consider yet another variant of Sen's *Lady Chatterley's Lover* case. As in the first variant used in Section 16.3 to crystallize a conceptual difficulty of Sen's approach, suppose that both Mr. P and Mr. L have a copy of *Lady Chatterley's Lover,* and their preference orderings over the set of feasible social states $\{(r, r), (r, n), (n, r), (n, n)\}$ are given by

$$R_P : (n, n), (r, n), (n, r), (r, r)$$

$$R_L : (r, r), (r, n), (n, r), (n, n).$$

As in the first variant, the issue of individual liberty contained in this situation may be captured neatly by the game form $G = (N, \{\{n, r\}, \{n, r\}\}, g)$, where $N = \{P, L\}$ and the outcome function g is such that $g(s_P, s_L) = (s_P, s_L)$, where s_P and s_L are taken from $\{n, r\}$. Unlike in the first variant, however, the preference profile $\boldsymbol{R} = (R_P, R_L)$ that defines a game $(G, \boldsymbol{R})$ has a *dominant strategy equilibrium* (n, r), which is Pareto-dominated by (r, n). Thus, the voluntary exercise of freedom of choice yields a social state that is Pareto-dominated by another feasible social state. This is the first instance in which Sen's impossibility of a Paretian liberal recurs in the context of realizing conferred game form rights.

As a matter of fact, Sen's impossibility recurs also in the context of initial conferment of game form rights. To show this possibility unambiguously, consider a situation where $N = \{C, D\}$ (C = consequentialist, D = deontologist). There are two issues to be decided on. The first issue is the religion, and there are two options: b = Buddhism and c = Christianity. The second issue is whether or not a book is to be read, and there are two options: r = "to read it" and n = "not to read it." Thus, the set A of physically possible social states consists of 16 alternatives. A typical element of A is denoted by $(c, n; b, r)$, which is a state where Mr. C believes in Christianity and does not read the book and Mr. D believes in Buddhism and reads the book. There are two feasible rights-systems: $\mathbf{G}^1 = \{G^1\}$ and $\mathbf{G}^2 = \{G^2\}$.[20] The game form $G^1 = (N, \{S_i^1\}, g^1)$, where S_i^1 is the Cartesian product of $\{b, c\}$ and $\{r, n\}$ for $i = C, D$ and $g^1(\boldsymbol{s}) = \boldsymbol{s}$ for all $\boldsymbol{s} = (s_1, s_2)$ such that s_i is in S_i^1 for $i = C, D$, is the one where the two persons are empowered to choose their religion as well as reading or not reading the book freely. In contrast, the game form $G^2 = (N, \{S_i^2\}, g^2)$, where $S_i^2 = \{r, n\}$ for $i = C, D$ and $g^2(\boldsymbol{s}) = \boldsymbol{s}$ for all $\boldsymbol{s} = (s_1, s_2)$ such that s_i is in S_i^2 for $i = C, D$, is the one where the two persons are only allowed to choose reading or not reading the book freely, the matter of choosing a common religion being decided by the society. If the social choice of a common religion is t in $\{b, c\}$ and the strategy pair $\boldsymbol{s}$ is chosen, then the social state will be given by $(t, s_1; t, s_2)$.

Let $\boldsymbol{Q} = (Q_C, Q_D)$ be the profile of extended individual preference orderings. Mr. C is a die-hard consequentialist who cares only about the outcomes of social interactions and nothing else. Thus, for all social state x in A, $(x, \mathbf{G}^1) I(Q_C)(x, \mathbf{G}^2)$ holds true, where $I(Q_C)$ is the indifference relation generated by Q_C. For each pair (u, v), where u (resp. v) refers to Mr. C's (resp. Mr. D's) religion, and for each $\mathbf{G} = \mathbf{G}^1$ and $\mathbf{G}^2$, let $Q_{C\mathbf{G}}(u, v)$ be defined by

$$Q_{C\mathbf{G}}(u, v) : (u, r; v, r), (u, n; v, r), (u, r; v, n), (u, n; v, n),$$

which, in turn, is used to define $Q_{C\mathbf{G}}$ by

$$Q_{C\mathbf{G}}: Q_{C\mathbf{G}}(b, c), Q_{C\mathbf{G}}(b, b), Q_{C\mathbf{G}}(c, b), Q_{C\mathbf{G}}(c, c).$$

20. Throughout this example, the feasible set A is fixed, which is why $\mathbf{G}^1$ as well as $\mathbf{G}^2$ consists of only one game form each.

Mr. D is a deontologist whose belief in the procedural justice in allowing people to choose their religion has such predominant importance that, for all x, y in A, he holds such preference as $(x, \boldsymbol{G}^1)P(Q_D)(y, \boldsymbol{G}^2)$. For each pair (u, v) of religions of Mr. C and Mr. D and for each $\boldsymbol{G} = \boldsymbol{G}^1$ and $\boldsymbol{G}^2$, we define $Q_{D\mathbf{G}}(u, v)$ by

$$Q_{D\mathbf{G}}(u, v)\colon (u, n; v, n), (u, n; v, r), (u, r; v, n), (u, r; v, r),$$

which, in turn, is used to define $Q_{D\mathbf{G}}$ by

$$Q_{D\mathbf{G}}\colon Q_{D\mathbf{G}}(c, c), Q_{D\mathbf{G}}(b, c), Q_{D\mathbf{G}}(c, b), Q_{D\mathbf{G}}(b, b).$$

Let us examine the game $(G^1, \boldsymbol{Q}_{G^1})$. It is easy, if tedious, to check that (b, r) is the dominant strategy for Mr. C and (c, n) is the dominant strategy for Mr. D. Thus, $(b, r; c, n)$ in A is the dominant strategy equilibrium in the game $(G^1, \boldsymbol{Q}_{G^1})$. In the situation where there exists a dominant strategy equilibrium, it is very natural to assume that $\tau(G^1, \boldsymbol{Q}_{G^1}) = ((b, r; c, n), \boldsymbol{G}^1)$. Turning to the game $(G^2, \boldsymbol{Q}_{G^2})$, it is again easy to confirm that r (resp. n) is the dominant strategy for Mr. C (resp. Mr. D) irrespective of whether the social choice of religion turns out to be b or c. Thus, $\tau(G^2, \boldsymbol{G}_{G^2}) = ((b, r; b, n), \boldsymbol{G}_2)$ or $((c, r; c, n), \boldsymbol{G}^2)$ depending on the social choice of b or c. Recollect that Mr. D holds a lexicographic preference for $(x, \boldsymbol{G}^1)$ against $(y, \boldsymbol{G}^2)$, whatever may be x and y. Thus, he must surely prefer $\tau(G^1, \boldsymbol{Q}_{G^1})$ to $\tau(G^2, \boldsymbol{Q}_{G^2})$. Mr. C being a consequentialist, he is indifferent between $\tau(G^1, \boldsymbol{Q}_{G^1}) = ((b, r; c, n), \boldsymbol{G}^1)$ and $((b, r; c, n), \boldsymbol{G}^2)$ and he prefers $((b, r; c, n), \boldsymbol{G}^2)$ to $((b, r; b, n), \boldsymbol{G}^2)$ as well as to $((c, r; c, n), \boldsymbol{G}^2)$. By transitivity of Q_C, Mr. C must then prefer $\tau(G^1, \boldsymbol{Q}_{G^1})$ to $\tau(G^2, \boldsymbol{Q}_{G^2})$. Thus, as long as the extended social welfare function Ψ satisfies the Pareto principle, $\boldsymbol{G}^1$ must be the rights-system to be conferred. However, if $\boldsymbol{G}^1$ is conferred and the game $(G^1, \boldsymbol{Q}_{G^1})$ is played, $(b, r; c, n)$ will be the social outcome, which is Pareto-dominated by another feasible social state $(b, n; c, r)$.

We have thus shown that Sen's Pareto libertarian paradox recurs not only in the context of realizing game form rights but also in the context of initial conferment of game form rights. It is in this sense that we contend that Sen's criticism against welfarism survives without losing an iota of its importance even if his articulation of libertarian rights should be replaced by the allegedly more proper game form articulation. We close this section by restating our conviction that the Sen impossibility problem "persists under virtually every plausible concept of individual rights."

16.6. Concluding Remarks

To argue for the *logical* relevance of Sen's criticism against welfarism is one thing, and to argue for *empirical* relevance in the actual context where welfare economics is set in motion is quite another. In this essay, we have confirmed that Sen's impossibility of a Paretian liberal does not lose its logical relevance even in light of the many criticisms recently raised against Sen's method of articulating individual liberty in terms of a person's decisive power in social choice. How about the empirical relevance? Is Sen's impossibility just a theoretical curiosity that is amusing as a logical exercise in the classroom yet can be safely neglected once we turn our attention to the pressing economic problems where the real bite of welfare economics is seriously tested? Quite to the contrary, it seems to us that there are many real situations where serious conflict occurs between the claim of individual rights and the desire for social efficiency.

Suffice it to visualize a local city where small and traditional retailers are engaging in hand-to-mouth business. From the viewpoint of improving social efficiency in retailing service in this city, it makes sense to allow a few large-scale organized retailers to enter this city. If we do so, however, those small retailers who have been doing business in this city over many years will almost surely be unable to cope with the large-scale retailers and will be expelled from the retailing business. Should we pursue the improvement in social efficiency at the cost of depriving small retailers of their "rights" of doing business? Or should we respect these "rights" at the cost of missing an opportunity to improve social efficiency in the retailing business? This is a typical and realistic situation where policy makers are confronted with the conflict between rights and efficiency.

To the extent that welfare economics claims to serve as the theoretical foundations of economic policy, there is no way of avoiding such conflict between two basic values—the welfaristic value of social efficiency, on the one hand, and the nonwelfaristic claim of individual rights, on the other. Although Sen [29] posed this serious problem in terms of a deceptively simple parable, the problem he thereby posed is neither simple nor unrealistic.

16.7. References

[1] Arrow, K. J., *Social Choice and Individual Values,* New York: John Wiley & Sons, 1951; 2nd edn., 1963.

[2] Bergson, A., "A Reformulation of Certain Aspects of Welfare Economics," *Quarterly Journal of Economics* **52**, 1938, 310–334.

[3] Berlin, I., *Four Essays on Liberty,* Oxford: Oxford University Press, 1969.

[4] Bernholz, P., "Is a Paretian Liberal Really Impossible?" *Public Choice* **20**, 1974, 99–107.

[5] Blau, J. H., "Liberal Values and Independence," *Review of Economic Studies* **42**, 1975, 395–402.

[6] Breyer, F., "Can Reallocation of Rights Help to Avoid the Paretian Liberal Paradox?" *Public Choice* **65**, 1990, 469–481.

[7] Deb, R., "Waiver, Effectivity and Rights as Game Forms," *Economica* **61**, 1994, 167–178.

[8] Deb, R., "Discussion of Hammond's Paper," in K. J. Arrow, A. K. Sen, and K. Suzumura, eds., *Social Choice Reexamined,* London: Macmillan, 1996, 96–99.

[9] Farrell, M. J., "Liberalism in the Theory of Social Choice," *Review of Economic Studies* **43**, 1976, 3–10.

[10] Feinberg, J., *Social Philosophy,* Englewood Cliffs, N.J.: Prentice Hall, 1973.

[11] Fudenberg, D., and J. Tirole, *Game Theory,* Cambridge, Mass.: MIT Press, 1993.

[12] Gaertner, W., P. K. Pattanaik, and K. Suzumura, "Individual Rights Revisited," *Economica* **59**, 1992, 161–177. Essay 15 of this volume.

[13] Gärdenfors, P., "Rights, Games and Social Choices," *Nôus* **15**, 1981, 341–356.

[14] Gibbard, A., "A Pareto Consistent Libertarian Claim," *Journal of Economic Theory* 7, 1974, 388–410.

[15] Gibbard, A., "Rights and the Theory of Social Choice," in L. J. Cohen, H. Pfeiffer, and K.-P. Podewski, eds., *Logic, Methodology and Philosophy of Science,* Amsterdam: North-Holland, 1982, 595–605.

[16] Hammond, P. J., "Liberalism, Independent Rights and the Pareto Principle," in L. J. Cohen, H. Pfeiffer, and K.-P. Podewski, eds., *Logic, Methodology and Philosophy of Science,* Amsterdam: North-Holland, 1982, 607–620.

[17] Hammond, P. J., "Social Choice of Individual and Group Rights," in W. Barnett, H. Moulin, M. Salles, and N. Schofield, eds., *Social Choice, Welfare, and Ethics,* Cambridge, UK: Cambridge University Press, 1995, 55–77.

[18] Hammond, P. J., "Game Forms versus Social Choice Rules as Models of Rights," in K. J. Arrow, A. K. Sen, and K. Suzumura, eds., *Social Choice Reexamined,* London: Macmillan, 1996, 82–99.

[19] Harel, A., and S. Nitzan, "The Libertarian Resolution of the Paretian Liberal Paradox," *Zeitschrift für Nationalökonomie* **47**, 1987, 337–352.

[20] Hayek, F. A., *The Constitution of Liberty,* London: Routledge & Kegan Paul, 1960.

[21] Luce, R. D., and H. Raiffa, *Games and Decisions,* New York: John Wiley & Sons, 1957.

[22] Nozick, R., *Anarchy, State and Utopia,* Oxford: Basil Blackwell, 1974.

[23] Pattanaik, P. K., "Rights and Freedom in Welfare Economics," *European Economic Review* **38**, 1994, 731–738.

[24] Pattanaik, P. K., "On Modelling Individual Rights: Some Conceptual Issues," in K. J. Arrow, A. K. Sen, and K. Suzumura, eds., *Social Choice Reexamined,* London: Macmillan, 1996, 100–128.

[25] Pattanaik, P. K., and K. Suzumura, "Rights, Welfarism and Social Choice," *American Economic Review: Papers and Proceedings* **84**, 1994, 435–439.

[26] Pattanaik, P. K., and K. Suzumura, "Individual Rights and Social Evaluation: A Conceptual Framework," *Oxford Economic Papers* **48**, 1996, 194–212.

[27] Samuelson, P. A., *Foundations of Economic Analysis,* Cambridge, Mass.: Harvard University Press, 1947; enlarged 2nd edn., 1983.

[28] Sen, A. K., *Collective Choice and Social Welfare,* San Francisco: Holden-Day, 1970; republished, Amsterdam: North-Holland, 1979.

[29] Sen, A. K., "The Impossibility of a Paretian Liberal," *Journal of Political Economy* **78**, 1970, 152–157.

[30] Sen, A. K., "Liberty, Unanimity and Rights," *Economica* **43**, 1976, 217–245.

[31] Sen, A. K., "On Weights and Measures: Informational Constraints in Social Welfare Analysis," *Econometrica* **45**, 1977, 1539–1572.

[32] Sen, A. K., "Personal Utilities and Public Judgements: Or What's Wrong with Welfare Economics," *Economic Journal* **76**, 1979, 537–558.

[33] Sen, A. K., "Utilitarianism and Welfarism," *Journal of Philosophy* **76**, 1979, 463–489.

[34] Sen, A. K., "Rights and Agency," *Philosophy & Public Affairs* **11**, 1981, 3–39.

[35] Sen, A. K., "Liberty and Social Choice," *Journal of Philosophy* **80**, 1983, 5–28.

[36] Sen, A. K., "Minimal Liberty," *Economica* **59**, 1992, 139–160.

[37] Sen, A. K., "Rationality and Social Choice," *American Economic Review* **85**, 1995, 1–24.

[38] Sugden, R., "Social Choice and Individual Liberty," in M. J. Artis and A. R. Nobay, eds., *Contemporary Economic Analysis,* London: Croom Helm, 1978, 243–271.

[39] Sugden, R., "Liberty, Preference, and Choice," *Economics and Philosophy* **1**, 1985, 213–229.

[40] Sugden, R., "Why Be Consistent? A Critical Analysis of Consistency Requirements in Choice Theory," *Economica* **52**, 1985, 167–183.

[41] Sugden, R., "Rights: Why Do They Matter, and to Whom?" *Constitutional Political Economy* **4**, 1993, 127–152.

[42] Suzumura, K., "On the Consistency of Libertarian Claims," *Review of Economic Studies* **45**, 1978, 329–342. Essay 13 of this volume.

[43] Suzumura, K., "A Correction," *Review of Economic Studies* **46**, 1979, 743. Incorporated in Essay 13.

[44] Suzumura, K., "Liberal Paradox and the Voluntary Exchange of Rights Exercising," *Journal of Economic Theory* **22**, 1980, 407–422. Essay 14 of this volume.

[45] Suzumura, K., "Equity, Efficiency and Rights in Social Choice," *Mathematical Social Sciences* **3**, 1982, 131–155.

[46] Suzumura, K., *Rational Choice, Collective Decisions and Social Welfare,* New York: Cambridge University Press, 1983. Reissued in paperback, 2009.

[47] Suzumura, K., "Alternative Approaches to Libertarian Rights in the Theory of Social Choice," in K. J. Arrow, ed., *Markets and Welfare. Issues in Contemporary Economics,* Vol. I, London: Macmillan, 1990, 215–242.

[48] Suzumura, K., "On the Voluntary Exchange of Libertarian Rights," *Social Choice and Welfare* **8**, 1991, 199–206.

[49] Suzumura, K., *Competition, Commitment and Welfare,* Oxford: Clarendon Press, 1995.

[50] Wriglesworth, J. L., *Libertarian Conflicts in Social Choice,* Cambridge, UK: Cambridge University Press, 1985.

PART V

CONSEQUENTIALISM VERSUS NONCONSEQUENTIALISM

Introduction to Part V

> Quite often good things have hurtful consequences. There are instances of men who have been ruined by their money or killed by their courage.
>
> —ARISTOTLE, *Nicomachean Ethics,* fourth century BC, Translated by J. A. K. Thomson

> Everything we do has a result. But that which is right and prudent does not always lead to good, nor the contrary to what is bad.
>
> —GOETHE, quoted in Johann Peter Eckermann's *Conversations with Goethe,* December 25, 1825.

> Half of the results of a good intention are evil; half the results of an evil intention are good.
>
> —MARK TWAIN, "The Devilish and the Offensive Stranger," *Europe and Elsewhere,* 1923

Kenneth Arrow, who founded his social choice theory on the informational basis of consequentialism, brought forward an interesting problem toward the end of the first edition of *Social Choice and Individual Values* (Arrow [1, pp. 89–90]): "Up to now, no attempt has been made to find guidance by considering the components of the vector which defines the social state. One especially interesting analysis of this sort considers that, among the variables which taken together define the social state, one is the very process by which the society makes its choice. This is especially important if the mechanism of choice itself has a value to the individuals in the society."[1] Observe that Arrow's suggestion to this effect is not meant to go against

1. In his interview with Arrow, Jerry Kelly [2, p. 22] asked whether he wants to allow preferences over processes. Arrow replied: "One of the things I fear is emptiness. You put preferences over enough things, then anything that happens can be defended. It destroys the idea of discourse. . . . This is why I'm a little unsympathetic to the rights issue—everybody just multiplies the rights all over the place and you get total paralysis."

the consequentialist basis of social choice theory and welfare economics altogether, but to allude that some complementary role may be played by procedural considerations in the evaluation of collective acts of social choice.

In sharp contrast with Arrow's allusion to the auxiliary role played by procedural considerations vis-à-vis consequential considerations, there are vigorous advocates of the procedural approach, such as James Buchanan [3; 4], Robert Nozick [7], and Robert Sugden [13; 14; 15; 16]. The contrast between Arrow and Buchanan et al. is sharp indeed. As Amartya Sen [12, p. 2] aptly pointed out, "[Buchanan's] emphasis on procedural judgments may be taken to suggest . . . that we should abandon altogether consequence-based evaluation of social happenings, opting instead for a procedural approach. In its pure form, such an approach would look for 'right' institutions rather than 'good' outcomes and would demand the priority of appropriate procedures (including the acceptance of what follows from these procedures)."[2]

To bring the contrast between a consequential approach and a procedural approach into clear relief, let X stand for the set of narrowly defined social alternatives and let $N = \{1, 2, \ldots, n\}$ $(2 \leq n < +\infty)$ be the set of individuals composing the society. Let $x, y \in X$ be two representative social alternatives, and let θ and μ be two representative game forms that express the decision-making procedures used in the society. We use Θ to denote the family of all game forms that are a priori conceivable. For each individual i, let $\succsim_i$ be i's weak preference ordering on the set $X \times \Theta$ such that, for any two pairs of consequences and procedures (game forms) (x, θ) and (y, μ), $(x, \theta) \succsim_i (y, \mu)$ means that, according to i's judgments, obtaining the social consequence x through the mediation of the procedure (game form) θ is at least as good as obtaining the social consequence y through the mediation of the procedure (game form) μ.[3]

2. See also Agnar Sandmo [9, p. 52], who underscored Sen's view in his review article on Buchanan's work of political economy: "[Buchanan's] view has strong implications for the way in which economists conceive of their own role in society. Rather than attempting to find 'optimal' solutions to economic problems they should concentrate on finding good decision rules, which all individuals and interest groups will find it in their own long-run interest to adopt for the solution of still unidentified conflicts over resource allocation."

3. What precisely do we mean by a social consequence to be obtained through the mediation of a procedure or a game form? In the full analysis of the extended social choice framework, we must introduce a profile of individual preference orderings (or payoff functions) over the set of consequences that provide each individual (or player) with his/her motivation for playing the

Once the Pandora's box of nonconsequential considerations in the context of social evaluation of economic policies and/or economic mechanisms is opened, nothing prevents us from exploring nonconsequential features of the world other than procedural features in the evaluative exercises.[4] A conspicuous example is the opportunity set that lies behind the final choice of outcomes. The importance of this aspect is emphasized by Sen [10; 11; 12], which can be illustrated as follows. Let $S \subseteq X$ be a typical example of a nonempty opportunity set available for choice. $\mathcal{S}$ stands for the family of nonempty opportunity sets. For each individual i, let $\succsim_i$ stand for i's weak preference ordering on the set $X \times \mathcal{S}$ such that, for any two pairs of consequences and opportunity sets (x, S) and (y, T), where $x \in S$ and $y \in T$, $(x, S) \succsim_i (y, T)$ means that, according to i's judgments, obtaining the consequence x from the opportunity set S is at least as good as obtaining the consequence y from the opportunity set T. People seem prepared to make judgments of this type. An impressive example due to Sen is that of the contrast between a death out of starvation in the miserable environment of a general famine, where the lack of availability of food and drink leads to the death with no choice, versus a death out of fasting, where the fasting individual voluntarily rejects the available food and drink in order to underscore the strength of his/her determination of political protest. From the viewpoint of social evaluation of the voluntary act of fasting vis-à-vis the involuntary act of death in a general famine, the widened conceptual framework, which allows room for opportunity aspects of choice environments to play an epistemic role, seems to be of crucial importance.

Part V consists of four essays that are concerned with the contrast between the consequential approach vis-à-vis the nonconsequential approach in social choice theory. Essay 17 ("Consequences, Opportunities, and

---

full-fledged game, as well as the equilibrium concept prevailing in the society. See Pattanaik and Suzumura [8] and Essay 28 of this volume for more details on the implications of this simple observation.

4. Proper recognition of the importance of procedural considerations along with consequential considerations, particularly when we are concerned with the issue of individual rights and freedom of choice, may occasionally be found in the literature. Assar Lindbeck [6, p. 295] acutely observed in his Joseph Schumpeter Lecture on individual freedom and welfare state policy that "the issue of 'individual freedom,' which is closely related not only to actual achievements but also to the process by which these are realized, is seldom squarely confronted in economic analysis." See Suzumura [17] for consequential and procedural approaches to the issue of individual rights and freedom of choice in the social choice theoretic framework.

Procedures") is meant to highlight the following two elementary points. In the first place, we would like to cast further light on the importance of nonconsequential considerations along with procedural considerations. This can be conducted by citing several concrete examples with real substance. As a matter of fact, instead of searching for scarce instances in vain, we are going to face an embarrassment of riches in this arena. In the second place, there is a widely held presumption that procedural considerations can be accommodated within the consequentialist conceptual framework by recharacterizing the concept of social alternatives. However, the necessary conceptual extension is neither trivial nor mechanical, and it is worthwhile to work out at least one example to see what is really involved in this plan of conceptual extension.

Essay 18 ("Characterizations of Consequentialism and Nonconsequentialism") makes use of the extended conceptual framework that includes the opportunity aspects of social evaluations and develops an axiomatic characterization of consequentialism and nonconsequentialism. Most, if not literally all, scholars on welfare economics and social choice theory are consequentialist in their conviction in the sense that their judgments on the goodness of economic policies and/or economic mechanisms hinge on whether their working leads to good consequences. However, it is undeniable that there do exist people who care not only about consequences of economic policies and/or economic mechanisms but also about nonconsequential features, such as their intrinsic procedural characteristics and/or the richness of opportunities they offer to individuals in the society where these economic policies and/or economic mechanisms are at work. Even those economists with strong consequential conviction should be ready to take the judgments of people with nonconsequential convictions into due account in order not to be paternalistic in their economic analysis. This essay develops several analytical frameworks that enable us to characterize the choice behavior of consequentialists and nonconsequentialists by means of a set of reasonable axioms.[5]

Observe that the concepts of consequentialism and nonconsequentialism defined and characterized in Essay 18 are *extreme consequentialism, strong*

5. Our axiomatic study of consequentialism versus nonconsequentialism in Part V should be regarded as a first step in this novel field of research, which opens the gate toward a rich field of future research.

consequentialism, extreme nonconsequentialism, and *strong nonconsequentialism.* These names clearly suggest that the characterized concepts are focused on rather extreme cases, where unequivocal priorities are given either to consequential features or to nonconsequential features. This observation applies not only to extreme consequentialism and extreme nonconsequentialism but also to strong consequentialism and strong nonconsequentialism. Essay 19 ("Consequences, Opportunities, and Generalized Consequentialism and Nonconsequentialism") is devoted to a more general framework, where active interactions between consequential considerations and opportunity considerations play essential roles, viz., we develop a framework that allows for the possibilities of a trade-off between the value of consequences and the value of the richness of opportunities.

The task of Essay 20 ("Welfarist Consequentialism, Similarity of Attitudes, and Arrow's General Impossibility Theorem") is to test the services rendered by our conceptual framework in the arena of Arrovian impossibility theorems. This test is worth performing for at least two reasons. In the first place, Arrow's own theorem is based on the epistemological foundations of the special class of consequentialism, which claims that social judgments on right or wrong actions should be based on the assessment of their consequential states of affairs, where the assessment of consequences is conducted exclusively in terms of people's welfare, their preference satisfaction, or their attaining what they want. What if we expand the conceptual framework and search over the wider field for acceptable rules of preference aggregation? This is certainly a proper question to ask.

In the second place, there exists a well-known thesis of Arrow's own to the effect that "the possibility of social welfare judgments rests upon a similarity of attitudes toward social alternatives" (Arrow [1, p. 69]). The validity of this thesis has been tested over many years in the context of the simple majority decision rule and its variants by such scholars as Kenneth Arrow and Duncan Black in the 1950s, Ken-Ichi Inada, Amartya Sen, and Prasanta Pattanaik in the 1960s, and many others. The expanded conceptual framework allows us to put Arrow's thesis in a quite different perspective. Suffice it to recollect that Arrow implicitly assumed that all individuals are ranking social alternatives in terms of their own welfare implications. In other words, Arrow's social choice theory is based on the implicit assumption that all individuals judge the goodness of social choice rules on the epistemological basis of *welfarist consequentialism* (or *welfarism* for short). By allowing individuals with consequentialist beliefs and individuals with nonconsequentialist beliefs to exist simultaneously, we may check the validity of Arrow's insight from wider perspectives.[6]

References

[1] Arrow, K. J., *Social Choice and Individual Values,* New York: John Wiley & Sons, 1st edn., 1951; enlarged 2nd edn., 1963. Republished with an Introduction by E. Maskin, New Haven, Conn.: Yale University Press, 2012.

[2] Arrow, K. J., and J. S. Kelly, "An Interview with Kenneth J. Arrow," in K. J. Arrow, A. K. Sen, and K. Suzumura, eds., *Handbook of Social Choice and Welfare,* Vol. II, Amsterdam: North-Holland/Elsevier, 2011, 4–24.

[3] Buchanan, J. M., "Social Choice, Democracy, and Free Markets," *Journal of Political Economy* **62**, 1954, 114–123.

[4] Buchanan, J. M., "Individual Choice in Voting and the Market," *Journal of Political Economy* **62**, 1954, 334–343.

[5] Dworkin, G., "Is More Choice Better Than Less?" in P. A. French, T. E. Uehling, Jr., and H. W. Wettstein, eds., *Midwest Studies in Philosophy,* Vol. VII, *Social and Political Philosophy,* Minneapolis: University of Minnesota Press, 1982, 47–61.

[6] Lindbeck, A., "Individual Freedom and Welfare State Policy," *European Economic Review* **32**, 1988, 295–318.

[7] Nozick, R., *Anarchy, State, and Utopia,* Oxford: Basil Blackwell, 1974.

[8] Pattanaik, P. K., and K. Suzumura, "Individual Rights and Social Evaluation: A Conceptual Framework," *Oxford Economic Papers* **48**, 1996, 194–212.

[9] Sandmo, A., "Buchanan on Political Economy: A Review Article," *Journal of Economic Literature* **28**, 1990, 50–65.

[10] Sen, A. K., *Commodities and Capabilities,* Amsterdam: North-Holland, 1985.

[11] Sen, A. K., *On Economic Inequality,* expanded edition, Oxford: Clarendon Press, 1997.

[12] Sen, A. K., "Rationality and Social Choice," *American Economic Review* **85**, 1995, 1–24.

[13] Sugden, R., *The Political Economy of Public Choice,* Oxford: Martin Robertson, 1981.

[14] Sugden, R., "Liberty, Preference, and Choice," *Economics and Philosophy* **1**, 1985, 213–229.

[15] Sugden, R., *The Economics of Rights, Co-operation and Welfare,* Oxford: Basil Blackwell, 1986.

[16] Sugden, R., "Rights: Why Do They Matter, and To Whom?" *Constitutional Political Economy* **4**, 1993, 127–152.

[17] Suzumura, K., "Welfarism, Individual Rights, and Procedural Fairness," in K. J. Arrow, A. K. Sen, and K. Suzumura, eds., *Handbook of Social Choice and Welfare,* Vol. II, Amsterdam: Elsevier, 2011, 605–685.

[18] Suzumura, K., and Y. Xu, "Consequentialism and Non-Consequentialism: Axiomatic Approach," in C. Puppe, P. Anand, and P. K. Pattanaik, eds., *Handbook of Decision Theory and Social Choice,* Oxford: Oxford University Press, 2008, 346–373.

6. In addition to Essay 18, Essay 19, and Essay 20, we refer interested readers to Suzumura and Xu [18] for a survey of this new vista.

ESSAY 17

Consequences, Opportunities, and Procedures

17.1. Introduction

In his characteristically lucid exposition of the celebrated general possibility theorem, Kenneth Arrow observed that "economic or any other social policy has consequences for the many and diverse individuals who make up the society or economy. It has been taken for granted in virtually all economic policy discussions since the time of Adam Smith, if not before, that alternative policies should be judged on the basis of their consequences for individuals" (Arrow [3, p. 124]). As a matter of fact, the informational parsimony of traditional normative economics is even more restrictive than consequentialism as such, as it allows for the description of consequences only in terms of welfare that "the many and diverse individuals who make

First published in *Social Choice and Welfare* **16**, 1999, pp. 17–40. This is the written text of the Plenary Session Lecture delivered at the Third International Meeting of the Society for Social Choice and Welfare, University of Maastricht, Netherlands, June 22–25, 1996. I am deeply indebted to Kenneth Arrow, Charles Blackorby, Peter Hammond, Hajime Hori, Serge Kolm, Eric Maskin, Herve Moulin, Prasanta Pattanaik, and Amartya Sen for their comments, encouragement, and suggestions over many years on the issues covered by this lecture. Thanks are also due to Timothy Besley, Birgit Grodal, Kevin Roberts, Maurice Salles, and Paul Samuelson for their comments and criticisms at various occasions. Last but not least, I am very grateful to St. Antony's College, Oxford University, and to the Centre for Philosophy of the Natural and Social Sciences, London School of Economics and Political Science. The completion of the original paper would have been much delayed without the warm hospitality of these institutions.

up the society or economy" entertain under each consequence.[1] It is true that Amartya Sen's justly famous criticism against the welfaristic foundations of normative economics, which capitalizes on his *impossibility of a Paretian liberal,* brings the importance of nonwelfaristic features of consequences into proper perspective, yet it still keeps us within the broad boundary of consequentialism.[2]

Starkly opposing the *consequentialist approach* to normative economics is the *procedural approach,* vigorously advocated most notably by James Buchanan [10; 11; 12; 13], Robert Nozick [40], and Robert Sugden [67; 68; 69; 70]. The purpose of the present essay is to fill in the gap between these two seemingly irreconcilable approaches by making the following two elementary points. In the first place, we contend that procedural considerations do matter in many important contexts of real substance, where welfare economics and social choice theory should have much to say, so that the traditional informational basis of normative economics cannot but be expanded to accommodate procedural information along with consequential information. To make this point, we need not look for far-fetched and/or concocted examples. Quite to the contrary, an embarrassment of riches is a real possibility here, and Sections 17.3–5 will be devoted to the three concrete problems that are meant to shed light on the separate aspects of the same coin. In the second place, there seems to exist a widely held presumption that procedural considerations can be combined with consequential considerations by recharacterizing the concept of social states more extensively. This is demonstrably the case indeed, but the necessary conceptual extension is neither trivial nor mechanical, and it is worthwhile to work out at least one example to see what is really involved in this conceptual extension. Section 17.6 is devoted to this task, focusing on the classical issue of welfare and rights posed by Sen's impossibility theorem as the field of our discourse. Section 17.7 concludes this essay with a few final observations.

1. On the informational parsimony of traditional welfare economics and social choice theory, see Sen [54; 55; 63] and Suzumura [77].
2. The amount of work that followed Sen's [51; 53] original criticism against welfarism in terms of the impossibility of a Paretian liberal is enormous. See Sen [55; 56; 61; 63] and Suzumura [72, Chapter 7; 75] for a succinct overview and evaluation of this large literature.

Before setting about pursuing the proper tasks of this essay, a preliminary observation on the concept of *opportunities* and *procedures* might be in order.

17.2. Opportunities and Procedures

Proper recognition of the importance of procedural considerations along with consequential considerations, particularly when one is concerned with the issue of individual rights and freedom, may not infrequently be found in the literature. To cite a salient example, in his Joseph Schumpeter Lecture on individual freedom and welfare state policy, Assar Lindbeck [38, p. 295] aptly pointed out that the issue of individual freedom is closely related not only to actual achievements but also to the process by which these are realized. However, Lindbeck's emphasis on the process by which consequential outcomes are realized quickly recedes to the background. Instead of formulating the *mechanism* or *procedure* that determines the process of choice explicitly, his attention becomes focused on the *opportunity set* from which the consequential outcomes are chosen. Presumably, this almost imperceptible shift of emphasis is motivated by his observation, which is certainly legitimate in itself, that "individual freedom has to do with the tightness of various types of constraints on the decisions and actions of individuals" (ibid., p. 295), so that "such freedom of choice will be analyzed . . . in terms of the *opportunity set* and/or the *potential options* of the individual" (ibid., p. 297). Thus, the procedural considerations enter into Lindbeck's analytical scenario only through the following two indirect channels: (i) the opportunity sets differ depending on how the various choice procedures constrain the decisions and actions of individuals; and (ii) "the attitude of the individual to constraints on his freedom of choice differ depending on *who* has imposed them" (ibid., p. 298).

The advocacy of using the opportunity set to capture the idea of freedom of choice in general, and the role of procedural considerations in analyzing freedom of choice in particular, finds additional support in Sen [65, p. 202]: "The value of [an opportunity] set need not invariably be identified with the value of the best—or the chosen—element of it. Importance can also be attached to having opportunities that are *not* taken up. This is the natural direction to go if the process through which outcomes are generated is of a significance of its own. Indeed, 'choosing' itself can be seen as a valuable functioning, and having an **x** when there is no alternative may be sensibly distinguished from choosing **x** when substantial alternatives exist."[3, 4]

Instead of subsuming procedural considerations indirectly through opportunity sets as in the Lindbeck-Sen approach, we adopt in this essay a direct approach whose origin can be traced back to Arrow [2, pp. 90–91]: "Among the variables which taken together define the social state, one is the very process by which the society makes its choice. This is especially important if the mechanism of choice itself has a value to the individuals in the society. For example, an individual may have a positive preference for achieving a given distribution through the free market mechanism over achieving the same distribution through rationing by the government."[5]

We may give analytical substance to Arrow's insightful observation in the following way. Instead of sticking to the traditional informational basis of normative economics, which focuses on individual preference orderings over the set X of conventionally defined social alternatives, we use an extended informational basis that consists of individual preference orderings over the Cartesian product of X and Θ, where Θ denotes the set of social decision-making mechanisms through which actual choices are going to be made. Let Q_i denote the extended preference ordering of individual i, and (x, θ^1) and (y, θ^2) be two representative elements of $X \times \Theta$. Then $(x, \theta^1)Q_i(y, \theta^2)$ means that, according to i's view, having an outcome x

3. See also Sen [57; 58].

4. Sen's [57; 58; 59; 60; 62] due emphasis on the importance of opportunity sets led to a huge literature on the evaluation of freedom in terms of the worth of opportunity sets. See, among many others, Arneson [1], Basu [6], Bossert, Pattanaik, and Xu [9], Fleurbaey [18], Gravel [22], Klemisch-Ahlert [34], Pattanaik and Xu [46], Puppe [47], and Sugden [71]. See also related earlier studies by Dworkin [16] and Jones and Sugden [32].

5. See also Sandmo, who wrote as follows: "Judging allocation mechanisms either by results or by the allocation processes themselves may not be a very fruitful contrast. . . . One problem with this approach is that it is not always clear how one should draw the distinction between outcomes and processes, because the individuals in the economy may have preferences that are partly defined over the processes themselves. Thus, one may prefer competitive markets to central planning because markets result in more consumption goods for everybody, but one may also have a preference for having one's consumption goods delivered by the market rather than by the central planning bureau" (Sandmo [49, p. 58]).

through the mechanism θ^1 is at least as good as having another outcome y through another mechanism θ^2.[6]

People seem prepared to make welfare judgments of this extended type, and it is in terms of this extended conceptual framework that we are going to incorporate procedural considerations along with consequential considerations.

17.3. Discrimination by Procedural Considerations: The Problem of Fair Cake Division

Back, then, to our main scenario. The first problem we examine is meant to shed light on the role procedural considerations may play in complementing purely consequential considerations when the latter fail to distinguish two situations that are relevantly different from the viewpoint of individual values and social welfare.

Example 17.1 (Suzumura [75, p. 31]). A father is to divide a cake among three children fairly. There are two methods to be examined. Method 1 is that the father divides this cake into three equal pieces and tells the children to take a piece each, or leave it. Method 2 is that the children are given the opportunity to discuss how this cake should be divided fairly among them, and cut it into three pieces in accordance with the conclusion they agree on. If they happen to conclude that the equal division is the fair outcome, and if we are informed only of the outcomes, we cannot but conclude that these two methods of division are the same. It is clear, however, that this is certainly inappropriate. In the case of method 1, the children are not provided with any right to participate in the process through which their distributive shares are determined, whereas in the case of method 2, they are indeed endowed with such an important right of participation.

---

6. In what follows, what we call a *mechanism* is to be interpreted as synonymous with a set of *institutional arrangements*, which, in its turn, is identified with a family of *game forms*. We will explain the meaning of these cryptic expressions in the specific context of individual libertarian rights in Section 17.5, leaving the general analytical details to Hurwicz [31]. See also Arrow and Hurwicz [4, Part I and Part IV] and Schotter [50] for related analyses.

The gist of this example is that the right to participate is an important procedural feature that we are unable to capture if our informational basis is narrowly confined to consequential outcomes and nothing else. To rectify this defect, we must enlarge the description of social states in such a way that, not only the social *outcomes*, but also the *procedures* or *mechanisms* through which such outcomes are chosen, are included.

The same point can be made in terms of a more serious-looking example to the following effect.

EXAMPLE 17.2 (PATTANAIK AND SUZUMURA [44, P. 437]). Consider a society endowed with a fixed bundle of commodities. Suppose that individuals are entitled to engage in voluntary exchange among themselves, and the outcome in the core will be socially chosen. We assume that the core is always nonempty and consists of a single allocation. Suppose that the social decision-making procedure is changed into the one where the central planning board assigns to each individual a consumption bundle that he/she would have chosen if the previous procedure were used. As far as the outcome of social decision-making procedures is concerned, the two situations are the same, yet the structure of individual freedom and rights is substantially different between the two situations.[7]

Thus, procedural considerations can help us discriminate two situations that cannot but be identified if our conceptual framework is narrowly confined to consequential considerations only.

17.4. Rectification by Procedural Considerations: Welfare and Competition

The second problem we analyze in order to shed further light on the services rendered by procedural considerations is the classic issue of competition and economic welfare. It goes without saying that competition is assigned an indispensable role in economics in general, and in welfare economics in particular. In the absence of market failures, it is *market-oriented competition* that is emphasized as the efficient and decentralized allocator of scarce

7. See also Sen [64, p. 14, footnote 20].

resources, whereas in the presence of market failures, it is *contest-based competition* within the public decision-making mechanism to cope with market failures that receives emphasis as a built-in safeguard against government failures.[8] In any case, there is a strong conventional belief in the welfare-enhancing effects of competition. This widespread belief may be traced back to Adam Smith, who wrote in *The Wealth of Nations* that "in general, if any branch of trade, or any division of labor, be advantageous to the public, the freer and more general the competition, it will always be the more so." Our first order of business is to see if and how this conventional wisdom can be vindicated.

With this crucial task in mind, we consider an oligopolistic industry producing a homogeneous product, where n firms compete in terms of quantities. Let $\pi_i(q_i; Q_{-i})$ be the profit of firm i, which is defined by

$$\pi_i(q_i; Q_{-i}) := q_i f(Q) - c(q_i) \quad (i = 1, 2, \ldots, n), \qquad (17.1)$$

where f is the inverse demand function for the product of this industry, q_i is the output of firm i, $Q_{-i} := \Sigma_{j \neq i} q_j$ is the aggregate output of firms other than i, $Q := Q_{-i} + q_i$ is the industry output, and c is the cost function that is common for all firms.

We assume that

(A.1). $f'(Q) < 0$ holds for all $Q > 0$.

(A.2). $c'(q) > 0$ and $c''(q) > 0$ hold for all $q > 0$.

(A.3). $(\partial^2/\partial q_i \partial q_j)\pi_i(q_i; Q_{-i}) < 0$ $(i \neq j; i, j = 1, 2, \ldots, n)$ holds for all $(q_i; Q_{-i}) > 0$.

Note that these assumptions are not pathological at all. To understand what is involved in (A.3), which is called the assumption of *strategic substitutability*, let the *reaction function* of firm i, to be denoted by $r_i(Q_{-i})$, be defined by

$$(\partial/\partial q_i)\pi_i(r_i(Q_{-i}), Q_{-i}) = 0. \qquad (17.2)$$

8. See Suzumura [76] for further details on this dual role of competition in the special context of developing market economies. See Stiglitz [66] and Vickers [81] for the theory of contest-based competition.

It is easy to check that *the reaction function is downward sloping if and only if the assumption of strategic substitutability is satisfied*.[9]

In what follows, we assume that *symmetric Cournot-Nash equilibrium* exists and is unique for each number of firms n. Let $q^N(n)$ and $Q^N(n)$ be, respectively, the individual firm's output and the industry output at the symmetric Cournot-Nash equilibrium with n firms. To see how $q^N(n)$ and $Q^N(n)$ will be affected by a change in n, we define the *cumulative reaction function*, to be denoted by $R_i(Q)$, by

$$q_i = R_i(Q) \quad \text{if and only if} \quad q_i = r_i(Q - q_i). \tag{17.3}$$

It is easy to confirm that *cumulative reaction function is downward sloping if and only if the reaction function is downward sloping*. Note also that, by definition, we have $q^N(n) = R_i(Q^N(n))$ for all $i = 1, 2, \ldots, n$. Adding up these n equations, we may obtain $Q^N(n) = \Sigma_{i=1}^n R_i(Q^N(n))$, which means that $Q^N(n)$ is nothing but the fixed point of the aggregate cumulative reaction function $\Sigma_{i=1}^n R_i$.

Figure 17.1 describes the displacement of Cournot-Nash equilibrium when the number of firms increases from n to $n + \Delta n$. As is clearly seen from this figure, we have $q^N(n) > q^N(n + \Delta n)$ and $Q^N(n) < Q^N(n + \Delta n)$. Analytical proof of these properties is available in Essay 21 of this volume, which is based on Suzumura and Kiyono [79]. See also Suzumura [74].

Turning to the long-run performance of the Cournot market, let $\pi^N(n)$ be the profit earned by each incumbent firm at Cournot-Nash equilibrium with n firms, which is defined by

$$\pi^N(n) := q^N(n) f(Q^N(n)) - c(q^N(n)). \tag{17.4}$$

If $\pi^N(n) >$ (*resp.* $<$) 0 holds, potential firms (resp. incumbent firms) will be motivated to enter into (resp. exit from) this industry, so that the *long-run Cournot-Nash equilibrium* will be attained when there are n_e firms in the industry, each producing the output $q^N(n_e)$, where n_e is defined by

9. This crucial assumption was first introduced by Bulow, Geanakoplos, and Klemperer [14] and soon became a standard tool in the analysis of oligopolistic interactions. See Suzumura [74] for the use of this assumption in various contexts of oligopoly and economic welfare.

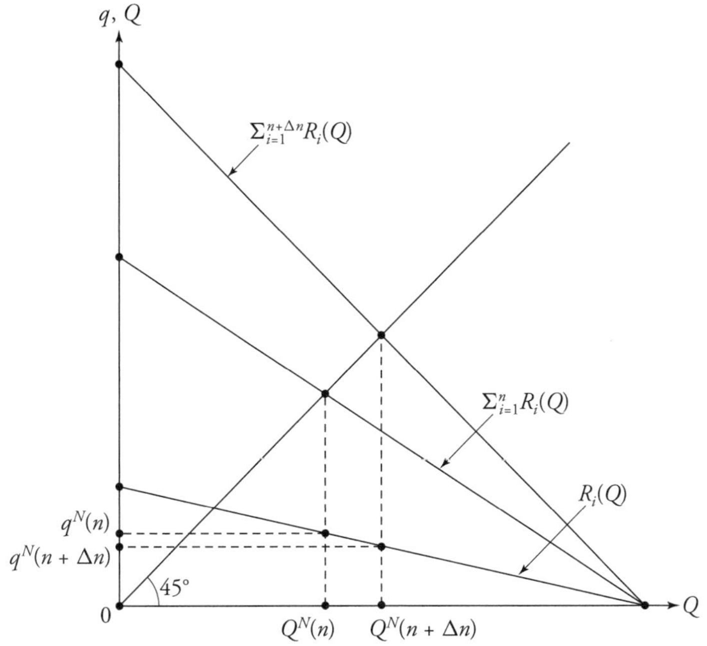

Figure 17.1. Firm entry and displacement of Cournot-Nash equilibrium

$\pi^N(n_e) = 0$. If this industry is left unregulated, this is the outcome we should expect to observe in the long-run Cournot market.

To understand the welfare implication of long-run competition in the Cournot market, let

$$V(x, y) = u(x) + y \tag{17.5}$$

denote the utility function of the representative consumer, where x and y stand, respectively, for the consumption of the good produced by the industry in question and that of the *numerative* good. The budget constraint of the representative consumer is given by $M = px + y$, where p is the price of the good produced by this industry, which not only gives us $u'(x) = p$ as the first-order condition for utility maximization but also allows us to rewrite (17.5) as $v(x) := V(x, M - px) = u(x) + M - px$, where M consists of the external income I and profits generated in this industry $\Sigma_{i=1}^{n} \pi_i(q_i; Q_{-i})$. Evaluating $v(x)$ at Cournot-Nash equilibrium and neglecting a term that is exogenous in our present analysis, we obtain the following welfare criterion:

$$W^N(n) := u(Q^N(n)) - nc(q^N(n)). \tag{17.6}$$

Suppose now that we are in the long-run Cournot-Nash equilibrium, and let there be a small decrease in the number of firms for whatever reason. This marginal change in n will affect the value of our welfare function by

$$(\mathrm{d}/\mathrm{d}n)W^N(n_e) = \pi^N(n_e) + n_e\{f(Q^N(n_e)) - c'(q^N(n_e))\}(\mathrm{d}/\mathrm{d}n)q^N(n_e) \tag{17.7}$$

at the margin. It is clear that the first term on the right side of (17.7) is zero by the definition of n_e, whereas the second term thereof is negative by virtue of (A.1), (A.2), and $(\mathrm{d}/\mathrm{d}n)q^N(n) < 0$. Thus, the social welfare measured by (17.6) *increases* when there is a marginal *decrease* in the number of firms from the long-run equilibrium level n_e, which vindicates that there is a *socially excessive* firm entry at the long-run Cournot-Nash equilibrium.[10]

If we are committed to the welfaristic, hence consequentialist, normative framework pure and simple, this simple result cannot but suggest that the traditional belief in the role of competition in the market economy must be rejected as a general truth. Should we acquiesce in a resigned view that "regulation by enlightened, but not omniscient, regulators could in principle achieve greater efficiency than deregulation" (Panzar [42, p. 313])? It is in this context that we should remind ourselves of the role we expect of competition much more in detail.

There are three *instrumental* roles of competition that seem to underlie the traditional belief. First, competition abhors wastes, just as nature abhors a vacuum. If wastes exist anywhere in the current allocation of scarce resources, an unambiguous signal is sent that there are unexploited profit

10. This result, which came to be known as the *excess entry theorem*, was discovered independently by Mankiw and Whinston [39] and Suzumura and Kiyono [79]. Since then, it has been generalized along several lines. To cite just a few salient examples, Konishi, Okuno-Fujiwara, and Suzumura [35] extended this proposition by allowing for general equilibrium interactions through factor markets, whereas Okuno-Fujiwara and Suzumura [41] extended the theorem to the three-stage game that subsumes strategic commitment with R&D in the second stage of oligopolistic interactions. These and other extensions are systematically expounded in Suzumura [74].

opportunities, and unfettered interfirm competition will soon drive them out. Thus, competition plays an instrumental role in promoting an intrinsic value of economic efficiency. Second, competition is a spontaneous mechanism through which new innovations are introduced into the market economy. Indeed, firms will be motivated to introduce new innovations in order to sharpen their competitive edge against their rivals, and also to protect themselves from rivals' challenges. In this sense, competition plays an instrumental role in promoting an intrinsic value of long-run economic progress. Third, competition is a *discovery procedure* in the sense of Friedrich von Hayek [28; 29; 30] through which a decentralized economic system may find a way to make an efficient use of dispersed and privately owned information. Since no agent in the decentralized economic system owns relevant information for calculating efficient use of resources at one stroke, it is left to market competition to find out who is most capable of meeting market demand in accordance with profit incentives and price signals. It is in this sense that competition plays an instrumental role in promoting an intrinsic value of privacy-respecting decentralized decision making.

In addition to these instrumental values, competition allegedly has an *intrinsic* value of its own. It is the unique mechanism through which each economic agent can try out her own life chance on her own initiative and responsibility. It is true that the mechanism of competition can be very cruel and wasteful in weeding out the winners from the losers. It is also true that freedom rendered by this mechanism is crucially conditioned by the initial distribution of assets and capabilities. However, these valid reservations do not change an iota of the fact that competition is a process that provides each agent with an equal and free opportunity to pursue his own aspirations in life. It is this intrinsic value of competition that the welfaristic concentration on consequential outcomes forces us to neglect.[11]

John Harsanyi once made an acute observation on value judgments to the following effect: "If I approve of using A as a means to achieve some end

11. Sen was absolutely right when he wrote that "the economic theory of market allocation has tended to be firmly linked with a 'welfarist' normative framework. The success and failures of competitive markets are judged entirely by achievements of individual welfare . . . , rather than by accomplishments in promoting individual freedom" (Sen [62, p. 519]). See also Lindbeck [38, p. 314].

B, I will do this on the assumption that A is causally effective in achieving B. Hence, my approval will be mistaken if this assumption is incorrect. Likewise, if I approve of A as an intrinsically desirable goal, I will do this on the assumption that A has some qualities I find intrinsically attractive. My approval will be mistaken if in fact A does not possess these qualities" (Harsanyi [27, pp. 792-793]). If we assume that A stands for the mechanism of competition and B for the enhancement of well-being of individuals, his argument helps us summarize the gist of our foregoing analysis briefly as follows: If we are committed to a consequential and instrumental approach to the value of competition, we cannot but disapprove this mechanism generally for its failure to achieve the proposed goal, whereas if we approve the same mechanism for its intrinsic value in terms of individual freedom, we are obliged to show that the competitive market mechanism is in fact capable of embodying such a value. It goes without saying that the normative analysis to this effect requires the expansion of our conceptual framework beyond consequentialism pure and simple.

17.5. Endorsement by Procedural Considerations: Restricted Trade and Welfare

The third context where procedural considerations play an essential role in normative economics is in bilateral trade restrictions and economic welfare. Among several possible issues we may select from this broad area, we focus in what follows on the welfare implications of *voluntary export restraints* (VERs). VER is a trade-restricting device that has been introduced at the request of the government of the importing country and is accepted by the exporting country to forestall other trade restrictions. It is a highly costly protective measure to the importing country. Indeed, a VER is a variant of an import quota where license is assigned to foreign exporters rather than to domestic importers.[12] This being the case, a natural question suggests itself: Why should this bilateral agreement be requested by the government

12. Instead of requesting a VER agreement, the importing country could use a tariff or import quota that would limit imports by the same amount. If these alternative import-restricting measures were invoked, rents earned by foreign exporters under VER would remain in the importing country either as tariff revenue or import license fees.

of the importing country, and why should it be "voluntarily" accepted by the exporting country? The answer is intuitively clear, yet depressing enough.

In the first place, by agreeing voluntarily to a VER, the foreign country may secure that rents will accrue to the exporters rather than remaining in the importing country. In the second place, domestic producers, who would otherwise have to face a challenge by foreign exporters, are protected by the VER-induced cartel, and can reap extra profits from the domestic price increase, which foreign exporters can likewise entertain. Thus, domestic producers as well as foreign exporters may be able to entertain a simultaneous increase in their profits *at the sacrifice of an overwhelming decrease in domestic consumers' benefits*. This is the reason why a VER arrangement, being strongly promoted by domestic (import-competing) producers, is agreed to in complete neglect of domestic consumers' concomitant losses.

To show that this intuitive conclusion is indeed inevitable, let us consider a simple duopoly model where a domestic firm h and a foreign firm f supply their products to the domestic market and compete in terms of prices.[13] Let $d_i(p_h, p_f)$ be the demand function for the good produced by firm i $(i = h, f)$. It is assumed that

(B.1). d_i is twice continuously differentiable. The goods produced by firms h and f are *substitutes* for each other, viz., $(\partial/\partial p_i)d_i(p_h, p_f) < 0$ and $(\partial/\partial p_j)d_i(p_h, p_f) > 0$ $(i \neq j; i, j = h, f)$ hold for all $(p_h, p_f) > 0$.

Let $c_i(q_i)$ be the cost function of firm i, which is assumed to satisfy the following:

(B.2). $c_i'(q_i) > 0$ and $c_i''(q_i) \geq 0$ hold for all $q_i > 0$ $(i = h, f)$.

The profit function of firm i $(i = h, f)$ is defined to be $\pi_i(p_h, p_f) := p_i d_i(p_h, p_f) - c_i(d_i(p_h, p_f))$, which each firm i maximizes with respect

13. The following analysis on the welfare effects of a VER agreement is a simplified version of Suzumura and Ishikawa [78]. Although we concentrate in the main text on the case of price competition, Suzumura and Ishikawa [78] have shown that essentially the same result holds true in the case of quantity competition as well. See also Bhagwati [8], Ethier [17], Harris [26], and Krishna [36; 37] for related analyses of the effects of a VER.

to its own strategic variable, viz., price p_i. The first-order condition for profit maximization is given by

$$\begin{aligned}(\partial/\partial p_i)\pi_i(p_h, p_f) &= d_i(p_h, p_f)\\ &\quad + \{p_i - c_i'(d_h(p_h, p_f))\}(\partial/\partial p_i)d_i(p_h, p_f)\\ &= 0\ (i \neq j; i, j = h, f). \qquad (17.8)\end{aligned}$$

Let $\{p_h^F, p_f^F\}$ be Nash equilibrium in prices, which is defined by the simultaneous solution for the first-order conditions (17.8) for $i = h$ and f. This is the *free trade price equilibrium* in our two-country model. Let us now suppose that a VER is imposed on the foreign firm at the free trade equilibrium level of exports, viz., $q_f^F := d_f(p_h^F, p_f^F)$, so that the feasible price configuration $\{p_h, p_f\}$ must satisfy the following constraint: $d_f(p_h, p_f) = q_f^F$. Under this VER constraint, we may define a function $\zeta(p_h)$ by

$$p_f = \zeta(p_h) \quad \text{if and only if} \quad d_f(p_h, \zeta(p_h)) = q_f^F \qquad (17.9)$$

for all $p_h > 0$. The meaning of the function $p_f = \zeta(p_h)$ should be clear. Since the VER cannot be violated once it is agreed to, the foreign firm cannot but choose $p_f = \zeta(p_h)$ when the domestic firm chooses p_h. In effect, the function $p_f = \zeta(p_h)$ describes how the foreign firm follows the domestic firm in choosing prices so as not to violate the VER. It is assumed that

(B.3). $(\partial/\partial p_h)d_h(p_h, \zeta(p_h)) + \zeta'(p_h)(\partial/\partial p_f)d_h(p_h, \zeta(p_h)) < 0$ holds for all $p_h > 0$.

This assumption requires that an increase in the price of domestic goods results in a decrease in the demand for domestic goods even when the price of foreign products undergoes a concomitant change so as to keep the VER unviolated. Differentiating $\zeta(p_h)$ and taking (B.1) into consideration, we can verify that

$$\zeta'(p_h) = -(\partial/\partial p_h)d_f(p_h, \zeta(p_h))/(\partial/\partial p_f)d_f(p_h, \zeta(p_h)) > 0 \qquad (17.10)$$

holds.

If firm h behaves in full awareness of the VER agreement, the profit function of firm h becomes $\pi_h^V(p_h) := \pi_h(p_h, \zeta(p_h))$, which is assumed to be a strictly concave function in p_h. If we define $p_h^V :=$ arg max $\pi_h^V(p_h)$, then $\{p_h^V, \zeta(p_h^V)\}$ represents the *VER equilibrium in prices*. Since p_h^V is characterized by $(d/dp_h)\pi_h(p_h^V, \zeta(p_h^V)) = 0$, we may obtain

$$d_h(p_h^V, \zeta(p_h^V)) + \{p_h^V - c_h'(d_h(p_h^V, \zeta(p_h^V)))\}\{(\partial/\partial p_h)d_h(p_h^V, \zeta(p_h^V)) + \zeta'(p_h^V)(\partial/\partial p_f)d_h(p_h^V, \zeta(p_h^V))\} = 0. \tag{17.11}$$

On the other hand, invoking (17.8) for $i = h$ at the free trade price equilibrium $\{p_h^F, p_f^F\}$, we may obtain

$$(d/dp_h)\pi_h(p_h^F, \zeta(p_h^F)) = \zeta'(p_h^F)\{p_h^F - c_h'(d_h(p_h^F, \zeta(p_h^F)))\}(\partial/\partial p_f)d_h(p_h^F, \zeta(p_h^F)). \tag{17.12}$$

Since $p_f^F > c_h'(d_h(p_h^F, \zeta(p_h^F)))$ follows from (17.8) for $i = h$, we can conclude on the basis of (17.12) that $(d/dp_h)\pi_h(p_h^F, \zeta(p_h^F)) > 0$, where use is made of (B.1) and (17.10), which implies in turn that $p_h^F < p_h^V$ by virtue of the strict concavity of $\pi_h^V(p_h)$. Since we have $d_f(p_h^V, \zeta(p_h^V)) = d_f(p_h^F, p_f^F) = q_f^F$ by virtue of (17.9), we may obtain

$$\pi_f(p_h^F, p_f^F) < \pi_f(p_h^V, \zeta(p_h^V)), \tag{17.13}$$

where use is also made of (17.10). Therefore, *profits of the foreign firm increase when a VER is imposed at the free trade equilibrium level of exports.* This being the case, we may assert that, *in an international duopoly with product differentiation, where a domestic firm and a foreign firm compete in terms of prices, a VER imposed at the free trade equilibrium level of exports is voluntarily complied with.*[14]

Turning to the consumer side of the home country, let $V_h(q_h, q_f) = u_h(q_h, q_f) + M_h - \Sigma_{i=h,f}\, p_i q_i$ be the utility function of the domestic representative consumer, where $M_h = I_h + \pi_h(p_h, p_f)$ denotes the

14. This part of our result vindicates the conclusion of Harris [26] in a generalized framework.

income of the representative consumer and I_h is his external income. By virtue of the first-order condition for utility maximization, u_h satisfies $(\partial/\partial q_i)u_h(q_h, q_f) = p_i$ $(i = h, f)$. Thus, our welfare measure can be specified by

$$W_h(d_h(p_h, p_f), d_f(p_h, p_f)) \\ := u_h(d_h(p_h, p_f), d_f(p_h, p_f)) - p_f d_f(p_h, p_f) - c_h(d_h(p_h, p_f)). \tag{17.14}$$

It then follows that

$$(d/dp_h)W_h(d_h(p_h, \zeta(p_h)), d_f(p_h, \zeta(p_h))) \\ = \{p_h - c_h'(d_h(p_h, \zeta(p_h)))\}\{(\partial/\partial p_h)d_h(p_h, \zeta(p_h)) \\ + \zeta'(p_h)(\partial/\partial p_f)d_h(p_h, \zeta(p_h))\} - \zeta'(p_h)d_f(p_h, \zeta(p_h)), \tag{17.15}$$

where $(\partial/\partial q_h)u_h(q_h, q_f) = p_h$, $(\partial/\partial q_f)u_h(q_h(p_h, q_f)) = p_h = \zeta(p_h)$, and $d_f(p_h, \zeta(p_h)) = q_f^F$ are all made use of.

As an auxiliary step in evaluating the effect of a VER on domestic welfare, we need a simple lemma.

Lemma 17.1. Let $\rho(p_h)$ be defined by $\rho(p_h) := p_h - c_h'(d_h(p_h, \zeta(p_h)))$. If $\rho(p_h^t) > 0$ $(t = 1, 2)$ holds, then $\rho(\theta p_h^1 + (1-\theta)p_h^2) > 0$ holds for any θ satisfying $0 < \theta < 1$.

Proof. Differentiating $\rho(p_h)$ we may verify that

$$\rho(p_h) = 1 - c_h''(d_h(p_h, \zeta(p_h)))\{(\partial/\partial p_h)d_h(p_h, \zeta(p_h)) \\ + \zeta'(p_h)(\partial/\partial p_f)d_h(p_h, \zeta(p_h))\} > 0, \tag{17.16}$$

where use is made of (B.2) and (B.3). Since $\rho(p_h^t) > 0$ $(t = 1, 2)$ by assumption and $\rho(p_h)$ is an increasing function, the assertion of the lemma immediately follows. ■

In order to compare the level of domestic welfare at the free trade equilibrium and that at the VER equilibrium, we now invoke the mean value theorem to assert that there exists a θ satisfying $0 < \theta < 1$ such that

$$W_h(d_h(p_h^F, p_f^F), d_f(p_h^F, p_f^F)) - W_h(d_h(p_h^V, \zeta(p_h^V)), d_f(p_h^V, \zeta(p_h^V)))$$
$$= (p_h^F - p_h^V)(d/dp_h)W_h(d_h(p_h(\theta), \zeta(p_h(\theta))), d_f(p_f(\theta), \zeta(p_h(\theta)))) \tag{17.17}$$

holds, where $p_h(\theta) := \theta p_h^F + (1-\theta)p_h^V$. It is clear that (17.8) for $i = h$ evaluated at $\{p_h^F, p_f^F\}$ entails $\rho(p_h^F) > 0$, whereas (17.11) entails $\rho(p_h^V) > 0$. Combining (17.15) for $p_h = p_h(\theta)$ with (17.17) and invoking Lemma 17.1 as well as the inequality $p_h^V > p_h^F$, which we have already established, we may finally obtain an unambiguous result:

$$W_h(d_h(p_h^F, p_f^F), d_f(p_h^F, p_f^F)) > W_h(d_h(p_h^V, \zeta(p_h^V)), d_f(p_h^V, \zeta(p_h^V))). \tag{17.18}$$

We have thus established the following remarkable result: *In an international duopoly with product differentiation, where a domestic firm and a foreign firm compete in terms of prices, a VER imposed at the free trade equilibrium level of exports cannot but decrease domestic welfare.*[15] This result is strongly reminiscent of Vilfredo Pareto's insightful observation to the following effect: "A protectionist measure provides large benefits to a small number of people, and causes a very great number of consumers a slight loss. This circumstance makes it easier to put a protection measure into practice" (Pareto [43, p. 379]).

In addition to the *welfaristic* criticism against the bilateral VER arrangements presented here, there is a *nonwelfaristic* or *procedural* criticism that also casts serious doubt on the legitimacy of bilateral trade restriction as a fair measure for international conflict resolution. More often than not, bilateral agreements are prepared and concluded in complete neglect of the third parties, which have no way of representing themselves in the procedure through which such agreements are designed and implemented between the two countries involved, even though the third parties would most likely

15. A recent study of Kemp, Shimomura and Okawa [33] examined the conditions under which this result holds in the presence of general equilibrium interactions.

be affected by spillover effects of the bilateral agreements thereby concluded. This problem would not be alleviated even when the nature of bilateral agreements in question was such that the third parties could equally entertain the beneficial *outcomes* of bilateral agreements in full accordance with the most-favored-nation treatment stipulated in the GATT/WTO agreements.[16] As was aptly observed by Sir Isaiah Berlin, "the desire to be governed by myself, or at any rate to participate in the process by which my life is to be controlled, may be as deep a wish as that of a free area for action, and perhaps historically older" (Berlin [7, pp. 15-16]). Recent proliferation of bilateralism is deeply lamentable, as it tends to deny this innate desire to the third parties, which are left outside the bilateral negotiation procedure. The problematic nature of bilateralism becomes even more lamentable when it is enforced by means of unilateral aggression and/or excessive extraterritorial applications of domestic laws. Needless to say, this concern is also rooted in procedural fairness considerations.

We have thus exemplified that there are cases where procedural considerations can add force to consequential considerations to strengthen the case for or against an economic or social policy under serious debate.

17.6. A Taste of Pudding: Welfare, Rights, and Social Choice Procedure

Enough has been said about the importance of procedural considerations in complementing, rectifying, and endorsing social welfare judgments based on

16. Our argument, which emphasizes the procedural fairness of trade dispute settlement mechanism, is in sharp contrast with Rudiger Dornbusch, who put forward a strongly consequentialist argument in favor of bilateralism to the following effect: "Bilateralism received a bad name when it was an instrument for restricting trade, but open bilateralism . . . can be an effective instrument for securing more open trade. Indeed, if trade is open in the sense of allowing conditional most-favoured-nation access, a bilateral initiative can become a vehicle for freer trade on a multilateral basis. Third countries excluded from an initial agreement should be welcome to enjoy its benefits on condition they adhere to its terms" (Dornbusch [15, p. 107]). See also Garten [21], who likewise tries to justify bilateralism along the lines we are arguing against in the text. Jeffrey Garten served as US Under Secretary of Commerce for International Trade until October 1995.

consequential considerations. What remains to be done is to exemplify the type of analysis that can be pursued on the basis of the extended conceptual framework introduced in Section 17.2.

Among many possible directions to explore, we have chosen to focus in what follows on the issue of logical compatibility between individual libertarian rights and Pareto efficiency, which was originally posed by Sen [51; 52] in terms of his *impossibility of a Paretian liberal*. However, unlike Sen, who articulated the concept of individual rights in terms of an individual's power (*local decisiveness*) to constrain the social choice rule, we articulate it as (i) the complete freedom of each individual to choose any admissible strategy and (ii) the obligation of each individual not to choose an inadmissible strategy for him/herself, and not to prevent anyone from choosing his/her admissible strategy. To be more precise, the concept of individual libertarian rights is articulated in our approach through a *game form,* which is a specification of a set $N := \{1, 2, \ldots, n\}$ of *players*, a set S_i of *admissible strategies* for each player $i \in N$, a set A of *feasible outcomes*, and an *outcome function* g_A, which maps each strategy profile $\boldsymbol{s}^N = (s_1, s_2, \ldots, s_n) \in \times_{i=1}^n S_i$ into a social outcome $g_A(\boldsymbol{s}^N) \in A$, viz., $G_A = (N, \{S_i | i \in N\}, A, g_A)$.[17]

Let us begin with a general remark. In any discussion on individual rights, three distinct issues should be carefully distinguished and separately addressed. The first issue is the *formal structure* of rights. As we have already observed in Essays 15 and 16 of this volume, the game form approach captures the formal structure of rights in terms of a game form G_A. Game form being nothing other than a game prior to the specification of players' preferences over outcomes, the formal structure of rights in the game form articulation is completely independent of players' preferences over outcomes. The second issue is the *realization* of conferred rights. The game form approach treats this issue in terms of a *game,* which is defined by a pair $(G_A, \boldsymbol{R})$ of a game form G_A and a profile $\boldsymbol{R} = (R_1, R_2, \ldots, R_n)$ of players' preference orderings over social outcomes. The game form approach regards the conferred individual rights to be fully realized if each player can freely

17. This *game form approach to individual rights*, so-called, originates in Nozick [40] and has been explored by Sugden [68], Gaertner, Pattanaik, and Suzumura [20], Pattanaik and Suzumura [44; 45], and Suzumura [73; 75]. Part IV of this volume is devoted to this and other important issues of welfare and rights.

exercise his/her admissible strategy in the actual play of the game $(G_A, \boldsymbol{R})$.[18] The third issue is that of the *initial conferment* of rights. It is in the context of treating this third issue within the game form approach that our extended conceptual framework plays an essential role.

To show how this issue can be treated in our framework, let us suppose that the decision-making mechanism is specified by the *rights-system* $\boldsymbol{G}$, which specifies a game form G_A for each set of feasible outcomes $A \subseteq X$, viz., $\boldsymbol{G} = \{G_A | A \in \mathcal{S}\}$, where $\mathcal{S}$ is the family of all feasible sets of outcomes. Let $\boldsymbol{Q} = (Q_1, Q_2, \ldots, Q_n)$ be the profile of extended individual preference orderings over the pairs of outcomes and rights-systems, viz., $(x, \boldsymbol{G}^1)$, $(y, \boldsymbol{G}^2)$, etc. Recollect that the intended meaning of $(x, \boldsymbol{G}^1)Q_i(y, \boldsymbol{G}^2)$ is that, according to the judgments of i, it is at least as good having an outcome x through a rights-system $\boldsymbol{G}^1$ as having an alternative outcome y through an alternative rights-system $\boldsymbol{G}^2$.

What precisely do we mean when we say "having an outcome x through a rights-system $\boldsymbol{G}$"? In particular, how do we formalize the concept of feasibility in our extended framework? To clarify our meaning, note that a rights-system $\boldsymbol{G}$ and an extended profile $\boldsymbol{Q}$ induce a restricted profile $\boldsymbol{Q_G} = (Q_{1G}, Q_{2G}, \ldots, Q_{nG})$ over the set X of conventionally defined social states in such a way that $x Q_{iG} y$ holds if and only if $(x, \boldsymbol{G}) Q_i (y, \boldsymbol{G})$ holds for all $x, y \in X$ and all $i \in N$. Let $G_A = (N, \{S_i | i \in N\}, A, g_A)$ be a game form that articulates the conferred rights when the feasible set $A \in \mathcal{S}$ prevails. Coupled with a restricted profile $\boldsymbol{Q_G}$, we have a *game* $(G_A, \boldsymbol{Q_G})$. The play of this game determines a set $T(G_A, \boldsymbol{Q_G})$ of *realizable extended social states*.[19] For the sake of simplicity in exposition, we assume in what follows that $T(G_A, \boldsymbol{Q_G})$ consists of a single outcome, say, $\tau(G_A, \boldsymbol{Q_G})$. In this case, a feasible extended social state is represented by a pair of an

18. It may well be the case that the game $(G_A, \boldsymbol{R})$ may not have an equilibrium when an equilibrium concept $\mathcal{E}$ is externally specified. This poses a problem for a theorist who wishes to analyze the interactions among individuals through this equilibrium concept, but the nonexistence of equilibrium does not mean in itself that the realization of individual rights is somehow hindered.

19. Let $C_{\mathcal{E}}(G_A, \boldsymbol{Q_G})$ be the set of pure strategy equilibria of the game $(G_A, \boldsymbol{Q_G})$, where $\mathcal{E}$ is the relevant equilibrium concept. If the set $g_A[C_{\mathcal{E}}(G_A, \boldsymbol{Q_G})]$ of pure strategy equilibrium outcomes is nonempty, it is quite natural to assume that $T(G_A, \boldsymbol{Q_G}) = g_A[C_{\mathcal{E}}(G_A, \boldsymbol{Q_G})]$. See Pattanaik and Suzumura [45, pp. 199–200] for the possible definition of $T(G_A, \boldsymbol{Q_G})$ when there exists no pure strategy equilibrium of the game $(G_A, \boldsymbol{Q_G})$.

outcome $\tau(G_A, Q_G)$ and a rights-system $\boldsymbol{G}$, viz., $(\tau(G_A, Q_G), \boldsymbol{G})$. We are now in the position to answer our previous question. Given a physically feasible set of states $A \in \mathcal{S}$ and an extended profile $\boldsymbol{Q}$, an extended social state $(x, \boldsymbol{G})$ is feasible in the sense that an outcome x is actually attainable through a rights-system $\boldsymbol{G}$, given $(A, \boldsymbol{Q})$, if and only if $x = \tau(G_A, Q_G)$ holds true.[20]

We are now ready to explain how the game form approach treats the issue of initial conferment of rights. Let Ψ be the *extended social welfare function* that maps each profile $\boldsymbol{Q} = (Q_1, Q_2, \ldots, Q_n)$ of extended individual preference orderings into an extended social welfare ordering: $Q = \Psi(\boldsymbol{Q})$. Given a set $A \in \mathcal{S}$ of feasible social outcomes, the *socially optimal conferment of rights* is nothing other than the rights-system $\boldsymbol{G}^*$ such that

$$(\tau(G^*_A, Q_{G^*}), \boldsymbol{G}^*)\Psi(\boldsymbol{Q})(\tau(G_A, Q_G), \boldsymbol{G}) \tag{17.19}$$

holds for any feasible rights-system $\boldsymbol{G}$.

An example may be helpful to make this abstract framework more intuitively understandable.[21] Consider a situation where $N = \{C, D\}$ (C = consequentialist, D = deontologist). There are two issues to be decided on. The first issue is the choice of religion, and there are two feasible options: b = Buddhism and c = Christianity. The second issue is whether or not a given book is to be read, and there are two options: r = "to read the book" and n = "not to read the book."

The set A of feasible social outcomes consists of 16 states. A typical element of A is denoted by $(c, n; b, r)$, which is the state where Mr. C believes in Christianity and does not read the book, and Mr. D believes in Buddhism and reads the book.

There are two feasible rights-systems: $\boldsymbol{G}^1 = \{G^1\}$ and $\boldsymbol{G}^2 = \{G^2\}$. The game form $G^1 = (N, \{S^1_i | i = C, D\}, A, g^1)$, where $S^1_i = \{b, c\} \times \{r, n\}$ for $i = C, D$ and $g^1(\boldsymbol{s}^N) = \boldsymbol{s}^N$ for all $\boldsymbol{s}^N = (s_1, s_2)$ such that $s_i \in S^1_i$ for

20. If $x \neq \tau(G_A, Q_G)$ holds, the extended alternative $(x, \boldsymbol{G})$ is not feasible, given $(A, \boldsymbol{Q})$. However, it still makes sense to talk about the preference for or against $(x, \boldsymbol{G}^1)$ vis-à-vis $(y, \boldsymbol{G}^2)$, just as we may meaningfully talk about preferences over the set of consumption plans irrespective of whether they can be attained under budget constraints.

21. The following analysis capitalizes on Essay 16 of this volume, which is based on Suzumura [75, Section 5].

$i = C, D$, is the one where the two persons are empowered to choose their religion as well as reading or not reading the book freely. In contrast, the game form $G^2 = (N, \{S_i^2 | i = C, D\}, A, g^2)$, where $S_i^2 = \{r, n\}$ for $i = C, D$ and $g^2(\boldsymbol{s}^N) = \boldsymbol{s}^N$ for all $\boldsymbol{s}^N = (s_1, s_2)$ such that $s_i \in S_i^2$ for $i = C, D$ is the one where the two persons are only allowed to choose reading or not reading the book freely, the matter of choosing a common religion being decided by the society. If the social choice of a common religion is $t \in \{b, c\}$ and the strategy pair $\boldsymbol{s}^N = (s_1, s_2)$ is chosen, the social state will be given by $(t, s_1; t, s_2)$.

Let $\boldsymbol{Q} = (Q_C, Q_D)$ be the profile of extended individual preference orderings. We assume that Mr. C is a die-hard consequentialist, who cares only about the outcomes of social interactions and nothing else. Thus, for all social states x in A, $(x, \boldsymbol{G}^1)I(Q_C)(x, \boldsymbol{G}^2)$ holds true, where $I(Q_C)$ is the indifference relation generated by Q_C. For each pair (u, v), where u (resp. v) refers to Mr. C's (resp. Mr. D's) religion, and for each $\boldsymbol{G} = \boldsymbol{G}^1$ and $\boldsymbol{G}^2$, let $Q_{C\boldsymbol{G}}(u, v)$ be defined by[22]

$$Q_{C\boldsymbol{G}}(u, v) : (u, r; v, r), (u, n; v, r), (u, r; v, n), (u, n; v, n), \quad (17.20)$$

which, in turn, is used to define $Q_{C\boldsymbol{G}}$ that orders 16 alternatives altogether by

$$Q_{C\boldsymbol{G}} : Q_{C\boldsymbol{G}}(b, c), Q_{C\boldsymbol{G}}(b, b), Q_{C\boldsymbol{G}}(c, b), Q_{C\boldsymbol{G}}(c, c). \quad (17.21)$$

We assume that Mr. D is a deontologist whose belief in the procedural justice in allowing people to choose their religion has such predominance that, whatever alternatives $x, y \in A$ are in fact at stake, he holds that $(x, \boldsymbol{G}^1)P(Q_D)(y, \boldsymbol{G}^2)$. For each pair (u, v) of religions of Mr. C and Mr. D and for each $\boldsymbol{G} = \boldsymbol{G}^1$ and $\boldsymbol{G}^2$, let us define $Q_{D\boldsymbol{G}}(u, v)$ by

$$Q_{D\boldsymbol{G}}(u, v) : (u, n; v, n), (u, n; v, r), (u, r; v, n), (u, r; v, r), \quad (17.22)$$

which, in turn, is used to define $Q_{D\boldsymbol{G}}$ by

$$Q_{D\boldsymbol{G}} : Q_{D\boldsymbol{G}}(c, c), Q_{D\boldsymbol{G}}(b, c), Q_{D\boldsymbol{G}}(c, b), Q_{D\boldsymbol{G}}(b, b). \quad (17.23)$$

---

22. Preference orderings are represented horizontally, with the less preferred alternative to the right of the more preferred alternative.

Let us examine the game $(G^1, \boldsymbol{Q}_{G^1})$. It is easy, if tedious, to check that (b, r) is the dominant strategy for Mr. C and (c, n) is the dominant strategy for Mr. D. Thus, $(b, r; c, n)$ in A is the dominant strategy equilibrium of the game $(G^1, \boldsymbol{Q}_{G^1})$. In the situation where there exists a dominant strategy equilibrium, it is very natural to assume that $\tau(G^1, \boldsymbol{Q}_{G^1}) = (b, r; c, n)$. Turning to the game $(G^2, \boldsymbol{Q}_{G^2})$, it is again easy to confirm that r (resp. n) is the dominant strategy for Mr. C (resp. Mr. D) irrespective of whether the social choice of religion turns out to be b or c. Thus, $\tau(G^2, \boldsymbol{Q}_{G^2}) = (b, r; b, n)$ or $(c, r; c, n)$ depending on the social choice of b or c. Recollect that Mr. D holds a lexicographic preference for $(x, \boldsymbol{G}^1)$ against (y, G^2) whatever may be x and y. Thus, he must surely prefer $(\tau(G^1, \boldsymbol{Q}_{G^1}), \boldsymbol{G}^1)$ to $(\tau(G^2, \boldsymbol{Q}_{G^2}), \boldsymbol{G}^2)$. Mr. C being a consequentialist, he is indifferent between $((b, r; c, n), \boldsymbol{G}^1)$ and $((b, r; c, n), \boldsymbol{G}^2)$ and he prefers $((b, r; c, n), \boldsymbol{G}^2)$ to $((b, r; b, n), \boldsymbol{G}^2)$ as well as to $((c, r; c, n), \boldsymbol{G}^2)$. By virtue of transitivity of Q_C, Mr. C must then prefer $(\tau(G^1, \boldsymbol{Q}_{G^1}), \boldsymbol{G}^1)$ to $(\tau(G^2, \boldsymbol{Q}_{G^2}), \boldsymbol{G}^2)$. Thus, as long as the extended social welfare function Ψ satisfies the Pareto principle, $\boldsymbol{G}^1$ must be the rights-system to be conferred. However, if $\boldsymbol{G}^1$ is conferred and the game $(G^1, \boldsymbol{Q}_{G^1})$ is played, $(b, r; c, n)$ will be the social outcome, which is Pareto-dominated by another feasible social state $(b, n; c, r)$.

We have thus exemplified in terms of the issue of initial conferment of game form rights what kind of analysis can be conducted through our extended conceptual framework, which endogenizes procedural considerations along with consequential considerations. In so doing, we have shown that Sen's Pareto libertarian paradox recurs in the context of initial conferment of game form rights in the sense that the Pareto principle imposed on the extended social welfare function, which is invoked in the initial conferment of game form rights, and the Pareto principle imposed on the conventionally defined social outcomes cannot be satisfied simultaneously in general. In this sense, Sen's original criticism against welfaristic foundations of normative economics survives even if his articulation of libertarian rights in terms of individuals' local decisiveness is replaced by the allegedly more proper articulation through game forms. We would like to conclude this section by repeating our conviction that Sen's impossibility problem "persists under virtually every plausible concept of individual rights" (Gaertner, Pattanaik, and Suzumura [20, p. 161]).

17.7. Concluding Remarks

No attempt will be made to summarize our main arguments presented in this essay. Instead, we would like to conclude this essay with several final observations.

In the first place, since the choice of a decision-making mechanism or procedure itself has to be made by a decision-making mechanism or procedure, it may be surmised that there must be some circularity in our conceptual framework. For example, in the concrete example through which we exemplified the working of this framework, the rights-system is chosen through the extended social welfare function, which, in itself, is a social decision-making mechanism. However, this does not cause any serious problem of logical circularity. To verify this fact, let x_1 denote the component of a social state that is not a decision-making mechanism. Let x_2 be the component of a social state that is a social decision-making mechanism to decide on x_1. In general, let x_t be the component of a social state that is a social decision-making mechanism to decide on $(x_1, x_2, \ldots, x_{t-1})$. Suppose that there exists a t^* and a social decision-making mechanism $x^*_{t^*}$ such that there exists unanimous support for $x^*_{t^*}$. In this case, the seeming logical circularity can be safely broken, and our exercise is on firm logical ground.[23] One cannot but recollect in this context a memorable passage from Jean-Jacques Rousseau to the following effect: "The law of plurality of votes is itself established by agreement, and supposes unanimity at least in the beginning."[24]

In the second place, the initial conferment of individual rights is determined in the game form approach by extended individual preference orderings through the extended social welfare function. A question may be asked if we are indeed prepared to change the initial conferment of rights each time people change their minds and express different preferences. Our answer is in the affirmative in a qualified sense. It would be absurd if we were to change the social choice of a rights-system each time people changed their preferences over *conventionally defined social outcomes*, but it would be likewise absurd if our social decision-making mechanism were totally insensitive to

23. This reasoning is a simple adaptation of Arrow's argument [2, p. 90].

24. J.-J. Rousseau, *The Social Contract*, English translation, New York and London: G. P. Putnam's Sons, 2nd edn., revised, 1906, pp. 165–166.

changes in people's preferences over *the pairs of outcomes and decision-making mechanisms*. People's perceptions of what should be the conferred rights do change over time, and it would be an unsatisfactory social decision-making mechanism indeed if it were unable to keep these changes properly on record.

In the third place, our method of incorporating procedural considerations, which capitalizes on an insightful observation due to Arrow, is by no means the only feasible method to serve that purpose. To cite just one salient example, Sven Hansson's [24; 25] recent attempt to explore social choice theory with procedural preferences is another method to capture the related, but distinct, idea. According to Hansson, "procedural preferences are no mere trifles in social decisions. To the contrary, they provide mechanisms for decisional stability in cases when preferences restricted to outcomes do not do this. Preferences for consensus, or preferences against ties, induce participants to take part in compromises that would not be motivated by their strictly consequential preferences" (Hansson [24, p. 273]). The gist of our attempt in this essay is not to advocate any particular method of analysis, but to call the readers' attention to the broad class of procedural issues that awaits our vigorous exploration.[25]

In the fourth and last place, we would like to keep on record our full agreement with Sen's assertion to the following effect: "The contrast between the procedural and consequential approaches is . . . somewhat overdrawn, and it may be possible to combine them, to a considerable extent, in an adequately rich characterization of states of affairs. The dichotomy is far from pure, and it is mainly a question of relative concentration" (Sen [63, p. 12]). The purpose of this essay would be served if we could bring this simple point home by exemplifying how such an "adequately rich characterization of states of affairs" could be implemented.

17.8. References

[1] Arneson, R. J., "Equality and Equal Opportunity for Welfare," *Philosphical Studies* **56**, 1989, 77–93.

[2] Arrow, K. J., *Social Choice and Individual Values*, New York: Wiley, 1951; 2nd edn., 1963.

25. See also related earlier work by Friedland and Cimbala [19] as well as Grofman and Uhlaner [23].

[3] Arrow, K. J., "Arrow's Theorem," in J. Eatwell, M. Milgate, and P. Newman, eds., *The New Palgrave: A Dictionary of Economics*, Vol. 1, London: Macmillan, 1987, 124–126.

[4] Arrow, K. J., and L. Hurwicz, *Studies in Resource Allocations Processes,* Cambridge, UK: Cambridge University Press, 1977.

[5] Baron, J., "Nonconsequentialist Decisions," *Behavioral and Brain Sciences* **17**, 1994, 1–42.

[6] Basu, K., "Achievements, Capabilities and the Concept of Well-Being," *Social Choice and Welfare* **4**, 1987, 69–76.

[7] Berlin, I., *Four Essays on Liberty*, Oxford: Oxford University Press, 1969.

[8] Bhagwati, J., *Protectionism*, Cambridge, Mass.: MIT Press, 1988.

[9] Bossert, W., P. K. Pattanaik, and Y. Xu, "Ranking Opportunity Sets: An Axiomatic Approach," *Journal of Economic Theory* **63**, 1994, 326–345.

[10] Buchanan, J. M., "Social Choice, Democracy, and Free Markets," *Journal of Political Economy* **62**, 1954, 114–123.

[11] Buchanan, J. M., "Individual Choice in Voting and the Market," *Journal of Political Economy* **62**, 1954, 334–343.

[12] Buchanan, J. M., *The Limits to Liberty: Between Anarchy and Leviathan*, Chicago: University of Chicago Press, 1975.

[13] Buchanan, J. M., *Liberty, Market and State*, New York: New York University Press, 1986.

[14] Bulow, J. I., J. D. Geanakoplos, and P. D. Klemperer, "Multimarket Oligopoly: Strategic Substitutes and Complements," *Journal of Political Economy* **93**, 1985, 488–511.

[15] Dornbusch, R. W., "Policy Options for Freer Trade: The Case for Bilateralism," in R. Lawrence and C. Schultze, eds., *An American Trade Strategy: Option for the 1990s*, Washington, DC: Brookings Institution, 1990, 106–141.

[16] Dworkin, G., "Is More Choice Better than Less?" in P. A. French, T. E. Uehling, Jr., and H. W. Wettstein, eds., *Midwest Studies in Philosophy*, Vol. VII, *Social and Political Philosophy*, Minneapolis: University of Minnesota Press, 1982, 47–61.

[17] Ethier, W., "Voluntary Export Restraints," in A. Takayama, M. Ohyama, and H. Ohta, eds., *Trade, Policy, and International Adjustments*, New York: Academic Press, 1991, 3–18.

[18] Fleurbaey, M., "Equal Opportunity or Equal Social Outcome?" *Economics and Philosophy* **11**, 1995, 25–55.

[19] Friedland, E. I., and S. J. Cimbala, "Process and Paradox: The Significance of Arrow's Theorem," *Theory and Decision* **4**, 1973, 51–64.

[20] Gaertner, W., P. K. Pattanaik, and K. Suzumura, "Individual Rights Revisited," *Economica* **59**, 1992, 161–177. Essay 15 of this volume.

[21] Garten, J. E., "Is America Abandoning Multilateral Trade?" *Foreign Affairs* **74**, 1995, 50–62.

[22] Gravel, N., "Can a Ranking of Opportunity Sets Attach an Intrinsic Value to Freedom of Choice?" *American Economic Review: Papers Proceedings* **84**, 1994, 454–458.

[23] Grofman, B., and C. Uhlaner, "Metapreferences and the Reasons for Stability in Social Choice: Thoughts on Broadening and Clarifying the Debate," *Theory and Decision* **19**, 1985, 31–50.

[24] Hansson, S. O., "A Procedural Model of Voting," *Theory and Decision* **32**, 1992, 269–301.

[25] Hansson, S. O., "Social Choice with Procedural Preferences," *Social Choice Welfare* **13**, 1996, 215–230.

[26] Harris, R., "Why Voluntary Export Restraints Are 'Voluntary,'" *Canadian Journal of Economics* **18**, 1985, 799–809.

[27] Harsanyi, J. C., "Value Judgements," in J. Eatwell, M. Milgate, and P. Newman, eds., *The New Palgrave: A Dictionary of Economics*, Vol. 4., London: Macmillan, 1987, 792–793.

[28] Hayek, F. A., *Individualism and Economic Order*, Chicago: University of Chicago Press, 1948.

[29] Hayek, F. A., *The Constitution of Liberty*, London: Routledge & Kegan Paul, 1960.

[30] Hayek, F. A., *New Studies in Philosophy, Politics, Economics and the History of Ideas*, London: Routledge & Kegan Paul, 1978.

[31] Hurwicz, L., "Institutions as Families of Game Forms," *Japanese Economic Review* **47**, 1996, 113–132.

[32] Jones, P., and R. Sugden, "Evaluating Choice," *International Review of Law and Economics* **2**, 1982, 47–65.

[33] Kemp, M. C., K. Shimomura, and M. Okawa, "Voluntary Export Restraints and Economic Welfare: A General Equilibrium Analysis," *Japanese Economic Review* **48**, 1997, 187–198.

[34] Klemisch-Ahlert, M., "Freedom of Choice: A Comparison of Different Rankings of Opportunity Sets," *Social Choice and Welfare* **10**, 1993, 189–207.

[35] Konishi, H., M. Okuno-Fujiwara, and K. Suzumura, "Oligopolistic Competition and Economic Welfare: A General Equilibrium Analysis of Entry Barriers and Tax-Subsidy Schemes," *Journal of Public Economics* **42**, 1990, 67–88. Essay 22 of this volume.

[36] Krishna, K., "Trade Restrictions as Facilitating Practices," *Journal of International Economics* **26**, 1989, 251–270.

[37] Krishna, K., "What Do VERs Do?" in R. Sato and J. Nelson, eds., *Beyond Trade Friction*, Cambridge, UK: Cambridge University Press, 1989, 75–92.

[38] Lindbeck, A., "Individual Freedom and Welfare State Policy," *European Economic Review* **32**, 1988, 295–318.

[39] Mankiw, N. G., and M. D. Whinston, "Free Entry and Social Efficiency," *Rand Journal of Economics* **17**, 1986, 48–58.

[40] Nozick, R., *Anarchy, State, and Utopia*, Oxford: Basil Blackwell, 1974.

[41] Okuno-Fujiwara, M., and K. Suzumura, "Symmetric Cournot Oligopoly and Economic Welfare: A Synthesis," *Economic Theory* **3**, 1993, 43–59. Essay 23 of this volume.

[42] Panzar, J. C., "Regulation, Deregulation, and Economic Efficiency: The Case of CAB," *American Economic Review: Papers and Proceedings* **70**, 1980, 311–319.

[43] Pareto, V., *Manual of Political Economy*, New York: A. M. Kelley, 1927.

[44] Pattanaik, P. K., and K. Suzumura, "Rights, Welfarism and Social Choice," *American Economic Review: Papers and Proceedings* **84**, 1994, 435–439.

[45] Pattanaik, P. K., and K. Suzumura, "Individual Rights and Social Evaluation: A Conceptual Framework," *Oxford Economic Papers* **48**, 1996, 194–212.

[46] Pattanaik, P. K., and Y. Xu, "On Ranking Opportunity Sets in Terms of Freedom of Choice," *Recherches Economique de Louvain* **56**, 1990, 383–390.

[47] Puppe, C., "An Axiomatic Approach to 'Preference for Freedom of Choice,'" *Journal of Economic Theory* **68**, 1996, 174–199.

[48] Rawls, J., *A Theory of Justice*, Cambridge, Mass.: Harvard University Press, 1971.

[49] Sandmo, A., "Buchanan on Political Economy: A Review Article," *Journal of Economic Literature* **28**, 1990, 50–65.

[50] Schotter, A., *The Economic Theory of Social Institutions*, Cambridge, UK: Cambridge University Press, 1981.

[51] Sen, A. K., "The Impossibility of a Paretian Liberal," *Journal of Political Economy* **78**, 1970, 152–157.

[52] Sen, A. K., *Collective Choice and Social Welfare*, San Francisco: Holden-Day, 1970; republished, Amsterdam: North-Holland, 1979.
[53] Sen, A. K., "Liberty, Unanimity and Rights," *Economica* **43**, 1976, 217–245.
[54] Sen, A. K., "Utilitarianism and Welfarism," *Journal of Philosophy* **76**, 1979, 463–489.
[55] Sen, A. K., "Personal Utilities and Public Judgements: Or What's Wrong with Welfare Economics," *Economic Journal* **76**, 1979, 537–558.
[56] Sen, A. K., "Liberty and Social Choice," *Journal of Philosophy* **80**, 1983, 5–28.
[57] Sen, A. K., *Commodities and Capabilities*, Amsterdam: North-Holland, 1985.
[58] Sen, A. K., "Well-Being, Agency and Freedom: The Dewey Lectures 1984," *Journal of Philosophy* **82**, 1985, 169–221.
[59] Sen, A. K., "Freedom of Choice: Concept and Content," *European Economic Review* **32**, 1988, 269–294.
[60] Sen, A. K., "Welfare, Preference and Freedom," *Journal of Econometrics* **50**, 1991, 15–29.
[61] Sen, A. K., "Minimal Liberty," *Economica* **59**, 1992, 139–160.
[62] Sen, A. K., "Markets and Freedoms: Achievements and Limitations of the Market Mechanism in Promoting Individual Freedoms," *Oxford Economic Papers* **45**, 1993, 519–541.
[63] Sen, A. K., "Rationality and Social Choice," *American Economic Review* **85**, 1995, 1–24.
[64] Sen, A. K., "Maximization and the Act of Choice," *Econometrica* **65**, 1997, 745–779.
[65] Sen, A. K., *On Economic Inequality*, expanded edition, Oxford: Clarendon Press, 1997.
[66] Stiglitz, J. E., *Whither Socialism?* Cambridge, Mass.: MIT Press, 1994.
[67] Sugden, R., *The Political Economy of Public Choice*, Oxford: Martin Robertson, 1981.
[68] Sugden, R., "Liberty, Preference, and Choice," *Economics and Philosophy* **1**, 1985, 213–229.
[69] Sugden, R., *The Economics of Rights, Co-operation and Welfare*, Oxford: Blackwell, 1986.
[70] Sugden, R., "Rights: Why Do They Matter, and To Whom?" *Constitutional Political Economy* **4**, 1993, 127–152.
[71] Sugden, R., "The Metric of Opportunity," *Economics and Philosophy* **14**, 1998, 307–337.
[72] Suzumura, K., *Rational Choice, Collective Decisions and Social Welfare*, New York: Cambridge University Press, 1983. Reprinted in paperback, 2009.
[73] Suzumura, K., "Alternative Approaches to Libertarian Rights in the Theory of Social Choice," in K. J. Arrow, ed., *Markets and Welfare*, Vol. 1 of *Issues in Contemporary Economics*, London: Macmillan, 1990, 215–242.
[74] Suzumura, K., *Competition, Commitment, and Welfare*, Oxford: Clarendon Press, 1995.
[75] Suzumura, K., "Welfare, Rights, and Social Choice Procedure: A Perspective," *Analyse & Kritik* **18**, 1996, 20–37. Essay 16 of this volume.
[76] Suzumura, K., "Industrial Policy in the Developing Market Economy," in E. Malinvaud, J.-C. Milleron, A. K. Sen, A. Sengupta, N. Stern, J. E. Stiglitz, and K. Suzumura, *Development Strategy and the Market Economy*, Oxford: Clarendon Press, 1996.
[77] Suzumura, K., "Paretian Welfare Judgements and Bergsonian Social Choice," *Economic Journal* **109**, 1999, 204–220. Essay 26 of this volume.
[78] Suzumura, K., and J. Ishikawa, "Voluntary Export Restraints and Economic Welfare," *Japanese Economic Review* **48**, 1997, 176–186.
[79] Suzumura, K., and K. Kiyono, "Entry Barriers and Economic Welfare," *Review of Economic Studies* **54**, 1987, 157–167. Essay 21 of this volume.
[80] Van Hees, M., "Libertarian Collective Decision-Making: A New Framework," *Social Choice and Welfare* **12**, 1995, 155–164.
[81] Vickers, J., "Concepts of Competition," *Oxford Economic Papers* **47**, 1995, 1–23.

ESSAY 18

Characterizations of Consequentialism and Nonconsequentialism

18.1. Introduction

It is undeniable that most, if not all, welfare economists are *welfaristic* in their conviction in the sense that they regard an economic policy or economic system to be satisfactory if and only if it is warranted to generate outcomes that score high on the measuring rod of social welfare.[1] It is equally undeniable, however, that there do exist people who care not only about welfaristic features of consequences but also about nonwelfaristic features of consequences, or even nonconsequential features of the procedure through which these consequences are brought about. Even those welfare economists with strong welfaristic conviction should be ready to take the judgments of people with nonwelfaristic convictions into account in order not to be paternalistic in their welfare analysis. The purpose of this essay is to develop several analytical frameworks that enable us to examine the choice behavior of nonwelfaristic people. More specifically, we develop several frameworks that can accommodate situations where an individual expresses his/her preferences of the following type: it is better for me that an outcome x is realized from the opportunity set A than another outcome y being realized from

---

First published in *Journal of Economic Theory* **101**, 2001, pp. 423–436 as a joint paper with Y. Xu. Thanks are due to an anonymous referee of *Journal of Economic Theory* whose incisive comments greatly improved the exposition of the original paper.

1. For a general observation on the concept and content of wefarism, see, among others, Sen [10; 11].

the opportunity set B.[2] Note, in particular, that he/she is expressing his/her intrinsic valuation of the opportunity for choice if he/she prefers choosing x from the opportunity A, where $x \in A$, rather than choosing x from the singleton opportunity set $\{x\}$. Using this analytical framework, we can put forward a concise definition of consequentialism and nonconsequentialism, and we can also characterize these concepts in terms of a few simple axioms.

The structure of this essay is as follows. In Section 18.2, we present the basic notation and definitions. Section 18.3 discusses the basic axioms that are assumed throughout this essay. Some simple implications of these axioms are also identified in this section. In Section 18.4, we define the concept of an *extreme consequentialist* and a *strong consequentialist*, and characterize them axiomatically. We then turn in Section 18.5 to the concepts of an *extreme nonconsequentialist* and a *strong nonconsequentialist* and their axiomatic characterizations. Section 18.6 concludes with some remarks.

18.2. Basic Notations and Definitions

Let X, where $3 \leq \#X < +\infty$, be the set of all mutually exclusive and jointly exhaustive *social states*. The elements of X will be denoted by $x, y, z, \cdots$, and they are called *outcomes*. $\mathcal{S}$ denotes the set of all finite nonempty subsets of X. The elements in $\mathcal{S}$ will be denoted by $A, B, C, \cdots$, and they are called *opportunity sets*. Let $X \times \mathcal{S}$ be the Cartesian product of X and $\mathcal{S}$. Elements of $X \times \mathcal{S}$ will be denoted by (x, A), (y, B), (z, C), $\cdots$, and they are called *extended alternatives*. Let $\Omega := \{(x, A) | A \in \mathcal{S} \text{ and } x \in A\}$. That is, Ω contains all (x, A) such that A is finite and x is an element of A. It

2. Much attention has been focused on the opportunity set evaluation, beginning with Sen [12; 13]. See, among many others, Bossert, Pattanaik, and Xu [2], Pattanaik and Xu [8; 9], Sen [14; 15], and Suzumura [16]. To the best of our knowledge, Gravel [4; 5] remains the unique precursor in analyzing the extended preference ordering on $X \times \mathcal{S}$, where X is the set of social states and $\mathcal{S}$ is the set of opportunity sets. However, his approach is quite different from ours in that he assumes that an individual has two preference orderings, one for ordering outcomes in X and another for ordering the choice situations in $X \times \mathcal{S}$. His analysis is focused on the possibility of conflict between these two orderings, and it has nothing to do with consequentialism and nonconsequentialism. Capitalizing on Arrow's [1; pp. 89–91] insightful observation, Pattanaik and Suzumura [6; 7] and Suzumura [16; 17] developed a conceptual framework for the analysis of nonconsequential features of the decision-making procedures through which consequential outcomes are brought about.

should be clear that $\Omega \subseteq X \times \mathcal{S}$, and for all $(x, A) \in \Omega$, $x \in A$ holds. For all $(x, A) \in \Omega$, the intended interpretation is the following: the alternative x is chosen from the opportunity set A.

Let $\succcurlyeq$ be a reflexive, complete, and transitive binary relation over Ω. The asymmetric and symmetric parts of $\succcurlyeq$ will be denoted by $\succ$ and $\sim$, respectively. For any $(x, A), (y, B) \in \Omega$, $(x, A) \succcurlyeq (y, B)$ is interpreted as "choosing x from the opportunity set A is at least as good as choosing y from the opportunity set B." Thus, in the extended framework, it is possible to give an expression to the intrinsic value of the opportunity set in addition to the instrumental value thereof. Indeed, the decision maker recognizes the intrinsic value of the opportunity of choice if there exists an extended alternative $(x, A) \in \Omega$ such that $(x, A) \succ (x, \{x\})$.

18.3. Basic Axioms and Their Implication

In this section, we introduce two basic axioms for the ordering $\succcurlyeq$, and examine the implication of combining them together.

Independence (IND). For all $(x, A), (y, B) \in \Omega$, and all $z \in X \setminus (A \cup B)$, $(x, A) \succcurlyeq (y, B) \Leftrightarrow (x, A \cup \{z\}) \succcurlyeq (y, B \cup \{z\})$.

Simple Indifference (SI). For all $x \in X$, and all $y, z \in X \setminus \{x\}$, $(x, \{x, y\}) \sim (x, \{x, z\})$.

IND corresponds to the standard independence axiom used in the literature (see, for example, Pattanaik and Xu [8]). Its requirement is simple: for all opportunity sets A and B, if an alternative z is not in both A and B, then the extended preference ranking over $(x, A \cup \{z\})$ and $(x, B \cup \{z\})$ corresponds to that over (x, A) and (y, B), independent of the nature of the added alternative z. SI requires that choosing x from "simple" cases, each involving two alternatives, is regarded as indifferent to each other.

The following result summarizes the implication of these two axioms.

Theorem 18.1. If $\succcurlyeq$ satisfies IND and SI, then for all $(x, A), (x, B) \in \Omega$, $\#A = \#B \Rightarrow (x, A) \sim (x, B)$.

Proof. Let $\succcurlyeq$ satisfy IND and SI. Let $(x, A), (x, B) \in \Omega$ be such that $\#A = \#B$.

First, consider the case where $A \cap B = \{x\}$. Let $A = \{x, a_1, \ldots, a_m\}$ and $B = \{x, b_1, \ldots, b_m\}$. Since opportunity sets are finite, $m < +\infty$ holds. From SI, clearly, $(x, \{x, a_i\}) \sim (x, \{x, b_j\})$ for all $i, j = 1, \ldots, m$. Applications of IND lead us to $(x, \{x, a_1, a_2\}) \sim (x, \{x, a_1, b_1\})$ and $(x, \{x, a_1, b_1\}) \sim (x, \{x, b_1, b_2\})$. From the transitivity of $\succsim$, $(x, \{x, a_1, a_2\}) \sim (x, \{x, b_1, b_2\})$ follows easily. By using a similar argument, we obtain $(x, A) \sim (x, B)$ from IND and the transitivity of $\succsim$.

Next, consider the case that $A \cap B = \{x\} \cup C$, where C is nonempty. From the preceding, noting that $\#(A \setminus B) = \#(B \setminus C)$, we must have $(x, (A \setminus C) \cup \{x\}) \sim (x, (B \setminus C) \cup \{x\})$. Since opportunity sets are finite, $(x, A) \sim (x, B)$ follows from IND. ■

18.4. Consequentialism

In this section, we define and characterize two versions of consequentialism: *extreme consequentialism* and *strong consequentialism*. First, we define extreme consequentialism and strong consequentialism, respectively, as follows.

Definition 18.1. $\succsim$ is said to be *extremely consequential* if, for all (x, A), $(x, B) \in \Omega$, $(x, A) \sim (x, B)$.

Definition 18.2. $\succsim$ is said to be *strongly consequential* if, for all (x, A), $(y, B) \in \Omega$, $(x, \{x\}) \sim (y, \{y\})$ implies $[(x, A) \succsim (y, B) \Leftrightarrow \#A \geq \#B]$, and $(x, \{x\}) \succ (y, \{y\})$ implies $(x, A) \succ (y, B)$.

Thus, according to extreme consequentialism, two choice situations (x, A) and (y, B) are judged exclusively on their consequences x and y, and the opportunity sets A and B from which these consequences are chosen are irrelevant. On the other hand, strong consequentialism stipulates that opportunity sets do not matter when the indiviudual has a strict preference over $(x, \{x\})$ and $(y, \{y\})$. Only when the individual is indifferent between $(x, \{x\})$ and $(y, \{y\})$ do opportunities matter.

To characterize extreme consequentialism and strong consequentialism, the following axioms will prove useful.

Local Indifference (LI). For all $x \in X$, there exists $(x, A) \in \Omega \setminus \{(x, \{x\})\}$ such that $(x, X) \sim (x, A)$.

Local Strict Monotonicity (LSM). For all $x \in X$, there exists $(x, A) \in \Omega \setminus \{(x, \{x\})\}$ such that $(x, A) \succ (x, \{x\})$.

LI is a minimal and local requirement of extreme consequentialism: there exists an opportunity set A in $\mathcal{S}$, which is distinct from $\{x\}$, such that choosing an alternative x from A is regarded as being indifferent to choosing x from the singleton set $\{x\}$. LSM requires that there exists an opportunity set A such that choosing x from A is strictly better than choosing x from the singleton set $\{x\}$. In other words, the individual values opportunities per se at least in this very limited sense.

Theorem 18.2. $\succcurlyeq$ satisfies IND, SI and LI if and only if it is extremely consequential.

Proof. If $\succcurlyeq$ is extremely consequential, then it clearly satisfies IND, SI, and LI. Therefore, we have only to prove that, if $\succcurlyeq$ satisfies IND, SI, and LI, then, for all $(x, A), (x, B) \in \Omega$, $(x, A) \sim (x, B)$ holds.

Let $\succcurlyeq$ satisfy IND, SI, and LI. First, note that from Theorem 18.1 we have the following:

$$\text{For all } (x, A), (x, B) \in \Omega, \#A = \#B \Rightarrow (x, A) \sim (x, B). \tag{18.1}$$

Hence, we have only to show that

$$\text{For all } (x, A), (x, B) \in \Omega, \#A > \#B \Rightarrow (x, A) \sim (x, B). \tag{18.2}$$

To begin with, we show that

$$\text{For all } x \in X \text{ and all } y \in X \setminus \{x\}, (x, \{x, y\}) \sim (x, \{x\}). \tag{18.3}$$

Let $x \in X$. Suppose for some $a \in X \setminus \{x\}$, $(x, \{x, a\}) \succ (x, \{x\})$ holds. Given SI, by the transitivity of $\succcurlyeq$ we have

$$\text{For all } y \in X \setminus \{x\} : (x, \{x, y\}) \succ (x, \{x\}). \tag{18.4}$$

Then, by IND, we obtain

$$\text{For all } z \in X \setminus \{x, y\} : (x, \{x, y, z\}) \succ (x, \{x, z\}). \tag{18.5}$$

Using an argument similar to that for (18.4) and (18.5), we can show that

$$\text{For all } (x, A) \in \Omega \text{ and all } m = 4, \ldots : \#A = m \quad \Rightarrow (x, A) \succ (x, \{x\}). \tag{18.6}$$

Equation (18.6), together with (18.4) and (18.5), is in contradiction with LI. Therefore, we cannot have $(x, \{x, a\}) \succ (x, \{x\})$ for some $a \in X \setminus \{x\}$. Similarly, if $(x, \{x\}) \succ (x, \{x, b\})$ for some $b \in X$, we can show that $(x, \{x\}) \succ (x, A)$ holds for all $(x, A) \in \Omega$ with $A \neq \{x\}$, another contradiction with LI. Hence, by the completeness of $\succsim$, (18.3) holds.

From (18.3), noting the finiteness of opportunity sets, and by the repeated use of IND, (18.1), and the transitivity of $\succsim$, (18.2) obtains. ■

Before turning to the full characterization of strong consequentialism, we note the following result, which will prove useful in establishing the remainder of our results in this essay.

Lemma 18.1. If $\succsim$ satisfies IND, SI, and LSM, then, for all $(x, A), (x, B) \in \Omega$, $\#A \geq \#B \Leftrightarrow (x, A) \succsim (x, B)$.

Proof. Let $\succsim$ satisfy IND, SI, and LSM. Note that, from Theorem 18.1, we have the following:

$$\text{For all } (x, A), (x, B) \in \Omega : \#A = \#B \Rightarrow (x, A) \sim (x, B). \tag{18.7}$$

Therefore, we have only to show that

$$\text{For all } (x, A), (x, B) \in \Omega : \#A > \#B \Rightarrow (x, A) \succ (x, B). \tag{18.8}$$

We first note that, by following an argument simlar to that in the proof of Theorem 18.2, the following can be established.

$$\text{For all } x \in X, \text{ all } y \in x \neq y \Rightarrow (x, \{x, y\}) \succ (x, \{x\}). \tag{18.9}$$

Now, from (18.9), by the repeated use of IND, we can derive the following:

$$\text{For all } (x, A) \in \Omega \setminus \{(x, X)\} \text{ and } y \in X \setminus A : (x, A \cup \{y\}) \succ (x, A). \tag{18.10}$$

Then, given the finiteness of the opportunity sets, it follows from (18.7) and (18.10) that (18.8) holds by virtue of the transitivity of $\succcurlyeq$. ■

To characterize strong consequentialism, we need an additional condition, which requires that, for all $(x, A), (y, B) \in \Omega$ and all $z \in X$, if the indiviudual ranks (x, A) higher than (y, B), then adding z to B while maintaining y being chosen from $B \cup \{z\}$ will not affect the individual's ranking: (x, A) is still ranked higher than $(y, B \cup \{z\})$. Formally, we introduce the following condition.

Robustness (ROB). For all $(x, A), (y, B) \in \Omega$ and all $z \in X$, if $(x, \{x\}) \succ (y, \{y\})$ and $(x, A) \succ (y, B)$, then $(x, A) \succ (y, B \cup \{z\})$.

We are now ready to put forward the following full characterization of strong consequentialism.

Theorem 18.3. $\succcurlyeq$ satisfies IND, SI, LSM, and ROB if and only if it is strongly consequential.

Proof. If $\succcurlyeq$ is strongly consequential, then it clearly satisfies IND, SI, LSM, and ROB. Therefore, we have only to prove that if $\succcurlyeq$ satisfies IND, SI, LSM, and ROB, then, for all $(x, A), (y, B) \in \Omega$, $(x, \{x\}) \sim (y, \{y\})$ implies $[(x, A) \succcurlyeq (y, B) \Leftrightarrow \#A \geq \#B]$, and $(x, \{x\}) \succ (y, \{y\})$ implies $(x, A) \succ (y, B)$.

Let $\succcurlyeq$ satisfy IND, SI, LSM, and ROB. Note that, from Lemma 18.1, we have the following:

$$\text{For all } (x, A), (x, B) \in \Omega : \#A \geq \#B \Leftrightarrow (x, A) \succcurlyeq (x, B). \quad (18.11)$$

Now, for all $x, y \in X$, consider $(x, \{x\})$ and $(y, \{y\})$. If $(x, \{x\}) \sim (y, \{y\})$, then, since X contains at least three alternatives, by IND, for all $z \in X \setminus \{x, y\}$, we must have $(x, \{x, z\}) \sim (y, \{y, z\})$. From (18.11) and by the transitivity of $\succcurlyeq$, we then have $(x, \{x, y\}) \sim (y, \{x, y\})$. Then, by IND, we have $(x, \{x, y, z\}) \sim (y, \{x, y, z\})$. Since the opportunity sets are finite, by repeated application of (18.11), the transitivity of $\succcurlyeq$ and IND, we obtain

$$\text{For all } (x, A), (y, B) \in \Omega : \text{ if } (x, \{x\}) \sim (y, \{y\}), \text{ then } \#A \geq \#B \Leftrightarrow (x, A) \succcurlyeq (y, B). \quad (18.12)$$

If, on the other hand, $(x, \{x\}) \succ (y, \{y\})$, then, for all $z \in X$, by ROB, $(x, \{x\}) \succ (y, \{y, z\})$. Since the opportunity sets are finite, by repeated use of ROB, we then have $(x, \{x\}) \succ (y, A)$ for all $(y, A) \in \Omega$. Therefore, from (18.11) and the transitivity of $\succsim$, we obtain

$$\text{For all } (x, A), (y, B) \in \Omega, \text{ if } (x, \{x\}) \succ (y, \{y\}), \text{ then } (x, A) \succ (y, B). \tag{18.13}$$

Combining (18.13) with (18.11) and (18.12), the proof of Theorem 18.3 is complete. ■

It is sasy to verify that the axioms IND, SI, and LI are independent and also that the axioms IND, SI, LSM, and ROB are independent. Thus, our characterization theorems, viz., Theorem 18.2 for extreme consequentialism and Theorem 18.3 for strong consequentialism, do not contain any redundancy.

18.5. Nonconsequentialism

In this section, we define and characterize two versions of nonconsequentialism, to be called *extreme nonconsequentialism* and *strong nonconsequentialism*, respectively. Their definitions follow.

Definition 18.3. $\succsim$ is said to be *extremely nonconsequential* if, for all $(x, A), (y, B) \in \Omega$, $(x, A) \succsim (y, B) \Leftrightarrow \#A \geq \#B$.

Definition 18.4. $\succsim$ is said to be *strongly nonconsequential* if, for all (x, A), $(y, B) \in \Omega$, $\#A > \#B \Rightarrow (x, A) \succ (y, B)$, and $\#A = \#B \Rightarrow [(x, \{x\}) \succsim (y, \{y\}) \Leftrightarrow (x, A) \succsim (y, B)]$.

According to extreme nonconsequentialism, consequences do not matter at all, and what is valued is the richness of opportunity involved in the choice situation. Thus, two extended alternatives, (x, A) and (y, B), are ranked exclusively according to the cardinality of A and B, and the consequences do not have any influence at all. In its complete neglect of consequences, extreme nonconsequentialism is indeed extreme, but it captures the sense in which people may claim, "Give me liberty, or give me death." On the other hand, strong nonconsequentialism pays attention to consequences if and only if two opportunity sets contain the same number of alternatives.

To give characterizations of extreme nonconsequentialism and strong nonconsequentialism, the following axioms will be used.

Indifference of No-Choice Situations (INS). For all $x, y \in X$, $(x, \{x\}) \sim (y, \{y\})$.

Simple Preference for Opportunities (SPO). For all distinct $x, y \in X$, $(x, \{x, y\}) \succ \{y, \{y\})$.

INS is simple and easy to interpret. It says that in facing two choice situations in which each outcome is restricted to choices from singleton sets, the individual is indifferent between them. INS thus conveys the message that in these simple cases, the individual feels that there is no real freedom of choice in each choice situation and is ready to express his indifference among these cases *regardless of the nature of the outcomes.* In a sense, it is the lack of freedom of choice that "forces" the individual to be indifferent among these situations. This idea is similar to an axiom proposed by Pattanaik and Xu [8] for ranking opportunity sets in terms of freedom of choice, which stipulates that all singleton sets offer the same amount of freedom of choice. On the other hand, SPO stipulates that it is always better for the individual to choose an outcome from the set containing two elements (one of which is the chosen outcome) than to choose an outcome from the singleton set. SPO thus displays the individual's desire to have some genuine opportunities of choice.

Theorem 18.4. $\succcurlyeq$ satisfies IND, SI, LSM, and INS if and only if it is extremely nonconsequential.

Proof. If $\succcurlyeq$ is extremely nonconsequential, then it clearly satisfies IND, SI, LSM, and INS. Therefore, we have only to prove that, if $\succcurlyeq$ satisfies IND, SI, LSM, and INS, then, for all $(x, A), (y, B) \in \Omega$, $\#A \geq \#B \Leftrightarrow (x, A) \succcurlyeq (y, B)$.

To begin with, from Lemma 18.1, we have the following:

$$\text{For all } (x, A), (x, B) \in \Omega,\ (x, A) \succcurlyeq (x, B) \Leftrightarrow \#A \geq \#B. \quad (18.14)$$

Now, for all $x, y \in X$, by INS, $(x, \{x\}) \sim \{y, \{y\})$. For all $z \in X \setminus \{x, y\}$, by IND, $(x, \{x, z\}) \sim (y, \{y, z\})$. It follows from (18.14) that $(x, \{x, y\}) \sim (y, \{x, y\})$, where use is made of the transitivity of $\succcurlyeq$. By the repeated use of (18.14), IND, and the transitivity of $\succcurlyeq$, and noting that all opportunity sets are finite, we can show that

$$\text{For all } (x, A), (y, B) \in \Omega, (x, A) \succcurlyeq (y, B) \Leftrightarrow \#A \geq \#B. \quad (18.15)$$

This completes the proof of Theorem 18.4. ■

Before presenting the characterization theorem for strong nonconsequentialism, we note the following result, which will prove useful in establishing the characterization theorem.

LEMMA 18.2. If $\succcurlyeq$ satisfies IND, SI, and SPO, then it also satisfies LSM.

PROOF. Let $\succcurlyeq$ satisfy IND, SI, and SPO. Let $x \in X$. For all $y \in X \setminus \{x\}$, by SPO, $(x, \{x, y\}) \succ (y, \{y\})$. Then IND implies $(x, \{x, y, z\}) \succ (y, \{y, z\})$ for all $z \in X \setminus \{x, y\}$. By SI, $(y, \{y, z\}) \sim (y, \{x, y\})$. The transitivity of $\succcurlyeq$ now implies $(x, \{x, y, z\}) \succ (y, \{x, y\})$. By SPO, $(y, \{x, y\}) \succ (x, \{x\})$. Then, $(x, \{x, y, z\}) \succ (x, \{x\})$ follows from the transitivity of $\succcurlyeq$. That is, LSM holds. ■

THEOREM 18.5. $\succcurlyeq$ satisfies IND, SI, and SPO if and only if it is strongly nonconsequential.

PROOF. If $\succcurlyeq$ is strongly nonconsequential, then it clearly satisfies IND, SI, and SPO. Therefore, we have only to prove that, if $\succcurlyeq$ satisfies IND, SI, and SPO, then, for all $(x, A), (y, B) \in \Omega$, $\#A > \#B \Rightarrow (x, A) \succ (y, B)$ and $\#A = \#B \Rightarrow [(x, \{x\}) \succcurlyeq (y, \{y\}) \Leftrightarrow (x, A) \succcurlyeq (y, B)]$.

Conversely, from Lemmas 18.2 and Lemma 18.1, we have (18.14). For all distinct $x, y \in X$, by SPO, $(x, \{x, y\}) \succ (y, \{y\})$. Then, from (18.14) and the transitivity of $\succcurlyeq$, for all $z \in X \setminus \{x\}$, $(x, \{x, z\}) \succ (y, \{y\})$. By IND, from $(x, \{x, y\}) \succ (y, \{y\})$, $(x, \{x, y, z\}) \succ (y, \{y, z\})$ holds for all $z \in X \setminus \{x, y\}$. Noting (18.14) and the transitivity of $\succcurlyeq$, we then have

$$\text{For all } (x, A), (y, B) \in \Omega, \text{ if } \#A = \#B + 1 \text{ and } \#B \leq 2, \text{ then } (x, A) \succ (y, B). \quad (18.16)$$

From (18.16), by the repeated use of IND, (18.14), and the transitivity of $\succcurlyeq$, coupled with the finiteness of all opportunity sets, we can obtain the following:

$$\text{For all } (x, A), (y, B) \in \Omega, \text{ if } \#A = \#B + 1, \text{ then } (x, A) \succ (y, B). \tag{18.17}$$

From (18.17), the transitivity of $\succcurlyeq$, and (18.14), we have

$$\text{For all } (x, A), (y, B) \in \Omega, \text{ if } \#A > \#B, \text{ then } (x, A) \succ (y, B). \tag{18.18}$$

Consider now $(x, \{x\})$ and $(y, \{y\})$. If $(x, \{x\}) \sim \{y, \{y\}\}$, following a similar argument as in the proof of Theorem 18.4, we can obtain

$$\text{For all } (x, A), (y, B) \in \Omega, \text{ if } (x, \{x\}) \sim (y, \{y\}) \text{ and } \#A = \#B, \text{ then } (x, A) \sim (y, B). \tag{18.19}$$

If, on the other hand, $(x, \{x\}) \succ \{y, \{y\}\}$, we can follow a similar argument as in the proof of Theorem 18.3 to obtain

$$\text{For all } (x, A), (y, B) \in \Omega, \text{ if } (x, \{x\}) \succ (y, \{y\}) \text{ and } \#A = \#B, \text{ then } (x, A) \succ (y, B). \tag{18.20}$$

Equation (18.20), together with (18.18) and (18.19), completes the proof. ■

It is easy to verify that the axioms IND, SI, LSM, and INS are independent and also that the axioms IND, SI, and SPO are independent. Thus our characterzation theorems, viz., Theorem 18.4 for extreme nonconsequentialism and Theorem 18.5 for strong nonconsequentialism, do not contain any redundancy.

18.6. Concluding Remarks

Using the analytical framework of extended preference orderings, where individuals express preferences over the pairs of outcomes and opportunity sets from which outcomes are chosen, we developed in this essay a simple analysis of consequentialism and nonconsequentialism. We have identified two types of consequentialism, extreme consequentialism and strong consequentialism, and two types of nonconsequentialism, extreme nonconsequentialism and strong nonconsequentialism. Although these identified types are rather extreme, they are meant to illustrate the kind of analysis in which we may talk about the similarity and dissimilarity of individual attitudes toward outcomes and opportunities. Such an analysis is presented in the companion essay, Suzumura and Xu [19] (Essay 20 of this volume), where we examined how and to what extent Arrow's general impossibility theorem hinges on his basic assumption of welfarist consequentialism, and whether or not Arrow's suggestion that "the possibility of social welfare judgments rests upon a similarity of attitudes toward social alternatives" (Arrow [1, p. 69]) can be sustained within a wider conceptual framework than Arrow's own.

It should be noted that, although individual attitudes toward outcomes and opportunities reflected in extreme and strong consequentialism and extreme and strong nonconsequentialism are quite diverse, they all satisfy IND and SI. More remarkably, strong consequentialism, extreme nonconsequentialism and strong nonconsequentialism have more in common: they all satisfy not only IND and SI but also LSM. With our axiomatic characterizations of extreme and strong consequentialism and extreme and strong nonconsequentialism, we hope that the contrast and similarity of these concepts have received some clarifications. These characterization theorems are summarized in Figure 18.1, where $A \oplus B$ indicates the logical combination of the two axioms A and B.

It is interesting to note that, despite their diverse attitudes toward opportunities and outcomes, extreme and strong consequentialism and extreme and strong nonconsequentialism all satisfy the following property.

Monotonicity (MON). For all $(x, A), (x, B) \in \Omega$, $B \subseteq A \Rightarrow (x, A) \succsim (x, B)$.

According to MON, the individual is not averse to richer opportunities; that is, choosing an outcome x from the opportunity set A is at least as good as choosing the same x from the opportunity set B, which is a subset of A.[3] Clearly, MON and LI, and MON and LSM are independent.

3. Note that we are neglecting decision-making costs and other factors, which may make a larger opportunity set a liability rather than a credit. In this context, see Dworkin [3].

$$\text{IND} \oplus \text{SI} \begin{cases} \oplus\, \text{LI} = \text{extreme consequentialism} \\ \oplus\, \text{LSM} \begin{cases} \oplus\, \text{ROB} = \text{strong consequentialism} \\ \oplus\, \text{INS} = \text{extreme nonconsequentialism} \\ \oplus\, \text{SPO} = \text{strong nonconsequentialism} \end{cases} \end{cases}$$

IND: Independence
SI: Simple Indifference
LI: Local Indifference
LSM: Local Strict Monotonicity
ROB: Robustness
INS: Indifference of No-Choice Situations
SPO: Simple Preference for Opportunities

Note: $A \oplus B$ indicates the logical combination of the two axioms A and B.

Figure 18.1. Characterization Theorems

It is hoped that our attempt in this essay will be suggestive enough to motivate further exploration of the analytical framework of extended preference orderings. To identify some possible directions to be explored, two final remarks may be in order.

First, the two basic axioms, viz., IND and SI, which are commonly invoked in our axiomatic characterizations of consequentialism and non-consequentialism, are not in fact beyond any dispute. Indeed, it is fairly common that an added alternative may have "epistemic value" in that it tells us something important about the nature of the choice situation. Sen [15, p. 753] provides us with a telling example: "If invited to tea (t) by an acquaintance you might accept the invitation rather than going home (O), that is, pick t from the choice over $\{t, O\}$, and yet turn the invitation down if the acquaintance, whom you do not know very well, offers you a *wider* menu of having either tea with him or some heroin and cocaine (h); that is, you may pick O, rejecting t, from the larger set $\{t, h, O\}$. The expansion of the menu offered by this acquaintance may tell you something about the kind of person he is, and this could affect your decision even to have tea with him." This means a clear violation of IND when $A = B$. SI is also not immune to possible exceptions. Take, for example, the case where X denotes the set of alternative measures of transportation for moving from city A to city B. If x and y stand, respectively, for exactly the same car except for the serial number, you may feel indifferent between choosing x and y, so that you may feel fine even if you must choose x rather than y from the opportunity set $\{x, y\}$. However, when the choice is between x and z, where z is a comfortable train connecting A and B, you may feel very unhappy if you are forced to choose x in the presence of z. Thus, you may express a preference for $(x, \{x, z\})$ against $(x, \{x, y\})$, which is a clear violation of SI.

Second, our axiomatizations of consequentialism and nonconsequentialism were concerned with rather extreme cases where unequivocal priority is given to consequences (resp. opportunities) not only in the case of extreme consequentialism (resp. extreme nonconsequentialim) but also in the case of strong consequentialism (resp. strong nonconsequentialism). It goes withoug saying that further research should be pursued so that active interactions between consequential considerations and procedural considerations are allowed to play an essential role. One possible approach retains IND and SI and invokes MON, which we have just observed to be the common property of extreme consequentialism, strong consequentialism, extreme nonconsequentialism, and strong nonconsequentialism. It can be shown that, for finite X and $\mathcal{S}$ being the set of all nonempty subsets of X, $\succcurlyeq$ satisfies IND, SI, and MON if and only if there exists a function $u : X \to \mathbb{R}$ and a function $f : \mathbb{R}^2 \to \mathbb{R}$ such that (a) for all $x, y \in X$, $u(x) \geq u(y) \Leftrightarrow (x, \{x\}) \succcurlyeq (y, \{y\})$; (b) for all $(x, A), (y, B) \in \Omega$, $(x, A) \succcurlyeq (y, B) \Leftrightarrow f(u(x), \#A) \geq f(u(y), \#B)$; and (c) f is nondecreasing in each of its arguments. It should be clear that the characterization theorems on consequentialism and nonconsequentialism that are developed in this essay can be located as special cases of this general theorem, which allows trade-offs between the value of consequences and the richness of opportunities. However, the full exploration of this general approach must be left for a future occasion.[4]

18.7. References

[1] Arrow, K. J., *Social Choice and Individual Values*, New York: Wiley, 1951; 2nd edn., 1963.

[2] Bossert, W., P. K. Pattanaik, and Y. Xu, "Ranking Opportunity Sets: An Axiomatic Approach," *Journal of Economic Theory* **63**, 1994, 326–345.

4. See Suzumura and Xu [18] (Essay 19 of this volume) for this generalization.

[3] Dworkin, G., "Is More Choice Better Than Less?" in P. A. French, T. E. Uehling Jr., and H. K. Wettstein, eds., *Midwest Studies in Philosophy*, Vol. VII, *Social and Political Philosophy*, Minneapolis: University of Minnesota Press, 1982, 47–61.

[4] Gravel, N., "Can a Ranking of Opportunity Sets Attach an Intrinsic Importance to Freedom of Choice?" *American Economic Review: Papers and Proceedings* **84**, 1994, 454–458.

[5] Gravel, N., "Ranking Opportunity Sets on the Basis of Their Freedom of Choice and Their Ability to Satisfy Preferences: A Difficulty," *Social Choice and Welfare* **15**, 1998, 371–382.

[6] Pattanaik, P. K. and K. Suzumura, "Rights, Welfarism and Social Choice," *American Economic Review: Papers and Proceedings* **84**, 1994, 435-439.

[7] Pattanaik, P. K., and K. Suzumura, "Individual Rights and Social Evaluation," *Oxford Economic Papers* **48**, 1996, 194–212.

[8] Pattanaik, P. K., and Y. Xu, "On Ranking Opportunity Sets in Terms of Freedom of Choice," *Recherches Economiques de Louvain* **56**, 1990, 383–390.

[9] Pattanaik, P. K., and Y. Xu, "On Diversity and Freedom of Choice," *Mathematical Social Sciences* **40**, 2000, 123–130.

[10] Sen, A. K., "Utilitarianism and Welfarism," *Journal of Philosophy* **76**, 1979, 463–489.

[11] Sen, A. K., "Personal Utilities and Public Judgements: Or What's Wrong with Welfare Economics," *Economic Journal* **76**, 1979, 537–558.

[12] Sen, A. K., *Commodities and Capabilities*, Amsterdam: North-Holland, 1985.

[13] Sen, A. K., "Freedom of Choice: Concept and Content," *European Economic Review* **32**, 1988, 269–294.

[14] Sen, A. K., "Markets and Freedoms: Achievements and Limitations of the Market Mechanism in Promoting Individual Freedom," *Oxford Economic Papers* **45**, 1993, 519–541.

[15] Sen, A. K., "Maximization and the Act of Choice," *Econometrica* **65**, 1996, 745–779.

[16] Suzumura, K., "Consequences, Opportunities, and Procedures," *Social Choice and Welfare* **16**, 17–40. Essay 17 of this volume.

[17] Suzumura, K., "Welfare Economics beyond Welfarist Consequentialism," *Japanese Economic Review* **51**, 2000, 1–32. Essay 27 of this volume.

[18] Suzumura, K. and Y. Xu, "Consequences, Opportunities, and Generalized Consequentialism and Nonconsequentialism," *Journal of Economic Theory* **111**, 2003, 293–304. Essay 19 of this volume.

[19] Suzumura, K. and Y. Xu, "Welfarist Consequentialism, Similarity of Attitudes, and Arrow's General Impossibility Theorem," *Social Choice and Welfare* **22**, 2004, 237–251. Essay 20 of this volume.

ESSAY 19

Consequences, Opportunities, and Generalized Consequentialism and Nonconsequentialism

19.1. Introduction

In recent years, people have gradually come to realize the importance of nonwelfaristic features of consequences in forming economic policy recommendations as well as in performing economic systems analysis. Some salient examples of nonwelfaristic features of consequences are individual and group rights, procedures through which consequences are realized, and opportunities from which outcomes are chosen.[1]

In a recent paper (Essay 18 of this volume), Suzumura and Xu [20] developed several analytical frameworks that can accommodate situations where an individual expresses his/her extended preferences of the following type: it is better for him/her that an alternative x is brought about from the opportunity set A rather than another alternative y being brought about from the opportunity set B. An important feature of these frameworks is the novel concept of *extended alternatives* in the form of (x, A) with the intended interpretation of x being realized from the opportunity set A, which is used to evaluate alternative economic policies. Within these proposed frameworks,

First published in *Journal of Economic Theory* **111**, 2003, pp. 293–304, as a joint paper with Y. Xu. We are indebted to the referee of *Journal of Economic Theory* for several substantial and expositional improvements.

1. There is an extensive literature addressing nonwelfaristic features of consequences. See, among others, Baharad and Nitzan [1], Bossert, Pattanaik, and Xu [3], Dworkin [4], Gravel [5; 6], Pattanaik and Suzumura [7; 8], Pattanaik and Xu [9; 10; 11], Sen [12; 13; 14; 15; 16; 17], Suzumura [18; 19], and Suzumura and Xu [20; 21].

they defined various concepts of consequentialism and nonconsequentialism and gave axiomatic characterizations of these concepts. The various concepts of consequentialism and nonconsequentialism defined and characterized in Suzumura and Xu [20] are *extreme consequentialism, strong consequentialism, extreme nonconsequentialism,* and *strong nonconsequentialism.*

However, their axiomatizations of consequentialism and nonconsequentialism were concerned only with rather extreme cases where unequivocal priority was given to consequences (resp. opportunities) not only in the case of extreme consequentialism (resp. extreme nonconsequentialism) but also in the case of strong consequentialism (resp. strong nonconsequentialism). The purpose of this essay is to pursue a more general framework so that active interactions between consequential considerations and opportunity considerations are allowed to play an essential role. In other words, we would like to develop a framework which allows trade-offs between the value of consequences and the richness of opportunities.

The structure of the essay is as follows. In Section 19.2, we present the basic notations and definitions. Section 19.3 discusses generalized consequentialism and nonconsequentialism in a simple framework in which the universal set is finite. In Section 19.4, we consider generalized consequentialism and nonconsequentialism in a context in which the universal set is infinite but opportunity sets are finite. Section 19.5 concludes the essay with some final remarks.

19.2. Basic Notations and Definitions

Let $\mathbb{Z}_+$ and $\mathbb{R}$ denote the set of all positive integers and the set of all real numbers, respectively. Let X, where $3 \leq \#X$, be the set of all mutually exclusive and jointly exhaustive alternatives.[2] The elements of X will be denoted by $x, y, z, \ldots$. $\mathcal{S}$ denotes a collection of nonempty subsets of X. The elements in $\mathcal{S}$ will be denoted by $A, B, C, \ldots$, and they are called *opportunity sets*. Let $X \times \mathcal{S}$ be the Cartesian product of X and $\mathcal{S}$. Elements of $X \times \mathcal{S}$ will be denoted by $(x, A), (y, B), (z, C), \ldots$, and they are called *extended alternatives*. Let $\Omega = \{(x, A) \mid A \in \mathcal{S} \text{ and } x \in A\}$. That is,

2. Throughout this essay, and for any finite subset A of the universal set X, $\#A$ denotes the cardinality of A.

Ω contains all (x, A) such that A is an element of $\mathcal{S}$ and x is an element of A. It should be clear that $\Omega \subseteq X \times \mathcal{S}$, and for all $(x, A) \in \Omega$, $x \in A$ holds. For all $(x, A) \in \Omega$, the intended interpretation is that the alternative x is chosen from the opportunity set A.[3]

Let $\succsim$ be a reflexive, complete, and transitive binary relation over Ω, viz., $\succsim$ is an ordering over Ω. The asymmetric and symmetric parts of $\succsim$ will be denoted by $\succ$ and $\sim$, respectively. For any $(x, A), (y, B) \in \Omega$, $(x, A) \succsim (y, B)$ is interpreted as "choosing x from A is at least as good as choosing y from B." Thus, in the extended framework, it is possible to give an expression to the intrinsic value of an opportunity set in addition to the instrumental value thereof. Indeed, the decision maker recognizes the intrinsic value of the opportunity of choice if there exists an extended alternative $(x, A) \in \Omega$ such that $(x, A) \succ (x, \{x\})$.

19.3. A Simple Framework

In this section, we confine our attention to the case where $\#X < \infty$, and $\mathcal{S}$ is the set of all nonempty subsets of X. We consider the following three axioms on the ordering $\succsim$, which are proposed by Suzumura and Xu [20].

Independence (IND). For all $(x, A), (y, B) \in \Omega$, and all $z \in X \setminus (A \cup B)$, $(x, A) \succsim (y, B) \Leftrightarrow (x, A \cup \{z\}) \succsim (y, B \cup \{z\})$.

Simple Indifference (SI). For all $x \in X$, and all $y, z \in X \setminus \{x\}$, $(x, \{x, y\}) \sim (x, \{x, z\})$.

Simple Monotonicity (SM). For all $(x, A), (x, B) \in \Omega$, if $B \subseteq A$, then $(x, A) \succsim (x, B)$.

IND has a parallel in the literature on ranking opportunity sets in terms of freedom of choice; see, for example, Pattanaik and Xu [9]. It requires that, for all opportunity sets A and B, if an alternative z is not in both

3. Depending on the context, one could also have alternative interpretations of the extended alternatives. For example, in the single agent case, (x, A) could be interpreted as having the alternative x from the set of alternatives that are produced by the procedure A. We owe this observation to the referee of *Journal of Economic Theory*.

A and B, then the extended preference ranking over $(x, A \cup \{z\})$ and $(y, B \cup \{z\})$ should correspond to the extended preference ranking over (x, A) and (y, B), regardless of the nature of the added alternative z. This axiom has been criticized in the literature. For example, one may argue that freedom of choice offered by an opportunity set is concerned about how diverse the alternatives are in the opportunity set. It may be the case that the added alternative z is very similar to some alternative in A but quite different from all the alternatives in B. As a consequence, the addition of z to A may not change the degree of real freedom of choice already offered by A, while adding z to B may vastly increase the degree of freedom of choice offered by B (see Pattanaik and Xu [10] for some formal analysis). If the individual cares about this aspect of opportunities, the individual may rank $(y, B \cup \{z\})$ strictly above $(x, A \cup \{z\})$ even though the same individual ranks (x, A) and (y, B) equally. SI requires that the individual ranks $(x, \{x, y\})$ and $(x, \{x, z\})$ equally as long as x and y are distinct, and x and z are distinct. It is clear that this property is vulnerable to similar criticisms as IND. Finally, SM is a monotonicity property requiring that choosing an alternative x from the set A cannot be worse than choosing the same alternative x from the subset B of A. It essentially reflects the conviction that the individual is not averse to richer opportunities. It may be argued that, in some cases, richer opportunities can be a liability rather than a virtue; see, for example, Dworkin [4]. In such cases, the individual may prefer choosing x from a smaller set to choosing the same x from a larger set. Thus, IND, SI, and SM are *not* axioms of uncompromising appeal, but they are *not* pathological axioms either. At the very least, they leave us with sufficient room for analyzing generalized consequentialism and nonconsequentialism within a simple operational framework.

The following simple implication of IND, SI, and SM proves useful.

LEMMA 19.1. Let $\succcurlyeq$ be an ordering over Ω and satisfy IND, SI, and SM. Then, for all $(a, A), (b, B) \in \Omega$, and all $x \in X \setminus A$, $y \in X \setminus B$, $(a, A) \succcurlyeq (b, B) \Leftrightarrow (a, A \cup \{x\}) \succcurlyeq (b, B \cup \{y\})$.

PROOF. Observe that, by Theorem 18.1 of Essay 18, the following is true:

CLAIM 19.1. For all $(a, A), (a, A') \in \Omega$, if $\#A = \#A'$, then $(a, A) \sim (a, A')$.

Let $(a, A), (b, B) \in \Omega$, $x \in X \setminus A$, $y \in X \setminus B$ and $(a, A) \succcurlyeq (b, B)$. Because $\succcurlyeq$ is an ordering, we have only to show that $(a, A) \sim (b, B) \Rightarrow (a, A \cup \{x\}) \sim (b, B \cup \{y\})$ and $(a, A) \succ (b, B) \Rightarrow (a, A \cup \{x\}) \succ (b, B \cup \{y\})$.

First, we show that

$$(a, A) \sim (b, B) \Rightarrow (a, A \cup \{x\}) \sim (b, B \cup \{y\}). \qquad (19.1)$$

Since $x \in X \setminus A$ and $y \in X \setminus B$, it is clear that $A \neq X$ and $B \neq X$. We consider three subcases, viz., (i) $A = \{a\}$; (ii) $B = \{b\}$; and (iii) $\#A > 1$ and $\#B > 1$.

(i) $A = \{a\}$: In this case, we distinguish two subcases: (i.1) $x \notin B$; and (i.2) $x \in B$. Consider (i.1). Since $x \notin B$, it follows from $(a, \{a\}) \sim (b, B)$ and IND that $(a, \{a, x\}) \sim (b, B \cup \{x\})$. By Claim 19.1, $(b, B \cup \{x\}) \sim (b, B \cup \{y\})$. Transitivity of $\sim$ then implies that $(a, \{a, x\}) \sim (b, B \cup \{y\})$. Consider now (i.2), where $x \in B$. To begin with, consider the subcase where $B \cup \{y\} = \{a, b\}$. Given that $x \in X \setminus A$ and $y \in X \setminus B$, we have $x = b$ and $y = a$, hence $B = \{b\}$. Since $\#X \geq 3$, there exists $c \in X$ such that $c \notin \{a, b\}$. It follows from $(a, \{a\}) \sim (b, \{b\}) = (b, B)$ and IND that $(a, \{a, c\}) \sim (b, \{b, c\})$. From Claim 19.1, $(a, \{a, b\}) \sim (a, \{a, c\})$, and $(b, \{b, c\}) \sim (b, \{a, b\})$. Then transitivity of $\sim$ implies $(a, \{a, b\}) \sim (b, \{a, b\})$; that is, $(a, \{a, x\}) \sim (b, B \cup \{y\})$. Turn now to the subcase where $B \cup \{y\} \neq \{a, b\}$. If $y \neq a$, starting with $(a, \{a\}) \sim (b, B)$, by IND, $(a, \{a, y\}) \sim (b, B \cup \{y\})$. By Claim 19.1, $(a, \{a, x\}) \sim (a, \{a, y\})$. Transitivity of $\sim$ implies that $(a, \{a, x\}) \sim (b, B \cup \{y\})$. If $y = a$, given that $\#X \geq 3$ and $B \cup \{y\} \neq \{a, b\}$, there exists $z \in B$ such that $z \notin \{a, b\}$. By Claim 19.1, $(b, B) \sim (b, (B \cup \{y\}) \setminus \{z\})$. From $(a, \{a\}) \sim (b, B)$, transitivity of $\sim$ implies $(a, \{a\}) \sim (b, (B \cup \{y\}) \setminus \{z\})$. Now, noting that $z \neq a$, by IND, $(a, \{a, z\}) \sim (b, B \cup \{y\})$ holds. From Claim 19.1, $(a, \{a, x\}) \sim (a, \{a, z\})$. Transitivity of $\sim$ now implies $(a, \{a, x\}) \sim (b, B \cup \{y\})$.

(ii) $B = \{b\}$: This case can be dealt with similarly to case (i).

(iii) $\#A > 1$ and $\#B > 1$: Consider $A', A'' \in \mathcal{S}$ such that $\{a, b\} \subseteq A'' \subseteq A'$, $\#A'' = \min \{\#A, \#B\} > 1$, $\#A' = \max \{\#A, \#B\} > 1$. Since $A \neq X$ and $B \neq X$, the existence of such A' and A'' is guaranteed. It should be clear that there exists $z \in X$ such that $z \in A'$. If $\#A \geq \#B$, consider (a, A') and (b, A''). From Claim 19.1, $(a, A') \sim (b, A'')$ follows from the construction of A' and A'', the assumption that $(a, A) \sim (b, B)$, and transitivity of

$\sim$. Note that there exists $z \in X \setminus A'$. By IND, $(a, A' \cup \{z\}) \sim (b, A'' \cup \{z\})$. By virtue of Claim 19.1, noting that $\#(A \cup \{x\}) = \#(A' \cup \{z\})$ and $\#(B \cup \{y\}) = \#(A'' \cup \{z\})$, $(a, A \cup \{x\}) \sim (b, B \cup \{y\})$ follows easily from transitivity of $\sim$. If $\#A < \#B$, consider (a, A'') and (b, A'). Following the similar argument as before, we can show that $(a, A \cup \{x\}) \sim (b, B \cup \{y\})$. Thus, (19.1) is true. The next step is to show that

$$(a, A) \succ (b, B) \Rightarrow (a, A \cup \{x\}) \succ (b, B \cup \{y\}). \qquad (19.2)$$

As in the proof of (19.1), we distinguish three cases: (a) $A = \{a\}$; (b) $B = \{b\}$; and (c) $\#A > 1$ and $\#B > 1$.

(a) $A = \{a\}$: (a.1) $x \notin B$. In this subcase, from $(a, \{a\}) \succ (b, B)$, by IND, we obtain $(a, \{a, x\}) \succ (b, B \cup \{x\})$. By Claim 19.1, $(b, B \cup \{x\}) \sim (b, B \cup \{y\})$. Transitivity of $\succcurlyeq$ implies that $(a, \{a, x\}) = (a, A \cup \{x\}) \succ (b, B \cup \{y\})$. (a.2) $x \in B$. If $B \cup \{y\} = \{a, b\}$, then, given that $x \notin A$ and $y \notin B$, we have $x = b$ and $y = a$. Since $\#X \geq 3$, there exists $c \in X$ such that $c \notin \{a, b\}$. It follows from $(a, \{a\}) \succ (b, \{b\}) = (b, B)$ and IND that $(a, \{a, c\}) \succ (b, \{b, c\})$. From Claim 19.1, $(a, \{a, b\}) \sim (a, \{a, c\})$ and $(b, \{b, c\}) \sim (b, \{a, b\})$. Transitivity of $\succcurlyeq$ implies $(a, \{a, b\}) \succ (b, \{a, b\})$; i.e., $(a, \{a, x\}) = (a, A \cup \{x\}) \succ (b, B \cup \{y\})$. If $B \cup \{y\} \neq \{a, b\}$, we consider (a.2.i) $y \neq a$ and (a.2.ii) $y = a$. Suppose that (a.2.i) $y \neq a$. From $(a, \{a\}) \succ (b, B)$, by IND, $(a, \{a, y\}) \succ (b, B \cup \{y\})$. By Claim 19.1, $(a, \{a, x\}) \sim (a, \{a, y\})$. Transitivity of $\succcurlyeq$ now implies $(a, \{a, x\}) = (a, A \cup \{x\}) \succ (b, B \cup \{y\})$. Suppose next that (a.2.ii) $y = a$. Since $\#X \geq 3$ and $B \cup \{y\} \neq \{a, b\}$, there exists $c \in B$ such that $c \notin \{a, b\}$. By Claim 19.1, $(b, B) \sim (b, (B \cup \{y\}) \setminus \{c\})$. From $(a, \{a\}) \succ (b, B)$, by transitivity of $\succcurlyeq$, $(a, \{a\}) \succ (b, (B \cup \{y\}) \setminus \{c\})$. Now, noting that $c \neq a$, by IND, $(a, \{a, c\}) \succ (b, B \cup \{y\})$. From Claim 19.1, $(a, \{a, c\}) \sim (a, \{a, x\})$. Transitivity of $\succcurlyeq$ implies $(a, \{a, x\}) = (a, A \cup \{x\}) \succ (b, B \cup \{y\})$.

(b) $B = \{b\}$. If $x \notin B$, it follows from $(a, A) \succ (b, B)$ and IND that $(a, A \cup \{x\}) \succ (b, \{b, x\})$. By Claim 19.1, $(b, \{b, x\}) \sim (b, \{b, y\}) = (b, B \cup \{y\})$. Transitivity of $\succcurlyeq$ now implies $(a, A \cup \{x\}) \succ (b, \{b, y\}) = (b, B \cup \{y\})$. If $x \in B$, then $x = b$. Consider first the case where $y = a$. If $A = \{a\}$, it follows from (a) that $(a, \{a, x\}) = (a, A \cup \{x\}) \succ (b, \{b, y\}) = (b, B \cup \{y\})$. Suppose $A \neq \{a\}$. Given that $x = b$, $y = a$, $x \notin A$, and $y \notin B$, and noting that $\#X \geq 3$, there exists $c \in A \setminus \{a, b\}$. From Claim 19.1, $(a, (A \cup \{x\}) \setminus \{c\}) \sim (a, A)$. From transitivity of $\succcurlyeq$ and noting that $(a, A) \succ (b, \{b\})$, $(a, (A \cup \{x\}) \setminus \{c\}) \succ (b, \{b\})$ holds. By IND,

$(a, A \cup \{x\}) \succ (b, \{b, c\})$. From Claim 19.1, $(b, \{b, y\}) \sim (b, \{b, c\})$. Therefore, $(a, A \cup \{x\}) \succ (b, \{b, y\}) = (b, B \cup \{y\})$ follows easily from transitivity of $\succcurlyeq$. Consider next that $y \neq a$. If $y \notin A$, then, by IND and $(a, A) \succ (b, \{b\})$, we immediately obtain $(a, A \cup \{y\}) \succ (b, \{b, y\})$. By Claim 19.1, $(a, A \cup \{y\}) \sim (a, A \cup \{x\})$. Transitivity of $\succcurlyeq$ implies $(a, A \cup \{x\}) \succ (b, \{b, y\}) = (b, B \cup \{y\})$. If $y \in A$, noting that $y \neq a$, $y \notin B$, and $x = b$, we have $\#((A \cup \{x\}) \setminus \{y\}) = \#A$. By Claim 19.1, $(a, A) \sim (a, (A \cup \{x\}) \setminus \{y\})$. Transitivity of $\succcurlyeq$ implies $(a, (A \cup \{x\}) \setminus \{y\}) \succ (b, \{b\})$. By IND, it then follows that $(a, A \cup \{x\}) \succ (b, \{b, y\}) = (b, B \cup \{y\})$.

(c) $\#A > 1$ and $\#B > 1$. This case is similar to case (iii) above, and we may safely omit it.

Thus, (19.2) is proved. (19.1) together with (19.2) completes the proof of Lemma 19.1. ∎

We are now ready to characterize completely the class of all orderings that satisfy IND, SI, and SM.

Theorem 19.1. $\succcurlyeq$ satisfies IND, SI, and SM if and only if there exist a function $u : X \to \mathbb{R}$ and a function $f : \mathbb{R} \times \mathbb{Z}_+ \to \mathbb{R}$ such that

$$\text{For all } x, y \in X,\ u(x) \geq u(y) \Leftrightarrow (x, \{x\}) \succcurlyeq (y, \{y\}); \qquad (19.3)$$

$$\text{For all } (x, A), (y, B) \in \Omega,\ (x, A) \succcurlyeq (y, B) \Leftrightarrow$$
$$f(u(x), \#A) \geq f(u(y), \#B); \qquad (19.4)$$

f is nondecreasing in each of its arguments and has the following property: For all integers $i, j, k \geq 1$ and all $x, y \in X$, if $i + k, j + k \leq \#X$, then (19.5)

$$f(u(x), i) \geq f(u(y), j) \Leftrightarrow f(u(x), i + k) \geq f(u(y), j + k). \qquad (19.6)$$

Proof. We first show that if $\succcurlyeq$ satisfies IND, SI, and SM, then there exist a function $f : \mathbb{R} \times \mathbb{Z}_+ \to \mathbb{R}$ and a function $u : X \to \mathbb{R}$ such that (19.3)–(19.5) of Theorem 19.1 hold.[4] Let $\succcurlyeq$ satisfy IND, SI, and SM. Since $\succcurlyeq$ is

4. According to (19.3), the function u can be construed as a utility function defined on the set of social states, whereas the function f weighs the value of consequential states, which is measured

an ordering, X is finite, and so is Ω, there exist $u : X \to \mathbb{R}$ and $F : \Omega \to \mathbb{R}$ such that

$$\text{For all } x, y \in X, (x, \{x\}) \succsim (y, \{y\}) \Leftrightarrow u(x) \geq u(y); \quad (19.7)$$

$$\text{For all } (x, A), (y, B) \in \Omega, (x, A) \succsim (y, B) \Leftrightarrow F(x, A) \geq F(y, B). \quad (19.8)$$

Clearly, (19.3) of Theorem 19.1 is satisfied. To show that (19.4) holds, let $(x, A), (y, B) \in \Omega$ be such that $u(x) = u(y)$ and $\#A = \#B$. From $u(x) = u(y)$, we must have $(x, \{x\}) \sim (y, \{y\})$. Then, by the repeated use of Lemma 19.1 if necessary, and noting that $\#A = \#B$, $(x, A) \sim (y, B)$ can be easily obtained. Now, define $\Sigma \subseteq \mathbb{R} \times \mathbb{Z}_+$ as follows: $\Sigma := \{(t, i) \in \mathbb{R} \times \mathbb{Z}_+ \mid \exists (x, A) \in \Omega : t = u(x) \text{ and } i = \#A\}$. Next, define a binary relation $\geq^*$ on Σ as follows: for all $(x, A), (y, B) \in \Omega$, $(x, A) \succsim (y, B) \Leftrightarrow (u(x), \#A) \geq^* (u(y), \#B)$. From the preceding discussion and noting that $\succsim$ satisfies SM and IND, the binary relation $\geq^*$ defined on Σ is an ordering, and it has the following properties:

(SM′). For all $(t, i), (t, j) \in \Sigma$, if $j \geq i$, then $(t, j) \geq^* (t, i)$;

(IND′). For all $(s, i), (t, j) \in \Sigma$, and all integers k, if $i + k \leq \#X$ and $j + k \leq \#X$, then $(s, i) \geq^* (t, j) \Leftrightarrow (s, i + k) \geq^* (t, j + k)$.

Since Σ is finite and $\geq^*$ is an ordering on Σ, there exists a function $f : \mathbb{R} \times \mathbb{Z}_+ \to \mathbb{R}$ such that, for all $(s, i), (t, j) \in \Sigma$, $(s, i) \geq^* (t, j)$ if and only if $f(s, i) \geq f(t, j)$. From the definition of $\geq^*$ and Σ, we must have the following: for all $(x, A), (y, B) \in \Omega$, $(x, A) \succsim (y, B) \Leftrightarrow (u(x), \#A) \geq^* (u(y), \#B) \Leftrightarrow f(u(x), \#A) \geq f(u(y), \#B)$. To prove that f is nondecreasing in each of its arguments, we first consider the case in which $u(x) \geq u(y)$ and $\#A = \#B$. Given $u(x) \geq u(y)$, it follows from the definition of u that $(x, \{x\}) \succsim (y, \{y\})$. Noting that $\#A = \#B$, by the repeated use of Lemma 19.1, if necessary, we must have $(x, A) \succsim (y, B)$. Thus, f is nondecreasing in its first argument. To show that f is nondecreasing in its second argument as well, we consider the case in which $u(x) = u(y)$ and $\#A \geq \#B$.

in terms of the utility of consequential states vis-à-vis the value of richness of opportunities, which is measured in terms of the cardinality of opportunity sets.

From $u(x) = u(y)$, we must have $(x, \{x\}) \sim (y, \{y\})$. Then, from the earlier argument, $(x, A') \sim (y, B)$ for some $A' \subseteq A$ such that $\#A' = \#B$. Now, by SM, $(x, A) \succcurlyeq (x, A')$. Then, $(x, A) \succcurlyeq (y, B)$ follows from the transitivity of $\succcurlyeq$. Therefore, f is nondecreasing in each of its arguments. Finally, (19.6) follows clearly from IND′.

To check the necessity part of the theorem, suppose $u : X \to \mathbb{R}$ and $f : \mathbb{R} \times \mathbb{Z}_+ \to \mathbb{R}$ are such that (19.3)–(19.5) of Theorem 19.1 are satisfied.

(SI). For all $x \in X$ and all $y, z \in X \setminus \{x\}$, we note that $\#\{x, y\} = \#\{x, z\}$, therefore, $f(u(x), \#\{x, y\}) = f(u(x), \#\{x, z\})$, which in turn implies that $(x, \{x, y\}) \sim (x, \{x, z\})$ holds.

(SM). For all $(x, A), (x, B) \in \Omega$ such that $B \subseteq A$, $f(u(x), \#A) \geq f(u(x), \#B)$ holds, since f is nondecreasing in each of its arguments and $\#A \geq \#B$. Therefore, $(x, A) \succcurlyeq (x, B)$.

(IND). For all $(x, A), (y, B) \in \Omega$, and all $z \in X \setminus (A \cup B)$, it follows from (19.6) that

$$f(u(x), \#A) \geq f(u(y), \#B) \Leftrightarrow f(u(x), \#A + 1) \geq f(u(y), \#B + 1)$$
$$\Leftrightarrow f(u(x), \#(A \cup \{z\})) \geq f(u(y), \#(B \cup \{z\})).$$

Therefore, $(x, A) \succcurlyeq (y, B) \Leftrightarrow (x, A \cup \{z\}) \succcurlyeq (y, B \cup \{z\})$. ■

Remark 19.1. Theorem 19.1 allows us to treat all the cases where the utility of consequential states and the value of richness of opportunities actively interact; it also covers the polar extreme cases of consequentialism and nonconsequentialism defined in Essay 18. Indeed, they can be obtained as special cases of Theorem 19.1 as follows:

Extreme Consequentialism. For all $(x, A) \in \Omega$, $f(u(x), \#A) = u(x)$.

Strong Consequentialism. For all $(x, A), (y, B) \in \Omega$, $(x, A) \succcurlyeq (y, B) \Leftrightarrow [u(x) > u(y) \text{ or } (u(x) = u(y) \text{ and } \#A \geq \#B)]$.

Extreme Nonconsequentialism. For all $(x, A) \in \Omega$, $f(u(x), \#A) = \#A$.

Strong Nonconsequentialism. For all $(x, A), (y, B) \in \Omega$, $(x, A) \succcurlyeq (y, B) \Leftrightarrow [\#A > \#B \text{ or } (\#A = \#B \text{ and } u(x) \geq u(y))]$.

19.4. Finite Opportunity Sets in the Infinite Universe

Although Theorem 19.1 provides us with a full characterization result for all orderings satisfying IND, SI, and SM, it hinges squarely on the restrictive assumption to the effect that the universal set X is finite. In many settings, for example, in microeconomics, the universal set X is often the consumption set, which is typically infinite. In this section, therefore, we discuss the case in which X contains an infinite number of alternatives, but $\mathcal{S}$ consists of the set of all finite nonempty subsets of X. Consequently, Ω contains all (x, A) such that A is finite and x is an element of A.

In this arena, the necessary and sufficient condition for an ordering over Ω to satisfy IND, SI, and SM can be identified as follows.

Theorem 19.2. $\succsim$ satisfies IND, SI, and SM if and only if there exists an ordering $\succsim^{\#}$ on $X \times \mathbb{Z}_+$ such that

$$\text{For all } (x, A), (y, B) \in \Omega, (x, A) \succsim (y, B) \Leftrightarrow$$

$$(x, \#A) \succsim^{\#} (y, \#B); \tag{19.9}$$

$$\text{For all integers } i, j, k \geq 1 \text{ and all } x, y \in X, (x, i) \succsim^{\#} (y, j) \Leftrightarrow$$

$$(x, i+k) \succsim^{\#} (y, j+k), \text{ and } (x, i+k) \succsim^{\#} (x, i). \tag{19.10}$$

Proof. First, we note that Claim 19.1 still holds; that is, for all (a, A), $(a, B) \in \Omega$, if $\#A = \#B$, then $(a, A) \sim (a, B)$. Next, we show the following.

Claim 19.2. For all $x, y \in X$ and all $(x, A), (y, A) \in \Omega$, $(x, \{x\}) \succsim (y, \{y\}) \Leftrightarrow (x, A) \succsim (y, A)$.

Let $x, y \in X$ and $(x, A), (y, A) \in \Omega$. If $x = y$, then Claim 19.2 follows immediately from reflexivity of $\succsim$. Let $x \neq y$. Suppose that $(x, \{x\}) \sim (y, \{y\})$. Let $z \in X \setminus \{x, y\}$. By IND, we have $(x, \{x, z\}) \sim (y, \{y, z\})$. From Claim 19.1, we must have $(x, \{x, z\}) \sim (x, \{x, y\})$ and $(y, \{y, z\}) \sim (y, \{x, y\})$. Then, by transitivity of $\sim$, we obtain $(x, \{x, y\}) \sim (y, \{x, y\})$. Noting that A is finite, by the repeated use of IND, we have $(x, A) \sim (y, A)$. Similarly, we can show that if $(x, \{x\}) \succ (y, \{y\})$, then $(x, A) \succ (y, A)$. Since $\succsim$ is an ordering, Claim 19.2 is proved.

We now show that, for all $(x, A), (y, B) \in \Omega$, if $(x, \{x\}) \sim (y, \{y\})$ and $\#A = \#B$, then $(x, A) \sim (y, B)$. Let $C \in \mathcal{S}$ be such that $\#C = \#A = \#B$ and $\{x, y\} \subseteq C$. From Claim 19.2, we have $(x, C) \sim (y, C)$. Note that $(x, C) \sim (x, A)$ and $(y, C) \sim (y, B)$ follow from Claim 19.1. By transitivity of $\sim$, we have $(x, A) \sim (y, B)$. Define a binary relation $\succcurlyeq^{\#}$ on $X \times \mathbb{Z}_+$ as follows: for all $x, y \in X$ and all positive integers i, j, $(x, i) \succcurlyeq^{\#} (y, j) \Leftrightarrow [(x, A) \succcurlyeq (y, B)$ for some $A, B \in \mathcal{S}$ such that $x \in A$, $y \in B$, $i = \#A$, $j = \#B]$. From the preceding discussion, $\succcurlyeq^{\#}$ is well defined and is an ordering. A similar method of proving (19.5) can be invoked to prove that (19.10) holds. ∎

Remark 19.2. Based on Theorem 19.2, the concepts of extreme consequentialism, strong consequentialism, extreme nonconsequentialism, and strong nonconsequentialism defined in Essay 18 can be expressed as in Remark 19.1 Section 19.3. Details may be left to the interested readers to spell out.

It should be clear that without imposing any other condition on the extended preference ordering $\succcurlyeq$, the value of consequential states may not be representable by any numerical function. In order for the value of consequential states to be numerically representable, further restrictions on $\succcurlyeq$ must be imposed. Assume, therefore, that $X = \mathbb{R}^n_+$ in the rest of this section,[5] and define the following property.

Continuity (CON). For all $x^i \in X$ $(i = 1, 2, \ldots)$ and all $x, y \in X$, if $\lim_{i \to \infty} x^i = x$, then $[(x^i, \{x^i\}) \succcurlyeq (y, \{y\})$ for $i = 1, 2, \ldots] \Rightarrow (x, \{x\}) \succcurlyeq (y, \{y\})$, and $[(y, \{y\}) \succcurlyeq (x^i, \{x^i\})$ for $i = 1, 2, \ldots] \Rightarrow (y, \{y\}) \succcurlyeq (x, \{x\})$.

Then we may assert the following proposition.

Theorem 19.3. Suppose that $X = \mathbb{R}^n_+$. Suppose also that $\succcurlyeq$ satisfies IND, SI, SM, and CON. Then there exist a continuous function $u : X \to \mathbb{R}$ and an ordering $\geq^*$ on $\mathbb{R} \times \mathbb{Z}_+$ such that

(a) For all $(x, A), (y, B) \in \Omega$, $(x, A) \succcurlyeq (y, B) \Leftrightarrow (u(x), \#A) \geq^* (u(y), \#B)$;

---

5. $\mathbb{R}^n_+$ stands for the nonnegative orthant of the Euclidean n-space, where n is a specified natural number.

(b) For all $x, y \in X$, $(x, \{x\}) \succcurlyeq (y, \{y\}) \Leftrightarrow u(x) \geq u(y)$;
(c) For all integers $i, j, k \geq 1$, and all $x, y \in X$, $(u(x), i) \geq^* (u(y), j) \Leftrightarrow (u(x), i+k) \geq^* (u(y), j+k)$; and $(u(x), i+k) \geq^* (u(x), i)$.

Proof. From Theorem 19.2, we know that there exists an ordering $\succcurlyeq^{\#}$ on $X \times \mathbb{Z}$ such that

$$\text{For all } (x, A), (y, B) \in \Omega,\ (x, A) \succcurlyeq (y, B) \Leftrightarrow (x, \#A) \geq^{\#} (y, \#B); \tag{F.1}$$

$$\text{For all integers } i, j, k \geq 1 \text{ and all } x, y \in X,\ (x, i) \geq^{\#} (y, j) \Leftrightarrow (x, i+k) \geq^{\#} (y, j+k); \text{ and } (x, i+k) \geq^{\#} (x, i). \tag{F.2}$$

Now, for all $x, y \in X$, define the binary relation R on X as follows: for all $x, y \in X$, $xRy \Leftrightarrow (x, \{x\}) \succcurlyeq (y, \{y\})$. Since $\succcurlyeq$ is an ordering and it satisfies CON, R on $X = \mathbb{R}^n_+$ is an ordering and it satisfies the following continuity property: for all $x \in X$, $\{y \in X | yRx\}$ and $\{y \in X | xRy\}$ are closed. Therefore, there exists a continuous function $u : X \to \mathbb{R}$ such that for all $x, y \in X$, $xRy \Leftrightarrow u(x) \geq u(y)$. From the definition of R, it is clear that for all $x, y \in X$, $(x, \{x\}) \succcurlyeq (y, \{y\}) \Leftrightarrow u(x) \geq u(y)$. Therefore, (b) of Theorem 19.3 holds. Given that (b) holds, it is straightforward to check that (a) and (c) hold as well. ■

If we go one step further and strengthen the condition of continuity in Theorem 19.3 to the following condition, to be called *strong continuity*, the binary relation $\succcurlyeq$ will be numerically representable altogether.

Strong Continuity (SCON). For all $(x, A) \in \Omega$, all $y, y^i \in X$ ($i = 1, 2, \ldots$), and all $B \in \mathcal{S} \cup \{\emptyset\}$, if $B \cap \{y^i\} = B \cap \{y\} = \emptyset$ for all $i = 1, 2, \ldots$, and $\lim_{i\to\infty} y^i = y$, then $[(y^i, B \cup \{y^i\}) \succcurlyeq (x, A)$ for $i = 1, 2, \ldots] \Rightarrow (y, B \cup \{y\}) \succcurlyeq (x, A)$, and $[(x, A) \succcurlyeq (y^i, B \cup \{y^i\})$ for $i = 1, 2, \ldots] \Rightarrow (x, A) \succcurlyeq (y, B \cup \{y\})$.[6]

6. It is clear that CON is a special case of SCON where $B = \emptyset$.

THEOREM 19.4. Suppose that $X = \mathbb{R}^n_+$ and that $\succcurlyeq$ satisfies IND, SI, SM, and SCON. Then, there exists a function $v : X \times \mathbb{Z}_+ \to \mathbb{R}$, which is continuous in its first argument, such that

(a) For all $(x, A), (y, B) \in \Omega$, $(x, A) \succcurlyeq (y, B) \Leftrightarrow v(x, \#A) \geq v(y, \#B)$,
(b) For all $i, j, k \in \mathbb{Z}_+$ and all $x, y \in X$, $v(x, i) \geq v(y, j) \Leftrightarrow v(x, i + k) \geq v(y, j + k)$ and $v(x, i + k) \geq v(x, i)$.

PROOF. From Theorem 19.2, we know that there exists an ordering $\geq^\#$ on $X \times \mathbb{Z}_+$ such that

$$\text{For all } (x, A), (y, B) \in \Omega,\ (x, A) \succcurlyeq (y, B) \Leftrightarrow (x, \#A) \geq^\# (y, \#B); \tag{G.1}$$

$$\text{For all integers } i, j, k \geq 1 \text{ and all } x, y \in X,\ (x, i) \geq^\# (y, j) \Leftrightarrow$$
$$(x, i + k) \geq^\# (y, j + k); \text{ and } (x, i + k) \geq^\# (x, i). \tag{G.2}$$

For all $(x, i) \in X \times \mathbb{Z}_+$ and all $j \in \mathbb{Z}_+$, consider the sets

$$U(x; i, j) = \{y \in X \mid (y, j) \geq^\# (x, i)\},$$
$$L(x; i, j) = \{y \in X \mid (x, i) \geq^\# (y, j)\}.$$

From (G.1), by SCON, it is clear that both $U(x; i, j)$ and $L(x; i, j)$ are closed. Note that $X = \mathbb{R}^n_+$. By Theorem 3 of Blackorby, Bossert, and Donaldson [2], there is a function $v : X \times \mathbb{Z}_+ \to \mathbb{R}$, which is continuous in its first argument, that represents $\geq^\#$. Therefore, part (a) of Theorem 19.4 follows. Part (b) of Theorem 19.4 follows from (a), (G.1) and (G.2). ■

19.5. Concluding Remarks

This essay has generalized our previous analysis reported in Essay 18 on extended preferences over consequences of choice and opportunities of choice that lie behind these consequences. Our previous analysis was the first attempt in the literature to axiomatize the concepts of consequentialism and nonconsequentialism, and it was concerned only with the special situations where no trade-off relationship exists between consequential considerations, which reflect the decision maker's intrinsic preferences over consequential outcomes, and nonconsequential considerations, which reflect his/her concern over the richness of opportunities from which alternatives are chosen. In this restricted analytical framework, axiomatic characterizations were given to the concepts of extreme and strong consequentialism as well as extreme and strong nonconsequentialism. Going beyond this concern with polar extreme cases of consequentialism and nonconsequentialism, we have characterized in this essay the extended preferences over consequences and opportunities of choice that embody active interactions between consequential considerations and nonconsequential considerations.

The universe of our discourse can be a finite set or an infinite set, but the family of opportunity sets is restricted to consist solely of finite sets. This analytical framework can be useful in generalizing some classical analyses of individual and social choices, where there is a pervasive, yet implicit, assumption to the effect that all individuals as well as society are concerned only with consequences of their choices. As a matter of fact, the traditional analysis is even more restrictive than consequentialism as such, since all individuals as well as society are implicitly assumed to evaluate consequences only through their effects on individual or social welfare. The effects of the existence of nonconsequentialists in the society on the Arrovian impossibility theorem are examined in Essay 20 on the basis of Essay 18, and it is an interesting exercise to see what difference, if any, the existence of active interactions between consequential considerations and nonconsequential considerations will exert on the results obtained in Essay 20. It is also interesting to examine how the traditional theory of consumers' behavior and general equilibrium analysis will have to be modified in the presence of nonconsequential considerations. To conduct this latter analysis, however, we must go beyond our current analytical framework, which restricts the family of opportunity sets to consist of finite sets. This task must be left for our future research.

19.6. References

[1] Baharad, E., and S. Nitzan, "Extended Preferences and Freedom of Choice," *Social Choice and Welfare* **17**, 2000, 629–637.

[2] Blackorby, C., W. Bossert, and D. Donaldson, "A Representation Theorem for Domains with Discrete and Continuous Variables," *Cahier* **16**, 2001, Centre de Recherche et Développement en Économique, Université de Montréal, 2001.

[3] Bossert, W., P. K. Pattanaik, and Y. Xu, "Ranking Opportunity Sets: An Axiomatic Approach," *Journal of Economic Theory* **63**, 1994, 326–345.

[4] Dworkin, G., "Is More Choice Better Than Less?" in P. A. French, T. E. Uehling Jr., and H. K. Wettstein, eds., *Midwest Studies in Philosophy*, Vol.VII, *Social and Political Philosophy*, Minneapolis: University of Minnesota Press, 1982.

[5] Gravel, N., "Can a Ranking of Opportunity Sets Attach an Intrinsic Importance to Freedom of Choice?" *American Economic Review: Papers and Proceedings* **84**, 1994, 454–458.

[6] Gravel, N., "Ranking Opportunity Sets on the Basis of Their Freedom of Choice and Their Ability to Satisfy Preferences: A Difficulty," *Social Choice and Welfare* **15**, 1998, 371–382.

[7] Pattanaik, P. K., and K. Suzumura, "Rights, Welfarism and Social Choice," *American Economic Review: Papers and Proceedings* **84**, 1994, 435–439.

[8] Pattanaik, P. K., and K. Suzumura, "Individual Rights and Social Evaluation: A Conceptual Framework," *Oxford Economic Papers* **48**, 1996, 194–212.

[9] Pattanaik, P. K., and Y. Xu, "On Ranking Opportunity Sets in Terms of Freedom of Choice," *Recherches Economiques de Louvain* **56**, 1990, 383–390.

[10] Pattanaik, P. K., and Y. Xu, "On Diversity and Freedom of Choice," *Mathematical Social Sciences* **40**, 2000, 123–130.

[11] Pattanaik, P. K., and Y. Xu, "On Ranking Opportunity Sets in Economic Environments," *Journal of Economic Theory* **93**, 2000, 48–71.

[12] Sen, A. K., "Utilitarianism and Welfarism," *Journal of Philosophy* **76**, 1979, 463–489.

[13] Sen, A. K.,"Personal Utilities and Public Judgements: Or What's Wrong with Welfare Economics," *Economic Journal* **76**, 1979, 537–558.

[14] Sen, A. K., *Commodities and Capabilities*, Amsterdam: North-Holland, 1985.

[15] Sen, A. K., "Freedom of Choice: Concept and Content," *European Economic Review* **32**, 1988, 269–294.

[16] Sen, A. K., "Markets and Freedoms: Achievements and Limitations of the Market Mechanism in Promoting Individual Freedom," *Oxford Economic Papers* **45**, 1993, 519–541.

[17] Sen, A. K., "Maximization and the Act of Choice," *Econometrica* **65**, 1996, 745–779.

[18] Suzumura, K., "Consequences, Opportunities, and Procedures," *Social Choice and Welfare* **16**, 1999, 17–40. Essay 17 of this volume.

[19] Suzumura, K., "Welfare Economics beyond Welfarist Consequentialism," *Japanese Economic Review* **51**, 2000, 1–32. Essay 27 of this volume.

[20] Suzumura, K., and Y. Xu, "Characterizations of Consequentialism and Nonconsequentialism," *Journal of Economic Theory* **101**, 2001, 423–436. Essay 18 of this volume.

[21] Suzumura, K., and Y. Xu, "Welfarist Consequentialism, Similarity of Attitudes, and Arrow's General Impossibility Theorem," *Social Choice and Welfare* **22**, 2004, 237–251. Essay 20 of this volume.

ESSAY 20

Welfarist-Consequentialism, Similarity of Attitudes, and Arrow's General Impossibility Theorem

20.1. Introduction

The purpose of this essay is to reexamine Arrow's *general impossibility theorem* with special reference to two basic features of his book *Social Choice and Individual Values*. The first feature is *welfarist consequentialism*, which claims that social judgments on right or wrong actions should be based on the assessment of their consequential states of affairs, where the assessment of consequences is conducted exclusively in terms of people's welfare, their preference satisfaction, or people getting what they want.[1, 2] Not only is Arrow's own analysis based squarely on welfarist consequentialism in this sense,

First published in *Social Choice and Welfare* **22**, 2004, pp. 237–251 as a joint paper with Y. Xu. We are grateful to Kenneth Arrow, Peter Hammond, Serge Kolm, Prasanta Pattanaik, and Amartya Sen for their helpful conversations and suggestions over many years on this and related issues. Thanks are also due to the anonymous referee of *Social Choice and Welfare,* whose incisive comments helped us improve our exposition, and to Yukinori Iwata, Toyotaka Sakai, and Masaki Shimoji for pointing out a logical flaw in an earlier draft of this essay. To cope with this logical flaw, a modified version of the independence condition, which was suggested to us by Toyotaka Sakai, was adopted in this essay. Needless to say, we are solely responsible for any errors and opaqueness that may still remain.

1. See Sen [16; 17; 19] and Sen and Williams [22] for a more detailed account of welfarist consequentialism and criticisms thereof. See also Arrow [2], Hammond [8], and Suzumura [25; 26; 27].
2. Welfarist consequentialism has been under intensive scrutiny and harsh criticism in recent years by, e.g., Bossert, Pattanaik, and Xu [4], Pattanaik and Xu [11; 12], Sen [18; 19; 20], and Suzumura [25; 26; 27]. It is often argued that individuals are ready to express preferences not only over outcomes but also over opportunity sets from which outcomes are chosen. It is not infrequently suggested that such an extended preference should be duly taken into consideration

but also this basic feature permeates the entire edifice of contemporary social choice theory.[3] The second feature is the perception that "the possibility of social welfare judgments rests upon a similarity of attitudes toward social alternatives" (Arrow [1, p. 69]). To substantiate this claim analytically, Arrow [1, p. 81] showed that "it is possible to construct suitable social welfare functions if we feel entitled to say in advance that the tastes of individuals fall within certain prescribed realms of similarity." It goes without saying that a large portion of the subsequent developments in social choice theory is devoted to the exploration of Arrow's important insight to this effect.[4]

To gauge the extent to which Arrow's impossibility theorem and its resolution hinge on these two basic features of his framework, this essay develops two extended frameworks in which individuals are supposed to express their preferences not only about consequential outcomes but also about opportunity sets from which outcomes are chosen. Two such frameworks are identified below: a *consequentialist* framework and a *nonconsequentialist* framework. It is shown that the counterpart of Arrow's impossibility theorem still holds in the consequentialist framework if the society is composed exclusively of individuals who show similar attitudes toward social alternatives, whereas a resolution of Arrow's impossibility theorem can be found if there is a diversity of attitudes among individuals. Thus, in the consequentialist conceptual framework, it is in fact a *dissimilarity* rather than a *similarity* among individuals that serves as a deus ex machina vis-à-vis Arrow's general impossibility theorem. In contrast with this verdict on the consequentialist framework, an interesting resolution of Arrow's general impossibility theorem exists in the nonconsequentialist framework, which may work even in

---

in the analysis of how socially right or wrong actions should be determined. However, most of the preceding attempts to respond to these arguments and suggestions are concerned with the *ranking of opportunity sets* in terms of the freedom of choice and/or overall well-being of individuals. To the best of our knowledge, the question as to how individuals' extended preference orderings over outcomes and opportunities should be aggregated into the social preference ordering has been left unexplored in this literature.

3. It is true that Sen's [14, Chapter 6*; 15; 16; 17; 19] well-known criticism against the welfaristic foundations of normative economics and social choice theory, which capitalizes on his *impossibility of a Paretian liberal*, sharply brought the importance of nonwelfaristic features of consequences to the fore. However, it still keeps us within the broad territory of consequentialism. See also Suzumura [23; 25].

4. See, among others, Black [3], Kuga and Nagatani [10], and Sen [14, Chapter 10*].

the *homogeneous* society where all individuals exhibit a similarity of attitudes toward outcomes and opportunities.

The structure of this essay is as follows. In Section 20.2, we lay the foundation of our analysis by introducing some basic notation and definitions. Section 20.3 is devoted to examining how Arrow's general impossibility theorem fares in the consequentialist framework, whereas Section 20.4 conducts the corresponding analysis in the nonconsequentialist framework. Section 20.5 describes how these results can be generalized, and Section 20.6 concludes this essay with several observations.

20.2. Basic Notation and Definitions

Let X be the set of all conventionally defined social states, which are mutually exclusive and jointly exhaustive. It is assumed that X satisfies $3 \leq \#X < +\infty$. The elements of X are denoted by $x, y, z, \cdots$, and they are called *outcomes*. $\mathcal{S}$ denotes the set of all nonempty subsets of X. The elements of $\mathcal{S}$ are denoted by $A, B, C, \cdots$, and they are called *opportunity sets*. Let $X \times \mathcal{S}$ be the Cartesian product of X and $\mathcal{S}$. The elements of $X \times \mathcal{S}$ are denoted by $(x, A), (y, B), (z, C), \cdots$, and they are called *extended alternatives*. The intended meaning of $(x, A) \in X \times \mathcal{S}$ is that the outcome x is chosen from the opportunity set A, but this interpretation will be vacuous if $x \notin A$. Thus, let $\Omega \subseteq X \times \mathcal{S}$ be such that $x \in A$ whenever $(x, A) \in \Omega$.

Let $N = \{1, 2, \cdots, n\}$ be the set of all individuals in the society, where $2 \leq n = \#N < +\infty$. Each individual $i \in N$ is assumed to have an extended preference ordering $\succsim_i$ over Ω, which is *reflexive, complete,* and *transitive*. For any $(x, A), (y, B) \in \Omega$, $(x, A) \succsim_i (y, B)$ is meant to imply that i feels at least as good when choosing x from A as when choosing y from B. The asymmetric part and the symmetric part of $\succsim_i$ are denoted by $\succ_i$ and $\sim_i$, respectively, which denote the strict preference relation and the indifference relation of $i \in N$.

Let $\mathcal{R}$ be the set of all logically possible orderings over Ω. Then a *profile* $\succsim = (\succsim_1, \succsim_2, \cdots, \succsim_n)$ of extended individual preference orderings, one extended ordering for each individual, is an element of $\mathcal{R}^n$. An *extended social welfare function* (ESWF) is a function f that maps each profile in some subset D_f of $\mathcal{R}^n$ into $\mathcal{R}$. When $\succsim = f(\succsim)$ holds for some $\succsim \in D_f$, $\sim$ and $\succ$ stand, respectively, for the social indifference relation and the social strict preference relation corresponding to $\succsim$. Given an ESWF f, the problem of social choice we envisage in this essay can be phrased as follows. Suppose that a profile $\succsim \in D_f$ and a set $S \subseteq X$ of feasible social alternatives are given. Then the best social choice from S can be identified to be an $x^* \in S$ such that $(x^*, S) \succsim (x, S)$ holds for all $x \in S$, where $\succsim = f(\succsim)$. To make this interpretation natural as well as sensible, we assume that each and every $x \in X$ denotes a *public* alternative, such as a list of public goods to be provided in the society or the description of a candidate in the public election.

20.2.1. Domain Restriction

In order to make our problem both analytically tractable and interesting, we assume that each individual's extended preference ordering $\succsim_i$ $(i \in N)$, which defines an admissible profile $\succsim = (\succsim_1, \succsim_2, \cdots, \succsim_n) \in D_f$, satisfies the following two conditions:

Independence (IND). For all $(x, A), (y, B) \in \Omega$ and all $z \in X \setminus (A \cup B)$,

$$(x, A) \succsim_i (y, B) \Leftrightarrow (x, A \cup \{z\}) \succsim_i (y, B \cup \{z\}).$$

Simple Indifference (SI). For all $x \in X$ and all $y, z \in X \setminus \{x\}$,

$$(x, \{x, y\}) \sim_i (x, \{x, z\}).$$

IND corresponds to the standard independence axiom used in the literature (see, for example, Pattanaik and Xu [11]). It requires that, for all opportunity sets $A, B \in S$, if an alternative $z \in X$ is not in both A and B, then the preference ranking over $(x, A \cup \{z\})$ and $(y, B \cup \{z\})$ corresponds to the preference ranking over (x, A) and (y, B). SI requires that choosing x from the two simple cases consisting of two alternatives each is regarded as indifferent no matter what alternative is added to x.

We may as well assume the following condition:

Monotonicity (MON). For all $(x, A), (x, B) \in \Omega$,

$$B \subseteq A \Rightarrow (x, A) \succsim_i (x, B).$$

MON makes an explicit use of information about the opportunity aspect of choice situations. It requires that choosing an outcome x from the opportunity set A is at least as good as choosing the same x from the opportunity set B, which is a subset of A. In the present context, this axiom seems very reasonable.

The following result summarizes the implication of these three conditions.

LEMMA 20.1. If $\succsim_i$ satisfies IND, SI, and MON, then for all $(x, A), (x, B) \in \Omega$, $\#A \geq \#B \Rightarrow (x, A) \succsim_i (x, B)$.

PROOF. Let $\succsim_i$ satisfy IND, SI, and MON. Let $(x, A), (x, B) \in \Omega$ be such that $\#A \geq \#B$.

If $\#A = \#B = 1$, then $A = B = \{x\}$. By reflexivity of $\succsim_i$, it follows immediately that $(x, A) \sim_i (x, B)$. If $\#A = \#B = 2$, then by $(x, A) \sim_i (x, B)$ follows from SI directly. Thus, we have proved the following:

$$\text{For all } (x, A), (x, B) \in \Omega, \text{ if } \#A = \#B \leq 2, \text{ then } (x, A) \sim_i (x, B). \tag{20.1}$$

To prove that $\#A = \#B = m > 2 \Rightarrow (x, A) \sim_i (x, B)$, we use the induction method. Suppose

$$\text{For all } (x, S), (x, T) \in \Omega \text{ such that } \#S = \#T < m, (x, S) \sim_i (x, T). \tag{20.2}$$

If there exists $y \in A \cap B$ such that $y \neq x$, then, from (20.2), $(x, A \setminus \{y\}) \sim_i (x, B \setminus \{y\})$. By IND, $(x, A) \sim_i (x, B)$ follows immediately. If $A \cap B = \{x\}$, then consider $C = (A \setminus \{a\}) \cup \{b\}$ where $a \in A \setminus \{x\}$ and $b \in B \setminus \{x\}$. From the previous argument, clearly, $(x, A) \sim_i (x, C)$ and $(x, B) \sim_i (x, C)$. Thus, by the transitivity of $\succsim_i$, $(x, A) \sim_i (x, B)$.

From (20.1) and (20.2), noting the finiteness of X, we have

$$\text{For all } (x, A), (x, B) \in \Omega, \text{ if } \#A = \#B, \text{ then} (x, A) \sim_i (x, B). \tag{20.3}$$

Consider now that $\#A > \#B$. If $\#B = 1$, that is, $B = \{x\}$, by MON, $(x, A) \succsim_i (x, B)$ follows immediately. Similarly, if $A = X$, then, by MON, $(x, A) = (x, X) \succsim_i (x, B)$. Let $\#X > \#A > \#B > 1$. Clearly, in this case, there exists $C \in \mathcal{S}$ such that $\#(B \cup C) = \#A$. From (20.3), $(x, C \cup B) \sim_i (x, A)$. By MON, $(x, C \cup B) \succsim_i (x, B)$. Hence, $(x, A) \succsim_i (x, B)$ follows from the transitivity of $\succsim_i$. ■

Thus, these simple conditions impose a mild restriction on each individual's extended preference ordering to the effect that *each individual is not averse to richer opportunities, viz. a larger opportunity set does not do any harm to him/her.*[5, 6]

Throughout Sections 20.3 and 20.4, we assume that each profile $\succsim = (\succsim_1, \succsim_2, \cdots, \succsim_n) \in D_f$ is such that $\succsim_i$ satisfies the conditions IND, SI, and MON for all $i \in N$.

20.2.2. Arrovian Conditions in the Extended Framework

In addition to the domain restriction on D_f introduced previously, we introduce several conditions on f, which are slight modifications of Arrow's own conditions. The first two conditions are well known, and require no further explanation.

Strong Pareto Principle (SP). For all $(x, A), (y, B) \in \Omega$ and all $\succsim = (\succsim_1, \succsim_2, \cdots, \succsim_n) \in D_f$, if $(x, A) \succ_i (y, B)$ holds for all $i \in N$, then we have $(x, A) \succ (y, B)$, and if $(x, A) \sim_i (y, B)$ holds for all $i \in N$, then we have $(x, A) \sim (y, B)$, where $\succsim = f(\succsim)$.

Nondictatorship (ND). There exists no $i \in N$ that satisfies $[(x, A) \succ_i (y, B) \Rightarrow (x, A) \succ (y, B)$ for all $(x, A), (y, B) \in \Omega]$ for all $\succsim = (\succsim_1, \succsim_2, \cdots, \succsim_n) \in D_f$, where $\succsim = f(\succsim)$.

There are various ways of formulating Arrow's independence of irrelevant alternatives in our present context. Consider the following:

5. It may be argued that the measurement of opportunity in terms of the cardinality of the opportunity set is naive, and one should take such information as similarities among outcomes into consideration. This can be done as in Pattanaik and Xu [13] using the minimum of the cardinalities of informationally equivalent classes rather than the cardinality of the opportunity set per se. It is for the purpose of keeping our framework as simple as possible that we are using in this essay the cardinality approach in measuring opportunity. See, however, Section 20.5
6. For some arguments that may cast reasonable doubts on the universal worth of having a larger opportunity set rather than a smaller one, the interested readers are referred to Dworkin [5].

Independence of Irrelevant Alternatives (i) (IIA (i)). For all $\succsim^1 = (\succsim_1^1, \succsim_2^1, \cdots, \succsim_n^1)$, $\succsim^2 = (\succsim_1^2, \succsim_2^2, \cdots, \succsim_n^2) \in D_f$, and for all (x, A), $(y, B) \in \Omega$, if $[(x, A) \succsim_i^1 (y, B) \Leftrightarrow (x, A) \succsim_i^2 (y, B)$ and $(x, \{x\}) \succsim_i^1 (y, \{y\}) \Leftrightarrow (x, \{x\}) \succsim_i^2 (y, \{y\})]$ holds for all $i \in N$, then $[(x, A) \succsim^1 (y, B) \Leftrightarrow (x, A) \succsim^2 (y, B)]$ holds, where $\succsim^1 = f(\succsim^1)$ and $\succsim^2 = f(\succsim^2)$.

Independence of Irrelevant Alternatives (ii) (IIA (ii)). For all $\succsim^1 = (\succsim_1^1, \succsim_2^1, \cdots, \succsim_n^1)$, $\succsim^2 = (\succsim_1^2, \succsim_2^2, \cdots, \succsim_n^2) \in D_f$, and for all (x, A), $(y, B) \in \Omega$ with $\#A = \#B$, if $[(x, A) \succsim_i^1 (y, B) \Leftrightarrow (x, A) \succsim_i^2 (y, B)]$ holds for all $i \in N$, then $[(x, A) \succsim^1 (y, B) \Leftrightarrow (x, A) \succsim^2 (y, B)]$ holds, where $\succsim^1 = f(\succsim^1)$ and $\succsim^2 = f(\succsim^2)$.

Full Independence of Irrelevant Alternatives (FIIA). For all $\succsim^1 = (\succsim_1^1, \succsim_2^1, \cdots, \succsim_n^1)$, $\succsim^2 = (\succsim_1^2, \succsim_2^2, \cdots, \succsim_n^2) \in D_f$, and for all (x, A), $(y, B) \in \Omega$, if $[(x, A) \succsim_i^1 (y, B) \Leftrightarrow (x, A) \succsim_i^2 (y, B)]$ holds for all $i \in N$, then $[(x, A) \succsim^1 (y, B) \Leftrightarrow (x, A) \succsim^2 (y, B)]$ holds, where $\succsim^1 = f(\succsim^1)$ and $\succsim^2 = f(\succsim^2)$.

IIA (i) says that the extended social preference between any two extended alternatives (x, A) and (y, B) depends on each individual's extended preference between them as well as each individual's extended preference between $(x, \{x\})$ and $(y, \{y\})$. IIA (ii), on the other hand, says that the extended social preference between any two extended alternatives (x, A) and (y, B) with $\#A = \#B$ depends on each individual's extended preference between them. Finally, FIIA says that the extended social preference between *any* two extended alternatives (x, A) and (y, B) depends on each individual's extended preference between them. It is clear that IIA (i) is logically independent of IIA (ii), and both IIA (i) and IIA (ii) are logically weaker than FIIA.

20.3. Arrovian Impossibility Theorems in the Consequentialist Framework

In this section, we discuss Arrovian impossibility theorems in the framework that is broader than welfarist consequentialism, yet lies within consequentialism. Following Essay 18, let us identify two types of an individual whom we have a reason to call a *consequentialist*:

EXTREME CONSEQUENTIALIST. An individual $i \in N$ is said to be an *extreme consequentialist* if, for all $(x, A), (x, B) \in \Omega$, it is true that $(x, A) \sim_i (x, B)$.

STRONG CONSEQUENTIALIST. An individual i is said to be a *strong consequentialist* if, for all $(x, A), (y, B) \in \Omega$,

(a) if $(x, \{x\}) \sim_i (y, \{y\})$, then $\#A \geq \#B \Leftrightarrow (x, A) \succsim_i (y, B)$; and
(b) if $(x, \{x\}) \succ_i (y, \{y\})$, then $(x, A) \succ_i (y, B)$.

Thus, an extreme consequentialist ranks two extended alternatives (x, A) and (y, B) simply in terms of their outcomes x and y, giving no relevance to the opportunity sets A and B from which x and y are chosen. In contrast, a strong consequentialist ranks two alternatives (x, A) and (y, B) in complete accordance with their outcomes x and y only if he/she has a strict preference between choosing x from the singleton set $\{x\}$ and choosing y from the singleton set $\{y\}$. If he/she is indifferent between choosing x from the singleton set $\{x\}$ and choosing y from the singleton set $\{y\}$, his/her preference ranking between (x, A) and (y, B) is in accordance with the cardinality comparison between A and B. It is to this limited extent that a strong consequentialist reveals his/her preference for opportunity, thereby exhibiting his/her impure consequentialist side.

As the following lemma shows, for an extreme as well as a strong consequentialist, imposing the conditions IND, SI, and MON does not in fact restrict his/her preferences at all.

LEMMA 20.2. An extreme as well as a strong consequentialist's extended preference orderings must always satisfy the three conditions IND, SI, and MON.

PROOF. It is easy to check that both an extreme and a strong consequentialist's extended preference orderings satisfy SI and MON. We now prove that IND is satisfied by an extreme and a strong consequentialist's extended preference orderings. ∎

EXTREME CONSEQUENTIALIST. Let i be an extreme consequentialist and $\succsim_i$ be her extended preference ordering. Let $(x, A), (y, B) \in \Omega$ and $z \in X \setminus (A \cup B)$ be such that $(x, A) \succsim_i (y, B)$ holds. By definition of an extreme consequentialist, we must have $(x, A) \sim_i (x, A \cup \{z\})$ and $(y, B) \sim_i$

$(y, B \cup \{z\})$. Then transitivity of $\succsim_i$ implies $(x, A \cup \{z\}) \succsim_i (y, B \cup \{z\})$. The converse implication may be similarly verified. Therefore, IND holds for an extreme consequentialist's extended preference orderings.

STRONG CONSEQUENTIALIST. Let j be a strong consequentialist and $\succsim_j$ be his extended preference ordering. Let $(x, A), (y, B) \in \Omega$ and $z \in X \setminus (A \cup B)$ be such that $(x, A) \succsim_j (y, B)$ holds. We distinguish three cases that exhaust all possibilities, viz., (a) $(x, A) \sim_j (y, B)$; (b) $x = y$ and $(x, A) \succ_j (y, B)$; and (c) $x \neq y$ and $(x, A) \succ_j (y, B)$. In case (a), according to the definition of a strong consequentialist, it must be that $(x, \{x\}) \sim_j (y, \{y\})$ and $\#A = \#B$. Then, by the definition of strong consequentialism, it follows that $(x, A \cup \{z\}) \sim_j (y, B \cup \{z\})$. In case (b), since $x = y$, by the definition of a strong consequentialist, we must have $\#A > \#B$. Clearly, $\#(A \cup \{z\}) > \#(B \cup \{z\})$. Hence, $(x, A \cup \{z\}) \succ_j (y, B \cup \{z\})$ follows from the definition of strong consequentialism. Finally, in case (c), we must have $(x, \{x\}) \succ_j (y, \{y\})$. Then $(x, A \cup \{z\}) \succ_j (y, B \cup \{z\})$ follows immediately from the definition of a strong consequentialist. The converse may be similarly verified. Hence, a strong consequentialist's extended preference orderings satisfy IND.

Let us now introduce three domain restrictions on f by specifying some appropriate subsets of D_f. In the first place, let $D_f(E)$ be the set of all profiles in D_f such that all individuals are extreme consequentialists. In the second place, let $D_f(E \cup S)$ be the set of all profiles in D_f such that at least one individual is an extreme consequentialist *uniformly* for all profiles $\succsim = (\succsim_1, \cdots, \succsim_n) \in D_f$ and at least one individual is a strong consequentialist *uniformly* for all profiles $\succsim = (\succsim_1, \cdots, \succsim_n) \in D_f$. Finally, let $D_f(S)$ be the set of all profiles in D_f such that all individuals are strong consequentialists.

We are now ready to present our results, beginning with the consequentialist framework. The first result is a simple restatement of Arrow's general impossibility theorem save for the restriction on the domain of the extended social welfare function and a slight strengthening of the Pareto principle.

THEOREM 20.1. Suppose that all individuals are extreme consequentialists. Then there exists no extended social welfare function f with the domain $D_f(E)$ that satisfies SP, ND, and either IIA (i) or IIA (ii).

Proof. Suppose that there exists an ESWF f on $D_f(E)$ that satisfies SP as well as IIA (i). Since all individuals are extreme consequentialists,

$$\forall i \in N : (x, A) \succsim_i (y, B) \Leftrightarrow (x, X) \succsim_i (y, X) \tag{20.4}$$

holds for all $(x, A), (y, B) \in \Omega$ and for all $\succsim = (\succsim_1, \succsim_2, \cdots, \succsim_n) \in D_f(E)$. Note that the conditions IND, SI, and SM impose no restriction whatsoever on the profile $\succsim = (\succsim_1, \succsim_2, \cdots, \succsim_n)$ even when, for each $i \in N$, $\succsim_i$ is restricted on $\Omega_X := \{(x, X) \in X \times \mathcal{S} | x \in X\}$. Note also that SP and IIA (i) imposed on f imply that the same conditions must be satisfied on the restricted space Ω_X. By virtue of the Arrow impossibility theorem, therefore, there exists a dictator, say, $d \in N$, for f on the restricted space Ω_X. That is, for all $\succsim = (\succsim_1, \succsim_2, \cdots, \succsim_n) \in D_f(E)$ and all $(x, X), (y, X) \in \Omega_X$, $(x, X) \succ_d (y, X) \Rightarrow (x, X) \succ (y, X)$, where $\succsim = f(\succsim)$. We now show that for all $(x, A), (y, B) \in \Omega$, $(x, A) \succ_d (y, B) \Rightarrow (x, A) \succ (y, B)$, viz., d is a dictator for f on the full space Ω. Note that, since d is an extreme consequentialist, we must have $(x, A) \succ_d (y, B)$ if and only if $(x, X) \succ_d (y, X)$. Since all individuals are extreme consequentialists, it must be true that $(x, A) \sim_i (x, X)$ and $(y, B) \sim_i (y, X)$ for all $i \in N$. Therefore, by SP, $(x, A) \sim (x, X)$ and $(y, B) \sim (y, X)$. By virtue of the transitivity of $\succsim$, it follows that $(x, X) \succ (y, X) \Rightarrow (x, A) \succ (y, B)$. That is, we have shown that $(x, A) \succ_d (y, B) \Rightarrow (x, A) \succ (y, B)$. In other words, d is a dictator for f on the full space Ω. Therefore, there exists no ESWF that satisfies SP, IIA (i), and ND.

A similar argument can be used to show that there exists no ESWF that satisfies SP, IIA (ii), and ND. ■

Thus, the similarity of attitudes among individuals in the sense that all individuals are extreme consequentialists brings back an essentially Arrovian impossibility result. The message of this theorem can be strengthened by proving the next theorem, which asserts that the impossibility result disappears if an extreme consequentialist and a strong consequentialist coexist in the society.

Theorem 20.2. Suppose that at least one uniform extreme consequentialist exists over $D_f(E \cup S)$ and at least one uniform strong consequentialist exists over $D_f(E \cup S)$ in the society.[7] Then there exists an extended social welfare function f with the domain $D_f(E \cup S)$ that satisfies SP, IIA (i), IIA (ii) and ND.

Proof. Let $e \in N$ be a uniform extreme consequentialist and $s \in N$ be a uniform strong consequentialist. By definition,

$$\forall (x, A), (x, B) \in \Omega : (x, A) \sim_e (x, B), \tag{20.5}$$

$$\forall (x, A), (y, B) \in \Omega : (x, \{x\}) \sim_s (y, \{y\}) \Rightarrow [(x, A) \succcurlyeq_s (y, B) \Leftrightarrow \#A \geq \#B], \tag{20.6}$$

and

$$\forall (x, A), (y, B) \in \Omega : (x, \{x\}) \succcurlyeq_s (y, \{y\}) \Rightarrow (x, A) \succcurlyeq_s (y, B) \tag{20.7}$$

hold. Now consider the following ESWF.

$$\forall (x, A), (y, B) \in \Omega:$$
$$(x, \{x\}) \succ_s (y, \{y\}) \Rightarrow [(x, A) \succcurlyeq (y, B) \Leftrightarrow (x, A) \succcurlyeq_s (y, B)];$$
$$(x, \{x\}) \sim_s (y, \{y\}) \Rightarrow [(x, A) \succcurlyeq (y, B) \Leftrightarrow (x, A) \succcurlyeq_e (y, B)],$$

where $\succcurlyeq \; = f(\succcurlyeq)$.

It may easily be verified that this ESWF satisfies SP and ND. To verify that it satisfies both IIA (i) and IIA (ii), we consider $(x, A), (y, B) \in \Omega$, and $\succcurlyeq = (\succcurlyeq_1, \succcurlyeq_2, \cdots, \succcurlyeq_n)$, $\succcurlyeq' = (\succcurlyeq'_1, \succcurlyeq'_2, \cdots, \succcurlyeq'_n) \in D_f(E \cup S)$. Let $\succcurlyeq = f(\succcurlyeq)$ and $\succcurlyeq' = f(\succcurlyeq')$.

To begin with, suppose that we have $(x, A) \succcurlyeq_i (y, B) \Leftrightarrow (x, A) \succcurlyeq'_i (y, B)$ as well as $(x, \{x\}) \succcurlyeq_i (y, \{y\}) \Leftrightarrow (x, \{x\}) \succcurlyeq'_i (y, \{y\})$ for all $i \in N$. If $(x, \{x\}) \succ_s (y, \{y\})$, then $(x, \{x\}) \succ'_s (y, \{y\})$, $(x, A) \succ_s (y, B)$, as well as $(x, A) \succ'_s (y, B)$. Then the ESWF gives us $(x, A) \succ (y, B)$ and $(x, A) \succ' (y, B)$. Secondly, if $(y, \{y\}) \succ_s (x, \{x\})$, then $(y, \{y\}) \succ'_s (x, \{x\})$, $(y, B) \succ_s (x, A)$, and $(y, B) \succ'_s (x, A)$. Then the ESWF gives us

7. A *uniform* extreme consequentialist over $D_f(E \cup S)$ is an individual who is an extreme consequentialist uniformly for all profiles in $D_f(E \cup S)$. The definition of a uniform strong consequentialist is similar.

$(y, B) \succ (x, A)$ and $(y, B) \succ' (x, A)$. Thirdly, if $(x, \{x\}) \sim_s (y, \{y\})$, then $(x, \{x\}) \sim'_s (y, \{y\})$. The ESWF implies that $(x, A) \succcurlyeq (y, B) \Leftrightarrow (x, A) \succcurlyeq_e (y, B)$ and $(x, A) \succcurlyeq' (y, B) \Leftrightarrow (x, A) \succcurlyeq'_e (y, B)$. Note that individual e is an extreme consequentialist. It is therefore clear that, in this case, if $(x, A) \succcurlyeq_e (y, B) \Leftrightarrow (x, A) \succcurlyeq'_e (y, B)$, then $(x, A) \succcurlyeq (y, B) \Leftrightarrow (x, A) \succcurlyeq' (y, B)$. Therefore, IIA (i) is satisfied.

Next, suppose that $\#A = \#B$ and that $[(x, A) \succcurlyeq_i (y, B) \Leftrightarrow (x, A) \succcurlyeq'_i (y, B)]$ for all $i \in N$. To show that $(x, A) \succcurlyeq (y, B) \Leftrightarrow (x, A) \succcurlyeq' (y, B)$ in this case, we observe that, when $\#A = \#B$, $(x, A) \succcurlyeq_s (y, B) \Leftrightarrow (x, \{x\}) \succcurlyeq_s (y, \{y\})$ and $(x, A) \succcurlyeq'_s (y, B) \Leftrightarrow (x, \{x\}) \succcurlyeq'_s (y, \{y\})$. Then the proof that the preceding ESWF satisfies IIA (ii) is similar to the proof showing that the ESWF satisfies IIA (i). We have only to note that individual e is an extreme consequentialist.

The binary relation $\succcurlyeq$ generated by this ESWF is clearly reflexive and complete. We now show that $\succcurlyeq$ is transitive. Let (x, A), (y, B), and $(z, C) \in \Omega$ be such that $(x, A) \succcurlyeq (y, B)$ and $(y, B) \succcurlyeq (z, C)$. Note that, since $(x, A) \succcurlyeq (y, B)$, by the ESWF constructed previously, we cannot have $(y, \{y\}) \succ_s (x, \{x\})$. Then, by the completeness of $\succcurlyeq_s$, there are only two cases to be distinguished and separately considered: (a) $(x, \{x\}) \sim_s (y, \{y\})$ and (b) $(x, \{x\}) \succ_s (y, \{y\})$.

Case (a). In this case, we must have $(x, A) \succcurlyeq_e (y, B)$. If $(y, \{y\}) \sim_s (z, \{z\})$, then it follows from $(y, B) \succcurlyeq (z, C)$ that $(y, B) \succcurlyeq_e (z, C)$. Then the transitivity of $\succcurlyeq_e$ implies $(x, A) \succcurlyeq_e (z, C)$. By the transitivity of $\succcurlyeq_s$, $(x, \{x\}) \sim_s (z, \{z\})$. Therefore, $(x, A) \succcurlyeq (z, C)$ if and only if $(x, A) \succcurlyeq_e (z, C)$. Hence, $(x, A) \succcurlyeq (z, C)$ follows from $(x, A) \succcurlyeq_e (z, C)$. If $(y, \{y\}) \succ_s (z, \{z\})$, then, by the transitivity of $\succcurlyeq_s$, it follows that $(x, \{x\}) \succ_s (z, \{z\})$. Therefore, $(x, A) \succcurlyeq (z, C)$ if and only if $(x, A) \succcurlyeq_s (z, C)$. Since s is a strong consequentialist, given that $(x, \{x\}) \succ_s (z, \{z\})$, we must have $(x, A) \succ_s (z, C)$. Therefore, $(x, A) \succ (z, C)$. Hence, $(x, A) \succcurlyeq (z, C)$ holds. Note that, given $(y, B) \succcurlyeq (z, C)$, we cannot have $(z, \{z\}) \succ_s (y, \{y\})$. Therefore, the transitivity of $\succcurlyeq$ holds in case (a).

Case (b). In this case, we must have $(x, A) \succ_s (y, B)$, hence $(x, A) \succ (y, B)$. Since $(y, B) \succcurlyeq (z, C)$, we must then have $(y, \{y\}) \succcurlyeq_s (z, \{z\})$. By the transitivity of $\succcurlyeq_s$, it follows that $(x, \{x\}) \succ_s (z, \{z\})$. Thus,

$(x, A) \succ_s (z, C)$ follows from s being a strong consequentialist. By construction, in this case, $(x, A) \succcurlyeq (z, C)$ if and only if $(x, A) \succcurlyeq_s (z, C)$. Hence, $(x, A) \succ (z, C)$. Therefore, the transitivity of $\succcurlyeq$ holds in case (b).

Combining cases (a) and (b), the transitivity of $\succcurlyeq$ is proved. ■

How about the society consisting only of strong consequentialists? Consistent with Theorem 20.1 as well as Theorem 20.2, we may assert the following.

Theorem 20.3. Suppose that all individuals are strong consequentialists. Then there exists no extended social welfare function f with the domain $D_f(S)$ that satisfies SP, IIA, and ND.

Proof. Since all individuals are strong consequentialists, we have the following for all $i \in N$: for all $(x, A), (y, B) \in \Omega$, if $(x, \{x\}) \sim_i (y, \{y\})$, then $\#A \geq \#B \Leftrightarrow (x, A) \succcurlyeq_i (y, B)$, whereas if $(x, \{x\}) \succ_i (y, \{y\})$, then $(x, A) \succcurlyeq_i (y, B) \Leftrightarrow (x, X) \succcurlyeq_i (y, X)$. Suppose that an ESWF f satisfies SP and FIIA, and consider all triples (x, A), (y, B), and $(z, C) \in \Omega$ such that x, y, and z are all distinct. Since all individuals are strong consequentialists and f has the domain $D_f(S)$, there exists no restriction on each individual's strict extended preference orderings over $\{(x, A), (y, B), (z, C)\}$. Thus, there is a dictator over the triple $\{(x, A), (y, B), (z, C)\}$. Note that the triple $\{(x, A), (y, B), (z, C)\}$, where $A \neq X$, coincides with the triple $\{(x, X), (y, B), (z, C)\}$ over the pair $\{(y, B), (z, C)\}$. Hence the dictator over the triple $\{(x, A), (y, B), (z, C)\}$ must in fact be independent of the set $A \in \mathcal{S}$. The same argument can be applied to $B \in \mathcal{S}$ as well as $C \in \mathcal{S}$. Hence, for *all* triples $\{(x, A), (y, B), (z, C)\}$, we must have a single dictator. Call him $d \in N$ and consider a triple (x, A), (y, B), and $(z, C) \in \Omega$ such that x, y, and z are all distinct. Consider any $(x, A^*) \in \Omega$, where $A \neq A^*$. If $A^* \subseteq A$, all individuals being strong consequentialists, SP implies that $(x, A) \succ (x, A^*)$, where $\succcurlyeq\ = f(\succcurlyeq)$. Similarly, if $A \subseteq A^*$, all individuals being strong consequentialists, SP implies that $(x, A^*) \succ (x, A)$, where $\succcurlyeq\ = f(\succcurlyeq)$. If neither A is a subset of A^*, nor A^* is a subset of A, all individuals being strong consequentialists, we must have $(x, A) \succcurlyeq_i (x, A^*)$ if and only if $\#A \geq \#A^*$. Then SP implies that $(x, A) \succcurlyeq (x, A^*)$ if and only if $\#A \geq \#A^*$, where $\succsim \; = f(\succsim)$. Hence, d is a dictator over Ω. Therefore, there exists no ESWF satisfying SP, FIIA, and ND. ∎

The message of these simple results seems clear. Within the consequentialist framework, if all individuals are either extreme consequentialists or strong consequentialists, we have essentially Arrovian impossibility results. As the society becomes diverse by having at least one uniform extreme consequentialist and at least one uniform strong consequentialist simultaneously, however, it is possible to design an extended social welfare function that satisfies a variant of the Arrow conditions. Thus, *it is the diversity of the society, or the heterogeneity of the population in the society, that plays a crucial role in resolving the Arrow impossibility theorem within the consequentialist framework.*

20.4. Arrovian Impossibility Theorem in the Nonconsequentialist Framework

Let us now turn to a nonconsequentialist framework. Our first task is to clarify what precisely we mean by nonconsequentialism. Following Essay 18, let us define an individual to be a nonconsequentialist as follows.[8]

NONCONSEQUENTIALIST. An individual $i \in N$ is said to be a *nonconsequentialist* if, for all $(x, A), (y, B) \in \Omega$, (a) $\#A > \#B \Rightarrow (x, A) \succ_i (y, B)$ and (b) $\#A = \#B \Rightarrow [(x, A) \succsim_i (y, B) \Leftrightarrow (x, \{x\}) \succsim_i (y, \{y\})]$.

Thus, a nonconsequentialist is a person whose preference ranking over two extended alternatives $(x, A), (y, B) \in \Omega$ are such that, whenever the opportunity set A contains more alternatives than the opportunity set B, (x, A) is ranked higher than (y, B). It is only when A and B contain the same number of alternatives that (x, A) and (y, B) are ranked exactly the same as $(x, \{x\})$ and $(y, \{y\})$. In this sense, a nonconsequentialist

8. In the terminology coined in Essay 18, a nonconsequentialist defined here is called a *strong nonconsequentialist*. Since this is the only category of nonconsequentialism that is relevant in the present essay, we have simplified our circumlocution by avoiding the adjective "strong."

is in sharp contrast with both an extreme consequentialist and a strong consequentialist.

The following lemma shows that, for a nonconsequentialist, imposing the conditions IND, SI, and MON introduced in Section 20.2.1 does not in fact restrict his/her preferences at all.

Lemma 20.3. A nonconsequentialist's extended preference orderings must satisfy the three conditions IND, SI, and MON.

Proof. It can be checked easily that a nonconsequentialist's extended preference orderings satisfy SI and MON. We now show that IND is also satisfied.

Let i be a nonconsequentialist. Let $(x, A), (y, B) \in \Omega$ and $z \in X \setminus A \cup B$. Suppose $(x, A) \succsim_i (y, B)$. There are two cases to consider: (a) $\#A > \#B$ and (b) $\#A = \#B$. In case (a), clearly, $(x, A) \succ_i (y, B)$ and $\#(A \cup \{z\}) > \#(B \cup \{z\})$. Hence, $(x, A \cup \{z\}) \succ_i (y, B \cup \{z\})$ follows from i being a nonconsequentialist. In case (b), we have $(x, A) \succsim_i (y, B)$ if and only if $(x, \{x\}) \succsim_i (y, \{y\})$ and $\#(A \cup \{z\}) = \#(B \cup \{z\})$. Then $(x, A \cup \{z\}) \succsim_i (y, B \cup \{z\})$ if and only if $(x, \{x\}) \succsim_i (y, \{y\})$ follows from i being a nonconsequentialist. Noting that $\succsim_i$ is complete, IND is therefore satisfied by $\succsim_i$. ■

Let $D_f(N)$ be the domain of an extended social welfare function f such that there exists at least one person, say, $n^* \in N$, who is a nonconsequentialist *uniformly* for all profiles $\succsim = (\succsim_1, \succsim_2, \cdots, \succsim_n) \in D_f(N)$. Such a person will be called a *uniform nonconsequentialist* over $D_f(N)$.

Theorem 20.4. Suppose that there exists at least one person who is a uniform nonconsequentialist over $D_f(N)$. Then there exists an extended social welfare function f with the domain $D_f(N)$ that satisfies SP, FIIA, and ND.

Proof. Let $n^* \in N$ be a uniform nonconsequentialist over $D_f(N)$. Then, for all $\succsim = (\succsim_1, \succsim_2, \cdots, \succsim_n) \in D_f(N)$ and all $(x, A), (y, B) \in \Omega$, $\#A > \#B$ implies $(x, A) \succ_{n^*} (y, B)$. Consider now the following ESWF f: for all $(x, A), (y, B) \in \Omega$,

$$\text{if } \#A > \#B, \text{ then } (x, A) \succ (y, B);$$

$$\text{if } \#A = \#B = 1, \text{ then } (x, \{x\}) \succcurlyeq (y, \{y\}) \text{ if and only if } (x, \{x\}) \succcurlyeq_1 (y, \{y\});$$

$$\text{if } \#A = \#B = 2, \text{ then } (x, A) \succcurlyeq (y, B) \text{ if and only if } (x, A) \succcurlyeq_2 (y, B);$$

$$\vdots$$

$$\text{if } A = B = X, \text{ then } (x, A) \succcurlyeq (y, A) \text{ if and only if } (x, A) \succcurlyeq_k (y, B), \quad \text{where } k = \min\{\#N, \#X\},$$

where $\succcurlyeq = f(\succcurlyeq)$. It is easy to verify that this f satisfies SP, IIA, and ND.[9] It is also clear that $\succcurlyeq$ generated by this ESWF is reflexive and complete. We now show that $\succcurlyeq$ is transitive as well. Let $(x, A), (y, B), (z, C) \in \Omega$ be such that $(x, A) \succcurlyeq (y, B)$ and $(y, B) \succcurlyeq (z, C)$. Then, clearly, $\#A \geq \#B$ and $\#B \geq \#C$. If $\#A > \#B$ or $\#B > \#C$, then $\#A > \#C$. By the constructed ESWF, $(x, A) \succ (z, C)$ follows easily. Thus, the transitivity of $\succcurlyeq$ holds for this case. Now, suppose $\#A = \#B = \#C$. Note that in this case, for all $(a, G), (b, H) \in \Omega$ such that $\#G = \#H = \#A$, $(a, G) \succcurlyeq (b, H)$ if and only if $(a, G) \succcurlyeq_k (b, H)$, where $k \in N$ and $k = \min\{\#N, \#A\}$. Therefore, the transitivity of $\succcurlyeq$ follows from the transitivity of $\succcurlyeq_k$. The preceding two cases exhaust all the possibilities. Therefore, $\succcurlyeq$ is transitive. ■

It is worthwhile to emphasize that, unlike the extreme consequentialist or the strong consequentialist, a nonconsequentialist is able to guarantee the existence of an Arrovian extended social welfare function *by him/herself*,

9. It may be worthwhile to note that the extended social welfare function constructed in this proof has some nice features. When $\#X + 1 \geq n$, every individual can dictate one "layer" of the extended social alternatives. Indeed, we assign the nonconsequentialist to dictate over (x, A) and (y, B) in Ω such that $\#A \neq \#B$. For each of all other individuals, we assign him/her to dictate over (x, A) and (y, B) in Ω such that $\#A = \#B$ coincides with his/her "index." When $\#X + 1 < n$, the number of "layers" is less than sufficient to assign each individual a "layer" for him/her to dictate. In this case, however, we can divide the population into two groups, group 1 and group 2. Group 2, which consists of $(\#X + 1)$ individuals including the nonconsequentialist, will dictate over specific extended social alternatives assigned to him/her. The remainder of individuals form group 1, which consists of $(n - \#X - 1)$ individuals, will decide who in group 2 should dictate which "layer" of alternatives, allowing the nonconsequentialist to dictate over (x, A) and (y, B) with $\#A \neq \#B$. In this fashion, all individuals are assigned to actively participate in the process of social decision making.

and his ability is not nullified even in the homogeneous society where all individuals are nonconsequentialists.

20.5. Generalizations

Although our analysis so far invoked the simple cardinality measure of the richness of opportunities, which is often criticized for its naiveté, some of our results can go far beyond this special measure. To see this, let Θ be a complete ordering over $\mathcal{S}$ such that, for all A, $B \in \mathcal{S}$, $A\Theta B$ holds if and only if A contains no less opportunity than B. $P(\Theta)$ and $I(\Theta)$ stand, respectively, for the asymmetric part and the symmetric part of Θ. The set X of all conventionally defined social states can be partitioned by $I(\Theta)$. Let $\mathcal{K}_\Theta$ denote the family of equivalence classes in accordance with Θ. For each $A \in \mathcal{S}$, let $E_\Theta(A) \in \mathcal{K}_\Theta$ be the equivalence class determined by A. We can then define a linear ordering Θ^* on $\mathcal{K}_\Theta$ by

$$\text{For all } E_\Theta(A), E_\Theta(B) \in \mathcal{K}_\Theta, E_\Theta(A)\Theta^* E_\Theta(B) \Leftrightarrow A\Theta B. \quad (20.8)$$

In what follows, we assume that $(\Theta, \mathcal{K}_\Theta)$ satisfies the following two basic requirements:

Assumption U. The richness measure of opportunities, Θ, is unanimously held by all individuals in the society.

Assumption R. There exist at least two equivalence classes in $\mathcal{K}_\Theta$.

The definitions of consequentialists and nonconsequentialists now read as follows:

Extreme Consequentialist. An individual $i \in N$ is said to be an *extreme consequentialist* if, for all (x, A), $(x, B) \in \Omega$, it is true that $(x, A) \sim_i (x, B)$.

Strong Consequentialist. An individual $i \in N$ is said to be a *strong consequentialist* if, for all (x, A), $(y, B) \in \Omega$,

(a) if $(x, \{x\}) \sim_i (y, \{y\})$, then $A\Theta B \Leftrightarrow (x, A) \succsim_i (y, B)$; and
(b) if $(x, \{x\}) \succ_i (y, \{y\})$, then $(x, A) \succ_i (y, B)$.

NONCONSEQUENTIALIST. An individual $i \in N$ is said to be a *nonconsequentialist* if, for all $(x, A), (y, B) \in \Omega$,

(a) $AP(\Theta)B \Rightarrow (x, A) \succ_i (y, B)$; and
(b) $AI(\Theta)B \Rightarrow [(x, A) \succsim_i (y, B) \Leftrightarrow (x, \{x\}) \succsim_i (y, \{y\})]$.

We can now generalize our results in Sections 20.3 and 20.4 for the framework discussed in this section as follows. The proofs of these results are similar to those of Theorems 20.1, 20.2, 20.3 and 20.4, and we may safely omit them.

THEOREM 20.5. Suppose that all individuals are extreme consequentialists. Then there exists no extended social welfare function f with the domain $D_f(E)$ that satisfies SP, ND, and either IIA (i) or IIA (ii).

THEOREM 20.6. Suppose that there exists at least one uniform extreme consequentialist over $D_f(E \cup S)$ and at least one uniform strong consequentialist over $D_f(E \cup S)$ in the society. Then there exists an extended social welfare function f with the domain $D_f(E \cup S)$ that satisfies SP, IIA (i), IIA (ii), and ND.

THEOREM 20.7. Suppose that all individuals are strong consequentialists. Then there exists no extended social welfare function f with the domain $D_f(S)$ that satisfies SP, FIIA, and ND.

THEOREM 20.8. Suppose that there exists at least one uniform nonconsequentialist over $D_f(N)$. Then there exists an extended social welfare function f with the domain $D_f(N)$ that satisfies SP, IIA, and ND.

Thus, our basic results in this essay do not in fact hinge on the somewhat controversial cardinality measure of the richness of opportunities.

20.6. Concluding Remarks

This essay developed two extended analytical frameworks of social choice theory in order to check how and to what extent Arrow's general impossibility theorem hinges on his basic assumption of welfarist consequentialism. Another motivation of our analysis was to see whether or not Arrow's observation that "the possibility of social welfare judgments rests upon a similarity of attitudes toward social alternatives" could be substantiated in the arena that is wider than welfarist consequentialism.

The starting point of our analysis was an extended individual preference ordering defined over the pairs of social states and opportunity sets to which these social states belong. This concept enabled us to formulate a wider conceptual framework for analyzing social choice, and we could identify two such frameworks: the *consequentialist framework* and the *nonconsequentialist framework*. The former is concerned with a society in which at least one consequentialist, either extreme or strong, exists, whereas the latter is concerned with a society in which at least one nonconsequentialist exists.

Within this consequentialist framework, it was shown that the Arrovian impossibility theorem strenuously comes back if all individuals are either extreme consequentialists or strong consequentialists, whereas a more diverse society resided in simultaneously by at least one extreme consequentialist and at least one strong consequentialist admits the existence of an Arrovian extended social welfare function. In this sense, it is the *diversity* rather than the *similarity* of individual attitudes toward social alternatives in the society that contributes to resolve the Arrow impossibility theorem within the consequentialist framework. The logical fate of the nonconsequentialist society is rather different. Indeed, within the nonconsequentialist framework, it was possible to guarantee the existence of an Arrovian extended social welfare function as long as there exists at least one nonconsequentialist in the society, and this ability is not nullified even if the society is *homogeneous* so that all individuals are nonconsequentialists. Although these results are first established by using a naive cardinality measure of the richness of opportunities, their validity does not hinge on this arguably controversial measure.

It is hoped that our results, though simple, would be suggestive enough to motivate further exploration of the wider conceptual frameworks of social choice theory.

20.7. References

[1] Arrow, K. J., *Social Choice and Individual Values*, New York: John Wiley & Sons, 1951; 2nd edn., 1963.

[2] Arrow, K. J., "Arrow's Theorem," in J. Eatwell, M. Milgate, and P. Newman, eds., *The New Palgrave: A Dictionary of Economics,* Vol. 1, London: Macmillan, 1987, 124–126.

[3] Black, D., *The Theory of Committees and Elections*, Cambridge, UK: Cambridge University Press, 1958.

[4] Bossert, W., P. K. Pattanaik, and Y. Xu, "Ranking Opportunity Sets: An Axiomatic Approach," *Journal of Economic Theory* **63**, 1994, 326–345.

[5] Dworkin, G., "Is More Choice Better Than Less?" in P. A. French, T. E. Uehling, Jr., and H. K. Wettstein, eds., *Midwest Studies in Philosophy*, Vol. VII, *Social and Political Philosophy*, Minneapolis: University of Minnesota Press, 1982, 47–61.

[6] Gravel, N., "Can a Ranking of Opportunity Sets Attach an Intrinsic Importance to Freedom of Choice?" *American Economic Review: Papers and Proceedings* **84**, 1994, 454–458.

[7] Gravel, N., "Ranking Opportunity Sets on the Basis of Their Freedom of Choice and Their Ability to Satisfy Preferences: A Difficulty," *Social Choice and Welfare* **15**, 1998, 371–382.

[8] Hammond, P. J., "Social Choice: The Science of the Impossible?" in G. R. Feiwel, ed., *Arrow and the Foundations of the Theory of Economic Policy*, London: Macmillan, 1987, 116–131.

[9] Iwata, Y., "A Variant of Non-Consequentialism and Its Characterization," *Mathematical Social Sciences* **53**, 2007, 284–295.

[10] Kuga, K., and H. Nagatani, "Voter Antagonism and the Paradox of Voting," *Econometrica* **42**, 1974, 1045–1067.

[11] Pattanaik, P. K., and Y. Xu, "On Ranking Opportunity Sets in Terms of Freedom of Choice," *Recherches Economiques de Louvain* **56**, 1990, 383–390.

[12] Pattanaik, P. K., and Y. Xu, "On Preference and Freedom," *Theory and Decision* **44**, 1998, 173–198.

[13] Pattanaik, P. K., and Y. Xu, "On Diversity and Freedom of Choice," *Mathematical Social Sciences* **40**, 2000, 123–130.

[14] Sen, A. K., *Collective Choice and Social Welfare*, San Francisco: Holden-Day, 1970; republished, Amsterdam: North-Holland, 1979.

[15] Sen, A. K., "Liberty, Unanimity and Rights," *Economica* **43**, 1976, 217–245.

[16] Sen, A. K., "Utilitarianism and Welfarism," *Journal of Philosophy* **76**, 1979, 463–489.

[17] Sen, A. K., "Personal Utilities and Public Judgements: Or What's Wrong with Welfare Economics," *Economic Journal* **76**, 1979, 537–558.

[18] Sen, A. K., *Commodities and Capabilities*, Amsterdam: North-Holland, 1985.

[19] Sen, A. K., "Rationality and Social Choice," *American Economic Review* **85**, 1995, 1–24.

[20] Sen, A. K., "Maximization and the Act of Choice," *Econometrica* **65**, 1996, 745–779.

[21] Sen, A. K., *Rationality and Freedom*, Cambridge, Mass.: Harvard University Press, 2002.

[22] Sen, A. K., and B. Williams, eds., *Utilitarianism and Beyond*, Cambridge, UK: Cambridge University Press, 1982.

[23] Suzumura, K., "On the Consistency of Libertarian Claims," *Review of Economic Studies* **45**, 1978, 329–342. Essay 13 of this volume.

[24] Suzumura, K., *Rational Choice, Collective Decisions and Social Welfare*, New York: Cambridge University Press, 1983. Reprinted in paperback, 2009.

[25] Suzumura, K., "Welfare, Rights, and Social Choice Procedure: A Perspective," *Analyse & Kritik* **18**, 1996, 20–37. Essay 16 of this volume.

[26] Suzumura, K., "Consequences, Opportunities, and Procedures," *Social Choice and Welfare* **6**, 1999, 17–40. Essay 17 of this volume.

[27] Suzumura, K., "Welfare Economics beyond Welfarist Consequentialism," *Japanese Economic Review* **51**, 2000, 1–32. Essay 27 of this volume.

[28] Suzumura, K., and Y. Xu, "Characterizations of Consequentialism and Nonconsequentialism," *Journal of Economic Theory* **101**, 2001, 423–436. Essay 18 of this volume.

PART VI

COMPETITION, COOPERATION, AND ECONOMIC WELFARE

Introduction to Part VI

To go beyond is as wrong as to fall short.
—CONFUCIUS, *Analects*, sixth century BC.
Translated by James Legge

You never know what is enough unless you know what is more than enough.
—WILLIAM BLAKE, "Proverbs of Hell," from his *The Marriage of Heaven and Hell*
Originally published in 1790

Paul Samuelson [7, Chapter VIII, p. 203] started his justly famous chapter on "Welfare Economics" with the following remark: "At least from the time of the physiocrats and Adam Smith there has never been absent from the main body of economic literature the feeling that in some sense perfect competition represented an optimal situation. . . . Although this doctrine is often thought to be conservative or reactionary in its implication and to reflect the 'kept' status of the economist, it is important to emphasize that it was 'radical' in the eighteenth century, and there is some evidence from events of the last decades . . . that it has become a thorn in the side of what are usually thought of as conservative interests."

Contrary to this long-lasting belief in the welfare-optimizing effects of competition, there has been a strenuous conventional belief in the *social excessiveness* of competition among public officials and the man or woman on the street in Japan. Suffice it to quote a firsthand testimony recorded by one of the most influential intellectuals at the dawn of modern Japan, Yukichi Fukuzawa, who had to confront a high-ranking public official in the Tokugawa shogunate regime:[1]

1. Fukuzawa [2, p. 190].

> I was reading Chamber's book on economics. When I spoke of the book to a certain high official in the treasury bureau one day, he became much interested and wanted me to show him the translation. . . . I began translating it. . . . When I came upon the word "competition" for which there was no equivalent in Japanese, and I was obliged to use an invention of my own, *kyoso*, literally, "race-fight."
>
> When the official saw my translation, he appeared much impressed. Then he said suddenly, "Here is the word 'fight.' What does it mean? It is such an unpeaceful word."
>
> "That is nothing new," I replied. "That is exactly what all Japanese merchants are doing. For instance, if one merchant begins to sell things cheap, his neighbor will try to sell them even cheaper. Or if one merchant improves his merchandise to attract more buyers, another will try to take the trade from him by offering goods of still better quality. Thus all merchants "race and fight" and this is the way money values are fixed. This process is termed *kyoso* in the science of economics."
>
> "I understood. But don't you think there is too much effort in Western affairs?"
>
> "It isn't too much effort. It is the fundamentals of the world of commerce."
>
> "Yes, perhaps," went on the official. "I understand the idea, but the word 'fight' is not conducive to peace. I could not take the paper with that word to the chancellor."

These two pieces of conventional wisdom regarding the welfare effects of competition have been influential ever since, and they have supplied sharply contrasting guidelines for the two facets of economic policies in Japan.[2] On the one hand, the guiding principle of Japanese industrial policy during the rapid growth era was allegedly provided by the conventional belief in the social excessiveness of competition.[3] On the other hand, the theoretical basis of Japanese competition policy, which was transplanted from the mother country of competition policy, viz., the United States of America, as an

2. I have long thought that this conventional belief in the social excessiveness of competition is indigenous to Japan, but I am convinced that it is rather widely held in many European countries and elsewhere as well.
3. See Itoh, Kiyono, Okuno-Fujiwara, and Suzumura [3], Komiya [4], and Komiya, Okuno, and Suzumura [5] for our research on Japanese industrial policy. See also Suzumura [9; 10] for the subsequent synthesis of the analysis of welfare and competition.

integral part of postwar economic democratization of Japan, has been widely believed to have its roots in the conventional belief in the welfare-enhancing effects of competition. No wonder that these two policies had not hit it off well with each other from the beginning up until now.

We seem to be confronted with an antinomy. Which one between these two assertions of conventional wisdom should we choose and enthrone to the status of the foundational guiding principle of microeconomic policy? Or is there any other way of resolving the confrontation between the two? Part VI consists of four essays on welfare and competition with the purpose of tackling the antinomy in question.

Essay 21 ("Entry Barriers and Economic Welfare") is meant to cast serious doubt on the validity of the welfare-enhancing effects of competition. The point of departure is an observation by William Baumol [1, p. 2] to the following effect: "The standard analysis [of industrial organization] leaves us with the impression that there is a rough continuum, in terms of desirability of industry performance, ranging from unregulated pure monopoly as the pessimal [sic] arrangement to perfect competition as the ideal, with relative efficiency in resource allocation increasing monotonically as the number of firms expands." By making use of Baumol's observation as a workable test hypothesis, we examine whether or not there is a well-defined meaning in which the social excessiveness of competition may make sense. Using a homogeneous-product Cournot oligopoly model as the canvas of our discourse, we answer our own question in the affirmative.

The basic *excess entry theorem*, so called, is established by means of a partial equilibrium model.[4] To gauge the robustness of this result, Essay 22 ("Oligopolistic Competition and Economic Welfare: A General Equilibrium Analysis of Entry Regulation and Tax-Subsidy Schemes") constructs a simple two-sector general equilibrium model, where one sector engages in oligopolistic competition, and the other sector is perfectly competitive. As is always the case with two-sector models of trade, tax, and/or growth, we need a hypothesis on the relative factor intensities between the two sectors. Both sectors use two factors of production, viz., capital and labor. The factor intensity condition in our mixed oligopolistic/perfectly competitive economy

4. Mankiw and Whinston [6] also proved a similar result. However, our excess entry theorem is completely independent of their work.

is more complicated than the case with overall perfect competition. However, we may identify the condition of *no capital intensity twist*, under which the message of the excess entry theorem can be kept intact even in the presence of general equilibrium interactions.

Another direction to explore the robustness of the excess entry theorem is to introduce a further stage of oligopolistic interactions. In the original model of Essay 21, there are only two stages of interactions. The additional stage introduced in Essay 23 ("Symmetric Cournot Oligopoly and Economic Welfare: A Synthesis") is that of R&D commitment, where those firms that have decided either to enter into or to stay within the industry decide on the R&D investment for cost reduction in order to sharpen their competitive edge against rival firms in the stage of market competition. The subgame perfect equilibrium of this three-stage model is examined, and the essence of the partial equilibrium prototype of the excess entry theorem is shown to be kept almost intact even in the presence of a further stage of R&D competition.

Viewed as a model of R&D investment by oligopolistic competitors, the model in Essay 23 lacks two important features. The first lacuna is that of R&D spillovers among firms, and the second lacuna is that of R&D collaborations among otherwise competitive firms. Needless to say, an explicit collaboration among competitive firms in the product market is an outright act of cartel and thus infringes upon competition law. This is not the case with R&D collaboration insofar as firms are committed to compete in the product market. Essay 24 is devoted to the welfare analysis of R&D collaboration among otherwise competitive oligopolistic firms in the presence of R&D spillovers. Hence the title "Cooperative and Noncooperative R&D in an Oligopoly with Spillovers."

Although the four essays in Part VI cover only a small part of welfare economics of micro-economic policies such as industrial policy and competition policy, it is hoped that they serve to exemplify the use and usefulness of welfare economics in action.

References

[1] Baumol, W. J., "Contestable Markets: An Uprising in the Theory of Industry Structure," *American Economic Review: Papers and Proceedings* **72**, 1982, 1–15.

[2] Fukuzawa, Y., *The Autobiography of Fukuzawa Yukichi*, 1899. English translation by E. Kiyooka with an Introduction by S. Koizumi, Tokyo: Hokuseisha Press, 1960.

[3] Itoh, M., K. Kiyono, M. Okuno-Fujiwara, and K. Suzumura, *Economic Analysis of Industrial Policy*, San Diego: Academic Press, 1991.
[4] Komiya, R., "Planning in Japan," in M. Bornstein, ed., *Economic Planning: East and West*, Cambridge, Mass.: Ballinger, 1975, 189–227.
[5] Komiya, R., M. Okuno, and K. Suzumura, eds., *Industrial Policy of Japan*, San Diego: Academic Press, 1988.
[6] Mankiw, N. G., and M. D. Whinston, "Free Entry and Social Efficiency," *Rand Journal of Economics* **17**, 1986, 48–58.
[7] Samuelson, P. A., *Foundations of Economic Analysis*, Cambridge, Mass.: Harvard University Press, 1947. Enlarged edn., 1983.
[8] Schmalensee, R., "Is More Competition Necessarily Good?" *Industrial Organization Review* **4**, 1976, 120–121.
[9] Suzumura, K., *Competition, Commitment and Welfare*, Oxford: Oxford University Press, 1995.
[10] Suzumura, K., "Excess Entry Theorems after 25 Years," *Japanese Economic Review* **63**, 2012, 152–170.
[11] von Weizsäcker, C. C., "A Welfare Analysis of Barriers to Entry," *Bell Journal of Economics* **11**, 1980, 399–420.
[12] von Weizsäcker, C. C., *Barriers to Entry: A Theoretical Treatment*, Berlin: Springer, 1980.

ESSAY 21

Entry Barriers and Economic Welfare

21.1. Introduction

Recent studies in the theoretical industrial organization have uncovered several instances that cast serious doubt on the reasonableness of "a widespread belief that increasing competition will increase welfare" (Stiglitz [14, p. 184]).[1] It has been shown that there are cases, which are not altogether unreasonable, where social welfare will be increased by strengthening, rather than weakening, the protection of incumbent firms from the threat of potential entry. This is in sharp contrast with the traditional belief.[2] What is not known, however, is how robust these "pathologies" in fact are. We intend

First published in *Review of Economic Studies* **54**, 1987, pp. 157–167 as a joint paper with K. Kiyono. We are indebted to Motoshige Itoh and Masahiro Okuno for their helpful comments on an earlier draft. Thanks are also due to an anonymous referee of *Review of Economic Studies* for his/her incisive comments, which helped us prepare the published version. Partial financial support from the Japan Economic Research Foundation and the Japan Securities Scholarship Foundation is gratefully acknowledged.

1. As Baumol [1, p. 2] has observed, "the standard analysis [of industrial organization] leaves us with the impression that there is a rough continuum, in terms of desirability of industry performance, ranging from unregulated pure monopoly as the pessimal arrangement to perfect competition as the ideal, with relative efficiency in resource allocation increasing monotonically as the number of firms expands." Baumol's contestable market theory casts serious doubt on the validity of this impression; so does our excess entry theorem to be established in this essay from a somewhat different angle.
2. Weizsäcker's analysis [17; 18] of the entry in a Cournot market is a good case in point. See also Dixit and Stiglitz [2], Kiyono [6], Spence [13], Suzumura [15], and Tandon [16].

to settle this problem by proving two "excess entry theorems" in the quasi-Cournot (parametric conjectural variations) homogeneous oligopoly model (Seade [11; 12]).

In the first place, we presuppose the existence of a strong ("first-best") government that could costlessly enforce the marginal-cost pricing principle by firms in an oligopolistic market and regulate new entry and/or exit in pursuit of "first-best" social welfare optimization. It is shown that the number of firms at the free-entry equilibrium exceeds the "first-best" welfare-optimizing number of firms. The result has already been noted by von Weizsäcker [17; 18] and others in terms of numerical examples. Our Theorem 21.1, presented in Section 21.3, asserts that this phenomenon always holds true for the family of quasi-Cournot models. An implication of this result is that the existence of entry barriers that protect incumbent firms from potential competitors is not necessarily welfare-decreasing, in sharp contrast with the traditional belief.

A problem remains with Theorem 21.1, however, in that an omnipotent first-best government does not exist in reality, and the first-best ideal is unrealizable in the actual economy.[3] Therefore, even if the intervention by a first-best government with a view to restricting the number of firms within an industry may be welfare-improving, it does not justify the intervention by a down-to-earth government that lacks the leverage of optimal price regulation. What is needed is an evaluation of the social gains from alternative feasible government actions. This is precisely what we intend to perform in Section 21.4 of this essay. In other words, we analyze an explicit "second-best" social welfare optimum in an oligopolistic economy and show that the "second-best" number of firms will fall short of the number of firms at the free-entry equilibrium if the marginal revenue of each firm decreases with an increase of the output of other firms taken together. By the "second-best" we here mean that oligopolistic (marginal cost equals marginal revenue) pricing is taken for granted by an entry-regulating government pursuing social welfare optimization. The implications of our analyses and several qualifications on our results will be discussed in the final Section 21.5.

3. See von Weizsäcker [17, p. 400] and Schmalensee [10] on this point.

21.2. The Model

In this section, we formulate a partial equilibrium model of oligopolistic interactions among a finite number of firms, where firms compete in terms of quantities produced. The basic assumptions, which are maintained throughout this Essay 21, are threefold. First, the product of the industry is homogeneous, and not differentiated. Second, the equilibrium concept that we use is the symmetric quasi-Cournot equlibrium, where each firm conjectures the competitive response of rival firms by means of the constant coefficient of conjectural variations. Third, if left unregulated, new firms (resp. incumbent firms) will enter into (resp. exit from) the quasi-Cournot market depending on whether profit is positive (resp. negative) at the quasi-Cournot equilibrium.

21.2.1. Quasi-Cournot Equilibrium: Definition and Characterization

We will be concerned with a model of an oligopolistic industry producing a homogenous good. All firms are assumed to be technologically as well as behaviorally identical. The number of firms in the industry will be denoted by n. The output of the ith firm is z_i $(i = 1, 2, \ldots, n)$ so that $Q := \Sigma_{i=1}^{n} z_i$ represents the industry output. The cost function of each firm and the inverse market demand function are denoted by $C(z_i)$ $(i = 1, 2, \ldots, n)$ and $p = f(Q)$, respectively. It is assumed that C and f are continuously differentiable as often as is required by the following analysis. The profit of the ith firm will then be given by

$$\pi_i(z_i; Q_i) = z_i f(z_i + Q_i) - C(z_i), \tag{21.1}$$

where $Q_i := \Sigma_{j \neq i} z_j = Q - z_i$ $(i = 1, 2, \ldots, n)$. Let μ denote the *coefficient of conjectural variations*, viz., $\mu := \partial Q / \partial z_i$ $(i = 1, 2, \ldots, n)$. The profit-maximizing output z_i of the ith firm corresponding to the output of all other firms taken together, Q_i, will then satisfy

$$f(z_i + Q_i) + \mu z_i f'(z_i + Q_i) - C'(z_i) = 0 \tag{21.2}$$

and

$$2\mu f'(z_i + Q_i) + \mu^2 z_i f''(z_i + Q_i) - C''(z_i) < 0. \tag{21.3}$$

Throughout this essay, we assume the following.

Assumption A1. The quasi-Cournot conjecture prevails, viz., μ is a positive constant that is less than n.[4]

Assumption A2. The inverse demand function satisfies $-M \leq f'(Q) < 0$ for some $M > 0$ and for all $Q > 0$.

Assumption A3. The cost function satisfies (i) $C'(z) > 0$ for all $z > 0$ and (ii) either $C(0) > 0$ or $\lim_{z \to 0^+} C''(z) := C''(0) < 0$.

Assumption A4. The marginal cost decreases, if ever it does, at a slower rate than the perceived demand curve, viz.,

$$\mu f'(z_i + Q_i) < C''(z_i) \tag{21.4}$$

for all $z_i > 0$ and $Q_i > 0$ $(i = 1, 2, \ldots, n)$.

Assumption A5. The marginal revenue of any firm is a decreasing function of the aggregate output of the other firms, viz.,

$$f'(z_i + Q_i) + \mu z_i f''(z_i + Q_i) < 0 \tag{21.5}$$

for all $z_i > 0$ and $Q_i > 0$ $(i = 1, 2, \ldots, n)$.

Assumption A6. For any n and μ satisfying assumption A1, a symmetric quasi-Cournot equilibrium uniquely exists, and is defined as triplet $\{z(n, \mu), Q(n, \mu), p(n, \mu)\}$ of the firm output $z(n, \mu)$, the industry output $Q(n, \mu)$, and the price $p(n, \mu)$, satisfying

$$f(nz(n, \mu)) + \mu z(n, \mu) f'(nz(n, \mu)) - C'(z(n, \mu)) = 0 \tag{21.6}$$

4. The gist of this assumption is that each firm can predict with confidence the effects of its action on the other firms taken together. Note that the Cournot conjecture, to the effect that each firm supposes that none of the other firms will deviate from their current course of action if the given firm deviates, is a special case of A1, where $\mu = 1$, whereas if all firms are fully aware of their interactions and collude as if they formed a cartel, we have another special case of A1, where $\mu = n$. It follows that $m := n/\mu$ may be construed to be the "effective" number of Cournot oligopolists. In general, $0 < \mu \leq 1$ (resp. $1 < \mu \leq n$) may be construed to correspond to the situation of "struggle" (resp. "collusion") among firms. We owe these observations to Seade [12].

and

$$Q(n, \mu) := nz(n, \mu), \quad p(n, \mu) := f(Q(n, \mu)). \tag{21.7}$$

21.2.2. Effective Number of Firms and Quantity Adjustment Process

To simplify our notation, let us introduce the following symbols:

$$m := \frac{n}{\mu}, \quad K(n, \mu) := 1 - \frac{C''(z(n, \mu))}{\mu f'(Q(n, \mu))}, \quad E(Q) := \frac{Qf''(Q)}{f'(Q)}. \tag{21.8}$$

In what follows, m will be referred to as the "effective" number of firms.[5] In these terms, (21.3) may be reduced to

$$E(Q(n, \mu)) + mK(n, \mu) + m > 0 \tag{21.9}$$

at the symmetric quasi-Cournot equilibrium.

Note that assumptions A1, A2, A4 and (21.8) together entail

$$K(n, \mu) > 0, \tag{21.10}$$

whereas assumptions A1, A2, (21.5), and (21.8) together entail

$$E(Q(n, \mu)) + m > 0. \tag{21.11}$$

Comparing (21.9) with (21.10) and (21.11), we may assert that assumptions A1, A2, A4 and A5 ensure that the second-order condition (21.9) for profit maximization is satisfied.

Note also that assumptions A4 and A5 are sufficient for an adjustment process in a quasi-Cournot market,

$$\dot{z}_i = \alpha_i \{z_i(Q_i) - z_i\}, \quad \alpha_i > 0, \tag{21.12}$$

5. See footnote 4.

to be dynamically stable, where $z_i(Q_i)$ is a solution to (21.2) for a given Q_i and $\dot{z}_i$ denotes the time derivative of z_i.[6]

21.2.3. Socially First-Best Output: Marginal Cost Principle

For each fixed number of firms n, the *socially optimal firm output* $z_*(n)$ may be defined as the unique maximizer of the market surplus function, viz.,

$$z_*(n) := \arg\max_{z>0} \left\{ \int_0^{nz} f(x)dx - nC(z) \right\}. \tag{21.13}$$

As is well known, $z_*(n)$ defined by (21.13) satisfies the *marginal cost principle:*

$$f(nz_*(n)) = C'(z_*(n)). \tag{21.14}$$

21.2.4. Entry-Exit Dynamics of the Quasi-Cournot Market

Finally, let us consider the entry-exit dynamics of the quasi-Cournot market. Suppose that each firm earns positive (resp. negative) profit at the symmetric quasi-Cournot equilibrium. Then there exists an incentive for a new firm (resp. an incumbent firm) to enter into (resp. to exit from) this industry. Treating the number of firms as a continuous variable, we formulate these entry-exit dynamics by a differential equation:[7]

$$\dot{n} = \beta\{f(nz(n, \mu))z(n, \mu) - C(z(n, \mu))\}, \quad \beta > 0, \tag{21.15}$$

where the expression within the curly brackets denotes profit, β is an adjustment coefficient, and $\dot{n}$ denotes the time derivative of n.

Let $n_e(\mu)$ denote the stationary point of (21.15) corresponding to $\mu > 0$, viz.,

$$f(n_e(\mu)z(n_e(\mu), \mu))z(n_e(\mu), \mu) = C(z(n_e(\mu), \mu)). \tag{21.16}$$

6. See Hahn [4] and Seade [11].

7. Treating the number of firms as a continuous variable is a common practice in the analysis of firm entry, which is followed by Dixit and Stiglitz [2], Okuguchi [7], Ruffin [9], Seade [12], and von Weizsäcker [17; 18], among many others. See Seade [12, p. 482] for an attempt to defend this common practice. See also Remark 4, in Section 21.5.

We relegate the proof of the uniqueness and stability of $n_e(\mu)$ to Appendix 21.A. In what follows, the symmetric quasi-Cournot equilibrium, viz., $\{z(n_e(\mu), \mu), Q(n_e(\mu), \mu), p(n_e(\mu), \mu)\}$ will be referred to as the *free-entry quasi-Cournot equilibrium*, whereas $n_e(\mu)$ will be called the *equilibrium number of firms*.

21.3. The First-Best Excess Entry Theorem

The task of this and next sections is to gauge the welfare performance of competition among oligopolistic firms. If we leave firms free to compete with each other under no outside interventions, the unconstrained competition will cease when and only when firms settle in the free-entry quasi-Cournot equilibrium among the equilibrium number of firms, to be called the free-entry equilibrium for short. To bring the welfare performance of the free-entry equilibrium into clear relief by contrast, we make use of two reference states, viz., the *first-best welfare optimum* and the *second-best welfare optimum.* Both states of affairs are identified by means of the market surplus function, the point of bifurcation being how powerful is the government in controlling the market behavior of oligopolistic competitors. The *first-best government* is able to enforce the marginal cost principle to all oligopolistic firms and control the entry-exit of firms from the point of view of social welfare optimization. In contrast, the *second-best government* is unable to enforce the marginal cost principle to all oligopolistic firms and leave each firm to freely pursue the private target of profit maximization. Subject to this freedom on the part of oligopolistic firms, the second-best government can still control the entry (resp. exit) of new (resp. incumbent) firms from the point of view of social welfare optimization.

Section 21.3 is devoted to the welfare performance of the free-entry equilibrium subject to the controlling power of the first-best government, whereas Section 21.4 is focused on the welfare performance of the free-entry equilibrium subject to the controlling power of the second-best government.

21.3.1. Performance of the First-Best Firm Output

Let us now set about analyzing the first-best welfare optimum. Our first order of business is to examine the property of the socially optimal firm output $z_*(n)$ vis-à-vis that of the equilibrium firm output $z(n, \mu)$.

LEMMA 21.1. For each $n > 0$ and $\mu > 0$, (a) $z_*(n) > z(n, \mu)$ holds true, and (b) $z(n, \mu)$ is a decreasing function of $\mu > 0$.

PROOF. See Appendix 21.B ∎

Several straightforward implications of Lemma 21.1 are worth mentioning at this stage. First, if we define $Q_*(n) := nz_*(n)$ and $p_*(n) := f(Q_*(n))$, we may conclude from assumption A2 and Lemma 21.1(a) that $Q_*(n) > Q(n, \mu)$ and $p_*(n) < p(n, \mu)$ hold true for all n and μ satisfying $0 < \mu < n$. Therefore, for any number of firms $n > 0$ and conjectural coefficient $\mu > 0$ such that the "effective" number of firms m exceeds one, the equilibrium industry output (resp. the equilibrium price) is less than (resp. greater than) the socially optimal industry output (resp. socially optimal price). Second, if we let μ converge to 0 fixing n, $z(n, \mu)$ increases by virtue of Lemma 21.1(b), and it is bounded from above by $z_*(n)$, thanks to Lemma 21.1(a). Therefore, $z(n, 0) := \lim_{\mu \to 0} z(n, \mu)$ exists. On the other hand, if we let μ converge to 0 in (21.6), taking the boundedness of $\{z(n, \mu)\}$ into consideration, we obtain by continuity that

$$f(nz(n, 0)) = c'(z(n, 0)) \tag{21.17}$$

holds true. Comparing (21.14) and (21.17) and noting the uniqueness of $z_*(n)$, we may conclude that

$$\lim_{\mu \to 0} z(n, \mu) := z(n, 0) = z_*(n) \tag{21.18}$$

holds true for every $n > 0$.[8]

21.3.2. Response of the Equilibrium Number of Firms to a Change in the Conjectural Coefficient

How about the effect of a change in n on the level of firm output? First, differentiating (21.14) with respect to n, we obtain

8. Letting μ converge to 0 corresponds to a situation where each and every firm becomes less and less aware of the effect of its own output change on the industry output. Therefore, (21.18) may be construed as implying that *the equilibrium firm output converges to the socially optimal firm output when the "subjective size" of a firm becomes infinitesimal.*

$$z'_*(n) := \frac{d}{dn} z_*(n) = -\frac{z_*(n)}{n - \frac{C''(z_*(n))}{f'(nz_*(n))}}, \tag{21.19}$$

which is negative for all n satisfying $n > \mu$. Therefore, *the socially optimal level of firm output decreases in response to the increase in the number of firms in the industry*. Secondly, differentiating (21.6) with respect to n, we obtain

$$z_n(n, \mu) := \frac{\partial}{\partial n} z(n, \mu) = -\frac{z(n, \mu)}{n} \frac{E(Q(n, \mu)) + m}{E(Q(n, \mu)) + m + K(n, \mu)}, \tag{21.20}$$

which is negative by virtue of (21.10) and (21.11). Therefore, *the equilibrium level of firm output decreases in response to the increase in the number of firms in the industry*.

21.3.3. Change of the Equilibrium and Optimal Firm Outputs in Response to a Change in the Number of Firms

How will the equilibrium number of firms $n_e(\mu)$ respond to a change in $\mu > 0$? We may easily verify the following:

LEMMA 21.2. $n'_e(\mu) > 0$ for all $\mu > 0$.

PROOF. See Appendix 21.C ∎

Roughly speaking, the message of this lemma may be summarized as follows: *The more collusive the interfirm relationship becomes, the more firms will there be in the industry at the free-entry quasi-Cournot equilibrium*. An intuitive reason for this result is that, as the industry becomes more collusive, the profit of each firm increases, thereby enticing more prospective firms to enter into this industry.

21.3.4. The First-Best Market Surplus Function and Its Maximization

So much for preliminaries. Let us now examine the consequence of the intervention by a price- and entry-regulating government in pursuit of first-best welfare optimization. Defining the *first-best market surplus function* by

$$W_f(n) := \int_0^{nz_*(n)} f(x)dx - nC(z_*(n)), \tag{21.21}$$

we define the *first-best number of firms* n_f by

$$n_f := \arg\max_{n>0} W_f(n). \tag{21.22}$$

In order to characterize n_f, we differentiate $W_f(n)$ to obtain

$$W_f'(n) = f(nz_*(n))z_*(n) - C(z_*(n)), \tag{21.23}$$

where use is made of (21.14) in deleting the terms involving $z_*'(n)$.

Differentiating (21.23) and making use of (21.14) and (21.19), we obtain

$$W_f''(n) = -\frac{\{z_*(n)\}^2 C''(z_*(n))}{n - \frac{C''(z_*(n))}{f'(nz_*(n))}}. \tag{21.24}$$

It follows that $W_f'(n) = 0$ holds true if and only if

$$f(nz_*(n)) = \frac{C(z_*(n))}{z_*(n)}, \tag{21.25}$$

viz., *price equals average cost*, whereas $W_f''(n) < 0$ holds true under assumptions A1, A2, and A3 if and only if $C''(z_*(n)) > 0$. Therefore, the first-best number of firms n_f is characterized by (21.25) if the marginal cost is increasing.

We are now at the stage of presenting the first main result of this essay.

THEOREM 21.1 (FIRST-BEST EXCESS ENTRY THEOREM). Assume that assumptions A1–A6 hold true. Assume further that (i) the marginal cost is increasing; and (ii) the nominal as well as the "effective" number of firms exceeds one at the free-entry quasi-Cournot equilibrium. Then the equilibrium number of firms $n_e(\mu)$ exceeds the first-best number of firms n_f.

PROOF. See Appendix 21.D. ■

Among the conditions A1–A6, which lie behind Theorem 21.1, A5 may seem to be rather stringent. However, we may replace it by a weaker assumption.

Assumption A5*.

$$E(Q(n,\mu)) + mK(n,\mu) + m > 0,$$
$$E(Q(n,\mu)) + K(n,\mu) + m > 0.$$

Note that the first part of A5* is nothing other than the second-order condition for profit maximization (21.9), whereas the second part is a necessary and sufficient condition, due to Seade [11; 12], for the dynamic stability of the process (21.12). To the extent that assumption A5* may replace A5, which may easily be verified, Theorem 21.1 can be placed on firmer ground.

21.4. The Second-Best Excess Entry Theorems

However desirable and appealing the first-best ideal may be, an actual, down-to-earth government may be unable to enforce the marginal cost principle, which is required by the first-best welfare optimization. Let us suppose, instead, that oligopolistic pricing has to be taken for granted by a down-to-earth government and try to see if the main message of our first-best excess entry theorem survives under this change in the leverage of a government.

21.4.1. The Second-Best Market Surplus Function and the Second-Best Excess Entry Theorem

As an auxiliary step, let us define the *second-best market surplus function* by

$$W_s(n,\mu) := \int_0^{nz(n,\mu)} f(x)dx - nC(z(n,\mu)), \qquad (21.26)$$

which enables us to define the *second-best number of firms* $n_s(\mu)$ by

$$n_s(\mu) := \arg\max_{n>0} W_s(n,\mu). \qquad (21.27)$$

In what follows, we show that $n_e(\mu) > n_s(\mu)$ necessarily holds true. Assume, to the contrary, that $n_s(\mu) \geq n_e(\mu)$ happens to be the case. Differentiating (21.26) with respect to n, we obtain

$$\frac{\partial}{\partial n} W_s(n, \mu)$$
$$= \mu\{z(n, \mu)\}^2 f'(nz(n, \mu)) \frac{E(Q(n, \mu)) + m}{E(Q(n, \mu)) + m + K(n, \mu)} + \pi(n, \mu), \tag{21.28}$$

where

$$\pi(n, \mu) := f(nz(n, \mu))z(n, \mu) - C(z(n, \mu)) \tag{21.29}$$

and use is made of (21.6) and (21.20). We then observe that

$$\frac{\partial}{\partial n}\pi(n, \mu)$$
$$= f'(nz(n, \mu))\{z(n, \mu)\}^2 \frac{mK(n, \mu) + E(Q(n, \mu)) + m}{E(Q(n, \mu)) + m + K(n, \mu)} < 0, \tag{21.30}$$

where use is made of (21.6), (21.10), (21.11), and (21.20). Since $\pi(n_e(\mu), \mu) = 0$ holds true by the very definition of $n_e(\mu)$, (21.30) implies that $\pi(n, \mu) < 0$ for all $n > n_e(\mu)$. It then follows that

$$\frac{\partial}{\partial n} W_s(n, \mu) < 0 \quad \text{for all } n \geq n_e(\mu), \tag{21.31}$$

where use is made of assumptions A2, (21.10), and (21.11). It follows from $n_s(\mu) \geq n_e(\mu)$ and (21.31) that $(\partial/\partial n)W_s(n_s(\mu), \mu) < 0$ holds true, in contradiction with the definition (21.27) of $n_s(\mu)$. By reductio ad absurdum, we may assert the following result.

Theorem 21.2 (second-best excess entry theorem). Assume that assumptions A1–A6 hold true. Then the equilibrium number of firms $n_e(\mu)$ exceeds the second-best number of firms $n_s(\mu)$.

Unlike Theorem 21.1, the validity of Theorem 21.2 hinges squarely on assumption A5. Indeed, if we replace assumption A5 by A5*, the assertion of Theorem 21.2 becomes untenable. Note also that each incumbent firm's profit is positive at the second-best optimum if assumption A5 is satisfied, viz., $\pi(n_s(\mu), \mu) > 0$, which may follow from (21.28) and $(\partial/\partial n)W_s(n_s(\mu), \mu) = 0$. Therefore, the financial viability of each firm at the second-best optimum is guaranteed.

21.4.2. The Second-Best Excess Entry Theorem at the Margin

An implication of (21.31) deserves special attention. It follows from (21.31) at $n = n_e(\mu)$ that $(\partial/\partial n)W_s(n_e(\mu), \mu) < 0$, viz., the second-best market surplus function $W_s(n, \mu)$ is a decreasing function of n at the equilibrium number of firms $n_e(\mu)$. Therefore, we have the following:[9]

THEOREM 21.3. Assume that Assumptions A1–A6 hold true. Then a small restriction in the number of firms at the free-entry quasi-Cournot equilibrium raises social welfare unambiguously.

The thrust of this result lies in the following fact: even if we cannot be sure where $n_s(\mu)$ is located exactly (e.g., because of uncertainty on the precise nature of the functions involved), we do know that "exit" is welfare-improving at the margin.

21.5. Concluding Remarks

In this essay, three excess entry theorems are presented. Presupposing the existence of a strong (first-best) government, the first theorem asserts that there are an excessive number of firms at the free-entry quasi-Cournot equilibrium vis-à-vis the first-best number of firms. The second theorem asserts that the main message of the first theorem essentially survives even if we presuppose a second-best government, which lacks the leverage of optimal price regulation, instead of an omnipotent first-best government. The third

9. Thanks are due to an anonymous referee of *Review of Economic Studies* who suggested this proposition to us.

theorem asserts that a marginal decrease of the number of firms at the free entry equilibrium always improves social welfare. In concluding this essay, several remarks are in order.

Remark 21.1. Our excess entry theorems are proved on the basis of a standard quasi-Cournot oligopoly model satisfying the stability conditions of Hahn [4] and/or Seade [11; 12]. As Seade himself observed, several counterintuitive results on entry into a Cournot market hold true only when the Cournot equilibrium is unstable. But the same charge cannot be raised against our excess entry theorems, which go counter to the widespread belief of the welfare-improving effects of increasing competitiveness.

Remark 21.2. Somewhat surprisingly, there are not many attempts in the literature to examine the second-best performance of the quasi-Cournot market. Harris [5] is a possible exception. Note, however, that Harris is concerned with the direct governmental control of the production decisions by private firms, subject only to the constraint that all firms are to be assured of nonnegative profit, in pursuit of the maximization of the market surplus function. In contrast, our second-best notion presupposes that the government is deprived of any direct control over the behavior of firms, leaving them to follow their own private incentives. Care should be taken with this contrast in comparing our results with those of Harris [5].

Remark 21.3. How does the first-best number of firms n_f compare with the second-best number of firms $n_s(\mu)$? We show in Appendix 21.E that no definite ranking is to be expected in general between n_f and $n_s(\mu)$. In contrast, the second-best number of firms in the sense of Harris [5] either coincides with or is less than the first-best number of firms, the difference in the latter case being exactly one.

Remark 21.4. Throughout this essay, we have followed a convention of treating the number of firms as a continuous variable. As a matter of fact, the continuous variables $n_e(\mu)$, n_f and $n_s(\mu)$ are to be regarded as continuous proxies to the discrete variables $N_e(\mu)$, N_f and $N_s(\mu)$, which are defined by $N_e(\mu) = [n_e(\mu)]$, $N_f = [n_f]$ (resp. $[n_f] + 1$) if $W_f([n_f]) \geq W_f([n_f] + 1)$ (resp. $W_f([n_f]) < W_f([n_f] + 1)$), and $N_s(\mu) = [n_s(\mu)]$ (resp. $[n_s(\mu)] + 1$) if $W_s([n_s(\mu)]) \geq W_s([n_s(\mu)] + 1)$ (resp. $W_s([n_s(\mu)]) < W_s([n_s(\mu)] + 1)$), where $[n]$ denotes the greatest integer that does not exceed n. Therefore, a qualification should be made to our excess entry theorems to the following effect: Although $n_e(\mu) > \max\{n_f, n_s(\mu)\}$ holds true quite strenuously, $N_e(\mu)$ may still fall short of N_f and/or $N_s(\mu)$ by the margin of at most one, reflecting the integer problem previously noted.

Remark 21.5. A final remark on the background of our interest in the problem at hand might not be out of place. Throughout the postwar period, a guiding principle of Japanese industrial policy has been the regulation of so-called excessive competition. To the extent that the meaning of this key concept has not been made precise, the debates on industrial organization and industrial policy have been rather cloudy to say the least. It is our hope that the analyses in this essay will help us crystallize a possible meaning of this strategic concept, thereby contributing to a more fruitful communication in the future.[10]

Appendix 21.A. Uniqueness and Stability of $n_e(\mu)$

The equilibrium number of firms $n_e(\mu)$ is defined by $\pi(n_e(\mu), \mu) = 0$, where $\pi(n, \mu)$ is given by (21.29). In view of (21.30), the uniqueness of $n_e(\mu)$ is clear.

Let $n_t := n(t, n_0)$ be the solution of the differential equation (21.15), where n_0 denotes the initial value of n. Define the distance between the solution path $\{n_t := n(t, n_0) \mid 0 \leq t < +\infty\}$ and the equilibrium number of firms $n_e(\mu)$ by $V_t := \frac{1}{2}\{n_t - n_e(\mu)\}^2$. It is clear that

$$\dot{V}_t = \{n_t - n_e(\mu)\}\dot{n}_t = \beta\{n_t - n_e(\mu)\}\pi(n_t, \mu). \qquad (21.1^*)$$

By virtue of (21.30), $\pi(n_t, \mu) > 0, = 0$, or < 0 accordingly as $n_t < n_e(\mu)$, $= n_e(\mu)$, or $> n_e(\mu)$. It then follows that $\dot{V}_t < 0$ as far as $n_t \neq n_e(\mu)$, whereas $\dot{V}_t = 0$ obtains if and only if $n_t = n_e(\mu)$. Therefore,

$$\lim_{t\to\infty} n(t, n_0) = n_e(\mu)$$

is guaranteed.

10. The interested readers are referred to Okuno and Suzumura [8] for our analysis of industrial policy.

Appendix 21.B. Proof of Lemma 21.1

(a) For any n, we define two functions $g_n(z) := f(nz) - C'(z)$ and $h_n(z) := f(nz) - C'(z) + \mu z f'(nz)$ of z. By virtue of assumptions A1 and A2, $\mu z f'(nz) < 0$ for all $z > 0$, so that we have $g_n(z) > h_n(z)$ for all $z > 0$. By definition of $z_*(n)$ and $z(n, \mu)$, we obtain $g_n(z_*(n)) = h_n(z(n, \mu)) = 0$. Furthermore, assumptions A2 and A4 entail $g_n'(z) = (n - \mu)f'(nz) + \mu f'(nz) - C''(z) < 0$, which is sufficient to ensure the uniqueness of $z_*(n)$ and the inequality $z_*(n) > z(n, \mu)$.

(b) Differentiating (21.6) with respect to μ, we may easily verify that

$$z_\mu(n, \mu) := \frac{\partial}{\partial \mu} z(n, \mu) = -\frac{z(n, \mu)}{\mu\{E(Q(n, \mu)) + m + K(n, \mu)\}} \tag{21.2*}$$

holds true, which is negative by virtue of (21.10) and (21.11). ■

Appendix 21.C. Proof of Lemma 21.2

Differentiating (21.16) with respect to μ, and taking (21.6) for $n = n_e(\mu)$ into consideration, we obtain

$$n_e'(\mu) = -\frac{z_\mu(n_e(\mu), \mu)}{z(n_e(\mu), \mu) + \{n_e(\mu) - \mu\} z_n(n_e(\mu), \mu)}. \tag{21.3*}$$

Substituting (21.2*) and (21.20) for $n = n_e(\mu)$ into (21.3*) and simplifying, we obtain

$$n_e'(\mu) = -\frac{z_\mu(n_e(\mu), \mu) m_e\{E(Q_e) + m_e + K_e\}}{z(n_e(\mu), \mu)\{m_e K_e + E(Q_e) + m_e\}}, \tag{21.4*}$$

where $E(Q_e) := E(Q(n_e(\mu), \mu))$, $m_e := n_e(\mu)/\mu$, and $K_e := K(n_e(\mu), \mu)$. By virtue of (21.10) and (21.11) for $n = n_e(\mu)$, (21.2*), (21.20), and (21.4*) ensure that $n_e'(\mu) > 0$ holds true for all $\mu > 0$. ■

Appendix 21.D. Proof of Theorem 21.1

To begin with, we prove that $n_e(0) := \lim_{\mu \to 0} n_e(\mu)$ exists and it satisfies $n_e(0) = n_f$. Note that

$$z(n_e(\mu), \mu) < z_*(n_e(\mu)) < z_*(1) \tag{21.5*}$$

holds true by virtue of Lemma 21.1(a), $z'_*(n) < 0$ and assumption (ii), viz., $n_e(\mu) > 1$. Note also that $(d/d\mu)z(n_e(\mu), \mu) = z_n(n_e(\mu), \mu)n'_e(\mu) + z_\mu(n_e(\mu), \mu) < 0$ holds true, where use is made of Lemma 21.2. Therefore, when μ decreases toward 0, $z(n_e(\mu), \mu)$ increases. Since $\{z(n_e(\mu), \mu)\}$ is bounded from above by $z_*(1)$, $\lim_{\mu\to 0} z(n_e(\mu), \mu) = z(\lim_{\mu\to 0} n_e(\mu), 0)$ exists. Let $n_e(0) := \lim_{\mu\to 0} n_e(\mu)$. Consider (21.6) for $n = n_e(\mu)$ and let μ converge to 0 to obtain

$$f(n_e(0)z(n_e(0), 0)) = C'(z(n_e(0), 0)), \tag{21.6*}$$

where use is made of assumptions A2 and A5*. In view of (21.18), (21.6*) may be rewritten as

$$f(n_e(0)z_*(n_e(0))) = C'(z_*(n_e(0))). \tag{21.7*}$$

Next, we let μ converge to 0 in (21.16) and take (21.18) into consideration to obtain

$$f(n_e(0)z_*(n_e(0)))z_*(n_e(0)) = C(z_*(n_e(0))). \tag{21.8*}$$

Coupled with (21.7*), (21.8*) yields $n_e(0) = n_f$, as desired.

Suppose now that $n_f \geq n_e(\mu)$ were true for some $\mu > 0$. By virtue of Lemma 21.2, we then obtain $n_f \geq n_e(\mu) > n_e(0) = n_f$, which is a contradiction. Therefore, $n_f < n_e(\mu)$ must be the case for all $\mu > 0$ satisfying $n_e(\mu) > \max\{1, \mu\}$, as was to be shown. ■

Appendix 21.E. Comparison between n_f and $n_s(\mu)$

Note that n_f, $n_s(\mu)$, and $n_e(\mu)$ are characterized by $\pi(n_f, 0) = 0$, $\pi(n_s(\mu), \mu) = \xi(n, \mu)$, and $\pi(n_e(\mu), \mu) = 0$, respectively, where $\pi(n, \mu)$ is defined by (21.29) and $\xi(n, \mu)$ is defined by

$$\xi(n, \mu) := -\mu\{z(n, \mu)\}^2 f'(nz(n, \mu)) \frac{E(Q(n, \mu)) + m}{E(Q(n, \mu)) + m + K(n, \mu)}, \tag{21.9*}$$

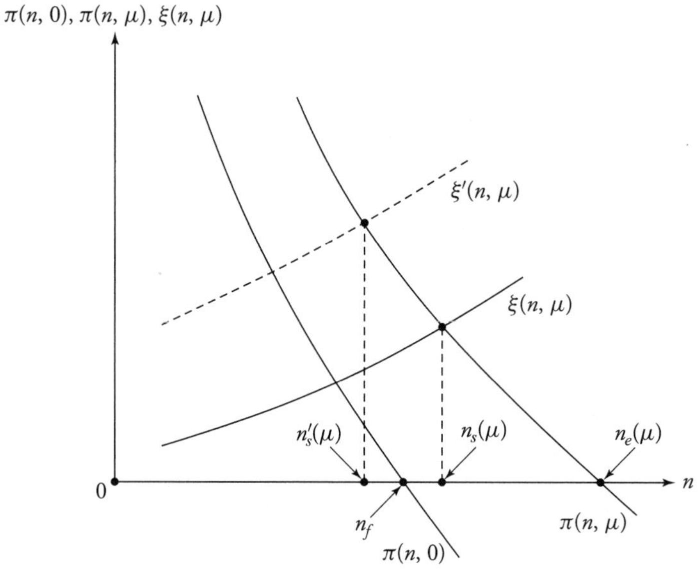

Figure 21.1. Comparison of n_f, $n_s(\mu)$, and $n_e(\mu)$

which is positive under our assumption. Note also that (21.30) guarantees that $(\partial/\partial n)\pi(n, \mu) < 0$, whereas Lemma 21.1(b) guarantees that

$$\frac{\partial}{\partial \mu}\pi(n, \mu) = (n - \mu)z(n, \mu)f'(Q(n, \mu))z_\mu(n, \mu) > 0. \quad (21.10^*)$$

We now draw the graphs of $\pi(n, 0)$, $\pi(n, \mu)$, and $\xi(n, \mu)$ for fixed $\mu > 0$ (Figure 21.1). As may easily be observed, $n_e(\mu) > n_f$ and $n_e(\mu) > n_s(\mu)$ hold true generally, whereas $n_s(\mu)$ may exceed or fall short of n_f depending on the relative position of $\xi(n, \mu)$ vis-à-vis $\pi(n, \mu)$. ■

References

[1] Baumol, W. J., "Contestable Markets: An Uprising in the Theory of Industry Structure," *American Economic Review* **72**, 1982, 1–15.

[2] Dixit, A., and J. Stiglitz, "Monopolistic Competition and Optimum Product Diversity," *American Economic Review* **67**, 1977, 297–308.

[3] Frank, Jr., C. R., "Entry in a Cournot Market," *Review of Economic Studies* **32**, 1965, 245–250.

[4] Hahn, F. H., "The Stability of the Cournot Market," *Review of Economic Studies* **29**, 1962, 329–331.

[5] Harris, R., "Price and Entry Regulations with Large Fixed Costs," *Quarterly Journal of Economics* **95**, 1981, 643–655.

[6] Kiyono, K., "Fundamental Nature of the Quasi-Cournot Oligopoly Markets." Paper presented at the annual meeting of the Japan Association of Economics and Econometrics, 1984.

[7] Okuguchi, K., "Quasi-Competitiveness and Cournot Oligopoly," *Review of Economic Studies* **40**, 1973, 145–148.

[8] Okuno, M., and K. Suzumura, "Economic Analysis of Industrial Policy: A Conceptual Framework through the Japanese Experience." In H. Mutoh, S. Sekiguchi, K. Suzumura, and I. Yamazawa, eds., *Industrial Policies for Pacific Economic Growth*, London: George Allen and Unwin, 1986, 23–41.

[9] Ruffin, R. J., "Cournot Oligopoly and Competitive Behaviour," *Review of Economic Studies* **38**, 1971, 493–502.

[10] Schmalensee, R., "Book Review: *Barriers to Entry* by C. C. von Weizsäcker," *Journal of Economic Literature* **21**, 1983, 562–564.

[11] Seade, J., "The Stability of Cournot Revisited," *Journal of Economic Theory* **23**, 1980, 15–27.

[12] Seade, J., "On the Effects of Entry," *Econometrica* **48**, 1980, 479–489.

[13] Spence, A. M., "Cost Reduction, Competition, and Industry Performance," *Econometrica* **52**, 1984, 101–121.

[14] Stiglitz, J. E., "Potential Competition May Reduce Welfare," *American Economic Review: Papers and Proceedings* **71**, 1981, 184–189.

[15] Suzumura, K., "Entry in a Cournot Market: Equilibrium versus Optimality," Discussion Paper No. 94, Institute of Economic Research, Hitotsubashi University, 1983.

[16] Tandon, P., "Innovation, Market Structure, and Welfare," *American Economic Review* **74**, 1984, 394–403.

[17] von Weizsäcker, C. C., "A Welfare Analysis of Barriers to Entry," *Bell Journal of Economics* **11**, 1980, 399–420.

[18] von Weizsäcker, C. C., *Barriers to Entry: A Theoretical Treatment*, Berlin: Springer-Verlag, 1980.

ESSAY 22

Oligopolistic Competition and Economic Welfare: A General Equilibrium Analysis of Entry Regulation and Tax-Subsidy Schemes

22.1. Introduction

The purpose of this essay is to make two contributions to the general equilibrium analysis of an oligopolistic economy with free entry.

First, we establish a general equilibrium extension of the excess entry theorem due to Mankiw and Whinston [13] and Suzumura and Kiyono [19], which establishes in a partial equilibrium framework that *a marginal decrease in the number of oligopolistic firms from the free-entry equilibrium level improves economic welfare*.[1] As is generally recognized, the advantage of using a partial equilibrium analysis lies in its simplicity, which enables us to crystallize a new theoretical insight. Since the new insight rendered by the excess entry theorem is somewhat paradoxical, it is reassuring that the theorem is essentially kept intact even in the presence of general equilibrium interactions. Indeed, the partial equilibrium verdict on the welfare effect of entry regulation in a free-entry oligopolistic economy is preserved in a general equilibrium setting

First published in *Journal of Public Economics* **42**, 1990, pp. 67–88, as a joint paper with H. Konishi and M. Okuno-Fujiwara. We are grateful to Anthony Atkinson, the editor, and two anonymous referees of *Journal of Public Economics* for their helpful comments. Financial support through a Grant-in-Aid for Scientific Research from the Ministry of Education, Culture, Sports, Science and Technology of Japan is gratefully acknowledged.

1. This theorem is called the second-best excess entry theorem at the margin in Essay 21 of this volume. There are two other versions of the excess entry theorem, which compares either the first-best number of firms or the second-best number of firms with the free-entry equilibrium number of firms. See Theorems 21.1 and 21.2 in Essay 21.

if the oligopolistic sector uses the same factor more intensively vis-à-vis the other factor than the competitive sector in the average as well as the marginal sense.

Note, however, that the excess entry theorem may be criticized in that a democratic government may lack sufficient leverage enabling it to impose direct entry regulation. Therefore, it is interesting to seek types of government policy instruments other than direct entry regulation. With this purpose in mind, the second task of this essay is to explore tax-subsidy schemes that guarantee an unambiguous Pareto improvement. Recall that the introduction of a tax-subsidy scheme into a perfectly competitive economy necessarily harms at least one economic agent, unless it is of the lump-sum variety. In contrast, the introduction of a tax-subsidy scheme can be welfare-improving if the market economy is imperfectly competitive. However, knowing that a tax-subsidy scheme *can be* welfare-improving is quite different from knowing when and precisely what kind of tax-subsidy scheme *is warranted* to be welfare-improving. It is interesting to identify several self-financing tax-subsidy schemes that guarantee Pareto improvement for sure, and this is precisely what we intend to accomplish.

At this juncture, some remarks on the related literature might be in order. In a partial equilibrium framework, Katz and Rosen [9] as well as Seade [17] analyzed the issue of tax shifting in oligopolistic competition, whereas the general equilibrium analysis of the incidence of a corporate profit tax in an imperfectly competitive economy was pioneered by Anderson and Ballentine [1], and analyzed further by Atkinson and Stiglitz [2, Chapter 7]. Their analyses differ from ours in several essential respects. First, unlike ours, Anderson and Ballentine analyzed the "short-run" incidence and welfare effect of corporate profit tax, where by "short-run" is meant that they fixed the number of Cournot oligopolists. Second, Atkinson and Stiglitz analyzed the model of monopolistic competition à la Dixit and Stiglitz [5], which subsumes our model of homogeneous-product oligopoly as a special case. Note, however, that they focused on a simplified case ($\gamma = 0$ in their notation) where the price-cost margin remains the same regardless of any change in exogenous environment because the residual demand of each firm has constant and identical elasticity. On the other hand, the price-cost margin is endogenous in our model, which enables us to analyze the welfare effects through prices as well as through other routes. Despite the formal generality, therefore, their model does not necessarily cover the area that our analysis focuses on. Besides, our focus is on short-run as well long-run welfare implications of various policies in contrast with their exclusive concern with the long-run incidence of corporate taxation.[2]

22.2. The Model

We consider a closed economy that consists of two sectors producing two goods, X and Y, using two factors of production, capital and labor. The endowment of these factors is fixed exogenously, and factors are freely mobile between two sectors. Good X is produced under increasing returns to scale due to the existence of fixed costs, which makes industry X oligopolistic. For simplicity, we assume that all firms in industry X are identical and behave as Cournot-Nash quantity competitors, so that we can work with the symmetric Cournot-Nash equilibrium. Good Y is competitively produced under constant returns to scale. We also simplify our model by supposing a single representative consumer, whose welfare is the central focus of our analysis. The consumer's income is taken as *numeraire*. Moreover, we confine our attention to the "long-run" equilibrium where entry and exit are free in the oligopolistic sector as well as in the perfectly competitive sector. This completes our informal description of the model.

22.2.1. Representative Consumer

Let $V(p_X, p_Y)$ be the indirect utility function of the representative consumer, where p_X (resp. p_Y) denotes the price of X (resp. Y) and the consumer's income is taken as numeraire. We assume quasilinearity of her

---

2. In what follows, we shall focus on the welfare effects of a change in the number of firms. In analyzing these effects, a crucial factor is the price-cost margin, which reflects the monopoly power of the firms. Using the Atkinson-Stiglitz framework with $\gamma = 1$, however, one cannot meaningfully analyze these effects as the price-cost margin remains the same even if the number of firms changes. On the other hand, the Atkinson-Stiglitz framework is quite suitable for analyzing the welfare effects of a change in the number of products. See also Besley and Suzumura [3], Myles [14], Robinson [15, Chapter 5], and Stern [18], among others, for different aspects of tax and welfare analyses in an oligopolistic economy.

preference for simplicity, which enables us to write the inverse demand function for X as[3]

$$p_X = p_Y \phi(X), \qquad \phi'(X) < 0. \tag{22.1}$$

Moreover, for expositional convenience, the price elasticity of demand for X, denoted by ϵ, is assumed to be constant, i.e.,[4]

$$\epsilon = -\frac{\phi(X)}{X\phi'(X)} = \text{const.} \tag{22.2}$$

22.2.2. Industry Y

Industry Y consists of perfectly competitive firms producing Y under constant returns to scale. Let $g(w, r)$ stand for the unit cost function of the representative firm, where r and w are, respectively, the rental rate of capital and the wage rate. Needless to say, g is homogeneous of degree one. The price of Y being p_Y, we should have

$$p_Y = g(w, r) \tag{22.3}$$

at equilibrium. Industry Y is assumed to be an untaxed sector.

22.2.3. Industry X

Industry X consists of identical and oligopolistically competitive firms. Let the *before-tax-subsidy* cost function of each firm be

$$C^*(q; w, r) = m^*(w, r)q + F^*(w, r), \tag{22.4}$$

where q is each firm's output of good X. Clearly, $m^*(w, r)$ and $F^*(w, r)$ denote, respectively, the marginal cost and fixed cost functions, which are

---

3. Quasilinearity is a strong assumption, which makes our analysis close to partial equilibrium analysis. However, this setup still allows us to discuss the crucial general equilibrium adjustment in factor markets in a straightforward way. In fact, weakening quasilinearity to homotheticity will not alter any essential results of this essay as we showed in Konishi, Okuno-Fujiwara, and Suzumura [11]. This paper is available to any interested reader on request.
4. The assumption of constant elasticity is made only for simplifying our presentation. Our results are valid even without this assumption as is clear from Konishi, Okuno-Fujiwara, and Suzumura [11].

homogeneous of degree one. Since we are concerned with the long-run analysis of the oligopolistic economy where firms enter into and exit from the oligopolistic sector, there is no sunk cost in our economy.

In this essay, we examine the welfare effects of various *infinitesimal* tax-subsidy schemes applied to the oligopolistic industry, which are represented by means of the following parameters:

s = production subsidy per unit output
s_w = rate of subsidy on the wage expenditure component of marginal cost
s_r = rate of subsidy on the capital expenditure component of marginal cost
t = lump-sum subsidy
t_w = rate of subsidy on the wage expenditure component of fixed cost
t_r = rate of subsidy on the capital expenditure component of fixed cost

Note that each of s, s_w, s_r, t, t_w, and t_r can be negative. If this is in fact the case, we are referring to a tax rather than to a subsidy. By the use of vector notation, let $\boldsymbol{S} = (s, s_w, s_r, t, t_w, t_r)$ be the overall tax-subsidy scheme, which is partitioned into the tax-subsidy scheme on the marginal cost part $\boldsymbol{s} = (s, s_w, s_r)$ and that on the fixed cost part $\boldsymbol{t} = (t, t_w, t_r)$.

Under the given tax-subsidy scheme, we can redefine the *after-tax-subsidy* cost function for X industry firms:

$$C(q; w, r, \boldsymbol{S}) = m(w, r, \boldsymbol{s})q + F(w, r, \boldsymbol{t}),$$

where $m(w, r, \boldsymbol{s}) = m^*(w - s_w, r - s_r) - s$, and $F(w, r, \boldsymbol{t}) = F^*(w - t_w, r - t_r) - t$.

Throughout this essay, we assume that the X industry is in Cournot-Nash competition in quantities. It follows that each firm solves the problem

$$\max_{q>0} \{p_Y \phi(X_{-i} + q)q - m(w, r, \boldsymbol{s})q - F(w, r, \boldsymbol{t})\}, \qquad (22.5)$$

taking the total output of other firms X_{-i}, the price p_Y of good Y, and that of production factors (w, r) and the tax-subsidy scheme $\boldsymbol{S}$ as given. The first-order condition for profit maximization becomes

$$p_Y \phi(X) \left\{ \frac{\phi'(X)}{\phi(X)} q + 1 \right\} = m(w, r, \boldsymbol{s}).$$

Under the assumption of identical firms, $X = nq$ holds at the symmetric Cournot-Nash equilibrium if there are n firms operative in industry X.

Using (22.2) and (22.3), we can derive the following equilibrium condition in industry X:

$$\phi(nq)\left(1 - \frac{1}{n\epsilon}\right) = \frac{m(w, r, \boldsymbol{s})}{g(w, r)}, \tag{22.6}$$

where $n > 1/\epsilon$ should be satisfied for the internal equilibrium solution to exist.

We also assume that entry and exit are free in industry X and focus on a long-run equilibrium of the economy. Thus, the output level of each firm and the number of firms in industry X are important determinants of the allocative efficiency of the economy.

The equilibrium number of firms is determined by the break-even condition. By virtue of (22.3), this condition is reduced to

$$\phi(nq)q = \frac{m(w, r, \boldsymbol{s})}{g(w, r)}q + \frac{F(w, r, \boldsymbol{t})}{g(w, r)}. \tag{22.7}$$

The integer problem on the equilibrium number of firms is assumed away following the customary practice in the literature (e.g., see Seade [16] and Suzumura and Kiyono [19]).

22.2.4. Consumer's Income

Recollect that the income of the representative consumer is taken as numeraire. Let K (resp. L) be the fixed supply of capital (resp. labor). Profit earned in industry X, if any, is distributed to the consumer. The resources, which are required to substantiate a tax-subsidy scheme, are collected from the representative consumer in a lump-sum fashion. When tax is collected from the oligopolistic sector, its revenue is distributed to the consumer in the same manner. Let T be the lump-sum subsidy (or tax if it is negative):

$$T = n\{(s + s_w m_w + s_r m_r)q + (t + t_w F_w + t_r F_r)\}.$$

In this expression, partial derivatives of the cost functions coincide with the levels of factor utilization in the marginal and fixed cost parts by virtue of Shephard's lemma.[5]

Finally, the normalization of the consumer's income implies

$$wL + rK + n\{g(w, r)\phi(nq)q - m(w, r, \boldsymbol{s})q - F(w, r, \boldsymbol{t})\} - T = 1. \tag{22.8}$$

Note that the third term on the left-hand side is equal to zero at equilibrium.

22.2.5. Factor Market Equilibrium

Capital and labor are allocated between industries through the adjustment of rental and wage rates. Both factor markets are assumed to be perfectly competitive. By the use of Shephard's lemma, total factor use in each industry can be written as

$$K_X = m_r(w, r, \boldsymbol{s})X + nF_r(w, r, \boldsymbol{t}), \quad L_X = m_w(w, r, \boldsymbol{s})X + nF_w(w, r, \boldsymbol{t}),$$
$$K_Y = g_r(w, r)Y, \quad L_Y = g_w(w, r)Y,$$

and the market-clearing conditions become

$$K_X + K_Y = K, \tag{22.9}$$

$$L_X + L_Y = L. \tag{22.10}$$

These six equations, (22.3) and (22.6)–(22.10), complete the general equilibrium system of our economy. The market-clearing condition for good Y is omitted because of Walras's law. There are six unknowns, s, q, n, p_Y, Y, w, and r.

---

5. Throughout this essay, a subscript to a function signifies partial differentiation with respect to the specified variable. For example, if the relevant function is given by $f(x, y)$, we denote $f_x = \partial f/\partial x$, $f_{xy} = \partial^2 f/\partial x \partial y$, and so on.

22.3. Welfare Criterion

In order to analyze this system, we first define the welfare criterion, which is the basis for evaluating the entry regulation policy and the tax-subsidy schemes to be examined later.

The welfare of the representative consumer is written as

$$V(p_X, p_Y) = V(g(w,r)\phi(nq), g(w,r)). \tag{22.11}$$

Total differentiation of (22.11) yields

$$\frac{1}{\lambda}dV = -\, g(w,r)X\phi'(X)dX - \{X\phi(X) + Y\}(g_w dw + g_r dr), \tag{22.12}$$

where use is made of Roy's Identity and λ represents the marginal utility of income ($\lambda > 0$).

In addition, total differentiation of (22.8) tells us that changes of variables are restricted by the following relation because of the normalization of the consumer's income:

$$\begin{aligned} &\{L - n(m_w q + F_w) + \phi(X)Xg_w\}dw + \\ &\{K - n(m_r q + F_r) + \phi(X)Xg_r\}dr \\ &+ g(w,r)\phi'(X)X(dX - dq) = 0, \end{aligned}$$

where (22.6) and (22.7) are applied. Note that the terms relating to the tax-subsidy parameters do not appear here because we are concerned only with the infinitesimal tax-subsidy schemes. Substituting (22.9) and (22.10), we can convert (22.13) into

$$\{Y + \phi(X)X\}(g_w dw + g_r dr) + g(w,r)\phi'(X)X(dX - dq) = 0. \tag{22.13}$$

Thus, using the restriction (22.14), we obtain the following welfare criterion in our economy:

$$\frac{1}{\lambda}dV = -g(w,r)X\phi'(X)dq. \tag{22.14}$$

The following useful theorem is now established.

THEOREM 22.1 (WELFARE CRITERION). The necessary and sufficient condition for a change in the number of oligopolistic firms and/or the introduction of an infinitesimal tax-subsidy scheme to be welfare-improving is that it induces an increase in the output of each oligopolistic firm.

The assertion of this theorem is intuitively clear. In a free-entry oligopolistic economy, average cost, which equals product price, exceeds marginal cost, which equals marginal revenue, so that there remain unexploited increasing returns. Hence, it is socially beneficial to expand the scale of production of each firm in the oligopolistic industry.

22.4. Perturbation of the General Equilibrium System

In this section we analyze our general equilibrium system using the so-called hat calculus and derive the relations that must hold at equilibrium among the output levels of each oligopolistic firm, the number of firms in the oligopolistic sector, and the relative factor price.[6] This is a customary procedure in the literature of tax incidence pioneered by Harberger [6].[7] To begin with, we examine the effect of a change in the number of firms, and later we investigate the effect of the introduction of a tax-subsidy scheme.

Consider (22.6), which is the Cournot-Nash equilibrium condition in industry X, and assume $\boldsymbol{S} = 0$. The right-hand side of (22.6) shows the relative marginal cost of industry X to that of industry Y. It is well known that the relative factor intensity between the two industries plays a central role in determining the relation between ω, the wage-rental ratio w/r, and the value of the right-hand side of (22.6); if the marginal cost part of industry X is more capital intensive than industry Y, an increase in ω decreases the value of the right-hand side of (22.6), and vice versa.

The left-hand side of (22.6), in turn, represents the marginal revenue of the oligopolistic sector in terms of the good Y. Clearly, it depends on the

6. For any variable x, we denote $\hat{x} = dx/x$.

7. See also Atkinson and Stiglitz [2] and Kotlikoff and Summers [12] for useful surveys.

equilibrium number of firms as well as the equilibrium output level of each oligopolistic firm. Using the hat calculus, we obtain the following equation of change:

$$-\frac{1}{\epsilon}\hat{q} - \frac{(n-1)\epsilon - 1}{\epsilon(n\epsilon - 1)}\hat{n} = \hat{m} - \hat{g}.$$

Let us now introduce a crucial assumption on the strategic behavior of oligopolistic firms: output levels are *strategic substitutes*. The property of strategic substitutes, first formulated by Bulow, Geanakoplos, and Klemperer [4], corresponds to the downward-sloping reaction curve for each oligopolistic firm, or equivalently, the negative partial derivative of the marginal revenue with respect to the output chosen by other firms. It is well known that the strategic substitutes property is a natural requirement when oligopolistic competition is fought in terms of quantities.

Note that the left-hand side of (22.6) is decreasing in q because of the second-order condition of profit maximization. Moreover, in our formulation, an increase in the number of firms will induce, *ceteris paribus*, an increase in other firms' output. The assumption of strategic substitutes, then, implies that the left-hand side of (22.6) is decreasing in n. Thus, the assumption of strategic substitutes and the existence of an internal solution imply that the number of firms, n, must satisfy $n > 1 + 1/\epsilon$ at the symmetric free-entry equilibrium.

The implied relation $(\hat{q}, \hat{n}, \hat{\omega})$ in (22.6) is now reduced to

$$-\frac{1}{\epsilon}\hat{q} - \alpha\hat{n} + A\theta^M\hat{\omega} = 0, \tag{22.15}$$

where $A = (wr/c)m_w L_Y > 0$, $\alpha = \{(n-1)\epsilon - 1\}/\epsilon(n\epsilon - 1) > 0$, and $\theta^M = (m_r/m_w) - (K_Y/L_Y)$.[8] θ^M denotes the difference in *marginal* capital intensity between two industries. If θ^M is positive (resp. negative), industry X's marginal cost is more capital (resp. labor) intensive than industry Y. Hence, an increase in the wage-rental ratio expands (resp. contracts) the output of each oligopolist if industry X is marginally more capital (resp. labor) intensive than industry Y. On the other hand, other things being equal, an

8. Note that, in the derivation of (22.15), the homogeneity property of the cost function is used.

increase in the number of firms in industry X reduces the output of each oligopolistic firm, regardless of the sign of θ^M.

Next, we apply the same procedure to the break-even condition (22.7) of industry X. The right-hand side thereof being the total cost of an oligopolistic firm in terms of the good Y, the value of the right-hand side determines the overall factor intensity. The implied relation of $(\hat{q}, \hat{n}, \hat{\omega})$ becomes

$$-(1/\epsilon)\hat{X} + \hat{q} = (mq/C)\hat{q} + (wr/C)L_Y L_X\{(K_Y/L_Y) - (K_X/L_X)\}\hat{\omega}.$$

By the use of (22.6), $mw/C = 1 - 1/\epsilon$, so that the preceding relation is reduced to

$$-\frac{n-1}{\epsilon}\hat{q} - \frac{1}{\epsilon}\hat{n} + B\theta^A\hat{\omega} = 0, \tag{22.16}$$

where $B = (wr/Cg)L_Y L_X > 0$ and $\theta^A = K_X/L_X - K_Y/L_Y$. θ^A denotes the difference in *average* capital intensity between two industries.[9] If it is positive, industry X is overall more capital intensive than industry Y and vice versa. Note that the average capital intensity is equal to the marginal intensity in industry Y because the industry is under constant returns to scale. By (22.16), if industry X is overall more (resp. less) capital intensive than industry Y, other things being equal, an increase in the output of each oligopolistic firm decreases the number of firms in industry X, and a rise in the wage-rental ratio induces new entry into (resp. exit from) industry X.

Finally, we must derive the factor market equilibrium relation of $(\hat{q}, \hat{n}, \hat{\omega})$, which is obtained by totally differentiating (22.9) and (22.10) and then eliminating dY. Since the calculation procedure is rather complicated, we shall state only the final result in the main text, relegating a detailed derivation to Appendix 22.A:

$$\lambda^M\hat{q} + \lambda^A\hat{n} + \Delta\hat{\omega} = 0, \tag{22.17}$$

where λ^M and λ^A are positively related to the difference in marginal and average factor intensities, θ^M and θ^A, respectively. Δ represents what is usually called the *factor substitution term* and is always positive.

9. The distinction between marginal and average factor intensities is due originally to Jones [8].

When the number of firms is fixed, interpretation of (22.17) is familiar in the theory of international trade and/or that of tax incidence. If in need, the reader is referred to the pioneering paper on the two-sector general equilibrium model by Jones [7].

Consider an increase in the wage-rental ratio. It induces firms in both industries to choose more capital-intensive technology, which brings about excess demand in the capital market and excess supply in the labor market. For both factor markets to clear, the output of the capital-intensive industry must decrease and that of the labor-intensive industry must increase; this is the renowned Rybczynski theorem. In our context, if industry X is marginally more capital intensive, the output of each oligopolistic firm must decrease and vice versa.

What is rather unfamiliar in (22.17) is the effect of an increase in the number of firms on the output of each oligopolistic firm under a constant wage-rental ratio. This depends on the difference not only in *marginal* factor intensities but also in *average* factor intensities between industries. Let us say that there exists a *factor intensity twist* in industry X when θ^M and θ^A are of opposite signs.[10] Figure 22.1(a) depicts the box diagram describing factor utilizations when there is no factor intensity twist at the given wage-rental ratio. Note that, in this figure, industry X is assumed to be overall more capital intensive than industry Y.

In Figure 22.1(a), E denotes the initial equilibrium. O^X and O^Y denote the origin of industry X and industry Y, respectively. Factor utilization of industry X, represented by the vector $O^X E$, can be decomposed into the fixed cost part and the marginal cost part:

$$(K_X, L_X) = (m_r, m_w)X + (F_r, F_w)n.$$

In this figure, $O^X F$ corresponds to the fixed cost part and FE to the marginal cost part. The slopes of both $O^X E$ and FE are steeper than that of $O^Y E$, reflecting the assumption of no factor intensity twist.

Now consider an increase in the number of firms in industry X. New equilibrium will occur at E', where factor utilization in the fixed cost part is expanded to $O^X F'$. However, if the production level of each oligopolistic

10. The crucial role played by the absence of the factor intensity twist was recognized by Atkinson and Stiglitz [2, Chapter 7] as well, although the nomenclature is ours.

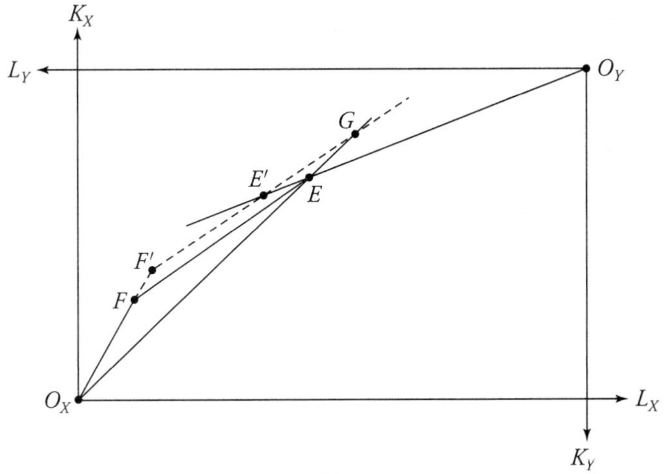

(a)

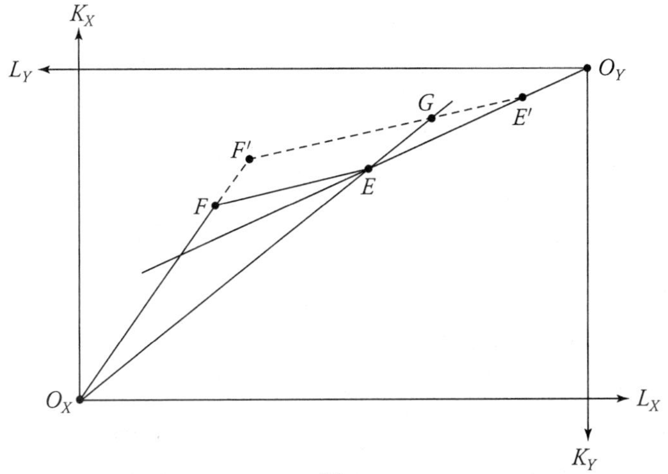

(b)

Figure 22.1. Factor Utilizations without Factor Intensity Twist [Case (a)] and with Factor Intensity Twist [Case (b)]

firm were to remain the same as before, industry X would utilize factors of $O^X G$. Hence, an increase in the number of firms leads to a fall in the output of oligopolists in industry X.

Figure 22.1(b) depicts the case with a factor intensity twist; the slope of $O^Y E$ is between those of $O^X E$ and FE. An increase in the number of firms changes the equilibrium from E to E', and the individual output level of the oligopolists increases because $F'G < F'E'$.

22.5. Excess Entry Theorem at the Margin

We are now ready to solve the equations of change, (22.15)–(22.17), and investigate the welfare effects of entry regulation.

Suzumura and Kiyono [19], using a partial equilibrium framework, examined the welfare effects of entry regulation in a free-entry quasi-Cournot oligopoly with fixed cost. They showed that a reduction in the number of firms leads to welfare improvement when the only available policy tool is the control of the number of firms. This result critically hinges on the assumption of strategic substitutability. Under this assumption, a reduction in the number of firms gives rise to an increase in the equilibrium output of each oligopolistic firm, which leads to a fall in the average cost of oligopolists due to the existence of unexploited increasing returns to scale.

However, a partial equilibrium result may not hold in a general equilibrium setting in general. One of the major aims of this essay is to show under what conditions entry regulation assures welfare improvement when we pay due attention to the general equilibrium interactions. In view of Theorem 22.1, we need only to know a sufficient condition for the output of each oligopolistic firm to increase when the number of firms is reduced marginally from the free-entry equilibrium level. Under entry regulations, n is fixed and the relation (22.16) no longer holds. Solving (22.15) and (22.17), we obtain

$$\hat{q} = -\frac{1}{\Omega}(\alpha\Delta + A\lambda^A\theta^M)\hat{n}, \qquad (22.18)$$

where $\Omega = (1/\epsilon)\Delta + A\lambda^M\theta^M > 0$. Thus, barring a factor intensity twist, a marginal reduction in the number of firms from the free-entry equilib-

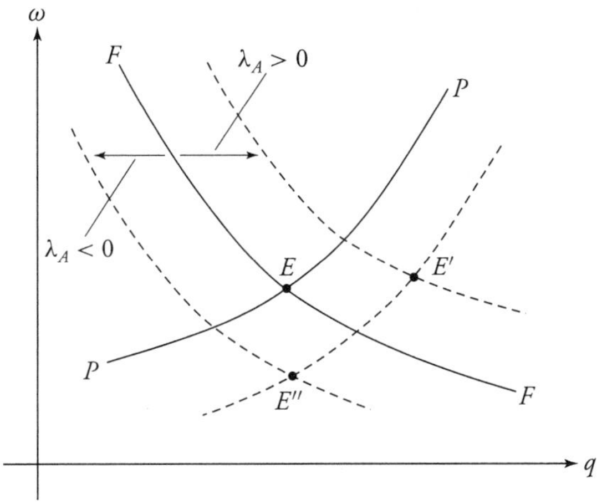

Figure 22.2. Excess Entry Theorem in General Equilibrium

rium level increases individual output in the oligopolistic sector. Invoking Theorem 22.1, we obtain the following.

THEOREM 22.2 (EXCESS ENTRY THEOREM IN GENERAL EQUILIBRIUM). Suppose that strategic substitutability and no factor intensity twist hold. Then a marginal reduction in the number of oligopolistic firms from the free-entry equilibrium level unambiguously improves economic welfare.

A diagrammatical exposition of Theorem 22.2 is given in Figure 22.2, which depicts the case of $\theta^M \lambda^M > 0$.

The downward-sloping schedule FF and the upward-sloping schedule PP are the implied relation of $(\hat{q}, \hat{\omega})$ in the factor market (22.17) and in the product market (22.15) with the assumption that $\hat{n} = 0$, respectively. The initial free-entry equilibrium is shown by E in the figure. When the number of firms in industry X is reduced marginally, the PP schedule moves to the right by the assumed strategic substitutability. The shift of the FF schedule depends on whether or not the factor intensity twist exists. If there is no factor intensity twist and $\theta^A \lambda^A > 0$, the FF schedule also moves to the right. It follows that an increase in q is always assured.

However, when there is a twist and $\theta^A \lambda^A < 0$, the response via factor markets to a reduction in the number of oligopolistic firms counteracts the expansion of the individual oligopolist's output. This is because a reduction in the number of firms induces a change in the wage-rental ratio, which worsens the marginal cost condition in industry X relative to that in industry Y. Thus, without the factor intensity twist, equilibrium moves to E' and an increase in q is entailed, but equilibrium may move to E'' and q may decrease with the factor intensity twist. The case of $\theta^M\lambda^M < 0$ can be examined similarly; we have only to notice that the relative position of the FF and PP schedules is reversed.

In concluding this section, we note that the relevance of Theorem 22.2 to the effect that restricting competitiveness of the oligopolistic sector directly would contribute to improve welfare may well be suspect, since it may be doubted how the government can directly regulate the number of firms in the oligopolistic sector. Assuming that the government's leverage against private incentives is indeed too weak to implement direct entry regulation, can we instead design tax-subsidy schemes that can induce welfare improvement indirectly? We now turn to this problem.

22.6. Welfare-Improving Tax-Subsidy Schemes

To analyze the effect of a tax-subsidy scheme in our model, the equations of change, viz., (22.15), (22.16), and (22.17), must be modified to include the tax-subsidy parameters. To avoid unnecessary complications, we will modify the equations of change with a familiar theoretical apparatus, the formal derivation of which is relegated to Appendix 22.A.

The Cournot-Nash equilibrium condition (22.15) in industry X will be modified by the introduction of tax-subsidy parameters as

$$-\frac{1}{\epsilon}\hat{q} - \alpha\hat{n} + A\theta^M\hat{\omega} = \frac{1}{m}m_S \cdot d\boldsymbol{S}, \tag{22.19}$$

where $m_S = -(1, m_w, m_r; 0, 0, 0)$ and $d\boldsymbol{S} = (ds, ds_w, ds_r, dt, dt_w, dt_r)$. It is clear from (22.19) that subsidies (resp. taxes) on the marginal cost increase (resp. decrease) the equilibrium output of each oligopolistic firm when the number of firms and factor prices is fixed.

Similarly, (22.16) can be modified by introducing tax-subsidy parameters as

$$-\frac{n-1}{n\epsilon}\hat{q} - \frac{1}{\epsilon}\hat{n} + B\theta^A\hat{\omega} = \frac{1}{C}C_S \cdot d\boldsymbol{S}, \tag{22.20}$$

where $C_S = -(q, qc_w, qc_r; 1, F_w, F_r)$. It follows from (22.20) that a cost reduction (resp. increase) in the oligopolistic sector induced by government subsidies (resp. taxes) brings about an increase (resp. decrease) in the number of firms when the individual output level and factor prices are fixed.

The effects of the introduction of taxes and subsidies into factor markets are familiar in the theory of tax incidence. For example, the number of firms and the output level of each oligopolistic firm being fixed, a subsidy on labor use in industry X, which brings about the factor substitution effect to cause excess demand in the labor market and excess supply in the capital market, increases the wage-rental ratio and so forth. Formally, the modified equation of change in factor market equilibrium becomes

$$\lambda^M\hat{q} + \lambda^A\hat{n} + \Delta\hat{\omega} = -\beta \cdot d\boldsymbol{S}, \tag{22.21}$$

where $\beta = (0, (1/w)\Delta^M, -(1/r)\Delta^M; 0, (1/w)\Delta^F, -(1/r)\Delta^F)$. Δ^M and Δ^F represent what we may call the substitution terms in the marginal cost and the average cost part, respectively. They are proved to be always positive.[11] Clearly, the production subsidy and the lump-sum subsidy do not directly affect factor market equilibrium. Since we are concerned only with the introduction of infinitesimal tax-subsidy schemes, the signs of λ^M and λ^A correspond to those of θ^M and θ^A, respectively.[12] Enumeration of the modified equations of change being now complete, we are ready to examine the welfare implications of several tax-subsidy schemes.

Consider the simultaneous equation system for $(\hat{q}, \hat{n}, \hat{\omega})$ defined by (22.19), (22.20), and (22.21):

$$\begin{bmatrix} -(1/\epsilon) & -\alpha & A\theta^M \\ -(n-1)/n\epsilon & -(1/\epsilon) & B\theta^A \\ -\lambda^M & -\lambda^A & -\Delta \end{bmatrix} \begin{bmatrix} \hat{q} \\ \hat{n} \\ \hat{\omega} \end{bmatrix} = \begin{bmatrix} (1/m)m_S \\ (1/C)C_S \cdot d\boldsymbol{S} \\ -\beta \cdot d\boldsymbol{S} \end{bmatrix}. \tag{22.22}$$

11. A formal derivation of (22.21) is contained in Appendix 22.A.

12. For the introduction of noninfinitesimal tax-subsidy schemes, see Atkinson and Stiglitz [2, Chapter 5] and the papers cited there.

Let H denote the determinant of the coefficient matrix in (22.22), i.e.,

$$H = -\frac{1}{\epsilon}\left(\frac{1}{\epsilon}\Delta + B\theta^A\lambda^A\right) + \frac{n-1}{n\epsilon}(\alpha\Delta + A\theta^M\lambda^A) - \lambda^M\left(-\alpha B\theta^A + \frac{1}{\epsilon}A\theta^M\right). \quad (22.23)$$

We prove in Appendix 22.B that the general equilibrium system is locally stable if $H < 0$. The rest of the analysis proceeds under this assumption of local stability.

Solving (22.22) for $\hat{q}$, we obtain

$$\hat{q} = \frac{\Delta + \epsilon B\theta^A\lambda^A}{\epsilon c H} \cdot m_S \cdot d\boldsymbol{S} - \frac{\alpha\Delta + A\theta^M\lambda^A}{CH} \cdot C_S \cdot d\boldsymbol{S} - \frac{A\theta^M - \alpha\epsilon B\theta^A}{\epsilon H} \cdot \beta \cdot d\boldsymbol{S}. \quad (22.24)$$

From this equation we can see how tax-subsidy schemes affect the equilibrium output level of each oligopolistic firm. The effect in question can be decomposed into three general equilibrium effects, each corresponding to a term in (22.24). We call them the *marginal cost effect*, the *total cost effect*, and the *factor substitution effect*, respectively, in accordance with the order of appearance in (22.24).

The marginal cost effect refers to the coefficient of $m_S \cdot d\boldsymbol{S}$, which is always negative. Therefore, other things being equal, a tax-subsidy scheme that brings the marginal cost down induces an expansion in the individual output of the oligopolistic firm. It is intuitively clear within a partial equilibrium framework that a reduction in marginal cost increases the output of each oligopolist if firms are symmetric. We have thus verified that, even when the general equilibrium interactions via factor markets are taken into account, such a partial equilibrium result remains true as long as the general equilibrium system is locally stable.

The total cost effect refers to the coefficient of $C_S \cdot d\boldsymbol{S}$. Suppose that the total cost is increased by the introduction of a tax subsidy. The effect on the output of each oligopolistic firm is two-fold. On the one hand, the output level of each oligopolistic firm will rise due to the exit of some firms from the oligopolistic industry (the excess entry theorem). On the other hand, the output level is also affected by an induced change in the factor price ratio; if industry X is more capital (resp. labor) intensive in the average sense, the wage-rental ratio goes up (resp. down). Thus, without the factor intensity twist, an increase in individual output of the oligopolistic firm is enhanced, while it is offset or may even be upset when there is a factor intensity twist.

Finally, the factor substitution effect refers to the coefficient of $\beta \cdot d\boldsymbol{S}$. A change in the relative factor price through substitution between factors affects the output level of each oligopolistic firm by changing the marginal cost condition and the number of firms. For example, consider the effect of the introduction of a subsidy on the wage expenditure component of marginal cost. Since it motivates the oligopolistic firms to substitute capital for labor, the wage-rental ratio must rise so as to adjust factor markets into equilibrium. When industry X firms are marginally more capital intensive but totally more labor intensive than industry Y, i.e., the factor intensity twist prevails, a rise in the wage-rental ratio necessarily expands the output of each oligopolistic firm as some firms are forced out of the industry. Without the factor intensity twist, however, it is ambiguous whether the output of each oligopolistic firm increases or not.

The following two observations might be in order here. First, those schemes that reduce total cost, i.e., $C_S \cdot d\boldsymbol{S} < 0$, may not lead to a welfare improvement because they always induce new entry into industry X. Second, the total cost effect and the factor substitution effect may conflict with each other in yielding an overall effect, for the former gives rise to an unambiguous change in q only *without* the factor intensity twist, while the latter only *with* it.

We say a tax-subsidy scheme is *self-financing* if $C_S \cdot d\boldsymbol{S} = 0$ holds. Note also that $\beta \cdot d\boldsymbol{S} = 0$ holds if and only if the tax subsidy is of the lump-sum category. It then follows from the previous remark that a tax-subsidy scheme induces an unambiguous welfare improvement only if it is either self-financing or of the lump-sum variety.

Invoking Theorem 22.1, we may now assert the following.

THEOREM 22.3 (WELFARE-IMPROVING TAX-SUBSIDY SCHEMES). Suppose that strategic substitutability, quasi-linear preferences, and local stability hold simultaneously. Then any tax-subsidy scheme that belongs to the following four fundamental categories is always welfare-improving:

(1) $m_S \cdot d\boldsymbol{S} < 0$, $C_S \cdot d\boldsymbol{S} = 0$, $\beta \cdot d\boldsymbol{S} = 0$

(2a) $m_S \cdot d\boldsymbol{S} < 0$, $C_S \cdot d\boldsymbol{S} = 0$, $\beta \cdot d\boldsymbol{S} > 0$ in the case of $\theta^M > 0$ and $\theta^A < 0$

(2b) $m_S \cdot d\boldsymbol{S} < 0$, $C_S \cdot d\boldsymbol{S} = 0$, $\beta \cdot d\boldsymbol{S} < 0$ in the case of $\theta^M < 0$ and $\theta^A > 0$

(3) $m_S \cdot d\boldsymbol{S} = 0$, $C_S \cdot d\boldsymbol{S} > 0$, $\beta \cdot d\boldsymbol{S} = 0$ in the case of $\theta^M \theta^A > 0$

A typical scheme that belongs to category 1 is an infinitesimal production subsidy accompanied by a self-financing lump-sum tax. Note that this scheme improves welfare independent of factor intensity conditions.[13]

A typical scheme that belongs to category 3 is a lump-sum tax, which improves welfare when factor intensity twist does not occur. This result is parallel to Theorem 22.2. What is added to the oligopolists' profit under entry regulation is transformed into tax revenue for the government.

Welfare-improving tax-subsidy schemes that belong to categories 2a and 2b are more complex. They guarantee welfare improvement when the factor intensity twist exists. To illustrate, consider the case where industry X is marginally more capital intensive but totally more labor intensive (category 2a). Accompanied by a self-financing lump-sum tax, the introduction of an infinitesimal labor subsidy, applied to both the fixed cost and the marginal cost at a uniform rate, is welfare-improving; if $d\boldsymbol{S} = (0, ds_w, 0; dt, ds_w, 0)$ with $ds_w > 0$ and $dt = -(qm_w + F_w)ds_w$, it belongs to category 2a.

Even when a self-financing lump-sum tax is not available to the government, it is possible to construct a welfare-improving tax-subsidy scheme if the government can distinguish between factors used in the marginal cost part and the fixed cost part of the oligopolistic production. In the case of category 2a, for example, the introduction of a production subsidy accompanied by a self-financing tax on the wage expenditure component of the fixed cost warrants welfare improvement. An infinitesimal subsidy on the capital

13. Although our analysis is confined to infinitesimal schemes, a combination of a noninfinitesimal production subsidy and a self-financing lump-sum tax appears to attain the first-best resource allocation. See Konishi [10].

expenditure component of the marginal cost accompanied by the same self-financing tax also satisfies category 2a. The reader is invited to examine the types of tax-subsidy schemes that satisfy category 2b.

22.7. Concluding Remarks

It goes without saying that the first-best policy in an oligopolistic economy such as ours is to simultaneously enforce marginal cost pricing and control the number of firms at the optimal level. However, this first-best policy is likely to be beyond the reach of any actual government. Still there might remain room for a second-best policy if the government, which is unable to control prices, can nevertheless control the number of firms to improve economic welfare.

In Section 22.5 of this essay, we reexamined and generalized the excess entry theorem at the margin by allowing general equilibrium interactions in factor markets. The assumption of strategic substitutability and quasi-linear preferences, upon which our generalization rests, is rather standard. Our main finding is that the validity of the theorem hinges crucially on whether or not the factor intensity twist exists. If there is a factor intensity twist, entry regulation in the oligopolistic sector may decrease welfare. We also noted that such a direct entry regulation may still be beyond the reach of the government. In Section 22.6 of this essay, we analyzed conditions for tax-subsidy schemes to be welfare-improving.[14] Our analysis delineates several types of tax-subsidy schemes that are unambiguously welfare-improving.

We should emphasize, however, that our model is based on several drastically simplifying assumptions, such as Cournot-Nash quantity competition, a single consumer (neglecting all the distributional issues), and the specific form of increasing returns to scale via the existence of fixed cost. It should also be noted that identifying capital (and wage) expenditures in marginal and fixed costs separately, which can be easily defined in theory, may be far from obvious in reality. The robustness of our results should be carefully examined before extracting any serious policy implications.

14. The second-best tax-subsidy scheme, rather than welfare-improving infinitesimal tax-subsidy schemes, is analyzed in Konishi [10].

Appendix 22.A. Derivation of Equations (22.17) and/or (22.21)

We use the following notation.

Cost shares:

θ_{XL}^{M} (θ_{XK}^{M}) $= wm_w/m$ (rm_r/m): marginal cost share of labor (capital) in industry X

θ_{XL}^{F} (θ_{XK}^{F}) $= wF_w/F$ (rF_r/F): fixed cost share of labor (capital) in industry X

θ_{XL}^{A} (θ_{XK}^{A}) $= w(m_w q + F_w)/F$ ($r(m_r q + F_r)/F$): total cost share of labor (capital) in industry X

θ_{YL} (θ_{YK}) $= wg_w/g$ (rg_r/g): cost share of labor (capital) in industry Y

Factor shares:

λ_{XL}^{M} (λ_{XK}^{M}) $= nqm_w/L$ (nqm_r/K): share of total labor (capital) used as variable input in industry X

λ_{XL}^{F} (λ_{XK}^{F}) $= nF_w/L$ (nF_r/K): share of total labor (capital) used as fixed input in industry X

λ_{XL}^{A} (λ_{XK}^{A}) $= L_X/L$ (K_X/K): share of total labor (capital) used in industry X

λ_{YL} (λ_{YK}) $= L_Y/L$ (K_Y/K): share of total labor (capital) used in industry Y

Elasticities of substitution:

$\sigma_X^M = -(\hat{m}_w - \hat{m}_r)/\hat{\omega}$: elasticity of substitution between variable inputs in industry X

$\sigma_X^F = -(\hat{F}_w - \hat{F}_r)/\hat{\omega}$: elasticity of substitution between fixed inputs in industry X

$\sigma_Y = -(\hat{g}_w - \hat{g}_r)/\hat{\omega}$: elasticity of substitution in industry Y

Total differentiation of (22.9) and (22.10) yields

$$\lambda_{XK}^{M}\hat{q} + \lambda_{XK}^{A}\hat{n} + \lambda_{YK}\hat{Y} - (\lambda_{XK}^{M}\theta_{XL}^{M}\sigma_X^{M} + \lambda_{XK}^{F}\theta_{XL}^{F}\sigma_X^{F} + \lambda_{YK}\theta_{YL}\sigma_Y)\hat{\omega}$$

$$= \lambda_{XK}^{M}\theta_{XL}^{M}\sigma_X^{M}\{(1/w)ds_w - (1/r)ds_r\} \qquad (22.A.1)$$

$$+ \lambda_{XK}^{F}\theta_{XL}^{F}\sigma_X^{F}\{(1/w)dt_w - (1/r)dt_r\}$$

and

$$\lambda_{XL}^{M}\hat{q} + \lambda_{XL}^{A}\hat{n} + \lambda_{YL}\hat{Y} - (\lambda_{XL}^{M}\theta_{XK}^{M}\sigma_{X}^{M} + \lambda_{XL}^{F}\theta_{XK}^{F}\sigma_{X}^{F} + \lambda_{YL}\theta_{YK}\sigma_{Y})\hat{\omega}$$

$$= -\lambda_{XL}^{M}\theta_{XK}^{M}\sigma_{X}^{M}\{(1/w)ds_w - (1/r)ds_r\} \qquad (22.A.2)$$

$$- \lambda_{XL}^{F}\theta_{XK}^{F}\sigma_{X}^{F}\{(1/w)dt_w - (1/r)dt_r\},$$

respectively. Eliminating $\hat{Y}$ from these two equations, we obtain

$$\lambda^{M}\hat{q} + \lambda^{A}\hat{n} + \Delta\hat{\omega} = -\beta \cdot d\boldsymbol{S}, \qquad (22.A.3)$$

where

$$\lambda^{M} = \lambda_{XK}^{M}\lambda_{YL} - \lambda_{XL}^{M}\lambda_{YK} = (1/K)\lambda_{XL}^{M}\lambda_{YL}\{(m_r/m_w) - (K_Y/L_Y)\},$$

$$\lambda^{A} = \lambda_{XK}^{A}\lambda_{YL} - \lambda_{XL}^{A}\lambda_{YK} = (1/K)\lambda_{XL}^{A}\lambda_{YL}\{(K_X/L_X) - (K_Y/L_Y)\},$$

$$\Delta = \Delta^{M} + \Delta^{F} + \lambda_{YL}\lambda_{YK}\sigma_{Y}$$

$$\Delta^{M} = \lambda_{XL}^{M}\lambda_{YK}\theta_{XL}^{M} + \lambda_{XK}^{M}\lambda_{YL}\theta_{XK}^{M},$$

and

$$\Delta^{F} = \lambda_{XL}^{F}\lambda_{YK}\theta_{XL}^{F} + \lambda_{XK}^{F}\lambda_{YL}\theta_{XK}^{F}.$$

Noting $d\boldsymbol{S} = 0$ yields (22.17), and this completes the derivation of (22.17) and (22.21). ■

Appendix 22.B. Local Stability of the System

To simplify the stability analysis, we assume that the wage and rental rates are adjusted instantly to equate demand and supply for labor and capital, respectively. Similarly, the market for Y is assumed to be cleared immediately. Thus, (22.3), (22.9), and (22.10) always hold along any adjustment path. We further assume that $\boldsymbol{S} = 0$.

We denote by ω^*, q^*, and n^* the equilibrium values of the wage-rental ratio, the individual output of each oligopolistic firm, and the number of firms, respectively. Assumptions on the adjustment process in the market for factors and for good Y warrant that

$$\frac{\omega - \omega^*}{\omega^*} = -\frac{1}{\Delta}\left\{\lambda^M \frac{q - q^*}{q^*} + \lambda^A \frac{n - n^*}{n^*}\right\} \tag{22.B.1}$$

and

$$p_Y = g(w, r) \tag{22.B.2}$$

hold in the neighborhood of equilibrium.

We next define the dynamic adjustment process by

$$\dot{q} = \kappa \left\{\phi(nq)\left(1 - \frac{1}{n\epsilon}\right) - \frac{m(w, r, 0)}{g(w, r)}\right\}, \tag{22.B.3}$$

$$\dot{n} = \eta \left\{\phi(nq)q - \frac{m(w, r, 0)}{g(w, r)}q - \frac{F(w, r, 0)}{g(w, r)}\right\}, \tag{22.B.4}$$

where $\dot{q}$ and $\dot{n}$ denote the time derivative of q and n, and $\kappa > 0$ and $\eta > 0$ are adjustment coefficients.

Linearly approximating (22.B.3) and (22.B.4) around the free-entry equilibrium and using (22.B.1), we obtain

$$\dot{q} = \kappa^* \left\{\left(-\frac{1}{\epsilon} - \frac{A}{\Delta}\theta^M \lambda^M\right)\frac{q - q^*}{q^*} + \left(-\alpha - \frac{A}{\Delta}\theta^M \lambda^A\right)\frac{n - n^*}{n^*}\right\}, \tag{22.B.5}$$

$$\dot{n} = \eta^* \left\{\left(-\frac{n^* - 1}{n^*\epsilon} - \frac{B}{\Delta}\theta^A \lambda^M\right)\frac{q - q^*}{q^*} + \left(-\frac{1}{\epsilon} - \frac{B}{\Delta}\theta^A \lambda^A\right)\frac{n - n^*}{n^*}\right\}, \tag{22.B.6}$$

where $\kappa^* = \kappa\phi(n^*q^*)\{1 - (1/n^*\epsilon)\} > 0$ and $\eta^* = \eta\phi(n^*q^*)q^* > 0$. Observe from these adjustment equations that the equilibrium is locally stable if

$$-\frac{1}{\epsilon} - \frac{A}{\Delta}\theta^M \lambda^M < 0$$

and

$$-\frac{H}{\Delta} = \left(-\frac{1}{\epsilon} - \frac{A}{\Delta}\theta^M\lambda^M\right)\left(-\frac{1}{\epsilon} - \frac{B}{\Delta}\theta^A\lambda^A\right) - \left(-\alpha - \frac{A}{\Delta}\theta^M\lambda^A\right)$$
$$\times\left(-\frac{n^*-1}{n^*\epsilon} - \frac{B}{\Delta}\theta^A\lambda^M\right) > 0.$$

The first inequality is always satisfied. Hence, $H < 0$ is sufficient for the local stability of equilibrium, as was to be verified.[15] ∎

References

[1] Anderson, R., and J. G. Ballentine, "The Incidence and Excess Burden of a Profit Tax under Imperfect Competition," *Public Finance* **31**, 1976, 159–176.

[2] Atkinson, A. B., and J. E. Stiglitz, *Lectures on Public Economics*, New York: McGraw-Hill, 1980.

[3] Besley, T., and K. Suzumura, "Taxation and Welfare in an Oligopoly with Strategic Commitment," *International Economic Review* **33**, 1992, 413–431.

[4] Bulow, J. I., J. D. Geanakoplos, and P. D. Klemperer, " Multimarket Oligopoly: Strategic Substitutes and Complements," *Journal of Political Economy* **93**, 1985, 488–511.

[5] Dixit, A. K., and J. E. Stiglitz, "Monopolistic Competition and Optimum Product Diversity," *American Economic Review* **67**, 1977, 297–308.

[6] Harberger, A. C., "The Incidence of the Corporation Income Tax," *Journal of Political Economy* **70**, 1962, 215–240.

[7] Jones, R. W., "The Structure of Simple General Equilibrium Models," *Journal of Political Economy* **73**, 1965, 557–572.

[8] Jones, R. W., "Variable Returns to Scale in General Equilibrium Theory," *International Economic Review* **9**, 1968, 261–272.

[9] Katz, M. L., and H. S. Rosen, "Tax Analysis in an Oligopoly Model," *Public Finance Quarterly* **13**, 1985, 9–20.

[10] Konishi, H., "Optimal Tax-Subsidy Structure in an Oligopolistic Economy with Free Entry." Paper presented at the annual meeting of the Japan Association of Economics and Econometrics, Kyoto University, 1988.

[11] Konishi, H., M. Okuno-Fujiwara, and K. Suzumura, "Welfare-Improving Tax-Subsidy Schemes in an Oligopolistic Setting," mimeograph, 1988.

[12] Kotlikoff, L. J., and L. Summers, "Tax Incidence," in A. J. Auerbach and M. Feldstein, eds., *Handbook of Public Economics*, Vol. 2, Amsterdam: North-Holland, 1987, 1043–1093.

---

15. Note that the asterisks are omitted in the main text.

[13] Mankiw, N. G., and M. D. Whinston, "Free Entry and Social Inefficiency," *Rand Journal of Economics* **17**, 1986, 48–58.
[14] Myles, G. D., "Ramsey Tax Rules for Economies with Imperfect Competition," *Journal of Public Economics* **38**, 1989, 95–116.
[15] Robinson, J., *The Economics of Imperfect Competition*, London: Macmillan, 1933; 2nd edn., 1969.
[16] Seade, J., "On the Effects of Entry," *Econometrica* **48**, 1980, 479–489.
[17] Seade, J., "Profitable Cost Increases and the Shifting of Taxation: Equilibrium Responses of Markets in Oligopoly," Warwick economic research paper, University of Warwick, Coventry, England, 1985.
[18] Stern, N. H., "The Effects of Taxation, Price Control, and Government Contracts in Oligopoly and Monopolistic Competition," *Journal of Public Economics* **32**, 1987, 133–158.
[19] Suzumura, K., and K. Kiyono, "Entry Barriers and Economic Welfare," *Review of Economic Studies* **54**, 1987, 157–167. Essay 21 of this volume.

ESSAY 23

Symmetric Cournot Oligopoly and Economic Welfare: A Synthesis

23.1. Introduction

Recent studies have revealed that competition may sometimes be socially "excessive." In particular, Mankiw and Winston [11] and Suzumura and Kiyono [21] have shown that socially excessive firm entry may occur in unregulated oligopolistic markets.[1] This happens because entry is occasionally more desirable to entrants than to the society, as new entry creates an incentive for incumbent firms to reduce their output. This result was established in a partial equilibrium framework for a symmetric Cournot oligopoly.[2]

First published in *Economic Theory* **3**, 1993, 43–59. Joint paper with M. Okuno-Fujiwara. This is the synthesized version of the two earlier papers, Okuno-Fujiwara and Suzumura [12] and Suzumura [19]. We are grateful to J. Brander, D. Cass, M. Majumdar, A. Postlewaite, J. Richmond, A. Sandmo, B. Spencer, and J. Vickers for their helpful comments and discussions on earlier drafts. Needless to say, they should not be held responsible for any remaining defects of this essay. Financial support from the Japan Center for Economic Research, Tokyo Center for Economic Research, a Grant-in-Aid for Scientific Research from the Ministry of Education, Culture, Sports, Science and Technology of Japan, and the Institute for Monetary and Economic Research, the Bank of Japan, is gratefully acknowledged.

1. See also Perry [13] and von Weizsäcker [22; 23].
2. Konishi, Okuno-Fujiwara, and Suzumura [9] have generalized this result with general equilibrium interactions, whereas Lahiri and Ono [10] have shown that this paradoxical result essentially survives with heterogeneous firms by proving that eliminating minor firms increases social welfare through the improvement of average production efficiency, which overwhelms the undesirable effect of a change in market structure.

The purpose of the present essay is to add a new dimension to this literature by looking into strategic aspects of cost-reducing R&D investment that may create incentives toward socially excessive investment. We consider an oligopolistic competition played in three stages. In the first stage, firms simultaneously decide whether or not to enter the market. In the second stage, firms make an irrevocable commitment to R&D investment, which affects production cost in the third stage where firms compete in quantities. Since R&D investment is a fixed commitment, firms' investment decisions are affected by strategic considerations.

In Section 23.2 and Section 23.3 of this essay, we analyze the second-stage game and the third-stage game, respectively, with a number of firms fixed. Brander and Spencer [2] analyzed these games in a Cournot *duopoly* setting and showed that the level of investment is higher at the strategic equilibrium than at the nonstrategic equilibrium. They also showed that investment is sometimes socially excessive as it exceeds the level that maximizes second-best social welfare.[3] In this essay, we identify the causes of this excessive investment and generalize their results in several respects. First, we shall focus on the excessive investment *at the margin* and decompose the welfare effect of an additional investment into the *commitment effect* and the *distortion effect*. Second, by invoking the concept of *strategic substitutes* due to Bulow, Geanakoplos, and Klemperer [4], we shall provide a clear interpretation of the excessive investment result.[4] Third, we shall establish that an increase in the number of firms is likely to cause a socially excessive investment.

In Section 23.4 of this essay, we shall consider the fully fledged three-stage game. Under a set of rather weak assumptions, we shall show that the excessive entry à la Mankiw-Whinston and Suzumura-Kiyono is extended even with the existence of strategic investment.

The structure of this essay is as follows. In Section 23.2, our model is formulated. Section 23.3 considers the second-stage game and the third-stage game with a fixed number of firms, and decomposes the welfare effect of a

3. Note, however, they assumed Cournot competition with product differentiation, while in this essay we assume Cournot quantity competition with homogeneous product. See also d'Aspremont and Jacquemin [5] and Suzumura [20], which analyzed the role of R&D spillovers and cooperative research associations in the framework of two-stage oligopoly models.

4. Brander and Spencer [2, p. 277] assumed, in effect, that products are strategic substitutes. See also Besley and Suzumura [1], Eaton and Grossman [7], and Fundenberg and Tiroie [8] for other contexts where this assumption plays an essential role.

change in R&D investment into the commitment effect and the distortion effect. In this section, we show that, under fairly mild conditions, the strategic R&D investment is socially excessive at the margin if the actual number of firms exceeds a certain critical level. Section 23.4 extends our analysis to the full three-stage model, and a marginal reduction of the number of firms from the free-entry level is shown to improve social welfare under a slightly more restrictive set of assumptions. Proofs are gathered in Section 23.5. Section 23.6 concludes.

23.2. Subgame Perfect Equilibrium of the Three-Stage Game

The cost reducing R&D is a crucial measure for firms competing in the oligopolistic industry. On the one hand, it is a powerful measure for potential firms trying to enter into the oligopolistic industry, as a successful cost-reducing R&D helps challengers to establish the competitive advantage vis-à-vis incumbent firms. On the other hand, it is a powerful measure for incumbent firms to defend themselves against the challenge from potential firms. Thus, both from offensive and defensive viewpoints, the cost-reducing R&D is a crucial factor in the analysis of oligopolistic competition. Apart from this aspect, there is another important aspect of the R&D activity, which may be called the *commitment aspect.* Investment in the cost-reducing R&D activity must be committed well ahead of time before the commencement of competition in the product market. In Essay 21 and Essay 22 in this volume, the welfare performance of the oligopolistic competition is examined without introducing the strategic commitment to R&D by incumbent firms and potential entrants. This essay is devoted to the analysis that fills in this conspicuous lacuna by considering the subgame-perfect equilibrium of the three-stage model of oligopolistic competition involving the strategic commitment with R&D.

23.2.1. Three-Stage Model of Oligopolistic Competition and Equilibrium Concepts

Consider an industry where operating firms produce a homogeneous product. Firms engage in three-stage competition. There are an infinite number of potential entrants. In the first stage, firms decide whether or not to enter the market in a predetermined sequential order. In the second stage, each firm makes a strategic commitment to cost-reducing R&D, whereas firms compete in terms of quantities in the third stage.

In this essay, we will utilize three different equilibrium concepts. Given any arbitrary number of firms and R&D investment profiles, the *third-stage Cournot-Nash equilibrium* is defined. Given an arbitrary number of firms, the *second-stage subgame perfect equilibrium* is defined when the relevant game is defined by the second and third stages of the entire game. Finally, the *first-stage free-entry equilibrium* is defined as a subgame perfect equilibrium of the entire game. The focus of our analysis is the welfare performance of the second-stage symmetric subgame perfect equilibrium and the first-stage free-entry equilibrium.

23.2.2. Basic Assumptions

The inverse demand function for the product is $p = f(Q)$, where p is the price and Q is the industry output. The cost-reducing R&D and the output level of firm i is denoted by x_i and q_i, respectively, and the variable cost function of firm i is represented by $c(x_i)q_i$, where the marginal cost function $c(\cdot)$ is assumed to be identical for all firms.

For each specified number of firms $n \geq 2$ and each specified profile of R&D commitments $\boldsymbol{x} = (x_1, x_2, \ldots, x_n) > 0$, the third-stage payoff function of firm i is given by

$$\pi^i(\boldsymbol{q}; \boldsymbol{x}; n) := \{f(Q) - c(x_i)\}q_i - x_i, \tag{23.1}$$

where $\boldsymbol{q} = (q_1, q_2, \ldots, q_n)$ and $Q = \sum_{j=1}^{n} q_j$. For notational simplicity, we assume that the R&D level x_i is measured by the expenditure for equipment installations. Let $\boldsymbol{q}^N(\boldsymbol{x}; n)$ denote the *third-stage Cournot-Nash equilibrium* corresponding to the specified $(\boldsymbol{x}; n)$.

We assume throughout that $\boldsymbol{q}^N(\boldsymbol{x}; n)$ is unique, symmetric and positive if the R&D profile $\boldsymbol{x}$ is symmetric and positive.[5] We also make the following assumptions.

5. An n-vector $\boldsymbol{y} = (y_1, y_2, \ldots, y_n)$ is *symmetric* if $y_i = y_j$ for all $i, j = 1, 2, \ldots, n$, whereas $\boldsymbol{y}$ is *positive* if $y_i > 0$ for all $i = 1, 2, \ldots, n$.

Assumption A1. $f(Q)$ is twice continuously differentiable and satisfies $f'(Q) < 0$ for all $Q \geq 0$ such that $f(Q) > 0$. Furthermore, there exists a constant $\delta_0 > -\infty$ such that[6]

$$\delta(Q) := \frac{Qf''(Q)}{f'(Q)} \geq \delta_0 \quad \text{for all } Q \geq 0 \text{ with } f(Q) > 0. \qquad (23.2)$$

Assumption A2. $c(x)$ is twice continuously differentiable and satisfies $c(x) > 0$, $c'(x) < 0$, and $c''(x) > 0$ for all $x \geq 0$.

For any output profile $\boldsymbol{q} = (q_1, q_2, \ldots, q_n)$, any R&D profile $\boldsymbol{x} = (x_1, x_2, \ldots, x_n)$, and any number of firms n, we define

$$\alpha_i(\boldsymbol{q}; \boldsymbol{x}; n) := \frac{\partial^2}{\partial q_i^2} \pi^i(\boldsymbol{q}; \boldsymbol{x}; n)$$

$$\beta_{ij}(\boldsymbol{q}; \boldsymbol{x}; n) := \frac{\partial^2}{\partial q_i \partial q_j} \pi^i(\boldsymbol{q}; \boldsymbol{x}; n) \; (i \neq j; i, j = 1, 2, \ldots, n).$$

Note that $\beta_{ij}(\boldsymbol{q}; \boldsymbol{x}; n)$ is the crucial term that determines whether the second-stage strategies are *strategic substitutes* ($\beta_{ij}(\boldsymbol{q}; \boldsymbol{x}; n) < 0$) or *strategic complements* ($\beta_{ij}(\boldsymbol{q}; \boldsymbol{x}; n) > 0$).[7] We make the following assumption.

Assumption A3. The second-stage strategies are strategic substitutes so that $\beta_{ij}(\boldsymbol{q}; \boldsymbol{x}; n) < 0$ holds for any $(\boldsymbol{q}; \boldsymbol{x}; n)$ $(i \neq j; i, j = 1, 2, \ldots, n)$.

Remark 23.1. A1 admits the following class of inverse demand functions with constant elasticity δ of $f'(Q)$:

$$f(Q) = \begin{cases} a - bQ^{\gamma} & \text{if } \gamma = \delta + 1 \neq 0 \\ a - b \cdot \log Q & \text{if } \delta = -1, \end{cases} \qquad (23.3)$$

where a is a nonnegative constant and b is a positive (resp. negative) constant if $\gamma < 0$ (resp. $\gamma > 0$). Note that (23.3) includes a linear demand ($\gamma = 1$)

6. The elasticity δ of the slope of the inverse demand function plays a crucial role in many contexts of oligopolistic interaction. See Besley and Suzumura [1], Seade [15; 16], Suzumura [19], and Suzumura and Kiyono [21], among others.

7. For the concept of strategic substitutes and complements, see Bulow, Geanakoplos, and Klemperer [4]. See also Eaton and Grossman [7] and Fudenberg and Tirole [8].

as well as constantly elastic demand ($a = 0$), so that it still accommodates a wide class of "normal" inverse demand functions.

Remark 23.2. The assumption of strategic substitutability is quite natural to require in our present context, since it is equivalent to assuming the downward-sloping reaction functions in the third-stage quantity game.

Remark 23.3. It is easy to verify that

$$\alpha_i(\boldsymbol{q}^N(\boldsymbol{x};n);\boldsymbol{x};n) = 2f'(Q^N(\boldsymbol{x};n)) + q_i^N(\boldsymbol{x};n) \cdot f''(Q^N(\boldsymbol{x};n)) \quad (23.4)$$

and

$$\beta_{ij}(\boldsymbol{q}^N(\boldsymbol{x};n);\boldsymbol{x};n) = f'(Q^N(\boldsymbol{x};n)) + q_i^N(\boldsymbol{x};n) \cdot f''(Q^N(\boldsymbol{x};n)) \quad (23.5)$$

hold, where $Q^N(\boldsymbol{x};n) = \sum_{j=1}^n q_j^N(\boldsymbol{x};n)$. If $\boldsymbol{x}$ is symmetric, α_i and β_{ij} are identical for all i and j. In this case, invoking (23.2), we can rewrite (23.4) and (23.5) as

$$\alpha(\boldsymbol{x};n) = n^{-1} \cdot f'(Q^N(\boldsymbol{x};n)) \cdot \{2n + \delta(Q^N(\boldsymbol{x};n))\} \quad (23.6)$$

and

$$\beta(\boldsymbol{x};n) = n^{-1} \cdot f'(Q^N(\boldsymbol{x};n)) \cdot \{n + \delta(Q^N(\boldsymbol{x};n))\}, \quad (23.7)$$

respectively, where we are using $\alpha(\boldsymbol{x};n) := \alpha_i(\boldsymbol{q}^N(\boldsymbol{x};n);\boldsymbol{x};n)$ and $\beta(\boldsymbol{x};n) := \beta_{ij}(\boldsymbol{q}^N(\boldsymbol{x};n);\boldsymbol{x};n)$ for notational simplicity. Therefore, A3 implies that

$$n + \delta(Q^N(\boldsymbol{x};n)) > 0 \quad (23.8)$$

for any $\boldsymbol{x}$ and $n \geq 2$, where use is made of A1. Note that (23.8) is satisfied for any $n \geq 2$ if and only if

$$2 + \delta(Q^N(\boldsymbol{x};n)) > 0 \quad (23.8^*)$$

holds. Note also that A1 and (23.8) guarantee that $\alpha(\boldsymbol{x};n) < 0$ holds for any $(\boldsymbol{x};n)$.

23.2.3. Properties of the Third-Stage Cournot-Nash Equilibrium

Under the assumption of an interior optimum, the third-stage Cournot-Nash equilibrium $\boldsymbol{q}^N(\boldsymbol{x}; n)$ is characterized by

$$f(Q^N(\boldsymbol{x}; n)) + q_i^N(\boldsymbol{x}; n) \cdot f'(Q^N(\boldsymbol{x}; n)) = c(x_i) \quad (i = 1, 2, \ldots, n). \tag{23.9}$$

The first aim of our analysis is to ascertain how the Cournot-Nash output $q_i(\boldsymbol{x}; n)$ behaves in response to a change in x_i, x_j $(i \neq j)$ and n. Defining $\omega(\boldsymbol{x}; n) := (\partial/\partial x_i)q_i^N(\boldsymbol{x}; n)$ and $\theta(\boldsymbol{x}; n) := (\partial/\partial x_j)q_i^N(\boldsymbol{x}; n)$ $(i \neq j)$, straightforward computations assert the following.

LEMMA 23.1. For each symmetric $\boldsymbol{x}$ and n,

$$(\partial/\partial n)q_i^N(\boldsymbol{x}; n) = -\frac{q_i^N(\boldsymbol{x}; n) \cdot \beta(\boldsymbol{x}; n)}{\alpha(\boldsymbol{x}; n) + (n-1)\beta(\boldsymbol{x}; n)} < 0, \tag{23.10}$$

$$\omega(\boldsymbol{x}; n) = \frac{c'(x_i)}{\Delta(\boldsymbol{x}; n)} \cdot \{\alpha(\boldsymbol{x}; n) + (n-2)\beta(\boldsymbol{x}; n)\} > 0, \tag{23.11}$$

and

$$\theta(\boldsymbol{x}; n) = -\frac{c'(x_i)}{\Delta(\boldsymbol{x}; n)} \cdot \beta(\boldsymbol{x}; n) < 0 \tag{23.12}$$

hold, where[8]

$$\Delta(\boldsymbol{x}; n) := \{\alpha(\boldsymbol{x}; n) - \beta(\boldsymbol{x}; n)\} \cdot \{\alpha(\boldsymbol{x}; n) + (n-1)\beta(\boldsymbol{x}; n)\} > 0. \tag{23.13}$$

---

8. Since $\beta(\boldsymbol{x}; n) < 0$ and $\alpha(\boldsymbol{x}; n) < 0$ hold under A1 and A3, it follows that

$$\alpha(\boldsymbol{x}; n) + (k-1)\beta(\boldsymbol{x}; n) < 0 \quad (k = 0, 1, \ldots, n) \tag{23.1*}$$

holds. Note that (23.1*) is a sufficient condition for the local stability of the myopic adjustment process

$$\dot{q}_i = \sigma \cdot \frac{\partial}{\partial q_i}\pi^i(\boldsymbol{q}; \boldsymbol{x}; n) \quad (i = 1, 2, \ldots, n), \tag{23.2*}$$

where $\dot{q}_i$ denotes the time derivative of q_i and $\sigma > 0$ stands for the adjustment coefficient.

23.2.4. Characterization of the Nash Equilibrium of the Second-Stage Game

We now turn to the second-stage game. For each specified n, the first-stage payoff function of firm i is given by

$$\Pi^i(\boldsymbol{x}; n) := \pi^i(\boldsymbol{q}^N(\boldsymbol{x}; n); \boldsymbol{x}; n). \tag{23.14}$$

If we denote the Nash equilibrium of the second-stage game by $\boldsymbol{x}^N(n)$, $\{\boldsymbol{x}^N(n), \boldsymbol{q}^N(\boldsymbol{x}^N(n); n)\}$ is nothing other than the *second-stage subgame perfect equilibrium* among n firms. We assume throughout that $\boldsymbol{x}^N(n)$ is unique, symmetric, and positive for each n.

Assuming an interior optimum, $\boldsymbol{x}^N(n)$ is characterized by

$$\begin{aligned} &\{f'(Q^N(\boldsymbol{x}^N(n); n)) - c(x_i^N(n))\} \cdot (\partial/\partial x_i) q_i^N(\boldsymbol{x}^N(n); n) + q_i^N(\boldsymbol{x}^N(n); n) \\ &\quad \cdot \{f(Q^N(\boldsymbol{x}^N(n); n)) \cdot (\partial/\partial x_i) Q^N(\boldsymbol{x}^N(n); n) - c'(x_i^N(n))\} \\ &\quad - 1 = 0 \quad (i = 1, 2, \ldots, n). \end{aligned} \tag{23.15}$$

Invoking (23.9) for $\boldsymbol{x} = \boldsymbol{x}^N(n)$, (23.15) may be reduced to

$$\begin{aligned} &- c'(x_i^N(n)) \cdot q_i^N(\boldsymbol{x}^N(n); n) - 1 = \{f(Q^N(\boldsymbol{x}^N(n); n)) - c(x_i^N(n))\} \\ &\quad \cdot \sum_{j \neq i} (\partial/\partial x_i) q_j^N(\boldsymbol{x}^N(n); n) \quad (i = 1, 2, \ldots, n), \end{aligned} \tag{23.16}$$

which proves to be crucially important in what follows.

23.2.5. First-Stage Free-Entry Equilibrium

Consider now the profits $\Pi^i(\boldsymbol{x}^N(n); n)$ earned by firm i at the second-stage subgame perfect equilibrium among n firms. According to the classical entry/exit dynamics, the number of firms n will increase (resp. decrease) whenever $\Pi^i(\boldsymbol{x}^N(n); n) > 0$ (resp. < 0), viz.,

$$\dot{n} > 0 \text{ (resp. } < 0) \Leftrightarrow \Pi^i(\boldsymbol{x}^N(n); n) > 0 \text{ (resp. } < 0), \tag{23.17}$$

where $\dot{n}$ denotes the time derivative of n.

Let the *equilibrium number of firms* n_e be defined as the stationary point of the dynamic process specified by (23.17):

$$\Pi^i(\boldsymbol{x}^N(n_e); n_e) = 0 \quad (i = 1, 2, \ldots, n_e). \tag{23.18}$$

Then $\{n_e, \boldsymbol{x}^N(n_e), \boldsymbol{q}^N(\boldsymbol{x}^N(n_e); n_e)\}$ constitutes the *first-stage free-entry equilibrium*.

23.2.6. Welfare Measure of Net Market Surplus

To gauge the welfare performance of the industry, we define the *net market surplus function* by

$$W(\boldsymbol{q}; \boldsymbol{x}; n) := \int_0^Q f(Z)dZ - \sum_{j=1}^{n} \{c(x_j)q_j + x_j\}, \tag{23.19}$$

where $Q = \sum_{j=1}^{n} q_j$.

If the government can control this industry in its entirety from the viewpoint of social welfare maximization, the best that can be done is to impose the socially first-best R&D, $x^F(n)$, and the socially first-best output, $q^F(n)$, on each incumbent firm and to choose the *first-best number of firms*, n_f. These are defined by

$$f(nq^F(n)) - c(x^F(n)) = 0, \tag{23.20}$$

$$-c'(x^F(n)) \cdot q^F(n) - 1 = 0, \tag{23.21}$$

and

$$n_f := \arg\max_{n \geq 1} W(\boldsymbol{q}^F(n), \boldsymbol{x}^F(n); n). \tag{23.22}$$

Realistically speaking, however, such a first-best policy is hard to implement, since firms are thereby imposed to produce at a deficit. If the government cannot control firms' competitive strategies, however, the best that can still be done may be to choose the *second-best number of firms:*

$$n_s := \arg\max_{n \geq 1} W(\boldsymbol{q}^N(\boldsymbol{x}^N(n); n); \boldsymbol{x}^N(n); n). \tag{23.23}$$

That is, let n_s firms freely compete to establish the second-stage subgame perfect equilibrium $\{\boldsymbol{x}^N(n_s); \boldsymbol{q}^N(\boldsymbol{x}^N(n_s); n_s)\}$.

In the short run, however, the government may not be able to control the number of firms. It may be forced to control the R&D level of each incumbent firm to the second-best level, $x^S(n)$, which is defined by

$$x^S(n) := \arg\max_{x>0} W(\boldsymbol{q}^N(\boldsymbol{x}; n); \boldsymbol{x}; n). \tag{23.24}$$

Despite its obvious relevance and appeal, such second-best policies may still be difficult to implement. Because of uncertainty on the precise nature of the functions involved, it may be prohibitively hard to identify where exactly $x^S(n)$ is located. What is required is a policy prescription that does not presuppose the availability of detailed knowledge on the nature of demand and cost functions involved. This is precisely what we look for in the next sections.

23.3. Social Excessiveness of R&D at the Margin

Observe that the present three-stage model of oligopolistic competition has three distinct concepts of equilibrium, depending on the constraint on the variables to be held fixed. For the sake of mnemonic convenience, the time span over which both the number of firms in the industry and the level of R&D commitment by firms are held fixed is called "short-run," the time span over which the number of firms in the industry is held fixed is called "medium-run," and the time span over which the number of firms in the industry, the level of R&D commitment, and the output level of each firm are not fixed at all is called "long-run." In this Section 23.3, we are concerned with the welfare performance of the medium-run subgame perfect equilibrium of the model, whereas in Section 23.4, we are concerned with the welfare performance of the long-run subgame perfect equilibrium of the model.

23.3.1. Commitment Effect and Distortion Effect

In this section, we assume the number of firms, n, is uncontrollable but R&D investment is under the government's control. Let $W^N(\boldsymbol{x}; n)$ be the net market surplus with output evaluated at the third-stage Cournot-Nash equilibrium:

$$W^N(\boldsymbol{x}; n) := \int_0^{Q^N(x;n)} f(Q)dQ - \sum_{j=1}^{n} \{c(x_j)q_j^N(\boldsymbol{x}; n) + x_j\}. \quad (23.25)$$

Suppose $(\partial/\partial x_i)W^N(\boldsymbol{x}(n); n) <$ (resp. $>$) 0. Then a marginal *decrease* (resp. a marginal *increase*) of firm i's investment at the second-stage subgame perfect equilibrium *increases* social welfare, so that the investment at the subgame perfect equilibrium is *socially excessive* (resp. *socially insufficient*) *at the margin*.

To understand what determines the crucial term $(\partial/\partial x_i)W^N(\boldsymbol{x}^N(n); n)$, it is useful to decompose it into the *commitment effect* $C_i(\boldsymbol{x}^N(n); n)$ and the *distortion effect* $D_i(\boldsymbol{x}^N(n); n)$. To be concrete, the commitment effect is defined by[9]

$$C_i(\boldsymbol{x}^N(n); n) := -c'(x_i^N(n)) \cdot q_i^N(\boldsymbol{x}^N(n); n) - 1, \qquad (23.26)$$

which, in view of (23.16), can be reduced to

$$C_i(\boldsymbol{x}^N(n); n) := \mu_i(\boldsymbol{x}^N(n); n) \cdot \sum_{j \neq i} (\partial/\partial x_i)q_j^N(\boldsymbol{x}^N(n); n), \quad (23.27)$$

whereas the distortion effect is defined by

$$D_i(\boldsymbol{x}^N(n); n) := \sum_{j=1}^{n} \mu_j(\boldsymbol{x}^N(n); n) \cdot (\partial/\partial x_i)q_j^N(\boldsymbol{x}^N(n); n), \quad (23.28)$$

where $\mu_j(\boldsymbol{x}^N(n); n) := f(Q^N(\boldsymbol{x}^N(n); n)) - c(x_j^N(n))$ denotes the *marginal distortion* of firm j, which is independent of firm index j at the

9. In the *absence* of strategic commitment, the problem of social welfare maximization takes the form of maximizing $\int_0^Q f(Z)dZ - \sum_{j=1}^n \{c(x_j)q_j + x_j\}$ with respect to $\{(q_i; x_i)\}_{i=1}^n$. The first-order conditions are then $f(Q) - c(x_i) = 0$ and $-c'(x_i)q_i - 1 = 0$ $(i = 1, 2, \ldots, n)$. Observe that the latter condition suggests that $C_i(\boldsymbol{x}^N(n); n)$ becomes nonzero *only by the presence of strategic commitment*.

symmetric equilibrium. By simply adding $C_i(\boldsymbol{x}^N(n); n)$ and $D_i(\boldsymbol{x}^N(n); n)$, we obtain the crucial term $(\partial/\partial x_i) W^N(\boldsymbol{x}^N(n); n)$.

In view of the symmetry of $\boldsymbol{x}$ and (23.11)–(23.13),

$$C_i(\boldsymbol{x}^N(n); n) = (n-1) \cdot \mu(\boldsymbol{x}^N(n); n) \cdot \theta(\boldsymbol{x}^N(n); n) < 0 \quad (23.29)$$

and

$$D_i(\boldsymbol{x}^N(n); n) = \mu(\boldsymbol{x}^N(n); n) \cdot \{\omega(\boldsymbol{x}^N(n); n) + (n-1) \cdot \theta(\boldsymbol{x}^N(n); n)\} > 0, \quad (23.30)$$

where $\mu(\boldsymbol{x}^N(n); n) := \mu_j(\boldsymbol{x}^N(n); n) > 0$. Therefore, $(\partial/\partial x_i) W^N(\boldsymbol{x}^N(n); n)$ consists of two components with opposite signs.

23.3.2. Graphical Illustration

It may be useful to illustrate our decomposition of the marginal welfare effect with the help of Figure 23.1. At the original symmetric subgame perfect equilibrium, each firm produces $q_i^* := q_i^N(\boldsymbol{x}^N(n); n)$ with the marginal cost $c^* := c(x_i^N(n); n)$, and the industry output is $Q^* := nq_i^*$. If firm i unilaterally increases its investment by a small amount $\epsilon > 0$, its marginal cost is reduced to $c^{**} := c^* - \epsilon \cdot \{-c'(x_i^N(n))\}$. Products being strategic substitutes, this increase in firm i's aggressiveness reduces other firms' output, so that firm i's residual demand curve shifts up, the industry output increases to Q^{**}, and the output of firm i increases to q_i^{**}.

The net welfare gain from this change consists of the following:

$$\text{change in consumers' surplus} = \text{area } Ap^{**}B' - \text{area } Ap^*B = \text{area } Bp^*p^{**}B',$$

and

$$\text{change in profits} = (\text{area } B'p^{**}c^*D' + \text{area } Cc^*c^{**}C' - \epsilon) - \text{area } Bp^*c^*D,$$

which, after neglecting terms of the second-order infinitesimal, boils down to (area $B'EDD'$) + (area $Fc^*c^{**}F' - \epsilon$). It is clear that the first term is noth-

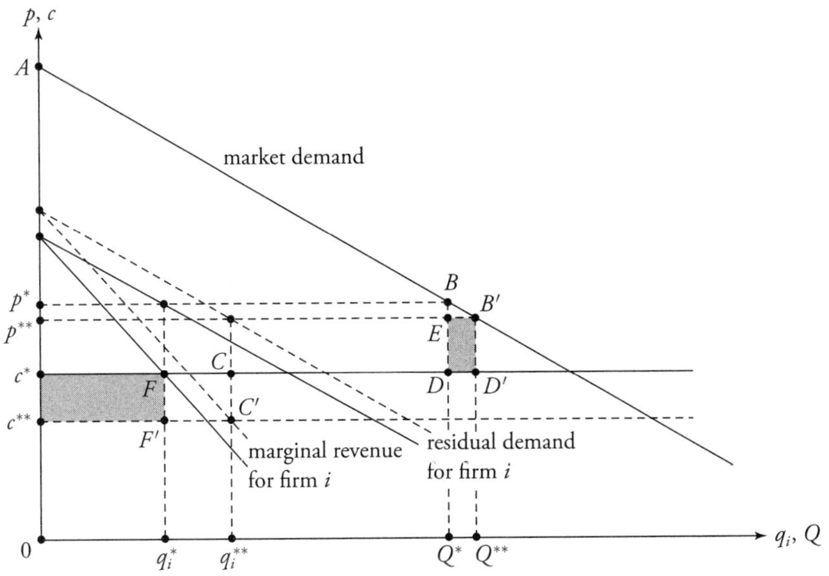

Figure 23.1. Distortion Effect and Commitment Effect

ing other than our distortion effect, whereas the second term corresponds precisely to our commitment effect.

Thus, the distortion effect, which is nothing but the familiar sum of marginal distortions, represents the welfare loss caused by the exercise of firms' monopolistic power on consumers. Clearly, an increase in investment that increases the industry's total supply will generate a positive distortion effect. On the other hand, the commitment effect measures the extent to which a firm can extract additional profits by capturing other firms' market share by taking advantage of a better third-stage game structure via an increase in investment in x_i. The total effect on economic welfare depends on the relative strength of these conflicting effects.

23.3.3. Excessive Investment Theorem at the Margin

In the rest of this section, we shall elucidate that the commitment effect is likely to dominate the distortion effect, so that the term $(\partial/\partial x_i)W^N(\boldsymbol{x}^N(n); n)$ is likely to become negative, if the number of firms is sufficiently large.

In view of (23.29), (23.30), (23.6), (23.7), (23.11) and (23.12), and noting A1 and (23.13), the condition for

$$(\partial/\partial x_i)W^N(\boldsymbol{x}^N(n);n) = C_i(\boldsymbol{x}^N(n);n) + D_i(\boldsymbol{x}^N(n);n) < 0$$

can be reduced to

$$1-(n-1)\cdot\left\{-\frac{(\partial/\partial x_i)q_j^N(\boldsymbol{x}^N(n);n)}{(\partial/\partial x_i)Q^N(\boldsymbol{x}^N(n);n)}\right\} < 0, \qquad (23.31)$$

which can be further reduced to

$$n^2 - 2n + (n-1)\delta(Q^N(\boldsymbol{x}^N(n);n)) > 0. \qquad (23.32)$$

By virtue of A1, (23.32) holds whenever $\lambda(n) := n^2 - 2n + (n-1)\delta_0 > 0$ is satisfied. Let $N(\delta_0) > 0$ be the largest root of the quadratic equation $\lambda(n) = 0$. Then $(\partial/\partial x_i)W^N(\boldsymbol{x}^N(n);n) < 0$ holds if $n > N(\delta_0)$. Thus we arrive at Theorem 23.1.

THEOREM 23.1. Under A1, A2, and A3, there exists a positive number $N(\delta_0)$ such that $(\partial/\partial x_i)W^N(\boldsymbol{x}^N(n);n) < 0$ holds, viz., the strategic cost-reducing investment is socially excessive at the margin if $n > N(\delta_0)$.

An important question still remains. How large is the critical number $N(\delta_0)$ that appears in Theorem 23.1? In the case of concave inverse demand functions, it is easy to see that $N(\delta_0) = 2$. In the case of constantly elastic inverse demand functions, $N(\delta_0)$ will increase as the elasticity η of the inverse demand function increases, but for all values of η satisfying $0 < \eta < 1$, we have $1 < N(\delta_0) < 2 + \sqrt{2}$. Thus, $N(\delta_0)$ remains fairly small for these important classes of situations.

23.3.4. Excessive Investment Theorem Illustrated

It may be useful to graphically illustrate why the number of firms, n, plays an important role in deciding social excessiveness of investment. Define the third-stage *reaction function* of firm i by

$$r_i(Q_{-i};x_i^0) := \arg\max_{q_i>0}\{f(q_i+Q_{-i}) - c(x_i^0)\}q_i, \qquad (23.33)$$

where $Q_{-i} := \sum_{j \neq i} q_j$, and an investment profile $\boldsymbol{x}^0 := (x_1^0, x_2^0, \ldots, x_n^0)$ is fixed. Then the *cumulative reaction function* $R_i(Q; x_i^0)$ is defined by

$$q_i = R_i(Q; x_i^0) \Leftrightarrow q_i = r_i(Q - q_i; x_i^0). \tag{23.34}$$

By construction, the industry output in the third-stage Cournot-Nash equilibrium $Q^N(\boldsymbol{x}^0; n)$ is the fixed point of the mapping $\sum_{j=1}^n R_j(Q; x_j^0)$, viz.,

$$Q^N(\boldsymbol{x}^0; n) = \sum_{j=1}^{n} R_j(Q^N(\boldsymbol{x}^0; n); x_j^0).$$

Figure 23.2 describes the original third-stage equilibrium E^0 as a point where the curve $\sum_{j=1}^n R_j(Q; x_j^0)$ cuts the 45° line.

Suppose now that firm i increases its investment marginally. Then the aggregate cumulative reaction curve will shift up to $\sum_{j=1}^n R_j(Q; x_j^1)$, where $R_j(Q; x_j^1) = R_j(Q; x_j^0)$ for all $j \neq i$, so that the industry output increases by $Q^N(\boldsymbol{x}^1; n) - Q^N(\boldsymbol{x}^0; n)$, whereas the output of firm j $(j \neq i)$ decreases by $q_j^N(\boldsymbol{x}^0; n) - q_j^N(\boldsymbol{x}^1; n)$, where $x_j^1 = x_j^0$ for all $j \neq i$. The ratio between the two, $[Q^N(\boldsymbol{x}^1; n) - Q^N(\boldsymbol{x}^0; n)]/[q_j^N(\boldsymbol{x}^0; n) - q_j^N(\boldsymbol{x}^1; n)]$, which closely approximates $-(\partial/\partial x_i)q_j^N(\boldsymbol{x}^0; n)/(\partial/\partial x_i)Q^N(\boldsymbol{x}^0; n)$ in (23.31) if an increase of firm i's investment is small enough, is provided by the slope of the cumulative reaction curve.

Figure 23.2 describes a situation where the inverse demand function is linear, so that the reaction curve is also linear *whose slope is independent of the number of firms n*. In this case, as n becomes large, $(\partial/\partial x_i)W^N(\boldsymbol{x}^0; n)$ clearly becomes negative, and the equilibrium investment becomes socially excessive at the margin.

23.3.5. The Case of Constantly Elastic Inverse Demand Function

Before closing this section, a final remark is in order. Since our welfare criterion need not be concave in general, a marginally welfare-improving investment may in fact be a "wrong" move from the global viewpoint. However, it is possible to compare the level of the second-best investment directly with that of the second-stage subgame perfect equilibrium if our

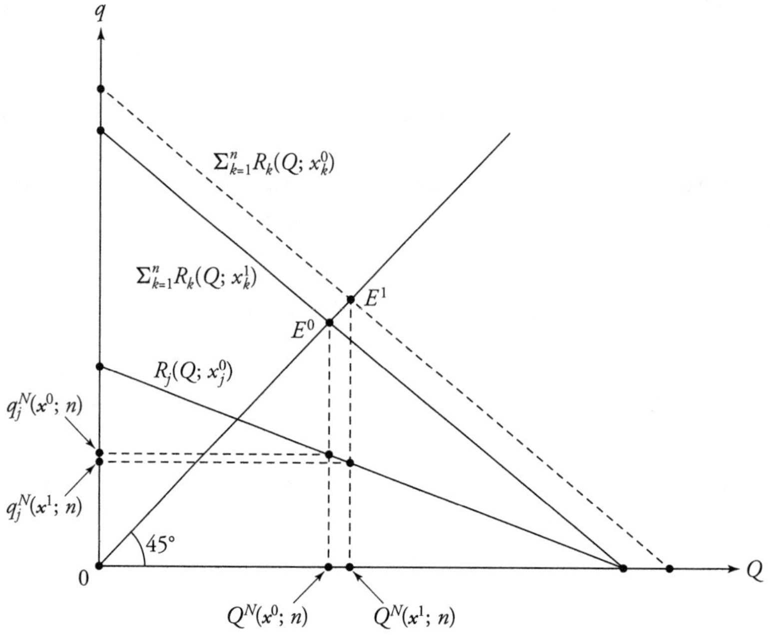

Figure 23.2. Cumulative Reaction Curves

model is parameterizable, viz., the inverse demand function as well as the cost function is constantly elastic. Quite consistent with our analysis so far, it can be shown that there exists a critical number of firms as a function of the elasticity η of the inverse demand function, say, $n^*(\eta)$, such that *the subgame perfect equilibrium level of investment exceeds the second-best level if* $n > n^*(\eta)$. The critical number is given by $n^*(\eta) := [(\eta + 3) + \sqrt{\{(\eta + 3)^2 - 4(\eta + 1)\}}]/2 < \eta + 3$, which remains fairly small for a wide range of η.

23.4. Excess Entry Theorem at the Margin in the Long Run

We are now in the stage of analyzing the subgame perfect equilibrium from the point of view of the welfare performance thereof. Theorem 23.2 asserts the first-best excess entry at the long-run subgame perfect equilibrium, whereas Theorem 23.3 asserts the second-best excess entry at the margin.

23.4.1. First-Best Excess Entry Theorem at the Margin

If the industry is left unregulated for a long time, the first-stage free-entry equilibrium with n_e firms, viz., $\{n_e, \boldsymbol{x}^N(n_e), \boldsymbol{q}^N(\boldsymbol{x}^N(n_e); n_e)\}$, will be attained. What, then, will be the welfare-improving policy that the government can enforce?

If the government can enforce marginal cost pricing, it is easy to verify that the welfare-maximizing policy is to restrict the number of firms to either zero or one and impose marginal cost pricing on the operating firm. Namely, we have the following:

THEOREM 23.2 (FIRST-BEST EXCESS ENTRY). Assume that A2 holds. Then a small reduction in the number of firms n unambiguously improves first-best social welfare in the sense that

$$(d/dn)W(\boldsymbol{q}^F(n); \boldsymbol{x}^F(n); n) < 0 \tag{23.35}$$

holds as long as $n \geq 2$. Indeed, the first-best number of firms n_f is either 0 or 1.

23.4.2. Second-Best Excess Entry Theorem at the Margin

Since enforcing the marginal cost principle is almost impossible for the actual government, we should examine how the second-best welfare function $W(\boldsymbol{q}^N(\boldsymbol{x}^N(n); n); \boldsymbol{x}^N(n); n)$ will be affected when the number of firms changes by a small amount.

Differentiating $W(\boldsymbol{q}^N(\boldsymbol{x}^N(n); n); \boldsymbol{x}^N(n); n)$ totally with respect to n, we obtain

$$\begin{aligned}
&(d/dn)W(\boldsymbol{q}^N(\boldsymbol{x}^N(n); n); \boldsymbol{x}^N(n); n) \\
&= \Pi^i(\boldsymbol{x}^N(n); n) + n \\
&\quad \cdot \{f(Q^N(\boldsymbol{x}^N(n); n)) - c(x_i^N(n))\} \cdot (\partial/\partial n)q_i^N(\boldsymbol{x}^N(n); n) \\
&+ n \cdot \{C(\boldsymbol{x}^N(n); n) + D(\boldsymbol{x}^N(n); n)\} \cdot x_i^{N'}(n).
\end{aligned} \tag{23.36}$$

Note that the first term on the right-hand side of (23.36) is zero when it is evaluated at $n = n_e$ by virtue of definition (23.18) of n_e, whereas the second term evaluated at $n = n_e$, viz.,

$$\mu(\boldsymbol{x}^N(n_e); n_e) \cdot (\partial/\partial n) q_i^N(\boldsymbol{x}^N(n_e); n_e), \tag{23.37}$$

is always negative by virtue of A1, (23.9) for $\boldsymbol{x} = \boldsymbol{x}^N(n_e)$, and Lemma 23.1. Note also that (23.37) is the crucial term that leads to the excess entry theorem of Mankiw and Whinston [11] and Suzumura and Kiyono [21] in the context of no strategic commitment.

The third term on the right-hand side of (23.36) is specific to the oligopoly models with strategic commitment. Its first component evaluated at $n = n_e$, viz., $C(\boldsymbol{x}^N(n_e); n_e)$, is what we called the commitment effect in Section 23.3. Its second component evaluated at $n = n_e$, viz., $D(\boldsymbol{x}^N(n_e); n_e)$, is the distortion effect.

As was shown in Section 23.3, $C(\boldsymbol{x}^N(n_e); n_e) < 0$ and $D(\boldsymbol{x}^N(n_e); n_e) > 0$, so that the presence of strategic commitment seems to introduce some ambiguity in signing (23.36). If we replace A1 by the following slightly stronger assumption A1*, however, we can establish an unambiguous result.

ASSUMPTION A1*. *$f(Q)$ is twice continuously differentiable with $f'(Q) < 0$ for all $Q \geq 0$ such that $f(Q) > 0$. Furthermore, the elasticity of $f'(Q)$ is constant, say, $\delta(Q) = \delta$.*[10]

With this, we can establish the following theorem.

THEOREM 23.3 (SECOND-BEST EXCESS ENTRY THEOREM AT THE MARGIN). Assume that A1*, A2, and A3 hold. Then a small reduction in the number of firms at the first stage free-entry equilibrium unambiguously improves the second-best social welfare at the margin in the sense that

$$(d/dn) W^N(\boldsymbol{q}^N(\boldsymbol{x}^N(n_e); n_e); \boldsymbol{x}^N(n_e); n_e) < 0 \tag{23.38}$$

holds as long as $n_e \geq 1 - \delta$.

10. See Remark 1 following the statement of A1.

Thanks to Theorem 23.3, under the assumed conditions, the exit of an incumbent firm at the first-stage free-entry equilibrium is welfare-improving at the margin in the second-best sense even if we do not know exactly where n_f and n_s are located. Note that the crucial inequality $n_e \geq 1 - \delta$ is obviously satisfied if the inverse demand function is concave, so that $\delta \geq 0$ holds.

23.5. Proofs

23.5.1. Proof of Lemma 23.1

Differentiating (23.9) with respect to n and rearranging terms using $\alpha(\boldsymbol{x}; n)$ and $\beta(\boldsymbol{x}; n)$, we obtain

$$\{\alpha(\boldsymbol{x}; n) + (n - 1)\beta(\boldsymbol{x}; n)\} \cdot (\partial/\partial n)q_i^N(\boldsymbol{x}; n) = -q_i^N(\boldsymbol{x}; n) \cdot \beta(\boldsymbol{x}; n), \tag{23.39}$$

which yields (23.10). The negative sign of $(\partial/\partial n)q_i^N(\boldsymbol{x}; n)$ is due to A1 and A3.

To prove (23.11) and (23.12), we differentiate (23.9) with respect to x_i and x_j $(i \neq j)$, respectively, and rearrange terms using $\omega(\boldsymbol{x}; n)$ and $\theta(\boldsymbol{x}; n)$ to obtain

$$\alpha(\boldsymbol{x}; n) \cdot \omega(\boldsymbol{x}; n) + (n - 1) \cdot \beta(\boldsymbol{x}; n) \cdot \theta(\boldsymbol{x}; n) = c'(x_i) \tag{23.40}$$

and

$$\beta(\boldsymbol{x}; n) \cdot \omega(\boldsymbol{x}; n) + \{\alpha(\boldsymbol{x}; n) + (n - 2)\beta(\boldsymbol{x}; n)\} \cdot \theta(\boldsymbol{x}; n) = 0. \tag{23.41}$$

Solving (23.40) and (23.41) for $\omega(\boldsymbol{x}; n)$ and $\theta(\boldsymbol{x}; n)$, we obtain (23.11) and (23.12). The signs of $\omega(\boldsymbol{x}; n)$, $\theta(\mathbf{x}; n)$ and $\Delta(\boldsymbol{x}; n)$ are determined by A3, (23.6), and (23.7). ■

23.5.2. Proof of Theorem 23.1

The sketch of the proof is given in the main text and hence it is omitted. ■

23.5.3. Proof of Theorem 23.2

Differentiating $W(\boldsymbol{q}^F(n); \boldsymbol{x}^F(n); n)$ totally with respect to n, we obtain

$$\begin{aligned}(d/dn)W(\boldsymbol{q}^F(n); \boldsymbol{x}^F(n); n) = &\{f(nq^F(n)) - c(x^F(n))\} \cdot q^F(n) - x^F(n) \\ &+ nq^{F'}(n) \cdot \{f(nq^F(n)) - c(x^F(n))\} \\ &+ nx^{F'}(n) \cdot \{-c'(x^F(n)) \cdot q^F(n) - 1\}.\end{aligned} \tag{23.42}$$

Invoking (23.20) and (23.21), we are then led to conclude that

$$(d/dn)W(\boldsymbol{q}^F(n); \boldsymbol{x}^F(n); n) = -x^F(n), \tag{23.43}$$

which is always negative, as was to be established. ■

23.5.4. Proof of Theorem 23.3

STEP 1. By virtue of A1, (23.9) for $\boldsymbol{x} = \boldsymbol{x}^N(n_e)$, (23.29), and (23.30), it can easily be verified that the sign of (23.36) coincides with that of

$$\begin{aligned}\Lambda(n) := &(\partial/\partial n)q_i^N(\boldsymbol{x}^N(n); n) + x_i^{N'}(n) \\ &\cdot \{\omega(\boldsymbol{x}^N(n); n) + 2(n-1) \cdot \theta(\boldsymbol{x}^N(n); n)\}\end{aligned} \tag{23.44}$$

at $n = n_e$. Invoking Lemma 23.1, $\Lambda(n)$ can be further reduced to

$$\begin{aligned}\Lambda(n) = &\frac{1}{\alpha^N(n) + (n-1)\beta^N(n)} \\ &\cdot \left\{ -q_i^N(\boldsymbol{x}^N(n); n) \cdot \beta^N(n) + \frac{\alpha^N(n) - n \cdot \beta^N(n)}{\alpha^N(n) - \beta^N(n)} \right. \\ &\left. \cdot c'(x_i^N(n)) \cdot x^{N'}(n) \right\},\end{aligned} \tag{23.45}$$

where $\alpha^N(n) := \alpha(\boldsymbol{x}^N(n); n)$ and $\beta^N(n) := \beta(\boldsymbol{x}^N(n); n)$ for short. By virtue of (23.6) and (23.7) for $\boldsymbol{x} = \boldsymbol{x}^N(n)$ and A1*, it follows that

$$\text{sgn } \Lambda(n) = \text{sgn } \{A + B \cdot x_i^{N'}(n)\}, \tag{23.46}$$

where

$$A = q_i^N(\boldsymbol{x}^N(n); n) \cdot f'(Q^N(\boldsymbol{x}^N(n); n)) \cdot (n + \delta) < 0 \tag{23.47}$$

and

$$B = c'(x_i^N(n)) \cdot \{n(n-2) + \delta(n-1)\}. \tag{23.48}$$

Note that $A > 0$ follows by virtue of (23.8), but the term $\{n(n-2) + \delta(n-1)\}$ is positive only when $n > N(\delta)$, as was shown in (23.32).

Step 2. We examine some properties of the second-stage payoff function $\Pi^i(\boldsymbol{x}; n)$, with the purpose of evaluating $x_i^{N'}(n)$ which appears in (23.46). To begin with, simple yet complicated computation using (23.2), (23.4), (23.5), A1*, and Lemma 23.1 establishes that

$$\begin{aligned} \Pi_i^i(\boldsymbol{x}; n) &:= (\partial/\partial x_i)\Pi^i(\boldsymbol{x}; n) \\ &= -c'(x_i) \cdot q_i^N(\boldsymbol{x}; n) \cdot \xi(n) - 1 \end{aligned} \tag{23.49}$$

holds, where

$$\xi(n) := 1 + \frac{n-1}{n} \cdot \frac{n+\delta}{1+n+\delta} > 0 \tag{23.50}$$

in view of (23.8).

Differentiating (23.49) partially with respect to x_i and x_j $(i \neq j)$, respectively, we obtain

$$\begin{aligned} \Pi_{ii}^i(\boldsymbol{x}; n) &:= (\partial^2/\partial x_i^2)\Pi^i(\boldsymbol{x}; n) \\ &= -\xi(n) \cdot \{c''(x_i) \cdot q_i^N(\boldsymbol{x}; n) + c'(x_i) \cdot \omega(\boldsymbol{x}; n)\} < 0 \end{aligned} \tag{23.51}$$

and

$$\begin{aligned}\Pi^i_{ij}(\boldsymbol{x};n) &:= (\partial^2/\partial x_i \partial x_j)\Pi^i(\boldsymbol{x};n)\\ &= -\xi(n)\cdot c'(x_i)\cdot \theta(\boldsymbol{x};n)\\ &= \xi(n)\cdot c'(x_i)\cdot \frac{c'(x_i)\cdot(n+\delta)}{f'(Q^N(\boldsymbol{x};n))\cdot n\cdot(n+1+\delta)} < 0 \quad (i \neq j)\end{aligned} \tag{23.52}$$

where the last equality of (23.52) is obtained in view of (23.6) and (23.7). Note that the second-order condition for profit maximization at the second-stage game requires that $\Pi^i_{ii}(\boldsymbol{x}^N(n);n) < 0$ holds, while A2, Lemma 23.1, and (23.52) ensure that $\Pi^i_{ij}(\boldsymbol{x};n) < 0$ $(i \neq j)$ holds for any $(\boldsymbol{x};n)$. Therefore, the second-stage strategies are warranted to be strategic substitutes if the third-stage strategies are.[11]

Differentiating (23.49) partially with respect to n and noting that

$$\xi'(n) = \frac{2n^2 + 2\delta n + \delta(\delta+1)}{n^2(1+n+\delta)^2} \tag{23.53}$$

follows from (23.50), we can finally obtain

$$\begin{aligned}&(\partial/\partial n)\Pi^i_i(\boldsymbol{x}^N(n);n)\\ &\quad = c'(x_i^N(n))\cdot q_i^N(\boldsymbol{x}^N(n);n)\cdot\frac{(1-n)\{2(n+\delta)^2+\delta\}}{n^2(1+n+\delta)^2}.\end{aligned} \tag{23.54}$$

Step 3. By definition, $\boldsymbol{x}^N(n)$ is characterized by

$$\Pi^i_i(\boldsymbol{x}^N(n);n) = 0 \quad (i = 1, 2, \ldots, n). \tag{23.55}$$

Differentiating (23.55) totally and invoking symmetry, we obtain

$$x_i^{N'}(n) = -\frac{(\partial/\partial n)\Pi^i_i(\boldsymbol{x}^N(n);n)}{\Pi^i_{ii}(\boldsymbol{x}^N(n);n) + (n-1)\Pi^i_{ij}(\boldsymbol{x}^N(n);n)}. \tag{23.56}$$

11. It is the latter half of A1* that is responsible for this nice property. In general, this property does not necessarily hold. See Besley and Suzumura [1] and Suzumura [19].

In view of (23.56), (23.46) is reduced to

$$\operatorname{sgn} \Lambda(n) = \operatorname{sgn} \left\{ \frac{A\Pi_{ii}}{\Pi_{ii} + (n-1)\Pi_{ij}} + \frac{(n-1)A \cdot \Pi_{ij} - B \cdot \Pi_{in}}{\Pi_{ii} + (n-1)\Pi_{ij}} \right\}, \tag{23.57}$$

where $\Pi_{ii} := \Pi^i_{ii}(\boldsymbol{x}^N(n); n)$, $\Pi_{ij} := \Pi^i_{ij}(\boldsymbol{x}^N(n); n)$ $(i \neq j)$, and $\Pi_{in} := (\partial/\partial n)\Pi^i_i(\boldsymbol{x}^N(n); n)$.

It follows that (23.47), (23.51), and (23.52) assure that the first term on the right-hand side of (23.57) is unambiguously negative. Thus, for the sign of $\Lambda(n)$ to be negative, a sufficient condition is

$$\Gamma(n) := (n-1)A \cdot \Pi_{ij} - B \cdot \Pi_{in} < 0. \tag{23.58}$$

Invoking (23.47), (23.51), (23.52), and (23.54), a straightforward calculation yields

$$\Gamma(n) = q_i(n) \cdot \{c'(n)\}^2 \cdot (n-1) \cdot \Omega(n), \tag{23.59}$$

where

$$\Omega(n) := \frac{(n+\delta)^2}{n \cdot (n+1+\delta)} \cdot \xi(n) + \frac{\{n(n-2) + \delta(n-1)\} \cdot \{2(n+\delta)^2 + \delta\}}{n^2 \cdot (1+n+\delta)^2}, \tag{23.60}$$

and $q_i(n) := q_i^N(\boldsymbol{x}^N(n); n)$ and $c'(n) := c'(x_i^N(n))$.

In view of (23.59), if $n > 1$, the sufficient condition for $\Lambda(n)$ to be negative boils down to the condition that $\Omega(n)$ to be negative. In view of (23.50), a straightforward computation yields

$$\Omega(n) = \phi_\delta(n)/\{n^2 \cdot (n+1+\delta)^2\}, \tag{23.61}$$

where

$$\phi_\delta(n) := -4n^3 - 8\delta n^2 - \delta(5\delta - 2)n - \delta^2(\delta + 1). \tag{23.62}$$

Step 4. The proof of Theorem 3 is complete if we can show that $\phi_\delta(n) < 0$ as long as $n \geq 1 - \delta$. Since $\phi_\delta(n) < 0$ holds for all $n > 0$ if $\delta \geq 0$, we have only to examine the case where $\delta < 0$. With this goal in mind, let $n^*(\delta)$ stand for the largest real root of the cubic equation $\phi_\delta(n) = 0$. The coefficient of the highest-order term of this cubic equation being negative, we have $1 - \delta > n^*(\delta)$ if all of $\phi_\delta(n)$, $\phi'_\delta(n)$, and $\phi''_\delta(n)$ are negative at $n = 1 - \delta$. This is indeed the case, as we have

$$\phi_\delta(1 - \delta) = 2(\delta - 2) < 0,$$

$$\phi'_\delta(1 - \delta) = -\delta^2 + 6\delta - 12 < 0,$$

and

$$\phi''_\delta(1 - \delta) = -8(3 - \delta) < 0$$

for $\delta < 0$. If $n \geq 1 - \delta$, we have $n > n^*(\delta)$, so that we obtain $\phi_\delta(n) < 0$, as was to be verified. ■

23.6. Concluding Remarks

In this essay, we have examined the welfare performance of oligopoly with strategic commitment, which culminated in the excess entry results. The second-best excess entry theorem at the margin, which is the main result of this essay, is based on three explicit assumptions. The first assumption is on the admissible class of inverse demand functions. Despite its restrictive nature, we should note that a wide class of demand functions satisfies this assumption, as it does accommodate all linear inverse demand functions as well as all constantly elastic inverse demand functions. The second assumption is on the nature of cost reduction technology, which seems to be on safe ground. The third assumption is on the nature of strategic interrelatedness of competitive measures. Within a model of quantity competition, the assumed strategic substitutability seems to be widely recognized as a normal case. Despite its rather paradoxical implications, therefore, our welfare verdicts cannot be flatly discarded as pathological. The fact that our results hold even in the presence of strategic commitment seems to enhance their relevance rather substantially.

It goes without saying that there are other implicit assumptions on which our results hinge. To cite just a few, quantity competition rather than price competition, exclusive focus on the symmetric equilibria, no uncertainty in cost-reducing R&D, and no product differentiation and no R&D spillovers can be referred to. It is almost certain, and in some cases demonstrably certain, that the mileage of our excess entry results are severely limited by these implicit assumptions. Nevertheless, the fact remains that the arena where our results do have their bites is in no sense negligible. Presumably, we are in need of more careful analyses of the role of competition as an efficient allocator of resources. The purpose of this essay would be served if it could succeed in bringing this simple point home.

23.7. References

[1] Besley, T., and K. Suzumura, "Taxation and Welfare in an Oligopoly with Strategic Commitment," *International Economic Review* **33**, 1992, 413–431.

[2] Brander, J. A., and B. J. Spencer, "Strategic Commitment with R&D: The Symmetric Case," *Bell Journal of Economics* **14**, 1983, 225–235.

[3] Brander, J. A., and B. J. Spencer, "Tacit Collusion, Free Entry and Welfare," *Journal of Industrial Economics* **33**, 1985, 277–294.

[4] Bulow, J. A., J. D. Geanakoplos, and P. D. Klemperer, "Multimarket Oligopoly: Strategic Substitutes and Complements," *Journal of Political Economy* **93**, 1985, 488–511.

[5] d'Aspremont, C., and A. Jacquemin, "Cooperative and Noncooperative R&D in Duopoly with Spillovers," *American Economic Review* **78**, 1988, 1133–1137.

[6] Dixit, A., "Comparative Statics for Oligopoly," *International Economic Review* **27**, 1986, 107–122.

[7] Eaton, J., and G. M. Grossman, "Optimal Trade and Industrial Policy under Oligopoly," *Quarterly Journal of Economics* **101**, 1986, 383–406.

[8] Fudenberg, D., and J. Tirole, "The Fat-Cat Effect, the Puppy-Dog Ploy, and the Lean and Hungry Look," *American Economic Review* **74**, 1984, 361–366.

[9] Konishi, H., M. Okuno-Fujiwara, and K. Suzumura, "Oligopolistic Competition and Economic Welfare: A General Equilibrium Analysis of Entry Regulation and Tax-Subsidy Schemes," *Journal of Public Economics* **42**, 1990, 67–68. Essay 22 of this volume.

[10] Lahiri, S., and Y. Ono, "Helping Minor Firms Reduces Welfare," *Economic Journal* **98**, 1988, 1199–1202.

[11] Mankiw, N. G., and M. D. Whinston, "Free Entry and Social Inefficiency," *Rand Journal of Economics* **17**, 1986, 48–58.

[12] Okuno-Fujiwara, M., and K. Suzumura, "Strategic Cost-Reduction Investment and Economic Welfare," Working Paper, All Souls College, Oxford University, 1988.

[13] Perry, M. K., "Scale Economies, Imperfect Competition, and Public Policy," *Journal of Industrial Economics* **32**, 1984, 313–333.

[14] Schmalensee, R., "Is More Competition Necessarily Good?" *Industrial Organization Review* **4**, 1976, 120–121.

[15] Seade, J., "The Stability of Cournot Revisited," *Journal of Economic Theory* **23**, 1980, 15–27.

[16] Seade, J., "On the Effects of Entry," *Econometrica* **48**, 1980, 479–489.

[17] Spencer, B. J., and J. A. Brander, "International R&D Rivalry and Industrial Strategy," *Review of Economic Studies* **50**, 1983, 707–722.

[18] Stiglitz, J. E., "Potential Competition May Reduce Welfare," *American Economic Review: Papers and Proceedings* **71**, 1981, 184–189.

[19] Suzumura, K., "Symmetric Cournot Oligopoly and Economic Welfare: A Synthesis," working paper, Department of Economics, University of Essex, Colchester, England, 1991.

[20] Suzumura, K.,"Cooperative and Noncooperative R&D in an Oligopoly with Spillovers," *American Economic Review* **82**, 1992, 1307–1320. Essay 24 of this volume.

[21] Suzumura, K., and K. Kiyono, "Entry Barriers and Economic Welfare," *Review of Economic Studies* **54**, 1987, 157–167. Essay 21 of this volume.

[22] von Weizsäcker, C. C., *Barriers to Entry: A Theoretical Treatment*, Berlin: Springer-Verlag, 1980.

[23] von Weizsäcker, C. C., "A Welfare Analysis of Barriers to Entry," *Bell Journal of Economics* **11**, 1980, 399–420.

ESSAY 24

Cooperative and Noncooperative R&D in an Oligopoly with Spillovers

The purpose of this essay is to examine the effects of cooperative R&D, wherein member firms commit themselves to a joint profit-maximizing level of R&D in a "precompetitive stage" but remain fierce competitors in the product market. As a standard of reference, this essay will also examine the characteristic features of noncooperative R&D, socially first-best R&D, and socially second-best R&D. Since the incentives for a firm to undertake R&D on its own depend on a sufficient degree of appropriability of the research outcomes (hence, a limited diffusion of knowledge), it is of particular interest and relevance to see how cooperative R&D fares vis-à-vis noncooperative R&D in the presence of R&D spillovers.

This analysis is conducted in terms of a two-stage model of oligopolistic competition. In the first stage, firms decide on their cost-reducing R&D either cooperatively or noncooperatively, whereas in the second stage they engage in quantity competition in the product market. Two-stage models of this type have been studied extensively by Timothy Besley and Kotaro Suzumura [2], James Brander and Barbara Spencer [3], Spencer and Brander

First published in *American Economic Review* **82**, 1992, pp. 1307–1320. Thanks are due to Paul David, Claude d'Aspremont, Terence Gorman, Akira Goto, James Mirrlees, Masahiro Okuno-Fujiwara, Agnar Sandmo, Stephen Turnbull, and John Vickers for their comments and discussion on this and related topics. I am also grateful to two anonymous referees of *American Economic Review* for their helpful comments, which substantially improved my exposition.

[17], and Masahiro Okuno-Fujiwara and Suzumura [13] in the absence of R&D coordination and R&D spillovers.[1]

Claude d'Aspremont and Alexis Jacquemin [6; 7] presented an interesting analysis of cooperative and noncooperative R&D in terms of a two-stage model of a *duopoly* with R&D spillovers. They make the interesting point that cooperative R&D agreements between otherwise competing firms may increase the R&D expenditure level relative to the fully noncooperative case, provided that the R&D spillovers are sufficiently large, although the cooperative R&D may still fall short of the socially first-best level. For at least two reasons, however, the robustness of their results is questionable. The present essay is meant to provide a careful examination of their findings with the purpose of locating them in a more appropriate perspective.[2] In so doing, it will develop a systematic method for analyzing the properties of a two-stage model of oligopolistic competition.

In the first place, d'Aspremont and Jacquemin [6] presented their results as surprising on the basis that cooperation should reduce excessive duplication of R&D efforts in the presence of large spillovers.[3] Note, however, that the R&D incentive of a single firm hinges squarely on the extent of appropriability of the R&D benefits, so that the presence of large R&D spillovers may drastically reduce the incentives for cost reduction, with the result that the R&D commitment made voluntarily by a firm tends to be socially too small. From this viewpoint, an enforceable agreement on cooperative R&D efforts seems to facilitate more commitments. The result of the net effect of the R&D cooperation hinges on the relative strength of these competing effects. It will be shown that the latter effect dominates the former not only in the duopoly example with the linear inverse demand function and linear marginal cost function assumed by d'Aspremont and Jacquemin [6], but

1. In contrast, Partha Dasgupta and Joseph Stiglitz [5], Richard Levin and Peter Reiss [12], and Michael Spence [16] analyzed one-stage models without strategic commitment to R&D, but with or without R&D spillovers.
2. Several salient features of cooperative research activities are analyzed by Michael Katz [11] and Jacquemin [10], among many others. Needless to say, there are several relevant features thereof that I had to leave out of this essay, but in the concluding remarks (Section 24.6), several directions in which the present analysis should be further developed will be pointed out.
3. Also, by participating in the cooperative R&D association, firms can conserve on the fixed costs of R&D equipment and administration.

also in a much wider class of oligopolistic industries, thereby supporting the robustness of their results.

In the second place, d'Aspremont and Jacquemin [6] invoked the first-best welfare (market surplus) function as their welfare criterion, but the relevance of this convention may be disputed in that the enforcement of the first-best arrangement may require considerable leverage on the government vis-à-vis private firms, something that may be hard to secure in reality. What is needed is an evaluation of the social gains from cooperative R&D within the alternative feasible arrangements. It will be shown that my results can be extended and made more relevant by invoking a second-best welfare (market surplus) function as an alterative welfare criterion.

24.1. The Model

Consider an industry with n firms ($2 \leq n < +\infty$) producing a homogeneous product. Let $p = f(Q)$ be the inverse demand function, where p and Q denote, respectively, the price and the aggregate output of this product. Let x_i and q_i denote, respectively, the amount of R&D and the output of firm i. The cost of production and that of R&D are assumed to be $c(x_i; \boldsymbol{x}_{-i})q_i$ and x_i, respectively, where $\boldsymbol{x}_{-i} := (x_1, \ldots, x_{i-1}, x_{i+1}, \ldots, x_n)$, assuming for the sake of notational simplicity that the amount of R&D is measured by its cost. Diminishing returns on R&D can be incorporated without affecting any of the results in this essay.

Throughout the analysis, I will assume the following:

Assumption A1. The inverse demand function $f(Q)$ is twice continuously differentiable with $f'(Q) < 0$ for all $Q \geq 0$ satisfying $f(Q) > 0$.

Assumption A2. The average variable cost function $c(x_i; \boldsymbol{x}_{-i})$ is twice continuously differentiable and satisfies $c(x_i; \boldsymbol{x}_{-i}) > 0$, $(\partial/\partial x_i)c(x_i; \boldsymbol{x}_{-i}) < 0$, and $(\partial/\partial x_j)c(x_i; \boldsymbol{x}_{-i}) \leq 0$ for any $\boldsymbol{x} = (x_1, x_2, \ldots, x_n) \geq \mathbf{0}$ $(i \neq j; i, j = 1, 2, \ldots, n)$. Furthermore, for any symmetric vector $\boldsymbol{x} = (x_1, x_2, \ldots, x_n) \geq \mathbf{0}$, $(\partial/\partial x_i)c(x_i; \boldsymbol{x}_{-i}) < (\partial/\partial x_j)c(x_i; \boldsymbol{x}_{-i})$ $(i \neq j; i, j = 1, 2, \ldots, n)$ holds.

No particular account is needed for A1. According to A2, a firm's R&D is cost-reducing and can benefit other firms without payment. However, the cost-reducing effect of a firm's own R&D outweighs the benefits accruing freely from other firms when all firms are spending the same amount on R&D.

In the model, firms are engaging in two-stage competition. In the first stage, firms make an irrevocable commitment to a level of R&D in full anticipation of the equilibrium that will be established in the second stage, where firms compete in the product market. The second-stage strategic variable is assumed to be the level of output.

Following d'Aspremont and Jacqemin [6], I will examine two types of equilibrium. The first equilibrium concept is noncooperative throughout the two stages, so that the equilibrium of the second stage is a Cournot-Nash equilibrium, and that of the entire game is a subgame perfect equilibrium. The second equilibrium concept is a mixed cooperative and noncooperative equilibrium; firms are supposed to coordinate their R&D in the first stage so as to maximize joint profits with the understanding that they engage in noncooperative competition in the second stage.

To characterize the second-stage equilibrium, let a profile of the amounts of R&D, $\boldsymbol{x} = (x_1, x_2, \ldots, x_n)$, be parametrically given. Then the profits of firm i in the second-stage game corresponding to an output profile $\boldsymbol{q} = (q_1, q_2, \ldots, q_n)$ are defined by

$$\pi_i(\boldsymbol{q}; x_i, \boldsymbol{x}_{-i}) := \{f(Q) - c(x_i; \boldsymbol{x}_{-i})\}q_i - x_i \quad (i = 1, 2, \ldots, n), \tag{24.1}$$

where $Q := \Sigma_{j=1}^{n} q_j$. In what follows, $\boldsymbol{q}^N(\boldsymbol{x}) = (q_1^N(\boldsymbol{x}), q_2^N(\boldsymbol{x}), \ldots, q_n^N(\boldsymbol{x}))$ denotes the Cournot-Nash equilibrium of the second-stage game corresponding to the specified first-stage R&D profile $\boldsymbol{x} = (x_1, x_2, \ldots, x_n)$. Assuming the interior optimum and second-order conditions, $\boldsymbol{q}^N(\boldsymbol{x})$ can be characterized by $(\partial/\partial q_i)\pi_i(\boldsymbol{q}^N(\boldsymbol{x}); x_i, \boldsymbol{x}_{-i}) = 0$ $(i = 1, 2, \ldots, n)$, viz.,

$$f'(Q^N(\boldsymbol{x}))q_i^N(\boldsymbol{x}) + f(Q^N(\boldsymbol{x})) - c(x_i; \boldsymbol{x}_{-i}) = 0 \quad (i = 1, 2, \ldots, n), \tag{24.2}$$

where $Q^N(\boldsymbol{x}) := \Sigma_{j=1}^{n} q_j^N(\boldsymbol{x})$. Throughout this essay, I focus on the symmetric equilibrium, so that $q_i^N(\boldsymbol{x}) = q_j^N(\boldsymbol{x})$ $(i, j = 1, 2, \ldots, n)$ holds if $x_i = x_j$ $(i, j = 1, 2, \ldots, n)$.

To lend substance to the oligopolistic interactions in the model, I now introduce a strategic assumption. Let $\alpha_i(\boldsymbol{q}; \boldsymbol{x})$ and $\beta_{ij}(\boldsymbol{q}; \boldsymbol{x})$ be defined for any R&D profile $\boldsymbol{x} = (x_1, x_2, \ldots, x_n)$ by

$$\alpha_i(\boldsymbol{q}; \boldsymbol{x}) := \frac{\partial^2}{\partial q_i^2}\pi_i(\boldsymbol{q}; x_i, \boldsymbol{x}_{-i}) \quad (i = 1, 2, \ldots, n)$$

and

$$\beta_{ij}(\boldsymbol{q}; \boldsymbol{x}) := \frac{\partial^2}{\partial q_i \partial q_j}\pi_i(\boldsymbol{q}; x_i, \boldsymbol{x}_{-i}) \quad (i \neq j;\ i, j = 1, 2, \ldots, n),$$

respectively. I can then state the following second-stage strategic assumption in a compact form.

ASSUMPTION A3. Firms' strategic variables in the second-stage game are strategic substitutes; that is, $\beta_{ij}(\boldsymbol{q}; \boldsymbol{x}) < 0$ $(i \neq j; i, j = 1, 2, \ldots, n)$ holds for any specified R&D profile $\boldsymbol{x} = (x_1, x_2, \ldots, x_n) \geq 0$.[4, 5]

Note that it is quite natural to invoke A3 in the present context of homogeneous-product Cournot oligopoly, as it corresponds to the assumption of downward-sloping reaction curves (see Bulow, Geanakoplos, and Klemperer [4]; Dixit [8]). Note also that A1–A3 are satisfied by d'Aspremont and Jacquemin's [6] example.

Turning to the first stage of the game, define the first-stage payoff function of firm i by

$$\Pi_i(\boldsymbol{x}) := \pi_i(\boldsymbol{q}^N(\boldsymbol{x}); x_i, \boldsymbol{x}_{-i}) \quad (i = 1, 2, \ldots, n). \tag{24.3}$$

---

4. The concept of strategic substitutes and complements was first introduced by Jeremy Bulow, John Geanakoplos, and Paul Klemperer [4] and is invoked quite widely in the recent literature on oligopoly theory. See, among others, Avinash Dixit [8], Besley and Suzumura [2], and Okuno-Fujiwara and Suzumura [13].

5. As Jesús Seade [14; 15] has aptly observed, perverse results often hold in oligopoly theory when the Cournot-Nash equilibrium is unstable. This being the case, it is reassuring that the myopic adjustment process à la Cournot that each firm increases (resp. decreases) its output marginally if marginal profitability is positive (resp. negative) can be shown to be locally stable under A1 and A3.

Then the Nash equilibrium of the first-stage game $\boldsymbol{x}^N = (x_1^N, x_2^N, \ldots, x_n^N)$ is characterized under the assumption of interior optimum and second-order conditions by $(\partial/\partial x_i)\Pi_i(\boldsymbol{x}^N) = 0$ $(i = 1, 2, \ldots, n)$; that is,

$$\sum_{j=1}^{n} \frac{\partial}{\partial q_j}\pi_i(\boldsymbol{q}^N(\boldsymbol{x}^N); x_i^N, \boldsymbol{x}_{-i}^N) \tag{24.4}$$

$$\cdot \frac{\partial}{\partial x_i} q_j^N(\boldsymbol{x}^N) + \frac{\partial}{\partial x_i}\pi_i(\boldsymbol{q}^N(\boldsymbol{x}^N); x_i^N, \boldsymbol{x}_{-i}^N) = 0 \quad (i = 1, 2, \ldots, n).$$

Note that $\{\boldsymbol{x}^N, \boldsymbol{q}^N(\boldsymbol{x}^N)\}$ is nothing but the subgame perfect equilibrium of the two-stage game, which is the central focus of subsequent analysis. By definition, $\boldsymbol{q}^N(\boldsymbol{x}^N)$ is the second-stage Cournot-Nash equilibrium, given $\boldsymbol{x}^N$. Throughout this essay, I focus on the symmetric $\boldsymbol{x}^N : x_i^N = x_j^N$ $(i, j = 1, 2, \ldots, n)$.[6]

Although A1–A3 will be maintained throughout this essay, there will be several occasions when A3 must be replaced by the following assumption for the sake of obtaining unambiguous verdicts.

Assumption A3*. The inverse demand function $f(Q)$ is concave; that is, $f''(Q) \leq 0$ holds for all $Q \geq 0$ such that $f(Q) > 0$.

---

6. To analyze in detail the structure of the first-stage game, define $\lambda_i(\boldsymbol{x}) := (\partial^2/\partial x_i^2)\Pi_i(\boldsymbol{x})$ and $\mu_{ij}(x) := (\partial^2/\partial x_i \partial x_j)\Pi_i(\boldsymbol{x})$ $(i \neq j;\ i, j = 1, 2, \ldots, n)$. As in the case of the second-stage game, the first-stage strategic variables are *strategic substitutes (resp. strategic complements)* if and only if $\mu_{ij}(\boldsymbol{x}) <$ (resp. $>$) 0 holds $(i \neq j;\ i, j = 1, 2, \ldots, n)$. Depending on the extent of R&D spillovers, both cases are a priori possible. It is easy to verify that the first-stage Nash equilibrium $\boldsymbol{x}^N$ is locally stable with respect to the myopic adjustment process $\dot{x}_i = \tau(\partial/\partial x_i)\Pi_i(\boldsymbol{x})$ $(i = 1, 2, \ldots, n)$, where $\dot{x}_i$ denotes the time derivative of x_i and $\tau > 0$ is the adjustment coefficient, if the inequality $\lambda + (k-1)\mu < 0$ $(k = 0, 1, \ldots, n)$ holds, where $\lambda := \lambda_i(\boldsymbol{x}^N)$ and $\mu := \mu_{ij}(\boldsymbol{x}^N)$. In the case of a duopoly where $n = 2$, this inequality boils down to $\lambda - \mu < 0$, $\lambda < 0$, and $\lambda + \mu < 0$. Note that the condition $\lambda < 0$ is nothing other than the second-order condition for the first-stage payoff maximization, whereas the other two conditions reduce to $-1 < \mu/\lambda < 1$; that is,

$$-1 < (\partial^2/\partial x_i \partial x_j)\Pi_i(\boldsymbol{x}^N)/(\partial^2/\partial^2 x_i)\Pi_i(\boldsymbol{x}^N) < 1 \quad (i \neq j;\ i, j = 1, 2),$$

which is precisely the condition analyzed by Irene Henriques [9] in the special context of the d'Aspremont and Jacquemin [6] duopoly example.

Note that A3* is the condition that guarantees the concavity of profit function $\pi_i(\boldsymbol{q}; x_i, \boldsymbol{x}_{-i})$ with respect to q_i, and it is clearly satisfied by the linear inverse demand function used by d'Aspremont and Jacquemin [6] as well as by many others. In the presence of A1, A3* implies A3, so that the set of A1, A2, and A3* is collectively stronger than the set consisting of A1, A2, and A3. Finally, note that $\alpha_i(\boldsymbol{q}; \boldsymbol{x})$ and $\beta_{ij}(\boldsymbol{q}; \boldsymbol{x})$ become independent of the firm indexes i and j $(i \neq j;\ i, j = 1, 2, \ldots, n)$ if they are evaluated at the symmetric $\boldsymbol{q}$ and $\boldsymbol{x}$. In such a case, it is possible to denote them simply as $\alpha(\boldsymbol{q}; \boldsymbol{x})$ and $\beta(\boldsymbol{q}; \boldsymbol{x})$.

This completes the description of the two-stage model of oligopolistic competition. Let us now set about analyzing the positive as well as the normative properties of the game.

24.2. R&D Spillovers and Output Response

To begin, I analyze how the individual firm's output and the industry aggregate output at the second-stage Nash equilibrium react to a change in the R&D expenditure by a firm in the first-stage game. With this purpose in mind, define $\omega(\boldsymbol{x}) := (\partial/\partial x_i)q_i^N(\boldsymbol{x})$ and $\theta(\boldsymbol{x}) := (\partial/\partial x_i)q_j^N(\boldsymbol{x})$ $(i \neq j;\ i, j = 1, 2, \ldots, n)$ for any symmetric R&D profile $\boldsymbol{x} = (x_1, x_2, \ldots, x_n)$. Clearly, $\omega(\boldsymbol{x})$ (resp. $\theta(\boldsymbol{x})$) denotes the effect of a marginal change in the first-stage R&D expenditure by firm i on the second-stage equilibrium output of firm i (resp. firm j), where $i \neq j$. By virtue of the symmetry of $\boldsymbol{x}$, $\omega(\boldsymbol{x})$ and $\theta(\boldsymbol{x})$ are independent of the firm indexes i and j $(i \neq j;\ i, j = 1, 2, \ldots, n)$. Clearly, the effect of a change in x_i on the equilibrium aggregate output $Q^N(\boldsymbol{x})$ is given by $(\partial/\partial x_i)Q^N(\boldsymbol{x}) = \omega(\boldsymbol{x}) + (n-1)\theta(\boldsymbol{x})$ $(i = 1, 2, \ldots, n)$.

In Appendix 24.A, I show that $\omega(\boldsymbol{x})$ and $\theta(\boldsymbol{x})$ can be calculated as

$$\omega(\boldsymbol{x}) = \frac{1}{\Delta(\boldsymbol{x})}\Bigg[\{\alpha(\boldsymbol{x}) - \beta(\boldsymbol{x})\}\frac{\partial}{\partial x_i}c(x_i; \boldsymbol{x}_{-i}) + (n-1)\beta(\boldsymbol{x})\left\{\frac{\partial}{\partial x_i}c(x_i; \boldsymbol{x}_{-i}) - \frac{\partial}{\partial x_j}c(x_i; \boldsymbol{x}_{-i})\right\}\Bigg] \tag{24.5}$$

and

$$\theta(\boldsymbol{x}) = \frac{1}{\Delta(\boldsymbol{x})}\left[\alpha(\boldsymbol{x})\left\{\frac{\partial}{\partial x_j}c(x_i;\boldsymbol{x}_{-i}) - \frac{\partial}{\partial x_i}c(x_i;\boldsymbol{x}_{-i})\right\}\right.$$
$$\left. +\{\alpha(\boldsymbol{x}) - \beta(\boldsymbol{x})\}\frac{\partial}{\partial x_i}c(x_i;\boldsymbol{x}_{-i})\right], \tag{24.6}$$

where $\alpha(\boldsymbol{x}) := \alpha(\boldsymbol{q}^N(\boldsymbol{x}), \boldsymbol{x})$, $\beta(\boldsymbol{x}) := \beta(\boldsymbol{q}^N(\boldsymbol{x}), \boldsymbol{x})$ for notational brevity and where $\Delta(\boldsymbol{x}) := \{\alpha(\boldsymbol{x}) - \beta(\boldsymbol{x})\}\{\alpha(\boldsymbol{x}) + (n-1)\beta(\boldsymbol{x})\}$ and $i \neq j$. One can then obtain

$$\begin{aligned}\psi(\boldsymbol{x}) &:= \omega(\boldsymbol{x}) + (n-1)\theta(\boldsymbol{x})\\ &= \frac{\alpha(\boldsymbol{x}) - \beta(\boldsymbol{x})}{\Delta(\boldsymbol{x})}\cdot\left\{\frac{\partial}{\partial x_i}c(x_i;\boldsymbol{x}_{-i}) + (n-1)\frac{\partial}{\partial x_j}c(x_i;\boldsymbol{x}_{-i})\right\}.\end{aligned} \tag{24.7}$$

It is easy to verify that

$$\alpha(\boldsymbol{x}) = 2f'(Q^N(\boldsymbol{x})) + f''(Q^N(\boldsymbol{x}))q_i^N(\boldsymbol{x}) \tag{24.8}$$

and

$$\beta(\boldsymbol{x}) = f'(Q^N(\boldsymbol{x})) + f''(Q^N(\boldsymbol{x}))q_i^N(\boldsymbol{x}) \tag{24.9}$$

so that $\alpha(\boldsymbol{x}) - \beta(\boldsymbol{x}) = f'(Q^N(\boldsymbol{x})) < 0$ by virtue of A1. It follows from A3 that $\alpha(\boldsymbol{x}) < 0$, which in turn guarantees that $\Delta(\boldsymbol{x}) > 0$. Therefore, $\omega(\boldsymbol{x}) > 0$ follows from (24.5), A2 and A3. In other words, *an increase in cost-reducing R&D by a firm unambiguously increases the equilibrium output of that firm.* In contrast, because of the R&D spillovers, an increase in cost-reducing R&D by firm i exerts two conflicting effects on the equilibrium output of firm j $(i \neq j)$. On the one hand, it tends to increase j's output by bringing j's cost down through spillovers of cost-reducing benefits. On the other hand, it tends to decrease j's output by strengthening i's competitive edge against j. I will say that *the R&D spillovers are sufficiently large if the former effect outweighs the latter so that $\theta(\boldsymbol{x}) > 0$ holds.*[7] Finally, it follows from (24.7) that

7. This definition is in concordance with the one adopted by d'Aspremont and Jacquemin [6]. Indeed, in their duopoly example, where $0 > (\partial/\partial x_j)c(x_i;\boldsymbol{x}_{-i}) = -\epsilon > -1 = (\partial/\partial x_i)c(x_i;\boldsymbol{x}_{-i})$

the industry aggregate output at the Cournot-Nash equilibrium always increases when one of the firms increases its cost-reducing R&D irrespective of whether the R&D spillovers are large or small.

24.3. Mixed Cooperative and Noncooperative Game

Let us turn now to the second two-stage game. In this game, firms coordinate their R&D in the first stage in order to maximize their joint profits, whereas they compete in the second-stage quantity game.

The cooperative equilibrium $\boldsymbol{x}^C = (x_1^C, x_2^C, \ldots, x_n^C)$ of the first-stage game can be characterized by $(\partial/\partial x_i)\Sigma_{j=1}^n \Pi_j(\boldsymbol{x}^C) = 0$ $(i = 1, 2, \ldots, n)$ under the assumption of interior optimum and second-order conditions. It is easy, although tedious, to reduce this condition to the following:

$$q_i^N(\boldsymbol{x}^C)\Bigg[(n-1)f'(Q^N(\boldsymbol{x}^C))\psi(\boldsymbol{x}^C) - \left\{\frac{\partial}{\partial x_i}c(x_i^C; \boldsymbol{x}_{-i}^C) + (n-1)\frac{\partial}{\partial x_j}c(x_i^C; \boldsymbol{x}_{-i}^C)\right\}\Bigg] - 1 = 0 \quad (i \neq j;\ i, j = 1, 2, \ldots, n). \tag{24.10}$$

Then the equilibrium of the whole game is given by $\{\boldsymbol{x}^C, \boldsymbol{q}^N(\boldsymbol{x}^C)\}$, which is also assumed to be symmetric.

24.4. First-Best Welfare Analysis

The welfare performance of $\boldsymbol{x}^N$ and $\boldsymbol{x}^C$ can be gauged and compared in terms of several alternative criteria. To begin, I invoke the *first-best welfare (market surplus) function* $W^F(\boldsymbol{x})$ à la d'Aspremont and Jacquemin [6]. For any R&D profile $\boldsymbol{x} = (x_1, x_2, \ldots, x_n)$ and output profile $\boldsymbol{q} = (q_1, q_2, \ldots, q_n)$, let the

---

$(i \neq j; i, j = 1, 2)$, $f(Q) = a - bQ$, $a > 0$ and $b > 0$, one may compute that $\theta(\boldsymbol{x}) = (2\epsilon - 1)/3$, which is positive if and only if $\epsilon > \frac{1}{2}$ (i.e., if and only if the R&D spillovers are "sufficiently large" in the sense d'Aspremont and Jacquemin [6] used the term).

market surplus function $W(\boldsymbol{x}, \boldsymbol{q})$ be defined by

$$W(\boldsymbol{x}, \boldsymbol{q}) := \int_0^Q f(Z)dZ - \sum_{j=1}^{n} \{c(x_j; \boldsymbol{x}_{-j})q_j + x_j\}, \quad (24.11)$$

where $Q := \Sigma_{j=1}^{n} q_j$, which is nothing other than the sum of the consumer's surplus and the producer's surplus.

For any symmetric R&D profile $\boldsymbol{x} = (x_1, x_2, \ldots, x_n)$, let $\boldsymbol{q}^F(\boldsymbol{x}) = (q_1^F(\boldsymbol{x}), q_2^F(\boldsymbol{x}), \ldots, q_n^F(\boldsymbol{x}))$ be the *socially first-best output profile* corresponding to $\boldsymbol{x}$, which is defined by

$$\boldsymbol{q}^F(\boldsymbol{x}) := \arg\max_{\boldsymbol{q}>0} W(\boldsymbol{x}, \boldsymbol{q}). \quad (24.12)$$

As is easily verified, $\boldsymbol{q}^F(\boldsymbol{x})$ is characterized by the familiar *marginal cost principle*:

$$f(Q^F(\boldsymbol{x})) = c(x_i; \boldsymbol{x}_{-i}) \quad (i = 1, 2, \ldots, n), \quad (24.13)$$

where $Q^F(\boldsymbol{x}) := \Sigma_{j=1}^{n} q_j^F(\boldsymbol{x})$. Comparing $\boldsymbol{q}^F(\boldsymbol{x})$ with $\boldsymbol{q}^N(\boldsymbol{x})$, one can obtain the following lemma.

LEMMA 24.1. For any symmetric R&D profile $\boldsymbol{x} = (x_1, x_2, \ldots, x_n)$, $q_i^F(\boldsymbol{x}) > q_i^N(\boldsymbol{x})$ holds $(i = 1, 2, \ldots, n)$.

(See Appendix 24.B for the proof.)

In terms of $\boldsymbol{q}^F(\boldsymbol{x})$, the first-best welfare (market surplus) function $W^F(\boldsymbol{x})$ is defined by

$$W^F(\boldsymbol{x}) := W(\boldsymbol{x}, \boldsymbol{q}^F(\boldsymbol{x})). \quad (24.14)$$

One straightforward way to apply the first-best welfare function $W^F(\boldsymbol{x})$ is to compare $\boldsymbol{x}^N$ and $\boldsymbol{x}^C$ directly with the socially first-best R&D, $\boldsymbol{x}^F$, which is defined by

$$\boldsymbol{x}^F := \arg\max_{\boldsymbol{x}>0} W^F(\boldsymbol{x}). \quad (24.15)$$

Unless the model is further specialized in detail so that one can actually compute $\boldsymbol{x}^N$, $\boldsymbol{x}^C$, and $\boldsymbol{x}^F$ as in the d'Aspremont and Jacquemin [6] duopoly example, however, such a direct application of $W^F(\boldsymbol{x})$ is hard to come by.

An alternative way to proceed is to evaluate the partial derivative $(\partial/\partial x_i)W^F(\boldsymbol{x})$ at $\boldsymbol{x}^N$ and $\boldsymbol{x}^C$ for any $i = 1, 2, \ldots, n$. If it so happens that $(\partial/\partial x_i)W^F(\boldsymbol{x}^N) <$ (resp. $>$) 0, then a marginal decrease (resp. increase) in x_i at $\boldsymbol{x}^N$ increases the value of $W^F(\boldsymbol{x})$ marginally, so that the cost-reducing R&D at $\boldsymbol{x}^N$ is socially excessive (resp. insufficient) at the margin in terms of the first-best welfare function $W^F(\boldsymbol{x})$. Similarly, one can gauge the marginal social excessiveness/insufficiency of the cost-reducing R&D at $\boldsymbol{x}^C$ by evaluating the sign of $(\partial/\partial x_i)W^F(\boldsymbol{x})$ at $\boldsymbol{x}^C$.

It is easy to verify that the crucial derivative to be evaluated, viz., $(\partial/\partial x_i)W^F(\boldsymbol{x})$, consists of two terms, which may be called the *commitment effect*,

$$\gamma^F(\boldsymbol{x}) := -\, q_i^F(\boldsymbol{x})\frac{\partial}{\partial x_i}c(x_i; \boldsymbol{x}_{-i}) - 1, \tag{24.16}$$

and the *spillover effect*,

$$\sigma^F(\boldsymbol{x}) := -\sum_{j \neq i} q_j^F(\boldsymbol{x})\frac{\partial}{\partial x_i}c(x_j; \boldsymbol{x}_{-j}). \tag{24.17}$$

The spillover effect $\sigma^F(\boldsymbol{x})$ is easy to interpret. A marginal increase in x_i reduces the marginal cost $c(x_j; \boldsymbol{x}_{-j})$ of firm j $(i \neq j)$ through the spillover of cost-reducing benefits, which will increase the first-best social welfare in proportion to j's output $q_j^F(\boldsymbol{x})$. Summing up these effects over all $j \neq i$, one immediately obtains $\sigma^F(\boldsymbol{x})$.

To motivate the commitment effect, consider the problem of social welfare maximization without strategic commitment and R&D spillovers. One is then working with the following alternative optimization problem:

$$\max_{\boldsymbol{q}, \boldsymbol{x} > 0} \left[\int_0^Q f(Z)dZ - \sum_{j=1}^n \left\{ c(x_j; \boldsymbol{x}_{-j})q_j + x_j \right\} \right], \tag{24.18}$$

where $Q := \Sigma_{j=1}^n q_j$. The first-order conditions for this maximization problem are

$$f\left(\sum_{j=1}^n q_j^*\right) = c(x_i^*; \boldsymbol{x}_{-i}^*) \quad (i = 1, 2, \ldots, n) \tag{24.19}$$

and

$$-q_i^* \frac{\partial}{\partial x_i} c(x_i^*; \boldsymbol{x}_{-i}^*) - 1 = 0 \quad (i = 1, 2, \ldots, n), \qquad (24.20)$$

where $\boldsymbol{q}^* = (q_1^*, q_2^*, \ldots, q_n^*)$ and $\boldsymbol{x}^* = (x_1^*, x_2^*, \ldots, x_n^*)$ represent the solution to (24.18). Comparing (24.16) and (24.20), one can maintain that $\gamma^F(\boldsymbol{x})$ captures the portion of the effect of R&D that can be nonzero only in the presence of strategic commitment to R&D (hence the use of the term "commitment effect").

It is shown in Appendix 24.C that both $(\partial/\partial x_i)W^F(\boldsymbol{x}^N) > 0$ and $(\partial/\partial x_i)W^F(\boldsymbol{x}^C) > 0$ hold in the presence of sufficiently large R&D spillovers.

Theorem 24.1. Suppose that A1–A3 hold. Then

(i) the noncooperative equilibrium R&D level is socially insufficient at the margin in terms of the first-best welfare criterion if R&D spillovers are sufficiently large; and
(ii) the cooperative equilibrium R&D level is socially insufficient at the margin in terms of the first-best welfare criterion irrespective of whether R&D spillovers are large or small.

According to Theorem 24.1, both x_i^N and x_i^C are socially insufficient at the margin in terms of the first-best welfare criterion. How, then, does x_i^N fare vis-à-vis x_i^C? To settle this, note that $\boldsymbol{x}^C$ is the maximizer of $\Sigma_{j=1}^n \Pi_j(\boldsymbol{x})$ and compute $(\partial/\partial x_i)\Sigma_{j=1}^n \Pi_j(\boldsymbol{x}^N)$. If A3* is used instead of A3, one can verify that $(\partial/\partial x_i)\Sigma_{j=1}^n \Pi_j(\boldsymbol{x}^N) > 0$ holds in the presence of sufficiently large R&D spillovers, leading to the following theorem.

Theorem 24.2. Suppose that A1, A2, and A3* hold. Then a marginal increase in R&D level at the noncooperative equilibrium increases firms' joint profits marginally in the presence of sufficiently large R&D spillovers.

(See Appendix 24.D for the proof.)

To highlight the role played by large R&D spillovers in the model, I will briefly examine the other extreme case of no R&D spillover. By definition, then, $(\partial/\partial x_j)c(x_i; \boldsymbol{x}_{-i}) = 0$ $(i \neq j; i, j = 1, 2, \ldots, n)$ and $\theta(\boldsymbol{x}) < 0$, so that the sign of $(\partial/\partial x_i)W^F(\boldsymbol{x}^N)$ is ambiguous in general. However, I prove in Appendix 24.E that $(\partial/\partial x_i)W^F(\boldsymbol{x}^N) < 0$ holds if A3* and $n \geq 3$ are satisfied. On the other hand, I have already shown that $(\partial/\partial x_i)W^F(\boldsymbol{x}^C) > 0$ holds regardless of the extent of R&D spillovers. It is shown in Appendix 24.E that $(\partial/\partial x_i)\Sigma_{j=1}^n \Pi_j(\boldsymbol{x}^N) < 0$ holds in the case of no R&D spillover.

Theorem 24.3. Suppose that A1–A3 hold and there is no R&D spillover. Then the following three statements hold:

(i) If A3* is satisfied in place of A3, the noncooperative equilibrium R&D level is socially excessive at the margin in terms of the first-best welfare criterion when $n \geq 3$.
(ii) The cooperative equilibrium R&D level is socially insufficient at the margin in terms of the first-best welfare criterion.
(iii) A marginal decrease in R&D level at the noncooperative equilibrium marginally increases firms' joint profits.

24.5. Second-Best Welfare Analysis

Despite its obvious intuitive appeal and the preceding utilization by d'Aspremont and Jacqumin [6] and many others, the relevance of the first-best market surplus function $W^F(\boldsymbol{x})$ as the welfare criterion must be called into question. Indeed, the assumed enforceability of the marginal cost principle, which underlies the use of $W^F(\boldsymbol{x})$ as a welfare criterion, is likely to run into problems of implementation for any government in a democracy. For this reason, it makes sense to invoke the *second-best welfare (market surplus) function* instead, which is defined by

$$W^S(\boldsymbol{x}) := W(\boldsymbol{x}, \boldsymbol{q}^N(\boldsymbol{x})). \tag{24.21}$$

Unlike $W^F(\boldsymbol{x})$, $W^S(\boldsymbol{x})$ presupposes that the oligopolistic competition in the second-stage quantity game lies beyond the regulatory power of the nonomnipotent government. In other words, $W^S(\boldsymbol{x})$ is one way to evaluate the second-best performance of the oligopolistic industry.

If $W^F(\boldsymbol{x})$ is replaced by $W^S(\boldsymbol{x})$, the crucial derivative $(\partial/\partial x_i)W^S(\boldsymbol{x})$ should be decomposed into three, rather than two, terms. In addition to the commitment effect,

$$\gamma^S(\boldsymbol{x}) := -q_i^N(\boldsymbol{x})\frac{\partial}{\partial x_i}c(x_i;\boldsymbol{x}_{-i}) - 1 \tag{24.22}$$

and the spillover effect,

$$\sigma^S(\boldsymbol{x}) := -\sum_{j\neq i} q_j^N(\boldsymbol{x})\frac{\partial}{\partial x_i}c(x_j;\boldsymbol{x}_{-j}), \tag{24.23}$$

there is an additional term, which may be called the *distortion effect:*

$$\delta^S(\boldsymbol{x}) := \sum_{j=1}^{n} [f(Q^N(\boldsymbol{x})) - c(x_j;\boldsymbol{x}_{-j})]\frac{\partial}{\partial x_i}q_j^N(\boldsymbol{x}). \tag{24.24}$$

Clearly, the distortion effect is nothing other than the sum of marginal distortions generated by a marginal change in x_i.

If $\gamma^S(\boldsymbol{x})$, $\sigma^S(\boldsymbol{x})$, and $\delta^S(\boldsymbol{x})$ are evaluated at $\boldsymbol{x}^N$, one obtains

$$\gamma^S(\boldsymbol{x}^N) = -(n-1)f'(Q^N(\boldsymbol{x}^N)) \cdot q_i^N(\boldsymbol{x}^N) \cdot \theta(\boldsymbol{x}^N), \tag{24.25}$$

$$\sigma^S(\boldsymbol{x}^N) = -(n-1)q_i^N(\boldsymbol{x}^N) \cdot \frac{\partial}{\partial x_j}c(x_i^N;\boldsymbol{x}_{-i}^N) \quad (i \neq j), \tag{24.26}$$

and

$$\delta^S(\boldsymbol{x}^N) = [f(Q^N(\boldsymbol{x}^N)) - c(x_i^N;\boldsymbol{x}_{-i}^N)] \cdot \psi(\boldsymbol{x}^N), \tag{24.27}$$

all of which are positive under A1–A3 in the presence of sufficiently large R&D spillovers. Therefore, $(\partial/\partial x_i)W^S(\boldsymbol{x}^N) = \gamma^S(\boldsymbol{x}^N) + \sigma^S(\boldsymbol{x}^N) + \delta^S(\boldsymbol{x}^N) > 0$.

On the other hand, evaluating $\gamma^S(\boldsymbol{x})$, $\sigma^S(\boldsymbol{x})$, and $\delta^S(\boldsymbol{x})$ at $\boldsymbol{x}^C$, one obtains

$$\gamma^S(\boldsymbol{x}^C) = -(n-1)q_i^N(\boldsymbol{x}^C) \tag{24.28}$$
$$\cdot f'(Q^N(\boldsymbol{x}^C))\psi(\boldsymbol{x}^C) + (n-1)q_i^N(\boldsymbol{x}^C) \cdot \frac{\partial}{\partial x_j}c(x_i^C;\boldsymbol{x}_{-i}^C),$$

$$\sigma^S(\boldsymbol{x}^C) = -(n-1)q_i^N(\boldsymbol{x}^C) \cdot \frac{\partial}{\partial x_j} c(x_i^C; \boldsymbol{x}_{-i}^C) \quad (i \neq j), \tag{24.29}$$

and

$$\delta^S(\boldsymbol{x}^C) = \{f(Q^N(\boldsymbol{x}^C)) - c(x_i^C; \boldsymbol{x}_{-i}^C)\} \cdot \psi(\boldsymbol{x}^C). \tag{24.30}$$

Since $\gamma^S(\boldsymbol{x}^C)$ cancels the second term of $\sigma^S(\boldsymbol{x}^C)$, one obtains

$$\frac{\partial}{\partial x_i} W^S(\boldsymbol{x}^C) = \Big[-(n-1)q_i^N(\boldsymbol{x}^C) f'(Q^N(\boldsymbol{x}^C)) + \{f(Q^N(\boldsymbol{x}^C)) - c(x_i^C; \boldsymbol{x}_{-i}^C)\}\Big] \cdot \psi(\boldsymbol{x}^C), \tag{24.31}$$

which is unambiguously positive under A1–A3, irrespective of whether R&D spillovers are large or small.

I have thus established the following theorem, which shows in effect that, when the R&D spillovers are sufficiently large, the social insufficiency of the amount of cooperative as well as noncooperative equilibrium R&D at the margin remains intact even if the first-best welfare criterion is replaced by the more realistic second-best welfare criterion.

THEOREM 24.4. Suppose that A1–A3 hold. Then

(i) the noncooperative equilibrium R&D level is socially insufficient at the margin in terms of the second-best welfare criterion if the R&D spillovers are sufficiently large; and
(ii) the cooperative equilibrium R&D level is socially insufficient at the margin in terms of the second-best welfare criterion irrespective of whether R&D spillovers are large or small.

By contrast, to crystallize the role played by the assumption of sufficiently large spillovers, examine the polar opposite case of no spillover. In the case of noncooperative equilibrium, $\gamma^S(\boldsymbol{x}^N) < 0$, $\sigma^S(\boldsymbol{x}^N) = 0$, and $\delta^S(\boldsymbol{x}^N) > 0$ from (24.25), (24.26), and (24.27) in the absence of R&D spillover, so that $(\partial/\partial x_i)W^S(\boldsymbol{x}^N)$ consists of two terms with opposite signs. Furthermore,

$$\frac{\partial}{\partial x_i} W^S(\boldsymbol{x}^N) = \delta^S(\boldsymbol{x}^N) \cdot \left[1 - (n-1) \left\{ \frac{-\frac{\partial}{\partial x_i} q_j^N(\boldsymbol{x}^N)}{\frac{\partial}{\partial x_i} Q^N(\boldsymbol{x}^N)} \right\} \right] \tag{24.32}$$

holds, where use is made of (24.2) for $\boldsymbol{x} = \boldsymbol{x}^N$. As Okuno-Fujiwara and Suzumura [13] have observed, the expression within the square brackets in (24.32) is independent of the number of firms n, so that (24.32) implies that the crucial term $(\partial/\partial x_i)W^S(\boldsymbol{x}^N)$ becomes negative as n increases.[8]

On the other hand, in the case of cooperative equilibrium, $\gamma^S(\boldsymbol{x}^C) > 0$, $\sigma^S(\boldsymbol{x}^C) = 0$, and $\delta^S(\boldsymbol{x}^C) > 0$ from (24.28), (24.29), and (24.30) in the absence of R&D spillover, so that $(\partial/\partial x_i)W^S(\boldsymbol{x}^C)$ is unambiguously positive.

In summary, one can assert the following

THEOREM 24.5. Suppose that A1–A3 hold and there exists no R&D spillover. Then

(i) if there is a sufficiently large number of firms in the industry, then the noncooperative equilibrium R&D level is socially excessive at the margin in terms of the second-best welfare criterion; and
(ii) the cooperative equilibrium R&D level is socially insufficient at the margin in terms of the second-best welfare criterion.

24.6. Concluding Remarks

The main conclusions of my analysis are succinctly summarized in Table 24.1 (large spillover case) and Table 24.2 (no spillover case), where a "+," "0," or "−" in any cell signifies that the partial derivative in the corresponding row is, respectively, "positive," "zero," or "negative" when it is evaluated at the R&D profile in the corresponding column. When the validity of a particular sign requires more than just the standard A1–A3, that fact is indicated in the table footnote. These marginal conclusions on the performance of $\boldsymbol{x}^N$ and $\boldsymbol{x}^C$ can

8. How large should the number of firms be for the validity of this assertion? It was shown by Okuno-Fujiwara and Suzumura [13] that the critical number of firms remains small for a wide class of models. Indeed, if the inverse demand function is concave (i.e., under A3*), it can be shown that the watershed number of firms is exactly two, so that my conclusion applies to *all* oligopoly models with concave inverse demand functions. If the inverse demand function is constantly elastic, the value of the watershed number of firms changes as the value of elasticity changes. However, for a wide range of the values of elasticity, the value of the watershed number of firms remains consistently less than 3.

be converted into global conclusions; that is, the ranking among x_i^N, x_i^C, x_i^F, and x_i^S, on the one hand, and the ranking among $Q^N(\boldsymbol{x}^N)$, $Q^N(\boldsymbol{x}^C)$, $Q^N(\boldsymbol{x}^S)$, and $Q^N(\boldsymbol{x}^F)$, on the other, can be obtained if the relevant welfare or joint profit function is guaranteed to be single-peaked.[9]

Comparison between Table 24.1 and Table 24.2 yields several policy-relevant conclusions:

(a) From comparison of the first and second rows in each table, it appears that the qualitative conclusions remain the same even if one uses the second-best welfare function instead of the first-best welfare function. Note, however, that the policy relevance of these conclusions is substantially increased by the use of the second-best welfare criterion.

(b) Comparing the first and second columns in Table 24.1, one sees that, in the presence of large spillovers, not only the noncooperative equilibrium R&D level but also the cooperative equilibrium R&D level is socially insufficient at the margin, so that the technology policy that facilitates further investment in R&D is marginally welfare-improving irrespective of whether firms cooperate or not.

(c) Comparing the first and second columns in Table 24.2, one sees that, in the absence of spillovers, while the cooperative equilibrium R&D level remains socially too small at the margin, the noncooperative equilibrium R&D level turns out to be socially excessive at the margin. Therefore, the marginally welfare-improving technology policy should facilitate (resp. restrict) investment in R&D if firms cooperate (resp. do not cooperate).

(d) From a comparison of the third row in Table 24.1 with the corresponding row in Table 24.2, it appears that an increase in R&D at the noncooperative equilibrium marginally increases (resp. decreases) joint profits if spillover effects are large (resp. small).

9. By the single-peakedness of a function $f(\boldsymbol{x})$, where $\boldsymbol{x} = (x_1, x_2, \ldots, x_n)$, I mean here that $f(x_i; \boldsymbol{x}_{-i})$ has a unique local (hence global) maximum with respect to x_i for an arbitrarily specified value of $\boldsymbol{x}_{-i} = (x_1, \ldots, x_{i-1}, x_{i+1}, \ldots, x_n)$ $(i = 1, 2, \ldots, n)$. Note that, in the duopoly example of d'Aspremont and Jacquemin [6], the first-best welfare function as well as the joint profit function is assured to be concave (hence single-peaked).

Table 24.1. Large Spillover Case

	R&D Profile	
Derivative	$\boldsymbol{x}^N$	$\boldsymbol{x}^C$
$(\partial/\partial x_i)W^F(\boldsymbol{x})$	$+$	$+$
$(\partial/\partial x_i)W^S(\boldsymbol{x})$	$+$	$+$
$(\partial/\partial x_i)\sum_{j=1}^{n}\Pi_j(\boldsymbol{x})$	$+^a$	0

Note: The vectors $\boldsymbol{x}^N$ and $\boldsymbol{x}^C$ denote, respectively, the noncooperative equilibrium R&D profile and the cooperative equilibrium R&D profile. The symbol "+" or "0" denotes, respectively, that the partial derivative in the corresponding row is "positive" or "zero" at the R&D profile in the corresponding column.
a. This requires A3*.

Table 24.2. No-Spillover Case

	R&D Profile	
Derivative	$\boldsymbol{x}^N$	$\boldsymbol{x}^C$
$(\partial/\partial x_i)W^F(\boldsymbol{x})$	$-^a$	$+$
$(\partial/\partial x_i)W^S(\boldsymbol{x})$	$-^b$	$+$
$(\partial/\partial x_i)\sum_{j=1}^{n}\Pi_j(\boldsymbol{x})$	$-$	0

Note: The vectors $\boldsymbol{x}^N$ and $\boldsymbol{x}^C$ denote, respectively, the noncooperative equilibrium R&D profile and the cooperative equilibrium R&D profile. The symbol "+," "0," or "−" denotes, respectively, that the partial derivative in the corresponding row is "positive," "zero," or "negative" at the R&D profile in the corresponding column.
a. This requires A3* and $n \geq 3$.
b. This requires that the number of firms is sufficiently large.

Several concluding remarks are in order concerning directions for future analysis of cooperative R&D. First, as Jeffrey Bernstein and Ishaq Nadiri [1] and Richard Levin and Peter Reiss [12] have emphasized, R&D undertaken by firms outside the industry (e.g., by material suppliers and equipment suppliers) may exert an influence on a firm's marginal cost. Such interindustry spillover effects should be taken into consideration along with the intraindustry spillover effects in order to obtain a well-balanced evaluation of the effects of R&D spillovers.

Second, one of the alleged functions of cooperative R&D is precisely to generate synergic effects by pooling various complementary resources, such as research information and experience, teams of researchers, and technological know-how. From this viewpoint, my formulation of R&D spillovers in terms of the average variable cost function, which remains the same irrespective of whether firms cooperate or not, may be seriously inadequate. For fuller analysis, one presumably should endogenize the spillover function by making the cost-reducing technology dependent on the extent to which firms pool their complementary R&D resources.

Third, the potential benefits of cooperative R&D are often related to an acceleration in the speed of invention and innovation by risk spreading and risk pooling. In discussing cost-reducing R&D, therefore, one should introduce an element of uncertainty into the analysis.

Fourth, my concentration on the second-stage quantity game and the assumption of symmetric equilibria are likely to restrict the generality of the conclusions. In particular, it may well be worthwhile to select a subgroup of cooperating firms and let this subgroup conduct R&D exclusively—subject to the cost-sharing agreements among all member firms—since the group as a whole can thereby conserve on the fixed cost of equipment installation and avoid unnecessary duplication of R&D efforts.

The policy implications of my results should be interpreted carefully in light of these qualifying observations. Nevertheless, I hope that the results, partial though they are, and the method of analysis that has been developed en route, will contribute to a better understanding of the complex issue of cooperative R&D.

Appendix 24.A. Derivation of the Formulas for $\omega(\boldsymbol{x})$ and $\theta(\boldsymbol{x})$

To derive formulas (24.5) and (24.6), let us differentiate the condition $(\partial/\partial q_i)\Pi_i(\boldsymbol{q}^N(\boldsymbol{x}); x_i, \boldsymbol{x}_{-i}) = 0$ characterizing $\boldsymbol{q}^N(\boldsymbol{x})$ with respect to x_i and x_h $(h \neq i)$ and use symmetry to obtain the following simultaneous equations for $\omega(\boldsymbol{x})$ and $\theta(\boldsymbol{x})$:

$$\alpha(\boldsymbol{x})\omega(\boldsymbol{x}) + (n-1)\beta(\boldsymbol{x})\theta(\boldsymbol{x}) = \frac{\partial}{\partial x_i} c(x_i, \boldsymbol{x}_{-i}) \qquad (24.\text{A}1)$$

and

$$\beta(\boldsymbol{x})\omega(\boldsymbol{x}) + \{\alpha(\boldsymbol{x}) + (n-2)\beta(\boldsymbol{x})\}\theta(\boldsymbol{x}) = \frac{\partial}{\partial x_j} c(x_i, \boldsymbol{x}_{-i}), \qquad (24.\text{A}2)$$

where $i \neq j$. Solving (24.A1) and (24.A2) for $\omega(\boldsymbol{x})$ and rearranging terms appropriately, one obtains (24.5) in the main text; solving for $\theta(\boldsymbol{x})$ and rearranging, one obtains (24.6). ■

Appendix 24.B. Proof of Lemma 24.1

Note that (24.2) and (24.13) yield

$$f(nq_i^F(\boldsymbol{x})) - f(nq_i^N(\boldsymbol{x})) = f'(nq_i^N(\boldsymbol{x}))q_i^N(\boldsymbol{x})$$

for any symmetric R&D profile $\boldsymbol{x} = (x_1, x_2, \ldots, x_n)$, so that there exists a positive number $\zeta(\boldsymbol{x})$, $0 < \zeta(\boldsymbol{x}) < 1$, such that

$$q_i^F(\boldsymbol{x}) - q_i^N(\boldsymbol{x}) = \frac{q_i^N(\boldsymbol{x}) f'(nq_i^N(\boldsymbol{x}))}{nf'(n[\zeta(\boldsymbol{x})q_i^F(\boldsymbol{x}) + \{1 - \zeta(\boldsymbol{x})\}q_i^N(\boldsymbol{x})])} \qquad (24.\text{B}1)$$

holds by virtue of the mean value theorem. Lemma 24.1 is an immediate consequence of (24.B1) and A1. ■

Appendix 24.C. Proof of Theorem 24.1

Taking the first-order condition (24.2) characterizing $q_i^N(\boldsymbol{x})$ and the symmetry of $\boldsymbol{x}^N$ into consideration, one can rewrite the first-order condition (24.4) characterizing $\boldsymbol{x}^N$ as follows:

$$\begin{aligned} &- q_i^N(\boldsymbol{x}^N)\frac{\partial}{\partial x_i}c(x_i^N; \boldsymbol{x}_{-i}^N) - 1 \\ &\quad = -(n-1) f'(Q^N(\boldsymbol{x}^N))q_i^N(\boldsymbol{x}^N)\theta(\boldsymbol{x}^N) \quad (i = 1, 2, \ldots, n). \qquad (24.\text{C}1) \end{aligned}$$

Comparing (24.16) at $\boldsymbol{x} = \boldsymbol{x}^N$ with (24.C1), one may obtain

$$\begin{aligned} \gamma^F(\boldsymbol{x}^N) = &- (n-1) f'(Q^N(\boldsymbol{x}^N))q_i^N(\boldsymbol{x}^N)\theta(\boldsymbol{x}^N) \\ &+ \left\{q_i^N(\boldsymbol{x}^N) - q_i^F(\boldsymbol{x}^N)\right\}\frac{\partial}{\partial x_i}c(x_i^N; \boldsymbol{x}_{-i}^N), \qquad (24.\text{C}2) \end{aligned}$$

which is positive in the presence of sufficiently large R&D spillovers, where use is made of Lemma 24.1 and A1 and A2. On the other hand, at $\boldsymbol{x} = \boldsymbol{x}^N$, (24.17) can be reduced to

$$\sigma^F(\boldsymbol{x}^N) = -(n-1)q_i^F(\boldsymbol{x}^N) \cdot \frac{\partial}{\partial x_j} c(x_i^N; \boldsymbol{x}_{-i}^N) \quad (i \neq j), \qquad (24.\text{C}3)$$

which is nonnegative by virtue of A2. It then follows that $(\partial/\partial x_i)W^F(\boldsymbol{x}^N) = \gamma^F(\boldsymbol{x}^N) + \sigma^F(\boldsymbol{x}^N) > 0$.

Turning to the cooperative R&D equilibrium $\boldsymbol{x}^C$ and invoking (24.10), we obtain

$$\begin{aligned}\gamma^F(\boldsymbol{x}^C) = & -(n-1)f'(Q^N(\boldsymbol{x}^C)) \\ & \cdot q_i^N(\boldsymbol{x}^C)\psi(\boldsymbol{x}^C) + \{q_i^N(\boldsymbol{x}^C) - q_i^F(\boldsymbol{x}^C)\} \\ & \cdot \frac{\partial}{\partial x_i} c(x_i^C; \boldsymbol{x}_{-i}^C) + (n-1)q_i^N(\boldsymbol{x}^C) \cdot \frac{\partial}{\partial x_j} c(x_i^C; \boldsymbol{x}_{-i}^C) \quad (i \neq j).\end{aligned} \qquad (24.\text{C}4)$$

Coupling (24.C4) with $\sigma^F(\boldsymbol{x}^C)$, which can be reduced to

$$\sigma^F(\boldsymbol{x}^C) = -(n-1)q_i^F(\boldsymbol{x}^C) \cdot \frac{\partial}{\partial x_j} c(x_i^C; \boldsymbol{x}_{-i}^C) \quad (i \neq j), \qquad (24.\text{C}5)$$

one obtains

$$\begin{aligned}\frac{\partial}{\partial x_i} W^F(\boldsymbol{x}^C) = & -(n-1)f'(Q^N(\boldsymbol{x}^C))q_i^N(\boldsymbol{x}^C)\psi(\boldsymbol{x}^C) \\ & + \{q_i^N(\boldsymbol{x}^C) - q_i^F(\boldsymbol{x}^C)\} \cdot \left\{ \frac{\partial}{\partial x_i} c(x_i^C; \boldsymbol{x}_{-i}^C) + (n-1)\frac{\partial}{\partial x_j} c(x_i^C; \boldsymbol{x}_{-i}^C) \right\},\end{aligned} \qquad (24.\text{C}6)$$

where $i \neq j$, which is positive by virtue of $\psi(\boldsymbol{x}^C) > 0$, Lemma 24.1, A1, and A2, irrespective of whether R&D spillovers are large or small. ■

Appendix 24.D. Proof of Theorem 24.2

Invoking (24.C1), one can compute that

$$\frac{\partial}{\partial x_i}\sum_{j=1}^{n}\Pi_j(\boldsymbol{x}^N) = (n-1)q_i^N(\boldsymbol{x}^N) \cdot \left\{ f'(Q^N(\boldsymbol{x}^N))\psi(\boldsymbol{x}^N) - \frac{\partial}{\partial x_j}c(x_i^N;\boldsymbol{x}_{-i}^N) \right\} \quad (24.\text{D}1)$$

holds, where $i \neq j$. Having recourse to (24.5) and (24.6), one is assured that

$$\text{sgn}\frac{\partial}{\partial x_i}\sum_{j=1}^{n}\Pi_j(\boldsymbol{x}^N) = \text{sgn}\left[\left\{ -(n-3)\alpha(\boldsymbol{x}^N) + 2(n-1)\beta(\boldsymbol{x}^N) \right\} \cdot \frac{\partial}{\partial x_j}c(x_i^N;\boldsymbol{x}_{-i}^N) - \alpha(\boldsymbol{x}^N)\frac{\partial}{\partial x_i}c(x_i^N;\boldsymbol{x}_{-i}^N) \right] \quad (24.\text{D}2)$$

so that $(\partial/\partial x_i)\Sigma_{j=1}^{n}\Pi_j(\boldsymbol{x}^N) >$ (resp. $<$) 0 holds if and only if

$$\Omega_i(\boldsymbol{x}^N) := \alpha(\boldsymbol{x}^N) + \{(n-3)\alpha(\boldsymbol{x}^N) - 2(n-1)\beta(\boldsymbol{x}^N)\} \cdot \frac{\frac{\partial}{\partial x_j}c(x_i^N;\boldsymbol{x}_{-i}^N)}{\frac{\partial}{\partial x_i}c(x_i^N;\boldsymbol{x}_{-i}^N)} > \text{(resp. } <\text{) } 0 \quad (24.\text{D}3)$$

holds, where $i \neq j$. Under the assumption of sufficiently large R&D spillovers,

$$\frac{\frac{\partial}{\partial x_j}c(x_i^N;\boldsymbol{x}_{-i}^N)}{\frac{\partial}{\partial x_i}c(x_i^N;\boldsymbol{x}_{-i}^N)} > \frac{\beta(\boldsymbol{x}^N)}{\alpha(\boldsymbol{x}^N)} \quad (24.\text{D}4)$$

obtains, where $i \neq j$. Note that an inequality $(n-3)\alpha(\boldsymbol{x}) - 2(n-1)\beta(\boldsymbol{x}) > 0$ is valid for any symmetric R&D profile $\boldsymbol{x} = (x_1, x_2, \ldots, x_n)$. To verify this fact, define $\kappa^N(\boldsymbol{x}) := Q^N(\boldsymbol{x})f''(Q^N(\boldsymbol{x}))/f'(Q^N(\boldsymbol{x}))$, which makes it possible to rewrite (24.8) and (24.9) as

$$\alpha(\boldsymbol{x}) = f'(Q^N(\boldsymbol{x}))\left\{2 + \frac{\kappa^N(\boldsymbol{x})}{n}\right\} \tag{24.D5}$$

and

$$\beta(\boldsymbol{x}) = f'(Q^N(\boldsymbol{x}))\left\{1 + \frac{\kappa^N(\boldsymbol{x})}{n}\right\}. \tag{24.D6}$$

It follows that

$$\begin{aligned}&(n-3)\alpha(\boldsymbol{x}) - 2(n-1)\beta(\boldsymbol{x})\\&= \frac{\alpha(\boldsymbol{x})}{2n+\kappa^N(\boldsymbol{x})}\cdot[-\{\kappa^N(\boldsymbol{x})+4\}n - \kappa^N(\boldsymbol{x})] > 0\end{aligned} \tag{24.D7}$$

whose sign is due to $\alpha(\boldsymbol{x}) < 0$ and $\kappa^N(\boldsymbol{x}) \geq 0$, which follows from A3*.

Putting (24.D4), (24.D5), and (24.D7) together and having recourse to A3*, one obtains

$$\Omega_i(\boldsymbol{x}^N) > \alpha(\boldsymbol{x}^N) + \frac{\beta(\boldsymbol{x}^N)}{\alpha(\boldsymbol{x}^N)}\cdot\{(n-3)\alpha(\boldsymbol{x}^N) - 2(n-1)\beta(\boldsymbol{x}^N)\}. \tag{24.D8}$$

Using (24.D5) and (24.D6), one can verify that

$$\begin{aligned}&\alpha(\boldsymbol{x}^N) + (n-3)\beta(\boldsymbol{x}^N) - 2(n-1)\frac{\{\beta(\boldsymbol{x}^N)\}^2}{\alpha(\boldsymbol{x}^N)}\\&= -\frac{f'(Q^N(\boldsymbol{x}^N))\kappa^N(\boldsymbol{x}^N)}{2n+\kappa^N(\boldsymbol{x}^N)}\cdot\{\kappa^N(\boldsymbol{x}^N)+n+1\} \geq 0.\end{aligned} \tag{24.D9}$$

One is thus led to conclude that $(\partial/\partial x_i)\Sigma_{j=1}^n \Pi_j(\boldsymbol{x}^N) > 0$. ■

Appendix 24.E. Proof of Theorem 24.3

In the case of no R&D spillover, $(\partial/\partial x_i)W^F(\boldsymbol{x}^N) = \gamma^F(\boldsymbol{x}^N)$, whose sign is indeterminate in general. However, if A3* is also adopted, one may obtain

$$\frac{\partial}{\partial x_i} W^F(\boldsymbol{x}^N) = \frac{\partial}{\partial x_i} c(x_i^N; \boldsymbol{x}_{-i}^N)$$
$$\cdot \left\{ \frac{n + \kappa^N(\boldsymbol{x}^N)}{n + 1 + \kappa^N(\boldsymbol{x}^N)} \left(\frac{n-1}{n}\right) q_i^N(\boldsymbol{x}^N) + q_i^N(\boldsymbol{x}^N) - q_i^F(\boldsymbol{x}^N) \right\}$$
$$\leq \frac{\partial}{\partial x_i} c(x_i^N; \boldsymbol{x}_{-i}^N) \cdot q_i^N(\boldsymbol{x}^N) \cdot \left\{ \frac{n + \kappa^N(\boldsymbol{x}^N)}{n + 1 + \kappa^N(\boldsymbol{x}^N)} \left(\frac{n-1}{n}\right) - \frac{1}{n} \right\}, \tag{24.E1}$$

where use is made of (24.B1), (24.C2), and (24.D5). Since the expression within the brackets is positive when $n \geq 3$, it follows from (24.E1) that $(\partial/\partial x_i) W^F(\boldsymbol{x}^N) < 0$ when $n \geq 3$. This proves part (i) of Theorem 24.3. Part (ii) of Theorem 24.3 needs no further proof, whereas part (iii) follows from (24.D2) by setting $(\partial/\partial x_j) c(x_i^N; \boldsymbol{x}_{-i}^N) = 0$ $(i \neq j)$. ■

24.7. References

[1] Bernstein, J. I., and M. I. Nadiri, "Interindustry R&D Spillovers, Rate of Return, and Production in High-Tech Industries," *American Economic Review: Papers and Proceedings* **78**, 1988, 429–434.

[2] Besley, T., and K. Suzumura, "Taxation and Welfare in an Oligopoly with Strategic Commitment," *International Economic Review* **33**, 1992, 413–431.

[3] Brander, J. A., and B. J. Spencer, "Strategic Commitment with R&D: The Symmetric Case," *Bell Journal of Economics* **14**, 1983, 225–235.

[4] Bulow, J. I., J. D. Geanakoplos, and P. D. Klemperer, "Multimarket Oligopoly: Strategic Substitutes and Complements," *Journal of Political Economy* **93**, 1985, 488–511.

[5] Dasgupta, P., and J. Stiglitz, "Industrial Structure and the Nature of Innovative Activity," *Economic Journal* **90**, 1980, 266–293.

[6] d'Aspremont, C., and A. Jacquemin, "Cooperative and Noncooperative R&D in Duopoly with Spillovers," *American Economic Review* **78**, 1988, 1133–1137.

[7] d'Aspremont, C., and A. Jacquemin, "Cooperative and Noncooperative R&D in Duopoly with Spillovers: Erratum," *American Economic Review* **80**, 1990, 641–642.

[8] Dixit, A., "Comparative Statics for Oligopoly," *International Economic Review* **27**, 1986, 107–122.

[9] Henriques, I., "Cooperative and Noncooperative R&D in Duopoly with Spillovers: Comment," *American Economic Review* **80**, 1990, 638–640.

[10] Jacquemin, A., "Cooperative Agreements in R&D and European Antitrust Policy," *European Economic Review* **32**, 1988, 551–560.

[11] Katz, M. L., "An Analysis of Cooperative Research and Development," *Rand Journal of Economics*, Winter 1986, **17**, 527–543.

[12] Levin, R. C., and P. C. Reiss, "Cost-Reducing and Demand-Creating R&D with Spillovers," *Rand Journal of Economics* **19**, 1988, 538–556.

[13] Okuno-Fujiwara, M., and K. Suzumura, "Symmetric Cournot Oligopoly and Economic Welfare: A Synthesis," *Economic Theory* **3**, 1993, 43–59. Essay 23 of this volume.

[14] Seade, J., "On the Effect of Entry," *Econometrica* **48**, 1980, 479–489.

[15] Seade, J., "The Stability of Cournot Revisited," *Journal of Economic Theory* **23**, 1980, 15–27.

[16] Spence, M., "Cost Reduction, Competition and Industry Performance," *Econometrica* **52**, 1984, 101–121.

[17] Spencer, B. J., and J. A. Brander, "International R&D Rivalry and Industrial Strategy," *Review of Economic Studies* **50**, 1983, 707–722.

PART VII

HISTORICALLY SPEAKING

Introduction to Part VII

> A further word on the subject of *issuing instructions* on how the world ought to be: philosophy, at any rate, always comes too late to perform this function. As the *thought* of the world, it appears only at a time when actuality has gone through its formative process and attained its completed state. . . . When philosophy paints its grey in grey, a shape of life has grown old, and it cannot be rejuvenated, but only recognized, by the grey in grey of philosophy; the owl of Minerva begins its flight only with the onset of dusk.
>
> —GEORG WILHELM FRIEDRICH HEGEL, *Elements of the Philosophy of Right*, 1820

In April 2001, I was engaged in research at Trinity College, Cambridge University, as a Visiting Fellow Commoner. One of my research projects was to complete the editorial work for *Handbook of Social Choice and Welfare*, Vol. I (Arrow, Sen, and Suzumura [1]) in collaboration with Kenneth Arrow and Amartya Sen. I was fortunate enough to be provided with a study in the Blue Boar Court in Trinity College as well as an office in the Faculty of Economics near Marshall Library.

One day I was resting in the faculty coffee room, taking a breather after an intensive day of working on the handbook's introduction.[1] An old acquaintance, Tony Lawson, approached me, and asked: "What are you working on nowadays?" My mind was still almost completely preoccupied with the historical origin of welfare economics and social choice theory. Thus, my spontaneous answer was, "I am writing a history of welfare economics." He seemed to be slightly taken aback, and murmured: "Well, that is a short history indeed."

His immediate response is understandable, particularly because this conversation took place in Cambridge University, where Arthur Pigou [8]

1. This introduction eventually matured into Essay 25 of this volume.

launched the construction of his "old" welfare economics, so-called, as recently as 1920. It should also be remembered that John Hicks [6, p. 218] made an authoritative remark to the effect that "[the] 'official' history [of welfare economics], of course, begins with Pigou, *The Economics of Welfare* (1920). For it was certainly Pigou who gave its name to the subject. If it existed before Pigou, it must have been called something else."

Technically speaking, Hicks was certainly right, but his observation could not literally mean that the substantial study of welfare economics was kicked off by Pigou from scratch. Quite to the contrary, there exists a long English tradition of moral philosophy, which can be traced at least as far back as to Jeremy Bentham.[2] Pigou's *Economics of Welfare* was nothing other than an attempted synthesis of this old tradition under the new title of welfare economics.

There are several authorities who are eager to trace back the historical origin of welfare economics far beyond not only Pigou but also Bentham. To cite just a few salient examples, Joseph Schumpeter and Paul Samuelson[3] emphasized "the hallowed antiquity of welfare economics," in the characteristic parlance of Schumpeter [14, p. 1069]. According to their verdicts, the historical origin of welfare economics can go back far beyond Pigou and his synthesis of English tradition of moral philosophy.[4] In spite of my strong respect for these great scholars in the history of economic analysis, I would like to emphasize that there is a clear distinction between the *instrumental concern* with concrete economic policies and/or economic systems, on the one hand, and the *theoretical concern* with their performance characteristics, on the other. Since this work is mainly concerned with the scholarly research focused exclusively on the latter concern, Part VII gathers only those papers that are related to the historical evolution of welfare economics in the tradition of Benthamite utilitarianism and its doctrinal offspring.

---

2. See Bentham [2].
3. Recollect that Samuelson [12, p. 223] once called himself a scholar "who before 1938 knew *all* the relevant literature on welfare economics." See also Agnar Sandmo [13, p. 398], who highly extolled Samuelson [11, Chapter VIII] for having written "a chapter on the history of welfare economics that is a masterly synthesis of the literature from the breakthrough of marginalism to the middle of the 1940s."
4. In Samuelson's [12, p. 203] own parlance, "Beginning as it did in the writings of philosophers, theologians, pamphleteers, special pleaders, and reformers, economics has always been concerned with problems of public policy and welfare."

Likewise, the origin of the *factual concern* with social choice rules and/or mechanisms can be traced back to the very beginning of human collaboration and division of labor organized for the sake of promoting common causes of the society. However, the main focus of essays in this volume is on the *theoretical performance* of actual or logically conceivable rules and mechanisms for collective decision making. It is for this reason that Part VII is mainly devoted to the historical evolution of social choice theory since the pioneering contributions by two eminent scholars around the time of the French Revolution, viz., Marie-Jean de Condorcet and Jean-Charles de Borda, and of normative economics since Benthamite utilitarianism. It is not an accident that Bentham in England and Condorcet and Borda in France were contemporaries across the English Channel.

I have selected four essays to be included in Part VII. The first, Essay 25, was prepared originally for the *Handbook of Social Choice and Welfare*, Vol. I, as the introduction, and turned into Essay 25 of the present volume under the title "Introduction to Social Choice and Welfare." It presents a succinct overview of the research areas of social choice theory and welfare economics with special emphasis on *ordinalist revolution* in welfare economics, on the one hand, and *economic planning controversy*, on the other. Both of these epoch-making events in the evolution of economic analysis took place in the 1930s. The former was the initial step in our current concern with the informational bases of social choice theory and welfare economics, whereas the latter was the first road map in the evolution of social choice theory.

The second essay, Essay 26, describes the historical evolution of the two schools of "new" welfare economics and their logical relationships under the title "Paretian Welfare Judgments and Bergsonian Social Choice." Both schools of thought tried to salvage the sound vestiges of Pigou's "old" welfare economics on the epistemological basis of ordinal and interpersonally noncomparable information on individual utilities or, more generally, welfare. The first school is founded on the compensation principles à la Nicholas Kaldor [7], John Hicks [4], Tibor Scitovsky [15], and Paul Samuelson [10], whereas the second school is founded on the concept of the social welfare function à la Abram Bergson [3] and Paul Samuelson [11, Chapter VIII; 12]. We try to identify a condition under which these two schools of thought can be logically compatible.

The third essay, Essay 27 ("Welfare Economics beyond Welfarist Consequentialism"), is an abbreviated version of my presidential address presented at the 1999 annual meeting of the Japanese Economic Association. It presents a brief account of social choice theory and welfare economics after the demise of old welfare economics à la Pigou under the devastating criticism by Robbins. It also describes a brief plan of reconstruction, which I have tried to develop over the years and summarized in other parts of the volume.

The fourth and last essay of Part VII, Essay 28 ("Informational Bases of Welfare Economics, Transcendental Institutionalism, and the Comparative Assessment Approach"), focuses on the two crucial points of departure in the theory of normative economics. The first point of departure is related to the bifurcation in the informational tree of normative judgments. As we have identified here, it was John Hicks who explicitly declared a farewell to the welfaristic informational basis of normative economics. In the first part of this last essay, we scrutinize how deeply rooted is Hicks's *Manifesto*, which goes not only against welfarism but also against consequentialism. The second point of departure is related to Amartya Sen's [16] identification of transcendental institutionalism and the comparative assessment approach in the theory of justice. In the second part of this essay, we contend that Sen's dichotomy has a strong relevance to the scope and method of normative economics as well, and bring the message of his dichotomy into clear relief in the arena of normative economics.

It is my modest hope that these four essays will put my overall work on social choice theory and welfare economics in better historical perspective.

References

[1] Arrow, K. J., A. K. Sen, and K. Suzumura, *Handbook of Social Choice and Welfare*, Amsterdam: North-Holland/Elsevier, Vol. I, 2002; Vol. II, 2011.

[2] Bentham, J., *An Introduction to the Principles of Morals and Legislation*, London: Payne, 1789. Reprinted in 1907 by Oxford: Clarendon Press.

[3] Bergson, A., "A Reformulation of Certain Aspects of Welfare Economics," *Quarterly Journal of Economics* **52**, 1938, 310–334.

[4] Hicks, J. R., "The Valuation of the Social Income," *Economica* **7**, 1940, 105–124.

[5] Hicks, J. R., "Preface—and a Manifesto," in his *Essays in World Economics*, Oxford: Clarendon Press, 1959. Reprinted with a revision in his *Wealth and Welfare*, Vol. I of *Collected Essays on Economic Theory*, Oxford: Basil Blackwell, 1981, 135–141.

[6] Hicks, J. R., "The Scope and Status of Welfare Economics," *Oxford Economic Papers* **27**, 1975, 307–326.

[7] Kaldor, N., "Welfare Propositions in Economics and Interpersonal Comparisons of Utility," *Economic Journal* **49**, 1939, 549–552.

[8] Pigou, A. C., *The Economics of Welfare*, London: Macmillan, 1st edn., 1920.
[9] Robbins, L., *An Essay on the Nature and Significance of Economic Science*, London: Macmillan, 1st edn., 1932; 2nd edn., 1935.
[10] Samuelson, P. A., "Evaluation of Real National Income," *Oxford Economic Papers* **2**, 1950, 1–29.
[11] Samuelson, P. A., *Foundations of Economic Analysis*, Cambridge, Mass.: Harvard University Press, 1947; enlarged edn., 1983.
[12] Samuelson, P. A., "Bergsonian Welfare Economics," in S. Resefielde, ed., *Economic Welfare and the Economics of Soviet Socialism: Essays in Honor of Abram Bergson*, Cambridge, Mass.: Cambridge University Press, 1981, 223–266.
[13] Sandmo, A., *Economics Evolving: A History of Economic Thought*, Princeton, N.J.: Princeton University Press, 2011.
[14] Schumpeter, J. A., *History of Economic Analysis*, New York: Oxford University Press, 1954.
[15] Scitovsky, T., "A Note on Welfare Propositions in Economics," *Review of Economic Studies* **9**, 1941, 77–88.
[16] Sen, A. K., *The Idea of Justice*, Cambridge, Mass.: Belknap Press of Harvard University Press, 2009.

ESSAY 25

Introduction to Social Choice and Welfare

25.1. Historical Background

Social choice theory is concerned with the evaluation of alternative methods of collective decision making, as well as with the logical foundations of welfare economics. In turn, welfare economics is concerned with the critical scrutiny of the performance of actual and/or imaginary economic systems, as well as with the critique, design, and implementation of alternative economic policies. This being the case, it goes without saying that the origin of social choice theory can be traced back all the way to antiquity. Indeed, as soon as multiple individuals participate in making decisions for their common cause, one or other method of collective decision making cannot but be invoked. As a reflection of this obvious fact, there are numerous examples in classic writings on the use and usefulness of alternative methods of collective decision making. Suffice it to quote Aristotle in ancient Greece and Kautilya in ancient India; they both lived in the fourth century BC, and explored

First published in K. J. Arrow, A. K. Sen, and K. Suzumura, eds., *Handbook of Social Choice and Welfare*, Vol. I, Amsterdam: Elsevier, 2002, pp. 1–32. Thanks are due to coeditors of the *Handbook of Social Choice and Welfare*, Kenneth Arrow and Amartya Sen, whose encouragement, comments, and persuasion enabled me to complete this essay. In preparing several drafts of this essay, I was greatly supported by helpful comments and encouragement provided by Nick Baigent, Walter Bossert, Marc Fleurbaey, Wulf Gaertner, Louis Gevers, Peter Hammond, Hervé Moulin, Maurice Salles, Koichi Tadenuma, John Weymark, and Yongsheng Xu.

several possibilities of collective decision making in their books, entitled, respectively, *Politics* and *Economics*.[1]

Likewise, as soon as any collective body designs and implements an economic mechanism and/or an economic policy, paying proper attention to the costs and benefits accruing to its constituent members, one or more social welfare judgments are unavoidable. In this sense, Joseph Schumpeter [108, p. 1069] was certainly right when he emphasized "the hallowed antiquity of welfare economics." He observed that "a large part of the work of Carafa and his successors as well as of the work of the scholastic doctors and *their* successors was welfare economics. We also know that the welfare point of view was much in evidence in the eighteenth century. . . . For Bentham and the English utilitarians generally this point of view was, of course, an essential element of their creed. Hence, the positive spirit of Ricardian economics notwithstanding, we find it also in the English 'classics,' particularly in J. S. Mill. So far as this goes, modern welfare economists merely revive the Benthamite tradition." It was in a similar vein that Paul Samuelson [101, p. 203] began his famous Chapter VIII on welfare economics in *Foundations of Economic Analysis* with the following remark: "Beginning as it did in the writings of philosophers, theologians, pamphleteers, special pleaders, and reformers, economics has always been concerned with problems of public policy and welfare."

Without contradicting these authoritative verdicts on the long historical background of social choice theory, we must nevertheless claim that the *instrumental concern* with concrete methods of collective decision making is one thing, and the *theoretical investigation* into their logical performance is another thing altogether. The former concern may be as old as the origin of human society, but the latter development seems to be of more recent origin. Indeed, it seems fair to say that the real origin of the theory of collective decision making can be attributed to the pioneering contributions by two eminent precursors around the time of the French Revolution, viz., Marie-Jean de Condorcet and Jean-Charles de Borda.[2] It was in the intellectual

1. See Sen [122, p. 350].
2. Iain McLean and John London [76, p. 107] maintained that they found "two medieval thinkers, hitherto unknown to historians of social choice [viz., Ramon Lull (c. 1235–1315), who proposed the Condorcet method of pairwise comparisons, and Nicolas Cusanus (1401–1464), who proposed the Borda method of rank-order comparisons], who anticipated the work of Condorcet, Borda and Dodgson by over 500 years." They aptly added, however, that "neither writer gives a

atmosphere of the European Enlightenment during the eighteenth century, with its conspicuous concern with human rights and the reasoned design and implementation of rational social order, that Condorcet [24] addressed the mathematical discipline of collective decision making in terms of simple majority voting and related procedures.[3] He discovered the *paradox of voting*, or the *Condorcet paradox*, to the effect that the method of pairwise simple majority voting may yield a social preference cycle—a social alternative A defeating another alternative B by a simple majority, B defeating the third alternative C again by a simple majority, and C in its turn defeating A by a simple majority. This paradox sent an unambiguous signal that the logical performance of voting and related procedures for collective decision making must be the subject of theoretical scrutiny. One of the logical implications of the Condorcet paradox is that, once a simple majority cycle occurs in the set of social alternatives $S = \{A, B, C\}$, there exists no *Condorcet winner*—a feasible alternative that is undefeated by any other feasible alternative—thereby excluding the possibility of basing social choice on the seemingly democratic method of collective decision making.

Condorcet's contribution seems to have been, at least partly and indirectly, inspired by an earlier work by Borda [19], who proposed what came to be known as the *Borda method* of rank-order decision making.[4] For each voter, this method assigns a score of zero to the last-ranked alternative, a

---

mathematical or logical justification for his scheme: such justifications had to await Condorcet and Borda" (McLean and London [76, p. 106]). It was for this reason that McLean [74] later christened the period over which Borda, Condorcet, and their contemporaries worked on the theoretical performance of voting schemes "the first golden age of social choice."

3. It is worthwhile to recollect that "Condorcet's work on social choice (1785–94) spans the most active constitution-making era in Western history until then, and the most active ever until 1989. Constitutions for the United States, Poland, and France were written, and Condorcet was connected with all three. . . . In 1792, Condorcet was made the chairman of a committee to draw up a Constitution for France. . . . After the Jacobin coup d'état of June 1793, Condorcet was out of power. His constitution was dumped in favor of one drawn up in great haste by Robespierre, who dropped all Condorcet's voting schemes" (McLean [74, pp. 23–26]). Condorcet's work on the theory of voting and human rights is translated into English by Iain McLean and Fiona Hewitt [75].

4. Borda's rank-order method was first proposed orally at the French Academy of Science in 1770, and remained unpublished until 1784. Condorcet was well aware of this method, and immediately recognized it to be an important challenge to his own pairwise comparison method. He stated in Condorcet [24, Discours préliminaire, p. clxxix] that he had heard of Borda's method orally, but that it was not published until after his own work was in press. According to McLean [74, p. 16], however, it was actually Condorcet himself who published Borda's work.

score of one to the penultimate alternative, and so on all the way up to the top-ranked alternative, which receives a score of $n - 1$ when there are n alternatives altogether. These individual scores are added for each candidate over all voters, and the candidate who earns the largest sum total becomes the overall winner in the contest. According to Duncan Black [15, p. 180], "soon after hearing Borda's paper in 1794 the [French] Academy [of Science] adopted his method in elections to its membership. It remained in use until 1800, when it was attacked by a new member and was modified soon afterwards. The new member was Napoleon Bonaparte."

The same rank-order voting procedure was obtained from slightly different premises by Pierre-Simon Laplace [66].[5] Laplace also acutely observed an obstacle to the use of this procedure to the effect that "its working might be frustrated by electors placing the strongest opponents to their favorite candidates at the foot of their list. This would give a great advantage to candidates of mediocre merit, for while getting few top places they would also get few lowest places" (Black [15, p. 182]). The same difficulty was confronted by Borda himself, who, when his procedure was opposed precisely for this reason of strategic vulnerability, had retorted by saying that his scheme is "only intended for honest men" (Black, [15, p. 182]). This episode seems to show us unambiguously that the apprehension about the *strategic manipulability of voting schemes* existed from the formative era of social choice theory.

There was intermittent exploratory work on voting schemes in the nineteenth century, most notably by Charles Lutwidge Dodgson [28; 29; 30], who is better known by his literary pseudonym (Lewis Carroll). His works were circulated only within a limited Oxford circle, and were virtually unknown in the outside world until Black [15, Appendix] made them widely accessible. Although ample circumstantial evidence (Black [15, pp. 192–194]) exists that Dodgson was acquainted neither with Borda [19] nor with Condorcet [24], he was clearly aware of the ubiquity of cyclical majorities as well as that of the rank-order method of voting, most probably through Isaac Todhunter [146, Chapters XVII and XIX], which every late Victorian scholar seems to have known about.[6] His major logical concern was to devise

5. For Laplace's theory of elections, those who are interested should refer to Isaac Todhunter [146, pp. 546–548] and Duncan Black [15, pp. 180–183].
6. Although Black [15, p. 193] went as far as to deny even the indirect influence of Borda and Condorcet on Dodgson's theory of committees and elections through Todhunter's [154]

a voting procedure that would enable him to choose the Condorcet winner if one exists, and to lexically supplement the simple majority voting if the Condorcet winner failed to exist. Black seems certainly right in concluding that "Dodgson had been caught in the grip of the theory of elections and committees and his understanding of the subject was second only to that of Condorcet" (Black [15, p. 212]).

In the last part of the nineteenth century and the first half of the twentieth century, some sporadic contributions such as those by Edward J. Nanson [80] and Francis Galton [38] notwithstanding, not much seems to have been done in the theory of collective decisions, the major breakthrough having been accomplished only in the late 1940s by Black [14]. He found a simple sufficient condition on the profile of voters' preferences, to be called the assumption of *single-peaked preferences*, under which simple majority voting can determine a social outcome, since there exists exactly one alternative that receives a simple majority over any other alternative, provided that the number of voters is odd, and Black's assumption of single-peakedness is satisfied. This assumption has a simple geometric representation whereby the utility indicators for the voters' preferences are such that the social alternatives can be represented by a one-dimensional variable and each of the graphs of voters' utility indicators has a single peak. Black's theorem is the first possibility result of this nature in social choice theory, and it opened the gate wide toward the modern development of the theory of voting.

Let us now turn to the welfare economics side of the coin. In this arena, too, it seems fair to say that the real origin of the critical and systematic approach to the mechanism design and policy evaluation belongs to the relatively recent past, and it may be safely attributed to the work of Bentham [10]. He was a contemporary in England of Borda and Condorcet. It is worthwhile to recollect that Condorcet wrote enthusiastically of the new society of the United States that "the spectacle of a great people where the rights of man are respected is useful to all others. . . . It teaches us that these rights are everywhere the same." He wrote as well of the French Revolution that it had "opened up an immense scope to the hopes of the

---

authoritative account of Borda's and Condorcet's contributions, which "every mathematical lecturer in the country ought to have studied" in Black's own admission, I found Black's argument less than persuasive.

human species. . . . This revolution is not in a government, it is in opinions and wills."[7] In sharp contrast, Bentham, a scholar in law and jurisprudence, was a stark critic of the concept of inviolable natural rights.[8] Indeed, it was in his harsh comment on the French "Declaration of the Rights of Man and the Citizen," which was embodied in the French Constitution of 1791, that he wrote the following famous passage: "Natural rights is simple nonsense: natural and imprescriptible rights, rhetorical nonsense—nonsense upon stilts" (Bentham [11, p. 501]). Instead of basing the economic policies on the concept of inviolable human rights, Bentham took recourse to the *greatest happiness principle*, so-called, to the effect that the ultimate criterion for judging the goodness of an economic mechanism and economic policy is that it can bring about the "greatest happiness of the greatest number." In accordance with this utilitarian view on the goodness of a state of affairs, the legislator's task is construed to arrange law and other social and economic institutions so that each person in pursuit of his or her own interest will be led to act so as to bring about the greatest happiness for all persons involved. This utilitarian basis of economic policies permeated the work of J. S. Mill, Edgeworth, and Sidgwick, and it served as a natural basis for the synthesis of this tradition by the hands of Pigou in the early twentieth century.

Pigou's so-called old welfare economics, being based on the Benthamite-utilitarian concept of economic welfare, presupposed that the utility of different individuals could be added to, or subtracted from, one another to define the social objective of total utility, viz., the greatest happiness.[9] It

7. Both citations from Condorcet are due to Rothschild [100, p. 6].

8. For Bentham, the only category of rights whose existence he could recognize at all were those that depended on law and legislation; a natural right was for him nothing other than a contradiction in terms: "There are no such things as natural rights—no such things as rights anterior to the establishment of government—no such things as natural rights opposed to, in contradiction to, legal; the expression is merely figurative: When used, in the moment you attempt to give it a literal meaning it leads to error, and to that sort of error that leads to mischief—to the extremity of mischief" (Bentham [11, p. 500]).

9. At this juncture, two remarks seem to be in order. In the first place, while Pigou in principle subscribed to the utilitarian viewpoint, careful reading of *The Economics of Welfare* reveals how discriminatingly was the use he actually made of it. Having said this, however, it should be pointed out that Pigou's discussions of tax-subsidy policies related to externalities, with which he is much associated, were directly derived through a utilitarian way of reasoning. It is true that Pigou's use of the utilitarian principle is not as conspicuous as Edgeworth's use. However, it was Pigou who inspired Hugh Dalton's [25] famous utilitarian measure of inequality. In the second

was against this epistemological basis of Pigou's old welfare economics that a harsh ordinalist criticism raged in the 1930s, which was kicked off by a famous essay by Robbins [94]. Note, however, that Robbins's criticism boils down to the categorical denial of the possibility of interpersonal comparisons of utility with interobserver validity; careful readings of Robbins [94, pp. 138–150; 95, pp. 636–637; 96, p. 5] convince us that he did not reject the possibility of making "subjective" interpersonal comparisons of utility, nor did he claim that economists should not make "subjective" interpersonal comparisons of their own. What he actually asserted is that "subjective" interpersonal comparisons cannot claim any "objective" interpersonal validity.

By the end of the 1930s, it became widely recognized that the foundations of Pigou's old welfare economics were hopelessly eroded, and new foundations for welfare economics had to be discovered on the basis of *ordinal* and *interpersonally noncomparable* utility information, and nothing else, in order to salvage something of substance from vestiges of Pigou's theoretical superstructure. This is the same informational basis as that of the Borda-Condorcet theory of collective decision making, which is a slightly ironic fact in view of the sharply contrasting background of the Borda-Condorcet theory of collective decision making, on the one hand, and the Bentham-Pigou theory of social welfare, on the other.

The first ordinalist response to this plea was to go back to the ordinalist tradition pioneered by Vilfredo Pareto [83; 84] and invoke the seminal concept of the *Pareto principle,* to the effect that *a change from one social state to another social state can be judged as socially good if at least one individual is*

---

place, unlike Bentham, who was strongly and outspokenly against the idea of natural rights, which goes squarely against the foundations of utilitarianism, Pigou [90, 1952 edn., p. 759] made an early use of the nonwelfarist notion of individual rights when he discussed people's claim to a "minimum standard of real income," which "must be conceived, not as a subjective minimum of satisfaction, but as an objective minimum of conditions." Pigou's characterization of "an objective minimum of conditions" is close to what came to be called the "basic needs," which consist of "some defined quantity and quality of house accommodation, of medical care, of education, of food, of leisure, of the apparatus of sanitary convenience and safety where work is carried on." Pigou might have thought that such rights could be justified on utilitarian grounds in the Benthamite tradition of regarding rights as intrinsically unimportant, but instrumentally crucial, but *The Economics of Welfare* is completely reticent concerning the utilitarian justification of these rights.

thereby made better off without making anybody else worse off in return. The characterization and implementation of Pareto-efficient resource allocation became the central exercise in this phase of the "new" welfare economics.[10] Note, however, that almost every economic policy cannot but favor some individuals at the cost of disfavoring some others, so that there would be almost no situation of real importance where the Pareto principle could claim relevance in isolation.

It was against this background that two distinct approaches were explored to rectify the unsatisfactory state of the post-Pigovian new welfare economics. The first approach was the introduction of *compensation criteria* by Kaldor [58], Hicks [50], Scitovsky [109], and Samuelson [102], which endeavored to expand the applicability of the Pareto principle by introducing hypothetical compensatory payments between gainers and losers from a change in economic policy.[11] According to Johannes de V. Graaff [43, pp. 84–85], "the compensation tests all spring from a desire to see what can be said about social welfare or 'real national income' . . . without making interpersonal comparisons of well-being. . . . They have a common origin in Pareto's definition of an increase in social welfare . . . but they are extended to situations in which some people are made worse off."

The second approach was the introduction of the concept of a *social welfare function* by Bergson [12] and Samuelson [101, Chapter VIII], which is deeply rooted in the belief that the pursuit of the logical consequences of any value judgments, irrespective of whose ethical beliefs they represent, whether or not they are widely shared in the society, or how they are generated in the first place, is a legitimate task of welfare economics. The social welfare function is meant to be the formal way of encompassing such an ethical belief. It was in terms of this concept of a social welfare function that Bergson and Samuelson tried to separate what belongs to the area of ethics, about

10. See, for example, Hicks [49].

11. According to John Chipman and James Moore [23, p. 548, footnote 2], Enrico Barone [8; 9] had developed the compensation principle much earlier than Kaldor and Hicks, "who mentioned it no less than four times." Barone's pioneering contribution was left unnoticed among English-speaking economists, however, even after the Italian original of his contribution was translated into English in von Hayek [150].

which economists qua scientists do not have any qualification to say anything objective whatsoever, from what belongs to the area of welfare economics, about which economists as scientists have every reason as well as obligation to say something of objective validity.[12]

Between these two schools of the new welfare economics, the former compensationist school met serious logical difficulties. Even before the scaffolds for construction were removed from the construction site, serious logical contradictions in the form of either the lack of asymmetry or the lack of transitivity were found in the social welfare judgments based on the Kaldor-Hicks compensation criteria by Scitovsky [109], Gorman [42], and many others, which fatally vitiated the credibility of new welfare economics of the compensationist school. The verdict on the Samuelson compensation principle, which was defined in terms of a uniform outward shift of the utility possibility frontier, is quite different. Indeed, the Samuelson compensation principle can always generate transitive social welfare judgments, so that its logical performance *in isolation* is impeccable. Nevertheless, it may still generate contradictory social welfare judgments *in combination with* the Pareto principle.[13] On the other hand, the second school of new welfare economics, which is founded on the Bergson-Samuelson social welfare function, has

12. The genesis of the Bergson-Samuelson social welfare function was traced as far back as Pareto [84] by Chipman [22] and Chipman and Moore [23]. True enough, Pareto was remarkably ahead of his time, and sympathetic eyes may catch the glimpse of social welfare function in Pareto's early writings. Nevertheless, it seems fair to say that, without Bergson [12] and Samuelson [101, Chapter VIII], the concept of the social welfare function could not have established itself as the central piece of modern welfare economics. It is in this sense that Samuelson [105, p. 248] is absolutely right when he wrote in a related context that "after, and only after, you have worked out a clear understanding of this subject are you able to recognize the bits of the puzzle that Pareto had already discerned."

13. Let P_p, P_s, and P stand, respectively, for the Pareto superiority relation, the Samuelson superiority relation, and the social preference relation. The social preference relation is said to respect the Pareto superiority relation as well as the Samuelson superiority relation if and only if it satisfies $P_p \subseteq P$ and $P_s \subseteq P$. It was shown by Suzumura [131; 134] that there exists a situation, which is not concocted at all, where we have four social states, say, x, y, z, and w, such that xP_py, zP_pw, yP_sz, and wP_sx hold. If the social preference relation respects the Pareto superiority relation as well as the Samuelson superiority relation, then we cannot but obtain xPy, yPz, zPw, and wPx, which clearly vindicate the social preference cycle. For more details, see Essay 26 ("Paretian Welfare Judgments and Bergsonian Social Choice") to follow.

been widely praised as the culmination of the ordinalist "scientific" approach to welfare economics.[14]

Broadly speaking, this was the intellectual atmosphere surrounding social choice theory and welfare economics when Arrow published his PhD dissertation, *Social Choice and Individual Values*, in 1951.

Quite apart from the Robbinsian criticism, which is epistemological in nature, there is a fundamental criticism of, and a proposal for a serious alternative to, Benthamite utilitarianism by John Rawls [92; 93], which is focused directly on the ethical nature of the Benthamite outcome morality. According to Rawls [93, p. 22], the main idea of classical utilitarianism is that "society is rightly ordered, and therefore just, when its major institutions are arranged so as to achieve the greatest net balance of satisfaction summed over all the individuals belonging to it." Not only is this classical principle based on *welfarism,* to the effect that "the judgment of the relative goodness of alternative states of affairs must be based exclusively on, and taken as an increasing function of, the respective collections of individual utilities in these states," but it also invokes the aggregation rule of *sum ranking,* to the effect that "one collection of individual utilities is at least as good as another if and only if it has at least as large a sum total" (Sen [119, p. 468]). Rawls criticizes the informational basis of welfarism and proposes the alternative informational basis of *social primary goods*, viz., "things that every rational man is presumed to want," which "normally have a use whatever a person's rational plan of life" (Rawls [93, p. 62]). Rawls also criticizes the utilitarian aggregation rule of sum ranking for its being "indifferent as to how a constant sum of benefits is distributed" (Rawls [93, p. 77]). Rawls's pro-

14. Thus, Samuelson [105, p. 223] could assert without any reservation the following: "As I write, the new welfare economics is just over four decades old. This subject, in its essentials as we know it today, was born when the 24-year-old Abram Bergson—then still a Harvard graduate student—wrote his classic 1938 *Quarterly Journal of Economics* article. To one like myself, who before 1938 knew *all* the relevant literature on welfare economics and just could not make coherent sense of it, Bergson's work came like a flash of lightning, describable only in the words of the pontifical poet:

Nature and Nature's laws lay hid in night:
God said, Let Newton be! and all was light."

posed alternative to Benthamite utilitarianism is such that "all social primary goods—liberty and opportunity, income and wealth, and the bases of self-respect—are to be distributed equally unless an unequal distribution of any or all of these goods is to the advantage of the least favored" (Rawls [93, p. 303]). His own justification of this principle of justice makes use of a hypothetical situation called the *original position*, where individuals choose the basic principles of the society behind the *veil of ignorance*, viz., without knowing their own position in the resulting social order as well as being ignorant of their personal identities. In such a situation of primordial equality, Rawls claims that his principles of justice would be generally accepted as a fair agreement in the absence of ethically irrelevant vested interests.[15]

The invocation of the logical device of a primordial stage of ignorance with the purpose of securing a fair field for designing a set of social rules is not original to Rawls. Other notable examples are William Vickrey [148; 149] and John Harsanyi [45; 46; 47], who respectively made use of the same device to find a justification for Benthamite utilitarianism. Vickrey [148] gave a brief, yet clear first statement of the original position idea. Harsanyi [46] proved the following important theorem: Suppose that social preferences as well as individual preferences satisfy the von Neumann–Morgenstern postulates of rationality, and if all individuals being indifferent implies social indifference, then social welfare must be the weighted sum of individual utilities. Under the additional requirement of anonymity, the Harsanyi representation for social welfare boils down to the unweighted sum total of individual utilities, viz., classical utilitarianism.[16]

---

15. Rawls's theory of "justice as fairness" exerted a strong influence on contemporary welfare economics in general and social choice theory in particular. But it is predominantly, if not exclusively, in the modified welfaristic version in which the Rawlsian concern with the well-being of the least favored individual is expressed with reference to the individual welfare levels, which are assumed to be interpersonally comparable. Needless to say, Rawls's own "difference principle" focuses directly on the minimal availability of "social primary goods" and not on the minimal individual welfare.

16. However, as Sen [116] acutely pointed out, utility is only used to represent preferences in the theorem of Harsanyi [46]. Thus, there is ample room for reservation on the claim that Harsanyi's argument can be interpreted as being an argument in support of utilitarianism. See also Pattanaik [85].

25.2. Social Choice and Individual Values

Without denying the importance of those pioneering contributions made by many precursors, it seems fair to say that Arrow's *Social Choice and Individual Values* elevated social choice theory to a stage that is qualitatively different altogether.

To lend concrete substance to this sweeping assertion, let us start by referring to the pioneering studies of voting schemes by Condorcet, Borda, Dodgson, Black, and many others again. Important though these celebrated works are, it is undeniable that their studies were concerned exclusively with some specified voting schemes, such as the method of simple majority voting, the Borda method, the Dodgson method, and so forth. In sharp contrast, Arrow [1; 2; 5; 6] developed an analytical method, which allowed him to treat all conceivable voting schemes simultaneously within one unified conceptual framework. To bring the importance of this development into clearer relief, consider the simplest imaginable society with only two individuals, say, 1 and 2, and three alternative social states, say, x, y, and z. Let us simplify our arena further by assuming away individual as well as social indifference relations altogether. It is clear, then, that there exist six distinct preference orderings of three social states:[17]

$$\alpha: x, y, z \quad \beta: x, z, y \quad \gamma: y, x, z \quad \delta: y, z, x \quad \epsilon: z, x, y \quad \zeta: z, y, x$$

Each one of these orderings can represent an individual preference ordering expressed by 1 and 2 over three social states. What Arrow christened the *social welfare function*, or *constitution* in his more recent terminology, is a function that maps each profile of individual preference orderings into a unique social preference ordering, which is meant to denote the process or rule for aggregating each profile of individual preference orderings into a social preference ordering. In other words, a social welfare function is a mapping defined on the Cartesian product $\Delta \times \Delta$, where $\Delta = \{\alpha, \beta, \gamma, \delta, \epsilon, \zeta\}$, and takes its values on Δ. Thus, even in our simplest conceivable society, there exist 6^{36} social welfare functions in the sense of Arrow, which

17. Alternatives are arranged horizontally, the more preferred alternative being to the left of the less preferred. Thus, the preference ordering α means that x is preferred to y, y is preferred to z, hence x is preferred to z.

is an astronomically large number indeed (roughly 10^{27}). It is clearly impossible to check all these Arrovian social welfare functions one by one for their democratic legitimacy, on the one hand, and for informational efficiency, on the other. Instead of attempting to cope with this clearly hopeless task, Arrow pioneered the axiomatic approach in social choice theory, which enabled him to analyze these 6^{36} Arrovian social welfare functions all at once, by imposing a set of axioms that are deemed necessary for the Arrovian social welfare functions to be reasonable, hence acceptable. It is this novel methodology that led him to the celebrated *general possibility theorem*, or *Arrovian impossibility theorem* in the currently prevailing terminology, which asserts that there exists no social welfare function satisfying a set of conditions necessary for democratic legitimacy and informational efficiency.

The novelty of Arrow's approach is no less conspicuous in the context of new welfare economics. For Bergson and Samuelson, their social welfare function was an analytical device for separating what should belong to economics from what should be relegated to ethics. According to Samuelson [101, pp. 220–221], "it is a legitimate exercise of economic analysis to examine the consequences of various value judgments, whether or not they are shared by the theorist, just as the study of comparative ethics is itself a science like any other branch of anthropology." It was as an analytical vehicle for implementing this "scientific" research program of new welfare economics that Samuelson invoked what came to be known as the Bergson-Samuelson social welfare function: "Without inquiring into its origins, we take as a starting point for our discussion a function of all the economic magnitudes of a system which is supposed to characterize some ethical belief—that of a benevolent despot, or a complete egoist, or 'all men of good will,' a misanthrope, the state, race, or group mind, God, etc. Any possible opinion is admissible. . . . We only require that the belief be such as to admit of an unequivocal answer as to whether one configuration of the economic system is 'better' or 'worse' than any other or 'indifferent,' and that the relationships are transitive."

In contrast with the Bergson-Samuelson social welfare function, which Bergson and Samuelson assumed to be given from outside of economics, Arrow was of the conviction that the process or rule through which the social value to be represented by the Bergson-Samuelson social welfare function is formed should also be the subject of logical scrutiny. In other words, in order for the economic analysis not to lose social relevance, it is necessary that the process or rule for constructing the Bergson-Samuelson social welfare function on the basis of individual judgments of the goodness of social states, viz., the Arrow social welfare function in this arena, must satisfy the minimal requirements of democratic legitimacy and informational efficiency. Interpreted in this new arena, the Arrow impossibility theorem turns out to be a basic criticism against the foundations of new welfare economics of the Bergson-Samuelson family. No wonder Arrow's theorem caused a stir among many reputable economists who created and promoted the Bergson-Samuelson new welfare economics. For example, Ian Little [68, pp. 423–424] contrasted Bergson's and Arrow's social welfare functions with the purpose of criticizing the latter as follows: "Bergson's welfare function was meant as a 'process or rule' which would indicate the best economic state as a function of a changing environment (i.e., changing sets of possibilities defined by different economic transformation functions), the individuals' tastes being given. . . . If tastes change, we must expect a new ordering of all the conceivable states; but we do not require that the difference between the new and the old orderings should bear any particular relation to the change of tastes which has occurred. We have, so to speak, a new world and a new order; and we do not demand correspondence between the change in the world and the change in the order. . . . Traditionally, tastes are given; indeed, one might almost say that the given individuals are traditionally defined as the possessors of the given tastes and that no sense is attached to the notion of given individuals with changing tastes."[18] Samuelson [104, p. 42], who has always been the most eloquent advocate of the Bergson-Samuelson school of new welfare economics, went as far as to declare that "the Arrow result is much more a contribution to the infant discipline of mathematical politics than to the traditional mathematical theory of welfare economics.

18. Little's criticism to this effect was strongly supported by Samuelson [104, pp. 48–49]: "For Bergson, one and only one of the . . . possible patterns of individuals' orderings is needed. It could be *any* one, but it is *only* one. From *it* (not from each of them all) comes a social ordering. . . . The only Axiom restricting a Bergson Social Welfare Function (of individualistic type) is a 'tree' property of Pareto-optimality type." It is this sharp contrast between the Arrow social welfare function and the Bergson social welfare function that created the widespread perception that the Arrow impossibility theorem, which requires the full force of multiple profiles of individual preference orderings, does not apply to the Bergson social welfare function, which is rooted in the single-profile framework.

I export Arrow from economics to politics because I do not believe that he has proved the impossibility of the traditional Bergson welfare function of economics, even though many of his less expert readers seem inevitably drawn into thinking so."[19]

What, then, are the axioms that Arrow demonstrated to be logically incompatible? In the 1963 revised version of the theorem (Arrow [3, pp. 96–97; 6]), there are four transparent axioms altogether. The first axiom is that each individual is free to form and express whatever preference ordering he/she cares to specify, which represents his/her evaluations of the goodness of social states, and the Arrow social welfare function must be robust enough to aggregate the profile of these individual orderings into a social ordering. The second axiom requires that the Arrow social welfare function must faithfully reflect the unanimous preferences expressed by all individuals over a pair of social states, which makes the process or rule of preference aggregation minimally democratic. The third axiom requires that the Arrow social welfare function must be informationally efficient in that, in deciding whether one social state is better than, or worse than, or indifferent to another social state, it is necessary and sufficient to know how individuals rank these two social states vis-à-vis each other. The fourth and the least controversial axiom requires that there should be no *dictator* in the society, who can decide a strict social preference for a state vis-à-vis another state by expressing his personal preference for the former against the latter.

These demonstrably contradictory axioms are nothing but the lineal descendants of what preceded *Social Choice and Individual Values*. Indeed, in the context of the methods of collective decision making, the simple majority voting rule satisfies all of the Arrovian conditions except that the generated social preference relation lacks the assurance of transitivity in view of the Condorcet paradox. In the alternative context of the foundations of welfare economics, the new welfare economics of the compensationist school, as well as of the Bergson-Samuelson school, is founded on the ordinal and interpersonally noncomparable informational basis; it is also rooted in

19. To keep the record straight, let us emphasize that the Arrovian impossibility theorem is not a theorem that negates the existence of the Bergson-Samuelson social welfare ordering; it is a theorem that negates the existence of a "reasonable" process or rule that can associate a Bergson-Samuelson social welfare ordering with each profile of individual preference orderings. See Suzumura [129; 134] and Arrow [4].

the Paretian tradition of requiring social preference to reflect unanimous individual preferences faithfully. Because it respects the preceding tradition, the Arrow impossibility theorem not only becomes more relevant but also sends a clear plea for systematic scrutiny of the logical contradiction thereby identified. In this sense, the message of Arrow's theorem is clearly positive rather than negative.

Arrow [2, Chapter VII] also made another important contribution by developing a systematic method of analyzing simple majority voting, which enabled him to pursue Black's geometric idea of single peaked preferences in the general case of any number of alternatives. This neat method enabled his successors to introduce some other restrictions on the admissible profiles of voters' preferences under which the simple majority voting rule can escape from the Condorcet paradox. Indeed, this method led Ken-Ichi Inada [55] and Sen and Pattanaik [125] to discover the necessary and sufficient conditions for its satisfactory working.

25.3. "Socialist Planning" Controversy

There was a harsh controversy of historical importance, which was fought mainly in the 1930s. Maurice Dobb [27, p. 183] expressed a cynical opinion on this controversy to the effect that "the old debate about *Wirtschaftsrechnung* . . . is nowadays sufficiently familiar . . . for any suggestion of revisiting it to invite disinclination rather than attention." Nevertheless, there are several lessons of this controversy with lasting importance in the evolution and orientation of the theory of decentralized planning procedures à la Edmond Malinvaud [69] and Geoffrey Heal [48], as well as of the related branch of social choice theory called implementation theory (or the theory of mechanism design) à la Leonid Hurwicz [52; 53; 54] and Eric Maskin [72; 73].

It was Ludwig von Mises [153] who kicked off this controversy. In his understanding, rational economic calculation is possible only when monetary prices exist, not only for consumption goods but also for production goods of any order, since it is monetary calculation that "affords us a guide through the oppressive plentitude of economic potentialities. . . . It renders their value capable of computation and thereby gives us the primary basis for all economic operations with goods of a higher order" (von Hayek [150,

p. 101]). According to von Mises, however, it is impossible to find necessary monetary prices for production goods of a higher order in a socialist state, because no production good will ever become the object of market exchange in a socialist state where, by definition, collective ownership prevails for all means of production.

It is clear that the impossibility thesis à la von Mises holds if and only if there are no prices for production goods in a socialist state with collective ownership of the means of production. It seemed obvious to Oscar Lange [64, p. 61] that the latter thesis was clearly false: "Professor Mises seems to have confused prices in the narrower sense, i.e., the exchange ratios of commodities on a market, with prices in the wider sense of 'terms on which alternatives are offered.' . . . It is only in the latter sense that 'prices' are indispensable for the allocation of resources. . . . " As Lange correctly pointed out, "prices in the generalized sense," or "efficiency prices" in the circumlocution of modern economic theory, exist irrespective of the ownership structure of the means of production. This fact alone was enough for Lange to refute the impossibility thesis à la von Mises.

However, the controversy resurged in the hands of Friedrich von Hayek [150; 151; 152], taking a more sophisticated form. Unlike von Mises, von Hayek never denied the theoretical existence of efficiency prices for all goods including the means of production, which, if made available, would enable a socialist state to attain a rational allocation of resources. The problem, which von Hayek pointed out and made the foundations of *his* impossibility thesis, was how such efficiency prices could be made available in practice: "This is not an impossibility in the sense that it is logically contradictory. But to argue that a determination of prices . . . being logically conceivable in any way invalidates the contention that it is not a possible solution, only proves that the real nature of the problem has not been perceived" (von Hayek [150, pp. 207-208]). To understand why, von Hayek urges us to visualize what the determination of efficiency prices by computational method would imply in practice: "It is clear that any such solution would have to be based on the solution of some such system of equations [for general economic equilibrium] as that developed in [Enrico] Barone's article (Barone [9]). . . . What is practically relevant . . . is not the formal structure of this system, but the nature and amount of concrete information required if a numerical solution is to be attempted and the magnitude of the task which this numerical solution must involve" . . . (von Hayek [150, p. 208]). In order to calculate efficiency prices by solving the general equilibrium equations, we must gather information about technology, primary and intermediate resources, and consumers' preferences, which are widely dispersed and privately owned by numerous economic agents. Given the nature and complexity of this private information, it would be prohibitively difficult, if not logically impossible, to motivate numerous private agents to comply with the request from the central planning board and submit this information faithfully for the purpose of computing efficiency prices. Thus, von Hayek concludes, "it is probably evident that the mere assembly of these data is a task beyond human capacity" (von Hayek [150, p. 211]). To make this situation even worse, "most of [the technical information] consists in a technique of thought which enables the individual engineer to find new solutions rapidly as soon as he is confronted with new constellations of circumstances" (von Hayek [150, pp. 210-211]). This is the essence of the impossibility thesis à la von Hayek.

Once again, Lange was ready to confront von Hayek's impossibility thesis. Capitalizing and elaborating on the earlier works by Barone [9] and Fred M. Taylor [145], Lange developed a sophisticated trial-and-error method of price adjustment in a socialist state. It is useful to see how he designed this scheme, which came to be called *Lange-Lerner market socialism* after Oscar Lange [63] and Abba Lerner [67], and how this scheme fares with respect to some performance criteria.

Lange assumed a socialist state where freedom of choice in consumption and freedom of choice of occupation are guaranteed. Thus, the preferences of consumers are the guiding criteria in production and allocation of resources. In this system, there exist market prices for consumption goods and labor services, but the prices for capital goods and productive resources other than labor are prices in the generalized sense, i.e., mere accounting prices. Some appropriate rules are applied to the distribution of social dividend to consumers. Subject to these rules of income formation and given market prices for consumption goods and labor services, consumers are free to choose their demand for consumption goods and supply of labor services. Likewise, some appropriate rules are applied to production units (in industries with many firms incurring setup costs) so that the average cost of production is minimized, and the marginal cost is made equal to the price of the product for each and every good produced. The accounting prices for capital goods and productive resources other than labor are formed and adjusted by the central planning board through the instrumental use of the Walrasian tâtonnement process, where the central planning board plays the role of the Walrasian auctioneer. The *modus operandi* of this successive trial-and-error process is exactly the same as the well-known Walrasian tâtonnement process, and the adjustment of the market price or the accounting price for each good and service are made in accordance with the aggregate excess demand for goods and services in question.

Two properties of this pseudo-Walrasian tâtonnement process deserve particular attention. In the first place, this process enables the central planning board to escape from the Hayekian task of gathering dispersed private information for computing accounting prices at the center, which von Hayek maintained to be practically impossible to perform, since the necessary computation is in effect performed by each holder of private information. In the second place, the accounting prices found at the equilibrium of this pseudo-Walrasian tâtonnement process in a socialist state "have quite the same objective character as the market prices in the regime of competition. Any mistake made by the Central Planning Board in fixing prices would announce itself in a very objective way—by a physical shortage or surplus of the quantity of the commodities or resources in question—and would have to be corrected in order to keep production running smoothly" (Lange [64, p. 82]). On the basis of these nice properties of his scheme, Lange concluded that "a substitution of planning for the functions of the market is quite possible and workable," and the immediate successors of the lessons of the controversy gladly concurred. Indeed, "as far as the economics profession is concerned," wrote Paul Sweezy [144, p. 232] in the Economics Handbook Series edited by Seymour Harris, "Lange's paper may be regarded as having finally removed any doubts about the capacity of socialism to utilize resources rationally." Upon careful scrutiny, however, this sweeping verdict turns out to be untenable.

To begin with, for the quasi-Walrasian tâtonnement process to serve as an algorithm for finding right market prices and accounting prices, it should be guaranteed to converge surely and rapidly to the system of general equilibrium prices. Unless some very special assumptions, such as gross substitutability, or the weak axiom of revealed preference, are imposed on the aggregate excess demand functions, however, there is no guarantee for the global stability of the Lange process of price adjustment.[20] In a postscript to the controversy written thirty years later, Lange [65, p. 158] wrote that "it was assumed without question that the *tâtonnement* process in fact converges to the system of equilibrium prices." Since there is no general guarantee of such a convergence property, the Lange-Lerner scheme of market socialism offers no assurance of nonwasteful workability.[21] More remarkably, Lange went on to maintain that "were I to rewrite my essay today my task would be much simpler. My answer to Hayek and Robbins would be: so what's the trouble? Let us put the simultaneous equations on an electric computer and we shall obtain the solution in less than a second. The market process with its cumbersome *tâtonnements* appears old-fashioned. Indeed, it may be considered as a computing device of the preelectronic age." This statement is truly remarkable, as it "proves that the real nature of the problem has not been perceived." Recollect that the impossibility thesis à la von Hayek was based not on the limitation of computational capacity on the part of the central planning board but on the prohibitive difficulty of gathering dispersed and privately owned information for the purpose of central computation. Needless to say, no computer with whatever capacity can work without being provided with the relevant data. Interestingly enough, Bergson [13, pp. 663–664] also posed the possibility of avoiding trial-and-error procedure by solving pertinent equations by means of mathematical techniques: "Both Lange and [Dickinson] wrote before the age of electronic computers. Given this technology, could not the [central planning board], in performing its cardinal task of fixing prices, confute Hayek after all simply by using mathematical techniques?" However, Bergson was far more careful in answering this question than Lange: "Should the Board seek to employ mathematical procedures in fixing prices comprehensively and in detail, its undertaking surely could become burdensome for managers of production units, who might be called on to predict

20. Herbert Scarf [107] constructed an explicit example where the competitive equilibrium is globally unstable. See also Takashi Negishi [82].

21. As far as the relative performance of the competitive market economy and Lange-Lerner market socialism are concerned, this objection is a double-edged sword; it applies not only to Lange-Lerner market socialism but also to the competitive market mechanism. But the basic fact remains that the Lange-Lerner scheme is not successful as a decentralized algorithm for computing a general equilibrium solution in a socialist state, as it was originally meant to be.

and articulate in inordinately concrete detail the complex and ever changing constraints and opportunities that confront them, and on this basis to communicate to the Board such data on these matters as the Board would require; and for the Board itself, which promptly would have to digest such information and to communicate the results of its deliberations to the managers. The capacities of managers as well as of the Board to grapple with these tasks might often be enhanced by use of computers, but not always."

Secondly, there is no systemic device in the Lange-Lerner scheme of market socialism to confront the possibility of strategic behavior by private agents. As Lange [64, p. 81] rightly observed, "on a competitive market the parametric function of prices results from the number of competing individuals being too large to enable any one to influence prices by his own action. In a socialist economy, production and ownership of the productive resource outside of labor being centralized, the managers certainly can and do influence prices by their decisions. Therefore, the parametric function of prices must be imposed on them by the Central Planning Board as an *accounting rule*. All accounting has to be done *as if* prices were independent of the decisions taken. For purposes of accounting, prices must be treated as constant, as they are treated by entrepreneurs on a competitive market." Since there is nothing in the Lange-Lerner scheme to make this accounting rule compatible with the private incentives of individual agents, we cannot but conclude that the Lange-Lerner scheme of market socialism lacks the important property of *incentive compatibility*.

Thirdly, Lange-Lerner market socialism is designed for the single-minded purpose of enabling a socialist state to use its endowed scarce resources efficiently. As was aptly observed by Sweezy [144, p. 233], "perhaps the most striking feature of Lange's model is that the function of the Central Planning Board is virtually confined to providing a substitute for the market as the coordinator of the activities of the various plants and industries. The truth is that Lange's Board is not a *planning* agency at all but a *price-fixing* agency; in his model production decisions are left to a myriad of essentially independent units, just as they are under capitalism." It is true that achieving the efficient use of scarce resources is a task of no mean difficulty, but "the common features of all collectivist systems may be described . . . as the deliberate organisation of the labors of society for a definite social goal. That our present society lacks such 'conscious' direction toward a single aim, that its activities are guided by the whims and fancies of irresponsible individuals, has always been one of the main complaints of its socialist critics" (von Hayek [151, p. 42]). If we take this observation at all seriously, we must go beyond mere efficiency and proceed to optimality with reference to the single social goal in order to have a full-fledged design of a rational collectivist society.

If we retain, as in the Lange-Lerner scheme of market socialism, the crucial value premise of consumers' sovereignty and want to orient a socialist state toward a definite social goal beyond the mere attainment of efficient allocation of scarce resources, we must find a process or rule to construct a conscious social goal on the basis of individual judgments on what constitutes social goods, since "the effect of the people agreeing that there must be central planning, without agreeing on the ends, will be rather as if a group of people were to commit themselves to take a journey together without agreeing where they want to go" (von Hayek [151, p. 46]). This is precisely the same problem posed and settled in the negative by Arrow in a related but distinct context of collective choice and social welfare. Interestingly enough, von Hayek [151, p. 44] observed that forming "a definite social goal" for its use in orienting central planning "would be impossible for any mind to comprehend the infinite variety of different needs of different people which compete for the available resources and to attach a definite weight to each."

These negative observations notwithstanding, it should be emphasized that the "socialist planning" controversy, in which both Lange and von Hayek played major roles, was the first serious attempt at designing an alternative economic mechanism with the purpose of satisfying some concrete performance characteristics. Through their efforts, Lange and von Hayek became the modern forerunners in the theory of decentralized planning procedures and the theory of mechanism design.

25.4. Significance of the Subject and Main Lines of Research

Enough has been said so far about the historical background of social choice theory and welfare economics. It remains for us to emphasize the significance of the subject, and identify the major lines of research in this broad and interdisciplinary area.

In our perception, there are three major lines of research, which we have identified in our account of the historical evolution of our subjct, that deserve to be highlighted: methods of collective decision making, the theoretical foundations of welfare economics, and the theory of incentive compatibility and mechanism design. To explain why these issues should be focused on, it is useful to go back to *Social Choice and Individual Values* once again.

To begin with, note that Arrow's theory tightly connected social choice with social preference ordering, which Arrow's social welfare function associates with each profile of individual preference orderings via the assumption of *collective rationality*. This crucial assumption has been one of the major targets for critics of the Arrovian framework of social choice theory.[22]

Two avenues of research were explored in response to this early criticism. One may want to discard the exacting requirement of transitivity of the indifference relation and retain only the more defensible requirement of transitivity of the strict preference relation, viz., Sen's *quasi transitivity*; one may go one step further and settle with the nonexistence of any strict preference cycle, viz., *acyclicity*. One may even discard the assumption of collective rationality altogether and focus directly on some choice-consistency properties. An important example of such a choice-consistency property is *path independence*: "the independence of the final choice from the path to it" (Arrow [3, p. 120]). The first avenue was pioneered and vigorously explored by Sen [110; 111, Chapter 4*; 117]; his path-breaking attempt was followed up by Mas-Colell and Sonnenschein [70]. The second avenue was suggested by Arrow himself, which was vigorously explored by Plott [91], Blair, Bordes, Kelly, and Suzumura [16, Essay 5 of this volume], and many others. Basically, however, this extensive research confirmed the robustness of Arrovian impossibility theorems.

The next crucial step in the search for an escape route from Arrow's impasse was to explore the use and usefulness of interpersonal comparisons of utilities, with or without cardinal measurability.[23] The context in which this potential escape route may make sense is where an ethical observer forms

22. See, in particular, Buchanan [20, p. 116] and Samuelson's witty remark on Buchanan's criticism in Suzumura [141, pp. 339–341].

23. Note, in passing, that cardinality of individual utilities without interpersonal comparability does not lead to any escape route from the Arrovian impossibility theorems. Indeed, it was shown by Sen [111, Theorem 8*2] that there exists no social welfare functional—which is "a mechanism that specifies one and only one social ordering given a set of individual welfare functions, one function for each individual (Sen [111, pp. 123–124])"—satisfying the following conditions: unrestricted domain, independence of irrelevant alternatives, nondictatorship, weak Pareto principle, cardinality, and noncomparability.

his own subjective interpersonal comparisons of utilities and makes use of this extended informational basis to define an essentially Arrovian social welfare function. A fruitful and systematic method of analysis was developed mainly in the 1970s by Sen [111; 120], Hammond [44], d'Aspremont and Gevers [26], and Maskin [71], among many others. These works brought about a neat axiomatization of the Rawlsian difference principle (in its welfaristic version) as well as of the Benthamite principle of utilitarianism. This may be a legitimate way out from the Arrovian impasse in the context of forming someone's social welfare judgments on the basis of his/her subjective interpersonal comparisons. However, this potential escape route is surely not available in the alternative context of collective decision making. Even in the context of forming social welfare judgments, the phantom of Robbins cannot be so easily exorcised; if there are multiple ethical observers who form their respective subjective interpersonal comparisons of utilities, their social welfare judgments may well conflict with each other so much so that some variants of the Arrovian impossibility theorems may come back. See Roberts [97; 98; 99] and Suzumura [136].

In passing, one particular type of interpersonal utility comparison deserves special attention: "People seem prepared to make comparisons of the form: State x is better (or worse) for me than state y is for you. . . . Interpersonal comparisons of the extended sympathy type can be put in operational form; the judgment takes the form: It is better (in my judgment) to be myself in state x than to be you in state y" (Arrow [3, pp. 114-115]).[24] This type of interpersonal utility comparison formed the informational basis of, e.g., an analysis of economic inequality by Sen [113], as well as of an axiomatization of the Rawlsian difference principle by Hammond [44] and Sen [116]. This is also the informational basis that enables us to extend the celebrated fairness-as-no-envy approach in the theory of resource allocation—developed most notably by Foley [36], Kolm [62] and Varian [147]—to the theory of social choice, which was initiated by Suzumura [132; 133].

Still centering around the original Arrow impossibility theorem itself, one may try to see how tight this remarkable theorem in fact is by carefully checking whether or not any one of the constituting axioms can be weakened without upsetting the validity of the theorem. One may also try to see the

24. The interpersonal comparisons of the extended sympathy type were first formulated with rich applications by Suppes [128].

trade-off relationship that may hold between different axioms, keeping the essential validity of the theorem intact. These ideas have been pursued, e.g., by Blau [18] and Wilson [156], on the one hand, and by Campbell and Kelly [21], on the other.

All the lines of research mentioned so far are, to a great extent, correctly describable as being the lineal descendants of Arrow's seminal work. There are some other lines of research that were mentioned, but not explored, in *Social Choice and Individual Values*. One salient example is the strategic aspect of collective decision making, which we have briefly mentioned in the context of the Borda-Laplace rank-order method of collective decision making. Arrow [2, p. 7] carefully pointed out that "once a machinery for making social choices from individual tastes is established, individuals will find it profitable, from a rational point of view, to misrepresent their tastes by their actions, either because such misrepresentation is somehow directly profitable or, more usually, because some other individual will be made so much better off by the first individual's misrepresentation that he could compensate the first individual in such a way that both are better off than if everyone really acted in direct accordance with his tastes." As a matter of fact, Samuelson [103, pp. 388–389] pointed out the ubiquity of strategic misrepresentation of preferences in the specific context of the efficient provision of public goods: "It is in the selfish interest of each person to give *false* signals, to pretend to have less interest in a given collective consumption activity than he really has." This *free-rider problem*, so-called, can be traced back much further to Knut Wicksell [155]: "If the individual is to spend his money for private and public uses so that his satisfaction is maximized, he will obviously pay nothing whatsoever for public purposes (at least if we disregard fees and similar charges). Whether he pays much or little will affect the scope of public service so slightly that, for all practical purposes, he himself will not notice it at all. Of course, if everyone were to do the same, the State would soon cease to function." In the context of social choice theory, however, the first general treatment of the strategic misrepresentation issue, of which Arrow was aware from the inception of social choice theory, but left unexplored, had to wait until the 1970s when Allan Gibbard [40] and Mark Satterthwaite [106] came up with a general theorem on the manipulability of voting schemes.[25]

25. See, however, an interesting earlier study on strategic behavior in voting by Robin Farquharson [35]. See also Pattanaik [86].

Recollect that a voting scheme is a social choice mechanism that assigns a single outcome to each profile of voters' preference orderings over outcomes. As long as there are at least three alternative outcomes and at least two voters, there exists no nondictatorial voting scheme that is free from strategic misrepresentation of preferences by individuals. It is worthwhile to point out that the Arrow theorem is closely related to the Gibbard-Satterthwaite theorem in the sense that the former theorem can provide the crucial step in proving the latter theorem. Given the validity of the basic Gibbard-Satterthwaite theorem on the ubiquity of strategic manipulation of voting schemes, it is natural that a huge body of literature was created in the search for either the escape route from the Gibbard-Satterthwaite impossibility theorem or directions in which their theorem may be generalized.

Since the strategic misrepresentation of preferences is demonstrably ubiquitous, there is a further problem to be tackled: "Even in a case where it is possible to construct a procedure showing how to aggregate individual tastes into a consistent social preference pattern, there still remains the problem of devising rules of the game so that individuals will actually express their true tastes even when they are acting rationally" (Arrow [2, p. 7]). It was precisely in response to this plea that a fruitful area of research, to be called the *implementation theory*, or the *theory of mechanism design*, was created by Leonid Hurwicz [52; 53; 54] and Eric Maskin [72; 73]. A mechanism is a game form, which is designed and managed by the helmsperson of the economy so that it can attain the social objective at the equilibrium of the game by assigning to each individual agent an appropriate set of admissible strategies and a payoff function. In view of the Gibbard-Satterthwaite theorem and Hurwicz's [53] theorem to the same effect in economic environments, the constructed game forms are such that the set of admissible strategies cannot be that of individual preference orderings, but that of a much wider nature. Although the public objective, which the helmsperson tries to optimize, is typically dependent on private information, it need not be concordant with the private incentives of individual agents. It follows that the requirement that individual agents within the designed mechanism should be so induced as to act to bring about the social objective optimization at equilibrium cannot but impose a constraint on the mechanisms to be designed and on the public objectives to be implemented.

Another game theoretic background of social choice theory deserves attention, which can be traced back all the way to the cooperative game theory of John von Neumann and Oscar Morgenstern [154]. Notable cooperative solution concepts to the axiomatic bargaining problem due to John Nash [81], such as the Nash bargaining solution or the Kalai-Smorodinsky [57] solution, as well as to the games of characteristic function forms, such as the Shapley value, the core, or the nucleolus, provide social choice theory with a rich class of reasonable (fair) compromises in the situation that mixes cooperation and competition among individual agents.

Not only Arrow's social choice theory but also the Gibbard-Satterthwaite theorem of the non-manipulability of voting schemes as well as the Hurwicz-Maskin theory on implementation and the cooperative game theoretic approach to fair compromises all make extensive use of axiomatic method. Many of the strengths and weaknesses of these theories hinge squarely on this common analytical character. As was observed by Arrow [2, p. 87], "one of the great advantages of abstract postulational methods is the fact that the same system may be given several different interpretations." In exchange for this great merit of versatility, however, the axiomatic method tends to be plagued with the potential weakness of a formal neglect of substantial issues. A case in point is a warning by Johansen [56] to the effect that the theoretically undeniable ubiquity of "playing down one's preferences for a public good in order to get a lower share in the costs of providing the good" does not seem "likely to succeed in an open political decision making process involving elected representatives." According to Johansen, "the two-tier system of electors and representatives tends to diminish the significance and relevance of the theoretical problem of unwillingness to reveal preferences for public goods." This warning urges us to examine in concrete detail the institutional structures of the society, political as well as economic, in search of the empirical relevance of purely theoretical results obtained in a general axiomatic framework. This is an interesting step to take if we want to verify that the paradox of voting is not just a theoretical curiosity but a phenomenon of substantial empirical relevance; it also motivates us to analyze the logical performance of representative democracy vis-à-vis direct democracy. Furthermore, instead of merging "voting, typically used to make 'political' decisions, and the market mechanism, typically used to make 'economic' decisions" (Arrow [2, p. 1]) into one and the same axiomatic system, it may prove useful to develop an idiosyncratic model of social choice in economic environments, along with developing a separate model of political decision making. All these steps have been taken vigorously in the contemporary social choice literature with rich ramifications of specific results.

There is yet another crucial point of departure from Arrow's original formulation of social choice theory. Not only traditional welfare economics, old as well as new, but also the Arrovian social choice theory itself, are deeply rooted in the philosophical approach of *welfarist consequentialism* in that they are based on the assessment of the goodness of states of affairs in terms of individual utilities obtained from these states of affairs. It was Sen's [111, Chapter 6*; 112; 114; 121] *impossibility of a Paretian liberal* that cast serious doubt on this long tradition by establishing an impossibility theorem to the effect that the weak welfaristic requirement of the Pareto principle cannot but conflict with the nonwelfaristic requirement of the respect for minimal individual liberty. Sen's seminal analysis can be traced back to the problem that J. S. Mill [77; 78] had to face in his simultaneous belief in utilitarian outcome morality, on the one hand, and in the sanctity of individual libertarian rights, on the other. In view of the remarkable pervasiveness of welfarist consequentialism in the whole spectrum of normative economics, it is natural to find many attempts in the literature to find an escape route from Sen's impossibility theorem, e.g., Gibbard [41], Blau [17], Sen [114, Sections III–XI], and Suzumura [130]; to gauge the robustness of Sen's liberal paradox, so-called, e.g., Kelsey [59; 60] and Sen [114, Section II and Appendix A2]; and to examine critically Sen's original articulation of individual liberty, e.g., Gärdenfors [39], Sugden [127], Gaertner, Pattanaik, and Suzumura [37, Essay 15 of this volume], and Pattanaik and Suzumura [87; 88]. The implications and relevance of these works on the impossibility of a Paretian liberal are critically evaluated by Suzumura [135], who distinguished the three related but distinct issues in the social choice theoretic analysis of welfare and rights: the issue of the analytical articulation of rights, the issue of the realization of rights, and the issue of the initial conferment of rights. There are also many criticisms of welfarist consequentialism in terms of the counterintuitive implications of this informational constraint in some paradigmatic cases, e.g., Ronald Dworkin [31; 33], Sen and Williams [126], Elster [34], Sen [120], and many others.

Once Pandora's box is opened and we are given a glimpse of possibilities that lie beyond the narrow confines of welfarist consequentialism, nothing prevents us from asking questions that can be properly posed only when we are ready to go beyond the traditional informational basis of welfarist consequentialism. In the analysis of individual well-being, for example, we need not necessarily analyze only through the looking glass of individual welfare. Alternative articulations of individual advantages have been proposed, which have opened new possibilities in welfare economics in general and social choice theory in particular. Representative proposals to this effect include *social primary goods* in Rawls's [93] theory of justice, *resources* in Dworkin's [31; 32] theory of equality, and *capabilities* in Sen's [120; 123] theory of well-being. The new vistas thereby opened have far-reaching implications with innovative perspectives on the theory and policy of economic development, as expounded in Sen [123]. We may even proceed beyond consequentialism as such, and pose some questions, such as the intrinsic value of opportunities to choose and/or the intrinsic value of procedures for choice, along with their instrumental values. Indeed, it is only with these new developments in clear perspective that we can gauge the true usefulness and limitations of the traditional informational basis of welfarist consequentialism. Some of these new vistas opened in this direction are expounded in Sen [124], Suzumura [137; 139; 140], and Suzumura and Xu [140; 142].

Overlapping partly with this trend to go beyond welfarist consequentialism as the informational basis of social welfare analysis, there were conspicuous developments in the theory of how to measure economic well-being. It was Kolm [61] and Atkinson [7] who kicked off the modern resurgence of interest in the measurement of income inequality. Soon afterward, Sen [115] axiomatized a new measure of income poverty, which went substantially beyond the crude traditional measure, such as the head count ratio, and incorporated a new distributional dimension into the measurement of poverty. More recently, Pattanaik and Xu [89] started a new area of research concerning how to measure freedom of choice. Each one of these seminal works generated substantial follow-up works of their own, which are enriching our theoretical toolbox for the measurement of well-being.

25.5. Concluding Remarks

It has been said that social choice theory is "a science of the impossible." This statement contains an element of truth only to the limited extent that the development of modern social choice theory received strong momentum from many impossibility theorems. Arrow's monumental theorem on the impossibility of democratic and informationally efficient preference aggregation procedures, Sen's theorem on the impossibility of a Paretian liberal, the Gibbard-Satterthwaite theorem on the impossibility of nonmanipulable and nondictatorial voting schemes, and the Hurwicz-Maskin theory of implementable social choice rules, to cite only a few most salient examples, have served us positively by sending an unambiguous signal that there are logical problems that await our careful scrutiny and serious attempts for resolution. In the process of understanding these impossibility theorems, we are brought to the far deeper perception of what underlies social conflicts of important values. Likewise, in the process of finding some meaningful escape routes from these logical impasses, we are brought to a much richer understanding of what makes several social values mutually compatible. In this sense, there is nothing intrinsically negative about social choice theory in general and impossibility theorems in particular.

It has also been said that welfare economics is plagued with elegance nihilism. In this context, it is worthwhile to recollect that Pigou's "old" welfare economics started with the following manifest: "The complicated analyses which economists endeavour to carry through are not mere gymnastic. They are instruments for the bettering of human life. The misery and squalor that surround us, the dying fire of hope in many millions of European homes, the injurious luxury of some wealthy families, the terrible uncertainty overshadowing many families of the poor—these are evils too plain to be ignored. By the knowledge that our science seeks it is possible that they may be restrained" (Pigou [90, p. vii]). Forty years later, however, Edward Mishan [79, p. 197] commenced his survey of welfare economics over the period from 1939 to 1959 with the following cold remark: "While it continues to fascinate many, welfare economics does not appear at any time to have wholly engaged the labors of any one economist. It is a subject which, apparently, one dabbles in for a while, leaves and, perhaps, returns to later in response to troubled conscience." Since Mishan's survey covered the period over which several staggering attempts were made to salvage the crumbling old welfare economics only to receive harsh criticisms on their own logical foundations, Mishan's cynicism may be understandable to some extent. However, as we have observed at the beginning of this essay, "as soon as any collective body designs and implements an economic mechanism and/or an economic policy, paying proper attention to the costs and benefits accruing to its constituent members, one or more social welfare judgments are unavoidable." Since social choice theory is partly concerned with the logical foundations of welfare economics, we cannot but maintain that the study of social choice theory and welfare economics is indispensable as long as one is interested in the problem of any economic policy, be that macroeconomic or microeconomic in nature. Pigou thought that welfare economics was a potent instrument for the bettering of human life. The same can be said of social choice theory.

References

[1] Arrow, K. J., "A Difficulty in the Concept of Social Welfare," *Journal of Political Economy* **58**, 1950, 328–346; reprinted with an introduction in *Collected Papers of Kenneth J. Arrow*, Vol. 1, *Social Choice and Justice*, Oxford: Basil Blackwell, 1984, 1-29.

[2] Arrow, K. J., *Social Choice and Individual Values*, 1st edn., New York: John Wiley and Sons, 1951.

[3] Arrow, K. J., *Social Choice and Individual Values*, 2nd edn., New York: John Wiley and Sons, 1963; with "Notes on the Theory of Social Choice, 1963."

[4] Arrow, K. J., "Contributions to Welfare Economics," in E. C. Brown and R. M. Solow, eds., *Paul Samuelson and Modern Economic Theory*, New York: McGraw-Hill, 1983, 15–30.

[5] Arrow, K. J., *Social Choice and Justice*, Vol. 1 of *Collected Papers of Kenneth J. Arrow*, Oxford: Basil Blackwell, 1984.

[6] Arrow, K. J., "Arrow's Theorem," in J. Eatwell, M. Milgate, and P. Newman, eds., *The New Palgrave: A Dictionary of Economics*, Vol. 1, London: Macmillan, 1987, 124–126.

[7] Atkinson, A. B., "On the Measurement of Inequality," *Journal of Economic Theory* **2**, 1970, 244–263.

[8] Barone, E., "Il Ministro della Produzione nello Stato Collectivista," *Gionale degli Economisti e Rivista di Statistica* **37**, 1908, 267–293.

[9] Barone, E., "The Ministry of Production in the Collectivist State," in F. A. von Hayek, ed., *Collectivist Economic Planning*, London: Routledge, 1935, 245–290.

[10] Bentham, J., *An Introduction to the Principles of Morals and Legislation*, London: Payne, 1789; republished, Oxford: Clarendon Press of Oxford University Press, 1907.

[11] Bentham, J., "Anarchical Fallacies," first published in English in J. Bowring, ed., *The Works of Jeremy Bentham*, Vol. II, Edinburgh: William Tait, 1843; republished, Bristol, UK: Theoremmes Press, 1995, 489–534.

[12] Bergson, A., "A Reformulation of Certain Aspects of Welfare Economics," *Quarterly Journal of Economics* **52**, 1938, 310–334.

[13] Bergson, A., "Market Socialism Revisited," *Journal of Political Economy* **75**, 1967, 655–673.

[14] Black, D., "On the Rationale of Group Decision-Making," *Journal of Political Economy* **56**, 1948, 23–34.

[15] Black, D., *The Theory of Committees and Elections*, Cambridge, UK: Cambridge University Press, 1958.

[16] Blair, D. H., G. Bordes, J. S. Kelly, and K. Suzumura, "Impossibility Theorems without Collective Rationality," *Journal of Economic Theory* **13**, 1976, 361-379. Essay 5 of this volume.

[17] Blau, J. H., "Liberal Values and Independence," *Review of Economic Studies* **42**, 1975, 395–401.

[18] Blau, J. H., "Semiorders and Collective Choice," *Journal of Economic Theory* **21**, 1979, 195–206.

[19] Borda (J.-C. de Borda), "Mémoire sur les Élections par Scrutin," *Mémoires de l'Académie Royale des Sciences Année*, 1781, 657–665; translated in English by A. de Grazia, "Mathematical Derivation of an Election System," *Isis* **44**, 1953, 42–51.

[20] Buchanan, J. M., "Social Choice, Democracy, and Free Markets," *Journal of Political Economy* **62**, 1954, 114–123.

[21] Campbell, D. E., and J. S. Kelly, "Trade-Off Theory," *American Economic Review: Papers and Proceedings* **84**, 1994, 422–426.

[22] Chipman, J. S., "The Paretian Heritage," *Revue Européene des Sciences Sociales et Cahiers Vilfredo Pareto* **14**, 1976, 65–171.

[23] Chipman, J. S., and J. C. Moore, "The New Welfare Economics 1939–1974," *International Economic Review* **19**, 1978, 547–584.

[24] Condorcet (M. J. A. N. de Condorcet), *Essai sur l'Application de l'Analyse à la Probabilité des Décisions Rendus à la Pluralité des Voix*, Paris: Imprimerie Royale, 1785; facsimile published, New York: Chelsea Publishing Company, 1972.

[25] Dalton, H., "The Measurement of the Inequality of Incomes," *Economic Journal* **30**, 1920, 348–361.

[26] d'Aspremont, C., and L. Gevers, "Equity and Informational Basis of Collective Choice," *Review of Economic Studies* **44**, 1977, 199–209.

[27] Dobb, M., *Welfare Economics and the Economics of Socialism*, Cambridge, UK: Cambridge University Press, 1969.

[28] Dodgson, C. L. (Lewis Carroll), *A Discussion of the Various Methods of Procedure in Conducting Elections*, imprint by E. B. Gardner, E. Pickard Hall, and J. H. Stacy, Oxford: Printers to the University, 1873; reprinted in D. Black, *The Theory of Committees and Elections*, Cambridge, UK: Cambridge University Press, 1958, 214–222.

[29] Dodgson, C. L. (Lewis Carroll), *Suggestions as to the Best Method of Taking Votes, Where More Than Two Issues Are to be Voted On*, imprint by E. Pickard Hall and J. H. Stacy, Oxford: Printers to the University, 1874; reprinted in D. Black, *The Theory of Committees and Elections*, Cambridge, UK: Cambridge University Press, 1958, 222–224.

[30] Dodgson, C. L. (Lewis Carroll), *A Method of Taking Votes on More Than Two Issues*, Oxford: Clarendon Press, 1876; reprinted in D. Black, *The Theory of Committees and Elections*, Cambridge, UK: Cambridge University Press, 1958, 224–234.

[31] Dworkin, R., "What Is Equality? Part 1: Equality of Welfare," *Philosophy and Public Affairs* **10**, 1981, 185–246.

[32] Dworkin, R., "What Is Equality? Part 2: Equality of Resources," *Philosophy and Public Affairs* **10**, 1981, 283–345.

[33] Dworkin, R., *Sovereign Virtue: The Theory and Practice of Equality*, Cambridge, Mass.: Harvard University Press, 2000.

[34] Elster, J., *Sour Grapes: Studies in the Subversion of Rationality*, Cambridge, UK: Cambridge University Press, 1983.

[35] Farquharson, R., *Theory of Voting*, New Haven, Conn.: Yale University Press, 1969.

[36] Foley, D. K., "Resource Allocation and the Public Sector," *Yale Economic Essays* **7**, 1967, 45–98.

[37] Gaertner, W., P. K. Pattanaik, and K. Suzumura, "Individual Rights Revisited," *Economica* **59**, 1992, 161–177. Essay 15 of this volume.

[38] Galton, F., "One Vote, One Value," *Nature* **75**, 1907, 414.

[39] Gärdenfors, P., "Rights, Games and Social Choice," *Noûs* **15**, 1981, 341–356.

[40] Gibbard, A. F., "Manipulation of Voting Schemes: A General Result," *Econometrica* **41**, 1973, 587–601.

[41] Gibbard, A. F., "A Pareto-Consistent Libertarian Claim," *Journal of Economic Theory* **7**, 1974, 388–410.

[42] Gorman, W. M., "The Intransitivity of Certain Criteria Used in Welfare Economics," *Oxford Economic Papers* **7**, 1955, 25–35.

[43] Graaff, J. de V., *Theoretical Welfare Economics*, London: Cambridge University Press, 1957.

[44] Hammond, P. J., "Equity, Arrow's Conditions and Rawls' Difference Principle," *Econometrica* **44**, 1976, 793–804.

[45] Harsanyi, J. C., "Cardinal Utility in Welfare Economics and in the Theory of Risk-Taking," *Journal of Political Economy* **61**, 1953, 434–435.

[46] Harsanyi, J. C., "Cardinal Welfare, Individualistic Ethics and Interpersonal Comparisons of Utility," *Journal of Political Economy* **63**, 1955, 309–321.

[47] Harsanyi, J. C., *Rational Behavior and Bargaining Equilibrium in Games and Social Situations*, Cambridge, UK: Cambridge University Press, 1977.

[48] Heal, G. M., *The Theory of Economic Planning*, Amsterdam: North-Holland, 1973.

[49] Hicks, J. R., "The Foundations of Welfare Economics," *Economic Journal* **49**, 1939, 696–712.

[50] Hicks, J. R., "The Evaluation of the Social Income," *Economica* **7**, 1940, 105–124.

[51] Hicks, J. R., "The Scope and Status of Welfare Economics," *Oxford Economic Papers* **27**, 1975, 307–326.

[52] Hurwicz, L., "Optimality and Informational Efficiency in Resource Allocation Processes," in K. J. Arrow, S. Karlin, and P. Suppes, eds., *Mathematical Methods in the Social Sciences 1959*, Stanford, Calif.: Stanford University Press, 1960, 27–46.

[53] Hurwicz, L., "On Informationally Decentralized Systems," in C. B. McGuire and R. Radner, eds., *Decision and Organization*, Amsterdam: North-Holland, 1972, 297–336.

[54] Hurwicz, L., "The Design of Resource Allocation Mechanisms," *American Economic Review* **58**, 1973, 1–30.

[55] Inada, K.-I., "The Simple Majority Decision Rule," *Econometrica* **37**, 1969, 490–506.

[56] Johansen, L., "The Theory of Public Goods: Misplaced Emphasis?" *Journal of Public Economics* **7**, 1977, 147–152; reprinted, in F. R. Førsund, ed., *Collected Works of Leif Johansen*, Vol. 2, Amsterdam: North-Holland, 1987, 663–668.

[57] Kalai, E., and M. Smorodinsky, "Other Solutions to Nash's Bargaining Problem," *Econometrica* **43**, 1975, 513–518.

[58] Kaldor, N., "Welfare Propositions in Economics and Interpersonal Comparisons of Utility," *Economic Journal* **49**, 1939, 549–552.

[59] Kelsey, D., "The Liberal Paradox: A Generalization," *Social Choice and Welfare* **1**, 1985, 245–252.

[60] Kelsey, D., "What Is Responsible for the 'Paretian Epidemic'?," *Social Choice and Welfare* **5**, 1988, 303–306.

[61] Kolm, S.-Ch., "Optimum Production of Social Justice," in J. Margolis and H. Guitton, eds., *Public Economics*, New York: Macmillan, 1969, 145–200.

[62] Kolm, S.-Ch., *Justice et Equité*, Paris: Editions du Centre National de la Recherche Scientifique, 1972; English translation, *Justice and Equity*, Cambridge, Mass.: MIT Press, 1997.

[63] Lange, O., "On the Economic Theory of Socialism," *Review of Economic Studies* **4**, 1936, 53–71; 1937, 123–142.

[64] Lange, O., "On the Economic Theory of Socialism," in B. E. Lippincott, O. Lange, and F. M. Taylor, eds., *On the Economic Theory of Socialism*, Minneapolis: University of Minnesota Press, 1938, 57–143.

[65] Lange, O., "The Computer and the Market," in C. H. Feinstein, ed., *Socialism, Capitalism and Economic Growth*, Cambridge, UK: Cambridge University Press, 1967, 158–161.

[66] Laplace, P.-S., "Leçons de Mathématiques, Données à l'École Normale en 1795," *Journal de l'École Polytechnique*, Tome II, Paris: Septième et Huitième Cahiers, 1812.

[67] Lerner, A. P., *The Economics of Control*, New York: Macmillan, 1944.

[68] Little, I. M. D., "Social Choice and Individual Values," *Journal of Political Economy* **60**, 1952, 422–432.

[69] Malinvaud, E., "Decentralized Procedures for Planning," in E. Malinvaud and M. O. L. Bacharach, eds., *Activity Analysis in the Theory of Growth and Planning*, London: Macmillan, 1967, 170–208.

[70] Mas-Colell, A., and H. Sonnenschein, "General Possibility Theorems for Group Decisions," *Review of Economic Studies* **39**, 1972, 185–192.

[71] Maskin, E., "A Theorem on Utilitarianism," *Review of Economic Studies* **45**, 1978, 93–96.

[72] Maskin, E., "Implementation and Strong Nash Equilibrium," in J.-J. Laffont, ed., *Aggregation and Revelation of Preferences*, Amsterdam: North-Holland, 1979, 433–439.

[73] Maskin, E., "Nash Equilibrium and Welfare Optimality," *Review of Economic Studies* **66**, 1999, 23–38. Originally circulated as MIT working paper in 1977.

[74] McLean, I., "The First Golden Age of Social Choice, 1784–1803," in W. A. Barnett, H. Moulin, M. Salles, and N. J. Schofield, eds., *Social Choice, Welfare, and Ethics*, Cambridge, UK: Cambridge University Press, 1995, 13–33.

[75] McLean, I., and F. Hewitt, *Condorcet: Foundations of Social Choice and Political Theory*, Hants: Edward Elgar, 1994.

[76] McLean, I., and J. London, "The Borda and Condorcet Principles: Three Medieval Applications," *Social Choice and Welfare* **7**, 1990, 99–108.

[77] Mill, J. S., *On Liberty*, London: Parker, 1859; reprinted in J. M. Robson, ed., *The Collected Works of John Stuart Mill*, Vol. 18, Toronto: University of Toronto Press, 1977.

[78] Mill, J. S., *Utilitarianism*, London: Collins, 1861.

[79] Mishan, E. J., "A Survey of Welfare Economics, 1939–59," *Economic Journal* **70**, 1960, 197–265.

[80] Nanson, E. J., "Methods of Election," *Transactions and Proceedings of the Royal Society of Victoria* **19**, 1882, 197–240; reprinted in British Government blue book, Misc. No. 3, Cd. 3501, 1997.

[81] Nash, J. F., "The Bargaining Problem," *Econometrica* **18**, 1950, 155–162.

[82] Negishi, T., "The Stability of a Competitive Economy: A Survey Article," *Econometrica* **30**, 1962, 635–669.

[83] Pareto, V., *Manuale di Economia Politica*, Milan: Societa Editrice Libraria, 1906; French translation (revised), *Manuel d'Économie Politique*, Paris: M. Giard, 1909; English translation, *Manual of Political Economy*, New York: A. M. Kelley, 1927.

[84] Pareto, V., "Il Massimo di Utilità per una Collettività in Sociologia," *Giornale degli Economisti e Revisita di Statistica* **46**, 1913, 337–341.

[85] Pattanaik, P. K., "Risk, Impersonality, and the Social Welfare Function," *Journal of Political Economy* **76**, 1968, 1152–1169.

[86] Pattanaik, P. K., *Strategy and Group Choice*, Amsterdam: North-Holland, 1978.

[87] Pattanaik, P. K., and K. Suzumura, "Rights, Welfarism and Social Choice," *American Economic Review: Papers and Proceedings* **84**, 1994, 435–439.

[88] Pattanaik, P. K., and K. Suzumura, "Individual Rights and Social Evaluation: A Conceptual Framework," *Oxford Economic Papers* **48**, 1996, 194–212.

[89] Pattanaik, P. K., and Y. Xu, "On Ranking Opportunity Sets in Terms of Freedom of Choice," *Recherches Economiques de Louvain* **56**, 1990, 383–390.

[90] Pigou, A. C., *The Economics of Welfare*, London: Macmillan, 1920.

[91] Plott, C. R., "Path Independence, Rationality, and Social Choice," *Econometrica* **41**, 1973, 1075–1091.

[92] Rawls, J., "Justice as Fairness," in P. Laslett and W. G. Runciman, eds., *Philosophy, Politics and Society*, 2nd series, Oxford: Basil Blackwell, 1962, 132–157; reprinted in S. Freeman, ed., *John Rawls: Collected Papers*, Cambridge, Mass.: Harvard University Press, 1999, 47–72.

[93] Rawls, J., *A Theory of Justice*, Cambridge, Mass.: Harvard University Press, 1971; revised ed., 1999.

[94] Robbins, L., *An Essay on the Nature and Significance of Economic Science*, 2nd edn., London: Macmillan, 1935; 1st edn., 1932.

[95] Robbins, L., "Interpersonal Comparisons of Utility," *Economic Journal* **48**, 1938, 635–641.

[96] Robbins, L., "Economics and Political Economy," *American Economic Review* **71**, 1981, 1–10.

[97] Roberts, K. W. S., "Possibility Theorems with Interpersonally Comparable Utility Levels," *Review of Economic Studies* **47**, 1980, 409–420.

[98] Roberts, K. W. S., "Interpersonal Comparability and Social Choice Theory," *Review of Economic Studies* **47**, 1980, 421–439.

[99] Roberts, K. W. S., "Valued Opinions or Opinionized Values: The Double Aggregation Problem," in K. Basu, P. K. Pattanaik, and K. Suzumura, eds., *Choice, Welfare and Development: A Festschrift in Honour of Amartya Sen*, Oxford: Clarendon Press of Oxford University Press, 1995, 141–185.

[100] Rothschild, E., *Economic Sentiments: Adam Smith, Condorcet, and the Enlightenment*, Cambridge, Mass.: Harvard University Press, 2001.

[101] Samuelson, P. A., *Foundations of Economic Analysis*, Cambridge, Mass.: Harvard University Press, 1947.

[102] Samuelson, P. A., "Evaluation of Real National Income," *Oxford Economic Papers* **2**, 1950, 1–29.

[103] Samuelson, P. A., "The Pure Theory of Public Expenditure," *Review of Economics and Statistics* **36**, 1954, 387–389.

[104] Samuelson, P. A., "Arrow's Mathematical Politics," in S. Hook, ed., *Human Values and Economic Policy*, New York: New York University Press, 1967, 41–52.

[105] Samuelson, P. A., "Bergsonian Welfare Economics," in S. Rosefielde, ed., *Economic Welfare and the Economics of Soviet Socialism: Essays in Honor of Abram Bergson*, Cambridge, Mass.: Cambridge University Press, 1981, 223–266.

[106] Satterthwaite, M. A., "Strategyproofness and Arrow's Conditions: Existence and Correspondence Theorems for Voting Procedures and Social Welfare Functions," *Journal of Economic Theory* **10**, 1975, 187–217.

[107] Scarf, H., "Some Examples of Global Instability of the Competitive Equilibrium," *International Economic Review* **1**, 1960, 157–172.

[108] Schumpeter, J. A., *History of Economic Analysis*, New York: Oxford University Press, 1954.

[109] Scitovsky, T., "A Note on Welfare Propositions in Economics," *Review of Economic Studies* **9**, 1941, 77–88.

[110] Sen, A. K., "Quasi-Transitivity, Rational Choice and Collective Decisions," *Review of Economic Studies* **36**, 1969, 381–393.

[111] Sen, A. K., *Collective Choice and Social Welfare*, San Francisco: Holden-Day, 1970; republished, Amsterdam: North-Holland, 1979.

[112] Sen, A. K., "The Impossibility of a Paretian Liberal," *Journal of Political Economy*, **78**, 1970, 152–157.

[113] Sen, A. K., *On Economic Inequality*, 1st edn., Oxford: Oxford University Press, 1973; expanded edn., with a substantial annexe by J. E. Foster and A. K. Sen, Oxford: Oxford University Press, 1997.

[114] Sen, A. K., "Liberty, Unanimity and Rights," *Economica* **43**, 1976, 217–245.

[115] Sen, A. K., "Poverty: An Ordinal Approach to Measurement," *Econometrica* **44**, 1976, 219–231.

[116] Sen, A. K., "Welfare Inequalities and Rawlsian Axiomatics," *Theory and Decisions* **7**, 1976, 243–262.

[117] Sen, A. K., "Social Choice Theory: A Re-Examination," *Econometrica* **45**, 1977, 53–89.

[118] Sen, A. K., "On Weights and Measures: Informational Constraints in Social Welfare Analysis," *Econometrica* **45**, 1977, 1539–1572.

[119] Sen, A. K., "Utilitarianism and Welfarism," *Journal of Philosophy* **76**, 1979, 463–489.

[120] Sen, A. K., *Commodities and Capabilities*, Amsterdam: North-Holland, 1985.

[121] Sen, A. K., "Minimal Liberty," *Economica* **59**, 1992, 139–159.

[122] Sen, A. K., "The Possibility of Social Choice," *American Economic Review* **89**, 1999, 349–378.

[123] Sen, A. K., *Development as Freedom*, Oxford: Oxford University Press, 1999.

[124] Sen, A. K., *Rationality and Freedom*, Cambridge, Mass.: Belknap Press of Harvard University Press, 2002.

[125] Sen, A. K., and P. K. Pattanaik, "Necessary and Sufficient Conditions for Rational Choice under Majority Decisions," *Journal of Economic Theory* **1**, 1969, 178–202.

[126] Sen, A. K., and B. Williams, eds., *Utilitarianism and Beyond*, Cambridge, UK: Cambridge University Press, 1982.

[127] Sugden, R., "Liberty, Preference, and Choice," *Economics and Philosophy* **1**, 1985, 213–229.

[128] Suppes, P., "Some Formal Models of Grading Principles," *Synthese* **6**, 1966, 284–306.

[129] Suzumura, K., "Remarks on the Theory of Collective Choice," *Economica* **43**, 1976, 381–390. Essay 6 of this volume.

[130] Suzumura, K., "On the Consistency of Libertarian Claims," *Review of Economic Studies* **45**, 1978, 329–342. "A Correction," *Review of Economic Studies* **46**, 1979, 743. Essay 13 of this volume.

[131] Suzumura, K., "On Distributional Value Judgements and Piecemeal Welfare Criteria," *Economica* **47**, 1980, 125–139.

[132] Suzumura, K., "On the Possibility of 'Fair' Collective Choice Rule," *International Economic Review* **22**, 1981, 307–320.

[133] Suzumura, K., "On Pareto Efficiency and the No-Envy Concept of Equity," *Journal of Economic Theory* **25**, 1981, 367–379. Essay 9 of this volume.

[134] Suzumura, K., "Social Welfare Function," in J. Eatwell, M. Milgate, and P. Newman, eds., *The New Palgrave: A Dictionary of Economics*, Vol. 4, London: Macmillan, 1987, 418–420.

[135] Suzumura, K., "Welfare, Rights, and Social Choice Procedure: A Perspective," *Analyse & Kritik* **18**, 1996, 20–37. Essay 16 of this volume.

[136] Suzumura, K., "Interpersonal Comparisons of the Extended Sympathy Type and the Possibility of Social Choice," in K. J. Arrow, A. K. Sen, and K. Suzumura, eds., *Social Choice Re-examined*, Vol. 2, London: Macmillan, 1996, 202–229.

[137] Suzumura, K., "Consequences, Opportunities, and Procedures," *Social Choice and Welfare* **16**, 1999, 17–40. Essay 17 of this volume.

[138] Suzumura, K., "Paretian Welfare Judgments and Bergsonian Social Choice," *Economic Journal* **109**, 1999, 204–220. Essay 26 of this volume.

[139] Suzumura, K., "Welfare Economics beyond Welfarist Consequentialism," *Japanese Economic Review* **51**, 2000, 1–32. Essay 27 of this volume.

[140] Suzumura, K., "On the Concept of Procedural Fairness," presidential address presented at the Society for Social Choice and Welfare, Alicante, Spain, July 2000.

[141] Suzumura, K., "An Interview with Paul Samuelson: Welfare Economics, 'Old' and 'New,' and Social Choice Theory," *Social Choice and Welfare* **25**, 2005, 327–356.

[142] Suzumura, K. and Y. Xu, "Characterizations of Consequentialism and Nonconsequentialism," *Journal of Economic Theory* **101**, 2001, 423–436. Essay 18 of this volume.

[143] Suzumura, K., and Y. Xu, "Welfarist Consequentialism, Similarity of Attitudes, and Arrow's General Impossibility Theorem," *Social Choice and Welfare* **22**, 2004, 237–251. Essay 20 of this volume.

[144] Sweezy, P. M., *Socialism*, New York: McGraw-Hill, 1949.

[145] Taylor, F. M., "The Guidance of Production in a Socialist State," *American Economic Review* **19**, 1929, 1–8; reprinted in B. E. Lippincott, O. Lange, and F. M. Taylor, eds., *On the Economic Theory of Socialism*, Minneapolis: University of Minnesota Press, 1938, 41–54.

[146] Todhunter, I., *A History of the Mathematical Theory of Probability from the Time of Pascal to That of Laplace*, London: Macmillan, 1865.

[147] Varian, H. R., "Equity, Envy, and Efficiency," *Journal of Economic Theory* **9**, 1974, 63–91.

[148] Vickrey, W. S., "Measuring Marginal Utility by Reactions to Risk," *Econometrica* **13**, 1945, 319–333.

[149] Vickrey, W. S., "Utility, Strategy, and Social Decision Rules," *Quarterly Journal of Economics* **74**, 1960, 507–535.

[150] von Hayek, F. A., ed., *Collectivist Economic Planning*, London: Routledge, 1935.

[151] von Hayek, F. A., *The Road to Serfdom*, London: Routledge and Kegan Paul, 1944.

[152] von Hayek, F. A., *Individualism and Economic Order*, Chicago: University of Chicago Press, 1948.

[153] von Mises, L., "Die Wirtschaftsrechnung im Sozialistischen Gemeinwesen," *Archiv für Sozialwissenschaften und Sozialpolitik* **47**, 1920; English translation, in von Hayek, F. A., ed., *Collectivist Economic Planning*, London: Routledge, 1935, 87–130.

[154] von Neumann, J., and O. Morgenstern, *Theory of Games and Economic Behavior*, 1st edn., Princeton, N.J.: Princeton University Press, 1944; 2nd edn., 1947.

[155] Wicksell, K., "Ein neues Prinzip der Gerechten Besteuerung," *Finanztheoretische Untersuchungen*, Jena, Germany, 1896; English translation, "A New Principle of Just Taxation," in R. A. Musgrave and A. T. Peacock, eds., *Classics in the Theory of Public Finance*, London: Macmillan, 1958, 72–118.

[156] Wilson, R. B., "Social Choice without the Pareto Principle," *Journal of Economic Theory* **5**, 1972, 14–20.

ESSAY 26

Paretian Welfare Judgments and Bergsonian Social Choice

In the wake of a harsh ordinalist criticism in the 1930s against the epistemological basis of the "old" welfare economics created by Pigou, several attempts were made to salvage the wreckage of Pigou's research agenda by reformulating welfare economics altogether on the basis of *ordinal* and *interpersonally noncomparable* welfare information and nothing else. The seminal concept of the *Pareto principle,* to the effect that a change from a state x to another state y can be construed as socially good if at least one individual is made better off without making anybody else worse off in return, came to the fore, and the characterization and implementation of Pareto-efficient resource allocation became the central exercise in the "new" welfare economics. However, since almost every economic policy cannot but favor some individuals at the cost

First published in *Economic Journal* **109**, 1999, pp. 204–220. Reprinted in Wood, J. C., and M. McLure, eds., *Paul A. Samuelson: Critical Assessments of Contemporary Economists*, 2nd series, London: Routledge, 2004, pp. 378–396. This essay capitalizes on Suzumura [29], and generalizes the main theorem that first appeared there. The basic idea was presented at the Fourth Osnabrück Seminar on Individual Decisions and Social Choice held at the University of Osnabrück, September 14, 1996, the Research Seminar at the Institute for Social and Economic Research held at Osaka University, January 22, 1997, the Far Eastern Meeting of the Econometric Society held at the Chinese University of Hong Kong, July 24–26, 1997, and the Fourth International Meeting of the Society for Social Choice and Welfare held at the University of British Columbia, July 3–6, 1998. I am grateful to Nick Baigent, David Donaldson, Wulf Gaertner, Philippe Mongin, Prasanta Pattanaik, Koichi Tadenuma, Yongsheng Xu, and Akira Yamazaki for their helpful comments and discussions at several stages of the evolution of this essay. Last but not least, my sincere thanks go to the editor in charge, Timothy Besley, and the two referees of the *Economic Journal* for their helpful comments and suggestions. Needless to say, I am solely responsible for any remaining defects.

of disfavoring others, there will be almost no situation of real importance where the Pareto principle can claim direct relevance.

Two distinct approaches were explored to rectify this unsatisfactory state of welfare economics. The first approach was the introduction of *compensation criteria* by Kaldor [12], Hicks [11], Scitovsky [19], and Samuelson [18], which endeavored to expand the applicability of the Pareto principle by introducing hypothetical compensation payments between gainers and losers. According to Graaff [8, pp. 84-85], "the compensation tests all spring from a desire to see what can be said about social welfare or 'real national income' . . . without making interpersonal comparisons of well-being. . . . They have common origin in Pareto's definition of an increase in social welfare—that at least one man must be better off and no one worse off—but they are extended to situations in which some people are made worse off." The second attempt was the introduction of the novel concept of a *social welfare function* by Bergson [3] and Samuelson [17, Chapter VIII], which is rooted in the belief that the analysis of the logical consequences of any value judgments, irrespective of whose ethical beliefs they represent, whether or not they are widely shared in the society, or how they are generated in the first place, is a legitimate task of welfare economics. The social welfare function is nothing other than the formal way of characterizing such an ethical belief, which is *rational* in the sense of being complete as well as transitive over the alternative states of affairs. A *Paretian* (or *individualistic*) social welfare function is one that judges in concordance with the Pareto principle if the latter does have relevance. It was Arrow [1, p. 108] who neatly crystallized the gist of this approach as follows: "The 'new welfare economics' says nothing about choices among Pareto-optimal alternatives. The purpose of the social welfare function was precisely to extend the unanimity quasi ordering to a full social ordering."

Capitalizing on Graaff's and Arrow's insightful observations on the nature and significance of these two schools of thought, where the concept of an *extension* of the Pareto quasi ordering plays a crucial role in both, this essay examines the logical performance of the new welfare economics. To be more precise, we synthesise the two approaches to the new welfare economics and identify a condition under which the new welfare economics is logically impeccable. The usefulness of our condition is twofold. In the first place, we may thereby check whether or not the hypothetical compensation criteria proposed by Kaldor, Hicks, Scitovsky, and Samuelson can serve as a useful preliminary step toward final rational social choices. In the second place, we can thereby cast a new light on some recent attempts to define several plausible quasi orderings on social welfare, including Suppes [23], Sen [20; 21], Fine [7], Blackorby and Donaldson [4], and Madden [15] vis-à-vis the analytical scenario of the new welfare economics.

It is hoped that the preceding attempts in the new welfare economics along various routes can be systematically understood and neatly evaluated with reference to our analysis in this essay.

26.1. Motivation and Illustration

To motivate our analysis intuitively, and to illustrate the nature of our central theorem neatly, let us begin by examining a situation where a policy maker should make democratic collective decisions by paying due respect for opinions expressed by citizens. For simplicity, suppose that there are only two citizens, say, 1 and 2, and only three options, say, x, y, and z. Citizens are free to express their preference orderings on $X = \{x, y, z\}$. Without loss of generality, assume that citizens can express strict preferences only. Then there are six logically possible preference orderings, say, α, β, γ, δ, ε, and ζ on X, which may be expressed.

Table 26.1 describes these possible preference orderings, where options are arranged vertically with the more preferred options being located above the less preferred ones. For example, α is one of the preference orderings, according to which x is preferred to y, y is preferred to z, hence x is preferred to z. Arranging these possible preference orderings vertically and horizontally, we may construct a box in Table 26.2 with 36 cells, where the vertical (resp. horizontal) list refers to citizen 1's (resp. citizen 2's) expressed preference orderings. Clearly, each and every cell in Table 26.2 represents a profile of the two citizens' expressed preference orderings. For example, the

Table 26.1. Possible Preference Orderings

α	β	γ	δ	ϵ	ζ
x	x	y	y	z	z
y	z	x	z	x	y
z	y	z	x	y	x

Table 26.2. Implications of the Pareto Principle

	α	β	γ	δ	ε	ζ
α	α	xPy xPz	yPz xPz	yPz	xPy	
β	xPy xPz	β	xPz		zPy xPy	zPy
γ	yPz xPz	xPz	γ	yPx yPz		yPx
δ	yPz		yPz yPx	δ	zPx	yPx zPx
ε	xPy	zPy xPy		zPy	ε	zPy zPx
ζ		zPy	yPx	yPx zPx	zPy zPx	ζ

cell (α, β) represents a profile in which citizen 1 expresses α and citizen 2 expresses β.

What we call a *Bergson-Samuelson social welfare ordering* is nothing other than a preference ordering from the society's viewpoint specified for each and every cell in Table 26.2, which guides the rational collective decision to be made by the policy maker. A Bergson-Samuelson social welfare ordering is *Paretian* or *individualistic* if it accepts everything that the Pareto principle tells us about the social desirability of one option vis-à-vis the other. For simplicity, we will refer to "what the Pareto principle tells us about the social desirability of one option vis-à-vis the other" collectively as *Paretian welfare judgments*. To be democratic, it is minimally required that the policy maker is ready to accept Paretian welfare judgments.

To what extent do Paretian welfare judgments restrict the admissible class of Paretian Bergson-Samuelson social welfare orderings to be filled in each cell? Clearly, the answer hinges squarely on the extent to which the two citizens agree on their individual preference orderings. Note that there are six cells (α, α), (β, β), (γ, γ), (δ, δ), $(\varepsilon, \varepsilon)$, and (ζ, ζ) along the main diagonal in Table 26.2, where the two citizens express exactly the same preference orderings α, β, γ, δ, ε, and ζ. Therefore, by virtue of the Pareto principle and nothing else, the Paretian Bergson-Samuelson social welfare orderings corresponding to these cells cannot but be α, β, γ, δ, ε, and ζ, so that nothing is left for any other principle to bridge the Paretian welfare judgments to the Paretian Bergson-Samuelson social welfare ordering. In all other cells in Table 26.2, the extent of interpersonal agreements of preferences among citizens is less than perfect. However, there are two distinct categories to be identified and separately addressed. The first category consists of those cells where only one pair of options is left to be socially ordered in order to bridge the Paretian welfare judgments to the Paretian Bergson-Samuelson social welfare orderings, whereas the second category consists of those cells where at least two pairs of options are left to be socially ordered before the Paretian welfare judgments can be completed into the Paretian Bergson-Samuelson social welfare orderings.

Take, for example, the cell (α, β), where the Pareto principle is enough to tell us that xPy and xPz, that is to say, the policy maker must accept that x is socially preferred to both y and z. Only one pair of options, viz., $\{y, z\}$, is left to be socially ordered before we arrive at a full-fledged Paretian Bergson-Samuelson social welfare ordering, so that this cell is of the first category. If y (resp. z) is judged somehow socially better than z (resp. y) in this cell, then we have xPy, yPz, and xPz (resp. xPz, zPy, and xPy), so that the Paretian Bergson-Samuelson social welfare ordering to be filled in this cell is uniquely determined to be α (resp. β). It is clear that the cells in Table 26.2 that compose the first category consist of (α, β), (α, γ), (β, α), (β, ε), (γ, α), (γ, δ), (δ, γ), (δ, ζ), (ε, β), (ε, ζ), (ζ, δ), and (ζ, ε). By definition, the step of deleting the residual indeterminacy in the cells of the first category is in fact nothing other than the *final* step rather than the *preliminary* step in the transition from Paretian welfare judgments to the full-fledged Paretian Bergson-Samuelson social welfare orderings. Since the asserted raison d'être of the new welfare economics lies in its preliminary role in expanding the Pareto principle in the presence of conflict of judgments among citizens without using anything that goes beyond intrapersonally ordinal and interpersonally noncomparable information on well-being, we will focus mostly on the cells (profiles) of the second category.[1]

1. The proportion occupied by cells of the second category over the total number of cells is $18/36 = 0.5$ in the situation with two citizens and three options, where citizens are allowed to express strict preference orderings only. It is easy, if tedious, to verify that this proportion increases to $120/169 \approx 0.71$ when two citizens are allowed to express occasional indifference among three options. For societies with more than two citizens and more than three options, this proportion will increase even further.

Consider the cell (α, δ), which is clearly of the second category. Since the Pareto principle tells us that yPz and nothing else in this cell, the feasible candidates for the Paretian Bergson-Samuelson social welfare ordering in this cell are limited to α, γ, and δ. Without loss of generality, suppose that α is the relevant social welfare ordering in this cell, and consider the set of partial welfare judgments that not only strictly extend the Paretian welfare judgments but also are strictly subsumed in the Paretian Bergson-Samuelson social welfare ordering α. It is easy to check that two partial welfare judgments exist, which satisfy these two requirements, viz., (i) Q^1, which says that y is socially better than z and x is socially better than z, and (ii) Q^2, which says that x is socially better than y and y is socially better than z. Note that, according to Q^1, the policy maker should not choose z, as it is dominated by x as well as by y in terms of social welfare. Likewise, according to Q^2, the policy maker should choose neither y nor z, as they are both dominated by x in terms of social welfare. It then follows that there is only one option in the set $X = \{x, y, z\}$ of all alternatives, viz., x, which is not excluded by any one of the two partial welfare judgments Q^1 and Q^2. As a matter of fact, this social choice of x is in full concordance with the choice according to the optimization of the Paretian Bergson-Samuelson social welfare ordering α.

This remarkable result is not an accidental outcome of our fortuitous choice of a cell of the second category, viz., (α, δ), nor is it due to our cunning choice of a particular Paretian Bergson-Samuelson social welfare ordering α. Indeed, what our main theorem guarantees is that this property is in fact a robust result that holds for all profiles of citizens' preference orderings of the second category in a society with an arbitrary number of citizens and options.

It is also important to realize the implication of this result. It suggests unambiguously that the research program of the new welfare economics is logically impeccable in the following sense: For each Paretian Bergson-Samuelson social welfare ordering R, the social choice set from any opportunity set S in accordance with the optimization of this R over S can be recovered by finding the undominated subsets of S for each and every partial preference relation that is a *strict subrelation* of R as well as a *strict extension* of Paretian welfare judgments, and taking the intersection of these undominated subsets. Thus, the preliminary step advocated by the new welfare economics serves us well in locating the rational choice exactly in terms of the Paretian Bergson-Samuelson social welfare ordering. In other words, the new welfare economics can indeed help the policy maker identify the rational social choice, at least in principle.

So much for the motivation and implication of our subsequent analysis. Let us now proceed to the proper analysis in a general setting.

26.2. Maximal Set, Greatest Set, and Extensions of a Binary Relation

To facilitate our analysis for a society with an arbitrary number of individuals and alternatives, let us summarize some basic properties of binary relations, maximal sets, and greatest sets and present an extension theorem for Suzumura-consistent—S-consistent for short—binary relations, which will play a crucial role in what follows.

Let X be the universal set of alternatives. A *binary relation* on X is a subset R of $X \times X$. It is customary to write, for all $x, y \in X$, xRy if and only if $(x, y) \in R$. When a binary relation R satisfies *completeness* (*for all* $x, y \in X, x \neq y$ *implies* $\{(x, y) \in R$ or $(y, x) \in R\}$), *reflexivity* (*for all* $x \in X$, $(x, x) \in R$), and *transitivity* (*for all* $x, y, z \in X$, $\{(x, y) \in R$ & $(y, z) \in R\}$ *implies* $(x, z) \in R$), we say that R is an *ordering* on X. If R satisfies reflexivity and transitivity, but not necessarily completeness, we say that R is a *quasi ordering*.

For any binary relation R on X, $P(R)$ and $I(R)$ denote, respectively, the *asymmetric part* of R and the *symmetric part* of R, which are defined by $P(R) = \{(x, y) \in X \times X \mid (x, y) \in R \ \& \ (y, x) \notin R\}$ and $I(R) = \{(x, y) \in X \times X \mid (x, y) \in R \ \& \ (y, x) \in R\}$. If R is transitive, $P(R)$ as well as $I(R)$ satisfy transitivity.

For any binary relation R and any nonempty subset S of X, an element $x \in S$ is an *R-maximal element* of S if $(y, x) \notin P(R)$ holds for all $y \in S$. The set of all R-maximal elements of S is the *R-maximal set* of S, to be denoted by $M(S, R)$. Likewise, an element $x \in S$ is an *R-greatest element* of S if $(x, y) \in R$ holds for all $y \in S$. The set of all R-greatest elements of S is the *R-greatest set* of S, to be denoted by $G(S, R)$.

The following lemma, which is a straightforward consequence of the definitions of a maximal set and a greatest set, will prove useful in our analysis.

A formal proof of this lemma is available in Sen [20, Chapter 1*]. See also Sen [22] and Suzumura [27, Chapter 2].

LEMMA 26.1.

(a) $G(S, R) \subseteq M(S, R)$ holds for all (S, R).
(b) $G(S, R) = M(S, R)$ holds for all (S, R) such that R is complete on $\mathcal{S}$.

A *choice function* C on a family $\mathcal{S}$ of nonempty subsets of X maps each and every $S \in \mathcal{S}$ into a nonempty subset $C(S)$ of S, which is called the *choice set* from the *opportunity set* S. A choice function C on $\mathcal{S}$ is *rational* if and only if there exists an underlying preference ordering R, to be called the *rationalization* of C, such that $C(S) = G(S, R)$ holds for all $S \in \mathcal{S}$. Thus, a *rational choice* is a choice in accordance with the optimization of an underlying preference ordering.[2]

For any binary relation R on X, a binary relation R^* on X is called an *extension* of R if and only if $R \subseteq R^*$ and $P(R) \subseteq P(R^*)$. Thus, an extension R^* of R retains all the information that R already contains, and goes possibly further. Note, in particular, that the asymmetric part $P(R)$ of R must be subsumed in the asymmetric part of R^*. When R^* is an extension of R, R is called a *subrelation* of R^*.

Let $\Sigma(R)$ denote the set of all subrelations of R. Then we have the following simple properties of the maximal sets and the greatest sets.

LEMMA 26.2. If $Q \in \Sigma(R)$, then $M(S, R) \subseteq M(S, Q)$ and $G(S, Q) \subseteq G(S, R)$.

PROOF. Obvious from the respective definitions of a maximal set, a greatest set, and an extension of a binary relation. ■

2. In the general theory of rational choice functions, a choice function is called *rational* if an underlying preference relation exists irrespective of whether the preference relation in question satisfies the axioms of an ordering. A rational choice function whose underlying preference relation satisfies the axioms of an ordering is called a *full rational* choice function. See, for example, Suzumura [24; 27, Chapter 2]. Since we are concerned in this essay only with a choice function that is rationalized by a Paretian Bergson-Samuelson social welfare ordering, however, we can do without introducing the concept of *degrees* of rationality altogether.

Under what conditions can there be an extension of a binary relation that satisfies the axioms of an ordering? As an auxiliary step in answering this crucial question of the existence of an *ordering extension*, we introduce the following two weaker versions of the transitivity axiom.

First, a binary relation R is *acyclic* if and only if there exists no finite subset $\{x^1, x^2, \ldots, x^t\}$ of X, where $2 \leq t < +\infty$, which satisfies $(x^1, x^2) \in P(R)$, $(x^2, x^3) \in P(R), \ldots, (x^t, x^1) \in P(R)$. Second, a binary relation R is *S-consistent* if and only if there exists no finite subset $\{x^1, x^2, \ldots, x^t\}$ of X, where $2 \leq t < +\infty$, such that $(x^1, x^2) \in P(R)$, $(x^2, x^3) \in R, \ldots, (x^t, x^1) \in R$. It is clear that the transitivity of R implies the S-consistency thereof, whereas the S-consistency of R implies the acyclicity thereof. The converse of each one of these implications is not true in general. Indeed, if we define R^1 and R^2 on $X = \{x, y, z\}$ by

$$R^1 = \{(x, y), (y, z), (z, y)\};\ R^2 = \{(x, y), (y, z), (z, y), (x, z), (z, x)\},$$

it is clear that R^1 is S-consistent but not transitive, whereas R^2 is acyclic but not S-consistent. If R is complete, however, R is S-consistent if and only if it is transitive.

We are now ready to state the following basic extension theorem.

Lemma 26.3 (Suzumura [24, Theorem 3; 27, Theorem A(5)]). A binary relation R has an ordering extension if and only if it is S-consistent.[3]

Let $\Omega(X)$ stand for the set of all reflexive and S-consistent binary relations on X. It is clear that $\Sigma(R) \subseteq \Omega(X)$ holds for any ordering R on X by virtue of Lemma 26.3. It is also clear that $R \in \Sigma(R)$ holds for any binary relation R, viz., any binary relation R is an extension of itself. Noting this fact, we call a binary relation $Q \in \Sigma(R)\backslash\{R\}$ a *strict subrelation* of R. R is then called a *strict extension* of Q.

So much for purely technical preliminaries. Let us now formally introduce our social choice problem.

---

3. Since transitivity is a sufficient but not necessary condition for S-consistency, this theorem is in fact a generalization of the classical extension theorem of Szpilrajn [30]. See also Arrow [1, p. 64] and Sen [20, Chapter 1*] for the role and importance of the extension theorems.

26.3. The Pareto Quasi Ordering and Bergson-Samuelson Social Welfare Ordering

Let $X := \{x, y, z, \ldots\}$ and $N := \{1, 2, \ldots, n\}$ be the set of all social states and the set of all individuals in the society, where $3 \leq \#X$ and $2 \leq n := \#N < +\infty$.[4] A *social state* means a complete description of economic, social, and all other features of the world that may possibly influence the well-being of individuals.

Each individual $i \in N$ is assumed to have a weak preference ("at least as good as") relation R_i on X, which satisfies the axioms of an ordering on X, such that $x R_i y$ holds if and only if x is judged by i to be at least as good as y. By definition, $P(R_i)$ and $I(R_i)$ stand for i's *strict preference relation* and his/her *indifference relation*, respectively.

Given a profile of individual preference orderings $\boldsymbol{R}^N = (R_1, R_2, \ldots, R_n)$, we define the *Pareto quasi ordering* $\rho(\boldsymbol{R}^N)$ by

$$\rho(\boldsymbol{R}^N) = \cap R_i \text{ over all } i \in N. \tag{26.1}$$

By definition, $(x, y) \in \rho(\boldsymbol{R}^N)$ if and only if $x R_i y$ for all $i \in N$, whereas $(x, y) \in P(\rho(\boldsymbol{R}^N))$ if and only if $x R_i y$ for all $i \in N$, and $x P(R_i) y$ for at least one $i \in N$. Within this conceptual framework, the problem confronted by the two schools of the new welfare economics may be neatly formulated as follows.

Recollect that the compensation criteria were designed to extend the applicability of the Pareto principle through hypothetical compensatory payments between gainers and losers. Let Q denote the generic binary relation representing the partial welfare judgments thus defined. The first task for this school of thought is to ensure that Q is a strict extension of $\rho(\boldsymbol{R}^N)$, viz., $\rho(\boldsymbol{R}^N) \in \Sigma(Q)\backslash\{Q\}$, since this school intends to go beyond the Pareto principle without losing what the latter principle already informs us of social welfare. But this is only half of the full story. Since the compensation criteria provide only a preliminary step toward final social choice, which should be rationalized by a Paretian Bergson-Samuelson social welfare or-

4. For each set A, $\#A$ stands for the number of elements in A.

dering, the mission will be left unaccomplished if what is meant to be a preliminary step turns out to preclude the possibility of final rational social choice. In other words, for the success of the compensationist school of thought, it is necessary that Q should be a strict subrelation of at least one Paretian Bergson-Samuelson social welfare ordering R so that we have $Q \in \Sigma(R)\backslash\{R\}$.

We have thus identified the research program of the new welfare economics as that of defining a principle of compensation between gainers and losers so as to generate partial welfare judgments Q such that (i) $\rho(\boldsymbol{R}^N) \in \Sigma(Q)\backslash\{Q\}$ and (ii) $Q \in \Sigma(R)\backslash\{R\}$ for some Paretian Bergson-Samuelson social welfare ordering R. It follows from this observation and Lemma 26.3 that this research program will be vacuous unless Q is guaranteed to be S-consistent. This is a useful remark, as it enables us to check whether the promise of the compensationist new welfare economics can be logically fulfilled.

26.4. The Recoverability Theorem

The research program of the new welfare economics can be located in a wider perspective with fruitful implications. Let R be a Paretian Bergson-Samuelson social welfare ordering corresponding to a given profile $\boldsymbol{R}^N = (R_1, R_2, \ldots, R_n)$ of individual preference orderings. Let $\Theta(\boldsymbol{R}^N, R)$ stand for the set of all partial welfare judgments, to be called the *test relations* for short,[6] which are *strict* extensions of $\rho(\boldsymbol{R}^N)$ as well as *strict* subrelations of R:

$$\Theta(\boldsymbol{R}^N, R) := \{Q \subseteq X \times X \mid \rho(\boldsymbol{R}^N) \in \Sigma(Q)\backslash\{Q\} \;\&\; Q \in \Sigma(R)\backslash\{R\}\}. \tag{26.2}$$

It is worthwhile to repeat why we should exclude $\rho(\boldsymbol{R}^N)$ and R from the set $\Theta(\boldsymbol{R}^N, R)$. The reason is squarely rooted in the very nature of the new welfare economics. Recollect that the research program of this school of welfare economics is to go beyond the Pareto principle and to provide

6. This convenient terminology was suggested to me by one of the referees of the *Economic Journal*.

a preliminary step toward the Paretian Bergson-Samuelson social welfare ordering that rationalizes the final social choice. Thus, $\rho(\boldsymbol{R}^N)$ as well as R cannot possibly qualify as the test relations in our analytical scenario, as $\rho(\boldsymbol{R}^N)$ (resp. R) does not in fact go beyond the Pareto quasi ordering (resp. is not in fact a preliminary step in locating R).

At this juncture of our analysis, it is useful to observe that Lemma 26.1 and Lemma 26.2 may assert that

$$G(S, R) = M(S, R) \subseteq M(S, Q) \tag{26.3}$$

holds for any $S \in \mathcal{S}$ and $Q \in \Theta(\boldsymbol{R}^N, R)$, so that we may assert that

$$\forall S \in \mathcal{S} : C(S) := G(S, R) \subseteq \cap\, M(S, Q) \text{ over all } Q \in \Theta(\boldsymbol{R}^N, R) \tag{26.4}$$

holds, where C is the *social choice function* on $\mathcal{S}$, which is rationalized by the Paretian Bergson-Samuelson social welfare ordering R. Thus, by defining the intersection of all the maximal sets with respect to each test relation $Q \in \Theta(\boldsymbol{R}^N, R)$, we can locate the area from which the final rational social choice in accordance with the Paretian Bergson-Samuelson social welfare ordering cannot escape.

Going one step further, suppose that (26.4) can be strengthened into the following set-theoretic equality:

$$\forall S \in \mathcal{S} : C(S) := G(S, R) = \cap\, M(S, Q) \text{ over all } Q \in \Theta(\boldsymbol{R}^N, R). \tag{26.5}$$

According to (26.5), *the social choice function C, which is rationalizable by the Paretian Bergson-Samuelson social welfare ordering R, can be exactly recovered by the maximization of each and every test relation* $Q \in \Theta(\boldsymbol{R}^N, R)$. Therefore, it makes sense to assert that the search for the test relations that are strict extensions of the Pareto quasi ordering $\rho(\boldsymbol{R}^N)$ as well as strict subrelations of the Paretian Bergson-Samuelson social welfare ordering R is a legitimate and effective preliminary step for final rational social choice if and only if (26.5) holds true. It is in this sense that the search for the conditions under which (26.5) holds true is of crucial importance for the logical completeness of the new welfare economics.

To orient our analysis, consider the following example.

Example 26.1. Suppose that $X = \{x, y, z\}$ and $\boldsymbol{R}^N = (R_1, R_2)$ are such that $R_1 = \Delta(X) \cup \{(x, y), (y, z), (x, z)\}$ and $R_2 = \Delta(X) \cup \{(y, x), (x, z), (y, z)\}$, where $\Delta(X) := \{(x, x), (y, y), (z, z)\}$ denotes the *diagonal binary relation* on X. Let the Paretian Bergson-Samuelson social welfare ordering be given by $R = \Delta(X) \cup \{(x, y), (y, z), (x, z)\}$. In this situation, we have $\rho(\boldsymbol{R}^N) = \Delta(X) \cup \{(y, z), (x, z)\}$ and there exists no binary relation Q that satisfies $\rho(\boldsymbol{R}^N) \in \Sigma(Q)\backslash\{Q\}$ and $Q \in \Sigma(R)\backslash\{R\}$. Thus, we have $\Theta(\boldsymbol{R}^N, R) = \varnothing$ for this $\boldsymbol{R}^N$ and R.

The message of this example is simple. If the degree of interpersonal difference of preferences is small enough as in Example 26.1, it may turn out that $\Theta(\boldsymbol{R}^N, R)$ is empty for the given profile $\boldsymbol{R}^N$ of individual preference orderings and the given Paretian Bergson-Samuelson social welfare ordering R. It is to confine ourselves to the interesting situations that we introduce the following assumption of *nontriviality*.

Assumption NT. $\Theta(\boldsymbol{R}^N, R)$ is nonempty for the given profile $\boldsymbol{R}^N = (R_1, R_2, \ldots, R_n)$ of individual preference orderings and the given Paretian Bergson-Samuelson social welfare ordering R.

Mild and innocuous though assumption NT may look, it enables us to prove the following recoverability theorem.

Recoverability Theorem. For any given profile $\boldsymbol{R}^N = (R_1, R_2, \ldots, R_n)$ of individual preference orderings, the rational social choice in accordance with the specified Paretian Bergson-Samuelson social welfare ordering R can be fully recovered by finding the maximal set for each and every test relation $Q \in \Theta(\boldsymbol{R}^N, R)$ and taking the intersection of these maximal sets if and only if assumption NT is satisfied.

It should be clear that the recoverability theorem verifies the general validity of what we have illustrated in Section 26.2 in terms of a simple case of two citizens and three options, and for the profile of citizens' preference orderings of the second category. Clearly, it also suffices to establish the logical completeness of the research program of the new welfare economics.

Since the proof of the recoverability theorem is slightly involved, it will be relegated to Section 26.5.

Some readers may be interested in knowing whether or not a stronger version of the recoverability property holds. Let $\Omega^*(X)$ be the set of all quasi orderings on X, and define the set $\Theta^*(\boldsymbol{R}^N, R)$ by

$$\Theta^*(\boldsymbol{R}^N, R) := \Omega^*(X) \cap \Theta(\boldsymbol{R}^N, R). \tag{26.6}$$

By construction, $Q \in \Theta^*(\boldsymbol{R}^N, R)$ holds if and only if (i) Q is a quasi ordering on X, (ii) Q is a strict extension of the Pareto quasi ordering $\rho(\boldsymbol{R}^N)$, and (iii) Q is a strict subrelation of R. Since it is clear that $\Theta^*(\boldsymbol{R}^N, R) \subseteq \Theta(\boldsymbol{R}^N, R)$ holds, we may assert that

$$\begin{aligned} \forall S \in \mathcal{S} : C(S) := G(S, R) &\subseteq \cap\, M(S, R) \text{ over all } Q \in \Theta(\boldsymbol{R}^N, R) \\ &\subseteq \cap\, M(S, R) \text{ over all } Q \in \Theta^*(\boldsymbol{R}^N, R) \end{aligned} \tag{26.7}$$

holds. Thus, if we could prove that the recoverability of $C(S)$ in terms of $\Theta^*(\boldsymbol{R}^N, R)$ holds, viz.,

$$\forall S \in \mathcal{S} : C(S) := G(S, R) = \cap\, M(S, Q) \text{ over all } Q \in \Theta^*(\boldsymbol{R}^N, R), \tag{26.8}$$

it would follow from (26.7) that the recoverability of $C(S)$ in terms of $\Theta(\boldsymbol{R}^N, R)$ must hold a fortiori. However, the recoverability property (26.8) is not true in general, as we can easily check in terms of Example 26.2 and Example 26.3 in Section 26.5. Plausible and desirable though it may look, the recoverability of Bergsonian social choice in terms of the maximization of each and every Paretian quasi ordering is a target that is unattainable in general.[7]

7. This is not to deny the possibility that some necessary and sufficient conditions can be identified for the recoverability property in terms of $\Theta^*(\boldsymbol{R}^N, R)$ to hold. For example, if the set of Pareto noncomparable pairs consists of only two pairs, we have succeeded in identifying the set of necessary and sufficient conditions for the recoverability property in terms of $\Theta^*(\boldsymbol{R}^N, R)$ to hold. Even in this simple case, however, the necessary and sufficient conditions in question are fairly complicated, and the proof of the recoverability property is rather involved.

26.5. Proof and Counterexamples

The purpose of Section 26.5 is two-fold. In Section 26.5.1, we provide a proof of the recoverability theorem. In Section 26.5.2, we show by examples that a plausible generalization of the recoverability theorem is in fact unsustainable.

26.5.1. Proof of the Recoverability Theorem

The "only if" part being obviously true, we have only to prove the "if" part of the recoverability theorem by reductio ad absurdum. Suppose to the contrary that there is an $S \in \mathcal{S}$ and an $x \in \cap\, M(S, Q)$ *over all* $Q \in \Theta(\boldsymbol{R}^N, R)$ such that $x \notin G(S, R)$, which means that

$$\exists z \in S : (z, x) \in P(R) \tag{26.9}$$

and

$$\forall Q \in \Theta(\boldsymbol{R}^N, R) : (z, x) \notin P(Q), \tag{26.10}$$

where use is made of the completeness of R. Thus

$$\forall Q \in \Theta(\boldsymbol{R}^N, R) : Q \subsetneq R \quad \text{and} \quad P(Q) \subsetneq P(R). \tag{26.11}$$

There are two cases to be considered.

Case 1. $Q^0 \cup \{(z, x)\} \subsetneq R$ for *some* $Q^0 \in \Theta(\boldsymbol{R}^N, R)$.

Case 2. $Q \cup \{(z, x)\} = R$ for *all* $Q \in \Theta(\boldsymbol{R}^N, R)$.

It should be clear that case 2 implies that $\Theta(\boldsymbol{R}^N, R)$ is in fact a singleton set, say, $\{Q^*\}$, where $Q^* \cup \{(z, x)\} = R$. However, it follows from the definition of $\Theta(\boldsymbol{R}^N, R)$ and assumption NT that there exist at least two distinct pairs, say, $\{a, b\}$ and $\{u, v\}$, such that, if we denote the relation between a and b (resp. u and v) in accordance with R by $(a * b)$ (resp. $(u * v)$), $Q^1 = \rho(\boldsymbol{R}^N) \cup \{(a * b)\}$ and $Q^2 = \rho(\boldsymbol{R}^N) \cup \{(u * v)\}$ must both belong to $\Theta(\boldsymbol{R}^N, R)$, which is a contradiction.

Consider now case 1 and define

$$Q^{**} = Q^0 \cup \{(z, x)\}. \tag{26.12}$$

Our task is to verify that $Q^{**} \in \Theta(\boldsymbol{R}^N, R)$. Since $Q^{**} \subsetneq R$ holds by definition, we have only to check that $\rho(\boldsymbol{R}^N) \in \Sigma(Q^{**})\backslash\{Q^{**}\}$ and $Q^{**} \in \Sigma(R)$. Note that $\rho(\boldsymbol{R}^N) \in \Sigma(Q^0)\backslash\{Q^0\}$ and (26.12) imply that $\rho(\boldsymbol{R}^N) \subseteq Q^0 \subsetneq Q^{**}$. To show that $P(\rho(\boldsymbol{R}^N)) \subseteq P(Q^{**})$, observe that $(a, b) \in P(Q^{**})$ if and only if either

$$(a, b) = (z, x), (b, a) \notin Q^0, \quad \text{and} \quad (b, a) \neq (z, x) \tag{26.13}$$

or

$$(a, b) \in P(Q^0), \quad \text{and} \quad (b, a) \neq (z, x) \tag{26.14}$$

holds, where use is made of (26.12). Suppose $(a, b) \in P(\rho(\boldsymbol{R}^N))$. It follows from $\rho(\boldsymbol{R}^N) \in \Sigma(Q^0)$ that $(a, b) \in P(Q^0)$, which implies that $(b, a) \notin Q^0$. If it happens to be the case that $(a, b) = (z, x)$, then $(b, a) = (x, z) \neq (z, x)$ holds, since otherwise $(a, b) = (x, z) \in P(Q^0) \subseteq P(R)$ in contradiction with $(z, x) \in P(R)$. Thus (26.13) must be the case, hence $(a, b) \in P(Q^{**})$ obtains. On the other hand, if $(a, b) \neq (z, x)$, then we cannot have $(b, a) = (z, x)$ since otherwise $(a, b) \in P(\rho(\boldsymbol{R}^N)) \subseteq P(Q^0)$ will have to imply $(x, z) \in P(Q^0) \subseteq P(R)$, a contradiction. Hence (26.14) must hold, so that $\rho(\boldsymbol{R}^N) \in \Sigma(Q^{**})\backslash\{Q^{**}\}$.

To verify that $Q^{**} \in \Sigma(R)$, note that $Q^0 \in \Sigma(R)$, $(z, x) \in P(R)$, and (26.12) imply $Q^{**} \subseteq R$. If $(a, b) \in P(Q^{**})$, either (26.13) or (26.14) holds. If (26.13) is the case, (26.9) implies that $(a, b) \in P(R)$. On the other hand, (26.14) and $Q^0 \in \Sigma(R)$ imply $(a, b) \in P(Q^0) \subseteq P(R)$. Thus $Q^{**} \in \Sigma(R)$ must be true.

We have thus shown that $Q^{**} \in \Theta(\boldsymbol{R}^N, R)$. However, since $(z, x) \in P(Q^{**})$ by definition, this contradicts (26.10) for this Q^{**}. Therefore, we obtain

$$\forall S \in \mathcal{S} : C(S) := G(S, R) \supseteq \cap\, M(S, Q) \quad \text{over all } Q \in \Theta(\boldsymbol{R}^N, R), \tag{26.15}$$

which completes the proof of (26.5) in view of (26.4). ∎

26.5.2. Counterexamples

Example 26.2. Let $S = X = \{x, y, z\}$, $N = \{1, 2\}$, and let a profile $\boldsymbol{R}^N = (R_1, R_2)$ of individual preference orderings be defined by $R_1 = \Delta(X) \cup \{(z, x), (x, y), (z, y)\}$ and $R_2 = \Delta(X) \cup \{(x, y), (y, z), (x, z)\}$. Clearly, the Pareto quasi ordering is given in this case by $\rho(\boldsymbol{R}^N) = \Delta(X) \cup \{(x, y)\}$. If a Paretian Bergson-Samuelson social welfare ordering R is specified by $R = \Delta(X) \cup \{(z, x), (x, y), (z, y)\}$, $\Theta(\boldsymbol{R}^N, R)$ consists of two relations Q^1 and Q^2 such that $Q^1 = \rho(\boldsymbol{R}^N) \cup \{(z, y)\}$ and $Q^2 = \rho(\boldsymbol{R}^N) \cup \{(z, x)\}$. It follows that we have $G(S, R) = \{z\} = M(S, Q^1) \cap M(S, Q^2)$, vindicating the recoverability theorem in terms of $\Theta(\boldsymbol{R}^N, R)$. Note, however, that $\Theta^*(\boldsymbol{R}^N, R)$ consists only of Q^1, because Q^2 will have to be expanded so as to include $\{(z, y)\}$ in order for it to satisfy the axiom of transitivity. However, doing this cannot but imply that the expanded Q^2 must coincide with R. Then we have $G(S, R) = \{z\} \subsetneq \{x, z\} = M(S, Q^1)$, so that the recoverability property does not hold in terms of $\Theta^*(\boldsymbol{R}^N, R)$.

Example 26.3. Let $S = X = \{x, y, z, w\}$, $N = \{1, 2\}$, and let a profile $\boldsymbol{R}^N = (R_1, R_2)$ of individual preference orderings be defined by $R_1 = \Delta(X) \cup \{(x, w), (w, y), (y, z), (x, y), (x, z), (w, z)\}$ and $R_2 = \Delta(X) \cup \{(w, x), (x, z), (z, y), (w, z), (w, y), (x, y)\}$. Clearly, the Pareto quasi ordering is given in this case by $\rho(\boldsymbol{R}^N) = \Delta(X) \cup \{(x, y), (w, y), (w, z)\}$. If a Paretian Bergson-Samuelson social welfare ordering R is specified by $R = \Delta(X) \cup \{(w, z), (z, x), (x, y), (w, x), (w, y), (z, y)\}$, $\Theta^*(\boldsymbol{R}^N, R)$ consists of the following three relations: Q^1, Q^2, and Q^3 such that $Q^1 = \rho(\boldsymbol{R}^N) \cup \{(w, x)\}$, $Q^2 = \rho(\boldsymbol{R}^N) \cup \{(z, y)\}$, and $Q^3 = \rho(\boldsymbol{R}^N) \cup \{(w, x), (z, y)\}$, so that $G(\{x, z\}, R) = \{z\} \subsetneq \{x, z\} = M(\{x, z\}, Q^1) \cap M(\{x, z\}, Q^2) \cap M(\{x, z\}, Q^3)$. Thus, the recoverability property does not hold in terms of $\Theta^*(\boldsymbol{R}^N, R)$.

26.6. Concluding Remarks

To assert the logical impeccability of the research program of the new welfare economics is one thing, and to assert the actual implementability of the logically impeccable program is quite another. This essay was mainly concerned with accomplishing the first task by establishing the recoverability of Pareto-compatible Bergsonian social choice through the maximization of Pareto-inclusive test relations. However, we could identify en route a condition to be satisfied by the eligible Pareto-inclusive test relations. The condition in question is the logical requirement of S-consistency, which was first introduced by Suzumura [25; 27, pp. 8–11], and it enables us to check whether or not various test relations proposed in the literature are capable of implementing the research program of the new welfare economics.

Take, for example, the hypothetical compensation principles proposed by Kaldor [12], Hicks [11], Scitovsky [19], and Samuelson [18]. The condition of S-consistency alone is sufficient to disqualify the Kaldor compensation principle, the Hicks compensation principle, and the Scitovsky compensation principle as workable guideposts for final rational social choice. Although the failure of these principles is well vindicated by Arrow [1, Chapter IV], Chipman and Moore [6], Graaff [8, Chapters IV and V], and Suzumura [26; 28; 29], among others, the essence of their failure can be neatly illustrated in Figure 26.1.[8] The three curves in this figure describe the utility possibility frontiers corresponding to three social states x, y, and z. According to each of the Kaldor, Hicks, and Scitovsky compensation principles, y is better than x, x is better than z, and z is better than y. Thus, these principles generate a test relation that is not acyclic, hence not S-consistent, so that these compensation principles are incapable of implementing the research program of the new welfare economics.

The verdict on the Samuelson compensation principle, which is defined in terms of a *uniform outward shift of the utility possibility frontiers*, is quite different. Indeed, the Samuelson principle can actually generate a test relation that is transitive, and hence S-consistent, but it fails to define a strict

8. The piecemeal welfare criteria à la Little [13; 14] and Mishan [16], which pay due attention to distributional equity considerations along with allocative efficiency considerations, can improve the logical score of the Kaldor-Hicks compensationist approach, but this progress is somewhat vacuous in the sense that the crucial value judgments on distributional equity are left completely unspecified. See Arrow [2, p. 927], according to whom "the hard problem . . . arises at the point where Little and everyone else stop. It is all very well to say that the effects of a proposed change on income distribution must be taken into account in deciding on the desirability of the change: but how do we describe a distribution of real income? Admittedly, the choice between two income distributions is the result of a value judgment; but how do we even formulate such judgment?" See also Chipman and Moore [6] and Suzumura [26; 29], among others, for critical examination of this line of thought.

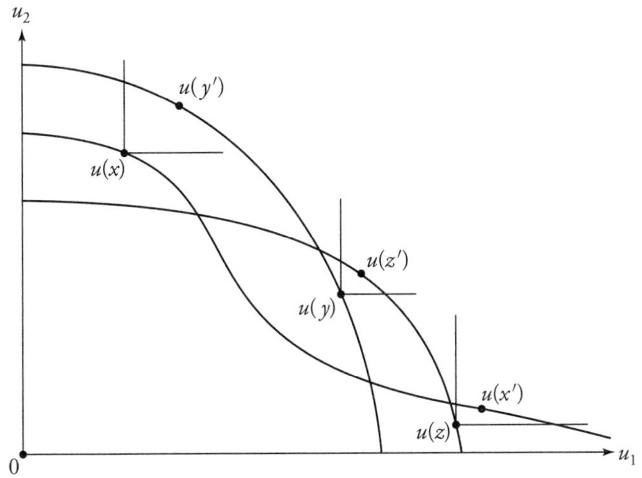

Figure 26.1. Inconsistency of the Kaldor, Hicks, and Scitovsky Compensation Principles. The curves drawn in this figure describe the utility possibility frontiers corresponding to various situations. Note that, according to each of the Kaldor, Hicks, and Scitovsky principles, y is better than x, z is better than y, but x is better than z.

extension of Pareto quasi ordering in general.[9] This failure is illustrated in Figure 26.2, which shows that the Samuelson compensation principle may generate a test relation that cannot be compatible with the Pareto principle.

How about many interesting proposals in the more recent literature, which tried to construct some relevant Pareto-inclusive quasi orderings? To cite just a few salient examples, the *grading principle of justice* à la Suppes [23] under the *axiom of identity* introduced by Sen [20, p. 156] or the *principle of acceptance* due to Harsanyi [10, p. 52], the *partial comparability approach* developed by Sen [21] and Fine [7], and some plausible quasi orderings introduced by Blackorby and Donaldson [4] immediately suggest themselves.[10] One may be led to think that an embarrassment of riches is a real possibility here, but a crucial problem still remains.[11] *All these proposed*

9. See also a recent work by Gravel [9], which shows how restrictive is the class of economies that are free from this logical difficulty of the Samuelson compensation principle.

10. See also Madden [15].

11. It should also be added that the recoverability of Bergsonian social choice in terms of the maximization of Pareto-inclusive quasi orderings does not hold in general.

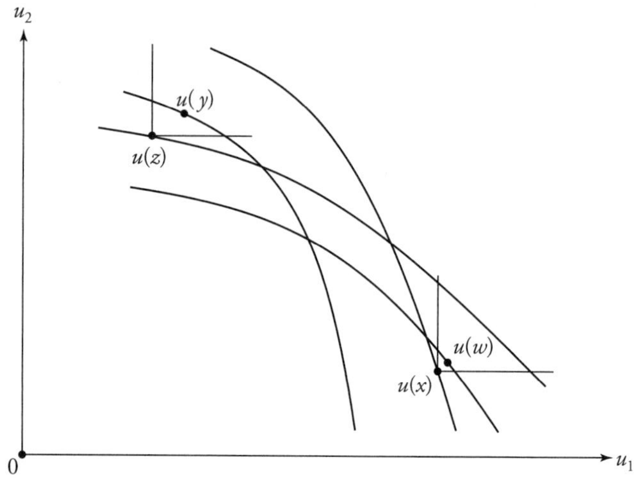

Figure 26.2. Incompatibility between the Pareto Principle and the Samuelson Compensation Principle. The curves drawn in this figure describe the utility possibility frontiers corresponding to various situations. If the Samuelson compensation principle is an extension of the Pareto principle, x is judged socially better than y, y is judged socially better than z, z is judged socially better than w, but w is judged socially better than x.

quasi orderings are based on interpersonal welfare comparisons in one form or the other. In this sense, they are not in fact in harmony with the informational basis of the new welfare economics.

It seems to us that defining the Pareto-inclusive test relations that can pass the crucial test of S-consistency without requiring anything beyond the informational basis characterized by *ordinalism* and *interpersonal noncomparability* is by no means an easy task.[12] This observation should not surprise anybody, however, as "nothing of much interest can be said on justice without bringing in some interpersonal comparability" (Sen [20, p. 150]).

12. In the same spirit, one referee posed an interesting question, which reads as follows: "It could be of interest to look at whether there are any criteria which utilise information similar to that used by compensation criteria (information about positions being compared and situations that can be reached through redistribution) that are both anonymous and satisfy the Pareto criterion. A negative answer would put the final nail into the 'new' welfare economics approach." This essay stops short of putting the final nail in the new welfare economics, but this suggestion is surely interesting to explore.

References

[1] Arrow, K., *Social Choice and Individual Values*, New York: Wiley, 1951; 2nd edn., 1963.

[2] Arrow, K., "Little's Critique of Welfare Economics," *American Economic Review* **41**, 1951, 923–934.

[3] Bergson, A., "A Reformulation of Certain Aspects of Welfare Economics," *Quarterly Journal of Economics* **52**, 1938, 310–334.

[4] Blackorby, C., and D. Donaldson, "Utility vs Equity: Some Quasi-Orderings," *Journal of Public Economics* **7**, 1977, 365–381.

[5] Chipman, J., and J. Moore, "The Compensation Principle in Welfare Economics," in A. Zarley, ed., *Papers in Quantitative Economics*, Vol. II, Lawrence: University of Kansas Press, 1971, 1–77.

[6] Chipman, J., and J. Moore, "The New Welfare Economics 1939–1974," *International Economic Review* **19**, 1978, 547–584.

[7] Fine, B., "A Note on 'Interpersonal Aggregation and Partial Compatibility,'" *Econometrica* **43**, 1975, 169–172.

[8] Graaff, J., *Theoretical Welfare Economics*, London: Cambridge University Press, 1957.

[9] Gravel, N., "On the Difficulty of Combining Actual and Potential Criteria for an Increase in Social Welfare," working paper, THEMA, Université de Cergy-Pontoise, 1997.

[10] Harsanyi, J., *Rational Behavior and Bargaining Equilibrium in Games and Social Situations*, Cambridge, UK: Cambridge University Press, 1977.

[11] Hicks, J., "The Valuation of the Social Income," *Economica* **7**, 1940, 105–124.

[12] Kaldor, N., "Welfare Propositions in Economics and Interpersonal Comparisons of Utility," *Economic Journal* **49**, 1939, 549–552.

[13] Little, I., *A Critique of Welfare Economics*, London: Oxford University Press, 1950; 2nd edn., 1957.

[14] Little, I., "Welfare Criteria, Distribution, and Cost-Benefit Analysis," in M. Boskin, ed., *Economics and Human Welfare*, New York: Academic Press, 1979, 125–131.

[15] Madden, P., "Suppes-Sen Dominance, Generalised Lorenz Dominance and the Welfare Economics of Competitive Equilibrium: Some Examples," *Journal of Public Economics* **61**, 1996, 247–262.

[16] Mishan, E., *Welfare Economics: An Assessment*, Amsterdam: North-Holland, 1969.

[17] Samuelson, P., *Foundations of Economic Analysis*, Cambridge, Mass.: Harvard University Press, 1947; enlarged edn., 1983.

[18] Samuelson, P., "Evaluation of Real National Income," *Oxford Economic Papers* **2**, 1950, 1–29.

[19] Scitovsky, T., "A Note on Welfare Proposition in Economics," *Review of Economic Studies* **9**, 1941, 77–88.

[20] Sen, A. K., *Collective Choice and Social Welfare*, San Francisco: Holden-Day, 1970; republished, Amsterdam: North-Holland, 1979.

[21] Sen, A. K., "Interpersonal Aggregation and Partial Comparability," *Econometrica* **38**, 1970, 393–409.

[22] Sen, A. K., "Maximization and the Act of Choice," *Econometrica* **65**, 1997, 745–779.

[23] Suppes, P., "Some Formal Models of Grading Principles," *Synthese* **16**, 1966, 284–306.

[24] Suzumura, K., "Rational Choice and Revealed Preference," *Review of Economic Studies* **43**, 1976, 149–158. Essay 1 of this volume.

[25] Suzumura, K., "Remarks on the Theory of Collective Choice," *Economica* **43**, 1976, 381–390. Essay 6 of this volume.

[26] Suzumura, K., "On Distributional Value Judgements and Piecemeal Welfare Criteria," *Economica* **47**, 1980, 125–139.

[27] Suzumura, K., *Rational Choice, Collective Decisions and Social Welfare*, New York: Cambridge University Press, 1983.

[28] Suzumura, K., "Social Welfare Function," in J. Eatwell, M. Milgate, and P. Newman, eds., *The New Palgrave: A Dictionary of Economics*, Vol. 4, London: Macmillan, 1987, 418–420.

[29] Suzumura, K., "Partial Welfare Judgements as Preliminaries for Rational Social Choice," discussion paper No. 437, Institute for Social and Economic Research, Osaka University, 1997.

[30] Szpilrajn, E., "Sur l'Extension de l'Ordre Partiel," *Fundamenta Mathematicae* **16**, 1930, 386–389.

ESSAY 27

Welfare Economics beyond Welfarist Consequentialism

Natural rights is simple nonsense: natural and imprescriptible rights, rhetorical nonsense—nonsense upon stilts.

—JEREMY BENTHAM, *Anarchical Fallacies* [3, p. 501]

Each person possesses an inviolability founded on justice that even the welfare of society as a whole cannot override.

—JOHN RAWLS, *A Theory of Justice* [24, p. 3]

Individuals have rights, and there are things no person or group may do to them (without violating their rights).

—ROBERT NOZICK, *Anarchy, State and Utopia* [20, p.ix]

27.1. Introduction

Welfare economics is a controversial subject, and its historical evolution is full of blind alleys and red herrings. Its "hallowed antiquity" (Schumpeter [31, p. 1069]) is surely respectable, but the standard history of this discipline

This is an abbreviated text of my presidential address delivered at the Japanese Economic Association held October 16–17, 1999, at the University of Tokyo. The full text was published in *Japanese Economic Review* **51**, 2000, 1–32. I am grateful to Kenneth Arrow, Rajat Deb, Allan Gibbard, Peter Hammond, Eric Maskin, Prasanta Pattanaik, Amartya Sen, Koichi Tadenuma, and John Weymark for their helpful comments and discussions over many years on this and related issues in welfare economics and social choice theory. An earlier draft was presented at the Economics and Human Values Workshop held at the Centre for Philosophy of Natural and Social Sciences, London School of Economics and Political Science.

almost surely begins with Arthur Pigou's monumental treatise, *The Economics of Welfare* [21]. Suffice it to observe that it was Pigou's path-breaking work that gave its name to this branch of economic analysis. As Hicks [16, p. 307] rightly observed, "if it existed before Pigou, it must . . . have been called something else." However, even the brief history of welfare economics after Pigou is full of many intricacies and perplexities.

One major perplexity is a huge gap between the passionate manifesto, with which Pigou [21] launched the old welfare economics, so-called, and the aloof remark, with which Mishan [18] commenced his survey of the new welfare economics, so-called, over the long period after Robbins's [23] criticism crushed the epistemological basis of Pigou's edifice. Pigou [21, p. vii] declared that "the complicated analyses which [welfare] economists endeavor to carry through are not mere gymnastic. They are instruments for the bettering of human life." This ardent declaration notwithstanding, Mishan [18, p. 197] began his survey of the new welfare economics over the period 1939–1959 with the following cool remark: "While it continues to fascinate many, welfare economics does not appear at any time to have wholly engaged the labors of any one economist. It is a subject which, apparently, one dabbles in for a while, leaves and, perhaps, returns to later in response to a troubled conscience." It is all too natural to ask why this huge cleavage evolved between the hot aspiration of the old welfare economics and the cool attitude of the new welfare economics over the brief but winding history of this intellectual discipline. In full awareness of this natural plea and capitalizing on the subsequent work on welfare economics and social choice theory, most notably by Arrow and Sen, this essay devotes itself to the reexamination of the logical foundations of the post-Pigovian welfare economics, old and new, with the purpose of finding several escape routes from the poverty of welfare economics.

27.2. Welfare Economics, Old and New

Pigou was a utilitarian, and his old welfare economics was based on the utilitarian concept of economic welfare. According to his famous definition, the *economic welfare* of a society is "that part of *social welfare* which can be brought directly or indirectly, into relation with the measuring-rod of money" (Pigou [21, p. 11]), which "consists in the balance of satisfaction from the use of the national dividend . . . over the dissatisfactions involved in the making of it" (Pigou [21 ,p. 85]). This definition presupposes that the satisfaction or welfare of different individuals can be added to, or subtracted from, one another. It was against this epistemological basis of Pigou's welfare economics that a harsh ordinalist criticism raged in the 1930s, beginning with Robbins [23], who forcefully negated the possibility of making *objective* interpersonal comparisons of welfare. However, a careful reading of Robbins [23, pp. 138–140, pp. 149–150; 24, pp. 636–637; 25, p. 5] reveals that he never negated the possibility of making *subjective* interpersonal comparisons of welfare, nor did he ever urge fellow economists to refrain from making subjective interpersonal comparisons of their own. His only assertion was that these subjective interpersonal comparisons cannot claim any interobserver validity.

By the end of the 1930s, if not earlier, it became widely accepted that "even if the satisfactions of a single individual were admitted to be measurable upon a cardinal scale . . . it would still be true that we should have no means of bringing the units of these scales into relation with one another. The satisfactions of different individuals are accordingly incapable of being added" (Hicks [16, p. 308]). Several attempts were made to fill in the conspicuous gap left wide open by the demolition of the utilitarian basis of the old welfare economics, and to salvage the wreckage of Pigou's research agenda by reformulating welfare economics on the informational basis of *ordinal* and *interpersonally noncomparable* welfare and nothing else. The salient concept of the Pareto principle that a change from a social state x to another social state y can be construed as socially good if at least one individual is made better off without making anyone else worse off came to the fore, and the characterization and implementation of Pareto-efficient allocation of resources became the central concern of the new welfare economics. However, since almost every economic policy favors some individuals at the cost of disfavoring others, there would be almost no situation of real significance where the Pareto principle could claim direct policy relevance. Something additional was clearly needed for the new welfare economics to contribute to the bettering of human life.

Two related but distinct avenues were explored to rectify this unsatisfactory state of the new welfare economics. The first avenue was the introduction of *hypothetical compensation criteria*. Kaldor [17], Hicks [15], Scitovsky [32], Samuelson [27], and others tried to expand the applicability of the Pareto principle by introducing hypothetical compensatory payments between gainers and losers from a policy change. According to the neat summary evaluation by Graaff [56, pp. 84–85], "the compensation tests all spring from a desire to see what can be said about social welfare . . . without making interpersonal comparisons of well-being. . . . They have a common origin in Pareto's definition of an increase in social welfare—that at least one man must be better off and no one worse off—but they are extended to situations in which some people are made worse off." The second avenue was the introduction of a *social welfare function* by Bergson [4] and Samuelson [26, Chapter VIII], who were firmly convinced that the economic analysis of the logical consequence of specified value judgments—irrespective of whose ethical beliefs they represent, whether or not they are widely held in the society, or how they are generated in the first place—is a legitimate task of welfare economics. The social welfare function was proposed as a theoretical device for characterizing such ethical beliefs about relative merits of alternative states of affairs. A *Paretian* social welfare function is one that judges in concordance with the Pareto principle when the latter has direct relevance. It was Arrow who crystallized the gist of this approach as follows: "[The] 'new welfare economics' says nothing about choices among Pareto-optimal alternatives. The purpose of the social welfare function was precisely to extend the unanimity quasi ordering to a full social ordering."

Graaff's and Arrow's insightful observations on the nature and significance of the new welfare economics help us examine the logical performance of the post-Pigovian welfare economics within a unified analytical framework. Capitalizing on Suzumura [45; 51], Essay 26 of this volume reiterates our verdict in this arena.[1]

---

1. Let us remind ourselves of the concept of *Pareto superiority* and the concept of *hypothetical compensation principles* due to Kaldor [17], Hicks [15], Scitovsky [34], and Samuelson [29].

Suppose that a policy change takes place and turns the *status quo ante* y into the *status quo post* x. We say that x is *Pareto superior* to y if all individuals judge x to be at least as good as y, and at least one individual judges x to be strictly better than y. This is the most basic concept of the new welfare economics, but there is almost no case of real importance where the Pareto superiority, by itself, can help us judge whether the policy change can be approved or not. Some device is called for in order to expand the applicability of Pareto superiority to the case where there are conflicts among individual judgments. As a deus ex machina, Kaldor and other "new" welfare economists take recourse to the hypothetical payment of compensation between gainers and losers from the policy change. Suppose that gainers (resp. losers) are able (resp. unable) to pay compensation to losers (resp. gainers) in such a way as to secure Pareto superiority of the

Let X and $N := \{1, 2, \ldots, n\}$ be the set of all social states and the set of all individuals in the society, where $3 \leq \#X$ and $2 \leq n < +\infty$. Given a profile of individual preference orderings $\boldsymbol{R}^N := (R_1, R_2, \ldots, R_n)$ on X, the *Pareto quasi ordering* $\rho(\boldsymbol{R}^N)$ is defined by $\rho(\boldsymbol{R}^N) := \cap R_i$ over all $i \in N$. Recollect that compensation criteria were introduced by the new welfare economics for the purpose of extending the applicability of the Pareto principle through hypothetical compensatory payments between gainers and losers. Let Q denote the binary relation representing the partial welfare judgments thus defined. Thus, the first task for this school is to ensure that Q is an *extension* of $\rho(\boldsymbol{R}^N)$, i.e., $\rho(\boldsymbol{R}^N)$ satisfies the following properties: (i) $\rho(\boldsymbol{R}^N) \subseteq Q$ and (ii) $P(\rho(\boldsymbol{R}^N)) \subseteq P(Q)$. By definition, any Q satisfying (i) and (ii) preserves all the information that the Pareto quasi ordering $\rho(\boldsymbol{R}^N)$ already contains, and goes possibly further. But this is only half of the full mission. The mission will be left unaccomplished if this preliminary step logically precludes the possibility of final rational social choice. For the success of this school, therefore, it is necessary that Q is compatible with at least one Paretian Bergson-Samuelson social welfare ordering (BS-SWO) R, i.e., Q must satisfy the following properties: (iii) $Q \subseteq R$ and (iv) $P(Q) \subseteq P(R)$. Thus, the research program of the new welfare economics may be boiled down to that of devising a principle of hypothetical compensation between gainers and losers so as to generate partial welfare judgments Q satisfying (i), (ii), (iii), and (iv) for some Paretian BS-SWO R.

---

policy-plus-compensation-induced state x^* (resp. no-policy-plus-compensation-induced state y^*) to be Pareto superior to the status quo ante y (resp. status quo post x). Then the status quo post x (resp. the status quo ante y) is called Kaldor (resp. Hicks) superior to the status quo ante y (resp. the status quo post x). An unfortunate fact is that both Kaldor superiority and Hicks superiority are not logically flawless. To save the day, Scitovsky introduced what came to be called the Scitovsky double test, according to which the status quo post x is Scitovsky superior to the status quo ante y if x is Kaldor superior to y, and that y is *not* Hicks superior to x. There is an insidious feature that commonly underlies Kaldor superiority, Hicks superiority, and Scitovsky superiority. These criteria use the utility distribution at the status quo ante and the status quo post as special standards of reference, paying no attention to the utility distribution at any other social state. It is in view of this lop-sided treatment of social states that Samuelson introduced a compensation principle of his own. The status quo post x is Samuelson superior to the status quo ante y if the utility possibility frontier passing through x lies uniformly above the utility possibility frontier passing through y.

More detailed analytical treatment of these hypothetical compensation principles can be found in Suzumura [47].

In fact, Q must satisfy $\rho(\boldsymbol{R}^N) \subsetneq Q$ and $Q \subsetneq R$. To see why, we have only to observe that a Q such that $Q = \rho(\boldsymbol{R}^N)$ (resp. $Q = R$) does not go beyond $\rho(\boldsymbol{R}^N)$ at all (resp. is not a preliminary step toward R). With this observation in mind, let $\Theta(\boldsymbol{R}^N, R)$ be the set of all eligible partial welfare judgments Q satisfying (i*) $\rho(\boldsymbol{R}^N) \subsetneq Q$, (ii) $P(\rho(\boldsymbol{R}^N)) \subseteq P(Q)$, (iii*) $Q \subsetneq R$, and (iv) $P(Q) \subseteq P(R)$.

In Essay 26 of this volume, which is based on Suzumura [53], the following negative verdicts are vindicated on the performance of the new welfare economics based on the hypothetical compensation principles.

(a) Among the well-known hypothetical compensation principles of historical importance, the Kaldor principle, the Hicks principle, and the Scitovsky principle are all disqualified as workable preliminary steps toward final rational social choice. The crucial reason for their failures lies in the fact that the preliminary welfare judgments generated by these principles fail to be Suzumura-consistent in general.

(b) The logical fate of the Samuelson compensation principle is different, but it fares no better than the Kaldor principle, the Hicks principle, and the Scitovsky principle. In contrast, the Samuelson principle always generates transitive, hence Suzumura-consistent, preliminary welfare judgments, but it fails to guarantee that these preliminary welfare judgments are capable of extending the Pareto quasi ordering.

Putting all these pieces together, we are now in a position to take stock and summarize the fate of the old welfare economics and the new welfare economics of the compensationist school. The old welfare economics of Pigou failed to elicit general support from economists because of its unwarranted—"unscientific"—informational basis, which is utilitarian in nature. The new welfare economics of the compensationist school, which endeavored to do without cardinality and interpersonal comparability of utilities or welfare, also failed to provide a consistent analytical framework. Indeed, the short history of the new welfare economics of the compensationist school is full of episodes in which the demolition activity took over immediately after the scaffold for the proposed new foundation was removed. It seems to us that the widely held apathy and cynicism toward welfare economics in general, and the new welfare economics in particular, have much to do with this Sisyphean labor expended by the compensationist school of the new welfare economics.

27.3. Arrovian Social Choice Theory and Welfarist Consequentialism

Recollect that the central task of the compensationist school of the new welfare economics was to generate preliminary social welfare judgments, which are capable of being extended to rational social choice, by means of the hypothetical payment of compensation between gainers and losers from a policy change. In contrast, the new welfare economics of the Bergson-Samuelson school was based on the concept of social welfare function, which is to be given from outside of economics. Recollect that the *Bergson-Samuelson social welfare function* (BS-SWF) u is nothing other than an order-preserving numerical representation of the *Bergson-Samuelson social welfare ordering* (BS-SWO) R such that, for all social states x and y, $u(x) \geq u(y)$ if and only if xRy. Since there is no general guarantee for the existence of a BS-SWF u corresponding to a BS-SWO R, the following discussion will be focused on the more basic concept of BS-SWOs rather than BS-SWFs.

To the extent that we focus our attention on the *Pareto-compatible* BS-SWO R, there is a constraint on the shape of R such that, for any profile $\boldsymbol{R}^N = (R_1, R_2, \ldots, R_n)$ of individual preference orderings, R must be an ordering extension of $\rho(\boldsymbol{R}^N) := \cap_{i \in N} R_i$. For Bergson and Samuelson, except for this Pareto-compatibility constraint, there is no other constraint to be imposed on the shape of BS-SWOs. In particular, there is no concern about the process or rule for generating a BS-SWO corresponding to the given profile $\boldsymbol{R}^N$. This point was made most explicitly by Samuelson [28, p. 221]: "Without inquiring into its origins, we take as a starting point for our discussion a function of all the economic magnitudes of a system which is supposed to characterize some ethical belief—that of a benevolent despot, or a complete egoist, or 'all men of good will,' a misanthrope, the state, race, or group mind, God, etc. Any possible opinion is admissible, including my own. . . . We only require that the belief be such as to admit of an unequivocal answer to whether one configuration of the economic system is 'better' or 'worse' than any other or 'indifferent,' and that these relationships are transitive." This is where Arrow parted from the new welfare economics of the Bergson-Samuelson school.

Contrary to Samuelson's bold declaration, Arrow [1; 2] believes that the aggregation process or rule f, through which a BS-SWO R is associated with the specified profile $\boldsymbol{R}^N$, viz., $R = f(\boldsymbol{R}^N)$, should be a legitimate analytical target of normative economics. Since Arrow's major theorem on the existence of a proper process or rule f is prima facie negative, many notable economists supporting the new welfare economics of the Bergson-Samuelson school denied strenuously the relevance of Arrow's general impossibility theorem, so-called, to welfare economics. Suffice it to quote the following passage from Samuelson [30, p. 42]: "the Arrow result is much more a contribution to the infant discipline of mathematical politics than to the traditional mathematical theory of welfare economics. I export Arrow from economics to politics because I do not believe that he has proved the impossibility of the traditional Bergson welfare function of economics."[2]

Samuelson's strong refutation notwithstanding, I firmly remain convinced that the problem identified by Arrow, viz., the inquiry into the nature and existence of the process or rule for amalgamating individual preference orderings into a social welfare ordering, is a legitimate task of normative economics. My belief to this effect is partly based on Arrow's [1, p. 108] observation that "one can hardly think of a less interesting question about [his] theorem than whether it falls on one side or another of an arbitrary boundary separating intellectual provinces."

Arrow christened the preference aggregation process or rule the "social welfare function." In order to prevent an inessential confusion with the related, but distinct, concept of the Bergson-Samuelson social welfare function, we will call Arrow's concept of preference aggregation process or rule the *Arrow social welfare function* (ASWF) in the rest of this essay. Given an ASWF f and any profile $\boldsymbol{R}^N$ of individual preference orderings, a BS-SWO R is determined by $R = f(\boldsymbol{R}^N)$. A BS-SWF u, if one exists, is nothing other than an order-preserving numerical representation of R.

Arrow's analysis of the class of ASWFs starts from the recognition that there is no meaning, which is relevant to social welfare judgments, in the measurability of individual utilities. The reason for this conviction can be traced back to "Leibniz's principle of the identity of indiscernibles," according to which "only observed difference can be used as a basis for explanation" (Arrow [1, p. 109]). In other words, it is because interpersonal comparisons of utilities are not based on any observable choice behavior that

2. See also Samuelson [31, p. 228] and Chipman [5, pp. 172–175].

the ASWF is made dependent only upon the interpersonally noncomparable individual preference orderings over the set of social states.

In addition to the requirement of an ordinal and interpersonally noncomparable informational basis, Arrow imposes (i) the condition of *unrestricted domain* on the class of ASWFs; (ii) a crucial condition, which he calls the *independence of irrelevant alternatives*;[3] (iii) the *Pareto principle* inherited from the new welfare economics; and (iv) the uncontroversial condition of *nondictatorship*. The culmination of his pioneering analysis was the justly famous *general impossibility theorem*, which states that there exists no Arrow social welfare function satisfying all four of his conditions. The appendix to this essay presents a simple backward induction proof of Arrow's theorem. Putting aside all technical details, let us here focus on the restrictive nature of Arrow's informational basis.

There is a sense in which Arrow's social choice theory may be construed as a lineal descendant of the Bentham-Pigou utilitarian tradition. Although Arrow dissociated himself from the cardinality and interpersonal comparability of utilities or welfare, he succeeded the utilitarian philosophy of basing social welfare judgments on the profile of individual utilities or welfare. This crucial remnant of utilitarian moral philosophy may be christened *welfarist consequentialism,* or *welfarism* for short. It boils down to the claim that the social judgments on right or wrong actions should be based on the assessment of their consequential states of affairs, where the assessment of consequences is exclusively in terms of people's welfare, their preference satisfaction, or people receiving what they want. Not only is Arrow's theory based on welfarism in this sense, but it also permeates almost the entire edifice of traditional welfare economics, old' as well as new, and contemporary social choice theory. It is this informational basis that, we contend, is to be held mainly responsible for the poverty of welfare economics.

3. This condition requires the following: if two profiles $\boldsymbol{R}^1$ and $\boldsymbol{R}^2$ coincide on a pair of social states $\{x, y\}$, then the social orderings R^1 and R^2 that correspond to $\boldsymbol{R}^1$ and $\boldsymbol{R}^2$, respectively, must also coincide on $\{x, y\}$. This can be construed as requiring the *informational efficiency* of the ASWF. Indeed, if the ASWF fails to satisfy this requirement, the society should gather information beyond individuals' opinions over the pair $\{x, y\}$ in determining whether x is socially better than y, or y is socially at least as good as x, with a result of inflating the gathering and processing cost of information much higher than otherwise.

27.4. What Is Wrong with Welfarist Consequentialism?

The use of the welfaristic informational basis has been so preponderant in the wide research areas of welfare economics, and the services thereby rendered have been so weighty, that we should be carefully on guard if we want to go against its ubiquitous use in normative economics. In this section, we would like to refer to the two major types of criticism on the use of the welfaristic informational basis.

The first type of criticism can be called *case implications criticism*. A major example thereof focuses on the phenomenon called *adaptive preference formation*. According to Elster [9, p. 25], "the adjustment of wants to possibilities—not the deliberate adaptation favoured by character planners, but a causal process occurring non-consciously"—cannot but undermine the credibility of welfarism as the informational basis of evaluations of, and judgments on, social justice and social welfare, because "behind this adaptation there is the drive to reduce the tension or frustration that one feels in having wants that one cannot possibly satisfy." To bring this point unambiguously home, let us cite another passage from Sen [41, pp. 21–22], which carries the same basic message: "Considerations of 'feasibility' and of 'practical possibility' enter into what we dare to desire and what we are pained not to get. Our mental reactions to what we actually get and what we can sensibly expect to get may frequently involve compromises with a harsh reality. The destitute thrown into beggary, the vulnerable landless laborer precariously surviving at the edge of subsistence, the overworked domestic servant working round the clock, the subdued and subjugated housewife reconciled to her role and her fate, all tend to come to terms with their respective predicaments. The deprivations are suppressed and muffled in the scale of utilities (reflected by desire-fulfillment and happiness) by the necessity of endurance in uneventful survival."

The second type of criticism may be called the *conflicting principles criticism*. Instead of exemplifying the problematic nature of welfarism by identifying some concrete contexts where it brings about intuitively repugnant conclusions, this criticism reveals that a basic value, which is deeply rooted in welfarism, cannot but conflict with another important value, which goes squarely against welfarism. Sen's [35, Chapter 6*; 36; 37; 42] justly famous *impossibility of a Paretian liberal* was presented as a criticism against welfarism in this spirit. To be precise, Sen exposed a serious logical conflict between the mild libertarian claim of individual rights, which is a basic nonwelfaristic value, and the welfaristic value of social efficiency in the form of the Pareto principle, by proving the nonexistence of the preference amalgamation process or rule that simultaneously satisfies these two essential values. To the extent that Sen's libertarian claim of individual rights is found appealing as a basic nonwelfaristic value, we are led to go against the unexceptional acceptance of the Pareto principle, which is arguably the most fundamental welfaristic value. Although many critics cast doubt on the legitimacy of the way Sen articulated libertarian rights, it seems fair to say that Sen's criticism against welfarism survives without losing its importance even if his articulation of libertarian rights is replaced by the allegedly more appropriate articulation in terms of *normal game forms,* as in Gaertner, Pattanaik, and Suzumura [12] and Sugden [45], or *games in effectivity function forms,* as in Deb [6], Deb, Pattanaik, and Razzolini [7], Gärdenfors [13], and Peleg [22].[4]

Dissatisfaction with welfarism was also forcefully voiced by Rawls [24], Dworkin [8], and Sen [35; 36; 39; 40; 41; 43], who urged that we should purge welfarism from its traditional status of the informational basis of normative analysis and replace it with some objective measures of individual advantages. Among these proposed alternative measures, Rawls's *social primary goods* and Dworkin's *resources* met harsh criticism from Sen [39; 41] to the effect that they focus on the means, rather than the ends, for the enhancement of an individual's well-being. As was pointed out by Sen, focusing on means is tantamount to committing a materialist mistake.

4. Jeremy Bentham was strongly against the idea of natural rights, as it goes squarely against the very foundations of utilitarianism. It is all the more interesting that Pigou [23, p. 759] had made an early use of the nonwelfaristic notion of individual rights when he discussed people's claim rights to "a minimum standard of real income," which "must be conceived, not as a subjective minimum of satisfaction, but as an objective minimum of conditions." His characterization of "an objective minimum of conditions" is in fact close to what we now call "basic needs," which consist of "some defined quantity and quality of house accommodation, of medical care, of education, of food, of leisure, of the apparatus of sanitary convenience and safety where work is carried on." Pigou must have had a firm belief that such rights could be justified on utilitarian grounds in the Benthamite tradition of regarding rights as intrinsically nonimportant but instrumentally essential. Unfortunately, *The Economics of Welfare* is completely reticent about the utilitarian justification of these rights. Thus, we cannot be sure how central was the consideration of individual rights in Pigou's old welfare economics. I owe this observation to Sen's remark in Gaertner and Pattanaik [11, p. 74].

To escape from the subjectivist mistake of welfarism,[5] as well as from the materialist mistake of Rawls and Dworkin, and to gear more directly with individual advantages per se, Sen proposed that we should focus on what he christened *functionings*: "A functioning is an achievement of a person: what he or she manages to do or to be. . . . [It] is . . . different both from (1) having goods (and the corresponding characteristics), to which it is posterior, and (2) having utility (in the form of happiness resulting from that functioning), to which it is . . . prior" (Sen [41, pp. 10–11]). The *capability* of a person is defined as the set of functioning vectors from which the person is capable of choosing. Thus, Sen's concepts of functionings and capabilities provide us with a vehicle by means of which we can examine the performance of alternative economic systems with the focus on individuals' opportunities to realize the life they value on deliberation.

Note, however, that Sen's space of normative analysis, i.e., the space of functionings, is no more than an alternative space of consequences. Indeed, the capability of a person is a measure of the consequential performance of an economic system in the form of an opportunity it enables him/her to pursue in the space of functionings. The fact that this measure is free from the subjectivist mistake of welfarism, as well as from the materialist mistake of Rawls and Dworkin, does not at all change the fact that Sen is still working within the boundary of *consequentialism*. Should we acquiesce in the consequentialist informational basis enriched by Sen's capability approach, or should we go even beyond consequentialism?

27.5. Preference for Opportunities

The question posed at the end of Section 26.4 may be rephrased as follows: *Is there any reason why we should go even beyond consequentialism as such?* As a matter of fact, there seem to be many reasons to explore the terrain beyond consequentialism pure and simple. A particularly illuminating discussion by Sen is worth citing in this context: "A well-established tradition in economics suggests that the real value of a set of options lies in the best use that can

---

5. Note that utilities are simply the subjective vindication of individual advantages, rather than the objective and interpersonally commensurable measure thereof. In this sense, to focus exclusively on individual utilities, as welfarism does, may well commit a subjectivist mistake.

be made of them, and . . . the use that is *actually* made. The valuation of the opportunity, then, lies in the value of one element of it (to wit, the best option or the actually chosen option). . . . On the other hand . . . the value of a set need not invariably be identified with the value of the best—or the chosen—element of it. Importance can also be attached to having opportunities that are *not* taken up. This is a natural direction to go in if the *process* through which outcomes are generated is of a significance of its own. Indeed, 'choosing' itself can be seen as a valuable functioning, and having an **x** when there is no alternative may be sensibly distinguished from choosing **x** when substantial alternatives exist" (Sen [44, pp. 201–202]).

A simple framework, which allows us to capture the *intrinsic value* of the opportunity for choice vis-à-vis the *instrumental value* thereof, may be given as follows. The key concept is the *extended preference ordering* $\succsim$ on $X \times \mathcal{S}$, where X is the set of all conventionally defined outcomes and $\mathcal{S}$ is the family of nonempty subsets of X. The intended interpretation of $(x, S) \in X \times \mathcal{S}$ is that an outcome x is chosen from the opportunity set S. For any $(x, S), (y, T) \in X \times \mathcal{S}$, $(x, S) \succsim (y, T)$ means that choosing x from S is at least as good as choosing y from T from the viewpoint of the decision-making agent. The strict preference relation and indifference relation corresponding to $\succsim$ are $\succ$ and $\sim$, respectively. Let Ω stand for the subset of $X \times S$ such that $(x, S) \in \Omega$ holds if and only if $x \in S$. This simple framework allows us to capture the intuitive concept of the intrinsic value of the opportunity for choice as follows: The decision maker recognizes the intrinsic value of the opportunity for choice if he/she prefers choosing x from S to choosing x from $\{x\}$, where $\{x\} \subsetneq S$, viz., $(x, S) \succ (x, \{x\})$.

By means of this simple framework, Suzumura and Xu [52, Essay 18 of this volume] introduced the definition of the concept of a *consequentialist* and that of a *nonconsequentialist*, and presented their axiomatic characterizations. Suzumura and Xu [53, Essay 20 of this volume] went further and explored the theoretical implication of the existence of at least one nonconsequentialist in the society in the context of Arrovian impossibility theorems. The essence of their work may be briefly stated as follows.

Let there be n individuals in the society, where $2 \leq n < +\infty$. Each individual $i \in N := \{1, 2, \ldots, n\}$ has an extended preference ordering $\succsim_i$ on Ω, together forming a profile $\succsim = (\succsim_1, \succsim_2, \ldots, \succsim_n)$ of individual extended preference orderings. An individual $i \in N$ is an *extreme consequentialist* if, for all $(x, S), (x, T) \in \Omega$, $(x, S) \sim_i (x, T)$ holds, whereas i is a *strong consequentialist* if, for all $(x, S), (y, T) \in \Omega$, the following two properties are satisfied:

(SC_1). If $(x, \{x\}) \succ_i (y, \{y\})$, then $(x, S) \succ_i (y, T)$ holds.

(SC_2). If $(x, \{x\}) \sim_i (y, \{y\})$, then $(x, S) \succsim_i (y, T)$ holds if and only if $\#S \geq \#T$.

Thus, an extreme consequentialist is one who ranks two extended alternatives (x, S) and (x, T) simply in terms of their consequences, paying no attention to opportunity sets from which these consequences are chosen. In contrast, a strong consequentialist ranks two extended alternatives (x, S) and (y, T) in complete accordance with their consequences x and y only if he/she happens to have a strict preference between $(x, \{x\})$ and $(y, \{y\})$. If he/she is indifferent between $(x, \{x\})$ and $(y, \{y\})$, his/her ranking of (x, S) vis-à-vis (y, T) is in accordance with the cardinality comparison between two opportunity sets S and T. It is to this limited extent that a strong consequentialist reveals his/her preference for the richness of opportunities behind his/her final choice.

Going to the other extreme, an individual $i \in N$ is an *extreme nonconsequentialist* if, for all $(x, S), (y, T) \in \Omega$, $(x, S) \succsim_i (y, T)$ if and only if $\#S \geq \#T$, whereas i is a *strong nonconsequentialist* if, for all $(x, S), (y, T) \in \Omega$, the following two properties are satisfied:

(SNC_1). If $\#S > \#T$, then $(x, S) \succ_i (y, T)$ holds.

(SNC_2). If $\#S = \#T$, then $(x, S) \succsim_i (y, T)$ holds if and only if $(x, x) \succsim_i (y, \{y\})$.

Thus, an extreme nonconsequentialist is one who does not care about consequences at all, and what he/she values is the richness of opportunities behind the chosen alternatives. A strong nonconsequentialist also does not care about consequences as long as two opportunity sets are strictly ranked in terms of the richness of opportunities. It is only when the richness of opportunities does not make a difference between two choice situations that his/her ranking faithfully reflects his/her preference between consequences.

Suzumura and Xu [54, Essay 18 of this volume] presented the characterization of the concepts of extreme and strong consequentialists and of extreme and strong nonconsequentialists. These clarifications are surely not without interest, but the real test to be imposed on this line of research is the impact it may exert on the preceding results that are derived on the implicit assumption that all individuals involved are consequentialists. As a partial answer to this challenging test, Suzumura and Xu [55, Essay 20 of this volume] applied the conceptual framework of consequentialism and nonconsequentialism to the Arrovian social choice theory. Exact technicalities aside, the results of their analysis may be summarized as follows:

(a) If all individuals in the society are extreme consequentialists, then there exists no extended social welfare function that satisfies the essentially Arrovian set of axioms.
(b) If there exists at least one extreme consequentialist and at least one strong consequentialist in the society, then there exists an extended social welfare function satisfying the essentially Arrovian set of axioms.
(c) If all individuals in the society are strong consequentialists, then there exists no extended social welfare function that satisfies the essentially Arrovian set of axioms.
(d) If there exists at least one strong nonconsequentialist in the society, then there exists an extended social welfare function satisfying the essentially Arrovian set of axioms.

According to these results, the similarity of attitudes among individuals in the sense that either all individuals are extreme consequentialists or all individuals are strong consequentialists strenuously brings back the Arrovian impossibility theorem even in this extended analytical framework. The impossibility result disappears, however, if either there exist an extreme consequentialist and a strong consequentialist simultaneously or there exists at least one strong nonconsequentialist.

Our analysis has shown that (i) there is a reason, which is rooted in individuals' intrinsic preference for the opportunity for choice, to go beyond consequentialism as such; (ii) the extended analytical framework allows us to give precise definitions of, and a concise axiomatization to, consequentialism vis-à-vis nonconsequentialism; and (iii) the existence of an Arrovian social welfare function may be secured if the society is heterogeneous to the extent that an extreme consequentialist and a strong consequentialist exist side by side or there exists at least one strong nonconsequentialist.

It is our modest hope that the exploration of nonconsequentialism along with consequentialism may be one avenue to be attempted in the future as a possible escape route from the poverty of welfare economics.

27.6. Consequences and Procedures

There is another case against the commitment to consequentialism even when the description of consequential outcomes is richly expanded. The point of departure of this argument is an ingenious passage from Arrow's *Social Choice and Individual Values* (Arrow [1, pp. 89–91]), which reads as follows: "Among the variables which taken together define the social state, one is the very process by which the society makes its choice. This is especially important if the mechanism of choice itself has a value to the individuals in the society. For example, an individual may have a positive preference for achieving a given distribution through the free market mechanism over achieving the same distribution through rationing by the government. If the decision process is interpreted broadly to include the whole socio-psychological climate in which social decisions are made, the reality and importance of such preferences, as opposed to preferences about the distributions of goods, are obvious."

To crystallize the reason why we believe that Arrow's argument goes against the narrow informational basis of consequentialism, let X be the set of conventionally defined social states and $\mathcal{M}$ be the set of all social decision-making mechanisms. To lend concreteness to our argument, let any $\mu \in \mathcal{M}$ be the *game form* $(N, \{\Sigma_i\}_{i=1}^n, g)$, where $N = \{1, 2, \ldots, n\} (2 \leq n < +\infty)$ is the set of all individuals in the society, Σ_i is the set of all *strategies* of $i \in N$, and g is the *outcome function* that sends each strategy profile $\sigma \in \times_{i=1}^n \Sigma_i$ to a conventionally defined social outcome $g(\sigma) \in X$. The crucial question to be answered is whether this expanded framework of analysis can be neatly articulated by the traditional analytical framework by means of the expanded definition of social states, viz., by treating the pairs (x, μ), (x^*, μ^*) and the like as the primitive concept of expanded social choice theory. For each $i \in N$, let R_i be the individual preference ordering on X, together forming the profile of individual preference ordering $\boldsymbol{R}^N = (R_1, R_2, \ldots, R_n)$. If $\mathcal{E}$ denotes the equilibrium concept prevailing in the society, the set of equilibrium outcomes of the game $(\mu, \boldsymbol{R}^N)$ is denoted by $g(\mathcal{E}(\mu, \boldsymbol{R}^N))$. Our contention is that we cannot accommodate the procedural considerations within the conventional analytical framework simply by expanding the description of consequences. To substantiate this assertion, we have only to examine the simple concept of *feasibility* of social outcomes. In the traditional framework, a consequential outcome x is feasible if and only if $x \in S$ holds, where $S \subseteq X$ stands for the set of conventionally defined feasible outcomes. In the expanded framework, an expanded outcome (x, μ) is feasible if and only if $x \in g(\mathcal{E}(\mu, \boldsymbol{R}^N))$ holds. In other words, just to see if an expanded outcome (x, μ) is feasible, we need the specification of the profile $\boldsymbol{R}^N$ of individual preference orderings and the equilibrium concept $\mathcal{E}$ prevailing in the society. Thus, the expanded concept of social choice requires the development of a novel theory of social choice.

To show that the expanded theory cannot be accommodated in the conventional theory is one thing, and to show that the novel theory has a raison d'être of its own is a different thing altogether. In this context, it may be worthwhile to recall the classical concept of *procedural justice*. Note that there are two contrasting approaches to the theory of fairness. The first approach presupposes an explicit *outcome morality*, which enables us to identify fair outcomes in the space of consequences. The concept of fair decision-making procedures is nothing other than a derivative of the concept of fair outcomes. This approach embodies the viewpoint of *perfect procedural justice* in the terminology of Rawls [24, pp. 85], which bestows on procedures only the instrumental value. In other words, the fairness of consequential outcomes is given logical priority over the fairness of decision-making procedures. In contrast, the second approach reverses the sequence of inference altogether, and construes a consequential outcome to be fair if it is brought about via the application of a fair decision-making procedure. This approach embodies the viewpoint of *pure procedural justice* in the terminology of Rawls [24, pp. 85–86], which bestows on procedures an intrinsic value of their own. In other words, the fairness of decision-making procedures is given logical priority over the fairness of consequential outcomes.

The viewpoint of perfect procedural justice associated with outcome morality such as Pareto efficiency and the no-envy concept of fairness has been dominant in the theory of welfare economics. The theory of welfare economics and social choice theory, which is based on the viewpoint of pure procedural justice, is much less developed up till now, but the relevance of this approach seems to be high in the context of fair conferment of individual rights, as well as in the context of taxation, competition, and welfare state policies. *Hic Rhodus, hic salta.*

27.7. Concluding Remarks

Instead of summarizing this long and contentious discussion issue by issue, I shall briefly recapitulate its central message. I have tried to identify the main culprit of the poverty of welfare economics, and have suggested that the informational basis of mainline welfare economics and social choice theory, viz., welfarist consequentialism, seems to be largely responsible for the present state of welfare economics. Even if people happen to agree that it is the informational parsimony of welfarist consequentialism that is to be blamed, however, they may disagree as to whether we should remain within the boundary of consequentialism if the description of consequences is substantially enriched beyond welfarism, or whether we should even go beyond consequentialism as such. I have contended that there exist at least two reasons, one based on the intrinsic value of the opportunity to choose and the other on the intrinsic value of the procedure for social choice, that seem to motivate us to go not only beyond welfarist consequentialism but also beyond consequentialism as such. Analytical frameworks were developed with the purpose of exploring the prospect of going beyond consequentialism, and the use and usefulness of such analytical frameworks were briefly exemplified in terms of some concrete economic analyses.

I am keenly aware that the analyses I have pursued in this and background essays are nothing more than the first few steps toward a fully fledged analytical framework that goes beyond consequentialism. Much depends on what these suggested avenues bring out in the future, especially in the applied arena with strong policy relevance. The modest purpose of this essay would be served if I were successful in calling readers' attention to this ongoing research program in pursuit of instruments for the bettering of human life.

Appendix 27.A. A Backward Inductive Proof of Arrow's Theorem

To improve the accessibility of the central theorem in social choice theory, viz., Arrow's general impossibility theorem, a short and self-contained proof will be given along the following scenario. It is shown that there should be an Arrovian social welfare function (SWF) for a society with $n - 1$ members, where $3 \leq n < +\infty$, if there is an Arrovian SWF for a society with n

members. By the repeated use of this property, it is assured that there is an Arrovian SWF for a society with 2 members if there is an Arrovian SWF for a society with 3 members. It is then shown that there exists no Arrovian SWF for a society with 2 members; hence there exists no Arrovian SWF for any society with any finite number of members.[6]

To facilitate our proof, let $I(n) := \{1, 2, \ldots, n\}$ be the set of individuals in the n-person society, where $2 \leq n < +\infty$. As in the main text, X denotes the set of all social states, where $3 \leq \#X$. A profile of individual preference orderings is denoted by $a = (R_1^a, R_2^a, \ldots, R_n^a)$, $b = (R_1^b, R_2^b, \ldots, R_n^b)$, and so on, and the set of all logically possible profiles will be denoted by A_n. An SWF for an n-person society is a function f_n, which maps each profile $a \in A_n$ into a social preference ordering $R^a = f_n(a)$. An SWF is *Arrovian* if it satisfies the following three axioms:

PARETO. For any $a \in A_n$ and any $x, y \in X$, if $x P_i^a y$ for all $i \in I(n)$, then $x P^a y$, where P_i^a is the strict preference corresponding to R_i^a, and P^a is the strict preference corresponding to $R^a = f_n(a)$.

INDEPENDENCE. If two profiles $a, b \in A_n$ coincide on $\{x, y\} \subseteq X$, then $R^a = f_n(a)$ and $R^b = f_n(b)$ coincide on $\{x, y\}$.

NON-DICTATORSHIP. There is no dictator for f_n, i.e., there exists no $d \in I(n)$ such that, for all $a \in A_n$ and all $x, y \in X$, $x P_d^a y$ implies $x P^a y$, where $R^a = f_n(a)$.

The following two lemmas are crucial for our proof.

DICTATOR LEMMA. Let f_n be an SWF satisfying Pareto and independence, where $2 \leq n < +\infty$. If there are $i \in I(n)$, $x, y \in X$, and $a \in A_n$ such that $x P_i^a y$, $(\forall j \in I(n) \setminus \{i\} : y P_j^a x)$ and $x P^a y$, where $R^a = f_n(a)$, then i is a dictator for f_n.

PROOF. Let $\{z, w\}$ be a distinct pair of social states such that $\{x, y\} \cap \{z, w\} = \emptyset$. The case where $\{x, y\} \cap \{z, w\} \neq \emptyset$ can be treated similarly.

6. The idea of this proof was originally explored in Suzumura [49]; however, the present version of the proof is slightly simpler.

Let $b \in A_n$ be such that $zP_i^b xP_i^b yP_i^b w$ and, for all $j \in I(n) \setminus \{i\}$, $zP_j^b x$, $yP_j^b x$, and $yP_j^b w$. There is no constraint on the ranking of z vis-à-vis w for each and every $j \in I(n) \setminus \{i\}$. Since a and b coincide on $\{x, y\}$ and $xP^a y$, we have $xP^b y$ by virtue of independence, where $R^b = f_n(b)$, whereas Pareto implies $zP^b x$ and $yP^b w$. R^b being transitive, it follows that $zP^b w$. Since i is the only person who prefers z to w at b, and there is no restriction whatsoever on R_j^b for all $j \in I(n) \setminus \{i\}$ over $\{z, w\}$, we may invoke independence once again and conclude that i is a dictator for f_n. ■

Reduction Lemma. If an Arrovian SWF f_n exists, where $3 \leq n < +\infty$, then there exists an Arrovian SWF f_{n-1}.

Proof. Let R^* be the universal indifference relation on X, i.e., $R^* := X \times X$, and define, for any $a \in A_{n-1}$, $f_{n-1}(a) := f_n(a, R^*)$. By definition, (a, R^*) is a profile for an n-person society, where each individual $i \in I(n-1)$ expresses R_i^a, and n expresses R^*. We show that f_{n-1} is an Arrovian SWF. It is clear that f_{n-1} inherits independence from f_n.

To show that f_{n-1} satisfies nondictatorship, suppose to the contrary that $d \in I(n-1)$ is the dictator for f_{n-1}. Let $x, y \in X$ and $a \in A_{n-1}$ be such that $xP_d^a y$ and $yP_j^a x$ for all $j \in I(n-1) \setminus \{d\}$. Since d is the dictator for f_{n-1}, $xP^a y$ holds, where $R^a = f_{n-1}(a) = f_n(a, R^*)$. Let $\{z, w\}$ be a disjoint pair of social states such that $\{x, y\} \cap \{z, w\} = \emptyset$. The case where $\{x, y\} \cap \{z, w\} \neq \emptyset$ can be treated similarly. Let $b \in A_n$ be such that $xP_d^b yP_d^b zP_d^b w$, $yP_j^b zP_j^b wP_j^b x$ for all $j \in I(n) \setminus \{d, n\}$ and $wP_n^b xI_n^b yP_n^b z$, where I_n^b denotes the indifference relation corresponding to R_n^b. By virtue of independence, $xP^b y$, whereas Pareto implies $yP^b z$, so that $xP^b z$ must hold by virtue of the transitivity of $R^b = f_n(b)$. R^b being complete, either $xP^b w$ or $wR^b x$ must be true. In the former case, the Dictator Lemma tells us that d is the dictator for f_n, whereas the latter case implies $wP^b z$ so that the Dictator Lemma tells us that n is the dictator for f_n. Since f_n is Arrovian by assumption, there can be no dictator for f_{n-1}.

To show that f_{n-1} satisfies Pareto, suppose that $x, y \in X$ and $a \in A_{n-1}$ are such that $xP_i^a y$ for all $i \in I(n-1)$ and $yR^a x$ holds, where $R^a = f_{n-1}(a) = f_n(a, R^*)$. Take any $z \in X \setminus \{x, y\}$ and let $b \in A_n$ be such that $xP_i^b zP_i^b y$ for all $i \in I(n-1)$ and $zP_n^b xI_n^b y$. By Independence, we have $yR^b x$, whereas Pareto on f_n entails $zP^b y$ so that $zP^b x$ holds by transitivity of $R^b = f_n(b)$. Then the Dictator Lemma tells us that n is the dictator for f_n, a contradiction. Thus f_{n-1} must satisfy Pareto. ■

ARROW'S GENERAL IMPOSSIBILITY THEOREM. There is no Arrovian social welfare function f_n, where $2 \leq n < +\infty$.

PROOF. If there exists an Arrovian SWF f_n, where $n \geq 3$, we may invoke the Reduction Lemma repeatedly to conclude that there exists a sequence of Arrovian SWFs $f_n, f_{n-1}, \ldots, f_2$. Let $x, y \in X$ and $a \in A_2$ be such that $x P_1^a y$ and $y P_2^a x$. $R = f_2(a)$ being complete, either $x R^a y$ or $y P^a x$ holds. In the latter case, 2 is the dictator for f_2 by the Dictator Lemma. In the former case, let $z \in X \setminus \{x, y\}$ and $b \in A_2$ be such that $x P_1^b y P_1^b z$ and $y P_2^b z P_2^b x$. Then independence and Pareto imply, respectively, that $x R^b y$ and $y P^b z$, which yield $x P^b z$ by the transitivity of $R^b = f_2(b)$, so that 1 is the dictator for f_2 by the Dictator Lemma. Thus, there is no Arrovian SWF f_2; hence there are no Arrovian SWFs $f_3, \ldots, f_n$. ■

References

[1] Arrow, K. J., *Social Choice and Individual Values*, New York: Wiley, 1st edn., 1951; 2nd edn., 1963.

[2] Arrow, K. J., "Arrow's Theorem," in J. Eatwell, M. Milgate, and P. Newman, eds., *The New Palgrave: A Dictionary of Economics*, Vol. I, London: Macmillan, 1987, 124–126.

[3] Bentham, J., "Anarchical Fallacies: Being an Examination of the Declarations of Rights Issued during the French Revolution," in J. Bowring, ed., *The Works of Jeremy Bentham*, Vol. II, Edinburgh: William Tait, 1843.

[4] Bergson, A., "A Reformulation of Certain Aspects of Welfare Economics," *Quarterly Journal of Economics* **52**, 1938, 310–334.

[5] Chipman, J. S., "Samuelson and Welfare Economics," in G. R. Feiwel, ed., *Samuelson and Neoclassical Economics*, Dordrecht, Germany: Kluwer Nijhoff Publishing, 1982, 152–184.

[6] Deb, R., "Waiver, Effectivity and Rights as Game Forms," *Economica* **61**, 1994, 167–178.

[7] Deb, R., P. K. Pattanaik, and L. Razzolini, "Game Forms, Rights, and the Efficiency of Social Outcomes," *Journal of Economic Theory* **72**, 1997, 74–95.

[8] Dworkin, R., "What Is Equality? Part 1: Equality of Welfare," *Philosophy & Public Affairs* **10**, 1981, 185–246.

[9] Elster, J., *Sour Grapes: Studies in the Subversion of Rationality*, Cambridge, UK: Cambridge University Press, 1983.

[10] Foley, D. K., "Resource Allocation and the Public Sector," *Yale Economic Essays* **7**, 1967, 45–98.

[11] Gaertner, W., and P. K. Pattanaik, "An Interview with Amartya Sen," *Social Choice and Welfare* **5**, 1988, 69–79.

[12] Gaertner, W., P. K. Pattanaik and K. Suzumura, "Individual Rights Revisited," *Economica* **59**, 1992, 161–177. Essay 15 of this volume.

[13] Gärdenfors, P., "Rights, Games and Social Choice," *Noûs* **15**, 1981, 341–356.

[14] Hicks, J. R., "The Foundations of Welfare Economics," *Economic Journal* **49**, 1939, 696–712.

[15] Hicks, J. R., "The Valuation of the Social Income," *Economica* **7**, 1940, 105–124.

[16] Hicks, J. R., "The Scope and Status of Welfare Economics," *Oxford Economic Papers* **27**, 1975, 307–326.

[17] Kaldor, N., "Welfare Propositions in Economics and Interpersonal Comparisons of Utility," *Economic Journal* **49**, 1939, 549–552.

[18] Kolm, S.-C., *Justice et Equité*, Paris: Centre d'Etudes Prospectives at d'Economie Mathématique Appliquées à la Planification, 1971; English translation, *Justice and Equity*, Cambridge, Mass.: MIT Press, 1997.

[19] Mishan, E. J., "A Survey of Welfare Economics, 1939–59," *Economic Journal* **70**, 1960, 197–265.

[20] Nozick, R., *Anarchy, State and Utopia*, Oxford: Basil Blackwell, 1974.

[21] Pattanaik, P. K., and K. Suzumura, "Individual Rights and Social Evaluation: A Conceptual Framework," *Oxford Economic Papers* **48**, 1996, 194–212.

[22] Peleg, B., "Effectivity Functions, Game Forms, Games, and Rights," *Social Choice and Welfare* **15**, 1998, 67–80.

[23] Pigou, A. C., *The Economics of Welfare*, London: Macmillan, 1920; 4th edn., 1952.

[24] Rawls, J., *A Theory of Justice*, Cambridge, Mass.: Harvard University Press, 1971.

[25] Robbins, L., *An Essay on the Nature and Significance of Economic Science*, London: Macmillan, 1st edn., 1932; 2nd edn., 1935.

[26] Robbins, L., "Interpersonal Comparisons of Utility," *Economic Journal* **48**, 1938, 635–641.

[27] Robbins, L., "Economics and Political Economy," *American Economic Review* **71**, 1981, 1–10.

[28] Samuelson, P. A., *Foundations of Economic Analysis*, Cambridge, Mass.: Harvard University Press, 1947; enlarged edn., 1983.

[29] Samuelson, P. A., "Evaluation of Real National Income," *Oxford Economic Papers* **2**, 1950, 1–29.

[30] Samuelson, P. A., "Arrow's Mathematical Politics," in S. Hook, ed., *Human Values and Economic Policy*, New York: New York University Press, 1967, 41–51.

[31] Samuelson, P. A., "Bergsonian Welfare Economics," in S. Rosefielde, ed., *Economic Welfare and the Economics of Soviet Socialism: Essays in Honor of Abram Bergson*, Cambridge, Mass.: Cambridge University Press, 1981, 223–266.

[32] Schumpeter, J. A., *Capitalism, Socialism and Democracy*, New York: Harper & Brothers, 1942.

[33] Schumpeter, J. A., *History of Economic Analysis*, New York: Oxford University Press, 1954.

[34] Scitovsky, T., "A Note on Welfare Propositions in Economics," *Review of Economic Studies* **9**, 1941, 77–88.

[35] Sen, A. K., *Collective Choice and Social Welfare*, San Francisco: Holden-Day, 1970; republished, Amsterdam: North-Holland, 1979.

[36] Sen, A. K., "The Impossibility of a Paretian Liberal," *Journal of Political Economy* **78**, 1970, 152–157.

[37] Sen, A. K., "Liberty, Unanimity and Rights," *Economica* **43**, 1976, 217–245.

[38] Sen, A. K., "Utilitarianism and Welfarism," *Journal of Philosophy* **76**, 1979, 463–489.

[39] Sen, A. K., "Equality of What?" in S. McMurrin, ed., *The Tanner Lecture on Human Values*, Vol. I, Salt Lake City: University of Utah Press, 1980; reprinted in A. K. Sen, *Choice, Welfare and Measurement*, Oxford: Basil Blackwell, 1982.

[40] Sen, A. K., "Well-Being, Agency and Freedom: The Dewey Lectures 1984," *Journal of Philosophy* **82**, 1985, 169–221.

[41] Sen, A. K., *Commodities and Capabilities*, Amsterdam: North-Holland, 1985.

[42] Sen, A. K., "Minimal Liberty," *Economica* **59**, 1992, 139–159.

[43] Sen, A. K., "Capability and Well-Being," in M. Nussbaum and A. K. Sen, eds., *The Quality of Life*, Oxford: Clarendon Press of Oxford University Press, 1993, 30–53.

[44] Sen, A. K., *On Economic Inequality*, expanded edition with annex, *On Economic Inequality after a Quarter Century* by J. Foster and A. Sen, Oxford: Clarendon Press, 1997.

[45] Sugden, R., "Liberty, Preference and Choice," *Economics and Philosophy* **1**, 1985, 213–229.

[46] Suzumura, K., "Remarks on the Theory of Collective Choice," *Economica* **43**, 1976, 381–390. Essay 6 of this volume.

[47] Suzumura, K., "On Distributional Value Judgements and Piecemeal Welfare Criteria," *Economica* **47**, 1980, 125–139.

[48] Suzumura, K., "On Pareto Efficiency and the No-Envy Concept of Equity," *Journal of Economic Theory* **25**, 1981, 367–379. Essay 9 of this volume.

[49] Suzumura, K., *Rational Choice, Collective Decisions and Social Welfare*, New York: Cambridge University Press, 1983. Reissued in paperback, 2009.

[50] Suzumura, K., "Social Welfare Function," in J. Eatwell, M. Milgate, and P. Newman, eds., *The New Palgrave: A Dictionary of Economics* **4**, London: Macmillan, 1987, 418–420.

[51] Suzumura, K., "Reduction of Social Choice Problems: A Simple Proof of Arrow's General Possibility Theorem," *Hitotsubashi Journal of Economics* **29**, 1988, 219–221.

[52] Suzumura, K., "Consequences, Opportunities, and Procedures," *Social Choice and Welfare* **16**, 1999, 17–40. Essay 17 of this volume.

[53] Suzumura, K., "Paretian Welfare Judgements and Bergsonian Social Choice," *Economic Journal* **109**, 1999, 204–220. Essay 26 of this volume.

[54] Suzumura, K., and Y. Xu, "Characterizations of Consequentialism and Nonconsequentialism," *Journal of Economic Theory* **101**, 2001, 423–436. Essay 18 of this volume.

[55] Suzumura, K., and Y. Xu, "Welfarist Consequentialism, Similarity of Attitudes, and Arrow's General Impossibility Theorem," *Social Choice and Welfare* **22**, 2004, 237–251. Essay 20 of this volume.

[56] van de Graaff, J., *Theoretical Welfare Economics*, Cambridge, UK: Cambridge University Press, 1957.

ESSAY 28

Informational Bases of Welfare Economics, Transcendental Institutionalism, and the Comparative Assessment Approach

Messenger Gracious Madam,
I that do bring the news made not the match.
Cleopatra Say 'tis not so, a province I will give thee,
And make thy fortunes proud: the blow thou hadst
Shall make thy piece for moving me to rage,
And I will boot thee with what gift beside
Thy modesty can beg.
—WILLIAM SHAKESPEARE, *Antony and Cleopatra*

28.1. Introduction

This long and winding pilgrimage in welfare economics and social choice theory is approaching its end. To conclude my personal collection and recollections, and to grope for the future direction to proceed for the sake of devising instruments for the betterment of human life, there are two crucial

In preparing this final essay, I had the great fortune of discussing its overall plan with Amartya Sen at Trinity College, Cambridge University, in 2011. I am also grateful to the University of Hyogo for enabling me to have access to Hicks's two unpublished documents (Hicks [8; 10]), which are kept as part of the Library and Papers of Sir John Hicks. Without this fortunate access, I may not have solidified my understanding of the meaning and reach of Hicks's stance on the issue of welfarism, consequentialism, and nonconsequentialism. An early draft of this essay was read in a seminar held at the University of Montreal on March 25, 2013. I am grateful to the participants of this seminar, including Walter Bossert, Lars Ehlers, and Iwao Hirose, for illuminating comments and discussions.

issues to be identified and explored. The first issue is the choice of informational bases of normative economics. It was John Hicks [9] who threw the first serious doubt on the traditional informational basis of normative economics, viz., welfaristic consequentialism, or welfarism for short.[1] In view of Hicks's major contribution (Hicks [5]; Hicks and Allen [13]) to the ordinalist revolution in microeconomic theory in the 1930s, as well as the role played by Hicks [6; 7; 11] in the evolution of new welfare economics, it is worthwhile to track down how deeply rooted is his farewell to welfarism. Section 28.2 is devoted to this investigation. The second issue is concerned with the basic approach of welfare economics, which underlies the standard understanding of the old welfare economics and the new welfare economics in common and has seldom, if ever at all, been challenged in the literature. The point to be made is closely related to the conceptual dichotomy in the theory of justice, which was introduced by Amartya Sen [26] in his monumental treatise, *The Idea of Justice*, viz., *transcendental institutionalism* versus the *comparative assessment approach*. In Section 28.3, we will contend that this conceptual dichotomy is acutely relevant in the theory of welfare economics and social choice theory as well, and bring the meaning and implication thereof into clear relief. What is at stake is the paradigm of social welfare maximization, which is held almost ubiquitously in welfare economics, old and new, as well as in major parts of social choice theory. Section 28.4 concludes this essay with a disclaimer and a plea for future work in normative economics.

28.2. Hicks's Farewell to Welfarism: How Deep-Rooted Is His Criticism?

As the point of departure of our discourse, let us refer back to the esoteric "Preface—and a Manifesto," with which Hicks [9] commenced his *Essays in World Economics* in 1959. With hindsight, this manifesto should have received far more serious attention than it actually did, as Hicks declared in this little piece his flat denial of the Pigovian tradition of *economic welfarism* for

1. See Section 7.1 of the introduction to this volume. See also the appendix to this essay for the informational tree of normative social evaluations, where the essential concepts of welfarism, nonwelfarism, consequentialism, and nonconsequentialism are expounded.

the first time in the history of welfare economics.[2] Let us briefly recapitulate the gist of Hicks's manifesto.

Hicks begins his excerpt of "Preface—and a Manifesto" in Arrow and Scitovsky [2] with the following remark: "The view which, now, I do *not* hold I propose (with every apology) to call 'Economic Welfarism'; for it is one of the tendencies which has taken its origin from that great and immensely influential work, the *Economics of Welfare* of Pigou. But the distinction which I am about to make has little to do with the multifarious theoretical disputes to which the notion of Welfare Economics has given rise. One can take any view one likes about measurability, or additivity, or comparability of utilities; and yet it remains undetermined whether one is to come down on one side or other of the Welfarist fence. The line between Economic Welfarism and its opposite is not concerned with what economists call utilities; it is concerned with the transition from Utility to the more general good, Welfare (if we like) itself." For the sake of facilitating later reference, the last sentence in this citation will be referred as "Hicks's statement A."

How should we understand the meaning and reach of Hicks's manifesto? It may help if we explicitly pose and settle the following two questions:

Q_1. Did Hicks's manifesto aim at economic welfarism as such, but not at welfarism more generally? In other words, was Hicks resigned to stay within the territory of welfarism even after he refused economic welfarism?

Q_2. How far was Hicks ready to go back along the informational tree of normative social evaluations? Was Hicks ready to cross over the boundary of welfarism toward the territory of nonwelfarist consequentialism, or even to cross over the boundary of consequentialism toward the territory of nonconsequentialism?

Since we are walking through a slippery area, let us begin with Pigou's definition of *welfare* in general and *economic welfare* in particular. According

2. To the best of my knowledge, it was not until Arrow and Scitovsky [2] edited their *Readings in Welfare Economics* and included an extract of Hicks's manifesto that it received a chance of being seriously scrutinized by the profession. It may not be out of place to point out that, even in November–December 2000 when I interviewed Paul Samuelson on behalf of *Social Choice and Welfare*, I was bitterly reminded that Samuelson was not at all ready to take Hicks's *antiwelfarist manifesto* seriously. See Suzumura [27, Section 2.7].

to Pigou [25, pp. 10–11], "Welfare . . . is a thing of very wide range. There is no need here to enter upon a general discussion of its content. It will be sufficient to lay down more or less dogmatically two propositions; first, that the elements of welfare are states of consciousness and, perhaps, their relations; secondly, that welfare can be brought under the category of greater or less. A general investigation of all the groups of causes by which welfare thus conceived may be affected would constitute a task so enormous and complicated as to be quite impracticable. It is, therefore, necessary to limit our subject-matter." The device that Pigou adopted for limiting the subject matter of welfare economics was straightforward: "In doing this we are naturally attracted toward that portion of the field in which the method of science seems likely to work at best advantage. This they can clearly do when there is present something measurable, on which analytical machinery can get a firm grip. The one obvious instrument of measurement available in social life is money. Hence, *the range of our inquiry becomes restricted to that part of social welfare that can be brought directly or indirectly into relation with the measuring-rod of money. This part of welfare may be called economic welfare.*"[3]

Pigou was not unaware of the difficulty of separating economic welfare from welfare in general. Thus, he wrote:[4] "It is not, indeed, possible to separate [economic welfare] in any rigid way from other parts [of general welfare], for the part which *can* be brought into relation with a money measure will be different according as we mean by *can*, 'can easily' or 'can with mild straining' or 'can with violent straining.' The outline of our territory is, therefore, necessarily vague. . . . Nevertheless, though no precise boundary between economic and non-economic welfare exists, yet the test of accessibility to a money measure serves well enough to set up a rough distinction. Economic welfare, as loosely defined by this test, is the subject-matter of economic science. The purpose of [the economics of welfare] is to study certain important groups of causes that affect economic welfare in actual modern societies."

With this background in mind, it may seem natural to surmise that what Hicks did was to reject Pigou's convention to separate economic welfare from general welfare, thereby joining hands with numerous critics of

3. Italics added.
4. See Pigou [25, p. 11].

Pigou in a similar spirit. We contend that this easy misperception of the nature of Hicks's far-reaching manifesto is mainly responsible for the long neglect that surrounded it. As a matter of fact, Hicks himself may have been partly responsible for this misperception. To illustrate how easily this misunderstanding could arise, let us quote the following passage from Hicks [9]:[5] "It is impossible to make 'economic' proposals that do not have 'non-economic aspects,' as the Welfarist would call them; when the economist makes a recommendation, he is responsible for it in the round; all aspects of that recommendation, whether he chooses to label them economic or not, are his concern." This citation from "Preface—and a Manifesto" will be called "Hicks's statement B" in what follows.

If we try to make Hicks's statement A and Hicks's statement B coherent, we may be naturally led to the following interpretation of Hicks's manifesto. To lay the sound foundations of sensible welfare economics, we should liberate ourselves from the artificial cage of economic welfarism and accept a wider informational basis for normative social evaluations. To give support to this interpretation, we have only to see the following "one strong example" presented by Hicks [12, p. 137] himself: "One of the issues that can be dealt with most elaborately by Welfarist methods is that of Monopoly and Competition: the theory of the social optimum which would be reached in a (practically unattainable) condition of all-round perfect competition, and of the departures from the optimum which must occur under any form in which a system of free enterprise can in practice be organised, is one of the chief ways in which the Welfarist approach has left its mark. I do not question that we have learnt a great deal from these discussions; but they leave me with an obstinate feeling that they have failed to penetrate to the centre of the problem with which they are concerned. . . . Why is it, for instance, that anti-monopoly legislation (and litigation) get so little help, as they evidently do, from the textbook theory? Surely the answer is that the main issues of principle—security on the one side, freedom and equity on the other, the issues that lawyers, and law-makers, can understand—have got left right out."

We are now ready to answer the questions (Q_1) and (Q_2) that we posed earlier in this essay. Our answer to (Q_1) is that *Hicks was prepared to go not only beyond economic welfarism but also beyond welfarism as such*. Our answer to

5. See Hicks [12, p. 137].

(Q_2) is that *Hicks revealed his willingness to go back along the informational tree of normative social evaluations all the way to nonconsequentialism*. This verdict is well vindicated by his emphasis of such nonconsequentialist features of the world as security, freedom, and equity. At this juncture of our discourse, we should call the reader's attention to the warning and reservation voiced by Hicks [12, p. 139]: "I have . . . no intention, in abandoning Economic Welfarism, of falling into the 'fiat libertas, ruat caelum' which some latter-day liberals seem to see as the only alternative. What I do maintain is that the liberal goods are goods; that they are values which, however, must be weighed up against other values."

The nonwelfarist manifesto by Hicks turned out to be so radical that it may be of some help if we dig deeper into the historical evolution of his welfare economics. Note that Hicks made repeated efforts to synthesize his multifaceted work in welfare economics into a comprehensive treatise, but he seems to have abandoned this long-awaited synthesis in the end. Indeed, his "Another Shot at Welfare Economics, Lecture I and Lecture II" (Hicks [8]) and his "The Real Product—A Revision of Welfare Economics" (Hicks [10]) were left eventually unpublished. Time seems ripe now for savoring Hicks's "Preface—and a Manifesto" again, and deliberating on his proposal to reconstruct welfare economics on a nonconsequentialist informational basis.

28.3. Seeking the Best Social Outcomes, or Devising Tools for Bettering Human Life

Let us now turn to the second issue identified in Section 28.1 of this essay. To prepare the ground of our discourse, it may not be out of order to reflect on the standard understanding of the research program of the old and new welfare economics. The standard understanding of the old welfare economics may be phrased as follows: "Design an institutional framework of the economy in such a way as to implement the solution $x^* \in S$ to the following constrained maximization problem:

$$\text{Max}\{u_1(x) + \cdots + u_n(x)\} \quad \text{over all } x \in S, \qquad \text{(B-P)}$$

where S is the set of feasible social alternatives, u_i $(i = 1, 2, \ldots, n)$ is the utility function of individual i, and (B-P) is the abbreviation of (Bentham

& Pigou)." Likewise, the main scenario of the Bergson-Samuelson school of new welfare economics may be phrased as follows: "Design an institutional framework of an economy in such a way as to implement the solution $x^* \in S$ to the following constrained maximization problem:

$$\text{Max}\, f(u_1(x), \ldots, u_n(x)) \quad \text{over all } x \in S, \qquad \text{(B-S)}$$

where f denotes a Bergson-Samuelson social welfare function, and (B-S) is the abbreviation of (Bergson & Samuelson)." Thus, the constrained maximization paradigm captures the essence not only of the old welfare economics but also of the new welfare economics of the social welfare function school.[6] The crucial difference between them can be reduced to the contrast between the sum total of individual utilities in the problem (B-P) and the value of a Bergson-Samuelson social welfare function in the problem (B-S). It is true that the replacement of the sum total of individual utilities by the value of a Bergson-Samuelson social welfare function was once considered to be a quantum leap in the history of welfare economics, with their concomitant contrast of informational bases, but they share the crucial feature of focusing on the maximization of social welfare subject to resource constraints.

The exclusive focus on the implementation of the socially first-best solution to the constrained maximization problem is also reflected in the theory of implementation à la Leonid Hurwicz [14; 15; 16; 17; 18; 19] and Eric Maskin [22; 23] that has received substantial attention in recent social choice theory.[7] For the sake of later reference, let us briefly summarize the gist of Hurwicz-Maskin implementation theory.

Let $N = \{1, 2, \ldots, n\}$ $(2 \leq n < +\infty)$ be the set of all individuals in the society, and let A be the opportunity set of feasible social alternatives.[8] Each individual $i \in N$ is free to form his/her preference ordering R_i on the set A, which is not known to the government in search of the first-best

6. The research program of the new welfare economics of the compensationist school may not be captured by the straightforward constrained maximization paradigm, such as (B-P) and (B-S). For the structure of the compensationist school of new welfare economics, see Essay 26 and Essay 27 of this volume.

7. See also Partha Dasgupta, Peter Hammond, and Eric Maskin [3], and Roger Myerson [24].

8. In what follows, we simplify our exposition by fixing the set A of feasible alternatives once and for all. This simplification does not affect substantial contents of the theory of implementation.

social outcome with respect to the social welfare ordering $R = f(\boldsymbol{R})$, where $\boldsymbol{R} = (R_1, R_2, \ldots, R_n)$ is the profile of individual preference orderings over A and f is an Arrovian social welfare function. The best that the government can do is to design a *game form* $(\boldsymbol{M}, g)$, where $\boldsymbol{M} = M_1 \times M_2 \times \ldots \times M_n$, M_i is the *message space* of individual $i \in N$, and g is the *outcome function* that maps each message profile $\boldsymbol{m} = (m_1, m_2, \ldots, m_n) \in \boldsymbol{M}$ into a feasible alternative $g(\boldsymbol{m}) \in A$, in such a way that, for each profile $\boldsymbol{R}$ of individual preference orderings, and given an equilibrium concept $\mathcal{E}$ prevailing in the society, the $\mathcal{E}$-equilibrium outcome of the game $((\boldsymbol{M}, g), \boldsymbol{R})$, viz., $g(\mathcal{E}((\boldsymbol{M}, g), \boldsymbol{R}))$, will attain the first-best social welfare maximization with respect to $R = f(\boldsymbol{R})$. Formally speaking, the game form $(\boldsymbol{M}, g)$ is said to *implement* the *social choice function* C that maps each profile $\boldsymbol{R}$ of individual preference orderings into the *social choice set*

$$C(\boldsymbol{R}) := \{x^* \in A \mid x^* R x \text{ for all } x \in A\},$$

where $R = f(\boldsymbol{R})$, if and only if the set of $\mathcal{E}$-equilibrium outcomes, viz., $O_{\mathcal{E}}((\boldsymbol{M}, g), \boldsymbol{R})$ of the game $((\boldsymbol{M}, g), \boldsymbol{R})$ satisfies

$$C(\boldsymbol{R}) = O_{\mathcal{E}}((\boldsymbol{M}, g), \boldsymbol{R}) := g(\mathcal{E}((\boldsymbol{M}, g), \boldsymbol{R})).$$

In this case, the socially first-best outcomes $C(\boldsymbol{R})$ can be attained through the decentralized play of the designed game $((\boldsymbol{M}, g), \boldsymbol{R})$ at $\mathcal{E}$-equilibrium.[9] The main problem that the theory of implementation grapples with consists of the following two parts:

IM_1. Find a set of conditions that characterizes the set of implementable social choice functions C.

IM_2. For each implementable social choice function C, design a game form $(\boldsymbol{M}, g)$ that can actually implement C.

Observe that the social welfare ordering R generated for each profile $\boldsymbol{R}$ of individual preference orderings via an Arrovian social welfare function f, viz., $R = f(\boldsymbol{R})$, can rank all social alternatives from the first-best, the second-best, and eventually to the worst alternative if the set of social alternatives is finite. However, implementation theory just focuses on the first-best

9. See Thomson [28] for some variations of the concept of implementation.

alternatives and neglects all other alternatives as socially irrelevant. In this sense, it has much in common not only with the old welfare economics captured by the scenario (B-P) but also with the social welfare function school of the new welfare economics captured by the scenario (B-S).

The exclusive concentration on the first-best alternative is widely shared by many other schools of thought in post-Pigovian ordinalist welfare economics. Suffice it to quote the *fairness-as-no-envy* approach à la Duncan Foley [4], Serge Kolm [20; 21], and Hal Varian [30; 31].[10] Let X be the set of conceivable social alternatives and let $N = \{1, 2, \ldots, n\}$ $(2 \leq n < +\infty)$ be the set of all individuals. Individuals are supposed to put themselves through imaginary exchange of circumstances into the position of each other individual, thereby forming an *extended preference ordering* in the following sense: $(x, j)\tilde{R}_i(y, k)$ holds if and only if, according to i's judgments, being in the position of individual j when the social alternative x prevails is at least as good as being in the position of individual k when the social alternative y prevails. This concept of extended preference ordering enables us to formulate the concept of equity-as-no-envy as follows. We say that i envies j at x if and only if we have $(x, j)P(\tilde{R}_i)(x, i)$, where $P(\tilde{R}_i)$ is the asymmetric part [strict preference part] of $\tilde{R}_i$. For each opportunity set $S \subseteq X$ and each profile $\tilde{\boldsymbol{R}}$ of extended preference orderings, an alternative $x^* \in S$ is said to be *no-envy equitable* if and only if nobody envies anybody else at x^* under $\tilde{\boldsymbol{R}}$. If x^* is no-envy equitable as well as Pareto efficient in S under $\tilde{\boldsymbol{R}}$, x^* is said to be *fair*.[11]

There is no a priori reason to expect that there exists a fair state in the specified environment. Even if there exists a fair state in the specified environment, there is no universally applicable mechanism that leads us into a fair state without infringing upon other values to be respected. Thus, the agenda of the fairness-as-no-envy approach may be boiled down to finding a set of conditions under which fair states are warranted to exist, on the one hand, and to design and implement a mechanism that is warranted to attain a fair state when and where one exists, on the other.

Not only did the proponents of this approach identify the fair state as the socially first-best target to be attained, but they also used this standard of reference for the sake of criticizing Arrovian social choice theory. To

10. A reference should also be made to Jan Tinbergen [29] as the precursor of this concept of equity.
11. See Essay 9 and Essay 10 in Part III of this volume for our analysis of the concepts of no-envy equity and fairness.

witness, Varian [30, p. 65] argued that "social [choice] theory asks for too much out of the [social aggregation] process in that it asks for an entire *ordering* of the various social states. . . . The original question asked only for a good allocation; there was no requirement to rank all allocations. The fairness criterion in fact limits itself to answering the original question. It is limited in that it gives no indication of the merits of two non-fair allocations, but by restricting itself in this way it allows for a reasonable solution to the original problem." Likewise, Kolm [20, p. 439] asserted that "the assumption of a social ordering, as well as the other weaker or alternative assumptions . . . are at odds with standard conceptions of equity and justice, and with consequences of rationality in the normal sense of 'for a reason'. . . . The requirement of a social ordering is indeed problematic at first sight: Why would we want to know the 193th best alternative? Only the first best is required for the choice."

To sum up our discussion in this section so far, it is argued that not only the standard understanding of the old welfare economics and the social welfare function school of the new welfare economics, but also the Hurwicz-Maskin theory of implementation and the no-envy approach in the theory of fairness, focus on the first-best alternatives in full neglect of other, less-than-the-first-best, alternatives. In fact, some major proponents of the no-envy fairness approach go as far as to criticize Arrovian social choice theory for its "irrelevant" concern about the ranking among socially less-than-the-first-best alternatives. Should we acquiesce in this criticism?

As an auxiliary step in finding our way to proceed, let us remind ourselves of an acute remark by Pigou to the effect that "the complicated analysis which economists endeavour to carry through are [to find] *instruments for the bettering of human life*."[12] Contrary to the standard understanding of Pigou's research program by means of the maximization problem (B-P), his old welfare economics was in fact focused on the design and implementation of instruments for the bettering of human life. In other words, Pigou's old welfare economics is not about the design and implementation of institutions so as to realize the socially first-best alternative, but about the design and implementation of institutions so as to improve human life in the down-to-earth world. Viewed from this standpoint, the role of the Arrow social

12. Italics added.

welfare ordering receives a new footlight. If our target is not to identify and implement the socially first-best alternatives but to devise and implement instruments for the bettering of human life in the down-to-earth world, we are in need of a social ordering among less-than-the-first-best social alternatives, which helps us find a way to proceed even when we are currently in a suboptimal state of the world. This insight, the origin of which may be traced back to Pigou's founding manifesto in the *Economics of Welfare*, is of crucial importance as it leads us to the overall reorientation of welfare economics.

This observation is closely reminiscent of the sharp contrast between *transcendental institutionalism* and the *comparative assessment approach* in the theory of justice, which Sen [26, pp. 5–6] introduced in *The Idea of Justice*: "There are two basic, and divergent, lines of reasoning about justice among leading philosophers associated with the radical thought of [the European Enlightenment in the eighteenth and nineteenth centuries]. One approach . . . concentrated on identifying just institutional arrangements for a society. This approach, which can be called 'transcendental institutionalism,' has two distinct features. First, it concentrates its attention on what it identifies as perfect justice, rather than on relative comparisons of justice and injustice. It tries only to identify social characteristics that cannot be transcended in terms of justice, and its focus is thus not on comparing feasible societies, all of which may fall short of the ideals of perfection. The inquiry is aimed at identifying the nature of 'the just,' rather than finding some criteria for an alternative being 'less unjust' than another. Second, in search for perfection, transcendental institutionalism concentrates primarily on getting the institutions right, and it is not directly focused on the actual societies that would ultimately emerge. . . . Both these features relate to the 'contractarian' mode of thinking that Thomas Hobbs had initiated, and which was further pursued by John Locke, Jean-Jacques Rousseau and Immanuel Kant. . . . The overall result was to develop theories of justice that focused on transcendental identification of the ideal institutions."

28.4. A Disclaimer and a Plea

In this essay, two rather unorthodox items on the agenda of normative economics are identified and proposed. The first item on the agenda is to liquidate a premature commitment to the welfaristic informational basis of normative social evaluations. On scrutinizing Hicks's "Preface—and a Manifesto," we came to the conviction that he was ready to go upstream the informational tree of normative social evaluations not only beyond the boundary of welfarist consequentialism and toward nonwelfarist consequentialism, but also beyond the boundary of consequentialism and toward conconsequentialism. In some parts of this volume, viz., Part IV and Part V, several attempts were made to pursue newly cultivated possibilities suggested by Hicks. The second item on the agenda is to reconsider the orthodox understanding of the scenario of welfare economics and social choice theory that focuses on the pursuit of the first-best social welfare maximization. An alternative scenario can be traced back to Pigou's preface to *The Economics of Welfare*, where he declared that "the complicated analysis which economists endeavour to carry through are . . . instruments for the bettering of human life." These two scenarios have a family resemblance with Sen's dichotomy in the theory of justice under the names of transcendental institutionalism and the comparative assessment approach. It is not our contention that these two items on the agenda are of dominant importance in the future agenda of normative economics, as there remain many fascinating and puzzling questions we may pose even in the conventional framework of welfare economics and social choice theory. If the aforementioned items on the agenda succeed in catching the fancy of present and future researchers, we would feel more than happy.

Having said this, however, I am hopeful that further explorations of the items on the agenda identified in this essay will prove truly worthwhile to pursue in the future. It is with this expression of our hope that we would like to close this long and winding pilgrimage.

Appendix 28.A. Informational Tree of Normative Social Evaluations

Suppose that we are engaging in normative social evaluations of alternative economic systems and/or economic policies. For the sake of making sensible evaluations, the agent in charge must be provided with relevant information about the performance of alternative systems and/or policies. To classify possible types of informational basis, let us introduce what we christen the *informational tree of normative social evaluations* (Figure 28.1).

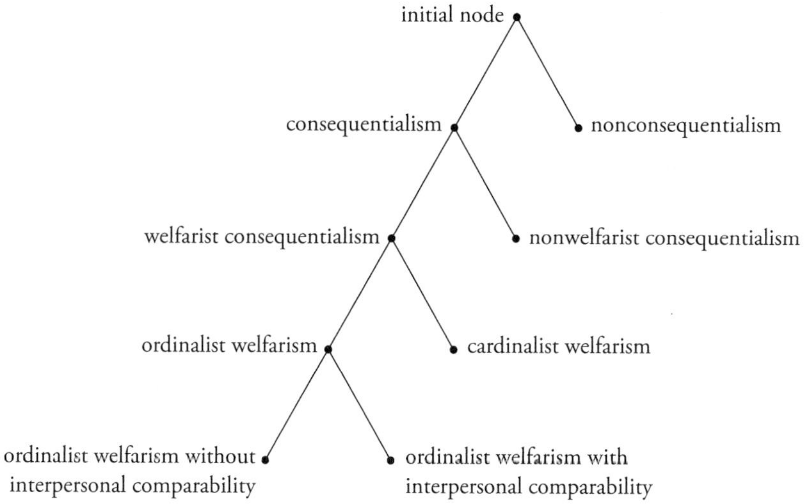

Figure 28.1. Informational Tree of Normative Social Evaluations

At the *initial node* of this tree, we are in the position of specifying the evaluating agent's informational requirement. Any sensible agent in charge of social evaluations surely requires information about *consequential outcomes* generated through alternative economic systems and/or economic policies. If the agent's informational requirement consists solely of consequential outcomes pure and simple, his/her stance is called *consequentialism*. If the agent requires some information beyond consequential outcomes, such as the *opportunity set* of culmination outcomes or *intrinsic procedural characteristics* of system and/or policy through which an outcome is socially chosen, his/her stance is called *nonconsequentialism*. Note that the nonconsequentialist stance does not necessarily neglect consequential information altogether; it just pays attention to some nonconsequential information in addition to consequential information. A special class of the nonconsequentialist stance is the *deontological stance*, which focuses solely on nonconsequentialist features of the world in complete neglect of consequentialist features of the world.

Suppose now that we are standing at the consequentialist node. Observe that there are several alternative ways of describing consequential outcomes by means of an economic system and/or economic policy. For example, we may focus on the welfare accruing to all individuals in the society at the consequential outcome of the system and/or policy, or we may require some nonwelfaristic description of the consequential outcomes. The former stance is called *welfarist consequentialism*, or *welfarism* for short, whereas the latter stance is called *nonwelfarist consequentialism*, or *nonwelfarism* for short.[13]

Suppose that we have proceeded to the welfarist node of the informational tree. Depending on whether we stick to the ordinal concept of welfare, or we are ready to accept the cardinal measurability of welfare, we are led either to the node of *ordinalist welfarism* or to the node of *cardinalist welfarism*. Suppose that we have proceeded to the node of ordinalist welfarism. Then we are standing at the last node of bifurcation in the informational tree. If we follow Lionel Robbins and reject the interpersonal comparability of individual welfare, we will arrive at the terminal node of *ordinalist welfarism without interpersonal comparability*. If, on the other hand, we are somehow ready to accept the interpersonal comparability of individual welfare, we will arrive at the terminal node of *ordinalist welfarism with interpersonal comparability*.

To conclude this appendix, two final observations are in order. In the first place, ordinalist welfarism without interpersonal comparability is the widely accepted stance among various schools of normative economics. Indeed, it is this stance that is accepted in common by the new welfare economics of the compensationist school, the new welfare economics of the Bergson-Samuelson school, and most, if not all, schools in social choice theory. In the second place, the evolution of post-Pigou welfare economics may be neatly described by means of the informational tree of normative social evaluations. Capitalizing on the long-lasting tradition of Benthamite utilitarianism, Pigou's "old" welfare economics was based on the epistemological basis of *cardinalist welfarism with interpersonal comparability*. This Pigovian informational basis was severely criticized by Robbins for its alleged lack of "scientific" foundations. To salvage the vestigial traces of Pigou's upper structure, two schools of "new" welfare economics were created in the late 1930s, viz., the *compensationist school* and the *social welfare function school*. To be free from Robbins's criticism on Pigou's epistemological basis, it was all too natural that both schools of new welfare economics as well as Arrovian social choice theory adopted the informational stance of ordinalist welfarism without interpersonal comparability. Viewed from this perspective, Hicks's

13. For example, we may describe the consequence of an income redistribution system by means of welfare distribution among individuals thereby created. Alternatively, we may describe the same consequence by means of such nonwelfaristic measures as the Lorenz curve or the Gini coefficient.

nonwelfarist manifesto seems to be all the more important. It may even be revolutionary.

References

[1] Arrow, K. J., *Social Choice and Individual Values*, New York: John Wiley & Sons, 1st edn., 1951; expanded 2nd edn., 1963. 3rd edn. with an introduction by Eric Maskin, New Haven, Conn.: Yale University Press, 2012.

[2] Arrow, K. J., and T. Scitovsky, eds., *Readings in Welfare Economics*, Homewood, Ill.: Richard D. Irwin, INC., 1969.

[3] Dasgupta, P., P. J. Hammond, and E. Maskin, "The Implementation of Social Choice Rules: Some General Results on Incentive Compatibility," *Review of Economic Studies* **46**, 1979, 185–216.

[4] Foley, D., "Resource Allocation in the Public Sector," *Yale Economic Essays* **7**, 1967, 45–98.

[5] Hicks, J. R., *Value and Capital*, Oxford: Clarendon Press, 1st edn., 1939; 2nd edn., 1946.

[6] Hicks, J. R., "The Foundations of Welfare Economics," *Economic Journal* **49**, 1939, 696–712.

[7] Hicks, J. R., "The Valuation of Social Income," *Economica* **7**, 1940, 105–124.

[8] Hicks, J. R., "Another Shot at Welfare Economics, Lecture I and Lecture II," unpublished typescript, 19 pages folio + 21 pages folio, diagrams in the text, no date; c. 1955.

[9] Hicks, J. R., "Preface—and a Manifesto," in his *Essays in World Economics*, Oxford: Clarendon Press, 1959. Reprinted in Arrow and Scitovsky [2, pp. 95–99] as well as in Hicks [12, pp. 135–141].

[10] Hicks, J. R., "The Real Product—A Revision of Welfare Economics," unpublished typescript, no date; c. 1963.

[11] Hicks, J. R., "The Scope and Status of Welfare Economics," *Oxford Economic Papers* **27**, 1975, 307–326. Reprinted in Hicks [13, pp. 218–239].

[12] Hicks, J. R., *Wealth and Welfare*, Vol. I of *Collected Essays on Economic Theory*, Oxford: Basil Blackwell, 1981.

[13] Hicks, J. R., and R. G. D. Allen, "A Reconsideration of the Theory of Value," Part I, *Economica* **1**, 1934, 52–76; Part II, "A Mathematical Theory of Individual Demand Functions," *Economica* **1**, 1934, 196–219.

[14] Hurwicz, L., "Optimality and Informational Efficiency in Resource Allocation Processes," in Arrow, K. J., S. Karlin, and P. Suppes, eds., *Mathematical Methods in Social Sciences,* Stanford, Calif.: Stanford University Press, 1960, 27–46.

[15] Hurwicz, L., "On Informationally Decentralized Systems," in R. Radner and C. B. McGuire, eds., *Decision and Organization*, Amsterdam: North-Holland, 1972, 297–336.

[16] Hurwicz, L., "On Allocations Attainable through Nash Equilibria," *Journal of Economic Theory* **21**, 1979, 140–165.

[17] Hurwicz, L., "Outcome Functions Yielding Walrasian and Lindahl Allocations at Nash Equlibrium," *Review of Economic Studies* **46**, 1979, 217–225.

[18] Hurwicz, L., "Institutions as Families of Game Forms," *Japanese Economic Review* **47**, 1996, 113–132.

[19] Hurwicz, L., "But Who Will Guard the Guardians?" *American Economic Review* **98**, 2008, 577–585.

[20] Kolm, S.-Ch., *Modern Theories of Justice*, Cambridge, Mass.: MIT Press, 1996.

[21] Kolm, S.-Ch., *Justice and Equity*, Cambridge, Mass.: MIT Press, 1998. English translation of the French original published in 1971.

[22] Maskin, E., "Nash Equilibrium and Welfare Optimality," *Review of Economic Studies* **66**, 1999, 23–38. Originally circulated as MIT working paper in 1977.

[23] Maskin, E., "Mechanism Design: How to Implement Social Goals," *American Economic Review* **98**, 2008, 567–576.

[24] Myerson, R. B., "Perspectives on Mechanism Design in Economic Theory," *American Economic Review* **98**, 2008, 586–603.

[25] Pigou, A. C., *The Economics of Welfare*, London: Macmillan, 1st edn., 1920; 4th edn., 1932.

[26] Sen, A. K., *The Idea of Justice*, Cambridge, Mass.: Harvard University Press, 2009.

[27] Suzumura, K., "An Interview with Paul Samuelson: Welfare Economics, 'Old' and 'New,' and Social Choice Theory," *Social Choice and Welfare* **25**, 2005, 327–356. Reprinted in J. Murray, ed., *The Collected Scientific Papers of Paul A. Samuelson*, Vol. 6, Cambridge, Mass.: MIT Press, 2011, 843–872.

[28] Thomson, W., "Concepts of Implementation," *Japanese Economic Review* **47**, 1996, 133–143.

[29] Tinbergen, J., *Redelijke Inkomensverdeling*, Haarlem, Netherlands: N.V. DeGulden Pers, 2nd edn., 1953.

[30] Varian, H. R., "Equity, Envy and Efficiency," *Journal of Economic Theory* **9**, 1974, 63–91.

[31] Varian, H. R., "Distributive Justice, Welfare Economics, and the Theory of Fairness," *Philosophy and Public Affairs* **4**, 1975, 223–247.

Index